AVID
READER
PRESS

ALSO BY GERALD POSNER

God's Bankers

Miami Babylon

Secrets of the Kingdom

Why America Slept

Motown

Killing the Dream

Citizen Perot

Case Closed

Hitler's Children

The Bio-Assassins

Warlords of Crime

Mengele

PHARMA

GREED, LIES, AND THE POISONING OF AMERICA

GERALD POSNER

Avid Reader Press
New York London Toronto Sydney New Delhi

Avid Reader Press
An Imprint of Simon & Schuster, Inc.
1230 Avenue of the Americas
New York, NY 10020

First Avid Reader Press hardcover edition March 2020

Manufactured in the United States of America

1 3 5 7 9 10 8 6 4 2

Library of Congress Cataloging-in-Publication Data is available.

ISBN 978-1-5011-5189-7
ISBN 978-1-5011-5204-7 (ebook)

To Trisha, my muse
and eternal love,
all things are possible
only with you

CONTENTS

PREFACE

James Phelan, a legendary reporter, gave me the idea for a book about the pharmaceutical industry over twenty years ago. In the 1990s, Phelan, an old-fashioned shoe-leather reporter, and I shared the same book editor, Robert Loomis. Phelan had a deserved reputation for cracking big cases. *The New York Times* had dubbed him one of the country's finest investigative journalists. Unmasking Clifford Irving's "autobiography" of Howard Hughes as a hoax was his biggest scoop.

I had met Phelan while researching *Case Closed*, my reinvestigation of the JFK assassination. In the late 1960s his groundbreaking reporting exposed that New Orleans district attorney Jim Garrison had falsified evidence in his criminal probe of whether there was a Big Easy conspiracy link to the assassination.

In the summer of 1997, I called him for some advice on my examination of the Martin Luther King Jr. assassination. We also talked about the state of investigative journalism. Phelan, not someone I knew to indulge in nostalgia, reminisced that he thought it had changed mostly for the worse. The trend toward ever-shorter deadlines made it tougher, he thought, to undertake long-term investigations. Even good reporters might return after a few months without a breakthrough. He cited examples from his own reporting, including one when military investigators had coerced a fake murder confession from an Air Force officer and another in which a California chiropractor had fleeced millions from patients with a bogus "cure." There was no certainty when he got those assignments that he would crack the story. The tips and strands of evidence that initially caught his attention might have turned into dead ends.

"That's a risk that most magazine and newspaper editors no longer want to take," he said. "You can at least still do it in books, there you have the time and space to get to the bottom of a good story."

He did not hesitate when I asked what subject he still considered challenging for a book.

"The pharmaceutical business. It's like throwing a dart at a storyboard."

Phelan said he was too old at eighty-five to undertake such a large project. He did not tell me he was also too sick. A few months later I learned he had died of lung cancer. Our last conversation planted in me the idea of one day looking into a book about the drug industry. In publishing, however, even good ideas can take years before they come to fruition.

It was January 2016 when I sent my editor, Ben Loehnen, a proposal with the no-frills working title "A History of the American Pharmaceutical Industry." I had read by then several dozen good books, each about some part of the story I hoped to cover in its entirety. There were histories of epidemics and pandemics, inspiring accounts of groundbreaking lab discoveries, biographies of storied scientists and pharma executives, even business histories of some companies. There was, however, no single volume that started with the wild anything-goes nineteenth-century era of homegrown "wonder remedies" to today's sprawling pharma conglomerates that sell a trillion dollars of drugs annually.

When I sent that proposal to Ben, I had not started my research in earnest. A proposal is sometimes not much more than selecting the book's topic. The finished manuscript might be radically different. *Pharma* proved to be a classic investigative story. Few will be surprised that a significant obstacle was the drug industry's zealous protection of its secrets. That forced me to find drug executives, scientists, and government regulators who were willing to talk, some of whom had never spoken on the record. Others, fearing retribution from their employers or the industry itself, agreed to help only on the condition of anonymity. Besides those interviews, uncovering the information at the heart of this book required sifting through tens of thousands of pages of overlooked government regulatory documents, hunting for evidence buried in the exhibits of massive pharmaceutical litigation, and examining remote and seldom accessed private archives.

I did not expect to find one person or a single family who provided a narrative thread through which to examine the industry's explosive growth after World War II. It was in those seventy postwar years that pharma transformed into a mega-industry.

The Lilly family, as well as the Mercks, Squibbs, and Johnsons, had left the industry as their companies became massive conglomerates. The term "Big Pharma" appeared first in news articles during the 1960s to describe a handful of dominant firms.[1] New titans arrived, but much later during the biotechnology revolution. I had always intended to write a chapter about three brothers, Arthur, Mortimer, and Raymond Sackler. They are best known today for buying in 1952 a small drug company, Purdue, that started manufacturing the opioid painkiller OxyContin in 1996.

During my research I discovered they played a much more extensive role in the drug business, often at critical junctures, starting in the 1940s. A largely unknown backstory of the Sacklers came alive in interviews and never-before-seen documents. In response to my Freedom of Information requests, FBI declassified files revealed the extent of the Sackler family's radical left-wing politics and the Bureau's suspicions about their loyalty to America. Notes and memos from a 1962 Senate committee had the details of what the investigative staff had uncovered about a hidden "Sackler empire." And, in late 2018, a small treasure trove of documents arrived at my office. They were in a sealed, plain manila envelope postmarked from New York and without a return address. Inside were copies of FDA and DEA documents with answers to some long-standing questions about how the Sacklers rose to such tremendous power and wealth.

Pharma opens a rare insider's window on the internecine battles between scientists and executives over drugs and money. It is about the secret world inside companies that are household names and how the quest for blockbuster drugs has at times crippled and distorted the industry's original mission to develop medications that treat the sick and save lives.

Pharma has plenty of heroes and villains. There are brilliant scientists, conniving business executives, compliant government regulators, and brave whistleblowers. Serendipitous lifesaving drug discoveries by scientists contrast with disturbing tales of criminal price-fixing, conspiracies to cover up tainted drugs, and a rigged regulatory system that too often serves as a compliant rubber stamp for drug companies.

Pharma is an industry like no other.

1

PATIENT ZERO

"Get the patient into isolation now," the doctor ordered. The patient was a woman in her mid-seventies from nearby Reno, Nevada. A few days earlier, she had arrived at the ER disoriented and running a fever. Temperatures that day had topped out at a stifling 100 degrees. The 2016 summer had been brutal even by the standards of a county that included a torrid stretch of Black Rock Desert.

When doctors learned she had recently returned from a trip to India they suspected that the rigors of a twenty-hour flight, coupled with the heat, had left her severely dehydrated.[1] A couple of days of intravenous fluids should make her as good as new.

They became increasingly alarmed, however, the following day. Her temperature spiked to 102, pulse raced at nearly 100 beats a minute, and breathing became labored. Blood tests revealed an abnormally high white blood cell count. That prompted a new diagnosis: systemic inflammatory response syndrome. Although her physicians could not identify an underlying infection, they thought it likely that her body's extreme immune response had somehow poisoned her own blood. They administered intravenous antibiotics to prevent irreversible organ damage.

There was no improvement. After another thirty-six hours, the doctors ordered more testing to hunt for the culprit they had missed in their initial blood and fluid screens. That test result startled her physicians. The infection was carbapenem-resistant Enterobacteriaceae (CRE), a typically benign intestinal bacterium that becomes a treacherous supergerm after it enters a patient's bloodstream or lungs. It then overwhelms the body's immune system.[2]

This CRE diagnosis was particularly alarming. Discovered only in

2008 in New Delhi, it had established itself in under a decade as the most lethal supergerm, killing half of the patients it infects.[3] The head of the Food and Drug Administration (FDA) described it as a "nightmarish bacteria." CRE has mutated into newer strains, some of which have enhanced resistance to the class of antibiotics that were traditionally the last line of defense.[4]

Doctors knew about superbugs for several decades but before the CRE variant most had dismissed their potential threat. No longer does anyone in medicine or pharmaceuticals underestimate supergerms. A series of sobering reports in medical journals laid bare the extent to which they have spread and wreaked havoc.[5] In 2010, the first year of reliable U.S. statistics, supergerms infected more than two million Americans and killed 23,000. Three years later the Centers for Disease Control and Prevention (CDC) issued an alert that the infection rate was accelerating much faster than epidemiologists had forecast. The president of the Infectious Diseases Society of America labeled CRE "an urgent threat" to America's health care system.[6] As bad as the crisis was in the United States, it was far grimmer in many poor countries where superbugs thrive in unsanitary conditions.[7]

The Nevada doctors understood that hospitals and nursing homes are ground zero for rapacious germs such as CRE. They are the ideal breeding environment for superbugs to infect patients at high risk, those with immune systems weakened by other illnesses or drug therapies. The supergerms also spread easily through breathing machines, IV needles, catheters, even blood pressure cuffs. CRE thrives on everything from light switches, doorknobs, and toilets, as well as the unwashed hands of health care workers.[8]

The typical five-to-seven-day dose of oral antibiotics usually prescribed for bacterial infections has no effect on CRE. Instead, doctors must overwhelm and eliminate all traces of it with a small class of ultra-powerful antibiotics dispensed through an intravenous drip. The Nevada treating physicians went from concern to alarm when additional tests showed the strain of CRE ravaging her body was resistant to all fourteen antibiotics the hospital stocked.

The state's senior epidemiologists dispatched a sample of the bug to CDC headquarters in Atlanta. There, scientists watched with dread as further testing demonstrated the Nevada strain was resistant to an additional twelve antibiotics, including some that had never before failed to stop a superbug.[9] The Nevada doctors were helpless as their patient deteriorated, went into septic shock, and died two weeks to the day after her ER admission.

Public health officials delayed reporting the death of Patient Zero until January 2017. The news of a superbug resistant to every available antibiotic kicked off sensational tabloid coverage with "end of the world" headlines. The resistant superbug overshadowed another pharma-related story that broke that same month. In January, states had begun reporting their drug overdose statistics for the previous year. They confirmed that America's multiyear opioid addiction crisis had worsened. Over 63,000 had died in 2016, a 20 percent spike from the previous year, which itself had been a record. More people died of drugs in 2016 than had in car accidents, gun violence, or AIDS during their peak years.[10] The state of emergency that two dozen governors had declared seemed to make little difference. Their overdose rates were up by double digits.[11] Opioid-based prescription painkillers were involved in two thirds of the deaths.

Addiction did not discriminate between rich and poor, black and white, men and women. It affected big cities—Philadelphia's medical examiner reported a grim record of thirty-five dead in three days—as well as some of the poorest stretches of Appalachia.

Just before the media was transfixed by Patient Zero and the invincible superbug, *The Washington Post* had run the final installment of a series on the opioid crisis. It was about Chillicothe, a historic Ohio town of 21,000 nestled along the Scioto River.[12] Residents used to call it "Mayberry," boasting that it was a postcard for the best of small-town American life. Easy access to prescription opioids changed it. A doctor who had run a local pill mill—where painkillers are dispensed for cash without any questions or exams—had been sentenced to four consecutive life sentences for those "patients" who had died from his reckless overprescribing. Chillicothe's forty drug deaths in 2016 were a record and triple the number of a couple of years earlier.

The city coroner said he dreaded talking "to one more parent who's lost a child." Firefighters, EMS workers, doctors, police, hospital workers, victims' families, all were succumbing to "opiate fatigue." The coroner had almost quit on a day he described as "the Zombie Apocalypse." Chillicothe's police and paramedics had responded to thirteen overdoses. A 911 call from a gas station attendant reported a woman passed out in the driver's seat of an idling car. When the police arrived, they found an infant girl in the backseat. That child was one of seven under the age of ten handed over that day to Child Welfare.

Chillicothe is part of the collateral damage for an industry that not only created the nation's most lethal drug crisis but allowed it to flourish mostly unchecked for twenty years. Its origins are in the addictive drugs that 150 years earlier were the core DNA of the pharmaceutical industry. Some of today's largest drug companies got their start selling then-legal heroin, morphine, cannabis, and cocaine-based medications that returned staggering profits.

Money, however, is only part of the answer. The pharmaceutical industry's relationship with its federal regulators at the FDA alternates between contentious and too cozy. And for sixty years it has prevailed in a bitter battle over whether laboratory discoveries should be rewarded with exclusive patents and long monopolies. Most important, the drug business has turned America into a medicated society. Successive waves over the decades of so-called wonder drugs, some real and some hyped, have resulted in huge profits while also creating tens of millions of dependent patients waiting for the next pill to solve an ever-expanding range of illnesses and disorders.

Big Pharma likes to portray itself as a quasi-public trust focused on curing illnesses and saving lives. Its profits, while large, come at great cost for research and development. Its critics cast pharma as a veritable evil empire in which money trumps health. Wild conspiracy theories have flourished, that the industry has developed and hidden a cancer cure or pushes autism-causing vaccines, all to make more money.

The truth about today's pharmaceutical companies and what truly motivates them is found in part through the history of their origins and growth. Understanding how today's dominant mega-companies developed explains why the creative science that was the industry's early hallmark is under assault.[13] Big Pharma resides at the intersection of public health and free enterprise. Only by knowing its history is it possible to fully appreciate how the battle between noble ambitions and greed is a permanent conflict.

2

THE POISON SQUAD

The American pharmaceutical industry emerged in the mid-nineteenth century in response to an unprecedented surge in demand for antiseptics and painkillers for combat troops. The Mexican-American War that ended in 1848 had taught the United States a painful lesson. Adulterated medications meant that frontline soldiers died needlessly; the failure to treat dysentery, yellow fever, infections, and cholera resulted in 87 percent of the fatalities.[1] Many who survived also suffered unnecessarily since the painkillers sent to treat battlefield wounds were often defective. No American company was then capable of large-scale manufacturing of morphine, the era's most powerful painkiller.

It had only been forty years since a twenty-one-year-old German pharmacist's apprentice had isolated the morphine alkaloid from the opium poppy. He called it Morpheus, after the Greek god of dreams, but his findings were mostly ignored after he published them in a little-read medical journal.[2] It was a decade before a French chemist realized its importance and not until the Roaring Twenties that Heinrich Emanuel Merck sold a standardized dose of morphine at his Engel-Apotheke (Angel Pharmacy) in Darmstadt, Germany. Morphine was inexpensive to produce and it became a key product at several new family-run German companies, including Ernst Christian Friedrich Schering's eponymously named Berlin company and Friedrich Bayer's chemical factory in Wuppertal.[3]

A year after the Mexican-American War, two German American cousins used $2,500 in savings and a $1,000 mortgage to launch Charles Pfizer and Company. It was a chemicals business in a two-story brick building on Brooklyn's Bartlett Street.[4] Their timing was good. Once the Civil War began, Pfizer had trouble keeping up with the demand for morphine.

Pfizer's competition came from Edward Robinson Squibb, who had opened E. R. Squibb & Sons, a pharmaceutical manufacturing plant, also in Brooklyn. Squibb was personally aware of the importance of quality and consistency in drug production. As a wartime naval surgeon he had personally tossed overboard crates of substandard medications sent to the front.[5] A year into the Civil War, pharmacist brothers John and Frank Wyeth opened a Philadelphia pharmacy and drug distributorship. The contract they got to supply medicine to the Union Army was so lucrative that after the war they sold their pharmacy and focused on mass-manufacturing drugs.[6]

Morphine was the most effective painkiller but not the only one. Dr. Samuel Pearce Duffield, chief of Detroit's health department, sold an ether and alcohol solution to Union troops. When he retired in 1871, an ex–copper miner turned investor, Hervey Coke Parke, and the company's twenty-six-year-old salesman, George Solomon Davis, incorporated Parke-Davis.

Eli Lilly, a chemist, missed the opportunity to cash in on the Civil War demand for morphine, but as a Union Army colonel he learned how critical medications were to the war effort. He left the military convinced that his future lay in the eponymously named laboratory that started manufacturing drugs in 1876.[7] Two other American pharmacists, Silas Mainville Burroughs and Henry Solomon Wellcome, also saw opportunity in the drug business. Deciding there was less competition in Britain than the U.S., they launched Burroughs Wellcome in London in 1880. It manufactured everything from cod liver oil to malt preparations to face creams to opiate-based pain compounds.[8]

Those pioneers entered a drug industry in its infancy. The highly addictive nature of their products, coupled with no government oversight and regulation, was good for sales. And they benefited also from the ignorance about what caused illnesses and chronic diseases or how to treat them. It had been only a few decades since French chemist Louis Pasteur had proven with a series of experiments on spoiled meat and sour milk the existence of microbes too small for the human eye to see. The emergence of "germ theory," that invisible microbes might cause disease, was greeted with considerable skepticism in the nineteenth century. Even if true, scientists did not know how to go about countering bacterial pathogens.

It took until 1882 before a German bacteriologist discovered that microorganisms caused tuberculosis; until then it was considered an inheritable illness.[9] In the U.S., cholera was thought to be a disease brought by immigrants, particularly the Irish. (The Immigration Act of 1891 addressed this by requiring a physical exam for all arriving migrants to exclude "all idiots, insane persons, paupers or persons likely to become public charges, [and] persons suffering from a loathsome or dangerous contagious disease.")[10] Before 1900, when an American Army surgeon, Walter Reed, demonstrated that mosquitoes spread yellow fever, it was thought to be passed only by contact with someone infected.[11]

Until 1900 there was no national medical licensing law; in most states anyone could call themselves a "doctor," open a practice, and treat patients.[12] The lack of basic medical knowledge meant there were few boundaries for promoting a drug. That was the case with the first inexpensive but powerful central nervous system stimulant, cocaine. It had been discovered by a German doctoral student whose chemistry dissertation was about how he had isolated the pure alkaloid from coca leaves. He named the alkaloid *cocaine*—from the Latin *ina*, *from*; it simply means *from coca.* (That student later went on to develop World War I's deadliest chemical warfare agent, mustard gas.)[13]

Merck, one of the first firms to concentrate on cocaine, touted it in products for everything from a numbing anesthetic to a cure for indigestion and hemorrhoids, even as an aid in eye surgery (it reduced bleeding by tightening blood vessels).[14] * [15] Cocaine was the officially sanctioned remedy of the United States Hay Fever Association.[16] The U.S. surgeon general said cocaine was effective for treating depression. Tobacconists sold cigars laced with 225 mg of cocaine for "soothing nerves," while dentists peddled cocaine-infused lozenges for toothaches. Asthma sufferers bought inhalants that were pure cocaine and instructed to "use them as needed."[17] A gram of pure cocaine cost on average 25 cents at any druggist.[18] The largest mail order catalog of the era, Sears & Roebuck, sold a hypodermic syringe—a Scottish doctor had invented it only a few decades earlier—and a small amount of cocaine for $1.50.[19]

The boom in cocaine-based remedies meant that over a two-year

---

* Many prominent public figures—Sigmund Freud, Pope Leo XIII, Robert Louis Stevenson, Queen Victoria, to name a few—waxed enthusiastic about the energy and fleeting euphoria cocaine produced. Its recreational use surged in the second half of the nineteenth century.

span Merck went from producing less than a pound of cocaine annually to more than 180,000 pounds a year.[20] Parke-Davis chemists patented a refined process that increased the drug's purity and extended its shelf life. It introduced coca cheroots, coca-leaf cigarettes, and an alcohol-and-cocaine-mixed syrup, all under the motto *Medicamenta Vera* (True Medicine).[21] Squibb manufactured and sold one of the strongest cocaine concentrations dissolved in a clear liquid base and used as a tincture. In less than a decade, cocaine became one of America's five top selling drugs.

Simply because cocaine had become popular did not mean U.S. pharma companies had lost their enthusiasm for opiates. Merck boasted of the purity of its powdered morphine and one of its most popular drugs was opium-laced cough lozenges.[22] Squibb and Pfizer sold nearly a dozen variations of opium tinctures.[23]

Drug firms such as Merck, Squibb, Pfizer, and others competed against each other. However, their stiffest competition came from so-called patent medicines, some fifty thousand homemade remedies marketed as miracle cures.[24] They were not actually patented (the U.S. did not start issuing chemical patents until 1925).[25]

Since there was no legal requirement that drugs substantiate any purported benefit—like today's supplement industry or legal cannabis markets, in which claims are unchecked—shameless pitches played on people's worst fears and ignorance. Compounding the problem was that there were no controls over ingredients, purity, or consistent dosing. While the nostrum makers used American copyright laws to protect their names, shapes of their bottles, and even the label designs, each kept their formulas secret. There was no requirement in the United States for a prescription for any medication. Nor was it necessary to see a doctor to get a drug.[26]

The best-selling nostrum companies bombarded consumers with a deluge of salacious ads in newspapers and magazines touting phenomenal healing powers.[27] Manufacturers secretly paid for breathless testimonials and advertised their "miracle elixirs" and tonics on tens of thousands of roadside billboards, posters strung along country fences, even makeshift yard signs.[28]

The owners of the most popular patent medicines earned huge personal fortunes. German immigrant William Radam became rich from his proprietary blend dubbed "Microbe Killer," which he claimed to "Cure ALL Diseases." The pink liquid was sulfuric acid diluted with red wine and returned a profit of 6,000 percent on each bottle.[29] Equally successful was a Quaker abolitionist, Lydia Pinkham, whose remedy of ground herbs and alcohol was made in her cellar kitchen in Lynn, Massachusetts, and marketed as a wonder remedy for women."[30] Dr. Jacob Hostetter's best-selling home-brewed remedy, "Hostetter's Celebrated Stomach Bitters," took advantage of the false but widespread belief that whiskey killed bacteria.[31] It was a market vegetable extract in 94-proof whiskey that promised a thorough detox as well as protection or cure against dozens of illnesses.[32] A Connecticut street peddler and former Texas farm hand used fire eaters and sharpshooter contests at traveling road shows to sell tens of thousands of "Indian Sagwa" to "purify the blood." It was moonshine mixed with common garden herbs for flavoring.[33]

Parents were particularly susceptible to nostrum pitches since 20 percent of all children did not survive to age five.[34] The company behind the top selling "Kopp's Baby Friend—*the King of Baby Soothers*"—checked daily newspapers for birth announcements and sent free samples to new mothers. Its secret formula was a solution of one-third pure opium, and over time it was responsible for dozens of lethal infant overdoses.[35]

Most pharmacists and doctors denigrated patent elixirs as the province of snake oil salesmen and traveling medicine shows. Trade publications such as *Druggists' Circular* exposed some of the most dangerous remedies. However, with a tiny circulation to medical professionals, those publications did nothing to slow the demand of enthusiastic lay consumers.[36] And despite the widespread scorn of many physicians and druggists, the money to be made was too tempting to a few who stocked top selling nostrums and marked up the price.[37] Crowded and filthy slums that were by-products of fast-growing cities in the late nineteenth century had become breeding grounds for a succession of epidemics, from smallpox, tuberculosis, typhus, and yellow fever to cholera. Each resulted in a deluge of profitable new nostrums, all promising instant cures.

In 1890, members of the American Pharmaceutical Association published the first *United States Pharmacopeia* and the *National Formulary* (*USP/NF*). Advances in chemical testing and machine manufacturing had made it possible for American pharmaceutical firms to produce drugs of improved purity and generally reliable quality.[38] The *USP/NF* was a somewhat rudimentary list of about two hundred "ethical pharmaceuticals" intended to be the gold standard for doctors and pharmacists.[39] * [40] The list was an easy guide for those wanting to avoid useless nostrums.[41]

Traditional pharmaceutical companies looked with disdain on their patent competitors. Still, the general lack of knowledge about the medicines they sold meant that ethical drugs could also sometimes be disasters. There was no better example than Heroin, a trademarked drug developed by Germany's Bayer. In 1898, the same Bayer research team credited with isolating salicylic acid (trademarked as Aspirin) added two acetyl groups to the morphine molecule and produced an opiate ten times as powerful. Bayer's director of pharmacology insisted the company not select "too complicated a name" so it chose the German *heroisch*, or "heroic."[42] Heroin went on sale in America in 1900 and was immediately listed on the *USP/NF.* Anyone over the age of eighteen could buy it. Bayer claimed it was much better at alleviating pain than morphine. It was ten times more effective for the relief of coughs and colds than codeine, contended Bayer, with only a tenth of codeine's toxic side effects.[43] The company also promoted it for treating epilepsy, stomach cancer, multiple sclerosis, asthma, and schizophrenia. Bayer's advertisements claimed it safe for children. It even sold it as a fast cure for morphine addiction, which by then was becoming a problem.[44]

Some states that had passed laws to cover adulterated foods also addressed drugs, but only with generic provisions that barred nostrum makers from selling lethal poisons.[45] The result was a hodgepodge of rules that were confusing, sometimes contradictory, and seldom enforced. It was impossible to address the booming interstate traffic without a federal law. Through the 1890s, Congress failed to pass a series of regulatory bills to empower federal oversight of both food and drugs.[46] The driving force behind the movement for a national law was a chemist and physician, Harvey Washington Wiley. He was the head of the Department of Agriculture's Division of Chemistry (a predecessor agency to the Food and Drug Administration).[47] Politicians and

* The term "ethical pharmaceuticals" made them sound as if they were more trustworthy medications than nostrums. The term later came to mean those not advertised to the public, a concept the American Medical Association pushed since it considered that ads directed to the public encouraged self-treatment and threatened the authority of doctors. Although there was no requirement yet for drug prescriptions, the AMA hoped that patients might seek the advice of physicians for selecting the right ethical drug.

industry lobbyists mostly ignored his zealous appeals to address the unreported dangers of adulterated food. They dismissed him as an inexperienced idealist and felt he was a powerless bureaucrat in an obscure government agency.

Wiley had, however, often been underestimated by others and repeatedly defied expectations. He was the deeply religious son of a self-educated Indiana farmer, Preston Wiley, who was also an evangelical preacher for a revivalist nineteenth-century Christian sect. The senior Wiley was the headmaster at the tiny town's single-room school.[48] His mother, Lucinda, worked the farm and tended to her seven children, all of whom she had given birth to on the dirt floor of the family's two-room log cabin (they had no running water, heater, or working toilet).[49] Second-generation Americans of Irish and Scottish ancestry, his parents worked long days on farmland outside Kent, a town of several hundred poor whites along the Kentucky border. It was a bare-bones, tough existence that had pushed many of Wiley's neighbors to the edge of desperation.[50]

Wiley grew up in a household where corporal punishment was meted out with a wooden rod for indulging in "devices of the devil," such as playing with other kids, singing, dancing, or celebrating holidays.[51] His parents expected him to take over the family farm when he turned eighteen. Instead, he surprised them by passing his college exams and even earning a scholarship. At twenty-six he received his medical degree and graduated near the top of his class at Indiana Medical College. When he moved east to study chemistry at Harvard he was captivated by the emerging science about diet and nutrition and a related study of safety concerns regarding food additives and preservatives.[52] In an era before refrigeration, as more food was shipped long distances from processing plants, producers constantly tested new preservatives. The food industry hired chemists to extend the transport and shelf life of perishable goods and to find chemicals that removed unpleasant odors and enhanced the color of food (red lead for beef, lead chromate for mustard, arsenic for green vegetables). Few scientists were studying the possible dangers in the new methods.[53]

Wiley had a reputation as a smart advocate for pure food. In a series of articles for *Popular Science Monthly* he highlighted potential risks in the U.S. food chain.[54] When he became the chief at the Division of Chemistry in 1883, the department had only six employees and a paltry budget of $40,000.[55] It seemed an unlikely place from which to launch a successful campaign for a pure food law or to wield influence to tame the unregulated pharma industry.

What the Division of Chemistry lacked in manpower and money, Wiley made up for with a talent for generating public attention for his campaign. He promoted his agenda in articles and testimony before congressional committees. Wiley traveled the country to dozens of women's clubs and social organizations delivering fiery speeches warning about the dangers of adulterated food.[56] At those events, Wiley seemed more an itinerant preacher than a scientist. The politicians and lobbyists who had dismissed him when he arrived in D.C. realized that his dramatic flair was a good complement to the quest of what he called "extensive and exhaustive investigations of adulterations and misbranding of foods."[57]

It was four years before Wiley and the Division of Chemistry published the first volume of a series of reports titled "Foods and Food Adulterants." The initial one focused on health risks to the nation's dairy products.[58] Half the milk samples tested had been thinned with water and chalk and were swarming with bacteria. Much of the butter sold contained no dairy at all. Over the next five years, Wiley and his small team of chemists issued nine more reports.[59] Among their findings was that nearly 90 percent of all ground coffee was adulterated, usually cut with sawdust and even dirt. "Embalmed beef" was sold in tin cans, made in part from lead, and infused with so many powerful preservative chemicals that it smelled like formaldehyde. There was a fury when children died in Nebraska and Indiana of contaminated milk. Some dairies used formaldehyde to mask the odor of sour milk and had sold it to orphanages.[60]

Wiley's reports—the first intensive federal investigation into potential health risks in the food supply—were a milestone. Flattering press coverage added to his reputation as an incorruptible champion for the common good.[61] *The Washington Times* was typical: "When he took up the gauntlet thrown down by a crowd of greedy parasites who were making huge fortunes by selling to the public foods not what they seemed, he determined to quash their nefarious practices."[62] The media attention cemented Wiley's public persona as "the pure food man," a lone government crusader arrayed against vast and powerful special interests intent on putting profits above safety.[63] He realized his popularity presented an opportunity to expand his influence. During his tenure, the secretary of agriculture upgraded his division to a bureau, a designation that imbued it with more autonomy. It grew from six to more than six hundred employees and its budget increased twenty-fold. The newly christened Bureau of Chemistry had its own building by 1902, and Wiley ran it as his personal fiefdom.[64]

That same year he convinced Congress to appropriate $5,000 to study potential health risks in common food preservatives and dyes.[65] Determined that the results would not get buried into some little-read official report that gathered dust on the back shelves of his Bureau of Chemistry, he planned a showstopper of a study. Relying on what he cited as inspiration from the biblical book of Daniel, Wiley decided to experiment not on animals but on humans.[66] He created a twelve-man "Hygienic Table Trial." Its volunteers, including a scientist, a former high school captain of a cadet regiment, and a Yale sprinter, were either employees from the Bureau of Chemistry or Georgetown Medical College students attracted by free room and board.[67] Before Wiley approved each, staffers screened them for good moral character, little or no alcohol use, and abstinence from medicines. "I wanted young, robust fellows, with maximum resistance to deleterious effects of adulterated food," he later noted.[68] The recruits promised to stay at least a year and waived all rights to sue the government if the trial proved harmful or deadly.

Wiley built a kitchen and dining room in the Bureau of Chemistry's basement. He bought all the food and drinks and served three meals daily for the twelve volunteers, all of whom dressed in formal attire for dinner. A chef, who boasted he had been the personal cook for the queen of Bavaria, prepared meals that included steadily increasing doses of preservatives and coloring agents that Wiley suspected as toxic.[69]

Wiley recorded the temperature and pulse of every man before each meal. He regularly checked their weight and collected urine and stool samples. He allowed some journalists from popular newspapers and magazines to observe the experiment. The ensuing coverage was sensational: "Young men of perfect physique and health" who were "martyrs of science," willingly ate potentially deadly food served by "a bespectacled scientist." The volunteers adopted the motto, "Only the Brave Dare Eat This Fare." A *Washington Post* reporter gave the project a name that stuck: *The Poison Squad*.[70] The element of danger totally captivated the public. Wiley worried that the popular frenzy might predispose the scientific community to dismiss the seriousness of his tests.

The Poison Squad, however, was far more than a hit turn-of-the-century reality show. The startling results over several years confirmed Wiley's worst fears about hidden dangers in America's food supply. Intensifying ailments afflicted his volunteers.[71] Preservatives such as borax and salicylic acid caused headaches and digestive problems. Formaldehyde that prolonged the life of dairy products caused weight loss, insomnia, and scarred kidneys. Benzoate caused severe heartburn and damaged blood vessels. Copper sulfate that enhanced the color of canned vegetables caused vomiting and liver damage.[72] Sulfites, the by-products of many preservatives used in wine, molasses, and cured meats, made the volunteers sick with dizziness and splitting headaches. Starting in 1904, Wiley released the first of five reports titled "Influence of Food Preservatives and Artificial Colors on Digestion and Health." In total, it was a damning one-thousand-page indictment.[73]

Wiley began winding down his audacious public spectacle in 1905 following the death of a weakened volunteer from tuberculosis. By then, however, the Poison Squad had earned an almost mythic place in American medical history. And Wiley knew it had reenergized his quest for a federal pure food law.

3

ENTER THE FEDS

Entrenched and well-connected food industry lobbyists did not sit idly while Wiley built his case for federal intervention. The most powerful ones represented canners, who relied on preservatives, and the profitable so-called rectified whiskey trade, in which distillers added coloring and flavor agents to cheap, impure alcohol and sold it as whiskey. Wiley had made rectifiers his number one target, charging that 90 percent of the country's whiskey was fake. Lobbyists argued that everything they added to liquor was harmless and that any federal regulation would be anti-American, decimate business, and force thousands out of work. Wiley, they argued, had no real-world experience in administering food laws and had cherry-picked evidence to draw inflammatory and misleading conclusions.[1] They also contended that Congress did not intend drinks and liquor to be covered by a law addressing *food*.

Wiley realized that Congress was unlikely to embrace any proposal that was too hard on the rectifiers. Between half to two thirds of all federal income came from a tax on alcohol; even fake whiskey makers paid it.[2]

Some consumer advocates were disappointed that the federal oversight and regulatory law Wiley envisioned was almost entirely about food and failed to address the dangers of pharmaceuticals. In fact, while he had assigned a small number of researchers in his Bureau of Chemistry to collect evidence of "advertising of fraudulent [patent] remedies," he favored excluding all patent drugs from any statute.[3] The one proposal he supported was more symbolic than substantive, an ambiguous provision to more efficiently inspect the two hundred or so *USP/NF* drugs.[4]

His reluctance surprised colleagues, some of whom knew that Wiley privately condemned patent medications as "the most vicious of the whole circus of medical frauds . . . which preyed on incurables."[5] A few friends knew about a childhood incident that helped form Wiley's opinion of nostrums. He fell ill with malaria when he was eleven, the result of a mosquito infestation in the southern Indiana lowlands. The Wileys were too poor to afford Abram's Pill, a proprietary "miracle cure" that promised "instant remedy" for malaria's high fever and bone-rattling chills. It turned out the Wileys were fortunate. Some neighbors died not from malaria but instead from Abram's Pill. Years later Wiley discovered the cure's main ingredient was arsenic.[6]

Why was he unwilling to take the lead when it came to a public health issue that matched so well with his expertise and interest in medicine and chemistry? The answer is in Wiley's personal letters and papers: his cold political calculus was that championing drug regulation reduced the chances of convincing Congress to pass a straightforward pure food law. Wiley thought he lacked the political capital to tackle two powerful lobbies simultaneously. He feared that adding drug oversight into the mix would be too complicated and doom any proposed legislation.[7]

However, in 1905, the year he started dismantling the Poison Squad, Wiley abruptly reversed himself. *Collier's* had begun publishing a blistering ten-part exposé of the dangers of bogus patent medications hawked as cure-all elixirs.[8] The opening paragraph of the first article set the tone: "Gullible America will spend this year some seventy-five million dollars in purchasing patent medicines. In consideration of this sum it will swallow huge quantities of alcohol, an appalling amount of opiates and narcotics, a wide assortment of varied drugs ranging from powerful and dangerous heart depressants to insidious liver stimulants; and far in excess of all other ingredients, undiluted fraud."[9]

The *Collier's* series sparked a fury over patent drugs. It shamed the American Medical Association to stop accepting nostrum advertisements in its journal, *JAMA*. It had been running lucrative patent drug ads while ostensibly debating the ethics of doing so.[10] In the wake of the *Collier's* publication it tried playing catch-up by reprinting the investigative series as an inexpensive booklet and distributing half a million copies.[11]

Wiley saw an unexpected opportunity in the great hue and cry. More than a dozen pure food bills had stalled in five previous Congresses. Maybe, he calculated, if he included drugs as part of any proposed law, the outrage over nostrums might help break the political stalemate. Politicians knew the *Collier's* series had struck a public nerve. Failure to act might provoke a voter backlash.[12]

To the distress of the nostrum makers, Wiley soon suggested the name of the proposed statute be changed from the Pure Food Act to the Pure Food and Drug Act.[13]

That proposal thrilled health advocates. By 1905, as Wiley drafted the bill that would be submitted to Congress, a plentiful and cheap supply of unregulated Heroin and cocaine had resulted in what he called the "tragic numbers": an estimated addiction rate as high as 2 percent of the population, upward of 1.5 million addicts.[14]

In one draft of the law, Wiley defined drugs as "any substance intended to be used for the cure, mitigation, or prevention of disease."[15] That was broad enough to encompass both *USP/NF* and patent drugs. He also proposed that patent remedies disclose all ingredients on their labels. As for any that included cocaine or alcohol—both of which he personally thought more dangerous than Heroin or opium—they should be dispensed only with a doctor's prescription.[16]

Those revisions sent a chill through the drug industry. At the turn of the century it was not a business dominated by a handful of mega-companies. Instead, there were hundreds of firms, ranging from established ones to many questionable operations that thrived selling nostrums. All disliked the idea of federal oversight. Conventional pharma firms hoped any statute might only go so far as to eliminate patent quackery. The influential Proprietary Medicine Manufacturers and Dealers Association of America, a consortium mostly of wealthy patent medicine businessmen, feared the law would target them.[17] Many of them had never made a nostrum but were naturally gifted promoters who wanted no restrictions on how they marketed their products to consumers.[18]

One strategy to fight the proposed law was to make Wiley himself the issue, casting him as a well-intentioned chemist who had exceeded his expertise and knowledge. There was a little-known counter-narrative to Wiley's selfless do-gooder image. The same considerable ambition that made it possible for him to attract a wide public following had spawned many bitter enemies.[19] Would Congress reject his statute if he was marked as someone who had cunningly manipulated his interests in food purity only to satisfy a lust for personal fame? The Proprietary Association knew Wiley had hired press agents to bolster his reputation for tirelessly battling corrupt businessmen to expose fraudulent labeling and fake products.[20] It also had uncovered evidence that he might have sometimes used his bureau's growing influence to benefit a handful of companies he favored.[21]

After a heated debate, however, the Proprietary Association decided Wiley was personally off limits. There was not enough evidence to make the case against him as a power-obsessed chameleon. The consensus was that going after him was too risky.

The Proprietary Association's final strategy was simple but inspired. Under the guise of public safety, it focused on deflecting the spotlight away from all patent drugs to only a handful of the most dangerous homemade nostrums.[22] Industries that had become dependent on patent remedies for revenue liked the idea that only a few outlier drugs were the problem. Dispensing physicians and pharmacists as well as wholesale suppliers of the ingredients joined the effort. Both the National Associations of Wholesale and Retail Druggists soon came aboard.[23]

The biggest indirect beneficiaries were the newspapers in which patent drugmakers advertised.[24] At the turn of the century, patent remedies brought in $50 million annually to more than four thousand papers.[25] It was half of all the income for newspapers, money that Wiley dubbed "blood money."[26] The newspapers dispatched a small army of lobbyists with the same message to Washington: don't damage a good industry because of the bad actions of a few. All the while, the Proprietary Association reminded congressional leaders of the federal 4 percent tax on the retail price of all patent drugs; any legislation that led to a reduction in the number of drugs sold would also reduce what had become a steady source of government revenue.[27]

The lobbying effort was relentless. Wiley rewrote the draft repeatedly to drum up congressional support. At times, he confided to a friend, he was so worried that lobbyists might kill the bill that he often knelt inside the closet of his office and prayed.[28]

Once the bill got to congressional committees, drug lobbyists redoubled their efforts. It was not long before most of the key revisions benefited the pharma industry. One amendment eliminated the requirement for prescriptions for cocaine and alcohol-based drugs.[29] Another diluted the language to punish drugmakers by freeing them of any responsibility so long as they could demonstrate their promotional claims were "made in good faith." Wiley had wanted a listing of all ingredients on every label but another change required they only had to show any of sixty "poisons." That was weakened further to require revealing just eleven ingredients deemed addictive or dangerous, including cocaine, opiates such as morphine, opium, and Heroin, alcohol, chloroform, and cannabis.[30] Even those judged "poisonous" were required only if they exceeded an arbitrary legal minimum.[31] Wiley fretted that allowing those drugs to be used without notice and at any dosage threatened to "simply make the bill a joke."[32]

The acrimonious debate continued for months. In early June, on the heels of the *Collier's* series, Wiley got some unexpected help in persuading last-minute holdouts in Congress. A socialist weekly ran a serialization of Upton Sinclair's novel *The Jungle*.[33] Sinclair wrote about the plight of poor immigrant workers in the U.S. He hoped his book might spark a revolt against capitalism. "The 'Uncle Tom's Cabin' of wage slavery!" wrote his friend and fellow socialist Jack London. "What 'Uncle Tom's Cabin' did for black slaves, 'The Jungle' has a large chance to do for the wage slaves of today."[34] Sinclair's political message was overshadowed, however, by the novel's fifteen stomach-wrenching pages about filthy conditions in Chicago's stockyards and meatpacking industry.[35] A revolted public read of putrefied meat deliberately mislabeled and sold. Worse was the disclosure that ground meat sometimes contained poisoned rats or dismembered body parts from accidents among the assembly line workers.[36] The outrage that followed that serialization compelled Congress to cobble together and approve the Meat Inspection Act. The Pure Food and Drug Act, informally known as the "Wiley Act," passed with it.[37] President Theodore Roosevelt signed both into law on June 30, 1906.[38]

The thrust of the new law, hailed as a milestone in consumer safety legislation, was "truth in labeling." That seemed straightforward since food and drug companies were not previously required to list *any* ingredients. And the landmark legislation put in place some long-overdue and commonsense regulations against misbranded and adulterated foods and drugs.[39]

The widespread enthusiasm might have been tempered if it had been known how the pharma lobby had weakened the provisions that applied to the drug industry. While the Pure Food and Drug Act appeared to deliver radical reform, it lacked the substance to enforce its hyperbolic promise. There were critical exceptions to universal truth in labeling. "The bill is not as good as we should like it," Wiley privately admitted to one colleague.[40] A last-minute amendment even permitted the sales of *USP/NF* medications that failed to meet the quality, strength, and purity claims on their labels.[41] Patent drug makers did not have to disclose any ingredients they did not tout in their marketing. The law's most devastating omission was its failure to address the fantastic but improbable therapeutic claims of nostrums. Wiley and other consumer advocates hoped the courts might liberally interpret the law's ban on "false labeling" to apply to unproven healing and curative claims. In *United States v. Johnson* in 1911, the Supreme Court dashed that by ruling that the bar on dishonest labeling did *not* cover therapeutic claims (the court upheld the right of a physician to sell six alcohol and herbal remedies as a cure for cancer).[42] * [43]

America's most popular patented medicines made minor changes to their labels and then trumpeted their compliance with the new law. Vin Mariani, a top selling nostrum marketed for maintaining "overall good health, energy and vitality," was typical. It was a French Bordeaux with 7.2 mg of pure cocaine per ounce. Vin Mariani, a favorite of Pope Leo XIII, claimed to have "over 7,000 written endorsements from prominent physicians in Europe and America." In the wake of the Pure Food and Drug Act it listed cocaine on its label but made no changes about the remedy's unproven curative powers.[44] Hundreds of other nostrum makers who featured cocaine or opium as primary ingredients did the same. Some even boasted that they reduced the concentration of opiates or alcohol in their nostrums, but those cuts were mostly negligible.[45] A few narrowed the breadth of what they promised. Hazeltine & Co. changed the tagline for its popular Piso's syrup—a solution of alcohol, cannabis, and chloroform—from "Cure for Consumption" to the more generic "Remedy for Coughs and Colds."[46]

Within a year of the law's passage, most nostrum makers included on their label, "Guaranteed under the Pure Food and Drug Act."[47] They hoped the public would conclude that tagline meant the drugs were not dangerous.[48]

---

* Dr. A. O. Johnson of Kansas City marketed Dr. Johnson's Mild Combination Treatment for Cancer. Every sale included a 125-page book of questionable testimonials from "cured patients." Congress addressed this statutory shortcoming in 1912, but the drug lobby weakened the final language to ban therapeutic claims that were "false and fraudulent." That meant enforcement actions had to establish "intent to defraud," a standard that proved nearly impossible as drug companies claimed they believed the claims to be accurate.

Although both the nostrum industry and traditional pharma had won many concessions in the law, it still empowered the Bureau of Chemistry with exclusive enforcement powers. Some wondered whether Wiley would push the limits of the law and tie up pharma firms in litigation. They did not know that Wiley had decided to concentrate on "battles attracting the attention of the whole nation." He wanted to target companies with which every American was familiar. Fortunately for pharma firms, none were that prominent. Although Bayer was a household name in Germany, it had not achieved that status yet in America. As a result, Wiley showed no interest in tackling its Heroin brand. A popular drug manual published by Squibb noted in 1903 that "Heroin has lost none of its prominence" and cited a small study in which it had demonstrated "decided advantages" in treating bronchial infections and without a "tendency to form a Heroin habit."[49] (It took sixteen years before the government required a prescription for Heroin and another decade before it placed restrictions on its sale. By then the country had added an additional quarter million addicts.) Wiley did not even open an investigation when Bayer announced its discovery of a new class of drugs, barbiturates. Potent and addictive sedatives, its first product, phenobarbital, went on sale under the brand name Luminal in 1908 without prescription.[50]

Moody's, the financial rating firm, reaffirmed to Wiley that he was right in judging the drug business too insignificant to generate daily headlines. When Moody's started publishing industry analyses in the U.S. in 1909, pharmaceuticals was so small it was not listed as a separate category. It took another twenty years before Moody's created one, ranking drug firms as the sixteenth most profitable American industry. There were hundreds of small companies vying for a piece of the nascent trade, none with more than 3 percent of the market.

Only 135 of the first 1,000 enforcement actions under the Pure Food and Drug Act were against drugmakers.[51] Most involved technical labeling infractions resulting in fines of less than $50.[52]

Wiley did bring some landmark actions. They involved corn syrup, saccharin, benzoate of soda, aluminum baking powders, and a multiyear battle over rectified versus pure whiskey[53] * [54] He declared caffeine

* Wiley's Boy Scout image was sullied years later when it was disclosed that he had not only accepted favors and gifts from some food industry giants, but that they influenced his decisions about whether to bring enforcement actions. A sugar industry lobbying

public enemy #1 and made Coca-Cola his highest-profile target. As Wiley correctly forecast, his campaign demonizing caffeine—which he claimed was more dangerous than strychnine—galvanized public attention. It was front-page news when he charged that Coca-Cola was a public health hazard that violated the law since it did not list caffeine as an ingredient. Wiley's "literal-mindedness about labels" was evident when he contended the company duped consumers by calling itself Coca-Cola despite having no cocaine—it had been removed entirely in 1904—and only a trace of cola.[55]

Wiley's animus against caffeine was sincere. His fundamentalist Christian parents had raised him to believe it was "a devil's stimulant."*[56] He was convinced caffeine caused mental defects and motor deficits as serious as alcohol and that it was "habit-forming and nerve-racking." Damning caffeine as "the most common drug in the country," he warned that "coffee drunkenness is a commoner failing than the whiskey habit. . . . This country is full of tea and coffee drunkards." He warned Congress that caffeine was toxic and in public speeches sounded the alarm: "I would not give my child coffee or tea any more than I would give him poison."[57]

With Wiley focused an caffeine, Congress acted on its own regard in 1909. It passed the first ever federal drug prohibition statute, the Opium Exclusion Act.[58] That targeted a smokable variety of opium favored by Chinese immigrants, whom Senate majority leader Henry Cabot Lodge had described as "uncivilized elements in America." The law did not address the opium used in patent medicines or traditional pharma drugs.[59] Its unintended consequence was that Chinese criminal gangs took control of the opium trade in San Francisco's and Los Angeles's Chinatowns, resulting in higher prices and a jump in crime.[60] Meanwhile, the American public interpreted the passivity of Harvey Wiley, who was admired for his zealous crusading, as evidence that

---

group employed his nephew in a sweetheart deal. He only moved against benzoate of soda after his benefactors at H. J. Heinz stopped using it; critics said he had conspired with Heinz to allow them to capture the catsup market. In one instance, he even testified in an adulterated coffee case on behalf of a businessman who had doled out favors to him and some of his family.

* Prohibition of caffeine remains a tenet for some Christian denominations. The Mormon-owned Brigham University finally yielded in September 2017 to appeals by non-Mormon students and permitted the sale of caffeinated soda.

drugs for sale had somehow passed safety and efficacy criteria under the Pure Food and Drug Act.

The Coca-Cola trial, *United States v. Forty Barrels and Twenty Kegs of Coca Cola*, in 1911, was the culmination of Wiley's career.[61] Prosecutors held the trial in Chattanooga, where Coca-Cola had a large bottling plant. The government's case cast Coca-Cola as a dangerous, addictive drink. Its caffeine stimulation was so well known, testified a Department of Agriculture chemist, that many consumers called it by the nicknames "coke" or "dope."[62] (Coca-Cola did not take a trademark on Coke until 1942.) In its defense, Coca-Cola called a series of leading chemists and research scientists who contended that the government had overstated the danger of caffeine, and in any case, the amount of caffeine in the soda was only a third of what was in an equivalent cup of coffee or tea.

Three weeks into the trial, Coca-Cola made a motion to dismiss the case. It argued that since caffeine had replaced coca-leaf extract in the soda recipe a year before the enactment of the Pure Food and Drug Act, it was not an added ingredient that qualified as an "adulterant or additive." Therefore the law did not apply. The trial judge stunned Wiley and the Justice Department by agreeing with Coca-Cola and dismissed the government's case.[63] It was a body blow the Supreme Court ultimately upheld.

Wiley's Bureau of Chemistry had committed enormous resources to the prosecution. By casting himself as the public face of the government's case he had put his reputation at risk. An internal federal investigation revealed that Wiley had so badly wanted to win that he had engineered an annual consulting arrangement for $1,600 with a Columbia professor who was the government's star trial expert about the evils of caffeine. Without that deal, the professor had been reluctant to agree to testify since the government paid its experts only $9 a day. Although Wiley had broken no laws with the consulting work-around, and his bosses had approved it, it looked bad after the case had imploded.[64]

After twenty-nine years at the Bureau of Chemistry, the combative and toxic environment had worn Wiley down. He resigned in 1912 and accepted a job at *Good Housekeeping* magazine for $10,000, double his government salary. As their director of foods, sanitation, and health, he still wielded influence with his monthly column about nutrition and food safety that reached 400,000 subscribers. The magazine built a modern testing lab for Wiley and initiated the Good Housekeeping Seal of Approval for products.[65]

Although Wiley had justifiably earned a place in history as the father of the Pure Food and Drug Act, he had little to boast about when it came to drugs. Business boomed for the traditional *USP/NF* medications. Worse was that sales of nostrums soared by 60 percent in a decade, for the first time crossing $100 million annually.[66] When Wiley later wrote his memoir, his failures were evident by his omissions. In 325 pages he attacked private lobbyists and government bureaucrats for diluting his landmark statute. He regaled his readers with insider details about his battles against saccharin manufacturers and whiskey rectifiers. He even re-litigated the Coca-Cola case. In Wiley's recounting of history, he was always right but somehow the government had repeatedly failed to do what was right.[67] But he never mentioned cocaine or heroin and only referred to patent drugs a single time—to claim that internal power struggles at the Bureau of Agriculture had "made it impossible to bring any cases."[68]

As Wiley stepped off the national stage, there was no doubt that pharma had emerged intact from the country's first landmark legislative effort at drug oversight. Its successful lobbying campaign had eviscerated much of the Pure Food and Drug Act. It would serve as a template for pharma battles with the government in the decades ahead.

4

THE WONDER DRUG

The federal government did put an end to patent medicines. It was not, however, the result of new laws or enforcement directed at nostrums. Instead the patent industry was decimated as the indirect result of historic legislation that outlawed its core ingredients, narcotics and alcohol. The first blow was the 1914 Harrison Narcotics Tax Act. The second was the Eighteenth Amendment to the U.S. Constitution five years later that kicked off thirteen years of alcohol prohibition.[1]

The Harrison Act was Congress's response to worldwide fears about skyrocketing demand for opiate-based painkillers. World War I had caused a seismic shift inside the pharmaceutical industry. The outbreak of hostilities in Europe in July 1914 led to the suspension of the International Opium Convention treaty, a sweeping anti-narcotics agreement signed a couple of years earlier by a dozen countries at The Hague.[2] Knowing that war was good for business and free of government regulation, drug firms ratcheted morphine production to record levels. Some, like Britain's Whiffen & Sons, doubled their annual output to twenty tons, much of it leaking to the black market. Overproduction in Swiss, Dutch, and German pharmaceutical companies also fed illegal syndicates.

Congress passed the Harrison Act only six months after the war started. It prohibited most distribution and use of cocaine as well as much of the importation of opiates. Bayer's lobbying, however, earned Heroin an exemption. The law created a national registry to track every person and company that dealt in opiate- or cocaine-based drugs. The AMA and other medical groups successfully petitioned to exclude physicians and hospitals that dispensed narcotic painkillers, so long as the drugs were not given to addicts (before the Supreme Court struck down that provision a decade later, 25,000 doctors were charged with violating the narcotics ban and 3,000 went to jail).[3]

The law sanctioned one class of opiate manufacturer and distributor: pharmaceutical companies. The only authorized purveyors were the manufacturers of drugs listed on the *USP/NF*. It was criminal for anyone else to import, make, or sell the same drugs.[4] The drafters of the Harrison Act mistakenly thought that making narcotics legal under the exclusive control of the medical/pharma industries would reduce the country's huge hunger for narcotics.

The underlying problem was the appetite pharmaceutical firms had developed for the staggering profits from their highly addictive products. It was an international malaise. When opiate production declined after World War I, drug companies turned to cocaine. French pharma firms conspired to divert their cocaine overproduction to drug traffickers for enormous profits. In Switzerland, one of the few countries to have opposed all drug treaties, a postwar report concluded the country's pharmaceutical industry had produced "100 times more [cocaine] than was required for [domestic] medical and scientific purposes." Anyone who simply attested to being a physician could buy ten kilos of cocaine from Swiss drug firms. Compounding the problem was that Switzerland was the only nation without any drug export controls. In Germany, Bayer, Merck, and competitors such as Hoechst AG had trouble keeping up with demand for cheap kilos of 99 percent pure cocaine.[5]

The situation was little different in the United States where narcotics provided upward of half all pharmaceutical profits. Barred by the Harrison Act from competing with the sanctioned pharma companies, and forbidden by Prohibition to use alcohol, most nostrum makers had finally given up. Philadelphia-based Smith, Kline and French, one of the most successful mail order companies, abandoned 5,800 of its 6,000 medications. It had enough left in its Eskay line of baby nutrition and food products to survive.[6] Meanwhile, for traditional drug companies, sales had increased since the demise of the patent remedy industry.

Press reports of addiction and overdoses with Heroin had spurred some companies to search for a less addictive substitute. In 1916, two German chemists had discovered Oxycodone, a synthetic opioid that was chemically similar to Heroin. They thought it was a "gentler codeine."[7] Four years later, two different German researchers developed hydrocodone, a semisynthetic opiate derived from codeine. The scientists believed both drugs matched Heroin's therapeutic benefits without the downside of addiction.

It was difficult, though, to wean the industry off its narcotics reliance since there were few other types of drugs to drive the market. "You could count the basic medications on the fingers of your two hands," noted a later president of Merck.[8] Most pharma companies were simply manufacturers who depended on research and discoveries in academic labs to find and license products.[9]

The pharma companies knew the drugs they sold cured virtually no disease. Although the public bought them for everything from smallpox to typhoid to diphtheria, the medications at best reduced symptoms and eased pain. Sales mattered more than cures to most pharma companies.[10] The most promising new drug category measured by revenues was barbiturates. Discovered in 1903 by Bayer, it had nothing to do with treating an illness but was marketed as "a new class of hypnotics" to provide relief for insomnia, anxiety, nerves, and depression. Overnight barbiturates replaced bromides, a cruder and more primitive class of patent drug sedatives.[11] Bayer released its most powerful version, phenobarbital, in 1912 (the press nicknamed it a "downer" because it made people drowsy).[12] Millions of patients flocked to barbiturates, all sold without prescription.

American companies that did not have their own branded barbiturate concentrated on getting their other medications listed on the *USP/NF*. Consumers believed the *USP/NF* drugs had the best quality control.[13] That allowed Merck, Lilly, Squibb, Pfizer, and others to charge several times more than the identical formula from small, family-run compounding pharmacies. When Bayer's copyright on Aspirin expired, the company's legal effort failed to stop others from manufacturing and selling it. So, Bayer's slogan became "Genuine Bayer Aspirin," and it sold for double the price of generic aspirin.[14] The same was true with Parke-Davis's Adrenalin, a compound of pure adrenaline it had patented. The company won a lawsuit in which a federal appeals court ruled that because of the similarity between the name of Parke-Davis's drug and the body's natural hormone, all other U.S. drug companies could only market their adrenaline medications as epinephrine. That ruling allowed Parke-Davis to charge triple the price of its competitors.[15]

A grim example of the downside of pharma's overall lack of innovation came during the deadly influenza epidemic of 1918. Called the

Spanish Flu since Spanish newspapers were the only ones in Europe that ran stories about it, it infected half a billion people, about a third of the world's population. By some estimates it killed 100 million over a brutal sixteen weeks. In comparison, the fourteenth-century bubonic plague had wiped out a quarter of the planet over ten years.[16] Pharma companies had nothing to slow or treat the pandemic. It stopped only after the lethal microbe had run its course.

The Spanish Flu spurred academic and private researchers to redouble their efforts to find treatments for contagious infections and illnesses. By this time, bacteriologists realized that the trillions of self-sufficient, single cell microbes, including those that make up about 70 percent of every human, are friendly. Or at the very least they had evolved to coexist with people.

What researchers did not yet know was that microbes, especially the predatory ones that cause disease, are the ultimate examples of Charles Darwin's survival of the fittest theory. Bacteria metamorphose incredibly fast to better replicate, sometimes in ways that rival science fiction. The germ responsible for tuberculosis, for instance, dies in about twenty-one days unless it can infect a new host. In many early cases, the TB germ attacked a patient's kidneys, lymph nodes, and sometimes even the skin. Over time that pathogen mutated so as to target the lungs. That resulted in a persistent cough and converted TB into an airborne pathogen that was easily spread in crowded cities. The same is true of other deadly bacteria. Rabies germs evolved to attack the part of the brain that controlled aggressive biting, making it more likely than an infected animal would try to pass it to other animals or humans by biting them. The microbes behind the Black Plague, *Yersinia pestis*, originally infected only rats but transformed over time so that fleas on those rats became the carriers to humans. It later morphed again so that humans who developed plague pneumonia spread the infection. When Lyme disease passed slowly from rats and deer, the infectious microbe evolved to infect ticks that fed on those animals. The ticks passed it much faster to people.[17]

Some pathogens lay dormant after an infection and then much later reappear as a different illness. Children infected by the chicken pox germ recover usually in a couple of weeks. The virus, however, hides in nerve cells along the spine and brain and often remerges decades later as shingles.[18]

The researchers made little headway on fighting infectious diseases. The hit drugs that came from the labs had nothing to do with eliminating pathogenic bacteria. A Los Angeles pharmacologist and chemist, Gordon Alles, was searching for an improved decongestant when he isolated the stimulant amphetamine sulfate.[19] He teamed with Smith Kline, who already marketed a cotton strip soaked in a slightly unstable liquid and sold it as a decongestant inhaler.[20] Smith Kline bought Alles's patent rights in exchange for a 5 percent royalty. The company's inhaler was wildly popular; 10 million sold in the first five years. And it was the first to market pure amphetamine pills, branded as Benzedrine Sulfate (*bennies* in street slang).

The most significant medical breakthrough was a treatment for diabetes, a deadly physiological condition. A team of University of Toronto researchers announced their discovery of insulin in 1922. The Indianapolis-based family who owned Eli Lilly won the exclusive right to develop and market insulin to diabetics in North and South America. The following year Lilly got a patent on its process to collect and extract large quantities pure enough for clinical distribution. The insulin market grew exponentially over a couple of decades.[21]

It was a second revolutionary drug discovery, however, that upended the pharmaceutical business. Penicillin might have remained undiscovered had it not been for some good luck in a science lab in 1928. A Scottish microbiologist, Alexander Fleming, returned from his summer vacation and noticed something unusual. His research involved growing bacteria and observing its behavior under different conditions. Along the edges of a stack of petri dishes he had left to be washed were colonies of staph bacteria. During his absence, a blue-green mold had grown on the plates. What caught his attention, though, was that staph bacteria near the mold on the plates had disappeared.[22] As a doctor at a British Army Hospital in northern France during World War I, Fleming had learned firsthand that bacteria were often as deadly as enemy shelling. He wondered whether some of the discharge from the mold had stopped the bacteria from growing.

Tests on his "mold juice" isolated it to a rare strain of the penicillium family.[23] Further tests were promising, demonstrating the mold killed a wide range of common microorganisms.[24] Fleming and his assistants could not, however, isolate a pure alkaloid from the chemically unstable mold juice. When Fleming wrote about his discovery in a 1929 scientific paper, he anglicized the Latin *penicillium* to *penicillin*, and he downplayed hope for possible therapeutic benefits. Penicillin went mostly unnoticed.[25]

A few other researchers also tried and failed to extract a pure alkaloid.[26] It took seven years before a team from Oxford's School of Pathology in 1936 chanced on Fleming's paper and restarted experiments. The previous year a German chemist had discovered Prontosil, a brick-red dye whose active ingredient was sulfonamide. That sulfa drug, and others that followed, were the first capable of combating streptococcal infections.*[27] Sulfa medications piqued the interest of the Oxford team to investigate the mold that Fleming had described as being lethal to dangerous microorganisms.[28]

Howard Florey, a Rhodes Scholar and Australian pathology professor, ran the Oxford lab. He assigned to the penicillin project a brilliant twenty-nine-year-old chemist, Ernst Chain, who had emigrated from Berlin in 1933. Chain's family were devout Jews and he had left Germany "because I felt disgusted with the Nazi gang. . . . I did not believe that the system would last more than six months at the most."[29] Initially, Chain, a self-described "temperamental Continental," seemed an odd fit with the small lab's more reserved Oxford- and Cambridge-trained researchers.[30] With his bushy black hair, thick mustache, and rumpled clothes, he seemed at times to relish his outsider status. Although his colleagues thought he was argumentative and brusque, they came to respect his considerable biomedical skills. In less than a year, Chain singlehandedly developed a process for extracting and purifying tiny amounts of penicillin.[31] It was twenty times more powerful in destroying colonies of bacteria than anything they had previously tested.

It took another four years, until 1940, before trials demonstrated penicillin shielded mice from deadly streptococci bacteria.[32] Still, the Oxford researchers worried that anything capable of so thoroughly

---

* Sulfa drugs stop bacterial infections by interfering with their metabolism. Antibiotics such as penicillin are more effective as they destroy the bacteria. The chemist who isolated the first sulfa drug, Gerhard Domagk, worked for the Bayer pharmaceutical subdivision of Germany's I. G. Farben conglomerate. When Domagk was awarded in 1939 the Nobel Prize in Medicine, Hitler—angry that a previous Nobel Peace Prize had gone to a German pacifist—barred Domagk from accepting the award. The Gestapo arrested Domagk and briefly jailed him because he had been "too polite" in the letter he had sent refusing the award.

obliterating bacteria might harm humans though it had not proven toxic to mice. The following January, Florey invited Charles Fletcher, a young doctor from Oxford's Radcliffe Infirmary, to meet his team. Florey asked Fletcher to "find a patient with some inevitably fatal disorder who might be willing to help."[33]

Fletcher recalled there "were no ethical committees in those days that had to be consulted, so I looked around the wards and found a pleasant 50-year-old woman with disseminated breast cancer who had not long to live."[34] She agreed to the experiment after Fletcher told her it was for a "new medication that could be of value to many people." That unnamed woman was the first of several terminally ill patients who volunteered over several weeks. Oral and rectal administration proved useless since tests revealed those procedures did not get enough penicillin into the blood. A stomach tube tried on another patient showed some promise. But doctors found the greatest concentration of the drug after an intravenous injection.

Fletcher hoped to next test penicillin's curative powers on a person seriously ill, but not at death's door as were the first group of patients. Fletcher found a forty three year old British policeman in the hospital's septic ward. He had scratched his face while pruning roses and the scratches had become infected. His face and arms were covered with abscesses. He had excruciating infections in his bones and was coughing up pus from lung cavities. Doctors had already removed his infected left eye. "There was all to gain for him in a trial of penicillin," recalled Fletcher, "and nothing to lose."[35]

On February 12, 1941, Fletcher started the treatment, 300 mg every three hours through an IV drip. In just a day the policeman felt better. By the fourth day "there was a striking improvement," and by the fifth he had made a miraculous recovery. His temperature was normal, he was eating regular meals, and the abscesses on his face, scalp, and arms were almost gone.[36] The problem was that the lab—still struggling with developing an efficient means of extracting purified penicillin—ran out of the drug. Florey watched in frustration as the bacteria roared back. The policeman died a few weeks later.

"We then decided to avoid using large amounts of the precious penicillin by concentrating on children and localized infections," recalled Fletcher. Five more patients, four of them children, were treated over the next few months. The serious bacterial infections cleared from each. There were few side effects and it did not have the toxicity associated with sulfa drugs.[37] Florey and his team realized by then that the drug might be one of the most important medical discoveries ever.[38]

By the time the Oxford team realized that penicillin was a momentous breakthrough, England had been at war with Nazi Germany for nearly two years. The constraints of a wartime budget left little money for an ambitious rollout of what many politicians considered an experimental drug. Even if Florey roused political support, war had consumed Britain's chemical industry. It had no spare capacity to produce the new drug. Florey's Oxford team continued its research on a tiny budget and with improvised equipment. Against the backdrop of what many expected to be an imminent Nazi land invasion of Britain, they prepared to destroy their lab and research files if the Germans arrived. Each of them rubbed some of the brown penicillin spores into their clothing; if one managed to evade capture by the Nazis, those spores would remain untraceable yet could be recovered years later.[39]

Chain tried to convince Florey to patent penicillin; at least it might bring in royalties to pay for more research. Florey asked the advice of two of Britain's leading authorities, Sir Edward Mellanby, director of the Medical Research Council, and Sir Henry Dale, a Nobel Laureate. Both were aghast at the idea of a patent, although their German, French, Swiss, and American counterparts did so regularly. Chain knew there had been little advancement on Prontosil, the sulfa drug discovered by Bayer. A German patent court had ruled its active ingredient—sulfanilamide—was in the public domain since it had been discovered and used in the dye industry in 1908. Some firms had figured out molecular modification to produce sulfanilamide derivatives, so-called me-too drugs.[40] Those chemical cousins qualified for patent protection.[41]

When Sirs Mellanby and Dale met with Chain, they were not moved by his impassioned argument. It was unseemly commercialization, they told him. If he persisted, they warned, it might not only scuttle his career but reflect badly on his fellow Jewish refugees.[42]

Forced to look for money abroad, Florey successfully lobbied for funding from the American-based Rockefeller Foundation, where he had had a fellowship a decade earlier.[43] Florey and one of his key researchers, Norman Heatley, planned a trip to the U.S. hoping the government and American pharmaceutical firms might help figure how to increase the yields of pure penicillin.

The day before departing for the States, Florey told Chain he was not included. Chain, shocked, thought it was an "underhand trick and act of bad faith."[44] He argued that the penicillin project had always been a "joint venture" only between him and Florey, and he cited reasons why he believed that Heatley had played a "very minor part." Florey refused to change his mind.

In the summer of 1941, Florey and Heatley were in Peoria, Illinois, where the Department of Agriculture had its Northern Regional Lab specializing in fermentation.[45] Heatley opted to stay there and work on increasing the yields while Florey lobbied U.S. pharma companies to commit resources to the project.

Over several weeks, the Peoria lab made progress. Substituting lactose for the sucrose used by the Oxford team produced significantly better yields. The Peoria lab next found that adding corn steep liquor during fermentation increased the results tenfold. Enhancements made to penicillin precursors again upped the yield. Still, it was a fraction of what was needed for the war. In late summer the Peoria researchers tried growing penicillin submerged in huge tanks. The Oxford strain still produced only small traces of the drug. So the Peoria lab launched an international search for a penicillium strain that might produce better yields. Soon, soil samples and produce with mold from around the world arrived at the small government lab. To the surprise of the researchers, the most productive strain came from the mold of an overripe cantaloupe a local housewife found at a Peoria fruit stand less than a mile from the lab. The Carnegie Institution used X-rays to create a modified and more powerful version of the cantaloupe strain. A team at the University of Wisconsin used ultraviolet radiation to boost its productivity even further.[46]

While Heatley and the American researchers in Peoria worked to mass-produce the drug, Florey was making little headway in his efforts to interest American pharmaceutical companies in the penicillin project. He knew that independent of the Oxford experiments, Merck, Eli Lilly, and Squibb had shown sporadic interest in the drug.[47] Florey's expectations were particularly high since he had enlisted the help of an old acquaintance, Alfred Newton Richards, a respected University of Pennsylvania pharmacology professor. Richards was chairman of the Committee on Medical Research, an influential branch of the Office of Scientific Research and Development (OSRD). Franklin Roosevelt had created the OSRD only a couple of months earlier (June 1941), and tasked it with prioritizing scientific and medical efforts needed to bolster national defense. If the OSRD deemed a project critical to the war effort—as it did with the atomic bomb—it could provide massive research and development funding. Civilian scientists served as key OSRD directors and Roosevelt cited national security to empower it to bypass most of the bureaucratic obstacles and contract directly with both universities and private industry.[48] Once Florey had persuaded Richards that penicillin was a breakthrough, Richards personally lobbied the drug firms.

Getting involved in penicillin would serve the national interest, Richards told senior management at each company. They were hesitant though to make any commitment. They had heard widespread tales of the difficulty in achieving significant yields with the existing fermentation methods. And they were concerned about whether the penicillin project would be subject to the regulations of the federal Food, Drug, and Cosmetic Act that had passed three years earlier, the first significant legislation about the drug industry since Harvey Wiley's 1906 Pure Food and Drug Act.[49] * [50] In fact, variations of the final law had been stuck in Congress for five years before a lethal drug disaster shamed Congress into acting (just as it had taken Upton Sinclair's stomach-wrenching *The Jungle* to get the 1906 law passed).[51] One hundred and seven people, mostly children, had died from Elixir Sulfanilamide, a sulfa-based cough syrup mixed with a chemical used in antifreeze and brake fluids to give it a sweetish flavor.[52] There was fury when the Tennessee-based patent drug maker maintained "we violated no law" since there was no legal requirement to test drugs for safety before selling them. The company was found guilty only on a minor violation: it marketed its lethal syrup as an elixir and by law elixirs had to contain alcohol; its did not.[53]

The new law was Congress's reactive effort to put a premium on safety regulations in medicine (medical devices and cosmetics joined drugs now under FDA oversight). New drugs had to be submitted to the FDA and demonstrated as safe before they could be sold to the pub-

---

* The 1938 statute also created limited powers for the FDA to certify food colorings as "harmless." Foods would be considered adulterated if they contained a coloring agent not approved by the government. While the 1938 law was the most sweeping legislation about drugs since the turn of the century, there had been a series of limited-scope laws during the 1930s that did reduce some of the remaining patent medicine abuse of opiates, cocaine, and marijuana. In 1937, marijuana was put under federal control with the Marihuana Tax Act.

lic. Another key provision was that the burden of proof to demonstrate safety shifted from the government to the drug company. It established the first ever rudimentary animal and human clinical testing for toxicity. Package inserts with dosing information and warnings about possible dangers had to be sent to pharmacists. The new law required all drug manufacturers to register with the FDA, which was now empowered to inspect factories and to recall medicines judged dangerous at the pharma company's expense.[54] That same year Congress also passed the Wheeler-Lea Act. It gave limited power to curb deceptive and false drug advertisements to the Federal Trade Commission (FTC), the government's agency created in 1914 for consumer protection and civil antitrust enforcement.[55]

American pharma companies detested any regulation. They had always operated in an industry built on the inviolable right of consumers to self-medicate.[56] What had them in a fury, though, was when the FDA issued operating regulations that proposed that some drugs deemed too dangerous should be prescription only since no warning label would be adequate.[57] It was the FDA's feeble attempt to rein in the explosive growth of barbiturates and amphetamines. There was ample evidence by the time of the 1938 law that both drugs were addictive and deadly in large doses. The law did not cover them since they were on sale before it was enacted. The FDA's effort failed. It managed to only mandate prescriptions for narcotic-based medication and powerful sulfa drugs.[58]

What about penicillin? The American pharma firms asked to help develop the drug worried what might happen if they were successful. Would penicillin be subject to a warning label by the FDA? Would it demonstrate some toxicity if developed and distributed widely, thereby becoming prescription only? The companies were particularly concerned because the FDA had managed to require prescriptions for sulfa meds. Those were antibacterials and marketed for some of the same infections that penicillin might target.[59] No drug company wanted to commit major resources to an experimental medication when the FDA might later try limiting its commercial use. Alfred Newton Richards tried inducing pharma to join the project by agreeing to put penicillin and all the related research for it outside the reach of the 1938 law.[60]

At an October 1941 meeting in Washington organized by Richards, although the drug chiefs were no longer worried about obstacles from the FDA, they were still ambivalent about making any commitment. Most looked to George Wilhelm Merck to take the lead.[61] Merck wielded great influence, even with his bitterest competitors. He had a widespread reputation as a pioneer who put research and drug innovation ahead of short-term profits.[62] When he opened the Merck Institute for Therapeutic Research in 1933, in the middle of the Great Depression, it was the industry's first research lab. It attracted some of the country's top academic chemists and pharmacologists.[63] They produced breakthroughs in antibiotics, hormones, sulfas, and vitamins (the discovery of B_{12} as an effective therapy for pernicious anemia accounted for 10 percent of Merck's sales in the mid-1930s).[64] Other companies followed; Lilly opened a research lab in 1934 and Abbott and Squibb christened theirs in 1938.

Given Merck's emphasis on drug innovation, Florey and his Oxford colleagues expected him to be their ally when it came to penicillin. They made the case that penicillin held the promise of fighting often lethal bacterial infections, including chicken pox, mumps, meningitis, rheumatic fever, pneumonia, and syphilis. The greatest cause of death for mothers was from infections following childbirth. Complications from simple contagions like tonsillitis were particularly deadly for children younger than ten. Fatalities from blood poisoning and gangrene, resulting often from a minor wound, accounted for about half of the 10 million soldiers who died in World War I.

Richards had warned Florey that Merck was "pessimistic" about penicillin.[65] He thought that was because Merck had little financial incentive to chase an experimental antibacterial. It was one of the first U.S. firms to obtain a license from Bayer to sell Prontosil, a sulfa drug targeted to fight pneumonia. Sales were strong.[66] What Florey and his team did not know was that Merck's company had little proficiency in fermentation, the part of the penicillin process that had stymied researchers. No one outside the company knew Merck's efforts to synthesize penicillin had gone poorly.[67]

At the October 1941 meeting, Merck surprised Florey. "We won't do it," he insisted.[68]

Everything changed two months later on December 7, when the Japanese launched a surprise attack on the American naval fleet at Pearl Harbor. Richards organized another meeting between Florey and a cross section of U.S. government scientists and pharma chiefs. They met in Manhattan ten days after Pearl Harbor. America had by then declared war on Japan and Germany. How many lives on the battlefield might be saved by penicillin was no longer a matter of idle speculation for the American drug executives. George Merck had overcome his reluctance. He surprised those at the meeting by announcing that if the yields reported by the Peoria lab could be replicated consistently, the American pharmaceutical industry would commit to a crash program.[69] One government official there thought that Merck's reversal marked the moment "a new pharmaceutical industry was born."[70]

To encourage their collaboration the government announced that the penicillin project was exempt from antitrust laws.[71] Merck and Squibb agreed to share all their research and to own equal shares in any patents and inventions from the work. Pfizer joined the following year after it resolved concerns that penicillin spores might contaminate the citric acid that was the backbone of its business.[72] Lilly, Abbott, Upjohn, and Parke-Davis soon entered their own information-sharing agreements.[73] The War Production Board enlisted the help of the U.S. Department of Agriculture and a broad cross section of government scientists.[74] The Office of Scientific Research and Development used public funds to sign fifty-six contracts with universities and research hospitals for penicillin-related studies.[75] Florey returned to Oxford while Heatley joined the team at Merck and worked with a noted chemist, Max Tishler (Tishler was also directing research on a synthetic hormone derived from the adrenal gland, cortisone).[76] The American drug firms discovered that the low yields that had frustrated the British researchers was a problem not easily solved.

It took until March 1942 to manufacture enough penicillin to treat the first American patient. Anne Miller, the thirty-three-year-old wife of Yale's athletic director, was in a New Haven hospital in critical condition from blood poisoning after a miscarriage. Such bacterial infections were especially lethal for young mothers. Every treatment her doctors tried—powerful sulfa drugs, blood transfusions, rattlesnake venom, even surgery—had failed.[77] A hospital physician was friends with Howard Florey, who had told him about the secret experimental antibiotic. Florey put him in touch with Max Tishler. Merck's team crashed around the clock for three days to purify 5.5 grams—a teaspoonful—of pure penicillin powder. It was half the entire stock in the U.S.[78] They rushed it by plane to Miller.[79] By the time the drug arrived, Miller was slipping in and out of consciousness. Her fever had spiked to 107. No one had any idea of what the correct dosage might be, so the physicians diluted a gram into her intravenous solution. Her astounding turnaround is recorded in her hospital chart (now a permanent part of the Smithsonian Museum). Miller's temperature was normal the following morning for the first time in a month, she was no longer delirious, and in less than a day she ate her first meal in a month. Her blood tested negative for bacteria only twenty-four hours after the first injection.[80] Miller's miraculous recovery was not only big news inside Merck, but it encouraged other U.S. pharmaceutical firms to redouble their efforts to find the best industrial process for mass-producing penicillin.[81]

Because of its potential military value, the penicillin work under way at the pharma companies was a national secret. That changed inadvertently that November following the deadliest nightclub fire in American history. Nearly five hundred died at Boston's Cocoanut Grove and hundreds were terribly burned. The federal government covertly asked for Merck's help. Tishler's lab worked around the clock. The best they could produce on such short notice was a diluted liquid containing some concentrated penicillin. What Merck sent to Massachusetts General was not of the clinical purity used to treat Anne Miller. Still its anti-infective qualities helped dozens of victims successfully fight the infections from their burns.[82]

By the time of the Cocoanut Grove fire, both the American and British governments had declared penicillin production a national security priority. In 1943, the War Production Board had two all-consuming priorities, developing an atomic bomb and mass producing penicillin.[83] The government knew that making it on an industrial scale required enormous federal resources and a collaboration of pharma firms with agricultural and chemical companies that specialized in fermentation. One hundred and seventy-five companies were evaluated. Seventeen made the final cut, including Merck, Squibb, Pfizer, Abbott, Eli Lilly, Lederle, Parke-Davis, and Upjohn. Once on board they learned that while making penicillin was their top mission, the government wanted them also to focus on developing antimalarials to slash the death rate for American troops fighting the Japanese in the Far East.[84] * [85] There

* As part of the frenzied research effort to perfect a drug to combat malaria, the Army-controlled Malaria Research Project conducted human experiments at four prisons, with the largest at Stateville Penitentiary outside Chicago. Prisoners were offered reduced sentences, cash stipends, and extra amenities for agreeing to be infected with malaria and then treated with experimental drugs. The prisoners were encouraged to keep meticulous notes. University of Chicago researchers selected 200 men, from 487

was also ongoing research for a new group of corticosteroids, originally fueled by false reports that the Nazis were using them to enable "super pilots" to fly at altitudes over forty thousand feet. When that research did not pan out, the Air Force bought millions of Smith Kline's Benzedrine pills and distributed them to bomber and fighter pilots. The Army stocked up on barbiturates, which were widely dispensed to sedate wounded soldiers, alleviate pain, and offset shock and anxiety in the battlefield.[86] (All the frenetic projects on corticosteroids and developing antimalarials led to unintended advances in immune globulins to fight infections and blood substitutes.)[87]

The government recruited researchers from thirty-six universities and hospitals.[88] It also approved and paid for six huge new penicillin manufacturing plants. The pharma firms, meanwhile, got tax incentives on all investments to retrofit their factories to maximize penicillin production. Lilly, for instance, reconfigured a plant used to produce two-quart milk bottles into penicillin manufacturing, complete with a three-thousand-gallon fermentation tank. Pfizer turned a former ice factory into a fermentation plant. Sensing the potential in penicillin, the previous year Pfizer had reincorporated in Delaware and went public with 240,000 shares of common stock.[89]

The results were dramatic. In the first five months of 1943, the government project produced 400 million units of penicillin, only enough to treat 180 severely sick soldiers. In the last seven months of the year, as the pharma firms got far more proficient, production increased 500 percent to more than 20 billion units. By D-Day, June 6, 1944, the joint effort churned out 100 billion units monthly, enough to treat 40,000 troops. By the end of the war in Europe, May 1945, American companies were producing a stunning 650 billion units monthly.[90]

volunteers, for two years of testing at the prison hospital. The trial drugs had toxic side effects that sickened many and resulted in one death. In 1947, defense attorneys for Nazi doctors charged with war crimes for human experimentation at concentration camps cited the malaria experiments in a failed effort for an acquittal.

5

"COULD YOU PATENT THE SUN?"

Three months after the end of the war in the Pacific, in December 1945, Alexander Fleming, Howard Florey, and Ernst Chain won the Nobel Prize in Medicine for their roles in the discovery of penicillin. Few outside the British medical research community knew that by then the three men had fallen out over mutual recriminations about which of them deserved most of the acclaim. By the time the Nobel was awarded, King George VI had knighted Fleming and the Australian Florey had been given a Knight's Batchelor. Chain recalled that during the frenzied wartime research at Oxford, he felt as if "Florey's behavior to me . . . was unpardonably bad."[1] Except for exchanging a few letters, Florey and Chain never spoke after the Nobel. Meanwhile, Florey stopped talking to Fleming after the British press had lavished the lion's share of credit for the drug on the Scottish researcher. Florey thought Fleming, who alone received honorary doctorates and medical association awards for penicillin, had not tried to correct the record.[2] As for Norman Heatley, who had been a key member of the Oxford team, being left out of the Nobel was the ultimate slight (it took fifty years before Oxford acknowledged his role by bestowing the first honorary Doctor of Medicine degree in its eight-hundred-year history, and today the penicillin researchers' original lab is the Heatley Laboratory).[3] * [4]

Many in the Oxford team had expected that since the British and

* A similar dispute over credit for insulin plagued the 1923 Nobel Prize in Medicine. It went to only two of the three researchers listed on the original Canadian patent as inventors.

American governments had provided the funding, most of the revenue that came from sales would go to public research for other significant drugs.[5] Some money, it was expected, might even find its way to the financially strapped academic research departments that had done the critical work when drug companies were uninterested. But pharma had no intention to share the spoils. The government had not insisted on any conditions to the tsunami of money it had doled out during the war. George Merck's view was typical of other CEOs: they might not have discovered penicillin, but without the ingenuity and capability of American pharmaceutical firms, the Oxford team would have still been conducting failed lab experiments to increase the yield. The companies deserved every dollar of profit, he contended. There was so much money to be made in penicillin with a surging worldwide demand that none of the pharma chiefs complained at the end of the war when Congress passed a law transferring quality control for the drug's production from the military to the FDA.[6]

The ways in which American pharma firms exploited penicillin after the war were the envy of foreign competitors. The British medical luminaries who had scolded Chain as "money-grubbing" when he had raised the patent question were incensed after the war when a U.S. government microbiologist, Andrew Moyer, acquired a U.K. patent for his method of manufacturing penicillin. Moyer was an anti-British isolationist who had worked with Oxford's Heatley at the Peoria lab and made his time there hellish. Chain's wartime prediction—without a patent that Britain would have to pay royalties to use the drug—came true.*[7] Sir Henry Harris, who had worked with Florey, said: "It is often said in the press here that they got the penicillin out at Oxford and the Americans pinched it."[8] In the U.S., Merck, Pfizer, Squibb, and others aggressively pursued "process patents" that protected unique methods for synthesizing, extracting, purifying, or manufacturing a drug. Eleven American pharma firms that manufactured penicillin after the war owned a remarkable 250 such patents.[9]

British pharmaceutical firms, meanwhile, were infuriated that the

* Moyer could not profit from the patent developed in Peoria since he was a government employee. However, he sold his foreign rights in the patent to Merck, Squibb, and Commercial Solvent. Because of the outcry, the British government created the National Research Development Corporation to make certain that discoveries and inventions by U.K. academics received patent protection.

American government sponsorship of a British invention had given a handful of U.S. firms a critical several years' head start on a blockbuster drug. Pfizer had concentrated on penicillin to the exclusion of other drugs in its pipeline. That paid off handsomely after the war since it was responsible for nearly half of the world's production. Squibb had doubled in size by becoming the only firm that manufactured, packaged, and sold penicillin directly to hospitals and pharmacists.

At the start of World War II, German pharmaceutical firms accounted for 43 percent of all drug sales.[10] After the war, as German industry struggled to recover, American pharma firms, fueled by their dominance in antibiotics, took the top spot, with nearly half the world market. In the U.S., fifteen firms selected by the War Production Board had 80 percent of all drug sales and a stunning 90 percent of profits.[11] Even sixty years later (2005), the top ten American pharmaceutical companies traced their rise to their selection for the wartime penicillin program.

The unprecedented federal role in penicillin also had an unintentional consequence for a handful of companies. The U.S. Department of Agriculture had acquired thirty-two key patents on fermentation methods.[12] The government's priority was producing a lot of penicillin, not making money. So, the USDA licensed those patents free of charge to companies interested in making the drug. The pharma firms had been granted a national security exemption from antitrust laws to encourage sharing their research with one another. When they developed mass fermentation for penicillin, it was a departure from the low-yield, synthetic chemistry that had defined the industry. Before World War II, no drug firm had imagined there could have been such a tremendous worldwide demand for any single medicine, much less that it could be mass-produced on an unprecedented scale. The influx of millions in direct federal subsidies changed everything. Drug companies expanded and retrofitted their plants with the large costly equipment required for commercial-scale production. Thirty-foot-tall steel tanks held penicillin mold, while submerged fermenters sterilized it, and enormous vats aerated the cultures at volumes exceeding ten thousand gallons to ready the drug for clinical use. In total, the pharma firms spent $23 million to build sixteen state-of-the-art antibiotics plants. Due to a special accelerated amortization provision, they recovered half their investments with savings on federal income tax. The government also sold to the drug companies—at less than half their investments—the six state-of-the-art penicillin production plants it had built at taxpayer expense during the war.[13]

Although penicillin had remade the industry, pharma companies were already looking for new and better drugs. That is because penicillin is a narrow-spectrum antibiotic, meaning that it is effective only against a limited range of bacteria (so-called Gram-positive).[14] While it was successful against many deadly illnesses, it failed to work against a long list of often lethal Gram-negative bacterial infections, such as tuberculosis, typhoid, cholera, meningitis, gonorrhea, salmonella, and certain pneumonias. The postwar Holy Grail for American pharma was to find a broad-spectrum drug, one that treated illnesses caused both by Gram-negative and Gram-positive bacteria.

That turned out to be streptomycin.[15] It was discovered as a microbe in a farmyard soil sample in 1943 by Selman Waksman, a Rutgers University soil microbiologist, and a PhD graduate student, Albert Schatz.[16] Waksman, who coined "antibiotic" the previous year to refer to chemicals taken from microorganisms that destroyed bacteria, was searching for a tuberculosis cure.[17] The lethal airborne pathogen dubbed the "Great White Plague" had killed an estimated two billion people in the preceding two centuries. Neither Waksman nor Schatz was medically qualified or licensed to do animal experiments. Waksman figured that since dangerous bacteria do not survive in soil, there were undoubtedly countless undiscovered microbes in dirt that killed bacteria. Since many of those antibiotic-producing organisms might also be toxic to humans, Waksman needed to conduct clinical tests. He used Merck's much better equipped laboratory only fourteen miles from Rutgers to extract enough of his drug to study at the Mayo Clinic. Those tests demonstrated that streptomycin might be the long-awaited first broad-spectrum antibiotic.[18]

The Office of Scientific Research and Development used its extraordinary wartime powers to classify it along with penicillin as a national security medication. That opened the federal money pipeline, fueling a crash research and development program. Three quarters of the drug's production in 1945 and 1946 went to the armed forces, and the remainder was set aside for drug trials at the National Research Council, which coordinated technological and scientific research between the military, private research laboratories, and universities.

Merck's contract with Waksman gave the company exclusive rights to any drug produced from his research. That meant Merck would have monopoly control of streptomycin once the government freed the drug for commercial sales.

As the war progressed, streptomycin was the only medication under development that had a chance of combating biological weapons—anthrax, yellow fever, or bubonic plague—that many feared the Japanese and Germans were developing. Besides his role on the National Research Council, George Merck was the chief of a secret civilian agency, the War Research Service. It was responsible for developing the American stockpile of bioweapons (Merck was later given the nation's highest civilian award, the Medal for Merit, for his wartime service).[19] Waksman appealed to George Merck, contending that no single company should have sole control of streptomycin as it was too important a public health discovery (*The New York Times* listed the streptomycin patent as "one of ten that shaped the world").[20] Merck agreed. In August 1944, he canceled the exclusive arrangement. The drug's rights returned to Rutgers.[21]

When the government lifted its controls on streptomycin at the end of 1946, eleven American pharma companies, including Merck, Squibb, Lilly, and Pfizer, began manufacturing and selling it. The early enthusiasm that it might eliminate tuberculosis had ebbed as it had proven capable only of controlling, not eradicating, the disease. However, clinical trials had demonstrated it was effective against meningitis, typhoid, and lung and bloodstream infections.[22] Streptomycin also tested as far less toxic than the sulfa drugs.[23]

Merck's attorneys, meanwhile, in early 1945, had filed an application for a patent in the names of the two Rutgers scientists, Waksman and Schatz. Until then, courts and the Patent Office had ruled that "products of nature" were in the public domain. The Patent Office had raised that prohibition when the streptomycin application arrived.[24] And while the application was pending, the Supreme Court issued a 7–2 decision denying the request of a company to patent a bacterial inoculant. The majority's decision seemed conclusive: "[P]atents cannot issue for the discovery of the phenomena of nature. The qualities of these bacteria, like the heat of the sun, electricity, or the qualities of metals, are part of the storehouse of knowledge of all men. They are manifestations of the laws of nature, free to all men and reserved exclusively to none."[25]

There was a small but vocal minority of American medical researchers who thought it was immoral for any firm to profit from a drug developed from nature. They contended that medications needed to stop fatal infections or crippling diseases should be royalty free. The best example of this noble view was the polio vaccine that stopped a disease that had previously left tens of thousands of children paralyzed annually. Edward R. Murrow asked the vaccine's inventor, Jonas Salk, who owned the patent. "Well, the people, I would say. There is no patent. Could you patent the sun?"[26]

It was true, admitted Merck's attorneys, that if all that was before the Patent Office was a microbe found in farm soil, then the patent should be denied. However, scientists and chemists had reworked that single microbe and had made "streptomycin available in a form which not only has valuable therapeutic properties but also can be produced, distributed, and administered in a therapeutic way." The unwavering conclusion of the Rutgers scientists? "This antibiotic is not a product of nature."[27]

Every pharma company knew that the issuance of a patent would change their industry. Earth is a microbial planet. For several billion years before humans appeared, trillions of microbes too small to see existed in everything from hot springs to Arctic snow, soil, rocks, oceans, air, plants, even on and inside animals. As with streptomycin, many of those microbes might turn into a new wonder drug. It meant that the industry, long mired in manufacturing a mishmash of ointments, plant extracts, and biologicals, all of which only occasionally alleviated symptoms, would have an opportunity to produce a range of drugs that delivered cures for the deadliest diseases. All drug companies embraced this theory.

It took three and half years, until September 21, 1948, for the Patent Office to grant Waksman and Schatz the first ever antibiotic patent, No. 2,449,866, for "streptomycin and process of preparation."[28] Since the two scientists had already assigned their commercial rights to Rutgers, the school was free to license it to drug companies in return for a royalty.[29] * [30]

At the close of 1948, penicillin and streptomycin accounted for 99.7

* The Nobel Prize in Medicine in 1952 went to Waksman for the discovery of streptomycin. It highlighted the tremendous rift between its creators about who deserved credit. The U.S. Patent Office listed Waksman and Schatz as equal co-owners. The patent affidavit they had submitted in 1945 listed both as joint discoverers. After the Nobel, however, Waksman dismissed Schatz as a disgruntled former graduate student. Schatz contended that not only was he the one who found the microbe in the throat of a chicken but that Waksman had ignored the discovery for months. Schatz eventually

percent of all U.S. antibiotic production.[31] Furious research had been under way for several years as pharma firms hunted for new broad-spectrum antibiotics they could patent. The industry was about to enter a new era in which a flood of "wonder drugs" would transform the way pharma did business.

---

sued Rutgers and Waksman for fraud. It turned out that while Waksman had gotten $350,000 in royalties from the drug's sales, he had sent a paltry $1,500 to Schatz. The parties settled. Rutgers's president issued a public statement confirming Schatz was the drug's co-discoverer, and paid Schatz $125,000 for his foreign patent rights. He got a 3 percent royalty on U.S. streptomycin sales in return for dropping the charges of fraud and duress against Waksman and Rutgers. The Nobel Committee, however, rejected Schatz's appeal to add his name to the 1952 award. Forty-two years later, Schatz received the Rutgers Medal for his role in discovering streptomycin.

6

AN UNLIKELY TRIO

Post–World War II America was a country with a newfound self-assurance. The Great Depression that ended in 1939 was a distant memory as total victory over Germany and Japan and a booming domestic economy resulted in what Rutgers historian William L. O'Neill dubbed the "American High." The fifteen-year span that began in 1945 was "our time of greatest confidence."[1] The pharma industry also emerged from war with a renewed sense of self-assurance. Its turn-of-the-century peddling of addictive drugs was long forgotten in the glow of its collaborative wartime penicillin program. The drug business also benefited from a widespread perception that technology and science were on the verge of a historic golden age. Physicist Alvin M. Weinberg later coined "Big Science" to describe the belief that everything from routine space travel to eradicating all disease was possible.[2]

Inventions and new products would come in a steady stream after the war. Some of the innovations included the microchip, videotape recorder, musical synthesizer, bar code, black box flight recorder, solar cells, optic fiber, supercomputers, and hard disks. A few of the least important inventions had the greatest impact on daily lives. People raved about the household revolution wrought by Teflon-coated cookware and super glue and halogen lamps. Power steering and radial tires added safety to cars while making it easier to drive. Transistor radios meant that broadcast programs and music no longer had to be listened to at home in a radio the size of a piece of furniture. And technology also introduced a way for people to buy the new devices, even if they did not have enough money to afford them: the first ever credit card (1950, Diners Club). And buy they did; in just five years after the war, Americans purchased 22 million cars, 20 million refrigerators, and 6 million stoves.

Medicine also flourished. Within ten years there would be a series of major breakthroughs: the first heart and lung machine; mechanical heart valve; discovery of DNA; open-heart surgery; introduction of a cobalt-ray machine to treat cancerous lung tumors; electric shock to revive a patient; kidney transplant and kidney dialysis equipment; microscopic brain surgery for seizures; ultrasound and coronary angiography; and the cardiac pacemaker.[3]

All the historic innovation created high expectations for the pharmaceutical industry. Antibiotics had reversed the public's pre–World War II opinion that drug companies profited with mediocre-at-best medications. A growing number of Americans had survived heart valve and bone infections, meningitis, scarlet fever, and other previously fatal diseases. Combined with plenty of press coverage over the many new in-house drug research departments, many hoped pharma would use science to conquer intractable diseases such as cancer.

C. Everett Koop, decades later Ronald Reagan's surgeon general, had been the custodian for the distribution of penicillin in Philadelphia when he was a surgical resident at the University of Pennsylvania in the late 1940s. He witnessed how penicillin saved lives: "I never lost the sense of wonder when I saw a youngster's fever and infection controlled by the antibiotic."[4] In his role as a surgeon he learned that almost all his patients thought that pharmaceutical breakthroughs "appeared to arise from nowhere," that they were accomplished "with ease." Although he knew that not to be true, it made Koop keenly aware that the industry's wartime achievements had created unrealistic public expectations that the pace of drug innovations would continue unabated.

Harry Truman and Dwight Eisenhower did their best to ensure the federal government helped make the pharma narrative a reality. They directed large federal investments into biomedical and drug research, much of it into the National Institutes of Health (NIH).[5] When Eisenhower created the Department of Health, Education, and Welfare in 1953 it was the first new cabinet level department in forty years.[6] HEW helped consolidate the NIH's various research agencies.

Although penicillin and streptomycin had made the pharma industry popular with the public, the two drugs were not having a good postwar effect on the firms' bottom lines. Production of penicillin and streptomycin outpaced demand. Prices had gone into a free fall.[7] A penicillin dose that cost $20 in 1944 had plummeted to only 30 cents three years later. Without any patent protection, the companies making and selling penicillin could only differentiate themselves by price. Each undercut the other to land orders. Streptomycin soon followed suit, dropping seventy-fold in price between 1946 and 1950.[8]

Despite the intense competition, Squibb's penicillin profit margins were 10 percent better than the average of its four top rivals. That was because it was the only vertically integrated firm, not only manufacturing the drug, but packaging it before selling it to hospitals, clinics, and physicians. Competitors only made it and then relied on packagers and wholesale distributors. Starting in the late 1940s, Pfizer, Merck, Lilly, and Parke-Davis created internal divisions to eliminate the middlemen.

Savvy CEOs knew, however, that changing their corporate structure would not alone boost their bottom line. What was needed were new patentable drugs that fueled big sales at higher prices. That required a two-pronged campaign. First, the firms cooperated in influencing Congress to pass laws that made it easier to obtain patent protection for laboratory discoveries. Next, they invested heavily in research and development as part of the frenzied race to find the next broad-spectrum antibiotic.

Merck hired some of the country's leading biochemists.[9] Pfizer and Lilly battled one another for recruiting noted scientists.[10] Pharma analysts predicted that one of the firms that had been at the forefront with penicillin and streptomycin—Merck, Squibb, Pfizer, Eli Lilly, Abbott, Upjohn, and Parke-Davis—would be the first with the next great antibiotic.

Scientists knew, however, that as penicillin had demonstrated, drug discovery sometimes required a bit of luck. History was about to be made at a place to which no one was paying attention. New Jersey–based Lederle was a small company that had been founded in 1906 by a former New York City health commissioner. Incorporated as Lederle Antitoxin Laboratories, it specialized in vaccines and antitoxins.[11] Chemical conglomerate American Cyanamid bought Lederle in 1930 and gave it an unusual degree of independence. Lederle had played a small role in the wartime penicillin project, never having made the manufacturing changes required to produce large quantities. Its antitoxin background, however, allowed it to provide the armed forces a quarter of all its blood plasma, a third of the flu vaccine, half of the tetanus inoculations, and half the gas gangrene antitoxin.

Lederle had one of the industry's smallest and least celebrated research departments. No one there was a Nobel Laureate or distinguished scientist. The company's researchers did not publish many articles in leading medical and pharma journals. Nor did Lederle have a formal relationship with the National Institutes of Health or any medical facility, such as the Mayo Clinic, by which promising lab discoveries could be tested clinically.

The three men who were ultimately responsible for the next drug breakthrough were quasi-outcasts; one a foreigner barred by U.S. immigration from becoming an American citizen, another judged too old by colleagues, and the third an African American surgeon at a time when the medical profession was nearly all white.

Lederle's chief of research was an Indian-born physiologist and physician, Yellapragada SubbaRow.[12] He was one of seven children from a poor family in Bhimavaram, an eastern Indian city best known as a major Hindu pilgrimage site. At thirteen, SubbaRow ran off to become a banana trader to the visiting pilgrims. His father, a tax collector, brought him home.[13] When his father died when SubbaRow was eighteen, he ran away again, this time to become a monk. His mother ordered him back to school, and local charities helped him afford Madras Medical College. But lack of money was always a problem. When he was twenty-four, he wed the fifteen-year-old granddaughter of a respectable merchant as part of an arranged marriage. His father-in-law paid for the last two years of tuition.[14]

SubbaRow was at school when the movement for Indian independence from Great Britain gained momentum inspired by Gandhi. He refused the British surgical gown given him at school and instead donned one made of a traditional and simple cotton *khadi*. That act of defiance cost him the college degree necessary to enter the State Medical College. Instead, he joined a local Ayurvedic college as an anatomy lecturer. It was there that an American doctor on a Rockefeller scholarship working on an anti-hookworm campaign encouraged SubbaRow to apply to Harvard's School of Tropical Medicine.

Harvard considered his Ayurvedic work disqualifying and rejected him. In 1922, he tried again, but then withdrew his application to help his mother and siblings after two brothers died from Tropical Sprue, a rare infectious digestive disease. Not dissuaded, he applied again the following year, emphasizing his anatomy training. Harvard accepted him.[15]

SubbaRow was twenty-eight when he left behind his wife, pregnant with their first child, and emigrated to the U.S. (his child, a son, died of a bacterial infection before he was one; not only did SubbaRow never see his child, he never again saw his wife).[16] He was ineligible for a scholarship because his Indian degree did not meet Harvard's standards. The same was true when he applied for an internship at Boston hospitals. He finally landed some odd jobs at one.[17] Industrious and hardworking, he earned his diploma in Tropical Medicine in 1924 and started on his PhD in biochemistry at Harvard Medical School.

In 1929, he coauthored his first scientific paper about his development of a simple color test to determine the amount of phosphorus in biological tissue.[18] The following year he was the first Indian in Harvard history to earn a biochemistry PhD and began working as a teaching fellow at Harvard Medical School. Although it was common for a scientist of his talent to use research assistants and collaborate with peers in the lab, Harvard directed he work alone. Although he made advances in phosphorus compounds connected to RNA synthesis, he was not allowed to publish his results.[19] In 1935, he had to disown the extent of his role in the discovery of the color test related to phosphorus, instead giving the credit to his coauthor, who was being considered for promotion to a full Harvard professorship.[20]

Denied tenure and tired of his second-class status, in May 1940 he accepted an offer to become Lederle's associate director of research at their lab in Pearl River, New York. When the previous director retired at the end of that year, SubbaRow became the chief.

SubbaRow had joined Lederle just in time to be part of the penicillin project. He was the company's representative when dealing with the government or other pharma firms. Although the penicillin work left little time in the laboratory, he was the first researcher to synthesize amethopterin, a chemical analog of folic acid. That research was prompted by a study that showed children with leukemia got significantly worse when fed a diet rich in folic acid. Scientists like SubbaRow wondered if an analog that was hostile to folic acid might have the opposite effect. Sidney Farber, a pathologist at Boston's Children's Hospital, made a breakthrough with SubbaRow's analog, developing in a few years the first effective chemotherapy agent.[21]

In 1942, SubbaRow hired seventy-year-old Benjamin Duggar, a plant physiologist, who had been forced to "retire" by the University of Wisconsin as he was "too old to teach."[22] Other pharma firms had politely turned Duggar away, saying there were no positions or that his specialty was not what they needed. SubbaRow saw experience in what others judged "too old" and he thought that in Duggar he might have found a valuable "antibiotic hunter."

At Lederle, coworkers came to know the Alabama native as amiable and eccentric. Every day at the lab Duggar slowly but methodically sifted through soil samples looking for antibiotic-producing fungi. At his suggestion, Lederle requested the Army have soldiers returning home bring a small amount of soil from wherever they had served. By 1944, a small shack outside the lab held thousands of samples from more than twenty countries on three continents. Duggar sometimes isolated antibiotic organisms from them. He and SubbaRow carried out tests to see if they had any effect in petri dishes on a broad range of bacterial pathogens.

Some days Duggar stayed away from the soil and instead reverted to the professor he had been for many years. He stopped by the lab but only to give a lecture to his younger colleagues.[23] Most evenings Duggar left no later than 5:30 so he could play golf at a country club before it got dark. A chain-smoker, he also spent free time tending to a makeshift garden he created near an abandoned stable. He shared little about his personal life with coworkers.

The fourth of five sons born near the end of Reconstruction, Duggar was raised in a devout Episcopalian household. His father, Reuben Henry Duggar, was a prominent physician.[24] No one in the Duggar family talked about the days before the "War of Northern Aggression." Union troops had seized their large plantation, Frederickton, outside of Macon. His father had served on the state medical board that passed on the fitness of volunteer doctors to serve as Confederate medical officers.

A savant at school, Duggar entered the University of Alabama at fourteen.[25] After he graduated from Cornell with a PhD, his father shared with him the only story he ever told about the Civil War. During the last year of fighting, he had served as a surgeon at a field hospital in Talladega, Alabama. Malaria was rampant. Thousands of mosquitoes from adjacent marshlands plagued the camp. Duggar ordered that all fires be built on the camp's windward side and then be extinguished at dusk. That caused the smoke to blow over the camp, clearing the mosquitoes. That was a couple of decades before science confirmed that mosquitoes were malaria carriers. The lesson, his father told him, was that even as a doctor, it was sometimes important to go with your intuition. Duggar recalled that lesson at Lederle.

One day in 1945, while extracting molds from soil samples from a dormant hayfield on the University of Missouri campus, he noticed one was an unusual gold color. Duggar had isolated hundreds of what he called "ultra-molds" during his three years at Lederle.[26] Somehow, he had a hunch this one was special. With SubbaRow overseeing his work, Duggar tested the mold he labeled A-377. To their elation, A-377 proved effective in halting the growth of both Gram-positive and Gram-negative bacteria, including the microbes responsible for bubonic plague, tuberculosis, typhus, and Rocky Mountain spotted fever.[27] They had discovered the first broad-spectrum antibiotic since streptomycin.

Although SubbaRow and Duggar put it on a fast track, that did not translate into much speed given Lederle's small staff and limited resources. It took three years of additional testing, until 1948, before Duggar was confident enough to publish a paper about his finding.[28] There, he dubbed the antibiotic organism he discovered *Streptomyces aureofaciens*, the "gold maker." Lederle executives liked that so much they gave the drug its brand name, Aureomycin (*áureo* is Latin for "gold").

Before there could be certainty that Aureomycin was a wonder drug, Duggar had to produce enough of a purified version for human testing. SubbaRow and Duggar picked New York's Louis Tompkins Wright to run clinical tests on the most important drug in the company's history. A decade earlier *Life* had dubbed Wright the "most eminent Negro doctor in the U.S. . . . [the] surgical director of Harlem Hospital, [and] only colored Fellow of American College of Surgeons."[29] A lower-caste Indian rejected for tenure at Harvard had selected the son of a Confederate officer and doctor, and together they picked the most famous black doctor in America—the son of a slave who had himself become a physician—to conduct the clinical trials.

The fifty-seven-year-old Wright grew up in rural Georgia where his family set the example that nothing was impossible because of the color of his skin. Although both his grandfathers were white, his father was born a slave. When his father died not long after Louis's birth, his mother met and married William Fletcher Penn, the first black graduate of Yale Medical School. Penn was one of only sixty-five black doctors in Georgia at the turn of the twentieth century.[30] Doctors nationwide had to be members of the American Medical Association to practice at most hospitals, but the AMA left membership decisions to local chapters. Those in the Deep South refused to admit black doctors (the AMA did not change its national policy until 1950). The result was that many black doctors began operating rudimentary clinics to serve local patients, sometimes even running them from their homes.[31]

After graduating as the valedictorian at nearby Clark University, Wright took a train to Cambridge. He had sent his college transcript and a cover letter to the admissions department at Harvard Medical School. An interview with the Medical School dean was set. The dean mistakenly thought the Clark University on the transcript was the exclusive whites-only university in Worcester, Massachusetts. Upon meeting Wright and realizing his mistake he sent him to the chair of the chemistry department. That professor was a tough, no-nonsense academic who, the dean thought, would disabuse Wright of any thought he had of attending Harvard Medical. The chemistry chair tried to get rid of him by giving him an oral exam on the spot. Wright secured his admission, however, by correctly answering every question.[32]

During his second year, he could not do his obstetrics clerkship at the traditional Boston hospital for Harvard medical students but instead had to complete it with a black physician. "That is the way all the colored men get their obstetrics," he was told.[33] Instead of going along quietly, he protested and rallied the support of classmates. Harvard reversed itself. It was only one of many racial barriers he encountered. Despite graduating fourth in his 1915 class, he failed to get an internship at the city's top hospitals.[34] Wright did not want to intern at one of Boston's black hospitals because he knew they had antiquated equipment and there was no opportunity to pursue clinical research, one of his passions.[35] Ultimately, he had no choice. When no white hospital allowed him to complete his internship, he left Boston and started at Washington, D.C.'s, blacks-only Freedmen's Hospital.[36]

Wright returned to Atlanta to work with his stepfather after his D.C. internship. Walter Penn had recently cofounded the Atlanta chapter of the National Association for the Advancement of Colored People. Maybe the NAACP could help change things, he told Wright, who joined (for Wright it was the start of thirty-six years of storied activism with the NAACP).[37] Frustrated, though, in Georgia, Wright joined the Army Medical Corps and was dispatched to France for the remainder of World War I.*[38]

After two years of frontline surgical experience, he left the Army and opened his own practice in Harlem. In New York Wright discovered that there were layers of segregation that were more subtle than the South's, but no less ingrained and rigid. Jewish and black doctors had their own hospitals and were mostly barred from integrated ones.[39] On January 1, 1920, Wright was the first African American to join the staff of Harlem Hospital. Although his job was the lowest possible for a physician—"clinical assistant in the Outpatient Department"—four white doctors resigned in protest. The person responsible for Wright's appointment was demoted to the information booth at Bellevue Hospital.[40]

Determined to demonstrate how good he was, Wright excelled. And soon it seemed "he was the first" had become part of his name. He was the first African American police surgeon in New York (1928); first admitted to the American College of Surgeons (1934); first director of surgery at Harlem Hospital (1943), and first president of the Hospital Board (1948).[41]

Lederle Laboratory's SubbaRow and Duggar probably cared little about Wright's trailblazing when it came to race and medicine. They chose him to conduct Aureomycin's clinical trials because they considered him eminently qualified. He had by then published nearly ninety papers in leading scientific journals, thirty-five of them about antibiotics.[42] And Wright, who had just returned to work after a three-year leave of absence to recuperate from a severe bout of tuberculosis, was enthusiastic about doing the testing. He had long been interested in LGV, a sexually transmitted infection of the lymphatic system. Aureomycin was his chance to discover whether a drug could help

---

*Wright watched in frustration as the federal government established the Veterans' Bureau in 1921 and opened a Veterans' Hospital for blacks only in Tuskegee, Alabama (a decision protested by the KKK in large street demonstrations). It was impossible, Wright knew, that a single hospital could meet the medical needs of the 385,000 black soldiers, overwhelmingly from the South. Eleven years later, that Veterans' hospital became one of three local clinics involved in the Public Health Service's notorious "Tuskegee Study of Untreated Syphilis in the Negro Male." It turned into a forty-year experiment on hundreds of black men about the ravaging effects of untreated syphilis. The men, many poor sharecroppers from Macon County, were never treated with any medications.

patients with the painful, chronic condition. Over two months in the spring and early summer of 1948 Wright conducted the first human experiments. Lederle's drug destroyed the chlamydia bacteria responsible for the disease. It was also effective on a nasty viral variant of pneumonia. Wright uncovered few side effects and certainly nothing toxic. His report to Lederle was that their drug was ready for public release.[43]

By the time Aureomycin was ready to go on sale in December 1948, Lederle's chief of research, Yellapragada SubbaRow, was not alive to savor it. He had died the previous August of a heart attack at the age of fifty-three.* SubbaRow would have liked Lederle's strong launch, advertising the drug as "the most versatile antibiotic yet discovered, with a wider range of activity than any other known remedy."[44] The company spent a record $2.4 million in promotion, including a first, 142,000 free samples to doctors nationwide.[45] It took until September of the following year before the U.S. issued Aureomycin patent number 2,482,055. That was what every pharma competitor had been waiting for. Lederle had proven that it was possible to obtain a patented monopoly on a broad-spectrum antibiotic. Its competitors were determined that Aureomycin would not have the market to itself for very long.

As for the three men responsible for discovering and testing Aureomycin, the public recognition they received for the accomplishment was imbalanced at best. After SubbaRow's death, Lederle named a library block on its campus for him, as well as a fungus (*Subbaromyces splendens*). The Indian government issued a commemorative stamp in 1995 on his birthday centennial. When Louis Wright was nominated in 1952 for a Distinguished Service Medal, he got only one vote from the National Medical Association. A few months later when he died unexpectedly at the age of sixty-one, his death went mostly unnoticed except in the African American press and some medical journals. *The New York Times* did not even run a stand-alone obituary, instead listing him with other deaths for that day.

---

* Few doctors then believed there was any connection between lifestyle and heart disease. If it had been a more prevalent theory, someone might have taken notice that SubbaRow had arrived in America as a practicing Hindu, a nonsmoking vegetarian. In the U.S., he adopted an American diet, high in saturated fat and lots of red meat. He had also become a heavy smoker.

In contrast, when Benjamin Duggar died in 1956, his passing was covered widely for his breakthrough drug discovery. This time the *Times* did a story in its national section, titled "Dr. Benjamin Duggar Dies at 84; Led in Discovery of Aureomycin; Conducted Antibiotic Research After Being Retired from a Teaching as Too Old."[46]

7

A ONE-ATOM DIFFERENCE

The 1948 launch of Aureomycin was the first in a rush of new antibiotics. Lederle's rivals marveled at how a single drug produced huge profits. In its first year it captured more than a quarter of all American antibiotic sales. Aureomycin's profit margin was an impressive 35 percent; that compared to a measly 3 percent on Lederle's nonantibiotic drugs.[1] Competitors were pushing as fast as possible the development of their own "wonder drugs."

Many doctors and patients thought of the drugs as a frontline defense not simply for serious bacterial contagions but also for sinus, urinary tract, and dental infections, acne, even prophylactically at the first signs of a fever, earache, scratchy throat, or runny nose. One microbiologist estimated that overenthusiasm about the new drugs meant they were prescribed unnecessarily more than 90 percent of the time.[2] The FDA did not seem overly bothered by the unrestrained dosing since there were few reported side effects.[3] Accounts of itching, nausea, upset stomach, and hives were dismissed as the inevitable sensitivity of a few patients. A handful of reports identified far more serious consequences, including fungal and bacterial superinfections as the drugs also killed off the body's good bacteria, antibiotic poisoning, and the beginning of drug resistance. That news was lost in the public's enthusiasm for antibiotics.[4]*

One reason for the FDA silence was that Walter Dunbar, the chemist who had become the FDA's commissioner in 1944, did not want

* No organized medical group existed to serve as a central repository for collecting and disseminating the risks and side effects as they were reported. The Infectious Diseases Society of America, the professional organization that is a critical resource for physicians and scientists, was not created until 1963.

the agency to be perceived as a bureaucratic obstacle to the rapid deployment of lifesaving antibacterials. Even if Dunbar had wanted to sound a cautionary note about the overuse of antibiotics, the FDA had few tools at its disposal. It was short on staff and Congress had cut its budget to $5 million. On average, the FDA managed to thoroughly review only one in every dozen new drug applications.[5] It was largely a bystander as the antibiotic gold rush became the most lucrative period in pharmaceutical history and upended the industry's sales and marketing practices.

Parke-Davis, whose previous hits had been the hormone Adrenalin, the anticonvulsant Dilantin, and the antihistamine Benadryl, was the first to release an Aureomycin competitor. In 1949, it announced the sale of Chloromycetin, a broad-spectrum antibiotic it had tested in its labs for two years. Parke-Davis set its largest advertising budget and doubled its sales force for a drug that *Collier's* praised "as the greatest antibiotic since penicillin."[6] In under a year, Parke-Davis bragged that with revenues of $138 million it had claimed the title of the world's largest drug company. Forty percent of that came from Chloromycetin (Parke-Davis continued marketing it despite occasional reports it sometimes induced a rare blood disorder).[7]

The success of Lederle and Parke-Davis only whet the appetite of John McKeen, Pfizer's hard-charging chairman. Born in Manhattan and raised in Brooklyn's Flatbush neighborhood, the no-nonsense forty-eight-year-old McKeen had joined Pfizer in 1926. A former star college quarterback, he had come to the attention of management when he developed a paint that solved the company's costly corrosion problem on its stainless-steel manufacturing equipment. Because he demonstrated a talent for cutting costs while increasing production yields, by 1937 he was in charge of quality control and plant construction.[8] By the time he became president in 1949, he was anxious to remake the small Brooklyn chemical and mining company into a fully integrated pharmaceutical firm. Before the wartime penicillin project, Pfizer was best known as a manufacturer of citric acid. It never marketed any medication under its own name but instead the few it produced were for other drug firms. Without its own broad-spectrum antibiotic, the company derived most of its revenue as the largest manufacturer of penicillin and streptomycin, which it sold under the brand names of rivals.[9] Both drugs were still popular, but their tumbling prices had put the company under tremendous pressure, cutting deeply into Pfizer's profit margins. There was no further room for discounting.

McKeen was impatient for a new product and wanted what one industry analyst dubbed "a speed record among antibiotics." [10] He assembled a team of virologists, biochemists, bacteriologists, chemical engineers, pharmacologists, and microbiologists, challenging them to accomplish in a year what had taken fifteen with penicillin.[11] Pfizer had been gathering and testing soil samples since 1945 at a state-of-the-art lab in Terre Haute, Indiana. There it had amassed more than 135,000 samples, some sent by foreign correspondents, pilots, even missionaries.[12] A Pfizer chemist later recalled that they collected "soil samples from cemeteries; we had balloons up in the air [to] collect soil that was windborne; we got soil from the bottom of mine shafts . . . [even] the bottom of the ocean." [13] Despite more than 20 million tests, the lab's microbiologists had not found a new and effective antibiotic culture.

By 1950, pharmaceuticals for the first time became the country's most profitable industry.[14] McKeen felt, however, as if Pfizer had missed the party. In a speech that March to the New York Society of Security Analysts, he was blunt: "If you want to lose your shirt in a hurry, start making penicillin and streptomycin. . . . From a profit point of view, the only realistic solution to this problem lies in the development of new and exclusive antibiotic specialties." [15] McKeen often referred to streptomycin as "distress-merchandise." [16]

Pharma's old guard, such as George Merck, did not believe that drug firms should put profits first. Merck thought it was possible to invest in research to produce drugs for the common good while also delivering the solid financial results demanded by investors. That philosophy was one of the reasons that *Fortune* cited Merck as the "most admired" company in America for a record seven consecutive years. In 1950, while McKeen was complaining about the poor returns on penicillin and streptomycin, Merck-associated scientists won the Nobel in Medicine for their synthesis of cortisone, the first of nearly two dozen subsequent Nobel awards.[17]

When George Merck addressed the graduating class of the Medical College of Virginia later that year, he set a high bar for the industry. "We try to remember that medicine is for the patient. We try never to forget that medicine is for the people. It is not for the profits. The profits follow, and if we have remembered that, they have never failed to appear. The better we have remembered it, the larger they have been."[18]

Those who knew Merck did not doubt his sincerity. He often spoke privately about his company as if it were a quasi-public trust. Many at that graduation ceremony accepted what Merck said in good faith. That was evidence of how much goodwill the industry had at the start of the second half of the twentieth century.

Not everyone was enamored, however, with Merck's "medicine is for the patient" philosophy. When McKeen heard it, he dismissed the words as a clever public relations ploy.[19] Executives in the McKeen mold believed that no drug was worthwhile if it did not return a hefty profit. One obstacle, thought McKeen, was that almost all the industry's scientists collected the same salary whether they made a Nobel Prize–winning discovery or found nothing in their testing. They very rarely got a bonus if a drug became a blockbuster, nor did they get their pay docked if something they invented failed in clinical tests. Their interests were pretty much the same as if they had worked for a university. McKeen believed that giving the researchers so much independence was a mistake. He wanted to empower the sales and marketing division with the authority to guide the scientists toward the medicines that might sell best. In McKeen's judgment, good marketing could sell even a mediocre drug.

Everything at Pfizer seemed to hinge on a yellow gold-colored powder its scientists had extracted from soil taken not far from the company's Terre Haute lab. It was labeled PA-76 (PA stands for Pfizer Antibiotic). Further testing demonstrated its effectiveness against more than a hundred Gram-positive and Gram-negative bacteria as well as even some fungi. The scientific tradition was that the discoverer named the drug. In the case of PA-76, McKeen took charge. From a list of several dozen names he chose Terramycin (Latin for "high land"). "I wanted a name connected with the earth," he later said, "and one that could easily be recalled by doctors, scientists and people in general."[20]

There was a small problem, however. Pfizer's scientists reported that the chemical structure of its drug appeared identical to Lederle's Aureomycin. It was as if each company had found and invented the same medication. Lederle had been a few steps ahead and had a patent on its drug. McKeen was not concerned whether they were the same. He needed someone to figure out how to make Terramycin different in a patent application. Differentiating the molecular structure of the two drugs had stymied Pfizer's chemists. McKeen hired Robert Burns Woodward, the world's best-known chemist. He had written hundreds of highly cited, peer-reviewed papers and earned every prestigious award except for a Nobel in his more than four decades at Harvard (he added a Nobel in Chemistry to his résumé in 1965).[21]

Woodward found Aureomycin was missing a single oxygen atom present in Terramycin.[22] It was a trifling difference, even for a chemist. It did not affect, Woodward said, the way the drugs worked in patients. But it was all McKeen needed. The extra oxygen atom allowed Pfizer's attorneys to file an application with the Patent Office.[23]

Pfizer pressed for expedited processing. In an affidavit included in its submission, McKeen noted that Pfizer had "spent large sums of money in the research and development" of Terramycin and said it "must decide in the near future" whether to "invest heavily" to manufacture and sell the drug.

He had made no effort to characterize his company's antibiotic research as motivated by a desire to better serve public health. He instead made it clear that Pfizer was looking for a solid return on its investment.[24] The Terramycin patent was issued in just seven months, a record. (The average drug patent at the time took three and a half years.)[25]

Pfizer had started clinical trials while the patent application had been pending. McKeen selected Gladys Hobby, a Columbia University microbiologist, to collate the results from over one hundred physicians nationwide. Hobby had led some of the early penicillin testing and she conducted her own trials on Terramycin that December at Harlem Hospital. It was the same place where Louis Wright had run the clinical trials the previous year for Aureomycin. By the time the patent was issued, Hobby had sent the stellar clinical results to McKeen.[26]

In preparation for Terramycin's sale, Pfizer's directors unanimously approved changes to the company's bylaws so it could bypass traditional drug distribution companies and instead itself sell directly "to retailers, wholesalers, and hospitals."[27]

FDA approval was the last hurdle before the eight newly hired "detail men" could start work in earnest.[28] Some of Pfizer's rivals had detail departments for more than a decade. The job entailed personal visits to doctors' offices for promoting the company's drugs. Good detail men boosted sales for a drug even though they did not take orders for them.

All they did was persuade physicians—the indispensable middle person in the pharmaceutical-to-consumer model—to write prescriptions for the company's brands.

In late February 1950, Pfizer submitted the drug to the FDA for approval. All eyes turned to Henry Welch, who had recently become the chief of the FDA's powerful Division of Antibiotics. Welch—who had a doctorate in bacteriology from Western Reserve—had joined the FDA in 1938 after the Food, Drug, and Cosmetic Act had expanded the agency's powers. During World War II he had overseen the division responsible for certifying the quality of penicillin manufactured by pharma companies.[29] In 1950, he had cemented his status as a prominent figure in the emerging world of antibiotics as the editor of a new publication, *The Journal of Antibiotics*. His editorial board had five Nobel Prize winners in medicine, including Alexander Fleming, Selman Waksman, and Howard Florey. In his new role as chief of the Division of Antibiotics, Welch single-handedly wielded influence to fast-track or delay an antibiotic application. A postponement could complicate any firm's well-planned drug launch, adding months to the rollout and costing millions in lost sales.

Welch recommended to the FDA commissioners that they accept Pfizer's clinical studies at face value and on March 23, 1951, the FDA approved Terramycin.[30] It was the first drug under the Pfizer label that the company had developed on its own, from discovery in the lab to sales to the public.[31]

Jack McKeen had his broad-spectrum antibiotic. But he knew that his company lacked the sales and marketing know-how to sell it. Some rivals thought that shortcoming would cause Pfizer to stumble. McKeen, however, had not invested so much time and money to let the drug fizzle. He turned for help to New York's Madison Avenue. No traditional ad agency, however, wanted the pharma business because the marketing was restricted by what drug companies considered respectable ways to promote their products. "Respectable" translated into boring by Madison Avenue standards. The ads that ran in specialized medical journals were often reproductions of the drug's packaging insert. The industry that had gotten its start with outrageous claims for dubious patent medicines, plastered in newspapers and on billboards across America, had morphed into the dullest business sector.

McKeen wanted someone capable of devising an unorthodox campaign that not only worked for Terramycin but could be the template for future Pfizer drugs. It took McKeen little time to settle on the right man, Arthur Sackler, an ad executive who was also a physician. Sackler was at the forefront of the embryonic medical advertising industry. There were only a handful of agencies staking out the fledgling market. McKeen had made a good choice. Sackler's aggressive and brilliant marketing would not only make Terramycin a blockbuster. In the process, he would forever transform how the pharmaceutical industry sold its drugs.

8

A "JEWISH KID FROM BROOKLYN"

As a self-described "Jewish kid from Brooklyn," Arthur Sackler did not advertise his Jewish roots in the WASP world of Madison Avenue.[1] One of Sackler's attorneys recalled how many times Sackler endured the ingrained anti-Semitism that was a hallmark of the 1950s New York ad business: "You would sit at meetings where they would tell Jewish jokes, anti-Jewish jokes, and you had to sit there and swallow it, and laugh along with the boys."[2] Sackler did not like it. He did not protest, however. Arthur instead decided his best revenge would be to beat his rival Mad Men, most of whom came from privileged families and boasted of Ivy League degrees, exclusive country club memberships, and listings in the society pages.

Arthur was born in Brooklyn in 1913 to Sophie and Isaac Sackler, Orthodox Jewish immigrants from Eastern Europe, who ran a small grocery store. They named him Abraham, after his grandfather (he later used that only on legal papers and opted instead for the less Jewish-sounding Arthur). When he was five, an influenza epidemic killed more than thirty thousand New Yorkers. The family's Flatbush neighborhood was hard hit. It was then, he later said, that he first thought of becoming a doctor.

After Sackler tested well on an IQ test, he joined a small class for gifted students at Brooklyn's Erasmus Hall High School. There were few Jews; and one of the teachers was overtly anti-Semitic.[3] Sackler kept a quiet profile, outperforming others while dividing his free time visiting the Brooklyn Museum or taking the subway to Manhattan to study with noted sculptor Chaim Gross at the Lower East Side's Educational Alliance Art School.[4]

After graduating from Erasmus, he enrolled in New York University's College of Arts and Sciences, then situated on top of a hill in the Bronx.[5] His major was English drama and at night he took classes on art history at tuition-free Cooper Union.[6]

His parents were hardworking. The savage downturn of the Great Depression, however, cost them their business and wiped out their savings, as it did for many of their neighbors and friends.[7] They had two more sons by then, Mortimer and Raymond. Unless Arthur found a job with a decent wage, he could not afford his NYU tuition, much less indulge his art interests. Ever practical, he added premed courses to his curriculum. "Unfortunately, early in life," he later recalled, "I realized my limitations."[8]

Given his financial pressures, art could not long compete with medicine as a career choice. The widespread belief among many recently arrived immigrants was that unrestrained capitalism had led to the economic collapse. That kindled Sackler's early attraction to left-wing politics.[9] Socialism was dominant in New York's Jewish neighborhoods. Sackler's parents had been part of the enormous wave of two million Jews from the Russian and Austro-Hungarian empires that arrived in America during a four-decade span ending in 1920. Living in overcrowded tenements and working long hours at factories in unsafe and harsh conditions, New York Jews became the force behind trade unions. Integral to the message about workers' rights were underlying socialist themes about developing a cooperative, classless society. Sackler's parents subscribed to *Forverts* (Forward), a socialist daily that, with a quarter million readers, was also the world's largest Yiddish newspaper. Many of their Brooklyn neighbors belonged to the United Hebrew Trades, an umbrella socialist organization designed to mobilize the Jewish workers who dominated the garment industry.[10] Jews accounted for 40 percent of New York's Socialist Party (not as shocking a figure as it might at first glance seem since Jews made up one third of the city's population).[11] The year before Arthur's birth, the Socialist candidate for president, Eugene V. Debs, garnered nearly a million votes (6 percent of the popular vote). Sixty percent of New York's Jewish voters voted for him.[12]

Arthur was one of a small group of committed Marxists at NYU. He had little opportunity, however, as an editor for the *Journal of the Medical Students Association* to indulge his politics. For protests over undergraduate rights, Sackler produced a "very crude strike bulletin."[13]

He also handled demands and negotiations with the college administration on behalf of his striking fellow students.[14] Mostly, however, to pay his bills he took a series of part-time jobs at Drake Business Schools, the *Medical Bulletin of Bellevue Hospital*, and even a few months at William Douglas McAdams, a four-person firm that specialized in the just emerging field of medical advertising. It sounded dull but germane to his studies. There Sackler learned he had a talent for writing ad copy.[15]

During his last year of medical school, he met Else Finnich Jorgensen, the daughter of a Danish family that had recently emigrated to America. After a short courtship he proposed. Sophie Sackler was crushed that her eldest son would marry a non-Jew. It was such a source of contention that Else converted to Judaism.[16] Sackler was only twenty-four when he graduated in 1937 from the NYU School of Medicine with specialties in psychiatry and neuroendocrinology. He began a rotating internship at Lincoln Hospital in the South Bronx, run by New York City's Department of Public Welfare.[17]

Arthur's younger brothers, Mortimer and Raymond, decided to follow him into medicine. Just a couple of months after Arthur's graduation, Mortimer got the bad news that he had failed to get one of the spots then allotted for Jews in New York's medical schools. So Mortimer instead sailed steerage to the U.K.[18] In Glasgow, the Jewish community helped him get admitted to the well-respected Anderson College of Medicine. Two years later the same happened to Raymond.[19]

During the spare time of his hospital internship, Arthur raised money to support Norman Bethune, a Canadian physician Sackler called his "moral exemplar."[20] Bethune was a committed communist who had volunteered as a battlefield surgeon for anti-fascist fighters in Spain before moving to China in 1938 to join the communist insurrection. Mao Zedong commissioned him to lead a mobile operating unit at the front. Arthur thought Bethune was a model for what a politically committed doctor might achieve.

By the time Arthur completed his residency in December 1939, however, Bethune was dead at forty-nine. He had cut himself during a battlefield operation and the resulting blood infection proved fatal. Years later everyone would know as much about Bethune as Sackler did; Chairman Mao made him a hero of the Communist Revolution by dedicating an essay to him.[21] And Arthur, when he visited China much later to sponsor medical conferences, told his Chinese hosts that nothing would be a greater honor for him than to be "a present-day Bethune."[22]

Bethune's death put Sackler into a funk. His parents were distressed to learn he had skipped the state medical exam, the final requirement before he could practice as a physician. Instead, the twenty-seven-year-old learned about a job at Schering, the American subsidiary of the German pharma company. Schering hired Sackler as the deputy to the director of its four-person Medical Information Division, the company's bare-bones ad department.[23] One of his jobs while working through school had been selling ads for Drake Business Schools and the *Medical Bulletin of Bellevue Hospital*.[24] He had told friends he thought many advertisers wasted their money since they did not know how to put a good sales pitch into a few columns of newsprint. The Schering post gave him a chance to prove he knew better. He tried jump-starting Schering's stagnant product line by creating the first graphic ads in medical journals. Before long he was pestering management in vain for a larger budget for a direct mail campaign.

World War II had been under way a few months by the time Arthur began working at Schering. He was one of the few in the forty-person executive suite who was not a native-born German.[25] Some recent arrivals, he learned, were German Jews, although none advertised that. Dr. Julius Weltzien, the CEO, was the son of a Christian schoolteacher father and a nonpracticing Jewish mother.[26] By Nazi race laws he was Jewish. Weltzien was one of seven "Jewish" managers and senior executives the German parent had transferred to America in 1938. By the end of that year, Schering in Germany had purged all Jewish directors in order to get a Certificate in Good Standing as an Aryan Company (the Nazi Ministry of Economics complained the following year that the U.S. branch was merely a subterfuge that kept Jews in management).[27]

America did not prove much of a safe haven for men like Weltzien.[28] Declassified FBI files obtained by the author reveal that the Bureau investigated German and Swiss pharmaceutical firms in America even before the U.S. formally entered the war after the attack on Pearl Harbor. It suspected that Schering, Hoffmann-La Roche, and Ciba Chemical were conduits for money to blacklisted countries. Schering, in particular, had obtained from several German conglomerates the exclusive patent rights for drugs the FBI considered "of great importance from the standpoint of national defense."[29] The U.S. military had concluded that its "adrenalin hormone which is used in the treatment of shock, especially shock resulting from severe burns and wounds, is of direct and immediate importance to our war efforts [and could] . . . have saved the lives of thousands of English soldiers after Dunkirk."[30]

The FBI suspected that Schering sold those drugs through "Panamanian dummy corporations" and then funneled the profits to "a Swiss Holding company." The FBI concluded the conspiracy had resulted in $2.5 million ($23 million in 2018) making its way to "Nazi controlled banks."[31] The British Ministry of Economic Warfare urged the U.S. to freeze Schering's accounts. The British charged that the company bankrolled a network of Nazi agents in foreign countries and its trade with South America was a sophisticated scheme to circumvent the British blockade of Europe.[32] As a result, the FBI pressured Weltzien and other executives, demanding they cooperate or be investigated for espionage.

FBI files reveal the Bureau had developed six confidential informants at Schering. One reported that during the previous year "a Jewish influence had been growing in the company . . . the management was Jewish." That unidentified source reported that Weltzien "denies the fact that he is a Jew" although the informant "feels sure he is."[33] To another, Weltzien admitted his mother was Jewish but insisted he was not, and that he was first and foremost a German.[34]

Hiding a Jewish family background was not unusual in Hitler's Germany. The Bureau had mistakenly thought that that fear would disappear for Germans who had recently emigrated to America. Yet they did not feel safe simply because they were several thousand miles away from Germany. They worried about the safety of relatives left behind. (Weltzien's mother later killed herself instead of being deported to a concentration camp.)[35]

If Weltzien was Jewish, the FBI wondered if that made it less likely that the New Jersey subsidiary played a key role in an elaborate scheme to funnel money to the Third Reich. According to the Bureau's chief informant, Weltzien and the other emigrant executives were "international Jews who would pour oil on both fires [Allied and Axis powers] if a profit was in sight."[36] Still, the FBI obtained information from Schering's few American Jewish employees, including Sackler. Declassified FBI files reveal that Arthur secretly helped the government agents: "Dr. Sackler is considered to be completely reliable and was of considerable assistance to the investigation."[37]

American socialists and communists were justifiably suspicious of the FBI; the Bureau treated membership in many left-wing organizations and political groups as proof of seditious intent. Sackler's cooperation is strong evidence that his distaste for Hitler's Third Reich trumped whatever apprehensions he had about helping the Bureau. (Arthur later told his family that he had volunteered to be drafted when the war broke out but had been rejected because of nearsightedness. The author was unable to verify whether he ever applied for military service.)[38]

During this period Arthur met Ludwig Wolfgang Fröhlich, a German who had emigrated to the U.S. in 1936 after a brief stopover in Bermuda.[39] Fröhlich, who applied the following year for American citizenship, would play a critical role in Sackler's life.[40] The same age as Arthur, he worked at the American subsidiary of a German typesetting firm. He Americanized his name to Bill and dropped the umlaut. If someone later asked what the *W* stood for, he said William. Frohlich was formal and charming. Colleagues and friends took notice of his tailored suits and talked about his refined sense of style.[41]

The no-nonsense Sackler with his sharp Brooklyn accent and the suave, softly spoken Frohlich would seem to have little in common. They shared a love of fine art, however, and were hugely ambitious in an era where such an admission was considered gauche. They became close friends.[42]

In the social watering holes on Manhattan's Upper East Side to which Frohlich gravitated, he focused on cultivating the right connections to gain entrée to New York's old-money crowd. He never talked about his past and steered away from conversations about the tumultuous events wracking Europe and his native Germany. An aura of mystery allowed plenty of rumors about him. At first, many thought he was a Jew who had fled Hitler. But that seemed less likely the more they got to know him. The friends he sought were from influential WASP families, many listed in the Social Register.

If Frohlich was not Jewish, then the gossipers wondered if he might be a Nazi. That rumor reached the FBI. The Bureau conducted a brief but intensive background check and failed to uncover any link to the Third Reich.[43]

Arthur Sackler was one of the very few who knew Frohlich was Jewish. Arthur understood the reasons why his new friend wanted it a secret. A surprisingly small number of colleagues knew that Sackler was Jewish.[44]

Hiding one's religion had not been easy in Nazi Germany. When applying in 1934 to Frankfurt's Goethe University, for instance, Frohlich filled an admissions form for "non-Aryans." On it, he noted that his family had lived in Germany since the fifteenth century and that his father fought for Germany in World War I. He also had to admit, however, that neither his parents nor grandparents were "of Aryan origin" (Nazis race laws considered anyone with one Jewish grandparent to be Jewish themselves).[45] The answer was also *no* as to whether his family had "renounced their Jewish faith."[46]

Frohlich had made a wide circle of well-placed friends before his younger sister, Ingrid, and their mother arrived in New York in 1938. His connections helped land the five-foot-eight Ingrid a coveted job as a couture model for Sophie Gimbel, the noted American designer who ran Saks Fifth Avenue's fabled Salon Moderne custom dress shop. Sophie was the first female clothing designer to make the cover of *Time*.[47] Only a wealthy clientele—including the Woolworths, du Ponts, Huttons, Dukes, and Loebs—could afford her steep prices, ranging from popular day dresses at $300 to $1,500 for hand-stitched evening gowns ($5,463 to $27,315 in 2019 dollars).[48]

Since working at Sophie's put Ingrid in touch with a rarefied crowd, the Frohlichs decided it was important to their new lives in America not only to deny their Judaism but to go out of their way to do so.[49] The author discovered that the last time either admitted to being Jewish was on their U.S. immigration papers, in which "German/Hebrew" is listed for both as nationality.[50] Ingrid, in particular, was insistent she was not Jewish.[51] "Christian" was her answer if asked about religion (later changed to "Lutheran" before finally becoming "Catholic"). A distant relative recalled years later that Ingrid often said, "Those Jewish people, I can't stand them."[52]

It worked. Ingrid became one of Sophie's top models. She was the personal favorite of Wallis Simpson, the American divorcée for whom the King of England, Edward VIII, had abdicated his throne. British intelligence was so concerned about Edward and Simpson's pro-German sympathies that the government exiled the couple to the Bahamas for five years. There, Edward served as the island's governor. Simpson battled boredom with regular shopping sprees to the U.S. Her carefree lifestyle angered many in Britain who endured constant German bombs, rockets, blackouts, and strict food rationing.

Sometimes Ingrid flew to Miami to model some of Sophie's designs for the duchess. During one trip she met her future husband, a wealthy Florida accountant, Thomas Burns. After they wed she became Kathleen Ingrid Burns and made an easy transition from the insular world of Sophie's salon to social seasons in New York and Palm Beach.[53] She joined the two most exclusive and prominent Palm Beach country clubs, the Bath and Tennis Club and Everglades Club, both of which enforced a "no Jews" admission policy.[54] In Manhattan, she became a member of the Colony Club, an all-women's club most famous for Eleanor Roosevelt's resignation after it rejected the membership application of Elinor Morgenthau, the wife of FDR's secretary of the treasury, Henry (the Morgenthaus were Jewish). The club was not apologetic about its exclusionary policy.[55]

Meanwhile, Ludwig joined Manhattan's University Club, which also barred Jews (that policy ended in 1962).[56] It was not long before he collected an eclectic and creative group of friends, including composer Aaron Copland and soprano Birgit Nilsson. When he later bought an East 63rd Street townhouse, he hosted parties that were coveted invites.[57] And with Ingrid, he purchased a small retreat in East Hampton. There he became a member of the Devon Yacht Club and both joined the exclusive Maidstone Club.[58]

Judaism was not L. W. Frohlich's only secret. Only a couple of his closest friends knew he was gay. For the rest of the world, he was one of New York's most eligible bachelors, often in the company of beautiful women.[59] "He will never settle down," was the common refrain from the gossipy dowagers who saw him with different dates at social events.

Two years after meeting Sackler, Frohlich left his job at the typesetting firm to launch his own art studio. Sackler tried helping him in his new venture by sending a lot of Schering's typesetting and graphics work.[60] Sackler was not only enjoying his work inside the ad department, but his medical degree gave him a role in drafting booklets that Schering sent to doctors from its Medical Research Division.[61]

That work at Schering was short lived. Not long after the December 1941 attack at Pearl Harbor, newspapers reported the Roosevelt administration was preparing to select an Alien Property Custodian. That had last happened during World War I, when the federal government seized assets of all significant German-owned properties in America. Arthur Sackler recognized that the only way Schering might avoid that same fate was if an American owned it.

Arthur had become familiar with Schering's strengths and weaknesses and was confident the right owner could turn it into a far more powerful pharmaceutical company than the one the government might seize. He arranged a meeting with Alfred Stern, the heir to a wealthy banking family, who had himself earned a small fortune in Chicago real estate. Stern's first marriage had been to one of the daughters of Julius Rosenwald, the part owner of Sears and Roebuck and one of the country's most progressive philanthropists. He had assumed control of the family's charitable foundation after Rosenwald's 1932 death. One of Stern's first endeavors was to fund the Institute for Psychoanalysis in Chicago, dedicated to research about the causes and treatment of mental illness. That intrigued Sackler, who had decided that if he ever became a practicing physician, it would be as a psychiatrist.[62]

By the time Sackler reached out to him, Stern had divorced Rosenwald's daughter and remarried. His new wife was Martha Dodd, the daughter of an American historian and diplomat. She had a secret. Soviet intelligence had recruited her as an agent while she was living with her father, the U.S. ambassador to Germany before World War II.[63] Martha soon converted Stern into an enthusiastic backer of left-wing causes, including Modern Age Books, an experimental paperback publisher of radical literature.[64] Stern had moved to New York, bought an East Side townhouse, and worked from an expansive office in Rockefeller Center. He became a director of New York's Citizens Housing and Planning Council, a haven for many left-wing intellectuals and militants fighting under the broad banner of "tenants' rights."

Sackler liked Stern's politics, activism, and his bank account. And Stern liked that someone who held only the number two spot in an underutilized part of Schering had the gumption to want to buy the company. But they could not act quickly enough. Beginning in January 1942, federal agents entered Schering and took physical control of its New Jersey headquarters.[65] The Alien Property Custodian was formally appointed the following month and straightaway seized all German-owned corporate assets in the U.S. (It took ten years before Schering was sold at public auction for $29 million—$281 million in 2019 dollars—to the Plough family and renamed Schering-Plough).[66]

Frohlich sold his design studio in early 1943 and launched L. W. Frohlich Inc., a medical advertising agency, at a nine-story brick townhouse at 34 East 51st Street. Parke-Davis became his first client. Sackler had introduced Frohlich to a senior vice president there. He knew they both shared a passion for opera and had season tickets to the Metropolitan.[67] Sackler correctly figured that would open the door to business.[68]

Arthur was uncharacteristically undecided about what to do next. It was an unplanned opportunity for him to spend more time with Else and their first child, Carol, born the previous August. He vacillated about taking the state medical exam. Although he had little desire to begin private practice, it would give an option of working one day with his brothers, Mortimer and Raymond. They were only several years away from getting their own MD degrees. While Arthur had worked at Schering toying with new marketing concepts, Mortimer had switched schools and finished his studies at Middlesex University School of Medicine in Waltham, Massachusetts (on land occupied now by Brandeis). Raymond, who had volunteered during the Battle of Britain serving as a plane spotter for the British Home Guard, followed his brother back to Middlesex. Their timing was auspicious. They got their degrees just before the school lost its accreditation, disqualifying some graduates from taking the state boards.[69]

On January 29, 1944, twenty-three-year-old Raymond married nineteen-year-old Beverly Feldman, a premed student at New York University. She was from a working-class Jewish family in the same Brooklyn neighborhood as the Sacklers.[70] Raymond and Beverly shared Arthur's hard-line leftist politics. A confidential informant had secretly taken photos of the 1944 membership list of the Communist Party of America (CPA) Kensington Club on Church Avenue in Brooklyn. Among the names were Raymond Sackler and Beverly Feldman, both of whom the FBI discovered were card-carrying party members. When the newlyweds moved temporarily to Boston that April so Raymond could finish his Middlesex studies, they transferred their membership to the party's Boston chapter.[71] On Raymond's graduation that September, the couple returned to Brooklyn. Beverly began studies at NYU Medical School while Raymond started as an intern at Harlem Hospital. Again, they requested their party memberships be returned to the local New York chapter.[72]

The couple had joined the Communist Party during its peak in the years following the Great Depression and World War II. The party had only 6,000 members before the 1929 stock market crash. A decade later it was 66,000.[73] In the 1930s and 1940s, half the members were Jewish, mostly Eastern European immigrant families like the Sacklers and Feldmans.[74] According to A. B. Magil, a card-carrying member of the

American Communist Party who later worked for Arthur, "a reliable source" told him that "all three Sacklers had been party members early on, but not for long."[75]*

Raymond and Beverly remained steadfast communists through a period that tested the faith of some party loyalists. Joseph Stalin's show trials of the old Bolshevik party leaders began in the mid-1930s. It was the start of Stalin's bloody and brutal "Great Purge." Germany's communists had helped the Nazis bring down the Weimar Republic. Stalin signed a nonaggression pact with Hitler and then joined the Nazis in conquering and dividing Poland in September 1939.

The file the FBI opened on Raymond and Beverly in 1944 remained active at least until 1968. The Bureau occasionally assigned agents to call or visit the Sacklers, always under some concocted story, to discover if their Communist Party affiliation made them security risks.[76] The family always refused to discuss any political allegiances with the FBI.[77]

---

* The FBI file for Beverly Sackler, née Feldman, is thus far only declassified in part. The FBI informed the author that at least one file on Raymond Sackler, created by the New York Field Office (100-NY-75887) was destroyed by the Bureau on November 12, 1970. That was, according to the FBI, done as a "periodic destruction of records pursuant to a legal schedule." The author consulted with an attorney specializing in the Freedom of Information Act. Pending the release of additional information now withheld by the FBI, it is not possible to verify if that purge of the New York field office file on Raymond Sackler was in accordance with the statutory requirements. The FBI identified to the author four additional, still-classified files, as potentially relevant to Raymond Sackler and/or Arthur Sackler. The author filed a public access records request for those files to the National Archives Special Access division. The Archives deemed that two, both from the Boston FBI—100-BS-15 and 100-BS-589—were "unresponsive to your request." Although they were about Americans who were Communist Party members in the Boston area, they had "no mention of any of the Sacklers." Two other files—100-HQ-340415 and 100-NY-75702—were responsive. They contain a total of approximately 350 pages about Arthur Sackler; the headquarters files (HQ) are an investigation into Arthur from March 1945 to July 1968, and the New York office file (NY) covers an FBI probe into him from November 1944 to July 1968. Although both files are in the Archives' first-tier processing queue, the Archives estimates that it is unlikely that a review and release of information shall take place before April 2020. The author became aware of another FBI file focused solely on Arthur Sackler—100-NY-75887—not in the possession of the National Archives but likely still in the Bureau's custody. A formal request for declassification of that file was made in April 2018 and it is pending with the Bureau's Freedom of Information Office. Finally, University of New Hampshire professor Ben Harris provided the author a copy of eighty-nine pages released by the FBI in 1999 subject to his request about Arthur Sackler (FOIPA No. 442908).

While Raymond and Mortimer were in their first-year residencies at Harlem Hospital in 1944, Arthur took a career detour. Frohlich told him there was an opening at William Douglas McAdams. Arthur had a part-time job there eight years earlier while working his way through New York University. William Douglas McAdams, a Chicago journalist, had started his agency in 1926 with consumer accounts that included Van Camp Beans and Mother's Oats. He later convinced Squibb it could sell more of its cod liver oil if it advertised to doctors in medical journals. That campaign doubled Squibb's cod liver oil sales in under a year.[78] McAdams boasted to Sackler that his agency was the nation's largest medical advertiser. He hired Arthur and gave him the impressive title of "medical and creative director."[79] It did not take Sackler very long to realize that being the country's biggest medical ad firm was not much to boast about given that the market was tiny.

In addition to his new McAdams job, Arthur also started a part-time residency that same year at Creedmoor Psychiatric Hospital in Queens, a seven-thousand-bed state mental institution.[80] The little free time he had vanished once he was promoted in record time to become vice president of McAdams.[81]

Mortimer and Raymond followed Arthur to Creedmoor. All three shared a belief that mental illness likely had biochemical roots that could be treated, or at least controlled, with medication.[82] That concept countered the prevailing Freudian theory that mental disorders were the result of people's experiences. The problem wasn't Freud, Arthur wrote years later in an essay about the future of psychiatry, but rather that the search for "an organic foundation" of mental illness "was obscured, if not lost, in the brilliance of his psychodynamics."[83] There was little funding for research into organic causes or pharmaceutical treatments.

The Sacklers saw little hope in earlier and cruder treatments, including electroshock and lobotomies. Instead, they hoped at Creedmoor to establish a research institute, supported by state funding, that concentrated on nascent drug therapies, primarily hormones.

American psychiatry, which was in its heyday in the 1950s, accommodated their left-wing politics. The FBI had placed an undercover informant inside the American Communist Party during the 1940s. In congressional testimony and public interviews the following decade, the informant disclosed that the party had a secret "professional unit" composed of "psychiatrists, psychologists, medical doctors and social, health and welfare workers."[84] "A huge percentage of young psychiatrists in the 1930s and 1940s considered themselves to be Marxists," history and psychology professor Ben Harris told the author.[85]

Arthur wanted to find work that would allow him to merge his medical knowledge and political zeal. During World War II, he got angry about the Red Cross's policy of refusing all blood donations from blacks, and later accepting them but segregating both the collection and dispensing of white and black blood. Although the Army's surgeon general realized there was no convincing medical reason for separating blood by race, he advised the assistant secretary of war that it was "psychologically important in America." Labor unions, some activist black newspapers, militant left-wing newsletters, and the American Communist Party were at the forefront demanding change. The communists condemned the blood drive segregation as "Barbarian Hitlerism." Sackler was outspoken, calling it ridiculous, and he might even have helped some students at Harlem's P.S. 43 with posters they distributed protesting the Red Cross policy. (The Red Cross ended its blood segregation policy in 1949. Arkansas required it until 1969 and Louisiana until 1972.)[86]

Sackler's activism brought him to the attention of the FBI in 1945. In a forty-nine-page memo sent to J. Edgar Hoover, the New York field office provided details about a February fundraising dinner at Times Square's Hotel Astor for the Joint Anti-Fascist Refugee Committee (it was soon placed on the attorney general's List of Subversive Organizations).[87] The ostensible purpose was to honor playwright Lillian Hellman, and to kick off a $750,000 fundraising drive to fight Spanish fascists (Pablo Picasso was an honorary chairman). Poet Dorothy Parker introduced Hellman, who had just returned from the Soviet Union. Hellman was one of the first Americans allowed to visit the Red Army at the front, and she regaled the audience with stories of how Russians fought for Soviet-style communism. There were several dozen banquet tables, each with ten paying guests; all proceeds went to the money drive. The FBI obtained a list of attendees. Table 72 was "Arthur and Else Sackler and Bill Frohlich."[88] Three months later, the FBI noted the Sacklers attended another Refugee Committee fundraiser, this time a "Doctor's Dinner" at the Hotel Commodore.[89]

The FBI understood that not everyone at left-wing fundraisers was a communist, much less a security threat. However, it also realized that while the American Communist Party had about 70,000 card-carrying members by 1945, there were many more supporters who were not formal members. When the Cold War got under way after World War II ended, the Bureau focused on Soviet espionage. At the top of the FBI's suspect list were committed communists and those sympathetic to the Red cause.

In 1947, Arthur pushed politics into the background to concentrate on his career. He took the state medical exam and received his license to practice as Abraham Sackler. Mortimer got his medical license a few months later, and Raymond got his the following year.[90] The author uncovered that just a couple of years before the trio got their professional licenses, they had incorporated Pharmaceutical Research Associates, their first joint business.[91] It was one of the earliest companies dedicated to conducting safety trials for new drugs. As the requirements for drug approval tightened in the coming decades, it designed and managed trials and prepared and submitted regulatory filings. Pharmaceutical Research Associates also bore a feature that would be a Sackler trademark in many future ventures: their ownership was secret.[92] Dr. Alfred Halpern, a Sackler family friend, was the only publicly listed name associated with the firm through the 1950s. Its address was 17 East 62nd Street, a five-story limestone townhouse that figured prominently in future Sackler ventures.[93]

It was not long after Arthur got his medical license that he told Mortie and Ray, as he called them, that he needed to reduce his Creedmoor workload.[94] He and his wife, Else, had saved enough to buy a one third share of William Douglas McAdams. It was one of the few companies in which the Sacklers could not remain anonymous. It was a prescient move; just as the breakthrough with antibiotics was revolutionizing the drug business, it would soon foster a competitive market tailor-made for modern advertising.*[95]

---

* The author discovered that one third remained with William McAdams, and one third was owned by Helen Haberman, the company's executive vice president. By 1953, McAdams's share was reduced to 10 percent and Arthur and Else had 46 percent with Haberman holding 44 percent.

9

MEDICINE AVENUE

By 1950, McAdams was the most successful agency of the handful that focused on medical advertising, a specialty that a John Hopkins professor later dubbed Medicine Avenue.[1] McAdams held that top spot for more than fifteen years until the big agencies played catch-up, after having mistakenly assumed the field would never take off.[2] Sackler and Frohlich—whose agencies dominated early on—had a friendship that superseded any business rivalry.[3] The duo, often joined by Arthur's wife, Else, attended art auctions and spent weekends trolling through flea markets and small antique shops. One day, Arthur later recalled, "I came upon some Chinese ceramics and Ming furniture. My life has not been the same since."[4] Sackler's awakening came at Transorient, a tiny Manhattan antique shop owned by a noted British art dealer, William Drummond.[5] That chance visit sparked in Sackler what became a lifelong passion.

The same year he told his brothers he was pulling back from Creedmoor, he created a not-for-profit corporation in New York called the Arthur M. Sackler Foundation.[6] It was the type of legal entity used by America's wealthiest families to shelter their art holdings and to make bequests to museums and public trusts.[7] * [8]

It was far more, however, than their shared interest in fine art that tied Frohlich and Sackler. They pooled information about clients, cooperated on drug launch strategies, and divided the market between them

* Mortimer and Raymond were then working on the medical staff at Creedmoor Psychiatric Hospital. They also incorporated their own charitable foundations in the 1960s. Much later they created parallel foundations and trusts in the United Kingdom. As of 2019, the author located twelve Sackler-named charitable foundations active in New York alone.

when firms released virtually identical drugs.[9] What no one then knew was that Arthur had secretly invested in Frohlich's agency and had a controlling interest.[10] When confronted years later, Sackler denied to *The New York Times* that he had any ownership stake in the Frohlich agency.[11] "That's because of conflicts of interest," Michael Sonnenreich, later Arthur's attorney and confidant, disclosed. "You couldn't represent two firms with competing products, so Frohlich's firm would handle a second product."[12] (Frohlich would later have his own secret ownership in a biweekly newspaper Sackler launched in 1960.)[13]

Although Arthur's secret link with Frohlich's agency gave him a step up on his other competitors, his rivals did not concern him. He was fully confident in his unorthodox vision for upending how pharma marketed its drugs. He pitched his novel ideas to one firm after another. No longer, he told them, should drug companies sell their products as if they were in a church and they could only whisper about it to the person in the adjoining pew. It was time, he contended, to develop sales departments capable of personally visiting thousands of doctors. Most physicians were so busy running their practices, he suggested, they did not have time to research which one of many drugs was the best to treat a patient's condition. Sackler believed a drug company had to win the doctor's loyalty for its entire product line. He brimmed with ideas. Promotions, drug conferences, advertisements in their favorite journals, exhibits at medical conventions, and saturating physicians with free samples. Although the FDA banned all direct drug advertising to the public, Arthur had a clever strategy for disguising product promotion as "news" covered in the consumer press.[14] It was possible in America's consumer culture to stoke a drug's popularity by getting patients to ask for it by its brand name. It turned out to be an inspired idea, although as Frohlich noted, "no physician relished the prospect of hearing about new drugs from his patients."[15]

Sackler had endless energy. His McAdams employees had no doubt he was a workaholic and perfectionist; one of his executives described him as "controversial, unsettling, [and] difficult."[16] Sackler was most demanding, however, on himself. Many who worked for him initially liked the highly charged atmosphere in which they competed to earn his approval.[17] Over time, some burned out and left unhappy, not only about the long hours but also the withering criticism to which Sackler sometimes subjected employees.[18]

Sackler thought his workers needed "a thicker skin."[19] And he was so preoccupied with work that there was little time for his family. His relationship with his wife, Else, and his daughter, Carol, suffered. They were often asleep by the time he got home late from the office. When not working, he was scouring antique stores and auction houses. Else had stopped joining him on those expeditions; their five-year-old daughter had little patience for a full day of hunting for Chinese collectibles and Else did not like leaving her with a baby-sitter.

One night in February 1947, Arthur went to a costume party at a hospital in Far Rockway, Queens, where Mortimer and Raymond were completing internships. Early that evening, a curvaceous woman dressed as a cabaret singer transfixed him. Who is that? he asked Mortimer. It was Marietta Lutze, herself a doctor, and one of the heirs to Dr. Kade, a privately owned 120-year-old German pharmaceutical firm.[20] Marietta had arrived in America only five months after the end of the war and began her medical internship at the same hospital as Sackler's younger brothers.[21]

Arthur struck up a conversation. He learned she was twenty-nine, six years younger than he. She came from a liberal Protestant and Catholic family and got her medical degree at the University of Berlin during the war. Arthur knew that school was the one the Nazi propaganda machine had selected for the great spectacle of burning twenty thousand "degenerate" books. By the time Marietta began her studies in 1939, 250 Jewish professors and administrators had been expelled and replaced with Nazi Party members who promoted racial eugenics.[22]

Marietta's first impressions of Sackler were his "professional air" and "his voice was very soft and persuasive, even comforting. I liked his blue eyes. . . . I don't know what we talked about but, whatever it was, it was intense, I can say that."[23] He asked her for a date, never once mentioning he was married. She liked him but was so "overwhelmed" at work that she said no.

Shortly after meeting Marietta, Arthur found time that March to attend the three-day Scientific and Cultural Conference for World Peace in New York. The sponsoring organization was the National Council of the Arts, Sciences, and Professions, a Communist Party front group. Sackler's connection to the event was Alfred Stern, the businessman he had tried to interest seven years earlier in buying Schering. The two had become friends. Arthur mixed at cocktail parties hosted by the Sterns at their sprawling Central Park West co-op and at intimate dinners at the couple's waterfront summer home in Connecticut.[24]

Arthur had an endless list of business ventures to pitch. In 1948 he again approached Stern, this time to see if he might be interested in helping Arthur buy Purdue Frederick, a small patent medicine company on New York's Lower East Side. Named after its nineteenth-century founders, Drs. John Purdue Gray and George Frederick Bingham, its annual revenues were only $20,000, less than Arthur had spent the previous year on Asian art.[25] It offered only a few "ethical over-the-counter" products; its top seller was Gray's Glycerine Tonic Compound, an alcohol-based "metabolic cerebral tonic."[26] Arthur thought an established drug company, even a tiny one like Purdue Frederick, could play a role in their future business projects. Stern was not convinced, and as he had when Sackler approached him about purchasing Schering during World War II, he passed.[27]

Less than a week after Stern turned him down, Arthur accepted an appointment as the deputy director of research at Creedmoor Psychiatric Center.[28] It was only part-time, he assured Mortimer and Raymond, who had wondered how he could manage all his responsibilities. Arthur assured them it was not a problem. In January 1949, Sackler created the Medical & Pharmaceutical Information Bureau (MPIB), the first company specializing in placing articles in the nonmedical lay press. It was part of his strategy designed to hype new drugs, sometimes before they even had FDA approval.[29] Sackler referred his McAdams drug clients to MPIB; most did not know he was its founder. Every week MPIB sent draft articles to editors and reporters with whom Sackler had developed good relationships. A Senate investigation would later find that MPIB planted stories in many publications, including *The Saturday Evening Post* and *Reader's Digest*. They were ostensibly about "new developments in medicine." Somewhere in each article, however, a "wonder drug" was invariably introduced. That generalized media coverage helped Sackler in creating public demand for a drug. Every time patients asked for "that marvelous drug I read about in the paper the other day" it buttressed the efforts of the pharmaceutical company's detail men and ads. Wall Street traders soon realized that MPIB's "news" sometimes provided an advance peek at a new blockbuster drug. A good MPIB article could cause a stock price to spike. (The same Senate probe later determined that Arthur Sackler traded stocks, including a large ownership position in Pfizer. Arthur sometimes made his buy and sell decisions on advance knowledge he had about what was in the

MPIB publication pipeline. The SEC did not enforce "insider trading" cases against private individuals until 1965.)[30]

Marietta came back into Arthur's life a few months after the birth of the Sacklers' second daughter, Elizabeth Anne. When her hospital internship ended, she had asked Raymond and Mortimer if they knew where she might find the second internship she needed before she could take the exams for her American medical license. They suggested she talk to Arthur as he was then directing a large research project on schizophrenia at Creedmoor.[31] After a brief stint at Queens General City Hospital, Marietta started working at Creedmoor with the Sacklers. Despite having discovered from his brothers that "he was married and had two children, [and] he'd had other relationships with women," when Arthur again asked for a date, Marietta agreed.[32]

She was about to learn one of Arthur's hardwired traits, a relentless focus on getting whatever he wanted. Daily flowers, gifts, surprise visits at all hours, "the intensity of the pursuit was overwhelming." In a few months, she told him over dinner that "you're the kind of man I could marry." What followed were angst-ridden discussions in which they each acknowledged their passionate fling was destructive for Arthur's wife and daughters. They decided to end their relationship. Their separation lasted only two weeks before the affair restarted.

In June 1949, Marietta returned to Germany to tend to her terminally ill grandmother. She had not felt well before her trip, battling fatigue and daily waves of nausea. "Even though I was a physician, I didn't think to diagnose my own pregnancy."[33] When her grandmother died that July, Marietta was the sole heir to Dr. Kade, her family's thriving pharmaceutical firm. It had emerged mostly unscathed from the devastation of World War II. Arthur sent her daily letters about how much he loved and missed her. In his note of June 30, he wrote: "When you come home, we will start a new life—it will be full of hope, joy and of passion."[34]

On Marietta's return to New York that fall, Arthur went to Mexico and got a fast divorce. Else retained custody of their daughters. To the surprise of many friends who expected Else to be furious with her husband's betrayal, she remained a distant part of Arthur's social circle. She was, as friends discovered, still attracted to his "maddening magnetism." Else also knew that remaining on good terms was best for their daughters. Arthur loved her, not as a wife, but as someone he trusted. He let her retain her ownership stake in William Douglas McAdams.[35]

Arthur and Marietta married hastily that December. Sophie Sackler gave her new German daughter-in-law a cool reception. The Orthodox Jewish matriarch of the Sackler family was distressed not only because she saw Marietta as a homewrecker, but also because of her German heritage. How could she have been unaware of what the Nazis were doing to German Jews when she was studying for her medical degree in wartime Berlin? "It was best to protect myself as others did," Marietta said, "much in the way the 'wise monkeys' hear no evil."[36] She tried to win over Sophie, but was not willing to convert to Judaism as had Else. Arthur was satisfied so long as his mother and new wife remained civil to each other, which they mostly did.

All the personal upheaval did not cause Arthur to lose any focus in his businesses. He had too many financial obligations to slow up. Just after they married, Marietta saw that he was under a "great financial burden." Arthur was subsidizing his own medical research and ad agency, supporting his mother and mother-in-law, his ex-wife and two children, and even aiding his brothers and their families. Everyone looked to him for money.

"I compared him to the Atlas in front of Rockefeller Center who carries the world," Marietta concluded. "To Arthur, that role may have felt natural."[37] What she did not realize then but soon saw was that Arthur envisioned himself as the sun in his own solar system; everyone else was merely "a planet . . . [who] could not step out of their separate non-intersecting orbits."

On February 9, 1950, he rushed Marietta to New York Hospital for the birth of their first child. While she was in labor, he apologized to the delivering doctor because he was scheduled to make the dedication at the Creedmoor Institute. He left the hospital before the birth of his first son, Arthur Jr.[38]

Missing his son's birth "marked the beginning of a pattern in our marriage," Marietta later observed. It rankled her that "Arthur continued seeing his former wife (without consulting me) and he allowed her needs to take precedence over mine and the children."[39] Marietta soon discovered that, for Arthur, family was less important than his career. In the late summer of 1950, just after he turned thirty-seven, Arthur was appointed chairman of the First International Congress of Psychiatry. While many people would have found all the disparate obligations overwhelming, he thrived on an ever more demanding schedule. He sold his interest in his two-year-old medical article placement firm, MPIB. With that money he opened a small competitor to MPIB, Medimetrics. He even encouraged his friend and sometimes business partner, Bill Frohlich, to establish his own MPIB competitor (Science Information Bureau).[40] This all happened while Arthur was preparing for the dedication of the Institute of Psychobiological Studies at Creedmoor.[41] Although it was eighteen years after his friend Alfred Stern had funded Chicago's Institute for Psychoanalysis, Arthur was proud that Creedmoor's center was the first American facility devoted to biological psychiatry.[42] The Sackler brothers saw it as an opportunity to further their research into possible connections between the endocrine system and mental illness.[43] The trio, alone and with collaborators, would eventually publish more than 150 scientific papers about human behavior, pharmaceuticals, biological psychiatry, and experimental medicine.[44] The Sacklers would be among the earliest to find a link between instances of psychosis and cortisone.

Complementing his work at Creedmoor, Arthur soon added to his responsibilities the editor-in-chief's role at *The Journal of Clinical and Experimental Psychopathology*; its board of directors included some prominent international researchers as well as his brothers.[45] Later he added the director's role at the College of Pharmacy in Long Island University as well as becoming a professor of therapeutic research there.[46]

Most people with the demanding professional responsibilities Arthur had assumed would have had little opportunity or desire to indulge personal pursuits. Sackler not only found the spare time but delved into it with the same intensity with which he approached his businesses. What begun innocently enough as an interest in Chinese antiquities had become a self-admitted "passion."[47] "When some people are frustrated, they go out and buy a new hat, or tie," he later said, "[so] my collections are in a sense the measure of my frustrations."[48] Marietta thought the compulsive collecting had less to do with his frustrations than with his overriding "necessity for prestige and recognition."[49] To his medical and advertising colleagues and fellow art collectors, Arthur Sackler was the epitome of a self-confident man who accomplished a great deal through discipline and organization. "A man of promethean intellect and energy," was the judgment of Harvard art historian John Rosenfield.[50]

"His public side, of course, was charming," noted Marietta. "A gifted intellectual, he could match anyone in debate. An engaging speaker and conversationalist, he moved people with his passion and intellectual power."[51]

Marietta, however, was witness to another side, "the fine line between fascination and obsession."[52] She saw the restlessness caused by his deep "need to achieve . . . that his name not be forgotten by the world." She was just beginning to understand how "his tremendous intellectual gifts were also his greatest demons, whipping him to produce ever more."[53]

"At night, he'd come home from the office," she recalled, "he would consume volumes on Chinese art and archaeology. I tried keeping up with him at first, but, soon, he outdistanced me. His speed of comprehension, his ability to integrate masses of material and his talent for turning all that knowledge into informed purchasing decisions were quite astonishing."[54] At an early moment of introspection, Arthur feared his collecting was "not always controllable."[55]

The dealers knew he was a serious and compulsive collector. They often enticed him to buy pieces he could not afford by financing his costlier acquisitions. Some of those arrangements, Marietta recalled, "extended over many years."[56] It created new obligations that kept him running ever harder in his professional life. Meanwhile, boxes of "ritual bronzes and weapons, mirrors and ceramics, inscribed bones and archaic jades" filled their home and spilled over to storage warehouses. "There was too much to open, too much to appreciate; some objects known only by a packing list."[57]

Arthur was in the early days of acquiring works of art that would become over time a stunning collection of Chinese and Asian antiquities, pre-Columbian and Iranian ceramics, Indian sculpture, Baroque terra-cottas, Postimpressionist paintings, Renaissance majolicas, and Piranesi drawings. A museum curator later dubbed him "a modern Medici."[58]

"I contracted the disease," he acknowledged later. "I was never able to develop an immunity to works of art."[59]

"As his knowledge grew, he became more and more passionate about it," said Marietta. "His fascination then turned in on itself and came to rule him."[60]

Marietta was not just Arthur's wife, she had become a psychiatrist after their marriage. She could not help but sometimes see him through her professional lens. "Addiction is a curse, be it drugs, women, or collecting."[61]

10

THE HARD SELL BLITZ

In 1951, the Sacklers published one of their most provocative theories, that schizophrenia might be identified by changes in blood as it clotted, and that ultrasonometry (the predecessor to ultrasound) could track physiological changes in schizophrenics.[1] They proposed the controversial thesis that histamines might effectively treat schizophrenics. Marietta worked with them extensively on that paper, but she was disappointed not to be listed as one of the authors. It took several years before she shared credit with the brothers, an overview of "psychiatric research perspectives at the Creedmoor Institute." It marked the one time four Sacklers were listed on a scientific publication.[2]

Marietta felt like an outsider to the family club. It was the same for Muriel Lazarus, Mortimer's wife, who was a researcher in biochemical genetics as well as a practicing psychoanalyst.[3] Another physician, however, who joined the brothers on scholarly collaborations, did become a trusted insider. Félix Martí-Ibáñez was a sociable and urbane Spanish psychiatrist. He and the Sackler brothers would go on to edit a remarkably ambitious book, *The Great Physiodynamic Therapies in Psychiatry: An Historical Reappraisal.* It was filled with contributions from some of the era's leading researchers opining about treatments for mental illness, from electroshock to insulin shock to lobotomies. The Sacklers and Martí-Ibáñez predicted that the treatment of choice would soon be "narcobiotics" (their vision of some yet-to-be-invented hybrid of tranquilizers as readily dispensed as antibiotics).[4] The four doctors considered themselves pioneers in the biological underpinnings of treating mental disorders. When they later discussed an ambitious book on "The Geography and the World Patterns of Schizophrenia and Other Mental Illnesses," Martí-Ibáñez wrote a letter to the Sacklers concluding, "The research and sociologic value of this project would be portentous. This might be Nobel Prize stuff. What do you say, boys?"[5]

Just as Arthur Sackler was more than a mere psychiatrist, Martí-Ibáñez was a self-described anarchist, historian, novelist, and entrepreneur. His résumé impressed even the Sacklers. He grew up in Cartagena, Spain; his mother was a noted pianist, his father a scholar and prolific author of dozens of books about education.[6] Martí-Ibáñez was a gifted student. He teased Arthur that he was only nineteen when he got his medical degree at the University of Madrid, five years faster than Sackler.[7] In another year he earned his doctorate in philosophy with a thesis about the history of the physiology and psychology of Indian mystics. After graduation, he traveled throughout Spain, lecturing at schools and social halls. As word spread about his ever-changing topics—rotating between medicine, art, graphic design, mythology, and even urban planning—he attracted ever-larger audiences. At twenty-one he published a scandalous short essay about "homosexuality throughout the history of the West."[8] He then set off a firestorm by condemning both the "dogmatic moralists" of the Catholic Church and Spain's growing fascist movement. Before long he championed other progressive and then unpopular campaigns, from the suffragist movement to proposing that a Marxist economy might be best for Spain. A government minister who attended one of his impassioned talks was so impressed that he named Martí-Ibáñez, then twenty-six, as the general director of public health and social service for Catalonia.[9] Two years later he became Spain's undersecretary of public health. By then, civil war wracked Spain. Neo-fascists led by General Francisco Franco battled the leftist government of the Second Republic. Martí-Ibáñez represented the Republic in the 1938 Universal Peace Congresses in Geneva, New York, and Mexico City. On returning to Spain he joined the air force's medical corps.[10] He suffered a shrapnel wound after only a few weeks and had barely recovered when the fascists captured Barcelona in January 1939. On Franco's wanted list, Martí-Ibáñez fled with the last contingent of Loyalist troops to the French Pyrenees. Some friends there helped him escape to America.[11]

The sociable polymath reinvented himself in New York. Six months after arriving in the U.S., Swiss-based Hoffmann-La Roche hired him as a consultant. In his free time, he assumed editorial roles at half a dozen medical, psychological, and psychopathological journals, as well as presenting his own papers at scientific conferences.[12] After three years he left

La Roche to become the medical director responsible for Latin American sales for U.S.-based Winthrop-Stearns. *The Journal of the American Medical Association* offered him the editor-in-chief's role for a proposed Spanish-language edition. He accepted instead an offer from Squibb for a post that put him in the middle of both drug development and marketing.[13] It was in that role that Martí-Ibáñez met Arthur Sackler and Ludwig (Bill) Frohlich in the embryonic world of medical advertisement.[14]

It is little wonder that the man who later wrote in his autobiography, "There is only one way to defeat death—to live fast," attracted the attention of Sackler and Frohlich.[15] Martí-Ibáñez admired Sackler's endless energy and willingness to take risks. In Sackler he had found a kindred soul for turning the medical status quo upside down. With Bill Frohlich, Martí-Ibáñez shared a genteel sophistication and love for arts and culture. At Frohlich's East Side townhouse parties, Martí-Ibáñez regaled the guests with tales of his offbeat travels to Africa and Asia or his musings about everything from medical philosophy in the Renaissance or the Spain of Don Quixote to the lost science of alchemy. He even presented his unorthodox theory that stress might cause disease. He used Frohlich's parties as an informal test market for his ideas. Those that provoked the best responses he turned into articles.[16]

Sackler wanted Martí-Ibáñez as a partner in his own ambitious plans to remake how the pharmaceutical world sold its products. The two spoke about it frequently but no early idea seemed quite right. When Martí-Ibáñez left Squibb, he opened a private psychiatric practice in Manhattan. He also became a regular lecturer at New York Medical College and Flower and Fifth Hospital.[17] Arthur hired him as a special consultant at the McAdams agency, and later made him a director of a wholly owned subsidiary, McAdams International.[18] In the spring of 1951, they formed MD Publications Inc., a shell company they agreed to keep inactive until the right opportunity arose. No one was aware that the Sacklers had put up most of the seed money and held a controlling stake. MD Publications shared office space with the McAdams agency.[19 * 20]

Neither Martí-Ibáñez nor Arthur Sackler hid their considerable am-

* In a *New York Times* profile thirty years later, Arthur Sackler denied any ownership in MD Publications, claiming instead he had been a consultant and had started a "well-known medical news magazine" for the company. Martí-Ibáñez was dead by the time of that interview. However, a Senate investigative staff later uncovered evidence that

bition. That sparked strong reactions from people who either admired their naked drive or considered it crass and overbearing. A series of seemingly unconnected events would soon put the duo into medical publishing, a venture that made them rich and presented an opportunity to wield unseemly power with the FDA.

In the marketing pitches Arthur had made to middle management at pharma firms, many thought his ideas too risky and him overconfident. He was, they concluded, trying to turn drugs into another lucrative ad business, like the ones that flourished for cars, tobacco, and consumer goods. Sackler did not endear himself to those midlevel managers when he tried going over their heads to top executives.[21]

When Sackler met Thomas Winn, Pfizer's sales director, he said that he would make Charles Pfizer a household name if the company gave him a big enough budget.[22] That decision could only be made by the company's CEO, John McKeen. It took another outsized personality like McKeen to embrace Sackler and trust him with something as critical as Pfizer's rollout of its much anticipated broad-spectrum antibiotic, Terramycin. McKeen set aside $7.5 million—then a record—for ads and promotion. The company even agreed to install a specially built telephone switchboard to handle what Sackler promised would be a record volume of calls.

On March 15, 1951, Pfizer sent over eight hundred telegrams to every drug wholesaler in the country alerting them to imminent FDA approval. It offered a deep discount for early buyers.[23] It was the start of what *Business Week* called "the Terramycin blitz."[24]

The eight-man "details team" group McKeen had hired stood at pay phones across the country, waiting for a call from headquarters to begin visiting doctors. Over several weeks, crisscrossing the country, they pitched Terramycin to several thousand physicians. Pfizer drafted seventy third-year medical students to assist the detail men.[25]

Arthur Sackler had funded the MD Publications start-up through his McAdams ad agency. Also, documents from Arthur's estate after his 1987 death confirmed that the Sackler brothers had indeed owned a majority interest in MD Publications.

The author discovered that the year before Arthur Sackler founded MD Publications, he had created the Angiology Research Foundation for the clinical testing of drugs for vascular diseases. The year after creating MD Publications, he incorporated the Inter America Medical Press and International Medical Press, both designed to help foreign drug companies promote their products in the U.S. The Sackler ownership interests remained secret.

Sackler knew no matter how hard they worked, the Pfizer field force was too small to reach every doctor. So he unleashed a blitzkrieg of direct mailers to clinicians and physicians, as well as pharmacists, including those at hospitals (about 85 percent of all hospitals had in-house pharmacies then).[26] Physicians known as heavy prescribers received two to three direct mail pitches daily for nearly a year.[27] Sackler employed a team of copywriters who worked on multiple campaigns, from letters to glossy brochures to Rolodex–ready file cards. One mailing was thousands of handwritten postcards that looked as if they were sent from exotic locations, such as India's Taj Mahal, Egypt's pyramids, and the Great Barrier Reef. Everyone had a brief story of how Terramycin was eradicating diseases in each country. Signed "Sincerely Pfizer," those cards quickly became collectibles.[28]

Pfizer soon introduced its in-house magazine, *Spectrum*, and had reprinted it as an eight-page glossy color insert in the prestigious *Journal of the American Medical Association*. Before Sackler released his advertising onslaught, *JAMA*'s pages were virtually free of branded drugs and featured mostly medical supplies. In the early 1950s, even tobacco companies placed cigarette ads.[29] Sackler saturated *JAMA* with his Pfizer campaign. Its ad pages jumped more than 500 percent over a couple of years, more ads than *Life*, and 75 percent of its antibiotic ads were for Terramycin.[30] At rates of more than $1,000 a page, and thousands of pages annually, *JAMA* and other premier medical journals grew dependent over time to pharma's promotion money. By the late 1960s, *JAMA*'s $15 million in ad revenues was 40 percent of the AMA's income.[31]

Pfizer agreed with Sackler's recommendation to concentrate the bulk of Terramycin's print campaign in *JAMA*. To advertise in a handful of other leading journals might have seemed a commonsense strategy. It was, instead, as with much connected to Arthur Sackler, more complicated and calculating. Arthur knew that Congress's legislative effort to curb false and misleading advertisements, the 1938 Wheeler Lea Act, bypassed the FDA by empowering the Federal Trade Commission with oversight of accuracy in drug ads. But there was a loophole: since doctors were judged capable of assessing the accuracy of drug promotion, ads in medical journals were free from oversight.[32] Sackler had focused on the medium in which the government was powerless to constrain his copy. Ads that boasted that Terramycin was "one of the most complex structures to ever be found in nature" were Sackler's way of making the drug appear to be far more innovative than it was.[33] * [34]

It was not long before Sackler was the first to experiment with radio ads. Some of his tactics became standard for the industry, including twenty-four-hour sales marathons and rich bonuses for sales reps. He helped persuade the American Medical Association that drug advertising would benefit if the companies had information about the prescribing habits of doctors. The AMA's Business Division started sending rudimentary monthly reports measuring the impact of ads on a cross-section of five hundred physicians nationwide.

Pfizer's McKeen told the New York Security Analysts Society that the company's great success was the result of "using vigorous promotional techniques."[35] That was an understatement. One of Sackler's Madison Avenue competitors, William Castagnoli, said it "is hard to quantify his influence on medical advertising, his impact was so great. . . . As head of McAdams, he took a chemical company new to the prescription drug market, Pfizer, and made it a force in the industry."[36] The Medical Advertising Hall of Fame later noted, "No single individual did more to shape the character of medical advertising. . . . His seminal contribution was bringing the full power of advertising and promotion to pharmaceutical marketing. . . . [His] campaign for Terramycin forever changed the industry's marketing model."[37]

Terramycin sales exceeded even McKeen's lofty expectations. Pfizer bought a surplus submarine shipyard in Groton, Connecticut, and converted it into the world's largest fermentation plant.[38] It operated at capacity to produce Terramycin around the clock. In under a year, Pfizer's detail team had ballooned from eight to three hundred (on its way to two thousand in five years).[39] Those most sought after were college graduates with chemistry, biology, or pharmacology degrees.[40] Still, they went through twelve months of training. They were taught that while technical knowledge was key, it was also important to cultivate a personal connection with the doctors they visited. Sales representatives asked for and remembered the details about families, outside

* When Pfizer released chlorpropamide in a few years, it targeted pre-diabetic patients who needed to stabilize their insulin levels. Sackler's promotion claimed an "almost complete absence of unfavorable side effects." In fact, Pfizer had commissioned a prerelease study that revealed "serious side effects" in 27 percent of test patients.

hobbies, and favorite sports. Half of physicians surveyed later said that the best of them were more like a friend than a salesman.[41] Each sales rep would be responsible for about three hundred doctors.[42]

McKeen made certain Pfizer's researchers and attorneys were relentless in getting FDA approvals for Terramycin in other formats, from pills to powders to eye drops, while expanding the conditions for which it could be prescribed to nearly forty. Americans were spending $100 million on broad-spectrum antibiotics like Terramycin, more than on penicillin, sulfanilamides, vitamins, nostrums, hormones, and botanicals combined.[43] Pfizer's profit margin was 50 percent, Lederle and Parke-Davis 40 percent and 35 percent, respectively. To handle the booming international demand for Terramycin, Pfizer opened offices in thirteen countries (some European countries had import duties that were incentives for American firms to open foreign subsidiaries).[44] Terramycin's success meant Pfizer accounted for a quarter of worldwide antibiotic sales, making it the number one firm in revenues in the pharmaceutical industry.[45]

Pfizer's aggressive marketing and sales tactics not only recast the company but transformed the industry. Traditionalists bitterly complained that Sackler's "hard sell" was unseemly and disturbing.[46] However, as competitors saw sales and profits set records for Pfizer, they did their best to copy the playbook. Rivals expanded sales departments and beefed-up marketing to doctors. Merck, playing catch-up, merged with Sharp & Dohme, a small firm well known for its experienced sales team.[47]

While Pfizer's Terramycin was a marketing wonder, it also benefited from the elevated regard with which the public still held the industry. Expectations for the latest drugs were high. Besides antibiotics, there were new medications to treat glaucoma, arthritis, and schizophrenia; a second generation of tranquilizers; oral contraceptives; and even a first to reverse an opioid overdose. Research was under way on an antianxiety that would kick off a revolution for meds marketed as "emotional aspirin." There was hope a polio vaccine might wipe out the disease made infamous in a country where most people had personal memories of how it had put Franklin Roosevelt into a wheelchair.

The public seemed unfazed when the first studies appeared indicating that lifestyle choices, not simply bacterial pathogens, might affect health and longevity. Smoking was tied to lung cancer for the first time in 1950 and later, when Pfizer released Terramycin, a report concluded diet might contribute to heart disease.[48] Arthur Sackler was in a tiny minority; he was so against smoking that he did not allow it inside the McAdams offices.[49] But most people, even many physicians, refused to believe that smoking and food could lead to chronic or fatal diseases. Even if true, however, the overriding faith in science and pharma was strong. Many shrugged it off; there would be a pill one day to take care of it, much as there was an antibiotic to treat infectious diseases.[50]

Pfizer and its rivals did not simply want to rely on a combination of public goodwill and a marketing blitz to keep antibiotic sales at record levels. They began a unified lobbying effort to get a major modification to the U.S Patent Law. The language they wanted would set a lower innovation threshold for granting a drug patent. It would give legal protection to antibiotics discovered through mass, routine screening of microbial soil samples.[51] When Congress modified the statute the following year (1952), it opened the door to a larger number of drugs on an ever-quicker pipeline from the lab to the marketplace.

That was the same year a Pfizer biologist got permission for "Project Piglet," in which he tested sub-therapeutic doses of antibiotics on pigs. The result? It accelerated their growth. Pfizer used those findings to market antibiotics to farmers who began using them in feed for cattle, pigs, and chickens.[52] CEO John McKeen liked that sales for farm animals were consistent and did not depend as they did with humans on epidemics or outbreaks of disease. Pfizer created the first separate sales and marketing team for agricultural products and other pharmaceutical firms followed. In a few years, bulk sales of antibiotics for agricultural uses accounted for a quarter of all production.[53] * [54] No one worried that daily exposures to antibiotics might kill only the weakest bacteria in animals and that the surviving organisms would become stronger and far more robust pathogens.[55]

---

* Research was even conducted for three years in New York on mentally deficient spastic children to determine whether low-dose antibiotics might boost childhood growth rates. It did, but pharma companies never sold their products to add quick bulk to children. In 1954, when penicillin discoverer Alexander Fleming visited the U.S., he was skeptical when he learned about that research. "I can't predict that feeding penicillin to babies will do society much good. Making people larger might do more harm than good." Although pharma did not market antibiotics to children for accelerated growth, children in the U.S. and Western Europe inadvertently ingested the drugs. Estimates are that through the 1950s, about 10 percent of every container of milk had penicillin residue from treated cows. At that time, farmers used the same penicillin developed for humans on cows.

The Terramycin launch was barely over when Arthur was again restless. It would be good, he thought, to have something on which he and his two brothers could work together. Arthur decided to buy the small New York drugmaker Purdue Frederick Company, the company he had pitched unsuccessfully in 1948 to his friend Alfred Stern. Not much had changed in four years. Purdue's annual revenues were still anemic and its best-selling product remained its "cerebral tonic," Gray's Glycerine Tonic Compound.[56] Operating out of a small office at 135 Christopher Street, the company was struggling to adapt to the rapid changes of the postwar pharmaceutical industry.[57]

Although Arthur had put up most of the money to buy Purdue Frederick in June 1952, the Sackler brothers agreed they owned it equally. None of their names, however, appeared on the New York State incorporation papers.

Mortimer asked what they would do with Purdue.

"We will sell what they have better than they did," Arthur said. "And then we will find our own products as we go along."

11

A HAVEN FOR COMMUNISTS

In the middle of Arthur Sackler's Terramycin campaign, Martí-Ibáñez had stumbled across what he thought was a terrific business opportunity. He had learned that the Washington Institute of Medicine, the publisher of the prestigious *Journal of Antibiotics*, was near bankruptcy. The FDA's chief of the Division of Antibiotics, Henry Welch, was the journal's editor. Because Welch only received a small honorarium, the FDA had given him its permission to act as editor in his spare time. They decided there was no conflict of interest since the amount of money was so small: $3,270 over three years.[1]

When Martí-Ibáñez called Arthur and told him about the Washington Institute's money problems, Sackler offered to pay its debts. MD Publications, the company they formed the previous spring, would become the new owner and publisher. It was worth doing, both agreed, only if Welch agreed to stay on as editor.

Martí-Ibáñez spoke to Welch. To entice him to remain, he and Sackler devised a generous offer. Welch would get 7.5 percent of all advertising income for any journal he edited, and 50 percent of net income from any reprints sold to pharmaceutical companies.[2]

Welch was so enthusiastic with the new terms that he even assigned his rights to a book, *Antibiotic Therapy*, on which he had been working.[3] Martí-Ibáñez and Welch agreed to introduce the first of a series of new journals; the initial one was a quarterly, *Antibiotics and Chemotherapy*. Sackler advanced $50,000 in start-up funding, enough to pay off the Washington Institute's debts and for a few operating months ($484,000 in 2019). Welch did not disclose the new financial arrangements with his FDA superiors.[4]

As with MD Publications, Martí-Ibáñez acted as if he owned the resurrected Washington Institute. Soon after the bailout he executed a contract entitling the Washington Institute to a flat "consulting fee" of $3,500 every time it published an MD Publication–branded journal. In a couple of years there were ten journals, translating into a fixed annual fee of $420,000 ($4.4 million in 2019).

The author uncovered that the Sacklers had a secret controlling stake in MD Publications. As with most businesses connected to the brothers, it was complicated. Arthur had become the editor-in-chief in 1950 of one of four quarterly publications then owned by the Washington Institute, *The Journal of Clinical and Experimental Psychopathology*. After Sackler's colleague, Joseph Borkin, became a part owner of the Washington Institute, responsibility for the psychiatric journal transferred to the Ophuijsen Center. That was the name of a research unit at Creedmoor Psychiatric Center, named after Johan van Ophuijsen, the Dutch director of the state hospital's medical trials.

The address listed for the Ophuijsen Center, however, was not its correct one in Queens, but 15 East 62nd Street, New York. The telephone number was (212) 832-7900. That is where Arthur moved the William Douglas McAdams Agency in 1954; it had the same phone number. The address was also listed in the Manhattan phone book for Mortimer and Raymond.[5] The author discovered that in later years 15 East 62nd Street, and that phone number, were used by a series of medical companies and charitable foundations controlled by the Sacklers.

Arthur stocked *The Journal of Clinical and Experimental Psychopathology* with his most trusted associates. Martí-Ibáñez was its international editor, and Mortimer and Raymond, along with the Washington Institute's Joseph Borkin, were directors. A series of stock transfers and option assignments resulted in Martí-Ibáñez, Borkin, and his partner Dr. Henry Klaunberg each owning 10 percent. The owner of the remaining 70 percent is not identified in any recorded legal document. However, the accountants for the anonymous buyer were Brooklyn-born brother and sister Louis Goldburt and Mary Siegel. The duo, operating from an office at 1440 Broadway, did tax withholding, payroll forms, and general accounting for other Sackler companies.[6] Louis was one of the three listed "owners" in New York State filings for Purdue Frederick. That covert 70 percent share returned a guaranteed minimum of $294,000 a year to the Sacklers, based only on the fixed reprint fees Martí-Ibáñez had created.

When the small Medicine Avenue partners speculated about what might be the next big development in the pharmaceutical industry, all agreed that it was certain to be tied to antibiotics. That market was in its early stages. Natural antibiotics and the first wave of broad-spectrum drugs had upended the industry.[7]

A problem they identified was that finding effective therapeutic organisms in millions of samples of soil or on decaying fruit was like playing the lottery. There had been, no doubt, major discoveries in some unexpected places. Cephalosporin was extracted from sewage waste, streptomycin located in a throat of a chicken, and fusidic acid, a topical antibiotic, found in Japanese monkey dung.[8] A few companies might get lucky and develop a blockbuster antibiotic, but it was unpredictable. That uncertainty might be acceptable for academic and scientific researchers. But it frustrated those responsible for bottom-line profits.

Sackler and Martí-Ibáñez saw those business issues through the prism of their medical backgrounds. The dream solution, both thought, was to find a way to synthesize improved antibiotics. That ran counter to accepted scientific wisdom that natural antibiotics were the best available because they had evolved over thousands of years by surviving countless strains of bacterium. Drug researchers believed it was not possible to create a synthetic drug more potent than what Mother Nature provided. A few efforts at modification had only decreased the drugs' benefits, producing weaker knock-offs of little value.[9]

Arthur Sackler knew that Pfizer was trying to change that. CEO John McKeen's hard-driving attitude had given the lab researchers an opportunity to pursue some long-shot theories.[10]

Lloyd Conover was a twenty-eight-year-old organic chemist who had been at Pfizer for two years. One of Conover's "scientific hunches" was that it was possible to modify natural antibiotics to enhance their therapeutic benefits. At Pfizer's Brooklyn lab, Conover worked with only a single assistant. He did not share any progress with his colleagues. "I didn't want an audience if we failed."[11]

Conover focused on the chemical structure of Pfizer's Terramycin and Lederle's Aureomycin. He was intrigued by what would happen if he manipulated two misaligned atoms. His experiments paid off in 1952 when he swapped a chlorine atom with an oxygen one. The result was a drug that was virtually the chemical twin of both Terramycin and Aureomycin but had more stability and potency as well as superior solubility. Pfizer's chemists named it tetracycline. Conover had invented the world's first semisynthetic antibiotic (he was ultimately inducted into the National Inventors Hall of Fame, joining five hundred other iconic American inventors including Henry Ford, Thomas Edison, and the Wright brothers).

Martí-Ibáñez and the Sacklers had predicted that synthetic antibiotics would herald a new age. Now they planned on how to profit. Exploiting the prestige and power of Welch's FDA position through their growing basket of journals gave them an unmatched advantage over competitors.

The Washington Institute, Welch's previous publisher, had run into financial difficulties because it refused ads it considered potential conflicts of interest with any of its scholarly content. The appearance of impropriety did not worry Martí-Ibáñez, Arthur Sackler, and Bill Frohlich. Sackler and Frohlich packed *The Journal of Antibiotics* with pharmaceutical ads.[12]

Martí-Ibáñez and Welch established an annual antibiotics conference that brought together more than six hundred clinicians and scientists. Welch convinced the Department of Health, Education, and Welfare to permit the FDA to co-sponsor it.[13] Pharma companies tried outdoing each other with lavish reception parties. President Eisenhower paid tribute to the event that "honored all those who, through their work in antibiotics, have made profound changes in the practice of medicine."[14] Welch and Martí-Ibáñez meanwhile skewed the papers selected for presentation to be those that favorably reviewed drugs from the biggest pharma firms, resulting in increased reprint sales. Sackler promoted those reprints as ideal for direct mail campaigns to physicians.[15] Every year the symposium proceedings were packaged and sold as a book titled *Antibiotics Annual*. Martí-Ibáñez and Welch established *MD Encyclopedia*, which became a widely accepted reference source about diseases, drugs, medical tests, and surgical procedures.[16]

No one at the FDA seemed concerned that the chief of the all-important Division of Antibiotics was so deeply involved in a commercial enterprise about the same drugs he regulated. Welch's superiors believed he was still only receiving a small honorarium. Martí-Ibáñez had assured him there was no way anyone could find out how much he earned from their private partnership.[17]

With Welch enmeshed as a partner in their publishing ventures, Sackler turned next to expanding Bill Frohlich's role. All Sackler's friends and business colleagues had heard him frequently complain that ad agencies such as his and Frohlich's were operating in the dark ages. Arthur contended that what was missing was prescribing data from physicians, pharmacies, and hospitals. That would be invaluable for pharma firms to target more accurately their drug ads. Frohlich and Sackler had already taken the first step. In 1950, Frohlich incorporated Intercontinental Medical Information Service in New York.[18] Now, based on renewed talks with Sackler, he was the owner on paper for two related companies and changed the name of the original business to International Marketing Services (IMS).[19]

In its early days, even though Frohlich promised that all patient data would be anonymized, most doctors resisted sharing information about which drugs they prescribed and for what ailments. Sackler suggested doctors and pharmacists might be more cooperative if Frohlich couched the requests under the guise that sharing information would help pharmaceutical companies develop better drugs. That helped. Still, however, IMS had to make small payments, between $25 and $150 monthly, to get the information it wanted.[20]

Although Frohlich was IMS's legal founder and owner according to the incorporation filings, the Sacklers had a hidden stake. Sackler wanted distance from IMS so his rivals could not complain that the collected market data gave him an unfair advantage in winning business for his McAdams agency. Arthur talked to Frohlich about the appearance of impropriety and that prompted Frohlich to open a separate office for IMS. At the beginning, it had shared the McAdams office. Although IMS had been Arthur's brainchild, he suggested it would be better if Mortimer and Raymond represented the Sackler family interest.[21]

Arthur's two younger brothers had the free time because in May 1953 they had been dismissed from Creedmoor. The FBI had shared some of its information about Raymond and Beverly Sackler's Communist Party membership.[22] It was during the height of the decade-long Red Scare, in which a series of congressional investigations whipped up a public frenzy over fears of communist influence and infiltration of the government and American businesses. The New York State commissioner of mental hygiene had the authority to fire the brothers since they were salaried employees at a state institution. Arthur, who still consulted there, was indignant and resigned. Psychiatric researcher Donald Klein, who arrived after the Sacklers were gone, recalled Arthur "had been thrown out by the Creedmoor Director on entirely political grounds."[23] An anonymous FBI source inside William Douglas McAdams later gave the FBI background on the Sacklers; Mortimer and Raymond had problems because of their "alleged involvement in subversive activity" reported by the FBI.[24]

The Creedmoor Psychiatric Institute's director, Johan van Ophuijsen, did not want it tarnished by news of the Sacklers' left-wing politics. The story that made its way to print in *The New York Times* was that while working on a research project for the Atomic Energy Commission on skin reactions to burns, Mortimer and Raymond had refused to sign an Army loyalty oath that would have required them to report any subversive conversations they overheard at work.[25] That was the public reason for their dismissal. The Bureau's McAdams informant said that privately Arthur had defended his brothers by claiming "it was contrary to a tenet of the Jewish faith to inform on anyone."[26]

Mortimer and Raymond wanted to devote all their efforts to building up Purdue Frederick. Arthur, however, convinced them there was much more than Purdue that needed their attention. Hiring the right professionals to run Purdue would give them freedom to take on other ventures. It would also allow them to stay in the background, something they all preferred.

Schneider recommended thirty-two-year-old Seymour Lubman, a pharmacist with corporate experience. He joined Purdue as a "sales administration assistant." It took only eight months for him to become the company's national sales manager.[27] The first key hire was sixty-year-old Benjamin Schneider, a pharmacist and sales manager at Harrower Laboratory, a California-based drug company founded by a pioneering endocrinologist, Henry Harrower.[28] Schneider was a Brooklyn native who grew up not far from the Sacklers. And Arthur admired the internal advertising department run by Harrower's parent, Lambert. The company had made its Listerine mouthwash a blockbuster by marketing it for halitosis, the medical term for bad breath. Lambert was one of the largest buyers of newspaper and magazine space and had elevated Listerine from $115,000 in sales in 1930 to nearly $20 million by the mid-1950s.[29] Schneider joined Purdue in June 1953 as an executive vice president, general manager, and board director.[30] The Sacklers made Schneider Purdue's president in under a year.[31]

The brothers were content to allow Schneider to be the company's public face. When *The New York Times* later did a story about four Lower East Side women who had worked at Purdue for nearly sixty years, the paper called Schneider "a master pharmacist" who "three years ago . . . took over Purdue and Frederick."[32] The double-column article did not mention the Sacklers. When Purdue announced the creation of an award "to encourage the international exchange of medical ideas on a physician-to-physician basis," Schneider was the only executive quoted in press coverage.[33] When the company sold its twenty-six-by ninety-foot parcel of land at 135 Christopher Street a few years later, Schneider was the one listed on the transfer papers.[34] * [35]

At IMS, Frohlich's medical data collection company, few knew that Mortimer and Raymond were helping or that Arthur had developed the business concept. A McAdams employee, David Dubow, who had also grown up in the same Brooklyn neighborhood as the Sacklers, left Arthur's ad agency to become IMS's president.[36] (Some histories of IMS mistakenly list Dubow as its founder.)

Arthur, more than his friends and siblings, relished the complicated business arrangements. For every new idea he created another company. Sometimes he was the owner, other times it was in the name of one of his wives, brothers, friends, or a trust for one of his children. When *The New York Times* later announced, for instance, that Purdue Frederick had retained Pharmaceutical Advertising Associates for all its brands, it seemed as if the Sackler-owned drug firm had deliberately avoided retaining the McAdams agency.[37] That was the simplest way of avoiding any potential conflict of interest between the products Purdue offered and those marketed by McAdams's powerful clients. But as the author uncovered, Pharmaceutical Advertising Associates was another Sackler-controlled entity they had founded in 1947 (it was separate from a company they created in 1945 with a similar name, Pharmaceutical Research Associates).[38]

Marietta did not know all the details of Arthur's corporate shell game, but she later wrote in her memoir that he was "entering into increasing numbers of business ventures that involved increasingly complex working arrangements with staff and associates. He'd come home exhausted from work. The slightest provocation would infuriate him." She observed that the "non-stop days and late-night meetings" were "more and more time consuming."[39]

* The first time the Sacklers decided to be the public face of Purdue was in 1960. The brothers had convinced the AMA to join them in launching the "Purdue Frederick–American Medical Association Presidential Award." It was for "contributions to science and the total welfare of the nation." The first one went to Dr. Louis Orr, the AMA's retiring president, and Mortimer Sackler presented it at the annual AMA convention.

The "complex working arrangements with staff and associates" that Marietta observed had attracted the attention of the FBI. Declassified documents obtained by the author through a Freedom of Information request reveal the Bureau investigated Sackler's web of companies. It was concerned Arthur's firms "may have become a haven for past or present members of the Communist Party."[40] Many left-wing journalists had been fired after they were subpoenaed before the House Un-American Activities Committee (HUAC) and refused to answer questions about their political affiliations by invoking their Fifth Amendment right against self-incrimination.[41] In a national frenzy started by Senator Joe McCarthy's congressional witch hunt for communists in the government and media, mainstream newspaper and magazine correspondents found little support from their employers. *The New York Times*, the *San Francisco Chronicle*, and United Press International were among the media outlets that terminated reporters for refusing to answer whether they were or had been Communist Party members.[42] Most of those sacked never again worked in journalism.[43] The FBI had zeroed in on Arthur Sackler because he had subsequently hired many of them.

In 1956, FBI agents met at New York's St. Regis Hotel with an unidentified informant who was a William Douglas McAdams employee. He warned the agents that Sackler himself had "pink sympathies."[44] The informant told them that in far-left political circles the word had spread that Sackler's companies were a safe place to earn a living while trying to rebuild shattered careers.

There were limits to how many Sackler could help. Walter Bernstein, for instance, was a screenwriter who had been blacklisted in Hollywood in 1950 after he was named as one of 151 actors, writers, and on-air journalists in *Red Channels: The Report of Communist Influence in Radio and Television*, a booklet that purported to unmask the "communist domination of the entertainment industry."[45] In September 1952, Bernstein showed up at 11 East 26th Street in New York, the location for four Sackler companies.[46] Bernstein met with Leo Davis, a film editor who got a job at Medigraphics after it was disclosed that he had signed the Communist Party petition for putting candidates on the New York ballot.[47] Bernstein was low on money and needed a loan and steady work. Davis knew that Bernstein, a talented screenwriter, would be an ideal fit for the promotional and instructional films Medigraphics developed for Sackler's pharmaceutical clients. The next month,

Davis told Bernstein that Medigraphics wanted to hire him. The FBI needed to first clear him.

Bernstein looked startled. "What would they want that for?"

"Medigraphics makes medical films for the U.S. Government."

Bernstein skipped the job.*

Bernstein was the exception; in most cases Sackler had no problem in hiring blacklisted journalists. The FBI informant told the Bureau that he suspected many of his McAdams coworkers had a Red connection. He pointed to a recent hire, David Gordon, a newspaper reporter. Gordon had been fired from New York's *Daily News* the day after he appeared before the Senate Internal Security Subcommittee and refused to answer if he had run the communist "shop paper" when he worked at the *Brooklyn Eagle*.[48]

The FBI confirmed that Gordon, going then by the name Alex Gordon, was a copywriter at Sackler's Medical Press.[49] The Bureau quickly discovered that many of the activists and writers it listed as communist sympathizers or former party members had gone unnoticed since Sackler gave them non-byline jobs at his newsletters and promotional publications.[50]

The New York Times had dismissed Jack Shafer, a foreign desk copy editor, after he invoked the Fifth Amendment before Congress when asked if he was a communist. He took a job at *Medical Tribune*, Sackler's biweekly free newspaper that went to 168,000 American doctors.[51] *Medical Tribune* was also where Max Gordon, a former city editor of the *New York Daily Worker*, found a job. The same was true for Melvin Barnet, a *Times* copy editor who had testified he was not a communist after 1942 but took the Fifth for the period before that. Although Barnet had an English and classics degree from Harvard and his thesis about Shakespeare won honors, his journalism career was finished. After the *Times* let him go, he ended up picking oranges in Florida and editing vanity books to pay his bills. Then a friend told him that Arthur

---

* Director Sidney Lumet helped Bernstein emerge from the blacklist three years later. Lumet hired him to write the screenplay in 1959 for the Sophia Loren film *That Kind of Woman*. He worked on *The Magnificent Seven* the following year but did not get credit. Then in 1964 he demonstrated his Red Scare past was truly behind him with the hit screenplay for *Fail Safe*.

Sackler at William Douglas McAdams "had hired others who had lost their job during the McCarthy era."[52] * [53]

The Bureau's probe gathered some momentum when it learned Peter Rhodes, who it had investigated for possible espionage, worked as a McAdams copywriter and editor. Rhodes had been a UPI reporter who had covered World War II for the Office of War Information. He lost his job after a special investigating unit of the House Un-American Activities Committee revealed he had signed petitions for the Communist Party for state and local elections in 1940 and had also listed fake addresses on the forms. During the war, an FBI surveillance team had tracked Jacob Golos, a Ukrainian-born Bolshevik revolutionary and Soviet intelligence operative who was a founding member of the American Communist Party, to Rhodes's Washington Heights apartment on West 173rd Street. Golos was in charge of recruiting foreign agents. Rhodes was never charged with espionage and after the war denied he was a Soviet asset.[54] The agents who worked his case thought he was lying.

The FBI learned from their McAdams informant that Rhodes had recently traveled to Europe and not returned; it was believed he was working there for McAdams International, which Sackler had opened to handle the promotion needs of his foreign pharma clients. Moreover, the informant said that Rhodes was responsible for Sackler hiring Jack Ryan, the former executive vice president of the New York local of the American Newspaper Guild. Ryan had resigned after witnesses publicly identified him as a Communist Party member (he never flatly denied it).[55] During his testimony before the House Un-American Activities Committee, when asked about work, Ryan said he was a self-employed horticulturist. At the time, he was on the payroll of Communications Associates, a McAdams subsidiary.[56]

The FBI informant warned the Bureau that he had become "increas-

---

* The author discovered that when Sackler did not have an opening for one of the blacklisted journalists, he sometimes asked Bill Frohlich for help. William Marx "Bill" Mandel, a reporter who was most famous for his heated exchanges with Senator McCarthy during the House Un-American Activities Committee hearings, got a job at L. W. Frohlich after Sackler made a personal request. The same was true for Carol Greitzer, a feminist activist who later became president of the National Abortion Rights Action League and in 1969 got elected to New York City Council. Once elected, she reduced her work at L. W. Frohlich to three days a week. Mandel's father, Hyman Robert Mandel, had served on New York's Citizen's Housing Council with Sackler's friend Alfred Stern.

ingly suspicious this summer [1956] when Dr. Arthur Sackler, Fritz Silber, two partners—Dr. De Forrest Ely [*sic*] and Dr. Felix-Ibanez [*sic*]—and the company accountant, Louis Goldburt, all visited Europe at the same time, ostensibly for pleasure trips." That was the first time Martí-Ibáñez's name came up. The Bureau knew that American leftists respected Martí-Ibáñez because he had fought the fascists in the Spanish Civil War.

Martí-Ibáñez traveled often to Switzerland to visit Dr. Henry Sigerist, a pro-Soviet physician who had left America after the FBI declared him a security risk.[57] Arthur Sackler, said the informant, "sees Rhodes while visiting there."[58] Some of Sackler's recent new hires—Fritz Silber and Heinz Norden—were "close associates of Ryan and Rhodes." That raised the specter of espionage. The memo sent to FBI headquarters noted: "The files of the NYO [New York Office] reflect that Dr. Arthur Sackler to have been an apparently close business contact of Alfred Kaufman Stern, a suspected Soviet agent."[59]

The FBI thought it odd that some of Sackler's companies shared the same address and telephone numbers.[60] The top executives overlapped.[61] The agents wondered whether the complexity was designed to hide the real owners and sources of funding.[62]

Relying on original incorporation, legal, and tax papers, the author cross-matched directors, attorneys, accountants, and shared office addresses and telephone numbers to unmask many of the previously secret Sackler enterprises. With some of their earliest ventures, the brothers were not hiding anything from the FBI but rather believed their odds for getting research grants were better if each company seemed independent when it applied to government and private foundations.

No Sackler was listed on the paperwork for the 1945 incorporation of Pharmaceutical Research Associates.*[63] It was formed to pursue drug research grants. Arthur Sackler did not appear as a director on a

* Pharmaceutical Research Associates initially listed its address as the law office of Brooklyn-born brothers Myron and Martin Greene. Martin incorporated the Sacklers' first charitable foundation in 1947. Both Greenes, and their office secretary, were listed as the sole shareholders for the February 1955 incorporation of Vard Pharmaceuticals (changed a month later to Bard Pharmaceuticals). Vard's address was also the Greenes' lower Broadway law office. After it became Bard, the address changed to 259 Broadway, the office of Louis Goldburt, Arthur Sackler's accountant.

corporate filing until 1957, the Laboratories for Therapeutic Research. It also pursued private and public research grants.[64]

The Sacklers's strategy worked. Time and again, both Pharmaceutical Research Associates and Laboratories for Therapeutic Research landed private and government funding without anyone realizing the Sacklers controlled both.

Even in instances in which the brothers used their names, they worked an angle. Arthur, for instance, was listed as the "Director of the von [*sic*] Ophuijsen Center [Creedmoor]," though he had not been formally with that research facility for years. Letterhead for the Ophuijsen Center discovered by the author listed its address as "130 East 50th Street, New York," the same as the McAdams agency. On another occasion, the electrochemicals department of DuPont de Nemours Company awarded Arthur a generous grant for a clinical trial about amino acids and gastric secretions. For his twenty-one-subject study he was aided by Dr. Lawrence Sophian, listed as the Ophuijsen Center's "Consultant Pathologist and Director of Research." There was no such position, although Sophian was real and employed as one of two doctors at the McAdams agency. Dr. Sophian was also one of the directors on the incorporation papers for the Laboratories for Therapeutic Research.[65]

Landing research grants was only one reason for the corporate maze the brothers created. Another was disseminating pharma-friendly information disguised as unbiased research.[66] Their new ventures mimicked the enormous success of Arthur's *Medical Tribune* newsletter. Arthur admitted to being the chairman of the board for Medical Press Inc., and president of the Medical Radio and TV Institute and the Physicians News Service (both of which shared with McAdams and other businesses three floors at 130 East 59th Street).[67] The author uncovered that Arthur, often with his brothers, had either a significant stake or full ownership in Brooklyn Medical Press (1942), Angiology Research Foundation (1950), Inter America Medical Press (1952), and International Medical Press (1952).[68]

Purdue Frederick, the patent drug company they bought in 1952, was at the center of most of their grand plans. Yet their Purdue ownership was not transparent, instead initially in the names of two of their lawyers and an accountant.[69] The same was true for a 1955 New York corporation, Bard Pharmaceuticals.[70] The trio opened their first foreign subsidiaries only three years after buying Purdue.[71] Mundipharma Limited (Latin for "world medicine") and Dagrapharm Limited (Urdu for "people's drugs") opened in August 1955 in London.[72] Those U.K. companies were followed soon by Mundipharma AG in Basel, Switzerland.[73] The author discovered that as was typical of their American operations, the two London companies shared the same address.[74] As for the Swiss firm, its address would be the same for fifteen future Sackler-connected Mundipharma-branded companies that opened in Switzerland through 2019 (twelve of which are still active).[75]

Despite its suspicions, the FBI never got the chance to probe the Sacklers' businesses. The Bureau was overwhelmed by a deluge of pending investigations about communist domestic infiltration and possible espionage. It had to do constant triage for prioritizing cases. Without any new evidence, the investigation into Arthur Sackler, his companies, and his employees, stalled. The case agents dutifully noted Arthur's left-wing leanings and his assistance to Communist Party members. The file on him and his brothers remained open.[76]

12

THE PUPPET MASTER

What the FBI did not know was that no matter who was listed as the owners on corporate registrations, Arthur was always in control. He was a natural puppet master for his tight circle of family, friends, and business associates.[1] It meant he gave far-flung advice on every aspect of their budding businesses. He encouraged Frohlich to create a string of new corporations with sometimes similar names, all of which might come in handy as they expanded.[*][2] Arthur convinced his brothers to add two successful products to the Purdue Frederick line, Cerumenex, a prescription earwax remover, and Senokot, a natural laxative. He also set goals for Mortimer and Raymond to continue clinical research into the organic causes of mental illness.

They occasionally bristled at his overbearing way. Help from Arthur was sometimes a euphemism for micromanagement. The wearying family dynamic was that after Arthur helped them—as he did by paying for their medical educations or funding Purdue Frederick—he made them feel as if they were bit players in his grand play.

In the meantime, everyone agreed Arthur had a knack for making money. He told Martí-Ibáñez and Frohlich that the 1955 launch of Pfizer's tetracycline was not only an opportunity for a redux to his smashing success with Terramycin but a chance to test the synergy in their parallel businesses.[3][†][4]

---

* In addition to L. W. Frohlich, there was soon Intercon Inc., Intercon International Inc., Intercon International Marketing Co. Inc., Shelfco Trading Co., IMI Liquidating, and IMTD Corp., most with their offices listed at 34 East 51st Street, New York, the same as Frohlich's advertising agency.

† While Pfizer and Sackler prepared for the tetracycline release, pharma competitors joined forces to wage a campaign against the discretion of pharmacists to substitute a similar drug for a prescribed one. What good was a drug patent that protected a firm's

Sackler and his McAdams agency pushed the limits of pharma advertising for tetracycline (Pfizer's brand name was Tetracyn). Frohlich furtively fed him prescribing data collected by IMS. It helped target those doctors who were big prescribers and most likely to be early adopters of new drugs. It also revealed that physicians were receptive to new Pfizer products because of "the reputation and image [the company] has created with the physician for quality and service."[5]

Martí-Ibáñez, who was so busy that he suffered from "headaches and insomnia," helped interpret the IMS data as a sub-rosa consultant for a McAdams subdivision. He was also publishing scholarly articles in *Medical Encyclopedia* that hyped tetracycline. Some researchers who published in Martí-Ibáñez's journals complained their work had been edited to include "repeated reference to Pfizer products" and it "gave the impression it was written for Pfizer rather than for physicians."[7]

Sackler's campaign, aided by Frohlich's prescribing data and the coverage in Martí-Ibáñez's journals, helped tetracycline sales far exceed Pfizer's already high expectations. In just over two years it became the most prescribed broad-spectrum antibiotic in America.[8]

When Lederle realized that tetracycline was a single atom modification of its Aureomycin, it sued Pfizer and simultaneously filed its own patent for tetracycline under the brand name Achromycin.[9] That encouraged other drug firms to reexamine their earlier lab research to determine whether their scientists had also isolated tetracycline but failed to recognize it as a stand-alone drug.[10] In what one industry analyst described as "an amazing coincidental discovery of the same substance," Bristol-Myers, Squibb, and Hayden Chemical filed lawsuits seeking to invalidate Pfizer's patent.[11] Each also filed for separate patents contending they were the rightful owners of their branded version of tetracycline.[12]

The firms prepared for a protracted legal battle. American Cyanamid, Lederle's parent, bought Hayden's patent for $600,000 more than its book value.[13] Squibb and Upjohn, two that did not have a scientific claim to a tetracycline patent, agreed to pay Bristol's litigation costs in return for a sizable discount on their bulk purchases of the drug should Bristol prevail.[14]

---

exclusive rights to sell it if pharmacists substituted a competitor's version? The pharma industry's intensive lobbying campaign succeeded in a few years to convince forty-four state legislatures to outlaw drug substitution by pharmacists.

As the industry approached the $2 billion milestone in annual sales by mid-decade, the legal battle over who owned the right to tetracycline attracted the attention of Congress.[15] * [16] The House Committee on Government Operations began a two-year probe into whether the FTC and FDA were doing enough to regulate the therapeutic claims made by pharma firms.[17] New York congressman Victor Anfuso called on the Federal Trade Commission to "conduct a full-scale investigation" to determine if the companies were putting profits ahead of patients and also to determine if there was genuine price competition.

The FTC had good credentials for such an investigation. Earlier in the decade it had conducted highly praised probes into the oil and steel industries. In fact, four years earlier the FTC had opened a preliminary probe into pharma. It had been sparked by a Yale law school professor who noticed, when he had filled a prescription for antibiotics at his local pharmacy, that three brands of the identical drug were priced the same. That puzzled him since the drugs were made by different companies with different manufacturing and development costs. That professor was married to an industrial economist at the FTC. She opened an official inquiry after he told her what he saw.[18] But the FTC did not give it the money and personnel to convert it into a serious probe. Anfuso and many of his fellow Democrats intended to change that. They authorized the budget the agency requested—$4.3 million—and by the end of 1955 the FTC had launched a vigorous new inquiry, in which it subpoenaed tens of thousands of company documents.[19] Those provided a rare look at how pharma rivals divided markets and blocked new companies' access to the market.

That FTC investigation was one of several public relations headwinds that pharma faced that year. It was proving difficult to maintain its postwar image of a selfless industry in which companies shared scientific research in pursuit of drugs that saved millions of lives. While there had been more laboratory breakthroughs—the antibiotic eryth-

* When the industry sales passed $2 billion, prescription drugs accounted for all but $3 million. The pharmaceutical companies had destroyed any vestige of patent drugs. They had not yet begun concentrating on the over-the-counter market for medications that would in coming decades be a significant part of revenues and profits.

romycin (1952), synthetic cortisone (1954), the antipsychotics Thorazine (1954) and Serpasil (1955), and oral anti-diabetic medications Orinase and Diabinese—none matched the excitement penicillin had generated.[20]

Another problem was that the importance of some 1950s innovations would not be immediately evident. It took more than forty years, for instance, before biotechnology firms turned Judah Folkman's research on the circulatory system into angiogenesis inhibitor therapies, drugs that prevent cancer tumors from using the body's blood vessels to grow.[21] At the University of Washington in 1953, an Italian physician, Rita Levi-Montalcini, isolated nerve growth factor (NGF) from cultures. Scientists at Stanford and Cornell used genetic engineering on NGF a quarter century later to develop drugs that treated cancer and eye conditions that led to blindness. It took until 1986 for Levi-Montalcini to get a Nobel for her discovery of NGF.[22] The same happened with two Burroughs Wellcome biochemists who had little success in blocking enzymes to develop an effective leukemia drug in 1953. Thirty-five years later the pair won the Nobel for their research, which led to immune-suppressive drugs that made organ transplants a reality and provided treatment for a broad range of severe autoimmune disorders.[23] And finally, a British researcher discovered interferon in 1957, but it took thirty years before gene-cloning technology allowed it to be converted into an effective drug against some cancers.[24]

Any laboratory advances were overshadowed in April 1955 when Cutter Laboratories, one of four pharma firms the government had selected to produce the polio vaccine, shipped vaccine lots contaminated with the live virus. More than forty thousand schoolchildren in five Western states fell ill, two hundred were permanently paralyzed, and ten died.[25]

Cutter—today best known for its insect repellants—had failed to follow Jonas Salk's protocol for deactivating the virus with formaldehyde. A National Institutes of Health epidemiologist responsible for testing the vaccines had found live virus in Cutter's version and warned the NIH director. He disregarded her findings.[26] Wyeth—which had been acquired by American Home Products, whose successful products included the over-the-counter analgesic Anacin, the hemorrhoid cream Preparation H, Black Flag insecticide, and Chef Boyardee canned ravioli—also produced vaccine with traces of live virus, but only the Cutter lots made people sick.[27]*

The fatal mistakes prompted the surgeon general's call for stricter testing and safety protocols for vaccine production. The NIH's division for regulating vaccines expanded in a year from 10 employees to 150.[28] In Congress, for the first time, pharma became a target. Repeatedly in debates over what safeguards should be implemented to prevent a repeat disaster, regulators rebuked drug firms for worrying that stricter safety regulations would be too costly.[29]

Following the lead of the FTC, the House Subcommittee on Intergovernmental Relations began a wide-ranging investigation of the firms that produced vaccines. The probe targeted not only whether they had cut safety to save money but also if they had fixed vaccine prices. The industry was justifiably concerned about the reputational damage that would be an inevitable by-product of two major government inquiries.

More bad news came in December 1955 in a scandalous New York criminal trial.[30] A jury found John G. Broady, an attorney and private investigator, guilty as the "prime mover" in a conspiracy that tapped the phones of prominent politicians and businessmen.[31] A subplot in the front-page coverage of City Hall dirty tricks involved corporate espionage at the highest levels of the pharmaceutical business.

One of Broady's clients was Robert Porter, Pfizer's general counsel. Porter had paid Broady $60,000 ($572,000 in 2018) to spy on dozens of Pfizer executives as well as tap phones at Squibb and Bristol-Myers headquarters.[32] Bristol seized on that testimony and tried to leverage it against Pfizer in the ongoing tetracycline litigation.[33] Pfizer's chief counsel denied under oath that he ordered any spying but Bristol threatened to sue claiming that Pfizer's tetracycline patent was the result of confidential data illegally obtained by the wiretaps.

Pfizer's CEO, John McKeen, held a summit with Bristol's vice president, Frederick Schwartz (in another eighteen months, Schwartz would be the company's first non-Bristol-family-member president).

* Fears over the safety of Salk's vaccine led to its replacement in 1963 with a live-virus vaccine developed by Dr. Albert Sabin. It had the benefit of oral administration, although it also was more dangerous since it occasionally produced polio in a small number of patients. Prior to its nationwide rollout in the U.S., human trials for that vaccine were given to about a million people in what was then the Belgian Congo.

McKeen convinced Bristol to pause its legal action while the five companies fighting over the rights to tetracycline redoubled their efforts to reach a negotiated settlement. Several months of intensive talks resulted in a sweeping March 1956 agreement that ended the litigation before the Patent Office and federal courts. Lederle, Squibb, Bristol, and Upjohn acknowledged the validity of Pfizer's patent. Pfizer and Lederle had secretly agreed that whichever of them prevailed on the patent claim, the other would withdraw its action in return for a favorable licensing agreement.[34] Pfizer executed a series of complex cross-licensing, assignment, and distribution agreements that allowed those firms to sell their own brands of tetracycline; Lederle got better terms than the others.[35] Industry analysts wondered whether the five rivals would soon be engaged in the same cutthroat price discounting that had decimated profits in the penicillin and streptomycin markets.[36] Tetracycline would only fulfill its bottom-line promise if its price remained stable.

In the wake of the settlement, all five firms offered a standard pack of tetracycline (sixteen capsules of 250 milligrams each) at $5.10. That was the price set by Pfizer and Lederle. It did not seem to matter that all had different production costs.[37] Upjohn and Squibb did not manufacture the raw material needed for the drug, instead buying it in bulk from Bristol, making manufacturing expenses for Upjohn and Squibb three times costlier than its competitors. Still, neither charged more for their tetracycline. No firm offered a discount.[38] All submitted the same prices when making sealed bids for federal and state government contracts. Nor did the prices vary in thirteen other countries where they sold the drug.[39] The five firms controlled the market and reaped hundreds of millions in earnings. That prices did not budge for the rest of the decade, concluded John Braithwaite, an Australian professor of business regulation and white-collar crime, was "either the result of price fixing or coincidence that defies belief."[40]

Confirmation that something was not right on the unmovable tetracycline pricing was what happened with the industry's second-biggest market, corticosteroids. Schering got a patent in 1955 on prednisone, which it claimed was several times more potent than previous patented versions of cortisone. Merck, Pfizer, Upjohn, and Parke-Davis filed for their own patents and contested the one granted to Schering. Just as had happened with tetracycline, the companies resolved the matter with a series of complex cross-licensing and royalty agreements. And the five supposed rivals kept their prices uniform at $17.90 per one hundred 5-milligram pills. It took a Mexican drug company, Syntex, to spark a price war by selling bulk prednisone at one fifth the price of the U.S. firms.[41]

There was no equivalent of Syntex for tetracycline. As a result, the gross profit margins for those firms topped 75 percent. Pfizer and Lederle between them boasted half of the broad-spectrum market.[42] Lederle antibiotics profits offset losses in the rest of its poorly performing drug division. Pfizer's revenues had increased 600 percent since the end of the war and tetracycline was responsible for more than 80 percent of its profits.[43] The companies used some of those gigantic returns to begin the expansion that in the next decade would transform them into powerful multinational conglomerates.[44]

13

FAKE DOCTORS

By the mid-1950s, Arthur Sackler and his Medicine Avenue partners were looking beyond promoting competing brands of tetracycline. As part of their hunt they focused on so-called fixed-dose combination antibiotics. The theory had both strong proponents and skeptical critics. Its advocates believed that when antibiotics were combined with other drugs, the resulting medications might have fewer side effects and more potency than either drug on its own. Some experts, like infectious disease researcher Hobart Reimann, thought fixed combinations could be more revolutionary than penicillin (his proposed name was multimycetin).[1] The naysayers believed the underlying science was flawed. The skeptics thought it was unlikely that any fixed combination would ever have better efficacy than the antibiotic on its own. Some voiced concerns that it was possible over time the combined drugs could become antagonistic to each other, resulting in serious long-term side effects.

It was not a new theory. In the late 1940s, a sulfa and penicillin mix had tested better in the lab at fighting some common infections. It never went on sale, however, since the sulfa component spiked adverse effects. Pharma researchers at half a dozen companies had tried hundreds of combinations since then and failed to get one from the lab to the marketplace.

Still, Medicine Avenue was enthusiastic. Martí-Ibáñez wrote to Sackler early in 1956, contending that fixed-dose combo antibiotics "are a defense against the current [downward] price trend in penicillin and streptomycin."[2] The reason for their confidence was that Pfizer was close to FDA approval of the industry's first fixed-dose combination antibiotic, Sigmamycin. It was a mixture of two parts tetracycline and one part oleandomycin, a weak relative of erythromycin.

Martí-Ibáñez held his annual Symposium on Antibiotics in New York in June 1956. Henry Welch, chief of the FDA's antibiotic division, gave the introductory remarks to the gathering of leading researchers, academicians, and clinicians.[3] He surprised many by enthusiastically endorsing fixed-dose combinations.[4] "It is quite possible that we are now in a third era of antibiotic therapy," he said.[5]

After he returned to Washington, Welch assigned a team inside his division to gather data that buttressed his bold conclusion.

No one outside a handful of friends knew that Welch's endorsement had been carefully orchestrated by Sackler on behalf of his client Pfizer. Arthur had convinced Martí-Ibáñez they would all benefit if Pfizer's advertising staff, and a few of his best McAdams copywriters, edited Welch's talk. Pfizer, Sackler said, would buy many reprints of a good speech since Sygmamycin was only months away from going on sale. Sackler himself coined the "third era of antibiotic therapy" to herald the drug's arrival, and it became the tagline in Pfizer's upcoming campaign (when it became a public scandal a few years later, a twenty-six-year-old medical student who paid his tuition by working as a copywriter in Pfizer's tiny marketing department took the blame for "jazzing up" Welch's address).[6]

Sackler delivered on his promise. Pfizer bought 238,000 reprints of Welch's opening remarks.[7] *Medical Encyclopedia*, launched by Martí-Ibáñez and Welch, was the publisher. The duo announced their paid-subscription *Antibiotic Medicine* would become a free-circulation journal. Its financing? "Who better than the pharmaceutical industry," asked Martí-Ibáñez in disclosing it would be supported by drug ads.[8] More than 160,000 copies of the first issue went to physicians and a select list of influential lay people.

Martí-Ibáñez and Welch also launched a new monthly, *The Medical Newsmagazine MD*. It was a glossy journal that promised the latest medical and pharmaceutical news.[9] Mortimer Sackler was appointed an editorial board director. The McAdams agency sold the ads.[10] Welch wrote to Sackler imploring him to give an "extra push" to all his pharma clients to make it a financial success.[11]

Welch's public endorsement of the science behind fixed-dose combination antibiotics excited Pfizer. It was perfectly timed for its November rollout of Sigmamycin. In lab tests the drug was particularly effective against the deadly *Streptococcus pneumoniae* bacterium. Arthur Sackler utilized the same aggressive tactics that had been so successful with Terramycin and tetracycline. In a massive nationwide direct-to-doctors mailing campaign, Pfizer eschewed randomized clinical trials to boast about its drug, instead relying on personal experiences by physicians. "Every day . . . everywhere . . . more and more physicians find Sigmamycin the antibiotic therapy of choice," was the headline on a flashy brochure that accompanied free samples.[12]

Pfizer ran a bold four-page ad in the November issue of *Antibiotic Medicine*. In an accompanying editorial, Welch praised the "stand out . . . synergism" of Sygmamycin's component drugs.[13] It was hard not to see his words as a product endorsement by the chief of the FDA's Division of Antibiotics.

That editorial sparked criticism of Welch's dual roles. Many scientists believed that no government watchdog agency should sponsor a private, for-profit symposium. Although the FDA would end its role in Martí-Ibáñez and Welch's annual Antibiotics Symposium the following year, it did not rein in Welch. It accepted his assurances that he still received only a small honorarium.

Sackler let Frohlich and Martí-Ibáñez assume responsibility for Welch successfully fending off any inquiries from his FDA supervisors. Arthur was not as involved since he was under tremendous personal stress, something he did not share with his business partners. Just a couple of months earlier a Hollywood producer had stunned the House Un-American Activities Committee with testimony that Alfred Stern and his wife, Martha Dodd, were Soviet spies. The couple had fled to Prague by that time (they never returned to the U.S.).[14] Sackler worried the FBI might pick up the trail of his friendship with Stern. He had reason to worry. The Ridgefield, Connecticut, summer house where Arthur sometimes visited them was where they also met with Soviet agents.[15] The FBI would come calling, but not for another four years.

In the meantime, as he fretted about the consequences of his friendship with the fugitive couple, Arthur relied on what one colleague called his "unwavering discipline" to refocus on business. In 1955, Mortimer and Raymond bought rights to L-Glutavite, four trademarked "therapeutical preparations," and eight product-related patents, from Boston's Gray Pharmaceutical Company.[16] L-Glutavite was a proprietary mixture that Gray touted as "optimal amounts of monosodium L-glutamate plus a therapeutic amount of the vasodilator niacin and co-enzymes and other essential elements."

"Broken down into ordinary layman's English," wrote John Lear, the no-nonsense science editor for *The Saturday Review*, "this means simply the familiar meat flavoring (MSG) plus vitamin B." With Arthur providing strategic advice, Mortimer and Raymond formed the Glutavite Corporation and approached the FDA about getting it approved as a drug.[17] The FDA said no approval was necessary since glutamate, its main chemical, was harmless, and vitamin B was sold over the counter. The agency warned the Sacklers not to make any therapeutic claims on advertisments to the public.[18]

Arthur figured out how to circumvent that. Although L-Glutavite required no prescription, the McAdams agency ran a promotional campaign directed only to doctors. Some industry observers thought it a waste of time and money to advertise an over-the-counter product to physicians who could not write a prescription for it. "That is a big misconception," says Richard Sperber, who later directed Schering-Plough's ethical OTC products, which included nasal spray Afrin and cold remedy Coricidin. "You need to build demand based on word of mouth. We promoted our OTC line widely, even to clinics, pharmacists, and nursing associations. There is a placebo effect that takes place for many consumers when a medical professional tells them about a pill."[19]

The first Sackler advertisements for L-Glutavite were illustrated with charcoal sketches of senile men and women. Arthur believed many physicians might be willing to dispense it for their patients who complained about conditions—a glum mood, faulty memory, or a general mental fogginess—that might not be serious enough for more powerful tranquilizers. The ads promised that a "rounded teaspoonful of powder in tomato or other vegetable juice" daily would "improve cerebral metabolism." *Saturday Review*'s John Lear noted, "The spectacle of three psychiatrists, members of a profession looked to with almost awesome respect for guidance in mental illness, concertedly pushing a flavoring extract mixed with vitamins as a means of arresting the pitiable deterioration of aging minds, is a painful experience."[20]

The American Medical Association's journal refused to carry the L-Glutavite ads. That was not a problem for the Sacklers. They formed a separate company that appeared to be an independent marketing firm (Medical Promotion Production Inc.).[21] It placed ads in Arthur's *Medical Tribune*, distributed free to the nation's doctors. L-Glutavite also featured in Arthur's recently launched *Medical News*, a weekly newsletter to another 35,000 physicians who were teachers at medical schools, held staff positions at hospitals, or served in the military.[22] Ads ultimately ran in fifteen medical journals to which the Sacklers had some business connection.[23]

L-Glutavite was a success from the moment the Sacklers began selling it. Inexpensive to manufacture and sold at a several hundred percent markup, it returned huge profits.

The Sacklers arranged for a clinical study of L-Glutavite at the Bedford, Massachusetts, Veterans Affairs Medical Center. Built in 1928 as a psychiatric asylum, Bedford had a large population of elderly patients diagnosed as schizophrenics. Mortimer and Raymond were friends with Dr. Louis Fincle, Bedford's chief psychiatrist.[24] The study involved several dozen patients averaging sixty-three years of age and twenty years of institutionalization. All were given a daily glass of tomato juice; L-Glutavite was mixed into half the drinks. No one, including Fincle, supposedly knew which patients got the spiked juice.

The results were dramatic. Fincle, joined by a Boston professor of psychology, Leo Reyna, reported "marked improvements" in 73 percent of the L-Glutavite patients. They had "improved behavior and outlook," some stopped quarreling, and others for the first time in years started dressing and feeding themselves. The progress was so marked for some patients that they were discharged to regular nursing homes. The researchers concluded that for "poor risk elderly patients" L-Glutavite was "safe and free of detrimental side effects."[25]

The Journal of Clinical and Experimental Psychopathology published the results in its March 1958 issue. A press release put it on the radar of newspapers and magazines across the nation: "Chemical in Juice Aids Mentally Ill" (*New York Times*), "Important New Drug for the Mentally Ill" (UPI), "A Boon to the Nation's Overcrowded Mental Hospitals" (AP).[26]

No one was aware of the many underlying conflicts of interest. The Sacklers owned *The Journal of Clinical and Experimental Psychopathology*. Arthur was its editor-in-chief and Felix Martí-Ibáñez its international editor. Mortimer and Raymond were listed on its letterhead as two directors.

On March 21, 1958, the same month that the Sacklers' psychiatric journal reported the results of the clinical trial, a stock listing was filed at the New York Stock Exchange. Application No. A-17508 listed seventy thousand additional shares of common stock of Chemway Corp., a home products manufacturer, for the purchase of Glutavite Corporation.[27] When the shares were issued that day at Chemway's market price of 7⅝, the Sacklers pocketed half a million dollars for their one-product company.[28] That was in addition to $1.5 million in sales over the three previous years.[29] Chemway placed L-Glutavite under its drug division, Crookes-Barnes. A Senate investigating committee later determined that Crookes-Barnes had been a "company partially owned by Sacklers." Chemway had bought it from Mortimer and Raymond Sackler in July 1955. Arthur Sackler was one of its directors.[30]

The clinical trial that showed such promise for L-Glutavite in treating or even reversing schizophrenia in elderly patients was the first of its kind and sealed the Chemway deal. That result, however, was never again duplicated. In recent years, researchers have concluded the opposite, that excess glutamate might be a trigger for schizophrenia.[31] Why was the L-Glutavite study conducted for the Sacklers, and published in a journal they controlled, such an outlier? No one can be certain so many years later. The author learned, however, that John "Jack" Brennan, one of the country's leading pharmacological experts, and the president of Gray Pharmaceutical at the time the Sacklers bought its products, had an opinion. He later told a colleague at Boston's Kendall Company that "someone had cooked the numbers."[32]

The inability to reproduce the success of the L-Glutavite trial did not concern the Sacklers. What mattered to the brothers was that L-Glutavite had returned over $2 million in under three years ($18.3 million in 2019).

Government regulatory agencies that might have taken notice were instead focused on investigating much larger companies and broader themes of competitiveness and pricing. While the Sacklers were orchestrating their Glutavite bonanza, the FTC was putting the finishing touches on a three-year investigation into the drug industry. Its highly critical 361-page "Economic Report on Antibiotics Manufacture" was released only a couple of months after the Sacklers sold Glutavite to Chemway.[33] The FTC's damning conclusion was that the years of uniform prices for all the tetracycline brands were not by chance but rather illegal collusion.

Bill Frohlich had boasted there was "a competitive zeal in the pharmaceutical industry which would have warmed Adam Smith's heart." That was put to the test the following month, when the FTC filed a sweeping antitrust complaint charging Pfizer, Lederle, Bristol-Myers,

Squibb, and Upjohn with conspiracy to fix tetracycline prices and using their cross-licensing agreements to exclude others from entering the market.[34] The FTC also accused Pfizer of fraudulently obtaining its patent monopoly by withholding critical information from the Patent Office. When its four competitors learned about that omission, instead of reporting it to regulators, the complaint contended they blackmailed Pfizer into partitioning the tetracycline market.[35]

On the heels of the FTC price-fixing charges, the Securities and Exchange Commission released a report that revealed the profits of pharmaceutical companies were, on average, more than double that of other manufacturing industries.[36]

Pharma firms deserved larger profit margins, argued Bill Frohlich, since drug sales had been flat through World War II before "increasing almost three times as much as the increase in the Gross National Product" during the 1950s. Half the biggest-selling medications were less than five years old, which according to Arthur Sackler meant that innovation drove profits.[37] While Sackler, Frohlich, and many of their colleagues shrugged at the SEC report, the part about pharma's immense profits was a lead story in the national press. It added to a growing perception that drug prices were too high.

Even a few prominent medical voices warned about the consequences of pharma's fixation on profits. Max Finland, an esteemed Harvard researcher who had led penicillin research on treating pneumonia, cautioned that the companies had lost sense of their original mission. At some point, Finland suggested, they should refocus on finding cures and stop judging success only by sales.[38] Finland correctly predicted that the failure to focus on what was best for the patient meant it was only a matter of time until pharma would cross a line that infuriated the public and result in more government regulation.[39]

Drug firms were on the defensive. The idea they were obsessed with profits was wrong, they countered. Finland's call to put public service ahead of profits was misplaced since they had spent $600 million on research and development since the end of World War II. They had also collectively introduced four hundred new medications in just three years.[40]

Those proclamations seemed hollow in light of an article by John Lear in *Saturday Review.* "Taking the Miracle Out of the Miracle Drugs" was published the same month the SEC reported about the industry's immense profits. Lear exposed that pharma firms were anything but noble. He presented a damning indictment of how "unduly enthusiastic and sometimes misleading . . . massive advertising pressure" had encouraged doctors to overprescribe antibiotics.[41] That widespread overuse had turned some ordinary microbes pathogenic. Lear revealed that between 1954 and the autumn of 1958, there had been five hundred hospital epidemics of resistant strains of staph infections. The deadliest outbreak killed twenty-two patients in a Texas hospital. Many doctors Lear interviewed acknowledged antibiotic resistance was a national problem. Yet he was the first to cover it in a national publication because "medical authorities discouraged writers from disseminating the fact on the grounds that people who needed hospital care would be frightened away."[42]

Lear was most critical of the advertisers and marketing companies who had encouraged overprescribing of antibiotics. He noted that while some drug companies were "traditionally cautious in advancing claims for their medicines," the industry had been "jostled and jolted . . . by the Madison Avenue 'hard sell'" which relied on "a great deal of money" and no "restraint in promotion."[43] The problem had been made worse since penicillin had not required a prescription during its first decade on the market.[44]

The marketing excesses, he charged, had reached a fever pitch with the introduction of fixed-dose antibiotics. Pfizer's Sigmamycin had been on sale for three years by the time of Lear's exposé. Rival companies had responded with their own brands, sixty-nine fixed-dose antibiotics.[45] Lear contended that studies showed that not a single compound offered therapeutic advantage over the underlying antibiotic on its own, and that the combinations were "sometimes dangerous."[46]

As for Sigmamycin, he was suspicious that all the clinical studies cited in the advertisements referred to reports published in Martí-Ibáñez's medical journals and edited by the FDA's Henry Welch. Arthur Sackler served as an advisor on those editorial boards.[47]

Lear met one evening with an unidentified "eminent research physician" at his laboratory. (Physician-historian Scott Podolsky believes the anonymous tipster was Harvard's Max Finland, whom Podolsky calls "the de facto Strep Throat.")[48]

"He pulled open several drawers that were full of drug samples and advertisements," Lear recalled. "'Just take a look at that stuff!' he told me, and then went on to say that a good part of the advertising was misleading—in fact, that some of it was downright fraudulent."

"Look, you're walking around a big story. Why don't you step into it?" the physician said to Lear.

"I might if I had enough information."[49]

The physician pulled from the drawer a folder with a banner of bold type that said, "Every day, everywhere, more and more physicians find Sigmamycin the antibiotic therapy of choice."

Lear said, "Below that were reproductions of what appeared to be the professional cards of eight doctors around the country, with addresses, telephone numbers, and office hours. The doctor said he had himself conducted some experiments with Sigmamycin, and at one point he had written to the eight doctors to ask the outcome of their use of the drug in clinical tests. As he told me this, he reached into one of the drawers and brought out eight envelopes, all stamped *Return to Writer—Unclaimed*. I asked him if I might report his experience, and he said that he couldn't get involved in any kind of exposé. He pointed out, however, that there was nothing to prevent me from writing to the doctors myself."[50]

When Lear wrote to them asking why they were enthusiastic about Sigmamycin, he encountered the same roadblock as his friend. The telephone numbers on the cards were false, the addresses made up. The "doctors" were fakes, none of them existed.[51]

Lear's discovery put Sackler and Pfizer's CEO, John McKeen, in an uncomfortable spotlight. McKeen visited Lear at the magazine's office and claimed he belatedly understood how the ad might be misleading. Pfizer had taken steps to avoid doing it again, he assured Lear. As for Sackler, Arthur blamed the fake doctors on an overly enthusiastic copywriter.[52] Lear interviewed Welch the following month and pressed him on whether his financial arrangements with Martí-Ibáñez was a conflict of interest given his role as the chief federal regulatory cop for antibiotics. Once again, as he did with his bosses at the FDA, Welch swore he only received a token honorarium for all his nongovernment work.[53]

The controversy kicked off by Lear's article forced the FDA to act. Welch's bosses decided that October that although he was an "outstanding scientist" who had "no conflict of interest," it would be better if he resigned from his outside editorial roles.[54] It was too little too late. Lear's searing exposé about the fake doctors prompted the FTC to bring its first ever unfair practice complaint against a drug company (the FTC trial examiner found Pfizer guilty, but refused to issue any penalty since Pfizer promised not to do it again).[55]

More bad news came in December 1959. The FDA announced three over-the-counter earwax removal products were "voluntarily withdrawn from the market." That decision had been forced by months of press accounts of patients who had developed alarming side effects. The recall included Cerumenex, the country's top selling eardrop solution. It was one of Purdue Frederick's most successful products. The Sacklers set about slightly reformulating the eardrops to get Cerumenex back on shelves (a "new and improved" version went on sale in a year and still topped the market).

The worst news for pharma that month was not, however, the recall of a few over-the-counter meds. It was instead that the entire industry had come into the crosshairs of the crusading and ambitious Tennessee senator Estes Kefauver. He wanted to find out if drug firms were more concerned with profits than in finding medications to cure illnesses. What followed was a watershed moment for the modern pharmaceutical industry.

14

A "SACKLER EMPIRE"

A 1950 investigation into organized crime made Senator Estes Kefauver famous.[1] Informally called the Kefauver Hearings, they had coincided with the introduction of television in the U.S. Networks were so new that they had little daytime programming. Providing live coverage of Kefauver's probe was a last-minute decision. It was a big gamble for the young industry. The six-foot-three, 220-pound Kefauver, his face partially hidden by his oversized eyeglasses, did not look like the prototype of a television hero. His strong Southern drawl combined with a tendency to mumble often made him difficult to understand.[2] Yet the daily soap opera about the Italian mafia, with a parade of colorful mobsters squirming and blustering before the subcommittee, became a national obsession. When Kefauver took his show to New York City for eight days of gripping testimony from top gangsters, *Time* noted it "will occupy a special place in history. . . . People had suddenly gone indoors into living rooms, taverns, and clubrooms, auditoriums and back-offices. There, in eerie half-light, looking at millions of small frosty screens, people sat as if charmed. . . . Dishes stood in sinks, babies went unfed, business sagged and department stores emptied while the hearings were on. . . . Never before had the attention of the nation been riveted so completely on a single matter."[3] Thirty million Americans tuned in to the hearings, about 90 percent of those with TVs. Kefauver became a public champion.[4]*

---

*Kefauver won an Emmy in 1952 for "outstanding public service on television." He was a celebrity guest on the highest-rated game show of the era, *What's My Line?*, and had a bit part in a Humphrey Bogart film, *The Enforcer*. He was one of the few Washington politicians recognizable wherever he went and his subsequent book about the hearings, *Crime in America*, was a *New York Times* best-seller.

Kefauver tried parlaying his fame into becoming president. He ran in 1952 and 1956, barely losing the Democratic nomination both times to Illinois governor Adlai Stevenson. In 1956, Kefauver ran as Stevenson's vice president, but Eisenhower trounced them. The following year he was appointed the chairman of the Senate's Antitrust and Monopoly Subcommittee. He used that platform to cultivate an appeal to "the little fellow" by launching high-profile investigations into the steel, auto, and bread industries (*Time* coined "In Kefauver we anti-trust" for his new role).[5]

Kefauver's drug probe got under way in December 1959. From the start he made it clear he was bothered by an industry where only a few firms dominated sales and had unfettered discretion to set prices.[6] Pharmaceuticals accounted for thirteen of the top fifty firms in America.[7] He intended to find out, he said, if they abused the patent system to control the pricing and the market for a few incredibly profitable medications.

Kefauver had assembled a small but experienced investigative team, led by two FTC veterans. John Blair was an economist who had proven on large FTC probes his talent for navigating through voluminous company files to compile evidence of wrongdoing. The general counsel was Paul Rand Dixon, a decorated World War II Navy pilot (he would be appointed the head of the FTC before the hearings finished). Both realized their staff of six economists and attorneys would be hard pressed to keep up with the drug industry's small army of publicists and lobbyists as well as teams of lawyers and seasoned expert witnesses.[8] The pharma firms had some powerful allies, including the American Medical Association, many chambers of commerce, and the nation's pharmaceutical associations. All feared that "politically inspired" hearings would result in more federal regulation, maybe even price controls. That had happened in Europe after World War II when many nations implemented national health care programs. Putting the governments into the role of buying drugs from the pharma industry led to the creation of panels of physicians and bureaucrats empowered to either get price concessions or block the sales of drugs judged too expensive. The United States, meanwhile, remained the only industrialized country that allowed pharmaceutical companies to set prices.[9]

The subcommittee's focus was on competition and pricing in different drug categories: antibiotics, hormones, tranquilizers, and diabetic medications. Subpoenas were served on nineteen companies. They ordered the testimony of key executives and the production of tens of thousands of internal files, including patent licensing contracts and purchase and sales agreements.

The hearings got under way with a string of top executives who all resented testifying.[10] Schering's president, Francis Brown, was first. He had served as general counsel to the Federal Deposit Insurance Corporation before his appointment to run Schering after the government seized it as a German asset during World War II. When the Plough family later bought Schering at public auction in 1952 for $29 million—$281 million in 2019 dollars—and renamed it Schering-Plough, it kept Brown at the helm.

Visibly irritated by the sharp questioning, Brown accused the senators of trying to exercise "thought control" and scolded them for "misconstruing" information to generate "headlines."[11] Schering's drug prices were "pretty reasonable," he contended. John Blair challenged that, since the company's brand of a hormone drug (prednisone) was marked up 1,118 percent of its production cost.[12]

Merck's president, John Connor, arrived flanked by two Nobel Prize–winning scientists and lectured the committee that its investigation would "slow the forward march" for better drugs.[13] Parke-Davis's CEO Harry Loynd did not hide his disdain for the "ridiculous proceedings."[14] Loynd, a trained pharmacist, had worked as a detail man for twenty years at Parke-Davis before rising to the top spot. He believed that good sales trumped poor drugs. "If we put horse manure in a capsule, we could sell it to 95 percent of these doctors," he once told his sales team.[15]

All the CEOs cited said their enormous research and development costs could only be recouped by the drug prices they charged. That excuse for the big markups would serve as the template for pharma's deflection in all future price investigations.

Dr. Austin Smith, president of the Pharmaceutical Manufacturers Association, complained that the senators had made the drug industry a "whipping boy" so they might open "the back door . . . to socialized medicine." Smith set a new low when he argued that the focus on pricing was misplaced: "All of us feel compassion for elderly people who find it difficult to pay for medication. . . . If the pharmaceutical industry is at fault here, it is because it has helped to create a pool of millions too old to work by prolonging their lives."[16] Even Smith's allies shook their heads in disbelief when he told the subcommittee that the costs of drugs were lower than funeral costs.[17]

Kefauver thought such arrogance would spark a backlash against the pharma bosses. Not many Americans, however, were paying attention. The nuances of patent and antitrust law, licensing deals, royalty arrangements, drug chemistry, and testimony from well-coached economists proved far less interesting than the colorful and often profane mobsters from whom Kefauver earned his fame.[18]

This time, no television network broadcast the hearings live. John Blair, the investigative staff's chief economist, noted that Kefauver himself "became increasingly concerned with getting to a wider audience" and that "a formidable problem" was that much of the investigation "had gone largely unreported by the press."[19] Kefauver was frustrated that not even a disclosure about Upjohn's 10,000 percent profit margin on one of its drugs got much press.[20] He could not understand why there was not more anger after Squibb's former medical director Dr. A. Dale Console testified that "more than half" of the drugs on the market, or "on the drawing board," were "useless." The only reason they were sold was because "they promise sales."[21] The number of reporters covering the hearings had dwindled by the time it got to the intricacies of the patent battle over tetracycline.

Kefauver knew that a quirk of World War II labor policies meant his drug hearings faced a hurdle in captivating public interest. Most Americans had health insurance coverage through their employers and few were affected directly by rising drug prices. Before the war, there had been only two nonprofit insurers, Blue Cross, created by a group of Texas hospitals in 1929, and Blue Shield, founded by doctors in 1939 in California. They provided catastrophic care insurance designed to lessen the financial impact of a major illness or prolonged hospitalization. Fewer than 10 percent of Americans had signed up by the time the U.S. entered the war. In 1942, Franklin Roosevelt invoked extraordinary wartime powers to freeze all private enterprise "salaries and wages, as well as bonuses, additional compensation, gifts, commissions, and fees."[22] With so many workers suddenly in the military there was a severe labor shortage. Businesses had competed for workers by raising salaries and offering incentive bonuses. FDR's order stopped that, but it had an exception. It allowed companies to grow "insurance and pension benefits . . . in a reasonable amount."[23]

That might not have seemed a big deal until later that same year, the

Revenue Act put into effect a punitive tax rate of 90 percent on "excess profits," defined as anything greater than what the company had earned the year before the war. The Revenue Act's silver lining was that it gave domestic companies a financial incentive to provide health insurance for their employees. The costs of such insurance became deductible to employers.[24] An IRS ruling the following year exempted employees from paying taxes on the value of their employer-provided health insurance. The perfect alignment of the different events meant that by mid-1943, corporate America addressed its labor crunch by luring workers with generous health insurance benefits. The number of Americans covered by health insurance jumped from the prewar 10 percent to 30 percent a year after the war (1946). The arrival in 1951 of the first for-profit insurers, Aetna and Cigna, kicked off the next wave of public enrollments.[25] By the time Kefauver started his hearings, 70 percent of all Americans had health insurance plans that also covered the most widely prescribed drugs, including antibiotics, tranquilizers, psychotropics, and sulfa meds.[26]

Kefauver's instincts about what the public wanted to hear were normally impeccable. While he was determined to push forward on his drug industry probe, he also directed his investigative staff to double their efforts to dig up more than price markups and possible collusion. Proof of how wide a net they cast is in an extraordinary March 16, 1960, memo in which John Blair wrote to the subcommittee's chief counsel, Paul Rand Dixon.[27] The subject was "Sackler Brothers."[28]

> During the course of the drug investigation I have from time to time heard the rumors of the "Sackler Brothers" or "Sackler Empire." At first I had been under the impression that this is something of a "fringe" operation, of passing interest because of its unique character but of little substantive importance. As I have gathered further information, however, I have been forced to modify this earlier impression.
>
> The Sackler brothers, among others, are both of the medical journals formerly edited by Dr. Welch, head of the Antibiotics Division of the F.D.A. Any outfit which has been able to establish such close ties with the most powerful man in government with respect to antibiotics is hardly a fringe operation. However, the clandestine manner in which they carry on their multitudinous activities also suggests there may be more here than meets

> the eye. Finally, the very number of organizations in every facet of the drug industry which are under their ownership, control or influence, is such that they must be regarded as constituting a relatively large-scale operation.

Blair identified Dr. Marietta Lutze, Arthur's second wife, as the group's "fourth member." Over two months the investigative staff drew the startling conclusion that "The Sackler empire is a completely integrated operation," including creating "new drugs in its drug development enterprise"; insuring that "various hospitals with which they have connections" do the clinical testing and produce "favorable reports"; "conceive the advertising approach and prepare the actual advertising copy"; make certain the ad campaign is "published in their own medical journals"; and to "prepare and plant articles in newspapers and magazines through their public relations organizations."[29]

Attached to the memo was a list of twenty companies his investigators believed "the Sackler brothers own or control" through proxies. That was no easy task, Blair acknowledged, "since the whole operation is cloaked in secrecy."[30] One of the earliest ventures, Pharmaceutical Research Center, was "a known 'cover' for Sacklers."[31] The web of interconnected firms with hidden interests and financiers, warned Blair, had become proficient at making money from many different parts of the pharmaceutical trade. Some Sackler-controlled companies tested, promoted, and sold new drugs; others cashed in on government grants from the National Institutes of Health; and a diverse group had carved out a lucrative niche with medical publications.[32] (The NIH funding for private industry drug and medical research reached $100 million annually in 1956 and would more than double to $250 million by the end of the decade.)[33] * [34]

As comprehensive as the list was—they had found Sackler's owner-

---

* Blair's team did not realize what the author discovered, that the addresses to which they tracked some of the companies—15 East 62nd Street and 139 East 59th Street, New York—were locations used for earlier ventures, including the phantom New York City branch of the Ophuijsen Center from Creedmoor. The Senate investigators did reveal, however, how the Sacklers transferred some entities to trusts created for their minor children, which they then managed on their behalf. And there was evidence the family owned an unnamed "photo-engraving firm which makes plates used in expensive advertisements for medical journals," a real estate company that owned properties leased to many of the Sackler firms, and "the company that makes Lysol." That was Lehn & Fink. Lysol was popular for decades with women for feminine hygiene. Some

ship stakes in the journals edited by the FDA's Henry Welch—they also missed some key connections. Sackler's equity in Bill Frohlich's ad firm and his IMS medical data collection company remained a well-guarded secret. And the investigators did not find any of the huge private company grants the Sacklers had obtained using outdated Creedmoor credentials.

Blair identified people who could help build a case against the Sacklers. They included the FDA's Welch; an unidentified New York college professor who doubled as a clinical writer at Pfizer; a "disenchanted" former McAdams executive; an investor known only by the last name "Collier" who had been cut out of his rightful share on an antibiotic; and a "well-known and respected" Mexican doctor who was furious that the Sacklers had used their influence to force the cancellation of his competing antibiotic symposium in Mexico. Blair also noted "that the Sackler brothers, perhaps through some dummy, are said to be large owners of the stock of Pfizer as well as other leading companies."[35]

A week later, Blair zeroed in on how Sackler and Martí-Ibáñez might have compromised the FDA's Division of Antibiotics.[36] Henry Welch had a heart attack shortly after the subcommittee asked for copies of the last decade of his tax returns. The reason for his fright became evident once the investigators got the records. Welch reported $287,142 in "honoraria" in six years of editing two journals for MD Publications ($3.2 million in 2019). His annual FDA salary was $17,500.[37] Welch had once told some FDA coworkers that his government salary barely covered his income tax. They did not report it since they thought he was joking.[38] A third of Welch's payments had come from what Arthur Sackler had promised, Pfizer's purchases of reprints of articles from the journals he edited.[39]

Welch and Martí-Ibáñez were scheduled for public testimony on May 17. Both canceled. Welch's doctor claimed he was too ill to be put under "any emotional or physical strain" and two physicians for Martí-Ibáñez said he had glaucoma and that "severe emotional stress and tension are known to aggravate glaucoma and may cause blindness."[40]

At a public hearing on May 18, Kefauver finally had a subject that got national attention. The subcommittee presented the evidence about how Welch had cashed in. The HEW secretary held a press confer-

---

used it as a mostly ineffective postcoital douche for birth control, but the FDA approval of the contraceptive pill in 1960 ended that often dangerous practice.

ence the next day and demanded Welch resign. In a resignation letter he submitted later that same day, Welch was defiant and blamed "politics" for his predicament. He claimed no one could find "any article, paragraph or sentence, which reflects a lack of editorial or scientific integrity."[41] Adding to the fury was the disclosure that the federal Civil Service Commission had approved Welch's request for a disability pension after his March heart attack. It was now not possible to deny him his full benefits.[42] The Welch debacle forced the HEW secretary to appoint an internal Special Investigative Unit to probe whether there were more widespread conflicts of interest inside the FDA. It concluded that Welch was an isolated case.[43] (The FDA's official historical timeline omits any reference to Welch.)[44]

The Sackler brothers were fortunate they did not get pulled into the Welch scandal. Arthur and his McAdams agency had edited Welch's big fixed-dose antibiotic speech, and most of Welch's money came from reprint purchases by Sackler's client, Pfizer. Moreover, Welch had told the *Saturday Review*'s John Lear that Martí-Ibáñez had shared with him that he had two secret investors. Welch insisted, however, that he did not know who they were. Lear's hunch was that it was Arthur Sackler and one of his brothers, but he could never prove it.[45] The Senate investigators also suspected the Sacklers owned a controlling stake in MD Publications but did not have the resources to investigate that.

Arthur Sackler did not appear worried about Kefauver's probe. Instead of following each twist and turn of the hearings, he spent more time on his growing art collection. He lobbied for and got an appointment to Columbia's prestigious Advisory Council of the Department of Art, History, and Archaeology, a position he kept for thirteen years.[46] Arthur had wanted that Columbia appointment so badly that he created Medimetrics International, a "scientific research and development" firm. He and his first wife, Else, owned a majority; but he gave Columbia a 39.1 percent bequest of the company about six weeks before he got picked for the Advisory Council.[47] Meanwhile, Sackler continued adding to a growing roster of pharma clients. When he had too much work, he sent the client to one of his "competitors." That happened with Parke-Davis, which ended up at Bill Frohlich's agency.

Sackler had founded *Medical Tribune* just before Welch's public meltdown. It promised a concise summary of important developments affecting their profession, everything from pharmaceuticals to politics. It was supported solely by drug ads. Arthur had pitched his idea for

Medical Tribune to Georges Doriot, a legendary entrepreneur and Harvard business school professor who is credited as the "father of venture capitalism."[48]

Arthur invited Doriot to make an investment in *Medical Tribune*. Doriot was one of the most respected names in the business world. One of Doriot's most quoted remarks was that "Someone, somewhere, is making a product that will make your product obsolete." Arthur pressed the idea that *Medical Tribune* was unlike anything else. Doriot not only invested but lent his name to it publicly. He praised *Medical Tribune* and announced it was one of only thirty ventures in which he had put his own money.[49] His backing for what he called "the first independent paper for doctors" attracted considerable attention in the financial press.[50]

Medical Tribune's masthead listed it as a wholly owned subsidiary of Medical and Science Communications Development Corporation. Only a handful knew that Arthur's first wife, Else, secretly controlled that company. It had been incorporated in Delaware, where shareholder secrecy is sacrosanct, in February 1960, only three months before Welch's humiliating denouement. The following month it was incorporated in New York and Nevada.[51] On its masthead, Sackler listed Doriot as the president, and Medical and Science Communications Development was "an affiliate" of Doriot's much admired venture capital firm, American Research and Development Corporation.

By the end of the decade, *Medical Tribune* would become one of Sackler's most successful businesses. In every issue, Arthur wrote a column, "One Man . . . and Medicine." It was his soapbox. He used it as a provocative forum for a wide range of topics. Sackler often attacked government regulators, ranted about the dangers of smoking and the need for mandatory car seat belts, and sometimes triggered a furious discussion in one of the medical disciplines, such as his "Does Schizophrenia Protect Against Cancer?" column, citing research at Creedmoor Psychiatric Center that he and his brothers had published in 1951 in a Sackler-controlled journal.[52] * [53]

Most of *Medical Tribune*'s success, however, came after Georges

---

* When Sackler bought McAdams in 1947, he made it a member of the American Association of Advertising Agencies (AAAA), which since 1917 had represented about 90 percent of the nation's ad firms. Arthur ran *Medical Tribune* from the same office as his McAdams agency. Sometimes, employees did work for both. That violated an

Doriot had sold his investment back to Arthur at a small profit.[54] Although Doriot thought Sackler was "fascinating, brilliant and likeable," he and his advisors were uncomfortable with Sackler's shuffling of ownership interests between family and friends. "We had a funny feeling about it," Doriot years later told *The Boston Globe*. "There was always something we didn't understand."[55]

What Doriot did not fully appreciate was that Arthur could have financed *Medical Tribune* on his own. Instead, Arthur knew that *Medical Tribune* got a priceless public relations boost if Doriot put his name to it.[56]

Medical Tribune debuted in the middle of the Kefauver hearings. The staff had had no opportunity to include it during its investigation. Instead, during the last four months of its public hearings, Kefauver's subcommittee focused on antibiotics prices. It was a replay of what happened earlier in the hearings when the spotlight was on hormones. Top CEOs were grilled about why they priced their medications as huge markups of their manufacturing costs. They stuck to their script: the government underestimated their research costs and overestimated their profits.[57]

That was the same excuse the pharma companies put forward when confronted about why their drugs were always significantly more expensive in America than anywhere else. Fifty tablets of a popular American-made tranquilizer cost $3.25 in the U.S. but only $0.75 in Argentina or $1.48 in the U.K. Lilly's antibiotic, Penicillin 5, was made and shipped from its Indianapolis plant and sold for $18 a lot in the U.S. but in Europe for an average of $7.25. The investigative staff discovered that the same pricing anomaly existed in all commercially successful drugs with a European origin. Swiss-based Ciba sold its hypertension medication, Resperine, at $40 a lot to European pharmacists, but its U.S. subsidiary charged American druggists $91. European pharmacists paid $10 for an allotment of French-based Rhône-Poulenc's hyp-

---

AAAA ethics rule that prohibited ad agencies and industry-related publications from sharing the same office or workers for fear that conflicts of interest would be unavoidable. About eighteen months after *Medical Tribune* was created, he withdrew from the AAAA. The only public explanation for the unusual decision to leave the advertising industry's premier trade group was not given for more than a quarter century; the AAAA's executive vice president would say only that McAdams had been a member in good standing before it left due to "differences with other members."

notic sedative, Largactil; when American licensee Smith Kline sold it in America, under the name Thorazine, the same amount cost $60.58.[58]

When confronted by the evidence that it did not matter whether the research and development was done in the U.S. or abroad, the pharma companies shifted their argument and blamed more expensive domestic labor costs for the higher prices.[59] If true, that costlier labor should have translated into smaller profits. Yet the U.S. sector averaged three to four times the average profit margin of other industries.[60] Moreover, Kefauver's staff confirmed that while European wages were lower than those in the U.S., American drug companies had "lower unit costs" than their European rivals because they were more efficient and used less labor because they had more automation.

If high drug prices were not from more expensive research, development, or labor costs, what was the culprit? Kefauver zeroed in on patents. "Unfortunately, monopoly pricing under patents is widespread in the drug industry."[61]

Kefauver had dispatched his chief economist, John Blair, to visit other countries to see how they regulated their pharma industries. Blair's finding was simple: the U.S. was the *only* nation that did not regulate drug prices or restrict their patents. Only twenty-seven of seventy-seven countries allowed any drug patent, and those that did granted much shorter exclusive periods. Switzerland and Germany did not permit patents on drugs but only on the processes to manufacture them. Blair had learned that the Oxford-based scientists responsible for penicillin had not patented it because they thought it was "too important to public health." European regulators told Blair they were troubled at how simple it was for pharma companies to get patent protection without having discovered a drug but simply making a few minor laboratory alterations to a rival's product.[62] In testimony before Kefauver's committee, Merck's president scorned the knock-off firms for not doing any original research but acting simply as "molecule manipulators" who got their patents by tagging along on the back of hard work and innovation by others.

Kefauver believed the legal threshold for obtaining the near copycat patents was far too low. And he was irked that when the knock-offs went on sale, they were frequently "priced to the last decimal like their predecessors. Thus the public pays for whatever research costs are involved but derives no benefits of price reduction."[63]

Blair suggested reducing American patent protection to five years from the current seventeen.[64] And any statute should require pharma firms with patents to license those drugs to all comers.[65] Kefauver liked both ideas. The information, he told Blair, would be important in drafting a law that might bring real competition to the pharmaceutical industry.

The hearings broke in September for a recess. There were only two months remaining in a tight presidential race between John Kennedy and Richard Nixon. Kefauver himself was in a tough reelection battle with a conservative state judge. The pharmaceutical lobby saw it as an opportunity to finish off the crusading senator. Drug firms poured money into direct mailers and radio ads suggesting that Kefauver's probe of the American drug industry was the predicate for the government to socialize medicine.[66] He was vulnerable in the South to charges that he was a closet liberal. In the past, he had refused to sign the Southern Manifesto against civil rights for blacks; introduced the censure bill for Red Scare senator Joe McCarthy; and cast the single no vote on a bill outlawing the Communist Party.[67]

Drug companies had good reason to fear Kefauver. His plans for reworking the patent system would end many of the pricing excesses that had become commonplace. That was bad enough, they thought, to make him an implacable foe. They might have been far more alarmed had they known that privately Kefauver shared with his investigative staff that he believed there was a good argument to make that drugs were an "essential commodity." That ruling would invest in the federal government the authority to regulate prescription prices as local and state governments set the allowable rates for public utilities.* [68]

---

* There was even some discussion of federal price controls. They had been implemented on basic food items during World War I to prevent price gouging. In World War II they were again imposed on food and expanded to gasoline. The idea of mandatory price caps has been revived in Florida senator Rick Scott's Transparent Drug Pricing Act of 2019. It would set the list price of U.S. drugs at the lowest retail list price in the U.K., France, Germany, Canada, and Japan. The Trump administration has proposed linking American drug prices to an index of fourteen nations. The pharmaceutical industry contends price caps would disincentivize innovation and result in Americans getting less access to cutting-edge drugs. In July 2019, Maryland became the first state to attempt to treat drug firms as public utilities, a move that pharma is contesting in the courts.

15

"BE HAPPY" PILLS

The scare campaign against Kefauver failed and he won in a landslide. It was bad news for pharma since he turned to preparing a final subcommittee report and also drafting legislation. While Kefauver had been fighting for his political survival, and the focus on pharma was on the fallout from the Welch/FDA scandal, a watershed moment had passed for the industry. The FDA approved Chicago's G. D. Searle's Enovid—put on sale three years earlier for "menstrual disorders"—to be dispensed as the first ever oral contraceptive.[1] Women could now control when and if they got pregnant. Objections from social conservatives and religious groups had delayed the FDA's decision for nearly two years. Some commissioners were uncomfortable with a medication for long-term daily use to otherwise healthy people. When the FDA finally said yes in 1960, they avoided any long-term safety questions by approving it for a maximum of twenty-four months. No one followed that directive once Enovid went on sale.[2] It was wrapped in such controversy, that the lay public and much of the press referred to Enovid and later me-too competitors as *the Pill*. Doctors and patients thought it was simple, safe, and reliable (it was three years before a Senate investigation revealed that the FDA made its momentous decision based on clinical studies of only 132 women who had taken the Pill for a year, sometimes a little longer).[3] * [4]

* Margaret Sanger, a nurse who coined the term "birth control," had opened America's first birth control clinic in 1916. She later battled religious and socially conservative opposition to the development of a female drug contraceptive. The organizations Sanger founded ultimately morphed into one as Planned Parenthood. Much of the money for the Pill's research came from Katharine McCormick, an heir to the International Harvester fortune. Sanger and McCormick were convinced that readily accessible and easy-to-use birth control was key to women's emancipation as house-

It was impossible at the time to fully appreciate how great an impact the Pill would have. It debuted only a few years before the 1960s sexual revolution and women's liberation movement (NOW, the National Organization for Women, was founded in 1966). Some saw in it a social tool to break the housewife-at-home-raising-a-family stereotype. As the first pharmaceutical reversible contraceptive, it introduced a newly minted term, "reproductive rights."

Searle took advantage of the Pill's sweeping promise in its advertising campaign. It featured Andromeda, a goddess of Greek mythology, breaking free of the chains around her wrists, symbolizing women breaking free of their worries of unwanted pregnancies.[5]

Many greeted the Pill enthusiastically. That was matched by the fervor of those opposing it on religious grounds. Sackler had intently followed the controversy. Bill Frohlich represented Ortho Pharmaceutical, one of the companies with its own oral contraceptive. Ortho was the first to offer the pills in a circular plastic container with a movable dial that made it much easier for women to remember when to take them (start on the fifth day of menstruation, then take one a day for twenty days, and then take a five-day break before restarting the cycle).[6] Arthur's idea about how to refine the promotion strategy seemed radical: do not directly mention the Pill or birth control. Frohlich thought at first it was counterintuitive to sell a product without talking about it, but Sackler won him over. Arthur thought that protestations about the Pill might taper off if the ads pitched the idea that it empowered families to choose how much time they wanted between children. Frohlich's full-page color ads ran in *Family Circle* and *True Story*. They featured a young woman talking to an older woman over a picket fence. "Don't plan your family over the back fence," was the headline at the top. At the bottom, it suggested that women talk to their doctors about ways to space pregnancies. "He can recommend a method that is dependable, simple, inexpensive, and best suited to the needs of you and your husband." The last line, in small print, read: "This message is sponsored by Ortho Pharmaceutical Corp., to whom medical methods of family planning are a particular concern."[7] The Sackler-inspired, Frohlich-designed campaign to soft-pedal the Pill as good family planning ran

---

bound spouses. When journalist Clare Boothe Luce learned about the FDA's approval of Enovid, she summed up the sentiment behind the movement: "Modern woman is at last free as a man is free to dispose of her own body."

into fierce opposition from the Catholic Church, which called it "immorality in advertising."[8] Priests used their pulpits across the country to urge parishioners to inundate the magazines with protests. In under a month, *Family Circle*, with a circulation of seven million, issued a statement from its advertising director: "The objections from readers was ferocious. We no longer are carrying the ads."[9] The magazine returned the $120,000 Ortho had paid for what was scheduled as a series of six ads. Other women's magazines followed.

Pharma companies and Medicine Avenue had underestimated the pent-up demand among women for something that at last gave them control over if and when to have children. They also misjudged the extent to which many social commentators and the mainstream press viewed the Pill as the progenitor of grand societal change. "If the Pill can defuse the population explosion," wrote *Time* in an article titled "Freedom from Fear," "it will go far for eliminating hunger, want and ignorance."[10] "It was the twentieth century's greatest technological advance," *The Economist* later concluded.[11] The Pill was groundbreaking for the reason that it had first stumped the FDA: it established the precedent that a drug need not address an infection or chronic condition. It was enough to help fulfill a personal lifestyle choice. That concept had been the pharmaceutical industry's Holy Grail, a medication separate from sickness.[12]

Even without ads in most major women's publications, the Pill was instantly a top seller. Searle's stock doubled in the year after it went on sale.[13] Ortho, with its clever packaging, sold more pills by 1962 than any other company. Its profits surged.

Sackler thought that if the Pill succeeded despite the fierce resistance, another lifestyle medication free of any moral controversy could be an even bigger blockbuster. His psychiatric training led him to conclude the next great challenge was developing a lifestyle medication for so-called mind drugs. It was possible, he speculated, that a hybrid, some type of "be happy" pill, might one day replace antibiotics as the industry sales leader. He focused on two broad classes of mind drugs: stimulants (uppers) that enhanced a patient's mood, and sedatives (downers) that targeted anxiety and mental illness.

Amphetamines, the stimulant gold standard, had long been promoted as a cure for all types of depression. The surging demand for amphetamines doubled after World War II following the AMA's approval to advertise them for weight loss.[14] Burroughs Wellcome introduced Methedrine to shed extra pounds. Abbott targeted narcolepsy with Desoxyn, its methamphetamine tablet. Ciba's entry was not an amphetamine, but a new drug that competed for the same market: Ritalin.[15] In 1950 Ciba had released Dexamyl, a combination of Dexedrine and Lilly's Amytal barbiturate that some doctors dubbed "among psychiatry's greatest hits."[16] Ads featuring all-American housewives touting it for treating "nervous tension, anxiety and agitation" had helped make it one of the most widely dispensed by general practitioners.[17] Rivals tried copying that success with their own amphetamine-sedative combinations, helping to expand the market throughout the 1950s.[18]

By the 1960s, the American amphetamine market hit a record eight *billion* pills annually. That output was constant for the rest of the decade. Authorities later discovered that about half that production was diverted illegally to street dealers or unscrupulous diet doctors. Some popular weight loss clinics were unmasked as virtual subsidiaries of generic amphetamine manufacturers. Their profits were enormous; 100,000 10 mg amphetamine pills cost the diet center $71 and were resold on average for $12,000. Its broad popularity had resulted in a spike in recreational abuse and adverse reactions.[19] That finally caught the media's attention. A series of national stories about former users recounting "amphetamine induced psychosis," antisocial behavior, and crippling paranoia added to the drug's darker narrative. The FDA had been slow to recognize the problems. It had such a benign view of stimulants that as late as 1963 it weighed approving Ciba's Dexamyl for over-the-counter sales.[20]

Sackler knew there had been little innovation in amphetamines in the thirty years since their discovery. And he had never found it useful during his Creedmoor research. He admired amphetamine's commercial success but he was skeptical about its long-term prospects and doubted it could be the basis for the hybrid mind/lifestyle drug he envisioned.

What about sedatives? The postwar barbiturate market was huge, second only to antibiotics.[21] There were 1,500 competing brands in the U.S. An estimated third of those manufactured were resold on the street—with names such as goofies, yellow jackets, and pink ladies—for recreational highs. They delivered big profits, rivaling the gross margins of the industry-leading antibiotics.[22] Barbiturates, as with amphetamines, had become a victim of their success. The federal Narcotics Bureau in 1947 listed them the most abused drug. Overdoses set a grim record in 1950 with one thousand dead.[23] The following year, *The New York Times* concluded that barbiturates "are more a menace to society than heroin or morphine."[24]

Congress responded with the Durham-Humphrey Amendment, meant to address the barbiturates problem by fixing vague language in the 1938 Food, Drug, and Cosmetic Act.[25] Before the amendment, prescriptions were required only for narcotics and sulfa drugs.[26] Thirty-six states had not waited for federal intervention, instead requiring prescriptions for barbiturates. The state rules were a confusing hodgepodge of regulations. More than half had no restrictions on the number of refills. The Durham-Humphrey Amendment invested the FDA with the power to deem any drug as dangerous "because of toxicity or other potentially harmful effect." Once the FDA made that threshold decision, the drug would be by prescription only.[27]

One of the law's omissions, however, was that it did not require drug companies to include side effect warnings to patients. Pharma firms only had to provide the drug data to pharmacists, who were then supposed to warn patients about potential abuse.

The Durham-Humphrey Amendment did not dent barbiturate sales. Because it did not have the resources, the FDA did not enforce its "prescription only" rule for six years, and then it went only after bromides, a cruder early-generation sedative.[28] Even then, requiring a prescription for barbiturates only meant that millions of habitual users began shopping for doctors willing to write prescriptions without asking too many questions.[29]

Sackler saw a glimmer of promise in the hypnotic qualities of strong barbiturates such as Lilly's Seconal. It could be useful in controlling seizures and constant agitation, two debilitating physical symptoms of mental illness. They were not optimized for serious mental disorders, however, and did not treat bipolar or schizophrenia. Smith Kline filled that market in 1954 in America when it rolled out Thorazine, a tranquilizer accidentally discovered in the late 1940s by a French surgeon who had been hunting for malaria cures. "Tranquilizer" was the new word in the pharma world, having appeared the first time the previous year in promotion for a hypertension drug from Ciba.* [30]

---

* In the nineteenth century, "tranquilizer" referred to the invention by a Philadelphia psychiatrist of a restraining chair into which agitated mental asylum patients were strapped.

Smith Kline marketed Thorazine as an antipsychotic.[31] It was so potent that in Europe it was informally dubbed "a medicinal lobotomy" and dispensed only to patients suffering severe psychosis.[32] Smith Kline's first ad featured a close-up of a man's head, electrodes attached to his forehead, and a large rubber stopper jammed into his mouth. It announced "Thorazine: Reduces Need for Electroshock Therapy." Psychiatrists, particularly those who worked in public asylums, wrote nearly 80 percent of the three million Thorazine prescriptions in its first year.[33] The drug arrived at a time when psychiatric institutions were increasingly vilified in scandalous public reports about cruelty and violence toward patients.[34] Thorazine marked the start of a pharmaceutical revolution in the treatment of those with disabling mental illness, moving away from the custodial-institutionalized care that had been the standard since the early nineteenth century. Thorazine's widespread use spurred a decline in the number of patients committed to New York's mental institutions—the largest state population—by 19 percent, the first reduction since records were kept.[35] Fewer patients meant lower costs, saving state governments $1.5 billion in the decade after Thorazine's introduction. The director of Washington, D.C.'s, eight-thousand-bed St. Elizabeth's Hospital heralded Thorazine as marking the end of "bedlamism," the word used by asylum workers to describe the chaos and disorder that was the hallmark of many insanity wards.[36]

Smith Kline trumpeted its success at the nation's mental hospitals, although no one seemed to have figured out the early taxpayer savings might be canceled out later by increased medical costs for the outpatient care of those who relapsed or whose illness worsened.[37] * [38]

---

* Thorazine and a succession of other tranquilizers were one reason that JFK had the confidence to announce the Mental Retardation Facilities and Community Mental Health Centers Act in 1963, an ambitious plan to release half of the 500,000 committed to state asylums. The savings were supposed to fund 1,500 community health centers to provide ongoing outpatient care to those released. States instead used most of the savings on matters unrelated to mental health. Fewer than half were built, and not one was fully funded. Between 1955 and 1980, "deinstitutionalization" reduced the population of American asylums from 558,922 to 130,000. *The New York Times* later reported the entire program to be "a vast failure." That was partly because federal and state governments had subsequently shifted the responsibility for serious mental illness to the prison system or to nursing homes. Medicaid allowed states to move the poor elderly to nursing facilities; by the mid-1980s, more than 600,000 of those two million nationwide residents had been diagnosed with mental illness. Ten times as

Despite the big sales numbers, Smith Kline worried there was a limit to the size of Thorazine's market. The better the drug worked, the greater the falloff in sales as patients were discharged from mental institutions. Smith Kline tried expanding the market by targeting doctors who cared for those patients who returned to society. Ads in *JAMA* featured a man fishing in a stream, personifying the mental calmness that was touted as the drug's hallmark. "Continuing therapy is almost always well tolerated, and is central to most patients' continued well-being," read the copy.[39] Smith Kline next tried adding "senile agitation" as a treatable condition. Ads, illustrated with an elderly man wielding his cane in a threatening manner, promised Thorazine would "control the agitated, belligerent senile" and "help the patient to live a composed and useful life."[40] It even tried marketing it for chronic nausea. But that was like using a sledgehammer to put a thumbtack on a corkboard. Few patients were so distressed by even the worst nausea to put up with side effects that could include difficulty breathing, severe fever and muscle pain, trembling, seizures, and even rarely, suicidal depression.[41]

Sackler was waiting for something more like a Thorazine-lite, a mood-altering medication that could offset anxiety while not being too sedating. He told his pharma clients about the great profit potential in a discovery of "emotional aspirin," a medication that treated a person's psychological well-being as well as antibiotics cured serious infections. Sackler knew from his tenure at Creedmoor that any drug that addressed anxiety or depression would have a greater side effect profile than aspirin. He hoped that by putting the concept of "emotional aspirin" into the research and development milieu, it might spark pharma firms to make it a laboratory priority.

Drug companies undoubtedly had the incentive for such a project. There was an enormous market for relieving the stress and anxiety that many Americans perceived as an unfortunate but integral part of twentieth-century life.[42] Magazines and newspapers ran stories about stress from the Cold War and how the fast pace of technology added to daily pressure. Composer Leonard Bernstein had in 1950 named his Second Symphony "The Age of Anxiety," after W. H. Auden's Pulitzer Prize–winning poem of the same title. The government provided

many people suffering from severe psychotic disorders were in prison by 2018, rather than in psychiatric clinics.

significant financial incentive for discovering a drug as Sackler envisioned. When the Mental Health Study Act was passed in 1955, it established a Psychopharmacology Research Center at the NIH. That new government division focused on biological psychiatry and had a multimillion-dollar research budget, which it shared with interested pharma firms.[43] Some drugs under review were still experimental although they showed promise in the lab. Lithium had been discovered in the early nineteenth century but clinical studies for treating mania had only begun in Denmark in the mid-1950s (the FDA did not approve it until 1970). The same was true for LSD-25, a synthetic compound discovered by a Swiss scientist in 1951, but only subjected to therapeutic testing for mental illnesses in the mid-1950s at the Rockefeller Institute for Medical Research.*[44]

The most advanced new class of drugs were the so-called minor tranquilizers. As had happened with Thorazine, it was another accidental discovery. Frank Berger, a Jewish Czech scientist who had emigrated to England when Hitler annexed Czechoslovakia, had chemically modified a disinfectant in the hope of finding a better preservative for penicillin. When he injected his altered compound into mice he noticed they remained awake and responsive at the same time that their muscles relaxed and they became passive.[45] When Berger moved to America in 1947, he took a job as a research professor at the University of Rochester Medical School. Two years later the patent drug and toiletries company Carter Products—whose most famous product was Carter's Little Liver Pills, a laxative with annual sales topping $450 million—hired him. They upped his university salary from $5,400 to $12,000 and gave him a 1 percent royalty on meds he discovered, up to a maximum of $75,000.[46] Carter's prescription drug sales were only $500,000 and it had only twenty employees in that department. Berger knew that two of Carter's other consumer products, Nair hair removal and Arrid deodorant, sold more in a week than the drug division did in a year.[47] After hiring Berger, Carter formed an alliance with Wallace Laboratories, a New Jersey–based medical research company. It

* Swiss-based Sandoz had the LSD patent and produced small batches for researchers. It asked the FDA for an "investigational exemption" in 1963. What the FDA should do with LSD was a heated topic, eventually coming under scrutiny by three different congressional committees. The issue was moot after the 1965 Drug Abuse Control Amendments; LSD was outlawed for any use.

also hired Bernie Ludwig, a respected organic chemist, as its medical director.

Berger and Ludwig tested hundreds of synthetic compounds before they found a promising one, meprobamate, in May 1950. In subsequent animal testing it was tranquilizing without being too much of a sedative. The two scientists thought they had found the right balance between the therapeutic qualities of Thorazine and its oppressive side effect profile. Two months later they submitted their drug for a patent. Carter's management was far less enthusiastic than its researchers since it was uncertain if there was sufficient demand for such a drug. Wallace Labs had conducted a study with two hundred doctors that showed most thought there was no use for such a medication. Three quarters said they could not think of any reason to prescribe it.[48]

Carter put the project on hold and delayed going to the FDA for approval. It took four years before Berger, armed with a battery of new clinical tests, convinced management that the drug was ready. It went to the FDA in December 1954. Faced with what category to apply for in its application, Carter feared "sedatives," which included barbiturates, carried too many negative connotations. "Tranquilizers" was also troublesome, especially as that category included Thorazine and other powerful hypnotics. Carter proposed a clever solution: the FDA would list the drug under tranquilizers, but Carter would market it as a "minor tranquilizer." While waiting for approval, Carter rejected a dozen brand names before settling on Miltown, the town where Wallace Labs performed the final testing on the product.*[49]

Even before the FDA approved Miltown, American Home Products bought a license from Carter to sell Miltown through Wyeth, its pharma subsidiary. Wyeth would sell the drug under the brand name Equanil. In May 1955, Miltown went on sale. Carter touted it as a less dangerous and toxic alternative to barbiturates and major tranquilizers, and emphasized it was effective for everyday "anxiety, tension and mental stress."[50]

---

*It took until the mid-1960s before psychotropic drugs were marketed with more specificity as antianxiety agents, antidepressants, or antipsychotics. "Antidepressant" was used in a 1947 ad for Edrisal, a Smith Kline combo drug of amphetamines and painkillers. By 1952, it referred only to tranquilizing drugs, but it did not become widely used by pharma companies until the mid-1960s. "Antipsychotic" was not even used to describe a drug until 1961. Sometimes the pharma marketing departments had more say than the scientists and medical directors.

The first edition of the American Psychiatric Association's *Diagnostic and Statistical Manual of Mental Disorders* (*DSM*) had been published only a few years earlier. It provided diagnostic criteria for identifying and treating many psychiatric illnesses. Instantly the bible for American psychiatrists, *DSM* had not listed anxiety as a stand-alone disorder (that would not happen until *DSM-III* in 1980).[51] Carter worried that psychiatrists might not think Miltown was necessary and general practitioners might think it addressed a condition too far removed from their own practice.

Carter had underestimated the pent-up demand among millions of Americans looking for a quick fix to anxiety and stress. Few thought of it as an illness but rather shrugged off anxiety as an inevitable by-product of a busy and productive life. Some boasted of it as evidence of hard work, ambition, and achievement.[52] The country was filled, concluded some psychiatrists, with "ambulatory psychoneurotics."[53] Miltown seemed ideally timed as an antidote to alleviate the occasional edginess and irritation caused by anxiety. A psychoanalyst welcomed it as the "penicillin of psychiatry."[54]

Miltown's sales took off. Three months after its release, *Time* noted that it "has become the fastest-selling pacifier for the frustrated and frenetic." Hollywood was the leading market for "Miltown mania." Celebrities from Tennessee Williams to Norman Mailer to Tallulah Bankhead created waiting lists at pharmacies for the "don't-give-a-damn" pills.[55] Sunset Boulevard's famed Schwab's Pharmacy sold 250,000 pills in four months before running out of stock. The frenzy in Hollywood spread to New York, Washington, and Boston. "It worked wonders for me," said comedian Milton Berle. "In fact, I'm thinking of changing my name to Miltown Berle."[56]

How successful was Miltown? In 1954 and 1955, Thorazine accounted for 99.6 percent of all tranquilizers sold in America. A year later, Miltown and its chemical twin, Equanil, went from less than 1 percent to 70 percent of sales.[57] In 1956, Carter and Wallace Labs sponsored a New York City conference on the drug.[58] Carter sent bound copies of those proceedings to 153,000 doctors.[59] Two years after it went on sale, one in twenty Americans had tried the pill. Doctors had dispensed 36 million prescriptions, a staggering one third of *all* prescriptions written.[60] The drug tripled Carter's gross revenue. The company felt flush enough to commission the surrealist Salvador Dalí to design its exhibit at the AMA's annual meeting in San Francisco in

1958. Dalí's wife and collaborator, Gala, was a Miltown patient. When she earlier had met Frank Berger, she suggested her husband could capture in art how the drug helped transform her anxiety to tranquility. The exhibit cost $100,000, of which $35,000 was Dalí's fee. Carter got its money's worth.[61] People marveled as they walked through Dalí's sixty-foot-long, wriggling white caterpillar made of parachute silk. *Time* concluded that "the monster stole the show" and it "was worth its weight in gold to Miltown."[62]

By the time Dalí created his Miltown exhibit, the surging demand for so-called peace of mind or happy pills resulted in a thriving black market for both the Carter and Wyeth brands as well as for counterfeits. In the absence of federal legislation, states began tightening rules for dispensing the drugs.[63] In early 1960, the Justice Department filed an antitrust action against Carter and American Home Products for price-fixing and conspiracy to exclude other firms from the market.[64] The CEOs of both firms denied gouging the public in testimony before Kefauver's Senate investigation. It was a mere coincidence, they claimed, that they had submitted identical bids for every government contract, and they protested that higher advertising costs in the U.S. were the reason their drugs cost six times more in America than Europe.[65]

What Arthur Sackler and other pharma insiders knew was that no matter how much the companies complained about their costs, the minor tranquilizers were profitable. Extremely so. Most prescription drugs in the late 1950s and early 1960s returned on average a very healthy 20 percent net profit. The tranquilizers and barbiturates did better, boasting returns of 35 percent to 55 percent, second only to antibiotics.[66] And most important in Sackler's view was that by 1960 about 75 percent of American physicians had written at least one Miltown prescription. Thorazine, in contrast, was still mostly the province of psychiatrists.[67]

As Miltown's success grew it attracted more scrutiny.[68] Some doctors questioned its efficacy, contending it was little better than a sugar pill. Other physicians warned it created tolerance since ever-larger doses were required to maintain any benefits. A few thought it might be addictive.[69] Previously unreported side effects flooded the FDA, everything from increased anxiety, impaired coordination, and confusion to tremors, muscle spasms, and vertigo.

Miltown was repeating a common pattern for blockbuster drugs, particularly those that created dependency and could be abused recreationally. Doctors and patients enthusiastically welcomed those medications when they first went on sale. Over time their popularity led to abuse, thriving black markets, counterfeits, and a steady upswing in reported side effects, sometimes even overdoses (toxicology reports on drug deaths showed that when Miltown was present, it was usually in tandem with copious amounts of alcohol, amphetamines, and barbiturates).

The FDA considered recalling Miltown. The drug's emerging darker narrative prompted a couple of dozen states to list Miltown on the same "no-refillable prescriptions" list that covered barbiturates.[70]

Sackler knew any headwinds Miltown faced opened the door to a competitor drug. In the mid-1950s neurophysiologist Ralph Gerard coined "psychotropic drugs" to refer to medicines developed for mental illness. Many pharma labs were working hard to find one that delivered enhanced therapeutic benefits with fewer side effects.

Swiss-based Hoffmann-La Roche had a secret research project under way at its New Jersey lab hunting for the next enhanced generation of Miltown.[71] Martí-Ibáñez had learned about it because he was friends with Leo Sternbach, a pharmacist who led the Roche team. Roche had transferred Sternbach, a Polish Jew, to the U.S. in 1941. (Roche was the only Swiss pharma firm that sent its Jewish researchers and German dissidents—what Sternbach called "all the endangered species"—to safety in jobs in America.)[72]

Even by Sackler's standards, Sternbach's research was ambitious. In the mid-1940s he had synthesized biotin, a water-soluble B vitamin that had resisted all earlier efforts for a commercially viable man-made version. Roche was then the world's top manufacturer of synthetic vitamins, so the discovery impressed even his more senior science colleagues. Beginning in the mid-1950s, he led a small team tasked with finding a drug that would win "the Great Tranquilizer War."[73] Roche made no pretense it was searching for a medication to eliminate deadly diseases or cure infections. It simply wanted to boost its bottom line by developing a better Miltown.[74]

The fastest route was to make a near therapeutic clone that had enough molecular changes so it did not violate Miltown's patent. That is what Roche's marketing department wanted. Sternbach, however, thought that a me-too drug was "boring."[75]

In Roche's Lab 303, Sternbach performed hundreds of modifications to dye chemicals, searching in vain for any sign of psychopharmacological activity. Biological chemists like Sternbach were called "backbench scientists" because they spent much of their time at benches and tables manipulating molecules (by the mid-1990s, computers generated the molecular changes in a fraction of the time and robots analyzed them for medicinal uses). For over two years Sternbach came up empty while half a dozen rival companies released me-too Miltown knock-offs.

Roche pharmacology chief Lowell Randall ordered Sternbach to end the project and shift to antibiotics.[76] Sternbach did start working on antibiotics, but in his off hours he continued researching tranquilizers. Near the end of 1956, Sternbach isolated a chemical compound that "crystallized nicely" and had the biological activity for which he had been searching.[77] The problem was how to tell Randall that he had not followed his order and stopped his tranquilizer research. Sternbach concocted a plan that would allow him to present his discovery as serendipity. On his birthday, May 7, 1957, he and his assistant, Earl Reeder, an organic chemist, announced they were setting aside the day for "a major spring cleaning" of their cluttered lab. It was, Sternbach later recalled, "covered with dishes, flasks, and beakers, all containing various samples and the working area had shrunk to almost zero."[78] During their cleanout, Reeder "found" two "discarded beakers" that bore the label "Ro5-0690." A hardened crystalline powder was on the bottom of each. Sternbach had it planted there. According to the lab notes he made, those beakers were leftovers of the tranquilizer work and had never been tested. That afternoon Sternbach sent them to his boss with his notes and said they had "just been found under all the mess."[79]

When Sternbach subsequently administered the compound to mice and cats, they relaxed as they did when fed other tranquilizers. The difference was the animals stayed active and alert. Every other tranquilizer, even Miltown, left them groggy and uncoordinated. Further testing demonstrated that Ro5-0690 "was vastly more potent [and] less toxic and sedating than any on the market."[80] A couple of months later, Sternbach again ignored company policy and tried the compound himself. That was not an unusual practice, many ambitious research scientists called themselves "two-legged rats."[81] His lab notes reveal that a couple of hours after ingesting it, he felt "slightly soft in the knees," was "cheerful," and also "pretty sleepy" all afternoon. He felt normal after ten hours.

Sternbach had discovered benzodiazepines, "benzos" for short, a new class of synthetic tranquilizers (it had an extra carbon atom in the inner ring structure as compared to Miltown).[82] Benzos would upend the market for happy pills. As another Roche researcher noted at the time, Sternbach's discovery had made him a "grand master of modern medicinal chemistry."[83] Roche named it Librium, from the last syllables of "equilibrium."

Roche undertook one of the largest and most diverse human clinical trials ever. Starting in 1958, it had more than two thousand doctors test Librium on some twenty thousand patients, from healthy undergraduate students to infirm elderly, psychiatric patients, premenopausal women, alcoholics, even drug addicts.[84] There was no risk in conducting too much testing. The FDA permitted pharma firms to choose which of their trials to submit in support of a drug's approval. If a study had a poor outcome, the company could withhold the results.[85] The onus fell on the FDA; it could order additional testing if it had reason to believe the firm was hiding bad news.[86]

The following year Roche presented Librium to the FDA. Under the rules then in place, Roche did not have to prove efficacy, only that Librium was safe. It had selected the result of 1,163 of the 20,000 patients to make its case. The handpicked test subjects showed no signs of drug tolerance. Nor were there signs of dependence. High doses caused some motor coordination loss and higher doses induced drowsiness. Still, it was one of the cleanest side effect profiles submitted in a new application. (Although doctors later split about whether benzodiazepines caused tolerance and addiction, there was no doubt they were much safer than barbiturates.)[87]

Roche went a step further, however. Although it was under no requirement to do so, the company wanted to brag about what the clinical trials demonstrated about efficacy. Librium effectively treated all types of anxiety, from mild and moderate to severe and acute. It also was a good muscle relaxant, anticonvulsive, sedative, and helped alleviate mild depression and eased alcoholism withdrawal.

Roche insisted Librium should be classified as a new class of "antianxiety medication." No one then understood why the drug had a more potent therapeutic profile (it took until 1977 before a Danish researcher discovered that benzodiazepines bind to brain receptors responsible for sending chemical messages related to anxiety and fear).[88]

The FDA gave Roche the approval to sell Librium in 1960, the same year that the Pill had become the industry's first lifestyle drug. That timing was fortuitous since it was when a German-born psychiatrist based in London developed the eponymously named Hamilton Rating Scale for Depression (it remains one of the most widely used reference guides). As part of his work he developed an "Anxiety Rating Scale," a simple fourteen-question survey intended as the first ever medical tool by which to measure a patient's anxiety.[89]

Hamilton's rating scale meant that anxiety was no longer something doctors had to diagnose subjectively as a mere feeling or state of mind described by a patient. Although Hamilton's test was somewhat rudimentary, it was a major step toward medicalizing anxiety as an accepted psychiatric disorder.[90] Roche later distributed the Hamilton tests to tens of thousands of doctors, calculating that physicians would prescribe more Librium if they felt they had a scientific basis for doing so. (Thirty-four years later, the Sackler family's launch of their timed release opioid product, OxyContin, would similarly benefit from a reanalysis of pain and addiction that included a ten-point system by which doctors could supposedly better measure patient pain.)

For Arthur Sackler, the benzodiazepines were *it*, the class of medications he thought might one day replace antibiotics as the drug industry's biggest seller. Roche picked him and his William Douglas McAdams agency to handle Librium's rollout. Sackler assigned his top account executives to monitor his other big clients—Pfizer, Glaxo, and Hoechst-Roussel—while he turned his full attention to Librium. He hired Irwin "Win" Gerson, a twenty-eight-year-old pharmacist with an MBA, to help with the market research. Gerson, who moved up fast through the executive ranks at McAdams, had been a detail man selling Wyeth's minor tranquilizer, Equanil.[91]

The $2 million campaign Sackler developed for Librium was a masterpiece, even by his exacting standards. Arthur kicked off the promotion with free coverage in the national press. He had figured out how to bypass the FDA's prohibition on advertising to consumers. His workaround was a so-called mat (master of aligned type), a press release disguised as legitimate journalism. It allowed newspaper and magazine editors to run stories about advances in health while the sponsoring pharma firm benefited from the coverage of its drug as "news," without being handcuffed by the disclaimers and warnings of traditional ads.

Those companies distributed copies of the clinical trials to Arthur's favorite science and medicine writers. Freelancers got detailed story outlines that only needed light editing before publication.

In the promotional packet Sackler had assembled, he highlighted two of Librium's most extreme clinical tests. The first involved violent prisoners in a Texas state prison. The "patients" in the second were wild animals at the Boston and San Diego zoos. The week Librium went on sale, the lead article in *Time* focused on those tests. The chief psychiatrist for Texas's Mental Health Board told *Time* that Librium had been dispensed to inmates at Huntsville Prison who were "classical psychopathic personalities with lifelong histories of antisocial behavior." They were regularly "mutilating themselves, setting fires, and starting fights." What happened after they took Librium? According to the prison psychiatrist, they became "placid and alert, despite their tension-provoking environment."[92] As for the zoo animals, *Time* reported a "lynx that had bloodied its nose in a savage dash against the side of its cage . . . was soon gamboling like an alley cat" after it was given Librium. Baboons, macaques, monkeys, a lion and a tiger, and Australian dingoes "calmed down the same way [but] most important, they were not knocked out to the point of being dopey, but remained active, with full muscular coordination, and apparently retained possession of whatever faculties nature gave them."[93]

Having established that Librium tamed wild animals and violent convicts, *Time* repeated much of Sackler's press release. There was "encouraging evidence that it will have the same effect on 70 percent or more of anxious, tense and hostile humans as it had on dingoes." Since the drug was new, finding the right dose for patients might be "admittedly tricky," but once established, "Librium comes close to producing pure relief from strain without drowsiness or dulling of mental processes." At high doses, while there might be some "impaired coordination," Librium otherwise demonstrated "unusual freedom from harmful side effects."[94]

Many national magazines had just begun regular columns devoted to medicine and health. Pharma companies correctly viewed those as additional outlets to sway public opinion, not just about specific drugs, but also about industry trends. (In 1983, Lilly became the first company to apply Sackler's prepackaged story concept to television for its new arthritis drug; the elaborate media kit included video interviews with clinical trial patients, scientists in the lab, and rheumatology experts, all ready to be edited and used in a "what's new in medicine" segment.)[95]

Sackler had tweaked and refined his promo tactics that he used for antibiotics. A month after Librium went on sale, he ran an eye-catching three-page ad in *Life*. It featured full-page pictures of the San Diego Zoo lynx before and after receiving Librium. "New Way to Calm a Cat" was the provocative headline.[96] After *Newsweek*, *National Geographic*, and *Esquire* lavished praise on the "breakthrough drug," Sackler sent tens of thousands of those magazines to doctors. He figured most would end up in patient waiting rooms. It was Sackler's way of circumventing the strict FDA ban on advertising directly to consumers. In another issue of *Time*, he ran a splashy special advertising insert, implying that Librium could prevent "nervous breakdowns" and "cure peptic ulcers." (When a Senate investigation later looked into that practice, Sackler and Roche defended the ad by noting the magazine insert had perforated edges so doctors could easily rip it out before placing it in their waiting rooms.)[97]

Sackler assumed that women would outnumber men as Librium patients, as they had with Miltown. He targeted *Cosmopolitan* and *Family Circle* for packaged stories.[98] The McAdams agency also offered newspapers Librium-positive short-shorts, small boxes of text that filled the empty space between main stories. Radio and television stations got featurettes, short broadcast segments that filled dead air. *Advertising Age* heralded the Librium campaign—which touted the drug as "the successor to the tranquilizers"—as "innovative" and "dazzling."[99]

Sackler also focused on the Roche detail team. Miltown had unwittingly provided the industry a cautionary tale about the importance of that personalized selling unit. Carter and Wallace Labs did not have a detail team. They relied on direct mailers to physicians, the ad campaign from their agency, Madison Avenue's Ted Bates, and word of mouth. In contrast, American Brands/Wyeth had 1,500 detail men and they blanketed the country, visiting doctors and pushing their chemically identical brand, Equanil. Despite the tremendous publicity for Miltown, Wyeth's Equanil surpassed Miltown in sales in 1956, only a year after they went on sale. Some pharma insiders thought that all the celebrity and Hollywood connections for Miltown made the drug less appealing to prescribing physicians. When many doctors went to dispense the latest minor tranquilizer, they increasingly wrote the Equanil prescription. Many traditional practitioners also considered

Carter a patent drugmaker and not part of the pharma club. By 1960, Equanil had pulled away, outselling Miltown three to one.[100]

Sackler coached Roche's detail team as if he were preparing them for a military operation. They should emphasize Librium's wide therapeutic benefits, especially its "muscle relaxant" and "anti-anxiety effect," which had gotten extensive coverage in the normally conservative *JAMA*.[101] What if a doctor was prescribing Miltown or Equanil, what was the best way to distinguish Librium? Sackler had already written the ad copy that proclaimed Librium was "completely unrelated chemically, pharmacologically, and clinically to any other tranquilizer. . . . [It was] as different from the tranquilizers as they were from the barbiturates."[102] That was similar to how he had distinguished Pfizer's Terramycin eight years earlier from a rival Lederle medication.[103]

Although Arthur was confident Librium was an antianxiety drug superior to anything that had preceded it, he recognized that some doctors would feel more comfortable sticking with Miltown since they were familiar with its benefits and risks after its five years on the market. Roche had to overcome that hesitation. In instances in which doctors were reluctant to switch to Librium, Sackler prepared a backup plan for the detail team: disparage Miltown and its me-too rivals. The salesmen were armed with reports of surging Miltown addiction, impairment that included considerable confusion and drowsiness, and even a spike in suicides among daily users.[104] They handed out reprints of a harsh review about Miltown that had run in the much respected *Medical Letter on Drugs and Therapeutics*, a nonprofit, peer-reviewed, bimonthly journal. It reinforced the core message that was part of every Roche product brochure, "benzodiazepines are unlike any other drug."[105]

Sackler designed the detail team guidelines with general practitioners in mind. He knew that psychiatrists would be acquainted with tranquilizers. Only a small fraction, however, of the consumers who Sackler and Roche hoped would become Librium patients had ever gone to a psychiatrist. Nathan Kline, who had replaced Sackler at Creedmoor, understood why Arthur saw so much potential in a small pill: "A lot of people shy away from the stigma of going to a psychiatrist. Their friends will say, 'He—or she—must be crazy.' But these same people are willing to take their problems to the family doctor. That is socially acceptable." Sackler was right. Psychiatrists ultimately wrote only 10 percent of Librium's prescriptions.[106]

Physicians wrote 1.5 million Librium prescriptions in its first month of sales. It was dispensed for alleviating anxieties and phobias, as well as illnesses then thought to have a link to stress, including high blood pressure, ulcers, acne, muscle pain, and headaches.[107] It was not public knowledge then, but even John Kennedy—wracked by lower back pain from his wartime injury—took Librium.[108] * [109] Miltown's maker, Carter-Wallace, saw its profits tumble nearly 20 percent.[110]

Roche gave Sternbach the $10,000 prize it offered for the discovery of a successful and profitable drug. The sum didn't change just because he produced the company's biggest ever blockbuster. But Sternbach was not disappointed. "I was a very happy scientist [since] I made the compound [but] it also made me."[111]

Before Librium, five medications, dominated by Miltown and Thorazine, accounted for 70 percent of the tranquilizer market.[112] In just three months, Librium was the best-selling tranquilizer in America. Sternbach's son, Michael, later recalled that his father was unusually emotional when he learned that his laboratory discovery had "buried Equanil [and] Miltown."[113] It was a spot Librium would not relinquish for eight years—to another Roche drug discovered by Sternbach and promoted by Arthur Sackler.[114]

* Kennedy, who also had colitis and Addison's disease, an adrenal gland insufficiency, was on eight daily medications and hormones. Max Jacobson, JFK's German-trained physician—nicknamed later by the press as "Dr. Feelgood"—also was the personal doctor of, among others, Tennessee Williams, Truman Capote, the Rolling Stones, and a who's who of Hollywood. In addition to Librium, JFK took barbiturates for sleep, and both codeine and Demerol for pain relief. Jacobson countered the sedative effects of those drugs by regularly administering 15 mg of methamphetamine to the president.

16

"THE THERAPEUTIC JUNGLE"

In April 1961, Kefauver's subcommittee introduced Senate Resolution 1552, a sweeping bill that proposed landmark changes to the patent, trademark, antitrust, and regulatory laws that applied to the pharmaceutical industry.[1] Its title was evidence of its ambition: the Drug Industry Antitrust Act.[2]

While pharma firms disliked the entire bill, they were most alarmed by a few provisions that promised to upend the way the industry priced its drugs. The seventeen-year exclusive selling monopoly granted by drug patents would be cut to five. Worse yet, after three years the patent holder would be required to license its drug to all comers for a royalty capped at 8 percent. Cross-licensing of patent rights, as the tetracycline manufacturers had done to fix prices, would be illegal. Companies that tried obtaining a patent by slightly modifying the chemical structure of an existing drug, a me-too drug, would have to prove that the alteration resulted in a "significant therapeutic benefit."[3] And that would also be the standard to extend patents on existing drugs. It would end abuses such as Lilly's use of minor alterations to dominate the insulin market for more than fifty years after the drug's 1920s release.[4]

As for trademarks, in addition to listing the brand name on all drug labels, the generic name—which the FDA would select—would be required in an equal-size font.[5]* And, to the particular consternation of

* At that time, pharma firms picked both the generic and brand names of any drugs they discovered. The Senate report concluded "they coined generic names so complex and unpronounceable as to virtually prohibit their use in the writing of prescriptions." A good example was Lederle's Kynex, an antibacterial to which Lederle gave the generic name sulfamethoxypyridazine. Once having created a long and difficult-to-remember generic name, pharma cited that complexity as a reason physicians should simply use their simpler brand names.

Arthur Sackler and his Medicine Avenue syndicate, the bill required that drug ads include full and accurate information about all reported side effects.[6] No other industry, claimed Dr. Hugh Hussey, the chairman of the AMA's Board of Trustees, required advertisers to tell "the whole truth."[7]

The proposed legislation provoked a massive pharma industry lobbying campaign. The drug companies condemned it as anti-American and unconstitutional since it limited patent rights for only one industry. If enacted it would harm science and innovation and slow the development of lifesaving medications. Sackler suggested a clever line of counterattack relevant to the ongoing Cold War (somewhat ironic given his leftist politics). If government regulators dampened the pharmaceutical industry's pioneering spirit, the Soviet Union would be the greatest beneficiary from any loss of American scientific leadership.

The Senate bill was not pharma's only problem. The FTC had opened a new investigation into the pricing and advertising practices of thirty-seven manufacturers and distributors. And a New York federal grand jury had returned indictments against Pfizer, Lederle's parent, American Cyanamid, and Bristol Myers, as well as their CEOs, charging criminal antitrust violations in the marketing of antibiotics.[8] The only good news was that an FTC examiner dismissed the charges the FTC had brought three years earlier against Pfizer, Lederle, Bristol-Myers, Squibb, and Upjohn for conspiring to fix tetracycline prices.[9] Few involved on either side of that litigation could have then imagined that the criminal and civil questions of whether those five drug companies had engaged in a highly profitable criminal conspiracy would not be resolved for another twenty-seven years.*

* As for the tetracycline price-fixing case, it took another two years, until 1963, before the full five-member commission reversed the examiner's dismissal. They ruled that the five companies had conspired to fix prices and that Pfizer and Lederle had also perpetrated a fraud on the Patent Office. Pfizer was ordered to license tetracycline at a discounted rate to any company that requested it. In 1967, a differently constituted five-member FTC commission reversed the finding of price-fixing but upheld the fraud count on the Patent Office. The Sixth Circuit Court of Appeals affirmed that ruling the following year. By then, there were more than 150 civil lawsuits; the plaintiffs included hospitals, union health funds, and government agencies seeking to recover what they had overpaid as a result of the price-fixing. The pharma firms collectively spent $250 million to settle all but fifty-eight cases prior to trial. The remaining lawsuits were consolidated into a class action that dragged through a byzantine course of discovery, procedural delays, and a seemingly endless battery of motions and appeals.

In June 1961, Kefauver's subcommittee released a damning 384-page final report, based on its public hearings of the previous year and tens of thousands of subpoenaed internal company documents.[10] It presented the case for why Congress should pass his proposed statute. Many of the entrenched problems about the pharmaceutical industry highlighted in the report would vex regulators and consumers for decades to come.[11]

Its conclusions were straightforward. "Drug prices are unreasonable" and resulted in "extraordinary margins and profits." The industry's "monopoly power" kept prices artificially inflated. The leading companies "abused patents" and deployed misleading and "exceptionally large advertising and sales promotion."[12]

Pharma was different from any other industry Kefauver had investigated: "He who orders does not buy; and he who buys does not order."[13] Doctors acted essentially as "purchasing agents" for consumers, who cannot price shop for a similar product since the physician's prescription locks them into buying a specific drug. "The consumer is 'captive' to a degree not present in any other industry."[14] Price increases do not affect the prescribing habits of doctors. Schering's president, Francis Brown, had illustrated the point during his testimony: "Unlike consumer marketing, Schering cannot expand its markets by lowering prices, Cortisone proved this. After all we cannot put two bottles of Schering medicine in every medicine chest where only one is needed, or two people in every hospital bed, where only one is sick. Marketing medicine is a far cry from marketing soft drinks or automobiles."[15]

The problem was amplified since the demand for medications was

---

In 1976, a Federal Appeals Court reversed the remaining FTC findings against the drug firms. *State of North Carolina v. Chas Pfizer & Co Inc.* 537 F. 2d 67 (4th Cir. 1976). That was four years after the tetracycline patent had expired and generic competitors had entered the market. That did not stop the litigation, however. In 1980, a different federal judge ruled against the Justice Department's effort to invalidate the Pfizer patent. That judge held the core of the government's case—the chief patent examiner's testimony that he would *not* have granted the patent in 1954 if he had known the information that Pfizer withheld, which was not reliable because so many years had passed since the events charged in the original complaint. And, even if Pfizer did give misleading data to the Patent Office, he ruled the government had failed to prove that Pfizer had acted with fraudulent intent. The Justice Department lost its final appeal in 1982. *U.S. v. Pfizer,* 676 F.2d 51 (1982). When all the civil cases were finished in 1986, the total payouts by the five tetracycline firms were a small fraction of what they had earned by fixing the price artificially high for so many years.

not responsive to price changes. Consumers bought drugs only when they were ill or had a chronic condition requiring treatment. Slashing the price of a hormone or antibiotic did not generate extra sales. Only the sick benefited while corporate bottom lines took a beating. The report noted the firms' internal files "left no room for doubt" that the industry exercised unparalleled pricing power over its products.[16] Although there were thousands of drugs on the market, just a few dozen were responsible for three quarters of all sales.[17] The top fifteen companies had gross margins approaching 80 percent and net profits that were double the average of nonpharma industries.*[18] The report blamed this outsized pricing power on the "private monopoly" that patents provided.[19]

Pharma executives had argued that drug innovation was possible because companies spent lavishly on R&D. The exclusive selling period afforded by a patent allowed them to recoup their costs and earn a profit. The Senate report countered that by listing important medications discovered at universities, foundations, nonprofit institutions, and clinics, all places where profits did not figure into the decision of whether or not to conduct new drug research.[20] Moreover, it emphasized that patents were originally introduced as a reward for the solo inventor but the drug industry had converted it into a search for products that held the greatest potential profit. The *inventors* for drugs were employees working in corporate laboratories and they had assigned all their rights to their employers. [21]

Kefauver's report sent shivers through the drug business. It raised the spectre the U.S. might adopt the European model of public health, one in which governments regulated prices.[22]

The report underscored an inherent shortcoming in the way drugs were developed, as relevant today as it was fifty-seven years ago: "The problem is with companies whose sole concern is business . . . the richest earning[s] occur when a new variety or variant of a drug is marketed before competing drugs can be discovered, improvised, named, and released." Secrecy before the rollout of a new medication was in-

---

*About six months before the report, Lederle, Bristol, and Parke-Davis reduced the price on their branded tetracycline by 15 percent, the drug's first ever discount. It was a preemptive move intended to demonstrate the willingness of companies to voluntarily cut prices even without any competitive impetus to do so. Kefauver and most of his Senate colleagues were not impressed and noted it in the report.

strumental to its success and to ensure rivals did not get an early start on developing a competitive product. The result was that most drugs were marketed after a "minimum of clinical trials" intended to do the very least required to demonstrate there were not any "potential dangers from toxicity."[23] The public, buying drugs prescribed by doctors, were effectively guinea pigs on whether the medications had long-term safety issues.

Kefauver's investigative staff had also focused on Medicine Avenue. "Abuses and corruption" were problematic in the visits to physicians by the detail men (20 million annually), direct mailers to doctors (750 million a year), free journals supported only by pharma advertising, and ever-grander exhibits at medical conventions.[24] Pharma companies had become addicted to the hard sell; the largest firms spent a robust quarter of all income on promotion (which the companies labeled "physician education"). One out of every six employees at the largest firms was a detail man. The promo and ad budgets were the fastest-growing expense for every firm, mushrooming from less than $100 million to $750 million over a decade.[25]

Arthur Sackler and his colleagues had taken advantage of an FTC loophole that exempted all ads directed to physicians from any oversight. Congress had created that exception believing that since doctors were knowledgeable they would not fall prey to misinformation or slick promotion. The Senate probe demonstrated that physicians were as susceptible to bad information as the general public. According to a three-year study of thousands of direct-to-doctor ads, more than half contained unreliable or misleading statements.[26] Some were not truthful, others deceptively ambiguous. Although every pharma firm had a physician as medical director, the ad departments frequently bypassed or overruled them when it came to more questionable promotions.[27]

In two thousand pages of ads run in leading medical journals, 40 percent "ignored side effects entirely" while the rest "dismissed the subject with some sort of reassuring phrase." The McAdams agency had introduced some of the most commonly used taglines: "virtually free of side effects," "with no irreversible side effects," "without clinically significant side effects," "relatively nontoxic," "few side effects to worry about," and "absence of serious side effects specifically noted."[28] The one that Arthur Sackler used the most was "side effects are generally of a transient and non-serious nature."[29]

Kefauver's subcommittee had found that doctors were overwhelmed by all the ads for the spiraling number of new medications, upward of five hundred a year. Many were slight chemical alterations of an existing drug and marketed with similar and easily confusable names. A busy physician had to sort through competing brand names and generics from foreign companies. The plethora of promotional materials was dubbed "the therapeutic jungle."[30]

That was no mistake by the drug companies. Internal marketing files from top firms boasted about how their products benefited from "the confusion technique," the perplexity caused by hundreds of ever-changing products. Sometimes the information overload caused physicians to keep prescribing the same pill with which they had been comfortable for years. That was especially true of those who had practiced for a long time. They had difficulty running their practices and keeping up with the flood of new information. Drug companies knew that was a reason to lock a doctor early on into a patented brand. Yet, in other cases, the new drugs served as "built in obsolescence." It forced physicians unable to keep abreast of all the latest developments to adopt whatever the detail men promoted as the latest and greatest.[31]

Few doctors thought they were to blame. Half of physicians polled reported that their earliest source of information about a new drug was not from ads but from the detail men.[32] Those pitches were always given in the privacy of the doctor's office and never put to paper. Often mixed into the presentation extolling the benefits of the new drug, the detail men raised fears about the safety and efficacy of competitors, particularly generics.[33] The government was so obsessed about lower prices, they claimed, that it had allowed generics without adequate safeguards for quality and safety.[34, 35]

It was difficult for physicians to determine if everything the detail man said was accurate science or mixed in with some hyperbole. The Kefauver panel had asked early on: "How often is the misrepresentation a matter of individual overzealousness and how often does it reflect deliberate company policy, codified into specific instructions to the detail man?"[36]

The internal files of Parke-Davis provided at least one answer to that question. It had marketed its successful antibiotic Chloromycetin for nearly a year when the first reports trickled in about some patients developing aplastic anemia, a rare and sometimes fatal condition affecting the bone marrow. The National Research Council had reported as early as 1952 that Chloromycetin was linked to nearly half the cases. It recommended a warning be sent to all prescribing physicians and hospitals that because of the potential severe adverse effects, "it is essential that adequate blood studies be made when prolonged or intermittent administration of this drug is required."[37]

What did Parke-Davis, and Bill Frohlich, whose ad firm was responsible for this account, send to doctors? They changed "essential" to "should" and suggested that Chloromycetin was "no more dangerous" than other strong antibiotics.[38]

The FDA intervened and ordered Parke-Davis to "revise labeling that would caution physicians explicitly against its indiscriminate use."[39] The detail men told doctors to ignore the substance of the FDA warnings. They turned the setback into a victory, boasting that the FDA's failure to ban the drug was "the *highest compliment* ever tendered the medical staff of our company" (emphasis in original).[40] That spin on the FDA's action undercut the prominent warning on the label and doctors' prescriptions for Chloromycetin remained the same.

Adding to all the discouraging revelations, the Senate report noted that even when doctors stayed up to date of the scientific press, many published papers "are written within the confines of the pharmaceutical houses concerned."[41] Upon closer inspection, the "allegedly scientific studies by doctors . . . amount in many cases to no more than testimonials of no scientific validity."[42] Arthur Sackler and Félix Martí-Ibáñez had refined the mixture of promotion and medical science into a veritable art.

Kefauver announced that beginning in January 1962, there would be a new round of public hearings on his proposed legislation. The first phase would focus on medical advertisements and promotion.

"The subcommittee has issued subpoenas to officials of two agencies that handle the bulk of the industry's advertising," reported *The New York Times*. "They are the William Douglas McAdams Agency and L. W. Frohlich Company [*sic*]."[43]

The first witness scheduled to testify was Arthur Sackler.[44]

17

"PAINT THE WORST POSSIBLE PICTURE"

On Tuesday, January 30, 1962, Arthur Sackler, responsible for devising the best strategies for many of the corporate executives who had previously testified, was himself in the spotlight. He was joined by McAdams president Dr. DeForest Ely, a Johns Hopkins–trained physician who had joined the agency in 1947, and Robert Barnard, a patent and trademark litigator and longtime friend.[1] * [2]

Arthur seemed confident as he settled in front of the subcommittee. The senators might have been more impressed with his demeanor had they known that the previous month, as revealed in documents obtained by the author, two special agents from the New York FBI field office had visited Sackler unexpectedly at the McAdams agency. They questioned him about his friendship with the fugitive Soviet spies Alfred Stern and Martha Dodd.[3] Sackler had nearly four years to prepare his answers since the couple had fled to Prague.[4]

He downplayed to the agents his relationship with the Sterns. As for business, he changed the story and cast Alfred Stern as the one who had first reached out to him. He claimed that Stern had initiated the discussion about buying Schering before the Alien Property Custodian confiscated it. The agents wondered why Stern called Sackler instead

* Preparation for his Senate testimony had not prevented Sackler from indulging new time-consuming pharma-related opportunities. He encouraged another of his attorneys, Stanley Wolder, to form a journal about the crossroads of medical science and law. The author discovered that five months after Sackler's Senate appearance, the International Academy of Law & Science was incorporated in New York. Wolder was a director, and the editor of its journal, *Lex et Scientia.* Arthur convinced a number of his own pharma clients to hire Wolder as a consultant.

of getting in touch with one of Schering's directors or senior executives. In their memo to headquarters, they noted: "Sackler mentioned that as an expert in the pharmaceutical field he is frequently consulted regarding the mark[et]ing, financing and promotion of pharmaceutical firms."[5] They somehow failed to realize that the Sackler and Stern meeting about putting together an investor group to buy Schering took place in 1941. It was twenty-seven-year-old Sackler's first job after completing his medical residency. He was an assistant to the chief of a four-person ad department. The agents, though, accepted his version.

Having convinced them that Stern sought his counsel in acquiring Schering, Sackler explained away their subsequent socializing—at their Central Park West co-op, summer home in Connecticut, and "a last minute" invitation to the Toscanini premiere—as all about business. When he spoke to Stern about buying another small pharma company in 1948, he insisted it was a brief conversation and only by telephone. What about the Sterns' political leanings? Arthur professed to be clueless. To clinch how casually he knew the Americans now wanted as spies, when shown a photo of Martha Dodd, he hesitated before claiming he could not positively identify her. This virtuoso performance left the agents persuaded that Arthur's connection to the Sterns was largely accidental and most likely innocent.*

Sackler was now prepared to repeat a convincing performance before Kefauver. He had carefully mapped out a strategy, first wanting to establish his own medical credentials and reputation. In documents he had provided to the subcommittee, there was a typed seven-page, single-spaced "bibliography." It listed fifty-nine scholarly articles he had written, one under way, and a copy of his 1956 book, *The Great Physiodynamic Therapies in Psychiatry*, done with his brothers and Martí-Ibáñez.[6] "A Brief Summary of Research Findings" was an attached sixty-page, two-part report extolling what he claimed he had anticipated and predicted before anyone else in "biologic psychiatry" and "physiology."[7] Sackler also attached letters from some medical luminaries who praised his work.[8]

His prepared statement emphasized his work as a "research psy-

* The agents were also initially concerned that Sackler had hired a former State Department employee, Mary Jane Keeney, dismissed as a security risk during the McCarthy hearings. The FBI had opened an espionage investigation into her husband but never built a case strong enough to arrest him.

chiatrist" who "has never had anything to do with testing or marketing of any drugs for clients of McAdams or for any pharmaceutical company."[9] He downplayed the influence of the McAdams agency. It handled, he claimed, only $15 million annually in "good ethical pharmaceutical advertising [that] plays a positive role in advancing the health of the community."[10] That was less than 2 percent of the $750 million pharma spent annually on promotion. "The cost of advertising material which we handle for our clients comes to less than 5 cents per prescription dollar for the drugs."[11]

Sackler emphasized that "no amount of money or promotional ingenuity can match demonstrated benefits for patients from good prescription drugs." The free market would dispose of drugs that failed to deliver what they promised. He reminded the senators that "the American people are healthier, not sicker; our children have less disease, not more, our lifespan has increased, not decreased."[12]

As for the subcommittee's focus on drug prices, Sackler contended that the type of promotion he did—informing doctors about new drugs from his pharma clients—"reduce[s] the cost of medical care even as it helps save lives and prevent suffering." Since the discovery of psychopharmaceutic drugs, he said, New York State spent $2.2 million on tranquilizers annually, while saving about $10 million in patient care and $170 million in new hospital construction. And just $16,000 in drugs to fight tuberculosis had saved New York City $16 million by converting sanitoriums to other uses.[13] Sackler wrapped up by addressing Kefauver's pending legislation. He believed it was unnecessary since the drug companies and ad agencies such as his had already voluntarily instituted everything the law proposed.[14]

Kefauver led off the questioning: what possible objection could there be to including a drug's side effects in any printed ads? Sackler said it would "impose an undue economic hardship upon the little manufacturer who cannot afford the necessary space."[15]

Herman Schwartz, the committee's staff counsel, tried rattling Sackler's cool demeanor. He brought up Upjohn's corticosteroid, Medrol, on which Sackler had done a nationwide ad campaign. Arthur was responsible for reporting, producing, and distributing *Scope Weekly*, Upjohn's in-house drug promotional that went to 175,000 physicians and all medical schools. Sackler earned $1.5 million annually just from *Scope Weekly*.[16]

The heart of the Medrol campaign was two side-by-side X-rays, the first labeled "Ulcerative Colitis" and the second "Ulcerative Colitis Following Treatment." One California radiologist, on close inspection, suspected that the X-rays were of two different people. When he wrote to Upjohn he discovered that not only were the X-rays of different patients, but he learned that neither had taken Medrol.

What followed was a combative half hour. The more Arthur was pressed, the more obstinate he became.

The ad was not misleading, insisted Sackler. The first X-ray was of "an irreversible condition" so the second X-ray could not be the same person since "you cannot reverse an irreversible condition."

That is why it is so misleading, countered Schwartz. The ad made it appear that Medrol cured the condition in six weeks.

Nowhere, Sackler argued, did the caption for the second X-ray claim, "Same patient as x-ray No. 1." At no time did the ad say "before" and "after." As for neither patient taking Medrol, Sackler said "It never said they did." Any doctor would know they were different people, he claimed, and the doctor who complained was the only one who did so out of 140,000 physicians.[17] The X-rays were only put into the ad as a "constructive service" to help inform physicians "of the total disease. . . . We were not with those x-rays trying to sell any medicine."[18]

"You were trying to get the doctors to prescribe the medicine?" asked Kefauver.

"We are trying to get the doctors to have available additional basic material."[19]

Sackler seemed irritated by and contemptuous of the questioning. He resented that the subcommittee did not have a single physician on staff. He told his attorneys that laymen could not understand the complexity of medical science and the finesse necessary to promote it.[20] The often sharp back-and-forth was as much an exposé about Sackler's "never admit a mistake" mind-set as it was about the flaws of what then passed as acceptable medical advertising practices.

Medrol had only been a warm-up for chief counsel Herman Schwartz. Next was MER/29, a cholesterol-lowering medication developed and patented by William S. Merrell, a small Cincinnati drug company and another McAdams client. Sackler and his team rolled out MER/29 with a million-dollar budget in March 1960.[21] McAdams sent 100,000 copies of a booklet extolling MER/29 to doctors nationwide. An eight-page color ad ran in prominent medical journals, followed by a deluge of full-page ads and more direct mail. The message:

MER/29 was the "first safe" and "nontoxic" drug that lowered cholesterol.[22] Merrell's detail men gave doctors a free 8mm movie that repeated the theme about MER/29's innovative status. It was a hit, with more than 300,000 users in a year. In October 1961, the Mayo Clinic sent Merrell a report that two patients using the drug had developed cataracts.[23] By December, eighteen months after the launch, the FDA required Merrell to send a "Dear Doctor" letter listing a page and a half of possible MER/29 side effects not previously reported; in addition to cataracts there were changes to reproductive organs, reduced adrenal gland function, severe dermatitis, and baldness, among others.[24]

As the number of adverse reactions piled up, the FDA subpoenaed Merrell's internal files. It discovered the company had lied about MER/29's success in animal testing. It had disposed of monkeys who died during the tests but listed them in the final report as having done well. Records of frequent incidents of gall bladder and liver damage, as well as dangerous weight loss, were either destroyed or omitted from the results submitted to the FDA for the drug's approval. Merrell had also somehow persuaded a group of Cleveland Clinic physicians to postpone their scientific paper disclosing the drug's "toxic side effects."[25] A week after the FDA had uncovered the evidence of Merrell's fraud, the company withdrew the drug from the market.[26] * [27]

The committee now wanted to know when Sackler had learned about MER/29's side effects. The McAdams promotional campaign had emphasized that "few toxic or serious side effects have been reported" in a prominent ad in the November 4, 1961, *JAMA*. Merrell knew by then that the FDA had ordered it to send a warning letter to doctors.

Sackler claimed that Merrell had not informed him until late October, and it was then too late to cancel or modify the *JAMA* ad. In any case, he said, he did not know what the big fuss was about.

That surprised the panel. Chief counsel Schwartz picked up the questioning. What about suppression of the adrenal gland function?

---

* Injured patients filed more than 1,500 civil suits against Merrell. Many were consolidated into a class action, one of the largest ever at that time against a drug company. While Merrell is estimated to have earned slightly more than $1 million in profits in the two years preceding the drug's recall, the civil settlements eventually cost much more, some $200 million. Compounding Merrell's problems, the Justice Department brought criminal charges against a vice president and three managers. They pled no contest to the charges.

"A good jigger or a few jiggers of whisky may also reduce adrenocortical output," Sackler replied.

What about the other side effects in the Merrell letter it was ordered to send to physicians?

"I do not believe that thinning of the hair is a toxic side effect," he quipped. "I'd prefer thin hair to thick coronaries."[28] It was vintage Sackler, a bombastic demeanor mixed in with a dash of condescension (there was no clinical evidence the drug prevented thickening arteries).

"Cataracts are certainly a serious side effect," Kefauver interrupted.

"There were four [cataract] cases in 300,000 patients," countered Sackler. Three of those were because the dosage was too high, he claimed. It was possible that the other patient who developed cataracts was simply "a chance finding."[29]

He reminded the subcommittee that he and his McAdams team did not write Merrell's warning letter to doctors. If they had asked for his opinion, he would have told them to fight the FDA directive since it was unnecessary. "There is no therapy which is totally without side effects," he said. Moreover, all the MER/29 ads he created had in small print: "Complete bibliography and prescription information available on request."[30]

No matter what the committee threw at him, Sackler was unfazed. If he was unable to deflect an issue he stonewalled or grew ever more combative. He chided the Senate's probe, "the whole thing isn't relevant."[31] When confronted with some of his own memos the investigative staff had obtained, but that he had failed to produce in response to a subpoena, he complained that the committee was trying to trap him instead of getting to the truth. Still, he offered to "testify on this blindfolded, so to speak" while complaining he had not been shown "this material until this morning."

What about the many documented instances the committee had compiled of misrepresentations and material omissions in the sales pitches by detail men? Sackler was adamant that "we cannot be responsible" for promotion "material which we do not prepare. . . . We act as agents. I could not in any way testify as to what a drug company does with its detail men unless I was preparing their material."[32] He assured the subcommittee he had nothing to do with any improper strategies for the detail squads.

It seemed the chief counsel might have a "gotcha-moment" when he produced a seventeen-page memo of opposition research prepared by

Pfizer, one of Sackler's main clients. The document, filled with negative data about a competitor's drug, was distributed to the detail men to use as needed to push doctors away from the rival medication and to instead prescribe the Pfizer brand. The subcommittee had uncovered letters from Sackler to Bill Frohlich discussing the memo in detail.[33] The American Medical Association and *JAMA*, among others, had strict prohibitions against using derogatory information about one drug to promote another. Arthur did not miss a beat.

"Someone sent this material to me, and I simply sent it back with a comment. We have *nothing* to do with it," he insisted.[34]

At another point, asked whether McAdams had suppressed the generic drug names by listing them in small fonts, he said, "Personally, I don't have any objection to 8 point type."[35] Shown ads in which McAdams had omitted the generic names, he claimed those were "mechanical" errors by a low-level employee. "We had the fewest [errors] of all agencies."[36] Confronted with letters from eight doctors who said that McAdams had used their names as endorsements in ads although they had expressly *refused* permission, Sackler blamed an employee who "is no longer with William Douglas McAdams."[37]

Only during the last hour of his testimony did Sackler lose his defiant stance. It involved questioning about whether he had violated the FDA's ironclad ban on "direct to consumers" ads. The subcommittee did not know about how Arthur circumvented the FDA prohibition in his celebrated Librium campaign. They did, however, have incriminating evidence about two other promotions they suspected were Sackler's handiwork. The first was Gray's Compound, the streamlined name Arthur had picked for Purdue Frederick's top selling Gray's Glycerine Tonic Compound. *Health Horizons*, a general circulation consumer health magazine, had run 178 clippings promoting Gray's Compound.

"Is Health Horizons an operation of McAdams?" asked Kefauver.

Sackler picked his words with the precision of an attorney. "Not to my knowledge, sir. I do not believe so."[38]

The chief counsel said the committee had determined that *Health Horizons* was owned by Medical and Science Communication Associates. That company had placed prepackaged ads disguised to look as if they were editorial stories into 171 newspapers and magazines about another Purdue product, the laxative Senokot. It seemed suspicious that its office was at the same midtown Manhattan address as the McAdams agency.[39] Kefauver pulled a file folder overflowing with documents from his briefcase. He flipped through some pages before holding one near the microphone.

"Is that company yours?" Kefauver asked.

Sackler said, "We used their services," but dodged a direct answer: "Senator, I have never had any stock in Medical Science Communications Associates."

"Was it a department [of yours]?" Kefauver asked.

"No sir, it was not. . . . And I was never an officer."

They were an independent company that paid for their own office space, Sackler averred, and whatever they did for drug ads or promotion, he played no role in it.

"Was this done for you?"

"No sir. . . . I would never approve the utilization of mats such as these in respect to the dissemination of prescription product information. . . . They were not clients of William Douglas McAdams, to the best of my knowledge."[40] Sackler became agitated when pressed. His voice rose.

"I would like to make it very clear. . . . Everything I have ever heard is that it is a violation of all the codes, it is unethical and everything else to advertise to the lay public, the idea being that the doctor ought to make the decision and that the patient should not be getting information so that he goes to the doctor and insist on getting the drug. And furthermore, these things don't set out the side effects, and the paper that takes it usually doesn't know that it is really advertising, it thinks it is just from a news service. And then the editors who might print an article of that sort of thing is just coming from some foundation or some organization of that sort, too."[41]

So, if that was true, why had Sackler incorporated in 1949 another company, Medical Pharmaceutical Information Bureau? It was dedicated to presenting drug research and information to journalists and editors.

"In the late 1940s we believed that a good information service would be valuable."

He claimed that when he realized the company sent out mats, he told the firm's president that "I personally felt the practice should stop." Sackler said he sold his interest in 1951 and declared since then he had "held no stock of any kind, directly or indirectly."

Kefauver again tried pinning him down about whether he had approved mats for his pharma clients.

"To the best of my knowledge, Senator, I cannot recall."

That was uncharacteristically vague for a man who prided himself on blunt and direct answers.

The Senate staff knew that Medical Science Communications Associates was owned by Arthur's ex-wife, Else, and Helen Haberman, the highest-ranking female executive at McAdams (the duo later merged it into Medical and Science Communications Development).[42] The obfuscation was vintage Sackler. He hid his own role and equity stake under different names, as he had done time and again in ventures with Bill Frohlich, Félix Martí-Ibáñez, and his brothers.[43]

In wrapping up his testimony, Sackler told the senators that the proposed legislation was not necessary. The government should instead stop overregulating the pharmaceutical industry and allow it to police itself. As Sackler prepared to leave, Nebraska's outspoken Roman Hruska apologized for the accusatory questioning. It was a shame, he said, that his colleagues had tried "to paint the worst possible picture" of drug advertising.[44]

Arthur was confident he had done a great job. Some of his friends were not as convinced. Bill Frohlich, who was scheduled to testify the following day, changed his mind after he learned about the aggressive questioning. He got a doctor to send the committee a letter by messenger that he had "an eye disorder which might be aggravated by his appearance, and that he is somewhere in Germany."

18

THALIDOMIDE TO THE RESCUE

Kefauver soon had more on his mind than Sackler. After the last witness testified in February 1962, the proposed legislation went to the Judiciary Committee for review. According to Kefauver, at "a secret meeting" with some other senators, the pharma industry "just about knocked the bill right out of the ring."[1]

The drug industry's lobbying was effective because few politicians feared voter backlash if they failed to control drug prices. The lack of public outcry over the hearings had emboldened the industry. The revised bill that emerged from the Judiciary Committee was "a mere shadow of" the original, Kefauver lamented.[2] Gone were key revisions of the patent law. Kefauver's two-and-a-half-year quest to change the way the pharmaceutical industry priced its drugs was on the verge of being scuttled.

Everything abruptly changed in mid-July. " 'Heroine' of FDA Keeps Bad Drug off Market," ran the front-page headline in *The Washington Post*.[3] It was the story of "how [the] skepticism and stubbornness of a government physician . . . a bureaucratic nitpicker . . . prevented what could have been an appalling American tragedy." The doctor was Frances Oldham Kelsey, an FDA approval officer. Merrell, the same firm that had faked studies for its MER/29 cholesterol drug, pressured Kelsey to approve thalidomide, a sedative sold over the counter throughout Europe as a nonaddictive sleep aid and a morning sickness treatment for expectant mothers.[4] At that time, a drug was automatically approved if the FDA took no action within sixty days of an application. Kelsey, however, had delayed the process by peppering Merrell with many requests for more information.[5] Despite the company's arguments, she was not convinced of the drug's safety.[6]

By the time of the *Washington Post* story, there was evidence of its dangers with some reports of horrible birth deformities in mothers who had taken the drug. (Eventually, thalidomide was blamed for more than ten thousand infants worldwide born with extreme underdevelopment of the arms or feet. Two thousand died of complications.)[7] * [8]

The tremendous fright caused by the thalidomide disaster revived overnight Kefauver's moribund legislation. The outcry sparked a bipartisan rush by politicians all wanting to take some credit for drug reform. A nationwide poll showed that 76 percent of those queried about "government control over drugs" thought it should be "more strict."[9] Kefauver embraced the newfound support even though he realized it meant abandoning his campaign to foster more competition and control pricing in favor of crafting a bill that focused on consumer safety.

Pharma was now on the defensive. It did not want to be cast as the villain by opposing a bill now framed as providing necessary safeguards to prevent the next thalidomide tragedy. The industry's main lobbying group, the Pharmaceutical Manufacturers Association, begrudgingly embraced some provisions that enhanced drug safety while resisting efforts to revive any of the antitrust and patent revisions.[10]

Adding to pharma's problems was a book published during the Senate hearings. Biologist Rachel Carson's *Silent Spring* indicted the dangers of unfettered pesticides in the environment and food chain. She warned about many health dangers, including possibly cancer.† [11] Carson's revelations about how American chemical companies often put profits ahead of people and the planet amplified similar concerns around thalidomide.[12] Polls showed it shook confidence in the post–World War II faith in science and medicine. Many Americans had faith in DuPont's slogan, "Better Living Through Chemistry." And an equal number had clung to a good opinion of pharmaceutical companies,

* Although Kelsey had prevented thalidomide from going on sale in America, Merrell had distributed the drug for clinical safety trials to some twenty thousand patients in the United States. No one is certain how many of those patients were pregnant, but the FDA later concluded that seventeen babies with thalidomide deformities were born in the U.S. In South America and some Asian countries it continued to be sold by foreign drug companies for another decade under different product names that never disclosed any thalidomide content.

† Carson's main culprit was DuPont's DDT, an insecticide often deployed by aerial spraying. It took activists a decade battling the chemical industry before the Environmental Protection Agency banned DDT in the U.S. The activist network spawned by *Silent Spring* was the driving force behind the 1970 creation of the Environmental Protection Agency.

believing that their mission of discovering cures somehow made them more altruistic.[13]

The public's anger emboldened the FDA's Young Turks, junior grade officials who believed the agency was hobbled by its insufficient powers. They lobbied Kefauver to include in his bill sufficient regulatory tools for the FDA to better keep tabs on the drug industry and its products. Kefauver offered to abandon his efforts to limit patents in order to get a few wavering senators to commit to giving the FDA significantly more authority.[14]

The legislation that had seemed dead only a few months earlier was passed unanimously by the Senate and House. President Kennedy signed it into law on October 10. It was the first major reform of the nation's drug laws since the 1938 Food, Drug, and Cosmetic Act and it marked the end to the hundred-year experiment in which the industry had policed itself and the public self-medicated. Consumer advocates hailed the law's safeguards.

The Kefauver Amendments marked the first time that all drug manufacturers had to register with the FDA, satisfy quality control standards, and agree to regular on-site inspections. The sixty-day time limit for an FDA examiner to respond to a new drug application was abolished. The FDA got the power to recall drugs it judged "an imminent hazard to the public health" or that failed to deliver their therapeutic claims.[15] The agency no longer had to wait until there was a trail of injured or dead patients for proof of a drug's danger. The statute also empowered the FDA, much to the consternation of Medicine Avenue, to ensure that advertisements to doctors struck a "fair balance" between promotional hyperbole and scientific accuracy.[16] The law did not define "fair balance," but left it to the FDA to figure out.[17]

While those changes were important, they paled in comparison to a few key provisions that made the Kefauver Amendments landmark legislation. Before the law, in order for a pharma firm to get its drug approved by the FDA, it only had to show the medication was reasonably safe. The FDA had no authority to consider whether the drug worked for what it was intended.[18] The focus only on safety resulted in therapeutically useless medications hitting the market. The technical distinction about the FDA's power was never clear to the public, which assumed that government approval meant a drug was safe *and* effective. *All* drugs now had to establish "substantial evidence" of efficacy based on "adequate and well-controlled studies." Each pharma firm had the burden of proof to demonstrate its drug "will have the effect it purports or is represented to have." The law did not define "adequate and well-controlled studies," again leaving the specifics to the FDA.[19]

If the intent of the Kefauver Amendments was to ensure that all future drugs actually worked, what about the more than nine thousand medications the FDA had approved between 1938 and 1962 when efficacy was not considered?[20] Some four thousand were still on the market, including a couple of hundred me-too drugs that had been approved with only an FDA advisory letter.[21] The Kefauver Amendments required that those pre-1962 medications had to also be examined for effectiveness. It gave two years for the pharma companies to assemble the evidence for the effectiveness of their early drugs.

Meeting the goals of the new law meant substantially more work for the FDA. That was not easy given its limited resources: the agency's budget allowed it to inspect drug factories on average only every five and a half years.[22] As an initial step, the FDA split its Division of New Drugs into five separate departments: the Investigational Drug Branch (evaluating the clinical studies pharma submitted); Controls Evaluation (reviewing product controls at research labs and manufacturing plants); Medical Evaluation (judging the safety and efficacy data in the New Drug Application forms); New Drug Status (working with manufacturers on the correct dosing levels); and New Drug Surveillance (compiling side effect reports).

Pharma companies feared that the law would make the drug approval process much longer, costlier, and more complex.[23] Pharma's apprehension soon turned to alarm. Frances Kelsey, the FDA medical officer who had refused to approve the sale of thalidomide in the U.S., was appointed the chief of the new Investigational Drug Branch.[24] Kelsey was a certified national hero. President Kennedy had awarded her the Distinguished Civilian Service Award, the highest honor for a government employee. Dozens of newspapers and half a dozen national magazines had published glowing profiles that made her the most recognizable face in FDA history.[25]

In January 1963, to eliminate ambiguity over the law's undefined "adequate and well-controlled studies," Kelsey announced a detailed protocol that every pharma company had to follow to demonstrate the efficacy of their proposed new drugs. Under Kelsey's rules, firms could not start human trials until they first convinced the Investigational Drug Branch that the proposed medication had no serious adverse effects and demonstrated therapeutic effectiveness in animal testing. Only then could they start the first of three phases for the human trials. The Kefauver Amendments gave the FDA the final say over the qualifications of the researchers and facilities chosen for those trials. The first phase, composed of several dozen volunteers, focused on safety. The second phase tested for therapeutic effectiveness on a minimum of several hundred patients. Kelsey's final stage was a backbreaker for pharma. It required randomized comparative testing against a similar drug or a placebo, using thousands of patients in many different locations. Kelsey made it evident that the FDA would give the most credence to double-blind trials, those in which neither the investigator nor the volunteer knew who received the drug and who got the placebo.[26] The 1963 rules would remain virtually intact for more than fifty years.

Pharma firms immediately withdrew about a quarter of the pending drug applications at the FDA, those that had not been approved before the Kefauver Amendments became law. They were medications judged to have a "low commercial priority" because they addressed rare illnesses and small numbers of patients. They did not seem profitable given the expense and time of the new clinical study requirements. Harry Shirkey, a leading pediatrician and chairman of the AMA's Council on Drugs, dubbed those medications "pharmaceutical orphans."[27] (Decades later the government would create a statute to revive them, turning the orphaned drugs from an abandoned category into the highest-priced sliver of the industry.)

The rigorous testing also had an unintended consequence that only became evident years later. It marked the beginning of the end for the era where individual researchers filtered tens of thousands of soil samples searching for antibacterial microbes or screening hundreds of compounds for signs of psychopharmacological activity. It was, of course, still possible for a lone scientist in a small lab to get lucky and discover an unknown and promising drug. And that did occasionally happen. But completing the FDA's three stages of clinical trials was incredibly more complex and took several years on average. Every company knew that no matter how promising a compound looked in a lab, it might be quite different when administered to patients. The high failure rate for innovative drugs was a reason why many pharma firms turned out me-too drugs.[28] Since 1960, the average pharma company put about 25 percent of its R&D budget into research for an entirely new class of drugs and 75 percent into developing me-too drugs.[29] Risk taking—starting—became an ever-rarer commodity in American pharma in the coming decades.[30]

It was not feasible to apply Kelsey's strict benchmarks for new drug approval to the four thousand pre-1962 medications still on the market. Research scientists estimated that reviewing all the published clinical information for those drugs would take between twenty-five and fifty years. Minnesota senator Hubert Humphrey, himself a pharmacist by trade, held hearings that summer about how federal agencies could better cooperate in regulating drugs.[31] One of the committee's final recommendations was that the AMA's Council on Drugs should take a more proactive role in providing unbiased drug information to doctors.[32] The Council on Drugs was game, but it had trouble keeping up even with just those drugs recently approved by the FDA. It managed on average to analyze only one of every three new medications fully. By the time doctors got the AMA information, it was often so late that newer drugs had replaced the ones the AMA had studied.[33] No matter how strong an exhortation the AMA received from Congress, it was evident the country's largest medical association could not keep up with the flood of drugs coming out of pharma labs.

The same was true at the FDA where the agency lacked the skilled staff and know-how to fully carry out its expanded powers.[34] Its annual budget was less than what some companies spent on introducing a single major drug.[35]

Pharma, meanwhile, complained publicly that the onerous regulations would stifle innovation. Privately they carped about how clinical testing would slow their products getting to the market and increase their costs. Pharma encouraged its allies to rally against the Kefauver Amendments in the hope that a future Congress might rein in some of the broader powers it granted to the FDA. At a midsummer 1963 international symposium in Chicago, many prestigious academicians, pharmacologists, and scientists expressed serious concerns about whether the new regulations would "snuff out the life of clinical pharmacology." A survey of medical school researchers that year revealed that 75 percent said the law had made them disinclined to finish their current projects and less likely to start new ones.

The *International Business and Financial Weekly* and other conservative financial publications ran editorials condemning the FDA's expansive new powers and urged Congress to "clip their wings."[36] The era's two leading libertarian economists, George Stigler and Milton Friedman, were adamant that only the free market should determine whether or not a product was effective. Drugs that did not work or were too expensive for the benefit they provided would lose out to more effective and lower-priced medications. The only role for the government, they declared, was to ensure that drugs were safe before they were sold to the public.[37]

Pharma had a superb confederate in the American Medical Association, which condemned the Kefauver Amendments for usurping the judgment of physicians. Just as Stigler and Friedman argued, the AMA contended the FDA's only focus in approving drugs was safety. Questions of efficacy should be the exclusive province of dispensing doctors who had firsthand experience with patients. The Pharmaceutical Manufacturers Association added to the firestorm by denigrating the qualifications of some of the FDA's newly hired medical officers when compared to renowned doctors. It was intended to raise doubts about the ability of the young government regulators, some just fresh from school, to pass judgment on drug effectiveness.[38]

Over time, pharma would point to a falloff in the number of annual drug approvals as evidence that the Kefauver Amendments had crimped innovation (the FDA's counterargument was that the lower number of approvals simply represented "a more measured scientific pace"). The slower approval process was dubbed "drug lag," and later kicked off a debate about whether the U.S. rules had allowed European pharma firms to surpass their American rivals.[39]

Drug industry executives shared a like-minded strategy, their belief that if the new regulations were onerous for pharma, they were crushing for the FDA. Their plan was simple. On every new drug application, they would bury the agency in dozens of three-ring binders crammed with information about clinical trials and laboratory minutiae.[40] Records from Parke-Davis show that its application for an epinephrine product in 1938 totaled twenty-seven pages. A decade later, it submitted seventy-three pages when applying for approval on a new expectorant. Its largest submission to the FDA before the Kefauver Amendments had been 430 pages in 1958. After the law, its 1962 application for a contraceptive was 8,500 pages. For a new anesthetic in a few years, Parke-Davis sent to the FDA a backbreaking 167 volumes, consisting of 12,370 pages.[41]

Pharma planned to appeal FDA decisions they did not like. Hiring more lawyers and outside medical experts would be part of the price of doing business in the post-Kefauver world. The FDA, however, was not naive about pharma's entrenched resistance. George Larrick, its commissioner, was a former senior federal food and drug inspector. Dwight Eisenhower had appointed him to run the FDA in 1954. He avoided the media and instead worked quietly during his tenure to build bipartisan support in Congress. Larrick's discreet lobbying was one of the chief reasons that Congress felt comfortable putting the enhanced drug enforcement powers of the Kefauver Amendments under the FDA. In 1954, when he took charge, there were 950 employees and the agency had a $6 million annual budget. Before Larrick left the FDA in 1965, its budget had increased tenfold to $50 million, and it had more than four thousand employees. Many of the new hires had medical degrees or doctorates in pharmacology.[42]

Larrick's problem, however, was his poor public image. His quiet, behind-the-scenes arm-twisting may have benefited his agency, but it did not lend itself to good press coverage. To the extent the public knew him, it was as the man who had been duped for several years by Henry Welch, the disgraced chief of the antibiotics division who had been business partners with Martí-Ibáñez. And even though the FDA had prevented a disaster with thalidomide, that credit went to Frances Kelsey. Consumer advocates criticized Larrick for an open-door policy that allowed pharma to have considerable access to and influence over FDA regulators, including the examiners responsible for approving drugs. He was, according to a lead editorial in *The Washington Post*, "an indifferent steward of an important post."[43]

Maybe the dismissive coverage was one of the reasons that Larrick decided to flex the FDA's new powers. He did not go out of his way to pick a fight. Nor did he, however, shy away from one. Larrick settled on a class of medications he considered an easy target: drugs containing an antibiotic in combination with antihistamines, decongestants, or analgesics, marketed "for the relief of symptoms and prevention of complications of the common cold."[44]

Medical studies in academic journals had overwhelmingly concluded those drugs were virtually worthless in fighting the viruses that caused colds. Arthur Sackler, however, had demonstrated that good promotion trumped the scholars when it came to sales. In 1955 he joined with his friend Bill Frohlich and took control of the campaign for Lederle's Achrocidin, a combination of tetracycline, antihistamine, and an analgesic. Its sales were then an anemic seven thousand annual prescriptions. The duo devised a typically aggressive direct-to-physician mailer. Their ads featured a picture of an obviously ill patient under the words "It Started With A Cold," noting that colds occasionally turned into upper respiratory infections. They cited a study that the odds were one in eight of developing a much more serious condition, such as pneumonia, bronchitis, sinusitis, and tonsillitis. They created the tagline "To protect and relieve the 'cold' patient: Achrocidin."[45]

The advertisements did not disclose that the cited study was from 1933. Nor did it make any reference to the twenty far more up-to-date scholarly articles concluding the drug was useless for treating a cold. Lederle's medical director was concerned the ads were misleading. Sackler and Frohlich had played with words and symptoms so that at a quick glance the product seemed a worthwhile remedy. Lederle's medical director formally objected but was overridden. The company mailed the ads to 140,000 physicians. They also ran them extensively in medical journals. For physicians without the time or inclination to do their own research, those pitches—combined with free samples and visits by the Lederle detail men—proved persuasive.

The new promotion made sales pop from the minuscule seven thousand prescriptions to over four million in 1962. Lederle's cold medication accounted for a remarkable 5 percent of all antibiotic sales in America.[46] Sackler's *Medical Tribune* later published the results of its own informal survey of doctors that supposedly ran ten to one in favor of prescribing antibiotics for the common cold.[47]

Larrick had watched intently when the Kefauver subcommittee investigated the Achrocidin ad campaign. The Senate panel had been frustrated since under the existing law, Sackler's ad did not violate rules for how drug companies sold their products. That ad was no longer being run. So Larrick decided that under the new law, the FDA should go after the drug itself.

In August 1963, the FDA announced its intent to "decertify" Achrocidin and other prescription cold remedies. Simultaneously, the agency challenged the efficacy of thirty less frequently used antibiotics, some of which were sold in over-the-counter mouthwashes, throat lozenges, and nose sprays. Larrick relied on the recommendation of a group of leading science advisors the FDA had appointed in conjunction with the National Academy of Sciences. Their conclusion was that all the antibiotic drugs targeted for removal were of "no value in preventing or treating colds."[48] *The New York Times* listed another reason for the FDA's move: "Frequent use can cause patients to develop resistance to the drugs, sometimes making them useless when the patient really needs them."[49] Those who opposed the move had thirty days to respond. The first battle in the post-Kefauver drug world had begun.

19

THE $100 MILLION DRUG

Sackler and his Medicine Avenue colleagues had their own concerns about the Kefauver Amendments. The law threatened to turn medical advertising into one of the most regulated fields of commercial promotion.[1] Labels and ads had to list all active ingredients and the drug's generic name. (The Pharmaceutical Manufacturers Association and thirty-seven drug companies sued the following year to invalidate the requirement for listing the generic name every time the brand name was mentioned; the FDA agreed to withdraw that provision after the case reached the Supreme Court in 1967.)[2] Even more irritating to Medicine Avenue was that the FDA would be the final arbiter of whether their promotions were "scientifically accurate." Ads also had to include a "brief summary" of the warnings and side effects from the package insert. No one knew what a "brief summary" meant in practice.

Sackler urged restraint to both rivals and friends. The agency could now recall any drug if its advertisements violated the new standards. Sackler reasoned that if Medicine Avenue did not unnecessarily provoke the government's only drug regulatory agency, it might not make advertising enforcement a top priority. There was little doubt the FDA had its hands full with approving new drugs and the fight to decertify fixed-dose cold remedies. The ad men hoped that all the new regulations would only affect future promotional campaigns, for drugs that were under development in laboratories.

To Medicine Avenue's relief, there were few changes initially. In the meantime, ad campaigns for antibiotics continued to be the most lucrative moneymakers for the agencies. No one then knew that the golden age of antibiotic discovery was coming to an end. Half of all the ones used today had already been discovered.[3]

Arthur Sackler had made his reputation in medical advertising a decade earlier with his aggressive rollout for Pfizer's Terramycin. Librium revealed what he would do next. Librium had become popular so fast that Hubert Humphrey's 1963 Senate investigation had made it a stand-alone part of their review of federal drug oversight. The disclosures about Librium were largely lost in the nearly one-thousand-page final report. The report noted that Roche's claims about Librium's "remarkable effectiveness and versatility" were from "completely uncontrolled studies" where no effort was made "to observe any of the established disciplines" for reliable trials. And a slow but steadily growing list of side effects—vertigo, drowsiness, impaired thinking, slurred speech, confusion, and sometimes hallucinations—were documented.[4] A study of thirty-six patients on high doses of Librium was the first to suggest it might cause dependence.[5] Another reported that the car accident rate of daily Librium users was ten times greater than average.[6]

Few physicians kept abreast of ever-changing drug updates much less had incentive to tackle a six-inch-thick government report. Despite Librium's spiking adverse effect profile, most doctors continued ranking it as one of the safest drugs on the market.[7] A nationwide poll of physicians provided the best evidence of the impact of Sackler's marketing: Librium was ranked as "one of the most significant advances in medical therapy." It was the top physicians' choice when asked "What drug is most useful in your own practice?" Librium also was the number one pick by doctors asked to select a drug that "was not used as primary therapy" but that "made the biggest contribution to easing the course of illness from the patient's perspective."[8]

Competitors worked furiously to create a rival drug. The results were more than a dozen me-too applications to the FDA, all chemical derivatives of Miltown.[9] Unlocking the chemistry of benzodiazepines and creating a serious Librium competitor proved far more challenging. Even before the FDA's 1960 approval of Librium, Roche had decided to protect its giant research lead in the new category by developing its own contender to its wonder drug. Leo Sternbach, the Roche scientist who discovered Librium, set about developing a successor. Sackler encouraged that strategy. He knew that every drug, no matter how indomitable it seemed when introduced, eventually lost market share to newer meds.[10]

This time, Sternbach's laboratory quest was simpler. Instead of testing hundreds of compounds in the improbable hunt for a new class of therapeutic treatments, he focused on "changing the molecule without losing the tranquilizing activity."[11] Roche wanted a better me-too Librium.[12]

Only a small team at Roche knew that on October 26, 1959, three months before the FDA had given Librium its final approval, Sternbach had found his improved benzo. Never before had a pharmaceutical firm devoted so many resources to developing a competing drug to one of its own brands, before that first one was even on the market. Sternbach gave his new drug the generic name diazepam. Roche finally settled on Valium for the brand, from the Latin *valere*, "to be strong and powerful."

Once again, Roche awarded Sternbach its $10,000 prize for an important discovery. He was only midway through a career that eventually garnered 241 drug patents (at one point, his discoveries accounted for a remarkable 40 percent of Roche's international sales). "After I won that award three or four times," Roche stopped giving it out every year.[13] * [14]

In its 1960 FDA submission, Roche claimed Valium to be more potent than Librium and with fewer side effects. Clinical testing confirmed that claim, demonstrating it was ten times stronger than Librium as an anticonvulsant and five times more powerful as a muscle relaxant and tranquilizer.[15] Valium had an additional marketing advantage since it did not have Librium's bitter aftertaste. Roche did not include that on its application since it was not required.

As opposed to Librium, which had been approved by the FDA before the 1962 Kefauver Amendments, Roche had to demonstrate "substantial evidence" of Valium's efficacy. The FDA was inundated with voluminous pending me-too variations of Miltown, and it was handicapped in reviewing mind drugs, as it had only two psychiatrists in its drug division.[16] It took three years before Valium was approved on November 15, 1963, ironically while the Senate hearings were under way about the undisclosed dangers of its chemical cousin, Librium.

The Senate scolding on Librium did not change Sackler's grandiose

---

* Several of Sternbach's subsequent benzo derivative discoveries became major sellers, including the tranquilizer Rohypnol, later notorious as a date rape drug; the sedative/hypnotic Alodorm; and the anti-insomnia Mogadon. As for two others, the long-acting sleep sedative Dalmane, and the antianxiety Klonopin, Roche patented them in 1963 and 1964, respectively. However, Dalmane was not marketed until 1970 and Klonopin did not go on sale until 1975. Roche did not want to introduce them in the mid-1960s as additional rivals to the market that Librium and Valium then dominated.

plans for Valium's rollout.[17] "Without question, Valium was the biggest," recalled Win Gerson, who had joined McAdams for the Librium campaign. "One of the great attributes of Valium was that it could be used by almost every specialty. There's an anxiety component in literally every phase of medicine."[18]

Roche had committed a record-setting $10 million for the drug's promotion. "That was unheard of," said Gerson. "Valium changed the way we communicated with physicians." Four-page pullout ads became eight pages, direct mail to physicians included three-dimensional inserts, video specials ran on the closed-circuit TV systems at hospitals.[19]

Librium had featured the San Diego Zoo lynx and many of the ads were an emotional pitch about the need for a medication to keep at bay modern life's insidious anxiety. For Valium, Sackler ditched the theatrics and concentrated on the drug's robust therapeutic profile. "Stronger is better" was the core message. And he emphasized the science behind the new pill.[20]

Roche's desire for an aggressive rollout aligned ideally with Sackler's style. In the summer of 1963, six months before the drug went on sale, the FDA had summoned Roche's chief of research, requesting that he bring the evidence to support its request to advertise Valium as a treatment for "nervousness."[21] Valium's clinical trials were conducted before the Kefauver Amendments required much stricter standards for testing. Matthew Ellenhorn, the FDA chief for the Division of New Drugs, was not impressed with Roche's trials. He suggested the company conduct more testing. Roche and Sackler ignored that advice. The first ad in *JAMA* that December touted Valium's effectiveness in treating "incapacitating symptoms of insomnia, nervousness, agitation, tension, irritability, and associated physical symptoms."[22]

The FDA called another meeting in which the New Drug Surveillance Branch asked Roche to remove one of Sackler's most prominent ad lines, "No serious side effects." The agency had received early reports that some patients developed ataxia, a loss of bodily functions. Roche said it would take the advice under consideration. Nothing changed in Sackler's ads.

Roche was determined to make Valium a bigger success than its record-setting Librium. It spent lavishly on the detail team, dispatching them not just to pitch individual doctors, but to sell to medical institutions, hospitals, mental clinics, government health care facilities, and the military. It also increased the budget for free samples, something Sackler thought particularly useful for introducing a lifestyle drug. Roche distributed so many free samples—in one year in Canada it gave away 82 million pills just to hospitals—that health advocates complained the drug was dispensed to many people who did not need it. (It took a decade before Roche responded to the criticism and announced it would distribute free samples only if doctors requested them by returning a prepaid postcard the company provided. After that change, it still gave away on average about 15 million tablets every year.)[23]

Sackler personalized the promotion for Valium based on information from Bill Frohlich and his data collection firm, IMS. It cross-referenced the doctors who subscribed to medical journals with their prescribing habits. Sackler convinced Roche to organize physician focus groups to gauge their responses to different ads.[24] The company also created a Sackler-inspired program explaining why benzodiazepines were the most effective drugs to counter the dangerous effects of too much stress. And it embraced Arthur's then radical idea to use emerging video technology to promote the benzos as part of an accredited program by which physicians could earn continuing education credits. Roche created a three-hour closed-circuit television course and spent more than a million dollars on financing the Network for Continuing Medical Education (Sackler had by then started his own CME courses). There was also a consumer version for journalists specializing in health and medicine.[25] Emphasizing Valium's benefits for countering the bad effects of stress allowed Roche to suggest its wonder pill should be dispensed for everything from migraines to ulcers to diabetes to obesity.

The ads in journals for gynecologists, for instance, targeted menopause; obstetricians, controlling muscle contractions in early labor; orthopedists, muscle spasms; neurologists, how it helped with epilepsy and cerebral palsy; cardiologists, control of hypertension and as an aid in regulating arrhythmia; surgeons, its use as a preanesthetic; and substance abuse specialists, how it reduced the severity of withdrawal symptoms for alcoholics.[26]

Sackler had opted to skip most journals directed to psychiatrics since he assumed they were aware of the benefits of benzos.[27] It worked. Although psychiatrists wrote large numbers of Valium and Librium prescriptions, most of Roche's success was through an astonishing 97 percent of general practitioners who dispensed them.[28]

Valium set a new standard for what a scientist later called "choose your mood medications."[29] Doctors had written more than 50 million prescriptions in the peak year for the minor tranquilizers Miltown and Equanil. That was far more than all antipsychotics and antidepressants, only behind barbiturates and antibiotics.[30] Librium's sales left Miltown in the dust. It had topped 70 million prescriptions annually. And Valium was in a class of its own, with more than 100 million per year to American consumers.[31]

"Miltown and Librium had created the right atmosphere," noted Gilbert Cant, *Time* magazine's medical editor. "In the crassest of clichés, Valium represented an idea whose time had come."[32] Fortunately for Roche, Sackler had helped to make Valium fashionable.

"Executive Excedrin" or "Psychic Aspirin" were its Wall Street nicknames. The Rolling Stones sang about it in their 1966 hit "Mother's Little Helper." "Mother needs something today to calm her down. And though she's not really ill, there's a little yellow pill . . ."[33] That same year novelist Jacqueline Susann called Valium "dolls" in her best-selling *Valley of the Dolls.*

Sackler's campaign made Valium the pharmaceutical industry's first $100 million drug.[34] "Astronomical at the time, particularly in those days when prices were not increased as often as they are today," said McAdams's Gerson.[35] Its success was so pervasive that for years its brand name was used in a broad sense to mean tranquilizer (the same as Xerox had in the 1950s and 1960s been used to mean photocopy).[36]

At Roche's New Jersey manufacturing plant, three enormous pill-stamping machines churned out 30 million pills every fifteen hours.[37] For what would become a record-setting stretch of thirteen years, as *The New York Times* noted, the world's top selling drug "is not, as might be expected, a hopeful remedy for some life-threatening or fatal condition like cancer or heart disease or a crippler like arthritis. Instead, it is a white or pastel-colored tablet generally prescribed for an emotional state vaguely described as anxiety."[38] * [39]

---

* For a decade after its introduction in 1963, Valium's new prescriptions outnumbered refills. That was the best evidence of an expanding market. In 1974, refills held a three-to-two advantage over new scrips. The silver lining was that the overall number of Valium prescriptions had not decreased, only more were going to existing patients. Roche knew that patients were loyal and felt the drug worked; studies reported that 95 percent of patients reported Valium helped them, an astonishing result for any drug, much less one that had been on the market for ten years at that stage.

Roche had worried that every Valium prescription might replace one that would have been dispensed for Librium. Instead, Valium expanded the market for tranquilizers by adding upward of a million new patients. When Valium became the country's top selling drug, Librium was still number three (the contraceptive pill was second). It had surpassed six billion total tablets in sales.[40] The two blockbuster benzos averaged about 80 percent of the tranquilizer market and made Roche the most profitable drug firm on the planet.[41]

"Every publicly traded drug company worried about a huge spike in revenues and profits from a blockbuster," recalls marketing executive Richard Sperber. "We all liked the success but not too much at once, it could not stay at that level forever. At some point, the year-over-year drop would look bad." Sometimes companies diverted sales income into so-called opportunity spending, a catchall for ambitious future projects. Accountants worked magic to keep some of it off the revenue ledger.[42]

There were not enough accounting tricks or phantom programs to hide the flood of money that poured into Roche from benzos. The company's stock peaked at a high of $73,000 a share, earning it the distinction as the most expensive publicly traded stock at that time. *Fortune* dubbed Valium "the greatest commercial success ever."[43]

20

LEGAL BUT SOMEHOW "SHIFTY"

Lost in the flood of good news about Valium and Librium were the first warning signs of problems with the drugs. It came in a final report in late 1963 from the President's Advisory Commission on Narcotic and Drug Abuse.[1] It seemed an unlikely forum to address the benzos since JFK had created the seven-person panel in January to study ways "to prevent abuse of narcotic and non-narcotic drugs." Its focus was amphetamine and barbiturate abuse, both of which had been the subject of alarming FDA warnings. Half the enormous annual pharmaceutical amphetamine production found its way to the illegal market.[2] News accounts demonized amphetamine "thrill pills" as the culprit for everything from increased road accidents for long-haul truckers to broken homes, porn and prostitution, and juvenile crime.[3] A sharp spike in overdose deaths was blamed on barbiturates (Marilyn Monroe's accidental overdose the previous year had made the topic a front-page story).

As part of its mandate, the Advisory Commission tackled the complicated issue of addiction. Scientists could not agree in the early 1960s about what qualified as drug addiction. There was a debate about differences between habituation, psychological, physiological, and physical dependence.[4] Adding to the challenge, only three of the prominent and well-connected directors had medical backgrounds.*[5]

---

*The commission's makeup demonstrated that political connections trumped the need for specialized scientific or medical knowledge. Elijah Barrett Prettyman, the chairman, was a respected federal judge. The other lay members were Henry Kimball, a powerful Michigan congressman; James Dumpson, New York City's first African American commissioner of welfare; and Austin MacCormick, a criminology professor. As for the three doctors, Rafael Sanchez-Ubeda was a general surgeon; James Dixon,

The commission's report was due sometime in November. Arthur Sackler and Roche knew it had gathered anecdotal information that Miltown and Librium might cause dependence. Few thought it had compiled enough evidence to make any firm conclusions about the so-called minor tranquilizers. Still, Sackler was on call in case the report included anything that needed to be rebutted about Roche's benzo.

Arthur hoped that the commission report might not be released until December, as he wanted to tend first to a personal matter. Sackler had devised a deal he wanted to make with New York's premier museum, the Metropolitan Museum of Art. It was common knowledge among New York art collectors and philanthropists that following the 1960–61 recession, the Metropolitan had a tough time raising money for a major renovation of its outdated galleries. Arthur had set a meeting with James Rorimer, the museum's director.

Sackler was not the type of mega-collector the Met usually courted. It concentrated on master Renaissance and Postimpressionist paintings and sculptures. The only museum to which Sackler had then given any of his artifacts was Phoenix's Art Museum a few months after it opened in 1959. His partial underwriting of a Laboratory of Art History and Archaeology at Columbia got him an appointment to an advisory panel in the art department. Sackler was conspicuously absent for any major grant to the nation's top museums, the Met, as well as its rivals, the Museum of Fine Arts in Boston, the Philadelphia Museum of Art, Chicago's Art Institute, and the Smithsonian and National Gallery in D.C.

The New York art world—dominated then by WASPs with patrician family ties that often traced their wealth to the Industrial Revolution—sneered at Sackler as a nouveau riche wannabe-patron. Robert Lehman, the banker who ran Lehman Brothers and himself a major art collector and contributor to the Metropolitan, considered the Met Trustees "an anti-Semitic club."[6] They noted Sackler had started assembling his Chinese antiquities in the late 1940s, when Asian art was out of style. The hard-line communist crackdown on arts and culture had tempered enthusiasm for the entire field.[7] A major reason the market for Chinese collectibles was depressed was not only that it was illegal for Ameri-

---

the president of the liberal arts Antioch College; and Roger Egeberg, a public health advocate and educator, was most famous for being General Douglas MacArthur's World War II doctor.

cans to do business with the mainland, but the communist leadership had banned all sales and exports to the West.[8] Sackler used middlemen to acquire the artifacts he secretly purchased in communist China and stored them at the German factory of Dr. Kade Pharmaceutical, the company Marietta had inherited.[9] * [10]

"To those who respected him, he was shrewd," said Thomas Hoving, later the director of the Met. "To those who detested him and his practices, he was slippery. And slippery was how he was regarded at the Met."[11] Maybe, some wondered, instead of possessing an intrinsic sense of style and culture, Sackler had chosen Asian art because he was a bargain hunter simply looking for the cheapest collectibles.[12] It was also well known among New York collectors that Arthur relied often on the advice of Dr. Paul Singer, a Hungarian-born, Vienna-schooled psychiatrist and self-taught Asian art authority.[13] He was the perfect complement to Arthur's focus on grand and much sought-after collectibles. Singer focused instead on rare, small archaeological objects found in digs throughout Asia and bypassed by dealers. He called them "the things that looters left behind."[14]

The two had psychiatric backgrounds and Judaism in common, and while neither had been to China nor spoke the language, they shared a passion for Chinese art.[15] Since 1957, when they first met, Sackler paid for the rent on Singer's Summit, New Jersey, apartment, a two-bedroom that was crammed floor to ceiling with antiques. Arthur also agreed to a monthly consulting fee as well as to secure off-site storage if Singer needed space for new acquisitions, all of which Sackler underwrote. The agreement allowed Singer to concentrate on hunting for artifacts without the pressures of fretting about how he might pay his monthly bills. Singer had no desire to display his collection in a museum, get a tax deduction, or see his name on a gallery that housed his collection. He agreed, meanwhile, that whatever he accumulated during his lifetime would pass to Sackler upon his death (when Singer died in 1997, his six-thousand-object collection was worth $60 million).[16]

Wen Fong, the chair of Princeton's Department of Art and Archae-

---

* Some Sino experts, such as the University of Washington's Roy Andrew Miller, thought "the highly questionable nature" of Sackler's acquisitions cast a pall over all of Sackler's Asian collectibles. Miller believed that if Sackler had tried to obtain "anything worth having" from the communist government, "they would never have allowed it to leave the country in the first place."

ology, and a consultant later to Sackler, wrote to a fellow art professor at Berkeley that Arthur's naked ambition meant he spent too little time on research and too much on simply accumulating.[17] "There's the danger of being tabbed as greedy or even vulgar," said the Met's Hoving.[18]

Notwithstanding the elitist snobbery that dismissed him as an unwanted interloper at the Met, Arthur wanted to put his plan into effect before he was consumed by defending Valium and Librium in the pending report from JFK's Advisory Commission on Narcotic and Drug Abuse. As far as Arthur was concerned, whatever the museum, any proposal from a potential donor was all about business. Did the museum want what he had to offer and what was it willing to give in return? The Met's financial pinch—the latest fundraising campaign had not even raised enough to complete its much needed air-conditioning—was a rare opportunity for Sackler to move from being a benefactor of second-tier museums like the Phoenix to becoming a patron at the fabled Metropolitan. He also knew that no matter how much the gossip inside the Met disparaged his collection, it was widely acknowledged that Far Eastern art was one of the museum's weakest holdings. "The Met sank enormous sums of money into Chinese paintings," said Professor Roy Andrew Miller, "that would have disgraced the collection of a chop suey shop."[19]

Earlier in the year the Sacklers had begun making contributions to the Met (1963 would be the first year they were listed in the museum's year-end published tribute titled "Donors and Lenders").* Sackler assured the Metropolitan's director, James Rorimer, that he was successfully encouraging unnamed professionals he knew to become Met donors for the first time. By reviewing the museum's annual published lists of "Donors and Lenders" since 1960, and then comparing the names to the corporate legal filings for the companies in which the Sacklers held overt or hidden interests, the author identified Sackler's "professionals." In 1963, the first time the Sacklers were listed, others in "Donors of Money & Securities" were Martin Greene, Myron J. Greene, and Louis Goldburt. Myron Greene was also a "Fel-

* The 1963 report for "Donors and Lenders" had "Dr. and Mrs. Arthur M. Sackler" and "Raymond Sackler" listed as having contributed an unspecified amount of "money and securities." Raymond was also under "Fellows in Perpetuity," which meant he had made a cash contribution of at least $5,000 to be included in an elite group of thirty-six donors.

low for Life" (minimum contribution of $5,000). All three were also on the 1964 compilation for gifts of "money and securities" and the Greenes were "Fellows in Perpetuity" (minimum of $20,000 each). Joining them was Lawrence Effman, an accountant who worked for Goldburt.[20]

The Brooklyn-born Greenes were brothers and attorneys who had represented the three Sackler brothers since 1947 when they incorporated the Sackler Foundation. They were listed as shareholders and directors of some early Sackler companies. Louis Goldburt, a Brooklyn-born accountant, together with Effman, did the payroll. Goldburt was also listed sometimes as a shareholder and he had helped conceal the Sacklers' ownership in the Washington Institute, the company to which Martí-Ibáñez and MD Publications paid $420,000 in annual consulting fees.[21] As for Effman, he was later listed on private ventures with Bill Frohlich and also served as a director for Frohlich's advertising agency.

It appears the Greenes, Goldburt, and Effman qualified for the Met's top-tier list by donating shares of privately held, Sackler-controlled companies. The Greenes, as attorneys, vouched for the legitimacy of the companies, and Goldburt and Effman, as the accountants, for the value of any gifted shares.[22] (The author was unable to determine whether the contributions were at inflated values—something that would have offset income for the Sackler companies while enhancing the family name at the Met—since the museum repeatedly refused the author's requests for details about the gifts).

Arthur knew, however, that money alone was not enough to get what he wanted from the Met. In his meeting with Rorimer, he spoke at length about his collection and how he envisioned it would be grander over time. They talked about a *New York Times* clipping from when Sackler had loaned some of his artifacts for the Columbia University exhibit.[23]

Having whet Rorimer's appetite, he moved to a new topic. Sackler surprised him by offering $150,000.[24] The money was for a complete renovation of a grand gallery on the second floor, just north of the Great Hall. The refurbished hall would house Chinese antiquities and be named the Arthur Sackler Gallery (in fifteen years it would be part of nine adjoining galleries under the Sackler Wing). Rorimer realized that Sackler had done his homework. The space he had selected had no formal name but was unofficially called the Rogers Hall. That was because most of the collectibles on display there had been acquired by the

Met as a result of one of its largest ever death bequests, $5 million in 1901 from railroad tycoon Jacob Rogers ($152 million in 2019). Rogers had directed the money be used for the "purchase of rare and desirable art objects and books for the library."[25] When banker J. P. Morgan became the Met's president three years later, he used the Rogers Fund to acquire a superb and diverse collection of Greek, Roman, and Egyptian antiquities; some Far Eastern objects; illuminated manuscripts; and seventeenth-century paintings by Dutch masters.[26]

Agreeing to naming rights for the $150,000 was the easy part. Sackler then raised another condition, one he considered creative and that struck Rorimer as unorthodox at best. Arthur had identified the Met's best Chinese sculptures and also a superb early wall painting. The museum had used the Rogers Fund to acquire them in the 1920s. Sackler insisted his entire gift depended on the Met selling him that art at the prices it had originally paid decades earlier. He would then "gift them back" to the museum. They would not even leave the Met. They would be displayed with the credit "Gifts of Arthur Sackler" instead of the existing "The Rogers Fund."[27] Rorimer did not take long to agree. He assured Arthur the museum would prepare quickly the paperwork for the "Dr. Arthur Sackler Gallery."[28] (Arthur later changed the credit on the great wall painting at the entrance to his gallery as a gift to the museum from his parents.)

It is not clear whether Rorimer knew that Sackler intended to take charitable tax deductions based on the current value of the fine artworks he bought from the Met. Thomas Hoving, the Met's future director, believed that Sackler "had figured that he would actually make money on the tax loophole he discovered—his deduction would be far more than the costs of the works and his donation."[29] Rorimer was desperate for the money and later complained to some colleagues the deal was "the biggest giveaway scandal in the history of the museum."[30]

Sackler came back later with a new request.[31] He let Rorimer know that in addition to the $150,000 bequest, the family was increasing its donations to the Met. Arthur and Marietta, as well as Sackler's first wife, Else, would qualify for inclusion as significant donors of "money and securities." "The Sackler Collection" would be listed as a "Lender of Objects of Art." And Arthur was on his way to be one of twenty-two "Benefactors," while Marietta and Else were separately listed as "Fellows in Perpetuity." Having laid the groundwork for the largesse, Arthur then presented his unusual idea. "He asked for a storeroom inside the museum to house his private collections, a rent-free space to which only he and his personal curator would have access," said Joseph Noble, the museum's administrative director.[32] In that enclave Sackler's curators would undertake the enormous task of cataloging the thousands of pieces in his collection.

Rorimer was initially hesitant but after a few days had decided it might benefit the Met as well as Sackler. The unprecedented arrangement might encourage Arthur to donate his Chinese collection one day to the Met. If Sackler's collection was stored at the museum, it would not be a great stretch to move it from that storeroom to permanent display in a Met gallery.[33] Arthur was noncommittal. He was smart enough, however, to say that if he could have the storeroom, everything was open to discussion.

The final deal involved a bit more than "a storeroom." It was about six hundred square feet of storage space that belonged to the Far East Department. The Met provided security and covered insurance and utilities expenses. At Sackler's request, the museum installed a telephone line that bypassed the main switchboard and rang only in that room. Remarkably, most of the museum's staff were unaware of the room's existence. It was not identified on charts or floorplans.[34]

The unusual concessions Sackler had won were legal, but somehow "shifty," according to Joseph Noble.[35] The general opinion of Sackler did not improve when he selected Lois Katz as his curator for his collection stored at the Met. Katz was an associate curator at the Brooklyn Museum's Department of Asian Art, having started there as an instructor in the Education Division.[36] Although she was well versed in Chinese bronzes, she was not a widely published Ivy League PhD, the background the Met relished. The Met directors were also not pleased when Sackler insisted that Paul Singer be the collection's "research fellow-consultant."[37]

Arthur Sackler wanted approval from institutions and businesses he respected. For the time being, however, he ignored the backbiting and chalked it up to jealousy. He had barely wrapped up the handshake agreement for the naming of the second-floor Sackler Gallery when the President's Advisory Commission released its final report on November 15, 1963. It contained an exhibit listing drugs "associated with physical dependence."[38] There was no surprise it included opiates, morphine, and barbiturates. The shocker was the inclusion of Miltown and Librium. The commission was so concerned about Librium and Miltown that it urged the creation of a special federal unit "to regulate . . . [such] dangerous drugs."[39] Adding to the confusion, the report classified amphetamines, cocaine, and marijuana as non-addictive.[40]

Roche and Sackler feared that listing Librium—the number one selling drug in America that year—as addictive and dangerous and riskier than cocaine and amphetamines was something that would receive widespread press coverage and spark considerable patient angst. A week after the report had been released, and while Roche and Sackler were finalizing a strategy for a public rebuttal, Lee Harvey Oswald assassinated President John Kennedy in Dallas. While the country reeled in shock and grief, there was a sliver of good news for Roche and Sackler: the report's damning conclusions about Librium got lost in the wake of JFK's murder.

21

TARGETING WOMEN

While Roche was relieved that few paid attention to the conclusions about Librium, internal memos reveal the company's senior executives correctly predicted that it was only the first volley in what would become a war between pharma and federal regulatory and narcotics agencies. The Advisory Commission Report kicked off a multiyear battle during which the federal government tried to rein in illicit drug use and prescription drug abuse. The following year, 1964, Connecticut senator Thomas Dodd introduced the Psychotoxic Drug Control Act, a sweeping bill aimed at beefing up the antidrug laws, the first such effort since the 1914 Harrison Act had banned opium imports.[1] To control the supply of barbiturates and amphetamines siphoned to the black market, Dodd's bill made it a crime if pharma firms, drug wholesalers, and pharmacists failed to maintain meticulous records of manufacturing, distribution, and sales. That was no small task given that the FDA estimated that the drug industry had churned out eight billion pills the previous year.[2] Dodd's bill would add law enforcement to the FDA's mission, with armed inspectors seizing illegal drugs and making arrests. (The Drug Enforcement Administration was created nine years later.)

Doctors and pharmacists opposed Dodd's bill, citing the onerous paperwork and raising concerns about the privacy of patient records. When a last-minute addition broadened the definition of drugs, pharma unleashed its full lobby.[3] Dodd's bill stalled. Congress did, nevertheless, pass the Drug Abuse Control Amendments the following year, expanding government authority to regulate barbiturates and amphetamines.[4] Although it gave the FDA the power to regulate any drug that had "a potential for abuse," the intensive pharmaceutical arm-twisting had succeeded in omitting any express mention of benzodiazepines.[5]

Advocates for the new law were concerned whether the FDA, which was already operating at full capacity, was capable of enforcing its new powers. In many instances, the agency seemed mostly reactive. Morale was low. The HEW secretary appointed an advisory committee tasked to make recommendations to reenergize the FDA. Named as chairman was James Goddard, a forty-two-year-old doctor with a master's in public health. Having joined the Public Health Service in 1951, Goddard had spearheaded federal research on the benefits of mandatory seat belts in autos. In 1962 he became the youngest chief ever of the Communicable Disease Center (the predecessor to the Centers for Disease Control and Prevention). He made no secret that he wanted to be surgeon general, so he accepted the role with the FDA advisory board on the understanding that it was temporary.[6]

Goddard thought that pharma had interpreted Commissioner Larrick's low-key regulatory approach as a sign of weakness. Drug companies made everything a battle on the assumption that Larrick would rather compromise than get into a nasty fight. That had happened with Larrick's much heralded August 1963 decertification of Achrocidin and other antibiotic combo cold remedy rivals. It faced vociferous opposition from pharma and the AMA's Council on Drugs. Larrick decided the battle was not worth the effort and withdrew the order.[7]

Incredibly, the FDA had not even begun the review required by the Kefauver Amendments of the efficacy of the four thousand pre-1962 medications still on sale to the public. The law had created a two-year waiting period between its enactment and when the FDA could start the review. That waiting period was intended to give the pharma firms the opportunity to do some testing and gather the data to convince the FDA that their early drugs were effective. No one in Congress had thought that the FDA would be too overwhelmed to fulfill its mandate under the Kefauver Amendments. Goddard was not sure how it could ever be taken seriously by the industry it was supposed to watch over. Instead of focusing, as Larrick had, on cooperating with other agencies on matters of public education and science, Goddard thought the FDA's top priority should be regulation.

As 1965 ended, Goddard's commission had assembled a long list of recommended reforms. Lyndon Johnson and the HEW secretary decided the most important change was who ran the FDA. George Larrick was out after eleven years and James Goddard was in, the first doctor in a generation and the first commissioner selected from outside the FDA.

Goddard decided to send a strong signal to the pharmaceutical industry that the change at the top of the FDA was substantive. The day after he took office, the agency announced formal hearings into whether Miltown and Equanil as well as Librium and Valium had a "potential for abuse." If they did, it would subject them to the strict controls in place on barbiturates and amphetamines.[8] Soon after Goddard's lightning directive, the contested administrative hearings got under way. Dozens of expert witnesses lined up by the government and the industry battled over what qualified as addiction. The lesson for Goddard was that few things were fast in the FDA bureaucracy. The hearings would drag on for years (Miltown and Equanil continued losing market share all that time to Roche's Librium and Valium).[9]

As part of his overall plan to recast the FDA as a more robust guardian of public health, Goddard also focused during his first weeks on the industry's runaway drug promotion. He was concerned that drug companies "trumpeted results of favorable research and have not mentioned unfavorable research; they have puffed up what was insignificant clinical evidence: they have substituted emotional appeals for scientific ones."[10] The FTC regulated medical ads before the Kefauver Amendments transferred this responsibility to the FDA. There were more than four million pages of ads annually just in medical journals.[11] Goddard knew the FDA did not have the resources to keep abreast of all of them. Still, he wanted to take early actions to at least emphasize to pharma that it was one of his priorities.

By the end of his first month he had gotten a "no contest" plea from Carter-Wallace in the FDA's first prosecution under the Kefauver provisions. It had advertised a combination drug, Pree MT, a mixture of Miltown and hydrochlorothiazide, a strong diuretic. In *JAMA* advertisements, the ad copy read, "Contraindications: None Known." In fact, the company knew its drug caused a sometimes fatal blood disease in addition to other side effects from gout to blood vessel constrictions. Carter-Wallace paid the maximum fine set by the new law, only $2,000.[12]

Encouraged by the Carter-Wallace plea, Goddard commenced

other "false advertising" cases. Merck and Wyeth had failed to report adverse effects causing temporary blindness in its animal testing of an experimental drug, DMSO, used as a preservative for transplants. Ciba was accused of having kept secret reports that demonstrated Elipten, its epilepsy drug, was responsible for masculinization of young girls. Merck, which had merged with Philadelphia-based Sharp & Dohme, hid "alarming" findings of breast cancer in four of six dogs on which it had experimented with a combination oral contraceptive.[13]

Another priority Goddard wanted to address was restricting how pharma targeted women for drugs that they often did not need.[14] It was an issue he became aware of a few years earlier when he ran the Communicable Disease Center. In 1963 he read Betty Friedan's *The Feminine Mystique*, a book credited as launching the second-wave feminist movement.[15] "Feminine mystique" was the notion—reinforced by everyone from Freudian psychoanalysts to Madison Avenue advertisers to women's magazines where the top editors were men—that women were fulfilled only as loving mothers and loyal, supportive housewives.[16] Friedan's best-selling book—it sold over a million copies—made a powerful case against the ingrained stereotype that those who wanted careers were neurotic and unhappy. What caught Goddard's attention was Friedan's conclusion that tens of millions of women were the ideal pharmaceutical customers because of boredom and lack of personal fulfillment.

"You wake up in the morning," Friedan wrote, "and feel as if there's no point in going on another day like this. So you take a tranquilizer because it makes you not care so much."[17]

Other feminist writers followed Friedan, furiously working to undo what they saw as centuries of societal distortion of female identity and diminution of self-worth.[18] American psychiatry, then dominated by Freudian-based psychoanalysts, got much of the blame. The writers condemned Sigmund Freud's theories as misogynistic, particularly his view that male was the norm and that fundamental differences with women were biological—"penis envy"—not the by-products of culture and environment.[19]

Goddard had studied the grim American medical history that had treated women differently than men when it came to ailments and care. Doctors in the eighteenth and nineteenth centuries believed women alone suffered from "treatable illnesses" of hysteria, nervousness, and excessive emotion.[20]* Physicians dispensed powerful sedatives. If those did not work, over twenty states allowed a husband to commit his wife to a mental asylum without a hearing.[21] A step beyond institutionalization was lobotomy. Nearly two thirds of all lobotomies in the U.S. were performed on women.[22] In the late 1940s and early 1950s, when lobotomies reached their zenith, the vast majority of patients were former housewives or living-at-home unmarried daughters.[23]

Goddard's interest in whether modern pharma had targeted and typecast women was perfectly timed. His arrival at the FDA coincided with Valium becoming America's top selling drug. Most of the customers for the hit tranquilizers were women.[24] That was no mistake. In the case of Valium and Librium, it was the strategy and skilled handiwork of Arthur Sackler. Arthur, as were his two brothers, was a Freudian-based psychiatrist.[25] Roche recognized that Sackler had an advantage over his lay Medicine Avenue competitors. As a doctor who had stayed active in laboratory trials and writing for scientific journals, he provided a unique perspective on how to best market drugs to other physicians.

How and why doctors should prescribe tranquilizers differently to men and women is laid out in an extraordinary eighty-page hardcover book, *Aspects of Anxiety*, that Roche sent to nearly ten thousand of the top prescribing physicians in the U.S. in 1965.[26] *Aspects of Anxiety* was Arthur's brainchild. No drug company had ever produced anything like it. There were twelve short chapters that laid out the different causes of anxiety and its physical and psychological toll. Produced on fine paper and with eye-catching charts and graphs, it was not only intended as a quick reference for doctors, but as a collectible to display in their offices.

Sackler had the idea when Librium was the only Roche benzo on the market. Roche had released Valium by the time it was published. It was too late to change the thrust of its focus on Librium, but Sackler thought it still a valuable doctor's guide for understanding anxiety and especially for directing them to Roche's benzodiazepines as the best treatment for most patients. A clever marketing ploy disguised as

---

* The word "hysteria" is from *hysterika*, Greek for "uterus." Ancient Greeks believed that an unhappy and "wandering uterus" led to uniquely female afflictions, and that concept persisted through the centuries and had become an accepted tenet of Western medicine.

an "informational tool," it sidestepped all FDA and FTC regulations.[27] Sackler convinced Professor Charles Henry Hardin Branch, the president of the American Psychiatric Association, to write the preface (they had met in 1953 while separately researching endocrine psychiatry and possible treatments for depression; both published medical journal articles about their parallel research the following year).[28]

Roche did not identify the author of *Aspects of Anxiety* but Sackler's handiwork is evident throughout.[29] The book was a combination of detailed medical and psychological jargon mixed with breezy passages that today seem a rudimentary *Men Are from Mars, Women Are from Venus* worldview.

Both sexes shared plenty of common worries and stress from major life events. However, the pressure on men—dubbed "executive neurosis"—was caused by the expectation that they had to be breadwinners for their families without showing any of the stress that led to ulcers and high blood pressure. Similar intense pressure on women did not morph into any organic illness but instead produced behavioral disorders such as neurosis, hysteria, anxiety, and depression.[30] * [31]

In a chapter titled "Anxiety and the Female Psyche," *Aspects of Anxiety* presented why women are prone to an "unstable emotional equilibrium" uniquely female. "In its most severe form, premenstrual tension may be characterized by panic states, suicidal tendencies and psychotic decisional episodes." Those who suffered from menstrual cramps often had "a low pain threshold . . . [and] this hypersensitivity increases their anxious anticipation." As women age, "menopause does represent deep psychological trauma, for the badge of femininity—menstruation—is now irretrievably lost." The feminist encouragement for women to get

* Sackler thought a series of Army experiments provided evidence to not only back his theory that untreated stress and anxiety caused organic diseases, but the resulting illnesses were different for each sex. The Walter Reed Army Institute of Research had conducted two years of experiments in the mid-1950s with hundreds of monkeys. In one series dubbed the "executive monkey trial," two monkeys were strapped into adjacent "restraining chairs," metal and glass contraptions that allowed limited movement only of their heads and arms. Electrodes attached to their feet delivered sharp electric jolts every twenty seconds. A lever situated next to one of the monkeys shielded both from the shocks when pressed. The "executive monkey" was the one with the responsibility to operate the lever in order to forestall the electric shocks. Every time the experiment was run, autopsies later revealed the executive monkeys developed acute intestinal and stomach ulcers while the control monkeys did not. The executive monkeys demonstrated what stress could do to men, Sackler and his colleagues concluded.

jobs outside their homes would "bring about an even greater denial of her biologic female role (childbearing and child-care contributions to society)." In fact, "numerous studies discuss the higher incidence of disorders in women who repudiate their roles as wives [and] mothers."[32]

Sackler and Roche cited eighty controlled studies and 162 clinical trials to encourage physicians to dispense Librium liberally for their patients reporting "anxiety and tension" as well as those complaining of everything from tension headaches, acne (evidence, said Roche, of a hormonal response to stress), gastrointestinal and cardiac problems, "behavior disorders in children," and "gynecologic, including premenstrual disorders."[33] *Aspects of Anxiety* made a shameless pitch toward male doctors—who then composed 95 percent of all American physicians—when it addressed premenstrual tension. "It has been said it is a condition known to many women but perhaps even better known to their husbands and children—victims of monthly personality change."[34]

Sackler and Roche were not the first pharma/advertiser combination to play on female typecasting in marketing a drug. Ads for phenobarbital, the 1960s best-selling generic barbiturate, featured always some slight variation of a harried housewife. One featured a woman screaming at her daughter, another was exhausted from mopping the floor, and still another at her breaking point toiling over a stove.[35] Amphetamine ads, meanwhile, emphasized that since women had to raise the couple's children, keep the house tidy, and cook dinner for their hardworking spouse, they might need a pharmaceutical jolt of energy to do all that and still be attentive to their husband's needs (sex was always implied, never directly addressed). Moreover, pharma added an inducement: speed might help keep them thin.

What differentiated Sackler's promotion of Librium, and especially of Valium, was it repackaged the same sexual stereotypes but in a sleeker and ostensibly smarter pitch. Flipping through medical journals in the 1960s, it seemed that for any man who was a driven overachiever, an ulcer was a casualty of success. Roche's benzos could tame the stress that was the culprit. Valium ads featured men from the worlds of business, sports, and entertainment, all telling their success stories. A typical one: "Have you heard the one about the traveling salesman? The strain of tracking down customers and living out of a suitcase—the family matters left unsolved at home—no joking matter to a man emotionally overreactive to stress and vulnerable to duodenitis [ulcers]." In this way Sackler pitched Valium as simply another indispensable tool for savvy businessmen on the way up.[36]

As for women, they were cast as responding to stress with emotional outbursts that took a gloomy toll on their own mental health as well as that of their husbands and children. Sackler therefore promoted Valium as pretty much an all-around female "fix." Roche ads encouraged doctors to prescribe Valium for exhausted moms, bored housewives, still-hoping-to-be-married single women over thirty, those moody and irritable during their menstrual cycle, and any depressed or anxious during menopause. Valium could tame the "unpredictable grouch," said one Sackler ad. For a "35, single and psychoneurotic" fictional spinster Sackler created, Valium alleviated her "alienation and hostility" and "neurotic sense of failure." It would also treat the depair of a "childless widow."[37]

Sackler's Valium campaign worked at every level. Through the 1960s, as sales boomed annually and set industry records, the drug was twice as likely to be dispensed to women than men.[38] Women got 63 percent of barbiturates, 68 percent of all antianxiety meds, 71 percent of the first generation of antidepressants, and 80 percent of all amphetamines.[39]

At that same time Roche and other pharma companies targeted women with psychotropics, Robert Wilson, a gynecologist colleague of the three Sackler brothers, was about to help make a hormone drug a blockbuster. Instead of playing to the subconscious biases of male physicians by emphasizing the emotional and fragile psyche of women, Wilson exploited their fears about losing their femininity and sexuality as they aged. Like the Sacklers, Wilson was born in Brooklyn and later moved his family and practice to Manhattan. The product he was tapped to sell was Premarin, made from the estrogen-loaded urine of pregnant horses (the brand name, approved by the FDA in 1942 to treat menopausal symptoms, is short for PREgnant MARes' urINe). Premarin was developed by a Canadian pharmaceutical firm, Ayerst, McKenna & Harrison. American Home Products (AHP) bought the company in 1943 and changed its name to Ayerst Laboratories.[40] In addition to his gynecological practice, Wilson got $1.3 million in the 1960s from Ayerst and other drug companies to conduct clinical studies on hormones and contraceptives.[41]

Bill Frohlich, Sackler's Medicine Avenue colleague and sometimes silent business partner, promoted many of the drugs for AHP's two drug subsidiaries, Ayerst and Wyeth. The company had much bigger plans for Wilson than having him offer a rave testimonial about Premarin in one of Frohlich's ads. Ayerst and Wilson had concocted a secret plan that Arthur Sackler would later acknowledge was an inspired way of circumventing the FDA's prohibition on direct-to-consumer advertising. Wilson had written several articles for medical journals extolling estrogen to offset bone loss and protect the heart during menopause.[42] In an expansive piece in 1962 in the *Journal of the American Medical Association*, his opening line read, "There is no convincing proof that estrogen has ever induced cancer in the human being." In that same article he became the first doctor to contend that estrogen actually *reduced* the incidence of cervical and breast cancers.[43]

In 1966, the same year that Goddard became FDA commissioner, Wilson published a book, *Feminine Forever*. Its cover proclaimed it as "one of medicine's most revolutionary breakthroughs": that "menopause is a hormone deficiency disease, curable and totally preventable. . . . And every woman, no matter what her age, can safely live a fully-sexed life for her entire life."[44]

No one knew that Ayerst had subsidized *Feminine Forever*, paid all Wilson's expenses, and even underwrote his national publicity tour.[45] It was decades before one of Wilson's sons disclosed the full extent to which pharma firms bought his father's endorsement. They paid for his Park Avenue office and eponymously named research foundation, as well as subsidizing his lectures to doctors' and women's groups.[46] Searle and Upjohn, both of which had their own hormone brands, paid him "consultation fees" so he would plug their products.

Sackler had already medicalized the best-known symptoms of menopause. Millions of women popped lots of Librium and Valium to keep hot flashes at bay, combat the blues, and fix disturbed sleep patterns. Roche's book, *Aspects of Anxiety*, sent the previous year to ten thousand doctors, had become the bible for physicians looking for any of a dozen reasons to dispense benzos. Those drugs, however, could not address some of the purely physical changes that many women experienced during menopause, including vaginal dryness, thinning hair, decreased muscle tone, dry skin, and loss of sexual desire.

Wilson zeroed in on a passage in every woman's life that he warned would turn them into nothing more than "the equivalent of a eunuch." He eschewed subtlety for dramatic overstatement. Menopause was a "living decay," he wrote, in which women were "desexed" and "dull-minded."[47] It was "a galloping catastrophe" for women fifty and older. Not only were women the "only mammal who cannot reproduce after middle age," Wilson ticked off a depressing list of twenty-six "debilitating symptoms" that left unmedicated menopausal women as "docile creatures missing life's values," allowing them only to "exist rather than live."

Wilson wrote that he had witnessed his own mother change through menopause from "a vital, wonderful woman who had been the focal point of our family into a pain-racked petulant invalid." He was not, however, all doom and gloom. He reported that one of his patients, a fifty-two-year-old unnamed woman, had started taking a "precious gift," Premarin. When he examined her two months later, she appeared much younger and more vibrant.

As presented in *Feminine Forever*, Wilson medicalized not only menopause but female aging as well. Premarin was a fountain of youth in a one-a-day pill. "Breasts and genital organs will not shrivel. Such women will be much more pleasant to live with and will not become dull and unattractive. . . . What is really at stake is a subtle and almost metaphysical factor—a woman's total femininity." As Wilson repeatedly emphasized, women were not introducing a new medication to their body but rather replacing a hormone that evolution had somehow forgotten to make last longer.[48] Wilson's pitch, as *The New York Times* described it, was that "women would be replacing a hormone they had lost at menopause just as diabetics replace the insulin their pancreas fails to make."[49]

Look and *Vogue* serialized *Feminine Forever*. It sold 100,000 copies in the first three months.[50] Other women's lifestyle magazines, some of which now dubbed estrogen the "Youth Pill," wrote glowingly about it.[51] *Feminine Forever* went from simply another "medical book about menopause" to a runaway best-seller in seventeen countries.[52]

Wilson's *Feminine Forever* created a huge demand for Premarin because women asked their doctors for it. That demand was fed by subsequent publications. One, *After Forty*, was an ode to estrogen written by Sondra Gorney, an actress and public relations executive. As it did for Wilson, Ayerst paid for her services, employing Gorney through a New York City front organization, the Information Center on the Mature Woman.[53]

The same year *Feminine Forever* was published, Goddard labeled Wilson an "unacceptable investigator" and took the rare step of barring him from undertaking any subsequent hormonal research.[54] That prompted his New York publisher to get in touch with the FDA to determine if *Feminine Forever* violated any federal regulations. Since the book recommended specific drugs for conditions for which they were not approved, the FDA said, the only limitation was that if the book was sold in drugstores, it could not be tied in to a promotion or made part of a sale of any prescription medication.[55] Goddard's frustration was that the FDA did not have any other way to curtail how Wilson marketed his book.

The problem with the entire estrogen revolution kicked off by *Feminine Forever* was that Wilson was wrong. Few suspected it, however. A New York cancer researcher, Saul Gusberg, sounded an early warning: "A human experiment has been set up in recent years by the widespread administration of estrogens to postmenopausal women."[56] When he was at Columbia in the late 1940s, Gusberg was alarmed to discover twenty-nine women taking estrogen pills had uterine cellular overgrowth and nine subsequently developed cancer. He suspected that estrogen might have been the culprit.

Gusberg's warnings were never covered in the mainstream press. In the meantime, Wyeth and Robert Wilson helped the market for menopausal hormones take off. In the decade after the publication of *Feminine Forever*, estrogen prescriptions tripled to over 30 million annually and the average brand name price doubled.[57] Premarin set company sales records. It accounted for 75–80 percent of the prescription estrogen market.[58] It was by far the firm's biggest profit maker. As Ayerst celebrated, Gusberg warned colleagues all the dosing could cause an explosive growth in cancer. Premarin and other estrogen drugs were a ticking time bomb, he predicted.[59] Few were listening.

22

DEATH WITH DIGNITY

While Goddard looked for ways the FDA could better regulate the approval and marketing of medications, a public debate played out in the United Kingdom about whether terminally ill cancer patients should have a say about their end-of-life care. Should they have a right to doctor-assisted suicide? Euthanasia was illegal in all European countries (the Netherlands was the first to legalize it in 2000).[1] A national reassessment would not get under way in the U.S. until the 1969 publication of Dr. Elisabeth Kübler-Ross's seminal book *On Death and Dying*.[2]

The policy debate in Britain, however, would change the way the Western world approached care for the dying. Cicely Saunders, an Oxford-educated nurse turned physician, spearheaded the drive for humane treatment of patients with end-stage cancer. She chanced upon a British drug company that had recently been acquired by the Sackler brothers. The ensuing debate sparked a partial reassessment about the use of opioids in controlling pain and the rights of the terminally ill to insist on treatment. What emerged was a concept of "death with dignity," leading to the birth of the modern hospice movement.

Saunders is justifiably credited as almost single-handedly introducing the rights of the dying. As a London nurse during the 1940s she became convinced there had to be a better way than the "wretched habits of big, busy hospitals where everyone tiptoes past the bed and the dying soon learn to pretend to be asleep." There she witnessed the prevailing medical ethos that focused only on healing patients. Those who were terminally ill and could not be cured were considered a sign of failure. Saunders was stunned when doctors repeatedly lied to terminally ill patients, withholding any information about their grim prognoses. Few questioned their physicians.[3]

In 1948, when she was thirty, Saunders had qualified as a medical social worker. Shortly after that she met a forty-year-old Polish-Jewish refugee who had escaped from the Warsaw Ghetto. He was dying of cancer.[4] In the terrible final weeks of his life in Whittington Hospital's cancer ward, the two formed a bond, something she described to friends as a deep, spiritual love. His death sent her spiraling into a "pathological grief." She found solace in a newfound belief that God had called her to care for the dying.

Over the next few years, Saunders tended to the dying at a north London hospital. One night she told a surgeon about her dream to open a home for the terminally ill, a place where medical knowledge would combine with compassion and love. He told her that neither patients nor doctors would listen to her. As a mere nurse she had no status in the rigid, hierarchical British medical community.

"Very well then," she told him, "I will become a doctor."[5]

Saunders worked her way through medical school over five years and earned her degree in 1957. She accepted a scholarship to study pain management in the pharmacology department at London's St. Mary's Medical School.[6] She also volunteered as an almoner at St. Joseph's, a Catholic-run clinic where forty-five beds were set aside for cancer patients whose prognoses were less than three months to live.[7] Saunders kept a journal of her observations. All the patients were in severe pain and she thought they were unnecessarily suffering. In conversations with them she discovered that the vicious cycle of such agony was debilitating fear, anxiety, and hopelessness. Untreated pain, she concluded, was the cause of all chronic end-of-life symptoms, including deep depression.

Fears about opioid addiction meant that her colleagues sparingly dispensed painkillers.[8] They provided at the most only four hours of relief. Instead of giving an additional dose when a patient complained about returning pain, doctors invariably wrote "p.r.n." on the charts, for the Latin *pro re nata*, "as required." Second doses the same day were rare.

She told the nurses in her ward that "constant pain calls for constant control . . . and the regular giving of drugs." According to Saunders, if a patient cried out from discomfort because the last painkiller had worn off, the nurses had failed in their treatment.[9]

She met stiff resistance from doctors at St. Mary's, leading her to conclude there was no intractable pain, only intractable physicians.

She did, however, make headway at St. Joseph's by emphasizing how her concept of aggressively treating patients' pain might be complementary with steadfast Catholic opposition to euthanasia. Saunders contended that "requests to end life are nearly always requests to end pain" and by relieving their physical discomfort and mental stress, patients would stop thinking about ending their own lives.[10] Another side benefit, she said, was that if patients no longer had to ask constantly for more medication, they were less dependent on the staff and that freed the nurses to attend to other care.[11] The St. Joseph's administration quietly approved her approach to see whether it worked as she expected.[12]

The narcotic most effective at alleviating severe pain was Heroin (diamorphine). She discovered that accidentally. Among the first five hundred patients she treated with her protocols at St. Joseph's, forty-two reacted badly to morphine.[13] They received heroin instead. "No other drug makes these patients look and feel so comfortable," she wrote. "In the doses we use, it does not cause changes in personality, frank euphoria or a 'could not care less' attitude, but it helps greatly towards our aim of keeping the patients feeling as well as possible for as long as possible."[14]

Saunders concluded that opioids were not nearly as addictive as doctors feared.[15] "Patients may indeed be physically dependent on the drugs but tolerance and addiction are not problems to us, even with those who stay longest." And she startled many physicians with the finding: "We have not found that diamorphine [heroin] has a greater tendency to cause addiction than any other similar drug. . . . We have several patients in the wards at the moment who have come off completely without any withdrawal symptoms."[16]

Saunders reported that for some patients the quality of life improved immeasurably. Several at St. Joseph's had demonstrated such "startling improvements," she wrote to the Royal Society, that they were "able to return for further palliative treatment or go home for a while."[17]

Heroin's major "drawback," in her view, was that "it may be rather short in action." She tried correcting that by increasing the doses. Instead of providing longer pain relief the higher doses only created more side effects. By trial and error, she learned it was better to add sedatives and tranquilizers. She also sometimes used a so-called Brompton cocktail, a mix of cocaine, gin, and Thorazine.[18]

Some physicians feared that her heavy narcotic regimen would turn her terminally ill patients into sedated zombies. Instead, it allowed some to briefly "come alive." The renewed vigor and mental clarity lasted from a few hours to several days or even weeks.

By 1959 she had completed a ten-page proposal for a sixty-bed hospice. It was a cloistral institution that she initially considered restricting to only Anglican patients. Although her concept was different from anything else that existed, it also adhered to the traditional British medical view that even end-of-life patients required treatments proven best by scientific researchers.

Saunders registered a charity in 1961 and began raising money the following year. She proved to be an indefatigable fundraiser, flying to America to lobby humanist organizations and the Ford Foundation, as well as crisscrossing England in search of contributions. At times she seemed a one-person movement for the incipient hospice crusade. She had by then written half a dozen articles on pain management in *Nursing Times*. It made her the national face for compassionate end-of-life care. By 1965, she had raised a remarkable £380,000 ($868,000 in 1965). It was enough to break ground on a South London location.[19] That was the same year Queen Elizabeth awarded her the honor of an OBE (Officer of the Most Excellent Order of the British Empire).[20]

St. Christopher's, the world's first modern hospice, opened with fifty-four beds in 1967. It did not look like a last stop for terminally ill patients. Its airy and open design instead resembled a quiet home in the countryside. It featured a large gathering room for families, a communal dining hall, and even a nursery for the children of staff members.

As its medical director, Cicely Saunders had total control over her palliative care research with patients. The hospice presented her an opportunity to test her observation about heroin's superiority as a pain reliever.[21] She invited another physician and researcher, Robert Twycross, to conduct a clinical study. Half the St. Christopher's patients got heroin while the others received morphine. Because of the high turnover rate in the hospice, in just over two years the study included seven hundred patients. The results demonstrated no significant difference between the painkillers.[22] The findings put Saunders on a mission to find a better painkiller than heroin or morphine. She wanted an analgesic that alleviated pain for a long period on a single dose with few side effects.

The year before St. Christopher's had opened, Arthur, Mortimer, and Raymond Sackler bought Cambridge-based H. R. Napp Pharmaceuticals. Napp, founded in 1923 by a Swiss chemist and pharmacist, had suffered several years of heavy losses from a slowing British economy and its own lackluster product line.[23] Napp's poor finances allowed the Sacklers to gain control at what Mortimer later bragged was a bargain.[24] The Sacklers had created Mundipharma in London eleven years earlier but had operated it only as a drug distributor with a sister Mundipharma in Switzerland. With the purchase of Napp, the brothers hoped to develop their foreign business in earnest. Mortimer soon bought a grand apartment in one of London's most fashionable neighborhoods in order to spend more time overseeing the turnaround they planned.[25]

They renamed the company Napp Pharmaceutical Group Limited. A couple of months later the brothers bought Scottish-based Bard Pharmaceuticals Co. (the same name as the drug company they had created in New York in 1955). They reconfigured Bard to serve as Napp's "Production and Supply Chain and Quality Division." Considering how little Napp had to sell, it was a sign of the ambitious plans the Sacklers had for their United Kingdom operations.[26]*

A small British drug company, Smith & Nephew Pharmaceuticals, had provided the morphine and heroin for the St. Christopher's trials. Original correspondence located in the archives of King's College, London, sets forth the efforts of Saunders and Smith & Nephew to find a better narcotic analgesic.[27] They collaborated with Saunders on developing questionnaires to distribute to hospice patients to judge the effect of different pain meds.[28] Smith & Nephew also prepared a more

---

*In the U.K., the Sacklers created the same complex business network as they had in the U.S. The author relied on public documents to unravel their labyrinth. They formed similar-sounding companies, often at the same addresses, and used them in related pharmaceutical endeavors. In the case of Napp, for example, some of the firms the Sacklers opened with only a slight modification of the original name include Napp Research Center Limited, Napp Pharmaceutical Holdings Limited, Napp Pharmaceuticals Ltd., and Napp Laboratories Ltd. (U.K.); Napp Chemicals Inc., and Napp Technologies (U.S.); and Napp Limited and Napp Company Ltd. (Thailand). As for Bard, future iterations included Bard Pharmaceuticals Ltd. (U.K.); Bard Pharmaceuticals Ltd. and Bard Pharmaceuticals Inc. (Canada); Bard Pharmaceuticals LLC and Bard Pharmaceuticals Inc, succeeded by Ikuwa Holdings Inc (U.S.). The Sacklers at times created new corporations with different names, passing the shares in a manner that made it difficult to follow the line of ownership. Napp Chemicals Inc., a Delaware corporation formed in 1970, for instance, did business in New Jersey as 195-203 Pine Products, then Lemke Chemicals, next it was Napp-Lodi Inc., then, finally, Napp Chemicals before subsequently changing to Napp Technologies Inc. In New York, Napp Chemicals instead became Purdue Pharma Technologies Inc.

extensive survey for physicians. It sought their input about how they diagnosed and treated pain.[29] Saunders pressed for questions that went beyond asking whether specific medications relieved a patient's physical pain. She wanted to know if the treatments affected the "mental stress and emotional problems of patients and relatives."[30] In the final questionnaire sent to 26,000 U.K. doctors, the survey included some rudimentary questions about the "morale" of both patients and their relatives.[31]

One of the major obstacles any company then faced in developing a more effective narcotic analgesic was the ignorance about how opioids relieved pain. It would be another six years (1973) before researchers discovered that opioids attached to several brain receptors.[32] It took until 1975 before scientists learned that some brain receptors produced natural opioids (endorphin and enkephalin) that blocked pain, slowed breathing, and had a calming effect. Their production was so limited, however, they were incapable of providing relief for moderate to severe chronic pain.[33] Synthetic opiates are initially effective because they fool the brain to recognize them as natural neurotransmitters. They attach to nerve cells and flood the brain with dopamine, producing the euphoria some patients describe. There is often nearly complete pain relief. At least until the pain receptors get accustomed to opioid and dopamine saturation. Continued exposure to opiates causes the receptors to start misfiring; the only way to make up for that is increasing the dose. When the drug therapy stops, the receptors are incapable of producing natural painkillers. Pain becomes intense. And patients crave that pleasurable zone opioids create. That was why, researchers speculated, it was addictive (the same sensations and cycle of abuse as with nicotine, alcohol, and cocaine).[34]

How and why opioids worked inside the body, however, were of less concern to Smith & Nephew than what the effect was on terminally ill patients in severe pain. Their focus was on providing enough narcotic in a single dose to alleviate the intensity of pain without causing sleepiness, motor coordination problems, and memory lapses. As important as getting the strength right, they hoped to be able to make each dose last longer.

Correspondence shows the company tried but failed to develop an analgesic that accomplished what Saunders wanted for her hospice patients. Instead of admitting outright failure, they dusted off a drug they had developed in 1960, Narphen. Smith & Nephew claimed it was three to ten times more powerful than morphine.* [35] When they had originally marketed it, the sales pitch was not only that it was powerful, but that it "has fewer and less serious side-effects than morphine . . . quicker acting and longer lasting . . . [and] less physical dependence." [36] Narphen's active ingredient was phenazocine, a synthetic opioid licensed from Sterling Drugs in the U.S. (the FDA did not approve it for sale in America until 1967).[37]

The year that Cicely Saunders opened St. Christopher's, the reports of a double-blind hospital study of Narphen showed it did provide fast and adequate mild to moderate pain relief with no reports of nausea or vomiting (one of the most persistent problems with morphine). It did, unfortunately, equal or surpass morphine's dangerous suppression of a patient's respiratory system.[38] There were also soon reports rebutting Narphen's claim it was not addictive.[39]

Smith & Nephew might have failed to develop a better end-of-life painkiller but that did not stop them from using the information they gleaned from their postal surveys to create a clever marketing campaign for Narphen. The company ran full-page ads with the trademarked tagline "Powerful Analgesic Without Sedative Effect" in *The British Medical Journal*, the *Lancet*, and other premier U.K. medical publications. The ads were tweaked to reach different markets of prescribing doctors by addressing the top concerns the physicians had listed in the pain surveys.[40]

Saunders thought Narphen was a decent enough painkiller, but it was certainly not the end-of-life pain treatment breakthrough for which she had hoped. That became ever more evident as Smith & Nephew promoted their drug for use "in emergencies, after accidents, and in orthopaedic and cardiac emergencies"; "as an adjunct to an-

---

* Pharmaceutical companies and government agencies (the CDC and FDA) often use morphine as the base drug by which to measure the strength of other narcotic painkillers. The comparisons are difficult since the therapeutic effects of the drugs vary widely depending on how quickly individuals metabolize them. Some are available only as pills while others are by injection, intravenous, or transdermal patch. Codeine is universally ranked as weaker than morphine; however, it can vary between one tenth to one third the strength for an equivalent dose. Hydrocodone is roughly the equivalent of morphine, but it is seldom as effective at pain relief. It is almost always prescribed as a pill with a nonopioid like acetaminophen. Limits on the amount of the nonopioid (no more than 3,000 mg daily for acetaminophen) restrict the amount of hydrocodone that can be prescribed. Oxycodone is one and a half to two times stronger than morphine, while heroin is three to five times more powerful.

aesthetics"; for "post-operative pain and restlessness"; and even for "obstetrics . . . reduces pain and apprehension during labor without interfering with uterine contraction."[41]

Inside the small world of independent British pharmaceutical companies, news spread that Saunders wanted a new medication that revolutionized pain control. It was the only way her patients might have a decent chance of spending their final days at home. When Mortimer Sackler learned about her quest, he assured Saunders that Napp had the scientific capability and know-how to develop the narcotic analgesic she wanted.[42] Mortimer and Napp's top executives did not know whether they could deliver on that bold promise. Still, they wanted to at least have a chance to do so; Smith & Nephew's stumble handed the Sacklers an opportunity they did not want to pass up. It was not long before Saunders and scientists at the newly configured Napp were exchanging ideas by mail and over the phone. The breakthrough at Napp, and its subsidiary Bard, was several years away. When it happened, however, it not only fulfilled the Sacklers' promise to revolutionize pain care for the terminally ill, but unwittingly provided the technology that would later fuel America's opioid crisis.

23

"GO-GO GODDARD"

While the debate in Britain was about end-of-life care, in the U.S., FDA commissioner James Goddard caused angst among the nation's big tobacco companies as he tried expanding his agency's authority to regulate their product. The surgeon general's report warning that smoking caused lung cancer had been released only eighteen months earlier (January 1964). In a country where 40 percent of adults were regular smokers, Congress had responded only by requiring that all cigarette packs include a generic warning label.[1] As with alcohol before Prohibition, lawmakers were reticent to do anything that might too severely crimp the huge tobacco tax revenues. They added more than $8 billion annually to the federal government, about 6 percent of its entire budget (another $3 billion went to states and cities with their own cigarette taxes).[2] Goddard contended the FDA should have jurisdiction over cigarettes since they had become a health issue. But without the science that unequivocally established nicotine's addictiveness, he could not make a winning case (it took forty-four years before the FDA got the authority to regulate tobacco).[3]

Although he failed to get control of tobacco, he cited it in staff meetings as proof of his intent to put an end to what he called the FDA's era of subservience. The agency had all the legal powers it needed, he said, but time and again had failed to use them. FDA general counsel William Goodrich thought Goddard was dramatically different from his predecessors. He was "very gung-ho," inspired by "the public interest movement," and "prepared to beat on the [pharma] industry."[4]

Word soon spread in Washington about the fiery new commissioner. *The New York Times* described him as "a wild-eyed crusader with a battle-ax flailing boldly."[5] Inside the agency his staff dubbed him "Go-Go Goddard."[6]

Goddard was not satisfied merely with picking a fight with the tobacco industry or with Roche and its blockbuster benzos. A few months into his tenure he delivered an unprecedented broadside to the Pharmaceutical Manufacturers Association, the industry's leading trade group, at its annual convention.

"Too many drug manufacturers," he said, "have obscured the prime mission of their industry: to help people get well."[7] While he was not against profits, he warned that the companies should stop trying "to slip something by us" in new drug filings. During his brief FDA tenure, he had been "shocked" at how many drug applications were shoddy and unprofessional. He promised to personally ensure that "amateur and unprofessional" submissions would be rejected. The FDA would no longer tolerate the "constant, direct, [and] personal pressure" the firms had long exerted on the review division.[8]

Goddard's frank and adversarial tone stunned those at the Pharmaceutical Manufacturers Association. He had cherry-picked a few bad examples, they contended, in order to smear the entire industry. Most left the convention convinced that Goddard was bad for business. They were abuzz about his final warning: if the industry did not try to resolve the problems he raised, pharma would be "altered beyond your present fear."[9]

Goddard turned out to be as much action as he was talk. Upon returning to Washington, he restarted his predecessor's recall of antibiotic combination cold remedies. Soon, the FDA expanded the number of drugs it wanted off the market from several dozen to 300.[10] Pharma got another jolt when Goddard created the Scientific Investigations Staff to examine "the work of clinical investigators suspected of performing improper research."[11] Adding to the industry's angst, he promoted Frances Kelsey, whom he considered "a sacred cow" for her role in preventing the sale of thalidomide in the U.S., to become the division's first director. And Goddard put a fright into pharma when he proposed that new drugs should be tested in clinical trials against meds in the same category that were already on the market. He contended that could ensure new medications were better than what was available already.

He did not get everything on his wish list. Drug companies quickly blocked his idea of testing new versus old drugs. Proving efficacy was enough of a hurdle for them to satisfy.[12] He was also frustrated he could not hold medical journals legally responsible if they ran drug ads that later turned out to be misleading.[13] *JAMA* had published an article citing thirty-five cases of birth defects from a Parke-Davis drug, and subsequently ran three months of advertisements that did not mention that (the ads were the handiwork of Bill Frohlich).[14]

And he failed to require clinical researchers to obtain detailed signed consent forms from all drug trial participants. It had been included in a draft of the Kefauver Amendments but deleted before it became law. Pharma had protested that full disclosure of all risks in experimental trials would frighten volunteers. Goddard's interest was because of a scandal eighteen months earlier. It concerned whether full disclosure had been made to hundreds of patients, most with cancer, who had been injected with live cancer cells to check immune response to new tumors.[15] The research was no secret. A team of cancer specialists, led by a leading authority, Dr. Chester Southam, had conducted the work for a decade at New York's prestigious Sloan Kettering. Many researchers on the team had given lectures or led symposiums about their work, and their results had been published over the years in eighteen peer-reviewed medical journals.[16] Beyond those patients at Sloan Kettering, the team had injected live cancer cells into patients at New York's Memorial Hospital, Brooklyn's Jewish Chronic Disease Hospital, and inmates who had apparently volunteered at Ohio State Penitentiary. What put the research on the front pages of the New York papers was that three doctors at the Jewish Chronic Disease Hospital refused to participate when they discovered that the informed consent form signed by the patients did not disclose that the injections contained live malignant cancer cells. Nor did it include anything about the risks. The three dissenting physicians, along with a hospital board director, resigned in protest when Southam went ahead anyway. "I don't want Nazi practices of using human beings as experimental guinea pigs," one said on departing. New York tabloids covered the story as if it was an American remake of the Nuremberg trials.[17]

An investigation by the New York State attorney general led to the state's Board of Regents finding Southam guilty of deceit, fraud, and unprofessional conduct. His license was suspended for a year.[18] Many of his colleagues thought he had been unfairly pilloried for the reason that the drug lobby fought Goddard's attempt at full disclosure: patients might have been scared away at words like "living malignant cells" or told about every risk, even the ones that were possible but unlikely. The best evidence that most in the medical establishment did not consider Southam's ethical violations egregious is that when he was again permitted to practice medicine in 1964, the American Cancer Society elected him their executive vice president.[19]

In the final regulations issued by the FDA the following year the agency made no mention of Goddard's desire for stricter and more transparent guidelines to protect research volunteers.[20] (It took the disclosure six years later of the shocking 1930s Tuskegee syphilis experiments on poor African Americans to force a meaningful revision of the informed consent rules.)

Although Goddard had an ambitious to-do list, he recognized that one matter took precedence: starting the ambitious review mandated by the Kefauver Amendments of the effectiveness of thousands of drugs approved between 1938 and 1962. The endeavor was beyond the FDA's capability, especially since he wanted the agency to devote more resources to expanded enforcement of existing regulations. Only a couple of months after becoming commissioner, he reached out for help to the National Academy of Sciences (NAS) and National Research Council (NRC). They struck an agreement, dubbed the Drug Efficacy Study, in June 1966. In exchange for $831,000 from the FDA, the NAS/NRC assigned their Division of Medical Sciences to undertake a broad evaluation of all the pre-1962 drugs. They divided the drugs into categories such as antibiotics, hormones, sulfas, and tranquilizers. Thirty panels composed of 185 scientific and medical experts would judge the drugs' efficacy.[21]

Harvard's Max Finland estimated that if the experts used Kefauver's standard of "substantial evidence," the panels would take twenty-five to fifty years to finish their work.[22] Goddard was a realist. He agreed to a more lenient standard of "the informed judgment and experience" of the medical experts.[23] Instead of requiring new and independent research, the panels would analyze every drug's published studies and data. Two hundred and forty pharma firms sent truckloads of information on over four thousand drugs to the reviewers.[24] The panels ranked each—effective, probably effective, possibly effective, and clearly ineffective—as to how it delivered on its therapeutic claims. Drugs deemed ineffective would be banned from the market unless the pharma company reformulated it and proved anew its efficacy.[25]

Fixed-dose combination antibiotics, introduced by the Pfizer-made/Sackler-promoted Sigmamycin, were the most controversial. Twenty percent of all medications under review were combinations.[26] In the ensuing debate the review panels added an additional finding: "ineffective as a fixed combination." That meant there was no evidence that the combined drugs were any more effective than each of the meds on their own.[27]

As Goddard waited for the Drug Efficacy Study to return with its final recommendations, the FDA's examiners in the administrative hearings on the mild tranquilizers returned in April 1967 with a partial judgment.[28] Relying on the 1965 Drug Abuse Control Amendments, both Miltown and Equanil met the definition of "potential for abuse" and should be subject to controls similar to those on amphetamines and barbiturates.[29] Drugmakers Carter and Wyeth had been prepared for an adverse ruling and immediately sued the FDA in federal court.

The FDA's hearings on Librium and Valium, meanwhile, were far from over. Roche was only halfway through presenting its defense. It had a long list of expert witnesses, mostly prominent researchers and noted psychopharmacologists. They testified that if the two benzos were used as intended, they did not produce debilitating or life-threatening side effects, were not addictive, and did not lead to an increase in suicide. Roche's attorneys dismissed the FDA's patient accounts of painful withdrawals from the drug as rare and not evidence of an underlying problem.[30]

The following month Goddard refocused on medical advertising. He had failed to interest a single pharma company with a proposal to replace all medical advertising with an annual FDA-produced compendium that included full labeling information.[31] Goddard wanted pharma to subsidize the cost. Drug executives thought it preposterous that they pay for a government-sponsored encyclopedia at the expense of abandoning their own advertisements.[32]

On May 17, the FDA issued a new set of regulations under the "fair balance" requirement for promotion. No drug could be advertised as superior to another unless the FDA approved the claim after the presentation of "substantial evidence." That rule was sparked by two instances in which companies advertised their birth control pills as safer (Mead Johnson) or that they caused less weight gain (Lilly), when neither was true.[33] The FDA also instituted a tougher requirement for listing side effects in an ad. They would have to be displayed in the promotional copy itself, not buried in a barely discernible font at the bottom.[34]

Finally, Goddard introduced measures to prevent a redux of what Sackler and Frohlich had done with Achrocidin, Lederle's fixed-dose antibiotic cold drug. In promoting that drug, Sackler and Frohlich had cited a 1933 clinical study to puff up the medication's supposed benefits, while ignoring twenty newer, more comprehensive studies indicating the exact opposite. Among a rash of new "dos and don'ts," obsolete data could no longer be used in promotion, published reports of side effects could not be ignored, and animal studies could not be cited as having any clinical significance.[35]

Pharma forcefully opposed the new rules. The president of Sackler's McAdams ad agency spoke for many on Medicine Avenue when he said the proposals "jeopardized freedom of the press."[36] Goddard did not budge. The FDA instead seized shipments of some medications in which it judged the ads misleading. Warner-Lambert's Peritrate, used for chest pain relief, was the first. The company had incorrectly relied on studies to boast about efficacy beyond what it had proved to the FDA.[37] The use of seizures was controversial and brought a howl of protest from drug companies who charged that under Goddard, the FDA's role had crossed from protecting the public to an abusive use of power.

Goddard created problems for pharma beyond simply the scope of FDA authority. He persuaded Lyndon Johnson that a stronger federal role was needed in keeping tabs on the drug industry. In 1967 LBJ endorsed legislation to restrict the $100 million that pharma spent on free samples to doctors annually. The final version of the Food and Drugs Safety Act passed that year was not as expansive, however, as Goddard had hoped. While the new law barred pharma from sending unsolicited drug samples through the mail, there was no limit on how many detail teams could distribute.[38] And to make up for losing the right to mail unsolicited samples, drug firms began adopting a wide range of new ways to provide doctors with perks, everything from weekend trips to the Bahamas to golf tournaments and cocktail parties.[39]

Not even the president could get all the legislation he wanted when it came to pharma. Two years earlier, Congress had passed the first ever government-sponsored health care programs, Medicare and Medicaid.[40] Both were part of LBJ's Great Society reforms. Medicare removed everyone over sixty-five from the individual health care insurance market. It focused on covering the costs of hospitalization. A prescription drug benefit was included in an early draft bill but dropped before the final vote "on the grounds of unpredictable and potentially high costs."[41] Eligibility for Medicaid, on the other hand, was not dependent on age. It was intended for Americans with limited incomes, defined as those living at or below the federal poverty line. Medicaid did cover prescription drugs.[42]

The Johnson administration was alarmed by the rapid increase in drug costs and how much pharmaceuticals exceeded what the government had budgeted. To control runaway prices, one LBJ-backed bill would have instituted "reasonable costs" as a pricing standard. Another would have mandated the government only buy generic medications.[43]

Those proposals set the drug industry on fire. The AMA joined in, arguing they would infringe on physician autonomy to decide which medication was best for a patient.[44] The Pharmaceutical Manufacturers Association flooded congressional offices with booklets warning generics were not safe.[45] Both bills died before making it out of their committees. In response, Lyndon Johnson appointed a Task Force on Prescription Drugs to determine whether drug coverage should be added to Medicare.*

Goddard, meanwhile, had the ear of some prescription-reform-minded Democratic senators, Wisconsin's Gaylord Nelson, Louisiana's Russell Long, and New Mexico's Joseph Montoya. Nelson had succeeded Estes Kefauver as the chairman of the Antitrust and Monopoly Subcommittee. Goddard repeatedly urged him to pick up where Kefauver stopped. Beginning in May 1967, Nelson opened an investigation—Competitive Problems in the Drug Industry—that focused on "the health and pocketbook of American citizens."[46] It was the first of what would be a record-setting thirty-four hearings over twelve years (generating seventeen thousand pages of final reports).[47] Nelson tried half a dozen times in the coming decade to enact some variation of compulsory generic drug legislation; pharma defeated it every time.

In January 1968, the Drug Efficacy Study panels finally reported their conclusions to the FDA. They had reviewed over 16,500 therapeutic claims for 4,000 pre-1962 drugs. Only 434, about 12 percent of those examined, delivered on all their promised claims.[48] Seven hundred and sixty-nine were marked as "ineffective"; that included most of

---

* That LBJ commission did not deliver its report for almost two years, during the first months of the Nixon administration. It recommended that Medicare should include a drug benefit program; Nixon relegated the idea to death by neglect. Adding drug coverage to Medicare would not be seriously considered again for thirty years.

the fixed-dose combination antibiotics.[49] Psychotropics were hit hard, with more than half marked as not working for the condition for which they were dispensed.[50] The biggest drug companies—Upjohn, Pfizer, Lederle, Lilly, Wyeth, and Merck—had the highest number of products judged "ineffective."[51]

The information in the final reports was so voluminous that Goddard established a Drug Efficacy Study Implementation (DESI) task force inside his Bureau of Drugs.[52] Its task was to recommend which drugs the FDA should decertify. It was also responsible for reviewing additional evidence drugmakers submitted to appeal the ratings, particularly the nearly 1,800 drugs marked as "possibly ineffective." Ultimately, the DESI task force upgraded to "effective" only an eighth of those.[53]

The failure of so many drugs to get passing marks from the scientific review panels was bad news for tens of millions of the drug-taking public. While many people had come to believe that pharma put profits above public health, a further shadow was cast over the industry's vaunted reputation for excellent research. Some national newspapers printed full-page summaries of the "ineffective" drugs.[54] How good was it if over half of all the therapeutic claims made for all pre-1962 drugs were not supportable? Few had known until those rankings that the "scientific evidence" many drug companies touted in ads were simply paid testimonials.

While the DESI was under way, Goddard was antagonizing pharma on new fronts. That February, during Senate hearings about the booming diet pill industry, he testified "there are no drugs which can safely control the problem of obesity."[55] That was a direct challenge to some five thousand physicians who specialized in treating obesity with diet pills. By the time of the Senate probe, Americans were spending $250 million annually on those doctors and another $120 million on so-called rainbow pills, named after the brightly colored tablets that had become a hallmark of weight loss clinics.[56] Goddard announced during his testimony that he had ordered the FDA to seize 43 million tablets from a dozen manufacturers.[57] The rainbow pill he targeted was a wildly popular combination of a desiccated form of the thyroid hormone mixed with the heart drug digitalis.

The drug in Goddard's crosshairs had been on the market for decades, but the FDA had only recently linked several deaths to it. "It is incomprehensible," said the president of Texas-based Lanpar, a manufacturer from whom federal agents seized $500,000 in pills, "that a product that has been marketed successfully for 30 years overnight becomes the target of the FDA."[58] Those drugs were lethal hazards, the commissioner told the Senate panel. And he cited the rainbow medications as a key reason why the FDA's review of which pre-1962 combination drugs should be recalled was vitally important.[59]

Goddard's rainbow pills seizures were front-page news. Many in the industry thought he was grandstanding. *Life* sent a thin reporter undercover to ten weight loss clinics, and while a couple told her she did not need to lose weight, the rest prescribed 1,500 amphetamine-based pills in two weeks.[60] While the manufacturers of rainbow pills were a handful of smaller firms that had been founded just for that purpose (New Jersey's Clark & Clark, Dallas's Lanpar Company, Denver's Western Research Laboratories, and St. Louis's Mills Pharmaceuticals), the seizures tarnished the entire industry.[61] News that March of the deaths of twelve Maryland women from rainbow pills prompted Senator Gaylord Nelson to add diet pills to his ongoing pharmaceutical inquiry.[62]

All of pharma agreed on one matter: they had to get rid of Goddard. For more than a year they had engaged in a whisper campaign designed to disparage him and undermine his support in Congress. They characterized him as driven by insatiable ambition, only interested in accumulating power as opposed to doing what was best for the public and drug industry. Business-friendly *Barron's* warned that the "FDA Has Become a Threat to U.S. Health and Welfare." The problem, according to *Barron's*, was that the agency was in "the doctrinaire hands of its Commissioner, James L. Goddard." His policies had so suppressed the development of lifesaving drugs in the country's pharmaceutical research labs, that "the medicine men of FDA, all unwittingly perhaps, are angels of death."[63]

Goddard unintentionally helped his enemies by saying things that weakened the support he had inside the Johnson administration. He irritated law enforcement officials in his 1968 testimony before a House subcommittee that was weighing whether to criminalize LSD. Goddard was the only administration voice to oppose the law, preferring instead to fund public education about the perils of drugs and treatments for addicts. His contention that local drugstores were not competitive and would one day be extinct irked one of his most ardent supporters, former pharmacist Vice President Hubert Humphrey.[64]

In May 1968, the embattled Goddard submitted his resignation.

According to *The New York Times*, his departure was "because of differences with the Administration over his policing of the purity of foods and the safety and efficacy of drugs. . . . He antagonized pharmaceutical manufacturers and many physicians."[65] Pharma was jubilant. Goddard's replacement, Dr. Herbert Ley Jr., the chairman of the Harvard School of Public Health's Epidemiology and Microbiology Department, started in July.*[66] But the celebration over Goddard's departure was short-lived as Ley disabused the industry that he would return to the less aggressive Larrick-era approach. He made it clear inside the agency as well that he was determined to follow through with most of Goddard's ambitious agenda, including the DESI recommendations regarding the pre-1962 drugs.

Thirty members of the National Academy of Sciences, all of whom had served on the drug panels, shared with Ley a draft of a scholarly article they wrote concluding that the FDA should decertify *all* fixed-dose combination antibiotic medications. They were almost never better than each of the constituent drugs alone, and in some cases demonstrably worse.[67] Drug companies used the combination meds to extend patents on expiring medications, or sometimes to develop combo products for which they charged considerably more than each drug on its own.[68] *JAMA* refused to publish the article, believing that removing the drugs cut the power of physicians. (The *NEJM* published it but not until the following year.)[69]

The chief target of the academic experts was Upjohn's Panalba, a patented combination of two generic antibiotics, tetracycline and novobiocin.[70] It had been a major success for Upjohn. With more than 750 million prescriptions in the decade since its release, it provided 20 percent of the company's American gross income.[71] The Drug Efficacy Study had concluded that Panalba was actually *less* effective than either stand-alone antibiotic because the duo often counteracted each other. As for side effects, Panalba was more toxic than just tetracycline, and one in five patients were allergic to novobiocin.[72] A dozen patients had died of Panalba complications.[73] And it had cost consumers at least $12 million more than if they simply had used just-as-effective tetracycline. What few knew was that Upjohn's internal testing had revealed

---

* Goddard had enough of government service. After leaving the FDA he initially took a job in Atlanta-based EOP Technology, a private data processing firm. He later moved to the Ford Foundation, and even did some consulting work for drug companies.

the drug was dangerous, capable of causing blood disorders and even liver damage.[74]

The reason for Panalba's success? Since its inception its promotion had been the brainchild of Arthur Sackler and his McAdams agency. Sackler had already gotten in trouble before the Kefauver subcommittee for his misleading campaign on Upjohn's corticosteroid.

With Panalba, Sackler developed something he dubbed the "rational approach to prescribing antibiotics." It was, as medical historian Scott Podolsky says, a "shoot first and ask questions later" philosophy. The ads urged doctors to use "Panalba promptly to gain precious therapeutic hours." Since taking a tissue culture to confirm whether an infection was bacterial was not always practical, "a rational clinical alternative is to launch therapy at once with Panalba, the antibiotic that provides the best odds for success." Sackler coined the description that Panalba was an "antibiotic-reinforced antibiotic" (the addition of novobiocin helped "protect against resistant staph").[75]

On Christmas Eve 1968, Commissioner Ley relied on the recommendation of his DESI task force and announced the FDA's intention to decertify Panalba. Ley knew if the agency was successful stopping the sale of the most successful fixed-dose combo antibiotic, it could move against the hundreds of others on the market. Ley provided thirty days for comments or input. Upjohn requested a full hearing to contest the decision, the same as Carter and Wyeth had done when they fought the Miltown/Equanil controls a few years earlier.

Ley said no. If every pharmaceutical company got a hearing to relitigate the merits of the DESI decisions, the agency would be bogged down for years. He was certain that the Kefauver Amendments' grant of power for reviewing the pre-1962 drugs was so broad that pharma would have to abide by whatever decision the agency reached. That proved a miscalculation. Panalba became the test case for the entire industry and turned into a much bigger fight than Ley had imagined. It sparked a Senate investigation (that ultimately judged fixed-dose antibiotics as useless and sometimes dangerous).[76] Upjohn filed a federal lawsuit contending the FDA ruling violated the doctors' constitutional free speech and exceeded its statutory authority. Upjohn insisted that the courts should in fairness order the FDA to hold administrative hearings for every drug it wanted to withdraw from public sale. Meanwhile, Panalba stayed on the market as the litigation wound its way to the Supreme Court. Some of Upjohn's rivals had by then filed their own lawsuits or briefs in support of the effort to quash the FDA's ability to demand effectiveness evidence for the pre-1962 drugs.

The battle over whether Congress intended the FDA to have such broad administrative powers in recalling drugs worked its way through the federal courts. The Supreme Court did not settle the matter for four years in a quartet of decisions. Justice William Douglas delivered the unanimous opinion in the main Panalba case.[77] It was a milestone for the FDA, a full-throated endorsement of the agency's powers. The court concluded that Congress meant exactly what it said in the 1962 law: it intended to give the FDA broad authority to remove drugs it considered ineffective, not just those deemed unsafe. When any drug is recalled, the court ruled it applied automatically to all the me-too versions. As for the question of whether the agency could use "administrative summary judgment" to withdraw drugs "for the protection of the public," the court ruled it did. All the FDA had to do was to "provide a formal hearing" in those instances when the company's newly submitted evidence met the agency's standard of "rigorous proof."[78] The Supreme Court's ruling in favor of the FDA's expansive power set the foundation for the FDA's gigantic second phase of the Drug Efficacy Study for 300,000 over-the-counter medications (which took twenty years to complete).[79] It also, concluded Edward Shorter, a social historian of medicine, transformed the FDA "from a sleepy little cop agency into a bureaucratic powerhouse."[80]

Many in the pharmaceutical industry, as had happened after the passage of every major previous drug law, warned that the court decision would cripple research and innovation. The problem for the drug companies was that they had lost their credibility on the "sky-is-falling" complaint. For every drug removed from the market in the U.S., manufacturers continued selling them for years in Latin America, Asia, Europe, and Africa.[81]

24

"HERE, EAT THIS ROOT"

The battle to remove Panalba and the other fixed-dose antibiotics had taken eleven years since the Kefauver subcommittee had zeroed in on the shortcomings of Pfizer's Sigmamycin, the drug that Arthur Sackler had advertised with testimonials from eight phantom physicians. Much of the media coverage about the FDA's victory was about the public savings of millions it would have otherwise spent on unnecessary and worthless drugs. The Supreme Court ruling meant the FDA did not have to ask for updated safety profiles before decertifying a drug. The agency was relieved because it thought it unnecessary and too time-consuming. The unintended consequences, however, of not requiring those safety profiles of the pre-1962 drugs was that the agency missed a chance to address the early stages of antibiotic drug resistance.

The FDA's miscalculation, reinforced by the widespread belief in the biomedical community, was to dismiss reports of drug resistance as anomalies that affected few patients. Laboratory tests in the late 1940s and through the 1950s predicted antibiotic resistance would rarely develop.[1] The tests showed that for bacteria to acquire resistance, they expended so much energy that it resulted in their self-destruction. And in the few instances in which bacteria did show evidence of resistance, its culture growth was slow. That reassured researchers, who cited it as evidence that even if antibiotic resistance developed in humans, "it would be unstable and short-lived."[2]

Two of the pioneers who developed penicillin were not as convinced. In his 1945 acceptance speech for the Nobel in Medicine, Alexander Fleming warned that if penicillin was dispensed too liberally it would be less capable of killing bacteria over time.

"There is the danger that the ignorant man may easily under dose himself and by exposing his microbes to non-lethal quantities of the drug make them resistant."[3]

Ernst Chain had an even more ominous warning. He feared bacterial pathogens were so adaptable that once they began evolving to resist antibiotics, it was only a matter of time until no drug could stop them.

Most researchers and academicians rejected those dire forecasts as overdramatic and unproven.[4] A mid-1950s report about a cluster of Japanese patients who did not respond to antibiotics because of resistant pathogens did not cause much concern among scientists. They dismissed it as an unexplainable anomaly. Doctors did not have the technology to diagnose why those patients had not responded to drug treatment.[5]

The early scientists worked from two incorrect assumptions. First, they thought that for there to be antibiotic resistance, some of the body's bacteria would have to develop that resistance. And they assumed the results they obtained in their controlled lab settings predicted what would happen when antibiotics were widely and repeatedly dispensed to millions of people.

It was several decades before researchers proved that by "random chance" some people's cells have genes capable of natural resistance to an administered antibiotic. The odds of resistant bacteria also increase when patients don't finish the full course of prescribed treatment. And the same is true when an antibiotic is dispensed for viral infections such as the common cold. Although useless against viruses, introducing the drug into the body activates so-called resistance genes (R genes). Biologists now estimate that humans have about twenty thousand potential R genes. [6] * [7]

Beginning in the mid-1950s, doctors liberally dispensed powerful broad-spectrum antibiotics. Their shotgun disbursement in the body meant they killed off good microbes in addition to any pathogenic

---

* In the late 1990s, the World Health Organization published an anonymous doggerel, titled "The History of Medicine," that summarized the evolutionary view that germs will always prevail: "2000 B.C.: – *Here, eat this root*; A.D. 1000 – *That root is heathen. Here, say this prayer*; A.D. 1850 – *That prayer is superstition. Here, drink this potion*; A.D. 1920 – *That potion is snake oil. Here, swallow this pill*; A.D. 1945 – *That pill is ineffective. Here, take this penicillin*; A.D. 1955 – *Oops . . . bugs mutated. Here, take this tetracycline*; 1960–1999 – *39 more "oops." Here, take this more powerful antibiotic*; A.D. 2000 – *The bugs have won! Here, eat this root.*"

bacteria. The germs left were those with natural resistance R genes, and they became more potent from having battled and survived the drug. The introduction of fixed-dose combination antibiotics in 1956 added to the overprescribing epidemic. Physicians dispensed those for common colds, sinus infections, sore throats, and runny noses. Every one of those needless prescriptions increased the odds for more resistant bacteria. Until the FDA removed them from the market in 1973, billions of doses of the combination antibiotics had been sold. Americans took more antibiotics every year in the 1950s and 1960s than all other prescription medications combined.[8]

Many also got extra antibiotics from the 30 million pounds of antibiotics used annually since the 1950s to fatten chickens, cattle, turkeys, and other animals used for meat, as well as protecting farmed fish from contracting diseases common in the overcrowded environments in which they were bred. They also became prevalent in plant agriculture, sprayed every spring for a week on fruit and vegetable crops to suppress the proliferation of otherwise destructive pathogens.[9] The constant exposure to antibiotics from different sources boosts the number and speed at which resistant genes proliferate.[10]*[11]

What was the result of the overprescription frenzy of the postwar decades? Researchers have now determined that ground zero for antibiotic drug resistance was during the early 1960s in America. A "core" population of resistant strains developed and took hold in susceptible patients. Scientists now realize that in some people, molecules of independently replicating DNA called plasmids (plasmid-mediated antibiotic resistance) develop. Those morphed into supercharged biological carriers capable of spreading resistant bacteria. Those plasmids, scientists believe, are how antibiotic resistance spread from America to every continent, including locations where antibiotics were used rarely.[12]†[13]

The grim ramifications of the FDA's decision not to update the safety profiles of the pre-1962 antibiotics only became apparent a de-

---

* The CDC and WHO have over the decades repeatedly warned doctors they should be judicious by limiting their antibiotic dispensing. Still, the CDC estimates that about 30 percent of the quarter billion antibiotics prescriptions written annually in the U.S. are unnecessary. An additional $50 billion of antibiotics are improperly administered in nursing home and hospitals.

† It was 2010 before British scientists concluded that MRSA, an opportunistic superbug infection caused by a resistant bacterial strain, also developed in the early 1960s.

cade later. The first indications of a problem were news reports of epidemic infection rates in developing countries of a common form of pneumonia and a sexually transmitted disease, neither of which responded to drugs.[14] During the mid- to late 1960s about 35,000 American troops in Vietnam got infected with a resistant strain of malaria that Army doctors said was a "recent mutant of more common types." It sparked a crash program by the National Institute of Science, the Walter Reed Army Research Institute, and leading tropical medicine physicians that failed to develop treatment (today, that mutant strain—falciparum malaria—is still the world's deadliest.)[15]

It would take thirty years before leading microbiologists had concluded that "The use of antibiotics by humans can be seen as an evolutionary experiment of enormous magnitude."[16] As is now evident, it was an experiment in which the odds—beginning in the 1960s in America—were unwittingly stacked in favor of the pathogens.

25

"THEY CLEAN THEIR OWN CAGES"

There were early warning signs that could not be ignored, however, for another blockbuster hormone drug created and marketed only to women: the contraceptive pill. In under a decade since the FDA approved it, Searle's Enovid had become an enormous success. Ten million women were regular users in the U.S. and another four million in another twenty countries. Searle liked to crow that one of every four married women in America was on the Pill.[1]

The Pill was undoubtedly a medical breakthrough that had empowered women to take charge of their reproductive options through a simple once-a-day tablet. In its first couple of years, physicians dispensed it as if there were no more side effects than aspirin. Searle's advertisements boasted, "It has been studied more thoroughly and for a longer continuous time in the same persons and in more women than any other drug."[2]

When patient complaints started trickling in of headaches, bloating, nausea, and breast tenderness, doctors were mostly dismissive, believing that women's bodies had to adjust to the pseudopregnancy stage the Pill induced. Through the mid-1960s, however, the number of reported side effects grew. It prompted the FDA to appoint an all-male panel of nine physicians to study whether the Pill made blood clots more likely, the adverse effect that raised the most concern, since it was potentially fatal. They found 272 reports of Enovid users who developed blood clots; thirty patients had died. The panel recommended that Searle add a warning to its label about the possibility of blood clots for those most at risk, women over thirty-five. Under intense pushback from Searle, the FDA overruled its committee, claiming the doctors had made a mathematical error in calculating the death rate from blood clots and the real risk for those on the Pill was "not statistically significant."[3] In 1966, in another concession to Searle's lobbying, the FDA lifted its forty-eight-month limit for how long a woman should stay on the Pill; there was now no time limit.[4]

From 1966 through 1969, the FDA documented another 1,034 instances of serious adverse effects, including 118 deaths, mostly from blood clots, but also a few from strokes and complications from hepatitis.[5] The FDA could not determine if the fatal illnesses resulted from the contraceptive or were merely a coincidence. By the late 1960s, the prescription package insert sent to pharmacists was a tiny booklet of three thousand words and five complex scientific tables that listed more than fifty side effects, including some potentially fatal ones.

Questions about the Pill's safety did not affect its commercial success. A five-year study concluded that 80 percent of women who stopped taking it did so because they were bothered by side effects such as bloating, cramping, and water retention, not because of fears about whether it might make them seriously ill. The market for the contraceptive kept expanding because so many more new patients between the ages of fifteen and forty-four replaced those who had discontinued it.[6] The number taking the Pill grew on average about half a million annually.

Patients never saw the prescription package inserts. Those only went to druggists and physicians who requested them. Most doctors dispensed the Pill with a generic "call me if something unusual occurs" assurance. There was a widespread sentiment among physicians that if patients received too much information about possible side effects, many "wouldn't understand it" or "it would scare the hell out of them."[7] In subsequent Senate hearings, Kansas senator Bob Dole questioned if telling women about the health risks might cause such anxiety they might end up "taking two pills . . . a tranquilizer and then the regular Pill."[8]

The University of Kentucky's Dr. David Clark believed the reason most of his colleagues were hesitant to criticize the Pill was that it had "diplomatic immunity." Its backers considered it as critical in everything from controlling overpopulation to ending poverty to reducing the divorce rate to improving sex lives by eliminating the fear of unwanted pregnancies, and emancipating women by giving them full and simplified control of their reproductive rights.[9] Peter Wyden, the editor of *Ladies' Home Journal*, rejected any critical stories about the oral contraceptive since he did not believe the magazine's readers wanted bad news.[10] Medical researchers at a 1965 World Health Organization conference were so worried about overpopulation that in the final report they omitted mentioning any of the Pill's side effects.[11]

The only information most women got was what they picked up in the "About the Pill" booklets that pharma companies printed by the tens of thousands. Those were distributed at Planned Parenthood, women's health clinics, hospitals, and private medical practices. No more than a few dozen pages each, they were reassuring in emphasizing that side effects were almost always minor and temporary. Searle ignored several FDA warnings and kept crossing the line between physician education and overzealous promotion. In its most widely distributed booklet, "A Prescription for Family Planning—The Story of Enovid," Searle totally ignored the most recent and disturbing adverse effects among its millions of consumers.[12] * [13]

The first cracks in the benign view of the Pill appeared slowly. "The Terrible Trouble with the Birth-Control Pill: Should You Stop Taking Them Immediately?" in the July 1967 *Ladies' Home Journal* was the first time millions read about the accumulating questions concerning long-term safety. It focused on new evidence of blood clot risks and a possible cervical cancer connection. Prominent medical journal editorials slammed the article for "sensationalism . . . half-truths . . . and quoting authorities out of context."[14]

A 1968 British study concluded that women on the Pill had a ninefold chance of developing blood clots, and they were seven times more likely to be fatal. The results received only passing coverage in the mainstream media.[15] The Pill's advocates dismissed the findings, contending that the risk, three deaths per 100,000 patients, was small when compared to the chances of death from other serious illnesses that women sometimes got during pregnancy.[16]

---

* Gynecologists, the same specialty responsible for dispensing most estrogen medications, wrote many of the oral contraceptive prescriptions. Menopause and birth control drugs consisted of different amounts of the same hormones. For contraception, it was estrogen and progesterone, while it was estrogen alone for the early menopause drugs. The "change of life" meds later added progesterone. They were designed so the Pill's estrogen suppressed a woman's natural production of hormones, while those aimed at menopause added to the body's declining levels. In terms of risk, however, there was no difference.

"A woman who takes oral contraceptives," said Dr. Malcolm Potts, Planned Parenthood's first medical director, "has more chance of being alive one year later than her sisters who choose to have a baby." The risk of death during childbirth was fifteen times greater than the risk of dying from the blood clots identified in the British study.[17]

The tide of public opinion, especially for those on the Pill, turned in 1969. Since the contraceptive was considered such an emancipating scientific advance for women, it seemed only fair that female critics expose the dangers to a wide audience. Barbara Seaman, a respected medical writer, published *The Doctors' Case Against the Pill.*[18] The bold tagline on the jacket gave all the preview necessary of the contents: "More than 100 medical specialists report how love with the pill can cripple and kill."[19] Her interviews with doctors and researchers resulted in some extraordinary warnings that the "public . . . and scientific scandal" of "pretending the Pill is safe" was at the precipice of a tsunami of cancer in those who had been using it for several years.[20]

Jane Brody, the *New York Times* medicine and biology reporter, followed Seaman the following year with an extensive front-page story that set the tone for much of the subsequent national press. In addition to accumulating accounts of patients with depression or loss of libido, Brody noted the Pill had been linked to "a long list of serious illnesses, among them blood clots, strokes, sight-threatening eye disease, sterility, seizures, diabetes-like upsets in sugar tolerance and even cancer." Most alarming was her inclusion of "two unpublished, highly controversial studies" by a New York gynecologist and researchers from Sloan Kettering Institute and the University of Chicago. In reviewing the records of 35,000 Planned Parenthood clients, the New York duo concluded that women on the Pill were twice as likely as diaphragm users to develop cancerlike changes in the cervix (carcinoma in situ). The Chicago researcher found the same risk was six times more likely for women over thirty-five.[21]

The question Brody posed is what millions of women in America were soon asking: "Is the woman who takes the Pill risking her life for the surety and convenience of this method of contraception?"[22]

In the spring and summer of 1969, on the heels of Brody's piece, the media was consumed with the dangers posed by the Pill. Dr. Roy Hertz, the chief of the National Institutes of Health's endocrine cancer research, predicted in a *Newsweek* cover story titled "The Pill and Cancer" that the Pill would cause a breast cancer crisis in a few years.[23] The warning from the National Conference on Breast Cancer that May was that if studies showed the Pill caused cancer in animals, then those studies applied to women: "The world stands on the threshold of a pill-caused cancer epidemic that will dwarf the thalidomide birth-deformity tragedy."[24] A leading Stanford pharmacologist, Sumner Kalman, said that "eight million women in this country alone now serve as guinea pigs."[25] Endocrinologists told reporters that since the Pill worked through the pituitary gland, it was "unrealistic to think that long-range effects will not be inevitable."[26] A New York gynecologist who treated more than fifty wives of physicians told the *Ladies' Home Journal* in another cover story that "not one of them is still on the Pill."[27] * [28]

All the doomsday coverage set off warning lights for government regulators. Louis Hellman, the chair of the FDA's Obstetrics and Gynecology Advisory Panel, had by 1969 changed from an avid proponent to publicly advising caution about the unknown effects of long-term use of "powerful synthetic hormones." Philip Corfman, the doctor in charge of the NIH's contraceptive research, admitted he would not prescribe the Pill in private practice unless a woman had no other option.[29] By June 1969, a medical malpractice insurance company in California was the first to require its sixteen thousand doctors to obtain signed disclosure forms from patients before prescribing the Pill.[30]

Not everyone was upset with the growing litany of side effects and serious illnesses. The author has learned that at least one pharmaceutical firm that did not have a contraceptive product in the market considered the Pill a "gateway drug" by which they could sell half a dozen of their own brands to mitigate the Pill's side effects. There were diuretics for bloating, antinausea and indigestion remedies, blood thinners to counter clotting, tranquilizers and benzos to reduce agitation or irritability, thyroid supplements or amphetamines to overcome fatigue, and antibiotics to treat the increased number of yeast infections. One

* To Arthur Sackler's credit, his *Medical Tribune* was one of the first to report in 1966 that clinical testing of a new contraceptive pill on 340 women "had been halted because of evidence of cancer in test animals (dogs) receiving the product." At the time, many doctors summarily dismissed results in animal studies by contending they did not apply to women. It took another three years before the alarm about whether the Pill caused cancer became mainstream. Sackler, of course, was always more than willing to undermine the business of pharmaceutical firms that were not his clients. McAdams had no drug firm selling an oral contraceptive.

Medicine Avenue antibiotic ad run made a direct pitch for the business of treating the contraceptive's side effects: "If she's on the Pill, she may need this tablet."[31]

The media and public focus, however, was not concerned about whether some drug firms had a mercenary strategy to take advantage of the Pill's woes. Instead, by the fall of 1969 the spotlight was on the FDA and questions about why it had not done a better job of alerting the public to the accumulating dangers. The British government had instituted stronger label warnings the previous year. When the FDA issued its second report on the Pill that September, it proved tone-deaf. Despite admitting a "small number" of women died annually from the medication, the benefits-to-risk ratio was high enough to keep its classification as a safe drug.[32]

The pressure was on the FDA to do something dramatic to make up for what seemed its laissez-faire oversight. Congressional and consumer advocacy critics agreed that Commissioner Herbert Ley bore the responsibility for the agency's failure to be more proactive. The last straw turned out not to be about the Pill but rather an announcement by the agency on November 10 that it had failed in two years to recall any of the two hundred fixed-dose antibiotics and cold remedies it had targeted for removal. Pharma firms had tied up the FDA in litigation, but that was lost mostly in news coverage that added to the agency's seeming incompetence under Ley.[33]

In early December, Ley was ousted, along with the agency's next two ranking officials, the deputy commissioner and the chief of compliance. The Nixon administration, less than a year in power, decided to change more than just the top few jobs. The secretary of HEW announced an overhaul of the 4,200-person agency. The FDA's Bureau of Science, Medicine and Compliance, which consumer advocates like Ralph Nader had excoriated for being too chummy with pharma, was disbanded and replaced with two streamlined departments. The entire agency was moved up in the HEW hierarchy, giving it expanded federal powers. Finally, a new commissioner was selected: Charles Edwards, a general surgeon who balanced a leadership role at the AMA with a part-time teaching post at Georgetown University Hospital. Edwards was also a vice president at the management consulting firm Booz Allen Hamilton.

With a reputation as a "hard-nosed, no nonsense decision-maker," Edwards viewed the disarray as an opportunity.[34] He knew that as the

FDA's powers got redefined, it would sometimes gain new authority and occasionally lose it. The previous year the FDA had lost its jurisdiction over illegal drugs to the Justice Department's newly formed Bureau of Narcotics and Dangerous Drugs. But it had also received expanded control over medicated feeds and animal drugs. The FDA had just gotten the green light from the Public Health Service to administer sanitation programs for shellfish, milk, and food services, and to the extent necessary for preventing poisoning or accidents at interstate travel facilities. The FDA also was in charge of antibiotic levels in milk, eggs, and food plants. However, Food Safety and Inspection Service was tasked with testing for antibiotic levels in poultry and meat.[35] The Environmental Protection Agency was given the oversight of antibiotic residues left on the outside of food plants, including fruits and vegetables.[36]

Edwards turned out to be good at bureaucratic chess. He got the right for the FDA to regulate biologics—serums, seasonal (antigenic) vaccines, and some blood products—taking them away from the NIH. After successfully getting Congress to double the FDA budget, Edwards established the National Center for Toxicological Research, dedicated to examining the biological effects of chemicals in the environment. The most important new power in a few years would be the Medical Device Amendments, by which the FDA got oversight of both the safety and efficacy of medical instruments and diagnostic products.[37]

On the other hand, Edwards could not prevail in every skirmish. The FDA lost to the Environmental Protection Agency the right to set tolerance limits for pesticides. The NIH's Division of Biologics Standards took the authority over the importation and distribution of foreign blood products. Nonmedical consumer goods such as home appliances and toys, as well as household chemicals, went to the newly created Consumer Product Safety Commission. Microwaves, however, went to the FDA because they emitted low levels of radiation. The biggest blow would be when HEW and Congress blocked the agency from setting standards and regulating vitamins, minerals, and supplements.[38]

As the power tug-of-war played out, Edwards knew that he had assumed control at a time when Congress intended to take the agency to task for the uproar over the Pill. Senator Gaylord Nelson—who had succeeded Kefauver as the Senate's crusader fighting abuses by big business—had pharma in his sights since 1967 with his Competitive Problems in the Drug Industry probe. Nelson thought that the FDA should be held responsible for their "abject failure" to protect American women from the health dangers of the Pill.[39] That was the focus of his investigation in January 1970. The following two months of public hearings riveted much of the country. Nearly 90 percent of *all* women between the ages of twenty-one and forty-five followed the hearings.

Nelson began with eight doctors and researchers (all men) specializing in birth control.[40] The first witness on January 14 was Hugh Davis, a Johns Hopkins professor of gynecology and the chief of its Contraceptive Clinic. Not only might the Pill cause breast cancer, he testified, but by the time a woman or her physician discovered a lump, it would have been there for many years.

The FDA's chief of the cell biology division, Dr. Marvin Legator, followed Davis by warning the subcommittee that the Pill made cellular and genetic changes that could lead to cancers or even inheritable mutations. It was difficult to identify those changes as they were indistinguishable from the ones caused by some other illnesses. As a result, Legator concluded, the Pill posed a more dangerous crisis than thalidomide.[41]

Dr. Herbert Ratner, a leading physician and author, was not able to hide his disdain for the extent to which women were at risk for unknown perils from the Pill. "The scientist in the laboratory has never had it so good. . . . [w]omen make superb guinea pigs—they don't cost anything. They clean their own 'cages,' feed themselves, pay for their own Pills and remunerate the clinical observer." [42]

The disclosures about blood clots and possible breast cancer and heart disease were not news to medical researchers. The Senate hearings were, however, the first time most women heard about them. All the facts and figures about risk versus benefits paled in insignificance when NIH scientist Roy Hertz testified to the committee that "estrogen is to cancer what fertilizer is to the wheat crop." [43] Women were stunned and infuriated. Two thirds of women in a Gallup poll said their physicians had never given them a single warning about any possible dangers.[44] Why had their doctors been silent?

Commissioner Edwards knew the FDA had to do something fast. Four days after the hearings got under way the agency sent a letter to the country's 381,000 doctors, urging them to advise their patients of the Pill's potential serious side effects.[45] Critics thought it too little too late. Edwards stumbled a couple of weeks later when he told a reporter that subject to different advice from their doctors, women "should continue to take" the Pill. At a contentious meeting with an activist group, D.C. Women's Liberation, members shouted questions at him about why there were not more women in authority at the FDA and why the agency had not pushed pharma to develop a male pill. Edwards stormed out before it finished.[46] * [47]

The pharma industry tried reversing the damning Senate narrative. It spread a rumor that Nelson's hearings were a prelude to the government banning the Pill and turning back the clock on women's reproductive rights.[48] A series of rebuttal witnesses went on the offensive before Nelson's subcommittee, accusing the investigation of creating "unwarranted and dangerous alarm . . . [and] panic."[49] They repeated a few key themes: the Pill was more effective than IUDs and diaphragms; no other form of birth control fully gave women the ability to plan their lives free of unwanted pregnancies; and the risks of death from blood clots caused by the Pill were statistically less than the number of women who died during childbirth or car accidents.[50] Other witnesses did not address whether the Pill was safe but instead emphasized its overriding social benefit.

Most women who followed the hearings were not interested in broad policy issues about curbing overpopulation. They were concerned about the degree to which pharma had put millions of them at risk by downplaying side effect reports for a decade. Was the Pill unsafe? A poll taken just two weeks after the Nelson inquiry had gotten under way showed that a sizable number of women answered yes: 18 percent with prescriptions had stopped taking it and another 23 percent were giving it "serious consideration."[51] At family planning clinics where it was dispensed to women too poor to otherwise afford it, upward of 30 percent stopped. After a month of public testimony, obstetricians and family clinics noted "a run on diaphragms."[52] Jane Brody reported in *The New York Times* that a check of pharmacies around New York confirmed a "significant increase in the sales of contraceptive foams, jellies and creams and condoms, and a definite falling off in sales of oral contraceptives."[53]

When a New York obstetrician later testified before the subcommit-

---

* Alice Wolfson, a Barnard graduate, founded D.C. Women's Liberation. Five years later, she was one of the cofounders of the nonprofit National Women's Health Network. By then, 1975, there were some 1,200 women's advocacy groups focused on women's health care rights.

tee, he castigated the panel for creating "dozens of unwanted pregnancies."[54] By March, the hearings' two-month point, Dr. Phyllis Piotrow, the director for the Population Crisis Committee, scolded the senators for "scaring [women] to death." Because so many were abandoning oral contraceptives, Piotrow predicted 100,000 unwanted "Nelson babies" by the end of the year.[55]

The warning of 100,000 unwanted "Nelson babies" proved wildly off target. A year later, even large, inner-city family clinics reported unwanted births in the hundreds, not in the tens of thousands. A lot of women had switched to different methods but they had not abandoned contraceptives. The biggest beneficiary of the fright over the Pill was not another drug, but rather a medical device, a uniquely designed IUD called the Dalkon Shield. Johns Hopkins's Hugh Davis had introduced it in 1969. By the time of the Nelson hearings it had sold 600,000 units.[56] That was the year A. H. Robins—the maker of ChapStick, Robitussin, and Dimetapp—bought the rights from Davis and marketed it as a "safe alternative" to the Pill. (Davis, who had excoriated the Pill when he was the leadoff witness before the Senate, was later condemned by colleagues for not disclosing his financial conflict of interest.)[57] * [58]

In the wake of Nelson's hearings there was a sharp drop in public confidence for the FDA, particularly among women. Eight years earlier with the thalidomide disaster, the FDA had been hailed for not approving a drug that left a trail of horrible birth defects in Europe.[59] The FDA emerged as the culprit from the Nelson hearings. Not only had it approved Enovid in 1960, the first of a radically new class of medications, but it had done so without any data about its long-term safety. Worse was its repeated failure to do anything as adverse effect reports poured in. While many expected the drug companies to bury bad news about their products, it was disturbing to see that pharma had so thoroughly outwitted and outmaneuvered the FDA regulators.

---

* At its peak, 3.5 million women in eighty countries, most formerly on oral contraceptives, relied on the Dalkon Shield. The first reports of blood poisoning, pelvic infections, and gynecological complications came to the FDA at the end of 1970. After four deaths were linked to the Dalkon Shield in 1974, Robins suspended sales. Two hundred thousand women eventually sued, forcing Robins into bankruptcy (American Home Products bought the company for a fraction of its pre-Dalkon value). Searle recalled its popular copper-7 IUD. An unintended benefit from the Dalkon Shield disaster was that, as it had in the past, it forced bipartisan Congressional action. The Medical Device Amendments to the 1938 Food, Drug, and Cosmetic Act gave the FDA authority over the approval and safety of medical devices.

Many women wondered that if the government watchdog had failed them on something as fundamental as birth control, what else might it have missed about the many other drugs on the market? One not very good answer came a few months after the Nelson hearings. Researchers linked diethylstilbestrol (DES), the first synthetic estrogen that had been dispensed since 1940 to women to prevent pregnancy complications, to a forty times greater risk of developing a rare vaginal cancer (clear-cell adenocarcinoma). Upward of 10 million women had used the more than one hundred DES-based drugs while pregnant. The FDA hurriedly sent letters to the nation's doctors directing they stop prescribing them. Researchers later concluded that DES was also responsible for birth deformities and even reproductive problems and increased instances of cancer in the daughters of women who had used it.[60] * [61]

Commissioner Edwards decided bold action was needed to restore public confidence. Citing a 1966 law requiring accurate labeling, he ordered that a message highlighting the Pill's major health risks be added to prescription inserts and distributed to patients. Edwards faced a torrent of opposition from physicians who thought that infringed on their autonomy to advise patients. Planned Parenthood rallied against it claiming that the Pill's dangers were greatly outweighed by its benefits and the insert might scare away patients. The pro-Pill lobby, led by the American Medical Association and the Pharmaceutical Manufacturers Association, got Edwards to slash his warning from six hundred words to one hundred. Still, the final version cautioned about possible blood clots. Pharma and the AMA were relentless, however, and forced another last-minute compromise. Instead of mandating the insert be in every package of oral contraceptives, the FDA allowed doctors to merely tell their patients about it.[62] Edwards, and activists like author Barbara Seaman, were justifiably concerned that many of the inserts to doctors would "land in 'circular files' (wastebaskets)." They were right. Physicians distributed only four million FDA warning inserts to ten million patients between 1970 and 1975.[63]

* The perception that male-dominated medical and pharmaceutical industries shortchanged women was one of the reasons for the enormous success of a 1967 book, *Our Bodies, Ourselves*. Published by the Boston Women's Health Book Collective, organized the previous year by a dozen young feminists, it helped women become educated consumers about their own health. The book sold more than four million copies.

Edwards was so incensed at the labeling fiasco that he ordered two birth control pills off the market for safety and quality concerns. Intended to show pharma that he would not be bullied, it was not very effective. Both companies were bit players with tiny sales.[64] A backup plan for showcasing the FDA's new aggressiveness had nothing to do with oral contraceptives. Edwards recalled nine of the country's best-selling mouthwashes, all of which had been advertised to "combat cold symptoms [and] destroy bacteria." The FDA announced they "were ineffective for preventative or therapeutic claims." Two of the nine, Betadine Mouthwash Gargle and Isodine, were Purdue Frederick products.[65] Large pharma firms, with fat profit margins earned from their top selling prescription drugs, paid little attention to the removal of the mouthwashes from the nation's drugstores.[66] Edwards followed up in November with a broader recall of several hundred prescription and over-the-counter drugs that the FDA judged "either ineffective or hazardous."[67]

Small drug firms with limited product lines, such as the Sackler-owned Purdue, took a short-term revenue hit from the FDA enforcement (one of Purdue's antiseptic solutions was also included in the November recall).[68] The overall industry, though, was unfazed by the FDA's actions. The sheer number of recalled drugs, reprinted in their entirety on full pages of the country's leading newspapers, seemed impressive to the lay public. Pharma, however, knew the medications were mostly unimportant. There was not a blockbuster on the list, not a single one in the top one hundred best-selling prescription drugs.[69]

As far as the industry was concerned, it had won the key battle, keeping most of the health risks about their oral contraceptives away from the women who took them. The next few years, however, showed that it was a Pyrrhic victory. There was a far more important battleground for the bottom line of the companies. Sales of birth control pills plummeted for five years before stabilizing. And the FDA responded with more stringent animal toxicology trials for oral contraceptives. The troubles over the Pill attracted attorneys specializing in consumer class action litigation (aggregated suits consolidating the claims of thousands of plaintiffs were only possible after a 1966 change in Federal Civil Procedure rules).[70]

The regulators, lawyers, and sinking sales meant that drug companies had little incentive to spend money for research and development for innovative new methods of birth control. The entire field went into hiatus at most pharmaceutical laboratories for the next two decades. Schering, for instance, had invested substantially during the 1960s into an injectable drug designed to provide three months of contraceptive protection. It shelved that work after the firestorm produced by the Nelson hearings. The same happened with collaborative 1960s research between Wyeth and the nonprofit Population Council on subdermal implants. That would have been useful for women who did not always remember to take a daily pill. That research was also halted after the Senate inquiry.* [71]

Eventually, the NIH prevailed on pharma to stop manufacturing any Pill that had more than 50 micrograms of estrogen. By then, clinicians estimated that 80 percent of all American women born after 1945 had at least tried the Pill. Pharma companies started searching for a "new generation pill" that might work with even less estrogen. Fifteen years later, following studies that showed adding low levels of progesterone reduced the odds for ovarian cancer, drug companies started mixing the two hormones.

"Only after millions of women had taken Enovid," Barbara Seaman later wrote, "and thousands had died or had been disabled by blood clots, was it discovered that the amount of hormones in the Pill was 10 times what was needed." [72] † [73]

---

* Pharma took more than twenty years to restart its work on the suspended 1960s research. Wyeth got FDA approval for Norplant, the first subdermal implant, in 1990. The FDA approved Schering's injectable contraceptive, Depostat, in 1992. The 1990s also marked the introduction of hormonal skin patch and vaginal ring. In some instances, the new ways of delivering hormones did not come without risks for the patients' health and the drug firms' bottom line. Fifty thousand women sued Wyeth over Norplant, contending the implant resulted in infections and debilitating fatigue; they settled for $100 million.

† On the fortieth anniversary of the sale of Searle's first Pill, Enovid, Barbara Seaman wrote in *The New York Times*: "I still frequently think about those women of an earlier generation who took the first Pill—unaware of their part in a still unfolding experiment—and died for love. I also think about the Tuskegee experiment on black men with syphilis, for which President Clinton apologized. Perhaps the families of those who died from Enovid deserve the same."

26

"SPLASHDOWN!"

Senator Gaylord Nelson's 1970 hearings about the dangers of the Pill had attracted the most intensive press coverage for a pharmaceutical story since the thalidomide scare eight years earlier. At the same time as the hearings, however, there was scant media interest in the Nixon administration's promise to introduce sweeping legislation to eliminate the duplication and confusion that hampered federal agencies tasked with enforcing the nation's drug laws. Nixon, who said that "America's Public Enemy No. 1 is drug abuse," had converted his battle on illegal drugs into a larger one about law and order. Some political analysts thought it was "arguably the decisive factor in his narrow triumph."[1]

The issue resonated with voters. Law and order had been the top worry in most preelection polls. The national violent crime rate doubled since 1960 and many middle-class voters were uneasy about increasing political and social unrest.[2] Nixon attacked the counterculture for embracing illegal drugs. He contended that antiwar activists, the Weather Underground radicals, hippies, and those who championed mind expansion with LSD or dropping out with marijuana, were behind the surge in crime as well as a spike in lethal overdoses. Heroin overdoses in New York City had quintupled over a decade to a record one thousand. Almost a quarter of arrests in big cities were drug-related. And as GIs returned from Vietnam, thousands were addicted to China White, a heroin so pure it was smokable. A year into his presidency (1971), Nixon called for a "war on drugs."[3] (Nixon was big on "wars" to fight public health issues; in 1971 he also declared a "war on cancer" and signed the National Cancer Act into law.)[4]

The idea that the existing hodgepodge of federal laws and regulations of drugs were ineffective and fragmented was not new. Lyndon Johnson had concluded during his last year as president that the "growing problem of narcotics and dangerous drugs . . . threaten[s] our Nation's health, vitality and self-respect." He urged Congress to reform federal drug laws that were "a crazy quilt of inconsistent approaches and widely disparate criminal sanctions."[5] Congress responded by folding the Treasury's Federal Bureau of Narcotics and HEW's Bureau of Drug Abuse Control into a newly created Bureau of Narcotics and Dangerous Drugs (BNDD) at the Justice Department. While that consolidated some enforcement duties in the federal bureaucracy, it fell far short of what Nixon envisioned.[6]

Not only did Nixon want to curb the importation and use of illegal drugs—he also wanted to strengthen the regulations over widely abused prescription medications. Previous crackdowns had focused on amphetamines and barbiturates and a rash of tough state laws had limited refills and dosing. Yet both classes of drugs remained popular. Their recreational availability seemed as widespread as ever. Stimulants and downers would undoubtedly get another review. The unanswered question when Nixon took office in January 1969 was whether his administration would take on mild tranquilizers, including the country's runaway best-selling drug, Valium. Arthur Sackler and Roche's top executives were disturbed at that possibility and held strategy meetings through the spring of 1969 to discuss how to prevent that from happening.[7]

Roche was Sackler's most important client and he made certain he was available whenever needed. That commitment put him under considerable stress because at the same time he was developing one of his greatest marketing ideas, one that could be transformative for his brothers and their drug company, Purdue Frederick. It revolved around Betadine, a distinctive orange-brownish liquid that combined a synthetic polymer (povidone) with iodine and killed bacteria on contact. The Sacklers had added Betadine to Purdue's offerings in 1966 when they bought Pittsburgh's Physician Products, a family-run drug company that held patents on several antiseptic products.[8] Arthur then had the clever idea of marketing Betadine to hospitals as an inexpensive disinfectant that doctors and nurses could use to clean their hands before all surgical procedures or contact with patients in intensive care, emergency, and recovery rooms. In 1968, the Sacklers won a lucrative Army contract to supply Betadine in bulk for wounded troops in Vietnam.[9]

Even Arthur, however, realized that his new idea was a long shot. He had learned a month after Nixon's election that NASA had an unusual concern about its planned summer space flight. If successful, two of the astronauts, Neil Armstrong and Buzz Aldrin, would become the first humans on the moon. The scientist worried that they might carry back to earth an extraterrestrial pathogen that could unleash an end-of-days pandemic. NASA planned to decontaminate the returning spaceship and all gear with a super bleach, as well as quarantining the astronauts for three weeks.[10] In a sealed room adjacent to the isolated astronauts, a group of germ-free mice would be exposed to moon soil. If the mice got ill or died, NASA expected the same would probably happen to the astronauts.[11]

Were those precautions enough? The answer to that might have been influenced by a book published only a few months before the Apollo 11 mission. It was the first best-seller by a doctor who had started writing fiction. Michael Crichton's *Andromeda Strain* was a terrifying tale of a deadly microorganism unwittingly brought back to earth by a military satellite. NASA decided it needed additional safeguards. Arthur Sackler managed to get Betadine before the space agency's senior scientists. They thought it was the ideal disinfectant.

When the astronauts splashed down in the Pacific on July 24, 1969, they put on biological isolation suits constructed from an innovative new nylon designed to prevent foreign microorganisms from attaching to their skin or hair. The history-making Apollo 11 team sprayed Purdue's Betadine on their space suits, the module's hatch, and their inflated rubber raft. NASA was confident that Betadine would kill alien microbes that hitched a ride to earth on any thin layer of moon dust that clung to the spacecraft or the men.

Anyone remotely familiar with Arthur Sackler's genius at promoting and selling drugs could have predicted what was next. Purdue ran dramatic full-age ads in the country's leading medical journals. "Apollo 11 Splashdown!" was the bold headline. "NASA Selects Betadine Antiseptic to Help Guard Against Possible Moon Germ Contamination."[12]

NASA had given Purdue a priceless sales pitch. Following the Apollo moon mission, the government increased its bulk purchases for the medical corps deployed in Vietnam.[13] The number of American hospitals relying on Betadine tripled, making it the country's most commonly used disinfectant. Better yet for the Sacklers, Betadine was cheap to make, pennies a gallon. Although the price to doctors and hospitals seemed reasonable, no one realized its enormous profit margins. Betadine was instantly Purdue's most lucrative product.

Mortimer and Raymond were ecstatic over Betadine's success, although they knew that since it had been Arthur's idea, they would have to endure him reminding them of why it was such a big hit. Seventeen years after they had bought Purdue, Mortimer and Raymond still worked under their brother's shadow. Marietta had observed that Arthur enjoyed turning everything into a competition, especially when it came to family.[14] He pushed himself, always taking on more work than anyone else, then insisting he did so because he did it better than anyone else. Once it was over, he goaded others by what he had achieved.

Mortimer and Raymond, for instance, had stopped conducting research studies and writing articles for medical journals (they had published almost all theirs with Arthur, between 1949 to 1959). Arthur, on the other hand, had continued his laboratory research and writing.[15] He never knew, he told them, when it might lead to a new Purdue product. And, in any case, it kept him grounded in the science he loved. Arthur had created the Laboratories for Therapeutic Research in 1957, and as its director pursued private and government research grants.[16] He had later hired Dr. A. Stanley Weltman as his senior research investigator.[17] Throughout the 1960s they not only got funding for ambitious clinical trials but the duo published their results in prominent medical journals. Many followed up on Sackler's earlier studies of how alterations in behavioral and endocrine levels affected mental illness.[18] Before the Betadine-moon project, Arthur became chairman of the International Task Force on World Health Manpower for the World Health Organization. The WHO expected he would concentrate on "advances in the drug therapy of mental illness." The author discovered that the WHO badly underestimated how broadly Arthur interpreted his mandate. He conducted studies to determine which workplace disturbances might negatively affect a worker's psyche and therefore their productivity. Sackler got funding from the Environmental Protection Agency to study the effect of loud noises in the workplace.[19] His conclusion in another study, delivered to the United Nations, was that a shortage of trained medical personnel led to the death or disability of 100 million people annually. It put Arthur back in *The New York Times*.[20] And he regaled in great detail to Mortimer and Raymond his annual keynote addresses in Geneva at the World Health Organization's World Workplace Health Day.[21]

The Laboratories for Therapeutic Research received about $800,000 in government or private foundation grants for clinical trials. There are no records available for how Sackler used the funding. Arthur did not get everything he applied for, however (he was particularly irked later by a failure to get a generous grant in 1971 from the Association for the Aid of Crippled Children).[22]

There was a certain prestige attached to a research scientist, especially one who chaired an international task force for the WHO. And Arthur never let Mortimer and Raymond forget it. He often needled them by recounting the details of what project was under way at the lab. On a later study, he told his brothers and Marietta about how he had chosen fifty rats, a "special breed that spontaneously develops high blood pressure." Then, twice a day, Arthur and Weltman strapped half the rats into a breadbox-sized plastic cage, attached them to a motorized shaker, and jolted them side to side 150 times a minute for half an hour. All the while, the rats were bombarded with sounds recorded from the New York subway system. After four months, four of those subjected to the shaking were dead. Autopsies revealed they had enlarged adrenals, the body's glands for generating hormones in response to stress.[23]

The results did not surprise Mortimer or Raymond, who thought it a waste of time. But Arthur had a knack of knowing when and how to promote something that seemed ordinary to others. He had gotten a grant from the Office of Noise Abatement and Control of the Environmental Protection Agency to study "transportation (rail and other), Urban Noise Problems and Social Behavior—Physiological and Psychological Effects."[24] Eventually, Weltman present their findings to the Federation of American Societies for Experimental Biology. *The New York Times* ran a prominent article because Arthur had figured out how to make the results interesting to the public. The *Times* headline was: "Scientists Advising Rats to Avoid Subway Rides."[25] It led with "Rats with high blood pressure should not ride the subways too often or too long. The stress of noise, vibration and crowding may kill some of them before their time. And, according to the scientists who tested the rats, similar studies should be conducted on human beings with high blood pressure to see whether they face the same hazard." Sackler was quoted, including his observation that "I don't think man was constructed to ride subway trains."[26]

Arthur did not need to say "I told you so" when he gave copies of the *Times* article to Mortimer and Raymond. It was not just about continuing clinical research that he kept haranguing them. He even prodded the two about why they were not filing more drug patents. He had several approved, all related to innovative and improved anatomical models for the brain and central nervous system, inventions that would be useful for medical students and researchers. Mortimer and Raymond did file for a series of patents, all related to Purdue products. Even then, Arthur lectured one or both about how they could have done it better. When Raymond had filed in 1966 for a chemical base that allowed for a considerably faster absorption rate for suppositories, Arthur lectured him about why it was smart to assign those rights to a Sackler company abroad. It might afford more legal protections and even a better tax rate should that patent become valuable. Raymond did assign "Novel Hydrogen Bonded Compounds and Pharmaceutical Compositions" to Mundipharma AG, the Swiss company the brothers had created in 1957.[27] Although Raymond made the transfer mostly to stop Arthur explaining why he should do so, it would turn out to have significant consequences when it later played a role in the development of Purdue's extended release coating for its narcotic painkiller, OxyContin. Putting trademarks, patents, designs, and copyrights—so-called IP, intangible or intellectual property—in a tax haven was an idea that not only became widespread in the pharmaceutical industry, but later allowed the Sacklers to save hundreds of millions in taxes when OxyContin became a blockbuster success.[28]

27

"TELL HIM HIS LAWYER IS CALLING"

In November 1969, Arthur's attention was abruptly brought back to Valium and Roche. The Fourth Circuit Court of Appeals, in Richmond, Virginia, ruled against drugmaker Carter-Wallace in its two-year-old lawsuit to overturn the FDA's decision that Miltown had the "potential for abuse."[1] The Fourth Circuit noted, "The evidence on this issue is in sharp conflict. It ranges from testimony of Carter-Wallace's experts that the potential for abuse of candy or aspirin is greater than for meprobamate to testimony from a government witness that he became so uneasy about alcoholics' affinity for the drug he stopped prescribing it for them."[2] Although the court acknowledged that the FDA's administrative judgment was "not supported by direct evidence," it was satisfied there was sufficient "circumstantial evidence, or indirect proof" of "future or potential abuse."[3] The unanimous verdict was bad news for Carter. Its broad language also did not bode well for Roche, whose appeal of the FDA's similar ruling against Librium and Valium was working its way through the courts.

Could the Nixon administration regulate the benzos while Roche's judicial appeal was pending? Roche and Sackler were not certain. They were not aware that a thirty-year-old Justice Department attorney, Michael Sonnenreich, was working on doing just that. He was drafting a law that would turn out to be Roche's feared worst-case scenario. Sonnenreich and Sackler did not know each other. In a few years, however, the young lawyer would play as important a role in Sackler's life as anyone, even becoming a closer confidant to Arthur than his own brothers.

Sonnenreich, born in 1938, was the second son in a middle-class

Jewish family in the mostly Italian neighborhood of Marble Hill, in the northernmost tip of Manhattan. His mother, Fay, who had graduated college with honors at only seventeen, was a former teacher. She was the first female administrator and executive secretary for Manhattan's Temple Israel.[4] Emmanuel (Manny), Sonnenreich's father, had a doctorate in ancient languages and had studied to be a rabbi before working at several New York social agencies. He became the membership director of B'nai B'rith, the world's oldest Jewish service organization. While the family was steeped in Judaism, Sonnenreich went to a public school.

A self-described "great test taker," he graduated near the top of his Bronx High School of Science class. Although he got a New York Regents "scholarship for academic excellence" to Cornell, he chose the University of Wisconsin ("I didn't want to stay in New York, and I liked Bob La Follette a lot)."[5] *

Without a scholarship Sonnenreich worked a series of odd jobs. Later his talent at duplicate bridge and billiards provided "just enough to pay" his bills. With majors in Applied Engineering, Mathematics, and History, he was the first American to spend a year abroad at the University of Spain.[6] There, he became a habitué of the Prado Museum's archives, indulging interests in art history and Thomistic philosophy. When he returned to Wisconsin for his senior year, he married a childhood friend four years his junior.[7]

Sonnenreich wanted a history doctorate but when he graduated from Wisconsin, he agreed to take the law boards to satisfy his father. "I bought a textbook about the law tests and that was all I needed," he recounted.[8] His aced the exams and was accepted at three schools to which he applied, Harvard, Yale, and Columbia. He selected Harvard. After graduating near the top of his law school class in 1963, he was drafted. His Harvard law degree meant the Army dispatched him to the Judge Advocate General's School in Charlottesville.[9] Two years later he was a civilian again and applied to some large New York firms.

---

* La Follette, nicknamed "Fighting Bob," was the founder of the Progressive Party under whose banner Teddy Roosevelt made his final run for the presidency in 1912. Under La Follette, a former Wisconsin governor, U.S. congressman, and senator, the progressives and the socialists fought for similar issues. La Follette advocated against the abuse of workers, the corruption of the moneyed industrial class, racial inequality, and suffrage. He ran for president in 1924, garnering 17 percent of the national vote. The Progressive Party dissolved after his death the following year.

"There was a long list of white-shoe law firms then that didn't hire Jews," he recalls, "so my choices were limited."[10] A traditionally WASPish breed, Abbott and Morgan made him an offer but he was not very interested in the bankruptcy, mergers, and business litigation that had become the mainstay for many large law firms in the 1960s. Sonnenreich accepted an offer in the Criminal Division of the Justice Department. As he had been in school, he proved a fast study. It was not long before his colleagues took notice of the young attorney with the eidetic memory capable of synthesizing complex issues into simple-to-understand talking points. Fred Vinson Jr., the Criminal Division's assistant attorney general, made him part of a team handling civil rights cases.

Sonnenreich's colleagues were by now accustomed to how he tackled assignments. Few could keep up when it came to working through a roomful of documents. He could read more than a thousand words a minute and retain them. By then he had gotten the attention of William Bittman, best known for his successful 1965 prosecution of Teamster boss Jimmy Hoffa.[11]

Sonnenreich would quickly be front and center in the debate over reforming the nation's drug laws. It was about a month later that John Dean, then an associate deputy under Nixon's attorney general, John Mitchell, walked into Sonnenreich's office. The two had met the previous year when Dean was the associate staff director to LBJ's National Commission on Reform of Federal Criminal Laws.

"I hear you rewrote the drug laws," Dean said to him.

"Yes."

It was not an empty boast. Later that year, the Government Printing Office would publish Sonnenreich's *Handbook of Federal Narcotic and Dangerous Drug Laws*.[12]

"Would you be willing to meet with the attorney general?"

"Yes."[13]

When Sonnenreich and Mitchell met, he told the attorney general that the "drug laws are archaic" and the enforcement and regulatory framework was a confusing and sometimes contradictory hodgepodge of laws and amendments that had been cobbled together over the decades. In 1951 Congress instituted the first mandatory minimum sentences for drug convictions and barred probation for first offenses.[14] Five years later a different Congress increased the minimum jail terms.[15] In 1965, faced with a wave of unknown psychedelic drugs, it criminalized manufacturing or possessing those hallucinogens and gave HEW enforcement responsibility.[16]

None of the laws addressed treatment, Sonnenreich told Mitchell. He believed it was not enough for reforms to curb supply. They should also cut the demand for drugs.[17] Mitchell asked Sonnenreich if he would meet with Nixon.

"Of course, I'd be willing to talk to the president."

A few days later in the Oval Office, Sonnenreich told Nixon about his idea for a commission to examine existing laws before making any final recommendations. Nixon liked that. Sonnenreich was transferred to the Bureau of Narcotics and Dangerous Drugs. There, as deputy chief counsel, he began drafting what would become the heart of the Controlled Substances Act. He established "schedules" by which drugs were listed, balancing their medical usefulness, if any, against their potential for abuse.

Sonnenreich was thirty-one years old and liked his work. He expected to to spend his career in government service. "My wife and I were happy; we had no problem in wanting more. We did everything we wanted to do. . . . One day this guy comes in with some Roche people and he says to me that 'If you schedule Librium or Valium, we're gonna challenge this, we're gonna challenge that.'"

It was Arthur Sackler. Sonnenreich had never heard of him.

"I welcome your challenge, it makes my day," Sonnenreich replied.

Sackler again warned that Roche would battle any effort to restrict the sale of its drugs.

"I'm going to do something better," said Sonnenreich. "I'm going to file an administrative action to put your drugs under control and put them on the three times prescription rule [a controlled substance limited to a maximum of three refills]."[18]

When Sonnenreich later held that administrative hearing to determine whether Roche's benzodiazepines should be covered in one of the Controlled Substances Act schedules, he recalls "they had all the big law firms there, the biggest D.C. powerhouses. They were wrong if they thought that might scare me. They didn't understand I was having a good time. They had just irritated me so much. I was still getting paid the same $7,900 a year, it didn't make any difference to me."

Sonnenreich and the Justice Department won the administrative action. "Arthur was obviously very, very upset," he recalls.[19]

Sonnenreich's draft of the Controlled Substances Act was at the heart of sweeping reorganization legislation—the Comprehensive Drug Abuse Prevention and Control Act—that the Nixon administration submitted to Congress in early 1970.[20]

In creating four schedules of "controlled substances," Sonnenreich had in part relied on extensive research and guidelines set out earlier that year by the World Health Organization.[21] The public initially misinterpreted those schedules to think the drugs were listed in order of danger. Sonnenreich had instead balanced the potential for abuse with whether a drug had "any currently accepted medical use." Although Cicely Saunders was then praising heroin as an effective pain reliever at her London hospice, it was judged to have no medical benefit. There was grim evidence of its abuse between hospital admissions and deaths from overdoses. It, along with LSD and ecstasy, were on Schedule I. So was marijuana, although that was a political compromise. The assistant secretary of health had suggested it be placed there temporarily until Nixon appointed a commission to recommend a final status.

Cocaine, methamphetamine, oxycodone, and fentanyl at least had demonstrated medical uses—cocaine in dental surgery as a topical anesthetic—and were listed on Schedule II, although they had a risk of "severe psychological or physical dependence." Drugs on Schedule III were those with recognized therapeutic benefits but with a moderate risk of "physical or high psychological dependence." That is where Miltown, along with amphetamines and barbiturates, was put. Schedule IV was designed to include combination drugs that had a "low potential for abuse."

What was notably missing from the statute sent to Congress was any mention of Librium and Valium. Sonnenreich had expected they would later be added to the same category as Miltown, the industry's original mild tranquilizer. Roche, however, argued that could not happen while its judicial appeal of the FDA's effort to regulate more strictly the benzos was still pending.[22]

A new round of administrative hearings attempted to settle the matter once and for all. Neil Chayet, the founder of the Law-Medicine Institute at Boston University and a member of the National Institute of Mental Health's Narcotic Addiction and Drug Abuse Committee, appeared in hearings as "an expert in legal medicine." He set forth Roche's position: Valium and Librium were not "drugs of abuse in the usual sense." Roche even presented eleven letters from police departments that stated that none had seen criminal problems associated with either Valium or Librium.[23]

Roche's lobbying worked. When Congress passed the law in the fall of 1970 it had a fifth grouping, what some called "the Roche schedule."[24] It covered drugs with the lowest potential for abuse, and it included Valium, Librium, and a few codeine-cased cough syrups that contained codeine.*

As Congress debated the bill, Neil Chayet called Sonnenreich. The two had been Harvard law school classmates. Chayet said he did legal work for Arthur Sackler and suggested the next time Sonnenreich was in New York, Sackler would like to meet him "to discuss Roche's drugs and federal oversight."[25]

"Why should I meet with that idiot?" Sonnenreich replied. ("Those are the types of things you say when you're very young," Sonnenreich told the author).[26]

Shortly after that conversation, Sonnenreich visited New York. Chayet arranged a dinner at Sackler's sprawling apartment at United Nations Plaza. The twin thirty-eight-story towers had opened only a couple of years earlier and had been designed by the same architects who did the United Nations. Sonnenreich knew it was home to some of New York's most prominent families.

"We had dinner," recalls Sonnenreich, "and during the discussion Arthur got frustrated and started yelling at me. Well, I don't respond well to being yelled at and I yelled back. Marietta was there and she got up from the table and left the room. Neil sat there quietly. And Arthur and I went on arguing for several hours. I had all the confidence and cockiness of a young guy and I kept telling him he was an 'old dog who didn't know the new things that had to be done.' He was trying hard to persuade me that I was wrong on the regulations. Neither of us convinced the other."[27]

The next day, when Sonnenreich was back at the Department of Justice, Sackler's secretary called.

"I got on the phone."

---

* The Schedules were amended repeatedly even after Nixon signed it into law on October 27, 1970. They were regularly updated with drugs added or removed and others transferred from one schedule to another. Barbiturates, originally on Schedule III, were reassigned to the more stringent Schedule II in 1972. In 1973, when the DEA was created, it upgraded the benzodiazepines to Schedule IV and moved Miltown there.

"You know I like you," Sackler started. "I would like you one day, if you leave the government, to do some work for me. Think about it."

"I am going to stay in the government," Sonnenreich told him. "This is what I'm happy doing, this is where I'm staying."[28]

Sonnenreich's career was moving fast. Nixon had embraced Sonnenreich's idea of a national commission to study and recommend how the government should address marijuana.[29] Going into private practice did not entice him.

The president appointed nine of the thirteen members on the National Commission on Marihuana and Drug Abuse. They included doctors, academics, psychiatrists, and attorneys. The congressional leadership appointed two U.S. senators, and two congressmen. Former Republican governor of Pennsylvania Raymond Shafer was its chairman (it was mostly referred to later as the Shafer Commission). Nixon tapped Sonnenreich to become the executive director, in charge of a staff of seventy-six.[30]

Nixon expected that the conservative Republican majority with which he had stacked the Shafer Commission would return with an uncompromising finding about the dangers of marijuana. Instead, after eighteen months of testimony from dozens of experts, Sonnenreich and Shafer knew they had reached a conclusion that Nixon was not likely to embrace: they had not found evidence that marijuana was physically addictive, nor was it a gateway drug.

"When I told them at the White House what we were planning to say," Sonnenreich told the author, "they thought I was crazy. They could not understand that we were going to recommend decriminalization."

"You need to take marijuana out of the criminal justice system," Sonnenreich argued in vain. "These young people are not criminals. You are degrading the criminal system. It can't handle all of them."[31]

Sonnenreich was not a proponent of the drug but thought criminalizing it was the wrong solution. He pointed out when Nixon had come into office, the government "spent a total of $66.4 million for the entire federal effort in the drug abuse area." That had ballooned to $796.3 million by 1972, and for the next budget it would exceed $1 billion.[32]

The administration hard-liners were furious with the interim report. They feared the public would interpret decriminalization as an endorsement for using marijuana. "From that moment on," Sonnenreich told the author, "I was cut off from the White House."[33]

The Shafer Commission did not finish its final report, with 3,700 pages of appendices, until 1973.[34] Nixon ignored its recommendations.*[35]

By that time, a special Senate committee had begun investigating the Watergate scandal. That fall, "Dean told me it was all going south," recalls Sonnenreich.[36]

It was evident later that year that the Nixon presidency was in trouble.

"I got a call from Arthur Sackler one day. And he says, 'Remember when I told you I wanted you to be my lawyer? Are you interested now?' "

"And then, in one of the great all-time stupid things I've said, I told him, 'If I was interested, you couldn't afford me.' "

"Try me," replied Sackler.

"I named a number, which I refuse to disclose," says Sonnenreich. "The next day, a check was on my desk."

What Sonnenreich did not know was that Sackler was more anxious than ever to hire him. It was not only because Sonnenreich was exceptionally smart, something Arthur considered an indispensable trait, but also because within eight months of each other the Sacklers had lost two of their most loyal confidants, Bill Frohlich and Félix Martí-Ibáñez. Frohlich was only fifty-eight when he died from a brain tumor on September 28, 1971. Just prior to his death, he had acquired a network of leading underground FM radio stations he christened the National Science Network.[37] And over several years, he oversaw IMS International's growth into one of the largest compilers of private medical and pharmaceutical information, with offices in thirty-two cities. He had expanded his eponymously named medical advertising agency in New York to seven countries. It had 340 employees.[38]

Martí-Ibáñez had just turned sixty when he died of a heart attack at his Manhattan townhouse only eight months after Frohlich. At the

---

* The "temporary" placement of cannabis on Schedule I, along with heroin, LSD, and ecstasy, became permanent once Nixon refused to follow his commission's decriminalization proposal. As anecdotal accounts accumulated over the decades that marijuana might have some medicinal properties, its advocates abandoned their effort to get it reclassified to a lower Controlled Substances schedule. Instead, starting in the 1990s a movement coalesced around legalizing medicinal marijuana. That opened the door for broader legalization arguments. As of December 2019, thirty-three states have approved medical marijuana and ten of those have legalized recreational use. The opioid crisis has created a possible market for medical cannabis as scientists debate mixed science about its pain-relieving properties.

time of his unanticipated death he was the editor of five international medical journals and the chairman of the History of Medicine Department at New York Medical College. Martí-Ibáñez was the author of several dozen illustrated histories of medicine, science, and philosophy, as well as half a dozen novels and several hundred academic articles and commercial short stories and essays (he left behind eleven unfinished manuscripts on varying projects).[39]

Marietta had hoped that the unexpected deaths of Frohlich and Martí-Ibáñez might serve as warning signal for Arthur. When she raised it, Arthur argued their deaths were unrelated to how hard the two had pushed themselves. Frohlich had the bad luck of developing cancer, he told Marietta. And Martí-Ibáñez was an inveterate smoker, he said, someone whose only exercise was lifting a martini glass every evening. Marietta was not surprised that Arthur tried brushing aside any suggestion that the death of his close friends should be a reason for him to slow down.

Although Arthur may not have seen a lesson in the early deaths of Frohlich and Martí-Ibáñez, he and his brothers mourned their passing. They had been two of their most trusted friends, as close to the brothers as family. The five had secretly owned stakes in each other's companies and all had more success than they could have imagined when they began. Now, their deaths had created a vacuum.

Having unexpectedly received the check from Sackler, Sonnenreich called Arthur's office. His secretary answered.

"I'd like to talk to Dr. Sackler."

"Who should I say is calling?"

"Tell him his lawyer is calling."[40]

28

A NEW DEFINITION OF BLOCKBUSTER

Long before the word "multitasking" morphed from the world of IBM mainframe computers to human behaviors, Arthur Sackler had an innate ability to juggle multiple projects simultaneously. While engrossed in the New York art world, he remained as busy as ever with Purdue Frederick, medical advertising, and publishing. There was a sea change under way in some key aspects of the pharmaceutical industry. He and his brothers monitored it closely; they did not want to be left behind.

Nixon had declared a "war on cancer" and Congress responded with the National Cancer Act in 1971. Oncology did not exist as a medical specialty and doctors knew remarkably little about the disease they were tasked to cure. Well into the 1970s, most physicians thought cancer was a single disease, defined by the organ in which it was discovered (for instance, breast or brain or lung cancer). No one understood the role gene mutations played. Today, cancer is recognized as approximately two hundred different and distinct diseases, each identified by unique molecular alterations, no matter where in the body it is found.[1]

The drug industry had been mostly a bystander in cancer treatment. The prevailing medical wisdom was that cancers could not be cured. However, the federal government's "war on cancer" created a big inducement for pharma: a lot of available research money. A year after Congress passed the act, the National Cancer Institute budget exceeded a billion dollars for the first time (the NCI's first budget in 1950 was a measly $2.1 million).[2]

Eighty-five percent of the new funding went to investigator-initiated research, mostly clinical testing for advanced chemotherapy drugs. Some promising earlier studies that had stalled for lack of funding restarted.[3] Those trials demonstrated that for early stage breast cancers chemotherapy after surgery was far more effective in eradicating tumors than either chemo or surgery alone.[4] Two follow-up studies showed the same was true for colorectal and testicular cancer.[5]

Some Arthur Sackler–minded promotion executives tried euphemistically calling chemotherapy "anti-tumor antibiotics." It never stuck. Seven new chemos, however, were developed from the new research, and the first reached the market in 1973.

The federal funding also led to breakthroughs outside of drugs. New diagnostic tools included colonoscopies for the early detection of colorectal cancer and CT scans and improved mammography for more precise tumor images. There was also noticeable progress on less invasive treatments once cancers were diagnosed. Radioactive seeds to treat prostate cancer replaced some surgeries, as did limited mastectomies for early stage breast cancer and targeted radiation for testicular cancer.[6]

The significance of some of the findings would not be apparent for a decade or more. Monoclonal antibodies, for instance, a technology for identical copies of an immune cell, was discovered in the lab in 1975. (It was not until the 1990s they were proven clinically useful in boosting the body's immune response to fight some cancers; the two scientists who discovered them won the Nobel in Medicine.)

Although many of the 1970s cancer treatments seem rudimentary in comparison to the targeted gene therapies that arrived decades later, the burst of research on the causes and treatments of cancer laid the foundation for what ultimately became significantly longer survival prognoses and lower death rates.

Not every drug firm was interested in producing a cancer drug. Some had grand ambitions in unrelated fields. Squibb had begun investigating in 1968 whether it was possible to create a synthetic compound that mimicked the peptides found in the venom of a poisonous Brazilian viper. It caused a fatal drop in blood pressure. Researchers discovered that the venom inhibited the production of a kidney chemical that regulated blood pressure. Squibb's researchers tested hundreds of chemical compounds before making a breakthrough in 1974 when they synthesized a molecule that mimicked the viper venom. They had put it together atom by atom.[7] The result was an orally active drug that in clinical trials showed promise at controlling blood pressure and treating congestive heart failure.

When Squibb put Capoten (captopril) on sale, it was the first ever ACE inhibitor.[8] Before its introduction, the medical advice for patients with congestive heart failure had been bed rest, diuretics (to help the heart pump fluid from the body), and digoxin (to relieve chest pain). Capoten was not a cure but it reduced the mortality rate and improved the quality of life for most patients.[9] Within a decade, half a dozen other pharma companies marketed competitive ACE inhibitors, transforming what had been a nonexistent market to more than 150 million annual prescriptions.[10]

While ACE inhibitors were big news, they paled in comparison to a new blockbuster class of medications targeting peptic ulcers. Doctors had for years known that ulcers, at times painful and in some cases deadly, were caused by excess acid in the digestive tract. Researchers were stumped, however, in how to treat them. The bland diets advised by most doctors did little to help. Over-the-counter alkalis, like Alka-Seltzer, provided temporary relief.[11] In severe cases, surgeons removed part of the stomach in the hope they excised the ulcerated portion.[12]

Ulcers were one of the conditions for which Sackler and Roche had pushed the limits of what the FDA had approved as the indications for its benzodiazepines. However, since the early 1960s, a growing number of researchers believed that the culprit was organic rather than emotional. They had discovered a single histamine molecule activated the production of acid when it locked on to a receptor in the stomach lining.[13] Doctors were familiar for decades with histamines, hormones produced by the immune system. They were mostly protective but sometimes caused inflammation, increased heart rate, allergies and hay fever, even pulmonary complications. A Swiss doctor, Daniel Bovet, had won the Nobel in Physiology and Medicine in 1957 because of his pioneering work in isolating and producing "histamine antagonists" (antihistamines to the lay public).[14]

A group of Smith Kline researchers knew that nothing stopped the histamine-stimulated acid that caused peptic ulcers. The team was led by Dr. James Black, a Scottish pharmacologist and physician. Black had won fame for developing the first beta blocker in 1962 while he was researching the effects of adrenaline on the heart (his discovery, called propranolol, was the first drug capable of controlling high blood pressure). Smith Kline had asked Black to find a cure for ulcers. That meant discovering, isolating, and then synthesizing an effective histamine antagonist. The problem was that the histamine responsible for ulcers bound itself to a type of receptor (the H2) that did not respond to antihistamines. After five years, in 1968, they had created more than seven hundred chemical composites but had nothing to show for their efforts.[15]

No one had ever produced a medication with a targeted biological pathway. The project was spared cancellation at the last moment when Black's team isolated some minor antagonist properties on a retest of one of their early compounds. It took another two years (1971) before the project produced a drug called metiamide. Black marveled as the ulcers on most test patients completely healed over several weeks of clinical trials in 1973. However, a third of those patients developed a serious blood disorder. Their white cells plummeted and made them susceptible to infections.[16] Back in the laboratory, Black's team made molecular alterations that produced a close chemical cousin to their original compound.[17]

Black and his researchers team gave it the generic name cimetidine. It passed clinical trials as effectively as had its predecessor in healing ulcers. This time there were no adverse effects. With a trouble-free approval process from the FDA, Smith Kline put Tagamet on the market in November 1976 in the U.K. and the following year in America (Smith Kline chose TAG from an*tag*onist and MET from ci*met*idine). It was a panacea for the millions suffering from peptic ulcers. Tagamet set a new standard by which to define a blockbuster. Black won a Nobel in Medicine. And Smith Kline was rewarded with spectacular profits. Tagamet became the first drug in history to sell a billion dollars in a single year.[18]

The receptor site medications would in another decade result in a series of other breakthrough drugs, including statins to lower cholesterol, nucleoside reverse inhibitors for HIV-AIDS, proton pump inhibitors for gastrointestinal reflux, and selective serotonin reuptake inhibitors for depression.[19] However, before the next wave of receptor site drugs arrived, research under way in northern California was about to open a window into technological and scientific advances that would be much more important for the pharmaceutical industry than any single blockbuster.

Since the discovery of penicillin, drug innovation in the laboratory had been a hit-and-miss process grounded in organic chemistry. Laboratories operated by so-called random drug discovery. Backbench scientists spent months looking for signs of biological activity in plants, soil, or other natural sources. The molecules that showed some possibility were isolated as potential compounds. For every 5,000 of those, 250 on average got to the next stage, testing on lab animals. That eliminated another half. Of the drugs that began human clinical studies, only 20 percent got FDA approval for sale to the public.[20]

In 1971, a Stanford biochemist, Paul Berg, developed a gene-splicing technique called recombination. Berg created a molecule from two different species (the results were not published until October 1972).[21] A year later, another Stanford professor, Stanley Cohen, teamed with Herbert Boyer, a University of California at San Francisco biochemist. They relied on Berg's gene-splicing method to clone genetically engineered organisms in foreign cells. The modified cells began replicating the new DNA as if it were its own. It was the birth of recombinant DNA (rDNA) technology.[22] Scientists mark the Cohen-Boyer discovery as the official beginning of genetic engineering. It kicked off a biotechnology revolution.

Many researchers, though, worried that there were unknown dangers to inserting rDNA from one organism to another. The science was moving fast and there were no restrictions on what could be done in a lab. What if some rDNA molecules later proved biologically hazardous? Much of the early focus was on *E. coli*, the intestinal bacterium that in one strain causes food poisoning. Its small genomic size, uncomplicated single set of chromosomes, and fast replication rate made it a versatile host for a range of recombinant DNA research. Would *E. coli* exchange genetic data with pathogenic bacteria, leading to unforeseen results in the gene combinations that might unintentionally unleash a human catastrophe?

The National Academy of Sciences' newly created Committee on Recombinant DNA Molecules comprised eleven of the world's leading biotech researchers, including Cohen and Boyer. Paul Berg was its chairman. In the July 1974 issue of *Science*, they signed a remarkable open letter titled "Potential Biohazards of Recombinant DNA Molecules." It warned of "emerging capabilities" risked the "creation of novel types of infectious DNA." One danger was if the rDNA in the lab contained a cancer-causing gene that metamorphosed into a transmissible human bacterium.[23]

A moratorium on genetic engineering went into effect.[24]

The Sacklers were convinced that the milestones in genetic research held the promise of big returns for any pharmaceutical company that could master recombinant DNA. They agreed to watch for opportunities so they might participate as investors. Writing a check to back a start-up was the most they could do. The brothers were barely keeping up with their own business demands.

The eldest sons of Arthur and Raymond found a way to have more time with their fathers. They went to work for them. Raymond's twenty-nine-year-old son, Richard, joined Purdue in 1971. He was also a physician, having graduated from New York School of Medicine and passing the licensing exams in both New York and Connecticut. Just before starting at Purdue with the newly created position "assistant to the president," he took Harvard Business School's intensive two-week Management Development Program. It was a crash course in how to hone "the skills to succeed in complex roles and shifting institutional and cultural landscapes." One of his first assignments was dealing with the FDA's determination that an antibiotic Purdue had in one of its ear-drop products was not potent enough to treat any infection. The FDA recalled those drops. Purdue blamed the manufacturer, Yonkers-based Bard Pharmaceuticals, which was covertly owned by the Sacklers.

As for Arthur, his son, Arthur Jr., had decided after graduating from Wisconsin's Lawrence College to join the family business. Arthur put his son to work in the McAdams marketing department. As opposed to Richard, who flourished under his father's guidance at Purdue, young Arthur was not as driven as his father and had difficulty meeting the high expectations set for him. Marietta thought that Arthur was too hard on his son. Soon he left McAdams and joined *Medical Tribune*. When that did not work out, Marietta arranged for her family firm, Dr. Kade Pharmaceutical, to sponsor Arthur Jr. for a certificate program in business administration at NYU. Following that, he accepted a director's position at Dr. Kade.[25]

Both sons knew how hard their fathers worked. There had been long periods growing up when they saw little of them. Still, it was not until they became employees that they realized how much was on the brothers' to-do list. Along with many other drug companies, the Sacklers were looking into opening a branch in Puerto Rico. A change in the tax code in the early 1970s exempted manufacturing firms from corporate income taxes on profits made in U.S. territories.[26] "There was a rush by many drug companies to set up manufacturing plants there," said Richard Sperber, a former Glaxo and Wyeth marketing director. "They would make the active substance of their drugs in Puerto Rico, then jack up the price and 'sell' it to another subsidiary that put it into final dosage form. Because the price on the drug's active ingredient was so expensive, little if any profit was earned. All the real money was at the untaxed manufacturing source."[27] In a few years the Sacklers opened Purdue Pharma in the capital of San Juan.*

The brothers, however, had bigger ambitions than creating subsidiaries to take advantage of changes in the tax code. They had long been interested in innovative delivery systems for oral and rectal medications. In the 1960s they had started researching technologies that might slow the rate at which a drug dispersed in the body, a rudimentary time release formula.[28] The author discovered ten patents Raymond and Mortimer had filed related to sustained release formulas for suppositories and tablets. The Sacklers were not alone. Plenty of pharmaceutical companies were pursuing some type of controlled release for medications.[29]

In 1969 and 1970, the Sacklers had also put the biochemists and pharmacologists at Mundipharma AG, their Swiss-based company, on a project to develop a time release technology. Mortimer and Raymond assigned all their 1960s patents to Mundipharma in Basel. That was also true of the legal rights for a co-inventor on four of those patents, Dr. Alfred Halpern (Halpern worked at Arthur Sackler's Pharmaceutical Research Associates, at 17 East 62nd Street, the address listed for half a dozen other Sackler businesses).[30]

The patents assigned by the Sacklers helped the Mundipharma team make progress in the lab. In 1971, Mundipharma filed for its own patent. The filing attracted little attention, even inside the pharma industry. As with many medical and science-related patents, it had a virtually indecipherable name: "Slow Release Formulation for Pharmaceutical Composition Containing a Fusible Carrier and Method for Producing the Same." Mundipharma soon filed two related patents for "Composition in Solid Dosage Form."[31]

That patent, and the underlying Mundipharma research, was the ideal complement to research then under way at two U.K. Sackler companies, Napp Pharmaceuticals and Bard Laboratories. The following year, Napp developed the first working compounds that the Sacklers

* Mortimer hoped that his twenty-year-old son, Robert, would also work for the family when he graduated from college. He died in an accident in 1975, at the age of twenty-five.

believed might be adaptable as a controlled release formulation applied to oral medications.[32]

The value of those Mundipharma patents, combined with others Napp subsequently filed, would not be evident until 1980 when Napp introduced a drug that had the first-of-its-kind sustained release coating. It was an invisible-to-the-human-eye chemical layer made of a dual-action polymer mix that turned to a gel when exposed to stomach acid. That allowed the drug, MST Continus (continuous), to release pure morphine at a steady rate over twelve hours.[33] Napp could adjust the release rate by fine-tuning the density of the coating's water-based polymer.[34]

MST Continus was the breakthrough painkiller for which Cicely Saunders had been searching for her end-of-life cancer and hospice patients since the mid-1960s. Its coating was also the technology that in the 1990s would help convert Purdue's opioid painkiller, OxyContin, into a much more widely prescribed medication. Doctors expected that a sustained release narcotic was less prone to addiction and abuse.

29

"KISS THE RING"

In the early days of his new job as Sackler's attorney, Michael Sonnenreich worked from an office at 15 East 62nd Street, the address where the Sacklers had listed more than a dozen companies since the 1950s. Sonnenreich used his talent as a fast study to learn everything possible about the brothers and their businesses.[1]

Before he left the Justice Department, Sonnenreich had met Bill Frohlich ("smart, he wanted me to be his lawyer") and Félix Martí-Ibáñez ("I found him a waste of time"). The Sacklers realized that if their new in-house attorney was going to be useful, they had to be honest with him. They filled him in on the secret deals that gave Arthur a stake in MD Publications and that he "basically owned the Frohlich Agency."[2]

In conversations with the brothers Sonnenreich realized there was an underlying friction between them that would likely worsen over time. Marietta had noticed their bickering for several years. It had started after their mother, Sophie, died from lung cancer at the age of sixty-nine in June 1963. She was the only one from whom, according to Marietta, Arthur "preferred to keep his distance, fearing her control."[3]

"The brothers remained close during their mother's illness," Marietta later recalled, "but their relationship began to decline after her death. It seemed to me that her strong, matriarchal force had maintained the vision of family togetherness. When she was gone, that vision began to dissolve."

The reasons behind the family tension seemed evident to Sonnenreich.

"Arthur basically got them through high school, college, medical schools in Edinburgh, and their medical residencies. He was the one that got them where they were, the one who put them into Purdue, the one who set everything up. And as older brothers tend to do, he wanted them to constantly kiss the ring. That's fine if you're in your twenties, maybe even if you are in your thirties. Then they reached a point where they didn't want to kiss the ring and then Arthur began getting very angry. They had big fights sometimes and would stop talking to each other for a while or talk about dividing things up. Then they would cool down and move on."[4]

It was not only Mortimer and Raymond with whom Arthur fought. "Arthur saw Else [his divorced first wife] every week, because they had kids, but he also liked her," recalled Sonnenreich. "That used to really aggravate Marietta."[5]

Notwithstanding the bickering, the Sacklers remained a tight-knit group wary of any outsiders. Sonnenreich earned their trust, especially Arthur's. The two had a special bond and were so similar that they sometimes clashed with each other.[6] The make-or-break moment for Sonnenreich with Arthur was not, however, about common traits. It was instead a challenge that Sonnenreich put to Arthur only a few months after becoming his attorney.

"You don't know how to run your business," Sonnenreich announced unexpectedly one morning. "You don't need a lawyer, you need someone to run your businesses."

"You think you can do it?"

"Arthur, I could lie on the floor and spit into the air and do better than you're doing."

"Okay, show me. Do it."[7]

Sackler had opened the door to bold proposals in an earlier conversation. "Arthur said to me once that when people look in a mirror they don't look to see what's on the other side. They only see their own reflection, they are not open to new ideas." Sonnenreich thought Sackler was "an advertising genius." However, he also recognized his limitations. Arthur was industrious at setting up a web of different enterprises but quickly lost interest and moved on to something else before finishing his last project. It was why some companies incorporated decades earlier were still inactive. Sonnenreich saw that the network of businesses Arthur had created was profitable, but he thought it was not realizing its full potential. He had reviewed the Sackler mini-empire and had marked the top targets.

Arthur had hired Sonnenreich with the understanding that he could do other work in the pharma field, so long as he always put the Sacklers first. Sonnenreich had accepted the president's job at the National Coordinating Council on Drug Education, the nation's largest non-profit, private drug education network.[8] He testified before congressional committees looking into drug and alcohol abuse.[9] And he had some clients besides the Sacklers, most prominently Dr. Sheldon Gilgore, then president of the pharmaceutical division of Sackler's biggest ad client, Pfizer (Sonnenreich negotiated the lucrative deal a decade later when Gilgore left Pfizer to become Searle's CEO).[10]

Sonnenreich assured the Sacklers that their businesses and personal affairs would always be his top priority. Arthur had confidence in the thirty-five-year-old, giving him a green light to first reorganize *Medical Tribune.* Sonnenreich streamlined some of the operations and impressed the brothers by reducing costs while boosting profits. He had a good eye for identifying unnecessary expenses and was unsentimental about eliminating them. That turned out to be a necessary trait when Arthur later decided to dismantle the union at *Medical Tribune.* Although Sackler had largely abandoned his youthful left-wing political passions, he had a soft spot for the former blacklisted journalists to whom he had provided safe-haven jobs during the height of the Cold War Red Scare. Because most of them had worked at daily newspapers under the Newspaper Guild of America, they asked Arthur to provide them with the protection of the union. As a result, *Medical Tribune* was the only unionized medical journal in the U.S. At first, Arthur did not want to do anything to change it, at least not while any of the former Red journalists worked there.[11]

There was only one left by the time Sonnenreich had started working for Arthur: Melvin Barnet, the copy editor dismissed by *The New York Times* in the mid-1950s for refusing to testify before Congress about his Communist Party past. He was the *Medical Tribune*'s associate editor. By then, Barnet was legally blind, but Sackler, "in kindness, kept him on long after he could see well enough to do the work." When Barnet retired in another year, Arthur allowed the hiring of freelance writers to "bust the union." Nine employees judged as too strongly aligned with the Newspaper Guild were dismissed. There was even an effort to induce students at the Columbia School of Journalism to submit articles for credit only.[12] The Guild called a strike. Sackler did not waver although Sonnenreich admits it "was a very difficult time" for Arthur. The union was finally broken at all the Sackler publications.[13]

While the shakeup at *Medical Tribune* was under way, Sonnenreich focused on unresolved matters left over from Frohlich's death. To ensure that Sackler's investments in Frohlich's advertising agency were protected, Louis Goldburt, Arthur's longtime accountant became one of the company's three directors. He brought with him another accountant from his firm, Lawrence Effman. Sackler had utilized both a decade earlier as donors at the Metropolitan Museum of Art and Effman had been selected to help Frohlich buy some independent radio stations on the West Coast. Shortly after the two accountants took control of the board, Frohlich's longtime president resigned, complaining the board was engaging in "subterfuge" and "deceit" and that it was "foolhardiness" to appoint an accountant who did not understand the agency's business. J. Walter Thompson, one of Madison Avenue's largest advertising agencies, appeared ready to purchase L. W. Frohlich International but client conflicts scuttled the deal.[14] It would be hard to hold the ad agency together without Frohlich at the helm. Three top executives had left a year after his death and formed their own ad firm, Lavey/Wolff/Swift.[15] A dozen division chiefs defected in 1973 to large agencies, all of which hoped to develop specialized subsidiaries for promoting pharmaceuticals and health care products.[16] The roster of Medicine Avenue expanded in the 1970s as L. W. Frohlich disintegrated.[17]

Sonnenreich at least succeeded in getting some of Frohlich's larger accounts, including Ciba's multimillion-dollar Vioform-Hydrocortisone campaign, switched to Sackler's McAdams.[18] Sonnenreich and Sackler not only susequently helped the Frohlich agency merge with a small medical ad firm, Sudler & Hennessey, they were instrumental in its sale to Young & Rubicam.[19]

Another pressing issue left from Frohlich's death were questions about a large bequest in his last will and testament. He had directed that Mortimer and Raymond were to get 85 percent of the proceeds from the 1.85 million shares he owned in IMS, whenever that company went public. Sonnenreich had learned that while "there was no paperwork for IMS," its start-up had been "all Arthur's money." To avoid any appearance of a conflict of interest, Arthur had stayed away, "but he put Mortie and Ray into it to watch over their investment."[20] Although Mortimer and Raymond were the only Sacklers named in the will, they intended to cut Arthur in on whatever payout they got.[21]

IMS began planning for an IPO a year after Frohlich's death.[22] No one could then have imagined that what seemed like a straightforward probate matter would turn into a quarter century of convoluted stock maneuvering, power plays on the IMS board of directors, and ploys that were masked as hostile takeovers.*[23] When there was eventually an IPO, the price was set at $25 per share. After deducting the underwriter's fee, Frohlich's estate, represented by his sister, Sophie, received $6.25 million. She was not happy that Mortimer and Raymond, with their 85 percent of her brother's shares, each received $37 million.[24]† Today IMS is valued at $20 billion, the world's leading firm in collecting and selling medical data.

It was not just business where Arthur Sackler and Michael Sonnenreich found common interests. The young attorney also had for more than a decade been buying art. Sackler had made it clear that was the one subject on which he did not want any advice. Sonnenreich concentrated on pre-Columbian and African art, staying far away from Sackler's interests. "I did not want to be told that I was doing something wrong," he recalled.[25]

What Sonnenreich had noticed about Arthur's collecting was that "he had done very little to publicly display his collections." Arthur was so focused on acquiring new pieces that he had little time to show his collections.

Sonnenreich knew that the Sacklers had given some of their early grants with their names attached to the gifts. Did they want that to continue? They said yes. That was important for Sonnenreich, who believed "strongly that if you put your name on something it is not charity, it's philanthropy. You get something for it. If you want your name on it, it's a business deal."[26]

The Sacklers wanted Sonnenreich to handle the business side of

---

* Sonnenreich had promised Arthur: "You are going to buy back IMS." The author discovered that Sonnenreich arranged for Arthur to initially buy 10 percent of IMS and then doubled that to 20 percent. "Then I went to Dubow [the IMS president]," Sonnenreich said, "and told him we wanted two directors for our 20 percent share." One was Bob Begondi, one of Sonnenreich's Harvard Law School classmates. The other was Robert Louis Dreyfus, heir to the eponymously named merchant banking dynasty. In 1998, Dreyfus oversaw the sale of IMS for $1.7 billion.

† Arthur was deceased by the time of that IPO, and Mortimer and Raymond had evidently forgotten about their assurances they would take care of their older brother. Arthur's children challenged the will, contending that "on a handshake with Bill Frohlich . . . he [Arthur] was entitled to one fourth." Mortimer and Raymond said they knew nothing about that, and the court rejected the argument put forth by Arthur's children since there was no written documentation to support the "handshake agreement."

their art bequests and gifts. When he was not working on their businesses, Sonnenreich urged the brothers to become major donors at the country's top museums.

"One day Marietta called me," Sonnenreich recalled. "She began excoriating me. 'You are worse than a mistress! He spends all his time with you!' "

"He's running a business, Marietta."

"He should be retiring," she replied.

When Arthur learned about Marietta's outburst, he smiled. That his wife was mad at Sonnenreich, he said, was a good sign that his new attorney and advisor was earning his pay.[27]

30

THE TEMPLE OF DENDUR

The short article titled "W. T. Grant Estate Sold," buried deep in the "Real Estate" section of the Sunday *New York Times* on June 3, 1973, was easy to miss. The $1,325,000 sale of the 12.3-acre Connecticut waterfront estate—built in 1948 for William Grant, the discount department store tycoon—was the most ever paid for a single residence in affluent Greenwich.[1] The house, put on the market months earlier at a $1.8 million asking price, had been designed by Edward Durell Stone, a pioneering modern American architect whose iconic New York works included the Museum of Modern Art and Radio City Music Hall. *The New York Times* described it as "one of the most spectacular private waterfront properties between New York and New Haven." Grant had died the previous year and bequeathed the estate to a local nonprofit hospital, which promptly put it up for sale.[2]

There were no buyers, however. The estate had huge upkeep costs. Grant employed nine full-time gardeners just to attend to his award-winning rose garden. And some potential buyers held off on making a bid since weak economic data through the spring of 1973 signaled an imminent downturn. Economists mark the ensuing recession, with high unemployment, runaway inflation, and a 40 percent drop in the stock market over eighteen months as the official end of the tremendous post–World War II expansion.

Who had the money and courage to pay a record price at a time the economy faced strong headwinds? No one knew. The anonymous buyer hid behind a real estate holding company that had created a PO box address for the deal. When a local reporter tracked down the holding company's Greenwich attorney, he refused to identify his client.[3] The lawyer disclosed that a shell corporation had provided $325,000 cash for the purchase. The additional $1 million came from a mortgage issued by a firm called Mundi-Inter. It was listed on the property deed as a New York corporation with a Norwalk, Connecticut, address.[4] When a *New York Times* reporter called the Mundi-Inter telephone number listed on the deed, an operator answered: "Good morning, the Purdue Frederick Company International."[5] When the journalist asked about Mundi-Inter, he was referred to Purdue's Manhattan headquarters. Upon calling Purdue, he was given the number of a New York lawyer. That attorney "declined to discuss any aspect of the purchase transaction."[6] No journalist followed Purdue Frederick back to the Sacklers. Their name did not appear in any story about the purchase of the Grant estate.

The house was for Raymond. Mortimer was spending much of his time abroad directing their rapidly expanding foreign operations. Arthur split his time between his midtown condominium and a four-story townhouse on East 57th Street in Manhattan's exclusive Sutton Place. He had bought that "on the spot" in 1960 at an estate sale. (Marietta Sackler later wrote, "Arthur surprised us with a townhouse that's too small for all of us but just right for him!")[7]

The big real estate purchases by the Sacklers were evidence of how well their ambitious business ventures were paying off. They were content as successful capitalists, their communist convictions a distant memory. None felt guilty about their newfound wealth. It was not the result of some clever invention or breakthrough drug. They had worked hard for it. Purdue's biggest-selling products were the laxative Senokot and antibacterial scrub Betadine.[8]

Arthur's McAdams agency had a larger roster of clients than at any other time in its history. In addition to Pfizer and Roche, he had added the Swiss multinational Ciba-Geigy after the two independent companies had merged in 1970. McAdams was approaching 150 employees and its billings were at a record, nearing $50 million annually.[9] Arthur's *Medical Tribune* was an international success. Bill Frohlich, to whom Arthur had given a small, then secret ownership stake, had used his excellent contacts in Germany to open the first foreign edition of *Medical Tribune* in 1967.[10] Seven other countries soon followed. Sackler's physician mailing list was unmatched.[11] Twice a week it reached more than a million doctors worldwide. In the U.S., ad pages cost $7,000, and annual profits were estimated at a million dollars.[12]

Arthur had also spun off a series of special supplements about psychiatry, cardiology, allergies, obstetrics and gynecology, pediatrics, and sexual medicine into six stand-alone magazines. To handle all his publications, he had created World Wide Medical Press and World Wide Medical News Service and Medical Tribune International (it later became Excalibur International Inc. and then Excalibur International Group).[13] The most successful of the new launches was *Sexual Medicine Today*. Arthur was listed as the publisher; his son, Arthur M., was the managing editor on later issues. Targeted toward psychiatrists, it straddled a precarious line between recent medical developments and quasi-tabloid coverage of then risqué subjects, including "Nazi Sexual Practices," "Do Sore Nipples Inhibit Sexual Foreplay?," "Medical Story of the Castrati," "Homosexual Prostitute: A Boy Prostitute," "Aphrodisiacs and Drugs," "Sex Change Surgery," and "Quest for the Ultimate Orgasm."[14]

Purdue Frederick had relocated its headquarters from New York City to Norwalk, Connecticut. In Connecticut, whose population had doubled in twenty years, an Economic Development Agency lured out-of-state businesses either to relocate or open branches. The Sacklers liked the state's lower business income tax rates and their move was sealed by an under-market rent at a new office building. With nearly three times the space as their cramped Greenwich Village headquarters, the brothers went on a hiring spree. For the first time Purdue surpassed two hundred employees.

The record-setting price paid in the late spring of 1973 for the Grant estate was not the only evidence of the family's financial success. The number and size of the bequests from their charitable foundations was further proof. Although the Sacklers went to considerable lengths to keep their names out of the news as buyers of the Grant estate, as patrons of the arts, education, and medicine starting in the mid-1960s they did so only on the condition their names *were* attached to major gifts.

It was logical that the brothers, involved as they were in so many aspects of medical publishing and pharmaceutical manufacturing, made their first major donations to medicine and education. In 1964 they underwrote construction of the Sackler School of Medicine in Tel Aviv (its American "admissions office" shared the same address and telephone number at one point as Arthur's McAdams agency).[15] When it opened in 1966, it attracted students who had moved to Israel and had completed at least three years of medical studies in their native countries. They could finish their education at the Sackler school and then do clinical training at other Tel Aviv hospitals (as of 2018, the Sackler School of Medicine in Tel Aviv is Israel's largest medical research and training facility, and has a unique arrangement with New York State whereby students who study there can be licensed as New York–qualified physicians).[16]

The Sacklers' debut in the world of elite philanthropy had been a $150,000 gift in 1963 to New York's prestigious Metropolitan Museum of Art. Now, a decade after Arthur had struck that deal with James Rorimer, the Met's director, he learned the museum was having difficulty finding a benefactor to finance the construction of a new wing to house the Egyptian Temple of Dendur. Egypt had given the two-thousand-year-old temple to the United States in gratitude for American assistance in building the Aswan High Dam. If the temple had not been moved piece by piece it would have been lost forever, submerged in the lake created by the dam.

Major American museums and universities wanted it. The National Foundation on the Arts and the Humanities established a commission to review all the applications. The Metropolitan was on a short list from the start.[17] The Met did a masterful job of explaining why the best way to preserve the monument was to build from scratch an ambitious new museum wing in which Dendur was reconstructed and displayed permanently.[18]

By the time the Met was awarded the temple in 1967, it had a new director. James Rorimer had died the previous year from a cerebral hemorrhage and the trustees had tapped Thomas Hoving as his replacement. Hoving, a charismatic art historian and New York's parks commissioner, learned that not much had happened since Egypt sent the dismantled six-hundred-ton temple by freighter to the U.S. The Met had stored the enormous 647 pieces in crates in an open-air building on its south parking lot.[19] The lack of progress was not for lack of desire. Hoving was a regular on New York's social A list and was tireless in charming the handful of ultra-wealthy philanthropists who might help underwrite the new wing.

He had tried all the usual suspects. Robert Lehman, heir to one of New York's great banking families, who had agreed to give the Met his 2,600 premier works of American and European art, was not interested. Nor was Michael Rockefeller, who had already made a gift of a major portion of his fine art collection. The same polite rejections came from other major Metropolitan benefactors, including André

Meyer (Lazard Frères), investment banker B. Gerald Cantor and his wife, Iris, and private equity titan Henry Kravis.[20]

At one point, Hoving was tantalizingly close to convincing Lila Acheson Wallace, the *Reader's Digest* cofounder, to write a check. She even tentatively said yes but then changed her mind. "It sometimes seemed the Temple of Dendur had fallen under King Tut's curse," Hoving later recounted.[21] As he went down the list of less likely donors, he stopped when he reached Arthur Sackler. The two had met shortly after Hoving had become the museum's director. Hoving had liked Arthur, judging him as "touchy, eccentric, arbitrary—and vulnerable, which made the game much more fascinating." And it had been in that meeting that Arthur surprised Hoving by announcing he was prepared to contribute another $150,000 to an acquisitions fund the director could use at his discretion. Sackler also wanted to underwrite the renovation of a special exhibitions gallery, adjacent to the one on the second floor named after his family. All he asked was that it should be named for his wife, Dr. Marietta Kade Sackler.[22]

Having run into a dead end on raising money for the Temple of Dendur wing, Hoving now remembered something else that Arthur said during their meeting six years earlier. Sackler "had mentioned his dream of uniting Egypt and Israel."[23] Figuring he had nothing to lose, Hoving called Sackler, who "surprised me by saying he would come to me, and he arrived less than a half hour later." Hoving told Sackler he was the "only one with the guts and the foresight" to pay for the Temple of Dendur and the Egyptian wing. Arthur knew he was not the museum's first choice; still he did not say so, instead allowing Hoving to pile on the compliments. After a few minutes, Hoving got to the bottom line. The Met needed $3.5 million ($21.5 million in 2019 dollars).

Hoving had hoped that Sackler might commit to give some of the money and help the museum raise the rest. He was not even certain whether Sackler was wealthy enough to make the bequest even if he wanted to do so.

Twenty seconds of silence elapsed. Hoving thought that Sackler was quiet because he was "embarrassed and was trying to figure out how to say no without making me feel like a fool."

"I'll do it," Arthur announced.

Hoving stared forward, not knowing for a moment what to say. He did not know that Arthur needed help from his brothers. Mortimer and Raymond agreed to join in underwriting the $3.5 million. They agreed it would come from their shares of Purdue Frederick profits.[24] So as not to put too much pressure on Purdue, the Sacklers wanted to put up as little cash as possible. Sonnenreich proved a tough and capable negotiator. It took a year of hard-nosed talks before there was a final deal.[25] The Met's biggest concession was allowing the brothers to spread their donation over twenty years, without interest. That translated into two decades of tax write-offs for the family.[26] The slow payout, Hoving later recalled, forced the Met "to borrow a few times from the endowment to pay the contractors."[27]

The Sacklers had agreed that besides the Dendur Temple they would bankroll new galleries for Egyptian Art, an archaeological and antiquities laboratory, and offices for the museum staff. The Raymond and Beverly Sackler Gallery for Assyrian Art was placed in a prime location, just to the left of the museum's main entrance.[28] The Mortimer and Theresa Sackler (his third wife) Gallery was dominated by three huge Tiepolo canvases and had a coveted location at the top of the Grand Staircase. The Temple of Dendur would be the first-floor portion of the newly named Sackler Wing. Each brother's name would be listed individually. The Sacklers had final say over press releases. The Met agreed that any further gifts they made would instantly be part of the museum's permanent collection. All catalogs, shows, photographs, or use of their galleries would feature their names.[29] "They insisted on having the M.D.'s on there," recalled Arthur Rosenblatt, the museum's vice director, saying later only partially in jest that only their office hours had been omitted.[30]

Old New York society had always sneered at the Sacklers as nouveau riche bargain hunters who bagged their naming rights from Rorimer at a fire sale price because the Met had then been desperate for money.[31] The arrangement for the Egyptian Wing and the Temple of Dendur did not require the Sacklers to donate any significant portion of their own art. Even their contribution—$3.5 million spread over twenty years without interest—seemed paltry compared to that of donors who underwrote their own wings, a low of $7 million from Gerald Cantor to $23 million for Lila Acheson Wallace.[32]

Arthur Sackler did not get a seat on the Met's Board of Trustees.[33] The sitting directors judged him too pushy. Sackler told his brothers that anti-Semitism kept him off and blamed the museum's general counsel, Ashton Hawkes.[34] Some of the patrician WASPs at the Met undoubtedly had dismissive and stereotypical views of self-made Jews such as the Sacklers. The evidence of that snobbery was that the Met's first Jewish trustee had decades earlier been George Blumenthal, the head of the U.S. branch of Lazard Frères. The refined German-born Blumenthal had built a mansion in Manhattan that occupied an entire city block. He needed the space to display a stunning art collection (most of which he bequeathed to the museum). He was also a generous philanthropist, writing a check for a million dollars to the Met in 1928 ($15 million in 2019), and equally large bequests to New York's Public Library and Mount Sinai Hospital.

Arthur would never have the right pedigree. On one occasion, C. Douglas Dillon, the Met's vice chairman, invited Sackler and Sonnenreich for lunch to his East 80th Street townhouse.[35] By then, Dillon was not only the chairman of an eponymously named international banking house, but he had served as Eisenhower's ambassador to France, treasury secretary for JFK and LBJ, and chairman of the Rockefeller Foundation and Brookings Institute.

"It felt like he [Dillon] was suffering our presence," Sonnenreich recalled to the author. "I would have left if I was not with Arthur."[36] When it was over and they had left, Sonnenreich told Arthur, "This was 'take a Jew to lunch day,' that's all this was. I'm just telling you bluntly."[37]

Arthur had not told Sonnenreich about his desire to become a museum director. Sackler knew he would have told him it was a waste of time. "Arthur had always tried to downplay his Jewish roots," Sonnenreich told the author. "He had even pretended he was Catholic for a while." Sonnenreich understood why it was such a sensitive matter; he had been at meetings at drug companies in which there were "all those kike jokes, you'd have to laugh with everyone else or it would have seemed strange you didn't think it was funny."[38]

However, not long after going to work for Sackler, Sonnenreich told him, "Let me explain something to you Arthur. If there is a pogrom, I don't care what you tell them you are, you are going to be in the same cattle car as I am. Stop the games. Stop them because they are not going to continue to work. You could marry all the Christian girls you want, it ain't going to work. They are still going to put you on the train and that's that."[39]

That pep talk had an impact on Arthur. Although he did not go out of his way to tell people he was Jewish, he no longer shied away from it whenever it came up.

Arthur Rosenblatt, the Met's number two, was Jewish. Rosenblatt thought the Met by then needed "every rich Jewish real estate mogul" since they had "run out of WASPs with money."[40] Still, the power brokers at the Met were slow to change.

Although Sackler did not become a trustee, he convinced Hoving to hire Princeton art historian Wen Fong as a special consultant to the Department of Asian Art.*[41] It had been Fong who had persuaded Arthur a few years earlier to donate to Princeton the largest collection of paintings by Tao-Chi, an important seventeenth-century artist.[42] The million-dollar gift created the Sackler Gallery for Chinese Art at Princeton. Maybe it was time, Sackler decided, to provide some not very subtle reminders to the Met that he had not yet decided where he would give the Chinese art stored in their basement.[43] He did little to hide meetings with university and museum directors who courted him. The National Gallery and Harvard's Fogg Art Museum were the most persistent.

Arthur would later donate $2 million for a therapeutic research lab at Long Island University, another $8 million for the Arthur M. Sackler Sciences Center at Clark University, and millions for the Sackler Institute of Graduate Biomedical Science at New York University and the Arthur M. Sackler Institute for Advanced Studies in Public Health, Medical Research and Communications at Tufts University. During his many travels to China, where he attended to his expanding *Medical Tribune*, he charmed government officials in the hope of getting permission to build the country's first post–Mao era museum at Beijing University.

Meanwhile, Mortimer and Raymond were expanding their bequests beyond the United States.[44] Mortimer led the way. He had in 1959 divorced his first wife, Dr. Muriel Lazarus Sackler, and married a much younger native Austrian, Gertraud (Gheri) Wimmer. Mortimer oversaw the family's Napp, Bard, and Mundipharma companies and split his time between homes in London, Gstaad, and the French Riviera.

* In July 1973, shortly after Sackler committed to donate $3.5 million for the Temple of Dendur, Hoving bought twenty-five tenth-century Chinese paintings and scrolls from C. C. Wang, a Hong Kong artist and dealer. Fong had recommended the purchase, which became embroiled for several years in a public controversy as to whether Fong and Hoving had been duped by high-quality fakes. The authenticity of another painting, *Travelers*, that Fong acquired for the Met was also disputed by some leading Asian art experts. Fong and the Met acquired it from Chang Dai-chien (Zhang Daqian), widely acknowledged as one of the twentieth century's most talented fine art forgers.

He soon added a ski chalet in the Austrian Alps and Rooksnest, a five-thousand-acre, sixteenth-century estate ninety minutes outside London. The following year he surrendered his American passport and became an Austrian citizen. His brothers were shocked. He chided them for remaining in America where the tax rates were significantly higher.[45] Whatever success the brothers had in the future, he would do better than they since he was free of U.S. taxes. At that time the top federal rate was 70 percent for couples earning more than $180,000.*[46]

While Arthur focused on China and the U.S., Mortimer and Raymond gave lavishly to London's Tate Modern, the British Museum, and the Royal Academy of Arts. Raymond, who was knighted by Queen Elizabeth in 1995 for his support of British arts and sciences, was later a major benefactor of an emerging field called convergence science, "the intersection of mathematical, engineering and physical sciences with biomedical science."[47]

Not to be outdone by his brothers, Arthur went on a buying binge, as if to further tease the Met and his brothers with notable additions to his collection. Marietta knew there was more behind it than simply taunting the Met and Mortimer and Raymond. "Arthur found safety and comfort in objects," Marietta later wrote. "They could not hurt him, they could not make demands on him. The irony, of course, was they made him their slave."[48]

---

* During subsequent divorce proceedings, Gertraud charged that Mortimer had given up his American citizenship because he wanted to avoid double taxation. After the couple reached a settlement and the divorce litigation records were sealed, Gertraud claimed that Mortimer's decision was not at all about taxes but only his love for Austria.

31

"VALIUMANIA"

Thomas Hoving and the Metropolitan's curator of Egyptian Art had underestimated the final costs for the Dendur design developed by architects Kevin Roche and John Dinkeloo. A reflecting pool offset by a spectacular wall of stippled glass along the north side was meant to evoke the temple's original location on a hillside near the Nile. It alone broke the budget. There were also big cost overruns for an underground employee parking garage, a reinforced loading dock, a protective environmental room for fragile antiquities, and a hydraulic lift designed to buttress the reassembled temple.

Hoving, however, not wanting to alienate Sackler further, did not ask him or the brothers to speed up their payout. Since the family would not allow any dilution of their extensive naming rights to the new wing, Hoving had to raise several million more from donors who were willing to do so without having their name "on a plaque on the wall." Almost two years after the Sacklers had agreed to donate $3.5 million, the construction on the new wing was not even at the one-third mark. The Sacklers were in no rush, however. They were busy on many other fronts.*[1]

While the Sacklers' increasingly high-profile lifestyle played out in the New York papers and art publications, their pharmaceutical ventures stayed out of public view. Arthur was still immersed in his pub-

* That same year, 1975, Arthur was again in the news when the New York attorney general sued him and Marietta in their role as trustees of New York's Museum of the American Indian. They were accused of not paying enough for museum artifacts they took and for a sweetheart deal on free storage at the museum of some of Arthur's collection. The Sacklers prevailed and the lawsuit was dropped, but the dustup reinforced the feeling in the New York art world that he was driven more by wheeling and dealing than collecting.

lishing empire and at McAdams, with its roster of top drug companies. Mortimer's focus was the trio's foreign operations while Raymond ran Purdue Frederick as its president.[2]

Arthur's cash cow was Roche and the Valium account. He had refined the promotion campaigns over time and had made Valium impervious to all competitors. It was the top-selling medication in the country by a wide margin, a spot it had held since 1968. Valium defied all odds by enlarging its lead over competitors by adding on average more than seven million new customers annually.[3] Librium, its chemical cousin, was not far behind, and in a dead heat with Ayerst's Premarin. Roche's blockbuster benzodiazepines were prescribed 103 million times in 1975, representing more than two billion pills.[4]

Sackler's enhanced marketing strategies that kept the benzos flying off the shelf did not come cheaply. Roche had set a record when it committed $10 million in 1963 for Valium's rollout. In 1975, it spent a staggering $400 million on Sackler-designed campaigns for its blockbuster benzos, about 40 percent of the industry's billion dollars allocated to marketing and promotion.

Roche and other companies paid for the enormous expenditures by keeping the prices high on their branded drugs sold in the United States. It was a windfall for Arthur. Michael Sonnenreich told the author that Sackler "made a lot of money in the beginning because he got bonuses based on sales volume. Later it changed to very large flat fees. Very large fees." The Swiss drugmaker, grateful to Sackler for the drugs' success, also provided him with millions in interest-free loans as advances against future advertising work, money he invested in the stock market.[5]

Roche did not mind paying Sackler huge fees because it understood how important he was in making the drug ubiquitous. "It would be very hard to find any group of middle-class women in which some aren't regularly on Valium," *Vogue* quoted a New York psychiatrist in 1975.[6] As patients reported to their doctors that the drug helped treat muscle spasms and cramps, inflamed and aching joints, convulsions, sleep, and anxiety, the list of ailments it treated had turned it into "Valium the Versatile."[7] And Sackler's promotion and Roche's detail team complemented its many therapeutic uses with the message about its benign side effect profile.

Millions of patients taking Valium were certain it was safe. Their doctors had assured them of that. And that so many friends were using it reinforced that comfort. The 1970s housewives who were Valium's core customers had heard horror stories about barbiturates from their mothers. Feminist psychologist Phyllis Chesler wrote in her seminal 1972 *Women and Madness* that Valium was a pharmaceutical strait-jacket, a chemical way of making women happy while keeping them locked into a subservient, second-class societal status.[8] Although the book was a commercial success and critically acclaimed, it did not hurt Valium's sales.

As the drug maintained its dominance, medical researchers debated whether patients developed a tolerance to benzos and therefore needed ever-higher doses to achieve the same therapeutic effect. In the early 1970s it seemed as if there was a new study every six months, each contradicting the findings of the preceding one. The scientific back-and-forth played out far away from the attention of the public. As with oral contraceptives, in which it had taken the voices of female activists and reporters to raise credible alarms, eventually women's publications and female journalists slowed Roche's juggernaut and began changing the widely held view that Valium and Librium were harmless be-happy pills.

McCall's raised a few concerns in autumn 1971 with "The Over-Medicated Women," as did *Ladies' Home Journal* with "Women and Drugs."[9] The turning point for the 30 million American women taking Valium did not happen until 1975 when a British clinical trial demonstrated that a significant percentage of long-term patients who abruptly stopped taking it suffered withdrawal symptoms. Millions of Valium patients could no longer ignore the controversy. Roche's contention that the study was flawed was lost in a deluge of mainstream press coverage that suddenly focused on the drug's risks.[10]

Vogue got everybody's attention with "Danger ahead! Valium—The Pill You Love Can Turn on You," in which a New York psychiatrist and addiction expert, Marie Nyswander, concluded that Valium could cause "a far worse addiction" than heroin.[11] Nyswander, according to *Vogue*, was in a position to say that since she specialized in using methadone to wean addicts off heroin. *Ms. Magazine* followed with "Do You Take Valium?," sobering first-person accounts of middle-class suburban women who described debilitating "physical and mental anguish" when they stopped taking the drug.[12]

Time's medical editor, Gilbert Cant, addressed the pros and cons in "VALIUMANIA," a cover story for *The New York Times Magazine*.[13] Valium, he noted, had become the symbol for a broad range of prescription medications charged with "turning America into an overtranquilized society of near zombies seeking peace of mind in a little bottle." Cant was the first to question whether Roche had "overmarketed" its best-selling drug, especially with its heavy-handed promotion to women.

He also cited Nyswander, the doctor who had raised "worse than heroin addiction" in *Vogue*. She was, he wrote, "a highly respected Manhattan psychiatrist" and noted that in her opinion "Valium is the most addictive drug in common, legal use. . . . She stands virtually alone." Still, Nyswander ramped up her doom-and-gloom forecast, warning there could eventually be two million Americans addicted to Valium, four times more than the number of heroin addicts. And she predicted that Valium would eventually prove lethal.[14]

That was a startling assertion given that Valium seemed quite tame in comparison to many other prescription and street drugs. Within a month of each other in 1970, Janis Joplin died from heroin and Jimi Hendrix from barbiturates. The following year a Paris medical examiner skipped an autopsy and ruled the cause of death of the Doors' Jim Morrison at twenty-seven was a heart attack. Rumors Morrison had died of a heroin overdose, though, gained traction within days.[15] Meanwhile, adding to the perception that Valium was not too potent, Ronald Reagan's national security advisor, Robert McFarlane, later tried killing himself with thirty Valium pills. It put him into a deep sleep and he woke up at a local hospital.[16]

Most physicians thought Nyswander was grandstanding by publicizing her contrarian views on the country's most popular drug. Some believed she was "riding to fame on the back of Valium," and dismissed her condemnations as baseless overstatements.*[17] Dr. Adam Lewenberg, the medical director for New York's Addiction Treatment Center, later said, only half in jest, "the definition of a Valium addict is a patient who takes more Valium than his doctor."[18]

The small but growing number of patients who had difficulty wean-

* It took almost two decades for uncontroverted evidence that Nyswander was mostly right: that the benzos were addictive and it was possible to overdose in extremely high doses. Benzodiazepines suppress the respiratory system the same as barbiturates, tranquilizers, sedatives, and opiates. They are most fatal when mixed in large quantities with other drugs that slow respiration (between 1996 and 2013, there was a sharp spike in benzo-related deaths, many times mixed with opioid painkillers).

ing off Valium pleaded with federal agencies to intervene on the benzos.[19] The FDA was on the sidelines but not for lack of will. It was locked in a multiyear legal battle with Roche over its proposal to put prescription limits on Valium and Librium.[20] The FDA had sought help from the Justice Department since the Controlled Substances Act had given Justice the power to restrict drugs subject to abuse.[21] The FDA passed along the data it had compiled about Valium's potential for dependence and abuse.[22]

In late 1975, the Justice Department did what the FDA could not do on its own. Valium and Librium were upgraded to Schedule IV, limiting the number of refills doctors could write. It also applied criminal penalties to diversion and illegal sales.[23] Even possessing the drug without a prescription could mean jail time. A visitor to an Illinois prison received a two-to-six-year sentence after guards at a security check found seven Valium pills. An Alabama man got four years after a policeman discovered he had nine Valium pills he had taken from his roommate's prescription supply.[24]

The FDA ordered Roche to add the "stress of everyday life does not require treatment with an [antianxiety] drug" on the Valium inserts sent to doctors and pharmacists. The government hoped that might reduce the widespread overprescribing.[25] Roche, as it always did, took the FDA to court. It would take five years to settle the standoff, with the agency agreeing to weaker language: "may not require" instead of "does not require."[26] While Roche had kept the FDA tied up in court over a few words on Valium's insert, it was unable to do much to delay changing public attitudes about its star drug. The drumbeat of news about possible dependence and unreported dangers fanned fears. Physicians became more cautious in dispensing the benzos after the DEA opened investigations into hundreds of so-called permissive prescribers.[27] States started removing benzos from formulary lists of drugs covered by Medicaid.[28] Restrictions on the number of refills forced devoted users to shop for doctors. As prescriptions got tougher to obtain, some patients found replacement meds, often riskier drugs such as barbiturates.[29]

The cumulative result was that Roche's juggernaut had slowed. Valium was still America's top selling drug, but its market was no longer expanding.

* * *

Nineteen seventy-five, when the media assault on Valium peaked, also marked a turning point for another blockbuster, Ayerst's Premarin. About half of all menopausal women in America were using it (30 million prescriptions).[30] On December 4, a report in *NEJM* made the front page of all major papers and was the lead story on the network evening newscasts.[31]

Two extensive clinical studies delivered alarming results about estrogen and uterine cancer.[32] Women taking estrogen for one to four years were 5.6 times more likely to develop that cancer than those not on the hormone. Women on estrogen for seven years had a fourteen-fold increased risk. In an accompanying editorial, Dr. Kenneth Ryan of the Boston Hospital for Women concluded the studies showed the estrogen risk for endometrial cancer was the same as the risk of lung cancer from smoking twenty or more cigarettes daily.[33] Dr. Harry Ziel, who directed one of the studies, told *The New York Times*, "This is not an innocuous drug that can be used like salt and pepper. Doctors should restrict its use to women with incapacitating symptoms, since it has a life-threatening risk."[34]

The FDA called an emergency meeting of its advisory panel on obstetrics and gynecology. It took a year to issue a new labeling requirement, a lengthy insert that pharmacists were supposed to distribute so that patients were aware of the increased risk of endometrial cancer and potential risks of abnormal blood clotting a breast and gallbladder cancers.[35]

Health activists and writers Barbara Seaman and Gary Null got a rare interview with Robert Wilson, the physician who had been at the forefront of medicalizing menopause and pushing Premarin. Seaman and Null met with Wilson after another article in *JAMA* had sparked a second round of national speculation about whether Premarin's undisclosed health risks made it too dangerous for long-term use. They asked Wilson for his thoughts about the latest science, particularly the studies showing a dramatically higher endometrial cancer risk for women on estrogen. Wilson was dismissive. "That's the worst lie in the world, the worst fallacy. I have over 40 doctors working all over the world, Switzerland, Czechoslovakia, all over the world, and we haven't seen one case of cancer!" That was not true, no doctors were working with him.

Did he still believe that women should take Premarin and other estrogen medications starting at age fifty?

"They say we should do nothing to retard menopause. Just think of that. Isn't that dreadful? The estrogen regimen should start at age 9. Nine to 90. It's necessary to begin then, and to check your estrogen levels all through life, so that it never leaves you. Don't allow it to."[36]

There was no support in the medical community for Wilson's extreme view that estrogen be dispensed from ages "9 to 90." The drug that he helped make a blockbuster (more than 35 million prescriptions in 1975) would be at the center of a debate between proponents who thought its benefits—symptomatic relief, stronger bones, and maybe some heart protection—outweighed the risks. Additional studies soon added weight to thc risk side of the equation. One raised the specter of a breast cancer link while another pointed to a higher risk for coronary disease.[37]

In the aftermath of the 1975 cancer studies, Premarin's sales plummeted by half over five years.[38] Women felt vulnerable since there was no screening test that might identify endometrial cancer in its earliest stages.*[39] Over time, however, fear faded as the drug companies spent millions to promote successfully a more refined version of Robert Wilson's "feminine forever" thesis. Paid celebrity endorsements—model Lauren Hutton and singer Patti LaBelle—pushed Premarin as a life-changing medication.[40] Popular women's magazines again ran stories about how hormones helped women over forty stay healthy, look better, and maintain active sex lives.[41] Gynecologists, many the recipients of large inducements from Ayerst, reembraced the drug. Premarin would, by 1990, again become the best-selling drug in the U.S. for a decade, exceeding by a third its mid-1970s pre–cancer scare peak.[42]

It took nearly twenty years for Prempro, a "new and improved" replacement, to reach the market. By then, Wyeth and Ayerst had merged into Wyeth-Ayerst Laboratories. Prempro was the first ever estrogen plus progestin pill. Progestin, a synthetic version of the natural hormone progesterone, had demonstrated its effectiveness in providing protection against uterine cancer. Wyeth-Ayerst was convinced that it needed the combination HRT to reach the market for women who

---

* The only screening test then recommended by the American Cancer Society (ACS) was an annual pap smear. The following year, 1976, the ACS added mammography breast exams to its list of recommended screening procedures. In 2013, researchers discovered that pap tests in some instances found cells that were useful in early detection of ovarian and uterine cancers.

avoided the company's hit Premarin because of cancer concerns. Prempro won FDA approval even though it had not conducted a randomized clinical trial.[43] It also became a best-seller. Between Premarin and Prempro, Wyeth-Ayerst dominated the HRT market; the two drugs accounted for two thirds of the annual 90 million HRT prescriptions.[44] Sales stayed strong until Prempo too was unmasked as putting millions of women at risk, the same as had happened with the Pill and with Premarin.[45]

Robert Wilson did not live to see the final chapters play out in the hormone saga. He died in 1981. And he thought he had taken a family secret to his grave. He would have succeeded if his wife, Thelma, had not confided it after his death to their younger son, Ronald.

Thelma was a registered nurse and had worked with her husband in his gynecological practice. In 1963, the couple had coauthored "The Fate of the Nontreated Postmenopausal Woman: A Plea for the Maintenance of Adequate Estrogen from Puberty to the Grave," in the *Journal of the American Geriatrics Society*. The first sentence set the tone: "The unpalatable truth must be faced that all postmenopausal women are castrates." The solution they suggested was for every woman to start taking estrogen beginning in puberty and continuing to death.[46 * 47]

Given their collaboration, it is no surprise that Thelma was on Premarin most of her life. After her husband's death, she told her son that she was battling breast cancer. He visited her at the family home in Cold Spring Harbor, New York. As he later told author Trisha Posner:

"This isn't the first cancer I've had."

He thought he had not heard her correctly. She could tell he seemed confused.

"It's not my first cancer."

"I heard you," he said slowly. He had left home to attend college and later had enlisted in the Air Force, spending years in Florida, far away from his family. But he had kept in touch with his mother and couldn't imagine that she had had cancer before and never told him.

"When?"

* Wilson was not the first to use "castrates" in referring to women. The prestigious *New England Journal of Medicine* published the work of three doctors in 1960 that suggested estrogen might help prevent heart disease in postmenopausal females they described as "castrated women."

"Over ten years ago," she said, her eyes cast downward. "I had breast cancer. I had a mastectomy then."

She could see the surprise on his face.

"Your father wanted me, no, needed me, to be a shining example of his work."

The couple feared that if news of her breast cancers became public, it would have ruined her husband's reputation.

Which of them had decided not to tell their own children?

"We all decided it."

"Who is all?"

"Me. Your father. Even the men at Wyeth. They urged us not to tell." *

* Thelma Wilson died in 1988 from complications of her breast cancer.

32

SWINE FLU

Before 100 million Americans got the polio vaccine starting in 1962, there were about fifteen thousand annual cases of polio, mostly in children. By the time the vaccination program finished three years later, there were fewer than five hundred new cases annually. That had fallen to only ten a year by the 1970s. Except for a single traveler who arrived in the U.S. in 1993 with polio, there has not been a case of the virus in North America since 1979.[1] * [2] The World Health Organization has long had the global eradication of the crippling disease as one of its primary goals. But polio has been difficult to eliminate in some developing countries.[3] The disease is endemic in Afghanistan and Pakistan where the Taliban ban aid workers, believing that Western countries conduct espionage under the guise of the health programs and that the vaccines are part of a covert CIA program to sterilize Muslim women.[4] In Central African countries, particularly Nigeria, there are fears fed by rumors that the injections caused AIDS and include cancer-inducing agents.[5] Health workers who have nevertheless tried administering vaccines have been attacked and killed.

While polio might be a distant memory in America, other contagious, and potentially deadly, diseases—measles, mumps, and rubella—have reappeared after medical science declared them eliminated. Doctors blame a modern-day anti-vaccine movement that was sparked by a

* A poliolike disease, acute flaccid myelitis (AFM), began to break out in 2014. Mostly children under the age of ten were infected. The CDC is still working to discover the cause of the breakout, but suspects three enteroviruses (A-16, A-71, and E-68) typically responsible for hand, foot, and mouth disease. As of December 2019, there is no treatment or vaccine and the CDC has confirmed 601 cases in all fifty states. Ninety percent of the infections have occurred in children.

1998 study published in Britain's prestigious *Lancet* medical journal. Twelve physician coauthors reviewed the cases of a dozen children hospitalized in London for inflamed digestive tracts and "regressive developmental disorder" (autism). Nine children lost their language skills after getting a combined vaccination for the three diseases. That was enough for the authors to conclude that "possible environmental triggers" (the vaccine) were connected somehow to the "developmental regression."[6]

Much of the media reported the results by converting a "possible" trigger into "vaccines cause autism." The study's lead author, Dr. Andrew Wakefield, reinforced the most sensational coverage. In public appearances and lectures he was far more provocative and confident about a vaccine-autism link than he and his colleagues were in their peer-reviewed *Lancet* article. It was not long before some prominent Hollywood celebrities and alternative medicine advocates embraced the anti-vaccine movement.[7] Lost in the tsunami of fear-mongering was that a year after the *Lancet* story, the U.K.'s Committee on Safety of Medicines completed a reappraisal of the evidence and concluded there was no link between the vaccines and autism.[8] It took another four years before a different British medical council discovered that the dozen children directed to the study, and some of the funding for it, came from "lawyers acting for parents who were involved in lawsuits against vaccine manufacturers."[9] That prompted ten of Wakefield's original coauthors to print a retraction in the *Lancet*, in which they stated, "No causal link was established between MMR vaccine and autism as the data were insufficient."[10] In 2010, the *Lancet* published a small, anonymous paragraph attributed only "on behalf of the editors."[11] It was extraordinary. The journal retracted the original paper and admitted it contained serious errors. Britain's General Medical Council concluded that Wakefield was guilty of scientific misrepresentation and ethical violations regarding the study's dozen children.[12]

The *British Medical Journal* delivered the coup de grâce with the disclosure that Wakefield and his coauthors falsified some of the supporting data and selectively chose results that only buttressed their conclusion.[13] Since then, dozens of other clinical research studies have failed to demonstrate any causal link between vaccines and autism or other mental disorders. Wakefield was struck off the medical register in the U.K.[14] Still, the anti-vaccine movement remains strong, with many parents hesitant to inoculate their children.* [15]

Although the modern-day anti-vaccine movement might have been sparked by a fraudulent 1998 scientific paper, the beginning of the public's loss of faith in vaccines happened more than twenty years earlier. It was February 4, 1976, when an eighteen-year-old Army recruit, David Lewis, collapsed unconscious during a five-mile hike with his Fort Dix–based platoon. Lewis and some of his fellow soldiers had been battling respiratory problems. He had gone on the midwinter march against the advice of the platoon's medical officer. His sergeant revived him with mouth-to-mouth resuscitation, but within a day Lewis was dead of pneumonia.[16]

An Army doctor sent samples of throat cultures from Lewis and eighteen sick soldiers to New Jersey's Department of Health. Most turned out to be a common influenza virus.[17] They could not, however, identify five cultures (that included the one from Lewis).[18] Researchers knew that the influenza virus mutated, and they then believed (incorrectly) that a severe influenza was likely about every decade. More than twenty thousand had died in 1957 in the U.S. from the Asian swine flu. It had been eight years since 1968's virulent Hong Kong bird flu killed forty thousand Americans.[19]

Worried that they might have stumbled across a new virulent influenza strain, the New Jersey Department of Health sent the mystery viruses to the Centers for Disease Control in Atlanta. There, alarmed researchers tested the sample positive for swine flu virus. Although swine virus was not isolated in a lab until the 1930s, most researchers thought it was responsible for the infamous Spanish flu that had killed upward of 100 million people in history's greatest pandemic in 1918.[20]

---

* When in March 2019 health officials in northern Kentucky banned unvaccinated students from school after an outbreak of more than thirty cases of chicken pox, one family sued on behalf of their son who refused the vaccine on religious grounds. The family, devout Catholics, said the vaccine "is derived from aborted fetuses and it goes against our Catholic faith." In fact, the chicken pox vaccine relies on cell lines from two fetuses aborted in 1964 and 1970, and no further abortions were done to keep those cell lines intact. The Vatican has grudgingly given its approval to the rubella vaccine, saying that the most important consideration of parents should be "to put the health of their children and of the population as a whole at risk." Still, legal experts believe the case is potentially precedent-setting since a religious exemption to vaccines could be claimed by many people without the ability of local governments or school districts to verify the truthfulness of such claims.

The Spanish flu had killed between 500,000 and 700,000 Americans, more than ten times the number who died in World War I.[21] *

If a close variant of the Spanish flu had returned after such a long absence, it would mean that no one under the age of fifty had any natural antibodies. What was most important was to determine if it was transmissible from person to person. There had been two cases of swine flu in 1974 and 1975 but both patients had worked in farms where they were in close contact with pigs. None of their friends, fellow workers, or family got sick and the two who were ill recovered fully.[22] More data was needed. Hospitals were put on notice to test all patients arriving at the emergency rooms for swine flu antibodies.

In several thousand blood tests taken at Fort Dix, close to five hundred tested positive for swine flu antibodies, including the sergeant who had done mouth-to-mouth resuscitation on Private Lewis. None had gotten sick yet. As for the four who had been ill with swine flu at the same time as Lewis, they had recovered. Lewis was so far the only fatality.[23] Still, CDC epidemiologists concluded that hundreds of exposures meant the bug they had isolated was almost certainly transmissible between people.

The first the public heard about it was in a February 19 press conference. The CDC's assistant director, Dr. H. Bruce Dull, read a prepared statement disclosing that the swine virus had been identified in a few patients at Fort Dix. There was little danger the virus would spark a "wildfire" epidemic, he said.[24] The statement avoided any reference to the 1918 pandemic. No one wanted to pass along "doom and gloom" and get ahead of the known facts.[25] Responding to a reporter's question, Dull did admit the CDC had confirmed that the Fort Dix cases were quite like the 1918 flu virus.

That opened the media floodgates. The next day's *New York Times* front-page headline was "U.S. Calls Flu Alert on Possible Return of Epidemic's Virus." The article, by the health and science reporter Harold Schmeck, started, "The possibility was raised today that the virus that caused the greatest world epidemic of influenza in modern history—the pandemic of 1918–19 may have returned."[26]

---

* The most deadly influenza year in the U.S. since the 1918 pandemic was 2018. An estimated eighty thousand Americans died, most of them elderly and with compromised immune systems. The problem, in part, was that the vaccination was not targeted for the strain that developed that year and provided little protection.

When the CDC's Advisory Committee on Immunizations met on March 10, there had not been a single case of swine flu reported anywhere in the world outside of Fort Dix. January and February are the peak months for influenza. New cases taper off starting in March. While it appeared there would not be any widespread outbreak for the current season, what about the next one? All agreed it was impossible to calculate precisely the odds for a swine flu pandemic. They decided the only "responsible approach" was to assume that "a pandemic was possible."

The CDC Advisory Committee concluded that the foolproof way of guarding against a catastrophic epidemic was a mass immunization program. It would take months, however, before such a plan might get the necessary approvals. Completing safety testing and then manufacturing tens of millions of vaccine doses would be a massive undertaking.[27] The public would have to be inoculated at the very latest several weeks before flu season kicked into high gear in mid-December (any vaccine needed two to three weeks to activate each person's immunity against swine flu).[28]

David Sencer, the CDC director, distributed a memo warning that an untreated national swine pandemic would be devastating. The World Health Organization had adopted a "wait and see" attitude.[29] Although a pandemic was certainly not inevitable, Sencer believed the government had to err on the side of public safety.[30] His bottom line was a "Combined Approach." Pharmaceutical companies would manufacture the vaccine from the swine virus isolated by the CDC. The Bureau of Biologics would handle all safety and efficacy testing, and the National Institute of Allergy and Infectious Disease would be responsible for oversight of the field trials. When vaccine production finished, the federal government would buy 200 million doses from the drug companies. At least 80 percent of Americans would get vaccinated at a network of assorted federal, state, local, and private medical facilities and clinics. It was an ambitious and complicated plan with an equally grand price estimate, $135 million.[31]

The HEW secretary forwarded Sencer's recommendation to the White House where President Gerald Ford hastily convened an advisory panel of esteemed infectious disease experts, including the inventors of the two competing polio vaccines, Jonas Salk and Albert Sabin.[32] They agreed that a swine epidemic was "possible" for the next flu season. They could not quantify if the chances were one in five or one in a million. A few suggested to start manufacturing the vaccine but waiting for more data before immunizing Americans. There was no time, unfortunately, for the more cautious approach. To produce the vaccine, pharma firms had to inject the CDC-isolated virus into millions of hen's eggs, where it was replicated, harvested, and purified. According to the CDC's Sencer, there were at most a couple of weeks to decide "go or no go."[33]

Faced with such a short window, the scientists voted to proceed with mass immunization. They had reached the same conclusion as the politicians: it was better to err on the side of safety given the catastrophic consequences from a pandemic.[34] Some of the scientists advising Ford later told the journal *Science* they felt the president was leaning to say yes before they even offered their advice.[35]

Ford had some reasons, totally separate from public medical and health considerations, to embrace bold action. The country was only four months from the two hundredth anniversary of the signing of the Declaration of Independence. The administration had planned grand celebrations for the Bicentennial and Ford hoped it might help reverse his abysmal approval ratings. They were the lowest of any president since World War II; he was the only one in Gallup history who did not top their "most admired man" list while in the White House.[36] Americans were desperate for some good news. It had been less than a year since the ignominious end to the country's military intervention in Vietnam. The images of civilians hanging on to the helicopter gunships that took off for the last time from the U.S. embassy, while North Vietnamese troops closed in on the capital, was a humiliating finish to the unpopular nineteen-year war. The previous year Ford had issued a controversial pardon to Richard Nixon for any crimes he may have committed while president. California governor Ronald Reagan thought that Ford was politically vulnerable and had challenged him for the nomination. Ford had started out strong, however, winning the first six primaries.[37]

On March 23, Reagan beat Ford in North Carolina. That panicked the president's political team. The following day, Ford addressed the nation from the White House: "I have been advised that there is a very real possibility that unless we take effective counteractions, there could be an epidemic of this dangerous disease [swine flu] next fall and winter here in the United States." He asked Congress "to appropriate $135 million, prior to the April recess, for the production of sufficient vaccine to inoculate every man, woman, and child in the United States."[38]

Ford correctly calculated that Congress would not stand in the bill's way. Without any dissenting debate, it authorized $135 million for "Preventive Health Services . . . for a comprehensive influenza immunization program" on April 15. Ford signed it in an Oval Office ceremony that same day.[39] Although the money was appropriated, none of the details had been worked out. The CDC submitted an ambitious timetable to start vaccine production by June and average 24 to 30 million doses monthly.[40] The FDA's Bureau of Biologics began selecting thousands of volunteers for what it called the "largest pre-certification field trials ever performed."[41]

The drug firms began "cultivating seed stock," the first step in growing millions of copies of the CDC-supplied virus in hen eggs.[42] After a few days, inspectors found that Parke-Davis had incorrectly recombined some of the virus's genetic elements. The equivalent of 2.6 million doses were useless. That caused a several-week delay as the CDC double-checked the technical procedures in place at each company.[43]

While that review was under way, an unexpected and more serious challenge came from the four pharmaceutical firms chosen to make the vaccines.[44] The executives from Merck's Sharp & Dohme subdivision, Merrell, Wyeth, and Parke-Davis, and the Pharmaceutical Manufacturers Association, were concerned about liability for adverse reactions to the swine flu vaccinations. The government had agreed to be fully responsible for a "duty to warn" all those who got the vaccine about its risks. However, eighteen months earlier, a federal appeals court sent chills through the pharma industry when it upheld a $200,000 verdict against Wyeth for partial paralysis in a Texas infant after she received an oral polio vaccine Wyeth had manufactured. The Texas Department of Public Health had bought the vaccine from Wyeth. Texas law required parents to vaccinate their children. A registered nurse at the Hidalgo County Department of Health Clinic had administered the vaccine to the child and the infant's mother had signed a liability release. When the child later developed poliolike symptoms, the mother sued, claiming that her primary language was Spanish and she had only a seventh-grade education.

Wyeth said it had satisfied its "duty to warn" as a manufacturer by including a large, detailed circular warning of possible side effects with every ten-dose batch. The nurse who administered the vaccine had not warned the plaintiff about the potential risks. Wyeth experts testified at the trial that the odds the infant's illness was from the vaccine was one in 5.88 million. Still, the court ruled that Wyeth's "duty to warn" extended past the date it sold the vaccine to any private or government agencies. It did not matter, concluded the court, whether the Texas mother would have changed her mind if she had gotten such a warning. What mattered was that Wyeth had not provided some means for that mother to have had easy access to the side effect printout.[45]

Little wonder that pharma firms believed that no matter how broadly the government assumed the "duty to warn," plaintiffs' lawyers would find a creative way to sue them. Major insurance underwriters agreed. They informed the drug firms they would not issue any liability coverage for the swine flu vaccinations. Given the huge size of the program and the expedited schedule, the insurers did not have time to calculate and price the potential risk.[46] Without insurance, the drug companies insisted on full indemnification from the government for defending lawsuits and settling cases that arose from side effects.[47]

Congress's $135 million emergency appropriations covered the costs for testing, manufacturing, and administrating the inoculations, but nothing for liability claims. Getting politicians to sign a blank check for the pharmaceutical industry in an election year was not easy. As a sign of good faith, the four pharma firms had began producing bulk amounts of the swine flu vaccine. They would not sell any of it to the government, however, until there was an indemnity agreement. Drug company attorneys did not budge in more than thirty summer meetings with federal health officials.[48]

The government finally capitulated, drafting legislation under which it assumed responsibility for all claims other than those resulting from the negligence of the drug firms. There was little support though for that in Congress, much to the anger of the drug firms.

By July 31, the pharma manufacturers had produced enough vaccine for 100 million doses. They still refused to sell any to the government.[49] HEW secretary F. David Mathews wrote to Ford: "Without a resolution of the liability issue, manufacturers are expected to stop vaccine production within a matter of days." Merrell and Parke-Davis had stopped buying eggs to make more vaccine.[50] Merrell announced it would soon withdraw from the program.[51]

Ford and CDC officials worried that the earlier sense of urgency had faded in Congress as the odds for a pending health crisis seemed more remote. Besides Private Lewis and the four Fort Dix soldiers who had gotten ill six months earlier, there had not been a single case of swine flu reported anywhere. Some health officials thought Congress might use pharma's indemnification demand as the excuse to scuttle the program. The public mostly blamed the delay on generalized bureaucratic inefficiency. Few realized the drug companies were the obstacle.

But as the thalidomide scare in 1962 had broken the impasse over the Kefauver Amendments, fear over an unrelated infectious outbreak in midsummer changed the dynamics in the swine flu stalemate. On August 2, Pennsylvania health authorities announced that dozens of military veterans who had attended a July American Legion convention in Philadelphia had become ill with high fevers, severe muscle aches, and in many cases pneumonia. The sicknesses were confined to one of the four hotels that hosted thousands of the veterans. Within a week of the convention, 221 veterans were seriously ill and 34 had died.[52] The lethal illness stumped state health officials. The press dubbed it "Legionnaire's Disease."

The news raised the prospect that the feared swine flu epidemic had started as those in charge were stuck debating who might pay for any injuries from adverse reactions. The CDC dispatched twenty epidemiologists to Philadelphia. *The New York Times* called it "the largest squad of medical detectives to investigate an outbreak in the federal agency's history."[53]

The news shook Congress from its torpor. No politician wanted to look as if they were risking the lives of Americans because of a money dispute over side effects that might affect a few people. Ford picked up his behind-the-scenes lobbying. In an August 4 letter he urged congressional leaders to "delay no longer," arguing "there is no excuse now . . . clinical tests show that the vaccine is safe and effective" and "the lives of many, many Americans" are at stake.[54] Only seventy-two hours after the first reports about Legionnaire's Disease, Congress appeared ready to approve the vaccine liability provisions. Just before the vote, the CDC director tried allaying public fears by announcing preliminary lab tests that showed it was "very unlikely" that swine influenza had caused the Philadelphia deaths. Congress postponed the vote.

Ford's advisors told him there was only a week left in which it was possible to restart vaccine production.[55] On August 6, only a few days before Congress's summer recess, Ford took his case to the public. He had considered charging that the drug companies were responsible for the impasse. Ford's advisors felt liability indemnity was too complex an issue to explain to the public. Congress was a much easier culprit. Ford, who had served in the House for twenty-four years before Nixon tapped him to become vice president in 1973, had good political instincts.

"I am frankly dumbfounded that Congress, which took the time and effort to enact ill-advised legislation to exempt its own members from certain State income taxes, has failed to act to protect 215 million Americans from the threat of swine flu. . . . There is no excuse . . . for any further delay."[56]

Ford's national address sparked public outrage that Congress had found the time recently to pass preferential tax treatment for its members while doing nothing about protecting citizens from a possible pandemic. *The New York Times* and a minority of newspaper editorial boards cited some dissident doctors and urged "a real public debate . . . on the few known facts instead of the bloodcurdling predictions being used to frighten the nation." It was too late for that. The public outcry meant there was little opposition in Congress.[57] The National Swine Influenza Immunization Program Act passed overwhelmingly the evening before the summer recess began and only a day before the Republican presidential convention. Ford signed it on live television.[58]

The bill put the federal government into the middle of the vaccine business for the first time. It alone assumed responsibility for all damages from personal injuries or deaths caused by the vaccinations. The attorney general was charged with defending any legal claims.

To reduce the likelihood of lawsuits, all patients had to sign informed consent forms that listed in detail the vaccine's benefits and risks.[59] Those forms, devised by the CDC, stated that swine flu had been tested extensively. Only a handful of people knew that the vaccine tested by the Bureau of Biologics and the National Institute of Allergy and Infectious Diseases had failed to develop any antibodies that would provide some immunity in children. As a result, the vaccine to be dispensed to the entire country—dubbed the X53a—had been reformulated to nearly twice the strength as the one in the clinical trials. X-53a had never been tested.[60]

While pharmaceutical companies were pleased that the government assumed all liability responsibility, they were irked by a clause that "eliminated any profit" from their production of the vaccine. What they got in exchange was authorization to earn "a reasonable profit" from the most commonly used version in annual influenza shots (the failure to define "reasonable" later led to considerable bickering between pharma and government officials).[61]

A Gallup poll showed that while a remarkable 94 percent of adult Americans were familiar with swine flu, only half were likely to be vaccinated.[62] Many worried about unknown side effects. Even more feared was the still-mysterious Legionnaire's. The CDC investigators had followed thousands of leads and conducted every possible test but were still stumped about what had caused it (in another four months, January 1977, the CDC determined the microbial culprit in the veterans' outbreak was from a bacterium found in dirty or sitting water; it spread through the invisible mist emitted by the hotel's air-conditioning units).[63]

The swine flu vaccinations got under way on October 1 even though there still had not been any more cases outside the small Fort Dix cluster.[64] Those most at risk, the elderly, children, and anyone with a suppressed immune system, were the priorities. Ten days after it had begun, the *Pittsburgh Post-Gazette* had a front-page story in its evening edition about three elderly people who had died shortly after getting their swine flu vaccinations at the Allegheny County Health Department. That story line—that the swine flu vaccine might have killed more people than the swine flu virus itself had nine months earlier at Fort Dix—took off.[65] Twenty-two additional deaths across the country were soon reported. The CDC's answer—they were "statistical anomalies" and the average age of "those who died was 72.1, and all but one had a history of heart disease"—was not reassuring to an already skittish public.[66] President Ford and his wife, Betty, tried tamping down the anxiety by getting their vaccine shots during a widely publicized photo opportunity.[67]

Forty million people, just under a fifth of the country, had been vaccinated by mid-October. Although it seemed an impressive number, health officials knew that if a pandemic was coming, it was too few people. They needed to double that and still allow enough time for the antibodies to develop to provide protection against an epidemic.[68]

Events worked against them. On November 2 Georgia governor Jimmy Carter defeated Ford in the presidential race. Four days later, Albert Sabin, one of Ford's highest-profile members of his blue-ribbon vaccine panel, wrote an op-ed for *The New York Times*. He said that "federal health agencies need public trust . . . but they are destroying it." According to Sabin, the government was "irresponsible to use scare tactics" by comparing the swine influenza to the Spanish pandemic of 1918. And he questioned the effectiveness of the vaccine with certain age groups. He concluded that it was "now highly probable" that "the epidemic does not come this winter," meaning that the vaccine would be "largely ineffective" if one should come the following year.[69]

Cities across the country had reported few cases of any strain of influenza during the first half of November. It was not because of the swine vaccine but because by chance, very few influenza viruses had developed that year in the U.S. Influenza-related deaths and pneumonia were at their lowest in years. Americans were increasingly skeptical as fears about a looming pandemic receded.

Fewer than five million people got the shot after November 1. For those still undecided, something that started during the third week of November helped them make up their minds. A Minnesota man who got the vaccine returned to his doctor complaining of weakness in his legs and arms. Initially, his feet and hands tingled but had since gone numb. His reflexes were poor. The physician recognized the symptoms: Guillain-Barré syndrome, a rare but serious disorder in which the immune system assaults healthy nerve cells. Most people recover but others have permanent nerve damage and paralysis. In some cases it is deadly.[70]

Although the CDC was aware that a mass immunization would result in adverse reactions for some, the government's epidemiologists had not expected to see much of Guillain-Barré.[71] Even those who suspected a link believed the risk was one or two cases for every million doses. The CDC-designed consent form everyone signed before getting the vaccination did not mention anything about neurological adverse effects. CDC director David Sencer later claimed that the omission was because he had not been told about the risk. A memo in July from Dr. Michael Hattwick, who ran the CDC's vaccine surveillance team, had raised that "neurological complications" were possible from any influenza vaccine. Somehow it had not been put into the consent form since some officials thought it would scare away too many people.[72]

Sencer issued an urged order to hospitals, doctors, and clinics to be on the lookout for Guillain-Barré. The problem was that there were no tests to detect the disease and doctors disagreed as to what symptoms confirmed a diagnosis.[73] It was not until December 14 that Sencer issued a press release disclosing that fifty-four vaccinated people were ill with Guillain-Barré. There were many calls to halt the program. Sencer suspended it for a month.

The CDC meanwhile kept investigating if there was a link between the vaccine and the unusual neurological disorder.[74] Efforts to explain away the infections as an "expected and normal rate" given the millions vaccinated, did little to allay public alarm.[75] Four days after the mass vaccinations were suspended, a *New York Times* editorial titled "Swine Flu Fiasco" concluded the entire effort had been a "sorry debacle" based "on the flimsiest of evidence." The CDC had exploited "Washington's panic" to "increase the size of its empire and multiply its budget."[76]

On January 20, 1977, Jimmy Carter was inaugurated as the thirty-ninth president of the United States. Guillain-Barré cases topped 1,100, with the swine flu vaccine responsible for most of them. More than one hundred patients were on respirators. Fifty-eight had died.[77] Carter wasted no time in selecting his own team to run the country's medical regulatory agencies. He appointed Joseph A. Califano Jr., Lyndon Johnson's top domestic advisor, as the HEW secretary . Two weeks later Califano dismissed David Sencer as the CDC's chief.

The first lawsuits on behalf of people claiming debilitating side effects were filed the same month the Carter administration took charge. There would ultimately be 4,181 claims asking for $3.2 billion in damages. The Justice Department, obligated by the National Swine Influenza Immunization Program Act, put ten lawyers full-time on defending the government. The White House Office of Management and Budget approved a multimillion-dollar emergency appropriation for the legal defense. The shortcomings in the legislation's indemnity clauses became clear. Liability was to be determined under the law of the state where the vaccine was dispensed, making it impossible to consolidate the cases into a single class action (they were merged for pretrial discovery only).[78] Instead, Justice Department attorneys had to juggle fifty different malpractice standards and product liability statutes.

The government paid $38 million to settle several hundred cases. More than 1,600 proceeded. The litigation lasted sixteen years, during which the government lost 109 cases. Taxpayer-funded judgments topped $100 million.[79]

The swine flu trials cost more than time and money. A lead attorney for the plaintiffs later commented that "permitting the government to step into the private world of the [pharmaceutical] manufacturers and defend the swine flu suits" meant that "the government has become the adversary of the citizens it originally acted to protect."[80] That tsunami of litigation also had a chilling effect on Congress, which steered far away for many years from approving any federal immunization programs. It also opened a Pandora's box. Some swine flu attorneys subsequently filed complaints for clients for all types of vaccines.[81]

The scientists involved in developing vaccines in the 1950s had hoped that mass immunization might not only prevent another influenza pandemic like the one that infected one third of the planet in 1918, but also eliminate typhus, polio, diphtheria, and whooping cough. Until swine flu, the U.S. produced about 80 percent of the *world's* annual supply of vaccine.[82] "Insurance carriers, politicians, drug companies, and the judicial system," writes science writer Laurie Garrett, "adhered to the basic principle that the rights of an immunized society superseded those of small numbers of individuals."[83]

The swine flu litigation, however, ended that cooperation. Federal courts became ground zero in an expanding controversy over individual rights versus the public health. District courts have at times issued orders overruling family objections and mandating vaccines for public school children or elderly relatives in nursing homes. In early 2019, the question of vaccines and immunizations reached a public crisis in several states due to an outbreak of measles. Officials in a hard-hit upstate New York county (Rockland) banned unvaccinated children from public places.[84] Washington and Oregon state legislators weighed overturning previous laws that allowed individuals to opt out of vaccines for "personal, religious or philosophical reasons."[85] (As of December 5, 2019, there were 1,276 reported infections in thirty-one states, the second highest on record since 2000, when the CDC had declared it eliminated.)[86]

The ghost of the swine flu debacle scared pharmaceutical companies and their liability insurers. In the coming years, more than a dozen drug firms that were in vaccine research and production abandoned the field. By 1993, there were only four American pharma companies left. Most are relieved to be out of the business. They were reminded of the perils of producing vaccines recently when major health problems were reported among three million children in the Philippines who had received the first ever vaccine against dengue fever. The three-dose shots made by French-based Sanofi had been under way since

2015. They resulted in adverse effects that often mimicked the disease it was supposed to prevent. For those who eventually contracted dengue, having had the vaccine made it a more virulent infection. The first lawsuits, charging that Sanofi's vaccine was responsible for a "runaway immune reaction," were filed in 2019. [87] * [88]

When Califano took charge at HEW, he ordered an outside investigation to determine what had gone wrong. It turned out there was no single error or miscalculation. There was, undoubtedly, a rush to judgment about the likelihood of a pandemic, based on too little data: five infections and a single death. Instead of methodically assessing the worst-case scenario, policymakers focused on the devastating outcome if they underestimated the possibility of a pandemic.

Adding to the sense of urgency was the fear that the time in which to deploy a vaccine was short. When the discussion turned to vaccine production and inoculation scheduling, policymakers had closed the door on debating the odds for a pandemic. Keiji Fukuda, a leading influenza epidemiologist, expressed a widely held consensus that the biggest error was the failure to realize the importance of no swine flu cases after the first ones at Fort Dix.

"If a new virus gets identified or reappears, you don't want to jump the gun and assume a pandemic is happening." [89] Many infectious disease physicians and researchers echoed that. Government health of-

---

* A subsequent example of the effect of litigation on the vaccine industry is Lyme disease, the bacterial infection that can cause debilitating arthritic conditions and was first spotted in 1976 in a cluster of children in Connecticut. Smith Kline got FDA approval for its LYMErix vaccine in 1998. In clinical trials it was 78 percent effective in preventing Lyme transmitted from infected ticks to humans. In the ten states that then accounted for 90 percent of the annual twenty thousand infections, Smith Kline dispensed 1.5 million vaccinations over eighteen months. The follow-up safety reports were good except for several dozen patients reporting either developing arthritis or that their existing arthritic condition worsened. Those claims caught the attention of the media. "Lyme Vaccine May Cause Problems"; "Concerns Grow over Reactions to Lyme Shots"; "Lyme Disease Vaccine's Safety Is Questioned." Anti–Lyme vaccine advocacy groups launched. Although no subsequent trial established a direct link from the vaccine to inducing arthritis, a class action lawsuit was filed in 2002. Smith Kline responded by withdrawing the vaccine. There have been 369,000 new infections of Lyme since then. The annual costs of treatment and lost productivity from disability in chronic cases is an estimated $75 billion annually. After Smith Kline canceled its product, Austrian-based Baxter Pharma abandoned its development of a Lyme vaccine that was in a combined Phase I/II trial. A French drug firm, Valneva, announced in 2018 it will start early trials of a vaccine like the one Smith Kline marketed twenty years ago. Until its expected approval in a few years, there is no Lyme vaccine.

ficials at the CDC acknowledged that swine flu had been a difficult lesson but one from which they learned. Unfortunately, it was a lesson learned at the wrong time. Within a decade, the mantra of "don't jump the gun and assume a pandemic is happening" would be one of the reasons for the slow and hesitant response to the emergence of a sexually transmitted lethal virus, HIV/AIDS.

33

"BLACK RIVER"

The news in the fall of 1976 from a small township in the Democratic Republic of the Congo was that villagers were suffering from high fevers, bone-rattling chills, and agonizing head and chest pains.[1] The gruesome details of the death of the town's headmaster, only a week after he fell ill, had spread fear throughout the remote region. Those tending to him reported how blood had filled the whites of his eyes, disfiguring blisters spread across his face and chest, and that he spasmed between coughing and vomiting. What they did not know was that a pathogen had ravaged his immune system and caused it to turn on him. The microbial invader had liquefied his organs. An autopsy revealed they had turned into a black liquid. No one then knew that the blood that poured from his mouth and nose when he died was packed with the lethal microbe, ready to infect its next victims. Within a month, 280 of the 318 villagers were dead (a nearly 90 percent mortality rate). For a backwater hamlet just across the border in South Sudan, a second outbreak had a 50 percent death rate.[2]

Blood samples of the dead were sent to Antwerp's Institute of Tropical Medicine.[3] Researchers there identified the microscopic culprit, a long wormlike virus. Its shape resembled the Marburg germ, a hemorrhagic fever virus discovered nine years earlier. Not certain if it was a new strain, the Belgians sent samples to both a British military lab and the American Centers for Disease Control. Epidemiologists at the CDC concluded that what was killing Africans so quickly and savagely was a "new organism . . . different than anything else we have seen."[4]

A team of physicians, epidemiologists, and microbiologists from the CDC, Antwerp, South Africa, and France traveled to the Congo.[5] The Congolese government had declared martial law and the military enforced a wide quarantine. Scientists and physicians in hazmat suits were soon the only ones visible in the ghost towns dubbed the "hot zones." Virologists narrowed the pathogen to a family of six related viruses native to fruit bats but that had spread over time to gorillas, chimpanzees, and monkeys.[6] The medical team thought it likely that the microorganism had jumped species from humans eating infected bush meat.[7] It was also possible that it passed to people from hunters who handled the raw meat when they had open cuts or scratches.[8]

An airborne virus would have a much higher infection rate. Their working assumption was that humans passed it by exchanging bodily fluids. That meant everything from sex to infected blood or perspiration penetrating an open wound or entering the mucous membranes in the nose, mouth, or eyes.[9] Local burial customs, it turned out, spread the pathogen since it put survivors in close contact with plague-ridden corpses.[10] Researchers did not know it then, but later determined that the virus that decimated those two African villages remained active in the blood and semen of survivors for up to forty days.[11]

The medical sleuths eventually solved how the outbreak had its quite accidental start. Belgian nuns at a local mission had been giving pregnant women vitamin shots. When they ran low on supplies, instead of stopping the injections, the nuns just kept reusing the same set of syringes and needles.[12] Once a woman carrying the deadly virus got an injection, every patient who followed got the bug.

One night, over a couple of bottles of Kentucky bourbon, the medical team that had been dispatched to Africa decided they should name the new microbial killer.[13] A French microbiologist from the Pasteur Institute suggested the Yambuku Virus, after the Congolese village it had wiped out. Others disagreed, saying that would forever stigmatize that village. That had happened before. In 1969 a virus struck Lassa, Nigeria. Later named the Lassa virus, it caused an exodus by many locals who mistakenly thought it was more likely to break out there than anywhere else.[14] A CDC researcher suggested that if they named it after something like a local river, that would make it geographically generic. Everyone liked that. The obvious choice was the continent's second-biggest river, the Congo, which snaked through the country. The problem was that a few years earlier a tick-borne viral disease had been designated Crimean-Congo hemorrhagic fever.[15] One of the doctors pulled a map from the wall and looked for the river that ran nearest to Yambuku. It was Ebola River, which in the local language meant "Black River."[16]

Ebola was not the only new deadly virus passed by sex and blood. A handful of people in Europe who had worked in or visited Central Africa were turning up at hospitals or clinics afflicted with a range of opportunistic infections. A Portuguese man who had returned after several years of managing a restaurant in the small West African nation of Guinea-Bissau was admitted in late 1976 to a London hospital. He was suffering from dehydration caused by chronic diarrhea. Tests revealed an intestinal infection caused by the microscopic *Cryptosporidium* parasite, common to tourists who drank untreated water or ate contaminated food.[17] Traveler's diarrhea passed, though, in a few days. That none of the antidiarrheal meds worked puzzled doctors.

A few months later, a Lisbon-born cabdriver who had served in the Portuguese navy in Angola and Guinea-Bissau was admitted to a Paris hospital complaining of chest pains and difficulty breathing. The diagnosis? Pneumocystis carinii, a rare but not lethal fungal lung infection that had jumped species in the 1940s from sewer rats to immunocompromised children who were Holocaust survivors at a Polish orphanage.[18] Again, physicians were stumped as to why antifungals did not clear it.

At the same time, a Greek fisherman showed up at an Antwerp hospital with Cryptococcal meningitis, caused by fungus found in soil and bird excrement that rarely affects humans. When the doctors learned he had worked at a commercial fishery at the Congo's Lake Tanganyika, they called Peter Piot, a twenty-seven-year-old microbiologist who had been one of the researchers dispatched to the Congo. He was a co-discoverer of the Ebola virus. The Antwerp physicians hoped that his experience might help diagnose what was wrong. Piot knew the fungus that had infected the patient's brain and spinal cord only flourished in people with compromised immune systems. Those were usually cancer patients undergoing chemotherapy or transplant surgeries in which doctors had weakened the body's immune response so it would not reject a donor's organ. That was not the case with the fisherman; Piot was perplexed that none of the antifungals slowed the infection.[19]

A few months later, Dr. Margrethe Rask, a Danish surgeon, returned to Copenhagen after five years at two Congolese clinics. She admitted herself to a hospital with trouble breathing and told the physicians she had battled fatigue, chronic diarrhea, and swollen lymph glands for a year. She tested negative for parasites but positive for oral thrush, a yeast contamination of the throat. Staph infections were multiplying in her blood. Tests revealed her body's natural disease-fighting T cells were almost depleted. The forty-seven-year-old physician was soon fighting the same rare Pneumocystis carinii pneumonia that had infected the Portuguese cabdriver in Paris.[20]

A German concert violinist checked in to a Cologne medical clinic because he was alarmed by dark purple lesions that had broken out across his chest and arms. It took doctors a week to diagnose Kaposi sarcoma (KS), a cancer so infrequent that one physician had to look it up in a textbook. It was generally benign and affected mostly older Italian and Jewish men. The same disease afflicted the sole survivor of a Canadian transport plane that had crashed in the Congo in 1976. He had required two units of locally sourced blood. A year later he developed some of the same immune problems encountered by the others, including Kaposi sarcoma. It took almost a decade for a husband-and-wife team of virologists at Columbia University to discover that the version of Kaposi affecting younger patients like the concert violinist was a new strain of herpes. As with hepatitis and Ebola, it passed from one person to another through exchanges of semen or blood.[21] * [22]

It was unfortunate serendipity that a surging demand in the United States and Europe for blood by-products was setting the groundwork for escalating the spread of any infectious agent. The culprit was the industry that had been built around plasma, a pale yellowish liquid that is about half a person's blood supply. It is packed with vital proteins, has excellent clotting components, and carries blood cells throughout the body. Doctors who understood why plasma was so vital also were aware of the dangers it posed when prepared or distributed improperly.

Plasma had become important during World War II because of the advantages it had over whole blood for emergencies. Not only did it keep longer without refrigeration, but it did not degrade when transported. Most important, it could treat shock and help wounds clot without worrying about matching blood type. There was no time in wartime field hospitals to check blood types and start searching for a

---

* In all the early instances that baffled doctors, the patients had died by 1979. In most cases, tissue samples were preserved for later study. In the 1980s, all were confirmed as positive for human immunodeficiency virus (HIV).

match among the whole blood bags. Plasma not only made it much faster but in situations where a standard transfusion could not be administered, it could be injected into muscles or even rubbed into the skin.

Before the war, it was difficult to separate plasma from blood. Charles Richard Drew, a thirty-five-year-old who was the only African American physician with a senior position in the wartime blood program, solved that problem in 1938. (After having earned an MD specializing in transfusion medicine, he was the first African American to earn a medical doctorate at Columbia. The "father of the blood bank," his doctoral thesis was "Banked Blood: A Study in Blood Preservation," and after the war he organized America's first national blood collection centers.)*

Drew's method for extracting plasma from blood was slow but effective. It involved spinning the blood to separate the sediment and then a series of steps applying ultraviolet light and sterile solutions.[23] The government wanted a crash program to use plasma as a blood substitute at the front lines. The Committee on Blood Substitutes was formed under the National Academy of Sciences. Millions of units of liquid plasma were shipped abroad in kits that included everything ready for battlefield infusion. The unintended consequence was that soldiers who got transfusions were fourteen times more likely to return home with hepatitis. In order to manufacture plasma in large enough quantities, it had been pooled from multiple donors.

When the Army realized it had a hepatitis problem, it ordered the pools to be no more than six donors and barred drawing blood from anyone with a history of jaundice. Still, the hepatitis infection rate stayed high. Laboratory efforts to kill the virus by heating or freezing plasma sometimes succeeded but invariably reduced its healing and clotting properties.

As opposed to penicillin, which was the dominant drug in the postwar pharmaceutical industry, plasma emerged from the war as a medical breakthrough that held great promise but had too many risks to justify widespread medical use. By the Korean War in 1950, the gov-

---

* Although Drew's work was instrumental in establishing the technology that made the American Red Cross flourish, he was barred as a black man from giving blood. That had been the segregated blood policy that Arthur Sackler railed against in the late 1940s.

ernment tried again to rid the plasma supplies of hepatitis, this time with a new process that relied on intense ultraviolet light. Its failure was measured in the postwar statistic that one in five soldiers who received plasma during the Korean conflict contracted hepatitis. That was three times the World War II infection rate.[24]

The civilian population in the U.S. was not faring much better. In the 1950s, almost a third of the blood supply was from prisoners. The rest came from nonprofit blood collection centers around the country. Three pharmaceutical firms had a monopoly on producing plasma from that collected blood (Cutter Laboratories, Hyland Labs, and Merck's Sharp & Dohme).[25] The overall hepatitis infection rate in six major cities grew in proportion to how much pooled plasma was used.[26]

Technology revolutionized plasma collection in the mid-1960s. The National Cancer Institute adapted the know-how used in dairy creamer separators for a much speedier, mechanized method for obtaining it (called modern plasmapheresis).[27] A needle or catheter drew whole blood from donors that was then put into a centrifuge machine that separated the plasma. That plasma was frozen while the red blood cells were reinjected into the donor.[28] The entire process took two to three hours, a fraction of the time it had taken to isolate plasma from harvested blood. Before plasmapheresis, men had waited a minimum of twelve weeks between blood draws and women sixteen weeks. Red blood cells needed time to rebuild. Giving blood too frequently raised the risk for anemia, a chronic and potentially debilitating illness. By reinjecting the donors with their own red blood cells, the body regenerated plasma much faster. Donors could give blood twice a week, a rate that resulted in a liter of plasma.[29]

There were some unexpected consequences from the scientific breakthroughs. Since donors could give blood more frequently there was considerably more money to be made by the faster turnaround. The blood industry was flooded, according to medical historian Douglass Starr, with "new classes of people . . . shadier buyers, more desperate sellers."[30]

European countries mostly banned paying for blood fearing that compensating donors attracted unhealthy ones, including alcoholics and drug addicts. The U.S. allowed the collection of "paid blood." Hundreds of independently owned plasma centers opened and offered anywhere from $4 to $8 a visit. Those clinics knew that people down on their luck were the ones most likely to be induced to donate blood for a few dollars. As a result, the plasma centers proliferated near big-city skid rows. They distributed tens of thousands of flyers in New York, Los Angeles, and Chicago to drug addicts, alcoholics, the homeless and destitute, telling them about the easy-to-be-had money.[31] A few clinics, led by the huge Doctors Blood Bank in Los Angeles, were more blatant in their pitch: donors received coupons redeemable at a local liquor store. The long lines desperate for cash or a drink formed early every day.*

Demand for plasma outstripped the supply. That was a result of scientific advances in the specialized blood products made from plasma. In 1965, for instance, a Stanford professor made a significant discovery about plasma's clotting components. She had examined the sludge that remained after thawing frozen plasma. That residue, at the bottom of each bag after transfusion, was considered useless waste material and blood banks had always discarded it. The professor found it was a dense, rich concentrate of Factor VIII, the name given to the set of proteins required for blood to clot. That residual slush became the key ingredient in a slew of new products for hemophiliacs who needed emergency or elective surgery.[32] It was not long before a concentrated white crystalline powdered form of Factor VIII transformed health care for hemophiliacs.[33] It was one hundred times more effective at clotting than regular plasma. In that way, the nation's ten thousand hemophiliacs no longer had to visit clinics or hospitals to get their plasma transferred from a bag.[34] The powdered concentrate in a salt-shaker-sized vial cost 11 cents a unit for a pharma company to produce.[35]

Beyond blood products for hemophiliacs, doctors and hospitals had begun relying on specialized plasma components to fight autoimmune illnesses, infections, and even as an aid in transplant surgeries. Fractionation, a process for extracting individual proteins such as albumin and gamma globulin from plasma, had been streamlined. Those proteins became concentrated derivatives and were in huge demand.

---

* Eventually, the FDA required blood centers to label their supplies as "volunteer" or "paid." That 1978 change eliminated the market for "paid blood" since American hospitals and clinics wanted only "volunteer" blood. They feared the consequences of buying riskier remunerated blood. However, the author learned that there was suspicion at some hospitals that what happened was that many of the less reputable blood clinics had merely marked all collected blood as "volunteer." That meant that some hospitals were still buying "paid" blood but paying the higher "volunteer" prices.

Obtaining enough for therapeutic doses required larger supplies of plasma.[36]

The plasma centers delivered the raw material for the specialized blood products. As more medical treatments became plasma intensive, demand exploded, requiring millions of liters a year. They could not process it fast enough unless they pooled all the donors. The plasma collection centers now mixed hundreds, even thousands of units from different donors. They sold it at 300 percent to 400 percent profit to hospitals and pharma manufacturers that then created the specialized products of clotting factors, gamma globulin, albumin, and others.

There was concern at the NIH and among some leading hematologists about the risks inherent in failing to screen the blood from "remunerated donors." Although a rudimentary test to spot hepatitis B antibodies was developed in 1964, the blood lobby had prevailed in stopping the FDA from requiring it. America's Blood Centers, the American Blood Resources Association, and the American Association of Blood Banks, national organizations that represented the country's for-profit and nonprofit blood centers, hospitals, and community blood banks, argued that the extra cost of the screening would be burdensome for the mom-and-pop blood collectors.[37]

The blood lobbyists contended, without any supporting evidence, that an infected single donor would be diluted by all the healthy donors in the pool. With that logic, the larger the pool, the better. It reduced the risk of any transmissible virus. Years later that was proven wrong. Researchers confirmed that a single patient with hepatitis could infect a pool of more than a million donors.[38]

Hepatitis infection rates across the country spiked starting in the mid-1960s. A 1968 study in *JAMA* reported that when the donors were "suspected narcotics addicts," it was seventy times more likely that a single transfusion resulted in a hepatitis infection.[39] In 1968 the federal government revoked all licenses for consumer sales of whole plasma from multiple donors (the FDA required hepatitis screening on blood and plasma supplies in 1972, but the test was only 15 percent effective).[40] A lot of the independent collection centers closed. Many of the remaining ones were bought by the four pharmaceutical firms that dominated the blood trade.[41]

It was a mistake to expect that eliminating most of the small operators might tamp the cowboy flavor of the American blood industry. The pharma firms now oversaw the plasma collection as well as processing it into a range of therapeutic products. Their incentive was to keep costs as low as possible. As a result they did not spend anything on making their products safer. Courtland and Hyland continued using skid row donors in large plasma pools. Hyland also set up plasma centers at U.S.-Mexico border towns, hoping to attract poor migrant donors. Cutter got into a fight with some hospitals over the right "to bleed prisoners."[42] A congressional investigation later obtained confidential documents from those companies, and from private blood collectors, that proved that for the next twenty years they often ignored, or at least delayed, readily available safety tests.[43] That only changed in the 1990s when AIDS made blood transfusions a matter of life and death.

Consolidating the plasma collection of the American blood industry under a handful of drug companies did not even result in more supply. They had not figured out how to induce more Americans to donate blood so demand continued to significantly outstrip production. The country's three largest blood organizations—the American Association of Blood Banks, the American Red Cross, and the Council of Community Blood Centers—had launched a promotion campaign to encourage more people to donate. It had a negligible effect.[44]

The gap in the supply of plasma was met by collection centers that opened in some of the poorest and most downtrodden urban slums in a dozen countries. The owners of the shuttered U.S. clinics ran some of them. By the end of the 1960s, blood centers in Costa Rica, El Salvador, the Dominican Republic, Mexico, Belize, Colombia, Haiti, and Nicaragua fed the American plasma market. The two largest collectors operated from Nicaragua and Haiti: Compañía Centroamericana de Plasmaféresis in Managua and Hemo-Caribbean in Port-au-Prince. They were in a class of their own, far outselling all offshore competitors in how much they sold monthly to the U.S.

There was, however, something unique about the Haiti center. It was the only one of the Third World collection operations with a link to the Democratic Republic of the Congo at a time when HIV was developing there. After the Congo declared independence from Belgium in 1960, a civil war wracked the country for four years. The U.N. secretary-general launched an ambitious project intended to recruit French-speaking engineers, physicians, nurses, teachers, and technicians to help stabilize the fledgling nation.[45] Although a lot of Belgian professionals had stayed in the country, the United Nations Educational, Scientific and Cultural Organization, UNESCO, wanted other nationalities than the one responsible for colonial rule. UNESCO offered housing and generous compensation packages and required a one- to four-year commitment. The largest contingent of French-speaking foreign professionals that arrived were between 4,500 and 6,000 Haitians.[46] They stayed on average twenty-four to thirty-six months before returning to Haiti. As they returned home, a few unknowingly were among the first people in the Western Hemisphere to have contracted HIV.[47]

The Hemo-Caribbean plasmapheresis center had opened in late 1970 in a two-story building in Rue des Remparts, a squalid street on the edge of the capital's infamous portside slums. An American stockbroker based in Miami, Joseph Gorinsteen, put up $250,000 to build it. An Austrian biochemist was its technical director.[48] Luckner Cambronne, the former head of the notorious Tonton Macoute police militia who had become the interior minister, had a secret stake. Aside from the island's autocratic president, François "Papa Doc" Duvalier, Cambronne was the most powerful man in Haiti.[49]

With Duvalier's blessing, Cambronne bypassed the country's minister of health and personally negotiated the contract that granted Hemo-Caribbean an exclusive ten-year contract for "plasma farming."[50] The center paid impoverished Haitians $3 per liter of plasma (2.1 pints). Those who queued before the doors opened daily at 6:30 were among the island nation's poorest, overwhelmingly illiterate and mostly unemployed. They could double or triple their average annual income of $75 by regularly giving blood.[51]

The Rue des Remparts center processed an average of 350 donors daily. There were usually some still waiting at its 8 p.m. closing. So many wanted to give blood that Hemo-Caribbean started building a second collection center in the capital capable of processing an additional five hundred daily.[52]

Although some hematologists criticized the center's poor hygiene and haphazard testing, it sold between five thousand to six thousand liters of plasma monthly to the American pharmaceutical companies licensed by the National Institute of Health's Division of Biologics Standards.[53] The frozen plasma, which returned a 500 percent profit, was flown to Miami on Air Haiti transports, an airline partly owned by Cambronne. Hemo-Caribbean's widespread plasma ventures had earned Cambronne a nickname in Port-au-Prince: "The Vampire of the Caribbean."[54] Once in Miami, the drug companies took the plasma and processed it into a lucrative range of therapeutic blood products.[55]

Werner Thill, Hemo-Caribbean's technical director, told a reporter that the blood center rejected 1 to 2 percent of its six thousand donors, judging them too weak or their hemoglobin count too low. What about donors who might be infected with hepatitis, malaria, or venereal diseases? Thill contended that it was foolish to worry about blood they collected since "Haiti has no drug-addict problem. . . . [and] most active blood sellers in the United States are drug addicts, many of whom have hepatitis."[56] As for anyone in Haiti "who may slip through the screening process," Thill claimed that Hemo-Caribbean had a unique freezing technique that "kills those bacteria" (that was wrong).[57]*

Even if the plasma it sold was contaminated, Thill asserted, "the companies that buy the plasma . . . are ultimately responsible for the product." The U.S. pharma and biologic companies were instead depending on the NIH's Division of Biologics Standards to randomly inspect blood products collected from paid donors in poor offshore countries with few stringent medical standards. When a *Los Angeles Times* investigation in 1972 raised troubling concerns about the safety procedures at Hemo-Caribbean, a California congressman, Victor Veysey, queried the Biologics Division. Federal regulators told him that "no imported plasma is being transfused directly into human beings." When pressed, they admitted that no one in the Biologics Division had verified that.[58] Instead, they relied on the assurances of the pharma companies distributing the Haitian plasma. Biologics also initially claimed there was no danger of the plasma transmitting hepatitis (HIV/AIDS was not yet identified) since it was broken into "its component fractions" for specialized treatments. When pushed by Veysey, the oversight agency admitted that the risk of passing on hepatitis or other infectious diseases "is not completely eliminated by this procedure."[59]

The author uncovered that one of Hemo-Caribbean's most dangerous cost-cutting measures was to reuse unsterile needles and sometimes catheters.[60] That is almost certainly why the clinic's donors had a high rate of injection site infections. In at least one instance, a worker became infected with hepatitis from handling the blood.[61] A former

* In fact, the only way to possibly kill such infectious viruses was the opposite, concentrated dry heat combined with solvent-detergents. After an advanced technology to heat plasma became available in the 1980s, the FDA pulled earlier versions from the U.S. market. Baxter International and Bayer continued to sell the recalled plasma to Asian, Latin American, and some European countries, despite an explicit FDA warning that those blood products might be contaminated with HIV.

Hemo-Caribbean lab technician (there were twenty-two at the company's peak of two hundred employees) later recounted there were some instances in which a donor's artery was mistakenly punctured instead of a vein, and others in which patients became sick to their stomach or short of breath. None of those was reported to the Ministry of Health.[62] Other times, in the lab, there were worries at the end of a second shift that the technicians and nurses were so tired that red blood cells taken from one donor had been "returned" to the wrong person. That could cause serious kidney and breathing problems as the body attacked the foreign cells as if they were invaders.

A sizable percentage of Hemo-Caribbean's weekly donors were sex workers, including men who regularly had sex with male tourists for pay, and ex-prisoners who had moved back to the neighborhood after their release from jail.[63] WHO and epidemiological studies later demonstrated that nearly three quarters of all sexually transmitted diseases in Haiti were then concentrated in those same demographic groups.[64]

By coincidence, eighteen months before Hemo-Caribbean opened its doors in Port-au-Prince there had been a medical breakthrough in the production of a highly concentrated form of Factor VIII. When the federal government had banned consumer sales of pooled plasma in 1968 over hepatitis fears, it exempted Factor VIII since there was no alternative for the nation's hemophiliacs. The thousands of monthly liters of pooled plasma that Hemo-Caribbean sold in the U.S. were distributed widely from California to New York to Indiana as finished Factor VIII.

In 1979 and 1980, a dozen men in Haiti were the first to be diagnosed with Kaposi sarcoma. The author was unable to confirm a report that ten of them had been Hemo-Caribbean donors.[65] A French geologist had his arm amputated after a car accident in 1979 while working in Port-au-Prince. He received eight pints of blood during surgery and eighteen months later developed Kaposi sarcoma (the first case of the new virus passing through a blood transfusion in the U.S. was that same year, 1979, to an eighteen-year-old hemophiliac in Pittsburgh).[66]

Expectant mothers started turning up with another herpes-related virus, cytomegalovirus (CMV). The symptoms—fatigue, fever, swollen lymph glands, and vision loss—created serious pregnancy complications. A thirty-four-year-old secretary for Air Zaïre checked in to a health clinic in Louvain, Belgium. She was ill with a severe CMV infection and toxoplasmosis, a parasitic disease normally found only in cats. Two of her daughters had died at six months of age from respiratory infections, and her three-month-old surviving daughter had oral candida, an opportunistic yeast throat infection. No medications helped. Against her doctors' advice, the secretary traveled to Zaire to visit her family. The doctors intended to perform additional testing when she returned to Belgium; she never did. There was no urgency or any follow-up; they considered her a puzzling medical anomaly.

No one could yet be expected to connect all the inexplicable reports in obscure journals about the cluster of young patients who had turned up at doctor's offices or emergency rooms with rare illnesses resistant to all traditional treatments. No one could imagine they were the harbinger of AIDS, the most lethal modern-day epidemic.* [67]

* Efforts to wean plasmapheresis centers off paying the poorest people for donating blood have failed repeatedly. The current demand for plasma, for which there is no synthetic substitute, is several times greater than it was in 1970. An investigation in 2018 in *The Atlantic* reported, "Americans are flooding into the country's blood-plasma donation centers in greater numbers than ever before, seeking to make up for low wages or small benefits checks, or even as their only source of cash income during a spell of extreme poverty. Their blood plasma—which historically has been collected disproportionately in the country's poorest communities—is fueling a multibillion-dollar worldwide industry."

34

"EVERYTHING CAN BE ABUSED"

The Sacklers paid little attention to the developments about Ebola or the scattered accounts of unexplained illnesses afflicting visitors to Africa. As doctors, they were naturally interested in the emergence of any new pathogen, but that was tempered by the knowledge that it did not present them any business opportunity. Purdue never had a product targeting infectious diseases. The immense research costs had made that field the province of much larger drug firms. Even Arthur's big pharma clients had shifted their scientists away from antibiotics and to new, more profitable classes of medications that targeted chronic diseases.

In 1978, the Sacklers rolled out Napp Chemicals in the U.S. and Pharma Technologies in the U.K. (no family member was listed as an owner on the incorporation papers).[1] The following year, they opened Mundipharma in Germany, the tenth country for the Mundi brand since its launch in Switzerland in 1957.*[2]

While Mortimer and Raymond worked on the family's pharma

---

* In 1978 one of the family's longest-serving attorneys, Martin Greene, opened a solo practice. The New York State Bar Association listed his address as 15 East 62nd Street in Manhattan and his telephone number as (212) 832 7900. That was the same address and number as a number of new Sackler-owned companies, including Terramar Research, Angiology Research Foundation, and the Raymond and Beverly Sackler Foundation. Listed next door at 17 East 62nd Street was the Mortimer D. Sackler Foundation, the Sackler Lefcourt Center for Child Development, the Sackler Family Foundation, and the U.S. office for the Sackler School of Medicine in Tel Aviv. Although some of the companies had changed over time, 15 and 17 East 62nd Street were the same addresses highlighted by the Kefauver subcommittee investigators in 1960 as "components of the Sackler empire . . . cloaked in secrecy."

components, Arthur was busy helping Roche scramble to figure out how to reverse the first ever drop in Valium sales.[3] Arthur was, as his brothers and colleagues knew, a blunt realist when it came to business. He did not sugarcoat Valium's prospects to Roche. Its past success was now part of its problem. An estimated 20 percent of *all* American adult women were regular users. Although revenue had declined in 1976, almost two billion pills had been prescribed.[4] Even without the Controlled Substances Act restrictions and the FDA limits, he contended, Valium had so saturated the market that it might be nearing its natural maximum penetration.[5]

Since there were still eight years left on Valium's patent, Sackler said, it would be foolish not to make every effort to stop it from slipping further. The upside to the aura around Valium meant it had crossed into popular culture and had a hold on the American psyche. It was, according to one medical writer, "one of the most praised drugs in history and one of the most maligned."[6] A decade after the Rolling Stones had sung about it, there were references to the drug in Neil Simon plays and Woody Allen films. A group of Upper East Side New Yorkers dubbed themselves the Valium Girls Club. Comedian Rodney Dangerfield boasted it was part of his daily regimen.

Valium's high profile also worked to its detriment whenever it figured in any much publicized story of celebrity addiction or overdose. Elizabeth Taylor admitted she was addicted to Valium and Jack Daniel's. Tammy Faye Bakker, half of an evangelical empire, claimed her reckless financial decisions were the result of her daily affection for a customized Valium nasal spray. Television producer Barbara Gordon's harrowing story of how she landed in a mental asylum after quitting Valium cold turkey became a best-selling book.[7]

When forty-two-year-old Elvis Presley died in August 1977, his autopsy was a toxicological snapshot of the era's most abused drugs: Valium was mixed with "significant" quantities of codeine, Quaaludes, Ethinamate, a popular sedative-hypnotic, and a barbiturate never confirmed but reportedly phenobarbital. He also had painkillers Demerol and morphine, another tranquilizer, Placidyl, and the antihistamine Chlorpheniramine.[8] *

* Years later, Valium lost some of its notoriety when much more powerful street drugs made a resurgence. In 1993, River Phoenix, the twenty-three-year-old actor that Hollywood had dubbed "the next James Dean," went into convulsions outside a West Holly-

Valium's sales stumbled. It was an opportunity for competitors to introduce new benzodiazepines they claimed had all of its benefits without the downsides. Arthur knew that Roche had a "better and improved" product, Klonopin (clonazepam). It was one of the "backup benzos" developed by Leo Sternbach, the scientist who had discovered Librium and Valium. Roche had patented it in 1964 and put it on the shelf. After Roche had both Librium and Valium on the market within three years of each other, it held back on releasing Klonopin for fear of cannibalizing the big sales of its first two benzos. With Valium under increasing attack, however, Roche agreed with Sackler. Thirteen years after the drug's discovery, Roche set aside $20 million for a national rollout of Klonopin in the U.S.[9]

Its release made other drug companies rush their competing benzos to market. Wyeth released Ativan in September 1977. It was a versatile benzo that was effective for insomnia, anxiety, and seizures. One dosing advantage it touted over Valium was a much shorter half-life, reducing the hangover effect about which some patients complained.[10] Warner Lambert followed in a month with Prazepam, another short-acting, antianxiety benzo.

Sackler adjusted Valium's advertising strategy. Data gathered by IMS showed that doctors were more inclined to write prescriptions for a premium pharmaceutical firm they judged to be at the forefront of research and development of a drug category.[11] As a result, Roche emphasized Valium's long history and the millions of case studies that demonstrated how safe and effective it was when used correctly. Did physicians want to gamble with their patients' health by dispensing newcomers that looked good in clinical trials but had little real-world experience?[12]

Valium sold a record 2.3 billion tablets the following year, 1978.[13] It became the first drug in the history of the pharmaceutical industry to surpass a billion dollars in accumulated sales.[14] That was the same year former first lady Betty Ford checked herself into rehab for an alcohol and Valium addiction.[15] Senator Ted Kennedy announced hearings before his Health Subcommittee to address the "nightmare of dependence" Valium had created for millions of Americans.[16] * [17]

---

wood nightclub. When his brother made a panicked call to 911, he said, "I'm thinking he had Valium." He died at the hospital of a heroin and cocaine overdose.

* Valium earned a dubious footnote in American history in March 1980 when a psychiatric outpatient tried assassinating Ronald Reagan. John Hinckley had been on a 15 mg

Sackler, however, could not rescue Valium. It was not ultimately possible to reverse the "health risk" story line that had reshaped the public's perception. He managed to delay its final reckoning, though. By 1980, Valium's annual prescriptions had fallen in half to 30 million. That was still enough to keep it in the top ten selling prescription drugs in America. Arthur had told Roche executives that if they wanted to revive the glory days when their benzos dominated the mild tranquilizers, the answer was to be found in their own labs.[18] Roche had hoped Klonopin might be the replacement but it did not have Valium's blockbuster appeal.

There were a couple of benzos in the FDA pipeline that Sackler thought were commercially very promising, but neither was a Roche product. Both were from Upjohn Laboratories in Kalamazoo, Michigan. Upjohn thought it had developed a Valium killer in a benzo it named Halcion.[19] It was fast acting and left no hangover. In small doses it was a good sedative and in higher strengths acted as a hypnotic tranquilizer. Upjohn submitted it to the FDA for approval in May 1976, as the tide against Valium was under way. The FDA review office had concerns about some efficacy claims but mostly about some adverse effects, including mental confusion, amnesia, and rebound insomnia in which abrupt discontinuation of a drug worsens a patient's sleeping problems.[20] Although the FDA's Psychopharmacologic Agents Advisory Committee recommended in 1977 that it be approved for sale, the FDA decided to order additional clinical testing. Halcion would not get approved for another five years (November 1982).

Upjohn had another drug, alprazolam, on which it had obtained a patent in 1971. It had intended to market it originally as a sleep aid. Additional clinical trials showed it was also effective in reducing anxiety, had promise as an antidepressant, and reduced panic attacks. Upjohn submitted the drug to the FDA only after Halcion's delay. And to Upjohn's surprise, in November 1981, alprazolam got approved while Halcion was still undergoing more testing. Upjohn put alprazolam on the market under the brand name Xanax.[21]

Arthur Sackler had been right. Valium's final denouement would not be because its large base of loyal patients became skittish about

---

daily dose of Valium. He took an additional 20 milligrams only hours before he shot Reagan. One of Hinckley's lawyers charged that giving more Valium to Hinckley was like "throwing gasoline on a lighted fire."

it; he had predicted they would leave for a medication they perceived as better. Xanax was a hit. As with Halcion, Xanax also metabolized in the body in about half the time required of Valium. Upjohn promoted it as the benzo that would not leave patients drowsy the next day. They also got lucky on another front. A year before the FDA gave Xanax a green light, the third edition of the *DSM* (*Diagnostic and Statistical Manual*)—the bible for diagnosing and treating psychiatric disorders—added "panic disorder" for the first time.[22] It was the first update of the *DSM* since 1968.

Although most researchers assumed that the other benzos—Librium, Valium, Klonopin—would probably be just as good in treating panic disorders, Upjohn was the only firm that had tested their drug for that condition and demonstrated its effectiveness.[23] When the FDA approved Xanax as the first ever drug to treat the disorder, some competitors sarcastically dubbed it "the Upjohn illness." No pharma rival underestimated the achievement in formally medicalizing panic disorder.[24] Xanax sales skyrocketed.[25] Into the mid-1990s, Xanax alone provided about a quarter of Upjohn's worldwide sales; that was no small feat considering it also had three other commercially successful drugs in unrelated categories.[26] * [27]

Upjohn had done more than create the drug that knocked Valium off its pedestal; by converting a *DSM* anxiety diagnosis and getting FDA approval for a biological solution on which it had a patent, it set the template rivals would follow. The 1980 edition of the *DSM*, which some Freudian psychiatrists criticized as "capitulation to computers and insurance company requirements," increased the number of recognized mental illnesses from 182 to 265.[28] A much wider range of emotional complaints suddenly seemed to have a *DSM* listing, making them subject to insurance coverage. Harvard psychiatric professor Arthur Kleinman thought the new *DSM* belittled the misery of people with serious mental illnesses at the cost of "medicalizing ordinary unhappiness."[29] Author and psychiatrist Peter Kramer dubbed it "diagnostic bracket creep."[30]

The *DSM III* separated depression from anxiety. It then provided a list of separate stand-alone mental illnesses under anxiety.

---

* Not even adding Xanax to Schedule IV of the Controlled Substances Act slowed its sales. In 1988 it was the world's top selling pharmacological drug. It dominated the more than one hundred benzodiazepine drugs on the market in the 1990s.

It put Upjohn's panic disorder alongside generalized anxiety disorder (GAD), obsessive-compulsive disorder (OCD), social phobias (SAD), and post-traumatic stress disorder (PTSD).

Vietnam vets and their advocates had lobbied hard for the inclusion of PTSD. A leading mental health journal estimated that upward of 700,000 of the three million who served in Vietnam had the disorder.[31] A later federal study thought the real number of vets suffering from PTSD was closer to 1.5 million, 85 percent of whom had been in combat. In a couple of years, PTSD was an increasingly common diagnosis for victims of domestic violence, rape, and child abuse.

Several pharmaceutical firms launched research to develop drugs that treated the new mental disorders in the *DSM*. By the end of the decade, some of the most dramatic results would be evident with the introduction of Prozac, a new class of antianxiety and antidepressant medications called serotonin reuptake inhibitors.

America's love-hate relationship with Valium was never more evident than in two quite different events in 1982. The inventor of the benzodiazepine class, Leo Sternbach, won the John Scott Legacy Medal for his pioneering work. That prestigious award, presented annually since 1816, is for an invention that "enhanced the comfort, welfare, and happiness of humankind." Previous winners included Marie Curie, Jonas Salk, Thomas Edison, and Nikola Tesla. At the same time Sternbach got that accolade, Ralph Nader's Health Research Group published *Stopping Valium*, a searing indictment that claimed Valium and its chemical cousins in the benzo class were responsible for an "unparalleled addiction and health crisis."[32]

Arthur Sackler found nothing incongruous about the Sternbach award and the Nader broadside. Nader focused on the worst statistics and assigned blame widely, all part of expanding his influence as a consummate consumer advocate. Nader and others blamed the pharmaceutical companies for discovering and then aggressively marketing their drugs. The more successful a drug, the more blame it got. In Sackler's view that was too simplistic. He agreed with Sternbach, who was asked by a reporter if he would have changed the drug were it possible to go back in time? "I can't get the feeling to be responsible for the drug's use. I'm responsible for the class of compounds. . . . But for its use, I mean, everything can be abused. So you cannot create things that will be abuse proof."[33]

Arthur clipped Gilbert Cant's famous *New York Times Magazine*

1976 cover story titled "Valiumania" The final paragraph read, "If Valium is a major reliance in what moralists and some sociologists complain is a hedonistic, sybaritic culture, losing its git-up-'n'-git-drive and seeking nirvana in a little bottle of tablets, its use is a symptom rather than a cause of this condition. Properly used by the medical profession, it has only medicinal properties. A drug has no moral or immoral qualities. These are the monopoly of the user or abuser." Arthur underlined the last two sentences. It not only applied to Valium, Sackler thought, but was true about drugs in general.[34]

35

THE AGE OF BIOTECH

Valium was the subject of thousands of stories in newspapers, magazines, and on television over a five-year period starting in 1975.[1] There were specials about the litigation between Roche and the federal government, the boom in illegal street use, and advance looks at how rivals were planning to dethrone Valium. A pharma story unrelated to the benzodiazepines received little coverage in comparison because most news editors considered it too technical for a lay audience. The embryonic biotech industry was laying the groundwork for technology that would have far greater long-term consequences for the pharmaceutical industry than which mild tranquilizer was American's best-selling drug.

A year into the voluntary moratorium on rDNA research, the fears had started receding about the likelihood that genetic testing might unleash an end-of-the-world virus. What was missing were guidelines for lab safety and containment. The National Institutes of Health finally stepped into the void. It took until July 1976, almost two years after the lockdown on genetic testing, before it released "Guidelines for Research Involving Recombinant DNA Molecules."[2] That detailed parameters for genetic laboratory testing and research. Since the NIH had no authority to regulate the industry, its guidelines were voluntary. When the National Academy of Sciences' Committee on Recombinant DNA Molecules endorsed the NIH guidelines, however, it was enough to lift the research and testing moratorium.

Some in Congress thought that no matter how small the odds that the new technology might produce something catastrophic, regulations should be mandatory. There were soon sixteen competing bills, most offering variations on creating a new biotech czar and department inside Health, Education, and Welfare. Dr. Donald Fredrickson, who had become the head of the NIH in 1975, lobbied the Carter White House to oppose any legislation. "Let's try to do it through a voluntary system," he pleaded. A committee appointed by the White House agreed. Fredrickson was relieved: "They recognized that you cannot regulate science by statute."[3]

Prior to the mid-1970s, only nonprofits were eligible for NIH research grants. Even then they came with a string attached: the NIH micromanaged the laboratory research it funded. It assumed that oversight was the best way assure that taxpayer money was well spent. By 1975, a new NIH administration was convinced that such tight control was detrimental to creative scientists.[4] Soon, the rules changed and allowed a "light touch" for research oversight. For the first time it also allowed private, for-profit companies to apply for research subsidies.[5] The changes were perfectly timed for the advent of biotechnology.

While the NIH played as significant a role in kick-starting the industry as did venture capitalists and academic research centers, the new science also remade the NIH into a powerhouse federal agency. Nixon's "war on cancer" in the early 1970s had bumped up its budget by a third but biotechnology helped it morph into the world's largest biomedical/genetic engineering lab. Within a decade of lifting the moratorium, the NIH comprised three thousand scientists overseeing biotech research in more than a thousand labs. And it still managed to give away most of its money to university and hospital research. Its budget had ballooned from $1 billion in the mid-1970s to $37 billion in 2019, a growth rate ten times faster than the budget-bloated Defense Department.[6]

The NIH even added an incentive to grants made to universities in biotech and genetic research. The schools would have the first option to patent any discoveries that had commercial potential. They could then license the patents to pharmaceutical firms and the earned royalties went to the schools.[7]

Some early biotech start-ups did not depend on federal funding. Just before rDNA research had restarted in 1976, a twenty-nine-year-old Silicon Valley venture capitalist, Robert Swanson, called Herbert Boyer, a biochemistry professor at the University of California at San Francisco.[8] Swanson was a partner in a Silicon Valley venture capital firm that had been cofounded only four years earlier by former executives from Hewlett-Packard and Fairchild Semiconductor.[9] Swanson hoped Boyer might have some ideas about how to commercially exploit the rDNA research he had co-discovered with Stanley Cohen. Boyer and

Cohen had applied for a patent on their rDNA work.[10] That was controversial since some universities and scientists contended that the results of academic research should be available to all. To deflect the criticism, the two scientists assigned their rights to their respective schools, Stanford and the University of California at San Francisco (UCSF). The patent was pending when Swanson called.

Boyer's medium-sized lab at UCSF was one of the world's most advanced in researching rDNA. He had little interest then in the commercial challenge of figuring out how to get biotech advances from the lab to the marketplace. Swanson, however, implored Boyer to meet for ten minutes and discuss it. When they got together, they talked for three hours, sharing ideas about how ongoing biotech research could transform the pharmaceutical industry. By the time they finished, the duo had decided to form the first biotechnology company. It would exploit the rDNA technology in the Boyer-Cohen pending patent.[11] Each invested $500 to "formalize" their agreement. Boyer even had an idea of what to name it: he took the first three syllables of GENetic ENgineering TECHnology to form Genentech.* [12]

Genentech did not seem formidable when it opened for business that April. Although Swanson's venture capital firm had contributed $100,000, the company had no lab equipment or assets, not even a secretary.[13] It had big ideas, though. A few months earlier, MIT biochemist Har Gobind Khorana, a Nobel Laureate in 1968 for his research on the genetic code, had synthesized the first artificial gene.[14] Boyer knew that a different UCSF lab than the one he worked in, as well as Harvard's Biology Laboratory, were using rodent insulin as a hormone in advancing their own gene sequencing research. Was it possible that

---

* The Boyer-Cohen patent was issued in 1980, after six years of contentious debate. That was the year the Supreme Court ruled on the case of a patent application for a genetically modified organism that absorbed crude oil cleanups. The Patent Office had rejected the application, but the Supreme Court overturned that, ruling that since the organism was "man-made," it could be patented. It was reminiscent of the 1940s battle by Merck for a patent on streptomycin, which the Patent Office had first denied as a "product of nature." The Boyer-Cohen patent became the most successful in pharmaceutical history. During its seventeen-year life span it was licensed to 468 companies, including premier drug firms such as Lilly, Merck, and Amgen. It was the basis for groundbreaking drugs in treating heart disease, cancer, diabetes, and HIV/AIDS. Stanford, which managed the patent and the University of California, has earned $320 million in licensing fees as of 2019.

one of those projects might find a way to create synthetic human insulin? An article in *Science* that fall suggested that genetically engineered insulin was possible by splicing an insulin gene into a self-replicating bacterium. Although it sounded simple, Boyer knew it was extremely ambitious.

Three research teams were in a race to be the first to develop a marketable synthetic insulin. Genentech was the underdog. Harvard's Biology Lab was run by Walter Gilbert, an eminent physicist who was one of the pioneers in DNA sequencing. The UCSF team was directed by Howard Goodman and William Rutter, both noted biochemists. Rutter was the department's chairman.

Although Genentech had to play catch-up with its rivals, Boyer knew the field was so new that their lead could not be too great. Boyer and Swanson tapped their $100,000 reserve. They reached out to two organic chemists at Southern California's City of Hope National Medical Center. The duo, Japanese-native Keiichi Itakura and Arthur Riggs, had been working on rDNA technology since its inception. They were immersed in a difficult project to synthesize somatostatin, a peptide hormone that was less complicated to modify than was insulin.

Boyer did not know that Itakura and Riggs had applied for an NIH grant for their gene research. When the NIH passed on their proposal they signed a contract with Genentech so they could continue their work. They convinced Boyer and Swanson that while there was no commercial market for somatostatin, their research could provide the technical road map for successfully synthesizing insulin. Instead of moving to Genentech's bare-bones headquarters, the duo stayed at their Los Angeles–area lab.

Boyer had not picked the duo by chance. He was well aware of the status of genetic research projects under way at major universities. He was confident that Itakura and Riggs were further along than the competition at Harvard or UCSF. Still, Boyer and Swanson did not want to take any chances. Genentech made its first full-time hires in late 1976 (it had a dozen employees by year end). David Goeddel, a twenty-five-year-old biochemist, had just earned his PhD in biochemistry when he became the company's third employee. Dennis Kleid, a twenty-nine-year-old organic chemist who had been working on DNA cloning at Stanford, became employee number five. They were both assigned to be the hands-on Genentech component of the Itakura and

Riggs team. That meant commuting from their homes in the Bay Area to Los Angeles, at the cost of sleep, regular meals, or time with their families.

In the spring of 1977, the Itakura team produced purified synthetic somatostatin DNA. It took another couple of months for them to refine a year-old technique and slash the time needed to synthesize the hormone from years to weeks.[15] By midsummer, they inserted their synthetic human protein into *E. coli* bacteria. It was a first. Boyer understood its importance. The process was completely synthetic and did not rely on any human genetic material. That meant it was exempt from the incredibly burdensome safety regulations established by the NIH for experiments involving human genetic cloning. The precautions covering containment and disposal were so strict that such experimentation had been almost exclusively the province of the Defense Department's biowarfare labs.[16] The costs for adhering to those guidelines was prohibitive for Genentech and would have spelled an abortive end to their insulin project.

Instead, by early 1978 Boyer was ready for Genentech to move to the next stages of research and testing. The breakthrough on synthetic somatostatin had the added benefit of bringing in a fresh wave of venture capital.

Genentech's rivals were not sitting idly by. Walter Gilbert, the physicist who ran Harvard's insulin rDNA project, had become one of the founding partners of Biogen, a Swiss-based firm that described itself as a "pharmaceutical company with an emphasis on breakthroughs in biology." Biogen had deep pockets from three venture capital firms and almost immediately signed an agreement to underwrite the Harvard research.[17]*

The University of California at San Francisco lab signed an ambitious funding agreement with Eli Lilly, the patent holder on human insulin since the 1920s. Not only was Lilly interested in synthetic insulin, but the contract also paid for parallel UCSF research into human growth hormone.[18] Lilly sent some of the University of California team

---

* Biogen became one of the most successful biotech firms. A year after its creation, its researchers cloned the first biologically active human interferon, and the company made a lucrative licensing deal for worldwide rights with Schering-Plough. That same year it was the first to synthesize hepatitis B antigens that would later be critical in developing a screening test for blood and plasma. And in 1980, Walter Gilbert won the Nobel Prize for his pioneering research in DNA sequencing.

to one of its labs in France where human genetic testing was permitted. The experiments failed due to accidental contamination.

In August 1978, Genentech's Dennis Kleid visited one of Lilly's insulin manufacturing plants on the outskirts of Indianapolis.

"There was a line of train cars filled with frozen pancreases," he recalled later.[19] The stockpile of cattle and pig pancreases was not surprising. Eight thousand pounds of pancreatic glands were necessary to produce a pound of insulin. The plant manager told Kleid that translated into about 23,500 animals. Lilly, which required about 56 million animals annually, was desperate for a synthetic insulin. Although they had signed a deal with the University of California, Boyer was confident that if Genentech made the breakthrough, Lilly would jump to license it.

Boyer was right. The Genentech team overcame a series of seemingly intractable laboratory hurdles and finally, on August 28, inserted the human insulin gene into *E. coli* bacteria. They synthesized enough for testing and sent it to Lilly. The report that returned was cause for celebration: Genentech's artificially created insulin was the identical twin of human insulin. Even better, it produced fewer allergic reactions than the animal-based product. Lily agreed to fund further Genentech research.

Still, it was not clear whether the Genentech insulin would become a usable drug or if it was just a scientific milestone with no practical use. No one had figured out how to manipulate the bacteria so it could yield fifty to sixty times what it ordinarily produced. That was required to convert it into an affordable, commercial product. After having seen firsthand the amount of animal pancreases used to manufacture insulin, Kleid was downcast. He told Swanson he did not think it was possible to get the required yields.

That became Genentech's priority for 1979. The breakthrough came with the development of a potent "control gene." That gene sent a signal to the intestinal bacteria and made it replicate rDNA insulin at record levels. Lilly was so confident in Genentech's synthetic insulin that it agreed to shepherd the drug through FDA approval and also began building two pilot manufacturing plants to prepare for what was certain to be a green light from the FDA.

The deal between Lilly and Genentech marked a turning point in the pharmaceutical industry. Lilly's licensing agreement permitted it to manufacture and market the recombinant insulin. It paid all the enormous costs to bring it to the market. Genentech had no financial risk. It only collected royalties on whatever sales Lilly made.

In 1980, Genentech had its IPO. At that point it still did not have FDA approval for its star discovery and had no income. What it did have, however, as internet companies would a decade later, were incredibly high investor expectations for a product they understood almost nothing about. Its offering was the most successful and frenzied IPO in a decade. It took only twenty minutes to sell out the million shares offered on its first trading day. The share price hit $88 during the day's trading before closing at $56, double its offering price of $35.

The Genentech-Lilly licensing contract served as a road map for other biotech firms that wanted to get a foothold in the pharmaceutical industry. The chief barrier to entry into the drug business had always been the huge start-up costs, a minimum on average of half a billion dollars.

In 1982, the FDA approved Genentech's synthetic insulin and Lilly began selling it the following year. It was an instant blockbuster.

Genentech was only the first of what would become a tsunami of biotechnology firms. More than 180 biotech start-ups opened in the year after the Genentech IPO, all hoping to produce a product that became a winning rDNA lottery ticket.[20] Scientists from top universities led the way with many of the start-ups that promised they would be "molecule to market" companies. Venture capital money flooded the sector. At a meeting of investors who were stumbling over one another to write checks to biotech start-ups, Paul Berg, who got a Nobel for his rDNA studies, asked, "Where were you guys in the '50s and '60s when all the funding had to be done in the basic science?"[21]

The early successes convinced many venture capitalists that investing in biotech was an easy way of making enormous profits. Wall Street underwriters lined up to bring biotech companies public. A leading broker at Goldman Sachs told *The New York Times*, "There's not enough to go around."[22] Next was Cetus, with its promise of an interleukin-2 inhibitor to reduce the chance of the body rejecting an organ transplant. Its IPO brought in $120 million, valuing the no-product start-up as a half-billion-dollar firm. At the time it was the "biggest industrial IPO in US corporate history."[23] Several dozen other biotech firms went public through the remainder of the decade, raising on average $20 to $30 million each.[24]

The companies invariably promised complex science innovations that sounded exciting on paper but which no one, not even the firms themselves, could be certain were possible. Few on Wall Street who bought biotech shares as fast as they were offered understood what was meant by "antibody-based formats," "cytotoxic potential of T-cells," or "connective tissue mesenchymal precursor cells." So-called momentum investors did not have to comprehend how it all worked, they just needed to have a market that traded up in a straight line. Many investors made so much early money that they dismissed the possibility the industry might ever have a correction, much less a bear market. Investors were buying companies that had no revenues based on a shared belief that in the future they might earn immense profits in a pharmaceutical industry and scientific medical world that most people were incapable of imagining (like the internet boom the next decade). The bull run in biotech was not slowed when Jack Bogle, the father of index investing, warned, "The first rule investors should understand is that what goes up must come down."[25]

Even some venture capitalists, without the sophistication of Swanson at Genentech, had little idea of the value of the company into which they were making substantial investments. What they did know, and what encouraged them to write checks, was that over the next decade half of the Nobel Prizes in Medicine went to researchers on the frontier of genetic engineering and biotechnology. In addition to Paul Berg's award for his genetic engineering research, scientists at Basel's Werner Arber University and Johns Hopkins later shared the Nobel for creating the first genetic map and Stanley Cohen got it for his discoveries of nerve and epidermal growth factors. Genentech, meanwhile, had projects under way on growth hormones, hepatitis vaccines, interferon, and a hormone that stimulated the body's disease-fighting cells. Advances in biotechnology demonstrated the importance of monoclonal antibodies, discovered in 1975, in enhancing the immune response to some cancers. That research opened a window to a new class of targeted drugs that held the promise of having as big an impact in the future as penicillin and lifesaving antibiotics had in the last century.

It is impossible to predict the specific trip wire that will send investors fleeing from a hot sector in panic. In 1987, when the FDA initially refused to approve Genentech's Activase designed to dissolve blood clots, the stock lost a billion dollars, a quarter of its value, the next trading day (Activase won FDA approval in 1996).[26] Investors lost faith in the many promises of a biotech miracle as the group fell into a crushing three-year bear market during a bull market for other American business sectors.[27] * [28]

In 1990, Genentech set a then record when it sold a 56 percent stake to Roche for $2.1 billion. Nineteen years later, the remaining 44 percent of Genentech cost Roche $47 billion. By then, a remarkable two thirds of Roche's revenues came from biologic cancer drugs developed by Genentech. Only twenty years earlier, Roche's benzodiazepines had accounted for the same oversized share of the company's revenues. The difference in Roche's best-selling drugs in those two decades made evident the transformative impact of biotechnology.

---

* The biotech industry is littered with instances in which investment banks issued *buy* recommendations and days later the bottom fell out of the share price because of some bad news about the company's drug. Even some of the savviest biotech venture capital investors can become infatuated with a product that sounds dazzling. A recent high-profile example is Theranos, a start-up built around a patented blood-testing device that was touted as the heart of "the laboratory of the future." The media cast its founder, Elizabeth Holmes, as the biomedical industry's equivalent of Apple's visionary Steve Jobs. Theranos attracted $700 million from some of the biggest private investors, all of whom were advised by industry specialists. Walgreens's pharmaceutical division was a major investor, as was a Stanford biotech dean. Only after Theranos, valued at $9 billion at its peak, crashed, was it disclosed that *not one* of the investors had asked for audited financial statements from an independent public accounting firm. In June 2018, the U.S. Attorney for the Northern District of California indicted Holmes and the company's president on multiple counts of wire fraud. Their trial is scheduled for August 2020.

36

A "GAY CANCER"

In June 1980, a few months before Genentech set Wall Street on fire, the Sackler-owned Napp Pharmaceuticals released in the United Kingdom the first extended relief oral, narcotic painkiller, MST Continus. It was the breakthrough palliative drug for which Cicely Saunders had searched since the mid-1960s. It had taken Napp several years of trial-and-error laboratory work, and dozens of tweaks to the underlying patent technology for the pill's delayed delivery system, to get it right. The result was an invisible dual-action polymer chemical coating that released pure morphine steadily over twelve hours. The speed at which the morphine was dispensed inside the body depended on how long it took stomach acid to penetrate the tablet, a feature Napp could fine-tune.

MST Continus meant that cancer patients who were not terminal could be discharged from the hospital and sent home to manage their pain with only two pills daily. Medical journals judged the drug as a significant advance in treating end-of-life pain. Oncologists and hospices did not seem concerned about a small-print warning Napp put on the package insert: "MST Continus tablets must be swallowed whole and not chewed." What that did not spell out was that if the pills were chewed, the entire dose of morphine—up to 100 mg per pill—would immediately be released. It was a precaution that the Medicines and Healthcare Products Regulatory Agency—Britain's equivalent of the FDA—thought wise but probably unnecessary. Few expected many seriously ill cancer patients would tamper with Napp's delayed release coating.

The same month, June 1980, that Napp put MST Continus on sale, five thousand miles away, San Francisco State University hosted a conference of gay physicians. It was timed to coincide with the city's

Gay Freedom Day Parade.[1] That was an annual event to commemorate three days of spontaneous demonstrations that had erupted after a June 1969 police raid on the Stonewall Inn, a Greenwich Village gay bar. Most social historians mark the Stonewall raid and public backlash as the catalyst for the 1970s Gay Liberation movement.

San Francisco may have only had 700,000 residents but its Gay Freedom Day Parade was the nation's largest, with a quarter million attending between spectators and marchers. By 1980, an estimated two of every five adult men in the city were openly gay, by far the highest number per capita in America.[2] Randy Shilts, then a reporter for the local public television station, KQED, noted in a report about the Stonewall commemoration that "after 10 years of gay freedom, the city that has come to represent that freedom is San Francisco."[3]

Many expressed their newfound freedom sexually, an indulgent celebration of liberties that had been illegal until 1975 when California excluded "private consensual activity" from statutes against sodomy and oral sex.[4] There was a crackdown in the early 1970s by the city's Italian American mayor. He had eyes on the governor's mansion and played to his morally conservative Catholic base. Police arrested some three thousand gay men for public sex felonies. Many convictions required registration as a sex offender.[5]

For many men who were for the first time publicly proud to be gay, promiscuous sex seemed an excusable element of social and political liberation. By 1980, it was also a $100-million-a-year business in thriving clubs and bathhouses that served as venues for anonymous sex.[6]

Many of the doctors at the June conference had come to San Francisco to join the two-mile Gay Freedom Day Parade celebration through the city's downtown. Their priority, however, was sharing information about a veritable explosion in sexually transmitted diseases that had become by-products of the sexual revolution that had remade gay life in some American cities. Bathhouses were breeding grounds for infections. Adding to the health risks for promiscuous gay men was the widespread use of recreational drugs, in particular, amyl and butyl nitrate. They were liquids legally dispensed to alleviate heart pain, but their street popularity was because of the short euphoric rush that increased the intensity of sex. Nicknamed poppers, they were inexpensive and available at head shops in many cities. No one then knew that their regular use suppressed the immune system and that they dilated the body's blood vessels, allowing viruses to enter more easily.[7]

Gay men accounted for more than half of all reported cases in 1980 in the U.S. of gonorrhea and syphilis.[8] Two thirds of the gay men at San Francisco's popular general clinic tested positive for hepatitis B, a liver infection spread sexually or through blood. Twenty percent of the sexually active gay men moving to San Francisco contracted hepatitis in their first twelve months. Within four years, the infection rate was virtually 100 percent.[9] No one yet realized it was a problem beyond those who got infected with hepatitis; blood bank officials estimated that in 1980 San Francisco gay men donated 5 percent to 7 percent of the city's blood. There was no test to screen for hepatitis.[10]

A Seattle study showed that an unusually large number of gay men had contracted shigellosis, a bacterial infection spread through contaminated food, water, or feces. Seventy percent of those infected had found their sex partners at bathhouses. A study in Denver found that gay men had on average three sexual encounters every time they went to a bathhouse. There was a one in three chance they left a bathhouse with gonorrhea or syphilis.[11] Chicago's Howard Brown Memorial Clinic recorded an epidemic infection rate of hepatitis B, about half of its gay patients. At the New York Gay Men's Health Project, a third had gastrointestinal parasites. In San Francisco, local clinics reported a stunning 8,000 percent increase in intestinal parasites over seven years, mostly young men in their thirties. It was so common by 1980 that medical journals dubbed it "Gay Bowel Syndrome."[12]

The doctors who gathered for the 1980 San Francisco conference knew that parasitic diseases like shigellosis, amebiasis, and giardiasis thrived in the feces of infected patients. Unprotected anal intercourse was one way the intestinal bugs spread. The other high-risk, yet popular, sex practice was rimming. The medical journals referred to that as "oral-anal intercourse."[13]

As Randy Shilts later wrote in *And the Band Played On*, his seminal book about AIDS and the deadly failure of the federal government to respond, "the success of the Gay Liberation movement which had started in the late-1960s, had by 1980, however . . . become a victim of its own success."[14]

By that summer, doctors started seeing an uptick in gay patients with multiple immune-related illnesses. In New York, Los Angeles, and San Francisco, clinics noticed young and seemingly fit gay men who were inexplicably ill with tuberculosis and rare atypical interstitial pneumonias (chronic swelling of the lungs' tiny air sacs).[15]

Gaëtan Dugas, a twenty-eight-year-old flight attendant for Air Canada, saw a Toronto specialist about purple lesions that had broken out on his back and face. His lymph nodes had been swollen for a year. A biopsy confirmed Kaposi sarcoma. Dugas kept working as an air steward, traveling thousands of miles annually to more than a dozen cities across the U.S., Canada, and Haiti. He later estimated to medical researchers that he had about 2,500 sex partners during the 1970s.*

A month later, a San Francisco resident, Ken Horne, was also diagnosed with Kaposi. Blood tests revealed his white blood cell count was extremely low and something undetermined was suppressing his immune system.

In July, a thirty-three-year-old German chef, who had worked in Haiti for three years, was admitted to the emergency room of Manhattan's Beth Israel Hospital. "He came to New York after he'd gotten sick in Haiti with weight loss and uncontrollable bloody diarrhea," recalled Dr. Donna Mildvan, then a thirty-five-year-old infectious disease specialist. A stool test revealed he had amoebic parasites, the type of intestinal bug common to travelers.

"He didn't get better. That was extraordinary," she recalled.

The chef kept going in and out of the hospital for the next six months.

"We'd get him a little more stabilized," Mildvan said, "he'd go home for a while, and then he'd be back." He kept losing weight, developed sores, and lost sight in one eye.[16]

Mildvan and her team were detectives hunting for the mystery of what their patient was so sick with. They ran dozens of tests and researched rare illnesses. They debated a wide range of treatments, including a massive dose of antibiotics, but feared if it was an immune disease, the antibiotics would hasten the disintegration.[17]

By the fall, Mildvan suspected a virus was the culprit. Beth Israel had

---

* Because he had so many sexual contacts and also traveled extensively while infected, Dugas was later referred to extensively as Patient 0 (zero), thought to be the person who almost single-handedly spread AIDS across North America. In fact, the letter assigned to him later by AIDS researchers was not a zero but an alphabetical *O*, shorthand for "Out of California." Dugas spent considerable time in San Francisco and Los Angeles, and some early researchers believed the strain of virus he carried was unique to the American West Coast. There was no patient zero, and according to scientists and epidemiologists, while Dugas might have spread the virus faster and farther than if he was not an infected, promiscuous flight attendant, he was not the first person ill with the disease in the U.S.

no virology lab. She and a colleague withdrew fluid from their patient's eye and rectal lesions and sent those to the lab at Montefiore Medical Center in the Bronx. Their report concluded that sexually transmitted herpes had caused the rectal lesions and herpes-related cytomegalovirus (CMV) was present in the eye fluid. Those viruses were not unusual. What astonished Mildvan was that they almost never caused illnesses as serious as the ones in her patient. Over the coming months, he continued deteriorating. He became blind when the CMV spread to the other eye. A CT scan showed his brain had shrunk like that of an elderly man with dementia.

"He curled up in a ball," recalled Mildvan, "staring blindly into the distance. He was incontinent. And he died."

Two weeks later she treated another gay male patient, a nurse with no foreign travel. He had the same CMV infection in an eye, but was deathly ill with Pneumocystis carinii. Mildvan knew that it was a rare pneumonia, only affecting those with compromised immune systems. He died after ten days at the hospital.

Across town, at New York University Medical Center, a leading dermatologist had begun seeing young men in otherwise good health who had the purple Kaposi sarcoma lesions. Dr. Alvin Friedman-Klein had been practicing for twenty-five years and the NYU skin clinic was America's largest. Still, he had only seen fifteen cases of Kaposi in his career. Now he had two dozen young patients in less than a month, none of them fitting the cancer's target demographic of older Jewish or Italian men.

"That's when it clicked," Mildvan recalls. "It's a new disease. Something's going on."

That same month, Ronald Reagan was inaugurated as the fortieth president of the United States. His successful campaign for the White House was in part based on a pledge to reduce the size and role of government. He delivered on that in January, proposing deep spending cuts. The proposed budget for the Centers for Disease Control was slashed in half.

It was not a good time to cut funding for the only government agency responsible for collating data and planning how to respond to any deadly transmissible new illness. For the next four years the medical community could agree on little, not even on whether the culprit was viral or bacterial. It is not always easy to tell. Infections that cause meningitis, pneumonia, and chronic diarrhea can be caused by either.

Chicken pox is a virus. Smallpox was a virus (past tense because it was the first deadly disease to be eradicated by a widespread twentieth-century vaccination program).

If the "new disease" that puzzled Mildvan and other doctors turned out to be from a bacterium, it would mean that some single cell microorganism that had coexisted with humans peacefully for thousands of years had somehow mutated into a virulent pathogen. That is what happened in the fourteenth century when bubonic plague killed 50 million people, 60 percent of Europe's population. Antibiotics are effective against bacteria because they interfere with their cell walls and either stop them from replicating or force them to self-destruct. The drugs accomplish that without inhibiting or damaging human cells.[18] Epidemiologists estimate that if antibiotics had existed during the bubonic plague, the death toll would have been cut by 90 percent.[19]

Antibiotics are useless, however, against viral invaders. Viruses do not have internal growth mechanisms that antibiotics destroy. They cannot survive alone but instead live inside human cells and hijack the reproductive mechanism of those cells. The 1918 Spanish influenza pandemic killed nearly 100 million people.[20] Pharmaceutical companies have discovered and marketed a series of antiviral medications since 1972, but they were effective only if dispensed early during an infection, and even then, only lessened the severity of symptoms and reduced the infection's duration.

Another weapon, vaccines, tricks the immune system into recognizing a virus and providing some "acquired immunity." Even if the new disease was a virus, Mildvan and her colleagues were familiar with the limitations of antivirals and knew that vaccines took many years to develop. Sometimes, a vaccine might not even be possible if the proteins on the surface of the virus mutate regularly. Slight modification in the proteins of the flu virus, for instance, means that last year's vaccine might not be effective against this year's influenza strain.

Whatever the cause, there was no disagreement that gay men were the first victims. In early 1981 there were stories about a "gay cancer" or "gay pneumonia," reported only in gay newspapers, the *New York Native*, *San Francisco Sentinel*, and Australia's *Sydney Star Observer*. Lawrence Altman, the *New York Times* medical correspondent, wrote his first article about it that July. Titled "Rare Cancer Seen in 41 Homosexuals," Altman began: "The rare and often rapidly fatal form of cancer . . . diagnosed among homosexual men." He quoted a CDC spokesman, Dr. James Curran, who added to the speculation that it might be a gay-only disease. "The best evidence against contagion," Curran told him, 'is that no cases have been reported to date outside the homosexual community or in women.'"[21] (*The Village Voice* condemned Altman's piece as a "despicable attempt of *The New York Times* to wreck the July 4 holiday break for every homosexual in the Northeast.")[22]

People began talking and writing more about the mystery symptoms. In Uganda, dubbed "Slim Disease," it left its victims terribly emaciated. Doctors treating men imprisoned at New York's Rikers Island named it after that prison, Rikers Island adenopathy (swollen lymph glands).[23] Most of the media stayed focused, however, on the gay nexus. Some wrote about the Gay Plague.[24]

When the doctors at the National Institutes of Health treated their first AIDS patient in June 1981, they named his condition as GRID, gay-related immune deficiency. Before that patient died in four months, seven different NIH divisions tried solving the mystery as to what had savaged his immune system. After his October death, the three departments with the most expertise in immunodeficiency disorders launched a joint project. It was directed by Samuel Broder, the chief of NIH's Clinical Oncology Division, Vincent DeVita, the head of the National Cancer Institute and the National Cancer Program, and Tony Fauci, chief of the Laboratory of Immunoregulation.[25]

In July 1982 the disease had a new name, one that would become the accepted medical standard: human immunodeficiency virus (HIV). The most critical, and often lethal stage of HIV infection was named acquired immunodeficiency syndrome (AIDS). The CDC used the word AIDS for the first time in a weekly report that September.[26]

The virus that led to AIDS was sexually transmitted, an equal opportunity infector of men and women. In Africa, where it had its genesis, and where scientists later discovered an almost exact primate strain they named simian immunodeficiency disease, it was overwhelmingly a heterosexual disease.*[27] That was the same in the early cases in Eu-

---

* In 1992, a journalist, Tom Curtis, kicked off a firestorm in *Rolling Stone* with a thesis that HIV in Africa was caused by the 1959 testing of a live polio vaccine on more than a million people in the Belgian Congo. Researchers dismissed it out of hand as a baseless conspiracy theory designed to sell magazines. In 1999, Edward Hooper, a BBC correspondent, wrote a densely sourced 1,000-page book, *The River*, published by Little, Brown. Hooper reached the same conclusion as Curtis had but had explosive new

rope as well as later for intravenous drug users and hemophiliacs. Gay men were not the reason AIDS started in the U.S. They were simply its first victims. HIV was an opportunistic disease that took advantage of immune systems already under assault from multiple sex partners, recreational drug use, and repeated infections of sexually transmitted diseases.[28]

Fear in heterosexual America was about whether they might "catch it" from a gay colleague or neighbor. The gay community, particularly men, were cast as scapegoats for the undiagnosed disease. In the coming years, confusion, misinformation, and rumor spread. People's fears fueled their worst prejudices.

The CDC did not help. In explaining how the disease was transmitted between people, the CDC said it was a result of the "exchange of bodily fluids." Did that mean vaginal or anal intercourse? Oral sex? Kissing? Perspiration from an infected person? Not even the best journalists were clear what that encompassed. *The New York Times*'s Lawrence Altman told *The Atlantic* in 2014: "The journalism community was behind for quite a while in not being more specific about what 'bodily fluids' meant. But also, public-health officials weren't explicit in what they meant by bodily fluids. It was a time when the words 'penis,' 'vagina,' 'sperm,' 'intercourse,' 'rectal intercourse'—those terms weren't part of the everyday public vocabulary. They may have been in private, but it wasn't as it is today."[29]

At the NIH, Broder, DeVita, and Fauci had assembled a public

---

reporting that a precursor of HIV had been accidentally introduced into the oral polio vaccine that had been administered in the Belgian Congo. Hooper charged the vaccine was grown in African chimpanzee cells, some of which were infected with simian immunodeficiency disease (SIVcpz), an almost identical strain to HIV. The doctors involved with the original research denied using chimpanzee cells in the vaccine. Papers published in *Nature* and *Science* examined stored samples of the 1959 vaccine and a molecular analysis revealed no chimpanzee DNA. There were no genetic traces of either HIV or SIV. In 2004, a study in *Nature* found that even if chimpanzee cells from the Congo had been used in the vaccine, the primates in that area had a virus genetically distinct from human HIV strains. Subsequent epidemiological studies dated the origin of HIV in humans to "at least 30 years prior to OPV (oral polio vaccines) in central Africa." The new data led Oxford's Edward Holmes, a preeminent virologist and evolutionary biologist, to conclude: "Scientifically, it is the end of the OPV theory." In 2019, scientists extracted a nearly complete HIV genetic code from a 1966 sliver of tissue from a deceased patient in the Republic of the Congo. By dating its genetic sequencing, they concluded that the virus that led to HIV emerged in humans a century ago.

health emergency team.[30] Although that effort drew little public attention, according to Broder "much of the critical work for perhaps the first three to four years of the AIDS epidemic originated with the NIH." In a later oral history, he expressed frustration that "some scientists and organizations that might have made a contribution, did not respond to the AIDS emergency."[31]

A few did not believe the virus would become widely transmitted. That view was reinforced when the CDC confirmed it was possible to get the disease through intravenous drug use.[32] Those new patients were overwhelmingly heterosexual. Since they were drug addicts, however, it only added to the perception that AIDS was a disease that affected the fringes of society. "People always ask when AIDS is going to spread to the general population, as they call it," asked Dr. Sheldon Landesman, an infectious disease expert. "That's absurd. It implies that those who have AIDS aren't part of the general population. It implies that *they* are giving it to *us*" (emphasis in original).[33] * [34]

Broder recalled that from 1982 to 1984 while the NIH researchers chased many theories, "there was an enormous sense of pressure and urgency, because there was so little known and so little we could do. As additional cases became known, there was a substantial level of stress and a certain public distrust and confusion, all of which made everyone's life more difficult."[35] Adding to the anxiety at the NIH, says Broder, was that there were "all sorts of crazy people, who in the Andy Warhol sense of the term, could obtain not only 15 minutes' worth of fame but possibly build a career [by] promoting ideas without a scientific foundation. This greatly confused the public and to some extent damaged science."[36]

The NIH researchers had developed tests to spot drugs that might suppress the AIDS virus in tissue cultures. They found none despite testing hundreds.

By 1984, Broder's team had focused on antiretroviral drugs, hoping they might hinder the virus from replicating in humans. Burroughs Wellcome, Pfizer, and Merck and Roche worked with those products in their labs. He did not have a receptive audience when he met with

---

* Infection from blood put the nation's ten thousand hemophiliacs at risk. Eventually, half would be infected with HIV and four thousand died of AIDS. Blood banks did not then screen donations for transmissible viruses or bacteria, but even if they had, there was no test yet to spot AIDS.

top management at the drug firms. "I went to one prestigious company, hat in hand," he later recounted. "I got about one minute and thirty seconds of a high-ranking officer's time. It was very disappointing for me. It was emblematic of the issue. There was no real interest in it."[37]

Dani Bolognesi, a Duke surgeon, arranged a meeting between Broder and scientists at Burroughs. Broder was interested in a twenty-two-year-old chemotherapy, Zidovudine, also known as azidothymidine (AZT). An academic with NIH funding had developed AZT in the mid-1960s but Burroughs later bought the rights to it. It had never been put on sale because it proved both toxic and ineffective.

There was some resistance in Burroughs to helping the NIH. AIDS was a terrible disease, Burroughs executives acknowledged to Broder, but it was too small a market.

"They made it clear that on the basis of 3,000 patients, there was no way they could practically get involved," Broder recalls. "As I left, I said, 'You know, we're going to have more than 3,000 cases. It is going to be commercially viable for you.' "[38]

They called him back to the conference room where he laid out some of the cataclysmic predictions the CDC had run. Broder said that nothing would get done unless the NIH had a private partner.

Burroughs finally agreed to help. Although the company owned the license to AZT, it had done so little with it that at first it could not even produce samples as it was missing a critical DNA constituent. The NIH sent the missing DNA strand to the company, who finally made enough of the drug for testing at the NIH. The results were good. It was the first drug, according to Broder, that "inhibited HIV viral replication" in the test tube.[39]

AIDS activists wanted human trials started as quickly as possible. For every day delayed, they contended, someone else died. They protested the failure of Ronald Reagan's administration to declare AIDS a health emergency capable of infecting anyone.[40] In the early years of HIV and AIDS, there were aftershocks from the 1976 swine flu fiasco. Dr. David Sencer, who had been the much maligned CDC commissioner during the swine flu debacle, had said after resigning his government post that if he was ever faced with scientific uncertainty over a possible infectious epidemic, he would err on the side of caution. Sencer had returned to public service as New York City's health commissioner. Activists accused him of "dragging his feet" when it came to the city's response to AIDS. At a time when action and speed were essential, Sencer fell short once again.

While once slow or negligent to cover HIV and AIDS, or to cast it as a fringe epidemic, mainstream media outlets by the mid-1980s raced to report that AIDS infections were about to explode. The front covers of national magazines fed a new fear. "Now No One Is Safe from AIDS" (*Life*); "AIDS: Fatal, Incurable, and Spreading" (*People*); "The Most Lethal Disease" (*Time*).[41] An American doctor writing in *The Lancet* compared its potential "vast scope of death" to the fourteenth-century bubonic plague.[42] Oprah Winfrey, in her first show about AIDS, passed along a dire prediction: "Research studies now project that one in five—listen to me, hard to believe—one in five heterosexuals could be dead from AIDS at the end of the next three years. . . . One in five!"[43]

Fifty million Americans did not die, of course, in the next three years. In the first fifteen thousand cases of AIDS in New York City, the Health Department listed only eight as having contracted the virus from heterosexual sex.[44] Still, the real numbers did not seem to matter. Fear often overruled reason. Mortuaries refused to handle bodies, hospitals turned away patients or put them in isolation. There was talk of whether sanitariums, or modern-day leper colonies, should house the sick. One debated "solution" was tattooing those infected so prospective sex partners had advance warning.[45]

Nationally syndicated columnist Pat Buchanan wrote in 1984 for *The American Spectator* that AIDS was "a killer disease . . . especially in cities like New York and San Francisco, the Sodom and Gomorrah of the Sexual Revolution." The sexual liberation that was an essential element in the Gay Liberation movement, according to Buchanan, "is ending, and it is revealed for what it always was: an egregious assault upon the ecology of the human body. Call it nature's retribution, God's will, the wages of sin, paying the piper, ecological kickback, whatever phraseology you prefer. The facts demonstrate that promiscuous homosexual conduct is utterly destructive of human health." Buchanan predicted that "short of some dramatic behavioral change, the gay community may self-destruct." And he warned that he was not spreading "scare talk," but that the HIV virus might mutate into the "real final epidemic" that would threaten "continuation of human life on this planet."[46]

Five months later Reagan appointed Buchanan as the White House director of communications and an assistant to the president.[47]

The heated rhetoric produced real results. Gay men, even some suspected of being gay, lost their jobs. There were campaigns to ban them as teachers or sports coaches. Some communities petitioned their local hospitals to exclude them from health care jobs.[48]

In the midst of the hysteria over AIDS, Samuel Broder and his NIH team had begun the human clinical trials on AZT in July 1985. Testing for an antiviral could take eight to ten years. The FDA approved AZT in a speed record of twenty months. For many Americans who had friends or relatives who were sick with HIV/AIDS, and unaccustomed to the snail's pace of modern drug approval, the twenty months seemed an eternity.[49]

To avoid any further delay over legal and commercial marketing rights, the government allowed Burroughs Wellcome to claim the patent. The company renamed the drug Retrovir. From its first day of sale, Burroughs marketed AZT as a "breakthrough" and as "finally light at the end of the tunnel."[50] National media covered AZT as effective for anyone who tested positive on the HIV antibody test.[51] Burroughs ignored advice from the FDA that because of the drug's toxicity it should be limited to the sickest patients, only those with full-blown AIDS.

Burroughs stunned AIDS families and activists, the medical community, and the NIH team that had developed the drug when it set the price at $10,000 per patient per year (not including transfusions and blood work). It was the most expensive drug in pharmaceutical history. Under tremendous public blowback, Burroughs cut the price to $8,000, still the highest-priced drug on the planet. Thirty-five percent of AIDS patients had no health insurance or had polices that did not cover the drug.[52] When Burroughs stuck with its exorbitant price tag, the federal government stepped in and subsidized the costs for many patients who would have otherwise been refused treatment.

"What makes the cost of AZT hard to swallow," wrote the *New York Times* editorial board in 1989, "is that all the invention and much of the risk was undertaken by the Federal Government."[53]

When a generic drug company announced it would make an inexpensive, generic copy of AZT, Burroughs sued and prevailed in federal court. During that litigation, which eventually wound its way to the Supreme Court, Burroughs contended that the NIH had no right to the patent. It described Broder's lab only as "a pair of hands" that had helped the company, nothing more.

Although North Carolina–based Burroughs was savaged in the press for its AZT pricing, and criticized in academic and government circles for its cynical framing of the drug's discovery, its shareholders were happy. AZT was the only large successful launch for the parent company, British-based Wellcome. It had gone public the year before AZT went on sale. In February 1987, the month Burroughs put AZT on the market, the company's share price shot up 500 percent. Its list price for AZT was so expensive that investors expected record profits. They were right. The share price doubled again in 1989. By then, AZT brought in a third of the company's $425 million profit. AZT itself passed $2 billion in sales by 1994.[54]

In San Francisco, AIDS had ravaged the Castro neighborhood, a vibrant hub of gay life. On January 25, 1988, the thousands who marched through city streets were not celebrating gay pride. They were protesting the exorbitant price of AZT. The handmade signs reflected the mood of the protesters. "Burroughs Wellcome AZT Scandal." "Greed Kills People."[55]

Wellcome met often with AIDS activists and victims' families. Its press spokesman said all the right things about compassion and mercy. It never discussed pricing or gave in to demands that it disclose its business records that would have shown what it cost the company to manufacture the drug.

Bristol-Myers started clinical trials in 1989 with a second AIDS drug, DDI (dideoxyinosine), which also showed promise in slowing the rate at which the virus replicated. It was evident the NIH and National Cancer Institute had learned their lesson from Burroughs's price-gouging. Under the terms of a contract with Bristol, the government could force it to license DDI, to generic manufacturers if it did not set a "reasonable price."

"Hallelujah," was the reaction from playwright Larry Kramer, the founder that year of the activist organization AIDS Coalition to Unleash Power (ACT UP). "I pray that this magnificent example by Bristol will be duplicated by the manufacturers of numerous other life-saving drugs."[56] Kramer and other activists might not have been happy with any of the drug companies that suddenly seemed eager to develop AIDS drugs if they had known that the pharma firms were earning millions more on every medication because of a little-known 1983 statute, the Orphan Drug Act. It was designed to encourage drug companies to develop medications to treat rare diseases, everything from multiple sclerosis to Huntington's to muscular dystrophy to ALS.[57] Many of the estimated two thousand diseases were genetic conditions but some were infections and autoimmune disorders, as well as rare cancers. They were dubbed orphaned since pharmaceutical companies avoided them because the tiny markets made it difficult to turn a profit. The FDA's Office of Orphan Products Development proposed that for a drug to qualify under the law, the disease it treated should not affect more than 0.05 percent of the U.S. population, at the time a maximum of 100,000 patients. However, when the FDA realized that excluded multiple sclerosis, Tourette syndrome, and narcolepsy, the agency eliminated measuring by a percentage of the population and instead set the maximum at 200,000. In practice, however, the number affected by an orphan disease frequently proved much smaller, usually under 10,000 and sometimes only a few hundred worldwide.[58]

The congressional sponsors of the Orphan Drug Act realized the government needed to offer substantial incentives in order to stimulate interest in the pharma industry. The law built financial inducements into every stage of orphan drug discovery and subsequent amendments made the tax credits and research subsidies even more generous. The act included four years of taxpayer grants of up to $500,000 annually to underwrite early research. Companies got a 50 percent tax credit on whatever they spent on R&D. The remaining 50 percent of costs were a deductible business expense. That meant that the federal government paid for about 70 percent of the R&D costs for orphan drug projects.[59] The law also simplified applying for academic and NIH co-sponsorship, waived processing fees, and expedited FDA approval. The gauntlet of three ever more rigorous trials was dramatically abbreviated.[60] The FDA also provided grants on a competitive basis for clinical trials it deemed important.

The Orphan Drug Act's final inducement—an exclusive seven-year selling monopoly—was an attempt to ensure the drug company had enough time to earn money without worrying about competitors.[61] Although shorter than the seventeen years for mass-market drugs, the orphan patent barred *all* competition. It not only banned generics but also me-too drugs, unless those meds offered a "major" improvement in safety or efficacy. Some pharmaceutical analysts called it a "platinum mini-me patent." It was one of the most unique and powerful pricing tools available to drug companies.[62] The mistaken assumption by the statute's drafters was that orphaned drugs would never be very profitable.[63] AIDS changed that.

In 1985, Burroughs applied for AZT to be designated an orphan drug for "the treatment of AIDS." The FDA approved that designation in July. It meant that in addition to all the assistance Burroughs had gotten from the NIH, it was now eligible for substantial additional subsidies and tax credits. Other drug companies realized that to get the same benefits, they had to artificially fragment the AIDS patient population into subgroups smaller than 200,000. In that way they created rare diseases small enough to qualify for orphan status. Within a decade, there were seventeen orphaned variations of antiviral HIV treatments, a dozen for AIDS-related Pneumocystis carinii pneumonia, nine for diarrheal and weight loss illnesses, and five each for Kaposi sarcoma, encephalitis, anemia, and tuberculosis, among others.[64]

Ellen Cooper, chief of the FDA's antiviral division, complained that the pharma companies were dividing the "AIDS related complex" population into arbitrary subclasses. There was nothing the FDA could do to stop it. The Orphan Act was clear that only Congress could make changes, and no elected official wanted to sponsor anything that might be interpreted as slowing the search for an AIDS cure.

The drug companies had learned to game the system. A study later determined that they "stack seven-year monopolies for the same drug on top of each other for indications that differ only negligibly." In other instances they "seek orphan designations for drugs that are barely modified versions of existing orphans and that offer little additional therapeutic improvement."[65] A large loophole the companies exploited was that once they got drugs approved for a small number of patients in the final stages of AIDS, they encouraged doctors to dispense it "off-label" for the much larger market of those infected with HIV. Off-label is when doctors dispense drugs to treat conditions other than the one for which the FDA approved it.[66] LyphoMed, for instance, got a 1984 approval for pentamidine to prevent and treat Pneumocystis carinii pneumonia for end-of-life AIDS patients. However, more than 80 percent of its sales was for the off-label treatment of pneumonia in HIV patients. LyphoMed increased its price 400 percent over two years. When its seven-year orphaned monopoly expired, it got another seven years for developing an aerosol version that qualified for new orphan status.

Nearly thirty years later not much has changed. As a new generation of AIDS drugs was introduced from biotech companies, they sought orphan protection. The most notable as of 2019 is Gilead's Truvada, a breakthrough pre-exposure prophylaxis when combined with safer sex practices (it is referred to widely as PrEP, pre-exposure prophylaxis).[67] It is not a new drug. Gilead, a California biotech company, had originally gotten FDA approval for it in 2004 for slowing the progression of HIV in those already infected.

The research that converted it to its current blockbuster status was done through government and private funding. The CDC in 2006 was researching medications to block HIV from infecting healthy people. Gilead sent free doses of Truvada to the CDC, where two years of lab work and tests on primates led to breakthroughs for which the CDC applied for a series of patents. A San Francisco AIDS researcher conducted parallel research with $50 million in federal grants.The NIH sponsored double-blind, placebo-controlled human clinical trials. The Bill & Melinda Gates Foundation contributed $17 million toward those trials.[68] Gilead again donated the medicine. The 2010 results of the clinical studies—up to a 44 percent reduction in the risk of HIV infections—drew national headlines.[69]

The U.S. government patented the new prophylactic use for Truvada in 2015. Gilead sued to block that, saying that it had given Truvada free of charge for the testing and its own scientists had created the old drug at the turn of the century.

Courts have so far sided with Gilead. Truvada costs $6 a month to manufacture. Gilead sells it to patients for $1,600 to $2,000 a month (a markup of 25,000 percent).[70] It has ranked every year since its release as a prophylactic in the top twenty drug sales in the United States, more than $3 billion annually, some $30 billion since it went on the market. Gilead's patent does not expire until 2021.

Two AIDS activists and a physician penned a 2018 *New York Times* op-ed. "The United States is failing miserably in expanding its [Truvada's] use. Less than 10 percent of the 1.2 million Americans who might benefit from PrEP are actually getting it. The major reason is quite clear: pricing. With a list price over $20,000 a year, Truvada, the only PrEP drug available in the United States, is simply too expensive to become the public health tool it should be. . . . In under 40 years, we've lost more Americans to H.I.V. than to combat in all of our wars combined. Science has delivered answers, but Gilead's greed and the government's inaction are keeping it from those who need it most. There's a pill that stops H.I.V. We can make it possible for everyone who needs that pill to get it."[71]

37

"NONE OF THE PUBLIC'S DAMNED BUSINESS"

In the early 1980s, Arthur Sackler followed the news about HIV but without much interest. Purdue Frederick had never researched antiviral drugs. It had nothing on the drawing board that might show promise in battling AIDS to submit to the NIH. Moreover, none of Arthur's pharma clients for the McAdams ad agency seemed to be rushing forward to develop a drug.

Working through the obstacles to a government-pharma-research partnership on AIDS was something that would have seemed to have been a natural for Sackler. When he worked at Schering during World War II he witnessed firsthand the gigantic joint effort by the government and a handful of pharmaceutical firms to convert penicillin from a promising lab compound into a wonder drug. Sackler, who was proud of his social activism that dated back to his efforts to end the Red Cross segregation of black and white blood in the 1940s, might have railed against the Reagan administration's reticence to make AIDS a public health priority because of its prejudices against the early victims, gay men and intravenous drug users. It was not just the emergence of AIDS and the political controversises around it, however, that failed to grab Arthur's attention. He was paying little heed to most of his businesses because he was consumed with a long-standing personal obsession: where to bequeath about one thousand of his rarest art objects.

All three Sackler brothers had a lofty view of themselves since the spectacular opening of the Metropolitan Museum's Sackler Wing, with its restored Temple of Dendur. The first exhibition were the glittering treasures from the tomb of the boy king Tutankhamen. It had been impressive, even by the standards of the Met, New York society, and the art world.[1] Arthur thought it an "epic debut." Mortimer claimed it "gave rise to the term 'blockbuster' exhibition."[2]

Thomas Hoving, who had been solicitous and amiable in courting Arthur and his brothers, had resigned as the museum's director. He made the Sacklers feel as if they were every bit as important as the Rockefellers or Lehmans. Hoving's replacement was the Met's vice director, Parisian-born Philippe de Montebello, the son of a French count and wartime resistance fighter. His family traced its heritage to Napoleonic aristocracy.[3]

The urbane Montebello had little patience with the Sacklers. Montebello had started at the Met as an assistant curator in European Paintings before Arthur had struck his first deal in 1966 for his named galleries and the basement storage to house his collection. Montebello was a witness to the many failed attempts of his predecessors to persuade Sackler to commit a significant portion of his superlative Asian collection to the Met. Arthur, whom he considered crass, irritated him and he had decided not to be cowed by Sackler's implied threat of donating the collection elsewhere. Few institutions rivaled the Met with a gravitas that would be illustrious enough for Arthur.

Montebello thought Arthur had a nonstop litany of "petty grievances" about how the museum used the temple. Sackler found the new director "a fogey, a Europhile, an elitist."[4]

Adding to the tension with the Met was a story that broke in *ARTnews* just before the Dendur inaugural. It exposed the special arrangement of Sackler's storage room in the Met's basement.[5] When called for a comment, the museum's general counsel told the reporter that whatever happened at the Metropolitan was "none of the public's damned business."[6] That was not quite true since the Met was publicly funded. The article piqued the interest of the New York attorney general, who opened an investigation into why the museum had over the years spent nearly a million dollars for storing Sackler's art.[7] Although unsubstantiated, Sackler was convinced the leak to the press was from Montebello.[8]*[9]

* Author Michael Gross reported in *Rogues' Gallery*, his 2009 social history of the Metropolitan Museum, that another factor that aggravated Sackler during this time was that he was "particularly vexed by the preponderance of homosexuals on the museum staff." A former business colleague of Sackler told the author that "Arthur didn't care one way or the other. If he liked you, it didn't matter what you were or did. If he didn't like someone, everything about that person was subject to criticism."

Marietta was convinced that Arthur was also afflicted with a "need for recognition."[10] The two had divorced and Arthur was courting British-born Jillian Lesley Tully, twenty-five years his junior.[11] Not long after they married in 1981, Arthur purchased one of New York's most iconic residences, a twenty-seven-room triplex at 666 Park Avenue. It had originally been commissioned by Mrs. William Vanderbilt in 1927 but she never moved in. *The New York Times* described it as "the greatest maisonette ever constructed in New York . . . [though] to call it a maisonette at all is rather like calling a Bugatti a runabout."[12]

Sackler now had four full-time curators working on his Asian collection. By 1980, they had compiled ten volumes of photos, descriptions, and provenance of 90 percent of his art. The following year Sackler initiated talks with the Vatican about exhibiting some of its historic collection in the U.S., what Arthur called an "art and faith" tour. The Metropolitan and the National Gallery had initially agreed to underwrite it jointly. Then the Metropolitan changed course and negotiated its own deal for a Vatican show. Sackler was furious.[13]

Carter Brown, the National Gallery's curator, saw an opportunity in the growing rift between Sackler and the Met. Washington, D.C.'s, Freer Gallery of Art began wooing Sackler in earnest. The Freer had been created at the start of the twentieth century after industrialist Charles Freer donated his significant collection of American and Asian art.[14] The Smithsonian Institution had taken over just before it opened to the public in 1923. As the first American museum funded by taxpayers, it was restricted from raising funds by borrowing money or striking lucrative arrangements with private donors in exchange for naming rights. In the 1960s and 1970s those restrictions made it difficult to compete with private museums in acquiring important private collections. The Freer was also desperate for more exhibition and storage space. Its fifty-year-old design was showing its design limitations.

"In effect, like Miss Havisham's mansion in *Great Expectations*, the Freer was frozen in time," noted Karl Meyer, who wrote a history of one hundred years of American interest in Chinese art.[15]

Congress approved an extra $500,000 in 1980 for the Smithsonian to start construction on two buildings to house African American and Asian art on the National Mall's Quadrangle. The Smithsonian put that project on hold the following year because it was short of funds to care for its existing buildings, much less oversee an expansion.

Sackler saw an opportunity in their problems. He asked Michael

Sonnenreich to negotiate a deal. In 1982, Sackler stunned Montebello and the Met by announcing a $4 million donation to the Freer and the donation of a thousand of his most prized collectibles, valued at $50 million. In return, the Smithsonian agreed to create the Arthur M. Sackler Gallery directly on the National Mall, adjacent to the Freer. It would be the first modern structure on the Mall to be named after a private person. Congress, with its oversight of the Smithsonian, held hearings on the bequest. Ultimately, no one in government wanted to be responsible for stopping the deal.

A month later, Sackler gave another $7.5 million for the Sackler Museum to be built at Harvard (eventually $10.7 million).[16] It was intended to complement Harvard's existing art museums, the Fogg and the Busch-Reisinger.

38

A PAIN MANAGEMENT REVOLUTION

Often in the drug industry, companies search for a discovery to treat a condition they believe can be treated by pharmaceuticals. Diabetes, high blood pressure, infectious diseases, and other illnesses and chronic ailments provided many profitable opportunities. However, there was one common complaint—chronic pain—that affected tens of millions of Americans and had stymied companies searching for an effective treatment.

That failure was not because of any lack of desire on the part of pharma. Instead, the plethora of remedies that started with patent drugs had demonstrated there were no good choices. Many drugs temporarily alleviated pain. Morphine, oxycodone, hydrocodone, and other opiates were effective pain relievers. They were listed, however, on the Controlled Substances Act because they had a notorious reputation for addiction.

A pharmacologist and a chemist at the National Institutes of Health had written in *Science* an overview about how years of academic and private company lab research had been devoted to finding a nonaddictive painkiller. Each ended in failure. The duo concluded it was unlikely such a medication was possible.

A few physicians, however, were intent on upending the traditional medical views about pain and how to treat it. Their reevaluation would encompass whether opioids had been unfairly judged and should be more widely dispensed. This movement inadvertently laid the groundwork for the Sacklers' 1996 opioid-based blockbuster painkiller, OxyContin.

Until the early 1980s, medical schools taught physicians that pain was only a symptom of some underlying physical condition. Physicians invariably searched for the cause of the pain rather than treating it as a stand-alone ailment. The specialty of "pain management" did not exist.[1] John Bonica, whom *Time* later dubbed "pain relief's founding father," was a leading voice challenging that conventional wisdom. Bonica was an Italian-born former professional wrestler, carnival strongman, and light heavyweight world boxing champion turned anesthesiologist. He suffered chronic shoulder and hip pain from his own sports career. His 1953 *The Management of Pain*, a 1,500-page monograph, was an unmatched resource.

Bonica believed doctors significantly underdiagnosed pain and, as a result, millions of patients suffered needlessly. In 1973, he organized a seven-day conference attended by 350 researchers from thirteen countries.[2] The following year, Bonica cofounded the International Association for the Study of Pain (its journal, *Pain*, is the field's leading publication).[3] Three years later a multidisciplinary group of doctors and clinical researchers relied on Bonica's research and created the American Pain Society (APS).[4]

The effort to prioritize pain was not long under way when a five-sentence "letter to the editor" in the January 10, 1980, *New England Journal of Medicine* sparked a parallel rethinking about conventional medical views on the risks of opioids. The authors were Dr. Hershel Jick and a graduate student, Jane Porter. They summarized their examination of 39,946 records of Boston University Hospital patients. Jick was a leading physician at the esteemed Boston Collaborative Drug Surveillance Program, financed in part by the NIH and the FDA. It was America's largest independent effort to determine the risks of adverse reactions and potential abuse in hundreds of widely used medications.[5] The duo reported that almost a third (11,882) of the patients had "received at least one narcotic preparation" but found only "four cases of reasonably well-documented addiction in patients who had no history of addiction." Their conclusion was as unorthodox as it seemed decisive: "Despite widespread use of narcotic drugs in hospitals, the development of addiction is rare."[6]

Jick and Porter's letter cited two previous drug surveillance studies. Both involved only hospitalized patients, all of whom were given small doses of opioids in a controlled setting. Only a handful took opioids for more than five days. None were given painkillers when discharged from the hospital.[7]

The prestigious *New England Journal of Medicine* had a deserved reputation for publishing peer-reviewed, pioneering health studies. That ninety-nine-word letter drew attention precisely because it was published in the *NEJM*. Yet not even its most avid readers could have predicted the impact it would exert in the coming reassessment of using opioids to treat pain. What few knew was that the *NEJM* almost never had outside experts to review "letters to the editor."[8] If they had subjected the Jick and Porter letter to peer review, the editors would have had a more precise and accurate conclusion by making it clear that "the development of addiction is rare" *in the controlled setting of a hospital*. Instead, during the next two decades that letter was cited over six hundred times in textbooks, medical journals, and other publications.[9] More than 80 percent of those who cited the Jick and Porter letter omitted any mention that it only studied hospitalized patients who took opioids for a few days. Instead it was mostly cited to buttress far broader conclusions about the safety profile of opioids.[10] * [11]

Whenever the consumer press mentioned the Jick and Porter study, it was invariably misdescribed to confer on it far more authority than it deserved. A Canadian psychologist writing in *Scientific American* called the 1980 letter "an extensive study" and altered its finding to be that "when patients take morphine to combat pain, it is rare to see addiction."[12] *Time* wrote that the "fear" of addiction "continues to hold sway over American medicine [and] is basically unwarranted." It called the Jick-Porter letter "a landmark study" (it is unlikely the *Time* journalist read the study he cited; he listed its publication as 1982 [it was 1980], said that "it followed almost 12,000 Boston hospital patients [none were followed for observation]," and that the study "had elim-

---

* In 2017, six researchers published in the *NEJM* the results of their review of all subsequent citations to the 1980 letter. "In conclusion, we found that a five-sentence letter published in the *Journal* in 1980 was heavily and uncritically cited as evidence that addiction was rare with long-term opioid therapy. We believe that this citation pattern contributed to the North American opioid crisis by helping to shape a narrative that allayed prescribers' concerns about the risk of addiction associated with long-term opioid therapy." The *NEJM* subsequently published a rare "Editor's Note," adding to its webpage with the original Jick-Porter letter: "For reasons of public health, readers should be aware that this letter has been 'heavily and uncritically' cited as evidence that addiction is rare with opioid therapy." Dr. Jick told the Associated Press in 2017: "I'm essentially mortified that that letter to the editor was used as an excuse to do what these drug companies did."

inated those with a history of addiction [it had not]."[13] A 1986 World Health Organization report, "Cancer Pain Relief," cited the ninety-nine-word letter as a scientific cornerstone for challenging decades of medical dogma that "the risks of widely prescribing opioids far outweighed any benefits."[14]

Six weeks after the WHO publication, the journal *Pain* published a startling report. The lead author of the "Chronic Use of Opioid Analgesics in Non-Malignant Pain" was Russell Portenoy, a thirty-one-year-old Memorial Sloan Kettering physician specializing in anesthesiology, neurology, pain control, and pharmacology. His coauthor was Kathleen Foley, a leading pain management specialist who was widely considered to be at the vanguard of palliative care.[15]

As had the WHO report, Portenoy and Foley cited the Jick-Porter letter. However, they did not rely on it. Instead, they presented the results of their own clinical study. It involved thirty-eight patients who had been administered narcotic analgesics—a third took oxycodone—for up to seven years. Sloan Kettering was one of the only American hospitals with a "formalized pain service . . . within the Department of Neurology."[16] Foley was its chief, and it was there that Portenoy had witnessed what Cicely Saunders had seen in London: opioids improved the quality of life for many terminally ill cancer patients. Two thirds of those studied had significant or total pain relief. There was "no toxicity," the two doctors reported, and only two patients had a problem with addiction, both of whom had "a history of prior drug abuse."[17]

"We conclude that opioid maintenance therapy can be a safe, salutary and more humane alternative to the options of surgery or no treatment in those patients with intractable non-malignant pain and no history of drug abuse."[18]

When they had begun their study, Portenoy and Foley expected that they might find the opposite, a higher addiction correlation. The results led them to conclude that the National Cancer Institute and the federal government were not interested in educating doctors about opioids. Instead, as Foley later said, the pharmaceutical companies became "our colleagues in education. . . . It was the drug company that wanted to improve pain management."[19]

The Portenoy-Foley paper helped kick off a contentious and at times acrimonious debate about whether opioids had been unfairly branded and therefore underutilized in pain management.[20] While Foley focused on palliative and hospice care, the charismatic Portenoy emerged as the unofficial spokesman for the embryonic movement to reevaluate opioids.[21]

Portenoy was a smart physician who relished clinical research. He believed he was at the forefront of reassessing antiquated views about opioids, and that by doing so, millions of patients suffering from untreated chronic pain might be helped. Although Portenoy had noted in his 1986 study that opioids should be considered an "alternative therapy" until there was further clinical research, that caution often got lost in his zealous fervor. He at times called opioids a "gift from nature" while occasionally castigating doctors whose "opiophobia" prevented them from dispensing the medications.

An eclectic and informal network of physicians, from New York neurologists to California psychiatrists to North Carolina pain physicians, contributed to the nascent reevaluation effort. The American Academy of Pain Medicine became the first organization for physicians specializing in pain management. It was followed by the American Society of Addiction Medicine (its slogan is "Addiction is a chronic brain disease"). The physicians at the vanguard of the movement encouraged their patients suffering from chronic pain to form advocacy groups and petition the FDA and Congress to loosen the dispensing restrictions on opioids.

In 1990, Dr. Mitchell Max, the president of the American Pain Society, wrote a widely read editorial in the *Annals of Internal Medicine* in which he bemoaned the lack of medical progress in diagnosing and treating pain. "Unlike 'vital signs,' pain isn't displayed in a prominent place on the chart or at the bedside or nursing station," he wrote. Doctors were "rarely held accountable" for failing to treat pain. "Pain relief has been nobody's job."[22]

Part of the failure was because patients often did not tell their doctors about their pain. Max thought the easiest fix was to make certain that physicians asked patients on every visit about whether they were in pain. For decades, physicians had kept watch of four vital signs when examining patients: blood pressure, pulse, temperature, and breathing. Dr. James Campbell, the president of the American Pain Society, suggested "Pain as the 5th Vital Sign."[23]

One reason doctors shied away from treating pain as a stand-alone condition was that there was no accepted diagnostic test, as there was for blood pressure or cholesterol. It was similar to evaluating psychiatric disorders, a somewhat subjective assessment based on the doctor's observations and the patient's descriptions of symptoms. In depression, anxiety, and other mental conditions, some patients were mildly affected in their daily lives whereas others had difficulty in functioning at all. The same was true with pain. What one patient described as moderate pain that restricted mobility might be excruciating to someone else.

As the Hamilton Rating Scales in the 1960s had become popular and simple tests by which to measure anxiety and depression, several "pain assessment" tools came into use in the mid-1980s. The McGill Pain Index had seventy-eight words related to pain divided into twenty sections. Patients picked the words that best described the state of their pain. The Memorial Pain Assessment Card had eight streamlined descriptions and included a single line on which patients marked the degree of pain intensity. A pediatric nurse and child life specialist in Oklahoma developed a chart with ten hand-drawn faces ranging from happy and laughing to angry and crying. The Wong-Baker Pain Rating Scale made it easy for children to pick the face closest to how their pain felt that day. Variations of that scale soon became a one to ten rating for adults, one being "very mild, barely noticeable," and ten signifying "unspeakable pain."

Although the pain tools were error prone since they relied on the patient's subjective assessment, they were hailed as the first rudimentary measurements by which doctors could determine if their patient's pain was getting better or worse. In that sense, it did not matter if a patient had a low or high pain threshold. What was important was whether their pain improved over time. The Joint Commission, an independent, not-for-profit organization responsible for accrediting 96 percent of all hospitals and clinics in the U.S, gave the first major endorsement for the concept that pain should be the fifth vital sign. When the Veterans Administration later embraced it, the practice did not take very long to move to the private sector.[24]

Portenoy's 1986 article that concluded that "opioid maintenance therapy can be a safe, salutary and more humane alternative" was the first of a couple of dozen that physician pain advocates published in medical journals over the next few years. Based always on small trials or anecdotal reports, they bolstered the dual arguments that opioids did not deserve their fearsome reputation and that they were extremely "effective in treating long-term chronic pain."[25] Buried in their scientific footnotes was that "long-term" usually meant twelve to sixteen weeks and "effective in treating" meant "superior to placebo."[26]

An anesthesiologist and dentist who specialized in pain management, J. David Haddox, pushed the boundaries of the reevaluation movement with a unique and controversial theory. He reported in *Pain* about the failure to treat the pain of a seventeen-year-old leukemia patient. According to Haddox, who went on to become the president of the American Academy of Pain Medicine and later worked for Purdue Pharma, the doctor's botched treatment had "led to changes similar to those seen with idiopathic opioid psychologic dependence (addiction)." Pseudoaddiction was a syndrome, he posited, over which the patient had no control. It was caused inadvertently when doctors failed to prescribe sufficient painkillers. That caused "behavioral changes" in patients that most doctors misinterpreted as signs of addiction. Haddox contended that was only evidence that the patient was desperate to get enough medication for pain relief. The solution to pseudoaddiction was to dispense more narcotic painkillers.[27]

The nation's three major pain associations embraced pseudoaddiction. In a joint statement they announced it "can be distinguished from true addiction in that the behaviors resolve when pain is effectively treated."[28] (It took twenty-five years before a comprehensive study revealed that in the 224 scientific articles in which the term was cited, only eighteen provided even the skimpiest anecdotal evidence to support the thesis. The study concluded that it was essentially a "fake addiction" and had "proliferated in the literature as a justification for opioid therapy for non-terminal pain.")[29]

The same month that pseudoaddiction entered the vocabulary, a dozen prominent physicians published "The Physician's Responsibility Toward Hopelessly Ill Patients" in *The New England Journal of Medicine.* Although it was about the treatment of terminally ill patients, their conclusion became a veritable slogan for the reevaluation movement: "The proper dose of pain medication is the dose that is sufficient to relieve pain and suffering. . . . To allow a patient to experience unbearable pain or suffering is unethical medical practice."[30]

The movement's progress could be measured by the number of states that adopted "intractable pain treatment" laws. Those statutes acknowledged patients had a right for treatment of their pain, and they shielded physicians from criminal or civil liability if the narcotics prescribed resulted in addiction. New Jersey was the first in 1984 to adopt such an act; eighteen others followed over a few years.[31]

Portenoy and colleagues contended that opioids should be the first treatment option "for patients with intractable nonmalignant pain and no history of drug abuse."[32] Instead of establishing a maximum dose, they posited that opioids should be dispensed until the patient's pain was relieved.[33]

Liberally dispensing opioids was the perfect complement to the emerging field of proactive pain management. Opioids alleviate pain by blocking the brain's receptors that send and receive pain signals. They do nothing to treat the underlying ailment that causes the pain. The twin themes—that not treating pain was negligent and that opioids were a reliable option for almost everyone—reinforced one another.[34]

The Sacklers would have been hard pressed to design a better lead-in to their release a decade later of OxyContin, their blockbuster opioid-based painkiller. When the pain reevaluation movement got under way in the mid-1980s, though, OxyContin was not yet on the drawing board. It was in the earliest stages of development by the time pain was on its way to becoming the fifth vital sign. Some suspect collaboration between Purdue and the leading physician advocates because they find it difficult to believe that they all were so utterly wrong about the diminution of the odds of addiction. That they were wrong, however, does not mean they were not sincere. The histories of medicine and the pharmaceutical industry are littered with practices and products that went from exalted pedestals to discarded dustbins.[35]

In the following decade, Purdue did what every other pharmaceutical company with an opioid-based product did: spent tens of millions in underwriting and subsidizing the physicians, advocacy groups, and pain societies at the forefront of the reevaluation movement.[36] Many doctors who were pioneers in the movement reaped big fees as company lecturers. Purdue and other drug firms funded medical school courses, professional conferences and conventions, pain management junkets, and even pain-focused continuing education classes. And, as with every other major drug introduction, some government officials, even a few from the FDA, went through a revolving door to work eventually for Purdue and other firms selling their own branded opioids. Purdue and its rivals spent money on those advocates only because they were *already* promoting ideas about pain treatment that the firms embraced.[37]

Whether the flood of pharma money made the early advocates more resistant to admitting their mistake as reports emerged much later that Purdue's opioid painkillers appeared far more addictive than any had forecast is a difficult assessment. They read the same news reports about the rising numbers of prescription opioid overdoses, illegal diversion, spiraling hospital admissions, and a surge in opioid-related crime. It was not just drug company money that kept them from admitting they had gotten it wrong. The leading pain management contrarians had built their reputations as physicians with the courage to challenge long-established medical dogma as archaic. Acknowledging that opioids were far more addictive than they had originally predicted would have shattered their careers.

At least publicly they clung to their old views even if privately they had second thoughts. The leading pain and opioid reevaluation proponent, Russell Portenoy, seemed never to waver from his early conclusions. By the time he appeared on *Good Morning America* in 2010, more than 300,000 Americans had died of opioid overdoses in the previous decade. Still, when asked about the risk of getting hooked, he assured ABC's four million viewers that "Addiction, when treating pain, is distinctly uncommon. If a person does not have a history, a personal history, of substance abuse, and does not have a history in the family of substance abuse, and does not have a very major psychiatric disorder, most doctors can feel very assured that that person is not going to become addicted."[38] Yet, that same year, in a more reflective mood and what he thought was a private setting, Portenoy confided to another doctor, "I gave innumerable lectures in the late 1980s and '90s about addiction that weren't true."[39]

39

ENTER GENERICS

In 1986, six years after MST Continus went on sale in the U.K., it was still not available in the United States. Because its active ingredient, morphine, was a Schedule II controlled substance, it got extra attention at the FDA. An even slower than normal approval process occurred. Raymond and Mortimer Sackler privately griped about the snail's pace. What bothered them was something common to all pharma executives: the time spent getting a drug to the market cut into its exclusive patent protection.[1] Before the 1962 Kefauver Amendments had required significantly more rigorous clinical trials, more than 90 percent of all drugs got approved in under a year after submission to the FDA. Since a patent's monopoly started ticking at the time of the invention, valuable years of sales were sometimes lost in the FDA's approval bureaucracy.*[2]

By the 1980s, it took on average between six and eight years for a drug to be approved from its date of invention.[3] Research and development cost several hundred million dollars.[4] Traditional pharmaceutical firms argued it was counterproductive to spend so much money and sometimes get so little exclusivity for selling new drugs.[5] Studies showed that once a drug patent expired, up to 80 percent of the top

* The United States was the last country that used the FTI (first to invent) standard for a patent. It was measured usually when the inventor filed a patent/trademark or copyright or sometimes by other evidence of when the invention was created. It did not matter if someone else filed for the patent. So long as an inventor could demonstrate they had the idea first, they would get the patent rights. In 2011, President Obama signed the America Invents Act, which converted the U.S. to the international standard of FTF (first to file). For patents filed prior to June 8, 1995, the term of the patent is twenty years from the first filing date or seventeen years from the issue date, whichever is longer. There are also different patent periods for biologics (twelve years) and small molecule drugs (usually pills with a simple organic composition, five to seven years).

brand-name sales disappeared within twelve months.[6] A decade later, Pfizer's cholesterol-lowering blockbuster, Lipitor, became the most cited example: it dropped from $5.3 billion in sales in its last year of patent protection to $932 million the year after.[7]

Pharma companies had tried speeding up the time from the lab to the market. Among the largest dozen drug firms, half had spent billions on new R&D technologies in combinational chemistry and genomics, both of which promised much faster drug discovery.[8] Instead of rebuilding their R&D from scratch, the other six companies scooped up biotech start-ups. It was the early days of what would become a decade-long pharmaceutical merger and acquisition boom.[9]

Spending billions on new research and development or acquiring biotech firms at inflated prices to get drugs out of the lab faster were not options for smaller drug companies such as Purdue. It is not surprising that they found ways—used by Big Pharma also—to extend the patent monopoly on their best-selling drugs. Instead of big expenditures on developing new medications, they simply recycled old ones. They could usually get patent extensions by changing how a drug was administered, the chemical composition of its coating, even its molecular makeup.

The nontherapeutic modifications were eligible for a three- to five-year patent extension, and occasionally pharma companies succeeded in convincing doctors and patients that it was worth paying a premium for those minor changes. However, winning a new patent and resetting the selling monopoly to day one required more than nontherapeutic alterations. It entailed demonstrating a "secondary medical use," evidence of its efficacy for a different therapy than the one for which it was approved originally.

The research divisions of pharmaceutical companies were always on the lookout for additional therapeutic uses for their existing product line. Surprisingly few, however, were discovered in the laboratory. Instead, most of the breakthroughs were the result of the unregulated power of doctors to dispense a company's drugs off-label. Physicians are presumed under the law to have enough expertise to use drugs as they deem fit. They can change the approved dosing, prescribe one approved drug to be taken in combination with others, or use it for conditions unrelated to the clinical testing for safety and efficacy conducted by the drug company.[10]

Estimates are that between a quarter to half of *all* prescriptions dispensed annually in the U.S. are for off-label use.[11] Doctors who prescribe drugs off-label are in effect conducting their own informal clinical trials. There is no requirement that physicians inform their patients that they are using a medication off-label. The AMA and other professional medical associations have made such disclosure discretionary, fearing that requiring it would make many patients skittish.[12]

At the very least, off-label seems an extraordinary circumvention of the FDA's power to examine drug safety and efficacy before patients use them.[13] Two Harvard Medical School professors who studied off-label dispensing in *The New England Journal of Medicine* noted that it bypasses all the "arduous testing required of drug companies" and "clinical trials . . . [to] determine whether a drug is safe and effective for an intended use."[14]

When doctors were empowered with off-label dispensing authority in 1938, there were fewer than twenty prescription drugs for sale in America. Entire classes of drugs—antibiotics, tranquilizers, hypertension meds—were yet to be invented. Drugs were not complicated, certainly nothing remotely like the later generations of biotech medications. Since 1938, the FDA has approved some 1,500 drugs.[15] In the far more complicated and fast-paced world of today's medical and pharmaceutical industries, the Harvard researchers warn that without the FDA "manufacturers could potentially bury physicians and patients in an avalanche of 'information' to promote drugs." While no single piece of data might be "technically fraudulent," the overall presentation might create a false appearance of safety or therapeutic benefit. No practicing physician has the time to independently verify the accuracy and context of the tsunami of information.[16]

The same unfettered discretion given to physicians, however, is strictly regulated when it comes to drug companies. It is a criminal violation for any pharma company or its employees to suggest any use of a drug that deviates from the strict terms of the FDA approval. Drug firms must submit a Supplemental New Drug Application and provide evidence of efficacy and safety before the FDA approves any changes.

Doctors, meanwhile, do not have to give any reason for their off-label dispensing. Oncologists often use chemotherapies off-label since one approved for a single type of cancer might show promise in treating other types of tumors. Cardiologists sometimes treat congestive heart failure and even anxiety with drugs approved for hypertension. And there is a disproportionate off-label dispensing of antipsychotic drugs to elderly patients, particularly those in long-term-care facilities.[17]

It does not matter to a firm's bottom line if a hit drug was prescribed 10 million times annually to treat the condition for which the FDA had originally approved it, or if half the sales were off-label. When the off-label prescribing reaches a tipping point, pharma companies then apply for "another medical use" to the FDA.

Many pharmaceutical companies have stories about how off-label dispensing led to hit drugs. Two hypertension drugs unexpectedly turned into popular "lifestyle" medications after doctors noticed patient side effects. The FDA approved Upjohn's Loniten (minoxidil) in 1979 to control high blood pressure. At the University of Colorado, a first-year resident asked the chief of dermatology to check on a patient in her forties with an odd skin reaction. Loniten had lowered her high blood pressure, but she had hair growth on her legs, arms, and along the hairline. The dermatology chief, only partly in jest, said, "Boy, this would be great stuff if we could apply it to the top of our heads."[18] Word that a possible hair growth medication was available spread. Balding men began asking their doctors about how they could get it. Starting in the early 1980s, the nation's dermatologists wrote on average twice as many Loniten prescriptions off-label than did cardiologists for hypertension. Several dozen "hair restoration" clinics sprang up across the country. When Upjohn had trouble keeping up with the demand, American doctors ordered it from foreign distributors.[19] It took Upjohn until 1988 before it got FDA approval for a totally reformulated prescription liquid called Rogaine.

A year after Rogaine hit the market, British Pfizer scientists discovered Rivatio (sildenafil citrate), a treatment for pulmonary arterial hypertension, a condition where blood pressure in the lungs is too high and causes shortness of breath, fatigue, and chest pain. It did not take treating physicians long to notice that male patients "did not want to give back the unused medication." A nurse later recalled that when she went to check on a patient's blood pressure during a clinical trial, all the men in the clinic were lying on their stomachs. Only then did she discover sildenafil's side effect was that it caused erections.

Pfizer could not ignore that the off-label prescribing for "enhanced sexual performance" boomed. It took off early on because a rumor went viral in the pre-internet world: many men mistakenly thought it increased penis size.[20] It also was in demand from recreational drug users, especially circuit parties where it was mixed with the club drug ecstasy and dubbed "sextasy." It took Pfizer until 1998 to obtain FDA approval for Viagra to treat the newly minted condition of "erectile dysfunction."[21] * [22]

Ortho-McNeil learned its Tri-Cyclen birth control pill had another use when doctors at Stanford reported that female students arrived at the campus clinic asking for "The pills that cure acne." The FDA allowed Barr Pharma to sell its Seasonale birth control to women who wanted fewer menstrual cycles ("menstrual suppression)." And extensive off-label dispensing allowed Bayer to get FDA approval for its oral contraceptive, Yaz, not only to treat acne but also for a premenstrual dysphoric disorder, a supercharged type of PMS that was identified only in 1987 as a stand-alone condition.

Allergan was mostly an ocular care company when it paid $8 million in 1991 to buy Oculinum, a drug developed by a San Francisco ophthalmologist.[23] † [24] The FDA had approved it in 1990 to treat two rare disorders, benign essential blepharospasm (BEB), a progressive neurological disorder that results in eyelid spasms, and strabismus, a misalignment of the eyes that causes them to wander and can lead to vision loss.[25] It was not long before doctors noticed that the drug, renamed Botox (short for BOtulinum TOXin), improved the appearance of wrinkles at the injection sites near the eyes. Botox took off. Dermatologists and cosmetic surgeons had trouble keeping up with baby boomers hoping to turn back the aging clock (10 percent of the users were men, leading to the nickname Brotox). Samantha Jones, the self-

* Rogaine's sales never lived up to the pre-release expectations; widespread media stories had touted it as a cure for baldness but its sales disappointed Upjohn after patients reported the results were slow and less dramatic. It was responsible only for $11 million of Upjohn's $776 million in revenues in the first six months it was on the market. Viagra, on the other hand, was an instant hit. On the first day of sales, March 27, 1998, pharmacists ran out of stock across the nation. Rivals called it the "Pfizer Riser." It went on to become a $2 billion drug for Pfizer over a decade and created a new drug category. Eli Lilly's erectile dysfunction drug, Cialis, shot right to the top after its 2003 release.

† Dr. Alan Scott, the ophthalmologist, had been searching for a cure for crossed eyes. He noticed that injections of the drug near the eyes of experiment monkeys had a side effect: it reduced forehead wrinkles. Decades later Scott told a reporter, "I really wasn't tuned into the practical, and valuable, aspect of that. . . . I was a pretty good doctor and not a bad lab worker, but I was not a great businessperson."

consumed publicist played by Kim Cattrall in the hit HBO series *Sex and the City*, helped make it part of the culture: "I don't really believe in marriage. Now, Botox on the other hand, that works every time."[26]

Most of that happened in the first decade while the drug was dispensed *only* off-label. It is unlikely that the hundreds of thousands of patients who paid $400 to $500 per session to lessen temporarily the appearance of their facial wrinkles were aware that it was not FDA approved for cosmetic treatment. Nor did they probably know that the CDC and military bioterrorism experts listed its active ingredient, botulinum toxin, as one of the world's deadliest nerve agents. When the San Francisco ophthalmologist had conducted his lab studies in the 1970s, he had to obtain the toxin from the military's biological warfare facility at Fort Detrick, Maryland. It was the same poisonous toxin that thrives in defectively canned food. When consumed it can cause paralysis and death.[27]

There was no better test case than Botox to demonstrate the inviolable natural right of U.S. doctors to prescribe drugs off-label. The FDA did not object to injections of the toxin around the eyes and in the forehead. There were no tests then about whether it could migrate into the central nervous system, where it would cause havoc. Was there a possibility the body might produce its own antibodies to a foreign toxin and over time use it to attack other cells spontaneously? Did injections every four to six months weaken the body's immune system?

Some other popular off-label drugs had proved disastrous.[28] Thalidomide had been approved in Europe in the late 1950s as a nonaddictive sleep aid. Doctors prescribed it off-label to control morning sickness for pregnant women. It was that unapproved use that led to the horrible birth deformities that became thalidomide's legacy.[29] Fenfluramine was a drug approved for weight loss for the morbidly obese. For off-label use it was often combined with a related drug, phentermine, and nicknamed fen-phen. It was dispensed not only to the morbidly obese but to two million patients who wanted a simple fix to shedding some extra pounds. It was pulled from the market after two years of accumulating reports that it caused a spike in cardiac valve disease and severe pulmonary hypertension.[30] Wyeth had to halt all off-label dispensing of its hormone replacement, Prempro, as "protective against heart disease," when a massive, multiyear study revealed it resulted in a significantly higher risk of breast cancer.

Allergan, in 2002, would finally get FDA approval for Botox for the "temporary improvement in the appearance of moderate to severe glabellar lines in adults aged 65 or younger." It was the first drug ever approved for a strictly cosmetic purpose. Botox, which was used in fewer than fifty thousand nonsurgical cosmetic treatments in 2001, broke four million annually in 2010. Its sales did not slow at all when the FDA ordered it to have a black box label warning about rare but potentially life-threatening complications (two children had died during trials for treatment of cerebral palsy). Since Botox was only dispensed at clinics or doctors' offices, patients never saw the warning on the box in which the vials were shipped. And few if any treating physicians mentioned it. Botox was, by the time of its black box warning, entrenched as Allergan's best-selling drug, a position it held for fifteen years. It consistently averages about 20 percent of the company's annual revenues ($3.2 billion in 2018).

Pfizer's Lyrica was approved originally for epilepsy and severe anxiety but was widely dispensed by doctors to treat spinal cord injury and diabetic nerve pain. Before its patent expired, Pfizer got the FDA's okay for it to treat those conditions.[31] That merely expanded the off-label uses for Lyrica, and its generic Pfizer cousin gabapentin. They are among the most widely used drugs for many types of pain, chronic cough, menopausal hot flashes, and even depression. A March 2019 *New England Journal of Medicine* review by two University of South Carolina doctors concluded that in "many well-controlled studies" Lyrica was little better than a placebo in treating pain.[32]

One of the researchers, Christopher Goodman, told *The New York Times*'s Jane Brody, "Patients and physicians should understand that the drugs have limited evidence to support their use for many conditions, and there can be some harmful side effects, like somnolence, dizziness and difficulty walking."[33]

Those caveats did not slow Lyrica's sales. Since 2011, off-label dispensing has provided about half of its annual revenues. During those eight years, Lyrica was mostly at or near the top ten selling drugs worldwide, and brought in $37.5 billion to Pfizer.[34]

The Sacklers had no such hopes that some enterprising doctors might find off-label uses for MST Continus and turn it into a blockbuster. The single restriction for off-label prescribing is that it is banned for all controlled substances.[35] Purdue had to concentrate on less ambitious ways of extending its patent. Together with Mundipharma, Napp, Bard, and other Sackler companies, Purdue researched how to alter

MST Continus just enough to qualify for an extension. Lab technicians tested dozens of different sustained release coatings in the hope of converting dosing from twice to once daily. Researchers examined dispersion methods to better control the drug's peak plasma level. That would allow custom-tuning of the pill to the patient's physical ailments. Suspension technology, the ability to dissolve the drug in a powdered form, was another line of research.

A ten-year study found that 80 percent of the top one hundred best-selling drugs had gotten at least one patent extension by using a "new and improved" application. More than half had multiple extensions.[36] (Purdue ultimately received thirteen new patents for its best-selling opioid painkiller OxyContin, released in 1996 and its exclusive sales rights extended through 2030).

Purdue and the Sacklers had backed the Pharmaceutical Manufacturers Association's efforts to get Congress to pass a seven-year extension for all patents. At twenty-four years it would have provided the world's longest patent protection and would save small drug companies like Purdue all the hard work and cost of developing "new and improved" versions. The PMA's thirty-five directors had lobbied for the longer patent at every legislative session since 1980. Congress nearly passed a PMA-drafted bill in 1982 but objections from generic drug manufacturers led to the vote's postponement. They contended that any agreement extending the exclusive time to sell a drug for traditional pharma firms should be part of more sweeping legislation that made generics more readily available.[37] Just as mainstream drug firms griped about how the Kefauver Amendments had made the FDA approval process torturous, generic drug companies grumbled about how that same law made it difficult for them to get their medications to market.[38]

After the thalidomide disaster, the Kefauver Amendments had concentrated on safety. That was the reason for the much more intensive clinical testing requirements for new drugs. All the safety and efficacy data were treated as if they were the proprietary information of the drug company that submitted it. Some shared it by publishing articles in scientific journals, but others kept it private. Except for antibiotics, which were exempted, that created a problem for generic manufacturers. The Kefauver statute required generic makers to submit a voluminous application with enough scientific literature to demonstrate convincingly that their copy was safe and effective. If they could not do that, their remaining option was to conduct their own costly clinical trials. Adding to the problems for generic manufacturers was that the FDA was so swamped with branded-name drug applications that it often pushed generic ones to the bottom of the pile.[39] The FDA, described by *The New York Times* as "the Federal Government's most criticized, demoralized and fractionalized agency," could not keep pace with the expanded powers it had gotten in the 1970s.[40]

Senator Ted Kennedy spearheaded an effort under the Carter administration to address shortcomings in the drug approval process. The result was the Drug Regulation Reform Act of 1978, which among other provisions gave the FDA more discretion to quickly approve a lifesaving breakthrough drug before the clinical trials were completed. It also expanded the agency's power to regulate pharma manufacturing processes as well as to require firms to conduct post-marketing studies of how their drugs were performing. And, spurred by a patient advocacy group for Huntington's disease, a fatal genetic brain disorder, Kennedy included in the new statute the creation of a National Center for Clinical Pharmacology. One of its missions was to address the dearth of research and development for so-called orphaned drugs.

The new law did not address how to speed up approvals for drug applications at the FDA.*[41] Most generics remained stuck in the slow lane. And there was not much the FDA could do to process drugs faster. Ronald Reagan had followed through on his campaign promise to cut the size of government agencies. During his first term, the FDA's budget was slashed, and it cut six hundred employees.[42] Drug approvals were not the only important understaffed division. Patient advocacy groups, backed by the Abuse and Mental Health Services Administration and the Department of Health and Human Services, had implored the FDA for several years to take action against Quaaludes (methaqualone), a barbiturate-type sleep aid. Rorer, the company whose most famous pre-Quaaludes product was the over-the-counter antacid Maalox, had started selling them in 1972. Before the end of the decade, the little white pills were one of the most popular and widely abused recreational club drugs. Pill mills that passed themselves off as "stress clinics" diverted tens of millions of tablets. By 1980, fewer than a dozen pill mills accounted for more than three fourths of all annually

* What did help beginning in 1992 was that drug companies agreed to pay the FDA special fees for "Accelerated Approval" or "Priority Review."

prescribed Quaaludes.[43] Ludes, disco biscuits, or quads, as they were called, led to an explosion in hospital admissions, date rapes, even lethal overdoses. The FDA never managed to put in place the dispensing restrictions that might have made a difference, instead only ordering some changes to the label that had little impact.

The Drug Enforcement Administration pushed the Food and Drug Administration out of the equation in 1984 by listing Quaaludes on Schedule I of the Controlled Substances Act, making their sale illegal in the U.S.[44]

That same year California congressman Henry Waxman and Utah senator Orrin Hatch brought the Generic Trade Association and the Pharmaceutical Manufacturers Association to the negotiating table. By the time they met, many generic manufacturers had given up on trying to make copies, even of a successful drug whose patent had expired. By 1984, there were nearly 150 brand-name medications that had come off patent and for which no generic version had FDA approval.[45] The few generic makers that tried going against the grain ran into the obstacles posed by Big Pharma legal departments. In 1984, Hoffmann-La Roche prevailed in a high-profile patent infringement suit against a generic firm, Bolar. The D.C. Circuit Court enjoined Bolar from even conducting its bioequivalence testing before Roche's patents expired. The court expressed sympathy for Bolar's contention that there should be an "experimental use" exemption to allow it and other generic companies to develop drugs that were ready for submission to the FDA the moment the patent expired on the brand-name medication. That was, the court ruled, a "legislative activity proper only for the Congress."[46]

The cost of such restricted generic competition was that patients paid anywhere from double to ten times more for brand-name drugs.[47] Waxman and Hatch hoped they could find common ground so a deal might benefit patients with more drug choices and competition.

In early talks, the standoff between the pharma companies and the generic makers seemed unbreakable. The momentum shifted to the generics after the FDA issued a report that estimated that more generics would save consumers about $1 billion over a decade.[48] Waxman and Hatch used the study to offer a compromise. Generics would only have to demonstrate to the FDA that they were the bioequivalent of the brand-name drug, meaning their copies offered the same strength, concentration, release pattern, and purity. They no longer would have to demonstrate efficacy but instead could rely on the studies provided in the original application for the brand they were copying. The Generic Trade Association enthusiastically endorsed the proposal. A lot of major drug companies thought it woefully insufficient.[49]

To appease the traditional drugmakers, the lawmakers offered extensions for drug patents, up to five years depending on a somewhat abstruse formula. The statute calls it "patent term restoration," and it can add a maximum of five years to make up for the time in regulatory review and half the period used for clinical trials. (In 1997, the FDA initiated a rule that allowed a six-month extension to any patent on which the drug company tested its product for pediatric use; two hundred companies have gotten that credit.)

Over a series of rancorous board meetings, the thirty-five directors of the Pharmaceutical Manufacturers Association debated an issue they knew was fundamental to the industry's future. The winning argument was that there was a real risk that Congress might pass the legislation even if the industry group presented a unified opposition. The groundswell of public support, combined with the lobbying by many "rare disease" patient groups, had brought the generics bill close to cracking the bipartisan support levels it needed to pass. If the drug industry was seen as only obstructive, protecting its own interests rather than focusing on what was best for patients, it might result in an even more punishing bill.

The vote by the drug reps was 22–12 in favor of the Hatch-Waxman compromise. Those voting against it included some of pharma's biggest names, including Hoffmann-La Roche, Merck, Schering-Plough, Johnson & Johnson, Squibb, Ciba-Geigy, Bristol-Myers, A. H. Robins, American Cyanamid, and American Home Products.[50] They were not standing on principle for the industry but focused on the impact the proposed law would have on their bottom lines. Ayerst Laboratories, a division of American Home Products, had a $300-million-a-year heart drug, Inderal, that was set to come off patent at the end of 1984. Roche's patent on Valium, still selling more than $250 million annually, was set to expire in 1985 (Roche offset the impact of losing Valium's patent by making a deal with Britain's Glaxo to help market the ulcer treatment Zantac. It became the world's biggest-selling drug.)[51] More than half of the country's top fifty selling drugs were set to come off patent in the coming decade.[52]

Upjohn thought that discounting a hit drug might scare away generic competitors. Its Motrin (ibuprofen) was the world's top selling nonaspirin and nonsteroidal anti-inflammatory and was scheduled to come off patent the following spring.* Motrin was responsible for ten percent of Upjohn's $2 billion in annual revenue and 40 percent of its profits. In July, Upjohn tried preempting any discounters by cutting its wholesale price for Motrin by 35 percent. The results were not good. In the short term, the stock market pummeled Upjohn's shares.[53]

A last-ditch lobbying effort by those opposed to the law failed. In September 1984, Congress passed comprehensive legislation that "created the modern US generic drug industry." That law, The Drug Price Competition and Patent Term Restoration Act, was informally known as the Hatch-Waxman Act.[54] The companies that had opposed the statute watched to see if the maneuvering by Upjohn in decreasing the price of Motrin, and directing its sales force to redouble its efforts to have pharmacies keep it as their first nonsteroidal anti-inflammatory drug, paid off. It did not. Rivals were prepared. The FDA had increased its Generic Division from thirty-two to fifty-four employees. It quickly approved several lower-strength over-the-counter versions. The shelves at local drugstores were soon stocked with Advil from American Home Products, Nuprin by Bristol-Myers, Thompson's Ibuprin, and Johnson & Johnson's Medipren. Motrin's sales plummeted 40 percent.

As for Inderal, Ayerst Labs' hypertension drug, within a year of it coming off patent in 1984, twenty generic versions had FDA approval. Some sold at half of Inderal's list price. Ayerst waged an aggressive multipronged campaign against the FDA-licensed copiers. It concentrated on doctors, since polls indicated that 80 percent thought that generics would fall short on delivering the same quality and efficacy as the brand-name medication.[55]

Ayerst paid for a dozen academic researchers to write articles for medical journals emphasizing the potential health risks of generics (only one disclosed Ayerst's backing). The company also sponsored a study in *JAMA* that picked a few outlying examples to conclude that the cost savings were negligible. It sent out "Dear Pharmacist" letters warning that if there were any quality problems with the copies of Inderal, druggists might be responsible for lawsuits by patients who had heart attacks as a result of switching medications.[56] And it offered free airline tickets anywhere in the U.S. for physicians who switched full-

* Motrin holds the title as the biggest-selling nonnarcotic prescription painkiller brand name in pharma history. More than half its sales were in the decade before the FDA approved an over-the-counter version at a lower strength.

time to prescribing only Inderal Long-Acting, a less popular extended release formula on which it still had a patent for another two years. Finally, Ayerst disseminated information that the FDA standards under Waxman-Hatch only required that the statistical variation between the efficacy of the brand-name drug and the generic be no more than 30 percent. Was it worth possibly saving a few dollars on a prescription to run the risk that the bargain medication could be close to one-third less effective? (The FDA tightened its standard to a 20 percent deviation in early 1987, although in practice the variation is often closer to 5 percent.)[57]

Despite Ayerst's campaign, in the two years following its patent expiration, Inderal sales were slashed by a third.[58]

The Waxman-Hatch Act had made generic manufacturers a force. The failure of Ayerst and other traditional companies to defend their off-patent best-selling brand drugs was evident in the industry's sales numbers. Before Waxman-Hatch, generics accounted for $1.5 billion of the $21 billion in annual drug sales. Two years after the legislation, generics had more than tripled to $5.1 billion, capturing 23 percent of the market.[59] That success was despite the lobbying efforts of the Pharmaceutical Manufacturers Association to enlist allies to raise questions about their safety and efficacy.[60]

Arthur Sackler thought Hatch-Waxman was a terrible development. Of course he had a personal stake in the outcome, since his McAdams advertising agency made its money from hundreds of millions spent on promotional campaigns for brand-name drugs, and generic manufacturers then did little advertising. Sackler tried to help his Big Pharma clients by publishing a series of articles in several of his most widely circulated medical journals, all passing along some supposedly terrible incidents about generics. One that received wide attention was "Schizophrenics 'Wild' on Weak Generic." It ran in the September 25, 1985, edition of *Medical Tribune*, distributed free to the nation's physicians. According to the article, when the psychiatric intensive care unit of the Charlie Norwood Veterans Administration hospital in Athens, Georgia, switched from the brand-name tranquilizer Thorazine to a generic, "11 previously stabilized patients ran amok and needed increased dosages until the hospital went back to Thorazine" a month later.[61] At that point, the patients returned to their previous calm states "as if a switch had been flipped."

When the FDA investigated, it discovered that half the patients had not received either tranquilizer. The other half did exhibit some behavioral problems, but not nearly as dramatic as the retelling in *Medical Tribune.* Moreover, those patients were on the generic for six months before there were any adverse indications, not the one month "as if a switch had been flipped" in the version Sackler published.

In that sensational article, the only person quoted about what supposedly had happened at the VA was the clinic's chief psychiatrist, Dr. Richard Borison. The FDA concluded in its probe that Borison had acted in good faith but the study lacked "the rigor of a truly scientific investigation." No one at the FDA put together that Borison and Arthur Sackler had long had professional ties. Not even Sackler could have imagined that a decade later a Georgia grand jury would issue a 172-count indictment against Borison and a colleague for having "developed and executed a scheme through which they systematically stole in excess of $10 million" and that they "routinely lied to conceal their crimes and endangered the safety of the patients and study participants they were employed to serve, protect and heal."[62] A CBS *48 Hours* report said the pair had "turned human drug trials into their personal money machine." One of the biggest scams, according to the indictment, involved AstraZeneca's antipsychotic Seroquel. They certified it as an effective pharmaceutical fix for post-traumatic stress disorder, although their clinical studies had demonstrated nothing of the kind.[63] Borison was ultimately convicted, sentenced to fifteen years in prison, fined $4.2 million, and stripped of his medical license.[64]

Long before Borison was brought to justice, Sackler cut back on publishing the "generics are dangerous" stories. It was tilting at windmills, he told a colleague. "Generics are here to stay." (Today they account for 80 percent of all prescription drugs dispensed.)[65]

40

SELLING HEARTS AND MINDS

•

The executives who ran the largest pharmaceutical companies believed the best way to push back against generics was to develop and patent groundbreaking drugs that gave them years of a selling monopoly. Competing against generics on price only meant lower profit margins. Firms redoubled their research efforts searching for new medications. Ever since the mega-success of Smith Kline's Tagamet, the focus had been on products that would similarly target specific cell receptors. The difference to a company's bottom line between a commercially successful drug and an epic seller was enormous. Merck had developed a series of hit drugs starting with Clinoril to treat arthritis in 1978. It had pushed sales up by 15 percent. The following year Merck released Mefoxin for bacterial infections. It too was a hit and sales growth went up by another 20 percent. And in 1980, a glaucoma treatment, Timoptic, went on sale and Merck got another 15 percent sales bump.

"But successful as they were," said Roy Vagelos, then the chief of Merck's research labs, "these drugs were not the kind of blockbusters that can change the sales and profit curves of a large corporation for a full decade."[1] The jump in sales was gone a year after the release of the third medication. And the increase in net income was only half the sales increase.

Tagamet's development highlighted the importance of technological and scientific breakthroughs in the laboratory. Advances in molecular modeling allowed Sandoz researchers to create 3D models that were indispensable in developing cyclosporine, an interleukin-2 inhibitor that reduced the chances of an organ transplant rejection. X-ray crystallography provided precise structural parameters for receptor inhibitor drug design. Parke-Davis developed the first robotic means of speeding the discovery of potential drug compounds (parallel synthesis). Glaxo made the automated techniques that got the most from combinational chemistry, enabling scientists to quickly make millions of structurally similar molecules that were then screened to isolate good drug candidates. Nuclear resonance imaging produced such detailed scans that scientists used them to study how their drugs encountered tissue and cells.

The new technology was not cheap. Only the largest companies could afford the hundreds of millions of dollars required to update their labs. Some swooped up tiny biotech firms to get a leg up on rivals. Eli Lilly acquired Agouron, at the forefront of 3D computer drug design, while Bristol-Myers bought Oncogen and Genetic Systems, both with patents on new techniques for analyzing nerve and brain cell therapies.

Pharma companies were aware, however, that it took more than buying the latest technology or purchasing some promising biotech. The key remained the quality of the researchers in the lab who used the new technology to discover and develop drugs. The richest firms competed to hire the best and brightest scientists. Merck, Squibb, and Glaxo raided university and government labs and offered huge salaries. Smith Kline, to protect its position at the top, joined in the frenetic hiring binge.

The top ten drug companies gambled an inordinate amount of their research budgets on trying to "hit the lottery" with one or two blockbusters. It occasionally worked. Smith Kline's H2 antagonist anti-ulcer drug, Tagamet, had no direct competition for six years after its 1977 introduction. Its sales accounted for a quarter of the company's revenue and an extraordinary 40 percent of profits.[2] But Smith Kline soon turned into a cautionary tale for the rest of the industry. It did not reinvest its profits into its research division. The company's researchers produced only a fraction of the scientific papers that came from Merck and Lilly. It had only twenty-eight drugs under development, less than a quarter of what some rivals had under way.

Glaxo introduced Tagamet's first direct challenge in 1983 with its anti-ulcer drug named Zantac. It had the advantage of twice-a-day dosing as compared to Tagamet's four times a day. Glaxo launched an Arthur Sackler–styled promotional campaign, emphasizing the results of clinical trials that demonstrated it had fewer side effects than Tagamet.[3] Tagamet's sales fell by nearly 20 percent in the first year after Zantac was released.

Smith Kline made developing a new and improved Tagamet its top priority. But the lab failed repeatedly. Three years after its release, Zantac climbed past Tagamet in sales. Smith Kline's profits were soon slashed in half.[4] Zantac not only became the second drug in history after Tagamet to earn $1 billion in annual sales, it did it twice as quickly as Tagamet. By the start of the 1990s, Zantac outsold Tagamet three to one.[5] Smith Kline's financial troubles were made worse since it did not have another lucrative product in its drug pipeline. In the wake of Tagamet's demise, the company was forced by the end of the decade into a merger with British-based Beecham by 1989 (the same year that Bristol-Myers and Squibb had a mega-merger).[6]*[7]

If Smith Kline in the 1980s exemplified the perils of overrelying on a blockbuster and failing to put enough money and guidance into science and research, Dr. Roy Vagelos, Merck's CEO, was shaping a company that was its antithesis. Vagelos believed that Merck's reputation for excellence in bringing new drugs to market should not be diminished by chasing only medications that the marketing department thought might be commercial hits.[8] Merck was then the only big pharma company that had never had a drug recalled. It was evidence, Vagelos contended, that its unmatched quality and standards were because of the people who chose to work there.

Vagelos was a bit of an anachronism. The New Jersey–born son of Greek immigrants who had lost their small candy store during the Great Depression, he was the only major drug CEO whose roots were as a research scientist. As somebody who preferred test tubes to spreadsheets, he had a different long-term view of the industry than many of his rivals. The self-effacing physician who considered it a compliment that

---

*There were smaller "one-drug" companies that ran into problems. Robins was bought by American Home Products after it was decimated by lawsuits over its Dalkon Shield contraceptive. Rorer fell back on Maalox after its hit Quaalude was banned as a Schedule I controlled substance. French-based Rhône-Poulenc bought Rorer at a discount in 1990. And Mexico's Syntex had a big hit with Naprosyn, its nonsteroid anti-inflammatory, which it produced from its Palo Alto subsidiary. It went from $800 million annual sales in the second half of the 1980s to less than 20 percent of that once its patent expired. Roche bought Syntex in 1995 and immediately laid off one third of the U.S. workforce.

he was called "a researcher's researcher" had become enamored with working in the laboratory after he got his medical degree in 1954 from Columbia and interned at Harvard's premier teaching hospital, Massachusetts General. From there he went to the NIH, where he worked with some leading biochemists.[9] Vagelos left the NIH in the mid-1960s to transform Washington University's biochemistry department into one of the country's premier research centers. In the early 1970s he accepted a consulting offer from Merck's chief of research to help "their scientists better understand what was going on at the cutting edge of biochemistry and enzymology."[10]

Vagelos liked what he saw at Merck's labs and was intrigued that they had independently found a possible drug compound that lowered blood cholesterol, although he noted "they didn't know the mechanisms of action at the molecular level."

Merck's organic drug research was the ideal complement to the intricate science background that Vagelos had developed over years of his own intense research on lipids. In 1974, Merck asked him to become president of all its laboratories and direct all new pharmaceutical projects.

Vagelos went into Merck with statins as his top priority. He knew that a couple of years earlier, a biochemist, Akira Endo, had assembled a small team at Tokyo's Sankyo Pharmaceuticals. Its mission was to develop a cholesterol-lowering drug. Since the 1960s, researchers knew that cholesterol was mostly manufactured by a single liver enzyme (HMG-CoA). What had stumped everyone, however, was that no one could locate a compound that inhibited that enzyme and thus caused it to produce less cholesterol.[11]

At the beginning of 1975, Endo's team, which had tested more than six thousand microbes, found one, compactin. It produced the long-sought enzyme inhibitor as part of its own natural defense against other germs in the body. Rumor of the breakthrough raced through biomedical and pharma labs worldwide. Tempering the enthusiasm, though, were reports that it caused debilitating muscle and tumor growth. Rumors were widespread that Endo had stopped his experiments since so many test dogs had died. Although those later turned out to be inflated accounts, they were serious enough to prevent Endo from conducting human testing. It also scared away several pharmaceutical firms from licensing deals with Endo.

Vagelos redoubled the effort at Merck. Three years passed before his team developed a high-speed process for screening thousands of soil microbes. In a common soil microorganism, they found biological activity that inhibited their target liver enzyme.[12] After the chemists isolated the active substance, lovastatin, Vagelos and his team realized their discovery was chemically quite similar to Endo's compactin. It took repeated testing before the Merck team was confident that lovastatin was a separate, stand-alone product.

It took another three years before the compound met Vagelos's exacting standards. Human clinical trials began in 1980. The cholesterol-lowering results bested the most optimistic calculations. "In the laboratories we were ecstatic," recalled Vagelos, and even the marketing group began expressing some excitement. Lovastatin had a brand name by then: Mevacor.

Overcoming all the FDA hurdles for the first drug of its type in an entirely new class of treatment was painfully slow. While it was tied up at the FDA, Vagelos became Merck's president.

He was in a unique position. Merck was about to release a series of important drugs. As the former chief of research, Vagelos had a familiarity with those drugs that no other pharma CEO had with their products. Anyone who thought that he was a science nerd who did not have the stomach for the hypercompetitive world of selling drugs was disabused of that notion when he oversaw the product launches. First up was Pepcid, Merck's entry into to the antacid and ulcer competition. Its campaign for Pepcid had been designed before Vagelos took charge. Tagamet and Zantac had a head start that Pepcid did not make up for, but it ended up with revenues exceeding a billion dollars a year.[13]

Vasotec, an ACE inhibitor that was the first rival to Squibb's big hit, Capoten, had been designed in Vagelos's lab and this was his first chance to influence how it was marketed. Merck settled on an understated pitch to cardiologists about clinical test results that demonstrated it was far superior to Squibb's drug. Vasotec took off after its 1986 release. It not only surpassed Capoten in sales within two years but became Merck's first ever drug to have revenues of a billion dollars in a single year. It had gotten to that watermark in half the time it had taken Squibb's drug.[14] When Vasotec made the billion-dollar club, Merck was the only pharmaceutical firm that had fourteen other drugs with annual sales of at least $100 million.[15]

Mevacor was in the final stages of FDA review as 1987 got under way. When it did get an okay later that year, its ten months from the submission of the application to the final approval was an FDA speed record. Merck had a specialized department consisting of 120 employees dedicated only to organizing all the data from clinical trials and preparing and stewarding the applications through the FDA.[16]

Before Mevacor was ready to release, Vagelos had to make a tough decision about another drug developed in the company's laboratory. What he decided would help to define his tenure, and Merck itself, as much as sales figures and profit margins. The drug was Mectizan, effective against river blindness and filariasis, parasites that were a scourge in the developing world. Since most of the sales would be to poor countries that had trouble affording it, Merck tried and failed to get the U.S. government and the WHO to subsidize its production and distribution costs.

When Vagelos raised the possibility of giving Mectizan free to any country that asked for it, and absorbing potentially tens of millions in costs, many executives objected. As a public company Merck had a duty to its shareholders. Launching a program that would cut into profits was not good business. Moreover, some contended, if Merck gave away Mectizan, it could set a dangerous precedent in which groups affected by virulent diseases, from malaria to HIV, might demand free drugs for those who could not afford them. All that would do, said the naysayers, was to end research on any medicines for such illnesses. Vagelos too worried about doing something with Mectizan that forced the company to do it time and again on future drugs. However, he concluded, "If we decided to sell Mectizan, it wouldn't reach those who needed it most regardless of how low we set the price."[17]

In the fall of 1987 Vagelos announced Merck would donate Mectizan free of charge to any country that asked for it. The WHO pitched in to help on the distribution. It marked the only instance in modern pharma history in which a leading firm gave away a drug they discovered and patented in order to eradicate a disease. It matched the spirit, he thought, when George Merck told the 1950 graduating class of the Medical College of Virginia that "medicine is for the patient . . . not [just] for the profits."[18] "(By the time the scientists who discovered Mectizan won the Nobel in Medicine in 2015, Merck had distributed over a billion doses in thirty-three countries.)[19] * [20]

* Some critics claim that Merck got tax credits for the value of the Mectizan it donated. Moreover, the company took advantage of the considerable good press it received as

When Mevacor launched that fall, it set its own sales record, the fastest drug in history to reach the $150 million to $200 million category.[21] That was just one record it notched on the way to becoming Merck's second billion-dollar-a-year drug.

While those medications went on sale, Merck's research and development teams were preparing their replacements. One of Vagelos's principles was that any successful drug should be replaced by a better and improved one by the time the first one lost its patent. Zocor, a second generation of Mevacor, was far along by the late 1980s. Prinivil would be version 2.0 of Vasotec. When Losec replaced Pepcid, Vagelos struck a partnership with consumer giant Johnson & Johnson, and the duo made Pepcid the most successful ever OTC acid-reducer. Besides the next generation of each star drug, the company had almost one hundred other medications in its pipeline it expected to dominate different categories.

Merck's remarkable success through the 1980s made Vagelos something of a legend. His peers thought of him as a throwback to the days when the focus was as much on cures as it was on profits. He somehow managed to do both better than his rivals.

Vagelos reinvested a large percentage of profits back into Merck's research labs, more than a billion dollars a year. It was far more than any of his predecessors. It helped generate the creative freedom he felt was the hallmark of his early years at the National Institutes of Health. Some competitors thought he was wasting Merck's profits. They spent their own money buying biotech firms or each other. Roche took Genentech, American Home Products bought American Cyanamid, and Pfizer spent $115 billion to acquire Warner-Lambert and $60 billion to get Pharmacia, which by then had merged with Upjohn.[22] Glaxo purchased Burroughs Wellcome and Smith Kline bought Beecham, Bristol-Myers. It was not long before Glaxo and SmithKline Beecham merged into the new Glaxo SmithKline.[23]

Some of Merck's top executives urged Vagelos to consider a merger with a rival. As the industry consolidated, the size and scope of the new firms might afford them significant advantages. The strengths of one would complement the weaknesses of the other so the combined

---

a result of Vagelos's altruism. Still, Merck has continued the good work to the current day, and as a result the WHO has forecast that by 2021 river blindness might be eliminated completely.

company would be a more formidable competitor. Vagelos's contrarian approach, however, paid off. He had predicted that the merger of different cultures would prove more difficult a challenge than the companies expected. Some wasted hundreds of millions on research projects that did not produce any new drugs. Others botched licensing and expansion opportunities, endured internal upheavals, defections of their best researchers, and clashes between the marketing departments of one firm with the research labs of another.

Pharmaceutical mergers and acquisitions were not the only industry trend that Vagelos monitored from a distance. American pharmaceutical companies had for decades benefited from unrestricted power in setting their drug prices. Employer-provided health insurance paid for 90 percent of brand-name prescriptions at their full list price. What caught Vagelos's attention was that an emerging group of new insurance providers, offering lower-cost options and more restrictive coverage, were challenging the generous private policies that had been a mainstay of American corporate benefits since World War II.

"Managed care was one of the domestic areas in which I thought Merck was responding too slowly," Vagelos later noted. "In 1988, about 30 million people were already enrolled in managed care, and our studies indicated that many more Americans would soon join them."[24]

"Managed care" had been virtually nonexistent before the Nixon administration marshaled the Health Maintenance Organization Act through Congress in 1973. It was a trial program to support the development of HMOs, independent networks of doctors and hospitals that provided services for a fixed annual fee paid up front. Medical costs were covered only if a patient stayed with health care providers in that network.

Nixon garnered bipartisan support from a Democratic-controlled Congress by pressing the case that managed plans like HMOs might slow the nation's accelerating health care costs. It was an opportune time to make that argument since rising drug prices had busted the Veterans Administration and Medicaid budgets for four consecutive years. As the country entered a recession in 1973, the economy was marked by stagflation, a term coined for the rare combination of a sluggish economy and high unemployment buffeted by escalating prices. Inflation jumped dramatically in 1973 from 3.4 percent to 9.6 percent, putting further pressure on finding a way to slow the upward pressure on drug prices.

Before the HMO Act, managed care insurers were a negligible part of the health care market. The first one, Kaiser Permanente Medical Care Program, had opened after World War II in San Francisco and most of its enrollees were unionized shipyard workers who were required to join.[25] Although Nixon made a good case for the lower fixed costs of managed care, no one then put together that Kaiser was founded by Henry Kaiser, the CEO of eponymously named industrial conglomerates in construction, shipbuilding, steel, and aluminum. Kaiser's son, Edgar, ran the HMO. The family backed Nixon in his unsuccessful runs for president in 1960 and California governor in 1962, and again in his successful races for the presidency in 1968 and 1972.*[26]

The 1973 statute directed millions of dollars in federal subsidies, loans, and grants to HMOs. The Nixon administration forecast that HMOs could cover as many as 50 million Americans in a decade. To achieve that goal it required that any employer who already offered medical insurance and had twenty-five or more employees had to present an HMO as a choice. Managed care policies had been off the radar for the country's employers. Once the law required it to be considered as an option, HMOs seemed attractive because they were priced at substantial discounts to the individual policies that had dominated the medical insurance marketplace. The early HMOs did not include prescription drug coverage. After a few years some covered a limited list of approved medications.[27]

The pharmaceutical industry was slow to respond to the ramifications HMOs might have on drug pricing. Even some of the smartest CEOs underestimated their impact. The greatest beneficiary was Kaiser Permanente, which had nearly 50 percent of all new enrollees in the

---

* The idea for HMO legislation was something Nixon discussed with his domestic affairs assistant, John Ehrlichman, during his first term. In 1971, the two talked about what Ehrlichman called "these health maintenance organizations like Edgar Kaiser's Permanente thing."

EHRLICHMAN: "Edgar Kaiser is running his Permanente deal for profit. And the reason that he can . . . the reason he can do it . . . I had Edgar Kaiser come in . . . talk to me about this and I went into it in some depth. All the incentives are toward less medical care, because . . ."

NIXON: [Unclear.]

EHRLICHMAN: ". . . the less care they give them, the more money they make."

NIXON: "Fine." [Unclear.]

EHRLICHMAN: [Unclear] ". . . and the incentives run the right way."

NIXON: "Not bad."

first decade. *The New York Times* later dubbed Kaiser "The King of the HMO mountain."[28] (It is still one of the nation's largest as of 2019, with nine million members and $22.5 billion in revenues.)[29]

An unintended consequence of the momentum toward managed health care was that it opened the door to a new service-oriented segment of the prescription drug industry. Just four years before Congress had passed the HMO Act, a small company called Pharmaceutical Card System (PCS) opened in Scottsdale, Arizona. It was not a health insurer but had adapted to prescription drugs the concept developed by payroll companies that processed employee wages, taxes, and withholding for corporations. PCS was the first firm to process prescriptions for medical insurance companies, maintain formulary lists, and reimburse pharmacies. It removed the burden of voluminous bureaucratic paperwork associated with drug benefits programs. PCS got paid by collecting a small fee for every claim it processed. It might have remained a mostly unknown company that had carved out a small niche of the medical insurance market had it not been for McKesson, the country's largest drug distributor. McKesson saw in the PCS business model an opportunity to create a new sector of the American pharmaceutical industry. In 1970, less than a year after PCS had opened, McKesson bought it.

McKesson used that acquisition to create pharmacy benefit managers (PBMs). The McKesson model was not simply a data processor that saved insurance companies time and paperwork. The PBMs McKesson envisioned would assemble vast patient networks and exert independent power as middlemen in the drug distribution network. Their profits would be the difference in discount prices they negotiated from manufacturers and lower reimbursement rates they paid to pharmacies. Pharmacy benefit managers emerged by serendipity when many of America's *Fortune* 500 companies were struggling to control soaring drug costs for their employees and retirees. Benefit programs for federal and state workers faced the same cost crunch.

More than a million customers came to PBMs from General Electric, IBM, and General Motors. Tens of millions more would become part of PBM patient lists in the coming decade. PBMs not only relieved the HMOs and other private medical insurance companies of the bureaucracy of processing their own benefit programs, they took over the responsibility for creating and maintaining the all-important drug formulary lists.

Over time they introduced mail order drug delivery programs that put pressure on the corner drugstores that had been the mainstay of how Americans had long filled their prescriptions. PBMs also developed computer software that increased the speed and accuracy of processing prescriptions. That forced national retail pharmacy chains to hire them as their own in-house service providers. All their different roles as middlemen meant that pharmacy benefit managers became repositories of the drug history for tens of millions of patients, able to provide potential side effect or contraindication data to pharmacists when patients switched doctors, went to work at a new company, or moved to another state.

Merck's Vagelos watched the power of PBMs increase through the 1980s. They were, he said, "revolutionizing the way many Americans purchased our medicines." By 1990, for instance, the largest PBM was seven-year-old Medco. It serviced 38 million patients, "an astonishing number for such a young enterprise," marveled Vagelos.[30] PBMs like Medco did much more than drive a hard bargain for the best prices from pharmaceutical companies. They could make or break a drug's commercial prospects by deciding whether it got listed on their formularies. Each PBM had a slightly different list of approved medications. Low prices were initially the most important factor in deciding whether a drug got on the list. When Congress passed the Hatch-Waxman Act in 1984 and opened the door to generic competition, the PBMs were situated to give patients the lower-cost copies on the formularies. If there was no generic in a category, the PBMs negotiated to find which pharma company was willing to discount its branded drug most heavily.

The largest drug companies slowly realized the PBMs were threats to their unrestricted pricing power.[31] That concerned Vagelos and other pharma CEOs. They worried about spending many years and hundreds of millions of dollars to develop a drug and then running into an obstacle with pharmacy benefit managers about whether it would be placed on a formulary for insurance coverage. Discounting list prices from the first day of sales to get on the formulary was anathema to the large pharma companies.

While Vagelos kept a wary eye on the growth of PBMs, it was not yet worrisome enough to mar what had become a golden era at Merck. Starting with Mevacor's release in 1987, *Fortune* ranked Merck as America's most admired company for a record seven consecutive years ("a stunning demonstration of managerial excellence").[32] *Fortune* concluded Merck was a "pioneer in discovering lifesaving drugs" and noted that Vagelos "has personally recruited some of the brightest academic researchers to work in his labs."[33]

Vagelos and Merck's executives relished the company's sterling reputation. It served as a magnet for recruiting the top scientists to its research labs at the same time as it encouraged doctors to dispense more Merck-branded drugs. At the halfway mark of what would be Vagelos's six-year tenure, the company's stock had risen 500 percent.[34]* Vagelos's decision to give Mectizan free to the developing world to eradicate river blindness, while at the same time turning out record profits, is why author Barry Werth said, "Merck was both the Arnold Schwarzenegger and Mother Teresa of American businesses."[35]

* While Vagelos had turned Merck into the industry's top profit earner, he was personally rewarded very well. Evidence is that since his retirement, he and his wife, Diana, have donated $450 million to his alma mater, Columbia University. A third of that is to pay for loans that students would otherwise have had to take.

41

"NO ONE LIKES AIRING DIRTY LAUNDRY IN PUBLIC"

The Hatch-Waxman Act that opened the door to robust generic competition caused considerable anxiety at Purdue. The FDA had not approved MST Continus for sale in the U.S. until 1987, seven years after it had gone on sale in the U.K. For the American market, Arthur thought MS Contin was a more commercial name than the Latin-based Continus. Purdue did not have the luxury of a pipeline of drugs ready for release every couple of years. The Sacklers would not mind Purdue Frederick being dubbed a one-drug company if its solo product was a smash hit.

Under FDA rules that the time for a drug patent ran from the date of discovery, Purdue had as little as five years before generics undercut MS Contin profits.[1] Such competition was not much of a concern before Hatch-Waxman.[2] The Sacklers had been in the industry long enough to know that any regulatory statute, no matter how well intentioned by those who crafted it, had loopholes. It did not take long to find one in Hatch-Waxman. That law required the FDA to freeze the approval process for any generic drug if the brand-name patent holder challenged it in court. The lawsuits quickly became a kitchen sink of allegations, everything from questioning the safety of the generic's manufacturing facilities to accusations of corporate espionage to claims of patent infringement. The legal costs were usually a fraction of what a drug company might earn by keeping the patent intact on its blockbuster medication. Bristol-Myers Squibb later lost its litigation but not before it blocked for two years any generic competition to its hit Taxol cancer drug. Bristol had earned hundreds of millions from Taxol while it kept the copycat drugs tied up in the courts for an estimated $20 to

$25 million in legal costs.[3] In other cases, parties avoided litigation with what the industry dubbed "pay for delay." Brand manufacturers paid generic companies to delay their drugs. Bayer paid $398 million to a competitor to postpone its generic rival to Bayer's Cipro antibiotic. Bayer earned nearly twice that by keeping Cipro unchallenged.[4]

MS Contin was profitable but not such a success that Purdue could afford to tie up would-be generic competitors in litigation. Richard Sackler—with the blessing of his father, Raymond—spearheaded a project that he hoped would protect Purdue from generic headwinds. Richard wanted an improved painkiller, one that might have much broader commercial appeal than MS Contin.[5]

Dr. Robert Kaiko, Purdue's vice president of clinical research, had been a key researcher on MS Contin. He agreed Purdue should concentrate on producing new "controlled-release opioids."[6] The company knew the field of narcotic painkillers well, said Kaiko, so there was no reason to take too far a detour for its next-generation product.

Both Sackler and Kaiko believed that MS Contin's active ingredient, morphine, was problematic if they hoped to reach a larger market. Morphine had too notorious a reputation. Purdue's own data showed that doctors dispensed MS Contin mostly to terminal cancer patients.[7] "It was an inhibition to the use of a product in every application," Richard Sackler later testified. "I believe the stigma . . . [was] that morphine was an end-of-life drug, if it was to be used at all."[8]

It did not take long before Purdue's science team settled on a different opioid, oxycodone, a chemical cousin of heroin. Two other drug companies were researching extended release narcotic painkillers but neither had focused on oxycodone.[9] While there were some oxycodone-based painkillers on the market—Percodan (oxycodone and aspirin) and Percocet (oxycodone and acetaminophen)—they were immediate release pills. If Purdue could master an extended release oxycodone-only pill, it would be the first of its kind.

This was the period during which the Sacklers filed several patents that provided a chemical roadmap for such a drug. To prevent competitors from easily finding out what they were up to, they assigned some of the patents to Mundipharma. Most, however, went to a company called Euro-Celtique. The author tracked Euro-Celtique to Luxembourg, where it was incorporated. It was an affiliate of Purdue Biopharma LP, a now defunct New Jersey–based subsidiary of Purdue Pharma LP.[10]

Napp in the U.K. was working in tandem with American Purdue. Napp had 30 percent of its Cambridge staff dedicated to research. After its success with MST Continus, that focus helped Napp obtain approval for additional narcotic painkillers, from Sevredol, an immediate release morphine tablet, to Palladone, a synthetic opioid several times stronger than heroin (pulled from the U.S. market in 2005 because of "serious and potentially adverse reactions can occur . . . [when] taken together with alcohol.").[11]

The good news for the Sacklers in the U.S. was that they knew any narcotic painkiller they developed would be well received by doctors. Oncologists liked MS Contin and had judged it a solid advance in palliative care. Purdue's medical department had sponsored nine multidose studies in Canada and Europe. The results were published in *Cancer* shortly after it went on sale in the U.S. Ninety-three percent of patients with "moderate to severe cancer related pain . . . achieved satisfactory to excellent analgesia on a twelve-hour regimen." The remaining 7 percent got "good results with eight-hour dosing." The bottom line was that MS Contin "was judged to be significantly more effective, and with significantly fewer side effects than both the pre-study opioid analgesics."[12]

There had been few options before MS Contin for treating the pain of terminally ill patients. Most short-acting opioid-based painkillers were mixed with aspirin or acetaminophen. Since the immune systems of cancer patients were compromised from chemotherapy or radiation, the mixed analgesics could result in life-threatening liver damage.

Besides lobbying his father and uncles for prioritizing an MS Contin successor, Richard Sackler also raised a more fundamental issue. The younger Sackler thought it was time to create a new company.[13] Most of Purdue Frederick's product line, he told them, was outdated and it did not have a reputation inside the industry for dramatic lab discoveries. Betadine and Senokot might be well known but they garnered little to no respect from rivals.

The elder Sacklers had a sentimental attachment to Purdue Frederick and liked it as it was. They were satisfied with the solid profits from a product line that did not depend on the fate of a single hit drug. The company they had bought in 1952 had never lost money. Sales had increased annually. Their international operations through Napp and the Mundipharma network were expanding rapidly.

Richard was not the only member of the next generation of Sacklers, however, who had grander plans.* The younger Sacklers felt burdened to live up to the expectations of their demanding, rags-to-riches parents. And it was tiring, the author learned, when at industry events someone looked at one of their business cards and said something to the effect of "Oh, the Betadine company."[14] They wanted to build a new Purdue beyond the imagination and vision of their fathers and none thought that was possible by relying on products such as laxatives, disinfectants, and MS Contin.

Arthur, Mortimer, and Raymond cautioned patience. Wait for the next painkiller from the labs, they suggested, before deciding. Maybe it was time instead to introduce Napp Pharmaceuticals to the United States? Since its 1966 founding, it had carved out a solid reputation in Britain and Europe for innovative laboratory research and quality products.

All the Sacklers agreed that the pharmaceutical industry in which Arthur, Mortimer, and Raymond had created their empire was undergoing rapid change. AIDS activists had shamed the FDA into putting a few experimental drugs on a faster approval track. Some pharma executives hoped quicker approvals might filter down to less important drugs.[15] That seemed unlikely, however, since the FDA's budget had been slashed even before it had the added responsibility for AIDS. That put the agency under great stress in the second half of the decade as it tried playing catch-up for its failure to respond aggressively earlier. The FDA's smaller size and added duties would lead over several years to what its commissioner, Dr. Frank Young, called a "partnership" with the drug industry. It no longer had the staff or budget to be as adversarial, even if it wanted to do so.

* The "next generation of Sacklers," in this instance, refers to Raymond's sons Richard and Jonathan and three of Mortimer's children, Mortimer A., Kathe, and Ilene. None of Arthur's four children ever had anything to do with Purdue Pharma. "The Sacklers," when used in reference to Purdue Pharma, covers all the Sackler family directors, including first-generation members Mortimer, Raymond, and his wife, Beverly. All declined through their attorneys or representatives to be interviewed for this book. Other Sacklers, including Arthur's children and some of the grandchildren of Mortimer and Raymond, did not answer interview inquiries. Beverly Sackler, Raymond's first wife and a Purdue director, died in October 2019, while my interview request was pending with her New York publicist. A different New York publicist representing Arthur's third wife, Jillian, asked for more information about my project, but this did not lead to an interview.

Some of its failures played out publicly. A blood screening test to detect HIV antibodies was not available until 1985, when the Reagan downsizing had decimated its ranks of blood supply inspectors. Plans for the blood industry to police itself proved unrealistic. Blood banks, including the Red Cross, repeatedly labeled and sold as safe blood products that had tested positive for HIV or hepatitis.[16] Pharmaceutical firms were not much better. Armour ignored the advice of one of its scientists and for two years sold infected blood that caused infections and deaths in the U.S., Canada, the Netherlands, and the U.K.[17]

Richard Sackler contended that if the FDA did not have the resources to regulate something as critical as the nation's blood supply during an era of AIDS, it meant that the approval bottleneck for non-lifesaving drugs would only worsen. Even if Purdue researchers developed a good MS Contin successor, it might get bogged down in the FDA's cumbersome bureaucracy.

Arthur was the only senior Sackler who did not totally dismiss the ideas of his nephews and nieces. He suggested the family should consider renaming Purdue Frederick as Sackler Pharma and spin it off. Then he proposed creating a new Purdue Pharma to assume the risks and rewards of future drug launches.[18] Arthur thought his solution was simple and ideal. Raymond and Mortimer were not enthusiastic. It had been many years since Arthur was able to dictate what they should do and when it came to Purdue, which was their fiefdom, they seemed almost instinctively to reject whatever he suggested.

While the Sacklers debated Purdue's future, Arthur had a couple of moments about which to brag to his brothers. *Scientific American* asked him in 1985 to join its board of directors, stocked with medical and pharmaceutical luminaries. Linus Pauling, the American biochemist who had won the Nobel in Medicine as well as the Nobel Peace Prize, dedicated his 1986 book, *How to Live Longer and Feel Better*, to him.[19] Mortimer and Raymond knew their brother and Pauling had been friends since the early 1960s when Pauling's political activism had gotten him branded a peace activist with communist sympathies (Pauling unsuccessfully sued the *National Review* and its editor, William Buckley, in 1965 for writing that he was a "fellow traveler" with the Soviets). Pauling and Sackler shared political passions in opposition to the Vietnam War and the growth of the American military.

The family discussions sparked by Richard Sackler's ambitious idea for a different kind of drug company were cut short the day after Memorial Day, May 25, 1987. A panicked telephone call came into the family before dawn. Arthur had fallen unconscious at his Manhattan home and was rushed to Columbia-Presbyterian Medical Center. The grim word came that afternoon from the treating physicians: seventy-three-year-old Arthur had died of a heart attack.[20]

It happened so quickly that no one in the family had a chance to prepare for his death and say, as one friend later said, "a proper goodbye." Mortimer, then seventy, and Raymond, sixty-seven, may have often bristled at Arthur's dismissive, know-it-all attitude, but they had not known a world without him.* [21]

Arthur's will was submitted for probate the following month. All his property and art was in two eponymously named trusts. Michael Sonnenreich, Arthur's friend, lawyer, and occasional business partner, was the executor. The probate court also appointed him in the important fiduciary role of independent trustee, whose responsibility was to ensure that the trust was administered as Arthur wanted.[22] The other trustees were Arthur's first wife, Else; his then wife, Jillian; and his four children from two marriages (Carol Master, Elizabeth Sackler, Arthur Jr., and Denise Marika). Marietta was conspicuous by her absence. Arthur was insistent she be excluded from any role overseeing the estate and she got no bequests.

The estate was very conservatively valued for tax purposes at $140 million. Mortimer, the author learned, laughed when he heard that valuation. He considered it at least twice that and said, "They must have divided by two."[23] German-based Springer, Europe's largest newspaper publisher, paid $75 million just for Arthur's *Medical Tribune*.[24] † [25]

---

* By the end of 1987, Mortimer and Raymond told friends it was a pity Arthur had not lived to see Eli Lilly release the world's first selective serotonin reuptake inhibitor (SSRI), Prozac. It kicked off a mental health revolution. Prozac—and the chemical copycats that followed—Zoloft, Celexa, Lexapro, among others—was as much a cultural watershed for the way people viewed clinical depression and its treatment as the contraceptive pill had been in 1960 for women to control reproductive rights. Prozac was the first SSRI to reach a billion dollars in annual sales. It and the SSRIs that followed were the fulfillment—in an updated and more sophisticated chemical composition—of the Holy Grail: a lifestyle mind drug that Arthur Sackler had searched for in the late 1950s. SSRIs replaced Valium, Xanax, and the benzodiazepines as the world's best-selling psychopharmacologic drugs.

† In 2006, the estate's value was reduced by $21 million from an original estimate in the value of Sackler's art collection. It made that adjustment based on a 1998 appraisal from Sotheby's. A smaller appraisal translated into lower estate taxes.

Arthur directed that all the income produced from the trust be paid annually to Jillian, who had only married Arthur six years earlier. That bequest infuriated his children, who split a single payment of $600,000. Sackler's will kicked off two decades of often nasty litigation between family members. They spent millions in legal fees over battles that left enmity between some of them to this day. Sonnenreich and Arthur's children brought Jillian to court in an unsuccessful suit to invalidate the trust.[26] She later sued the trust when it denied her request to loan some of Arthur's art collection for an exhibition she planned and also to use a sixteenth-century Chinese bed and several other collectible pieces of furniture on display at her home.[27] She prevailed initially but the judgment was overturned on appeal.[28] Jillian also failed later to stop the sale of some of Arthur's collection, including his Renaissance ceramics (majolica), and some terra-cottas and bronzes.[29] She later refused to pay $2 million of a $3.5 million bill from her original lawyers, Breed, Abbott and Morgan. They sued for their fee and she counterclaimed for malpractice.[30] At another point, Else Sackler had to sue to get $2 million from the trust over a contested promissory note Arthur had created before he died.[31] Even a dispute over $54,000 in a bill submitted by a previous guardian ad litem (appointed for any interest Arthur's grandchildren might have had in the estate) ended up in court (the judge awarded half the amount).[32] The squabbling did not stop even after Else's death in 2000. Arthur's children from their marriage, Carol and Elizabeth, were appointed as the trustees for their mother's estate. They were soon part of a bitter lawsuit, a 2007 action in which they all had different takes on the executor's commission.[33]

While most of the estate litigation pitted Arthur's children against his third wife, Jillian, they also sometimes joined forces against Mortimer and Raymond. Sonnenreich told the author that the first problem arose from Bill Frohlich's IMS. "It was Arthur's creation," Sonnenreich says. "Arthur had removed himself so there was no appearance of any conflict of interest between his advertising agency and IMS. He put Mortie and Ray into it. And they had all agreed that if Frohlich ever sold it, his share would be split four ways."[34] Instead, Mortimer and Raymond got $37 million each when Dun & Bradstreet acquired IMS in 1988, a year after Arthur's death. There were heated meetings about whether Arthur's family would receive anything from the IMS sale.

"Mortie and Ray knew about the Frohlich agreement, but they pretended they didn't," Sonnenreich recalled.[35] Raymond relied in part on advice from the New York law firm of Chadbourne & Parke. A partner there, Stuart Baker, had been the chief outside counsel for Purdue Frederick since the late 1970s. Mortimer had also retained an American law firm in case the Frohlich dispute went to court. (Since he lived abroad, Mortimer relied on a British solicitor, Christopher Benbow, who represented the family's U.K. pharma firms.)*

Ultimately, it was not possible to challenge Mortimer and Raymond since both Frohlich and Arthur were dead. There was no documentation to support the "handshake agreement."[36] Arthur's children were not the only ones furious at their uncles. Jillian complained that the duo had taken millions in outsized profits from Purdue Frederick, money that should have been split with Arthur. "There was supposed to be a three-way agreement with Purdue Frederick, and they have taken gigantic sums out of that," Jillian complained to Sonnenreich.[37] The final, bitterly contested buyout of Arthur's one-third share in Purdue Frederick was $22,353,750 (when OxyContin became a blockbuster after its 1996 release, that would be less than a week of its sales). Following the family tradition of insisting on long payment schedules for their philanthropic gifts, Mortimer and Raymond demanded and got one: the last installment to Arthur's estate was November 1997, more than a decade after he had died.[38]

All the family battles that followed Arthur's unexpected death stayed out of the press. The Sacklers were not yet famous enough to attract lurid coverage from New York's tabloids. That was good news for the family, says Sonnenreich. "No one likes airing dirty laundry in public."

---

* Both Baker and Benbow were directors of Sackler companies before Arthur's death (Baker incorporated Mundipharma Inc. in New York in 1979 and Benbow had been a director of Napp in the U.K. since the mid-1970s). Benbow resigned nearly fifteen of his director's positions on different Sackler-owned foreign corporations in 2016 and 2017. As of 2019, the author confirmed that Stuart Baker was inactive as a director on some twenty companies, but was an active director on more than a dozen, including Britain's two Napp companies, five Mundipharma firms in the U.K., and others in India, Denmark, and Myanmar (files in collection of author). Neither attorney has ever been named in any complaint filed against a Sackler company nor ever accused of any wrongdoing by plaintiffs who subsequently sued Purdue over its aggressive marketing of OxyContin, its blockbuster narcotic painkiller.

42

"THE SALES DEPARTMENT ON STEROIDS"

Richard Sackler got his wish, a new company to "take on the risk of new products."[1] Purdue Pharma Inc. incorporated in 1991, five years before it launched the successor to MS Contin. Raymond Sackler's sons, Richard and Jonathan, as well as two of Mortimer's daughters, Kathe and Ilene, became Purdue Pharma directors. Raymond's wife, Beverly, and Mortimer's third wife, Theresa, as well as another of Mortimer's seven children, Mortimer Jr., joined the board a year before the company's new drug went on sale.[2]

That oxycodone-based drug was still an unnamed product. Its first clinical trial had only been completed in 1989.[3] Purdue would not even apply for a patent until 1992. The drug's development was under the aegis of Purdue Frederick but only until it went on sale; it would then become a holding company.[4] The marketing and sales meanwhile were split between Purdue Pharma Inc. and Purdue Pharma LP, another company the Sacklers created in 1990.[5] They also incorporated PF Laboratories as the manufacturer. As for asset protection and tax mitigation, the family stuck to what the senior Sacklers had done since the 1960s and assigned key patents on the pills' enhanced extended release coating to their Swiss-based Mundipharma AG.

Richard Sackler later admitted that while the corporate structure was indecipherable to outsiders, at times even he found it "confusing and complex." Years later, in a deposition, he could not recall whether the directors of the many companies were the same or different.[6] Nor was he certain whether sales representatives were employed by Purdue Frederick or Purdue Pharma.[7] When asked, "How many Purdue entities are there?" he replied, "I don't know." He could not even provide a guess as to how many Sackler-owned companies existed.[8] * [9]

What was not in doubt was that a privately held and family-controlled drug company of Purdue's size was increasingly rare.[10] The pharmaceutical industry had been swept up in a mania of mergers and acquisitions that started the previous decade. There were $500 billion in deals over ten years. The Sacklers had watched with some envy as biotechnology companies only a fraction of Purdue's size had successful public offerings on not much more than a dream encapsulated in a single product that existed only on paper. By the mid-1990s the largest ten firms accounted for half of all drug sales versus only 20 percent at the start of the consolidation.[11]

Only the large pharma conglomerates could afford research and development costs that had multiplied more than sixfold since the 1970s.[12] Despite all the significant progress in chemistry and biology, it was still virtually impossible for scientists to be certain how a drug synthesized in the laboratory would react in people. Only about fifteen of every thousand lab compounds made it to clinical trials.[13] After a GAO report found that nearly half the 209 drugs the FDA approved between 1976 and 1985 had caused serious and unexpected side effects, the agency set stricter guidelines.[14] That meant human studies were more complex and expensive than ever. By the 1990s, each clinical trial for a mass-market drug included about five thousand subjects, more than double what had been required in the 1970s.[15] Yet the success rate for the drugs that began those trials remained the same dismal 10 to 20 percent.[16]

Purdue had spent $40 million in developing and testing its MS Contin successor, which it had named OxyContin.[17] While that was a fraction of what Big Pharma paid on major drugs, it was almost ten times

---

* Mortimer and Raymond followed Arthur's playbook and incorporated multiple Purdue-named entities during several years before and after OxyContin's release. The author located nearly seventy post-1990 "Purdue Pharma" companies, most concentrated in the Northeast. In Delaware, there were twenty-six Purdue-named companies, sixteen in Connecticut, and another five in New York. An additional Arthur-inspired strategy was using similar company names. In half a dozen instances, the only difference were the letters at the end of the name indicating its legal status, as with three separate Purdue Neuroscience companies, one a Corp., another an Inc., and the third an LP. The same business addresses often overlapped for some, including Purdue AO Pharmaceuticals Inc., Purdue Biopharma, Purdue Healthcare Tech, Purdue Pharma Manufacturing Inc., Purdue Associates, Purdue Land, and Purdue Products.

more than the Sacklers had ever committed to a product.[18] Richard Sackler kept assuring them it was a worthwhile investment.

OxyContin held the promise for all their dreams. In its November 1992 patent application, Purdue presented its drug as a breakthrough because a single dose lasted twelve hours to "control pain in approximately 90 percent of patients."[19] The emphasis on its twelve-hour duration was at the heart of Purdue's strategy to set OxyContin apart from rivals. In pre-sales surveys, Purdue learned that patients with chronic pain rated as "very important" whether a treatment might require less frequent dosing. Its twelve-hour effectiveness was also the drug's only tangible benefit on which Purdue could focus. Clinical trials had demonstrated that OxyContin did not have *any* therapeutic advantage over other opioid-based painkillers. The FDA later concluded in its review that OxyContin provided no better relief than immediate release generic oxycodone dispensed four times daily.[20]

Few outside of Purdue and the FDA knew that even the claim of twelve-hour pain relief had been cast into doubt in half a dozen clinical trials the company had sponsored. A third of the subjects needed another dose to offset pain before twelve hours expired.[21] Under FDA regulations, however, only half of those in a trial had to get twelve hours of relief for the company to make the claim. About 55 percent of the trial subjects got the full relief Purdue promised.

In 1995, as the OxyContin application was pending at the FDA, Purdue geared up for what the Drug Enforcement Administration would later describe as "the most aggressive campaign for an opioid in U.S. history."[22] The Sacklers had opened up their checkbooks even before FDA approval to exert influence in the opioid and pain reevaluation movement. Purdue created a speakers bureau that attracted some of the leading pain management advocates, including two of the pioneers, Drs. Portenoy and Haddox.[23] That speakers bureau was only a warm-up. Before and immediately after OxyContin's 1996 release, Purdue spent millions on grants to patient/pain advocacy groups and sponsored over twenty thousand pain management educational programs. It subsidized dozens of conferences at which some five thousand doctors and pharmacists got all-expense-paid trips to listen to company representatives praise OxyContin as a "breakthrough painkiller."[24]

One of Purdue's most innovative ventures was creating special pain management curriculums at leading universities. It trained a future generation of physicians in the philosophy of "pain as the fifth vital sign" and that "not all opioids are bad."[25] At Tufts University, Purdue funded a master's program titled "Pain, Research, Education and Policy" and was one of the biggest donors to the Tufts School of Medicine.[26] An annual "Sackler Lecture" featured internationally renowned pain specialists. Tufts later appointed Richard Sackler a director of its medical school and when it gave his father, Raymond, an honorary degree, its president said, "It would be impossible to calculate how many lives you have saved."[27] At Massachusetts General, Harvard Medical School's largest teaching hospital , the company spent millions on the Purdue Pharma Pain Program. It rolled out similar initiatives at Northeastern, Boston Universities, and the Massachusetts College of Pharmacy.

Purdue also spent money on medical associations that advocated for more liberalized dispensing of opioids.[28] It provided 80 percent of the funding for the American Pain Foundation, a pain management organization of which Portenoy was a director.[29] The University of Wisconsin's Pain and Policies Studies Group depended on Purdue's largesse.[30] The company also wrote big checks to the American Pain Society and the American Academy of Pain Medicine. (A year after OxyContin's release Purdue gave them $400,000, and through 2017 contributed an additional $2.1 million).[31] * [32]

---

* The heavy spending not only continued but increased until 2016 when it dropped for the first time. From 2013 through 2017, Purdue spent $49 million on doctors and a broadly defined category "Research Payments," the latter comprising mostly grants to teaching hospitals. The author calculated that about 70 percent of those funds were directly for promoting OxyContin, and more than 95 percent for Purdue's stable of opioid-based drugs. The payments to doctors were primarily consulting fees, but also included approximately $3 million for "food and beverage," another $900,000 for speaking fees, and $750,000 for "travel and lodging."

Purdue's $49 million was a small part of the industry's overall $9 billion spent on 900,000 doctors over the same time. Details on the the promotion money paid by pharmaceutical companies, broken down by specific drugs, became public in August 2013, as required by the Affordable Care Act (it was included in a provision of the statute aptly titled "Physician Payments Sunshine Act"). The federal government's Centers for Medicare and Medicaid Services has compiled huge raw data information files for public review (https://openpaymentsdata.cms.gov), and *ProPublica* has entered it into a single searchable database. Also, there is public information about payments from 2009 to 2013 for seventeen drug companies that were required to disclose it as a result of litigation settlements. Those companies represented about half the drug sales in the U.S. Purdue was not one of them.

Purdue, of course, was not the only pharmaceutical company with an opioid drug that dispensed money to the professional pain societies, as well as doctors and patient advocacy groups. Knoll Pharma (Vicodin), Ortho-McNeil (Tramadol), and Janssen Pharmaceuticals (Duragesic) provided about 40 percent of the associations' annual budgets in the 1990s and more than a million dollars through promotions often disguised as public service education about pain.[33]

Beefing up the detail team was another pre-sales priority. Purdue doubled its sales force to six hundred before the drug launch.[34] A good sales rep's one-on-one pitch to a doctor was an unmatched way of creating a best-selling drug. The senior Sacklers knew firsthand that a detail team was indispensable. They recalled how in the 1950s, American Brands/Wyeth had knocked off Carter-Wallace's number one selling tranquilizer, Miltown.[35] The two companies marketed chemically identical drugs under different brand names. Although Miltown had the advantage of being first on the market, Carter-Wallace could not maintain the sales momentum since it had no detail team. American Brands, on the other hand, had its 1,500 salesmen saturate the country.[36] The success of American Brands sparked a boom in detail teams. Into the 1970s the drug industry spent twice as much on promotion and marketing as it did on research and development.[37]

There was another benefit to one-on-one pitches. Since there was no record of what was said in the doctor's office it was impossible for competitors or government regulators to determine if the salesmen adhered to the efficacy limits the FDA had set for the drug or provided adequate warning about side effects. Sales representatives were careful not to leave notes at the doctor's office. Purdue's internal documents reveal that management constantly reinforced to the detail squad that they "commit nothing to a permanent record." Anyone making such a mistake would be subject to "immediate dismissal."[38]

In March 1995, the sales and marketing divisions gathered at the company's Norwalk headquarters to strategize about how to best promote OxyContin.[39] First, they were told, it was not simply MS Contin version 2.0. "We do not want to niche OxyContin for cancer pain," a marketing executive said in leading off the presentation.[40] They had to generate enthusiasm about the drug. That required marketing it as the industry's long-awaited miracle pain reliever, a narcotic analgesic with longer-lasting benefits and fewer risks than any predecessor.

Purdue had discovered in focus groups that general practitioners still balked at dispensing opioids for anything other than end-of-life pain. An independent study showed many were reluctant even then. Half the patients who died in hospitals received no pain medication during their final week. Another report showed that only a quarter of elderly cancer patients in nursing homes were given *any* medication.[41] That opioid-based painkillers were not being used even in hospitals and nursing homes served as a sharp reminder to the sales team of the challenge they faced. It was disappointing that despite a decade of the pain and drug reevaluation movement many doctors stubbornly clung to what the Sacklers thought were outdated views of pain and the risks of addiction from opioids.

Since it was not possible to dodge the issue, Purdue reps were instructed to raise "concerns about addiction" before the physician did.[42] Patients developed "a normal physiologic response [but] tolerance and physical dependence [were] not the same as addiction."[43] That only happened, they said, when "a susceptible individual" got the drug and ignored the doctor's dosing instructions.[44] It was understandable that no matter how wonderful a drug, "a small minority" of patients "may not be reliable or trustworthy" for narcotic painkillers.[45] If the doctors remained skeptical, the detail team was to show them the drug's FDA-approved label that stated if OxyContin was used as prescribed for treating moderate to serious pain, addiction was "very rare."[46]

To emphasize the point, flashy charts prepared for the sales team illustrated how each pill released oxycodone into the bloodstream at a steady rate over twelve hours. That gave the sales reps a chance to tout OxyContin's patented, controlled release coating, an improved version of the one that worked so well with MS Contin. That coating, Purdue claimed, made it impossible for addicts to get the rush they chased. Without a high, patients would not want more of the drug as it wore off. Those charts would prove to be powerful aids that bolstered the company's claim that there was little chance of OxyContin abuse.[47] The odds of addiction were "much less than one percent," the detail squad hammered, so long as the "pain patients are treated by doctors."[48] * [49] One of Purdue's cleverest marketing lines was that OxyContin provided "relief—not a 'high' . . . [when] taken as directed."[50]

---

* No one was aware that Arthur had drawn the opposite conclusion about the addictiveness of narcotic painkillers. The author discovered 1966's *The Anatomy of Sleep*, a

There was a problem with those charts, however, that would remain a Purdue secret for nearly a decade: the data downplaying the odds of addiction had been skewed.[51] Worse, the company approved it although its own clinical trials demonstrated that for some patients up to 40 percent of oxycodone was released into the bloodstream in the first hour or two.[52] That was fast enough to cause a high, and for some resulted in a crash that required another pill to feel better.

To tilt the odds in favor of its "low risk of addiction" sales strategy, Purdue later underwrote several studies that reported addiction rates from long-term opioid treatment between only 0.2 percent and 3.27 percent. Rigorous independent studies never confirmed them. It was not rare in the drug industry for a company-sponsored study to return a result that echoed the marketing. A review of a thousand clinical trials over ten years among many different classes of drugs reveals that pharma-funded studies produced favorable results far more often than government-sponsored trials. Depending on the drugs and years, the pharma-subsidized trials produced positive results about a minimum of 50 percent more frequently and for some drugs an eye-popping twenty times more often.[53] Those results explain why clinical studies paid for by drug companies, which were only a quarter of all trials in the 1980s, were more than half by the late 1990s.[54] And it explains why Purdue financed its own to obtain the right "risk of addiction" numbers so the sales team could tell doctors that "Oxy was non-habit forming."[55] Even as late as 2019, a former Purdue director, Richard's son, David, when asked in an interview about OxyContin's addiction rate, cited a 2018 study in the *British Journal of Anaesthesia* that put it at 4.7 percent. "I think a fair number is somewhere between 2 and 3 percent."[56]

The author learned there was at least one later instance in which a Purdue employee at the Stamford headquarters asked whether it was possible the studies had a flawed methodology that led to the underestimating the real-world opioid addiction rate. A division manager

135-page book about the physiology and pharmacology of sleep. Arthur helped Roche Laboratories prepare the book. It was designed to subtly promote Librium and Valium as useful sleep aids, although the FDA had not approved them for that purpose. In discussing other pharmaceutical aids, it stated: "If sleeplessness is pain-related . . . primarily, narcotics are prescribed for relief of pain. . . . The addiction potential of narcotics is well recognized in our century, as it was not always in the past."

closed off any discussion; that question reflected a defeatist attitude, he said, and would not be tolerated.[57] * [58]

After OxyContin's release, Purdue got help in promoting the "low risk of addiction" from the American Academy of Pain Medicine and the American Pain Society.[59] Both were beneficiaries of generous funding and subsidies from Purdue and other opioid drug manufacturers.[60] They issued a consensus statement emphasizing that opioids were effective for treating nonmalignant chronic pain and reiterating that it was "established" that there was "less than 1 percent" probability of addiction."[61] Purdue had developed its own simplified pain rating scale, a sheet of facial expressions ranging from smiling and happy to frowning and sad. It distributed tens of thousands to physicians.[62] Allowing a patient to leave a medical appointment with untreated pain, Purdue sales representatives told doctors, bordered on negligence.

In order for the detail team to concentrate on those physicians likely to write the most prescriptions, Purdue went to IMS (International Marketing Service). Advances in computers and software had changed medical data collection in the near forty years since Bill Frohlich and Arthur Sackler had founded IMS.[63] Instead of manually entering data obtained from those pharmacists willing to share it for a small fee, "information technology" allowed IMS and its rivals to collect virtually all prescription information from pharmacies and hospitals. The American Medical Association, representing more than half the nation's physicians, cooperated by licensing the dispensing information in its "Physician Masterfile."[64]

Initially Purdue only bought lists of doctors, sorted by zip code, who were heavy prescribers of existing painkillers such as Vicodin, Percocet, Lortab, and Percodan.[65] Those records covered about 5,000 of the country's 800,000 active physicians.[66] According to the charges set forth later in a complaint by the Massachusetts attorney general, that was enough for the sales squad to focus on what Purdue internally dubbed the "core dispensers," the physicians it believed "could be influenced to increase opioid prescriptions the most."[67] The author

* That concern later turned out to be right. All the studies had excluded patients with preexisting mental health disorders or previous substance abuse. Those were the very patients who were far more likely to develop addiction problems. Later studies that included those patients also followed them over a year or more of outpatient treatment. The reported addiction rates in those studies ranged from a low of 32 percent to as high as 80 percent.

discovered that Purdue later spent more than a million dollars to buy IMS's Cornerstone 3.0 software. It was the only system then capable of providing the sales team real-time updates on prescriptions written by doctors in their sales territory.[68] That software "put the sales department on steroids," recalled an assistant marketing manager.[69]

Purdue did not expect its detail team to make a generic pitch to doctors for more liberal dispensing. The marketing team had targeted specific patient groups in the hope of tapping into a much wider market than the one for MS Contin. Geriatrics topped the list. Sales reps told doctors that OxyContin improved "the quality of life" for seniors. They played off the phrase "performance enhancing drugs" that described anabolic steroids used by athletes, to suggest that Oxy could "enhance personal performance."[70] There were no studies that supported their "quality of life" or "personal performance" claims. And they did not mention those studies that showed patients older than sixty-five on opioid painkillers had increased risks for falls and bone fractures.[71]

A second part of the geriatric strategy was pushing Oxy for an indication not approved by the FDA, osteoarthritis. Purdue had tested OxyContin for it and failed to find any benefit. Why misrepresent it as effective in relieving arthritic pain? It is the most common age-related disease, affecting more than 80 percent of those older than fifty-five. And the last element in the geriatric sales strategy was to focus on nursing homes and long-term-care facilities. Purdue thought it possible to "maximize demand" there since they were essentially "open formularies" (they have few limitations on access to medicines).[72]

Veterans were the next priority. Purdue had accumulated a file of anecdotal evidence that chronic pain was one of the most common complaints at VA hospitals. The Department of Veterans Affairs later released figures that confirmed that 60 percent of vets returning from Afghanistan and Iraq suffered from chronic pain. Fifty percent of veterans from previous deployments had the same complaint. Purdue created separate publications and pamphlets for vets and later contracted with a decorated combat veteran for a book that urged veterans returning from combat zones to ask their physicians for opioids and lobby hesitant prescribers. Opioids were not addictive, claimed the book, unless someone was "predisposed" because substance abuse ran in their family.[73]

The author learned that there was some discussion inside Purdue that the high rate among returning veterans of substance abuse (estimated at 20 percent) might make them more vulnerable to OxyContin addiction.[74] While the focus on veterans later paid off financially for Purdue, it did translate into an addiction rate for veterans much higher than other OxyContin patients. And ultimately, they were twice as likely as the national average to die of a drug overdose.

Aside from geriatrics and veterans, Purdue had a catchall category, those who had never tried opioids. Marketing dubbed them "opioid naive." The detail team called them OVS (opioid virgins). It was a huge market. Purdue was prepared to distribute hundreds of thousands of brochures that suggested OxyContin could treat many different conditions (none of them expressly approved by the FDA). One of its most popular was "How You Can Be a Partner Against Pain and Gain Control Over Your Own Pain." It suggested that patients discuss with their physicians if OxyContin was the right remedy for backaches, migraines, sore knees, even tooth extractions.

The second-generation Sackler directors knew that the detail team's success could make or break the drug. That did not mean, however, that they planned to rely only on direct sales. Purdue authorized the development of modern promotion strategies to coincide with the launch. OxyContin Physicians Television Network was an online video service in which paid medical consultants hyped the drug.[75] Purdue set aside a budget large enough for dispatching hundreds of physicians across the country encouraging their medical colleagues to learn about the advantages of dispensing OxyContin for chronic pain. It also funded half-day courses aimed at general practitioners. Purdue needed them to write a lot of OxyContin prescriptions if the drug was to become a blockbuster.[76]

Online promotion was also a priority. One website, In the Face of Pain, targeted health care professionals looking for information about pain treatment. The content was presented as unbiased professional testimonials, but Purdue did not disclose that it had paid $250,000 to the eleven featured "advocates."[77] Another website, Partners Against Pain, conducted a poll of a thousand chronic pain sufferers. A third of the respondents ranked their pain as "debilitating" while 15 percent said it was so unbearable that they had contemplated suicide.[78] Partners Against Pain was where Purdue mastered the art of disguising straightforward public relations as a public service about pain management. The company's Pain Assessment Scale was the site's most visited page. Another page claimed that pure opioid agonists such as oxycodone, morphine, heroin, or fentanyl had "no ceiling dose."[79] That meant that a patient in severe pain will always get additional relief from higher doses of opioid painkillers; there is no analgesic ceiling.[80] The downside at those high doses is an increased possibility of death since the opioids suppress the respiratory system.[81] Purdue did not list that on Partners Against Pain and internal company files reveal it realized consumers were likely to misinterpret "no ceiling dose" to mean that opioids were safe at high doses.[82] (It eventually spent $8 million subsidizing Partners Against Pain.)*[83]

As the date approached for OxyContin to go on sale, Purdue moved its promotion campaign into high gear. Some of the strategies were old-school ones developed by Arthur decades earlier and that had since become standard for drug companies rolling out highly anticipated medications. They included slick brochures, newsletters, magazine inserts, flashy mailings to doctors, big ad spreads in medical journals, and sponsored programs at medical schools. The detail team got ready to distribute millions of dollars in Oxy-branded swag to doctors, pain clinics, hospitals, and nursing homes in their sales territories. There was everything from luggage tags to baseball caps and sweatshirts, notepads, binders and pens, coffee mugs with heat-activated sensors, even stuffed toys for children. Two favorites, for which Purdue had to place reorders repeatedly, was a pedometer stamped: "OxyContin—A Step in the Right Direction," and a CD, "Swing in the Right Direction with OxyContin," in which a couple danced over a giant Oxy logo.[84]†[85]

---

* Software programmers added a feature to Partners Against Pain that made it easier for patients to find a local "pain specialist." Referrals were provided based on the patient's address. What the patients did not know was that the website was coded to display the contact information only for doctors who were heavy prescribers of narcotic painkillers (information Purdue knew from its IMS data files). Before OxyContin's release, Purdue had compiled a database of tens of thousands of patients who were searching for pain specialists. That became part of a special promotion file Purdue aggressively utilized once the pill was on sale.

† Some gifts by sales reps in other drug companies became the examples of what *not* to do. A Pfizer detail man once paid a doctor an "unrestricted educational grant" of $35,000. Both knew it was so the doctor, a top prescriber, could build a swimming pool in his backyard. The larger debate was whether doctors were unduly influenced by modest drug company gifts. Studies reveal that physicians who accept perks and gifts are more likely to write prescriptions for that company. That is a statistical coincidence, claim defenders of the gifts policy. Bert Spilker, a senior VP of the drug industry trade group PhRMA, wrote in an editorial in *Health Affairs*, "I find it hard to imagine that any of my colleagues would compromise professional concern for their patients . . . [by] 'selling their souls' for a pack of M&M candies and a few sandwiches and doughnuts." Social scientists who have studied drug detail teams believe that even when the

All that money was well spent. A later study in New York State demonstrated that for every dollar in promotional goods, entertainment, or travel that a doctor received "he or she prescribes at least $10 of additional opioids." Purdue expected that the more they spent and lavished on high-prescribing doctors, the greater the return on their money. That proved to be right beyond the most optimistic internal forecasts. The New York study showed that the "top 1 percent of Oxy prescribing doctors got 80 percent of the money paid by Purdue."[86] A study published in *JAMA* later showed that even something as simple as buying a meal for a doctor resulted in increased opioid prescribing.[87]

A week before OxyContin went on sale, Russell Portenoy and Dr. Ronald Kanner published a 357-page book titled *Pain Management: Theory and Practice*.[88] Purdue had been expecting it. A dozen well-known physicians, in specialties from rheumatology, anesthesia, behavioral medicine, surgery, psychiatry, and rehabilitation, contributed to what became recognized as the definitive guide to the latest research about diagnosing pain and how to treat it. Opioids, they concluded, were unfairly pilloried because of their "association with drug abuse."[89] Citing 176 studies and journal articles to support their thesis, Portenoy and Kanner methodically dismissed concerns about long-term opioid use. "Misconceptions about tolerance and dependence are common and reflect the stigma associated with opioid drugs."[90]

While Portenoy and Kanner admitted there were "unfortunately, no systematic studies of the addiction liability associated with the long-term medical use of opioid drugs," they were confident their review of "the evidence suggests that the risk of addiction is extremely low in the typical patient with no prior history of drug abuse who is prescribed an opioid for a painful medical condition."[91] * [92]

The American Pain Society followed the Portenoy and Kanner book with a pamphlet, "Treatment of Pain at the End of Life." It drew the startling conclusion that distressed patients would not turn as frequently to suicide if opioid painkillers were dispensed more freely.[93]

---

gifts are modest, they create a subconscious sense of debt for the physician, one they repay by writing more prescriptions for the sales rep's drug.

* Portenoy and Kanner explained away one study that reported a high addiction rate of 19 percent. They contended it was from a pain management program in which many patients had "a prior history of drug abuse, personality disorder, younger age, and chaotic family life."

43

"$$$$$$$$$$$$$ IT'S BONUS TIME IN THE NEIGHBORHOOD!"

"New Hope for Millions of Americans Suffering from Persistent Pain" was the headline on the May 31, 1996, press release from Purdue that announced the on-sale date of OxyContin.[1] "The first and only 12-hour oxycodone" was heralded as "a significant advance in the treatment of persistent pain." OxyContin was, according to the release, the end of patients enduring "anxious 'clock-watching' when pain must be controlled over long periods." (No regulations required that Purdue disclose that a third of patients in clinical trials did not get twelve hours of pain relief.)[2] Pushing the limits of the conditions for which the FDA had approved the drug, Purdue claimed Oxy was for "moderate to severe pain lasting more than a few days . . . such as the pain associated with arthritis, cancer, injuries, lower back problems, and other musculoskeletal problems."[3] According to the press release, "drug dependence is treatable . . . and 'addiction' to opioids legitimately used in the management of pain is very rare."

The detail team fanned out across the country for its sales blitzkrieg. The Sacklers knew that money was the best motivator for sales representatives. Purdue made it simple. Most drug companies paid their reps based on how many prescriptions the physicians they had visited later wrote. For OxyContin the sales force's compensation was based on the dollar amount of the prescriptions dispensed by the doctors each had visited. The IMS Cornerstone 3.0 software Purdue bought eliminated the difficulty of figuring out if a sales rep had influenced a doctor to write more scrips. Through the 1980s, a physician's dispensing data were a quarterly snapshot. By the time of OxyContin's release, drug companies tracked the exact number of scrips written daily.

In high-volume states, salesmen visited each "core dispenser" a minimum of two hundred times annually.[4] Some called daily. Each one-on-one visit cost Purdue about $200.[5] That translated into $40,000 for *each* top-tier doctor, an amount that added into the millions. The Massachusetts attorney general in a complaint filed in 2019 against Purdue and the Sackler-family directors noted that "Purdue did not spend $40,000 per doctor so sales reps could watch doctors write prescriptions that they were already going to write anyway. Instead, Purdue paid to lobby these doctors because Purdue knew its reps would convince them to put more patients on opioids, at higher doses, for longer periods. Those extra prescriptions paid back Purdue's investment many times over."[6]

Carl Elliott, a doctor and professor of bioethics, has reviewed decades of the changing relationships between drug reps and physicians. He noted that over a five-year period starting in 1996, the year OxyContin went on sale, the number of industry detail reps doubled to ninety thousand. This era introduced what old-timers disparaged as Pharma Ken and Pharma Barbie, attractive young reps whose pharmaceutical know-how was not as important as their ability to sell. For drugs exceeding $200 million annually in sales, which OxyContin achieved, the average return was tenfold for every dollar spent on the detail team.[7]

Purdue's revised compensation meant that the sales team, especially top performers, were among the highest paid in the pharmaceutical industry. Large bonuses sometimes doubled a sales rep's annual salary and became a much sought-after incentive for generating the largest OxyContin sales.[8] Purdue had fulfilled a promise set out in an internal memo to the "Entire Field Force" just after the drug went on sale. Employing an analogy from *The Wizard of Oz*, it assured the detail team that for those reps who sold the most, "A pot of gold awaits you 'Over the Rainbow.'"[9] Two months later, a memo that reminded sales reps to encourage the more profitable, higher-dose pills was titled: "$$$$$$$$$$$$$ It's Bonus Time in the Neighborhood!"[10]

Purdue was not alone in empowering its sales force. Many of the biggest companies had long capped how much reps could earn. When Anthony Wild, a former Sandoz chemist, became Parke-Davis president in 1995, one of his first directives was to remove the limits on detail team bonuses. "Why not let them get rich?" he answered to some long-serving executives who questioned the decision. Wild's view was that the more the sales team made, the more Parke-Davis earned. When he announced the decision at a San Francisco company conference, "the sales force went nuts!" he later recounted.[11]

It took little time before the sales team realized there was more profit for Purdue and more money for them by pushing higher doses of OxyContin. When it first went on sale, there were three strengths: 10, 20, and 40 milligrams. An 80 mg tablet was released a month later (15, 30, 60, and 160 mg would arrive in a few years).[12] Purdue's production costs across the board were virtually the same since oxycodone, the active ingredient, was cheap to manufacture. However, it charged more for each higher strength.[13] On average, a bottle of 20 mg pills cost twice as much as the 10 mg variety. Eighty milligrams were about seven times more expensive than the low-dose. If a patient took 20 mg pills twice a week, internal documents put Purdue's profit at less than $40. The same patient prescribed 80 mg pills twice a week returned over $200 to the company, a 450 percent increase (that profit exceeded $600 a bottle in another five years).[14] Prescribing physicians typically had no idea what Oxy cost, nor did most care. Since they did not pay for the drugs, they passed the worry to patients and their medical insurance companies.[15] * [16]

Purdue created a campaign it called "Individualize the Dose" to help the detail team push the strongest doses. Sales reps told doctors that the company's own studies showed that instead of starting patients on low strengths to see if that worked, it was best to start on a medium to higher dose. That way the drug would relieve pain faster and allow the patient to stop using it quicker. Moreover, in any instances in which doctors reported that they were dispensing OxyContin three or even four times daily because their patients were not getting the promised twelve hours of pain relief, sales representatives assured doctors that higher doses would make the drug last longer.[17] The detail team had been instructed not to ever suggest more than twice-a-day dosing. Purdue feared that would be the fastest way for the company to run afoul of the FDA. And insurance companies and hospitals that had agreed to

---

* Twenty years later, when the CDC pressed for explicit warnings and voluntary prescription limits on the highest doses, Purdue calculated how much money it would lose if physicians followed the recommendations.

cover OxyContin had done so on the basis it was a twelve-hour drug. If it proved otherwise, insurance companies might stop paying for it.[18]* [19] The higher doses, Purdue representatives assured physicians, could be dispensed even to people who had never used opioids, all without adverse effects. The field reps contended that the higher-dose pills were no more likely to cause addiction.[20]

That was not true. Internal documents later revealed that Purdue's detail team knew that stronger doses carried a much higher likelihood of dependence, addiction, even respiratory suppression that could be lethal. While the company's press releases claimed that "dose was not a risk factor for opioid overdose," internal communications are replete with references to the dangers of "dose-related overdose."[21]

Besides encouraging physicians to dispense higher doses, Purdue ran a parallel campaign to extend OxyContin's treatment period for as long as possible. Sales reps told doctors that a common error was putting patients on the drug for too short a period since that resulted in a rebound in pain.[22] Longer treatment was a gold mine for Purdue and the sales reps. A patient given 80 mg pills twice a day brought Purdue $200 profit. The company earned $11,000 if that patient stayed on the drug for a year. Internal correspondence reveals that patients were 30 times more likely to die of an overdose if they took OxyContin for three months, 46 times more likely after six to eleven months, and 51 times more likely to die if they remained on OxyContin more than a year.[23]

All the aggressive promotion took place without any public objection from the FDA. Although the FDA does not have to preapprove ads, pharmaceutical companies are required to submit all promotional material to the agency before using it. At the time, the office assigned that responsibility was understaffed and overwhelmed. Thirty-nine employees oversaw some 35,000 promotional items annually.[24] In the case of OxyContin, the FDA would not complain to Purdue for two years, and when it finally did so, it was about a video distributed to doctors that had not been sent first to the agency. Purdue claimed it

---

* In 2004, Purdue paid $10 million to settle a lawsuit filed by the West Virginia attorney general. The suit demanded reimbursement for the extra costs incurred by the state on its prescription benefit programs for the elderly and poor. Purdue's twelve-hour dosing claim, contended the attorney general, was deceptive marketing. In the settlement, Purdue admitted no wrongdoing.

was an oversight and submitted it. The FDA did not review that video for another four years, at which time it ordered it withdrawn for minimizing the risks of OxyContin and overstating its benefits. There was no penalty for Purdue having made the false claims, just a promise not to do it again.

As the sales team encouraged doctors to extend their prescriptions of OxyContin, the company introduced a savings card that encouraged chronic pain patients to at least try the drug. It offered a substantial discount on their first prescription (later it offered one free refill).[25] A long-term Purdue planning document concluded that "more patients remain on OxyContin after 90 days." The card got them started. It worked better than even the company's most optimistic forecast for its return on investment. For each million dollars Purdue spent on the freebies, the patients who tried the drug and stayed with it brought in $4.28 million in additional sales.[26]

The same year OxyContin went on sale, Purdue hired Dr. J. David Haddox. As the company's medical director, Haddox became the public face for Oxy at physicians' conferences and training courses. He reassured his colleagues that the risk of addiction was only "one-half of one percent," something that was "exquisitely rare."[27] Many who heard Haddox make the case for OxyContin were not pain specialists but general practitioners who had not paid close attention to the opioid reevaluation movement. For them, his presentation was new and persuasive.

Haddox also developed a separate strategy that would have made Arthur Sackler proud. Some in the detail team were not sure how to handle instances in which physicians raised the possibility that one or more of their patients on OxyContin might be addicted. Most doctors, Haddox told them, misinterpreted pseudoaddiction as true addiction.[28] Those doctors were likely just observing their patients' reaction to severe pain and the stress of failed treatments. The only way to eliminate pseudoaddiction was to eliminate the underlying pain. That meant whenever physicians thought patients showed signs of addiction, the sales representatives recommended they stay with the drug and increase the dose.[29] That persuaded a surprising number of doctors. For physicians who were reluctant to sometimes double the dose, some dispensed the same strength but increased the frequency.

One topic forbidden in Purdue was what might happen if someone scraped off Oxy's patented coating or crushed the pill. Purdue had conducted its own tests before OxyContin's release and knew what would happen. When someone bypassed the extended release shell, about 70 percent of the oxycodone, as opposed to the time released 10 percent, went straight to the brain. That produced a euphoric high that rivaled heroin.[30] The FDA thought it had addressed the matter by requiring that Purdue put an all-caps warning on the prescription insert: "TABLETS ARE TO BE SWALLOWED WHOLE, AND ARE NOT TO BE BROKEN, CHEWED OR CRUSHED. TAKING BROKEN, CHEWED OR CRUSHED TABLETS COULD LEAD TO THE RAPID RELEASE AND ABSORPTION OF A POTENTIALLY TOXIC DOSE OF OXYCODONE."[31] It took the Centers for Disease Control twenty years to determine that was a deadly flaw in the pill's design.[32]

Although there were no supporting studies or empirical evidence, the FDA also had allowed Purdue to claim on the drug's insert that OxyContin's delayed absorption was "believed to reduce the abuse liability."[33] It was the first time the FDA had approved such an assertion. It accepted Purdue's theory that since drug addicts needed a narcotics rush, they would always want fast-acting painkillers such as Vicodin and Percocet. "That contention proved disastrously wrong," later wrote Barry Meier, the *New York Times* reporter who covered Purdue and OxyContin.[34]

Purdue realized that the FDA language was invaluable and a presales marketing memo said it might serve as the drug's "principal selling tool."[35] No wonder Richard Sackler was so confident that he promised his family directors and Purdue executives that "the launch of OxyContin Tablets will be followed by a blizzard of prescriptions that will bury the competition. The prescription blizzard will be so deep, dense, and white."[36] An initial marketing plan set forth a goal that seemed like hyperbole but demonstrated how ambitious the plans were for Oxy: "Purdue Pharma's corporate goal is to be one of the Top 10 pharmaceutical companies by 2010."

Richard Sackler was right. OxyContin was a big hit.[37] Doctors wrote more than half a million prescriptions for non-cancer-related pain in its first year. Dr. Curtis Wright, the FDA official who had approved OxyContin for sale, left his government post and joined Purdue the year after it was on sale. His hire likely added to the perception that OxyContin was on its way to changing how physicians treated pain. Two years after it went on sale Oxy returned a remarkable 80 percent of Purdue's profits and was double MS Contin's top revenue year.[38] Sales soared from $48 million in 1996 to $1.1 billion in 2000, the first drug in Purdue's history to join the pharmaceutical industry's small billion-dollar-in-sales club.[39] By then, Purdue's detail team was earning over $40 million in year-end bonuses.[40]

44

TALKING STOMACHS AND DEAD PRESIDENTS

A watershed moment in the pharmaceutical industry came in 1997 when the FDA made a controversial decision to lift restrictions on direct-to-consumer advertising (DTCA) by drug companies.[1] (The U.S. and New Zealand are the only countries that allow it.)[2] Arthur Sackler had not lived to see it become a reality. He had found loopholes, mostly prepackaged promotional write-ups placed into the health sections of papers and magazines as if they were news. Sackler had also refined the art of running eye-catching, foldout inserts in national magazines that were likely to end up in the waiting rooms of physicians nationwide. That ad was intended for the doctor, he said when challenged once by a Senate panel. If the physician put the magazine into the patient waiting room, the inserts always had perforated edges, so the doctor could tear it from the magazine. Sackler knew, of course, that no physician could be bothered ripping out drug ads from *Time*, *Newsweek*, *Family Circle*, *National Geographic*, and *Life*.[3]

Until 1962, the Federal Trade Commission had power over drug ads.[4] That year, the Kefauver Amendments passed to the FDA the jurisdiction over pharma advertising.[5] Direct-to-consumer ads were not an issue to which the FDA paid attention. The concept seemed far-fetched and dangerous. Policymakers believed that consumers did not have the medical expertise to make informed decisions about prescription drugs. Ads would cause confusion and might persuade many to ask for a drug based simply on clever promotion. Only doctors, it was thought, were smart enough to evaluate and cut through overhyped advertisements. When some studies during the 1970s revealed that physicians were not much better than patients at making sense of pharmaceutical advertising, it oddly bolstered the case against allowing the industry to advertise to consumers.[6]

It took until 1969 for the FDA to issue its first comprehensive advertisement regulations. All prescription ads had to be a "true statement of information" that summarized a "fair balance" of the drug's effectiveness versus risk.[7] The FDA checked all ads, 90 percent of which were run in medical journals, to make certain they were not misleading or unbalanced.[8] There was no mention of advertisements to the public.[9] There were, however, a couple of small paragraphs that attracted little attention but became important years later. According to the 1969 regs, all ads by phone, radio, or television (there were no TV ads then for drugs) had to include the medication's side effects "in the audio and visual parts of the presentation." However, if the drug company could make an "adequate provision" to somehow pass along the side effect information separate from the ad, that was allowed. "Adequate provision" was not defined.[10] The second part that seemed unimportant but later proved key were so-called "reminder advertisements," in which a drug company did not have to mention side effects if it omitted the brand name or did not make claims about safety or efficacy.

Beginning in June 1970, the door to DTCA opened a little with efforts by consumer advocacy groups. The four-year-old National Welfare Rights Organization, an activist group dedicated to expanding government support for the poor, issued the first ever list of "patients' rights." Most of the twenty-six "rights" focused on privacy and confidentiality, nondiscrimination for medical services, and community representation on the governing boards of hospitals. Its core message was that patients should be fully informed about their diagnoses and treatment options.[11] Two years later the American Hospital Association, representing most of the nation's hospitals, relied on the language that came from the National Welfare group and adopted the first Patient Bill of Rights. That kicked off a wave of patients' rights statutes at the state level.[12]

Several consumer groups, led by Ralph Nader's Public Citizen and the Health Research Group, petitioned the FDA in 1975 and urged that the agency order that drug labels and inserts be included in all prescriptions dispensed to patients.[13] Those package inserts, over which the FDA and drug firms often battled, were only included by pharma companies to pharmacists. Just as it was theoretically the obligation of a physician to know all the risks and benefits before writing a prescription, pharmacists were supposed to summarize verbally all the warning labels and inserts for the patient.

The same year that consumer groups asked the FDA for the right to the drug's inserts, the nation had its first major "right to die" case. Twenty-one-year-old Karen Ann Quinlan had lapsed into a coma after mixing Valium, Quaaludes, and alcohol. The family sued after doctors refused to turn off her respirator at her father's request. The often heated ensuing public debate was resolved when the New Jersey Supreme Court ruled for the family and the hospital removed the life support the following year. The debate over Quinlan fueled the growth of patients' rights movements (she lived another ten years in a vegetative state).

As the Quinlan case had wound through the courts, the FDA held the first of three public hearings about "patient-packet inserts" (PPI). After three years of study, it issued a regulation requiring inserts in every dispensed prescription. Pharma companies expected that ruling since the public testimony and the questions and comments by FDA officials made it clear the government watchdog was in favor of "patients' rights." The Pharmaceutical Manufacturers Association immediately filed an administrative appeal and contended that the requirement was costly and an unfair burden since drug companies already provided that identical information to pharmacists. That prompted a one-year delay, until 1979, after which the FDA modified its regulation and limited it only to ten classes of prescription drugs.[14]

Ronald Reagan had only been president for four months when he appointed a new FDA director, Dr. Arthur Hayes Jr., in April 1981. Hayes took another look at the patients' package insert rules. Drug firms opposed it. Besides the costs, they argued it was an unnecessary government interference. Physicians were also against it, contending it interfered with the "sanctity of the doctor-patient relationship."[15] Doctors wanted the discretion to decide which adverse effects to disclose, contending that as medical professionals they knew their patients best and that not all side effects were likely. (The FDA later determined that doctors reported only the most serious side effects, sometimes as few as one percent of what they observed.)

Hayes canceled the patients' package insert program in 1982. The FDA replaced it with a pharma-recommended plan by which the companies voluntarily distributed all required information to patients.[16] A British drug company, Boots, had a short run of TV spots in 1981 for its generic competitor to Upjohn's Motrin. It was the first drug ad on American television. Merck entered the new marketing arena the following year, running a series of "are you aware of the pneumonia vaccine?" ads. Aftermarket research showed that only a small percentage of adults over sixty-five who should get the vaccine even knew about it.

FDA officials were split about television drug ads. One contingent thought that the more information the consumer had, the less likelihood they could be easily misled. Others countered that the 1969 rules had not seriously weighed the benefits and downsides of allowing drug companies to promote their products directly to consumers over TV. Twenty professional medical associations opposed direct television ads. In a poll taken by the AMA, 84 percent of physicians thought it was a bad idea.[17]

Commissioner Hayes leaned toward okaying DTCA. His only hesitation was whether adding oversight of direct-to-consumer ads to the long list of FDA responsibilities might be too much for the agency to handle. Its 1982 budget was $329 million, while prescription drug sales in America topped $15 billion annually. That did not include the approximately 300,000 heavily promoted over-the-counter products under FDA jurisdiction. A quarter of all FDA employees were in non-drug oversight such as cosmetics, food, medical devices, diagnostic products, and veterinary remedies.[18] Ronald Reagan's 1981 budget cuts had hit the FDA hard.[19]

Democrats had picked up twenty-six seats in the House in the 1980 election and had a solid majority. Michigan congressman John Dingell, chairman of the House Subcommittee on Oversight and Investigations, set public hearings to examine DTCA.[20] Hayes ordered a moratorium on any direct-to-consumer advertising until the subcommittee issued recommendations.

When the hearings got under way, few seemed enthusiastic about DTCA. While there was no surprise that doctors overwhelmingly opposed it, what raised eyebrows were FDA-sponsored studies demonstrating most consumers wanted more drug data but did not think that drug advertisements were the best way to get it. Almost two thirds believed it would be difficult to near impossible to evaluate the risks of a drug in a thirty-second television spot.[21] When asked if they felt confident to make an informed decision about whether to take a prescription medication, three quarters said no. Two thirds said they doubted they could tell whether a drug ad was misleading.[22] The underlying loss of faith in the drug industry made many Americans skeptical about how pharma might package drugs in advertisements. In a 1966 poll, three quarters of Americans had a "great deal of confidence" in both medicine and pharmaceuticals. That had fallen by half as the DTCA hearings got underway (it bottomed out at less than a quarter of the public by 1990).[23]

Leading consumer groups, from the American Association for Retired Persons (AARP) to the Health Research Group, asked for a permanent ban on all direct drug advertising in print, radio, and television. Consumers, they contended, deserved more information about the medications they used, but not filtered through a Madison Avenue sales pitch. Spending money on consumer ads could raise drug prices, warned the AARP, and the public would be susceptible to thinking minor drug changes were important ones.

The pharmaceutical industry surprised the subcommittee. Its executives were unified in opposition. Schering's senior vice president thought it "is not in the public interest"; Upjohn's chairman said "it would be detrimental to the pharmaceutical industry and, more importantly, a potentially disruptive element in our medical delivery system"; Eli Lilly's executive vice president said that "drugs embody a complex set of factors," and direct advertising was "both unwise and inappropriate."[24] The only industry in favor, of course, was the advertising industry. Ad execs tried turning the "lack of sophistication" consensus about the public into a reason for DTCA. It would give the public much more exposure to drug information, they contended. The most creative argument pushed by Medicine Avenue was that a more informed consumer might even help spot diseases earlier.

Dingell's committee took more than two years to complete its final report, "Prescription Drug Advertising to Consumers." By the time it was published in September 1984, Arthur Hayes had been replaced at the FDA with a less industry-friendly commissioner, Dr. Frank Young, the dean of the University of Rochester's medical school.

The subcommittee's report concluded that "the perils of popularizing prescriptions" and "creating new consumer demand" would lead to "unnecessary prescriptions . . . and the use of potent drugs by those who do not need them." Its bottom line was that "if the industry wants a better educated public" there were better ways than through product advertising.[25] To most industry observers, that seemed the end of drug companies advertising directly to consumers.

In 1985, Commissioner Young startled just about everybody by lifting the moratorium on consumer ads. He thought it was only a symbolic change. Young directed that any ads to consumers had to meet the same legal requirement as when pharma advertised to physicians.[26] Over time the "brief summary" of the drug's label had become anything but brief. Young thought that made television ads impossible. Only in print might it be possible to include required warning information in a tiny font.

Over the next five years, only twenty-four drug products were pitched to consumers. Most, like Merck's series to inform seniors about the pneumonia vaccine, concentrated on passing along information, not on a hard sell. Young had promised pharma he planned on taking another look at loosening the ad restrictions, so long as it seemed they were helpful for the public. Before he could do that, Young got tied up in a scandal at the FDA. Congress ordered the Department of Health and Human Services inspector general in 1988 to investigate reports of corruption in the generic approval process. It exposed a cabal of approval officers who accepted hundreds of thousands of dollars in gifts and cash in return for faster drug approvals. In some instances the generic makers had falsified the information to demonstrate they were the biological equivalents of the brand name. Others waited until their drugs were approved and then switched to cheaper coloring agents, fillers, and extenders. That altered their chemical stability of other drugs and made them less effective.[27] The Justice Department eventually obtained convictions or guilty pleas from five FDA employees—three approval officers and two chemists—and twenty-four generic company executives, on multiple counts of fraud, racketeering, and obstruction of justice. The scandal prompted major changes in the generic review process, including uniform guidelines and a backup system intended to catch wayward approvals. It also cost Young his job.[28]

In November 1990, President George H. W. Bush picked David Kessler as the new FDA commissioner. He took charge in the wake of the generics corruption scandal. The FDA was in disarray and veteran employees demoralized. The agency was still coping with the aftershocks of the Reagan-era budget cuts and seemed adrift. Kessler, who had a medical degree from Harvard and law degree from the University of Chicago, was a relentless advocate that the FDA should proactively use its expansive powers to protect Americans from dangerous drugs and reckless pharmaceutical and food companies. He was persuasive, likable, and telegenic. Kessler's frequent appearances on news programs made him for most Americans the face of a previously anonymous bureaucracy. His tenure was, as *The New York Times* described it, "tumultuous."[29]

Kessler was inexhaustible in politicking on behalf of the FDA. And he seemed particularly energized when he was on the attack during a fight with Big Pharma or Big Tobacco. His critics thought he was a power-hungry self-aggrandizer whose naked ambition would be his undoing.[30] However, all admitted he was smart. In the six years before his appointment as FDA commissioner, he taught at both New York's Albert Einstein College of Medicine and Columbia Law School at the same time he ran a 431-bed teaching hospital.

He was in office five months when he showed how serious he was about getting tougher on the accuracy of food labels. Federal agents swooped into a Minnesota warehouse and seized two thousand cases of Procter & Gamble's "Fresh Choice" orange juice because it "was misleading since it was made from concentrate." Kessler told a food industry conference, "The time has come to end the din of mixed messages and partial truths on food labels in this country."[31]

His FDA predecessors had always amicably resolved such labeling matters by correspondence. They never contemplated going after a $3 billion food and beverage company just to "make a point." But for Kessler, that was the point—only by going after a giant like P&G would the rest of the industry pay attention.

The moratorium he supervised on silicone breast implants kicked off thousands of lawsuits that ultimately forced Dow Corning to file bankruptcy.*[32] The following year he set the supplement and vitamin industry on fire by trying to regulate their products for safety and efficacy (Congress put an end to any possible meddling by the FDA by passing the Dietary Health and Education Act of 1994; it explicitly separated supplements from drugs and food additives). And he caused a furor when he tried extending the FDA's jurisdiction to the promotion and labeling of tobacco.[33]

When it came to the question of direct-to-consumer drug ads, Kessler realized that his predecessors had kicked it down the road. He

---

* Three independent government reviews later concluded that there was no link between silicone breast implants and any autoimmune illness. The moratorium was lifted after sixteen years.

wanted to update the FDA's 1969 ad rules. He instinctively tilted toward consumer protection and was skeptical that slickly packaged Madison Avenue ads could ever be genuinely informative. Kessler believed they were just another tool in pharma's promotional arsenal to make Americans buy more medications.

He did not favor an outright ban without studying it more. Kessler was sensitive that patients wanted more transparent medical data. He did not want the FDA to appear out of step with the changing times by denying information to consumers. A couple of thousand patient advocacy groups, most of them disease-specific, lobbied Congress for everything from rights to privacy over medical records to increased research funding for diseases to easier-to-understand consent forms for surgery.[34] And being a more informed patient was undoubtedly getting easier. America Online, Microsoft Network, and CompuServe were all fairly rudimentary online services when they got under way in the 1980s, but by the mid-1990s, surveys showed that consumers were searching for medical information online and visiting their doctors armed with a list of questions.[35]

Kessler increased the budget of the department that regulated drug advertising. In November 1994, any reform strategy he had envisioned was derailed. The Republicans swept to power in Congress. The new Speaker of the House, Newt Gingrich, attacked Kessler and the FDA and charged that it deliberately failed to approve good drugs and promising medical devices. That discouraged innovation, charged Gingrich, who called the FDA the "number 1 job killer." As for Kessler, Gingrich called him "a bully and a thug."[36] Gingrich even floated a plan that would have privatized the drug approval process and taken it away from the FDA.

A growing number of pharmaceutical firms wanted to run more direct-to-consumer ads. They were frustrated by the 1969 rules that had not contemplated television. What had prevented TV ads was the requirement that companies pass along a substantial part of the drug's warning label. They were so long that it would eat up most of the airtime. Pharma firms thought that fundamental limitation meant any campaign would be ineffective.

In 1996, Schering-Plough developed a groundbreaking television advertisement for Claritin, its just released prescription allergy medication. The thirty-second spot had attractive people skipping through a field of flowers. A man and woman talked over each other to an upbeat soundtrack: "Claritin. It's time. It's time. Don't wait another minute for Claritin. Claritin, I'll ask my doctor. It's time to see your doctor. At last, a clear day is here. I want to know more about Claritin. Ask your doctor for a trial of Claritin and for free information and a $5 coupon toward a prescription for Claritin. Call 1-800-CLARITIN."

Schering-Plough's ad had everyone asking, "What is Claritin?" A poll by the *New York Post* showed most people thought it was an antidepressant since everyone seemed so happy. That spot received accolades from Madison Avenue. It also challenged the FDA. Would Kessler shut the door for all direct ads or would Schering's spot force him to loosen the regulations?

While an FDA special committee considered that, Kessler surprised all of Washington by announcing his resignation in January 1997. He said it was for "family reasons." That was true. His wife, Paulette, had implored him for months to quit. Watching him get "ripped to shreds for all the negative editorials, it gets wearing," she told reporters.[37]

With Kessler gone, drug companies that had opposed direct-to-consumer ads suddenly lobbied the FDA to relax the regulations. Upjohn and Pfizer led the charge. The successful introduction of Rogaine for Upjohn and Viagra for Pfizer had changed their minds about the potential value of advertising to consumers. Several other pharma firms had well-known drugs—Tagamet, Zantac, and Pepcid—that were about to go off patent and then on sale over the counter.[38]

In the summer of 1997, the FDA made a landmark ruling. Instead of banning direct to consumer ads, the agency relaxed the guidelines and made it easier for television advertisements. There was no longer a requirement to explain the warning label. The ads would have to direct viewers to a toll-free number, a website, even a magazine ad.[39] The pent-up demand in the pharmaceutical industry for TV advertising exploded. "Ask your doctor," one of the lines from the breakthrough Claritin ads, became a widely used tagline in many of the new spots.

Veteran Madison Avenue ad men recall that the drug companies inundated their agencies with demands to get their products on TV. The FDA ruling, however, had caught the advertisers off guard. Even agencies such as Arthur Sackler's McAdams or William Frohlich's shop were not sure how to adapt their traditional print and direct mail campaigns to a quite different medium. Since buying ad time was so expensive, no company wanted to pay for agencies to learn on the job. Still, pharma was shelling out a lot of money to pitch its best products on TV. Just before Kessler left the FDA in 1997, there was about $35 million a year in DTCA ads. A year after the rule change, it was $1.17 billion, almost all in television campaigns.[40] The evidence that the torrent of money had caught the ad industry unprepared is that in the first few years there were a lot of bad ads.[41] There were talking stomachs, Abe Lincoln at a playground with beavers, Andrew Jackson praising a wonder ointment, even eerie animated characters that morphed into toenail fungus.

Consumer activists complained that the ads relied on celebrities and were heavy on imagery and light on information. In the battle over elevated cholesterol, for instance, Bristol-Myers used Kirk Douglas, Sylvester Stallone, and Angela Bassett for Pravachol, Merck relied on Atlanta Falcons head coach Dan Reeves for Zocor, and Pfizer picked Olympic figure skater Peggy Fleming for cholesterol-lowering Lipitor. Football great Joe Montana pitched Novartis's Lotrel for hypertension against Jack Nicklaus for King's Altace. Debbie Reynolds had the overactive bladder market to herself as the face of Pfizer's Detrol.[42] In the 2004 Super Bowl, two of the three erectile dysfunction drugs faced off against one another, one with ex–Chicago Bears coach Mike Ditka and the other featuring former senator Bob Dole.

Ad companies realized that sometimes celebrityhood gave the appearance of authority and expertise consumers wanted. Bayer's sales of branded aspirin increased by 30 percent after it hired America's most trusted family doctor: television's Marcus Welby. Robert Young, who had played Welby for seven hit seasons, appeared in his white lab coat and gave the disclaimer, "I'm not a doctor, but I play one on TV."

Schering-Plough signed *Good Morning America*'s co-host Joan Lunden, herself an allergy sufferer, for a $40 million Claritin campaign. She appeared in ads reading copy that made it appear as if she were simply the likable morning anchor presenting the news. Claritin's sales soared 50 percent that first year, to $2.3 billion (it stayed over $2 billion annually until it lost its patent in 2002).[43]

Pfizer mastered the new medium for Lipitor, its cholesterol-lowering statin that became part of its product lineup after it bought Warner-Lambert in 2001 for $90 billion.[44] Although Lipitor was late to the cholesterol-lowering drug market—Merck's Mevacor and Zocor were billion-dollar drugs for almost a decade by then—Pfizer set aside a stunning $258 million for promotion and hired Robert Jarvik as its spokesman. *Time* called Jarvik a "national hero" when it put him on its 1982 cover after the first successful transplant into a patient of a self-contained artificial heart. The Lipitor ads portrayed Jarvik as the inventor of the artificial heart and as a busy medical practitioner who dispensed Lipitor to his patients. They ended with him disclosing that he used the drug himself. Lipitor was on its way to being the pharmaceutical industry's most successful drug ever, with more than $15 billion in sales in a single year. The problem revealed in a later congressional investigation was that Jarvik, it turned out, had graduated from medical school but never got a license to practice. He was not a cardiologist and never prescribed the drug to anyone. He had taken it himself, but only briefly. And in some ads in which he was shown paddling a canoe, it was a body double. He was one of several medical engineers responsible for the artificial heart, not its inventor. By then, Pfizer had run the ads for five years.[45]

AstraZeneca decided it did not need to pay a celebrity or package someone as an authority. It used the capsule's color to sell Prilosec, the market's first proton-pump-inhibitor (PPI) to combat acid reflux. It became a megahit through a campaign that branded it only as "the little purple pill."[46] One of the most popular ads was a swarm of giant purple pills gently falling out of a brilliant blue sky, like a rain of candy from the heavens. The drug's name was never mentioned. Prilosec was released in 1996. By 2000, AstraZeneca had spent $108 million in direct-to-consumer ads. Prilosec's sales were $4.1 billion, the company's biggest ever seller.

What did AstraZeneca do when Prilosec's patent expired the following year? It sold Prilosec over the counter and rolled out Nexium as its prescription replacement. The FDA had approved Nexium although it was essentially Prilosec. The only chemical alteration was it did not have one of Prilosec's less important mirror-image isomers. The drugs worked almost identically and clinical tests repeatedly demonstrated that the equivalent dose of each had the same efficacy.[47] The only visible difference to the public was that Nexium was a brighter shade of purple than its predecessor.[48]

AstraZeneca knew, however, that there was an important difference between the two pills. Nexium, at $4 each, cost 600 percent more than the over-the-counter Prilosec.[49] Its $200 million ad campaign worked. Consumers moved to Nexium. It became a billion-dollar drug faster than any other medication in the ulcer and acid-reducer class. Nexium stayed on top of that drug category for a decade, puzzling many industry analysts who thought it was "ripe for price competition" since there were so many inexpensive rival generics.[50] Consumer groups filed dozens of lawsuits against AstraZeneca, claiming its advertising was false since it marketed essentially the same drug under a different name and color shade. AstraZeneca prevailed on all cases, although it took a decade. The company's defense rested on the FDA approval of Nexium as a stand-alone drug.[51]

Who was vetting drug ads for their accuracy? No one, it turned out. The pushback against direct-to-consumer promotion reached a crescendo in 2004 when Merck pulled the ads for Vioxx, its hit painkiller (figure skater Dorothy Hamill, an arthritis sufferer, was the drug's face on TV). The nonsteroidal anti-inflammatory COX-2 inhibitor was at the center of a scandal about how the company had ignored warnings that its drug increased the risk for heart attacks and strokes. Its aggressive marketing of Vioxx for treating menstrual cramps, osteoarthritis, and muscle pain had turned it into a $2-billion-a-year pill since its 1999 release.[52] Merck yanked it from the market just days before the FDA issued a mandatory recall. Vioxx broke Merck's perfect record of never having had a drug recalled.* [53]

The Vioxx scandal prompted a concerted pushback against consumer drug ads. Bristol-Myers announced they would voluntarily withhold any direct-to-consumer ads for its new products. David Kessler, now the dean of the Yale School of Medicine, directed his words to the executives who had done their best to undermine him when he was at the FDA: "Your companies likely will face lawsuits eventually about the claims they make for their products in television commercials. One day in a courtroom, I assure you, one of you is going to have your DTC ads played."[54]

There were calls from consumer groups that another moratorium be put on all direct drug ads. The FDA considered a one- to two-year freeze while it conducted hearings. Instead, in only two months, the agency bowed to industry pressure. The FDA issued only some minor revisions to its guidelines. The one it touted was that it had protected America's children by ordering that erectile dysfunction medications

* As the Vioxx scandal worsened—faked results in some of the clinical trials and senior executives who buried alarming reports about adverse effects—Merck faced hundreds of class action lawsuits. It ultimately settled most of them in 2007 for $4.85 billion, and then paid another $950 million in 2011.

only be advertised between 10 p.m. and 6 a.m.[55] Activists dismissed that as inconsequential and predicted the FDA's surrender would reinvigorate pharma's appetite for TV ads. Not even the consumer activists could have imagined that in a few years there would be $200 million annually in cringe-worthy ads for incontinence and overactive bladders.[56]

45

"WE HAVE TO HAMMER ON THE ABUSERS"

Although the Sacklers and Purdue executives knew about early reports of abuse with OxyContin in late 1997 or early 1998, the first media stories—mostly in rural newspapers—did not appear until 1999. Small-town police forces scattered across six Appalachian states stretching from Kentucky to Maine reported a surge in drug dealers arrested with OxyContin and pharmacies robbed at knife- or gunpoint.[1] There was also a spike in Oxy-related hospital admissions.[2] The drug had begun showing up in toxicology reports of overdose autopsies (although it varied by year, on average there were twenty-five emergency room visits related to opioids for every lethal overdose).[3]

Steven Passik was then a clinical psychologist in pain management and palliative care at the University of Kentucky's School of Medicine. He had written about pain and opioids. Kentucky was one of the states hard hit early on by OxyContin. There would soon be nine counties in America that had an opioid-related overdose death rate greater than 20 per 100,000. Four of those were in eastern Kentucky. Passik described it as a region "marked by poverty and 20 percent unemployment among laborers with lots of chronic pain. This environment was ripe for prescription drug abuse."[4]

Passik had no idea then of the extent to which Purdue had targeted poverty-scarred working-class whites in rural America as a prime market. Although a few small towns felt under siege from OxyContin, there was little evidence the problem extended much beyond a dozen counties in a handful of states. Health and Human Services' "Drug Abuse Warning Network," which relied on reports from hospital emergency rooms and medical examiners, reported a 93 percent jump in "oxycodone mentions" in 1998. It was written off as a cyclical spike common with illegal drug supply and demand.[5] No one could have then imagined they were witnessing the national opioid epidemic in its infancy.

In the fall of 1999, Jay McCloskey, Maine's U.S. attorney, noticed state police arrests for illegal possession or distribution of prescription narcotics had jumped ninefold in four years. McCloskey was the first public official to realize that OxyContin was behind the surge; it was involved in more than half the arrests. He met that October in Washington with a group of citizen advocates who were trying to raise awareness of what they claimed were OxyContin's unrecognized dangers.[6] They included parents of addicted children and others who themselves had become dependent on the drug. Three months later McCloskey sent a letter to all Maine's practicing doctors "warning them about the increasing problems with illegal diversion and abuse of OxyContin."[7] That got the attention of the Sacklers and Purdue.

OxyContin had become Purdue's best-selling drug ever. Just a few months earlier, chief operating officer Michael Friedman had sent Richard Sackler an email with the news that its sales exceeded $20 million weekly. It was well on its way to becoming a billion-dollar drug. Sackler's semisatirical response? "Blah, humbug. Yawn."[8] In fact, the Sacklers were ecstatic at the numbers. And when they learned of McCloskey's letter, they wanted to make certain that any bad press was nothing more than a public relations speed bump.[9]

In a strategy meeting, the Sackler-family directors and their top executives decided to confront the problems in Maine. A few weeks later, J. David Haddox, Purdue's medical director, called McCloskey. Haddox seemed genuinely interested to learn more about what had prompted the warning letter to the state's doctors. He asked if he and several Purdue colleagues could meet McCloskey but the U.S. attorney declined. "I found it difficult to envision how the manufacturer could help stop the illegal diversion and abuse of OxyContin," he later testified before the Senate.[10]

It took several months before McCloskey concluded that "traditional law enforcement techniques alone would have very little impact." Counties in northern Maine had reported 2.5 times as many arrests for prescription narcotics as the rest of the state. There were a lot of first-time offenders. Breaking and entering and strong-arm robberies were up 70 percent.[11] McCloskey asked Purdue if it would help "reach an audience of health care providers to whom law enforcement generally did not have access."[12] Purdue dispatched Haddox, its chief operating officer, Michael Friedman, and legal counsel Howard Udell to meet with prosecutors, federal and state law enforcement officials, and local police chiefs at a conference McCloskey arranged.

McCloskey thought the trio seemed sincerely surprised at the "extent of the diversion." They told the conference that during the thirteen years in which Purdue had sold a "similar product," MS Contin, they "had not experienced any serious diversion problems."[13] That was not true, but no one besides the three Purdue executives knew that. Internal documents that became public years later as part of a 120-page Justice Department report revealed that in the late 1980s Purdue's management knew there was a diversion and abuse problem with MS Contin. Michael Friedman received a memo that showed a $51 prescription of MS Contin (thirty tablets of 60 mg each) sold on the street for $1,050 (about $35 a pill).[14] In 1990, Cincinnati police reported that MS Contin had surpassed heroin as the city's most abused opioid. Other cities reported addicts either chewing the tablets or liquefying them for injection.[15]

"They pledged that they would do whatever they could to assist the efforts of law enforcement officials to address the illegal diversion of OxyContin," McCloskey later recalled. Howard Udell told the conference, "We want to do what is right."

"I remember these words very distinctly," McCloskey later recalled, "and although I did not give any special weight to them at the time, I later recalled them on several occasions as I observed all that Purdue Pharma later did, and offered to do, in an effort to reduce OxyContin abuse."[16] Within a month, Purdue hired half a dozen consultants and instructed them to devise better ways for physicians to identify addicts and potential abusers. The detail team was told to end their sales pitches by reminding doctors that opioid-based painkillers such as Oxy were "common targets for both drug abusers and drug addicts."[17]

Richard Sackler had become Purdue's president the previous year, (evidently over the objections of Mortimer Sr.).[18] The board promoted Mortimer D., Jonathan, and Kathe to vice presidents. The second generation was in charge. Purdue needed to be publicly as concerned as anyone in America at reports about OxyContin abuse.[19] There was no contradiction in assuring public officials that the company would do its best to prevent diversion at the same time it aggressively marketed the drug. Those twin strategies would inevitably collide. The more successful the promotion and sales, the greater the likelihood of abuse and diversion. Yet, in 2000, Purdue believed it could have it both ways.

While the public relations department went into high gear with its "we are all in this together" message, Purdue applied for approval to the FDA for a 160 mg pill, double its then maximum dose.[20] The FDA gave its okay that spring, intending it to be dispensed to a small number of patients who had developed tolerance to lower-dose opiates because of long-term treatment. To discourage patients who filled prescriptions and then sold the pills, physicians had to warn that such a mega-dose could prove dangerous, even fatal, for someone unaccustomed to opioids.[21]

When the 160 mg OxyContin went on sale in July, Purdue launched an ad campaign in medical journals, trade shows, and online videos, promoting it for both cancer and noncancer patients to treat a wide variety of musculoskeletal and postsurgical pain.[22] Purdue hoped that it might capture some of the market for pain relief from the 700,000 annual knee replacements, 650,000 tendon repairs, and 500,000 lower back surgeries. (A later study demonstrated that patients who used opioids after surgery were twice as likely as the general population to misuse them eventually.)[23]

While Purdue saturated its top prescribers with a sales pitch for Oxy's 160 mg version, it dispatched spokesmen nationwide to reassure local politicians and police that "we strongly support . . . law enforcement efforts to combat the abuse and misuse of OxyContin and other pain medications."[24] It announced a program to help physicians better identify drug dependence. Television and print ads in some of the hardest-hit markets warned teenagers not to abuse prescription drugs. Purdue also rolled out an outreach program, "Painfully Obvious," that provided educational materials to parents and teachers.[25]

The Sackler-family directors hoped the news of OxyContin abuse might stay limited to the dozen small regional newspapers and television stations that had covered it. Although Dr. Robert Kaiko, OxyContin's co-inventor, had warned only a year after the drug went on sale that it was "highly likely that it will eventually be abused," Richard Sackler wanted instead to focus on how to "substantially improve your sales."[26] The first notice the Sacklers got of how naive it was to think that news of OxyContin abuse might remain a regional Appalachian story came in November when Michael Friedman, Purdue's COO, learned a *New York Times* correspondent was "sniffing about."[27]

That the *Times* was interested made the Sacklers anxious. At their next board meeting they adopted a strategy to "deflect attention away from the company owners."[28] It was a theme, the author learned, inspired by Raymond Sackler. He had urged Richard to emulate the National Rifle Association motto: "Guns don't kill people, people kill people."[29] J. David Haddox represented the company when reporters called. The board thought as medical director he should concentrate on the pain relief benefits of OxyContin while steering clear of talking about the pill's incredible commercial success (prescriptions had increased twentyfold in just four years).[30]

The February 9, 2001, front-page story, titled "Cancer Painkillers Pose New Abuse Threat," was the first *New York Times* article to mention OxyContin. The 1,200-word story by Francis X. Clines with Barry Meier included firsthand accounts from law enforcement officials and health care workers at the front lines in seven states. Oxy abuse had "been tracked over the past 18 months" and some of America's poorest districts had become the equivalent of legally sanctioned dope exchanges. "Addicts have been paying about $1 a milligram for the drug," reported the *Times*. The hardest-hit regions were those in which heroin was too expensive or in short supply. Oxy was soon dubbed "hillbilly heroin" in remote areas of Kentucky and West Virginia (in other states it became "OxyCotton" or "OC").[31] * [32]

According to the *Times*, OxyContin had in just a few years come from nowhere to become the favorite drug for addicts who "have learned to circumvent its slow time-released protection and achieve a sudden, powerful morphine-like high."[33] In some cities, Oxy was muscling aside heroin and it was behind a sharp uptick in overdoses, car accidents, workplace injuries, and even suicides.[34]

"I personally counted 59 deaths since January of last year that local police attributed to addicts using the drug," Joseph Famularo, the U.S. attorney in Kentucky, told the *Times*. "And I suspect that's pretty conservative." The paper quoted Haddox disputing the number of overdose deaths and warning that "inflammatory statements like that"

* Patients covered under Medicaid and retirees with Medicare soon discovered that the government listed OxyContin as a covered drug. So did private medical insurance for the large number of the miners and construction workers in those early-hit states. In June, Britain's *Guardian* reported a Medicaid patient who paid $3 for a prescription of one hundred 80 mg pills could earn $8,000. That was a third of what the average person earned annually in those West Virginia and Kentucky counties.

might cause doctors to withhold the drug from patients suffering from chronic pain.[35] Richard Sackler's reaction to the article was relief. "That is not too bad. It could have been far worse."[36]

Still, the Sackler-family directors felt as if the paper had picked on OxyContin because of its great success. According to one assistant marketing manager, they believed the press coverage was "patently unfair." Law enforcement vilified popular prescription drugs in order to get bigger enforcement budgets.[37] Benzodiazepines and amphetamines in the 1970s had given way to Quaaludes, then Adderall. Americans consumed the most opioids by far on the planet (a 2009 study confirmed by how much the U.S. was in the lead: 81 percent of the world's oxycodone and 99 percent of all hydrocodone).[38]

Although OxyContin was Purdue's top seller, it was then less than 10 percent of the opioid market. Johnson & Johnson, Janssen, Cephalon, and Endo Pharmaceuticals had their own narcotic pain relievers and their ads were as "aggressive" as any from Purdue. Their sales teams also pitched them for neck and back pain, and the companies subsidized many of the same nonprofits and patient advocacy groups as did Purdue. Janssen had even managed to get FDA approval in 1990 for the first ever fentanyl patch to treat severe pain. Fentanyl was then the most potent synthetic opioid, one hundred times stronger than morphine and 1.5 times more powerful than oxycodone.[39] Two years after the FDA had given a green light to OxyContin, it approved Cephalon's Actiq, a fentanyl "lollipop," for cancer patients whose intense pain did not respond to other narcotics.[40] Fentanyl patches and Actiq pops had been diverted illicitly for big profits and sometimes had deadly side effects. There were widespread rumors inside the industry that Cephalon's detail team was pushing its lollipops off-label as "ER on a stick" for generalized chronic pain. It is understandable that the Sacklers wondered why the media was not writing about their rivals.*[41]

Inside Purdue there was a widespread belief that if OxyContin be-

---

* By 2005, oncologists wrote only 1 percent of Actiq's 187,076 retail pharmacy prescriptions. Eighty percent of the patients given the drug did not have cancer. One of Cephalon's sales representatives was so concerned about the detail team's off-label marketing that he contacted the FDA and later wore a surveillance wire to a sales conference to help the U.S. attorney gather evidence. In 2008, Cephalon paid $375 million to settle civil charges of Medicare and Medicaid fraud and a separate $50 million for a single criminal count of illegal off-label marketing. The court awarded Bruce Boise, the detail rep turned whistleblower, $17 million.

came the target of a "media frenzy," sensational coverage itself might become a self-fulfilling prophecy. A media blitz that damned the relatively unknown drug as a modern-day scourge was much more likely to attract the attention of addicts and even casual drug users who wanted to see if it lived up to its notoriety.[42]

Only a month before the *Times* story, the Justice Department's National Drug Intelligence Center had issued its first systemwide Information Bulletin concluding that "diversion and abuse of the prescription pain reliever OxyContin is a major problem, particularly in the eastern United States." The bulletin warned that addicts were frequently substituting it for heroin and that the problem would worsen.[43]

In an internal Purdue email distributed the same month as the *Times* story, Richard Sackler said: "We have to hammer on the abusers in every way possible. They are the culprits and the problem. They are reckless criminals."[44] Sales representatives were instructed again that "patients were to blame for abuse and addiction, not the drug."[45] It was a more aggressive version of a defense that had been used by drug companies since Miltown came under scrutiny in the 1950s.[46*]

Hope of a respite from mainstream press coverage about OxyContin, however, was dashed a month later. Another front-page *Times* story, "Sales of Painkiller Grew Rapidly, But Success Brought a High Cost," marveled at Oxy's commercial success while extensively reporting more about its emerging dark side.[47] "In a little over four years, OxyContin's sales have hit $1 billion, more than even Viagra's. Although the drug has helped thousands of people in pain, its success has come at a considerable cost." A DEA official blamed the drug "in the deaths of at least 120 people, and medical examiners are still counting."[48]

The tone of the *Times* coverage had changed in the month between the two stories. The first quoted police and doctors about OxyContin's excesses and abuses. The second put the spotlight on Purdue by questioning if its aggressive marketing was partially responsible for the

* The blunt language in many of Richard Sackler's emails and memos became a weak spot for the company as it defended itself in hundreds of lawsuits. Richard's son, David, himself a Purdue director from 2012 to 2018, tried defending his father in a 2019 *Vanity Fair* interview: "He just cannot understand how his words are going to land on somebody. . . . For a person like that, email is about the worst medium possible to communicate in, because there is no other cue. And so he's saying things that sound incredibly strident and sound incredibly unsympathetic, and that's not the person that he is."

growing problem. A Maine pain treatment physician who threw a Purdue salesman out of his practice told the reporters, "They were pushing it for everything." A pain specialist at New York's Mount Sinai Hospital noted that while "all companies market . . . these people were in your face all the time." A West Virginia pharmacist said, "The problem with this drug is the company."[49]

The *Times* revealed that Purdue had paid for all-expenses-paid junkets for two to three thousand physicians to Florida, California, and Arizona. Hundreds of others were paid hefty speaker's fees at some seven thousand Purdue-sponsored "pain management seminars."[50] The article also had the first brief background about the Sacklers, from the founding of Purdue Frederick by Arthur, Mortimer, and Raymond to the family's "illustrious ties to the arts and sciences."

The family directors refused interview requests. Haddox stuck to talking points emphasizing that Purdue was "as surprised as anyone" at OxyContin's abuse. He disclosed that the company was researching how "to reformulate OxyContin" so it was more difficult for patients to abuse. That was true. Purdue was spending a lot of money to develop a way to foil, or at least make it tougher, to tamper with the pill's time release technology. It tried adding a small amount of a narcotic blocker, naloxone, to counter the effects of the oxycodone. That might turn off users looking for a euphoric rush. The obstacle the researchers ran into was that no matter how they adjusted the dose and release time of the naloxone, it blocked too much of OxyContin's pain relief.[51] Purdue experimented next with converting Oxy from a tablet to a capsule and inserting microscopic beads of a different narcotic blocker, naltrexone. By the time Haddox had his second interview with the *Times*, that combination showed some promise, but it was in very early research.[52]

What caused the most anxiety inside Purdue from the March 5 *Times* story were a few sentences indicating that Oxy had attracted unwanted attention from several critical federal agencies. An unnamed DEA official told the paper that "no other prescription drug in the last 20 years had been illegally abused by so many people so soon after it appeared." Dr. Cynthia McCormick, director of the FDA's Anesthetics, Critical Care, and Addiction Drug Products, admitted the FDA had not adequately considered the many ways patients bypassed Oxy's protective coating. "We've learned something from this," she admitted. And finally, the *Times* reported, "Last Thursday, officials of five states met in Richmond, Va., to discuss ways to halt illegal traffic in OxyContin."

The news might have been worse if reporters had followed the Sacklers' pharmaceutical ownership to the U.K. There, MST Continus, OxyContin's predecessor, had been on sale since 1980. The British government had charged Napp Pharmaceuticals with exercising monopoly powers in the U.K.'s narcotic painkiller market. Thousands of pages of filings spelled out the details of how Napp executives conspired to use discounts to 90 percent of British hospitals so that the low prices did not attract competitors. Then Napp charged up to ten times the list price when selling to the country's National Health Service for individual patients. Mortimer Sackler oversaw Napp's operation. The prosecutor's case, which resulted in a $7.5 million fine and a strict consent agreement, provided a roadmap for how Napp had cut corners and skirted the law in pursuit of ever-bigger profits.[53]

The Sacklers soon had their hands full in the U.S. Purdue and its marketing of OxyContin were the subject of two preliminary investigations, one at the DEA and one by the U.S attorney in Virginia. Both would have wide-ranging consequences.

Laura Nagel, a twenty-two-year veteran of the DEA, had been promoted the previous year from the Criminal Division to become the deputy assistant administrator of the Office of Diversion Control. That was government-speak for the agent in charge of investigating the enormous illicit trade in prescription meds. Drugs subject to abuse came in and out of fashion. The DEA intervened when they began showing up in large quantities on the black market. Nagel knew there were plenty of ways that legal drugs got diverted. Doctors sometimes got greedy and operated pill mills; users forged or altered physician prescription pads or robbed drug company warehouses and pharmacies; free samples at doctor's offices were sold to crooked pharmacists; health care workers stole from supplies at hospitals or nursing homes; and sometimes there was theft at the source, the pharmaceutical company's manufacturing and distribution centers.

As Nagel settled into the new role, OxyContin was at the top of her list.[54] The veteran agents in Diversion Control told Nagel that they believed Purdue was not doing anything to warn physicians and patients that their best-selling drug was far more addictive than what it claimed in its promotion.[55]

The DEA was aware Purdue had a problem at PF Laboratories, its Totowa, New Jersey, manufacturing plant. Nagel had reports the company could not account for small batches of pills at the end of some manufacturing runs. Were there compliance problems at PF Laboratories? She knew that a chemical explosion at New Jersey–based Napp Technologies in 1995 had killed five and injured forty-eight. Napp made MS Contin there. The Occupational Safety and Health Administration had considered filing criminal charges against the company for willful safety violations but ultimately brought only an administrative proceeding and settled for a $127,000 penalty.[56] Except for local papers, the story had gotten lost under saturation coverage of the terror bombing at the Murrah Federal Building in Oklahoma City two days earlier. The Sacklers had authorized general counsel Howard Udell to settle all civil claims from the Napp explosion. OxyContin approval was then pending before the FDA and the family wanted no bad press that might in any way delay its release.[57]

Nagel had reviewed the OSHA report on the Napp explosion. The company's fire brigade never had proper emergency training. The guidelines for mixing the volatile chemicals were ignored.[58] Nagel wondered if there were similar shortcomings at PF Labs. There were strict protocols under federal law for manufacturing controlled substances.

In April, Nagel and some of her Diversion Control team met with Purdue COO Michael Friedman, the new medical director, Paul Goldenheim, and Howard Udell. Richard Sackler attended for the first half of a two-hour discussion. When Nagel asked about PF Laboratories, Udell said he did not know of any problem. That was a lie, the author learned. The reports of diversion had reached him at the Stamford headquarters.[59] Purdue had hoped to keep the diversion at their New Jersey plant an internal matter, since the company was preparing to open a second manufacturing plant in North Carolina to meet the booming Oxy demand.

The DEA next presented evidence that abuse and deaths were up significantly since OxyContin went on sale in 1996. The troubling numbers tracked Oxy's success from 300,000 prescriptions in its first year to nearly 6,000,000 by 2001.

At one stage, Nagel told Richard Sackler that "People are dying. Do you understand that?"[60] All the Purdue executives disagreed that OxyContin was behind the spike in overdose deaths. The meeting ended in a stalemate, neither side able to agree on what measures Purdue should undertake. Nagel offered a final suggestion: Purdue should voluntarily limit Oxy sales to select pharmacies and restrict the detail team to oncologists and certified pain management specialists. The three Purdue executives stared at her blankly. Udell finally gave the noncommittal "We'll take it under advisement."[61]

Purdue knew the only federal agency with the power to regulate how it sold Oxy was the FDA. Still, as a sign of good faith to the DEA, a few weeks after that meeting, Purdue announced its "temporary suspension" of its mega-dose 160 mg pill. A press release said it was because the company was "concerned about the possibility of illicit use of tablets of such high strength." Much of the evidence the DEA had provided about diversion and abuse involved that dosage. It had gotten the nickname "Oxy-Coffin."[62] Its potency meant it was much sought after by addicts, and drug dealers priced it at a huge premium compared to lower-strength Oxy street pills.[63]

Nagel wondered whether Purdue's withdrawal of it was a temporary public relations play and it would reintroduce it when there was not as much scrutiny. To keep up the pressure, Nagel began drafting a "national strategy" to fight OxyContin abuse. She wanted to document the crisis with evidence that Purdue could not ignore or brush aside as "mere anecdotal stories." She huddled with Frank Sapienza, chief of the Drug & Chemical Evaluation Section, Christine Sannerud, senior scientific advisor in the Diversion Control Division, and David Gauvin, a pharmacologist who was a senior drug science officer. They asked the National Association of Medical Examiners to collect and send to the DEA up to two years of autopsies in which there had been "oxycodone positive toxicologies."[64]

While the science team analyzed those autopsies, Nagel kept the pressure on Purdue. In May, she publicly released her proposal asking the company to voluntarily limit its dispensing of Oxy.[65] That caused an unexpected, sharp pushback from doctors who thought the idea draconian. There were so few licensed pain management specialists it almost certainly would force patients with chronic pain to go untreated.

The first private lawsuits charging that OxyContin had been overprescribed as a result of Purdue's deceptive marketing were filed in Ohio, Kentucky, Virginia, and West Virginia. Most of the plaintiffs were outraged families who had relatives die while prescribed OxyContin.[66] In early July, two employees at the Sackler-owned PF Laboratories were arrested and charged with theft of two thousand pills, worth an estimated street value of $160,000.[67] That came shortly after fourteen arrests in a syndicate that forged prescriptions and got eight thousand pills covered by insurance.[68] * [69]

By the time of the July arrests, the Sackler-family directors and top executives were not paying much attention to anything but their negotiations under way at the FDA. Curtis Wright, who had left the agency to work at Purdue as its medical officer for risk assessment, had stayed in touch with his former colleagues and had reported that the FDA was reviewing the OxyContin label it had approved in 1995. Some state prosecutors and victims' families had petitioned the FDA to reevaluate the wording in light of emerging evidence of abuse and diversion. Purdue grudgingly cooperated in the hope it might influence any revisions to its label.[70] There are no records of the private meetings between Purdue executives and FDA regulators. All that is available is the result of those talks. In July the FDA acted.[71] It seemed as if the FDA had cracked down on Purdue's hit drug, because it ordered the addition of a so-called black box warning. The bold font warning was a reminder to doctors that OxyContin was "a Schedule II controlled substance with an abuse liability similar to morphine." No drug company liked having a black box warning added to its label, but as the author learned, Purdue was not that distressed since it considered the language a good compromise. One marketing executive remarked later, "It is black box lite."[72] It merely reiterated what most physicians knew already about OxyContin.

Many victims groups and prosecutors thought the original 1995 label had helped fuel OxyContin's big sales. Although Purdue had not conducted any clinical trials to see whether OxyContin was less likely to be addictive or abused than other opioid painkillers, the FDA had approved the wording, "Delayed absorption as provided by OxyContin tablets, is believed to reduce the abuse liability of a drug."[73] The detail team highlighted that extraordinary sentence to persuade doctors it was a safer narcotic than its rivals. The FDA finally deleted that sentence on its 2001 label.[74]

---

* Two ex-employees sued Purdue, charging that the manufacturing plant's supervisors had forced them sometimes to bypass security protocols that required all batches of the drug always be kept on the assembly line, and even had them fake counts of vials and caps to cover up pills missing in the final inventory.

The 1995 label declared that "iatrogenic addiction [one that resulted from treatment by a physician] is rare." Purdue had also relied extensively on that in its promotion. The FDA's 2001 revision was that addiction in "managed patients with pain has been reported to be rare."[75] That was a great disappointment to those who had expected the FDA to rely on recent studies that demonstrated the risk of addiction was "moderate to high." Finally, on the 1995 label, the FDA had given Purdue a significant victory with the language that OxyContin was for "constant, moderate-to-severe pain that is expected to last a long time." That was despite the existing science having only studied its active ingredient, oxycodone, for short-term safety and efficacy. Purdue cited that language to encourage doctors to prescribe Oxy for chronic ailments like back pain or arthritis.[76] In the FDA's 2001 revision, the label stated: OxyContin was "for the management of moderate to severe pain when a continuous, around the clock analgesic is needed for an extended period of time."[77]

That provoked a furious reaction from victims' families and patient advocacy groups.

"The label change was a blank check," according to former FDA commissioner David Kessler, "one the drug industry cashed in for billions and billions of dollars. Now, Big Pharma had a green light to push opioids to tens of millions of new pain patients nationwide."[78]

"If you're taking them around the clock every day," says Andrew Kolodny, co-director of the Opioid Policy Research Directive at Brandeis University, "you quickly become tolerant to the pain-relieving effect. In order to continue getting pain relief, you'll need higher and higher doses."[79] That fit with Purdue's marketing strategy of maximizing profits by getting physicians to dispense OxyContin for longer periods at ever-higher doses.

Ed Thompson, a drug manufacturer who made opioid products for several pharmaceutical companies for over a quarter century, told *60 Minutes* in 2019 that changes such as the ones the FDA made on the 2001 OxyContin label "determine whether [a drug] can make $10 million or a billion dollars. . . . It opened the floodgates. It was the decision of no return for the FDA."[80]

Inside Purdue the Sackler-family directors and marketing and sales departments were ecstatic. "The action by the FDA . . . has created enormous opportunities" was the conclusion of a widely distributed internal memo. Purdue's advertisements to doctors soon reflected the emphasis on long-term dispensing. Sales tripled over the next two years.[81]

A month after their victory on the revised OxyContin label, the Sacklers sent COO Michael Friedman, general counsel Howard Udell, and senior physician Paul Goldenheim to testify before the House Subcommittee on Oversight and Investigations. Law enforcement officials told the committee that OxyContin was surpassing heroin and cocaine to become the top choice among addicts.[82]

The Purdue trio stuck to a prepared script, with more than half their time packaged as a veritable infomercial for OxyContin, replete with a tutorial about how pain had been historically undertreated and how Oxy had improved the lives of millions. The executives claimed they had no reason to expect there would be any abuse or diversion because there had been none with Purdue's predecessor, MS Contin: "We had no reason to expect otherwise with OxyContin." Friedman, Goldenheim, and Udell were smooth and no matter how hard the subcommittee pressed, they fell back on the theme that Purdue was doing everything possible to fight any abuse, which was, they insisted, exaggerated. They reminded the panel that "While all of the voices in this debate are important, we must be especially careful to listen to the voices of patients who, without drugs like OxyContin, would be left suffering from their untreated or inadequately treated pain."*

The trio had honed their defense of OxyContin in more than one hundred presentations around the country. The only difference this time was that they were in front of a congressional committee. When they returned to Purdue headquarters, they received a standing ovation for their Capitol Hill performance.

The 9/11 terror attack on the World Trade Center and Pentagon took the focus far off Purdue for several months. By December, however, OxyContin was again in the news, and none of it was good. An $800,000 shipment of Oxy from the factory was stolen while in transport to Cardinal Health.[83] An Indiana doctor who was in demand as a member of Purdue's speakers bureau was arrested for illegally dispens-

* Friedman also disclosed that Purdue had discussions with the FDA about developing a version of OxyContin that included an opioid antagonist: "We have developed several technologies that should enable us to achieve the goal of having an opioid medicine that is resistant to abuse by the oral route as well as by injection."

ing more than a million dollars in OxyContin to a drug ring and the state's Medicaid program.[84] CBS's prime-time *48 Hours* got its highest ratings for the year with an investigation into "OxyContin, a prescription painkiller that contains a synthetic opium and has become a lethal street drug." MTV did the same with its *True Life* reality series and "I'm Hooked on OxyContin."[85] There were calls from state medical association directors in New York, Florida, Nevada, and Kentucky to develop prescription-monitoring programs that could more quickly identify overprescribing physicians and problem patients.[86] The president of Odyssey House, a leading drug rehab center in New York City, warned that while it treated more crack cocaine and heroin addicts, "if this drug is not sufficiently controlled, that could change fast."[87]

The low point came on December 12 before another congressional subcommittee. Asa Hutchinson, the chief of the DEA, blamed Purdue's aggressive marketing for making OxyContin a drug of "disproportionate abuse."[88] Two hundred and eighty-two people had died from OxyContin overdoses in a nineteen-month period, charged Hutchinson. Purdue had dispatched the same executives who had testified before the House in August. Paul Goldenheim "vehemently disputed any suggestion that the company had inappropriately marketed" OxyContin.[89]

Harold Rogers, a congressman from a Kentucky district that was hit hard by OxyContin, pressed Goldenheim about instances in which physicians had greatly overprescribed. Why did Purdue not cut them off from getting the drug? "We don't control what they prescribe," said Goldenheim. "We can't stop them from prescribing our product."

"*We* can," said Rogers.

The Sacklers did not take the threat of government restrictions lightly. They knew that Rogers had taken a hard-line stance since his district had so many OxyContin-related problems. Still, there was the chance that such sentiment could build. That was why Purdue wanted to always give the impression that it was leading the fight against abuse and diversion.[90]

Although 2001 was a troubled year for Purdue, there was one area that was stellar. OxyContin sales and profits hit a new record. Sales were up 41 percent year over year, bringing in $1.45 billion in revenue. It would break its own record again for the coming year (2002), with $1.59 billion in sales and accounting for 80 percent of Purdue's business. Although OxyContin was under attack from government agencies and angry patients, it had become the top selling brand-name, controlled substance drug ever (a title it holds still as of 2019).[91]

The entire pharmaceutical industry was booming that year. It seemed in some ways as if OxyContin was just one of many drugs surging in sales. The top ten drug companies in the *Fortune* 500 had more combined profits than the other 490 companies.[92]

The DEA was using every tool not only to track the amount of OxyContin sales, but to know from which doctors and pharmacies it was prescribed and for which ailments. It was, Drug Enforcement claimed, a better indicator of the drug's effect across the country. Were the number of prescriptions rising in tandem with the jump in revenue or was Purdue just charging more since it had a patent monopoly? In the case of OxyContin, it was both. Not only had the revenues soared, but so had the numbers of prescriptions. In its first full year (1997), doctors had written 920,000 scrips. In 2002 it ballooned to 7.2 million.[93] What most alarmed those who believed that OxyContin was prescribed far too easily: only one million were for cancer-related pain. Nearly half the drug's prescribers were primary care doctors. OxyContin had gone mainstream.[94]

46

"GIVING PURDUE A FREE PASS"

Purdue's internal files reveal that the Sacklers thought their star drug could transform their company into one of the country's most profitable pharmaceutical firms. Even if that was just wishful thinking, or mentioned to motivate employees, it explains in part why they were not satisfied when Oxy broke a billion dollars in sales. That was only the first milestone. They wanted much more. Marketing files show that 75 percent of the $400 million Purdue spent promoting OxyContin came after 2000. That is the year that executives from the company later claimed in congressional testimony they first learned of reports about the drug's abuse.[1]

A few pharmacists had alerted Purdue nearly two years earlier about a Myrtle Beach pain clinic operating as a pill mill (usually a cash-only doctor or clinic where narcotic prescriptions are dispensed to anyone for any reason).[2] Purdue did nothing to investigate those reports although the volume of sales to that clinic was far greater than what it needed for treating the local population. Purdue did not even question why sales in Myrtle Beach had surged by an extra million dollars in the first quarter of 2001, by far the largest increase in OxyContin revenue in the nation.[3] As its executives later contended, the company had no legal obligation to alert the FDA or any law enforcement agency.

It was December 2001 before the DEA raided that Myrtle Beach clinic and suspended the license of six doctors who had written thousands of OxyContin prescriptions weekly.[4] What no one outside the company then knew was that the three sales representatives responsible for that pill mill continued to collect bonuses based on the sales it had produced. Raymond Sackler and a senior executive made that decision personally. They reasoned that Purdue had earned its profits on pills sold to the shuttered clinic, even if Oxy had been dispensed improperly. It was out of the question that they might return those profits, so withholding the sales reps' bonuses might demoralize the team.[5]

The detail team understood the top priority was how many pills they sold. The Sackler-family directors and their top executives supported plans to persuade more doctors to prescribe more OxyContin at ever-higher doses and for longer periods. The stars at Purdue were not the scientists in the research lab looking for new medications. The stars were those detail squad members who managed to crush their quarterly sales quotas.

Going forward, there were very few instances in which the detail squad reported an incident where they thought a doctor or clinic in their sales territory improperly dispensed Oxy. Instead, the detail squad concentrated on the "high value target" prescribers, internally listed as SP (super prescribers). Courting the super prescribers paid off with spectacular results for the company's bottom line and the detail team's annual bonuses. In OxyContin's thirteen top markets a few hundred SPs wrote more prescriptions than there were people.[6] Nationally about 55 percent of all opioids were prescribed by 3 percent of all physicians.[7]

Purdue was not blind to overprescribing. It had identified the sales territories where it suspected that illegal dispensing contributed to the outsized volume of sales in relation to the population. That area was internally dubbed "Region Zero." Law enforcement would eventually arrest some of the most reckless prescribers and shut down pill mills, but never as a result of a tip from Purdue. The company did not warn any state or federal agency that a West Virginia doctor wrote 335,000 prescriptions over eight years, a rate of 130 daily, seven days a week.[8] Purdue was silent about its star prescriber in Massachusetts who penned 347,000 OxyContin prescriptions over five years. He stopped only when the state stripped him of his medical license.[9] Purdue instead awarded both those doctors, and others like them, lucrative speaker's contracts at sponsored symposiums about pain and pharmaceutical treatments.[10] Some eventually lost their licenses. Others went to prison.

Employees who reported likely overprescribing met resistance. Purdue executives rejected a plea from one employee that the company do the "right and ethical thing" by providing insurance companies with a list of likely illegal prescribers. "If it reduces abuse and diversion of opioids," she wrote in an email, "then it seems like something we should be doing."[11] In another instance, a member of the detail team, Mark Ross, alerted his sales manager that one doctor's office in his territory was packed with drug addicts. The manager's response was fast and direct: Ross's job was to sell the company's drugs, not to play detective to determine if a "doctor was a drug pusher."[12]

As if Purdue's failure to act on the warning signs from the sales data it compiled were not egregious enough, internal files show the detail squad sometimes pressed those suspect doctors to write prescriptions for drug addicts who had been turned away by other physicians.[13]

In January 2002 the problems posed by OxyContin abuse drew increased attention from the country's politicians. A government advisory committee concluded that opioid pain medication abuse was on the verge of becoming a public health crisis. In February, the Senate Committee on Health, Education, Labor and Pensions held public hearings on "Balancing Risks and Benefits of OxyContin." In the coming decades, as OxyContin worsened from a "problem" to an "epidemic," the Senate and House held more than a dozen hearings into the causes of the crisis and to discuss possible solutions. The Government Accountability Office produced multiple reports that provided detailed snapshots that in retrospect are a sad commentary on the slow bureaucratic response to the most lethal prescription drug scourge in modern American history.[14]

The DEA's Laura Nagel, meanwhile, had arranged for an extraordinary summit meeting with representatives from Purdue and the FDA at Drug Enforcement's Washington headquarters. Nagel was joined on April 12, 2002, by the DEA's senior science officer, David Gauvin, Frank Sapienza, chief of the Drug & Chemical Evaluation Section, and Christine Sannerud, the senior scientific advisor in the Diversion Control Division. The FDA sent Deborah Leiderman, director for controlled substances in the Center for Drug Evaluation and Research. Purdue again dispatched Friedman, Goldenheim, and Udell.

The Purdue executives were unaware that behind the scenes Nagel and Leiderman were at odds about how to best respond to the OxyContin problems. As far as the FDA was concerned, it had approved Oxy as effective and the drug demonstrated real-world usefulness for many patients. Issues of diversion and abuse were the DEA's job. The problem, though, at Drug Enforcement was that its authority was limited to go after drug dealers and syndicates, pill mills, and doctors who had broken the law. Nagel was convinced that arrests and enforcement alone could not resolve the crisis. Only the FDA had the power to restrict the otherwise legitimate production and distribution of a controlled substance. Nagel wanted the FDA to restrict how OxyContin was dispensed, as it had previously done for barbiturates, amphetamines, and benzodiazepines. Leiderman had shown no interest yet in that.

Unable to reach an understanding on how to proceed before the meeting, Nagel hoped that at least the two government agencies would present a united front to Purdue. If they did that, she hoped, the company might agree to some voluntary restrictions on OxyContin to avoid more stringent federal regulation. Nagel had something she expected would help push the parties toward an agreement: the DEA's science team had completed its internal review of the autopsy reports and the results showed that previous estimates of nearly three hundred OxyContin overdose deaths nationwide were significantly understated.[15]

As the meeting got under way, Gauvin distributed a forty-five-page PowerPoint presentation of their findings (the author obtained a printout of that unpublished presentation).[16] Medical examiners had sent 1,304 autopsies during the previous two years in which there had been "oxycodone positive toxicologies."[17] Gauvin presented the methodology used by the science team. That was critical since overdose-death autopsies that flagged the presence of OxyContin often included a combination of other legal and illegal drugs as well as alcohol. He and Sapienza had filtered the information to exclude those autopsies not verifiable as being "directly" or "most likely" associated with OxyContin.*[18]

The DEA's presentation was a damning overview of the deepening OxyContin crisis. The science team had reevaluated all the laboratory

* One hundred and thirty-four of the autopsies were deaths from gunshots, traffic accidents, AIDS, and cancer. Although oxycodone was present in each, Gauvin excluded them. He also omitted another 221 in which the "summary statements" from the medical examiner were "incomplete." As for the remaining 949, Gauvin had "464 deaths linked to single entity oxycodone products." He split those into "OxyContin verified" and "OxyContin-likely." The uncategorized remainder all showed medium to high blood levels of oxycodone. Although the science team believed those were also OxyContin-related, the directive from Nagel had been to err on the side of a conservative analysis to make it tougher for Purdue to ignore the data.

data, toxicology reports, and therapeutic drug profiles to confirm their accuracy. Included in the PowerPoint were five-year charts that tracked the number of emergency room visits that coincided with the increase in OxyContin sales. The DEA had also obtained Veterans Administration data showing that a quarter of all patients treated with Oxy for pain ended up abusing the drug. Primary care doctors said the abuse number was closer to a third of their civilian patients. Police departments provided information demonstrating that OxyContin was among the top ten most popular street drugs in the nation's fifteen largest cities.

Gauvin told the stone-faced Purdue representatives that he had begun a review of a number of OxyContin deaths across the nation that had been classified as suicides. They could add to the total number of overdose deaths attributed to the drug.

Gauvin finished his presentation with an unexpected finding. Only twelve of the deaths were attributed to injecting, snorting, or chewing Oxycodone. Ninety-eight percent of those who had died had taken it orally, as approved by the FDA and as intended by Purdue.[19] That made the point, according to the DEA, that the overdose deaths did not measure the full extent of OxyContin abuse. The chronic opiate abusers would have developed a tolerance to the drug that would make it far less likely for them to die of an oral overdose. That meant the hardcore abusers were still driving the market for Oxy's diversion and illicit trade.

Goldenheim, as Purdue's senior medical officer, made an abbreviated rebuttal. He complained that Purdue had not been given full access to all the DEA data. That made it impossible, he said, for Purdue to uncover any errors or misjudgments by the medical examiners. He also contended it was not possible to determine "OxyContin verified" deaths since the toxicology reports usually did not list exact levels of the other drugs at the time of death.[20]

Drug and Chemical chief Frank Sapienza reminded Goldenheim that the DEA marked a death as "OxyContin verified" only if the level of OxyContin in the bloodstream was high enough to be deadly on its own.[21]

"Assuming the measurements were accurate, how do we know that?" asked Goldenheim.

Gauvin leaned forward. "Do you think patients have a legal right to opiates? Or an inalienable right to be drug dependent?"

All three Purdue executives agreed with the right to opiates but said the second question was moot since patient dependence was not a widespread problem with Oxy.

Gauvin directed them to a copy of the World Health Organization and U.N. treaty in which "everyone had a right to reduced pain," but "pain by opiates was not an inalienable right." Pointing to a several-inch-thick stack of data from the autopsies, Gauvin said, "It is a direct attack on modern pharmacology to promote opioids as you do in the United States."[22]

That is when, according to one of the DEA officials in attendance, Deborah Leiderman surprised everyone by declaring she tended to agree with Purdue. The autopsy results were inconclusive, or at least not as definitive as the DEA had presented them. The FDA also, she said, had not received copies of all the data the DEA had analyzed.[23] Nagel and Gauvin looked at each other in disbelief. The meeting broke up soon after that.

A retired DEA officer familiar with what transpired next told the author that Nagel and Gauvin were so incensed by Leiderman's intervention on the side of Purdue that they discussed whether she might have sabotaged their investigation. They had no evidence of any wrongdoing and did not think she was in Purdue's pocket.[24] Instead, they wondered if it was Leiderman's way of pushing back against the DEA for overreaching its authority by seeking prescription restrictions.

Nagel's backup plan in case Drug Enforcement did not get the FDA's backing was to release the science team's conclusions publicly: "Recent media reports of 'hundreds of deaths' attributed to OxyContin can now be substantiated by credible scientific evidence." Few outlets picked it up. What did make news, however, was when the FDA publicly took issue with the DEA conclusions.

Three days after the failed meeting, a front-page *New York Times* story was headlined "OxyContin Deaths May Top Early Count." Barry Meier reported the DEA findings. The paragraph that got attention was: "But an F.D.A. official said that agency had not reviewed the reports underlying the D.E.A. analysis and appeared to express caution about it. That official, who spoke on the condition of anonymity, said the Food and Drug Administration's own review of data involving OxyContin was continuing but so far had not produced evidence that the drug posed a threat to people who took it as prescribed. 'We don't believe there is cause for panic,' the F.D.A. official said."[25]

"We knew where it had come from," an ex-DEA official told the author. "It was as if they were going out of their way in giving Purdue a free pass. What the hell was going on over there [at the FDA]?"[26]

The DEA team knew after the *Times* article that they had to win not only the tug-of-war with the FDA but also the fight for public and professional opinion. For a month they drafted an article setting out their evidence that OxyContin was proving increasingly lethal. They submitted it that summer to *The New England Journal of Medicine*. One of the DEA officials involved in that article told the author the *NEJM* rejected it as "too alarmist." An editor said it "was too early in post marketing surveillance to make claims of risks/hazards."[27]

While Nagel, Gauvin, and others huddled to decide their next move, the issue of OxyContin abuse and diversion had finally drawn the interest of the Justice Department. John Brownlee was the recently appointed U. S attorney for the Western District of Virginia. Neighboring West Virginia was one of the hardest-hit OxyContin states. The thirty-six-year-old Brownlee had been an assistant U.S. attorney in Washington, D.C., before George W. Bush had nominated him.

When Brownlee got to the Virginia prosecutor's office he was at first surprised it was "a pretty small shop."[28] That was true by the standards of Washington where he had been one of 350 attorneys with a support staff of nearly 400.[29] The Western District of Virginia had only 23 of the country's 5,300 federal prosecutors.[30] Four worked civil cases and the 22-person support staff included only two investigators. Its size, though, did not dissuade Brownlee from opening two ambitious preliminary investigations a month after taking charge. One was a national security probe into whether the ITT Corporation might have illegally transferred classified technology to other countries. The second was into Purdue and OxyContin. Brownlee wanted to find out whether the drug's maker had any legal responsibility for the budding epidemic.[31] Over the next few years he directed his Oxy task force, eventually composed of nine state and federal agencies, from a strip mall.*[32]

---

* To learn more about how OxyContin had hit West Virginia like a plague, Brownlee read Barry Meier's *Pain Killer*. He later heard that Purdue had complained bitterly to the *Times* and that resulted in Meier being taken off that story (he was not allowed to cover it for four years). That piqued Brownlee's interest in what the drug company might have to hide. Purdue's general counsel, Howard Udell, had convinced the *Times* public editor that Meier's reporting cast the company as the villain since it guaranteed more coverage by the newspaper. Meier's byline had appeared on fourteen stories, many on the front page, since the first ran on February 9, 2001. His 2003 book was evi-

No one at Purdue's Stamford headquarters initially paid much attention to the investigation operating from the heart of Appalachia and with a prosecutor who had never directed a major case. Purdue was getting accustomed to aggressively defending itself on simultaneous fronts. It prevailed that year (2002) with dismissals and winning jury verdicts in the first wave of private lawsuits claiming OxyContin made them addicts.[33] Howard Udell boasted, "We have not settled one of these cases, not one. Personal injury lawyers who bring them in the hopes of a quick payday will continue to be disappointed."[34]*

Raymond Sackler and his son Richard were not so sanguine. The DEA was a problem. However, it could not bring an indictment or cause the type of legal havoc that a U.S. attorney hell-bent on a mission might produce.

"Who better to represent Purdue?" Raymond Sackler asked at an informal meeting at the firm's Norwalk headquarters.[35] Rudy Giuliani was "America's mayor." He was riding high after two terms as New York's mayor and just months after he was widely praised for his calm leadership in the aftermath of the 9/11 terror attacks on the World Trade Center. His 9/11 role had earned Giuliani *Time*'s Man of the Year and an honorary knighthood from Britain's Queen Elizabeth. When he returned to private life in January 2002, he opened Giuliani Partners, a consulting firm. Giuliani was selling access and influence. As a former United States attorney for the prestigious Southern District of New York, he was friendly with many top-ranking Justice Department officials. He knew Asa Hutchinson, the Drug Enforcement Administration director, for twenty years. Maybe, thought the Sacklers, Giuliani might find a way to put a check on Brownlee's Virginia probe.

There was no dissent from Purdue's directors or the top executives. In May 2002, the company retained Giuliani Partners. It was the ex-

---

dence, Purdue claimed, that Meier had a financial interest in keeping the story alive by concentrating on the most sensational and damaging news. "Their agenda was to shut me down," Meier later said.

* Until 1978, Udell had been the law partner of Myron and Martin Greene, the brothers who were attorneys and proxy owners of companies that formed the basis of the Sackler labyrinth of companies in the 1950s and 1960s. Martin Greene went into a solo legal practice in 1978 after Myron Greene died of a heart attack. The address and telephone number listed in the Manhattan yellow pages for his solo law firm was the same as half a dozen Sackler-owned businesses. Udell went to Purdue Pharmaceutical that same year (1978) and became its general counsel.

mayor's first major client. While the fee agreement remains a secret since both Purdue and Giuliani Partners refuse to disclose it, documents produced later by Purdue in litigation reveal it was paying about $3 million a month to all its high-powered attorneys.[36] It could certainly afford it. Oxy was bringing in $30 million per week, about 90 percent of its profits.[37]

Purdue was direct with Giuliani: it had hired him to extinguish the brewing firestorm in Washington.[38] When Laura Nagel heard the news, "My reaction was that they went around me. They went and got Rudy. . . . They thought they were buying access and insight into how to manage things politically."[39]

Giuliani assigned Bernard Kerik, New York's former police commissioner who had also joined Giuliani Partners, to oversee a security appraisal of Purdue's Totowa, New Jersey, manufacturing plant. That was the plant where unaccounted-for Oxy had attracted police attention. And Giuliani set an August meeting with the DEA.

"The mayor and I met with Asa Hutchinson, the director of the DEA; his staff; and people from Purdue [general counsel Udell]," Kerik told *New York* magazine a few weeks later. Karen Tandy, the associate attorney general responsible for Drug Enforcement oversight, also attended.[40] "We don't want Purdue put in a position where it winds up being taken over by the courts," said Kerik. "Or they get put out of business. What I'd like to see come out of this is we set model security standards for the industry."[41]

A week before the first anniversary of 9/11, Giuliani joined Hutchinson and Attorney General John Ashcroft at the opening of a DEA exhibit on terrorism and drug trafficking. Giuliani gave a speech that raised $20,000 for the Drug Enforcement Museum Foundation. When he finished, Hutchinson asked Laura Nagel to join him with the ex-mayor. A week later they gathered in Giuliani's twenty-fourth-floor office overlooking Times Square. The OxyContin team that Giuliani had assembled ran through a thirty-minute PowerPoint they had developed "to keep OxyContin out of the wrong hands." It was built around the concept that Purdue had a good drug and was doing its best to abide by all the necessary rules and regulations. What was needed were better tools to earlier spot abuse and diversion. The DEA pair said little. "We were receivers of the information," Hutchinson later said.

Nagel was anxious to return to headquarters. When she did, colleagues recall that she railed against that "dog and pony show."[42] She soon took notice that Purdue had adopted another tactic popular with pharmaceutical companies: silencing critics by hiring them. Dr. Louis Sullivan, former chief of Health and Human Services, became a Purdue consultant developing courses for medical schools about pain treatment. Jay McCloskey, the Maine prosecutor who had been the earliest federal critic of Purdue's promotion and extravagant doctors' junkets, was a legal consultant. The FDA official who oversaw the OxyContin approval process, Dr. Curtis Wright, had become Purdue's senior medical director.[43]

That autumn, Purdue confronted a wide-ranging investigation under way at the Florida attorney general's office.[44] Richard Sackler, Michael Friedman, and J. David Haddox planned a counterstrategy. Mortimer, eighty-five, and Raymond, eighty-one, kept abreast of the developments.[45]

In November, Purdue made its second "big hire" in its counteroffensive to the ongoing government investigations. Burt Rosen was a familiar and well-connected pharmaceutical lobbyist in the corridors of D.C. power. The Sacklers had lured Rosen from Novartis where he was senior vice president for communications and governmental relations. The amiable, backslapping Rosen had gotten his taste for politics as a law student at the University of South Carolina, where he clerked as an aide to the state's long-serving senator Fritz Hollings. After getting his law degree, he became Pfizer's youngest ever director of government relations. Rosen had a talent for the socializing and dealmaking required to navigate Washington agencies and lawmakers. After Pfizer, he ran Government Relations for three years at Bristol-Myers Squibb, then for eight years ran "Government Affairs" at SmithKline Beecham before joining Novartis. Purdue created a new position for him: vice president of federal government affairs.

Rosen joined the company at a time the Sacklers were increasing their own contributions to politicians ($2.3 million since 1996 to over three hundred candidates and political groups; the author discovered even Arthur Sackler is listed on public records as having made contributions after his death, sometimes Marietta Sackler donating in her deceased husband's name).[46] As Purdue and other opioid manufacturers came under increasing scrutiny, the companies opened up their wallets to lobby Congress and statehouses. Over a decade, drug companies selling an opioid product spent $746 million on state and federal lobbying. They spent another $80 million on state and federal candidates; that was split almost equally between Democrats and Republicans.[47] Rosen directed Purdue's lobbying. He oversaw a little-publicized group, the Pain Care Forum, a group of pharma companies that spent more than $700 million in a decade on lobbying for expanded opiate dispensing and for the FDA to loosen dispensing regulations.[48]

After several months of talks, Giuliani managed to settle the Florida investigation. The Florida attorney general agreed to drop the probe in return for Purdue agreeing to pay up to $2 million to develop a "prescription monitoring program" that allowed the state to maintain digital records of all doctors who dispensed narcotic prescriptions and the patients who filled them.[49] Purdue, however, never developed that software. And inexplicably Florida returned the money the company advanced toward the project. Letting Purdue off so lightly turned out to be a great error. Over the next eight years, law enforcement nicknamed the high concentration of pill mills in Florida's Broward County as the Oxy Express. Over a thousand dispensing clinics sold more OxyContin than any other county in the nation (at its peak, 89 percent of all the OxyContin in America).[50] "The illegal sale of prescription drugs, and oxycodone in particular," concluded the *New York Times* in 2011, "boomed in Florida because of the absence of a widely used prescription drug monitoring system." That was the software Purdue had failed to deliver after agreeing to do so in its 2002 deal with the state's attorney general.[51]

Giuliani also helped Purdue emerge unscathed from hearings called by Ted Kennedy before his Health, Education, Labor and Pensions Committee. Physicians and patients urged government intervention to stop the "misprescribing and overprescribing of this drug."[52] The committee, though, had no appetite for singling out OxyContin. Christopher Dodd, the senator from corporate Purdue's home state, Connecticut, seemed to help Purdue whenever the questioning got too heated. He insisted that the counties reporting the highest levels of OxyContin abuse were places that had long-standing prescription drug problems.[53]

As the Senate probe finished without any breakthroughs, Bernard Kerik announced rigorous changes at Purdue's New Jersey OxyContin plant. Laura Nagel had built a damning case against the cavalier way the company handled the manufacturing of a controlled substance. It was the only one of the 257 OxyContin abuse and diversion cases she initiated over two years connected directly to Purdue.[54] Still, Giuliani had managed to make certain Purdue faced only civil charges. Once the feds signed off, Purdue paid a $2 million civil penalty for its lapses in security and failure to enforce regulations that allowed the drug to be diverted to the black market. By then, OxyContin sales were up twentyfold since its introduction and it was on its way to $2 billion in annual sales. Two million dollars was not an insignificant amount, but it was, as one Purdue executive boasted, "less than a day's [OxyContin] revenue."[55] * [56]

* Kerik resigned from Giuliani Partners the following year. President George W. Bush had nominated him to become the secretary of homeland security on Giuliani's recommendation. Kerik later pled guilty in 2010 to eight felonies, including lying to White House officials and tax fraud, and was sentenced to four years in prison.

47

"YOU MESSED WITH THE WRONG MOTHER"

The string of victories in deflecting most of the regulatory and legal challenges left the Sacklers overconfident. Purdue seemed invincible. Competing narcotic painkillers from other pharma companies had not dented OxyContin's record sales. Florida had closed its wide-ranging investigation, the FDA remained almost completely passive, the DEA probe had stalled, and more than half of the one hundred lawsuits filed by victims' families had been dismissed.[1] John Brownlee, the Virginia U.S. attorney, was the last worry. Although a federal criminal probe was cause for concern, the Sacklers doubted that Brownlee could muster much of a case from his tiny Western Virginia district.

The victories would prove short-lived. Everyone at Purdue underestimated the growing fury, determination, and commitment among the families of Oxy victims.

Twenty-nine-year-old Jill Carol Skolek was a single mom in Phillipsburg, New Jersey. April 29, 2002, was the first time her six-year-old son, Brian, had come back from school and not found her waiting for him at the bus stop near their house. When he got home he discovered his mother in bed, in what he thought was a deep sleep. He fixed a snack, spent a few hours watching cartoons and playing with toys, and then crawled beside her and fell asleep. The next morning, when she still seemed asleep, he shook her and kept yelling "Mommy." Finally, he called 911. "I need your help. I think my mommy's heart stopped."[2] Only when the EMS arrived did they realize that Jill had been dead since the previous day.

Jill's mother, Marianne Skolek, a part-time nurse, lived thirty minutes away in Readington. The unexpected death of her daughter left her to care for her grandson.[3] Marianne could not understand why her daughter died. Her only physical problem was a herniated disk from lifting furniture the previous year. The funeral three days later was a small gathering of family. The obituary in the *Courier-News* read in part: "Jill, I love you with all my heart and am truly proud of the way you raised your son. Rest in peace precious daughter until we can be together again. Love Mommy."

One morning, a week after Jill's funeral, Brian startled his grandmother.

"Mommy changed."

"What do you mean?"

"She changed after taking that pill."[4]

He had gone with his mother on visits to a family doctor and remembered how her back felt much better after she got something the doctor called "oxy."

Marianne, who worked weekend shifts at the oncology unit at Somerset Medical Center, was familiar with OxyContin. She dispensed it herself to end-of-life cancer patients.[5] "I turned to my grandson and said, 'Mommy didn't take OxyContin, honey.'"[6] Marianne was stunned when the medical examiner's toxicology report confirmed that Jill had died of respiratory arrest. The cause? Heart failure due to OxyContin. The death was ruled accidental.[7]

"Anyone who is responsible for this is going to be held accountable," she vowed."[8]

It was time to start digging into what happened to her daughter. She wanted answers as to why the drug she administered to terminally ill cancer patients was prescribed to Jill for back pain. Marianne was no stranger to research. In 1991 she had been the top student and president of her graduating nurse class. She had a paralegal certification and had served on the local Community Service Board for Gannett's *Courier-News*. Her articles about the many problems faced by AIDS patients, coupled with her volunteer service at an AIDS support group, earned her a Community Service Award in 1993 from a local HIV/AIDS Task Force.[9]

She tracked down a couple of other patients familiar with the doctor's practice where Jill had been a patient. One told her that after the first appointment with the physician, subsequent ones were with the receptionist, who wrote the Oxy refills. That prompted Marianne to write to the New Jersey and Pennsylvania medical boards where the physician was licensed. State investigators interviewed her and opened a case. Meanwhile, she met with lawyers at a Philadelphia-area firm that friends had recommended. They seemed confident there was a wrongful death action for what had happened to Jill. They worked for weeks with Marianne on preparing a complaint.[10]

A few days before the complaint was scheduled to be filed, one of the attorneys called. They could not proceed. He claimed they did "not have the resources for it."

It made no sense to her that lawyers who had been so hot to take the case dropped out without a good reason. At home that evening she sat at her dining room table. It doubled as a work desk, half of it filled with a computer, printer, and fax. What could they have meant by "we don't have the resources"? Then it dawned on her.

"I said aloud, 'It's not the doctor—it's the pharmaceutical company!' "[11]

Her first online search was to learn more about the company that made OxyContin. Every night she explored the web for information about the executives who ran Purdue and the history of OxyContin. "It was becoming more and more evident to me as I dug that it was a web of deceitful marketing."[12]

Promising herself that her daughter's death would not be in vain, Marianne Skolek became a one-person advocate on behalf of Jill and other OxyContin victims. She delved into how the drug was being dispensed nationwide. Her grandson, Brian, sometimes asked, "Did you get the bad guys yet?"[13]

For six months she peppered the FDA with letters providing examples in which she thought Purdue was mass-merchandising its powerful painkiller. She also called local reporters in New Jersey and Pennsylvania and encouraged them to look into the company and its best-selling painkiller. A few small-town newspapers in areas hard hit by OxyContin reported that "Marianne has launched her own investigation into her daughter's death."[14] New Jersey's *Courier-News* let her write an op-ed in which she listed her phone number and asked others who "are interested in starting a grass-roots campaign" to get in touch.[15]

She did not then know it, but her letters helped move the FDA to issue a January 2003 "warning letter" to Purdue. It read in part, "Your journal advertisements omit and minimize the serious safety risks associated with OxyContin, and promote it for uses beyond which have been proven safe and effective."[16] In particular, the FDA highlighted osteoarthritis, which Purdue's detail team pushed as a treatable condition at the same time downplaying the drug's potential addictiveness. Purdue supervisors had also drafted an article published in a medical journal without any disclosure of the company's role. It claimed that patients taking less than 60 milligrams per day can stop the drug "abruptly without withdrawal symptoms." The detail team cited that extensively in sales pitches.

The FDA had enough evidence of misconduct to commence a false advertising hearing. That would allow the agency to punish Purdue with restrictive labeling requirements and restrictions on refills. Giuliani, however, met half a dozen times with FDA officials and again managed to make it go away. Ultimately, Purdue did not make any public admission of wrongdoing or remove OxyContin from pharmacy shelves. It only had to promise not to do it again.[17]

The month after the FDA letter to Purdue, Skolek drove to New York for a conference at Columbia University's National Center for Addiction and Substance Abuse.[18] She had decided to attend after seeing a notice that Purdue was sending medical director J. David Haddox. "I wanted to see what made this company tick," she later wrote.[19] She read about Haddox before the conference and learned he was the dentist turned doctor who had invented the theory of pseudoaddiction. Besides Haddox, Marianne got a chance to see the DEA's Laura Nagel, who warned about the abuse potential for "hillbilly heroin."[20] Richard Blumenthal, Connecticut's attorney general (and now U.S. Senator), was also a panelist. Purdue's Stamford headquarters were in Blumenthal's jurisdiction.

Marianne sat in the front row. She had bought off eBay an OxyContin "window shade" pen that had been one of the many small gifts the detail team distributed to doctors by the tens of thousands. She had wanted that pen because the FDA had ordered it pulled from the market since some of the dispensing information on the pullout shade was wrong.

In Haddox's presentation, he extolled Oxy's pain relief benefits and glossed over its potential for addiction. Marianne stared at him and played with the pullout shade. "The lies, the lies he was spewing in front of a packed audience grated on me."[21]

When the conference ended, Haddox walked through a makeshift aisle between dozens of rows of folding chairs. As they passed one another, Skolek said she "did not hear the word 'now' but felt the word 'now.'" The one-hundred-pound Skolek rammed Haddox with her shoulder and sent him crashing into the folding chairs.

"Now you know how the victims of OxyContin feel when they hit the depths of addiction and are on their knees fighting the horrific effects of the withdrawing from the drug," she said as she walked past.[22]

After Haddox hurriedly left the hall, the only remaining Purdue executive was Robin Hogen, the company's soft-spoken press spokesman (his official title was vice president of public affairs). He had witnessed Marianne's body block of Haddox. Some reporters had gathered around Hogen. He was easy to spot, sporting a different colorful bow tie every day.

The Purdue press office was familiar with Marianne. Initially they had avoided saying anything publicly about her. It was a no win, they concluded, to get into a public fray with a grieving mother. A couple of months before the Columbia conference, however, Hogen's deputy press director, James Heines, told reporters that Skolek had "raised a lot of fear and concern based on misinformation. . . . The death of her daughter is tragic, but I don't know the real circumstances behind it and I haven't seen the autopsy report. . . . She [Marianne] might be a well-meaning person, but I don't believe she is an expert in pain management."[23]

As the Columbia conference broke up, Hogen indicated that he had additional information about Skolek's daughter. "We think she [Jill] abused drugs."[24] Bob Braun, a *Courier-News* reporter, noted the medical examiner's report had not mentioned that. "That's a pretty heavy charge to make against a young woman who died, leaving behind a 6-year-old son . . . because Jill can't defend herself." Hogen shrugged, smiled, and said he "really doesn't know."[25]

But Hogen had done what he wanted to do, planted a seed of doubt. Maybe Jill Skolek was not as often described as an adoring and innocent mother. Purdue had gotten dozens of lawsuits dismissed with its aggressive defense that put the victims on trial. It claimed the plaintiffs were often addicts who had latched on to the painkiller to satisfy their drug habits.

Braun wrote about Hogen's "disclosure" in his *Courier-News* column a few days later. What Hogen said was important "because it might lead journalists—like me—to avoid writing about her mother's efforts to hold a big pharmaceutical house accountable. No one wants to create sympathy for a junkie. But Jill was no junkie."[26] * [27]

Hogen and others at Purdue misjudged Marianne Skolek if they thought she would abandon her search for answers if they tarred her daughter's reputation. "I told Hogen that you messed with the wrong mother."[28] She redoubled her commitment to expose Purdue as "an out of control, greedy pharmaceutical company."[29] Two weeks after Braun's column, Purdue's chief operating officer, Michael Friedman, wrote to the newspaper. His statement read in part, "I write on behalf of Purdue Pharma L.P. to repudiate the comment about Jill Skolek made by our employee, Robin Hogen, as reported in Bob Braun's March 5 column. Hogen regrets having made the remark and has acknowledged in a letter to Jill Skolek's mother, Marianne, that he was wrong to do so. . . . Hogen's inappropriate remark is inconsistent with our values and our commitment, and we sincerely regret that it was made."[30]

The diminutive grandmother became a regular at local hearings and she refined her investigation and writing skills. When she learned that Purdue had asked the FDA to approve OxyContin to treat postpartum pain for new mothers who were breastfeeding their infants, Skolek "flooded the country with emails and faxes to Attorneys General and the media reporting." She told them "we had enough devastation in the country without addicting infants to OxyContin." Purdue withdrew its request for expanded approval.

At the end of 2002, investigators working for U.S. Attorney John Brownlee got in touch with Marianne. She had written to all fifty state attorneys general and dozens of federal prosecutors beseeching them to investigate Purdue and offering whatever help she could provide.[31] The timing was ideal for Brownlee. He had just started his probe.

By telephone and email she remained in daily contact. Skolek gave

* After the conference, Braun had also interviewed Connecticut attorney general Richard Blumenthal. During the panel discussion, Blumenthal said his office had "an ongoing inquiry" about Purdue. Braun asked whether that "constituted an investigation." "Well, yes, you can call it an investigation," Blumenthal said. "It might not be a criminal investigation, but it's an investigation." Purdue's Hogen had overheard the exchange and left Braun a voicemail a few hours later. "There is no investigation under way." He claimed Blumenthal had only asked for some Purdue marketing documents, "but that does not constitute an investigation, and that would be inaccurate for you to report tomorrow that the attorney general of Connecticut has launched an investigation of Purdue Pharma."

his investigators some early leads. Marianne had found an employee in Purdue's legal department when buying some OxyContin promotional items on eBay. Marianne and her son drove to Stamford to meet with her at a Starbucks. There they discovered that a Purdue employee had "become addicted to OxyContin and was fired. . . . She had worked for Purdue Pharma for close to 25 years." Although the ex-employee "was petrified of Purdue Pharma and their power, what a story she had to tell." Skolek put her in touch with "Delta Force," her nickname for the Brownlee task force.

Marianne seemed to be everywhere. She set up a website, oxydeaths .com, as a resource for those who wanted to share stories about the drug's dangers.[32] In Iowa, she teamed up with Chelly Griffith, an outspoken mother of two who had become an addict after being prescribed OxyContin for a herniated disk. She was furious that the FDA had failed to require Purdue to include the word "addictive" on Oxy's label instead of the more obtuse notice that it has "an abuse liability similar to morphine."[33] And Skolek got Purdue to remove from their website a press release titled "65–0: OxyContin Cases Against Purdue Pharma Dismissed at a Record Rate." She "told them it was very bad taste to call them an OxyContin victory and to gloat over it."[34]

Skolek was a key source for reporter Doris Bloodsworth's seminal front-page, five-part *Orlando Sentinel* series titled "OxyContin Under Fire: Pain Pill Leaves Death Trail." The first installment appeared on October 19, 2003. The *Columbia Journalism Review*, in a later analysis of early media coverage about OxyContin, noted that "The *Sentinel*'s coverage was more ambitious [than earlier reporting]. At its core was a claim that posed a serious threat to Purdue's business: Taking OxyContin as prescribed could lead to dependence, addiction, and death."[35]

Instead of countering with facts, Purdue looked for mistakes in the series. "In retrospect, despite the Sentinel's prescience, journalistic carelessness caused the project to backfire, and thus miss its target. Within days, serious reporting errors in the series emerged." Two "innocent victims" were in fact drug addicts.[36] Bloodsworth's conclusions from her analysis of the autopsy reports were overstated; instead of 573 fatal overdoses "solely from OxyContin" in Florida during 2001 and 2002, only 25 percent of those were from Oxy alone. As the *Sentinel* made a series of corrections, Purdue used the "unforced errors" to "attack the Sentinel in a PR campaign ultimately aimed at avoiding a regulatory crackdown and ensuring a bonanza of profits."[37] Bloodsworth resigned the following February and the city editor was reassigned.*[38]

In 2004, OxyContin officially earned the dubious distinction as the most abused drug in the United States.[39] A former Purdue assistant marketing manager told the author that he never heard anyone mention that dark milestone at its Stamford headquarters. "It was as if we did not talk about it, it hadn't really happened." A coworker joked once to him that the news reports made it seem like there was a "*pain*demic" in the making. "He thought it was funny. If anyone in a supervisory position heard that, he would have been terminated. It was not a joking matter."[40]

Meanwhile, the Sacklers kept the Purdue team focused on news that avoided any discussion of the growing OxyContin health crisis. The company championed the "Global Day Against Pain." That was a World Health Organization–sponsored event to make pain relief a basic human right. Canada and Sweden were the first countries to go along. This emerging view of pain treatment was, as some experts noted, an "inflection point" in which "failure to provide pain management was professional misconduct and . . . poor medicine."[41]

The Sacklers and Purdue, however, could not ignore the accumulating bad news forever. John Brownlee was busy putting the finishing touches on what he was certain was a substantial and damning case. He had focused on a narrow aspect of federal criminal law. Misbranding or fraudulently marketing OxyContin was a felony. The statute did not require proof of intent or any damages. Simply doing it was the crime. Although that was the minimum count Brownlee wanted to file, his task force was confident it had gathered enough evidence for charges against Purdue money-laundering, wire and mail fraud, and defrauding the government.[42]

Under Justice Department regulations, Brownlee's superiors in Washington had to sign off on his case. He forwarded it to headquarters in 2006.[43] The Criminal Division career prosecutors who reviewed it recommended the most serious charges. One reason for their confidence was a confidential Department of Justice memorandum prepared by Brownlee's team that determined that senior Purdue executives were

* The *Sentinel* never retracted the story but did assign two senior reporters who worked for three months before the paper printed a 2,500-word article on what had gone wrong in Bloodsworth's reporting and the paper's editorial and fact-checking oversight.

aware of OxyContin's abuse problems within months of its 1996 on-sale date, not five years later as they claimed.[44]

When Purdue learned that Brownlee was far enough along to send a draft complaint to headquarters, Giuliani called James Comey, the deputy attorney general.[45] Purdue's lawyers had assembled what they claimed was proof that Brownlee's team had abused its investigatory powers. When Comey called Brownlee to ask whether it was true, Brownlee immediately drove to Washington to make his case in person. Comey was satisfied after they met that there was no wrongdoing. He sent Brownlee back to Virginia and told him, "Do your case."

Purdue kept scrambling for ways to derail it. Howard Udell, its general counsel, convinced a senior DOJ lawyer to telephone Brownlee at home shortly before he was about to seek a sealed grand jury indictment. He suggested Brownlee wait since Purdue wanted to settle the matter without formal proceedings. Brownlee was certain it was another delay tactic.

Brownlee and his team met with Giuliani and Purdue's defense lawyers over two days in September. As a former U.S. attorney, Giuliani was intimately familiar with how the process worked. Although he had no intention of bringing the case to trial since public opinion was turning against his client and its product, Purdue's defense team blustered they would turn the case into a humiliating public defeat for the government. Brownlee was unimpressed.[46] A few weeks later, defense attorneys met with senior Justice Department officials in Washington and failed to convince them there was not enough evidence to bring charges against Purdue and some top executives.[47]

Only years later would internal Purdue documents demonstrate that while its legal team negotiated with federal prosecutors, it continued most of the same bad behavior that had gotten the company into trouble. In the first three months of 2007, during plea bargaining negotiations, the Sackler-family directors learned that more than five thousand "adverse events" had been reported to Purdue. They came from doctors, pharmacists, health clinics, hospitals, and law enforcement. Over one hundred consumers had called Purdue's compliance hotline reporting everything from suspected illegal sales to overdoses. It was a record number of alerts, more than triple that of any previous quarter.

The FDA defined "adverse events" as "any undesirable experience associated with the use of a medical product in a patient." Drug companies are required to report "serious" ones to the government, including when a drug is suspected of causing death, hospitalization, disability, and birth defects. The FDA has a catchall category, "Other Serious," which includes such trigger events as anything "requiring treatment in an emergency room . . . [and] the development of drug dependence or drug abuse."[48]

Purdue's compliance team only investigated twenty-one cases from the flood of calls and reports. They cherry-picked the ones that appeared less serious. Then, based on those, they concluded there was no widespread diversion or abuse problem with Oxy. They did not report a *single* call from the hotline or the five thousand adverse events to the FDA, even though those reports indicated that as many as two thirds involved hospitalization or visits to the ER or raised questions about OxyContin dependence or abuse.[49] They did not inform the DEA or any other federal, state, or local drug and law enforcement agency.[50]

In early summer, Brownlee got bad news from headquarters. Top DOJ officials, including Alice Fisher, then the Criminal Division's chief, decided against filing the expanded charge and instead authorized Brownlee to bring only the less serious misbranding case.[51] That was a clean and straightforward prosecution. "They decided at HQ to go for the low-hanging fruit," a case investigator confided to the author.[52] Brownlee later told Joseph Rannazzisi, a DEA official, that the DOJ decision had put him into an untenable position. By eliminating the most serious charges, it forced him to settle the case without going to trial. Otherwise, he told Rannazzisi, Purdue's large, well-funded legal team might well overwhelm his small group of prosecutors. "He told me he was outgunned," Rannazzisi told *The New York Times*.[53]

On May 10, Purdue's Michael Friedman (now president), Howard Udell, and its former medical director Paul Goldenheim, and a team of nearly a dozen lawyers, arrived at a federal courthouse in Abingdon, Virginia. Giuliani and Purdue's lawyers had hashed out a plea agreement with Brownlee.

Brownlee had agreed not to seek jail time for the three executives in exchange for their guilty pleas to the misbranding charges. The Sackler-family directors voted unanimously that Purdue Frederick, the drug firm Arthur, Mortimer, and Raymond had bought in 1952, would plead guilty to a felony for deceptive and fraudulent marketing practices in misbranding OxyContin as less addictive and subject to abuse than immediate release opioids.[54] It was a clever strategy. Purdue Frederick's plea effectively put it out of business while protecting Purdue LP and Purdue Inc., the two entities primarily responsible for OxyContin since its 1996 release. Avoiding a guilty plea also ensured that Purdue Pharma retained its ability to do business with government health care agencies such as Veterans Affairs, Medicaid, and Medicare.[55]

In the Virginia courthouse, Purdue's lawyers admitted that starting a year before OxyContin's release, its "supervisors and employees, with the intent to defraud or mislead, marketed and promoted OxyContin as less addictive, less subject to abuse and diversion, and less likely to cause tolerance and withdrawal than other pain medications."[56] Friedman, Udell, and Goldenheim pled guilty to criminal fraud in marketing OxyContin.[57] Purdue was fined $634.5 million. Some legal analysts questioned whether that was a big enough penalty considering that Purdue had $9.6 billion in sales of Oxy in the previous six years. The three executives also got fined: Friedman $19 million, Udell $8 million, and Goldenheim $7.5 million.

In the Consent Agreement, Purdue agreed that going forward it "shall not make any written or oral claim that is false, misleading, or deceptive" in marketing OxyContin. The court ordered the company to give doctors and patients an evenhanded presentation of the dangers and benefits of the drug. It agreed to present the risks of taking OxyContin for longer periods and at higher doses, including the likelihood of addiction and possibly death.

In a separate Corporate Integrity Agreement, Purdue agreed to adhere strictly to rules and regulations that banned the type of deception that had been its trademark OxyContin promotion. The Sacklers and top management committed to a training course to ensure they understood and would comply with all the requirements. The agreement obligated Purdue and its directors and employees to promptly report to the government any signs of deceptive or false marketing.[58]

The company also agreed to create an "abuse and diversion detection program" designed to identify high-prescribing physicians. When Purdue became suspicious of "potential abuse or diversion," it was required to stop promoting and selling OxyContin to those doctors and promptly report it "to appropriate medical, regulatory or law enforcement authorities."[59]

Although the Sackler family escaped without any personal admission of guilt, the settlement required that Richard, Jonathan, Mortimer,

Beverly, Ilene, Kathe, and Theresa Sackler certify in writing that each had read and understood the rules and swore to follow them.[60] The Sacklers had reluctantly agreed to a sentence on which Justice Department prosecutors were insistent: "Purdue is pleading guilty as described above because Purdue is in fact guilty." (In 2019, an ex-family director, David Sackler, played down the extent of the company's culpability: "It is conduct that the company engaged in, yes. A number of sales reps took the language on the label and overdid the safety. We wish it never happened. For sure the company should have had a more robust compliance framework, and should have weeded out the reps that were misbranding the medication. For sure.")[61]

Brownlee had asked Marianne Skolek to present a victims' impact statement at the sentencing hearing. She was furious that the three defendants would leave the court as free men. "As I walked in front of the defense table Friedman, Udell and Goldenheim, surrounded by their flock of high-profile attorneys glared at me. I stood 3-feet from them and said, 'You are sheer evil. You are bastards.' "

She began to move toward them, thinking about reaching out and slapping one. "They deserved it." But she did not do it.[62] Instead, she gave an impassioned plea during which the courthouse fell silent. She did not convince the judge, however, to change his mind by sending the trio to jail or to issue an order that "they should not be gainfully employed again in the pharmaceutical industry."[63]

Federal prosecutors and public health advocates hailed the 2007 judgment as the end of the criminal misconduct at Purdue. Pharmaceutical industry analysts forecast that OxyContin had been stopped in time to avoid a more serious and deadly epidemic.[64]

The DEA's Laura Nagel, who had tried building a case against Purdue for five years, was one of those who did not join in the celebration. "I would not have been happy unless we put them in shackles in front of the courthouse."[65] Marianne Skolek was also not pleased. "I knew that the evil I witnessed that day was not going away. . . . They would continue their need for greed and be successful at it."[66]

Brownlee and his fellow prosecutors had been so impressed with Skolek's impact statement that they asked her to present it again two months later before the Senate's Judiciary Committee hearings into whether the Purdue plea deal was adequate enough punishment. Skolek appeared with her eleven-year-old grandson. She wanted him to see where the fight to get justice for his mother had brought them. The Senate chamber fell hushed when Marianne settled at the large oak table and pulled out a few sheets of paper with handwritten notes. Before she began, she noticed that only two seats away was Jay McCloskey, who had been the U.S. attorney from Maine from 1993 to 2001. He had been the first federal prosecutor to take notice of problems with OxyContin abuse. "He was relentless in exposing Purdue Pharma," Marianne thought to herself. "He was not seated at the table with me as an ally though. McCloskey was now a hired consultant for Purdue Pharma and he was defending them."

She told the senators that "Pain patients from various pain societies will speak of the merits of OxyContin and their quality of life being restored because of the drug. These pain societies throughout the country, are funded by Purdue Pharma."[67]

Her voice picked up tempo. "Anything that is imposed against these convicted criminals will not give us back Jill, but I will guarantee that Purdue Pharma will never forget the name Jill Skolek. . . . I want to know why 12 warning letters were sent by the FDA to Purdue Pharma about their marketing of OxyContin and to this day, they are not required to put 'highly addictive' or 'addictive' on the label of the drug. I want to know why the FDA deleted without reading so many of my emails about the marketing of OxyContin until this last month. I want to know why Curtis Wright, while employed by the FDA, played an intricate part in the approval of OxyContin and then was hired by Purdue Pharma. . . . I want to know how Rudy Giuliani could be the 'big star' hired by Purdue Pharma to play down the abuse and diversion of OxyContin and also get paid by the DEA for work performed for them. I want to know why the Sackler family has not been held accountable for their involvement with Purdue Pharma and the mass marketing of OxyContin. Eventually Purdue Pharma will introduce another blockbuster drug similar to OxyContin. . . . My advice to Purdue Pharma is when you are ready to introduce another drug such as OxyContin . . . look behind you, because I will be right there. I will be working at having Howard Udell disbarred for his criminal activities and Paul Goldenheim's medical license revoked for what amounts to white collar drug trafficking. I will be actively working at Friedman, Udell and Goldenheim never being able to work in the pharmaceutical industry again because they are convicted criminals who criminally marketed

OxyContin. I will accomplish this . . . do not doubt me at not being successful at achieving this. Her name was Jill Carol Skolek. She did not deserve to be prescribed OxyContin and die because of the criminal activities of individuals of Purdue Pharma. Please give my family justice and investigate the criminal activity of Purdue Pharma."[68]

48

PROFITS AND CORPSES

The strict terms of the Consent Agreement signed by the Sackler-family directors should have been the end of OxyContin's nationwide trail of destruction. The worst was yet to come, however. What seemed like a persistent problem in 2007 would over the coming decade develop into a full-blown national epidemic, a public health crisis that has claimed several hundred thousand American lives. The most lethal years and the greatest abuse would all come *after* the 2007 guilty plea.

Purdue apparently decided to break most of its promises to the federal government. The company did not report dangerous prescribers. It did not even order that the detail team stop visiting them.[1] Instead, it expanded OxyContin's deceitful promotion and sales campaign for the sole purpose of selling ever-more drugs for the longest possible period and at the highest dosages.

A few months before the plea agreement, the Sackler-family directors received a report that forecast a 2007 profit of $407 million. At a July 15 board meeting, just two months after their legal settlement, they learned that estimate was too low by 50 percent. Net sales in 2007 would top a billion dollars and produce profits of more than $600 million.[2] OxyContin was responsible for ninety percent of all revenue.

The main reason for the huge spike in the bottom line? "Sales effort," according to internal memos. At the time, Purdue had 301 sales representatives (compared to 34 in drug research). The detail team's focus on getting physicians to write higher-strength prescriptions had paid off. More than half of the 2007 record-setting revenue was from sales of the 80 mg pill, at the time the most powerful OxyContin.[3] Over the coming decade, Purdue more than doubled the size of its detail team, hiring hundreds of new reps to keep up with the drug's surging demand.[4]

The Sackler-family directors were not remote board members with little idea of what was happening inside the company. Internal documents reveal the extent to which many Purdue executives and managers who reported to them complained about their micromanagement, particularly from Richard Sackler. Once he overruled a recommendation from one of the company's outside counsel that it keep a wide distance from the three executives who had pled guilty. Why? he asked. They had made a public statement of contrition and paid large personal fines.[5] Although Goldenheim had left the company, Friedman visited regularly and Howard Udell had moved back into his corner office and helped sometimes with in-house legal matters. Also, after their guilty plea, the Department of Health and Human Services had banned the trio for twenty years from doing business with any taxpayer-subsidized health care (Medicare, Medicaid, etc.). Richard Sackler had spearheaded the effort to hire a premier law firm that appealed that ruling and got the ban reduced to twelve years. (Their effort to get it lifted entirely was rejected in 2010 by a Washington, D.C., judge.)[6]

The Sacklers approved several million dollars in payments to the convicted executives (the largest was $3 million to Michael Friedman).[7] That money helped offset most of the impact from the fines that had been levied against them. The Massachusetts attorney general later charged that the help to the three men was "to maintain their [the three executives] loyalty and protect the Sackler family."[8]

The author uncovered that, in the wake of the bad publicity from the criminal guilty plea, Purdue relied increasingly on influencing the "key physician opinion leaders" as it tried to maintain the momentum of Oxy's sales. An example was *Advances in Pain Management*, launched near the time of the plea agreement. It was jointly sponsored by the University of Kentucky Colleges of Pharmacy and Medicine and Remedica Medical Education and Publishing. Purdue had flooded Kentucky medical and pharmaceutical school curriculums with grants and subsidies. The Kentucky Pharmacists Association had opposed stricter dispensing rules for OxyContin in 2001.[9] Remedica was a London-based medical publisher that had been founded the same year Purdue released OxyContin.[10]

It might seem unlikely that a London publisher ended up as a partner with an accredited college of pharmacy located in a ground zero state for OxyContin abuse and diversion.[11] Who were its editors? Russell Portenoy, a leading voice for the pain and opioid reevaluation movement, was the journal's editor-in-chief. In a small-print footnote in the first issue, Portenoy listed forty-two "relevant financial relationships" with pharmaceutical companies, including Purdue.[12] The associate editor was Ricardo Cruciani, an Ivy League–trained chair of the neurology department at Philadelphia's Drexel research university. Portenoy and Cruciani reversed positions on the masthead in late 2008. One of the journal's featured writers was Lynn Webster, a Utah-based anesthesiologist who was an advocate of pseudoaddiction and had created the Opioid Risk Tool, a bare-bones five-question assessment intended to ferret out patients at risk of abusing opioids.[13] For doctors not up-to-date on the latest developments in pain management, that one-minute screening contributed to a false sense that liberalized dispensing of opioids was not risky. Purdue, and other opioid manufacturers, featured it on their websites.[14] The CDC ultimately concluded that Webster's screening test was ineffective; it had "insufficient accuracy" and was "extremely inconsistent."[15]

Was it a coincidence that *Advances in Pain Management* published articles that at times seemed as if they were taken from Purdue's marketing playbook?[16] Portenoy and Cruciani received more than $2 million over time for consulting, lectures, and research from Purdue and other opioid manufacturers.[17] Lynn Webster's Lifetree Pain Clinic in Salt Lake City had also received millions in research; an investigation by *The Salt Lake Tribune* later reported that Webster ranked "among the top 50 for single largest payments received" from drug companies, "behind marquee hospitals, such as the Mayo Clinic, Cleveland Clinic and Duke and Harvard Universities."[18] Portenoy and Cruciani were not far behind as recipients of drug company largesse (the money spigot to Cruciani was cut off in late 2017 after seventeen of his female patients in three states accused him of sexual assault and rape; he was convicted the following year and is serving a ten-year sentence).[19]

Webster's Lifetree Pain Clinic closed after the DEA raided it in 2010 and discovered a file cabinet labeled "deceased patients." More than twenty of his patients who were prescribed massive doses of OxyContin had died under his care. (The U.S. attorney did not file criminal charges, something a DEA agent described as the "most frustrating event of his career.")[20] Webster's problems did not mean that Purdue distanced itself from him. It continued paying hundreds of thousands to Webster as he continued echoing the party line for liberalized opioid dispensing. With Purdue's backing, Webster later became the president of the American Academy of Pain Medicine and a senior editor of *Pain Medicine*, a journal that relied only on advertising from Purdue and other drug companies with narcotic painkillers.[21]

Working with key physicians in the reevaluation movement and lobbying for good coverage in pain specialty periodicals was just one strategy that Purdue rolled out to prevent OxyContin's sales from plateauing after its 2007 federal guilty plea. The following year, it added over one hundred new sales representatives and introduced an opioid savings card that discounted the first five prescriptions (induced by those discounts, 160,000 people tried OxyContin for the first time and 44,000 became repeat patients). The marketing and promotion budget doubled to $160 million.

Still, the Sacklers worried about more than simply a slowing of Oxy's momentum. Purdue was a one-drug company whose future success lay in selling as much OxyContin as possible for as long as possible. Richard sent a private memo to his relatives on the board in mid-2008 and warned about "a dangerous concentration of risk." He raised the possibility that they might want to sell Purdue; OxyContin's success meant they could get a great price. That idea fell flat with other family-directors who instead wanted to "milk the profits."[22]

At four board meetings in 2008, the Sackler directors voted to distribute $850 million to themselves from Oxy's record profits.[23] According to "some people close to the family," the *Wall Street Journal* later reported, how much and when to take profits was a matter on which the directors did not always agree. The unidentified sources told the *Journal* that Raymond Sackler and his relatives—Richard, Jonathan, and David—wanted to reinvest the profits into the business while Mortimer and his relatives—particularly Kathe and Mortimer D.—insisted the money be paid to the family.[24] At the September 2008 board meeting, the Sackler directors voted themselves $199 million in profits. At the following month's meeting they got a report that acknowledged OxyContin abuse and diversion was a nationwide problem. One hundred and sixty-three tips about excessive prescribing and diversion had come into Purdue's hotline the previous month. None were reported to law enforcement or the FDA. With that unpleasant discussion over, the Sacklers focused on a new "Toppers Club Sales Contest." The five sales representatives who managed the biggest increases in revenues in their territories stood to win the largest bonuses ever paid by the company.[25]

The competition resulted in another year of record revenues. That translated into huge bonuses more than double the expected quotas for the entire sales force. At the same March 2009 board meeting at which the Sacklers approved the Toppers Club Sales Contest, they voted another $200 million for themselves.[26] Two months later they were informed that the company had violated the Corporate Integrity Agreement that had been part of their 2007 guilty plea. Purdue's managers had ignored their obligations to oversee the detail team and prevent misrepresentations in the pitches to doctors. The Sacklers' response? They fired three salesmen. They also approved another $162 million in payments to themselves.[27] A couple of months later they voted to pay the family $173 million despite a flurry of internal correspondence showing that both Richard and Mortimer were concerned about a sales department prediction that OxyContin's revenue was flattening and might soon decline. To reinvigorate sales, in 2010 Purdue introduced a "new and improved" tamper-resistant OxyContin. David Sackler later claimed the two-year project cost the company $1 billion. Purdue touted the new version as more difficult to crush, snort, or inject. The company knew its reformulated version helped in only a small minority of instances in which someone did that to get an immediate high.[28] Upward of 90 percent of patients misused OxyContin by swallowing the pills.[29]

The company had conducted two small trials, run by three employees and a paid consultant. In one, recreational drug users thought the tamper-resistant coating made Oxy less desirable. In a second study, twenty-nine subjects, for seven days, snorted crushed tamper-resistant Oxy while others got a placebo. Purdue concluded from the ratings given by the volunteers that the tamper-resistant version had "a reduced abuse potential compared to the original formulation."[30]

From years of accumulating data, the FDA knew the two Purdue studies proved little. The agency's officials informed the company that during its field tests of the new version, there was "no effect" in reducing the addiction and overdose potential. Still, the FDA approved the tamper-resistant OxyContin.

The author learned the reason Purdue wanted the new coating was not about reducing the deadly fallout from its star drug, but to obtain a patent extension to prevent generic competition. Once the FDA approved it, Purdue rolled out a campaign titled *Opioids with Abuse Deterrent Properties*.[31] It spent millions on sponsoring and touting its crush-resistant formulation as the first ever narcotic pain reliever that reduced the chances for abuse and slashed the addiction rate.[32]

The campaign worked. Many doctors believed it and picked up their prescribing pace. That physicians were susceptible to pseudoscience, of course, was something Mortimer and Raymond had learned decades earlier from Arthur and his major drug launches at the McAdams agency.

In 2010, Purdue spent a record $226 million on marketing and promotion, mostly for its "new and improved" OxyContin. Some of the marketing budget was for the release of a new FDA-approved drug Purdue had worked on for nearly three years. Butrans was a narcotic patch the company claimed delivered a five-day dose of buprenorphine, a synthetic opioid twenty-five to forty times more powerful than morphine. Although its clinical tests demonstrated it was ineffective in treating osteoarthritis, at a board meeting the Sacklers asked if it was possible for the sales reps to omit that failed study. The detail team later mentioned osteoarthritis in over a third of their doctor visits without citing the negative trial results.[33]

The Sacklers pushed the sales team to its limits. Each rep had to meet escalating target quotas for how often they visited physicians. The average was 7.5 visits daily. In 2010, that translated into more than half a million one-on-one sales pitches. Starting the following year, with yet a larger detail squad, the number of visits hit three quarters of a million.[34] Dozens of internal emails and memos reveal that the Sackler-family directors believed the sales team could always do more as well as do it better.[35]

The one matter on which there were no complaints from the Sacklers was how much money they got from Oxy profits. At four board meetings during 2010, they approved an additional $890 million for themselves ($249 million in February, $141 million in April, $240 million in September, and $260 million in December).[36] They also ratified a remarkably ambitious ten-year plan that included doubling the detail team and increasing opioid sales by 20 percent annually. It projected that the profits to the Sackler family from 2010 through 2020 would be "at least $700,000,000 each year."[37]

In 2011, four years after the criminal guilty plea by Purdue and three top executives, OxyContin gained the dubious distinction as the country's most deadly drug, surpassing the combined fatalities from heroin and cocaine overdoses.[38] The Sacklers worried about the increasing media coverage that blamed the company for how aggressively it fed the demand and ignored the "danger to public safety." The family believed it encouraged more legal complaints against Purdue. A few months earlier they had approved $22 million to settle several dozen private lawsuits. While those civil suits were a nuisance, what was more worrying to the Sacklers was renewed interest from law enforcement. Purdue had managed to keep the FDA at bay during its 2007 criminal plea for misbranding Oxy. It might not be so fortunate the next time.

Purdue's compliance department had informed the Sacklers that the number of complaints about abuse or diversion to the company's hotline had broken a record in the last quarter of 2010. Purdue again did not report to the FDA any instances in which the sales representatives might have underplayed OxyContin's addictive power in their pitches to doctors.[39] Later, when one of the key elements in the lawsuits brought by dozens of state attorneys general was Purdue's overzealous marketing of OxyContin, the company's legal defense was to shift the responsibility for the drug being dispensed and abused so widely to the doctors who wrote the prescriptions.[40]

The Sacklers turned to legal matters in their first board meeting in January 2011. They authorized Purdue to pay all legal costs for an extended group of Purdue executives and sales managers. The Sacklers wanted to send a signal to employees that the family "had their backs."

It had been John Crowley, the company's executive director of Controlled Substances Act compliance, who had brought to the board's attention that some key producers on the detail team worried about the consequences of getting dragged into legal contests, even if only as witnesses or for depositions. Legal fees could be devastating. Crowley was concerned for good reason. A sales manager, Michele Ringler, had emailed him in 2009 about her suspicions that a Los Angeles pill mill was ordering an inordinate amount of OxyContin from distributors. Lake Medical was a two-room "pain clinic" that an ex-felon and his physician partner had opened the previous year. Most pharmacies in Ringler's L.A. sales territory ordered an average of 1,500 OxyContin pills monthly. Lake Medical averaged that every week.[41] "I feel very certain this is an organized drug ring," Ringler told Crowley. "Shouldn't the DEA be contacted about this?"

Crowley did nothing. Ringler's suspicions were right. By the time the DEA closed down Lake Medical in another year, it had distributed more than a million OxyContin pills to the Crips gang and Armenian traffickers. Only after the clinic was shuttered and its owners indicted did Crowley tell the DEA what Purdue knew.[42]

"They had an obligation, a legal one and a moral one," said Joseph Rannazzisi, the DEA agent who had replaced Laura Nagel in 2005 as chief of the agency's Office of Diversion Control, responsible for oversight of the pharmaceutical industry.[43] Inside Purdue, detail team managers mocked the idea they should be bound by some ill-defined and nebulous concept of *moral obligations*. Apparently, the Sackler-family directors thought it was foolish to expect moral parameters to limit acceptable industry business practices. In the cutthroat world of pharmaceutical sales, any company that enforced "moral obligations" would be pulverized by competitors. The only rules to follow were those few on which they had no discretion. That was not as simple a maxim as it appeared. Virtually every rule that appeared ironclad was subject to legal interpretation. The DEA's Rannazzisi had both law and pharmacy degrees; he construed the Controlled Substances Act to require pharma companies and drug distributors to reject and report "suspicious orders" if they had reason to believe the drugs might be illegally diverted.[44] Purdue's general counsel, Phil Strassburger, gave legal cover to Crowley and others in the compliance department. "It would be irresponsible to direct every single anecdotal and often unconfirmed claim of potential misprescribing to these organizations," contended Strassburger.[45]

While Rannazzisi had expected to get stonewalled by Purdue or Johnson & Johnson, he had hoped he might get some voluntary compliance from the distributors, the big companies in between the pharma firms and the pharmacies, hospitals, and doctors' clinics. "Cardinal Health, McKesson, and AmerisourceBergen," he said, "control probably 85 or 90 percent of the drugs going downstream." The distributors maintained precise data for how many pills go to each pharmacist for whom they fulfilled orders. Rannazzisi knew there were instances in which the distributors had ignored warning signs that were impossible to miss unless they did so intentionally. There was one pharmacy, for instance, in Kermit, West Virginia, a town of 392 people. It ordered over nine million OxyContin in two years. Neither Purdue nor the distributors filed any timely report to authorities about that pill mill.[46] "There were just too many bad practitioners, too many bad pharmacies, and too many bad wholesalers and distributors," concluded Rannazzisi.*[47]

The legal headaches were the inevitable costs, contended the Sacklers, of being the market leader on a drug that was a controlled substance. What about the fallout from Vioxx a few years earlier? they asked rhetorically. FDA officials had estimated that Merck's nonnarcotic painkiller had killed sixty thousand Americans, more than had died during the Vietnam War.[48] Independent statisticians contended Vioxx might have been responsible for half a million deaths by increasing the risks for a lethal heart attack for those patients who were genetically susceptible.[49] Vioxx had indeed caused a national uproar. It tarnished Merck's sterling reputation. It led to calls to invest the FDA with authority to review the safety of medications it had previously approved. Thousands of lawsuits were filed; Merck settled them in 2007 for $4.85 billion, then a record for pharmaceutical litigation.[50]

The insulated "circle the wagons" mentality was reinforced by every media story that portrayed Purdue as the villainous face of the opioid industry. There was also a perception, the author has learned, among the Sacklers and top management that plaintiffs' lawyers and government investigators had focused on Purdue because it was the only privately owned company then selling a successful opioid painkiller. Its competitors were well-known publicly traded firms selling everything from extended release pills mixing opioids and anesthetics to fentanyl patches (among others, Johnson & Johnson had Nucynta, Pfizer made Embeda, Janssen Pharma had Duragesic, Cephalon/Teva had Actiq,

* The DEA ultimately fined McKesson and Cardinal Health $341 million for filling millions of OxyContin from "suspicious orders." After that, the distributors bypassed Rannazzisi and went to his superiors. "They complained to Congress that DEA regulations were vague," recalled Rannazzisi, "and the agency was treating them like a foreign drug cartel." By 2013, he recalls, "there was a sea change in the way prosecutions of big distributors were handled. Cases . . . that once would have easily been approved, now weren't good enough." McKesson, Cardinal, and AmerisourceBergen were subsequently named as plaintiffs in the consolidated opioid litigation in federal courts. In April 2019, they reached their first settlement agreement. West Virginia got $37 million from McKesson, $20 million from AmerisourceBergen, and $16 million from Cardinal. The trio only paid the fines, none admitted any wrongdoing. In late October, on the eve of the first opioid trial scheduled in Ohio, McKesson, AmerisourceBergen, and Cardinal agreed to pay $215 million to the two plaintiffs, Cuyahoga and Summit Counties. Another defendant, Israel-based Teva Pharmaceutical Industries, settled at the same time for $20 million cash and $25 million in addiction-treatment medications. None admitted wrongdoing.

and Bio Delivery Sciences had Onsolis). The opioid painkillers sold by large publicly traded companies were a small part of their diversified product lines. While those painkillers were profitable, the companies did not depend on them. Without OxyContin, Purdue would close shop. That made it simpler in a court of public opinion to portray Purdue as nothing more than a legally sanctioned drug dealer.

The DEA's Joseph Rannazzisi was an eyewitness to better treatment that some enormous public corporations got as compared to small companies. McKesson, AmerisourceBergen, and Cardinal Health were all *Fortune* 500 companies (ranked 6, 12, and 15, respectively). They had pushed back against Rannazzisi's aggressive enforcement for hundreds of instances where they failed to report and reject "suspicious orders." Rannazzisi's Justice Department superiors grilled him about his tactics against the distributors. That had "infuriated" Rannazzisi, who refused to change his attitude that "this is war. We're going after these people and we are not going to stop." The distributors, according to Rannazzisi, lobbied to get the DEA to change course. And it did. It stopped using its strongest remedy, the ability to freeze distributors' shipments of drugs, against any of the largest companies.

"So the question is," asked Rannazzisi, "why would it be any different for these companies as compared to the small mom-and-pops that we had done hundreds of times before? The difference is, they have a lot of money, and a lot of influence."[51]

"With a privately run company, the owners become the face of the business," a lawyer friendly with the Sacklers told the author. "What do you think worried the Sacklers? What do you think juries in Appalachia might think if they got the idea that a family of New York Jews made a fortune from a drug that some lawyer tells them was to blame for all the misery in their communities?"[52] * [53]

What most distressed the Sackler-family directors in 2011, how-

* In dozens of cases filed against Purdue since 2016, state attorneys general included Johnson & Johnson, Ortho-McNeil Janssen, Endo Health, Allergan, and Watson Pharmaceuticals in their complaints. In February 2019, the Oklahoma attorney general filed a suit charging that Johnson & Johnson had acted as "a kingpin behind the public-health emergency, profiting at every stage." Besides making and selling its own opioid-based products, the Oklahoma AG said the reason J&J had acted like a drug kingpin was that it had used foreign subsidiaries in Tasmania to grow and process raw opium that it then sold to other drugmakers for the ingredients used in two thirds of all painkillers. On August 26, 2019, a judge ruled against Johnson & Johnson. He found the company liable for overhyping the benefits of its opioids and downplaying the risks.

ever, was a midyear report that OxyContin sales were hundreds of millions less than had been forecast. All the bad news about opioids was taking its toll on the dispensing habits of doctors, who were writing lower-strength prescriptions. The two strongest Oxy doses, 60 mg and 80 mg, were off by 20 percent. They had Purdue's biggest profit margins. By the end of the year, the Sacklers had "only" paid themselves $551 million. Although it was an enormous payout, it was a third of a billion dollars less than what they drew the previous year.[54] As a result, the Sacklers (with a new family director that July, David Sackler, Richard's son) exhorted the sales team in 2012 and 2013 to meet ever-higher targets. Richard Sackler blamed a sales dip over Christmas because many reps had taken off for the holidays. The company launched a quantitative research project that focused on patients who were long-term users of prescription opioids. Richard Sackler thought it might help give the detail team some fresh ideas about selling more Oxy at higher doses for longer periods.[55] The company also produced and promoted videos encouraging doctors to prescribe liberally, kicked off a new marketing campaign called "Individualize the Dose," and hired McKinsey consultants to develop innovative ways to generate more sales.[56]

The detail team reported that their one-on-one pitches were increasingly met with more questions, sometimes skepticism, especially from general practitioners. It had not helped that in May 2012, the Senate Finance Committee had launched an investigation into the degree to which money from Purdue, Johnson & Johnson, and Endo Pharmaceuticals had influenced seven of the country's leading pain foundations.[57] The probe was the idea of the committee's chair, Montana's Max Baucus, and the ranking minority member, Iowa's Chuck Grassley. Both states were hard hit by the opioid epidemic.

The top target was the American Pain Foundation (APF), the country's largest nonprofit dedicated to pain management. It promoted the idea that opioid painkillers were not the problem and the fault was overprescribing physicians. The APF was an industry mouthpiece that masqueraded as a patient advocacy organization. Over 90 percent of its revenue came from opioid manufacturers, with Purdue giving more than double any of its rivals.[58] The day that the Senate Finance Com-

---

It was fined $572 million. That was reduced in November to $465 million. Johnson & Johnson has appealed.

mittee announced its probe, the American Pain Foundation closed. In its final public release, it claimed that "due to irreparable economic circumstances" it could not remain "operational."[59] The widespread speculation was that the APF preferred shutting down rather than answer subpoenas for the production of documents that would expose the extent to which Purdue and its rival opioid manufacturers had controlled and manipulated it. The Senate investigation and the APF closure were front-page national news.*[60]

In March 2013, Purdue circulated an internal report with grim statistics and a frightening prediction. Not only had drug overdose fatalities in the U.S. tripled over a decade, but the tens of thousands who had died were just "the tip of the iceberg." For everyone who died, there were over a hundred others battling dependence or abuse with prescription opioids.[61] Purdue's executives worried that such figures would prompt doctors to instinctively pull back further on their opioid prescribing.

There was a single bright spot for the company in the otherwise steady stream of negative news. On April 16 a small celebration broke out at its Stamford headquarters. Burt Rosen, Purdue's Washington-based chief lobbyist, had called Richard Sackler with the news that the FDA had rejected the application of several manufacturers to approve a generic version of OxyContin.[62] The patent that had expired on that same day was the one Purdue got in 1995 on the original formulation of OxyContin. Purdue had stopped manufacturing the original and replaced it in 2012 with its "new and improved" version featuring the abuse-deterrent coating.[63] That version had a new patent that precluded generic competitors until 2025 (according to David Sackler, all the timing was a coincidence, something that seems very unlikely given that the patent monopoly was worth billions in extra years of profits).[64]

---

* It took a year of hearings and document production before its draft conclusions were ready. Those have never been released. In January 2014, Baucus left to become President Obama's ambassador to China and Grassley switched to the Judiciary Committee. Their replacements, Utah's Orrin Hatch and Oregon's Ron Wyden, kept the report sealed. That it is secret years after its completion has spawned dozens of conspiracy theories including one that the U.S. government has covered up a Sackler/OxyContin and Sinaloa Mexican Cartel/heroin alliance. In fact, the progressive Senator Wyden, no friend to the pharmaceutical industry, has explained that the Senate rules "prohibit the release of documents collected in the course of an investigation outside the context of an official report."

Purdue had been justifiably worried that a decision to allow generics would slash its selling price. Losing its unchallenged pricing power, the company forecast, would cause the average cost of a bottle of one hundred 40 mg pills to plummet from $450 to less than $100.[65] The generic manufacturers had been joined by some pain management experts and patient advocates in arguing unsuccessfully that a denial was rewarding Purdue for having had an unsafe drug on the market for thirteen years before it developed the abuse-deterrent coating.

Not only was the FDA ruling a win for Purdue's bottom line but it was the first time the drug agency had ever permitted a pharmaceutical company to make the claim on its label that its drug has "tamper-resistant properties."[66] In making that controversial ruling, the FDA said it had reviewed additional data submitted by Purdue that "was enough to show that the new version of OxyContin was safer, in its abuse resistance, than the original version."[67]

By midsummer, it was back to disappointing news. Oxy year-over-year sales were almost $100 million less than expected. That was just in time for McKinsey's finished report in August, *Identifying Granular Growth Opportunities for OxyContin: First Board Update*. It provided recommendations for how Purdue might "turbocharge the sales engine." Among the short-term solutions, it suggested an increase in the annual quota for sales reps' one-on-one doctor visits by 20 percent. The company had lost its laserlike concentration on courting the most "prolific prescribers." Visits that tried to get low dispensers to write more prescriptions resulted in little increased revenue. According to McKinsey, the "more prolific group 'write 25 times as many OxyContin scripts' as the less prolific prescribers." Moreover, McKinsey determined that after a Purdue sales rep visited one of the high-volume prescribers, they wrote even more scrips for opioids.[68] (In 2015, Purdue tightened its compensation rules for the detail team; sales reps who did not visit enough "high value" prescribers lost bonus pay.)[69]

Finally, McKinsey suggested the detail team push OxyContin's savings cards in neighborhoods with a high concentration of Walgreens pharmacies. Oxy sales were down 18 percent across all Walgreens pharmacies. The country's second-largest retail pharmacy chain had two months earlier pled guilty to breaking the law by filling tens of thousands of illegitimate Oxy prescriptions. As part of its plea deal with federal prosecutors, Walgreens agreed to institute a long list of safeguards to ensure it could not happen again. The only way to boost the sales at the chain, said the McKinsey report, was for the Sacklers to lobby the top management at Walgreens to relax some of those new regulations for OxyContin.[70]

CVS, the nation's largest retail pharmacy chain, was in the same predicament. The Sacklers discussed what to do at their September board meeting. They first voted another payment to themselves, bringing their 2013 total to $400 million.[71] Then all agreed if they were not successful at getting the two retail chains to find a workaround for the government-imposed safeguards, Purdue should look into placing its star drug into mail order pharmacies or even consider selling Oxy directly. The last idea was not realistic. No pharmaceutical firm had ever been allowed to sell a controlled substance straight to consumers.

Before the year ended, Burt Rosen, Purdue's in-house lobbyist, approached Richard Sackler about a sensitive matter, "concerns over our internal documents."[72] Rosen worried that Purdue's files might contain incriminating information. The multiplying lawsuits and government probes made it ever more likely those documents might one day be subpoenaed and made public. Richard Sackler did not seem too troubled. Rosen then raised it with Jonathan Sackler, who also seemed unperturbed.

Richard Sackler had had several small strokes by this time and his health was not good. Purdue brought in five outside directors to serve with the nine Sackler directors. The most persistent rumor was that David Sackler, Richard's son, might replace his father as Purdue's chief.[73] It was evident that whoever took control of the family-run drug empire was going to be safeguarding one of America's largest personal fortunes. The Sackler family entered the *Forbes* "Richest Families" list with an estimated net worth of $14 billion in 2014.[74] The magazine noted that twenty years of sales of Purdue's wildly popular opioid product was "why they edged out families like the Busches, Mellons and Rockefellers."[75]

Copies of *Forbes* passed around headquarters. Some of the family thought it was aspirational and might encourage top Purdue executives and the sales team to redouble their efforts. No one at the company mentioned that the same year the Sacklers cracked the elite *Forbes* list, a record nineteen thousand Americans had died of prescription opioids, mostly OxyContin. David Sackler, a Purdue director for six years starting in 2012, was the only family member who later commented on the drug's deadly legacy. In a 2019 interview in *Vanity Fair* in which he tried to do some belated damage control for the much besieged family, he claimed, "We have so much empathy. . . . We feel absolutely terrible."[76]

49

GAMING THE SYSTEM

OxyContin dominated the sales of narcotic painkillers through 2014 despite competition from opioids released by Johnson & Johnson, Pfizer, Endo, and Janssen. None, however, offered therapeutic or dosing advantages significant enough to induce users to switch. While rivals tried breaking Oxy's grip on the top selling spot, they did not compete on price. Comparable doses of all extended release prescription opioids were priced within a few cents of one another.[1] Discounting would have likely increased a firm's market share but at the expense of profits.

With the bulk of their sales in the United States, all the narcotic painkillers had robust profit margins. There was no more lucrative market than America, the world's largest consumer of prescription drugs per capita. In 2013, prescription drugs accounted for 20 percent of American health care spending, about $850 per citizen, more than double the average of nineteen advanced industrialized nations.[2] U.S. pharmacies dispensed the equivalent of seventy tons of pure oxycodone. Americans used 83 percent of the world's supply.[3] Most important, pharma companies charged significantly more for their drugs in the U.S. A thirty-day supply of OxyContin cost $265 on average in the U.S. The same prescription averaged $72 in Europe and even less in South America and Asia.[4]

By pricing its blockbuster at 400 percent more in the U.S. than what it charged elsewhere, Purdue was typical of all American pharma firms. A comparison in 2014 of the twenty top grossing drugs, which accounted for 15 percent of all global prescription spending, revealed U.S. prices were on average three times higher than Europe, six times higher than Brazil, and sixteen times higher than India, the lowest-priced nation.[5]

Selling drugs at high prices in America has been part of the industry's DNA since the end of World War II. In 1959, Senator Estes Kefauver began his three-year investigation into why U.S. companies sold their drugs for "much lower prices in foreign countries than in the U.S."[6] The pharmaceutical industry had contended that its more expensive domestic research and development costs explained the pricing disparity. Kefauver's subcommittee proved that wrong. The reason for the pricing inequality was easy to pinpoint: the U.S. was the only country that allowed pharma companies to set their own prices. Every other industrialized nation used price caps or indirect controls to limit prices.

The effects of the unfettered pricing discretion are magnified in the U.S. since it is also where patents provide the world's longest sales monopoly. Mylan's CEO, Heather Bresch, the daughter of West Virginia senator Joe Manchin, was remarkably candid in a 2016 CNBC interview when asked why the company's best-selling EpiPen product sold for $608 in the U.S. but only $100 to $150 in Europe. "We [the United States] do subsidize the rest of the world, and as a country we've made a conscious decision to do that. And I think the world's a better place for it."[7]

Mylan had raised the price of EpiPen, a lifesaving autoinjector to counter severe allergic reactions, fifteen times since it bought the rights to the product in 2007 from a Pfizer subsidiary.[8] Revenues over that time had jumped fivefold from $200 million to a billion dollars. EpiPen provided 40 percent of Mylan's profits and its margins ballooned from 8 percent to 55 percent.[9] Bresch's salary tracked EpiPen's accelerating price chart; it went from $2.5 million when Mylan bought EpiPen to $19.5 million in five years. Mylan eventually paid $465 million to settle charges it had bilked Medicaid by deliberately misbranding cheaper EpiPen versions as more expensive ones.[10]

Most Americans blame greedy drug manufacturers for the price-gouging. That is undoubtedly a key factor. In the year in which the Sacklers broke onto the *Forbes* list of wealthiest American families, pharmaceutical prices increased 12.2 percent, one of the fastest ever year-over-year escalations.[11] The problem is more complicated, however, than industry executives setting high prices and counting profits as their products fly off pharmacy shelves. There are unique features of the U.S. drug distribution system that encourage artificially high and uncompetitive drug prices to flourish.

A key element, and one about which the public knows little, is the role of pharmacy benefit managers (PBMs). They had begun as a tiny niche providing processing benefits and paperwork for medical insurance companies. McKesson, the industry's largest drug distributor, bought the first PBM in 1970 and transformed it from a simple service provider into an independent powerhouse. As the number of PBMs proliferated during the 1970s and 1980s, they came to control drug formularies, negotiate discounts directly with manufacturers, and reimburse pharmacists. Drug companies, which had initially dismissed PBMs as mere paper pushers, came to see them as an emerging threat to their pricing hegemony.[12] In the 1980s, Merck's CEO, Roy Vagelos, noted the largest PBM, Medco, could on its own "shift market share within a class of drugs to their preferred product."[13] Drug manufacturers were forced to deal with the PBMs since they had become the middlemen between pharma and medical insurers. So Vagelos decided it might be better for Merck to own its own PBM. It bought Medco in 1993 for $6.6 billion. That kicked off a rush by rivals to buy their own pharmacy benefit manager. Eli Lilly scooped up the industry founder, PCS, for $4.1 billion. SmithKline Beecham spent $2.3 billion for Diversified Pharmaceutical Services. Bristol-Myers Squibb formed an alliance with Caremark and Pfizer did the same with ValueRx.[14] There was a flurry of mergers and acquisitions among the remaining independent PBMs through the 1990s.[15] Rite Aid in 1998 decided the fastest way to expand its presence in the HMO and managed care market was to buy its own PBM; it paid Lilly $1.5 billion for PCS.

In 1999, PBMs covered half of all insured Americans. That year, Bill Clinton proposed a prescription drug benefit for Medicare. It had been thirty years since an LBJ-appointed commission had recommended that prescription drug coverage be available to the nation's seniors. Health care had been a priority in the Clinton administration. An ambitious effort at a quasi-national health insurance plan failed in 1993. Four years later the administration managed to pass the Children's Health Insurance Program (CHIP) as part of the Balanced Budget Act. It expanded Medicaid assistance to "uninsured children up to age 19 in families with incomes too high to qualify them for Medicaid."

The 1999 Clinton drug plan would pay half of the first $5,000 in medication costs and 100 percent of everything over that. As opposed to the extensive government control in the administration's 1993 proposal, PBMs would manage in the new one. But it proved impossible to get any legislative momentum in the last year of Clinton's presidency. It took another four years, and a dozen variations on a series of bills, before a Republican-led Congress got enough bipartisan support to pass George W. Bush's Medicare Prescription Drug, Improvement, and Modernization Act.[16]

When the law went into effect in 2006 it was the first time prescription drug benefits were available to *all* the country's 41 million seniors. Unfortunately, as with the Clinton plan, PBMs had a central role. The pharmaceutical industry lobbied to ensure that the legislation explicitly prevented the government from negotiating drug prices.[17] * [18]

Making drugs available to tens of millions of patients without empowering the government to negotiate or cap prices was a boon for companies that had a role in manufacturing, distributing, and selling prescription medications to Americans. The expanded coverage put the pharmacy benefit managers in a powerful position because they controlled the drug formularies. Only those medications on the lists were eligible for medical insurance reimbursement. What resulted was a complex and obscure scheme of "rebates" by which drug manufacturers paid PBMs to get their drugs on the formularies. The costlier the brand-name medication, the larger the rebate demanded by the PBM.

Rebates are legal but controversial. They ensure that many drugs on the formularies are not chosen for the best interests of the patients or keeping a cap on health care costs. Rebates foster a system riddled with conflicts of interest. The "pay for listing" system serves as an incentive for pharma to raise list prices so it can offer larger rebates to the PBMs.†

PBMs are the only unregulated part of the pharmaceutical supply chain. There are no requirements for public transparency. Nor do they have any legal obligation to disclose to anyone the rebates they received from pharma companies. PBMs do not use those rebates to offset retail

---

* Federal statute prohibits the secretary of Health and Human Services from negotiating prescription drug prices. Only Congress can change that. However, even if the government had the authority to negotiate prices, it would be unlikely that alone would result in substantial discounts. The pharmaceutical industry would have no incentive to lower prices unless the government also had the power to remove certain drugs from its approved formulary or to cap prices at a certain amount.

† According to Linda Cahn, an attorney who helps health insurers negotiate with PBMs: "Let's say there are two drugs in the same therapeutic category—one for $500 and one for $350. Which manufacturer can promise more rebates? Obviously the one with the $500 drug." A larger rebate from the more expensive drug would get it listed on the formulary at the same time its rival's cheaper medication was delisted. Medical insurance carriers and patients with copays would pay more based on the artificially high list prices of the rebated drug.

drug prices or lower the cost of patient insurance premiums. Studies demonstrate that pharma rebates to PBMs increase the average costs on many popular medications by about one third.[19] Yet patients filling prescriptions at retail pharmacies are in the dark. They are clueless that undisclosed rebates are often why PBMs direct them to a costlier brand-name drug instead of one better suited and cheaper. Sometimes, pharmacy benefit managers switch patients to different brands than the ones prescribed by the physician. Other times they make it more difficult to get a drug by requiring a "letter of medical necessity" from the dispensing physician.[20] A "gag clause" prevents pharmacists from telling patients if there is a comparable and cheaper drug available (in 2018, President Trump signed two bills passed by Congress that were supposed to eliminate the gag clause. The legislation did not, however, require pharmacists to inform patients about lower-priced drugs. Patients have to ask).[21]

The Obama administration's 2010 Affordable Care Act (ACA) was the first time in U.S. history that prescription drug coverage was defined by statute as "an essential health benefit." All medical insurance companies were required to offer drug coverage in order to be ACA compliant. Before the ACA, Medicaid covered drugs for Americans at or below the federal poverty line ($31,721 for a family of four). The ACA expanded Medicaid eligibility by raising the income level to 133 percent of the poverty line. That translated into another 10 million people eligible for Medicaid (71.2 million total). The ACA also increased the scope of drug coverage for those in the Children's Health Insurance Program, adding another two million. And the Affordable Care Act reduced the so-called donut hole in Medicare's prescription drug plan; that is a coverage gap that required seniors to pay some drug costs out of pocket beyond their deductibles or co-insurance.[22] It also expanded Medicare's "Low-Income Subsidy" that offers additional coverage for the thirteen million who barely missed qualifying for Medicaid.[23] The federal government is legally required in all its drug benefit programs to cover *every* FDA-approved drug, whether a prescription was written for an inexpensive generic or an exorbitantly priced biologic.[24] * [25]

It is unlikely that anyone who drafted the Affordable Care Act in-

---

* For most of its aid programs, the federal government buys drugs at 20 percent to 22 percent off list price. The ACA also established a complicated formula for reducing the

tended to help the pharmaceutical industry increase its revenues and profits. That was the result, however, of expanding drug coverage without also establishing more restrictive formularies or empowering the government to somehow control prescription pricing. Little wonder that pharma companies greeted the ACA as an unintended gift.

Prescription drug spending increased dramatically in the wake of the Affordable Care Act. In Medicaid alone it rose over two years by 25 percent to $40 billion. More than 90 percent of Medicaid's drug expenditures by 2015 were for brand names instead of generics.[26] From 2006, when Medicare's prescription drug plan went into effect, through 2010, Medicare spending on prescription medications ranged between 2 percent and 5 percent of the total U.S. spending on drugs. After the ACA, from 2011 through 2017, Medicare's share of all national expenditures on prescriptions soared to 30 percent. It is now the second-largest contributor to drug spending after private insurance companies.[27] When Medicaid and other government drug benefit programs are included, the federal government pays a remarkable 45 percent annually of all the retail prescription costs in the U.S.[28]

The combination of high prices and ever-expanding insurance coverage is reflected in the number of billion-dollar-selling drugs. There had been only eight such drugs in the history of the industry before 2000. Since then, there have been more than a hundred, with a handful regularly selling between $10 and $15 billion annually.[29]

Pharmacy benefit managers have also become more influential, a $250-billion-annually sector of the pharmaceutical industry. PBM drug plans now cover 253 million Americans, 95 percent of the country's eligible population. The big three—Express Scripts, United Health's OptumRx, and CVS's Caremark—are listed in the top twenty of the *Fortune* 500. Those three alone have about 180 million customers.[30]

Pharmacy benefit managers are in a powerful position since they are the only segment of the drug distribution system that knows what everyone else is paying and getting paid. They have separate contracts with their own clients—HMOs, large corporations, and government aid programs—as well as with independent drugstores and pharmacy chains. Those contracts are complex and obtuse, making it difficult to

share of drug costs the government paid in the future. And it opened the door to states creating and fine-tuning drug formularies.

know the precise amount of their administrative fees and considerable "incidental costs." It also has given them an opportunity to squeeze more profits through another legal yet controversial scheme.[31] PBMs bill for prescriptions filled by patients. They also control the amount reimbursed to retail pharmacies that dispense the drugs. Advanced software scans millions of prescription orders for so-called spread pricing. That is when PBMs bill the insurers more than they reimburse pharmacists. The PBMs pocket the difference.[32] Opportunities for spread pricing are most common with generics sold to government agencies. Bloomberg analyzed the ninety most dispensed generic medications in Medicaid in 2017: PBMs took $1.3 billion in spread pricing out of the $4.2 billion Medicaid insurers spent.[33] Spread pricing is possible for the same reason that rebates flourish: there is no federal oversight of pharmacy benefit managers.

The country's 22,000 community pharmacists, who dispense about 40 percent of America's retail prescriptions, are the most vocal PBM critics. Pharmacists feel left out of the industry gravy train. PBMs regularly push pharmacy reimbursements as low as possible to increase their own profits. Sometimes PBMs force pharmacies to forgo any reimbursement by threatening abusive audits or penalizing druggists for minor typos on insurance claims. Independent pharmacists have lobbied, without much headway thus far, for legislation requiring that PBMs report *all* financial data. That would stop spread pricing. It would also either end secret rebates or put pressure on the PBMs to pass them back to health plans, reducing the overall cost of individual medical insurance policies.[34]

The Pharmaceutical Care Management Association, the leading PBM trade group, claims that in the coming decade PBMs will save Americans half a billion dollars because of streamlined methods for delivering drugs and cutting red tape. Saving patients money was the promise of the pharmacy benefit managers when they entered the industry in 1970. That promise remains unfilled. Prescription drugs are the single fastest rising component of American health care costs. They have soared 1,100 percent during the quarter century starting when PBMs began wielding measurable influence.[35]

In the last five years, during a period of historically low inflation, drug costs for Medicare and Medicaid rose between 10 percent and 15 percent annually.[36] Over that same period, the adjusted profit per prescription for the nation's largest PBM, Express Scripts, rose by 500 percent ($3.87 to $5.16). Its closest competitors, OptumRx and Caremark, had comparable jumps in per-prescription profits.[37] Internal documents from Express Scripts reveal the company was well aware its profit ratios far outstripped those in other industries. The list prices for the nation's top brand-name medications increased 127 percent over those five years, compared to an 11 percent rise in a basket of common household goods.[38]

When Mylan's CEO Heather Bresch was on the defensive in 2016 over her company's 600 percent price increase on its lifesaving product, EpiPen, the House Oversight and Government Reform Committee grilled her. One important aspect of her testimony was mostly overlooked. A chart presented into evidence broke down EpiPen's $608 list price. Just over half went to pharmacy benefit managers, insurers, retailers, and other wholesalers. Buddy Carter, the only congressman who was also a pharmacist, asked Bresch if she knew how much the PBM received of the EpiPen list price.

"I don't specifically know the breakdown," admitted Bresch.

"Nor do I," replied Carter. "And I'm the pharmacist. . . . That's the problem, nobody knows."[39]

Journalist David Dayen, in writing about pharmacy benefit managers, called them "a black box understood by almost no one." Pharma's byzantine pricing bureaucracy, with multiple levels of red tape regulated only by PBMs, pharmacies, drug companies, and insurance providers, allows each to blame the other when pressed on why prices are so much higher in America than elsewhere.

Richard Sackler, in a 2015 deposition in the lawsuit filed against Purdue by the Commonwealth of Kentucky, was asked about OxyContin.

"What are the gross sales?" It seemed a straightforward enough query given that Oxy accounted for 90 percent of Purdue's revenue.

Sackler, however, said "I don't know." The reason, he claimed, was that in the drug industry, "a lot of money is inherently rebated back to purchasers, insurance companies, hospitals, et cetera, through wholesalers, in rebate agreements, which are negotiated."[40]

Brand-name drugs are not the only ones with upward price pressure. A 2016 Government Accountability Office report revealed that more than three hundred generic drugs had price increases in the previous twenty-four months. More than half had at least doubled. Ten percent had increased more than 1,000 percent. Three widely prescribed hypertension medications on the market for more than fifty years were suddenly 2,500 percent higher.[41]

The spike in the prices of generics hit the United States harder than other countries since they account for 90 percent of all drugs dispensed in America (versus 70 percent in the U.K. and closer to 60 percent in the rest of Europe).[42] It would not be a crisis were generics not on average far more expensive in the U.S.[43]

Pharmaceutical companies fight every effort to make it simpler for patients to compare prices when they fill prescriptions. A Trump administration regulation that ordered drugmakers to include their list prices in television ads was struck down by a federal judge in July 2019. Pharma firms prevailed on the argument that Health and Human Services did not have the authority to issue a decree and that, in any case, it violated their First Amendment rights.[44]

When Estes Kefauver had investigated the drug industry seventy years ago, he discovered that five leading firms conspired to keep their tetracycline prices identical even though they all had different manufacturing and distribution costs. In May 2019, history repeated itself. Forty state attorneys general filed a five-hundred-page lawsuit against the largest generic drugmakers, charging a multiyear, systematic conspiracy that resulted in substantially higher drug prices that had cost consumers billions of dollars. The suit listed 1,215 generic drugs whose prices had jumped on average more than 400 percent in the previous year. Included were some lifesaving drugs. One for severe asthma had soared 4,000 percent.[45]

When the state attorneys general filed their lawsuits, the pharmaceutical companies seemed to pull some stock replies from their archives. There was no truth to the charges. Prices went up because in some cases, like insulin, there were drug shortages. In other instances, market forces were responsible. One of the attorneys general who had filed the price-fixing lawsuit, Connecticut's William Tong, knew personally about how soaring drug costs made it unaffordable for many patients. He took a medication for a skin condition. It had jumped in a single year over 8,000 percent, from $20 to $1,820 a bottle. When told of how the pharma industry brushed off the charges, Tong became heated in a *60 Minutes* interview. "It's a $100 billion market.

We're talking about the drugs that America takes every day to live. And they're profiteering off of that in a highly illegal way. They're just taking advantage. . . . It wasn't about product shortages. It was about profit. It was about cold, hard greed."* [46]

---

* High drug prices are one of the leading topics in the 2020 presidential race. Every Democratic candidate has a plan. Some want the federal government to manufacture generics and sell them at cost. Others allow Americans to buy cheaper drugs from foreign countries. Elizabeth Warren and Bernie Sanders proposed eliminating all private insurance and making the government subsidize expensive drugs.

In December 2019, the House of Representatives passed a drug plan sponsored by California congresswoman Nancy Pelosi. *STAT*, the leading medicine and pharmaceutical online journal, described it as "dramatically more aggressive than expected." Under the Pelosi plan, Medicare would negotiate directly with drug firms on prices for 250 medications that do not have competition from at least two generics or biosimilars. No drug in America could be more than 1.2 times the average price of the same medication in Japan, Germany, France, Canada, Australia, and the U.K. Failure to comply would result in a punitive tax of 75 percent on a company's gross sales. The provision that was most unsettling for pharma was that the federal government would have the power to claw back profits earned from drug price hikes since 2016 in cases in which those increases were greater than the rate of inflation. That translates into potentially hundreds of billions in profits. It was, according to one commentator, "déjà vu" for what Estes Kefauver had tried to do sixty years ago.

The Pelosi bill is expected to stall in the Republican Senate. There, bipartisan support has built for a bill that caps out-of-pocket drug costs for Medicare at $3,100 annually.

50

BILLION-DOLLAR ORPHANS

Pharmacy benefit managers are not, of course, the only reason for exorbitant drug prices in America. Even if PBMs did not exist, there would still be instances of eye-popping price increases by pharma companies. Compared to the largely anonymous and mostly unfathomable world of PBMs, when a drug company sets an outrageous price, there is often an unlikable CEO cast by the media as the face of pharmaceutical greed. That feeds a widespread perception that the main culprits in rising drug costs are pharma companies themselves. Public sentiment has changed dramatically since the early 1960s. Most Americans were then unaffected by overpriced drugs and few paid attention to Estes Kefauver's Senate investigation. Today, many feel the effects of the rising costs of medication. The drug prescription component of what Americans spend annually on health care passed a milestone of $1,000 per person in 2015. That was by far the highest of any developed nation, with drugs responsible for nearly 20 percent of all costs.[1]

Separate from the avarice of pharmacy benefit managers, the pharmaceutical industry's secret is that exorbitant drug prices often result from widespread exploitation of the quarter-century-old Orphan Drug Act. The manipulation that began with AIDS drugs in 1987 has only picked up pace, fed by pharma's appetite for ever-larger profits. The industry is so skilled at milking every possible advantage from the Orphan Drug Act that publicly traded biotech companies have seen one-day share price spikes of 30 percent simply on the news of obtaining an orphan designation.[2]

If success is measured by the number of orphans approved by the FDA, the act has been a success. In the decade before the statute, only three companies had released ten medications for orphaned diseases. After the law, two hundred companies have developed nearly five hundred orphans, with half since 2012.[3] They are no longer the industry's poor stepchild. Seventy orphan drugs approved by the FDA in the last decade were for successful, mass-market medications whose patents were about to expire. Pharma companies had found ways to "repurpose" the medications for a rare disease.[4] Eight others have been approved for more than one orphaned disease.* Half the FDA approvals in the last five years have been secondary ones, what the FDA's Office of Orphan Products Development calls "multiple bites of the apple."[5]

As of 2018, the median annual cost for an orphan drug treatment per patient is $98,500, compared with $5,000 for nonorphan drugs. The startling price difference has lured many companies to search for orphan drug designations for their products. Since 2015, half of all new medicines approved annually by the FDA are for orphans.[6] That same year, orphan drugs broke $100 billion in sales.[7] Analysts project $176 billion by 2020, double the growth rate of the worldwide prescription market.[8] Orphans will account then for 20 percent of all global prescriptions, up from only 5 percent in 2000.[9]

"The industry has been gaming the system by slicing and dicing indications so that drugs qualify for lucrative orphan status benefits," according to Martin Makary, a Johns Hopkins surgery professor who has written about how "unintended and misplaced [Orphan Drug Act] subsidies and tax breaks fuel skyrocketing medication costs." The misuse of the statute, says Makary, means that "funding support intended for rare disease medicine is diverted to fund the development of blockbuster drugs."[10] "By "slicing and dicing" Makary refers to when drugmakers take a disease and break it into smaller subsets of patients, qualifying each as a stand-alone disorder eligible for orphan drug status. That had begun with AIDS when drug companies, over the protests of the FDA, arbitrarily created subcategories of "rare diseases" related to HIV and AIDS patients. Evidence of "slicing and dicing" is that there were some two thousand orphaned diseases identified by scientists and the FDA in 1983 when the Orphan

* A half dozen of the most profitable pharmaceutical firms have gotten their drugs designated as treatments for up to nine orphaned diseases. After the drug is developed the first time, research and development costs drop substantially for future approvals. While the companies must conduct clinical trials, because the targeted diseases are so rare the FDA sometimes only requires a single study with as few as a dozen subjects. Despite much lower R&D costs, pharma companies still receive all the monetary benefits of the Orphan Drug Act for every drug they get designated to another rare disease.

Drug Act passed. Today there are more than seven thousand.[11] Multiple approvals also provide a loophole around the law's cap on the number of patients per disease. So long as each disease has fewer than 200,000 patients, there is no limit on how many rare diseases a single orphan drug can treat. And if a drug is approved for a rare disease that later affects more than 200,000, it retains its orphan status (that happened with nineteen drugs that got orphan approvals for treating AIDS; when the number of people infected with AIDS passed 200,000 in 1993, they kept their orphan benefits until their individual patents expired).

Pharma companies and biotechs get help navigating the Orphan Drug Act and the FDA's unique approval process from a couple of consulting firms founded by former FDA officials who ran the orphan drug division and are intimately familiar with its idiosyncrasies. Drug firms pay for what Tim Coté, the ex–FDA orphan drug director, boasted on his company's website was "the inside track."[12] He told NPR in 2017 that his Coté Orphan sent more orphan submissions to the FDA than anyone else. "We write the entire application."[13] Coté's competition is Haffner Associates, founded in 2009 by Marlene Haffner, an internist and hematologist who had directed the FDA's Office of Orphan Products Development for twenty-one years. Haffner is often acknowledged as the "mother of orphan drugs." When she took charge in 1986 the Orphan Drug Act was only three years old.[14] She left the government in 2007 to become Amgen's executive director of global regulatory policy. After two years there she established her own consulting firm. On her LinkedIn profile, Haffner notes, "Have extensive experience in writing orphan designation requests, Fast Track, pediatric vouchers and basically every enhanced approval product for the development of new products for rare diseases."[15]

Coté and Haffner oversaw nearly three hundred orphan drug applications when they were at the FDA. Both know how to expedite the orphan application process. Starting in 2015, every year a remarkable seven to eight of the top ten selling drugs in America are orphans. Genentech and Biogen, for instance, developed rituximab, a monoclonal antibody therapy the FDA approved as an orphan in 1994 to treat follicular B-cell non-Hodgkin's lymphoma. It was a cancer estimated to affect about fourteen thousand Americans. Since then, rituximab has gotten eight additional orphan approvals. Some are smaller subsets of the original disease.[16] Through 2018, it is the sixth best-selling drug of all time, with almost $90 billion in sales.[17]* [18]

Many of the drugs submitted by large pharmaceutical companies to the FDA are orphans in name only. They were never developed to eradicate a rare disease but are repackaged mass-market medications. The FDA approved Amgen's Repatha in 2013. Amgen developed it to treat a genetic condition, FH (familial hypercholesterolemia), that resulted in "very high LDL [bad cholesterol] . . . that can lead to premature cardiovascular disease as well as other complications." The number of Americans with FH ranges from 600,000 to Amgen's estimate of 11,000,000.[19] Amgen priced Repatha at $14,000 a year per patient. On the same day, the FDA approved Repatha as an orphan drug to treat a much smaller genetic subset, HoFH (homozygous familial hypercholesterolemia). It covered patients who had inherited the faulty gene from both parents, affecting between 900 and 2,200 people in the United States.[20]

The underlying genetic condition of extremely high LDL cholesterol was the same. The treatment was also the same. The only difference was that the vast majority of patients with FH inherited only a single dominant gene from one parent.[21] Their LDL cholesterol levels run two to three times higher than what doctors deem safe. In the small subgroup in which both parents pass on the genes, LDL cholesterol levels are three to six times greater than normal.

If Amgen had not gotten the separate orphan designation, those afflicted with HoFH would have simply taken the regular Repatha prescription. However, by simultaneously processing the drug as an orphan, Amgen got a multimillion-dollar tax credit and additional write-offs for its huge research costs.[22]

AstraZeneca went one step further when it tried to repurpose Crestor, its successful cholesterol-lowering medication, as an orphan. It was a last-ditch effort to stave off generic competition. In 2016, Crestor was the second most widely prescribed drug in America (Syn-

---

*In 2014, Genentech made its branded version of rituximab available only through specialty distributors instead of the industry's regular wholesalers. It did the same for two other blockbuster cancer biologics, Avastin and Herceptin, both of which had a slew of orphan drug approvals. Genentech claimed the move was to "improve the efficiency and security of the supply chain." In fact, its action meant that hospitals and oncology clinics lost out on traditional industry discounts, resulting in an effective overnight price hike of $300 million annually.

throid, a thyroid medicine, was at the top). Crestor was about to come off patent. A slew of generic competitors were prepared with products when AstraZeneca surprised the industry by applying to the FDA for Crestor to treat pediatric HoFH. It was the same genetic disorder that Amgen had relied on a couple of years earlier except that AstraZeneca had "sliced and diced" a pediatric subset that affected anywhere from three hundred to one thousand children.* [23]

The Orphan Drug Act had special incentives for companies to create drugs for pediatric diseases. The Rare Pediatric Disease Priority Review Voucher Program provides a voucher to any pharmaceutical company "who receives an approval for a drug or biologic for a 'rare pediatric disease.'" The drug company can redeem that voucher "to receive a priority review of a subsequent marketing application for a different product." It was the equivalent of an expedited pass for the firm's next drug application, even if that was for a mass-market therapeutic.

Besides the voucher program, the FDA has two others—the Orphan Products Clinical Trials Grants and the Pediatric Device Consortia Grants Program—both of which underwrite most of the research costs for pediatric rare illnesses. A drug that targeted a pediatric disease on the list qualified automatically for a six-month extension to its seven-year exclusive selling period.[24] Finally, the 21st Century Cures Act, which President Obama signed into law in 2016 with the intent of encouraging more pharmaceutical lab research, gave an extra six months of protection from generic competition to any existing drug if it got approved for an orphaned disease.[25]

When the FDA approved Crestor for HoFH it did not initially seem important since it only gave Crestor a seven-year selling monopoly for the several hundred affected children. AstraZeneca, however, cleverly argued to the FDA that its seven-year mini-patent should extend the expiring patent on mass-market Crestor to its 21 million patients. Ge-

* Crestor is a good example of the often substantial difference between what the FDA requires for clinical testing for a mass-market drug, and what it requires for an orphan drug, even when the drug treats the same condition. Fifteen years earlier, for mass-market Crestor, AstraZeneca conducted the largest ever New Drug Application for a statin. It submitted twenty-seven Phase II/III clinical trials from 12,569 patients. Crestor for those affected by pediatric HoFH was based on a single clinical study of fourteen children, in which Crestor was given to half. Their cholesterol was tested only once, after six weeks of treatment, and those who had taken the pill had a slightly lower bad (LDL) cholesterol level.

neric drugmakers and public advocacy groups petitioned the FDA to reject Crestor's claim. It was, they contended, a flagrant abuse of the Orphan Drug Law.[26] In fact, in 2002, Congress had passed a statute prohibiting drug companies from extending their patents on a brand-name drug originally approved for adults by simply reapplying to have it okayed for children.[27] That law did not specifically preclude, however, a pharma company from applying for their drug to treat a pediatric orphaned illness.[28] As a result, it took a federal court to determine whether the law applied. The court rejected AstraZeneca's novel argument, but it still pocketed all the financial incentives from the Orphan Drug Act.[29]

AstraZeneca is not alone. Otsuka Pharmaceuticals avoided the patent expiration on its hit antipsychotic, Abilify, by getting it approved for an orphaned diseased, Tourette syndrome. Genentech got two orphan drug extensions for its cancer blockbuster, Herceptin.[30]

Not every pharma company is satisfied at getting one orphan designation for their hit mass-market drug. Novartis's Gleevec was the first targeted cancer biologic approved in 2001 to treat chronic myelogenous leukemia, a blood-cell cancer that starts in the bone marrow and affects nine thousand patients in the U.S. It was priced at a then unprecedented $26,400 per year.[31] By the time its patent expired in 2013, Novartis had more than quadrupled the price to $120,000.[32]* [33] Gleevec has gotten eight additional orphan designations for closely related cancers as well as immune disorders, resulting in several billion dollars in revenues.[34] All that "repurposing" of a single drug for nine orphan illnesses has little scientific benefit. It flies in the face of the Orphan Drug Act's original intent of one new drug for one untreated rare disease. The law, contends Johns Hopkins professor Martin Makary, was never intended to allow drugs like Gleevec to be designated for an orphan population. Instead, Gleevec had become a star example of how a drug company returned to the FDA with the same medication again and again, each time testing it against a related but "new" rare disease.

Humira is one of the most profitable prescription drugs ever. Hu-

---

* When Gleevec's patent was about to expire, Novartis introduced Tasigna, an almost structurally identical drug, and launched a massive advertising campaign to coax oncologists to prescribe the drug. Tasigna had a list price of $115,000 per patient annually, and is under patent protection until 2026. It became a $2 billion drug within a year of its 2014 release.

mira (HUman Monoclonal antibody In Rheumatoid Arthritis) was the first monoclonal antibody made from entirely living cells instead of synthetic chemicals. The FDA approved it in 2002 to treat rheumatoid arthritis. Humira was the result of an ambitious multiyear joint venture between a group of British academics, a small U.K. biotech (Cambridge Antibody Technology), and Germany's largest chemical conglomerate (BASF). Much of the research funding came from the government-funded U.K. Medical Research Council. The pharmaceutical company Abbott spent $6.9 billion to buy all the patents to Humira and then shepherded it through the FDA.[35]

Humira, as are most biologics, was always expensive. When it went on sale in 2003 it cost $13,200 a year. Abbott forecast $250 million in revenues in its first year and the marketing department predicted sales could build to a peak year of $1 billion annually.[36] Humira blew past the most optimistic projections. Its strength was its dosing advantage over two competitive biosimilars. Humira was a "self-injection pen" used at home every two weeks. Johnson & Johnson's Remicade required a weekly visit to a clinic. Amgen's Enbrel was an autoinjector, but required twice-a-week dosing. All three drugs are among the top ten selling in pharma history: Enbrel, #7, Remicade, #4, and Humira, #2. The three have more than $300 billion in sales.[37]

After its 2002 debut for rheumatoid arthritis, Humira got a near-record eight orphan drug approvals. Three of those were for orphaned diseases that were tiny pediatric subcategories of illnesses it had already been approved to treat for adults (rheumatoid arthritis, Crohn's disease, and ulcerative colitis).[38] Humira's original patent for treating rheumatoid arthritis was set to expire in 2013. An approval for an orphaned illness in 2011, pediatric ulcerative colitis, extended it. That year Humira's price jumped from $13,200 annually to $19,000. Three additional orphan drug approvals in 2014 and 2015 again added some "pediatric patent extensions." By 2018, Humira's price had doubled to $38,000. From the time of its first orphaned approval for pediatric ulcerative colitis in 2011, through 2018, Humira has had $108.5 billion in sales. It holds the record as the drug with the most consecutive years of sales exceeding $10 billion a year (six, from 2013 through 2018).[39]

Another manipulation of the Orphan Drug Act is when drug companies either use an orphan approval to expand off-label dispensing or use an orphan drug to later get approval for a mass-market therapy. Eighty firms have done so during the last decade. One, Allergan, managed to do both at once. When Botox was developed in 1990 it was submitted and approved for two orphan illnesses related to involuntary eye muscle spasms. Allergan, which had distributed the drug for its ophthalmologist inventor, bought the rights the following year.[40] A decade later, Allergan got Botox approved to treat another orphaned diseased, cervical dystonia, a condition marked by neck and shoulder muscle spasms that result in an abnormal head position. Allergan used that orphan approval to grow its off-label sales illegally. It dispatched sales representatives nationwide to convince doctors to dispense more Botox to treat headaches and generalized pain, conditions for which it was not approved. The company disingenuously claimed that cervical dystonia was "greatly underdiagnosed" and that even when physicians "did not see any cervical dystonia" in their patients, Botox was an effective therapy to relieve *any* "pain in the head, neck, and shoulders." Allergan's detail team focused on the most prolific off-label dispensers: physicians. It held workshops demonstrating how to disguise off-label Botox injections when billing insurance companies in order to get reimbursed. Allergan paid for weekend getaways, physician conferences, workshops, and dinners, all concentrating on expanding off-label therapies. It created an online "patient information" organization that tilted its advice to recommending off-label Botox use. Doctors were mostly receptive because Botox was dispensed in their clinics or offices. By cutting out retail pharmacies, there was more money to be made by physicians, who bundled fees for their services into the price they charged patients for the drug.[41]

In 2010, after a two-year Department of Justice investigation, Allergan pled guilty to a single criminal misdemeanor for "misbranding" Botox with its off-label promotion. It was the same criminal violation that Purdue pled guilty to in 2007 over its misuse of OxyContin. Allergan paid a criminal fine of $375 million, and a separate civil settlement with the federal government and the states cost the company an additional $225 million. The civil settlement was because Allergan had helped doctors file false claims to Medicare, Medicaid, Veterans Affairs, and other government-funded prescription drug programs.

Allergan, as did Purdue with its OxyContin settlement, executed a Corporate Integrity Agreement that instituted a strict compliance program. Any further "material breach" would result in Allergan being excluded from federal health care programs.[42] The Corporate Integrity Agreement did not prohibit Allergan from submitting Botox for additional orphaned diseases. Subsequent to its criminal plea, the FDA approved Botox for other orphan diseases, including severe primary axillary hyperhidrosis (excessive sweating in the armpits), Meige syndrome/oral facial dystonia (lip spasticity), urinary incontinence resulting from neurologic conditions such as spinal cord injury and multiple sclerosis, and adult upper and lower limb spasticity.[43] * [44]

Because of the Orphan Drug Act, taxpayers had offset much of Allergan's R&D for each of its orphan drugs. Every time the FDA approved Botox for another orphaned disease, Allergan got a new round of government tax credits, subsidies, fee waivers, and extended exclusive selling periods.

Allergan next did something that was a first in the drug industry. It used its orphan drug research to focus on getting mass-market approvals for Botox. It has succeeded over time in getting the FDA to approve Botox for treating overactive bladders, migraines, and its best-known therapy, cosmetic improvements of facial wrinkles.[45] Because of its many financial breaks as an orphan drug, what Allergan paid for its R&D as a cosmetic treatment was a fraction of what a typical drug would have cost.

Allergan has another advantage over rivals in its applications. No competitor has figured out Botox's complex chemical structure. Instead of protecting its precise formulation with a patent, Allergan holds it as a trade secret. It is as critical to Botox as Coca-Cola's secret formula is to its soda. Fewer than a dozen Allergan employees know all the reagents utilized and the exact settings of its anaerobic fermentation process. So long as it alone knows that recipe, it will continue to apply for new disease subsets of its existing orphaned drugs, getting the financial benefits of the law as well as additional seven-year selling monopolies on each. After a voluntary hiatus in the wake of two children with cerebral palsy who died in Botox trials in 2008, as of 2019, Allergan is testing Botox for a dozen additional orphaned illnesses.[46]

The problem under the Orphan Drug Act—even for the best-

---

* Allergan has been creative in satisfying the statute's requirement that an orphaned disease cannot affect more than 200,000 patients. While more than a million people eighteen and older suffer from upper limb spasticity, Allergan only tested Botox for stiffness in seven muscles in the elbow, wrist, and one finger. It later sought and received FDA approval to treat two additional fingers. All the slicing and dicing of symptoms and treatment areas was to satisfy the limitations for the number of patients in an orphan disease.

intentioned biotech companies using gene mapping technology to produce treatments for different cancers, muscular dystrophy, and cystic fibrosis—is the temptation to make outsized profits during its seven-year sales monopoly by setting often a jaw-dropping price.[47] The world's most expensive drug from 2011 until December 2017 was Soliris, developed by Connecticut-based Alexion Pharmaceuticals. The FDA approved Soliris for atypical hemolytic uremic syndrome (aHUS), a genetic illness in which the body's immune system attacks blood platelets and cells. It affects an estimated six to seven hundred Americans.[48] When it went on sale in 2011 it was priced at $18,000 a dose, $500,000 annually.[49]

Soliris was dethroned as the world's most expensive drug in December 2017 when the FDA approved Luxturna, a novel gene therapy to treat a genetic eye disease that leads to progressive loss of vision for 1,500 to 2,000 affected patients.[50] The price was set at $850,000. Luxturna lost its "most expensive" title in May 2019 when Novartis introduced Zolgensma to treat pediatric spinal muscle atrophy for a one-time treatment cost of $2.1 million (at one stage it had considered setting the price as high as $5 million).[51] In defending its pricing, Novartis claimed it had priced its drug at less than half the cost of chronic medical care in the first years of an afflicted child's life. After discussions with fifteen American insurance companies, Novartis announced the industry's first ever installment plan by which the insurance firms would pay for it over five years.[52]

Not every orphan drug that promises an innovative treatment of a rare disease that had previously stumped researchers enters the market at a record-setting price. But when real-world use confirms the drug is in fact a radical breakthrough, companies frequently race to raise their prices. When Genzyme, for instance, introduced Cerezyme in 1991 to treat Gaucher disease, a progressive genetic disorder of the liver and spleen, its annual cost was $150,000 per patient. Its popularity meant that by 2014, Cerezyme's price had more than doubled to $310,000.[53] Similarly, Vertex got approval in 2012 for Kalydeco, a bioengineered drug targeting a genetic mutation carried by 1,200 of the 30,000 with cystic fibrosis. Vertex priced it at $294,000. Six months later it raised Kalydeco to $307,000. In another year it was $373,000.[54]

Academic researchers and scientists were angered about the Kalydeco price hikes. Twenty-eight scientists and physicians who treated cystic fibrosis signed a letter to Vertex's CEO condemning its pricing as "unconscionable."[55] They were particularly enraged because significant portions of Kalydeco research funding, as is the case for many novel biosimilar orphans, was possible only because of National Institutes of Health grants. Between 2010 and 2016, *every* one of the 210 drugs approved by the FDA had early research partly funded by the NIH, more than $100 billion in total.[56] (Since the 1930s, the NIH has invested $900 billion into research that drug companies used to patent brand-name medications).[57]

That taxpayer money was often indispensable for biotechs with an ambitious idea but not the money to develop it. What researchers found particularly distressing was how many ways the companies relied on the federal grants and assistance and then kept all profits. In the case of Vertex, buzz over Kalydeco made its stock pop more than $6 billion in one day. The company's executives raked in over $100 million when they cashed in stock options. All the time they kept increasing the drug's price, not lowering it.

Nothing in the Orphan Drug Act requires pharma companies to reimburse the government for research funding or to share any profits with either the National Institutes of Health or the National Cancer Institute. Several legislative efforts to close the loopholes exploited in the Orphan Drug Act have failed.[58]

Not all extravagantly priced orphan drugs are from biotech labs. Some of the most notorious are decades old, approved by the FDA before the Kefauver Amendments required the agency to rely on clinical trials. These are instances in which companies stopped making the older medications because the market was too small. It took number-crunching Wall Street entrepreneurs to realize that notwithstanding a small market, the way to make an orphaned drug profitable was to set a high enough price.

Acthar was such a drug, approved in 1952 by the FDA primarily to treat West syndrome, an uncommon but often fatal epileptic disorder that strikes infants younger than one. Acthar's main ingredient was a hormone extracted from the pituitary glands of slaughtered pigs. It was discovered by the drug division of meatpacking giant Armour.[59] Sanofi Aventis bought it and through the 1990s unsuccessfully tried expanding the therapies for which it was dispensed.

Acthar was priced at $40 per vial.[60] After losing money every year, Sanofi stopped making it. In 2001, Questcor, a small and unprofitable drug company that was looking for new products, bought the rights at a fire sale price of $100,000.[61] Over the next few years it raised Acthar from $40 to $1,650 a vial.[62] Still, the patient market was so tiny that Questcor lost money and considered abandoning the drug.[63] That changed in 2007 when Don Bailey became Questcor's CEO. He was a business executive with no drug industry experience but a great résumé as a turnaround artist for struggling firms. For Bailey, Acthar was not a difficult problem to solve. He knew the company's costs and how many patients were in the market. The only calculation Questcor had gotten consistently wrong, he concluded, was the price necessary to turn a good profit. If the price he picked was too high and the drug failed, then at least Questcor would know with certainty that nothing could save its drug.

One of the first things Bailey did was to raise the per-vial price to $23,000. He was unapologetic about the stratospheric increase, telling Wall Street analysts that "We have this drug at a very high price right now because, really, our principal market is infantile spasms. And we only have about 800 patients a year. It's a very, very small—tiny—market."[64]

Bailey got the FDA to give his slightly reformulated Acthar Gel a seven-year orphan drug patent. Under Bailey, Questcor expanded the indications for which Acthar could be dispensed to nineteen autoimmune and inflammatory illnesses. Its biggest promise was possibly treating multiple sclerosis patients who did not respond to more traditional IV steroids.[65] It also had tentative FDA approval for nephrotic syndrome (kidney disorder), rheumatoid arthritis, and lupus. In the five years after Bailey had set the $23,000 price, Questcor's stock went from 60 cents to $50, one of the top ten performing stocks in the entire market. (Insiders sold more than $100 million of stock over two years.)[66]

Smart CEOs like Bailey knew how to limit or avoid patient protests about high prices. As do many other companies selling exorbitantly priced drugs, Questcor gave some of its drugs free to those in need. It had a separate department devoted to helping patients get assistance with copays. The company's profit comes from the 70 percent of sales to private insurance companies and to Medicare, Medicaid, the Children's Health Insurance Program (CHIP), and Veterans Affairs.[67]

In the case of Acthar, Questcor not only managed to pull off the price increase from $40 to $23,000, but it turned into a profitable company that won accolades in the business world. In 2013 it was ranked as #1 on *Forbes*'s "Best Small Companies in America." The company that had been losing money before it bought the rights to Acthar had a market cap of $3.5 billion.

The following year its stock reached $92.35 just as it was acquired for $5.6 billion by Mallinckrodt Pharmaceuticals.[68] Mallinckrodt was best known for a complicated tax inversion that left its headquarters in St. Louis but its tax domicile in Ireland. Some of the money saved in taxes went to CEO Mark Trudeau, whose annual salary jumped from $6 million to $14 million. At at the same time Mallinckrodt raised a vial of Acthar to $38,892 and then to $43,000.[69]

A study in *JAMA* disclosed that Acthar dispensing in Medicare had increased several hundred percent, driven by a very small number of physicians. Those doctors were prescribing it to more patients and with greater frequency even though there were comparable generics that cost thousands of dollars less per treatment.[70] The government paid more than $2 billion from Medicare on over 45,000 Acthar prescriptions from 2011 to 2016.

"I was shocked for my profession," said Dr. Dennis Bourdette, one of the study's authors and chairman of neurology at Oregon Health and Science School of Medicine. Since some of Acthar's competitors cost one fiftieth as much, Bourdette said, "It's a mystery to me why someone would be prescribing the drug."[71] One reason is that the U.S. rights to an almost identical Canadian drug, Synacthen, which sells for $33 for a comparable dose, were bought by Mallinckrodt and killed.[72] About 60 percent of the big spike in Acthar's sales to seniors in Medicare were for off-label ailments including rheumatoid arthritis. A researcher told *60 Minutes* in 2018 there was "no evidence" Acthar helped treat arthritis. Saate Shakil, a UCSF professor, wrote a blistering accompanying editorial to the *JAMA* study, highlighting the "lack of high-quality evidence" to support Acthar's supposed benefits and called the price increases "unconscionable."[73]

In April 2019, under increasing scrutiny about its Acthar marketing, Mallinckrodt announced it would change its corporate name to Sonorant Therapeutics. Two months later the Justice Department announced an investigation of Mallinckrodt based on two whistleblowers who reported the company bribed doctors to overprescribe Acthar (two months later it settled the matter for $15.4 million).[74] Fortunately for Mallinckrodt, not many people outside the drug industry know who CEO Mark Trudeau is or what he looks like. For firms trying to squeeze the last dollar from an old grandfathered drug, the personality of the CEO can affect public perceptions. When Martin Shkreli, a thirty-two-year-old ex–hedge fund manager, raised the price of an inexpensive orphan drug that was long off patent by 5,000 percent in 2015, he became overnight the villainous poster boy for unconscionable drug prices.[75] Denounced in both mainstream and social media, Shkreli appeared before Congress where he invoked his Fifth Amendment right against self-incrimination. All the time, he smirked at lawmakers on live television. It was bad enough that Shkreli had paid $55 million for the rights to Daraprim (the FDA approved it in 1953) and raised its price from $13.50 to $750 a pill. What made it somehow worse was that the pill treated a rare parasitic infection that affected immunosuppressed infants and HIV/AIDS patients. Daraprim was indispensable for some two thousand patients: there were no generic competitors.

Shkreli was arrested in December 2015 on securities fraud and conspiracy charges unrelated to the pricing of Daraprim. Pharmaceutical Research and Manufacturers of America (PhRMA), the drug trade's powerful lobbying association, knew the outspoken and unapologetic Shkreli was bad for an industry already held in low esteem by a majority of Americans (a 2019 Gallup poll revealed that Americans had a more negative opinion of the pharmaceutical business than any other industry).[76] "I think the image of the sector has been hijacked by some bad actors, and we have to do a better job of telling our story," said Stephen Ubl, PhRMA's president, when he announced a $60 million ad campaign that emphasized "more lab coat, less hoodie" (a reference to the gray hoodie Shkreli wore when he was arrested).[77]

Shkreli, who was convicted in 2017 of two counts of security fraud, is serving a seven-year prison sentence.[78] Although he mostly dropped out of the news after his conviction, Turing, the drug company of which he had been CEO, quietly kept Daraprim's price at $750 a pill. The federal government continued paying $35,556.48 for a month's supply for Medicaid patients.[79] The same prescription had cost $608 before the price increase.

What happened with Daraprim was condemned as heartless. It was not, however, against the law.* [80] Legislators and the FDA have com-

* Some states have tried controlling prices, but most substantive drug regulation is a federal power. Vermont, for instance, in 2016 became the first to require drug manufacturers to demonstrate cause for price hikes. If the pharmaceutical companies do not

plained about that since Burroughs's price-gouging thirty-two years ago with AZT, the first drug to combat AIDS. To industry veterans familiar with the Orphan Drug Act, none of the news from AZT to Botox to Shkreli is surprising. Marlene Haffner, who ran the FDA's Office of Orphan Products Development for twenty-one years before she opened her own successful orphan drug consulting firm, believes it was all to be expected.[81]

"What we are seeing is a system that was created with good intent being hijacked," according to Bernard Munos, an ex–corporate strategy consultant at Eli Lilly who reviewed the FDA Orphan Drug databases as part of a 2017 investigation by Kaiser Health News. It is "quite remarkable that it has gone on for so long."[82]

---

comply, they can still sell their drugs, but are subject to a $10,000 fine. Also in 2016, California voters defeated a proposition that would have capped drug prices at whatever Veterans Affairs paid. The industry spent $120 million to defeat it.

51

THE COMING PANDEMIC

In 2015, there was no mainstream media reporting that seven of the top ten selling medications in America were orphan drugs. Although high prescription prices were frequently discussed, the complex reasons behind the price-gouging were something only covered in industry publications and by patient advocacy groups. One of the pharmaceutical stories that dominated the year's media coverage was antibiotic resistance. A study commissioned by the U.K. delivered sobering news. At least fifty thousand people died annually in the U.S. and Europe from antimicrobial-resistant infections.[1] Upward of 50 percent of bloodstream infections were the result of drug-resistant strains.[2] Not only was the use of antibiotics up (rose by 40 percent from 2000 to 2010), but the ease of international travel translated into superbugs spreading to every country. The report predicted that by 2050, 10 million people would die annually from drug-resistant bacteria, more than from cancer.[3] If governments did not address it as a major health crisis, modern health care that relied heavily on antibiotics would "be undermined" and could lead to "a return to the dark age of medicine." The WHO later emphasized that: "A post-antibiotic era [is one] in which common infections and minor injuries . . . can once again kill."[4]

In March, President Obama urged Congress to double the budget to fight antibiotic-resistant bacteria. Doctors write a quarter billion antibiotic prescriptions annually to Americans.[5] That is twice the rate of Europeans and the CDC says that a third of those dispensed are "unnecessary."[6] In May, the United Nations and the World Health Organization unanimously adopted plans to develop better tools to spot cases of resistance and to commit enough funding to develop new antibiotics.[7]

Sally Davies, the U.K.'s chief medical officer, concluded that the threat posed by antibiotic-resistant bacteria was as great as terrorism. She had overseen a government report that concluded superbugs were the top public health emergency. "We may be a bit late," she told *The New York Times*. "If you look at the trajectories of rising antimicrobial-resistance, increasing use of antibiotics and a lack of new antibiotics, this could be a catastrophe."[8]

Since that warning, a series of sobering reports in medical journals exposed the extent to which antimicrobial-resistant infections have spread and wreaked havoc. In 2017, the same year that the CDC announced the death of the Nevada woman who was a victim of a resistant strain that did not respond to any antibiotics, superbugs infected 3,000,000 Americans and killed more than 24,000. Worldwide, an estimated 700,000 died.[9]

It took the CDC three years to develop a system to identify superbugs.[10] When five hundred CDC workers fanned out across the country in 2018 to collect random samples, the results were not good. There were 221 instances in which so-called nightmare bacteria—germs with already high levels of resistance—had developed "unusual" and "novel" antibiotic-resistant genes. CDC researchers worry that upward of a quarter of those might spread their resistance to other germs. If that happens, antibiotic resistance will not just be an evolutionary question of how long it takes germs to survive when faced with new drugs. Instead, superbugs might convert otherwise vulnerable bacteria into dangerous clones.[11]

The CDC and FDA are also worried about the widespread use of antibiotics in the food chain.[12] A remarkable 80 percent of antibiotics manufactured in the U.S. are not dispensed to patients but used by livestock farmers. The drugs have been used since the 1950s to spur faster growth in cows, pigs, and chickens and are a cheap substitute for hygiene in overcrowded and unsanitary conditions. The Obama administration addressed that in 2015 by having the FDA set stricter reporting requirements from pharma companies that make the drugs for animals. That only clarified the size of the problem. In 2017, farmers gave 141,000 tons of antibiotics to food animals. That was when the U.N. released the first of two studies concluding the widespread use of antibiotics in livestock had created a "rise of AMR [antimicrobial resistance] in zoonotic pathogens, including to last-resort drugs. . . . [It] is an important challenge for human medicine because it can lead to untreatable infections."[13] The FDA responded finally in 2017 by banning all antibiotics used on livestock for "growth promotion and feed efficiency."[14] Tremendous lobbying by the farming and food industries allowed them to keep using the drugs for "health maintenance."

An equally worrying development is the agricultural use of antibiotics. Florida's $7.2 billion citrus industry has been fighting "citrus greening disease," a bacterial infection that arrived in 2005 and makes fruit too bitter for commercial use. It is spread by a flying insect originally from China. Efforts to control it with pesticides had mixed success. In 2016, the Environmental Protection Agency under the Obama administration approved the limited spraying of two vintage antibiotics, streptomycin and oxytetracycline. The FDA and CDC objected, fearing the widespread use of those antimicrobials could fuel drug resistance. In Europe and Brazil, they are banned for agricultural use.

In May 2019, under the Trump administration, the EPA approved an expansion of the use of those two antibiotics to three quarters of a million acres in Texas, California, and other citrus-producing states. Once again, it was over strenuous protests from the FDA and CDC. Under the current guidelines, while Americans will consume about 15,000 pounds of those drugs annually, some 650,000 pounds will be sprayed on citrus crops.[15] The objections from the two regulatory agencies with oversight on health were straightforward. It is not even clear after three years of use in Florida that the drugs stop the citrus greening disease. Studies showed that pathogenic bacteria in soil became resistant to them over time. That is most likely with streptomycin, which stays active in dirt for weeks.[16] The drugs spread to people through groundwater and accelerate human resistance.[17]

The EPA stuck to its position. It cited studies from pesticide manufacturers who claimed the antibiotics would be "quickly dissipated in the environment."[18] While the EPA eventually agreed there was a "medium" risk from the expanded use of the drugs, it did not ban them since it concluded there was no conclusive research on "whether a massive increase in spraying would affect the bacteria that infect humans."[19] In response to the concerns from federal health regulators, the EPA said it would implement additional monitoring of the spraying and also require new approvals every seven years.

The CDC released an alarming report in November 2019 in which it concluded that drug-resistant germs presented a much greater "public health threat" than it had previously forecast. Its latest analysis revealed that, on average, every eleven seconds someone in the U.S. is infected by a superbug, and every fifteen minutes, someone dies.[20]

"No one knows where it [the next pandemic] will come from," says Karen Bush, a biology professor who had worked for nearly forty years in antibacterial development at a succession of large pharma companies. "Only when it arrives can we look back and identify what sparked it." Some of her colleagues worry about avian or swine flu that might morph into more deadly strains in humans. Cross-species transmissions have been the cause of every major epidemic from the bubonic plague (rats and fleas) to the 1918 influenza (birds), malaria (mosquitoes), and HIV/AIDS (primates). Scientists have identified eighty-four diseases that pass from animals to humans. The one about which they are most concerned is the one that has not yet jumped species. "We won't know that until it happens," says Bush. Reports in 2019 that an African swine fever had killed 150 million of China's 440 million pigs attracted considerable attention from epidemiologists and infectious disease experts. A story about its devastation in *Bloomberg* noted, "The good news is it can't infect humans. The bad news is that nobody knows when it will stop spreading."[21]

Exacerbating fears over the growth of supergerms is that few pharmaceutical companies are developing new antibiotics. "In 1980, there were thirty-six U.S. and European companies in the antibiotic business," notes Bush. "Today there are fewer than six."[22]

In 1968, Smith Kline had introduced Proloprim, a combination sulfonamide and synthetic antimicrobial agent. It took thirty-one years before there was a new class of antibiotics, oxazolidinones.[23] Every antibiotic used to fight infectious bacteria in the interim was a chemically similar me-too clone of an earlier drug. In the last decade, the FDA approved only nine new antibiotics.[24] In contrast, explosive advances in nanotechnology, stem cells, and deciphering the microbiome have led to almost a hundred new anti-cancer drugs over the same period.[25] Those are credited with survival rates having doubled since the 1970s.[26]

"Innovation, especially in the antibacterial area, is certainly not what it used to be," says Barry Eisenstein, the senior vice president in charge of Scientific Affairs at Cubist.[27] "Part of this problem is that anti-infectives can be notoriously difficult to make," says Mike Skoien, a former marketing executive in charge of Merck's anti-infective program.

There is less profit too. "The cost of production is much higher and the return almost always lower," says Skoien.[28] Some highly anticipated biotech antibiotic startups filed for bankruptcy in 2019 while others that were in desperate need of cash had difficulty finding investors. "Antibiotic treatment used to be seven days, and is now five or less," notes Eisenstein. "On the other hand, drugs that treat high cholesterol, hypertension, diabetes, depression, and other chronic conditions yield much bigger profits for the long-term bottom line."[29]

"The problem is that we cured most patients and did it too quickly and cheaply," says Steven Projan, head of infectious diseases at Astra Zeneca's MedImmune.[30]

"Without a renaissance in antibiotic development," says Eisenstein, "the very preservation of society as we know it will be at risk."[31]

The prediction of a coming pandemic, unstoppable because the pharmaceutical industry has put profits over its duty to develop drugs for the public good, is no wild-eyed conspiracy theory heavy on drama and light on evidence. "It is not a question of if," warns Professor Bush, "it is a question of when."[32]

52

"ESSENTIALLY A CRIME FAMILY"

While antibiotic resistance was a popular story in the media in 2015, it paled in comparison to interest in the opioid epidemic. The federal government released yet another study. The news was grim. Opioid prescription rates were triple the number dispensed in 1999.[1] Enough Oxy had been prescribed that year to medicate every American for nearly a month.[2] It had killed more people than had fatal car crashes and guns combined (52,000). The lethal overdoses from Purdue's blockbuster surpassed the peak year of HIV/AIDS deaths (1995). Statisticians blamed OxyContin for the first decline in more than twenty years in the life expectancy of Americans.[3] A report from the CDC confirmed what some doctors had suspected: prescription opioid users were forty times more likely to become heroin addicts, making meds like Oxy the most effective gateway drugs into heroin. The Veterans Administration released a report that highlighted the danger of higher dosing. It sampled five years of chronic pain patients on OxyContin and found that those who died of an opioid overdose took on average 60 mg daily. There were few deaths for patients on 30 mg a day.[4]

The escalating epidemic prompted the CDC to urge doctors either to "carefully justify" or "avoid" prescribing more than 60 mg daily. Still, the guidelines were voluntary. Only seven states had passed legislation to limit the duration and number of prescriptions.[5] That was the same year the author learned that a party took place at Purdue's Stamford headquarters to celebrate a national survey released by Johns Hopkins. It revealed the extent to which Purdue's different messages had caused confusion among primary care physicians, the country's top prescribers of opioids. Nearly half erroneously believed that Purdue's tamper-resistant pill was less likely to cause addiction than standard formulations from its rivals.[6]

In 2016, OxyContin and the opioid epidemic had become a topic on the presidential campaign. More than 200,000 Americans had died of opioid overdoses since the government began collecting statistics in 1999.[7] Purdue felt pressured again. Although OxyContin sales had fallen 40 percent since their 2012 peak, it was the brand name the public associated with the crisis. The Joint Commission, responsible for accrediting hospitals and clinics, reversed its 2001 position and declared that it "does not endorse pain as a vital sign."[8] Purdue thought it was only a matter of time before its painkiller came under stricter FDA regulation. As a result, it executed a contingency plan to expand aggressively overseas. The Sacklers used their Mundipharma network. Arthur, Mortimer, and Raymond had established a single Mundipharma Limited in London in August 1955. By 2016, through licensing agreements, distribution deals, and family ownership stakes sometimes hidden in offshore tax havens, Mundipharma consisted of ninety-seven companies operating in more than one hundred countries. Richard Sackler admitted in a 2015 deposition that the Sackler family owned Mundipharma.

The OxyContin expansion strategy concentrated on countries where opioids were underused. China, Brazil, and India were at the top of Purdue's list. The plan was to launch a slightly modified version of the same aggressive campaign as the company had in the 1990s in the U.S. The core message again was that the "silent epidemic of pain" was undertreated. As Purdue had done in the U.S., Mundipharma hired leading industry lobbyists in each country. It proved "very good at co-opting regulators," said Stanford's Keith Humphreys, who is familiar with Mundipharma's growth.[9] There is evidence of its success. In the past three years, OxyContin sales are higher by up to 700 percent in half a dozen European and South Asian countries. Mundipharma was ranked as one of the fastest-growing pharmaceutical firms in Brazil's pain market.[10]

When the *Los Angeles Times* brought the Mundipharma expansion to the attention of former FDA commissioner David Kessler, he immediately recognized Purdue's strategy. "It's right out of the Big Tobacco playbook. As the United States takes steps to limit sales here, the company goes abroad."[11]

In 2017, top public health experts at ten universities gave forecasts about opioid deaths in the coming decade. The grim consensus was "it will get worse before it gets better."[12] The most dire scenario was that as many as an additional 650,000 Americans will die by 2027, more than the entire population of Boston and almost as many Americans as would die from prostate and breast cancer over the same time.[13]

The Sackler-family directors had launched a belated effort to burnish their reputation and that of Purdue. December 2017 marked the start of the company's national ad campaign in which it endorsed the CDC guidelines for safe opioid prescribing. In January, it announced an initiative to put pill disposal boxes in pharmacies and health clinics, began a radio campaign to warn of the dangers of abusing opioid painkillers, rolled out a training program to provide EMS workers with supplies of an overdose antidote (naloxone), and introduced a new medication to combat the common opioid side effect of constipation.[14] In February, not long after forty-one state attorneys general had subpoenaed more internal Purdue marketing and promotion documents, the company announced its intent to slash its sales force by half. And it would no longer directly market Oxy to individual physicians, instead concentrating on hospitals and clinics. Industry analysts noted that Purdue had softened its long-standing message that "we're not the drivers of the problem, the addicts are the drivers of the problem."[15]

The financial press reported Purdue was also attempting to wean itself from its addiction to OxyContin revenues and profits. At its peak in 2012, the drug accounted for 94 percent of the company's sales. As of 2018, it was still 84 percent. The Sacklers were looking for alliances with drug firms specializing in oncology and sleep meds.[16]

In March 2018, the national focus returned to the lethal fallout from Purdue's star drug. President Trump announced the outlines of a new push to resolve the opioid crisis as "a public health emergency." There were 115 overdose deaths daily.[17] Congress had by then passed more than sixty short-term fixes during the past decade. Although throwing more money at the problem has never worked, it evidently allowed politicians to demonstrate that if they were not ending the crisis, they were at least studying and talking about it a lot.

At the same time that American politicians were wondering what to do about its "public health emergency," British politicians were embarrassed by revelations that the Sacklers had not only run their foreign OxyContin operations from the U.K., but had taken advantage of a loophole to avoid paying $1.4 billion in taxes over twenty-five years (it stopped in 2016 after the law changed). Napp Pharmaceuticals, founded by Arthur, Mortimer, and Raymond in 1966, was the manufacturer for the OxyContin shipped to most countries other than the United States. Together with Mundipharma, Sackler-manufactured OxyContin accounts for 70 percent of the drug used in Britain. Under the scheme, Napp produced the OxyContin and then "sold" it at cost to Mundipharma in Bermuda. Bermuda Mundi then "sold" it for distribution to other Mundipharma companies worldwide. On paper, all the profit was earned in Bermuda and that is where it stayed. Bermuda-based companies do not pay taxes on income from sales.

But Napp never shipped the OxyContin to Bermuda. All the transfers and sales were phantom ones that existed only on paper.[18]

Adding to the outrage in the U.K., by crafting the elaborate arrangement, Mortimer avoided paying millions in personal income, capital gains, and inheritance taxes on his international holdings. He contended he was not "domiciled in the UK," despite having been a resident there for thirty-six years before his 2010 death. His British third wife and the couple's three British-born children were raised in the U.K. (the tax domicile rules were changed as a result of the outrage over how Mortimer had worked the system).*[19]

A month after those disclosures in Britain, seven members of the Sackler family resigned as Napp Pharmaceuticals directors. None made any public comment. Napp issued a statement that said: "As part of ongoing and regular operational reviews, changes have been made to Napp's board of directors."

In 2019, the momentum picked up against the Sacklers in the U.S. Purdue was in the crosshairs of angry patients, dozens of the country's best class action attorneys, almost all state attorneys general, and Justice Department prosecutors.[20] More than two thousand civil lawsuits

* In the 1980s, Mortimer had purchased the five-thousand-acre Rooksnest Estate outside London. It is where Theresa, his wife, lives today. The couple also had a grand flat in London. When British tax authorities tried proving that Rooksnest Estate was Mortimer's main home, there was no evidence that he or any other Sackler owned it. The owners were instead five companies, three based in Bermuda. Some of the estate farming contracts are with a company in the Channel Islands (Beacon Co.). Earls Court Farm Limited, another Bermuda company, managed the property. The author found that a previous director on that board was Christopher Mitchell Benbow, the solicitor who was a director of Napp Pharmaceuticals and represented the Sacklers on most of the U.K. business ventures.

filed by cities and counties had been consolidated under the jurisdiction of a federal district judge in Ohio.[21]

In March, the Massachusetts attorney general filed an amended complaint different from all others.[22] It was the first to rely on Purdue's own records to charge that the Sackler-family directors had personally "created the epidemic and profited from it through a web of illegal deceit."[23] The complaint named eight Sacklers who had served on Purdue's board as defendants. They were the widows of Raymond and Mortimer, along with five of their children and one grandchild.[24]

"Eight people in a single family made the choices that caused much of the opioid epidemic. The Sackler family owns Purdue, and they always held a majority of the seats on its Board. Because they controlled their own privately held drug company, the Sacklers had the power to decide how addictive narcotics were sold. They hired hundreds of workers to carry out their wishes, and they fired those who didn't sell enough drugs. They got more patients on opioids, at higher doses, for longer, than ever before. They paid themselves billions of dollars. They are responsible for addiction, overdose, and death that damaged millions of lives. They should be held accountable now."

A few weeks after the Massachusetts complaint, the New York attorney general not only named the Sackler-family directors as defendants, but she was the first to contend they had transferred hundreds of millions in assets to offshore tax havens (a billion dollars through Swiss bank accounts). New York, according to the complaint, "wants to claw back some of the profits earned by the family over the decades."[25]

Through their lawyers, the Sacklers named as defendants vehemently denied the charges and vowed an aggressive defense. They were no longer only battling lawsuits seeking tens of billions in damages. The Sacklers were now trying to salvage the family's public reputation. Although they had been well known inside the pharmaceutical industry and the worlds of art and philanthropy, it was mostly in the wake of the 2019 lawsuits naming them individually that they became familiar to millions of Americans who had never taken an OxyContin pill and never heard of Purdue. The opening night when New York's A-list paid tribute to the Sacklers at the Metropolitan Museum's Temple of Dendur seemed a long-forgotten memory as the family's role in the opioid epidemic attracted episodes on *60 Minutes* and PBS's *Frontline* and investigations by *The New York Times*, *Boston Globe*, and *Los Angeles Times*.

Gossip columnists reported that New York society shunned the

Sacklers. Purdue's banker, JPMorgan Chase, declined to do business with the company and some of the family. Hildene Capital Management cut ties with them.

It had seemed hyperbole when an unnamed plaintiff's lawyer told Britain's *Guardian* in December 2018 that the Sacklers were "essentially a crime family . . . drug dealers in nice suits and dresses."[26] In 2019, however, such a statement was longer mere litigation posturing. John Coffee, Columbia University Law School's director of its Center on Corporate Governance, had been retained by Utah's Division of Consumer Protection. It wanted his opinion as to whether Richard Sackler, and his cousin Kathe, could be held civilly or criminally responsible for how they ran Purdue. Coffee's sixty-one-page report, submitted in July and initially sealed by the court, concluded that "the Sackler-family dominated club . . . is dysfunctional corporate governance, and there is little to distinguish the control the Sacklers exercised over Purdue from the control that the Godfather held over his Mafia family."[27]

Not even the family's legendary art philanthropy was safe. Some of Arthur's family tried protecting his legacy from the backlash over OxyContin, a drug that went on sale nine years after his death. "The opioid epidemic is a national crisis and Purdue Pharma's role in it is morally abhorrent to me," Elizabeth, his second daughter, said in a statement sent to an art magazine. Herself a noted art and culture philanthropist, she drew distance from her cousins who had served as Purdue directors. "None of his [Arthur's] descendants have ever owned a share of Purdue stock nor benefitted in any way from it or the sale of OxyContin."[28] Jillian, Arthur's third wife, wrote an op-ed in the *Washington Post*, in which she said Arthur had "been found guilty by association—along with the rest of what is referred to by the blanket designation 'the Sackler family'—because of some family members' association with Purdue Pharma, the maker of OxyContin."[29] * [30] But the tsunami of anger over the contrast between the accumulating body count and the billions in profits reaped by the Sacklers spared no one.[31] Some institutions that had received millions in Sackler bequests distanced

* Since Arthur's 1987 death, Jillian Sackler has become a Dame of the British Empire and was awarded the National Academy of Sciences' "Einstein" Award in 2005. She carried on his philanthropy as the president of the Dame Jillian and Dr. Arthur M. Sackler Foundation for the Arts, Sciences and Humanities. In a February 2018 statement, she said, "Passing judgment on Arthur's life's work through the lens of the opioid crisis some 30 years after his death is a gross injustice."

themselves from the family. Public petitions with tens of thousands of signatures submitted to Harvard and Tufts asked the schools to remove the Sackler name, which Tufts announced it would do. Oregon's Senator Jeff Merkley requested their name be eliminated from the Smithsonian, where Arthur's art collection is on permanent display.

Photographer Nan Goldin, herself in recovery from an OxyContin addiction, organized widely publicized demonstrations to force Sackler-funded institutions to stop accepting any more of their money. Elizabeth Sackler supported her.[32] It has worked in some instances. London's Tate and New York's Guggenheim announced they would no longer accept Sackler bequests. Britain's National Portrait Gallery canceled a planned $1.3 million gift from the Sackler Trust. A small museum in South London returned a donation. The biggest blow was when the Metropolitan Museum joined the "no more Sackler money" contingent, although the Met, for the time being, says it has no plans for renaming the Sackler Wing that houses the Temple of Dendur.

In an effort to reverse the bad press, in March 2019, a couple of days after the New York attorney general had filed the complaint seeking to claw back the family's early profits, Purdue announced it had reached a settlement with the Oklahoma attorney general in a case that had been scheduled to be the first to trial by early summer. Purdue agreed to pay $270 million. Although no Sacklers were named in that case, the family announced it made a $75 million "goodwill" contribution to Oklahoma State University's Center for Wellness and Recovery.[33] * [34]

It was a gesture that for most Americans, especially the relatives of those who died from OxyContin, seemed calculated and far too little too late. The Sacklers had bought their way out of the 2007 federal prosecution. The Oklahoma settlement spurred speculation that the family had developed another escape strategy. Some legal experts thought Purdue was preparing to settle a few major lawsuits before de-

* Teva Pharmaceuticals had also settled the Oklahoma suit before the trial. Johnson & Johnson, through its subsidiary Janssen, was the only company to go to trial. On August 26, 2019, when a judge ruled against J&J and ordered it to pay $572 million to the state, he relied on Oklahoma's century-old public nuisance law. "The harm it [the opioid crisis] has wrought, and the threat it continues to pose to the health, safety and welfare of the State, make it the worst nuisance Oklahoma has ever known." That law traditionally covered instances in which there was interference with the use of public property. Applying it to commercial activity was a first. Judges in Connecticut and North Dakota had earlier rejected public nuisance claims against opioid manufacturers.

claring bankruptcy. Others said that given the legal hurdles involved in suing corporate directors, the family might be able to protect a significant part of its personal fortune. The idea that the Sacklers were trying to shield their OxyContin wealth got momentum with news that some family members had sold their New York homes for large estates in Florida, a state where homesteading laws protect all residences from creditors.[35]

Richard Sackler's son, David, was the president of an LLC that bought a West Palm Beach office building for $6.8 million and was about to spend $7.4 million on a Boca Raton mansion.[36] Those Florida purchases were not known when David tried to soften the family's image in a summer *Vanity Fair* interview.[37] He said his four-year-old had returned from nursery school one day and asked, "Why are my friends telling me that our family's work is killing people?" According to Sackler, he and his relatives were tired of "vitriolic hyperbole" and "endless castigation."[38] Instead of putting a human face on the Sacklers the interview added to the growing anger against them. The *Daily Mail* headline was typical: "Heir to $13B OxyContin Fortune Says Son, 4, Asked if Family Kills People, Rejects Blame for Opioid Crisis and Plays Victim in Interview."[39]

One of the themes David Sackler pressed was Purdue's long-standing claim that OxyContin had such a small share of all prescription opioids that it was impossible for it to have been primarily responsible for the opioid crisis. Oxy is, Sackler said, a "tiny, niche little product with tiny market share." On Purdue's website, a page titled "Common Myths About OxyContin" listed its "small percentage of the total opioid market." A DEA report unsealed during the summer seemed to bolster the assertion; Purdue had only 3.3 percent of the prescription opioid market from 2006 to 2012. Those measurements include, however, instant release opioid painkillers, most of which are available as inexpensive generics. The instant release opioids account for 90 percent of all sales. The remaining 10 percent for extended release opiates accounts for 60 percent of all revenues ($25.4 billion in 2018). Oxycodone dominates that segment. Moreover, the studies on market share do not consider potency. A September 2019 *ProPublica* analysis revealed that based on the amount of oxycodone sold, Purdue had 16 percent of the market, the third-largest opioid seller in the U.S.[40]

If the Sacklers believed a single interview might help stem the tide of public anger, they misjudged the power of the case presented by dozens of state attorneys general. Those complaints rely on Purdue's files to persuasively argue that its wrongdoing was not a few isolated instances that could be ascribed to the unauthorized behavior of some errant executives. The 51 million pages of documents Purdue has produced in response to subpoenas detail a course of conduct likely to result in civil racketeering and fraud charges against former executives and possibly even some Sackler-family directors.[41]

In September 2019, an insider to the negotiations between Purdue and a couple of dozen lead plaintiffs leaked the outline of an offer the Sacklers had made and that they valued between $10 billion and $12 billion.[42] In exchange for ending all pending lawsuits, the Sacklers would pay $3 billion in cash and put Purdue into a structured bankruptcy.[43] Court-appointed trustees would select a board of directors to run a for-profit Purdue as a public-benefit corporation.[44] Overdose and addiction mitigation drugs in Purdue's pipeline would be distributed free of charge to communities affected by the opioid epidemic.[45]

The lead plaintiffs were divided. The Massachusetts and New York attorneys general insisted the family pay more cash up front, about $4.5 billion. The Sacklers could manage that if they agreed to immediately sell their interests in Mundipharma.[46] But the family resisted, claiming that if buyers knew Mundipharma had to be sold at a fire sale price, it would fetch less than half what it was worth a couple of years earlier.[47]

Not only did the Sacklers refuse to personally offer more than $3 billion cash, they insisted they pay it over seven years of installments. The largest contributions, more than half, would come in years five through seven.[48] They wanted the same seven years to unload their Mundipharma stake.[49]

One thing evident despite all the argument over how much cash the family should pay was that the Sacklers would be left with upward of $4 billion of their OxyContin profits. That estimate of how much wealth the Sacklers would retain seemed low when, a few weeks later, court documents revealed that Purdue had paid the Sackler-family directors $12 to $13 billion in profits.[50] "This apparent settlement is a slap in the face to everyone who has buried a loved one due to this family's destruction and greed," said Josh Shapiro, Pennsylvania's attorney general. "It allows the Sackler family to walk away billionaires and admit no wrongdoing."[51]

There was also considerable skepticism about the financial numbers and projections the Sacklers provided. Although the family had shown what auditors said were complete finances, veteran attorneys and investigators have had trouble getting an accurate accounting of the extent of Sackler ownership in Imbrium and Adlon Therapeutics, two limited partnerships launched by Purdue in early 2019. Both share the company's Connecticut headquarters and are run by former Purdue executives. Adlon recently got FDA approval for an ADHD medication and Imbrium has signed a joint marketing deal with a Japanese drug company for an insomnia pill in the FDA approval pipeline.[52] Besides U.S. holdings that are opaque to investigators, there are offshore trusts, holding companies, and limited partnerships in international tax havens. Many of the foreign OxyContin distributorships are wrapped in a series of contracts between shell companies based in Cypress, Bermuda, Switzerland, Singapore, and the Channel Islands. Whatever ownership stake the Sacklers might have is nearly impossible to determine given the corporate secrecy laws of those tax haven jurisdictions. Even the family's nonpharmaceutical holdings are difficult to assess. Their stake in Cap 1 LLC, a closely held company that owns and manages ski resorts, is estimated to be worth close to $2 billion. Its balance sheets are not public, however.[53]

When Purdue's Sackler-family directors had voted themselves four billion dollars in company profits from 2008 to 2016, the money was distributed to a dozen entities and trusts they controlled and then in many cases transferred to Swiss financial institutions.[54] One frequently used company, Rosebay Medical, is listed in twenty countries, from Australia to Germany, as owning some Sackler medical firms.[55] No one paid much attention to Rosebay's U.S. address. It is run from an office in Oklahoma City, the same one that Arthur, Mortimer, and Raymond had used decades earlier as a mailing address for some of their drug companies (and the same address listed for David Sackler in 2018 when he spent $22 million to buy a Bel Air mansion).[56] * [57]

The complex corporate chess game in which Arthur Sackler excelled

---

* In Purdue's 2007 $635 million guilty plea and settlement with the federal government, the Consent Agreement required the company to list all companies in which it had any ownership interests. It listed 215 entities. Only later did prosecutors realize that the Sacklers had omitted nearly two dozen firms that oversaw investments and property management for the family. Four months after the plea agreement, Rhodes Pharmaceuticals opened in Coventry, Rhode Island, and began producing painkillers based on oxycodone, morphine, and hydrocodone. It has become one of the largest

has for decades become how the Sacklers arrange their finances. That byzantine structure is the reason for such great distrust among plaintiffs' attorneys and victims' relatives. Given how the Sacklers and Purdue lied over the marketing of OxyContin, few believe the figures the family's lawyers and accountants rely on to account for $4 billion to $5 billion of purported value in the settlement.[58] Two overdose and addiction mitigation drugs in Purdue's pipeline, for instance, are estimated to be worth at least $4.4 billion over a decade.[59] Nalmefene is an older drug that Purdue is modifying to a new version that counteracts opioid overdoses. The second drug is an over-the-counter naloxone nasal spray.[60] The problem is that the FDA has not approved either. Although they are on a fast track, when they reach the market they will enter a competitive field dominated by Narcan and Teva's recently approved generic nasal spray.[61] The robust sales figures projected by the Purdue attorneys are anything but certain.

Maryland's attorney general, Brian Frosh, dismisses the billions promised in the sales of drugs not even on the market as "vaporous. I have not seen a deal that would yield anywhere close to those types of returns."[62] Others are irritated that Purdue has crafted a way to use drugs that would mitigate the deadly effects of OxyContin as a way to finance a settlement. "This family started a national fire," said New York attorney general Letitia James. "An arsonist should never be able to give advice on fire prevention."[63]

There was another feature of the proposed settlement that caused significant consternation. Purdue would continue selling OxyContin. Although it would be a fraction of its former sales, and without the promotion that had made it America's most abused drug, it is a sticking point. Since it is Purdue's only commercially successful drug, its sales are needed to keep the public trust version of the company afloat until the two treatment drugs get FDA approval.[64]

The settlement offer from the Sacklers was high-stakes poker. The family's attorneys had indicated they were likely to file a "free-fall" bankruptcy if the offer was not accepted. Without any agreement about the details of a reorganization, there would be far more extensive litigation as the plaintiffs battled over Purdue's remnants. Some

---

manufacturers of off-patent, generic opioid painkillers. The Sacklers concealed their ownership stake of Rhodes. It came to light in 2015 when the FDA followed a patent assignment to Rhodes back to Purdue.

state attorneys general feared a free-fall filing might ultimately provide $1.2 billion for the states and cities, a tenth of the Sackler offer.[65] The clock against which the parties negotiated was an October 21 trial date in an Ohio court for the so-called multidistrict litigation. It had been brought by cities and counties, hospitals, even Indian tribes, against Purdue and other manufacturers, as well as drug distributors and pharmacy chains.

On September 12, 2019, the executive committee representing the two thousand plaintiffs recommended accepting the Sackler offer. In addition to the $3 billion in cash, the Sacklers had agreed to put toward the settlement any amount over $3 billion when they eventually sold Mundipharma.[66] Twenty-three states, four U.S. territories, and most of the cities and counties agreed. But the sharp divisions that had split the plaintiffs during the negotiation now came to a public head. California, New York, Pennsylvania, and twenty-four other states opposed the deal.

Purdue filed for bankruptcy protection on Sunday, September 15. It put all litigation against the company on hold. It made it unlikely that Purdue, with a rapidly shrinking balance sheet, will itself ever be on trial. The dissenting state's attorneys instead will focus on pursuing Sackler-family directors. While the Sacklers had been willing to contribute financially to an overall settlement, they made it clear they would not admit any personal liability. Moreover, they would spend whatever is necessary of their considerable fortune to keep intact their perfect record of never having a civil judgment against any family member who served as a Purdue director. That standoff means those state investigations and resulting private civil lawsuits could take years.[67]

There is a widespread and understandable sentiment among the victims' families that the company and the Sacklers must be punished. Purdue and OxyContin have deservedly become the public face for the near–quarter million victims. Still, no matter how severely they are ultimately held to account, few believe it will result in full justice in the opioid crisis. It will not answer questions about all those responsible for the deadly epidemic nor will it hold many of them liable. By putting the responsibility for the crisis so squarely on Purdue and the Sacklers, there is a risk others who played material roles in creating and feeding the epidemic may not pay a price. That is the hope among thousands of others, sales representatives and executives of rival pharma companies with their own opioid products, overprescribing doctors, FDA bureaucrats who did not want to restrict OxyContin, pharmacists who diverted prescriptions to the black market, and pain management experts who preached that opioids were not addictive when prescribed for pain.

A real solution will take much more than money and free treatment drug giveaways. Besides the human toll, cities and states have spent more than a trillion dollars since 2000, everything from the additional cost of health care to criminal justice, social services, and drug treatment, as well as lost productivity and earnings from those who died.[68] Litigation alone cannot fix the problem. A multidisciplinary solution that focuses on education for patients and doctors, pain medicine alternatives, and addiction treatment can work but will require patience and commitment from policymakers.

Hopefully, the energy the government and the public have focused on Purdue and the Sacklers will not fade once they are held accountable. The cost has been too high for anyone to walk away unpunished from the trail of destruction left by prescription opioids.

ACKNOWLEDGMENTS

Writing about the American pharmaceutical industry posed some unique challenges. Three years proved a short time for what turned out to be far more extensive research than I envisioned. I put great demands on many people to obtain information. It would take a chapter to thank all who helped. I want to acknowledge here those who made a distinct contribution to the success of this investigation.

One hurdle was that pharmaceutical insiders were frequently reluctant to cooperate with a journalistic account of their industry. Decades of stinging criticisms from congressional investigations, criminal and civil litigation, and a string of whistleblowers made it difficult to persuade some to talk on the record. Several key interviewees spoke only on the condition of anonymity. Some of those unwilling to be identified still worked in the drug business and were concerned about being blackballed or violating nondisclosure agreements. Others had worked at Purdue Pharma, the company at the center of the opioid epidemic, or had friendships or professional relationships with the Sacklers, Purdue's owners. They wanted to avoid being dragged into the couple of thousand lawsuits pending during the project's research. A final group comprised former government employees, mostly law enforcement, the FDA, and CDC officials, who did not want to publicly violate the trust of still-serving colleagues.

Whenever information obtained from any of those unattributed interviews is used in this book, it is identified as such. More important, in every instance, I corroborated its accuracy either by independent documentary sources or from others in a position to know.

As for the dozens who spoke to me for attribution, I could not have gotten the complete story without the assistance of some industry veterans who had personal oversight of how the pharmaceutical business had changed in recent decades. Instrumental in understanding why drug companies have largely abandoned antibiotic research and development and the dangers that creates for a possible pandemic were Barry Eisenstein, Mike Skoien, Richard Baltz, Prabha Fernandes, Karen Bush, Lynn Silver, Steven Projan, Joyce Sutcliffe, Richard Happel, and Richard White. I am not only deeply grateful that Marianne Skolek agreed to once again review the painful details of her daughter's unnecessary overdose death from OxyContin, but I am indebted to her for sharing her moving unpublished memoir. Finally, a special note of thanks to Michael Sonnenreich. Between his different roles in government service, then as a private attorney and sometimes business partner with Arthur Sackler, and finally as a successful pharmaceutical entrepreneur, he was incredibly patient in many hours of interviews with me and my wife, Trisha. His insights about key figures in the industry proved invaluable. Thanks to Peter Sonnenreich for opening the door to his father.

Besides interviews, the history presented in this book is the result of research in voluminous government and private archives on two continents. Sometimes I benefited from the good journalism of others, including papers that became public only after lawsuits were filed by *The New York Times* and Kaiser Health News. Once, I was aided in paperwork by an anonymous source. In February 2019, a sealed brown manila envelope without a return address arrived at my Miami-area office. It was postmarked from New York. It contained copies of FDA and DEA documents that helped fill in pieces of the puzzle about why the government had not taken earlier and more forceful action to stop the prescription opioid epidemic from becoming the nation's most deadly ever.

I requested under the Freedom of Information and Privacy Acts many previously classified files that included important background about how the Sackler family came to such prominence. Tens of thousands of pages of litigation files, court records, and FDA administrative hearings, including decades of contemporaneous testimony from key figures, provided the equivalent of a hidden oral history of the pharmaceutical industry.

In obtaining documentation, I am indebted to the diligence and patience of archivists who assisted with my repeated inquiries. As with previous books, the excellent staff at the National Archives in Washington, D.C., and College Park, Maryland, were indispensable. Particular thanks to Richard Peuser, chief of Textual Reference Operations; Adam Berenbak, archivist, Center for Legislative Archives; Dr. Amanda Weimer and John Perosio, archivists, Special Access and FOIA; and Jessie Hartman, information specialist. Questions about which documents might be relevant to a specific FOIA request never devolved into a dispute thanks to Martha Wagner Murphy, public liaison in the Accessioned Executive Branch Records in Washington, D.C.

I was aided in the production of Freedom of Information and Privacy requests by Leanna Ramsey, Public Information Officer, Record/Information Dissemination Section, FBI-Records Management Division, Winchester, Virginia. The FBI FOIA Negotiation Team at the Information Management Division worked efficiently to narrow the scope of my requests in order to process them expeditiously.

The FDA History Office is a great repository of information, not only about the agency itself but also its predecessor, the Bureau of Chemistry. Its research files, originally curated by FDA historian Suzanne Junod, provided the background on regulatory history and pharmaceutical legislative proposals as well as FDA policy changes. Its records include interviews with former commissioners, early inspectors, research scientists, medical publishers, pharmaceutical executives, and officials from some important drug lobbying groups. Transcripts of the oral histories maintained at the National Library of Medicine at the Bethesda, Maryland, campus of the National Institutes of Health were instrumental in re-creating the contemporaneous settings for milestone pharmaceutical events.

I am grateful to Jack McPeters, New York State Archives. And I owe special thanks to several university and private collections: Sarah Coggrave, Archives Services Officer at King's College London Archives, and Chris Olver, Archives Project Officer at King's College London Archives, for the assistance with the papers of Cicely Saunders; the Center for the History of Medicine at Harvard's Countway Library; Morgan Swann at the Rauner Special Collections Library at Dartmouth; Dylan Claussen for his assistance with the Marietta Lutze Sackler manuscript; Genevieve Coyle and Jessica Dooling for the Félix Martí-Ibáñez papers at Yale University's Manuscripts and Archives; Deborah Shapiro at the Smithsonian Institution Archives; Jenna Mocklis at Crain Communications; the reference staff at the American Philosophical Society Library; and Rachel Gould at Oxford University Press.

Although I prefer reviewing files at a library or archive, quality online databases are increasingly necessary for a project of this scope. Special thanks to Jennifer Bourque at SAGE Knowledge; and Tara Bauer at Casetext who helped navigate their online database of legal cases, attorneys' briefs and filings, and statutory and regulatory law. Equally helpful was Lauren Mattiuzzo at William S. Hein, whose digital database included many of the government hearings and legislative histories I required.

Professors Alan Wald and Ben Harris were very helpful in putting into perspective the Sacklers' communist sympathies against the backdrop of the 1950s Red Scare. The late Roy Andrew Miller, professor of Asian studies and literature at the University of Washington, saved me many hours in assessing the value of Arthur Sackler's Asian collection that was bequeathed to the Smithsonian.

Paul Rosenblatt was patient with my many attempts to locate his father's oral history. I could not have gotten the complete story without the assistance of Drs. Leslie Baumann and Steve Mandy, Richard and Judy Wurtman, Dr. Vinay Prasad, Harry Martin, Diane Dimond, Nick Spill, Victoria Narkin, Mark Shapiro, Mark Zaid, Lynne Pauls Baron, Jessica Packer, Chip Fisher, Adam Tanner, and Sean Cassidy. Rick Lippin was tireless in finding relevant stories in often obscure medical journals and blogs.

Three friends, Christopher Petersen, Frank DelVecchio, and Ann Froelich, generously agreed to read early manuscript drafts and their insights made it a better book. Drs. David and Jane Cohen were kind enough to take the time from running their private practices to check that the manuscript was free of medical errors.

I am fortunate to be represented by David Kuhn and Nate Muscato at Aevitas Creative Management. Their sage advice and enthusiasm for the project was always appreciated.

I am lucky to have Simon & Schuster, and its new imprint Avid Reader Press, as my publisher. Simon & Schuster's president, Jonathan Karp, and Ben Loehnen, Avid Reader's editor-in-chief, took a risk on *Pharma*. They realize that the subjects of my book proposals are mostly mysteries to me. What I get from them is the faith that given enough time I will dig up a story worthy of a book. For that I am forever grateful.

I owe thanks at my publisher to Carolyn Kelly, editorial assistant. Fred Chase had the unenviable task of copyediting this book, as he did my last, *God's Bankers*. Fred has a great eye for consistency and detail.

Jonathan Evans, Associate Director of Copyediting, not only oversaw the editorial production, but served at times as everything from a vital fact checker to a much needed enforcer of consistency and style. His extraordinary efforts and incredibly long hours meant the project met its tight deadline.

Ben Loehnen is a sublime editor. His line editing cleaned and tightened the text without ever stepping on my voice. If he ever expresses doubts or second thoughts when I send a manuscript more than double the size he expected, he is kind enough not to take me to task for it. Most important, his edit and advice helped me stay focused on the story, keeping me from too many detours. This would not be remotely as good a book without him.

Anyone familiar with my work knows that *Pharma* would not be possible without my wife, the author Trisha Posner. She had completed her own book in 2017, one with a different pharmaceutical theme. *The Pharmacist of Auschwitz* was the first nonfiction account of the Bayer druggist who ran the dispensary at the largest Nazi death camp. Trisha might have liked a break before going directly from the dark tale of Nazi medicine to the often disturbing history of the American pharmaceutical industry. If that was the case, she never mentioned it. Instead, she once again threw herself enthusiastically into this project, sifting thousands of pages of documents and sharing with me every interview. It was her idea to convert the only blank wall in our home office into a whiteboard. With its dozens of arrows and circles and groupings it looked at times more like the schematic for a complex criminal investigation than the outline for a book about the drug industry.

This was, at times, all-consuming. For days on end, we did not leave our apartment but stayed in our "book cave" to meet a seemingly endless series of self-imposed deadlines. When a friend asked once how long we expected to spend on the story of American pharma, Trisha had a ready answer. "It's a six-year project, but we are doing it in three."

Putting Trisha's name on the front cover as a coauthor would do her justice. Until she agrees to that one day, this public acknowledgment shall have to suffice in showing that *Pharma* is as much hers as mine.

SELECTED BIBLIOGRAPHY

Books

Achilladelis, Basil, Ralph Landau, and Alexander Scriabine. *Pharmaceutical Innovation: Revolutionizing Human Health*. Philadelphia: Chemical Heritage Press, 1999.

Adomakoh, C. C. *Advances in the Drug Therapy of Mental Illness*. Geneva, Switzerland: World Health Organization, 1976.

Alwood, Edward. *Dark Days in the Newsroom: McCarthyism Aimed at the Press*. Philadelphia, PA: Temple University Press, 2007.

The Anatomy of Sleep. Nutley, NJ: Roche Laboratories, 1966.

Anderson, Oscar E., Jr. *The Health of a Nation: Harvey W. Wiley and the Fight for Pure Food*. Chicago: University of Chicago Press,1958.

Angell, Marcia. *The Truth about the Drug Companies: How They Deceive Us and What to Do About It*. Melbourne, Australia: Scribe, 2006.

Anxiety and Allergy. Nutley, NJ: Roche, 1966.

Bate, Roger. *Phake: The Deadly World of Falsified and Substandard Medicines*. Washington, DC: AEI Press, 2014.

Bernstein, Walter. *Inside Out: A Memory of a Black List*. New York: Alfred A. Knopf, 1996.

Blaser, Martin J. *Missing Microbes: How the Overuse of Antibiotics Is Fueling Our Modern Plagues*. New York: Henry Holt and Company, 2014.

Blum, Deborah. *The Poison Squad: One Chemist's Single-Minded Crusade for Food Safety at the Turn of the Twentieth Century*. New York: Penguin Press, 2018.

Bobst, Elmer Holmes. *Bobst: The Autobiography of a Pharmaceutical Pioneer*. New York: D. McKay, 1974.

Bowden, Mary Ellen, Amy Beth Crow, and Tracy Sullivan. *Pharmaceutical Achievers*. Philadelphia, PA: Chemical Heritage Press, 2003.

Braithwaite, John. *Corporate Crime in the Pharmaceutical Industry*. New York: Routledge, 2013.

Breggin, Peter Roger. *Medication Madness: A Psychiatrist Exposed the Dangerous Moon-Altering Medications*. New York: St. Martin's Press, 2008.

Brody, Howard. *Hooked: Ethics, the Medical Profession, and the Pharmaceutical Industry*. Lanham, MD: Rowman & Littlefield, 2008.

Carpenter, Daniel P. *Reputation and Power: Organizational Image and Pharmaceutical Regulation at the FDA*. Princeton, NJ: Princeton University Press, 2010.

Castagnoli, William. *Medicine Avenue: The Story of Medical Advertising in America*. Huntington, NY: Medical Advertising Hall of Fame, 1999.

Clark, Ronald. *The Life of Ernst Chain: Penicillin and Beyond*. Originally published in London: Weidenfeld & Nicolson Limited, 1985; Kindle edition by Bloomsbury Press, 2011.

Clark, Roscoe Collins. *Three Score Years and Ten, A Narrative of the First Seventy Years of Eli Lilly and Company, 1876–1946*. New York: Lakeside Press, R. R. Donnelly & Sons, 1946.

Collins, James C., and Jerry I. Porras. *Built to Last: Successful Habits of Visionary Companies*. New York: HarperCollins, 2009.

Coney, Sandra. *The Menopause Industry: A Guide to Medicine's "Discovery" of the Mid-Life Woman*. London: The Women's Press, 1995.

Coppin, Clayton A., and Jack High. *The Politics of Purity: Harvey Washington Wiley and the Origins of Federal Food Policy*. Ann Arbor, MI: The University of Michigan Press, 1999.

Crawford, Dorothy H. *Virus Hunt: The Search for the Origin of HIV/AIDS*. Oxford, UK: Oxford University Press, 2015.

Crunden, Robert M. *Ministers of Reform: The Progressives' Achievement in American Civilization 1889–1920*. New York: Basic Books, 1982.

Daemmrich, Arthur A. *Pharmacopolitics: Drug Regulation in the United States and Germany*. Chapel Hill, NC: The University of North Carolina Press, 2004.

Dowbiggin, Ian Robert. *The Quest for Mental Health: A Tale of Science, Medicine, Scandal, Sorrow, and Mass Society*. New York: Cambridge University Press, 2011.

Dupree, Hunter A. *Science in the Federal Government: A History of Policies and Activities to 1940*. Cambridge, MA: Belknap Press of Harvard University Press, 1957.

Dutfield, Graham. *Intellectual Property Rights and the Life Sciences Industry*, 2nd ed. Singapore: World Scientific Publishing, 2009.

Eban, Katherine. *Bottle of Lies: The Inside Story of the Generic Drug Boom*. New York: Ecco, 2019.

England, Paul. *Intellectual Property in the Life Sciences: A Global Guide to Rights and Their Applications*. London: Globe Law and Business, 2015.

Espejo, Roman. *The Pharmaceutical Industry: Opposing Viewpoints*. Detroit: Greenhaven Press, 2012.

Florey, Howard, et al. *Antibiotics: A Survey of Penicillin, Streptomycin, and Other Antimicrobial Substances from Fungi, Actinomycetes, Bacteria, and Plants*, vols. 1 and 2. London: Oxford University Press, 1949.

Fumento, Michael. *The Myth of Heterosexual AIDS*. New York: New Republic/Basic Books, 1993.

Galambos, Louis, Roy P. Vagelos, Michael S. Brown, and Joseph L. Goldstein. *Values and Visions: A Merck Century*. Whitehouse Station, NJ: Merck & Co., 1991.

Gambardella, Alfonso. *Science and Innovation: The US Pharmaceutical Industry during the 1980s*. Cambridge, UK: Cambridge University Press, 1995.

Gamble, Vanessa Northington. *Making a Place for Ourselves: The Black Hospital Movement, 1920–1945*. New York: Oxford University Press, 1995.

Garrett, Laurie. *The Coming Plague: Newly Emerging Diseases in a World Out of Balance*. London: Penguin Books, 1996.

Goldacre, Ben. *Bad Pharma: How Drug Companies Mislead Doctors and Harm Patients*. New York: Farrar, Straus & Giroux, 2013.

Gøtzsche, Peter C., Richard Smith, and Drummond Rennie. *Deadly Medicines and Organised Crime: How Big Pharma Has Corrupted Healthcare.* London: Radcliffe Publishing, 2013.

Greene, Jeremy A. *Generic: The Unbranding of Modern Medicine.* Baltimore, MD: Johns Hopkins University Press, 2014.

Greenwood, David. *Antimicrobial Drugs: Chronicle of a Twentieth Century Medical Triumph.* Oxford, UK: Oxford University Press, 2008.

Gross, Michael. *Rogues' Gallery: The Secret Story of the Lust, Lies, Greed, and Betrayal That Made the Metropolitan Museum of Art.* New York: Random House, 2009.

Hare, Ronald. *The Birth of Penicillin.* Sydney, Australia: Allen & Unwin, 1970.

Harris, Richard. *The Real Voice.* New York: Macmillan, 1964.

Harris, Richard F. *Rigor Mortis: How Sloppy Science Creates Worthless Cures, Crushes Hope, and Wastes Billions.* New York: Basic Books, 2018.

Harrison, Joanne K., and Grant Harrison. *The Life and Times of Irvine Garland Penn.* Philadelphia, PA: Xlibris, 2000.

Hawthorne, Fran. *Inside the FDA: The Business and Policies Behind the Drugs We Take and Food We Eat.* New York: John Wiley & Sons, 2015.

———. *The Merck Druggernaut: The Inside Story of a Pharmaceutical Giant.* Hoboken, NJ: John Wiley & Sons, 2003.

Hayes, J. N. *Epidemics and Pandemics: Their Impacts on Human History.* Santa Barbara, CA: ABC-CLIO, 2005.

Healy, David. *Let Them Eat Prozac: The Unhealthy Relationship between the Pharmaceutical Industry and Depression.* New York: New York University Press, 2006.

Herzberg, David L. *Happy Pills in America: From Miltown to Prozac.* Baltimore, MD: Johns Hopkins University Press, 2008.

Higby, Gregory J., and Elaine C. Stroud. *The Inside Story of Medicines: A Symposium.* Madison, WI: American Institute of the History of Pharmacy, 1997.

Hooper, Edward. *The River: A Journey to the Source of HIV and AIDS.* Boston, MA: Back Bay Books, 2000.

Hoving, Thomas. *Making the Mummies Dance: Inside the Metropolitan Museum of Art.* New York: Simon & Schuster, 1994.

Kang, Lydia, and Nate Pedersen. *Quackery: A Brief History of the Worst Ways to Cure Everything.* New York: Workman Publishing, 2017.

Kefauver, Estes, and Irene Till. *In a Few Hands: Monopoly Power in America.* New York: Pantheon, 1965.

Kinsella, James. *Covering the Plague AIDS and the American Media.* New Brunswick, NJ: Rutgers University Press, 1990.

Kleinman, Daniel Lee. *Politics on the Endless Frontier: Postwar Research Policy in the United States.* Durham, NC: Duke University Press, 1995.

Kleinman, Daniel Lee, Abby J. Kinchy, and Jo Handelsman. *Controversies in Science and Technology.* Madison, WI: University of Wisconsin Press, 2005.

Kolata, Gina. *Flu: The Story of the Great Influenza Pandemic of 1918 and the Search for the Virus That Caused It.* New York: Farrar, Straus & Giroux, 1999.

Law, Jacky. *Big Pharma: Exposing the Global Healthcare Agenda.* New York: Avalon Publishing Group, 2006.

Lax, Eric. *The Mold in Dr. Florey's Coat: The Story of the Penicillin Miracle.* New York: Henry Holt, 2005.

Le Fanu, James. *The Rise and Fall of Modern Medicine.* New York: Carroll & Graf Publishers, 1999.

Lesch, John E. *The First Miracle Drugs: How the Sulfa Drugs Transformed Medicine*. Oxford, UK: Oxford University Press, 2007.

Li, Jie Jack. *Laughing Gas, Viagra, and Lipitor: The Human Stories Behind the Drugs We Use*. New York: Oxford University Press, 2006.

Liebenau, J. *Medical Science and Medical Industry: The Formation of the American Pharmaceutical Industry*. London: Palgrave Macmillan, 1987.

Long, Edward V. *The Intruders: The Invasion of Privacy by Government and Industry*. New York: Frederick A. Praeger, 1967.

Lutze, Marietta. *Who Can Know the Other?: A Traveler in Search of Home*. No. 29 of 225 copies. Lunenburg, Vermont: Marietta Lutze Sackler, 1997; reprint 2002. Author viewed edition in the Special Collections of Dartmouth Library, Rauner Presses Collection, control number: ocm80453625.

Macy, Beth. *Dopesick: Dealers, Doctors, and the Drug Company That Addicted America*. New York: Back Bay Books, 2019.

Maeder, Thomas. *Adverse Reactions*. New York: William Morrow and Company, 1994.

Marks, Lara. *Sexual Chemistry: A History of the Contraceptive Pill*. New Haven, CT: Yale University Press, 2010.

Marshall, Walter Gore. *Through America; or, Nine Months in the United States*. London: S. Low, Marston, Searle & Rivington, 1881.

Martí-Ibáñez, Félix. *The Epic of Medicine*. New York: Bramhall House, 1962.

———. *Journey around Myself: Impressions and Tales of Travels around the World: Japan, Hong Kong, Macao, Bangkok, Angkor, Lebanon*. New York: Potter, 1966.

May, Elaine Tyler. *America and the Pill: A History of Promise, Peril, and Liberation*. New York: Basic Books, 2010.

McGreal, Chris. *American Overdose: The Opioid Tragedy in Three Acts*. New York: Public Affairs, 2018.

Meier, Barry. *Pain Killer: A Wonder Drug's Trail of Addiction and Death*. New York: Rodale Books, 2003; updated edition, *Pain Killer: An Empire of Deceit and the Origin of America's Opioid Crisis*. New York: Random House, 2018.

Meyer, Karl E., and Shareen Blair Brysac. *The China Collectors: America's Century-Long Hunt for Asian Art Treasures*. New York: St. Martin's Press, 2015.

Meyers, Morton A. *Happy Accidents: Serendipity in Major Medical Breakthroughs in the Twentieth Century*. New York: Skyhorse Publishing, Inc., 2011.

Mez-Mangold, Lydia. *A History of Drugs*. Basel, Switzerland: Hoffmann-La Roche, 1989.

Mines, Samuel. *Pfizer: An Informal History*. New York: Pfizer, 1978.

Moynihan, Ray, and Alan Cassels. *Selling Sickness: How the World's Biggest Pharmaceutical Companies Are Turning Us All into Patients*. New York: Nation Books, 2006.

Nesi, Thomas J. *Poison Pills: The Untold Story of the Vioxx Drug Scandal*. New York: St. Martin's Press, 2008.

Offit, Paul A. *The Cutter Incident: How America's First Polio Vaccine Led to the Growing Vaccine Crisis*. Hartford, CT: Yale University Press, 2007.

———. *Pandora's Lab: Seven Stories of Science Gone Wrong*. Washington, DC: National Geographic Society, 2017.

———. *Vaccinated: One Man's Quest to Defeat the World's Deadliest Diseases*. Washington, DC: Smithsonian Books, 2008.

Oppenheimer, Jerry. *Crazy Rich: Power, Scandal, and Tragedy Inside the Johnson & Johnson Dynasty*. New York: St. Martin's, 2014.

Oshinsky, David M. *Polio: An American Story*. Oxford, UK: Oxford University Press, 2006.

Pekkanen, John. *The American Connection; Profiteering and Politicking in the "Ethical" Drug Industry*. Chicago: Follett Pub. Co., 1973.

Pepin, Jacques. *The Origin of AIDS*. Cambridge, UK: Cambridge University Press, 2012.

Petersen, Melody. *Our Daily Meds: How the Pharmaceutical Companies Transformed Themselves into Slick Marketing Machines and Hooked the Nation on Prescription Drugs*. New York: Picador, 2009.

Podolsky, M. Lawrence. *Cures Out of Chaos: How Unexpected Discoveries Led to Breakthroughs in Medicine and Health*. Amsterdam: Harwood Academic Publishers, 1997.

Podolsky, Scott H. *The Antibiotic Era: Reform, Resistance, and the Pursuit of a Rational Therapeutics*. Baltimore, MD: Johns Hopkins University Press, 2015.

Portenoy, Russell K., and Ronald M. Kanner. *Pain Management: Theory and Practice*. Philadelphia, PA: F. A. Davis Comp., 1996.

Pringle, Peter. *Experiment Eleven: Dark Secrets behind the Discovery of a Wonder Drug*. New York: Bloomsbury, 2013.

Quammen, David. *The Chimp and the River: How AIDS Emerged from an African Forest*. New York: W. W. Norton & Company, 2015.

Quick, Jonathan D., and Bronwyn Fryer. *The End of Epidemics: The Looming Threat to Humanity and How to Stop It*. New York: St. Martin's Press, 2018.

Quinones, Sam. *Dreamland: The True Tale of America's Opiate Epidemic*. London: Bloomsbury Press, 2015.

Rasmussen, Nicolas. *On Speed: The Many Lives of Amphetamine*. New York: New York University Press, 2009.

Redwood, Heinz. *Pharmapolitics 2000: Key Issues for the Industry*. Richmond, Surrey, UK: Oldwicks Press, 1997.

Rodengen, Jeffrey L. *The Legend of Pfizer*. Fort Lauderdale, FL: Write Stuff Syndicate, 1999.

Rosen, William. *Miracle Cure: The Creation of Antibiotics and the Birth of Modern Medicine*. New York: Viking, 2017.

Rosenbaum, Lee. *The Complete Guide to Collecting Art*. New York: Alfred A. Knopf, 1982.

Rost, Peter. *The Whistleblower: Confessions of a Healthcare Hitman*. Brooklyn, NY: Soft Skull Press, 2006.

Rothstein, William G. *American Physicians in the Nineteenth Century: From Sects to Science*. Baltimore, MD: Johns Hopkins University Press, 1992.

Sackler, Arthur M., Mortimer D. Sackler, Raymond R. Sackler, Felix Marti-Ibanez, and Ugo Cerletti, eds., *The Great Physiodynamic Therapies in Psychiatry: An Historical Reappraisal*. New York: Hoeber-Harper Medical, 1956.

Salzman, Carl. *Benzodiazepine Dependence, Toxicity, and Abuse: A Task Force Report*. Washington, DC: American Psychiatric Association, 1990.

Schur, Edwin M. *Labeling Women Deviant: Gender, Stigma, and Social Control*. New York: McGraw-Hill, 1984.

Schwarcz, Vera. *Place and Memory in the Singing Crane Garden*. Philadelphia, PA: University of Pennsylvania Press, 2014.

Schwartzman, David. *Innovation in the Pharmaceutical Industry*. Baltimore, MD: Johns Hopkins University Press, 1976.

Schwarz, Alan. *ADHD Nation: Children, Doctors, Big Pharma, and the Making of an American Epidemic*. New York: Little, Brown and Company, 2017.

Seaman, Barbara. *The Doctor's Case against the Pill*. Alameda, CA: Hunter House, 2000.

———. *The Greatest Experiment Ever Performed on Women: Exploding the Estrogen Myth*. New York: Seven Stories, 2009.

Shilts, Randy. *And the Band Played On: Politics, People, and the AIDS Epidemic*, 20th Anniversary Edition. New York: St. Martin's Griffin, 2007, Kindle Edition, 2007.

Shook, Robert L. *Miracle Medicines: Seven Lifesaving Drugs and the People Who Created Them*. New York: Portfolio, 2014.

Shorter, Edward. *Before Prozac: The Troubled History of Mood Disorders in Psychiatry*. Oxford, UK: Oxford University Press, 2009.

Shryock, Richard. *American Medical Research Past and Present*. New York: Commonwealth Fund, 1947.

———. *The Development of Modern Medicine: An Interpretation of the Social and Scientific Factors Involved*. New York: Alfred A. Knopf, 1936.

Silverman, Milton, and Philip R. Lee. *Pills, Profits and Politics*. Berkeley, CA: University of California Press, 1974.

Smith, Mickey C. *Pharmaceutical Marketing: Strategy and Cases*. New York: Informa Healthcare, 2009.

———. *Principles of Pharmaceutical Marketing*. Philadelphia, PA: Lea & Febiger, 1983.

———. *A Social History of the Minor Tranquilizers: The Quest for Small Comfort in the Age of Anxiety*. London: Pharmaceutical Press, 1991.

Spink, Wesley W. *Infectious Diseases: Prevention and Treatment in the Nineteenth and Twentieth Centuries*. Minneapolis, MN: University of Minnesota Press, 1978.

Starr, Douglas P. *Blood: An Epic History of Medicine and Commerce*. New York: Harper Perennial, 2002.

Starr, Paul. *The Social Transformation of American Medicine: The Rise of a Sovereign Profession and the Making of a Vast Industry*. New York: Basic Books, 2017.

Stelzer, Irwin M. *Selected Antitrust Cases: Landmark Decisions*. Homewood, IL: Richard Irwin, 1981.

Stoller, K. Paul. *Incurable Me: Why the Best Medical Research Does Not Make It into Clinical Practice*. New York: Skyhorse Publishing, 2016.

Sullivan, Mark. *Our Times: The United States 1900–1925*. Vol. 2 of *America Finding Herself*. New York: Charles Scribner's Sons, 1927.

Tanner, Adam. *Our Bodies, Our Data: How Companies Make Billions Selling Our Medical Records*. Boston: Beacon Press, 2017.

Tanner, Ogden. *25 Years of Innovation: The Story of Pfizer Central Research*. Lyme, CT: Greenwich Publishing Group, 1996.

Temin, Peter. *Taking Your Medicine: Drug Regulation in the United States*. Cambridge, MA: Harvard University Press, 1980.

Tobbell, Dominique A. *Pills, Power, and Policy: The Struggle for Drug Reform in Cold War America and Its Consequences*. Berkeley, CA: University of California Press, 2012.

Tone, Andrea. *The Age of Anxiety: A History of America's Turbulent Affair with Tranquilizers*. New York: Basic Books, 2012.

Tone, Andrea, and Elizabeth Siegel Watkins. *Medicating Modern America: Prescription Drugs in History*. New York: New York University Press, 2007.

Vagelos, Roy, and Louis Galambos. *Medicine, Science, and Merck*. New Cambridge, UK: Cambridge University Press, 2004.

Vagelos, Roy, Louis Galambos, and Pindaros Roy. *The Moral Corporation: Merck Experiences*. Cambridge, UK: Cambridge University Press, 2006.

Verg, Erik, Gottfried Plumpe, and Heinz Schultheis. *Milestones: The Bayer Story, 1863–1988*. Leverkusen, Germany: Bayer AG, 1988.

Villafana, Frank. *Coercion as Cure: A Critical History of Psychiatry*. Abingdon-on-Thames, UK: Routledge, 2017.

Wald, Alan M. *American Night: The Literary Left in the Era of the Cold War*. Chapel Hill, NC: University of North Carolina Press, 2014.

Weinberg, Eric, and Donna Shaw. *Blood on Their Hands: How Greedy Companies, Inept Bureaucracy, and Bad Science Killed Thousands of Hemophiliacs*. New Brunswick, NJ: Rutgers University Press, 2017.

Welch, Henry, and Félix Martí-Ibáñez. *The Antibiotic Saga*. New York: Medical Encyclopedia, 1960.

Whitaker, Robert. *Anatomy of an Epidemic: Magic Bullets, Psychiatric Drugs, and the Astonishing Rise of Mental Illness in America*. New York: Crown, 2010.

Wiley, Harvey W. *An Autobiography*. Indianapolis, IN: The Bobbs-Merrill Company, 1930.

———. *The History of a Crime against the Food Law*. Washington, DC: Harvey W. Wiley, 1929.

Wolpe, Joseph. *Orientation to Behavior Therapy*. Nutley, NJ: Hoffmann-La Roche, 1971.

Young, James Harvey. *The Medical Messiahs: A Social History of Health Quackery in Twentieth-Century America*. Princeton, NJ: Princeton University Press, 1967.

———. *Pure Food: Securing the Federal Food and Drugs Act of 1906*. Princeton, NJ: Princeton University Press, 1989.

———. *The Toadstool Millionaires: A Social History of Patent Medicines in America before Federal Regulation*. Princeton, NJ: Princeton University Press, 1961.

Articles, Reports, and Other Publications

Achenbach, Joel. "Once 'So Mayberry,' a Town Struggles with Opioid Epidemic." *The Washington Post*, December 30, 2016.

Adams, Rebecca, and Kate Shuler. "Lawmakers Weigh Incentives for High-Risk Vaccine Business." *Congressional Quarterly Weekly Report* 61, no. 41 (October 30, 2004).

Adams, Samuel Hopkins. "The Great American Fraud." "The Nostrum Evil." October 7, 1905; "Peruna and the Bracers." October 28, 1905; "Liquozone." November 18, 1905; "The Subtle Poisons." December 2, 1905; "A Fraud's Gallery." January 13, 1906; "The Fundamental Fakes." February 17, 1906. *Collier's*.

Alleyne, Richard. "Widespread Antibiotic Use in 1960s Sparked MRSA." *The Telegraph*, January 22, 2010.

Altman, Lawrence K. "In Philadelphia 30 Years Ago, an Eruption of Illness and Fear." *The New York Times*, August 1, 2006.

Amaral-Zettler, L., L. F. Artigas, J. Baross, L. Bharathi, A. Boetius, D. Chandramohan, G. Herndl, K. Kogure, P. Neal, C. Pedros-Alio, A. Ramette, S. Schouten, L. Stal, A. Thessen, J. de Leeuw, and M. Sogin. "A Global Census of Marine Microbes." In *Life in the World's Oceans: Diversity, Distribution and Abundance*, edited by Alasdair D. McIntyre. Oxford, UK: Blackwell Publishing Ltd, 2010.

Angst, J. "Panic Disorder: History and Epidemiology." *Eur Psychiatry* 13, no. S2 (1998): S51–55.

"Antibiotics at Risk." Editorial, *The British Medical Journal* 2, no. 5971 (1975): 582.

Armstrong, Terry. "Distribution in Jig Time: The Story of Terramycin." *Sales Management* 66 (1951).

"ASPMN Backs Pain Champion: Russell Portenoy." *Pain Management Nursing* 14, no. 1 (January 22, 2013).

Austin, T. "Mixed Drug Overdosage with Phenelzine, Amytal and Chlordiazepoxide. A Case Report." *Anaesthesia* 21, no. 2 (1966): 249–52.

Bachhuber, M. A., S. Hennessy, C. O. Cunningham, and J. L. Starrels. "Increasing Benzodiazepine Prescriptions and Overdose Mortality in the United States, 1996–2013." *American Journal of Public Health* 106, no. 4 (2016): 686–88.

Balch, Robert J., and Andrea Trescot. "Extended-Release Morphine Sulfate in Treatment of Severe Acute and Chronic Pain." *Journal of Pain Research* 3 (September 21, 2010): 191–200.

Barber, Mary. "Staphylococcal Infection Due to Penicillin-Resistant Strains." *The British Medical Journal* 2 (1947).

Barber, Mary, and Mary Rozwadowska-Dowzenko. "Infection by Penicillin-Resistant Staphylococci." *The Lancet* 255 (1948).

Bassett, M. T., and M. Mhloyi. "Women and AIDS in Zimbabwe: The Making of an Epidemic." *International Journal of Health Services* 1, no. 21 (1991): 143–56.

Bax, Richard P. "Antibiotic Resistance: A View from the Pharmaceutical Industry." *Clinical Infectious Diseases* 24 (1997).

Bedard, Nicholas A., Andrew J. Pugely, et al. "Opioid Use after Total Knee Arthroplasty: Trends and Risk Factors for Prolonged Use." *The Journal of Arthroplasty* 32, no. 8 (August 2017).

Belongia, Edward A., and Allison L. Naleway. "Smallpox Vaccine: The Good, the Bad, and the Ugly." *Clinical Medicine and Research* 1, no. 2 (2003).

Bennet, Amanda, and Anita Sharpe. "Federal AIDS Campaign Neglects High-Risk Groups." *The Wall Street Journal*, May 1, 1996.

Berndt, Ernst R., and Murray Aitken. "Brand Loyalty, Generic Entry and Price Competition in Pharmaceuticals in the Quarter Century after the 1984 Waxman-Hatch Legislation." *International Journal of the Economics of Business* 18, no. 2 (July 2011).

Bero, L., F. Oostvogel, P. Bacchetti, and K. Lee. "Factors Associated with Findings of Published Trials of Drug–Drug Comparisons: Why Some Statins Appear More Efficacious than Others." *PLOS Medicine* 6, no. 4 (June 5, 2007): e184.

Boehma, Garth, et al. "Development of the Generic Drug Industry in the US after the Hatch-Waxman Act of 1984." *Acta Pharmaceutica Sinica B* 3, no. 5 (September 2013).

Boffey, Philip M. "Worldwide Use of Valium Draws New Scrutiny." *The New York Times*, October 13, 1981.

Bogdan, Herman A. "Félix Martí-Ibáñez—Iberian Daedalus: The Man behind the Essays." *Journal of the Royal Society of Medicine* 86 (October 1993): 593–96.

Borger, Julian. "Hillbilly Heroin: The Painkiller Abuse Wrecking Lives in West Virginia." *The Guardian* (UK), June 24, 2001.

Brady, Joseph V. "Ulcers in 'Executive' Monkeys." *Scientific American*, October 1958.

Brody, Jane E. "Birth Control Pills: A Balance Sheet on Their National Impact." *The New York Times*, March 23, 1969.

Bryan, Jenny. "From Snake Venom to ACE Inhibitor—the Discovery and Rise of Captopril." *The Pharmaceutical Journal* (April 17, 2009).

Bud, Robert. "Antibiotics, Big Business, and Consumers: The Context of Government Investigations into the Postwar American Drug Industry." *Technology and Culture* 46, no. 2 (2005): 329–49.

———. "Resisting Antibiotics: The Social Challenges of Drug Reform." *Boston Review*, October 27, 2015.

———. "Upheaval in the Moral Economy of Science? Patenting, Teamwork and the World War II Experience of Penicillin." *History and Technology* 24, no. 2 (2008).

Burrows, Adam. "Palette of Our Palates: A Brief History of Food and Its Regulation." *Comprehensive Reviews in Food Science and Food Safety* 8 (2009).

Bush, Karen. "The Coming of Age of Antibiotics: Discovery and Therapeutic Value." *Antimicrobial Therapeutics Reviews* (December 23, 2010).

Cacciapaglia, Frank, and Howard B. Rockman. "The Proposed Drug Industry Antitrust Act: Patents, Pricing, and the Public." *George Washington Law Review* 30, no. 5 (June 1962).

Calcaterra, Nicholas E., and James C. Barrow. "Classics in Chemical Neuroscience: Diazepam (Valium)." *ACS Chemical Neuroscience* 5, no. 4 (2014).

Cant, Gilbert B. "Valiumania." *The New York Times Magazine*, February 1, 1976.

Castagnoli, William G. "There Were Giants in Those Days." *Medical Marketing & Media*, March 1, 1997.

———. "Remembrance of Kings Past." *Medical Marketing & Media* 31, no. 7 (July 1, 1996): 44.

Castro, K. G., A. R. Lifson, C. R. White, et al. "Investigations of AIDS Patients with No Previously Identified Risk Factors." *JAMA* 259, no. 9 (1988).

Catan, Thomas, and Evan Perez. "A Pain-Drug Champion Has Second Thoughts." *The Wall Street Journal*, December 17, 2012.

Cavers, David F. "The Food, Drug, and Cosmetic Act of 1938: Its Legislative History and Its Substantive Provisions." *Law and Contemporary Problems* 6 (Winter 1939), 2–42.

Chelminski, P. R., et al. "A Primary Care, Multi-Disciplinary Disease Management Program for Opioid-Treated Patients with Chronic Non-Cancer Pain and a High Burden of Psychiatric Comorbidity." *BMC Health Services Research* 5, no. 1 (2005): 3.

Cicero, T., J. Inciardi, and A. Munoz. "Trends in Abuse of OxyContin and Other Opioid Analgesics in the United States: 2002–2004." *The Journal of Pain* 6 (2005): 662–72.

Clines, Francis X., and Barry Meier. "Cancer Painkillers Pose New Abuse Threat." *The New York Times*, February 9, 2001.

Cobb, W. Montague. "Louis Tompkins Wright, 1891–1952." *JAMA* 45 (March 1953).

Cohen, David. "The Opioid Timebomb: The Sackler Family and How Their Painkiller Fortune Helps Bankroll London Arts." *The Evening Standard*, March 19, 2018.

———"The Sackler Files" (Multi-part investigation into tax avoidance). *The Evening Standard*, May 11, 2018. See the entire series at http://www.standard.co.uk/opioids.

Cohen, Jon. "Searching for the Epidemic's Origins." *Science* 288, no. 5474 (June 23, 2000).

Cohen, Kelly, R. L. Semple, P. Bialer, A. Lau, A. Bodenheimer, and I. Galynker. "Relationship between Drug Company Funding and Outcomes of Clinical Psychiatric Research." *Psychological Medicine* 36, no. 11 (2006): 1647–56.

Cohen, Pieter A., Alberto Goday, and John P. Swann. "The Return of Rainbow Diet Pills." *American Journal of Public Health* 102, no. 9 (2012).

Comfort, Nathaniel. "The Prisoner as Model Organism: Malaria Research at Stateville Penitentiary." *Studies in History and Philosophy of Biological and Biomedical Sciences* 40, no. 3 (2009).

Cooper, Arnie. "An Anxious History of Valium." *The Wall Street Journal*, November 15, 2013.

Cooperstock, Ruth. "Sex Differences in the Use of Mood-Modifying Drugs: An Explanatory Model." *Journal of Health and Social Behavior* 12, no. 3 (1971).

Costello, Peter M. "The Tetracycline Conspiracy: Structure, Conduct and Performance in the Drug Industry." *Antitrust Law & Economic Review* 1 (1968): 13–44.

Cramp, Arthur J. "Nostrums and Quackery: Collected Articles on the Nostrum Evil and Quackery." Reprint by *JAMA*. Chicago: American Medical Association Press, January 1, 1912.

Crane, George E. "Advances in the Drug Therapy of Mental Illness." *American Journal of Psychiatry* 134, no. 6 (June 1977).

Davis, Michael Henry, Peter S. Arno, and Karen Bonuck. "Rare Diseases, Drug Development and AIDS: The Impact of the Orphan Drug Act." *Milbank Quarterly* 73, no. 231 (1995).

Dehner, G. "WHO Knows Best?: National and International Responses to Pandemic Threats and the 'Lessons' of 1976." *Journal of the History of Medicine and Allied Sciences* 65, no. 4 (2010).

Delaney, Martin. "Double Jeopardy for Gallo." *Science* 296, no. 5573 (May 31, 2002).

Deschamps, J. R. "The Role of Crystallography in Drug Design." *The AAPS Journal* 7, no. 4 (2005): E813–19.

De Sousa, João Dinis, et al. "Enhanced Heterosexual Transmission Hypothesis for the Origin of Pandemic HIV-1." *Viruses* 4, no. 10 (2012): 1950–83.

Di Justo, Patrick. "The Last Great Swine Flu Epidemic." *Salon*, April 28, 2009.

DiMasi, Joseph A., and Cherie Paquette. "The Economics of Follow-On Drug Research and Development: Trends in Entry Rates and the Timing of Development." *PharmacoEconomics* 2, no. S2 (2004).

Doern, G. V., M. J. Ferraro, A. B. Brueggemann, and K. L. Ruoff. "Emergence of High Rates of Antimicrobial Resistance Among Viridans Group Streptococci in the United States." *Antimicrobial Agents and Chemotherapy* 40 (1996): 891–94.

Donohue, Julie. "A History of Drug Advertising: The Evolving Roles of Consumers and Consumer Protection." *The Milbank Quarterly* 84, no. 4 (2006): 659–99.

Drews, Gustav. "Federal Drug Regulation Act." *Brooklyn Law Review* 29, no. 1 (December 1962): 91–97.

Drucker, E., P. G. Alcabes, and P. A. Marx. "The Injection Century: Massive Unsterile Injections and the Emergence of Human Pathogens." *The Lancet* 358, no. 9297 (December 8; 2001): 1989–92.

Duggar, Benjamin M. "Aureomycin: A Product of the Continuing Search for New Antibiotics." *Annals of the New York Academy of Sciences* 51 (1948).

Dunklin, A. "The Reality of Prescribing Opioids in Texas: An Interview with a Drug Agent." Interview by Anita L. Comley. *Baylor University Medical Center Proceedings* 13, no. 3 (2000).

Eccles, R. G. "Radam's Microbe Killer." *Druggists Circular and Chemical Gazette* 33 (1889).

Edlund, Mark J., Mark Sullivan, Diane Steffick, Katherine M. Harris, and Kenneth B. Wells. "Do Users of Regularly Prescribed Opioids Have Higher Rates of Substance Use Problems Than Nonusers?" *Pain Medicine* 8, no. 8 (November 1, 2007).

Eggertson, Laura. "Lancet Retracts 12-Year-Old Article Linking Autism to MMR Vaccines." *Canadian Medical Association Journal* 182, no. 4 (2010): E199–200.

Ehrenkranz, N., et al. "Pneumocystis Carinii Pneumonia among Persons with Hemophilia A." *Morbidity and Mortality Weekly Report* (1982).

Elliott, Carl. "The Drug Pushers." *The Atlantic*, April 2006.

Epstein, Richard Seth. "The Isolation and Purification Exception to the General Unpatentability of Products of Nature." *Columbia Science and Technology Review*, January 15, 2003.

Esbjörnsson, Joakim, et al. "HIV-1 Molecular Epidemiology in Guinea-Bissau, West Africa: Origin, Demography and Migrations." Edited by Sheila Bowyer. *PLOS One* 6, no. 2 (2011): e17025.

Facchinetti, N. J., and W. M. Dickson. "Access to Generic Drugs in the 1950s: The Politics of a Social Problem." *American Journal of Public Health* 72, no. 5 (1982).

Fair, Richard J., and Yitzhak Tor. "Antibiotics and Bacterial Resistance in the 21st Century." *Perspectives in Medicinal Chemistry* 6 (2014): 25–64.

"The Federal Trade Commission Act of 1938." *Columbia Law Review* 39, no. 2 (1939): 259–73.

Feldman, Robin, Evan Frondorf, Andrew Cordova, and Connie Wang. "Empirical Evidence of Drug Pricing Games—A Citizen's Pathway Gone Astray." *Stanford Technology Law Review* 20, no. 1 (2017).

Ferner, Robin. "A Short History of Pharmaceutical Marketing." *The BMJ* 345, no. 7884 (2012).

Fineberg, Harvey V. "Swine Flu of 1976: Lessons from the Past." *Bulletin of the World Health Organization* 87, no. 6 (June 2009).

Fishbain, David A., Brandly Cole, John Lewis, Hubert L. Rosomoff, and R. Steele Rosomoff. "What Percentage of Chronic Nonmalignant Pain Patients Exposed to Chronic Opioid Analgesic Therapy Develop Abuse/Addiction and/or Aberrant Drug-Related Behaviors? A Structured Evidence-Based Review." *Pain Medicine* 9, no. 4 (May 1, 2008).

Fitzpatrick, Michael. "The Cutter Incident: How America's First Polio Vaccine Led to a Growing Vaccine Crisis." *Journal of the Royal Society of Medicine* 99, no. 3 (2006).

Fleming, M. F., J. Davis, and S. D. Passik. "Reported Lifetime Aberrant Drug-Taking Behaviors Are Predictive of Current Substance Use and Mental Health Problems in Primary Care Patients." *Pain Medicine* 9, no. 8 (2008).

Fletcher, Charles. "First Clinical Use of Penicillin." *The BMJ* 289 (1984).

Foley, K. M., J. J. Fins, and C. E. Inturrisi. "A True Believer's Flawed Analysis." *Archives of Internal Medicine* 171, no. 9 (2011).

Frohlich, L. W. "The Physician in the Pharmaceutical Industry in the United States." *Proceedings of the Royal Society of Medicine* from April 11, 1960, London. 53, sec. 1 (August 1960): 579–86.

Fugh-Berman, Adriane, and Shahram Ahari. "Following the Script: How Drug Reps Make Friends and Influence Doctors." *PLOS Medicine* 4, no. 4 (2007).

Fullerton, W. S. "The Objectionable Influence of Proprietary Medicines Upon the Young Practitioner." *Journal of the Minnesota State Medical Association and the Northwestern Lancet* 26 (October 15, 1906).

Galambos, L., and J. L. Sturchio. "Transnational Investment: The Merck Experience,

1891–1925." In Hans Pohl, ed., *Transnational Investment from the 19th Century to the Present*. Stuttgart, Germany: Franz Steiner Verlag, 1994.

Gardner, M. N., and A. M. Brandt. "The Doctors' Choice Is America's Choice: The Physician in US Cigarette Advertisements, 1930–1953." *American Journal of Public Health* 96, no. 2 (2006).

Gaughan, Anthony. "Harvey Wiley, Theodore Roosevelt, and the Federal Regulation of Food and Drugs." Third-Year Paper at Harvard Law School (Winter 2004).

Gaul, Gilbert M. "How Blood, the 'Gift of Life,' Became a Billion-Dollar Business." *The Philadelphia Inquirer*, March 12, 1989.

Gaydos, J., R. Hodder, et al. "Swine Influenza A at Fort Dix, New Jersey (January–February 1976), II. Transmission and Morbidity in Units with Cases." *The Journal of Infectious Diseases* (December 13, 1977): S363–68.

Glacek, Christopher. "The Secretive Family Making Billions from the Opioid Crisis." *Esquire*, October 16, 2017.

Glueck, Grace. "An Art Collector Sows Largesse and Controversy." *The New York Times*, June 5, 1983.

———. "Dr. Arthur Sackler Dies at 73; Philanthropist and Art Patron." *The New York Times*, May 27, 1987.

———. "Sackler Art Museum To Open At Harvard." *The New York Times*, October 18, 1985.

Godlee, F. "The Fraud Behind the MMR Scare." *The BMJ* 342 (2011): 22.

Gong, Z., X. Xu, and G. Z. Han. "Patient '0' and the Origin of HIV/AIDS in America." *Trends in Microbiology* 25, no. 1 (January 2017): 3–4.

Gormus, B. J., L. N. Martin, and G. B. Baskin. "A Brief History of the Discovery of Natural Simian Immunodeficiency Virus (SIV) Infections in Captive Sooty Mangabey Monkeys." *Frontiers in Bioscience* 9 (January 1, 2004): 216–24.

Gottlieb, M. S., R. Schroff, H. M. Schanker, J. D. Weisman, P. T. Fan, R. A. Wolf, and A. Saxon. "Pneumocystis Carinii Pneumonia and Mucosal Candidiasis in Previously Healthy Homosexual Men: Evidence of a New Acquired Cellular Immunodeficiency." *The New England Journal of Medicine* 305, no. 24 (December 10, 1981): 1425–31.

Gøtzsche, Peter C. "Big Pharma Often Commits Corporate Crime, and This Must Be Stopped." *The BMJ* 346, no. 7894 (2013): 26.

Grabowski, Henry. "The Evolution of the Pharmaceutical Industry over the Past 50 Years: A Personal Reflection." *International Journal of the Economics of Business* 18, no. 2 (July 2011).

Greene, J. A., and D. Herzberg. "Hidden in Plain Sight: Marketing Prescription Drugs to Consumers in the Twentieth Century." *American Journal of Public Health* 100, no. 5 (2010): 793–803.

Greene, Marion S., and R. Andrew Chambers. "Pseudoaddiction: Fact or Fiction? An Investigation of the Medical Literature." *Current Addiction Reports* 2, no. 4 (2015): 310–17.

Gürtler, Leon. "Merck in America: The First 70 Years from Fine Chemicals to Pharmaceutical Giant." *Bulletin for the History of Chemistry* 25, no. 1 (2000).

Gürtler, Leon, and J. Eberle. "Aspects on the History of Transmission and Favor of Distribution of Viruses by Iatrogenic Action: Perhaps an Example of a Paradigm of the Worldwide Spread of HIV." *Medical Microbiology Immunology* 206, no. 4 (August 2017): 287–93.

Hadland, S. E., M. Cerdá, Y. Li, M. S. Krieger, and B. D. L. Marshall. "Association of Pharmaceutical Industry Marketing of Opioid Products to Physicians with Subsequent Opioid Prescribing." *JAMA Internal Medicine* 178, no. 6 (2018): 861–63.

Hahn, Beatrice H., et al. "AIDS as a Zoonosis: Scientific and Public Health Implications." *Science* 287, no. 5453 (January 28, 2000).

Hall, Wendell H. "The Abuse and Misuse of Antibiotics." *Minnesota Medicine* 35 (1952).

Haller, John S., Jr. "Antibiotic Era." *Pharmacy in History* 56, nos. 1–2 (2014).

Hamowy, Ronald. "The Early Development of Medical Licensing Laws in the United States, 1875–1900." *The Journal of Libertarian Studies* 3 (1979).

Harding, Herbert. "The History of the Organization among Manufacturers and Wholesale Dealers in Proprietary Articles." *American Druggist* 36 (1900).

Harris, Gardiner. "How Merck Survived while Others Merged—Drug Maker Relied on Inspired Research." *The New York Times*, January 12, 2001.

Hart, F. Leslie. "A History of the Adulteration of Food Before 1906." *Food, Drug, Cosmetic Law Journal* 7 (1952).

Heit, H. A. "Addiction, Physical Dependence, and Tolerance." *Journal of Pain & Palliative Care Pharmacotherapy* 17, no. 1 (2003).

Helm, Katherine A. "Protecting Public Health from Outside the Physician's Office: A Century of FDA Regulation from Drug Safety Labeling to Off-Label Drug Promotion." *Fordham Intellectual Property, Media and Entertainment Law Journal* 18, no. 1 (2007): article 9.

Herper, Matthew. "The Best Selling Drugs in America." *Forbes*, April 19, 2011.

———. "A Biotech Phoenix Could Be Rising." *Forbes*, September 25, 2002.

———. "Solving the Drug Patent Problem." *Forbes*, May 2, 2002.

Herxheimer, Andrew, Cecilia Stålsby Lundborg, and Barbro Westerholm. "Advertisements for Medicines in Leading Medical Journals in 18 Countries: A 12-Month Survey of Information Content and Standards." *International Journal of Health Services* 23, no. 1 (January 1993).

Hicks, Jesse. "Fast Times: The Life, Death, and Rebirth of Amphetamine." *Distillations*, Science History Institute, April 14, 2014.

Higano, R., W. N. Robinson, and W. D. Cohen. "Effects of Long-Term Administration of Estrogens on Serum Lipids of Postmenopausal Women." *The New England Journal of Medicine* 263: 828–31.

"History of Federal Regulation: 1902–Present: Food, Drug, and Cosmetic Act of 1938." FDAReview.org, A Project of the Independent Institute. http://www.fdareview.org/01_history.php.

Ho, J. M., and D. N. Juurlink. "Considerations When Prescribing Trimethoprim-Sulfamethoxazole." *Canadian Medical Association Journal* 183, no. 16 (2011): 1851–58.

Hollister, Leo E., Francis P. Motzenbecker, and Roger O. Degan. "Withdrawal Reactions from Chlordiazepoxyd (Librium)." *Psychopharmacology* 2, no. 1 (January 1961): 63–68.

Hønge, Bo Langhoff, et al. "High Prevalence and Excess Mortality of Late Presenters among HIV-1, HIV-2 and HIV-1/2 Dually Infected Patients in Guinea-Bissau—A Cohort Study from West Africa." *The Pan African Medical Journal* 25 (2016): 40.

Hooper, Edward, et al. "Search for the Origin of HIV and AIDS." *Science* 289, no. 5482 (August 18, 2000).

Horowitz, Nathan. "Arthur M. Sackler, MD." *Medical Tribune* 25, no. 22 (June 10, 1987).

Houck, J. A. "'What Do These Women Want?': Feminist Responses to Feminine Forever." *Bulletin of the History of Medicine* 77, no. 1 (Spring 2003).

Howell, Mary C. "What Medical Schools Teach About Women." *The New England Journal of Medicine* 291 (August 8, 1974).

Inciardi, James, and Jennifer Goode. "OxyContin and Prescription Drug Abuse." *Consumer's Research* (July 2003).

Isis, Doogab Yi. "Who Owns What? Private Ownership and the Public Interest in Recombinant DNA Technology in the 1970s." The University of Chicago Press on behalf of the History of Science Society 102, no. 3 (September 2011).

Jacobs, Andrew. "Citrus Farmers Facing Deadly Bacteria Turn to Antibiotics, Alarming Health Officials." *The New York Times*, May 17, 2019.

Jawetz, Ernest. "Infectious Diseases: Problems of Antimicrobial Therapy." *Annual Review of Medicine* 5 (1954).

Jayawant, Sujata S., and Rajesh Balkrishnan. "The Controversy Surrounding Oxycontin Abuse: Issues and Solutions." *Therapeutics and Clinical Risk Management* 1, no. 2 (2005).

Jones, C. M., E. B. Einstein, and W. M. Compton. "Changes in Synthetic Opioid Involvement in Drug Overdose Deaths in the United States, 2010–2016." *JAMA* 319, no. 17 (2018): 1819–21.

Joseph, Andrew. "Purdue Cemented Ties with Universities and Hospitals to Expand Opioid Sales, Documents Contend." *STAT News*, January 16, 2019.

Jurtshuk, Peter, Jr., et al. "Biochemical Responses of Rats to Auditory Stress." *Science*, May 22, 1959.

Kaiko, Robert F., et al. "The United States Experience with Oral Controlled-Release Morphine (MS Contin Tablets), Parts I and II. Review of Nine Dose Titration Studies and Clinical Pharmacology of 15-mg, 30-mg, 60-mg, and 100-mg Tablet Strengths in Normal Subjects." *Cancer* 63 (June 1, 1989): 2348–54. Note: team of writers from the Medical Department of the Purdue Frederick Company, Norwalk, CT, and Yonkers, New York.

Karki, L. "Review of FDA Law Related to Pharmaceuticals: The Hatch-Waxman Act, Regulatory Amendments and Implications for Drug Patent Enforcement." *Journal of the Patent Trademark and Office Society* 87 (2005).

Keefe, Patrick Radden. "The Family that Built an Empire of Pain." *The New Yorker*, October 23, 2017.

Kent, Francis B. "Rising Criticism—Haiti: Jobless, Poor Line Up to Sell Blood." *Los Angeles Times*, January 27, 1972.

Khazan, Olga. "The New Heroin Epidemic." *The Atlantic*, October 30, 2014.

Kiang, M. V., S. Basu, J. Chen, and M. J. Alexander. "Assessment of Changes in the Geographical Distribution of Opioid-Related Mortality across the United States by Opioid Type, 1999–2016." *JAMA Network Open* (2019).

Kingston, William. "Streptomycin, Schatz v. Waksman, and the Balance of Credit for Discovery." *Journal of the History of Medicine and Allied Sciences* 59 (2004).

Kirby, T. J. "Cataracts Produced by Triparanol. (MER-29)." *Transactions of the American Ophthalmological Society* 65 (1967): 494–543.

Kitt, G. W. "Benjamin Minge Duggar: 1872–1956." *Mycologia* 39, no. 3 (May–June 1957).

Korber, B., et al. "Timing the Ancestor of the HIV-1 Pandemic Strains." *Science* 288, no. 5472 (June 9, 2000).

Kornbluth, Jesse. "The Temple of Sackler." *Vanity Fair*, September 1987.

Krause, Richard. "The Swine Flu Episode and the Fog of Epidemics." *Emerging Infectious Diseases* 12, no. 1 (January 2006).

Kreston, Rebecca. "The Public Health Legacy of the 1976 Swine Flu Outbreak." *Discover*, September 30, 2013.

Krupka, L. R., and A. M. Vener. "Gender Differences in Drug (Prescription, Non-Prescription, Alcohol and Tobacco) Advertising: Trends and Implications." *Journal of Drug Issues* 22, no. 2 (April 1992).

Lall, Sanjaya. "Multinational Companies and Concentration: The Case of the Pharmaceutical Industry." *Social Scientist* 7, no. 8/9 (1979).

Larkin, Timothy. "The New Flu: What It Is and What Is Being Done About It." *FDA Consumer* 10, no. 4 (May 1976).

Laven, Stuart A. "Invalid Patents: Removing Statutory Protection from Improperly Granted Monopolies." *Case Western Reserve Law Review* 21, no. 2 (1970).

Lear, John. "The Certification of Antibiotics." *Saturday Review* (February 7, 1959): 43–48.

———. "Do We Need a Census of Worthless Drugs?" *Saturday Review* (May 7, 1960).

———. "Taking the Miracle Out of the Miracle Drugs." *Saturday Review* 42 (January 3, 1959).

Lenzner, Robert. "A Financial Man and the Fogg." *The Boston Globe*, February 16, 1982.

Leung, Pamela T. M., Erin M. Macdonald, Matthew B. Stanbrook, Irfan A. Dhalla, Li Ka Shing, and David N. Juurlink. "A 1980 Letter on the Risk of Opioid Addiction." *The New England Journal of Medicine* 376 (June 1, 2017): 2194–95.

Levin, Tamar. "Drug Makers Fighting Back Against Advance of Generics." *The New York Times*, July 28, 1987.

Liebeskind, J. C. "Pain Can Kill." *Pain* 44, no. 1 (January 1991).

Lombardino, Joseph G. "A Brief History of Pfizer Central Research." *Bulletin for the History of Chemistry* 25, no. 1 (2000).

López-Muñoz, Francisco, Ronaldo Ucha-Udabe, and Cecilio Alamo. "The History of Barbiturates a Century after Their Clinical Introduction." *Neuropsychiatric Disease and Treatment* 1, no. 4 (2005): 329–43.

Mandell, D. T., et al. "Pathogenic Features Associated with Increased Virulence upon Simian Immunodeficiency Virus Cross-Species Transmission from Natural Hosts." *Journal of Virology* 88, no. 12 (June 2014): 6778–92.

Mangano, Michael F. "A Multi-Disciplinary Approach to Problem Solving: The Generic Drug Scandal." *The Government Accountants Journal* (Fall 1992).

Mant, A., and D. Darroch. "Media Images and Medical Images." *Social Science & Medicine* (1975).

Martí-Ibáñez, Félix. "The Artist as Physician; Medical Philosophy in the Renaissance." *International Record of Medicine and General Practice Clinics* 167, no. 4 (April 1954): 221–42.

———. "Doctors Must Tell." *International Record of Medicine and General Practice Clinics* 172 (October 1959): 651–52.

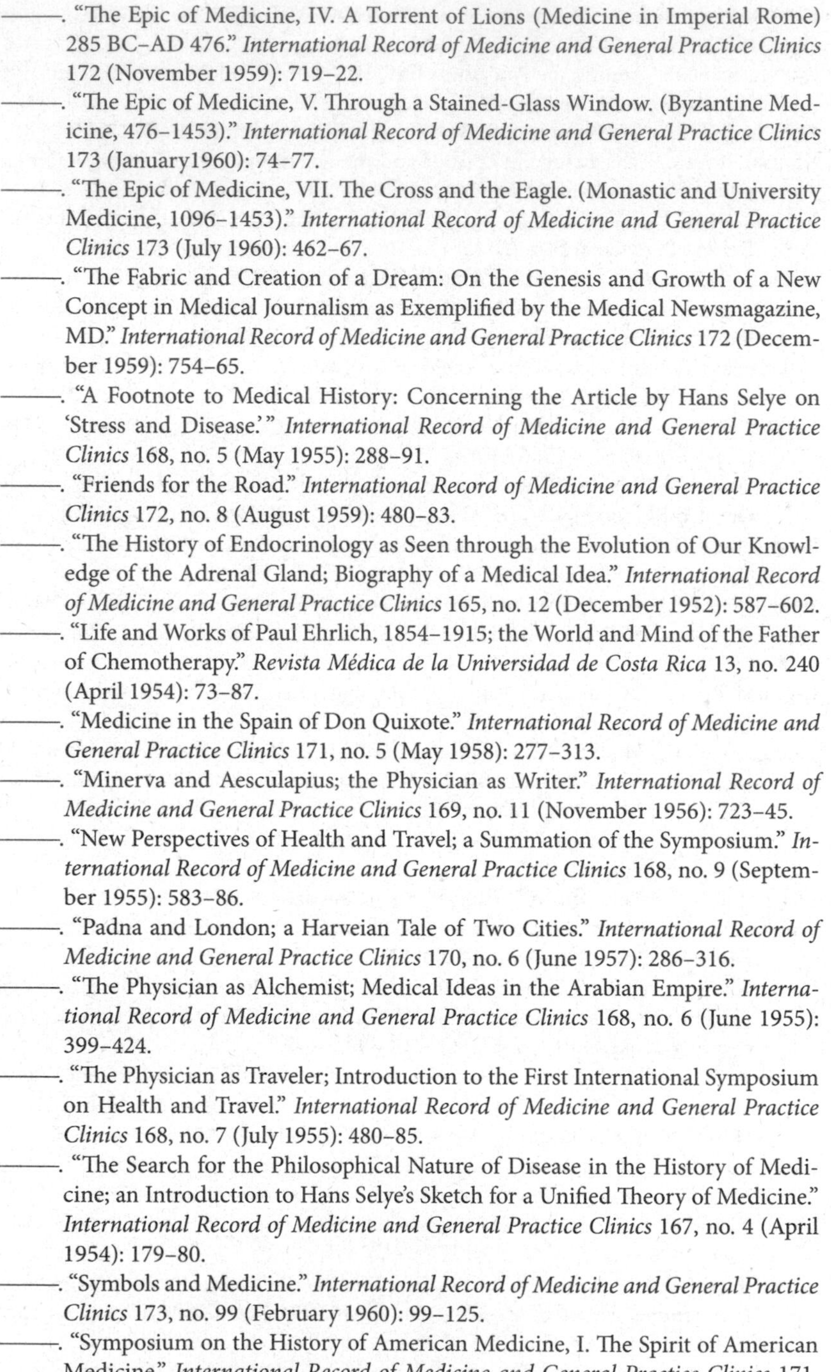

———. "The Epic of Medicine, IV. A Torrent of Lions (Medicine in Imperial Rome) 285 BC–AD 476." *International Record of Medicine and General Practice Clinics* 172 (November 1959): 719–22.

———. "The Epic of Medicine, V. Through a Stained-Glass Window. (Byzantine Medicine, 476–1453)." *International Record of Medicine and General Practice Clinics* 173 (January1960): 74–77.

———. "The Epic of Medicine, VII. The Cross and the Eagle. (Monastic and University Medicine, 1096–1453)." *International Record of Medicine and General Practice Clinics* 173 (July 1960): 462–67.

———. "The Fabric and Creation of a Dream: On the Genesis and Growth of a New Concept in Medical Journalism as Exemplified by the Medical Newsmagazine, MD." *International Record of Medicine and General Practice Clinics* 172 (December 1959): 754–65.

———. "A Footnote to Medical History: Concerning the Article by Hans Selye on 'Stress and Disease.'" *International Record of Medicine and General Practice Clinics* 168, no. 5 (May 1955): 288–91.

———. "Friends for the Road." *International Record of Medicine and General Practice Clinics* 172, no. 8 (August 1959): 480–83.

———. "The History of Endocrinology as Seen through the Evolution of Our Knowledge of the Adrenal Gland; Biography of a Medical Idea." *International Record of Medicine and General Practice Clinics* 165, no. 12 (December 1952): 587–602.

———. "Life and Works of Paul Ehrlich, 1854–1915; the World and Mind of the Father of Chemotherapy." *Revista Médica de la Universidad de Costa Rica* 13, no. 240 (April 1954): 73–87.

———. "Medicine in the Spain of Don Quixote." *International Record of Medicine and General Practice Clinics* 171, no. 5 (May 1958): 277–313.

———. "Minerva and Aesculapius; the Physician as Writer." *International Record of Medicine and General Practice Clinics* 169, no. 11 (November 1956): 723–45.

———. "New Perspectives of Health and Travel; a Summation of the Symposium." *International Record of Medicine and General Practice Clinics* 168, no. 9 (September 1955): 583–86.

———. "Padna and London; a Harveian Tale of Two Cities." *International Record of Medicine and General Practice Clinics* 170, no. 6 (June 1957): 286–316.

———. "The Physician as Alchemist; Medical Ideas in the Arabian Empire." *International Record of Medicine and General Practice Clinics* 168, no. 6 (June 1955): 399–424.

———. "The Physician as Traveler; Introduction to the First International Symposium on Health and Travel." *International Record of Medicine and General Practice Clinics* 168, no. 7 (July 1955): 480–85.

———. "The Search for the Philosophical Nature of Disease in the History of Medicine; an Introduction to Hans Selye's Sketch for a Unified Theory of Medicine." *International Record of Medicine and General Practice Clinics* 167, no. 4 (April 1954): 179–80.

———. "Symbols and Medicine." *International Record of Medicine and General Practice Clinics* 173, no. 99 (February 1960): 99–125.

———. "Symposium on the History of American Medicine, I. The Spirit of American Medicine." *International Record of Medicine and General Practice Clinics* 171, no. 6 (June 1958): 317–22.

———. "Words and Research." *Antibiotic Medicine and Clinical Therapy* 4, no. 11 (New York: November 1957): 740–47.

Martin, Douglas. "James L. Goddard, Crusading FDA Leader, Dies at 86." *The New York Times*, January 2, 2010.

Martin, W. R., C. G. Eades, J. A. Thompson, R. E. Huppler, and P. Gilbert. "The Effects of Morphine- and Nalorphine-Like Drugs in the Nondependent and Morphine-Dependent Chronic Spinal Dog." *Journal of Pharmacology and Experimental Therapeutics* (1976).

Max, M. B. "Improving Outcomes of Analgesic Treatment: Is Education Enough?" *Annals of Internal Medicine* 113, no. 11 (December 1990).

May, Charles D. "Selling Drugs by 'Educating' Physicians." *The Journal of Medical Education* 36, no. 1 (January 1961).

Mayo, Caswell, and Keenan Thomas. "American Druggist and Pharmaceutical Record: A Semi-Monthly Illustrated Journal of Practical Pharmacy." New York: American Druggist Publishing Co.: 1906–1907.

McEvilla, Joseph D. "Competition in the American Pharmaceutical Industry." PhD diss., University of Pittsburgh, 1955.

McFadyen, Richard E. "Estes Kefauver and the Drug Industry." PhD diss., Emory University, 1973.

———. "The FDA's Regulation and Control of Antibiotics in the 1950s: The Henry Welch Scandal, Félix Martí-Ibáñez, and Charles Pfizer & Co." *Bulletin of the History of Medicine* 53, no. 2 (Summer 1979).

McGibney, David. "The Future of the Pharmaceutical Industry." *RSA Journal* 147, no. 5489 (1999).

McLean, Bethany. "We Didn't Cause the Crisis." *Vanity Fair*, August 2019.

Meed, Steven, Phyllis M. Kleinman, and Thomas G. Kantor. "Management of Cancer Pain with Oral Controlled-Release Morphine Sulfate." *American College of Clinical Pharmacology* (February 1987).

Meier, Barry. "At Painkiller Trouble Spot, Signs Seen as Alarming Didn't Alarm Drug's Maker." *The New York Times*, December 10, 2001.

———. "Opioid Makers Are the Big Winners in Lawsuit Settlements." *The New York Times*, December 26, 2018.

———. "Origins of an Epidemic: Purdue Pharma Knew Its Opioids Were Widely Abused." *The New York Times*, May 29, 2018.

———. "Why Drug Company Executives Haven't Really Seen Justice for Their Role in the Opioid Crisis." *Time*, June 15, 2018.

Meier, Barry, and Melody Petersen. "Sales of Painkiller Grew Rapidly, But Success Brought a High Cost." *The New York Times*, March 5, 2011.

Melzack, Ronald. "The Tragedy of Needless Pain." *Scientific American* 262, no. 2 (February 1990).

Mikami, Koichi. "Orphans in the Market: The History of Orphan Drug Policy." *Social History of Medicine* 32, no. 3 (August 2019).

Mintz, Morton. "'Heroine' of FDA Keeps Bad Drug Off Market." *The Washington Post*, July 15, 1962.

Morone, Natalia E., and Debra K. Weiner. "Pain as the Fifth Vital Sign: Exposing the Vital Need for Pain Education." *Clinical Therapeutics* 35, no. 11 (2013).

Morrell, Alex. "The OxyContin Clan: The $14 Billion Newcomer to Forbes' 2015 List of Richest U.S. Families." *Forbes*, July 1, 2015.

Mosher, H. "Portrayal of Women in Drug Advertising: A Medical Betrayal." *Journal of Drug Issues* (1976).

Munch, James C., and James C. Munch Jr. "Notices of Judgment—the First Thousand." *Food Drug Cosmetic Law Journal* 10 (1955).

Musto, David F. "An Historical Perspective on Legal and Medical Responses to Substance Abuse." *Villanova Law Review* 18 (May 1973): 808–17.

Nagendrappa, Gopalpur. "Yellapragada SubbaRow: The Man of Miracle Drugs." *Resonance* (June 2012).

Nahas, G. G., and A. Greenwood. "The First Report of the National Commission on Marihuana (1972): Signal of Misunderstanding or Exercise in Ambiguity." *Bulletin of the New York Academy of Medicine* 50, no. 1 (1974).

Nathanson, Neal, and Alexander D. Langmuir. "The Cutter Incident. Poliomyelitis Following Formaldehyde-Inactivated Poliovirus Vaccination in the United States during the Spring of 1955: I and 2. Background." *American Journal of Epidemiology* 78, no. 1 (July 1, 1963).

———. "Thalidomide in America: A Brush with Tragedy." *Clio Medica* 11 (Spring 1976): 79–93.

Nelson, M. L., and S. B. Levy. "The History of the Tetracyclines." *Annals of the New York Academy of Sciences* 1241 (2011): 17–32.

Nelson, Valerie J. "Dr. James L. Goddard: 1923–2009." *Chicago Tribune*, August 25, 2018.

Neushul, Peter. "Science, Government, and the Mass Production of Penicillin." *Journal of the History of Medicine and Allied Sciences* 48 (October 1993).

Neustadt, R. E., and H. V. Fineberg. "The Swine Flu Affair: Decision-Making on a Slippery Disease." D, Selected Documents. (Washington, DC: National Academies Press: 1978).

Nevius, James. "The Strange History of Opiates in America: From Morphine for Kids to Heroin for Soldiers." *The Guardian*, March 15, 2016.

Norberg, Peter, Maria Bergström, Vinay Jethava, Devdatt Dubhashi, and Malte Hermansson. "The IncP-1 Plasmid Backbone Adapts to Different Host Bacterial Species and Evolves through Homologous Recombination." *Nature Communications* 2 (2011): 272.

Palo, Nishit, et al. "Effects of Osteoarthritis on Quality of Life in Elderly Population of Bhubaneswar, India: A Prospective Multicenter Screening and Therapeutic Study of 2,854 Patients." *Geriatric Orthopaedic Surgery & Rehabilitation* 6, no. 4 (2015): 269–75.

Papadopoulos, Stelios. "Evolving Paradigms in Biotech IPO Valuations." *Nature Biotechnology* 19 (2001): BE18–19.

Parker-Pope, Tara. "Drug Resistance, Explained." *The New York Times*, March 27, 2008.

Parthasarathy, R. "Discoverer of Miracle Medicines." "Science and Technology." *The Hindu*, March 13, 2003.

Perch, Michael Morten Sodemann, Marianne S. Jakobsen, Palle Valentiner-Branth, Hans Steinsland, Thea K. Fischer, Dina Duarte Lopes, Peter Aaby, and Kåre Mølbak. "Seven Years' Experience with Cryptosporidium Parvum in Guinea-Bissau, West Africa." *Annals of Tropical Paediatrics* 21, no. 4 (2001).

Perrone, Matthew, and Ben Wieder. "Pro-Painkiller Echo Chamber Shaped Policy Amid Drug Epidemic," Part 2 of 3. The Center for Public Integrity, copublished with The Associated Press, September 19, 2016.

Perrone, Matthew, Liz Essley Whyte, and Geoff Mulvihill. "Drugmakers Push Profitable, but Unproven, Opioid Solution," Part 3 of 3. The Center for Public Integrity, copublished with The Associated Press, December 15, 2016. See under Liz Essley Whyte for Part 1.

Pestka, Sidney. "The Interferons: 50 Years after Their Discovery, There Is Much More to Learn." *The Journal of Biological Chemistry* 282, no. 28 (July 13, 2007).

Pisano, Gary P. "Can Science Be a Business?: Lessons from Biotech." *Harvard Business Review*, October 2006.

Plunkett, Matthew J., and Jonathan A. Ellman. "Combinational Chemistry and New Drugs." *Scientific American*, April 1997.

Podolsky, Scott H. "Antibiotics and the Social History of the Controlled Clinical Trial, 1950–1970." *Journal of the History of Medicine and Allied Sciences* 65, no. 3 (2010): 327–67.

Podolsky, Scott H., and J. A. Greene. "Keeping Modern in Medicine: Pharmaceutical Promotion and Physician Education in Postwar America." *Bulletin of the History of Medicine* 83, no. 2 (Summer 2009).

Portenoy, R. K. "Appropriate Use of Opioids for Persistent Non-Cancer Pain." *The Lancet* 364, no. 9436 (2004): 739–74.

———. "The Use of Opioids for the Treatment of Chronic Pain." *The Journal of Pain* 6, no. 1 (Spring 1997): 77–79.

Portenoy, R. K., and K. M. Foley. "Chronic Use of Opioid Analgesics in Non-Malignant Pain: Report of 38 Cases." *Pain* 25, no. 2 (May 1986): 171–86.

Prather, J., and L. Fidel. "Sex Differences in the Content and Style of Medical Advertisements." *Social Science & Medicine* (1975).

Quest, T. L., J. O. Merrill, J. Roll, A. J. Saxon, and R. A. Rosenblatt. "Buprenorphine Therapy for Opioid Addiction in Rural Washington: The Experience of the Early Adopters." *Journal of Opioid Management* 8 (2012): 29–38.

Quianzon, Celeste C., and Issam Cheikh. "History of Insulin." *Journal of Community Hospital Internal Medicine Perspectives* 2, no. 2 (2012).

Quinn, Roswell. "Rethinking Antibiotic Research and Development: World War II and the Penicillin Collaborative." *American Journal of Public Health* 103, no. 3 (2013).

Ransom, Alicia Burnett. "Direct-to-Physician Advertising, Depression, and the Advertised Female Patient." PhD diss., University of Tennessee, 2017.

Rao, T. S. Sathyanarayana, and Chittaranjan Andrade. "MMR Vaccine and Autism: Sensation, Refutation, Retraction, and Fraud." *Indian Journal of Psychiatry* 53, no. 2 (2011).

Rasmussen, Nicolas. "America's First Amphetamine Epidemic 1929–1971; A Quantitative and Qualitative Retrospective with Implications for the Present." *American Journal of Public Health* (June 2008).

Regier, C. C. "The Struggle for Federal Food and Drugs Legislation." *Law and Contemporary Problems* 1, no. 1 (1933).

Reynolds, Preston P. "Dr. Louis T. Wright and the NAACP: Pioneers in Hospital Racial Integration." *American Journal of Public Health* 90, no. 6 (June 2000).

Rheingold, Paul D. "The MER/29 Story—an Instance of Successful Mass Disaster Litigation." *California Law Review* 56, no. 1 (1968).

Rheingold, Paul D., and Clifford J. Shoemaker. "The Swine Flu Litigation." *Litigation* 8, no. 1 (1981).

Rickels, K., et al. "Controlled Psychopharmacological Research in Private Psychiatric Practice." *Psychopharmacologia* 9, no. 4 (1966).

Rita, R. "Court Upholds Injunction on Sale of Sackler Art." *The New York Times*, January 7, 1993.

Romm, Cari. "'The Disease of the Century': Reporting on the Origin of AIDS." *The Atlantic*, December 5, 2014.

Rosenbaum, Lee. "The Met's Sackler Enclave: Public Boon or Private Preserve?" *ARTnews*, September 1978, 56–57.

Rosenberg, Charles, and Carroll Smith-Rosenberg. "The Female Animal: Medical and Biological Views of Woman and Her Role in Nineteenth-Century America." *Journal of American History* (1973): 60.

Rosenblum, Andrew, Lisa A. Marsch, Herman Joseph, and Russell K. Portenoy. "Opioids and the Treatment of Chronic Pain: Controversies, Current Status, and Future Directions." *Experimental and Clinical Psychopharmacology* 16, no. 5 (2008): 405–16.

Ruge, R. B. "Regulation of Prescription Drug Advertising: Medical Progress and Private Enterprise." *Publishing Entertainment Advertising Law Quarterly* 9, no. 3 (1969): 261–99.

Ruoff, K. L. "Miscellaneous Catalase-Negative, Gram-Positive Cocci: Emerging Opportunists." *Journal of Clinical Microbiology* 40, no. 4 (2002): 1129–33.

Ryan, Harriet, Lisa Girion, and Scott Glover. "OxyContin Goes Global—'We're Only Just Getting Started,'" *Los Angeles Times*, December 18, 2016.

———. "'You Want a Description of Hell?' Oxycontin's 12-Hour Problem." *Los Angeles Times*, May 5, 2016.

Ryan, Kenneth J. "Cancer Risk and Estrogen Use in the Menopause." *The New England Journal of Medicine* (December 4, 1975): 293.

Sackler, A. M. "Taboos of the Past and Perspectives for the Future in Social Psychiatry." *International Journal of Social Psychiatry* 19, nos. 1–2 (1973): 4–9.

Sackler, Arthur M., and Lawrence H. Sophian. "The Effects of the Ingestion of Amino Acid on Gastric Secretion, with Particular Reference to L-Lysine Monohydrochloride." *American Journal of Clinical Pathology* 28, no. 3 (September 1, 1957): 258–63.

Sackler, M., F. Martí-Ibáñez, R. Sackler, and A. Sackler. "The Challenge of Bio- and Chemotherapy in Psychiatry." *The Journal of Clinical and Experimental Psychopathology* 17, no. 1 (January–March 1956): 15–18.

———. "Contemporary Physiodynamic Therapeutic Trends in Psychiatry." *The Journal of Clinical and Experimental Psychopathology* 15, no. 4 (October–December 1954): 382–400.

———. "Neuroendocrinologic Basis for a Metabolic Concept of Several Psychiatric Disorders." *International Record of Medicine and General Practice Clinics* 166, no. 3 (March 1953): 81–90.

———. "On Tolerance to and Craving for Alcohol in Histamine-Treated Schizophrenics; A Physiodynamic Interpretation of Observations on Histamine-Adrenocortico-Hormonal Equilibrations." *The Psychiatric Quarterly* 26, no. 4 (October 1952): 597–607.

———. "The Philosophy of Organicism in Psychiatry." *The Journal of Clinical and Experimental Psychopathology* 15, no. 3 (July–September 1954): 179–90.

———. "Psychiatric Implications of Sex Differences in Thyroid-Histamine Interrelationship; A Clinical and Laboratory Study." *The Journal of Clinical and Experimental Psychopathology* 17, no. 3 (July–September 1956): 297–307.

———. "Quantitated Identification of Psychosis by Blood Sample, I. Instrumentation of

Ultrasound for Biologic Quantitation." *The Journal of Clinical and Experimental Psychopathology* 12, no. 4 (October–December 1951): 283–87.

———. "Quantitated Identification of Psychosis by Blood Sample, II. Ultrasonometry: A New Modality in Biology and Medicine." *The Journal of Clinical and Experimental Psychopathology* 12, no. 4 (October–December 1951): 288–303.

———. "Quantitated Identification of Psychosis by Blood Sample, III. Ultrasonometry: A New Modality in Biology and Medicine." *The Journal of Clinical and Experimental Psychopathology* 12, no. 4 (October–December 1951): 304–22.

———. "The Quest for Freud." *The Journal of Clinical and Experimental Psychopathology* 17, no. 2 (April–June 1956): 117–27.

———. "Tests for Pathophysiologic Identification and Classification of Psychoses." *The Journal of Clinical and Experimental Psychopathology* 19, no. 1 (January–March 1958): 1–6.

———. "Theory and the Future of Research in Psychiatry." *The Journal of Clinical and Experimental Psychopathology* 18, no. 4 (October–December 1957): 319–22.

———. "Toward a Unifying Concept in Psychiatry." *The Journal of Clinical and Experimental Psychopathology* 19, no. 2, S1 (April–June 1958): i–iv.

Sackler, M. D., et al. "Psychiatric Research Perspectives at the Creedmoor Institute for Psychobiologic Studies." *Journal of Clinical Experimental Psychopathology* 15, no. 2 (April–June 1954): 119–29.

Sackler, R. R., et al. "Eosinophile Levels in Hospitalized Psychotics during Combined Testosterone-Estrogen Therapy." *Proceedings of the Society for Experimental Biology and Medicine* 76, no. 2 (1951).

Sarayloo, Kimiya. "A Poor Man's Tale of Patented Medicine: The 1962 Amendments, Hatch-Waxman, and the Lost Admonition to Promote Progress." *Quinnipiac Health Law Journal* 18 (2015).

Saunders, C. "The Treatment of Intractable Pain in Terminal Cancer." *Proceedings of the Royal Society of Medicine* 56, no. 3 (1963).

Schatz, Albert, Elizabeth Bugie, and Selman Waksman. "Streptomycin, a Substance Exhibiting Antibiotic Activity Against Gram-Positive and Gram-Negative Bacteria." *Proceedings of the Society for Experimental Biology and Medicine* 55 (1944).

Schechtman, Leonard M. "The Safety Assessment Process—Setting the Scene: An FDA Perspective." *ILAR Journal* 43, no. 1 (January 2002).

Scherer, F. M. "The F.T.C., Oligopoly, and Shared Monopoly." Faculty Research Working Paper Series, Harvard Kennedy School, RWP13-031, September 2013.

Scherer, F. M., and William S. Comanor. "Mergers and Innovation in the Pharmaceutical Market." Faculty Research Working Paper Series, Harvard Kennedy School, RW11-043, November 2011.

Schmeck, Harold M. "Congress Votes Flu Vaccine Liability Bill." *The New York Times*, August 11, 1976.

Schneider, A. Patrick, Christine M. Zainer, Christopher Kevin Kubat, Nancy K. Mullen, and Amberly K. Windisch. "The Breast Cancer Epidemic: 10 Facts." *The Linacre Quarterly* 81, no. 3 (2014).

Schobelocka, Michael J., et al., "Multiple-Dose Pharmacokinetic Evaluation of Two Formulations of Sustained-Release Morphine Sulfate Tablets." *Current Therapeutic Research* 56, no. 10 (October 1995).

Scholl, L., P. Seth, M. Kariisa, N. Wilson, and G. Baldwin. "Drug and Opioid-Involved

Overdose Deaths—United States, 2013–2017." *Morbidity and Mortality Weekly Report* (2019): 67.

Schulte, Fred. "How America Got Hooked on a Deadly Drug." "Kaiser Health News." *The Washington Post*, June 13, 2018.

Schulte, Fred, and Nancy McVicar. "OxyContin Ads Were Aggressive, Records Show." *Florida Sun-Sentinel*, February 21, 2003.

———. "OxyContin Was Touted as Virtually Nonaddictive, Newly Released State Records Show." *Florida Sun-Sentinel*, March 6, 2003.

Schwartz, L. M., and S. Woloshin. "Medical Marketing in the United States, 1997–2016." *JAMA* 321, no. 1 (2019): 80–96.

Schwartzman, David. "Innovation in the Pharmaceutical Industry." (Baltimore, MD: Johns Hopkins Press, 1976).

"SciTech Tuesday: Sir Alexander Fleming's Ominous Prediction." *See & Hear*, The National WWII Museum blog, January 11, 2017.

Scroop, Daniel. "A Faded Passion? Estes Kefauver and the Senate Subcommittee on Antitrust and Monopoly." *Business History Conference* 5 (2007).

Sencer, David J., and J. Donald Millar. "Reflections on the 1976 Swine Flu Vaccination Program." *FDA Consumer* 12, no. 1 (January 2006).

Severo, Richard. "Impoverished Haitians Sell Plasma for Use in the U.S." *The New York Times*, January 28, 1972.

Shah, Manish S., Erin R. Holmes, and Shane P. Desselle. "The Use of Persuasion in Print DTC Advertisements of Prescription Drugs: A Content Analysis of Leading Consumer Magazines from 1995–2000." *Journal of Pharmaceutical Marketing & Management* 15, no. 3 (2003): 23–43.

Shapiro, Edward S. "Jews with Money." *Judaism* 36, no. 1 (Winter 1987).

Sharp, Paul M., and Beatrice H. Hahn. "Origins of HIV and the AIDS Pandemic." *Cold Spring Harbor Perspectives in Medicine* 1, no. 1 (2011).

Sharp, Paul M., et al. "Origins and Evolution of AIDS Viruses: Estimating the Time-Scale." *Biochemical Society Transactions* 28, no. 2 (February 1, 2000): 275–82.

Shorter, Edward. "The Liberal State and the Rogue Agency: FDA's Regulation of Drugs for Mood Disorders, 1950s–1970s." *International Journal of Law and Psychiatry* 31, no. 2 (2008): 126–35.

Siegel, Ronald K. "Repeating Cycles of Cocaine Use and Abuse." In *Treating Drug Problems, Volume 2: Commissioned Papers on Historical, Institutional, and Economic Contexts of Drug Treatment*. Institute of Medicine, Committee for the Substance Abuse Coverage Study. (Washington, DC: The National Academies Press, 1992.)

Simons, J. "Lilly Goes Off Prozac: The Drugmaker Bounced Back from the Loss of Its Blockbuster, but the Recovery Had Costs." *Fortune*, June 28, 2004.

Smith, Michael J., Susan S. Ellenberg, Louis M. Bell, and David M. Rubin. "Media Coverage of the Measles-Mumps-Rubella Vaccine and Autism Controversy and Its Relationship to MMR Immunization Rates in the United States." *Pediatrics* 121, no. 4, e836–43 (April 2008).

Smith, Mickey C., and Lisa Griffin. "Rationality of Appeals Used in the Promotion of Psychotropic Drugs." *Social Science & Medicine* (1977).

Sneader, Walter. "The Discovery of Heroin." *The Lancet* 352, no. 914 (1998).

Snyder, Solomon H. "Arthur M. Sackler and Science." *Proceedings of the National Academy of Sciences of the United States of America* 98, no. 20 (2001).

So, Anthony D., Neha Gupta, and Otto Cars. "Tackling Antibiotic Resistance: Concerted Action Is Needed to Provide New Technologies and Conserve Existing

Drugs." *The BMJ* 340, no. 7756 (2010): 1091–92. http://www.jstor.org/stable/40702199.

Speaker, Susan L. "From 'Happiness Pills' to 'National Nightmare': Changing Cultural Assessment of Minor Tranquilizers in America, 1955–1980." *Journal of the History of Medicine and Allied Sciences* 52, no. 3 (July 1, 1997).

Steele, Henry. "The Fortunes of Economic Reform Legislation: The Case of the Drug Amendments Act of 1962." *The American Journal of Economics and Sociology* 25, no. 1, January 1966.

Steere, A. C., et al. "Vaccination against Lyme Disease with Recombinant *Borrelia burgdorferi* Outer-Surface Lipoprotein A with Adjuvant." *The New England Journal of Medicine* (1998): 339. https://www.nejm.org/doi/full/10.1056/NEJM199807233390401.

Stengren, Bernard. "He Takes Pulse of 150,000 U.S. Physicians." *St. Louis Post-Dispatch*, June 13, 1960.

Sternbach, Leo H. "The Benzodiazepine Story." *Journal of Medicinal Chemistry* 22 (1979): 1–7.

———. "The Discovery of Librium." *Agents and Actions* 2, no. 4 (1972).

Sullivan, Mark D., and B. Ferrell. "Ethical Challenges in the Management of Chronic Nonmalignant Pain: Negotiating through the Cloud of Doubt." *The Journal of Pain* 6, no. 1 (2005): 2–9.

Sullivan, Mark D., and Catherine Q. Howe. "Opioid Therapy for Chronic Pain in the United States: Promises and Perils." *Pain* 154, no. S1 (2013).

Tanne, Janice Hopkins. "Fighting AIDS: On the Front Lines Against the Plague." *The New York Times Magazine*, January 12, 1987.

Tomer, Adam. "The Secret Life of the Gay Jewish Immigrant Whose Company Sells Your Medical Information." *The Forward*, January 12, 2017.

Temin, Peter. "The Evolution of the Modern Pharmaceutical Industry." Working paper no. 223, Department of Economics, Massachusetts Institute of Technology, 1978.

Tuck, Lon. "Dr. Arthur Sackler: Art and Frustrations." *The International Herald Tribune*, September 27–28, 1986.

Urdang, George. "The Antibiotics and Pharmacy." *Journal of the History of Medicine and Allied Sciences* 6, no. 3 (1951).

"U.S. False Ad Drive Cites Journal of AMA." *Los Angeles Times*, March 4, 1966.

Valium Mainstream Health Alerts: "Tired? Nervous? Here's a Pill." *McCall's*, April 1973; "Danger Ahead! Valium—The Pill You Love Can Turn On You." *Vogue*, February 1975; Nolen, William. "Tranquilizer Use and Abuse." *McCall's*, May 1976; "What's Good about Tranquilizers?" *Vogue*, April 1976.

Vallely, Paul. "Drug That Spans the Ages: The History of Cocaine." *The Independent* (UK), March 2, 2006.

Van Boeckel, Thomas P., et al. "Reducing Antimicrobial Use in Food Animals." *Science* 357, no. 6358 (September 29, 2017): 1350–52.

Van Miert, A. S. "The Sulfonamide-Diaminopyrimidine Story." *Journal of Veterinary Pharmacology and Therapeutics* 17 (1994): 309–16.

Van Zee, A. "The Promotion and Marketing of OxyContin: Commercial Triumph, Public Health Tragedy." *American Journal of Public Health* 99, no. 2 (2009).

"VA's Opiate Overload Feeds Veterans' Addictions, Overdose Deaths." *The Center for Investigative Reporting*, September 28, 2013.

Wainwright, Milton. "Streptomycin: Discovery and Resultant Controversy." *History and Philosophy of the Life Science* 13, no. 1 (1991).

Wakefield, A. J., et al. "Ileal-Lymphoid-Nodular Hyperplasia, Nonspecific Colitis, and Pervasive Developmental Disorder in Children." *The Lancet* 351, no. 9103 (February 28, 1998): 637–41.

Wakefield, Anne E. "Biology of Plagues: Evidence from Historical Populations." 1st Edition, by Susan Scott, Christopher J. Duncan.

———. "*Pneumocystis carinii* Role in Childhood Respiratory Infections." *British Medical Bulletin* 61, no. 1 (March 1, 2002).

Wallace, Mike. "Swine Flu." CBS *60 Minutes*, November 4, 1979.

Walters, Joanna. "America's Opioid Crisis: How Prescription Drugs Sparked a National Trauma." *The Guardian*, October 25, 2017.

Wanzer, Sidney H., et al. "The Physician's Responsibility Toward Hopelessly Ill Patients." *The New England Journal of Medicine* (March 30, 1989).

Watanabe, Myrna. "AIDS 20 Years Later." *The Scientist*, June 11, 2001.

Watkins, Elizabeth Siegel. "How the Pill Became a Lifestyle Drug: The Pharmaceutical Industry and Birth Control in the United States Since 1960." *American Journal of Public Health* 102, no. 8 (August 2012): 1462–72.

Watson, Bruce. "The Poison Squad: An Incredible History." *Esquire*, June 27, 2013.

Webster, L. R., and P. G. Fine. "Approaches to Improve Pain Relief While Minimizing Opioid Abuse Liability." *The Journal of Pain* 11, no. 7 (2010): 602–11.

Weinberg, Alvin M. "Impact of Large Scale Science on the United States." *Science* 134, no. 3473 (July 21, 1961).

Weinstein, Louis. "The Spontaneous Occurrence of New Bacterial Infections during the Course of Treatment with Streptomycin or Penicillin." *American Journal of Medical Science* 214 (1947).

Weisberger, Bernard A. "Doctor Wiley and His Poison Squad." *American Heritage* 47, no. 1 (February/March 1996).

Weissman, D., and David J. Haddox. "Opioid Pseudoaddiction—an Iatrogenic Syndrome." *Pain* 36, no. 3 (March 1989).

White, G. C. "Hemophilia: An Amazing 35-Year Journey from the Depths of HIV to the Threshold of Cure." *Transactions of the American Clinical and Climatological Association* 121 (2010): 61–73; discussion S74–5.

Whitebread, Charles. "The History of Non-Medical Use of Drugs in the United States." *Journal of Cognitive Liberties* (Fall 2000).

Whyte, Liz Essley, Geoff Mulvihill, and Ben Wieder. "Politics of Pain: Drugmakers Fought State Opioid Limits Amid Crisis," part 1 of 1. The Center for Public Integrity, copublished with The Associated Press, September 18, 2016.

Winn, Thomas J. "The Antibiotics Market." *Drug and Cosmetic Industry* 67 (1950).

Winslow, Charles-Edward A. "The Conquest of Epidemic Diseases: A Chapter in the History of Ideas." (Princeton, NJ: Princeton University Press, 1943).

Wirtschafter, Jonathan Dine. "The Genesis and Impact of the Medical Lobby: 1898–1906." *Journal of the History of Medicine and Allied Sciences* 13, no. 1 (January 1958).

Wistrand-Yuen, Erik, et al. "Evolution of High-Level Resistance during Low-Level Antibiotic Exposure." *Nature Communications* 9, no. 1 (2018).

Wolfram, Charles W. "The Antibiotics Class Actions." *American Bar Foundation Research Journal* 1, no. 1 (1976): 251–363.

Wong, Stacy. "Thrust Under Microscope: Stamford Drug Company's Low Profile Shattered by Controversy over Abuse of Painkiller OxyContin." *Hartford Courant* (New Haven, CT), September 2, 2001.

Wood, Donna. "The Strategic Use of Public Policy: Business Support for the 1906 Food and Drug Act." *The Business History Review* 59, no. 3 (Autumn 1985).

Worley, John K. "Problems of Compliance with the Drug Amendments of 1962." *The Business Lawyer* 19, no. 1 (1963).

Worobey, M., et al. "Direct Evidence of Extensive Diversity of HIV-1 in Kinshasa by 1960." *Nature* 455, no. 7213 (2008): 661–64.

Yasmin, Seema, and Madhusree Mukerjee. "The Dengue Debacle." *Scientific American*, April 2019.

Young, James Harvey, and George Griffenhagen. "Old English Patent Medicines in America." *Chemist and Druggist* (London), June 29, 1957.

Yuli, Yang. "U.S. Doctor's Generosity to China." *Beijing Review*, May 13–19, 1992.

Zajac, V. "Evolutionary View of the AIDS Process." *The Journal of International Medical Research* 46, no. 10 (2018): 4032–38.

Zhang, Sarah. "The One-Paragraph Letter from 1980 That Fueled the Opioid Crisis." *The Atlantic*, June 2, 2017.

Zhu, T., B. Korber, A. Nahmias, E. Hooper. P. M. Sharp, and D. D. Ho. "An African HIV-1 Sequence from 1959 and Implications for the Origin of the Epidemic." *Nature* 391, no. 6667 (February 1998): 594–97.

Ziporyn, Terra. "The Food and Drug Administration: How 'Those Regulations' Came to Be." *Journal of the American Medical Association* 254 (1985).

Government Hearings and Publications

Administered Drug Prices: Report of the Committee on the Judiciary, Subcommittee on Antitrust and Monopoly, pursuant to S. Red. 52, to Study the Antitrust Laws of the United States and Their Interpretation, Study of the Administered Prices in the Drug Industry. 87th Cong., 1st sess. (Washington, D.C.: U.S. Government Printing Office, 1961).

Administered Prices Hearings before the Subcommittee on Antitrust and Monopoly of the Committee on the Judiciary, U.S. Senate, 86th Cong., 2nd sess., part 23 (Washington, D.C.: U.S. Government Printing Office, 1957).

Alcohol, Drug Abuse, and Mental Health Administration. National Institute on Drug Abuse Division of Research.

Benzodiazepines: A Review of Research Results. Ed. oversight Stephen I. Szara and Jacqueline P. Ludford. National Institute on Drug Abuse, NIDA Research Monograph 33 A RAUS Review Report, Department of Health and Human Services Public Health Service.

Biomedical Politics. Division of Health Sciences Policy Committee to Study Biomedical Decision Making, Institute of Medicine. (Washington, D.C.: The National Academies Press, 1991).

Decisions of Courts in Cases under the Federal Food and Drugs Act. Full text, vol.1 (Washington, D.C.: U.S. Government Printing Office, 1934).

Economic Report on Antibiotics Manufacture. Federal Trade Commission. (Washington, DC: U.S. Government Printing Office, 1958).

Evaluating the Propriety and Adequacy of the Oxy-Contin Criminal Settlement. Hearing Before the Committee on the Judiciary, U.S. Senate, 110th Cong., 1st sess. (July 31, 2007). (Washington, D.C.: U.S. Government Printing Office, 2008).

"Examination of the Pharmaceutical Industry, 1973–74." Committee on Labor and

Public Welfare. *Hearings Before the Subcommittee on Health*, 93rd Cong., 1st and 2nd sess., 1973–1974, part 3.

"Foods and Food Adulterants: Dairy Products," vol. 1, no. 13, U.S. Department of Agriculture, Division of Chemistry (Washington, D.C.: Government Printing Office, 1887).

"Foods and Food Adulterants: Spices and Condiments," vol. 2, no. 13, U.S. Department of Agriculture, Division of Chemistry (Washington, D.C.: U.S. Government Printing Office, 1887).

"Foods and Food Adulterants: Fermented Alcoholic Beverages, Malt Liquors, Wine, and Cider," vol. 3, no. 13, U.S. Department of Agriculture, Division of Chemistry (Washington, D.C.: U.S. Government Printing Office, 1887).

"Foods and Food Adulterants: Lard and Lard Adulteration," vol. 4, no. 13, U.S. Department of Agriculture, Division of Chemistry (Washington, D.C.: U.S. Government Printing Office, 1889).

"Foods and Food Adulterants: Baking Powder," vol. 5, no. 13, U.S. Department of Agriculture, Division of Chemistry (Washington, D.C.: U.S. Government Printing Office, 1889).

"Foods and Food Adulterants: Sugar, Molasses and Sirup, Confections, Honey and Beeswax," vol. 6, no. 13, U.S. Department of Agriculture, Division of Chemistry (Washington, D.C.: U.S. Government Printing Office, 1892).

"Foods and Food Adulterants: Tea, Coffee, and Cocoa Preparations," vol. 7, no. 13, U.S. Department of Agriculture, Division of Chemistry (Washington, D.C.: U.S. Government Printing Office, 1892).

"Foods and Food Adulterants: Canned Vegetables," vol. 8, no. 13, U.S. Department of Agriculture, Division of Chemistry (Washington, D.C.: U.S. Government Printing Office, 1893).

"Foods and Food Adulterants: Cereals and Cereal Products," vol. 9, no. 13, U.S. Department of Agriculture, Division of Chemistry (Washington, D.C.: U.S. Government Printing Office, 1898).

"Foods and Food Adulterants: Preserved Meats," vol. 10, no. 13, U.S. Department of Agriculture, Division of Chemistry (Washington, D.C.: U.S. Government Printing Office, 1902).

"Foods and Food Control," (W. D. Bigelow, chief, Division of Foods), U.S. Department of Agriculture, Bureau of Chemistry, revised to July 1, 1905 (Washington, D.C.: U.S. Government Printing Office, 1905).

Freer, Robert E., chairman, Federal Trade Commission, "Truth in Advertising (with Specific Relation to the Broadcasting Industry)," talk before the Radio Executives Club of New York, November 20, 1944.

Hearings Before the Committee on Interstate and Foreign Commerce of the House of Representatives on the Pure-Food Bills H.R. 3044, 4527, 7018, 12071, 13086, 13853, and 13859, for Preventing the Adulteration, Misbranding, and Imitation of Foods, Beverages, Candies, Drugs, and Condiments in the District of Columbia and the Territories, and for Regulating Interstate Traffic Therein, and for Other Purposes, 59th Cong., 1st sess., House Committee on Interstate and Foreign Commerce (Washington, D.C.: U.S. Government Printing Office, January 1, 1906).

Hussey, H. H. *Statement of the American Medical Association Re: S.1552*, 87th Cong. Drug Industry Antitrust Act. *JAMA* 177, no. 3 (1961): 190–95.

"Influence of Food Preservatives and Artificial Colors on Digestion and Health: Boric Acid and Borax," vol. 1, no. 84, U.S. Department of Agriculture, Division of Chemistry (Washington, D.C.: U.S. Government Printing Office, 1904).

"Influence of Food Preservatives and Artificial Colors on Digestion and Health: Boric Salicylic Acid and Salicylates," vol. 2, no. 84, U.S. Department of Agriculture, Division of Chemistry (Washington, D.C.: U.S. Government Printing Office, 1906).

"Influence of Food Preservatives and Artificial Colors on Digestion and Health: Sulphurous Acid and Sulphites," vol. 3, no. 84, U.S. Department of Agriculture, Division of Chemistry (Washington, D.C.: U.S. Government Printing Office, 1907).

"Influence of Food Preservatives and Artificial Colors on Digestion and Health: Benzoic Acid and Benzoates," vol. 4, no. 84, U.S. Department of Agriculture, Division of Chemistry (Washington, D.C.: U.S. Government Printing Office, 1908).

"Influence of Food Preservatives and Artificial Colors on Digestion and Health: Formaldehyde," vol. 5, no. 84, U.S. Department of Agriculture, Division of Chemistry (Washington, D.C.: U.S. Government Printing Office, 1908).

Halcion: An Independent Assessment of Safety and Efficacy Data. Institute of Medicine (US) Committee on Halcion: An Assessment of Data Adequacy and Confidence. (Washington, D.C.: National Academies Press, 1997).

"Incentives and Focus in University and Industrial Research: The Case of Synthetic Insulin". Institute of Medicine (US) Committee on Technological Innovation in Medicine; N. Rosenberg, A. C. Gelijns, and H. Dawkins, eds. *Sources of Medical Technology: Universities and Industry* (Washington, DC: National Academies Press, 1995). 7,

Meyers, E. B., ed. *Journal of Proceedings of the Seventh Annual Convention of the National Association of State Dairy and Food Departments,* vol. 7 (Washington, D.C.: State Dairy and Food Departments, January 1, 1903).

"Prescription Drugs: Oxy-Contin Abuse and Diversion and Efforts to Address the Problem," GAO-04-110 (Washington, DC: General Accounting Office, December 2003).

"Pulse Check. Trends in Drug Abuse. January-June 2001 Reporting Period. Special Topic: Synthetic Opioids." (Washington, D.C.: Office of National Drug Control Policy, 2001).

Pure Food Legislation: Hearings Before the Committee on Interstate and Foreign Commerce of the House of Representatives on Bills H.R. 3109, 12348, 9352, 276 and 4342, Poviding [sic] Against the Adulteration or Misbranding of Foods, Beverages, Drugs, Etc., in the District of Columbia and the Territories, and for Regulating Interstate Traffic in Such Products. (Washington, D.C.: U.S. Government Printing Office, January 1, 1902).

"Vaccine Supply and Innovation." National Research Council (US) Division of Health Promotion and Disease Prevention. *Liability for the Production and Sale of Vaccines.* (Washington, D.C.: National Academies Press, 1985), 6.

Private Papers and Archival Collections

A. H. Robins Company, Virginia Museum of History & Culture, 1885–2004 (Mss3 R5535a FA2), Virginia Historical Society, Richmond, VA.

American Medical Association, Archives and Manuscripts Division, Chicago, IL.

Bonita, John. Management of Pain and Oral History, History of Pain Collection, University of California at Los Angeles, CA.

Burroughs-Wellcome Papers. Wellcome Library for the History of Medicine, London, England.

The Collection of Louis Tompkins Wright Papers. 1879, 1891–1997, Center for the History of Medicine, Francis A. Countway Library of Medicine, Boston, MA.

Drug Efficacy Study records. National Academy of Sciences Archives, Washington, DC.

Drug Industry Digital Archive. Archives and Special Collections, University of California, San Francisco, Library.

Duggar, Dorothy. "Our Lineage." Thirteen-page typewritten document about Duggar's recollections, and details about her grandparents, Dr. Reuben Henry Duggar and Margaret Louisa Minge. Undated, collection of author.

Finland, Maxwell. Papers. Archives and Special Collections, Countway Medical Library, Harvard Medical School, Boston, MA.

Guide to the Communist Party of the United States of America Records. TAM.132, Tamiment Library and Robert F. Wagner Labor Archive, Elmer Holmes Bobst Library, New York, NY.

Kefauver, Estes. Papers. Hoskins Special Collections Library, University of Tennessee, Knoxville, TN.

Lasagna, Louis C. Papers. Department of Rare Books, Special Collections and Preservation, Rush Rhees Library, University of Rochester, NY.

Martí-Ibáñez, Félix. Papers. Yale University Archives, New Haven, CT.

Mayo Foundation History of Medicine Library, Mayo Clinic, Rochester, MI.

Murti, Kasturi Suryanarayana. Transcript of interview by S. P. K. Gupta in Kakinada, India, August 1954; collection of author.

Parke-Davis Regulatory Affairs Office and Company Library, Ann Arbor, MI.

Scherer, F. M. "The F.T.C., Oligopoly, and Shared Monopoly." Faculty Research Working Paper Series, Harvard Kennedy School, Boston, MA, September 2013.

Upjohn Company records, Kalamazoo Public Library, Kalamazoo, MN.

Government Collections

FDA Library, U.S. Food and Drug Administration, Rockville, MD.

Florey, Howard Walter. Catalog of Papers. "Howard Walter Florey, Baron Florey of Adelaide Pathologist (1898–1968)." Royal Society, London.

Goddard, James L. Papers. History of Medicine Division of the National Library of Medicine, Bethesda, MD.

Harvey Washington Wiley Papers, Library of Congress Manuscript Division, Washington, DC.

John C. Liebeskind History of Pain Collection, History & Special Collections, UCLA Louise M. Darling Biomedical Library, Los Angeles, CA.

Letterbrooks, General Correspondence, Bureau of Chemistry, National Archives.

National Archives and Records Administration. Washington, D.C., and College Park, MD, Records of the FDA, RG 88.

———. Records of the Secretary of Agriculture, RG 16.

———. Committee on Manufactures, Records of the Senate, RG 46.

———. Records of the National Institutes of Health, RG 433.

National Archives of the United Kingdom. Records of the Committee on the Safety of Drugs, Kew, London, UK.

Oral History Collection for the FDA, History of Medicine Division, and Oral History Collection, National Institutes of Health, Historical Office, both at the National Library of Medicine, Bethesda, MD.

Records of the U.S. Department of Health, Education and Welfare (partial). John F. Kennedy Presidential Library, Boston, MA.

Swine Flu, James M. Cannon Files, Gerald R. Ford Presidential Library, University of Michigan, Ann Arbor, MI.

Welch, Dr. Henry. FDA Materials Correspondence (10 of 10), RG 46, National Archives.

Wiley, Anna Kelton. Papers. Coolidge-Consumerism Collection, Manuscript Division, Library of Congress, Washington, D.C.

Wiley, Harvey Washington. Papers. Library of Congress Manuscript Division, Washington, D.C.

Trial Transcripts, Proceedings, Hearings

Administered Prices: Drugs, Report of the Committee on the Judiciary, Subcommittee on Antitrust and Monopoly, 87th Cong., 1st sess. (Washington, D.C.: U.S. Government Printing Office, 1961).

American Cyanamid Company, Petitioner, v. Elliot L. Richardson, Secretary of Health, Education and Welfare, et al., Respondents, 456 F.2d 509, No. 71-1388, United States Court of Appeals, First Circuit, Heard December 14, 1971, Decided December 16, 1971.

Antibiotic Resistance Threats in the United States, CDC (Washington, D.C.: U.S. Government Printing Office, 2013).

Biotechnology Law Report 24, no. 6, Purdue Pharma L. P., The Purdue Frederick Company, The P. F. Laboratories, Inc., and *The Purdue Pharma Company and Euro-Celtique S.A. v. Endo Pharmaceuticals Inc. and Endo Pharmaceuticals Holdings Inc.* (04-1189, 04-1347, 04-1357). Published online: December 8, 2005.

Carter-Wallace, Inc., Petitioner, v. John W. Gardner, Secretary of Health, Education, and Welfare, and James L. Goddard, Commissioner of Food and Drugs, Respondents, 417 F.2d 1086 (4th Cir. 1969), U.S. Court of Appeals for the Fourth Circuit—417 F.2d 1086 (4th Cir. 1969). Argued October 31, 1968. Decided November 4, 1969.

"Circulation of Antibiotics: Journeys of Drug Standards, 1930–1970." Papers presented from June 16–18, 2009, Madrid, Spain. European Science Foundation, Centro de Ciencias Humanas y Sociales Consejo Superior de Investigaciones Científicas (CSIC). Romero, Ana Christoph Gradmann, and Maria Santemases, eds. (Oslo, Norway, May 2010).

"Competitive Problems of the Drug Industry, Summary and Analysis." Subcommittee on Monopoly, Prepared by the Congressional Research Service, Select Committee on Small Business, 90th and 91st Cong. (Washington, D.C.: Library of Congress, November 1972).

"The Competitive Status of the U.S. Pharmaceutical Industry: The Influences of Technology in Determining International Industrial Competitive Advantage." Edwards, Charles C., chairman.

Control of Psychotoxic Drugs: Hearing Before the Subcommittee on Health of the Committee on Labor and Public Welfare, U.S. Senate, 88th Cong., 2nd sess., on S. 2628, a bill to protect the public health (August 3, 1964).

"Declaration of Montréal: Declaration That Access to Pain Management Is a Fundamental Human Right." International Pain Summit of the International Association for the Study of Pain. *Journal of Pain and Palliative Care Pharmacotherapy* 25, no. 1 (2011): 29–31.

Department of Health, Education, and Welfare, FDA. "Report Including Recommended Findings and Conclusions re: Potential for Abuse of the Drugs Librium and Val-ium." April 7, 1967, Manufacturers Files No. AF14–324, re Hoffmann-La Roche, Federal Drug Administration History Office.

Final accounting by the executors of the decedent's estate, Matter of Sackler, 0249220/2007 (September 28, 2007).

Follow the Money: Pharmaceutical Manufacturer Payments and Opioid Prescribing Patterns in New York State. New York State Health Foundation Publication, June 2018.

GAO report number GAO-03–177, "Prescription Drugs: FDA Oversight of Direct-to-Consumer Advertising Has Limitations." Released December 04, 2002.

Generic Drug Enforcement and Approval Process: Hearings before the Subcommittee on Oversight and Investigations of the Committee on Energy and Commerce, House of Representatives, 102nd Cong., 1st sess., March 7 and June 5, 1991.

Hoffmann-La Roche, Inc., Petitioner, v. Richard G. Kleindienst, Attorney General of the United States, and John E. Ingersoll, Director, Bureau of Narcotics and Dangerous Drugs, United States Department of Justice, Respondents, 478 F.2d 1 (3d Cir. 1973), U.S. Court of Appeals for the Third Circuit—478 F.2d 1 (3d Cir. 1973), Argued June 25, 1971. Decided March 28, 1973, as Amended July 3, 1973.

Impact of Direct-to-Consumer Drug Advertising on Seniors' Health and Health-Care Costs: Hearing before the Special Committee on Aging, United States Senate, 109th Cong., 1st sess., Washington, D.C., September 25, 2004.

Institute of Medicine (US) Forum on Microbial Threats. "Microbial Evolution and Co-Adaptation: A Tribute to the Life and Scientific Legacies of Joshua Lederberg." Workshop Summary. (Washington, DC: National Academies Press, 2009).

Lacy Glenn Thomas, Rapporteur, Prepared by the Pharmaceutical Panel, Committee on Technology and International Economic and Trade Issues, Office of the Foreign Secretary, National Academy of Engineering Commission on Engineering and Technical Systems, National Research Council (Washington, D.C.: National Academies Press, 1983).

Medina, Jose L., and Seymour Diamond. "Drug Dependency in Patients with Chronic Headaches." *Headache,* March 1977.

Memoranda of Philip and Mary Jane Keeney, "FBI Silvermaster File 65–56402," serial 2127; Testimony of Philip O. Keeney and Mary Jane Keeney and Statement Regarding Their Background: Hearings. U.S. House Committee on

Un-American Activities (Washington, D.C.: U.S. Government Printing Office, 1949).

Memorandum from Dr. A. M. Sackler to Dr. Félix Martí-Ibáñez, December 14, 1956, "Subj: Geography and World Patterns of Schizophrenia and Other Mental Illnesses," MS 1235, Box 2, Folder "S" 1957, Papers of Félix Martí-Ibáñez, Yale University, Manuscripts and Archives, New Haven, CT.

Napp Pharmaceutical Holdings Limited and Subsidiaries v. Director General of Fair Trading, In the Competition Commission, Appeal Tribunal, Before Sir Christopher Bellamy, Professor Peter Grinyer, and Harry Colgate, New Court, London, Case No 1001/1/01, January 15, 2002.

Plea Agreement dated November 1, 2002, between the Office of the Attorney General, Department of Legal Affairs, State of Florida, and Purdue Pharma L. P. and Purdue Frederick Company, 9 pages, and Exhibits A and B and a 3-page amendment dated April 25, 2003.

"Prescription Drug Advertising to Consumers," Staff Report Prepared for the Use of the Subcommittee on Oversight and Investigations of the Committee on Energy and Commerce," House of Representatives, 98th Cong., 2nd sess. (Washington, D.C.: U.S. Government Printing Office, September 1984).

"Prescription Drugs: OxyContin Abuse and Diversion Efforts to Address the Problem." General Accounting Office. (Washington, D.C.: U.S. Government Printing Office, December 2003).

Present Status of Competition in the Pharmaceutical Industry, Part 30 of the Competitive Problems in the Drug Industry Hearings Before Subcommittee on Monopoly and Anticompetitive Activities of the Select Committee on Small Business, United States Senate, 94th Cong., 2nd sess., April 28, May 10 and 24, 1976.

Proceedings of the Seventh Annual Convention of the National Association of State Dairy and Food Departments Held at St. Paul, Minnesota, Containing Proceedings of the Seventh Annual Convention. The Dairy and Food Laws of All the States and Territories with State and United States Supreme Court Decisions Thereon. Also Rulings and Tables of Standards Adopted by the State and Government Commissions. Published Under the Personal Direction of the National Association of State Dairy and Food Departments H. B. Meyers, Editor and Compiler, 1903.

Public Hearings on Noise Abatement and Control, vol. VII—Physiological and Psychological Effects, October 28–29, 1971, conducted by the Office of Noise Abatement and Control, January 1, 1972.

"The Rate of Addiction by Pain Patients Who Are Treated by Doctors, Is Much Less Than 1 Percent." "I Got My Life Back." Purdue Pharma L. P., video presentation by Dr. Alan Spanos, 1998.

Records of the U.S. Senate, Committee on the Judiciary, Subcommittee on Antitrust and Monopoly, 86th and 87th Cong., RG 46.15, sub 13.115, NARA.

See Matter of Estate of Sackler, 149 Misc.2d 734, 564 N.Y.S.2d 977, 980 (N.Y. Sur. Ct. 1990); Matter of Sackler, (September 28, 2007), 2007 NY Slip Op 33226(U) (N.Y. Misc. 2007).

OxyContin: Balancing Risks and Benefits. Hearing of the Committee on Health, Education, Labor, and Pensions, United States Senate, 107th Cong., 2nd sess., "On Examining the Effects of the Painkiller OxyContin, Focusing on Federal, State and Local Efforts to Decrease Abuse and Misuse of This Product While

Assuring Availability for Patients Who Suffer Daily from Chronic Moderate to Severe Pain," February 12, 2002. Printed for the use of the Committee on Health, Education, Labor, and Pensions, 77–770, U.S. Government Printing Office.

Senate Judiciary Subcommittee on Antitrust and Monopoly Hearings, Part 6, Advertising Provisions, January 30, 1962.

"Subcommittee on Reorganization and International Organizations of the Committee on Government Operations, U.S. Senate, 88th Cong., 1st sess., Agency Coordination Study, (Pursuant to S. Res. 27, 88th Cong., as Amended)," Review of Cooperation on Drug Policies Among the Food and Drug Administration, National Institutes of Health, Veterans' Administration, and Other Agencies, March 20-June 26, 1963; *Hearings Before Subcommittee on Monopoly and Anti-competitive Activities of the Select Committee on Small Business,* U.S. Senate, 90th through 93rd Cong., 1967–1975.

United States Attorney's Office Western District of Virginia [news release]. Available at: http://www.dodig.osd.mil/IGInformation/IGInformationReleases/prudue_frederick_1.pdf.

Use and Misuse of Benzodiazepines: Hearing Before the Subcommittee on Health and Scientific Research of the Committee on Labor and Human Resources, United States Senate, 96th Cong., 1st sess., September 10, 1979.

U.S. Congress: Senate: Treatment and Rehabilitation of Juvenile Drug Addicts. Subcommittee to Investigate Juvenile Delinquency, Committee on the Judiciary. Hearings, pursuant to S.R. 173 and S.R. 303, December 1956, 984: 2, Washington, D.C., 1957.

U.S. House, Committee on Government Operations, Subcommittee on Legal and Marketing Affairs (1958).

U.S. Senate, Committee on Government Operations, Subcommittee on Reorganization and International Organizations, Interagency Coordination in Drug Research and Regulation (Washington, D.C.: U.S. Government Printing Office, 1964), 1.

U.S. v. Chas. Pfizer & Co., et al. Defendants, United States District Court, Southern District New York, 245 F. Supp. 801 (1965), September 9, 1965.

U.S. v. Chas. Pfizer & Co., et al. Defendants, United States District Court, Southern District New York, 367 F. Supp. 91 (1973), No. 61 Cr. 772, November 30, 1973.

WHO Expert Committee on Addiction-Producing Drugs. Thirteenth report. Geneva, World Health Organization, 1964 (WHO Technical Report Series, No. 273); The ICD-10 Classification of Mental and Behavioral Disorders. Clinical Descriptions and Diagnostic Guidelines. Geneva, World Health Organization, 1992; WHO Expert Committee on Drug Dependence. Twenty-Eighth report. Geneva, World Health Organization, 1993 (WHO Technical Report Series, No. 836).

World Health Organization, International Task Force on World Health Manpower & Symposium on Advances in the Drug Therapy of Mental Illness (November 21–23, 1973, Geneva).

Unpublished Manuscripts and Papers

Mc-Crea, Frances B. "Politics and Medicine in the Estrogen Replacement Controversy: A Comparative Analysis of the United States and Great Britain." Master's Thesis, Graduate College of Western Michigan University, August 1981.

Skolek Perez, Marianne. "You Messed with the Wrong Mother: One Mother's 17-Year Personal Account Exposing Purdue Pharma, Maker of Oxy-Contin in Fueling the 'Manufactured' Opioid Epidemic Crippling the U.S." Unpublished manuscript last modified October 2019. Cited here by courtesy of the author.

NOTES

Preface

1. Katherine A. Helm, "Protecting Public Health from Outside the Physician's Office: A Century of FDA Regulation from Drug Safety Labeling to Off-Label Drug Promotion," *Fordham Intellectual Property, Media and Entertainment Law Journal*, volume 18, number 1, 2007, Article 9, 142.

Chapter 1: Patient Zero

1. As for increased risks of dehydration among the elderly that require hospitalization, see generally J.M. Schols et al., "Preventing and Treating Dehydration in the Elderly During Periods of Illness and Warm Weather," *Journal of Nutrition, Health & Aging*, volume 13, number 2, 2009.
2. Pashtana Usufzy, "'Superbug' Resistant to All Available Antibiotics Killed Elderly Northern Nevada Woman," *Las Vegas Review Journal*, January 12, 2017.
3. It is New Delhi Metallo-beta-lactamase-1, abbreviated usually to NDM-1. Centers for Disease Control and Prevention, National Nosocomial Infections Surveillance (NNIS) system report, data summary from January 1992–June 2001, *American Journal of Infection Control* 2001; 29:404–21. See also generally Monte Morin and Eryn Brown, "Superbug: What It Is, How It Spreads, What You Can Do," *Los Angeles Times*, February 10, 2015.
4. Helen Branswell, "A Nevada Woman Dies of a Superbug Resistant to Every Available Antibiotic in the US," *STAT*, January 12, 2017.
5. See generally Patricia A. Bradford et al., "Emergence of Carbapenem-Resistant *Klebsiella* Species Possessing the Class A Carbapenem-Hydrolyzing KPC-2 and Inhibitor-Resistant TEM-30 ß-Lactamases in New York City," *Clinical Infectious Diseases* (CID) 2004:39 (1 July); A. Hossain et al., "First report of plasmid-encoded carbapenem hydrolyzing enzyme KPC-2 in Enterobacter cloacae [C1–264]" in Program and abstracts of the 43rd Interscience Conference on Antimicrobial Agents and Chemotherapy (Chicago) (Washington, D.C.: American Society for Microbiology, 2003), 75.
6. Ari Frenkel and Paul Cook, "Current Issues in Approaches to Antimicrobial Resistance," *Gastroenterology & Endoscopy News*, volume 65, number 12, December 31, 2014, 48–53.
7. See generally J.J. Yan et al., "Outbreak of infection with multidrug-resistant Kleb-

siella pneumoniae carrying bla (IMP-8) in a university medical center in Taiwan," *Journal of Clinical Microbiology* 2001: 39:4433–39.

8. Marie Abdallah et al., "Rise and fall of KPC-producing Klebsiella pneumoniae in New York City," *Journal of Antimicrobial Chemotherapy* 2016, June 26, 1093–97; D. Landman et al., "Transmission of carbapenem-resistant pathogens in New York City hospitals: progress and frustration," *Journal of Antimicrobial Chemotherapy* 2012; 67: 1427–31. See generally Morin and Brown, "Superbug."
9. According to Alexander Kallen, a CDC doctor, that sample from Nevada "was tested against everything that's available in the United States," and was "not effective." Branswell, "A Nevada Woman Dies Of A Superbug." See also Lei Chen, senior epidemiologist with Washoe County Health District quoted in Branswell, "It was my first time to see a [resistance] pattern in our area."
10. The peak years for deaths: car accidents, 1972; gun violence, 1993; HIV/AIDS, 1995.
11. "Drug Overdose Death Data," Centers for Disease Control and Prevention, https://www.cdc.gov/drugoverdose/data/statedeaths.html. See generally "Analysis of Overdose Deaths in Pennsylvania, 2016," Joint Intelligence Report, between the Drug Enforcement Administration and the University of Pittsburgh.
12. Joel Achenbach, "Once 'so Mayberry,' a town struggles with opioid epidemic," *Washington Post,* December 30, 2016, 1.
13. Penicillin was the first milestone drug but there were earlier important discoveries that were not cures but treatments. Those include smallpox vaccine (1796), the antiseptic carbolic acid (1860), the antipyretic phenazone (1884), hypnotic barbiturate Veronal (1903), syphilis treatment arsphenamine (1911), and the antibacterial sulfamidochrysoidine (1935).

Chapter 2: The Poison Squad

1. Fran Hawthorne, *Inside the FDA: The Business and Policies Behind the Drugs We Take and Food We Eat* (New York: John Wiley & Sons, 2015), Kindle Edition, 925–943 of 7181.
2. When Friedrich Sertürner isolated the alkaloid morphine he tested it on himself and his dogs. Joseph Louis Gay-Lussac was the French chemist who realized the importance of the discovery. He named it morphine, in accord with a widespread practice of using the suffix "ine" for drugs. There were several suffixes that evolved over time by drug category; antivirals get the suffix "vir," "illin" for most antibiotics, "arbital" for barbiturates, etc. Sertürner's work led in the following century to new alkaloids such as atropine, quinine, codeine, and cocaine. A. P. Klockgether-Radke, "F. W. Sertürner und die Entdeckung des Morphins," *Anästhesiol Intensivmed Notfallmed Schmerzther* 2002; 37(5): 244–49.
3. Bayer made dyes from coal tar. Within a decade, he patented low-cost technologies to mass-produce them. After he discovered they contained antiseptic qualities, he remarketed them as pharmaceuticals. Many German drug companies began as unintended offshoots of the chemical industry. See Erik Verg, with Gottfried Plumpe and Heinz Schultheis, *Milestones: The Bayer Story, 1863–1988* (Leverkusen, Germany: Bayer AG, 1988), 14–29; Christopher Kobrak, "Politics, Corporate Governance, and the Dynamics of German Managerial Innovation: Schering AG between the Wars," *Enterprise & Society* 3, no. 3 (2002): 429–61.
4. They were twenty-five-year-old Charles Pfizer and twenty-eight-year-old Charles

Erhart. Joseph G. Lombardino, "A Brief History Of Pfizer Central Research," *Bull. Hist. Chem.*, Vol. 25, Number 1 (2000), 10–15. See also Jeffrey L. Rodengen, *The Legend of Pfizer* (Fort Lauderdale, FL: Write Stuff Syndicate, 1999), 13.

5. J. Liebenau, *Medical Science and Medical Industry: The Formation of the American Pharmaceutical Industry* (London: MacMillan, 1987), 8–9.
6. Business history and timeline of Wyeth at http://www.fundinguniverse.com/company-histories/wyeth-history/.
7. See generally Roscoe Collins Clark, *Three Score Years and Ten: A Narrative of the First Seventy Years of Eli Lilly and Company, 1876–1946* (New York: Lakeside Press, R. R. Donnelly & Sons, 1946).
8. Gilbert Macdonald, *In Pursuit of Excellence: One Hundred Years Wellcome, 1880–1980* (London: Wellcome Foundation, 1980).
9. Thomas D. Brock, *Robert Koch: A Life in Medicine and Bacteriology* (Washington, D.C.: ASM Press, 1999).
10. J. N. Hayes, *Epidemics and Pandemics: Their Impacts on Human History* (Santa Barbara, CA: ABC-CLIO, 2005), 216–19.
11. Besides being in the dark about diseases and how they spread, there was little understanding in science and medicine of what was necessary for good health. Good nutrition was an unexplored field. The word "vitamin" was not coined until 1911. "History Timeline Transcript, Yellow Fever: History, Epidemiology, and Vaccination Information, Department of Health and Human Services," Centers for Disease Control and Prevention, Office of Surveillance, Epidemiology, and Laboratory Services, 2016, 2. See also Hunter A. Dupree, *Science in the Federal Government: A History of Policies and Activities to 1940* (Cambridge, MA: Belknap Press of Harvard, 1957), 269.
12. Ronald Hamowy, "The Early Development of Medical Licensing Laws in the United States, 1875–1900," *Journal of Libertarian Studies* 3 (1979).
13. The German student was Albert Niemann. Also, an Italian neurologist and anthropologist, Paolo Mantegazza, learned about cocaine while traveling in South America. In 1859, he wrote about his experiments with coca leaves and is often credited with popularizing the pure alkaloid Niemann isolated. See Albert Niemann, "Über eine neue organische Base in den Cocablättern," *Archiv der Pharmazie*, 153(2): 129–256, 1860; Paolo Mantegazza, *Sulle Virtù Igieniche e Medicinali della Coca e sugli Alimenti Nervosi in Generale* (On the Hygienic and Medicinal Properties of Coca and on Nervous Nourishment in General), *Annali Universali di Medicina* 167, 1–76, 1859.
14. Dwight Garner, "The Lure of Cocaine, Once Hailed as Cure-All," *New York Times*, July 19, 2011; Paul Vallely, "Drug That Spans the Ages: The History of Cocaine," *Independent* (UK), March 2, 2006.
15. Vallely, "Drug That Spans the Ages."
16. Paul M. Gahlinger, *Illegal Drugs: A Complete Guide to Their History, Chemistry, Use and Abuse* (New York: Plume, 2003), 40.
17. Ronald K. Siegel, "Repeating Cycles of Cocaine Use and Abuse," *Treating Drug Problems: Volume 2: Commissioned Papers on Historical, Institutional, and Economic Contexts of Drug Treatment*, Institute of Medicine, Committee for the Substance Abuse Coverage Study (Washington, D.C.: The National Academies Press, 1992).
18. David F. Musto, "Illicit Price of Cocaine in Two Eras: 1908–14 and 1982–89," *Pharmacy in History* 33, no. 1 (1991): 3–10.

19. Alexander Cockburn and Jeffrey St. Clair, *End Times: The Death of the Fourth Estate (Counterpunch)* (Chico, CA: AK Press, 2006), 141. During World War I, London's Harrods department store sold a leather-bound kit it described as "A Welcome Present for Friends at the Front." It consisted of a vial of powdered cocaine, morphine, syringes and needles. "Drug that Spans the Ages: The History of Cocaine," *Independent*, March 2, 2006.
20. T. Appelboom, "Consumption of Coca in History," *Verh K Acad Geneeskd Belg.*, 53(5):497–505, 1991.
21. See generally *Complete Catalogue of the Products of the Laboratories of Parke, Davis & Company, 1900–1901, 1904–1905, 1907–1908*. For instance, the catalog highlighted 1-ounce solutions in which cocaine was reduced to an injectable liquid. "These solutions will remain sterile and active for an indefinite period—a distinct advantage for those who desire to have a reliable Cocaine Solution always available without the trouble of preparing same in each instance," (511). William Rosen, *Miracle Cure: The Creation of Antibiotics and the Birth of Modern Medicine* (New York: Viking, 2017), 242; and Edward Shorter, *Before Prozac: The Troubled History of Mood Disorders in Psychiatry* (Oxford: Oxford University Press, 2009), Kindle Edition, 262, 276 of 4159.
22. As for Merck's products, see "Chemicals And Drugs Usual In Modern Medical Practice Compiled from the Most Recent Authoritative Sources," *Merck's 1899 Manual of the Materia Medica* (Merck & Co.: New York, 1899).
23. *Squibb's Materia Medica* (Brooklyn: E. R. Squibb & Sons, 1900).
24. "Proprietary Association of America," *California State Journal of Medicine*, January 1906, 5, in PubMed Central at U.S. National Library of Medicine, National Institutes of Health. See also "Hearings Before the Committee on Interstate and Foreign Commerce of the House of Representatives on the Pure-Food Bills H.R. 3044, 4527, 7018, 12071, 13086, 13853, and 13859, for Preventing the Adulteration, Misbranding, and Imitation of Foods, Beverages, Candies, Drugs, and Condiments in the District of Columbia and the Territories, and for Regulating Interstate Traffic Therein, and for Other Purposes," U.S. Congress (Washington, D.C.: Government Printing Office, 1906).
25. Their name came from a seventeenth-century practice by which British royals issued "letters patent," endorsements, to their favorite nostrums. English settlers brought the trade to the colonies. The shortcomings in science and medicine opened the door to the patent drug boom. Historian Richard Shryock described it as a time when Americans believed in "inalienable rights to life, liberty, and quackery." Liebenau, *Medical Science and Medical Industry*, 35; Shryock, *The Development of Modern Medicine*, 255.
26. Temin, *Taking Your Medicine*, 23.
27. Ibid., 24–27; James Harvey Young, *The Toadstool Millionaires: A Social History of Patent Medicines in America before Federal Regulation* (Princeton, NJ: Princeton University Press, 1961), 82, 226.
28. The price for a testimonial varied widely. Popular local politicians, for instance, usually commanded $5 for a local councilman and up to $50 for a small-town mayor. A British writer who chronicled his 1870s travels in America observed that "one of the first things that strike the stranger as soon as he has landed in the New World: he cannot step a mile into the open country, whether into the fields or along the high roads, without meeting the [nostrum ads] disfigurement." Young, *The Toadstool Millionaires*, 122.

29. Wirtschafter, "The Genesis and Impact of the Medical Lobby," 40; R. G. Eccles, MD, "Radam's Microbe Killer," *Druggists Circular and Chemical Gazette*, volume 33, 1889, 195–96; James Harvey Young, *The Medical Messiahs: A Social History of Health Quackery in 20th Century America* (Princeton, NJ: Princeton University Press, 1967), 28.
30. Pinkham's slogan was "Only a woman can understand a woman's ills." She was famous for personally answering every customer inquiry; the company kept her death a secret and sent handwritten letters with her "signature" until it was exposed by *Collier's* twenty-two years after she had died.
31. William G. Rothstein, *American Physicians in the Nineteenth Century: From Sects to Science* (Baltimore, MD: Johns Hopkins University Press, 1992). According to Rothstein, alcohol, especially whiskey and brandy, was "probably the most important medicinal agent of the second half of the [nineteenth] century." See also Young, *Pure Food*, 115–16.
32. The advertised listing for "Hostetter's Celebrated Stomach Bitters" in the 1867 United States Almanac claimed it did not just "prevent" illness "but [is a] cure."
33. Young, *The Toadstool Millionaires*, 192–93.
34. Most died from whooping cough, scarlet fever, diphtheria, or diarrheal ailments, the last one a result of drinking water in cities that was contaminated with human sewage. Martin J. Blaser, *Missing Microbes: How the Overuse of Antibiotics Is Fueling Our Modern Plagues* (New York: Henry Holt and Company, 2014), 62–63.
35. See a partial list of some infant deaths from Kopp's poisoning at Arthur J. Cramp, *Nostrums and Quackery: Collected Articles on the Nostrum Evil and Quackery*, reprint by the *Journal of the American Medical Association* (Chicago: American Medical Association Press), 1912, 425; "Poisoning by Kopp's Baby Friend," *JAMA*, February 10, 1906, XLVI(6):447–48.
36. See for example *Druggists' Circular*, 33 (1889); also, Young, *The Medical Messiahs*, 28.
37. W. S. Fullerton, "The Objectionable Influence of Proprietary Medicines upon the Young Practitioner," *Journal of the Minnesota State Medical Association and the Northwestern Lancet*, volume 26, October 15, 1906, 446–47.
38. German pharma companies were far ahead of their U.S. counterparts in consistency and standardization. Young, *Pure Food*, 116–18, 120.
39. Eleven doctors at a meeting in Washington, D.C., in 1820 had established the *United States Pharmacopeia*, but it did not include descriptions of the drugs or any guidance about therapeutic applications. Liebenau, *Medical Science and Medical Industry*, 21; Donohue, "A History of Drug Advertising," 664.
40. Julie Donohue, "A History of Drug Advertising: The Evolving Roles of Consumers and Consumer Protection," *Milbank Quarterly*, 2006; 84(4), 664.
41. Ibid., 665.
42. The name Aspirin likely is from the "A" in acetyl chloride, the "spir" in spiraea ulmaria (the plant from which salicylic acid is derived), and "in" was one of the common suffixes for drugs. A widely told story about its name is that Bayer's chief pharmacologist, Heinrich Dreser, a devout Catholic, named it after St. Aspren of Naples, a first-century convert. Dreser mistakenly thought he was the patron saint of headaches. (In fact, that distinction belonged to the sixteenth-century St. Teresa of Avila, herself a migraine sufferer.) Aspirin was developed by a team led by Bayer's chief of pharmaceutical science, Arthur Eichengrün, a scientist with forty-seven patents to his credit. His team had discovered acetamin-

ophen (Tylenol) a year earlier but had mistakenly found it unsafe in lab tests. When Bayer published an official history of Aspirin in 1934, it omitted the Jewish Eichengrün, instead crediting one of his assistants with the discovery. Under the Third Reich, companies like Bayer purged Jews from their labs and executive ranks. Eichengrün, who later survived a wartime concentration camp, appealed in vain to I.G. Farben, Bayer's parent, about the misplaced credit. He died in 1948 without any acknowledgment for his role. In 1999, a Scottish clinical pharmacologist and historian relied on original Bayer laboratory and research reports to reach the now universally accepted conclusion that Eichengrün had in fact developed Aspirin. David B. Green, "This Day in Jewish History 1899: Bayer Patents Aspirin, Will Pretend It Hadn't Been Invented by a Jew," *Haaretz*, March 6, 2016; Walter Sneader, "The Discovery of Heroin," *Lancet*, Vol. 352, Issue 914, 1698.

43. R. Askwith, "How Aspirin Turned Hero," *Sunday Times* (London), September 13, 1998.
44. William Stewart Halsted, one of the physician founders of Johns Hopkins Hospital in 1889, was a morphine addict who continued to do surgery until his death from an overdose in 1922. "Heroin werbt in spanischer Zeitung," Pressemitteilung, 14, November 2011, Koalition gegen BAYER Gefahren (Deutschland). Bayer struck lucrative licensing deals with other small drug companies. Fraser Tablet Company and the Martin H. Smith Company mixed Bayer's Heroin with glycerin and sugar to produce a palatable syrup sold primarily for coughs, asthma, migraines, and pneumonia. As for the German physician addiction rate to morphine, see Eric Hesse, *Narcotics and Drug Addiction*, 41.
45. Hawthorne, *Inside the FDA*, 947 of 7151. Twenty-three states approved food legislation between 1874 and 1895.
46. From 1879 to 1906, almost a hundred bills that addressed some aspect of food or drug purity failed to pass Congress. See Fran Hawthorne, *The Merck Druggernaut: The Inside Story of a Pharmaceutical Giant* (Hoboken, NJ: John Wiley & Sons, 2003), 21.
47. Formed originally as the Division of Chemistry, after July 1901 the department was renamed the Bureau of Chemistry. It became the Food, Drug, and Insecticide Administration in July 1927 and three years later the Food and Drug Administration. The FDA was part of the Department of Agriculture until June 1940, when it was moved under the newly created Federal Security Agency. In April 1953, the FDA was transferred to the Department of Health, Education, and Welfare (HEW). In 1968, it was put under the control of the Public Health Service inside HEW. Finally, in May 1980, the FDA was moved to a new division, the Department of Health and Human Services.
48. Wiley's father was a Campbellite preacher, a movement named after Thomas Campbell and his son Alexander. The Alexanders were Baptist preachers who advocated a strict adherence to the New Testament only and argued that American Christianity needed reformation.
49. Harvey W. Wiley, *An Autobiography* (Indianapolis: The Bobbs-Merrill Company, 1930), 14.
50. Ibid., 50.
51. Ibid., 27, 30.
52. Ibid., 101, 117.
53. Mark Sullivan, *Our Times: The United States 1900–1925, Volume II, America Finding Herself* (New York: Charles Scribner's Sons, 1927), 483–492, 501–4.

54. Wiley, *An Autobiography*, 151.
55. Bruce Watson, "The Poison Squad: An Incredible History," *Esquire*, June 27, 2013; Weisberger, "Doctor Wiley and His Poison Squad"; Michael Robert Patterson, "Harvey Washington Wiley, Corporal, United States Army, Government Official." See also Wiley, *An Autobiography*, 155–58.
56. Some of his colleagues thought those talks were useless since politicians did not fear women since they could not vote. Women got the right to vote in 1920 with the ratification of the Nineteenth Amendment. Weisberger, "Doctor Wiley and His Poison Squad."
57. Wiley, *An Autobiography*, 177.
58. "Foods and Food Adulterants, Dairy Products," No. 13, Vol. 1, U.S. Department of Agriculture, Division of Chemistry (Washington D.C.: Government Printing Office, 1887).
59. Vol. 1, "Dairy Products," 1887; Vol. 2, "Spices and Condiments,"1887; Vol. 3, "Fermented Alcoholic Beverages, Malt Liquors, Wine, and Cider," 1887; Vol. 4, "Lard and Lard Adulteration," 1889; Vol. 5, "Baking Powder," 1889; Vol. 6, "Sugar, Molasses and Sirup, Confections, Honey and Beeswax," 1892; Vol. 7, "Tea, Coffee, and Cocoa Preparations," 1892; Vol. 8, "Canned Vegetables," 1983; Vol. 9, "Cereals and Cereal Products," 1898; Vol. 10, "Preserved Meats," 1902 (Washington, D.C.: Government Printing Office).
60. Deborah Blum, *The Poison Squad: One Chemist's Single-Minded Crusade for Food Safety at the Turn of the Twentieth Century* (New York: Penguin Press, 2018), 59.
61. It is a legacy that many who have studied him and the Pure Food and Drug Act have concluded is accurate. See generally C. C. Regier, "The Struggle for Federal Food and Drugs Legislation," *Law and Contemporary Problems* 1, no. 1 (1933), 6. Also Clayton A. Coppin and Jack High, *The Politics of Purity: Harvey Washington Wiley and the Origins of Federal Food Policy* (Ann Arbor, MI: The University of Michigan Press, 1999), 4, 15, 60–61.
62. "The Man Who Is Leading the Fight for Pure Food," *Washington Times*, November 20, 1904, 5.
63. Ibid. See also a sampling of favorable coverage of Wiley in "Three More Deaths Result from Effects of Infected Antitoxin," *St. Louis Republic*, November 2, 1901, 1; "Vaccination Scare in Philadelphia," *Scranton Tribune* (Scranton, PA), November 19, 1901; "Dr. Wiley's Poison Squad Enlisted from Expert Topers," *St. Louis Republic*, December 6, 1903, 12; "How the Beef Trust Has Poisoned Peoples' Food," *Commoner* (Lincoln, NE), June 8, 1906, 7.
64. "The Man Who Is Leading the Fight for Pure Food," *Washington Times*, November 20, 1904, 5. See also Hunter A. Dupree, *Science in the Federal Government: A History of Policies and Activities to 1940* (Cambridge, MA: Belknap Press of Harvard), 1957, 176–83; chapter 1 in Peter Temin, *Taking Your Medicine: Drug Regulation in the United States* (Cambridge, MA: Harvard University Press, 1980); Anthony Gaughan, "Harvey Wiley, Theodore Roosevelt, and the Federal Regulation of Food and Drugs" (2004 third-year paper, Harvard Law School, Winter 2004), https://dash.harvard.edu/handle/1/8852144. The *New York Sun* called Wiley the "chief janitor and policeman of the people's insides." Sullivan, *Our Times*, 520.
65. He had at least succeeded, as he said, in "forcing congressional leaders to gradually recognize it [pure food legislation] as a serious problem." Wiley, *An Autobiography*, 203; Young, *Pure Food*, 152.

66. Wiley thought the Bible included the first ever study of food served to royals against a diet of only vegetables and water. Young, *Pure Food*, 152.
67. Wiley wanted only men, believing women were not strong enough to be subjected to a diet filled with toxic substances. No volunteer got individual credit for their contribution. Most of their names are still unknown. Watson, "The Poison Squad: An Incredible History."
68. Wiley, *An Autobiography*, 220.
69. Carol Lewis, "The 'Poison Squad' and the Advent of Food and Drug Regulation," *U.S. Food and Drug Administration Consumer Magazine*, November–December 2002. See also for the chef—known only as Perry—Watson, "The Poison Squad: An Incredible History."
70. The reporter was twenty-three-year-old George Rothwell Brown. His daily political column, "Post Scripts," was later syndicated by Hearst newspapers. Watson, "The Poison Squad: An Incredible History." See also Lewis, "The 'Poison Squad' and the Advent of Food and Drug Regulation."
71. Wiley, *An Autobiography*, 225–26.
72. Benzoate is commonly used today as a pesticide. Watson, "The Poison Squad: An Incredible History"; Coppin, *The Politics of Purity*, 55–56. See also Wiley, *An Autobiography*, 204.
73. "Influence of Food Preservatives and Artificial Colors on Digestion and Health," Vol. 1, "Boric Acid and Borax," 1904; Vol. 2, "Salicylic Acid and Salicylates," 1906; Vol. 3, "Sulphurous Acid and Sulphites," 1907; Vol. 4, "Benzoic Acid and Benzoates," 1908; Vol. 5, "Formaldehyde," (Washington, D.C.: U.S. Government Printing Office, 1908).

Chapter 3: Enter the Feds

1. Wiley, *An Autobiography*, 267.
2. Every year from 1876 to 1904, the tax on drinking alcohol provided more than 50 percent of all federal income. See Young, *Pure Food*, 165. The alcohol tax was important because the federal government did not then have the authority to levy an income tax (that power came in 1913 with the passage of the Sixteenth Amendment to the Constitution).
3. Wiley, *An Autobiography*, 205.
4. National Association of State Food and Dairy Officials, *Proceedings of the Annual Convention* (Washington D.C., 1904), 295–97; Coppin and High, *The Politics of Purity*, 70.
5. Wiley, *An Autobiography*, 207.
6. Ibid., 53.
7. Letter from Wiley to James R. Mann, March 19, 1906, Letter Book 180, No. 305; Letters from Wiley to George Simmons, February 20, 1906 and March 2, 1906, Letter Book 178, Nos. 113 and 495; Letter from Wiley to Samuel Adams, Letter Book 179, No. 476, March; Wiley to George Simmons, March 2, 1906, Letter Book 179, No. 476; all in Record Group 97, National Archives and Records Administration (hereafter cited as "NARA").
8. Samuel Hopkins Adams, "The Great American Fraud," consisting of "The Nostrum Evil," October 7, 1905; "Peruna and the Bracers," October 28, 1905; "Liquozone," November 18, 1905; "The Subtle Poisons," December 2, 1905; "Preying on the Incurables," January 13, 1906; "The Fundamental Fakes," February 17, 1906;

"Quacks and Quackery," July 14, 1906; "The Miracle Workers," August 4, 1906; "The Specialist Humbug," September 1, 1906; "The Scavengers," September 22, 1906; all in *Collier's*. As for the amount of federal revenue provided by alcohol between 1870 and 1915, see "1913" at https://inpud.wordpress.com/timeline-of-events-in-the-history-of-drugs/.

9. Adams, "The Great American Fraud," 14. Seven of the twelve articles that appeared before Congress passed the Pure Food and Drug Act the following year.
10. Before the *Collier's* series forced a change, the AMA had focused its lobbying on fighting vivisection bans and encouraging states to adopt uniform admission rules for physicians. The AMA's influential Committee on Medical Legislation had worked on securing federal funds to wage a campaign against malaria and yellow fever, which was rampant among American workers building the Panama Canal. Jonathan Dine Wirtschafter, "The Genesis and Impact of the Medical Lobby: 1898–1906," *Journal of the History of Medicine and Allied Sciences*, Vol. 13, No. 1, January 1958, 17–18; Wirtschafter, "The Genesis and Impact of the Medical Lobby," 31–39, 42.
11. A 1905 lead editorial in *JAMA* condemned nostrums as "a business that is both infamous and despicable; a business in which few men will, without blushing, acknowledge that they are engaged; a business that thrives on misrepresentation and fraud, that fattens on the gullibility and credulity of the ignorant, and that prospers by deceiving the sick and afflicted." "The Power And Influence Of The Proprietary Association Of America," *JAMA* Vol. XLV, No. 21 (November 18, 1905), 1577. See also Young, *The Toadstool Millionaires*, 224–25; Robert M. Crunden, *Ministers of Reform: The Progressives' Achievement in American Civilization 1889-1920* (New York: Basic Books, 1982), 176.
12. Wiley wrote most of the proposed statute. The bill was introduced into the Senate by Idaho's Weldon Heyburn. See also James Harvey Young, *Pure Food: Securing the Federal Food and Drugs Act of 1906* (Princeton, NJ: Princeton University Press, 1989), 5–6, 146–51. As for legislative defeats of a pure food bill in previous Congresses, see generally Gaughan, "Harvey Wiley, Theodore Roosevelt, and the Federal Regulation of Food and Drugs." As for the stalled bills in previous Congresses, see Crunden, *Ministers of Reform*, 187.
13. Wiley, *An Autobiography*, 210, 217, 219, 231, 239, 241, 247.
14. Some estimates were as high as 3.5 million addicts. Charles Whitebread, "The History of Non-Medical Use of Drugs in the United States," *Journal of Cognitive Liberties*, Fall 2000; Wiley, *An Autobiography*, 206–7.
15. For a brief history of the battle of an acceptable definition of drugs, see Young, *Pure Food*, 168–170.
16. Harvey Wiley, pamphlet reprinted in "Drugs and their Adulterations and the Laws Relating Thereto," *Washington Medical Annals*, 2, 1903. See also Clayton A. Coppin and Jack High, *The Politics of Purity: Harvey Washington Wiley and the Origins of Federal Food Policy* (Ann Arbor, MI: The University of Michigan Press, 1999), 60.
17. Coppin and High, *The Politics of Purity*, 62–63; "The Power and Influence of the Proprietary Association of America," *JAMA*.
18. Herbert Harding, "The History of the Organization among Manufacturers and Wholesale Dealers in Proprietary Articles," *American Druggist* 36, 1900, 190–93.
19. Journalist Mark Sullivan concluded, "Hardly any man in the United States, ex-

cepting only [President Theodore] Roosevelt himself, has a larger or more powerful group of enemies than Wiley." Sullivan, *Our Times*, 520–21.

20. Coppin and High, *The Politics of Purity*, 4. As for the power of the Proprietary Association, see generally C. C. Regier, "The Struggle for Federal Food and Drugs Legislation," *Law and Contemporary Problems* 1, no. 1 (1933), 7–8.
21. See generally Coppin and High, *The Politics of Purity.*
22. Oscar E. Anderson, Jr., *The Health of a Nation: Harvey W. Wiley and the Fight for Pure Food* (Chicago: University of Chicago Press, for the University of Cincinnati, 1958), 161–64.
23. Jonathan Dine Wirtschafter, "The Genesis and Impact of the Medical Lobby: 1898-1906," *Journal of the History of Medicine and Allied Sciences*, Vol. 13, No. 1, January 1958, 15–49. See also Coppin and High, *The Politics of Purity*, 59–60, 76–77.
24. Temin, *Taking Your Medicine*, 24–27; Young, *The Toadstool Millionaires*, 82, 226.
25. The explosion in the number of newspapers nationwide was spurred by plummeting prices for newsprint. In 1862 cotton rag newsprint cost 24 cents a pound. In 1900, an improved newsprint made from wood pulp, cost 2 cents a pound. See generally George B. Waldron, "What America Spends in Advertising," *Chautauquan*, 38 (October 1903), 156. See also Young, *The Medical Messiahs*, 22; Sullivan, *Our Times*, 511.
26. Wiley, *An Autobiography*, 208. For the percentage of income to newspapers from patent medicines, see Donohue, "A History of Drug Advertising," 664.
27. Young, *The Toadstool Millionaires*, 107–08.
28. Wiley to Sullivan, *Our Times*, note 2, 519.
29. Wiley to James Mann, March 19, 1906, Letter Book 180, No. 305; Wiley to Samuel Adams, March 12, 1906, Letter Book 179, No. 476; in Record Group 97, NARA.
30. The other "poisons" required to be listed were the sedative chloral hydrate, the anesthetic eucaine, and acetanilide, used as an analgesic but with toxic side effects. Chloral hydrate is known on the street as a "Mickey Finn," or "knockout cocktail." As for the other ingredients considered poisonous, see generally Young, *The Medical Messiahs*, 54.
31. Young, *The Toadstool Millionaires*, 240–42. See generally Ezra J. Kennedy, *The Pharmaceutical Era,* Proprietary Association of America Vol. XLIX (New York: D. O. Haynes & Co., January to December 1916). See also Young, *Pure Food*, 170–71.
32. Letters from Wiley to Congressman James Mann, March 23 and April 2, 1906, *Congressional Record*, 59 Congress, Session 1, 8892–8897, 9340, Bureau of Chemistry, General Correspondence, RG 97.2, NARA.
33. The weekly was the Kansas-based *The Appeal to Reason.*
34. London wrote an enthusiastic review of *The Jungle* in the same paper that serialized the book. See Walter B. Rideout, *The Radical Novel in the United States, 1900-1954: Some Interrelations of Literature and Society* (Cambridge, MA: Harvard University Press, 1956), 30.
35. Macmillan had canceled Sinclair's book contract after receiving his manuscript in 1905 and concluding the book was "gloom and horror unrelieved." Doubleday, Page & Co. published it after its newspaper serialization. Expectations for sales were low. Public interest, however, translated into 160,000 sales the first year and translations into seventeen languages. Blum, *The Poison Squad*, 124, 142.
36. Martin Leonard, "The safety assessment process—Setting the scene: An FDA per-

spective," *ILAR journal / National Research Council, Institute of Laboratory Animal Resources* 43 Suppl. S5–10 (February 2002).

37. "The Pure Food and Drug Act," Historical Highlights, June 23, 1906, History, Art & Archives, U.S. House of Representatives, http://history.house.gov/HistoricalHighlight/Detail/15032393280. See Coppin, *Politics of Purity,* 81–82. See also "Upton Sinclair Tells About the Sufferings of the Women in Packingtown," *Evening World,* June 9, 1906, 3; Donna J. Wood, "The Strategic Use of Public Policy: Business Support for the 1906 Food and Drug Act," *Business History Review,* Vol. 59, no. 3, 1985, 403–432.
38. The Pure Food and Drug Act was the first comprehensive federal statute to regulate adulterated or misbranded foods or drugs. In 1848, Congress had passed the Drug Importation Act. Despite its sweeping name it was a feeble and mostly unenforced effort to restrict the importation of dangerous drugs, many of which had adversely affected American troops during the Mexican-American War. Federal Food and Drug Act of 1906, (The "Wiley Act"), Public Law Number 59-384, 34 STAT. 768 (1906), 21 U.S.C. Sec 1-15 (1934), (Repealed in 1938 BY 21 U.S.C. Sec 329 (a)).
39. A *New York Times* editorial was typical of the unchecked excitement and high expectations: "The purity and honesty of the food and medicines of the people are guaranteed," July 1, 1906, 24.
40. Wiley quoted in Young, *Pure Food,* 271.
41. Young, *Pure Food,* 265.
42. *United States v. Johnson,* 221 U.S. 488 (1911). See also Wallace F. Janssen, "Cancer Quackery: Past And Present," *FDA Consumer,* July–August 1977.
43. "FDA Focus: The Sherley Amendment," *The Pharma Letter,* October 11, 2014.
44. Garner, "The Lure of Cocaine, Once Hailed as Cure-All." As for the claim of medical and Pope Leo XIII endorsements, see *Harper's Magazine,* March 1984, full-page advertisement.
45. Young, *The Medical Messiahs,* 43–44.
46. See *Standard Remedies,* Vol. 4 (Chicago: The Standard Remedies Publishing Co., 1918).
47. Young, *The Medical Messiahs,* 46–47.
48. Ibid., 36.
49. Squibb started publishing *Ephemeris of Materia Medica* in 1885. It competed with the *U.S. Pharmacopeia* as a resource for drug information. As for Heroin, see E. H. Squibb, *An Ephemeris of Materia Medica: Pharmacy, Therapeutics and Collateral Information* (Brooklyn, NY: E. R. Squibb & Sons, 1903), 80. See also G. W. Wood, "A Study of the Indications and Contra-Indications of Heroin," *Cincinnati Lancet-Clinic* Vol. XLVII (November 16, 1901), 529.
50. Francisco López-Muñoz, Ronaldo Ucha-Udabe, and Cecilio Alamo, "The history of barbiturates a century after their clinical introduction," *Neuropsychiatric Disease and Treatment* 1.4 (2005): 329–343.
51. See generally Gaughan, "Harvey Wiley, Theodore Roosevelt, and the Federal Regulation of Food and Drugs." See also "The Man Who Is Leading the Fight for Pure Food," *Washington Times,* November 20, 1904, 5; Dupree, *Science in the Federal Government,* 176–83; chapter 1 in Temin, *Taking Your Medicine.*
52. The Post Office was more active against nostrums than Wiley's Bureau of Chemistry. It brought several dozen mail fraud cases against nostrum makers who touted cures for cancer or drug addiction and used the mail to ship the products.

See Liebenau, *Medical Science and Medical Industry*, 92–93; James C. Munch and James C. Munch, Jr., "Notices of Judgment—The First Thousand," *Food Drug Cosmetic Law Journal,* 10 (1955), 219–42; "Decisions of Courts in Cases under the Federal Food and Drugs Act," Full Text: Vol.1. (Washington, D.C.: Government Printing Office, 1934); Coppin and High, *The Politics of Purity*, 97–99; Young, *The Medical Messiahs,* 41, 45.

53. Coppin and High, *The Politics of Purity*, 99, 118, 134, 161. See also Wiley, *An Autobiography*, 268.
54. Clayton A. Coppin, "John Arbuckle: Entrepreneur, Trustbuster and Humanitarian," *Market Process* 7, No. 1, Spring 1989, 11-15; Gaughan, "Harvey Wiley, Theodore Roosevelt, and the Federal Regulation of Food and Drugs," 26; Coppin and High, *The Politics of Purity*, 85–87.
55. John Pemberton, a Confederate soldier and pharmacist, created Coca-Cola after the Civil War as a tonic he hoped might cure the morphine addiction he developed while recovering from a wartime saber wound. He called his original formula French Wine Coca and mixed coca leaves with alcohol and kola nuts. In 1886 he patented Coca-Cola, a nonalcoholic version that included a trace of cocaine. Pemberton sold it exclusively in a single Atlanta pharmacy. Shortly before his death in 1888, Pemberton sold Coca-Cola to Asa Candler, an Atlanta businessman who had publicly endorsed Wiley's Pure Food and Drug Act as good for the food industry. It was Candler who marketed the drink as a thirst quencher with ads promoting it as "Delicious. Refreshing. Exhilarating. Invigorating." Candler also changed Coca-Cola's label to include "extractives from coca leaves (cocaine removed)" and replaced the cocaine with caffeine. See Ludy T. Benjamin, "Pop psychology: The man who saved Coca-Cola," *American Psychological Association,* 2009, Vol. 40, No. 2, 18; Paul Vallely, "Drug That Spans the Ages: The History of Cocaine," *Independent* (UK), March 2, 2006; Blum, *The Poison Squad*, 218; David F. Musto, "An historical perspective on legal and medical responses to substance abuse," *Villanova Law Review*, 18:808–17, May 1973; 43.

    The caffeine war kicked off by Wiley's 1906 Pure Food and Drug Act inspired a German merchant, Ludwig Roselius, to patent in 1908 a process for extracting caffeine from coffee beans. He was the first to sell decaffeinated coffee, under different names worldwide. In France, it was Sanka (sans caffeine), while in the United States Merck marketed it as Dekafa. Mark Pendergrast, *Uncommon Grounds: The History of Coffee and How It Transformed Our World* (Revised Edition, New York: Basic Books, 2010), 104–5.
56. Peggy Fletcher Stack, "12 Myths About Mormons," *Salt Lake Tribune*, November 5, 2012; T. Rees Shapiro, "Caffeinated Sodas Heading to Brigham Young Campus," *Washington Post*, September 21, 2017.
57. Wiley cited newspaper accounts that asserted one in three regular coffee drinkers were at risk of blindness. When he visited England, he claimed to have seen women who missed their afternoon tea break "would become almost wild." He was, however, more tolerant of caffeine in tea and coffee than in Coca-Cola since it was an indigenous ingredient. Pendergrast, *Uncommon Grounds*, 95, 103–4. See also Oscar E. Anderson, Jr., *The Health of a Nation: Harvey W. Wiley and the Fight for Pure Food* (Chicago: University of Chicago Press, 1958), 2–8.
58. House Resolution 27427, Public No. 221, Sixtieth Congress, Chs. 100, 101, February 9, 1909.
59. The focus on the variety of opium imported from China was more about Amer-

ican foreign policy than drug prohibition. Teddy Roosevelt wanted to start business trade with China. Since China chafed constantly at British pressure to sell opium, Roosevelt decided that banning Chinese opium in the U.S. might win favor with the Chinese government. Dale Gieringer, "The Opium Exclusion Act of 1909," *Counterpunch*, February 6, 2009.

60. Albert F. Nathan, "Drug Fiends Make 'Crime Wave,'" *Los Angeles Times*, November 30, 1919, 1.
61. United States v. Forty Barrels and Twenty Kegs of Coca Cola Co., 241 U.S. 265, 281–83, 36 S. Ct. 573, 60 L. Ed. 995.
62. Blum, *The Poison Squad*, 239.
63. Ibid., 243. In dismissing the case, the judge said: "I am constrained to conclude that the use of the word 'added,' when applied to poisonous and deleterious ingredients . . . cannot be considered meaningless."
64. Blum, *The Poison Squad*, 246. The $1,600 is $43,643 in 2019 dollars.
65. Pendergrast, *Uncommon Grounds*, 104; Blum, *The Poison Squad*, 282.
66. Rosen, *Miracle Cure*, 75; Young, *The Medical Messiahs*, 57.
67. Blum, *The Poison Squad*, 282.
68. Wiley, *An Autobiography*, 238–39. Harvey Wiley died at his home in Washington in 1930 and was buried in Section 13 of Arlington National Cemetery. Michael Robert Patterson, "Harvey Washington Wiley, Corporal, United States Army, Government Official," Arlington National Cemetery, http://www.arlingtoncemetery.net/hwwiley.htm.

Chapter 4: The Wonder Drug

1. Different dates are sometimes cited for the passage of Prohibition. Congress approved it on December 18, 1917, but it took until January 16, 1919, before the states ratified it. Many histories use 1919 as the start date. However, Section 1 of the Amendment states that liquor will not become illegal until "one year from the ratification" (January 1920).
2. See "Germany—The International Opium Convention," signed at The Hague, January 23, 1912, and subsequent relative papers [1922], LNTSer 29; 8 LNTS 187, League of Nation Treaty Series. An effort in the U.S. in 1910 to pass a congressional antinarcotics act, the Foster Bill, had failed. Vermont senator David Foster's bill would have eliminated all medical drug traffic in opium, cocaine, marijuana, and chloral hydrate, a widely abused sedative. Renata Limón, "Dens of Bureaucracy," *The New Inquiry*, April 25, 2013. See also Eva Bertram et al., *Drug War Politics: The Price of Denial* (Berkeley: University of California Press, 1996).
3. The Harrison Act also required increased record-keeping for doctors or pharmacists who dispensed opiates. Nathan, "Drug Fiends Make 'Crime Wave,'" 1; "How Did We Get Here? History Has a Habit of Repeating Itself," *Economist*, July 26, 2011. See also "Without Opium, Chinamen Die," *Los Angeles Times*, August 17, 1909; Dale Gieringer, "The Opium Exclusion Act of 1909." As for the Supreme Court ruling that "Direct control of medical practice in the states is beyond the power of the federal government," see Linder v. United States, 268 U.S. 5 (1925); Lawrence Kolb, "Drug Addiction: A Study of Some Medical Cases," *Arch NeurPsych*, 20(1), 1928.
4. Bertram et al., *Drug War Politics*, 66–67.
5. It took the 1925 Geneva Convention, coupled with threats of an economic boycott

by other countries, before European countries restricted drug firms to manufacture only enough narcotics to satisfy their domestic consumption. See generally V. Berridge, "War Conditions and Narcotics Control: The Passing of Defence of the Realm Act Regulation 40B," *Journal of Social Policy* 7.3 (1978), 285–304; T.M. Parssinen, *Secret Passions, Secret Remedies: Narcotic Drugs in British Society, 1820–1930* (Manchester, 1983); Frances R. Frankenburg MD, *Brain-Robbers: How Alcohol, Cocaine, Nicotine, and Opiates Have Changed Human History* (ABC-Clio, 2014).

6. Liebenau, *Medical Science and Medical Industry*, 131.
7. Sneader, *Drug Discovery*.
8. The drugs mentioned were "morphine, quinine, digitalis, insulin, codeine, aspirin, arsenicals, nitroglycerin, mercurial, and a few biologicals." M. Lawrence Podolsky, *Cures out of Chaos: How Unexpected Discoveries Led to Breakthroughs in Medicine and Health* (Amsterdam: Harwood Academic Publishers, 1997), 59.
9. They did not advertise to doctors because until 1938 any nonnarcotic medication could be bought without a prescription. As for narcotic-based drugs that required a prescription, about half were made in compounding pharmacies, cutting into pharma profits.
10. Antitoxins and vaccines had shown promise with tetanus and rabies, and syphilis responded to an arsenic-based drug. See Testimony, "The Competitive Status of the U.S. Pharmaceutical Industry: The Influences of Technology in Determining International Competitive Advantage," Committee on Labor and Public Welfare, Hearings on the "Examination of the Pharmaceutical Industry, 1973–74," before the Subcommittee on Health, 93rd Congress, 1st and 2nd Sessions, 1973–1974, Part 3.
11. The anticonvulsant potassium bromide was the oldest and most popular nineteenth-century sedative. Its drawback was toxicity. A German pharmacology professor invented so-called knock-out drops, a more powerful sedative, in 1869, and it remained in use until the mid-twentieth century. Novelist Virginia Woolf was addicted to chloral hydrate to treat her bipolar and insomnia; she wrote the drug was "that mighty prince with the moth's eyes and the feathered feet." See Shorter, *Before Prozac*, 287 of 4159; Dowbiggin, *The Quest for Mental Health* (Cambridge: Cambridge Essential Histories, Cambridge University Press), Kindle Edition, 146–47. See also Helen Salter, "The Madness and Modernism of Virginia Woolf," HCBooksOnline, https://www.hcbooksonline.com/the-madness-and-modernism-of-virginia-woolf/.
12. Bayer named its first barbiturate Veronal, after the Italian city Verona. Its primary ingredient was barbital, a sleep-inducing agent. David L. Herzberg, *Happy Pills in America: From Miltown to Prozac* (Baltimore: Johns Hopkins University Press, 2008), Kindle Edition, 124–25.
13. Liebenau, *Medical Science and Medical Industry*, 45–46.
14. Peter Temin, "The Evolution of the Modern Pharmaceutical Industry," Working Paper, Department of Economics, Massachusetts Institute of Technology, No. 223, 1978, 4; Podolsky, *Cures out of Chaos*, 38.
15. Parke-Davis and Co. v. H.K. Mulford and Co., 189 Fed. 95 (S.D.N.Y. 1911) affirmed, 196 Fed. 496 (2nd Cir. 1912). See also Graham Dutfield, *Intellectual Property Rights and the Life Sciences Industry*, 2nd edition (Singapore: World Scientific Publishing, 2009), 114–18.
16. Joan Trossman Bien, "The Swine Flu Vaccine: 1976 Casts A Giant Shadow," *Pa-*

cific Standard, December 4, 2009; John M. Barry, "The Site Of Origin Of The 1918 Influenza Pandemic And Its Public Health Implications," *Journal of Translational Medicine* Vol. 2, No. 3 (January 2004).

17. Blaser, *Missing Microbes*, 49, 60, 62–63.
18. Some microbes act as bacterial zombies, altering the behavior of the infected host in order to either replicate or enhance their ease of transmission to others. See Michael Chao, "Zombies: Microbial Mind Control," *Microbiology*, February 11, 2016; Blaser, *Missing Microbes*, 61.
19. Jesse Hicks, "Fast Times: The Life, Death, and Rebirth of Amphetamine," Distillations, *Science History Institute*, April 14, 2014. Amphetamine compounds were discovered earlier but not turned into a modern drug. MDA was synthesized in a lab in 1910. Four years later Merck patented MDMA (best known decades later as the club drug ecstasy). A Japanese chemist in 1919 discovered methamphetamine (speed). Shorter, *Before Prozac*, 391 of 4159.
20. Shorter, *Before Prozac*.
21. The firm was then run by Eli Lilly III, the somewhat eccentric, philanthropist grandson of the company's founder. Celeste C. Quianzon and Issam Cheikh, "History of Insulin," *Journal of Community Hospital Internal Medicine Perspectives* 2.2 (2012). See also Dutfield, *Intellectual Property Rights and the Life Sciences Industry*, 112.
22. The bacteria on those petri dishes was *Staphylococcus*, a strain that caused abscesses, sore throats, and even boils.
23. It was *Penicillium notatum*. See James Le Fanu, *The Rise and Fall of Modern Medicine* (New York: Carroll and Graf, 1999), 7.
24. Fleming and his two assistants, Frederick Ridley and Stuart Craddock, tested it initially on meningococcus, streptococcus, and diphtheria bacillus.
25. Alexander Fleming, "On the Antibacterial Action of Cultures of a Penicillium, with Special Reference to their Use in the Isolation of B. influenza," *British Journal of Experimental Pathology*, June 1929,10(3): 226–36. See also Fanu, *The Rise and Fall of Modern Medicine*, 8–9; Eric Lax, *The Mold in Dr. Florey's Coat: The Story of the Penicillin Miracle* (New York: John Macrae/Owl Book/Henry Holt, 2005), 28–31.
26. The most notable attempt was an intensive effort by Harold Raistrick, a biochemistry professor at the London School of Hygiene and Tropical Medicine. It took until 1964 before one of Fleming's former assistants, Ronald Hare, solved the mystery of why Fleming had succeeded where others had failed. Fleming's nine-day holiday away from the lab coincided with a historic cool front in London. That weather was ideal for the growth of the particular penicillin strain that had found its way from the adjacent lab of a fungus researcher. Fleming had left the uncovered petri dishes stacked in a corner of his lab, where they got no sunlight. "Without the nine cool days in the summer of 1928, Fleming would not have discovered penicillin." Ronald Hare, *The Birth of Penicillin* (Sydney, Australia: Allen & Unwin, 1970); Lax, *The Mold in Dr. Florey's Coat*, 13–17, 47–48; Clark, *The Life of Ernst Chain*, Kindle Edition, 521 of 3834; Podolsky, *Cures out of Chaos*, 186–89.
27. A. S. van Miert, "The sulfonamide-diaminopyrimidine story," *Journal of Veterinary Pharmacology and Therapeutics*, 17: 309–316.
28. Temin, *Taking Your Medicine*, 62–63.
29. His wrong calculation about Hitler's longevity was personally costly. By the time Chain tried to get his mother and sister out of Germany, the Nazis had stopped

the emigration of Jews. Both died in the Theresienstadt concentration camp in 1942. Ronald Clark, *The Life of Ernst Chain: Penicillin and Beyond* (originally published in London: Weidenfeld & Nicolson Limited, 1985; Kindle Edition by Bloomsbury Press, 2011), 139 of 3834.

30. Clark, *The Life of Ernst Chain*, 17 of 3834.
31. Lax, *The Mold in Dr. Florey's Coat*, 80–81.
32. Eight mice were injected with the bacteria and four administered penicillin. The four that got the drug were the ones that survived. The results of the experiment happened to fall on May 26, the first day a flotilla of small ships started the evacuation of 300,000 British troops who were trapped by the German army in the French seaport of Dunkirk. Clark, *The Life of Ernst Chain*, 911–19 of 3834.
33. Charles Fletcher, "First Clinical Use of Penicillin," *British Medical Journal*, Vol. 289, 1984, 1721.
34. Ibid.
35. Ibid.
36. Ibid., 1721–23.
37. May and Baker (M&B) 693 and Prontosil were the first sulfas, introduced in 1936. M&B was briefly heralded as a "wonder drug" after it was credited with twice saving Winston Churchill's life in 1943 when he was infected with bacterial pneumonia. Although both drugs were effective in fighting some infections, the list of alarming side effects accumulated in the first few years of use. Penicillin replaced both drugs. Gregory J. Higby and Elaine C. Stroud, *The Inside Story of Medicines: A Symposium* (Madison, WI: American Institute of the History of Pharmacy, 1997), 101–19. As for the others treated with penicillin by the Oxford team, see Florey, H., et al, "Penicillin in Action," *Lancet*, Aug. 16, 1941; Charles Fletcher, "First Clinical Use of Penicillin," *British Medical Journal*, Vol. 289, December 22–29, 1984.
38. Florey and his team did not realize that Penicillin would also create a therapeutic revolution for effective treatment of nonlethal chronic infections of the joints, bones, and sinuses. Fanu, *The Rise and Fall of Modern Medicine*, 5.
39. Lax, *The Mold in Dr. Florey's Coat*, 3.
40. J. E. Lesch, *The First Miracle Drugs: How the Sulfa Drugs Transformed Medicine* (Oxford: Oxford University Press, 2007). M. Lawrence Podolsky, *The Antibiotic Era: Reform, Resistance, and the Pursuit of a Rational Therapeutics* (Baltimore, MD: Johns Hopkins University Press, 2015), 18.
41. Milton Silverman and Philip R. Lee, *Pills, Profits and Politics* (Berkeley, CA: University of California Press, 1974), 4–5.
42. Graham Dutfield, *Intellectual Property Rights and the Life Sciences Industry*, 2nd Edition (Singapore: World Scientific Publishing, 2009), 135; Clark, *The Life of Ernst Chain*, 1062–82 of 3834; Podolsky, *Cures out of Chaos*, 203; Lax, *The Mold in Dr. Florey's Coat*, 163.
43. The Rockefeller Foundation agreed to a two-year grant; £1,250 per year ($5,000). They later extended it to a five-year grant. Podolsky, *Cures out of Chaos*, 199.
44. Clark, *The Life of Ernst Chain*, 1275 of 3834.
45. It was renamed the National Center for Agricultural Utilization Research in 1990. The medical and scientific community, however, still calls it the Northern Lab, the name by which it played its central role in the penicillin project.
46. The penicillin yields the Oxford researchers had before Peoria averaged 4 units per milliliter of culture broth. The cantaloupe found by the housewife yielded 250

units per milliliter. The University of Wisconsin turned out 50,000 units with its enhanced technology. Every strain of penicillin produced since World War II is a direct descendant of that Peoria cantaloupe strain. Blaser, *Missing Microbes,* 73–75. See also Lax, *The Mold in Dr. Florey's Coat*, 180–87.

47. Podolsky, *Cures out of Chaos*, 194–95; Lax, *The Mold in Dr. Florey's Coat*, 146–47.
48. Daniel Lee Kleinman, *Politics on the Endless Frontier: Postwar Research Policy in the United States* (Durham, NC: Duke University Press, 1995), 51.
49. "Prohibited Acts and Penalties," Subchapter III of Chapter 9, "Federal Food, Drug and Cosmetic Act."
50. "Good Medicine, Bad Behavior: Drug Diversion in America: The History of Prescription Drugs," Drug Enforcement Administration museum display, Springfield, VA.
51. The FDA, created in 1931, wanted Congress to revise the outdated 1906 Food and Drug Act, under which the FDA was virtually powerless. It tried building support by getting press coverage for its "Chamber of Horrors," photos of horrible side effects caused by deceptively packaged or dangerous medications and cosmetics. Pharma managed to kill the bill every year. Kathryn C. Zoon and Robert A. Yetter, "The Regulation of Drugs and Biological Products by the Food and Drug Administration," in *Principles and Practice of Clinical Research* (New York: Academic Press, 2007); Robert E. Freer, Chairman, Federal Trade Commission, "Truth in Advertising (With Specific Relation to the Broadcasting Industry)," talk before the Radio Executives Club of New York, November 20, 1944; Leonard M. Schechtman, "The Safety Assessment Process—Setting the Scene: An FDA Perspective," *ILAR Journal*, Volume 43, Issue Suppl. 1, 2002, S5–S10.
52. Although the law passed in 1938, the legislation had been drafted in 1933 and stalled. The Elixir Sulfanilamide disaster provided the impetus for Congress to finally act. Temin, "The Evolution of the Modern Pharmaceutical Industry," 9; Jef Akst, "The Elixir Tragedy," *Scientist*, June 1, 2013. The poisonous compound was diethylene glycol. Elixir Sulfanilamide was a solution of 10 percent sulfanilamide, 16 percent water, and a deadly 72 percent diethylene glycol.
53. Carpenter, *Reputation and Power*, 85–89, 98–101.
54. A drug could be recalled, for instance, if it turned out to be dangerous to patient health at the dosage recommended on the label. Zoon and Yetter, "The Regulation of Drugs and Biological Products by the Food and Drug Administration"; Freer, "Truth in Advertising" talk; Schechtman, "The Safety Assessment Process."
55. David F. Cavers, "The Food, Drug, And Cosmetic Act Of 1938: Its Legislative History And Its Substantive Provisions," 6 *Law and Contemporary Problems*, 2–42 (Winter 1939). See also Zoon and Yetter, "The Regulation of Drugs and Biological Products by the Food and Drug Administration."
56. "History of Federal Regulation: 1902–Present: Food, Drug, and Cosmetic Act of 1938," FDAReview.org, a project of the Independent Institute, http://www.fdareview.org/01_history.php.
57. Peter Temin, "The Origin of Compulsory Drug Prescriptions," *Journal of Law and Economics*, Number 222, Massachusetts Institute of Technology, September 1977.
58. The FDA later put warnings on two powerful barbiturates, Seconal and Nembutal.
59. Bayer's Prontosil was the first commercially sold sulfa medication; the company marketed it to combat blood infections and some strains of bacterial pneumonia.

60. Aldridge et al., "The Discovery and Development of Penicillin, 1928–1945," *The Alexander Fleming Museum,* November 19, 1999, 5. See also Lax, *The Mold in Dr. Florey's Coat*, 185–86.
61. His full name was George Wilhelm Herman Emanuel Merck. He told *Time* magazine in a 1952 cover profile, "Named after all my uncles, who had to give me silver presents for ten years." "Medicine: What the Doctor Ordered," *Time*, August 18, 1952.
62. James C. Collins and Jerry I. Porras, *Built to Last: Successful Habits of Visionary Companies* (New York: Harper Business,1994).
63. Some of them included Hans Molitor from Austria, and the University of Wisconsin's Karl Folkers and Harvard's Max Tishler. Before Merck established that lab, the American Society for Pharmacology and Experimental Therapeutics barred the admission of anyone who worked for private industry. L. Galambos and J. L. Sturchio, "Transnational Investment: The Merck Experience. 1891–1925," in H. Pohl, Ed., *Transnational Investment from the 19th Century to the Present* (Stuttgart: Franz Steiner Verlag, 1994), 232–35; "Medicine: What the Doctor Ordered."
64. Besides B_1, Merck developed in order, B_2 for pellagra, B_{12} for anemia, vitamin C for colds, and vitamin A for eyesight. Gortler, "Merck in America," 4; "Medicine: What the Doctor Ordered." See also Rodengen, *The Legend of Pfizer*, 44.
65. Aldridge, "The Discovery and Development of Penicillin."
66. Bayer had developed an earlier process for developing the same chemical for which it later discovered therapeutic benefits. Although its patent on that process had expired, it managed to obtain patents in the U.S. and U.K. on Prontosil. While Merck preferred to use Bayer's premium-priced drug, any pharma firm was free to make and sell medicines with its active ingredient, sulfanilamide. John E. Lesch, *The First Miracle Drugs*, 153–54. Also see Dutfield, *Intellectual Property Rights and the Life Sciences Industry*, 91.
67. Leon Gortler, "Merck in America: The First 70 Years From Fine Chemicals to Pharmaceutical Giant," *Bulletin for the History of Chemistry*, Volume 25, Number 1, 2000, 6; "Medicine: What the Doctor Ordered."
68. George W. Merck quoted in "Medicine: What the Doctor Ordered."
69. Aldridge, "The Discovery and Development of Penicillin," 6.
70. The official was Robert Coghill, the chief of the Department of Agriculture's Fermentation Department. Peter Neushul, "Science, Government, and the Mass Production of Penicillin," *Journal of the History of Medicine and Allied Sciences* 48 (October 1993), 388.
71. "Penicillin Data Exchange Exempted from Antitrust Laws," *Oil, Paint, and Drug Reporter*, December 20, 1943.
72. Pfizer's experience with deep fermentation for manufacturing citric acid gave them an advantage when it came to mastering penicillin production. See Rodengen, *The Legend of Pfizer*, 18–19, 53–58.
73. Roswell Quinn, "Rethinking Antibiotic Research and Development: World War II and the Penicillin Collaborative," *American Journal of Public Health* 103.3, (2013): 426–34.
74. Ibid.
75. U.S. Federal Trade Commission, "Economic Report on Antibiotics Manufacture," (Washington, D.C.: Government Printing Office, 1958), 47–60.
76. Lewis H. Sarett and Clyde Roche, Chapter on Max Tishler in *Biographical Mem-*

oirs, V. 66, Office of the Home Secretary, National Academy of Sciences (Dulles, VA, The National Academies Press, 1995), 353–70. See also Amy K. Saenger, "Discovery of the Wonder Drug: From Cows to Cortisone," *Clinical Chemistry* 56 (8) (August 2010), 1349–50.

77. Lax, *The Mold in Dr. Florey's Coat*, 1.
78. Ibid., 1–2.
79. Jie Jack Li, *Triumph of the Heart: The Story of Statins* (Oxford: Oxford University Press, 2009).
80. Miller was released after two weeks. She died in 1999 at the age of ninety.
81. Wolfgang Saxon, "Anne Miller, 90, First Patient Who Was Saved by Penicillin," *New York Times*, June 9, 1999, A27.
82. The *Boston Globe* broke the news about the existence of penicillin, although the paper did not know its name. It reported that "police escorts from four states accompanied a consignment of an as yet unnamed drug rushed to the Massachusetts General Hospital. . . . A 32-liter supply of this drug, described as priceless by a laboratory technician, will be used to prevent infection from the burns. The mercy vehicle arrived at 4:30 this morning after a seven-hour, 368-mile drive through steady rain." *Boston Globe*, December 2, 1942.
83. Lax, *The Mold in Dr. Florey's Coat*, 206–7.
84. Kleinman, *Politics on the Endless Frontier*, citing a 1946 article in *Fortune*, 69.
85. Nathaniel Comfort, "The Prisoner as Model Organism: Malaria Research at Stateville Penitentiary," *Studies in History and Philosophy of Biological and Biomedical Sciences* 40.3 (2009), 190–203.
86. Andrea Tone, *The Age of Anxiety: A History of America's Turbulent Affair with Tranquilizers* (New York: Basic Books, 2012), 23.
87. Le Fanu, *The Rise and Fall of Modern Medicine*, 20–21.
88. Robert Bud, "Upheaval in the moral economy of science? Patenting, teamwork and the World War II experience of penicillin," *History and Technology* no. 2 (2008).
89. Rosen, *Miracle Cure*, 218, 358.
90. Although Merck led American pharma into the penicillin project with the government, and benefited from the federal funding, it was not the largest wartime penicillin producer. Squibb and Pfizer manufactured more than their rivals. The business shifted postwar and Merck competed for the top spot in penicillin sales. Gortler, "Merck in America," 6. The penicillin project was the first but not last in which American pharma was dependent on government or charitable largesse. The polio vaccine in the 1950s, for instance, was the result of public funding. And Planned Parenthood underwrote the initial research for the contraceptive pill. Basil Achilladelis, Alexander Scriabine, and Ralph Landau, *Pharmaceutical Innovation, Revolutionizing Human Health* (Philadelphia: Chemical Heritage Press, 1999), 15–16. See also Michael Hiltzik, "The Origins of Big Science," *Boom*, Fall 2015, Vol. 5, No. 3.

Chapter 5: "Could You Patent the Sun?"

1. Chain quoted in Clark, *The Life of Ernst Chain*, 853 of 3834.
2. Lax, *The Mold in Dr. Florey's Coat*, 80–81, 211–23, 238–43.
3. Clark, *The Life of Ernst Chain*; Lax, *The Mold in Dr. Florey's Coat*, 261.
4. Controversy in a Nobel award was not always contingent on leaving out a key

contributor. Portuguese physician Egas Moniz was controversial in 1941 because many doctors were not convinced that his development of a prefrontal lobotomy to treat serious mental illness was an advance worthy of the prize. About forty thousand Americans were lobotomized, the peak period was from just after World War II and into the early 1950s. Dowbiggin, *The Quest for Mental Health*, 112; Dutfield, *Intellectual Property Rights and the Life Sciences Industry*, 112–13.

5. Ernst Chain told *The New York Times* in late 1945: "No one in our group has received a penny out of this but firms are making millions of dollars. . . . I don't see why a commercial development should get so much money. I thought the governments would take over the production of penicillin and there would be no great profits." Lax, *The Mold in Dr. Florey's Coat*, 246–47; Clark, *The Life of Ernst Chain*, 1996 of 3834.
6. Temin, *Taking Your Medicine*, 56.
7. Andrew J. Moyer and Robert D. Coghill, "The Effect of Phenylacetic Acid on Penicillin Production," *Journal of Bacteriology*, 1947 Mar; 53(3): 329–41. See also "Application for United State Patent 2476107, "Method for Production of Penicillin," July 12, 1949, U.S. Patent Office, Washington, D.C.; Wesley W. Spink, MD, *Infectious Diseases: Prevention and Treatment in the Nineteenth and Twentieth Centuries* (Minneapolis, MN: University of Minnesota Press, 1978), 101.
8. Henry Harris quoted in Lax, *The Mold in Dr. Florey's Coat*, 251.
9. See Table 63, "Antibiotic Patents Acquired by the United States and 11 Principal Producers of Antibiotics, 1942–1956," in the U.S. Federal Trade Commission, "Economic Report on Antibiotics Manufacture" (Washington, D.C.: Government Printing Office, 1958), 234–35. Typical was Squibb's development and patenting of a unique process by which it mixed penicillin with peanut oil and beeswax. It claimed prolonged absorption at the injection site. The drug's short half-life was a concern since it required more frequent dosing to maintain the therapeutic levels. Squibb abandoned it after an "unacceptable rate of allergic reactions." Karen Bush, "The coming of age of antibiotics: discovery and therapeutic value," *Antimicrobial Therapeutics Reviews*, Annals of The New York Academy of Sciences, Decmber 23, 2010, 3. See also Quinn, "Rethinking Antibiotic Research and Development."
10. Dutfield, *Intellectual Property Rights and the Life Sciences Industry*, 75–76.
11. The top four firms controlled 28 percent of all sales. *Economic Report on Antibiotics Manufacture*, Federal Trade Commission (Washington, D.C.: Government Printing Office, 1958), 47–49, 92–95. See also U.S. Bureau of the Census, Census of Manufactures (Washington, D.C., Government Printing Office, 1947–1957), 3; George J. Stigler, *Capital and Rates of Return in Manufacturing Industries* (Princeton: Princeton University Press for the National Bureau of Economics Research, 1963), 58–62; Walter Adams, (ed.), *The Structure of American Industry* (4th ed. New York: Macmillan, 1971), 166.
12. Quinn, "Rethinking Antibiotic Research and Development."
13. The government spent \$7.6 million on the plants and sold them for \$3.4 million. Elmer L. Gaden, Jr., *Fermentation Process Kinetics*, presented at the 134th National Meeting of the American Chemical Society, Chicago, September 1958, reprinted in *Journal of Biochemical and Microbiological Technology and Engineering*, Vol. 1, No. 4, pp. 413–29 (1959). For the ways in which the government helped the drug industry, see U.S. Federal Trade Commission, "Economic Report

on Antibiotics Manufacture" (Washington, D.C.: Government Printing Office, 1958, 6, 13; Temin, "The Evolution of the Modern Pharmaceutical Industry," 12.

14. Bacteria is either Gram-positive or -negative depending on its reaction to a chemical stain developed in 1884 by Hans Christian Gram, a Danish bacteriologist.
15. All antibiotics ending with "mycin" are natural products or derivatives obtained from soil microbes. Antibiotics ending with "micin" are those obtained from plant microbes.
16. Waksman extracted streptomycin from a microorganism that was known for thirty years but had never been screened for antibiotic properties. Dutfield, *Intellectual Property Rights and the Life Sciences Industry*, 142; Albert Schatz, Elizabeth Bugie, and Selman Waksman, "Streptomycin, a Substance Exhibiting Antibiotic Activity Against Gram-Positive and Gram-Negative Bacteria," *Proceedings of the Society for Experimental Biology and Medicine* 55 (1944): 66–69; Peter Pringle, *Experiment Eleven: Dark Secrets Behind the Discovery of a Wonder Drug* (London: Bloomsbury, 2012, Kindle Edition).
17. A British medical statistician, Sir Austin Bradford Hill, designed the first randomized double-blind controlled clinical trial in 1946. It showed conclusively streptomycin's effectiveness in combating tuberculosis. Hill's clinical trial format remains the gold standard today for testing new drugs for safety and therapeutic value.
18. Peter Pringle, *Experiment Eleven,* 4, 62.
19. Ibid., 60.
20. Stacy Jones, "Ten Patents That Shaped the World," *New York Times Magazine*, September 17, 1961. The other nine patents chosen by the *Times* were: the telephone, moldable plastics, Thomas Edison's lamp, gasoline, rockets, synthetic fibers, the vacuum tube, powered flight, and nuclear power.
21. Rutgers agreed to pay Merck $500,000 from future royalties on streptomycin to compensate the company for what it had spent on research. See "Circulation of Antibiotics: Journeys of Drug Standards, 1930–1970," papers presented from June 16–18, 2009, Madrid, Spain, European Science Foundation, Centro de Ciencias Humanas y Sociales Consejo Superior de Investigaciones Científicas (CSIC), edited by Ana Romero, Christoph Gradmann, and Maria Santemases, Oslo, Norway, May 2010, 126–27. See also Temin, "The Evolution of the Modern Pharmaceutical Industry," 15.
22. Pringle, *Experiment Eleven*, 99.
23. J. P. Garrod, "Obituary of Waksman," *British Medical Journal* (1973), 506.
24. Richard Seth Epstein, "The Isolation and Purification Exception to the General Unpatentability of Products of Nature," *Columbia Science and Technology Review*, January 15, 2003; Pringle, *Experiment Eleven*.
25. Funk Brothers Seed Co. v. Kalo Inoculant Co., 333 U.S. 127 (1948).
26. Jonas Salk quoted in Brian Palmer, "Jonas Salk: Good at Virology, Bad at Economics," *Slate*, April 13, 2014.
27. Selman Waksman, response to patent examiner's objections, June 5, 1946, in Patent Application no. 577,136, February 9, 1945. See Parke-Davis & Co. v. H. K. Mulford & Co., 189 F. 95 (C.C.S.D.N.Y. 1911); Kuehmsted v. Farbenfabriken of Elberfeld Co., 179 F. 701 (7th Cir. 1910).
28. Two months earlier, Merck chemist Robert Peck got a patent for a process that extracted crystalline salts from streptomycin. Merck's lawyers did the patent work

free of charge for Rutgers; it was part of the joint agreement that nullified Merck's exclusive right to the drug. U.S. Patent Office patent No. 2,449,866; Sept. 21, 1948.

29. The average royalty rate was 6 percent of sales. Because of its business arrangement with Waksman, Merck got a preferred rate of 2.5 percent. It also got that low royalty for any drug that Waksman discovered. Pringle, *Experiment Eleven*, 30.
30. Milton Wainwright, "Streptomycin: Discovery and Resultant Controversy," *History and Philosophy of the Life Science*, Vol. 13, No. 1 (1991), 97–124; J. H. Comroe, "Retrospectroscope, Pay Dirt: The Story of Streptomycin," Part 1 "From Waksman to Waksman"; Part 2 "Feldman, Hinshaw, Lehman," both in *American Review of Respiratory Diseases* (1978), 117, 773–81, 957–68). See also Peter A. Lawrence, "Rank Injustice," *Nature*, Vol. 415/February 21, 2002, 835.
31. The other 0.3 percent was from sales of gramicidin 10 and bacitracin, peptidic antibiotic ointments. Bush, "The coming of age of antibiotics," 1–4. See also *Economic Report on Antibiotics Manufacture*, 67.

Chapter 6: An Unlikely Trio

1. William L. O'Neill, *American High: The Years of Confidence, 1945–1960* (Florence, MA: Free Press, 1986).
2. Alvin M. Weinberg, "Impact of Large Scale Science on the United States," *Science*, Vol. 134, Issue 3473, July 21, 1961, 161–64.
3. Le Fanu, *The Rise and Fall of Modern Medicine*, xvii. The first open-heart surgery in 1953 was an eleven-year-old Philadelphia girl doctors put into a freezer to lower her body temperature to 88 degrees. That allowed them to stop her blood flow for five minutes so they could close a hole in her heart wall. "'Deep Freeze' Surgery," *Time*, April 20, 1953, 127.
4. C. Everett Koop, "Keynote Address: Medicines in American Society—A Personal View," in Gregory J. Higby and Elaine C. Stroud, *The Inside Story of Medicines: A Symposium* (Madison, WI: American Institute of the History of Pharmacy, 1997), 9.
5. The NIH was created in 1897. Most of its modern components were more recent. The National Cancer Institute was formed in 1937. After World War II, there was the National Institute of Mental Health (1946) and the National Heart Institute and National Dental Institute (1948). Congress added about $15 million a year to the NIH budget under Eisenhower. By 1956, its budget had reached $100 million. By 1960, the NIH was spending $250 million on 10,000 research projects at 220 universities and medical schools. As of 2019, the NIH has spent $900 billion on research grants. Wesley W. Spink, *Infectious Diseases: Prevention and Treatment in the Nineteenth and Twentieth Centuries* (Minneapolis, MN: University of Minnesota Press, 1978), 43–49; Kleinman, *Politics on the Endless Frontier*, citing a 1946 article in *Fortune*, 151–52.
6. The Department of Labor had been created in 1913.
7. U.S. Federal Trade Commission, "Economic Report on Antibiotics Manufacture," (Washington, D.C.: Government Printing Office, 1958), 7, 8.
8. Dutfield, *Intellectual Property Rights and the Life Sciences Industry*, 143, 146. See also U.S. Federal Trade Commission, "Economic Report on Antibiotics Manufacture" (Washington, D.C.: Government Printing Office, 1958), 17.
9. Vagelos and Galambos, *Medicine, Science, and Merck*, 39.

10. Joseph G. Lombardino, "A Brief History Of Pfizer Central Research," *Bull. Hist. Chem.*, Vol. 25, Number 1 (2000), 11–12.
11. Liebenau, *Medical Science and Medical Industry*, 101–3.
12. SubbaRow's name is spelled differently in many books and publications. When the Smithsonian had an exhibit in 2014, titled "Beyond Bollywood: Indian Americans Shape the Nation," the spelling was Subbarao. However, in all his scientific publications, including his first in 1929 in *The Journal of Biological Chemistry*, he spelled his surname as SubbaRow. One Indian writer believes SubbaRow was "an attempt to anglicize his name so non-Indian speakers didn't butcher it as much." The author checked public records. The U.S. Naturalization entry card is Subbarow; 1936 Boston telephone listing is "Dr. Y Subbarow," and the 1948 Orangetown, New York, death listing is "Subbarow." On a 1942 World War II Draft Registration card, the name is listed as SubbaRow and it is signed by him as "Yellapragada SubbaRow." See "The Indian-American I didn't know: Yellapragada Subbarao," May 24, 2014, at http://wildtypes.asbmb.org/2014/03/24/the-indian-american-i-didnt-know-yellapragada-subbarao/.
13. Gopalpur Nagendrappa, "Yellapragada SubbaRow: The Man of Miracle Drugs," *Resonance*, June 2012, 539.
14. He was presented with a choice between two cousins in the same family. He chose one a year younger hoping he might not have to start a family immediately and thereby have more time to devote to his studies. Nagendrappa, "Yellapragada SubbaRow," 540; Transcript of Kasturi Suryanarayana Murti, interviewed by S P K Gupta, at Kakinada in August 1954, collection of author.
15. In the few months before he left for America, neighbors thought it peculiar that SubbaRow spent an hour or more on a swing in a rusted and abandoned playground. It was his way of preparing for his sea voyage to America. It worked; he never got seasick. More troublesome was that his father-in-law had not bought him even a third class ticket, which would have entitled him to so-called steerage in the bottom of the ship. Instead he had to stay on the deck, exposed to the elements. As the only vegetarian passenger, he had trouble eating well. Transcript of Kasturi Suryanarayana Murti, interviewed by S P K Gupta, at Kakinada in August 1954, collection of author.
16. As for the death of his child, SubbaRow told friends he had predicted it through astrological calculations he had done before the child was born. Another son born the following year died before his first birthday from a bacterial infection. SubbaRow never saw that child, either. See Nagendrappa, "Yellapragada SubbaRow," 538–57; R. Parthasarathy, "Discoverer of miracle medicines," *Science and Technology*, *The Hindu*, March 13, 2003.
17. Transcript of Kasturi Suryanarayana Murti, interviewed by S P K Gupta, at Kakinada in August 1954, collection of author. See also Parthasarathy, "Discoverer of miracle medicines."
18. C. H. Fiske, and Y. SubbaRow, "The Colorimetric Determination of Phosphorus," *Journal of Biological Chemistry* 66, 1929, 375–400.
19. This is according to George Hitchings, one of SubbaRow's lab mates, who in 1988 was awarded the Nobel Prize in Medicine.
20. Harvard's excuse for the shoddy treatment was that while the State Department permitted him to stay in America because of his professional pursuits, his visa had to be renewed biannually and he was not eligible for American citizenship.

The school claimed that uncertainty about his status prevented him from becoming a faculty member. Nagendrappa, "Yellapragada SubbaRow," 545–46.

21. Farber's discovery was in 1947 and most doctors refused to believe his results on children with acute leukemia could be replicated. There had never been any treatment for a blood or bone marrow cancer. The only previous treatments had been surgery and radiation, both of which were at much cruder stages than what would be available between immunotherapy and targeted therapies in several decades. Denis R. Miller, "Sidney Farber: The Father of Modern Chemotherapy," *British Journal of Haematology*, Vol. 134, Issue 1 (2006).
22. Before Wisconsin, Duggar had been Professor of Botany at the University of Missouri as well as Chair of Plant Physiology at Cornell, and Acting Professor of Biological Chemistry at Washington University Medical School. Nagendrappa, "Yellapragada SubbaRow," 551. See "Dr. Benjamin Duggar Dies at 84; Led in Discovery of Aureomycin," *New York Times*, September 11, 1956, 35.
23. Since attendance was not mandatory, sometimes he would be talking to only one clinician.
24. Dorothy Duggar, "Our Lineage," thirteen-page typewritten document about Dorothy's recollections and details about her grandparents, Dr. Reuben Henry Duggar and Margaret Louisa Minge, undated, collection of author.
25. G. W. Kitt, "Benjamin Minge Duggar: 1872–1956," *Mycologia*, Vol. 39, No. 3, May–June 1957, 434–38.
26. M. L. Nelson and S. B. Levy, "The history of the tetracyclines," *Annals of the New York Academy of Sciences*, 1241, (2011), 18.
27. Ibid., 18–19.
28. Benjamin M. Duggar, "Aureomycin: a product of the continuing search for new antibiotics," *Annals of the New York Academy of Sciences*, 51 (1948), 177–81.
29. W. Montague Cobb, "Louis Tompkins Wright, 1891–1952," *Journal of the American Medical Association*, March 1953, 130–46. See *Life*, 1938, 53.
30. Karen Jordan, "The Struggle and Triumph of America's First Black Doctors," *Atlantic*, December 6, 2016.
31. Wright's view on race was formed in large part from a traumatic event when he was fifteen, in 1906. A story that some black men assaulted white girls sparked three deadly days of riots by marauding white mobs. His stepfather handed him a shotgun and instructed him to guard the family home. After the riots, young Wright came across the corpse of a lynched black man in the woods near his school. It seemed to Wright that the chasm between the races would never be mended. "The Higher Education of Louis Tompkins Wright," *Journal of Blacks in Higher Education*, April 30, 2001.
32. Ibid.
33. Vanessa Northington Gamble, *Making a Place for Ourselves: The Black Hospital Movement, 1920–1945* (Oxford, UK: Oxford University Press, 1995), 60.
34. Massachusetts General, Peter Bent Brigham, and Boston City rejected him. Although he graduated cum laude from Harvard Medical School, he was not allowed to march with the other honors students and had to stay in the rear.
35. Gamble, *Making a Place for Ourselves*, 60.
36. In 1916, when Woodrow Wilson planned a huge parade for peace in Washington, the Freedman's Hospital staff was included in the event. Wright refused to participate because all the black marchers were assigned to the rear.
37. Gamble, *Making a Place for Ourselves*.

38. Ibid., 70–89; U.S. Public Health Service Syphilis Study at Tuskegee, Centers for Disease Control and Prevention, https://www.cdc.gov/tuskegee/timeline.htm.
39. David Warmflash, "Profiles in Science: Louis Tompkins Wright: Surgeon, Scientist, Civil Rights Activist," VisionLearning, Vol. SCIRE-3 (5), 2017; Gamble, *Making a Place for Ourselves*, 62.
40. History of Harlem Hospital Center, General Surgery Department, General Surgery Residency Program, http://www.cumc.columbia.edu/harlemhospital/surgery-residency/generalsurgerydept/History%20of%20Harlem%20Hospital%20Center.
41. Podolsky, *The Antibiotic Era*, 23.
42. Warmflash, "Profiles in Science."
43. Rosen, *Miracle Cure*, 216; Podolsky, *The Antibiotic Era*, 21–22.
44. Podolsky, *The Antibiotic Era*, 25–26. See also "A Review of the Clinical Uses of Aureomycin" (New York: Lederle Laboratories, 1951), 9.
45. U.S. Federal Trade Commission, "Economic Report on Antibiotics Manufacture," (Washington D.C.: Government Printing Office, 1958), 130, 139. See also Charles E. Silberman, "Drugs: The Pace is Getting Furious," *Fortune* (May 1960), 140.
46. *New York Times*, October 11, 1952, 19; *New York Times*, September 11, 1956, 33; Vanessa Northington Gamble, *Making a Place for Ourselves: The Black Hospital Movement, 1920–1945* (New York: Oxford University Press, 1995).

Chapter 7: A One-Atom Difference

1. Podolsky, *The Antibiotic Era*, 26–27.
2. Ernest Jawetz, "Infectious Diseases: Problems of Antimicrobial Therapy," *Annual Review of Medicine* 5 (1954): 1–2. See also Podolsky, *The Antibiotic Era*, 204–5.
3. Blaser, *Missing Microbes*, 77–78.
4. An Australian study of patients in a hospital ward provided the first evidence in 1945 of resistance to penicillin. Two further studies published in the late 1940s in British medical publications demonstrated the Australian cases were not an anomaly. It took a decade for scientists to understand how pathogenic bacteria mutated to become resistant to antibiotics. And it was another decade before they realized that some disease-causing microbes have a variant gene that allows them to survive an antibiotic. Those genetic variants then multiply, giving the impression that the emerging bacterial strain is resistant to drugs. As for the bacteria without the resistant gene, once each microbe realizes an antibiotic will overcome it, its cell activates what one doctor has dubbed a "bacterial hara-kiri." Blaser, *Missing Microbes*, 76–78. See generally Louis Weinstein, "The Spontaneous Occurrence of New Bacterial Infections during the Course of Treatment with Streptomycin or Penicillin," *American Journal of Medical Science* 214 (1947): 56–63; Mary Barber, "Staphylococcal Infection Due to Penicillin-Resistant Strains," *British Medical Journal* 2 (1947): 863; Mary Barber and Mary Rozwadowska-Dowzenko, "Infection by Penicillin-Resistant Staphylococci," *Lancet* 255 (1948). There were published reports of patient resistance only a year after Lederle's release of Aureomycin. See C. M. Demerec, "Patterns of bacterial resistance to penicillin, aureomycin, and streptomycin," *Journal of Clinical Investigation*, 28, 1949, 891–93. For more comprehensive warnings in the early to mid-1950s, see Wendell H. Hall, "The Abuse and Misuse of Antibiotics," *Minnesota Medicine* 35 (1952), 629; Jawetz, "Infectious Diseases," 1–2.

5. Interview with William W. Goodrich, part of the FDA Oral History Program, October 15, 1986;1:4–8; Edward Shorter, "The Liberal State and the Rogue Agency: FDA's Regulation of Drugs for Mood Disorders, 1950s–1970s," *International Journal of Law and Psychiatry* 31.2 (2008): 126–35.
6. "Editorial: Significance of Chloromycetin," *Therapeutic Notes* 56 (July–Aug. 1949): 157; Rosen, *The Creation of Antibiotics*, 247.
7. Merck did not have a broad-spectrum antibiotic yet was second with $120 million in revenue derived from its sulfas, hormones, penicillin and streptomycin, and vitamins. Only three patented antibiotics were produced under Merck's name. Otherwise, it provided drugs for other companies. "Medicine: What the Doctor Ordered," *Time*, August 18, 1952; Tom Mahoney, *Merchants of Life* (Riverdale, NY: Ayer Co., 1980), 68–70. As for Chloromycetin and what led to its recall from the market, see Carpenter, *Reputation and Power*, 148–49.
8. Rodengen, *The Legend of Pfizer*, 45–48.
9. Rosen, *Miracle Cure*, 218.
10. John E. McKeen, "Antibiotics and Pfizer & Co.," *Armed Forces Chemical Journal*, Vol. III, No. 8 (April 1950), 37–38.
11. *Chemical Engineering*, November 1950, 162, cited in U.S. Federal Trade Commission, "Economic Report on Antibiotics Manufacture" (Washington, D.C.: Government Printing Office, 1958), 231.
12. Samuel Mines, *Pfizer: An Informal History* (New York: Pfizer, 1978), 107–21.
13. Jeffrey L. Rodengen, *The Legend of Pfizer*.
14. By a different metric, total gross sales, pharma had become the largest industry in 1948 and reigned supreme for twenty years. See Rosen, *Miracle Cure*, 169.
15. John McKeen quoted in *Business Week*, March 26, 1950, 26; see Robert Bud, "Resisting Antibiotics: The Social Challenges of Drug Reform," *Boston Review*, October 27, 2015; Pringle, *Experiment Eleven*.
16. U.S. Federal Trade Commission, "Economic Report on Antibiotics Manufacture" (Washington, D.C.: Government Printing Office, 1958), 230.
17. Hawthorne, *The Merck Druggernaut*, 25–26.
18. Transcript of speech by George W. Merck, "Medicine Is for the Patient, Not for Profits," December 1, 1950, available in full at https://www.merck.com/about/our-people/gw-merck-doc.pdf. See also James C. Collins and Jerry I. Porras, *Built to Last: Successful Habits of Visionary Companies* (New York: Harper Business, 1994).
19. Merck stepped down that year as the company's president and became the chairman, a position from which he was less involved in daily operations. In his years as president, Merck's sales had boomed from $24 million annually to $171 million. A fifth of all its revenue came from foreign markets. Hawthorne, *The Merck Druggernaut*, 25–26.
20. Rodengen, *The Legend of Pfizer*. Also see Ogden Tanner, *25 Years of Innovation: The Story of Pfizer Central Research* (Lyme, CT: Greenwich Publishing Group, 1996).
21. Rosen, *Miracle Cure*, 218–19.
22. Stephens, C.R., et al., "Terramycin. VIII. Structure of Aureomycin and Terramycin," *Journal of the American Chemical Society*, 1952, 74: 4976–77.
23. Woodward remained a consultant to Pfizer through 1952, and they relied on his further research to enhance the therapeutic claims they made in advertisements.
24. Affidavit of John E. McKeen, president of Chas. Pfizer & Co., February 20, 1950.

25. U.S. Federal Trade Commission, "Economic Report on Antibiotics Manufacture," (Washington, D.C.: Government Printing Office, 1958), 232, n. 20.
26. Clinical tests then did not involve the use of placebos, formal techniques for randomization, or so-called blinding, in which test patients did not know what therapeutic agent they received. Instead, Wright, Hobby, and other doctors administered the test drug to patients who were sick with a wide range of bacterial infections and then monitored and recorded what happened. See generally Arthur A. Daemmrich, *Pharmacopolitics: Drug Regulation in the United States and Germany* (Chapel Hill, NC: The University of North Carolina Press, 2004).
27. Terry Armstrong, "Distribution in Jig Time: The Story of Terramycin," *Sales Management* 66 (1951): 74–78. See also Joseph D. McEvilla, "Competition in the American Pharmaceutical Industry," PhD dissertation, University of Pittsburgh, 1955, 143.
28. J.A. Greene and S. H. Podolsky, "Keeping modern in medicine: pharmaceutical promotion and physician education in postwar America," *Bulletin of the History of Medicine*, The American Association For The History Of Medicine, The Johns Hopkins Institute of the History of Medicine, Vol. 83, No. 2 (Summer 2009), 343.
29. It was called the Division of Penicillin Control and Immunology. Richard E McFadyen, "The FDA's Regulation And Control Of Antibiotics In The 1950s: The Henry Welch Scandal, Félix Martí-Ibáñez, And Charles Pfizer & Co," *Bulletin of the History of Medicine*, The American Association For The History Of Medicine, The Johns Hopkins Institute of the History of Medicine, Vol. 53, No. 2 (Summer 1979), 160.
30. E. King to Chas. Pfizer & Company, 9 March 1951, FDA Files, AF 12-118. See also Thomas Maeder, *Adverse Reactions* (New York: William Morrow, 1994), 54; Rosen, *Miracle Cure*, 223.
31. Rodengen, *The Legend of Pfizer*, 50.

Chapter 8: A "Jewish Kid from Brooklyn"

1. Jackson Lears, *Fables of Abundance: A Cultural History of Advertising in America* (New York: Basic Books, 1995).
2. An Austrian ad exec who worked for Sackler was Catholic but had a Jewish mother. "It was certainly a very embarrassing subject," he later recalled. "I didn't want to talk about it." Lears, *Fables of Abundance*, 7.
3. Lutze Marietta, *Who Can Know the Other? A Traveler in Search of Home* (Lunenburg, Vermont: Marietta Lutze Sackler, 1997, reprint 2002), no. 29 of 225 copies, in the Special Collections of Dartmouth Library, Rauner Presses Collection, 167.
4. The Arthur M. Sackler Collections, http://arthurmsacklerfdn.org/the-sackler-collection/#prettyPhoto. The Educational Alliance was a nonprofit organization established in 1889 to help Jewish immigrants settle in America.
5. The Heights campus, now the Bronx Community College of CUNY, was open from 1894 to 1973, when the university had to close it during a major national recession. http://www.nyuuniversityheights.com.
6. http://arthurmsacklerfdn.org/the-sackler-collection/#prettyPhoto.
7. "Arthur M. Sackler, M.D.," *Medical Tribune*, Vol. 25, No. 22, June 10, 1987, 1.
8. Lon Tuck, "Dr. Arthur Sackler: Art and Frustrations," *International Herald Tribune*, September 27–28, 1986.
9. Letter from A. B. Magil to Professor Alan M. Wald, September 4, 1991, transcript provided to the author in an email from Professor Wald, March 27, 2017.

10. Tony Michels, *Jewish Radicals: A Documentary History* (New York: NYU Press Scholarship, March 2016), 2.
11. Ibid., 2, 6.
12. Ibid., 2, 5–6.
13. Letter from A. B. Magil to Professor Alan M. Wald, September 4, 1991, transcript provided to the author in an email from Professor Wald, March 27, 2017. See also http://arthurmsacklerfdn.org/the-sackler-collection/.
14. Letter from A. B. Magil to Professor Alan M. Wald, September 4, 1991, transcript provided to the author in an email from Professor Wald, March 27, 2017. Arthur had also been the business and advertising manager for his high school paper. See Lutze, *Who Can Know the Other?*
15. Sackler believed promotion and sales were in the family genes. Arthur's younger brother Mortimer followed Arthur into ad sales for his high school newspaper, and persuaded Chesterfield cigarettes to place a weekly ad in the paper. Mortimer got a $5 weekly commission from those ads ($101 in 2019). http://arthurm sacklerfdn.org/the-sackler-collection/#prettyPhoto. See also Bruce Weber, "Mortimer D. Sackler, Co-Owner of Purdue Pharma, Dies at 93," *New York Times*, March 31, 2010, and J. Rosenfield, "Arthur Mitchell Sackler (1913–1987)," *Archives of Asian Art*, Vol. 41 (2011), 93.
16. See Esther (Else) Jorgensen, New York Marriage License Record Indexes, 1907–1995, September 13, 1938, New York, New York, Spouse: Abraham Sackler.
17. Rotating internships have fallen out of favor in recent decades as medical students have concentrated on residency programs for specialized practices. In Sackler's era, the program was an introduction to a broad range of general medicine. As a house pediatrician at Lincoln, he had to practice under the supervision of another physician. Lincoln had opened in 1839 as the Home for the Colored Aged, then became the Colored Home and Hospital, before renamed in 1899 in honor of Abraham Lincoln. By the time Sackler interned there, New York City's Department of Public Welfare owned it.
18. Many private medical schools in the U.S. had admission quotas for Jews. Cornell, Pennsylvania, Columbia, and Yale were the most notorious. At Yale Medical School, for instance, in 1935, 76 students were accepted to the first-year class from 501 applicants. Five Jews were among those admitted. Dean Milton Winternitz had told the admission director: "Never admit more than five Jews, take only two Italian Catholics, and take no blacks at all." Gerard N. Burrow, *A History of Yale's School of Medicine: Passing Torches to Others* (New Haven, CT: Yale University Press, 2008), 107ff.
19. Phil Hal, "Dr. Raymond Sackler, co-owner of Purdue Pharma, dies at 97," *West Fair*, July 23, 2017; Phil Davison, "Drugs mogul with a vast philanthropic legacy."
20. Vera Schwarcz, *Place and Memory in the Singing Crane Garden* (Philadelphia: University of Pennsylvania Press, 2014), 193.
21. "In Memory of Norman Bethune" was one of Mao's early essays and became part of the "Three Articles to Be Constantly Read," the small handful that were judged ideologically correct for Chinese communists. https://chineseposters.net/themes /98ethune.php.
22. Yang Yuli, "U.S. Doctor's Generosity to China," *Beijing Review*, May 13–19, 1992, 29–34. See also Schwarcz, *Place and Memory in the Singing Crane Garden*, 193.
23. See biographical information summary on Arthur Sackler in FBI report, File No. 65-1935, July 18, 1941, "Newark NJ office, re: Espionage, Schering Corpora-

tion, Dr. Gregory H. Stragnell, with aliases Gregor Straglovich, Gregory Passover, Nathan Pinkus." See also report of June 23, 1942, part of FBI FOIPA response and release March 30, 1999, subject "Arthur M. Sackler," FOIPA 442908, 89 pages.

24. http://arthurmsacklerfdn.org/the-sackler-collection/.
25. File No. 65-1935, July 18, 1941, Newark NJ office, NARA 65-HQ-4851, 10.
26. When Weltzien joined the firm, it was Chemische Fabrik auf Aktien. It changed its name after World War I to Schering.
27. Christopher Kobrak, "Julius Weltzien and the Interwar Transatlantic Business Dilemma: Nationalism and Internationalism Corrupted (1889–1950)," *Immigrant Entrepreneurship*, ESCP, Federal Ministry of Economics and Technology, Germany, December 3, 2012, File No. 65-1935, July 18, 1941, Newark NJ office, NARA 65-HQ-4851, 131.
28. Christopher Kobrak, *National Cultures and International Competition: The Experience of Schering AG, 1851–1950* (Cambridge: Cambridge University Press, 2002), 217–44.
29. "The most important products . . . are in the sex hormone field. The male and female sex hormone preparations manufactured by Schering are of extreme importance to the medical profession. . . . The Corporation is the sole source of most hormone preparations, and its other products are one of higher potency and purity than those manufactured by its competitors. The Corporation also holds the patent for certain sulpha products which are of a great importance because they are non-toxic." FBI Memorandum from Sherman Culbertson, "CHANGED: SHERING [*sic*] COPORATION [*sic*], 86 Orange Street, Bloomfield, New Jersey, Dr. GREGORY H. STRAGNELL, with aliases Gregor Straglovich, Gregory Passover, Nathan Pinkus And Canan Passover," June 23, 1942, File. No. 65-1935, 25 pages, 65-HQ-4851, V. 3, Serial 73, NARA, 2. For instance, according to the FBI, Schering had recently introduced a cortisone-based medication, Cortate, a "new hormone product . . . considered valuable in post-operative shock. According to officials in Washington . . . [this] anti-shock hormone is regarded as extremely important in war time." FBI report, File No. 65-1935, July 18, 1941, Newark NJ office, NARA 65-HQ-4851, 9, 11, 18.
30. FBI Memorandum from Sherman Culbertson, June 23, 1942.
31. It was five months before Pearl Harbor. There was evidence German shareholders in the U.S. subsidiary had sold their American stock but avoided any block on the funds by transferring it to the Swiss Bank Corporation in Basel. FBI report, File No. 65-1935, July 18, 1941, Newark NJ office, re: Espionage, Schering Corporation, Dr. Gregory H. Stragnell, with aliases Gregor Straglovich, Gregory Passover, Nathan Pinkus. See also report of June 23, 1942, part of FBI FOIPA (Freedom of Information and Privacy Act) response and release March 30, 1999 regarding subject "Arthur M. Sackler," FOIPA 442908, 89 pages.
32. FBI Memorandum, From Charles H. Kimball, "CHANGED: SHERING (sic) COPORATION (sic), 86 Orange Street, Bloomfield, New Jersey, Dr. GREGORY H. STRAGNELL, with aliases Gregor Straglovich, Gregory Passover, Nathan Pinkus," July 18, 1941, File. No. 65-1935, 33 pages, 65-HQ-4851, V. 1, Serial 21, NARA, 19.
33. The FBI reports misspell Weltzien as Weltzein.
34. The FBI learned that Weltzien had been a close friend of Gregor Strasser, an early Nazi Party member. Strasser was a chemist and Weltzien met him through joint pharmaceutical ventures. Hitler considered Strasser a rival and ordered him mur-

dered in 1934. Memorandum from Charles H. Kimball, "CHANGED: SHERING (sic) COPORATION (sic), 86 Orange Street, Bloomfield, New Jersey, Dr. GREGORY H. STRAGNELL, with aliases Gregor Straglovich, Gregory Passover, Nathan Pinkus," July 18, 1941, File. No. 65-1935, 33 pages, 65-HQ-4851, V. 1, Serial 21, NARA.

35. Kobrak, "Julius Weltzien and the Interwar Transatlantic Business Dilemma," 2.
36. FBI report, File No. 65-1935, July 18, 1941, Newark NJ office, NARA 65-HQ-4851, 20–21.
37. Ibid.
38. Lutze, *Who Can Know the Other?*, 168.
39. Sackler and Fröhlich met in late 1938 or early 1939; the precise date is not known. Adam Tanner, *Our Bodies, Our Data: How Companies Make Billions Selling our Medical Records* (Boston: Beacon Press, 2017). See also Castagnoli, "There Were Giants in Those Days."
40. The 1936 date is based on records from the Immigration and Naturalization Service. The *New York Times* obituary incorrectly listed his move to the U.S. as 1931. Fröhlich had visited the U.S. for the first time in 1935.
41. Tanner, 23–24.
42. Castagnoli, *Medicine Avenue*, 31.
43. A March 13, 1943, note made part of the Bureau's investigation says: "Subj. has close relatives in Germany & was a member of the German ARBEITSDIENST a student working camp in Germany in 1933." See Tanner, *Our Bodies, Our Data,* 175.
44. Frohlich's top employees were Jewish. "I never asked him about his religion," says Schering's Richard Sperber, who had worked with Frohlich's agency. "Never thought about it," says Sperber, himself Jewish. "I just assumed he was Jewish because all the top guys who worked there were."
45. Adam Tanner, "The Secret Life of the Gay Jewish Immigrant Whose Company Sells Your Medical Information," *Forward*, January 12, 2017; Tanner, *Our Bodies, Our Data*, 25–26. Frohlich had also been in the Reich Labour Service (Reichsarbeitsdienst), set up by Hitler to fight unemployment with public service work. Up to March 1, 1937, it allowed Jewish members. Egon Harings, *Germany and Two World Wars: From the German Reich to the End of the Nazi Regime* (Hamburg, Germany: Tredition, 2018), 26.
46. Tanner, "The Secret Life of the Gay Jewish Immigrant Whose Company Sells Your Medical Information."
47. Besides Gimbel's own elaborate seasonal gowns and evening dresses, she ran the Saks Fifth Avenue couture department for forty years. "Fashion: Counter-Revolution," *Time*, September 15, 1947.
48. Eric Wilson, "An Unheralded Muse of Midcentury Fashion," *New York Times*, January 16, 2013. See also Enid Nemy, "Sophie Gimbel, Leading American Designer for 40 Years, Dies at 83," *New York Times,* November 29, 1981.
49. Tanner, "The Secret Life of the Gay Jewish Immigrant Whose Company Sells Your Medical Information."
50. By the time she traveled to the U.S. she had become Ingrid, and added Lilly as a middle name a year later once settled in America.
51. Tanner, "The Secret Life of the Gay Jewish Immigrant Whose Company Sells Your Medical Information."
52. Lars Ericson quoted in Tanner, "The Secret Life of the Gay Jewish Immigrant Whose Company Sells Your Medical Information."

53. "Kathleen Ingrid Burns," obituary listing, *New York Times*, January 2, 2010.
54. Lisa Rab, "Don't Ask, Don't Tell: Details on the Everglades Club's Policy Toward Jews," *Broward Palm Beach New Times*, July 22, 2009. Also see Mark Seal, "How Donald Trump Beat Palm Beach Society and Won the Fight for Mar-a-Lago," *Vanity Fair*, December 26, 2017.
55. "Discrimination Remains a Policy and a Practice at Many Clubs," *New York Times*, September 13, 1976.
56. "Number of Clubs Barring Jews from Membership Sharply Decreasing," *Jewish Telegraphic Agency*, December 13, 1965.
57. Tanner, *Our Bodies, Our Data*, 23–24.
58. Tanner, "The Secret Life of the Gay Jewish Immigrant Whose Company Sells Your Medical Information."
59. Ibid.
60. Information about Frohlich's businesses is from Julian Farren, the L. W. Frohlich agency's executive vice president, to the Senate Judiciary Subcommittee on Antitrust and Monopoly hearings, Part 6, Advertising Provisions, January 30, 1962, 3142.
61. Three composed a clinical guide to "Female Sex Hormone Therapy," and the fourth was how the hormone extracted from pregnant mares might offer "treatment of sterility" for men and women. See "Female Sex Hormone Therapy: A Clinical Guide: Part One: The Follicular Hormone," "Part Two: Corpus Luteum Hormone," "Part Three: Male Sex Hormone," Medical Research Division, The Schering Corporation, January 1, 1941 (158 pages total); "Anteron: The Gonadotropic Hormone of Pregnant Mare Serum, For the Treatment of Sterility in Male and Female," The Schering Corporation, 1942 (4 pages total), in collection of author.
62. "Psychoanalysis Institute Opens Here Monday," *Chicago Tribune*, September 30, 1932, 9.
63. Allen Weinstein and Alexander Vassiliev, *The Haunted Wood* (New York: Modern Library, 1999), 51–52.
64. Michael Denning, *The Cultural Front: The Laboring of American Culture in the Twentieth Century* (Brooklyn: Verso, 2011), 226.
65. Kobrak, "Julius Weltzien and the Interwar Transatlantic Business Dilemma."
66. Although Nikola Tesla was an American citizen when he died in 1943 at the New Yorker Hotel in Manhattan, the Alien Property Custodian confiscated most of his research from his hotel room. It was only released after an investigation determined nothing threatened U.S. national security if it fell into enemy hands. "Tesla—Master of Lightning: The Missing Papers," PBS, 2008. See 131.3 Headquarters Records of the Office of Alien Property and its Predecessors Relating to Activities Arising from World War II, 1878–1965 (bulk 1930–49), NARA. See also Kobrak, "Julius Weltzien and the Interwar Transatlantic Business Dilemma"; Harris, *The Real Voice*, 56.
67. Frohlich operated his agency as an unincorporated sole proprietorship. He incorporated it in 1970, two years before his death, and changed the spelling of his name by adding an *e* after the *o*. See NY Department of State, Division of Incorporations, William Frohlich Associates, DOS ID 297752, November 2, 1970.
68. William G. Castagnoli, "There Were Giants in Those Days," Medical Advertising Hall of Fame, *Medical Marketing and Media*, Haymarket Media, March 1, 1997.
69. "What was Middlesex University," From the Brandeis Archives, February 14, 2009, http://brandeisarchives.blogspot.com/2009/02/what-is-middlesex.html.

70. The couple married in January, in a civil wedding in Yonkers presided over by a city judge. In April, they had a religious ceremony in Brooklyn, officiated by Rabbi Jacob Bosniak. Both were listed on their wedding certificate filed with the city. Federal Bureau of Investigation, Dr. Raymond Raphael Sackler, Beverly Sackler, report by Special Agent John V. Barnes, Security Matter C, 3 pages, Re: Beverly Feldman, Security Matter – C, from Special Agent William C. Courtney, New York Office, June 23, 1945, in FBI file 100-NY-73194_1, Special Access Division, NARA, 7-8, 9, 13.
71. Memo, Re: Beverly Feldman, Security Matter – C, from Special Agent William C. Courtney, to New York Office, March 14, 1945, in FBI file 100-NY-73194_1, Special Access Division, NARA, 2–3. See also Memo, Re: Beverly Feldman, Security Matter—C, from Special Agent William C. Courtney, to New York Office, March 13, 1945, 8–9.
72. Federal Bureau of Investigation, "Dr. Raymond Raphael Sackler, Beverly Sackler," report by Special Agent John V. Barnes, 7–10.
73. The party's peak was 1947 when it had 75,388 members. Many members became alienated when reports of Stalin's brutal crackdown on dissidents in the Soviet Union filtered to the West. By 1950, the national membership had dropped by half. http://depts.washington.edu/moves/CP_map-members.shtml; https://jwa.org/encyclopedia/article/communism-in-united-states.
74. Historians estimate that for each "card-carrying" communist, there were three to four others who took part in party-led events but did not formally join. Priscilla Murolo, "Communism in the United States," *Jewish Women's Archive*, https://jwa.org/encyclopedia/article/communism-in-united-states.
75. Letter from A. B. Magil to Professor Alan M. Wald, September 4, 1991, transcript provided to the author in an email from Professor Wald, March 27, 2017.
76. There are forty-four pages about the surveillance of Beverly and Raymond Sackler, including reconnaissance of their international travel during the 1950s and 1960s, in FBI file 100-NY-73194_1, Special Access Division, NARA.
77. In 1958, for instance, when an FBI agent visited Beverly Sackler concerning her application for a passport, he noted in his report to headquarters that "Mrs. Sackler did not answer questions relating to present and past membership in the CP." Federal Bureau of Investigation, "Dr. Raymond Raphael Sackler, Beverly Sackler, report by Special Agent John V. Barnes, 16.
78. Stuart Elliott, "McAdams Forms Division to Focus on Latest Drugs," *New York Times*, December 16, 1991, D9. See also William G. Castagnoli, "Remembrance of Kings Past," *Medical Marketing & Media*, 31(7): 44. July 1, 1996, 30. The company was operated as a sole proprietorship until it was incorporated in New York on September 27, 1945. Also, Dr. DeForest Ely, president of McAdams, gave a brief history of the company during Senate testimony in 1962. See Drug Industry Antitrust Act, Hearings before the Subcommittee on Antitrust and Monopoly, Senate Committee on the Judiciary, Part 6 Document No. 6, January 31, 1962, 3071–72.
79. "Arthur M. Sackler," MAHF Inductees, Medical Advertising Hall of Fame, 1997; "Arthur M. Sackler, M.D.," *Medical Tribune*, Vol. 25, No. 22, June 10, 1987, 1.
80. Biography of Arthur M. Sackler, Drug Industry Antitrust Act, Hearings before the Subcommittee on Antitrust and Monopoly, Senate Committee on the Judiciary, Part 6 Document No. 6, January 30, 1962, 3064. See also Philip Shenon, "Fear and Brutality in a Creedmoor Ward," *New York Times*, June 18, 1984, A1, B6.

81. Biography of Arthur M. Sackler, 3064.
82. "Arthur M. Sackler, M.D.," *Medical Tribune*, Vol. 25, No. 22, June 10, 1987, 1. See also NY Department of State, Division of Incorporations, Laboratories for Therapeutic Research, Inc, DOS ID 166868, August 9, 1957, inactive and dissolved November 12, 1992.
83. Sackler, A. M. "Taboos of the Past and Perspectives for the Future in Social Psychiatry," *International Journal of Social Psychiatry* (1973), 1.
84. Matt Cvetic, "The Thought Control Brigade," *American Mercury*, October 1958, 137–38.
85. Email to author from Professor Ben Harris, May 6, 2018; also interview of Ted Reiss by Ben Harris, 1983, courtesy of Ben Harris; see also Arnold D. Richards (2016), "The Left and Far Left in American Psychoanalysis: Psychoanalysis as a Subversive Discipline," *Contemporary Psychoanalysis*, 52:1, 111–29.
86. Arthur Sackler's role in stopping the Red Cross blood segregation policy was minor at best. An introduction to a 2016 profile of his second daughter, Elizabeth, said, "As a testament to the nature instilled by the elder Sackler, a man responsible for New York City's first integrated blood bank, she has used her powerful position to make room for those typically marginalized: women, American Indians, the Jewish community, and incarcerated people." The author's repeated requests to Elizabeth Sackler for an interview have gone unanswered. Ali Maloney, "Art and activism: The compass points of Elizabeth Sackler's storied career," *Women in the World*, January 8, 2016; Josh Rosenau, "How Science Students Helped End Segregated Blood Banks," *National Center for Science Education*, August 5, 2015; Thomas A. Guglielmo, "When the Red Cross refused to accept 'Negro blood,'" *Week*, December 22, 2015; Dwight Jon Zimmerman, "The American Red Cross African-American Blood Ban Scandal," *DefenseMediaNetwork*, January 21, 2012.
87. The Joint Anti-Fascist Refugee Committee sued the attorney general in 1948, arguing that there was no evidence to support the listing. The question of whether an organization had the right to challenge a security listing made its way to the Supreme Court in 1951. The justices ruled that the Joint Anti-Fascist Refugee Committee could challenge its inclusion on the subversive list. It took another twelve years before a D.C. circuit court ruled that the evidence against the group was "negligible." It was of interest to historians and legal scholars but had no practical effect since the Refugee Committee had disbanded in 1955. Joint Anti-Fascist Refugee Committee v. McGrath, 341 U.S. 123, 1951.
88. FBI Memorandum, To the Executive Director of the President's War Relief Control Board, from J. Edgar Hoover, "Re Joint Anti-Fascist Refugee Committee, with attachment, 6/20/45, Edward J. Mooney, Special Agent, Report Re Joint Anti-Fascist Refugee Committee also known as Spanish Refugee Appeal," NY File No. 100-3642, 100-HQ-7061, V. 50, Serial 1071, NARA, 9.
89. FBI Memorandum, To the Executive Director of the President's War Relief Control Board, from J. Edgar Hoover, 14.
90. Abraham M. Sackler, License No. 045772, date of licensure, 2/6/1947; Mortimer D. Sackler, License No. 046790, date of licensure, 10/09/1947; Raymond R. Sackler, License No. 047200, date of licensure, 2/19/1948, Office of the Professions, New York.
91. Pharmaceutical Research Associates, Inc., filing date New York State June 25, 1945, DOS ID. 56217.

92. In 1962, a Senate investigative panel looking into competition in the drug industry listed Pharmaceutical Research Associates as possibly controlled by the Sacklers. The author located files in the New York State Division of Corporations revealing that when the company went inactive in 2004, the registered agent was an attorney who sometimes represented Purdue, Stuart Baker. He was then with the Manhattan law firm of Chadbourne & Parke (as of this writing, he is a partner at New York's Norton Rose Fulbright). In 1994, Baker remained at Chadbourne & Parke while serving as a director and officer of Purdue Pharma. Business profile of Pharmaceutical Research Associates, Inc., at https://www.bloomberg.com/research/stocks/private/snapshot.asp?privcapId=4279695.
93. Dr. Halpern published academic papers that sometimes were thinly disguised endorsements of products sold by a drug firm that the Sacklers bought in 1952 (Purdue Frederick). Typical was "The Peripheral Vascular Dynamics of Bowel Function," *Angiology*, October 1, 1960. It concluded that potential coronary risks associated with "straining at stool" could be avoided with a stool softener. The product used in the small trial tests was *Senokot*. A footnote in the article noted it was "supplied by the Purdue Frederick Company."
94. At the bottom of a memo from Arthur Sackler to Félix Martí-Ibáñez in 1956, Sackler copied his brothers simply as "Mortie & Ray." See Memorandum from Dr. A. M. Sackler to Dr. Felix Marti-Ibanez, December 14, 1956, Subj: "Geography And World Patterns Of Schizophrenia And Other Mental Illnesses," MS 1235, Box 2, Folder "S" 1957, Papers of Félix Martí-Ibáñez, Yale University, Manuscripts and Archives, New Haven, CT.
95. "Her Ambitions Demand Toll," *Salt Lake City Tribune*, July 8, 1945, 28; "She Was Clever but She Lacked Sense of Values," *Daily Times* (Davenport, Iowa), March 1, 1947, 3. Haberman, while still at McAdams, later served in the New York City Department of Mental Health and Mental Retardation Services in the 1960s and 1970s, appointed by both Mayors Wagner and Lindsay. "Mental Health Aid," *New York Daily News*, June 10, 1960, 379; "Mental Health Agency Adds 8," *New York Daily News*, January 8, 1970, 315.

Chapter 9: Medicine Avenue

1. Harry Phibbs, a former Burroughs Wellcome salesman, opened the first agency that concentrated only on ethical drugs in Chicago in 1926. The Harry C. Phibbs Advertising Company was followed in Chicago later that year by William Douglas McAdams. McAdams moved his agency to New York in the 1930s and soon had competition. In 1934, two Squibb promotion executives, Arthur Sudler and Matthew Hennessey, formed an art studio and ad firm that focused on drugs. Paul Klemtner, who had worked as an accountant for pharmacists, opened his own agency in 1942 in New Jersey. See generally Castagnoli, *Medicine Avenue*, 14–15, 22, 110–11. As for the use of Medicine Avenue, see "Doctor's Dilemma," *New England Journal of Medicine* 266:1335 (June 21, 1962).
2. John Lear, "The Struggle for Control of Drug Prescriptions," SR/Research/Science & Humanity, *Saturday Review*, March 3, 1962, 36.
3. See Castagnoli, *Medicine Avenue*, 29.
4. Karl E. Meyer and Shareen Blair Brysac, *The China Collectors: America's Century-Long Hunt for Asian Art Treasures* (New York: St. Martin's Press, 2015), 56.
5. "William Drummond: Gently anarchic art dealer with a talent for sniffing out

junk shop gems who employed a young Sarah Ferguson as his assistant," *Times* (London), April 13, 2018.

6. New York Department of State, Division of Corporations, The Sackler Foundation Inc. DOS ID 69974, March 18, 1947.
7. Arthur created his own foundation in 1965. The Arthur M. Sackler Foundation incorporated in New York State on October 18, 1965, DOS ID# 191762.
8. The Mortimer D. Sackler Foundation incorporated in New York State on December 8, 1967, DOS ID# 217072. Raymond did not incorporate in New York, but instead a year earlier in Delaware. Also: The Serpentine Trust, No. 298809, March 21, 1988, Charity Commission, UK; The Dr. Mortimer and Theresa Sackler 1988 Foundation, Co. No. 327863, July 12, 1988, Charity Commission, UK; Raymond and Beverly Sackler 1988 Foundation, Co. No. 327864, July 12, 1988, Charity Commission, UK; The Napp Educational Foundation, Co. No. 05346056, January 26, 2005, Companies House, UK; The Sackler Trust, Co. No. 1132097, October 13, 2009, Charity Commission, and No. 0702224, Sept. 17, 2009, Companies House, UK; Raymond and Beverly Sackler Foundation, Co. No. 06802986, January 27, 2009, Companies House, and No. 1128918, March 31, 2009, Charity Commission, UK; The Dr. Mortimer and Theresa Sackler Foundation, Co. No. 06802998, January 27, 2009, Companies House, and No. 1128926, April 1, 2009, Charity Commission, UK.
9. Attorneys Richard Leather and Michael Sonnenreich to Adam Tanner, *Our Bodies, Our Data,* 24–25.
10. Michael Sonnenreich told the author that "Frohlich's firm basically was Arthur's." Interview with author, January 19, 2019.
11. Grace Glueck, "An Art Collector Sows Largesse and Controversy," *New York Times*, June 5, 1983; Tanner, *Our Bodies, Our Data,* n. 7, 175.
12. Michael Sonnenreich interview with author, January 19, 2019.
13. Adam Tanner, based on his interviews with former executives at Frohlich businesses as well as the attorneys for both Sackler and Frohlich, concluded that Frohlich owned a 50 percent interest in the international editions of *Medical Tribune.* See Tanner, *Our Bodies, Our Data,* N. 19, 175.
14. Castagnoli, "There Were Giants in Those Days."
15. In Milton and Lee, *Pills, Profits and Politics* (22), a physician complains: "My patients read the latest issue of *Reader's Digest* and then tell me what to prescribe." See also L.W. Frohlich, "The Physician in the Pharmaceutical Industry in the United States," Proceedings of the Royal Society of Medicine, from April 11, 1960, London, Vol. 53, Sec. 1, August 1960, 584.
16. William G. Castagnoli, "Remembrance of Kings Past," *Medical Marketing & Media*, 31(7): 44. July 1, 1996.
17. Castagnoli, "There Were Giants in Those Days."
18. A 1982 profile of Sackler in *The Boston Globe* noted, "Former employees complain about his treatment. Nevertheless, despite rumor and harsh opinion, the accusations have never been turned into legal judgments against him." Robert Lenzner, "A Financial Man and the Fogg," *Boston Globe*, February 16, 1982, 49.
19. Michael Sonnenreich, interview with author, January 19, 2019.
20. The full name is DR. Kade Pharmazeutische Fabrik GmbH.
21. "They looked so much alike," Marietta wrote later in a memoir, "they'd sometimes pretend to be the other, especially when one of them needed to show up for some routine hospital duty." Lutze, *Who Can Know the Other?*, 100.

22. Arye Carmon, "The Impact of the Nazi Racial Decrees on the University of Heidelberg," Shoah Resource Center, Yad Vashem.
23. Lutze, *Who Can Know the Other?*, 99.
24. FBI Confidential Memorandum from the New York Office to Washington Headquarters, "IS-PO Registration Act," January 31, 1963, FOIPA 442908: FBI files regarding Arthur Sackler released March 30, 1999 (89 pages), 37.
25. Stacy Wong, "Thrust Under Microscope: Stamford Drug Company's Low Profile Shattered by Controversy Over Abuse of Painkiller OxyContin," *Hartford Courant* (New Haven, CT), September 2, 2001, 1.
26. Gray's Glycerine Tonic Compound was 11 percent alcohol. Phil Davison, "Drugs mogul with a vast philanthropic legacy," *Financial Times*, April 23, 2010; author interview with Richard Sperber, March 26, 2019, about the category of sales called "ethical over-the-counter."
27. FOIA collection on documents released pursuant to the request of Professor Ben Harris, 1999, 5.
28. Biography of Arthur M. Sackler, Drug Industry Antitrust Act, Hearings before the Subcommittee on Antitrust and Monopoly, Senate Committee on the Judiciary, Part 6 Doc. No. 6, January 30, 1962, 3064.
29. Lear, "The Struggle for Control of Drug Prescriptions," 36. Sackler sold his interest in Medical & Pharmaceutical Information Bureau to a friend, science writer Richard Sigerson, in 1952. The Senate investigated medical advertising a decade later. In public testimony, John Weilburg, the president of MPIB, admitted that he had returned to Sackler all his files despite a Senate subpoena to provide all documents to the investigative staff. Weilburg said that when Sackler's attorneys had requested Arthur's files, he had complied as "the terribly naïve guy I am." "Testimony of John Weilburg, President, Medical and Pharmaceutical Information Bureau, Administered Prices, Drug Industry Antitrust Act, Hearings on S. 1552, Part 7, Advertising Provisions" (Washington, D.C., U.S. Government Printing Office, 1962), 3216–17.
30. Ibid., 3212–21. Congress outlawed many types of stock manipulation in the 1934 Securities and Exchange Act, however it took eight years before the SEC adopted Rule 10b-5, applying fraud elements to purchases as well as sales of securities. Although 10b-5 became the enforcement tool against insider trading, the term is not defined in the rule. It took SEC actions and court rulings for the concept to evolve. It was not until 1965 that the SEC sued thirteen executives at a Texas energy and mining company for relying on private information to profit from buying the firm's stock. See Eileen Shanahan, "S.E.C. Insider Suit Names Texas Gulf Sulphur Aides," *New York Times*, April 20, 1965, 1; "Timeline: A History of Insider Trading," *New York Times*, December 6, 2016.
31. Lutze, *Who Can Know the Other?*, 100.
32. Ibid.
33. Ibid., 103.
34. Ibid., 106.
35. "Deaths: Sackler, Else," *New York Times*, March 17, 2000.
36. Lutze, *Who Can Know the Other?*
37. Ibid., 110.
38. Ibid., 112.
39. Ibid., 164.
40. See Lear, "The Struggle for Control of Drug Prescriptions."

41. Adolf Meyer, John Hopkins's influential psychiatrist-in-chief, introduced "psychobiology," what he called a "newer psychiatry." It theorized there were biological underpinnings to some mental illness, a notion Freudians rejected. Meyer was responsible also for the word "psychiatry," replacing the nineteenth-century "alienism," which had been used for the mentally ill, people considered to be alienated from their own natural state. "Psychiatrist" had mostly replaced "alienist" by the early nineteenth century. Dowbiggin, *The Quest for Mental Health*, 114; see also "Raymond Sackler," *Artforum International*, 2017.
42. Edward Shorter and Max Fink, *Endocrine Psychiatry: Solving the Riddle of Melancholia* (Oxford University Press, 2010), 38.
43. "Arthur M. Sackler, M.D.," *Medical Tribune*, Vol. 25, No. 22, June 10, 1987, 1. See also NY Department of State, Division of Incorporations, Laboratories for Therapeutic Research, Inc, DOS ID 166868, August 9, 1957, inactive and dissolved November 12, 1992; Rosenfield, J. (1988). Arthur Mitchell Sackler (1913–1987), *Archives of Asian Art*, 41, 93, from http://www.jstor.org/stable/20111186.
44. One of their most widely discussed papers was written with Dutch psychiatrist Johan van Ophuijsen; it suggested that injections of histamines, a naturally occurring body chemical responsible for allergies, might be more effective than electroshock in treating mental illness. Tuck, "Dr. Arthur Sackler." "Problems of Insanity Concern Both Statesmen and Scientists," *Life*, March 13, 1950, 161; "Medicine: All in the Mind," *Time*, May 23, 1949.
45. Arthur Sackler to Dr. M. F. Ashley Matagu, Princeton University, from the *Journal of Clinical and Experimental Psychopathology*, May 15, 1955, collection of author.
46. Biography of Arthur M. Sackler, Drug Industry Antitrust Act, Hearings before the Subcommittee on Antitrust and Monopoly, Senate Committee on the Judiciary, Part 6 Document No. 6, January 30, 1962, 3064.
47. Tuck, "Dr. Arthur Sackler."
48. Ibid.
49. Lutze, *Who Can Know the Other?*, 152.
50. J. Rosenfield, "Arthur Mitchell Sackler (1913–1987)," *Archives of Asian Art*, 41, 1988, 93.
51. Lutze, *Who Can Know the Other?*, 166.
52. Ibid., 153.
53. Ibid., 165–66.
54. Ibid., 153.
55. Tuck, "Dr. Arthur Sackler."
56. Lutze, *Who Can Know the Other?*, 207
57. Ibid., 155
58. Meyer and Brysac, *The China Collectors*, 354–55; Tuck, "Dr. Arthur Sackler."
59. Arthur Sackler quoted in Rosenfield, "Arthur Mitchell Sackler."
60. Years later Marietta tried joining him on his collecting. She discovered that while she "could appreciate . . . his love for art," it was "not as a partner, for he was far too self-absorbed for that." Lutze, *Who Can Know the Other?*, 149, 153, 156.
61. Ibid., 149, 156.

Chapter 10: The Hard Sell Blitz

1. M. Sackler, F. Martí-Ibáñez, R. Sackler, and A. Sackler, Co-Tui FW, Mittleman, MB, "Quantitated identification of psychosis by blood sample. I. Instrumentation of ultrasound for biologic quantitation," *The Journal of Clinical and Experimental Psychopathology*. 1951 Oct–Dec;12(4), 283–7 and 288–303. The Sacklers also had an exclusive design on an early ultrasound machine and sold the rights in 1958 for a tidy profit. See Schwarcz, *Place and Memory in the Singing Crane Garden*, 193–94; Glueck, "An Art Collector Sows Largesse and Controversy."
2. She took the name Marietta Lutze Sackler, both professionally and personally. Lutze, *Who Can Know the Other?*, 125. As for her collaboration with the Sackler brothers, see Sackler Md, Sackler Rr, Tui Co, Sackler Ml, Sze Lc, Sanders Rh, Martin Cr, Steinman K, Jacobi E, Nicoll A, Sackler Am, Laburt Ha, "Psychiatric research perspectives at the Creedmoor Institute for Psychobiologic Studies, 1953," *Journal of Clinical and Experimental Psychopathology*, 1954 Apr–Jun;15(2):119–29. Marietta also wrote two articles without any Sackler contribution: "Xanthine oxidase from liver and duodenum of the rat: histochemical localization and electrophoretic heterogeneity," Sackler ML., *J Histochem Cytochem*, 1966 Apr;14(4):326–33; "Haemochromatosis and hepatic xanthine oxidase," Mazur A., Sackler M., *Lancet*. 1967 Feb 4;1(7484):254–55.
3. Marietta said the Sackler brothers had a "closeness [that] was unusual, one from which all wives were excluded." It was a "complicated dependency . . . that led to tremendous interpersonal strains." Lutze, *Who Can Know the Other?*, 117, 169. See also Muriel L. Sackler, *New York Times*, October 9, 2009.
4. Insulin-induced hypoglycemia, later dubbed insulin shock, was the first of three therapies developed around 1930 intended to jolt the brain into a less agitated and more coherent state. There were some notable successes. The 1994 Nobel Prize laureate for economics, American mathematician John Nash, had ICT treatment to treat paranoid psychosis not long after he obtained his PhD at Princeton. Vaslav Nijinsky, one of the twentieth century's greatest ballet dancers, underwent two hundred insulin shock sessions during his career. The second shock procedure substituted a camphor-style drug, Metrazol, for insulin. The final one was electroconvulsive therapy (ECT). All three treatments fell out of favor not only because of side effects but also because they were made somewhat obsolete with the introduction of Thorazine in 1954. A lighter and more refined ECT procedure has had a resurgence starting in the late 1980s. Dowbiggin, *The Quest for Mental Health*, 114–18; Arthur M Sackler (Ed), Mortimer D Sackler (Ed), Raymond R Sackler (Ed), Félix Martí-Ibáñez (Ed), Ugo Cerletti (Ed), *The Great Physiodynamic Therapies in Psychiatry: An Historical Reappraisal* (New York: Hoeber-Harper Medical, 1956).
5. Office Memorandum from Felix Marti-Ibanez, M.D., to Doctors Arthur, Mortimer and Raymond Sackler, December 6, 1956, "re: NEW PROJECT—OUR PAPER AND MONOGRAPH ON 'THE GEOGRAPHY AND THE WORLD PATTERNS OF SCHIZOPHRENIA AND OTHER MENTAL ILLNESSES,'" MS 1235, Box 2, Folder "S" 1957, Papers of Félix Martí-Ibáñez, Yale University, Manuscripts and Archives, New Haven, CT.
6. "Dr. Felix Marti-Ibanez Is Dead; Psychiatrist and Publisher, 60," *New York Times*, May 25, 1972.

7. "Personal, August 10, 1945–December 1945," || Box 2, Papers of Félix Martí-Ibáñez, Yale University Archives, New Haven, CT, also "CV."
8. "Considerations about Homosexuality," Félix Martí-Ibáñez, "Consideraciones sobre el homosexualismo," *Estudios* 145, September 1935, 3–6.
9. Herman A. Bogdan, "Félix Martí-Ibáñez—Iberian Daedalus: The Man Behind the Essays," *Journal of the Royal Society of Medicine*, Vol. 86, October 1993, 595.
10. Ibid., 595–96.
11. Ibid., 596.
12. He traveled widely for the International Congresses on the History of Science, Psychiatry, and Psychology; Bogdan, "Félix Martí-Ibáñez," 595–96.
13. Ibáñez to Morris Fishbein, 8/24/45; Ibáñez to Fishbein, 10/3/45; Ibáñez to Fishbein, 11/2/45, "Personal, August 10, 1945 - December 1945," Box 2, Papers of Félix Martí-Ibáñez, Yale University Archives, New Haven, CT.
14. "CV," Box 3, and "Personal, January 1943 - October 1943" Box 2, FMIP. And see Ibanez to Arthur M. Sackler, 8/19/52, "William Douglas McAdams," Box 5, Yale University Archives, New Haven, CT.
15. Félix Martí-Ibáñez, *Journey Around Myself.*
16. See for instance Félix Martí-Ibáñez, "The artist as physician; medical philosophy in the Renaissance," *Int Rec Med Gen Pract Clin.* 1954 Apr;167(4):221–42; "The physician as alchemist; medical ideas in the Arabian Empire," *Int Rec Med Gen Pract Clin.* 1955 Jun;168(6):399–424; "Symposium on the history of American medicine. I, The spirit of American medicine," *Int Rec Med Gen Pract Clin.* 1958 Jun;171(6):317–22; "The physician as traveler; introduction to the First International Symposium on Health and Travel." *Int Rec Med Gen Pract Clin.* 1955 Jul;168(7):480–85; "Minerva and Aesculapius; the physician as writer," *Int Rec Med Gen Pract Clin.* 1956 Nov;169(11):723–45; "The search for the philosophical nature of disease in the history of medicine; an introduction to Hans Selye's Sketch for a unified theory of medicine," *Int Rec Med Gen Pract Clin.* 1954 Apr;167(4):179–80; "Words and research," *Antibiotic Med Clin Ther* (New York). 1957 Nov;4(11):740–7; "Symbols and medicine," *Int Rec Med.* 1960 Feb;173:99–125; "Medicine in the Spain of Don Quixote," *Int Rec Med Gen Pract Clin.* 1958 May;171(5):277–313; "A footnote to medical history: concerning the article by Hans Selye on 'Stress and disease," *Int Rec Med Gen Pract Clin.* 1955 May;168(5):288–91; "New perspectives of health and travel; a summation of the symposium," *Int Rec Med Gen Pract Clin.* 1955 Sep;168(9):583–6; "Friends for the road," *Int Rec Med Gen Pract Clin.* 1959 Aug;172(8):480–3; "The epic of medicine. (V). Through a stained-glass window. (Byzantine medicine, 476–1453)," *Int Rec Med.* 1960 Jan;173:74–7; "The epic of medicine. IV. A torrent of lions (medicine in Imperial Rome) (285 B.C.–A.D. 476), *Int Rec Med.* 1959 Nov;172:719–22; "The epic of medicine. (VII). The cross and the eagle" (Monastic and university medicine, 1096–1453)," *Int Rec Med.* 1960 Jul;173:462–7; "The fabric and creation of a dream: on the genesis and growth of a new concept in medical journalism as exemplified by the medical newsmagazine, *MD*," *Int Rec Med.* 1959 Dec;172:754–65; "Doctors must tell," *Int Rec Med.* 1959 Oct;172:651–2; "Life and works of Paul Ehrlich, 1854–1915: the world and mind of the father of chemotherapy," *Rev Med Costa Rica.* 1954 Apr;13(240):73–87; "Padna and London; a Harveian tale of two cities," *Int Rec Med Gen Pract Clin.* 1957 Jun;170(6):286–316; "The history of endocrinology as seen through the evolution of our knowledge of

the adrenal gland; biography of a medical idea," *Int Rec Med Gen Pract Clin.* 1952 Dec;165(12):587–602.

17. Six years later he became the Chair of the History of Medicine at New York Medical College. "DR. FELIX MARTI-IBANEZ: Appointed professor of history of medicine and director of new department by New York Medical College," *Antibiotic Med Clin Ther* (New York), 1956 Jun;3(1):75. See also Bernard Stengren, "He Takes Pulse of 150,000 U.S. Physicians," *St. Louis Post-Dispatch*, June 13, 1960.
18. Some previous publications claim that Sackler hired Martí-Ibáñez at the McAdams agency. A 1960 profile on Martí-Ibáñez reported that Sackler had brought him to the agency in part because his "facility with words and experience in editing made him a particularly valuable asset." Stengren, "He Takes Pulse of 150,000 U.S. Physicians," 39. Podolsky, *The Antibiotic Era*, 79–80, lists Martí-Ibáñez as an "employee of the William Douglas McAdams agency." Also, in a March 10, 1954, letter from Marti-Ibáñez to Dr. Henry Welch, Chief of the Antibiotics Division at the FDA, Marti-Ibáñez told Welch that he was "extremely hurried with the moving of McAdams International to 15 East 62nd Street, which by the way, is a most pleasant and convenient location." He urged Welch to stop by the new offices when he next visited New York. It was the address also for the relocated McAdams ad agency, as well as the business address listed in the phone book for Mortimer and Raymond Sackler. See John Lear, "The Struggle for Control of Drug Prescriptions," SR/Research/Science & Humanity, *Saturday Review*, March 3, 1962, 37.
19. As for the sharing of office space, see Barry Maier, *Pain Killer: An Empire of Deceit and the Origin of America's Opioid Crisis* (New York: Random House, 2018), 212.
20. Glueck, "An Art Collector Sows Largesse and Controversy." And see a final accounting by the executors of the decedent's estate, Matter of Estate of Sackler, 149 Misc.2d 734, 564 N.Y.S.2d 977, 980 (N.Y.Sur. Ct. 1990); Matter of Sackler, (9-28-2007), 2007 NY Slip Op 33226(U) (N.Y. Misc. 2007). See also New York Department of State, Division of Corporations, Angiology Research Foundation, Inc., DOS ID #78434, May 10, 1950; Inter America Medical Press, Inc., DOS ID #84349, June 20, 1952; International Medical Press, Incorporated, DOS ID# 83791, April 7, 1952. Blair-Dixon Memorandum, collection of author.
21. Castagnoli, "There Were Giants in Those Days."
22. Sam Quinones, *Dreamland: The True Tale of America's Opiate Epidemic* (London: Bloomsbury Press, 2015), 29.
23. "Pfizer Put an Old Name on a New Drug Label," *Business Week*, October 13, 1951, 134.
24. Ibid., 136.
25. U.S. Federal Trade Commission, "Economic Report on Antibiotics Manufacture" (Washington, D.C.: Government Printing Office, 1958), 142. Also see "Company History," Pfizer, 1951, https://www.pfizer.com/about/history/all.
26. U.S. Federal Trade Commission, "Economic Report on Antibiotics Manufacture," (Washington, D.C.: Government Printing Office, 1958), 145.
27. Tom Fortunato, "The Origin of Pfizer Cards," June 18, 2005, http://www.deardoctorpostcards.com/art-2005pfizer.html.
28. Quinones, *Dreamland*, 29. See also Donohue, "A History of Drug Advertising," 34; Fortunato, "The Origin of Pfizer Cards."
29. Rosen, *Miracle Cure*, 228–29.

30. Podolsky, *Antibiotics Era*, 35–36. Any medical device or drug ad that ran in *JAMA* prior to 1955 had to have the Seal of Approval from the AMA's Council on Drugs. That requirement was dropped so that *JAMA* could fill its pages with a much more diverse assortment of drug ads. The AMA—under pressure from some of the largest pharma firms—soon dropped its Seal of Approval program. Carpenter, *Reputation and Power*, 207; Drug Industry Antitrust Act (n. 39), p. 131. See also Milton and Lee, *Pills, Profits and Politics*, 109.
31. May, "Selling Drugs by 'Educating' Physicians," 12; Milton and Lee, *Pills, Profits and Politics*, 68.
32. Donohue, "A History of Drug Advertising"; "The Federal Trade Commission Act of 1938," *Columbia Law Review*, vol. 39, no. 2, 1939, pp. 259–73; James Harvey Young, PhD, *The Medical Messiahs: A Social History of Quackery in 20th-Century America*, chapter 14.
33. Donohue, "A History of Drug Advertising," 33.
34. R. B. Ruge, "Regulation of Prescription Drug Advertising: Medical Progress and Private Enterprise," *Publishing Entertainment Advertising Law Quarterly* 9(3):261–99, 1969.
35. Podolsky, *Antibiotic Era*, 36.
36. Castagnoli, "There Were Giants in Those Days."
37. Castagnoli, *Medicine Avenue*, 18.
38. Rodengen, *The Legend of Pfizer*, 50.
39. Lombardino, "A Brief History of Pfizer Central Research," 12; Mahoney, *Merchants of Life*, 237–50.
40. Tone, *Age of Anxiety*, 70.
41. Donohue, "A History of Medical Advertising," 668–69.
42. Since the 1990s, many sales forces at the largest pharma conglomerates are split into subspecialties. Some sell only to oncologists, others to internists, OB-GYN practitioners, even dermatologists. Studies demonstrate that concentration allows for better one-on-one sales.
43. Thomas Winn, Sales Manager of the Antibiotics Division for Pfizer, quoted in note 96, Podolsky, *Antibiotic Era*, 39.
44. Robert L. Shook, *Miracle Medicines: Seven Lifesaving Drugs and the People Who Created Them*. See also Robin Walsh, "A History of the Pharmaceutical Industry," *Pharmaphorum*, February 16, 2017.
45. Pfizer had surpassed Lederle's Aureomycin sales, with 23 percent of the worldwide market. Parke-Davis's Chloromycetin had fallen sharply in sales after reports emerged linking it to aplastic anemia, a rare and debilitating bone marrow disease. Rosen, *Miracle Cure*, 224–25.
46. John Lear, "Taking the Miracle out of the Miracle Drugs," *Saturday Review* 42 (Jan. 3, 1959). Lear followed with "The Certification of Antibiotics," February 7, 1959, and "Do We Need a Census of Worthless Drugs?" May 7, 1960.
47. Sharp & Dohme had earlier acquired a Philadelphia-based drug firm, H. K. Mulford, that specialized in vaccines. Louis Galambos et al., *Values and Visions: A Merck Century* (Whitehouse Station, NJ: Merck & Co., 1991), 28–30; Dutfield, *Intellectual Property Rights and the Life Sciences Industry*, note 139, 103.
48. The smoking–lung cancer study was published by R. Doll and A. Bradford Hill, "Smoking and Carcinoma of the Lung," *British Medical Journal*, September 30, 1950, 739–48; the link between diet and coronary disease was by A. Keys, "The Cholesterol Problem," *Voeding* (13), 1952, 539–55.

49. Quinones, *Dreamland*, 28.
50. The breakthroughs in vaccines and cardiovascular drugs were not only good for the public, but also the industry's bottom line. Sales went from $150 million in 1940 to more than $2 billion by 1960. At that time, the industry plowed an estimated $194 million into research and development for new drugs and some $210 million into promotion (*not* including money spent on medical conventions or medical journal ads). See John Lear, "Do We Need a Census of Worthless Drugs?" SR/Research/Science & Humanity, *Saturday Review*, May 7, 1960, 57. The American Medical Association (AMA) and National Association of Radio and Television Broadcasters tried to ensure that the public's faith in science was not easily abused. Beginning in 1953, in television and radio ads, actors were prohibited from playing physicians without being identified as actors, and restrictions were introduced on the use of words such as "safe" and "harmless."
51. The American pharma industry engaged the New York Patent Bar Association to draft the language eventually adopted in the Patent Act of 1952. See legislative history of the act at http://www.ipmall.info/sites/default/files/hosted_resources/lipa/patents/patentact.asp. Also see Dutfield, "Intellectual Property Rights and the Life Sciences Industry," 85–86.
52. Denise Gellene, "Lloyd Conover, Inventor of Groundbreaking Antibiotic, Dies at 93," *New York Times*, March 12, 2017; Rosen, *Miracle Cure*, 233.
53. U.S. Federal Trade Commission, "Economic Report on Antibiotics Manufacture," (Washington, D.C.: Government Printing Office, 1958), 78–79. Fleming quoted in Pagan Kennedy, "The Fat Drug," *New York Times*, March 8, 2014; Rosen, *Miracle Cure*, 235.
54. Fleming quoted in Kennedy, "The Fat Drug."
55. In later years, those surviving bacteria morphed into super versions of salmonella on farms and a related form of staph infections in hospitals. Kennedy, "The Fat Drug."
56. Phil Davison, "Drugs mogul with a vast philanthropic legacy," *Financial Times*, April 23, 2010.
57. Purdue Frederick was at 15 Murray Street in Manhattan's immigrant Lower East Side. Before World War I, the company moved to 298 Broadway. And in 1922 it relocated to 135 Christopher Street, in the West Village. That was its location when the Sacklers bought it. See "About New York: A Paean to 4 Ageless Girls Who Happily Defied the Storms of a Changeful Era," *New York Times*, October 24, 1956, 58. See also Stacy Wong, "Thrust Under Microscope: Stamford Drug Company's Low Profile Shattered by Controversy Over Abuse of Painkiller OxyContin," *Hartford Courant* (New Haven, CT), September 2, 2001, 1.

Chapter 11: "A Haven for Communists"

1. "Administered Drug Prices," Report of the Committee on the Judiciary, Subcommittee on Antitrust and Monopoly, 12323.
2. US v. Chas. Pfizer & Co., et al Defendants, United States District Court, Southern District New York, 245 F. Supp. 801 (1965), September 9, 1965.
3. Administered Prices Hearings before the Subcommittee on Antitrust and Monopoly of the Committee on the Judiciary, U.S. Senate, 86th Cong. 2nd sess., Part 23 (Washington, D.C.: US Government Printing Office, 1957), 12261–86, 12949–51.

4. See Lear, "The Struggle for Control of Drug Prescriptions," 37.
5. Ibid.
6. Ibid., 38–40.
7. Podolsky, *Era of Antibiotics*, 3.
8. David Greenwood, *Antimicrobial Drugs: Chronicle of a Twentieth-Century Medical Triumph* (Oxford, UK: Oxford University Press, 2008), 245.
9. Nelson, "The History of the Tetracyclines," 21.
10. John E. McKeen, "Antibiotics and Pfizer & Co.," *Armed Forces Chemical Journal*, Vol. III, No. 8 (April 1950), 37–38.
11. Lloyd Conover quoted in Abe Zaidan, "Inventors To Be Inducted Into Hall Of Fame: Chemist Says Luck Played Role In Wonder Drug," *The Plain Dealer* (Cleveland, OH), April 24, 1992, 1B.
12. McFadyen, "The FDA's Regulation and Control of Antibiotics in the 1950s," 161.
13. "Administered Drug Prices," Report of the Committee on the Judiciary, Subcommittee on Antitrust and Monopoly, Part 23, 12949.
14. Symposia Registration, Box 1089, Miscellaneous (2 of 6), RG 46; Dwight Eisenhower to Henry Welch, 10/28/54, in preface to *Antibiotics Annual* (1954–1955).
15. McFadyen, "The FDA's Regulation and Control of Antibiotics in the 1950s," 161.
16. Lear, "The Struggle for Control of Drug Prescriptions," 38.
17. Administered Prices Hearings before the Subcommittee on Antitrust and Monopoly of the Committee on the Judiciary, U.S. Senate, 86th Cong. 2nd sess., Part 23 (Washington, D.C.: US Government Printing Office, 1957), 12678–79.
18. New York State, Division of Incorporations, DOS ID 65755, May 11, 1950. Frohlich opened a branch in his native Germany, in collaboration with Thieme Medical Publishing, under the name Institut für Medizinische Statistik. It soon expanded in Europe. The companies, as was the habit with Frohlich and the Sacklers, changed over time with new ones formed with slight name variations. The original was Intercontinental Medical Information Service, Inc., New York Department of State, Division of Corporations, DOS ID May 11, 1950, Dissolution December 23, 1992. Intercontinental Medical Book Corp, DOS ID 92644, was incorporated November 13, 1953, and on that same date so was Stratton Intercontinental Medical Book Group, DOS ID 92644. Intercontinental Medical Statistics International Ltd was not incorporated until October 23, 1973 (DOS ID 236752), followed by Intercontinental Marketing Corporation, March 2, 1982, DOS ID 754499 and Intercontinental Marketing Group, Inc. April 21, 1983, DOS ID 836630, and Intercontinental Marketing Source, Inc. May 1, 1998, DOS ID 2255205, and finally Intercontinental Medical Statistics International Inc, April 24, 1998, DOS ID 2252767.
19. New York State, Division of Incorporations, Stratton Intercontinental Medical Book Corp, DOS ID 92644, November 13, 1953, and Intercontinental Medical Book Corp, DOS ID 92644, November 13, 1953, both with Thieme Medical Publishing listed as the registered agent. Thieme acquired both companies in 1985.
20. Tanner, *Our Bodies, Our Data*, 27–28.
21. Michael Sonnenreich interview with author, January 19, 2019.
22. FOIA collection on documents released pursuant to the request of Professor Ben Harris, 1999.
23. Interview with Donald F. Klein, by John M. Davis, in Boca Raton, Florida, December 12, 2007, for *An Oral History of Neuropsychopharmacology, The First Fifty*

Years, Peer Interviews, Vol. 9: Update, Thomas A. Ban Ed, (Brentwood, TN: ACNP Publisher, 2011), 269.

24. Memorandum from Supervisor in Charge, New York, to Director, FBI, Subject: Changed, David Alex Gordon, SM-C, July 5, 1956, 12 pages, 100-HQ-419511 v. 1 Serial 6, NARA, 4.
25. "2 Doctors to be Privates: Dropped by Hospital for Refusal to Sign Army Loyalty Oath," *New York Times*, May 8, 1953.
26. Memorandum from Supervisor in Charge, New York, to Director, FBI, Subject: Changed, David Alex Gordon, 4.
27. "Business Notes," *New York Times*, July 25, 1954, 116; "Executive Changes," *New York Times*, July 1, 1958, 47; "Seymour Lubman," Obituaries, *New York Times*, November 30, 1982, 44.
28. T. B. Schwartz, "Henry Harrower and the turbulent beginnings of endocrinology," *Ann Intern Med,* 1999 Nov. 2;131(9):702–6.
29. Listerine was developed for the dental profession and not sold over the counter to the public until 1914. Jordan Wheat Lambert, a pharmacist, named his mouthwash after a British surgeon, Joseph Lister. Lister was most famous for his nineteenth-century discovery of carbolic acid, which became the most widely used germ killer in hospitals and medical practices. http://adage.com/article/adage-encyclopedia/lambert-pharmaceutical/98741/. See also Podolsky *Cures Out of Chaos,* 377–78.
30. "Vice-President, Director of Purdue Frederick, Co.," *New York Times*, June 13, 1953, 24. Schneider moved to Purdue too early to enjoy the benefits of a 1955 merger between Lambert and another company Schneider had worked at, Warner Drugs. Warner-Lambert doubled in size by that merger. It later added Parke-Davis (1976) before Pfizer bought the company in 2000. See also "Practical Pharmacy Edition," *Journal of the American Pharmaceutical Association,* Vol. 21., No. 2, February 1960.
31. "Elected to Presidency of Drug Manufacturer," *New York Times*, May 8, 1954, 25.
32. "About New York: A Paean to 4 Ageless Girls Who Happily Defied the Storms of a Changeful Era," *New York Times*, October 24, 1956, 58. The *Times* mistakenly referred to him as "Dan" instead of "Benjamin" Schneider.
33. See "Medical Award Set Up," *New York Times*, June 22, 1957, 23.
34. "Manhattan Transfers," *New York Times*, December 25, 1957, 47.
35. "Top Medical Award," *New England Journal of Medicine*, July 7, 1960, 263:46.
36. Tanner, *Our Bodies, Our Data*, 22, 29.
37. "News of Advertising and Marketing," *New York Times*, March 27, 1956, 58.
38. Pharmaceutical Research Associates, Inc. Filing Date New York State June 25, 1945, DOS ID. 56217. Pharmaceutical Advertising Associates, Inc. Filing Date New York State May 9, 1947, DOS ID 62641. The telephone number listed for Pharmaceutical Advertising Associates in the Yellow Pages Directory was (212) 223-0368. That was the main business line for the American "office of admissions" for an eponymously named School of Medicine the Sacklers incorporated in 1964 in Israel. Both entities shared the same office at 17 East 62nd Street.
39. Lutze, *Who Can Know the Other?,* 141, 162, 164.
40. FOIA collection on documents released pursuant to the request of Professor Ben Harris, 1999, 5, 19.
41. Wisconsin senator Joe McCarthy was the moving force on the committee starting

in the late 1940s. He was out, however, by 1954, censured by his colleagues for his smear tactics. FOIA collection on documents released pursuant to the request of Professor Ben Harris, 55–57.

42. With only a few exceptions, one at the *San Francisco Chronicle* and three at *The New York Times*, journalists were dismissed for refusing to cooperate with the congressional Red investigations. Edward Alwood, *Dark Days in the Newsroom: McCarthyism Aimed at the Press* (Philadelphia: Temple University Press, 2007), 149.
43. It was concern about possible espionage that put the former journalists on the FBI's radar in the 1950s. A decade earlier the Bureau had intercepted a September 13, 1939, Soviet cable to American Communist Party leaders in the U.S., emphasizing the importance of recruiting "journalists of a solid bourgeois newspaper who will be able to live in Europe and to move from one country to the other." While journalists who traveled to Europe frequently were under the most suspicion, the Bureau and HUAC also put a high priority on newspaper editors because they often had the power to affect the slant of content in their papers. Alwood, *Dark Days in the Newsroom*, 95, 100; Haynes and Klehr, *Venona*, 79; Nigel West, *Venona: The Greatest Secret of the Cold War* (New York: HarperCollins, 1999), 279–80.
44. A. B. Magil, a Communist Party member who later got a job at *Medical Tribune*, had first applied after he heard from a "reliable source" that upward of a dozen blacklisted writers and journalists were working there. Memorandum from Supervisor in Charge, New York, to Director, FBI, Subject: Changed, David Alex Gordon, 5.
45. Bernstein's name had been uncovered by the National Security Agency intercept of a Soviet cable discussing American communist assets. The so-called Venona Papers comprise twenty-one volumes of KGB archival material, nine notebooks written by a Russian espionage historian, Alexander Vassiliev, and twelve compilations of Soviet telegraphic cables deciphered by the U.S. National Security Agency from 1943 to 1980. The project became public in 1995. Historians generally agree that those named were likely contacts or informants for Soviet intelligence. Most Americans in the papers were never charged with any crime and in many instances there is no independent evidence other than the Venona Project to determine what role they might have had. West, *Venona*.
46. The companies at that address were Medical Press, Medical Science and Communications, World Wide Medical News Service, and Medigraphics.
47. See also Signers of 1939–40 Communist Party Petitions for State and City Elections, Boroughs of New York City: Official Report, the Names and Addresses of the Signers of Petitions for Candidates of the Communist Party for State and City Elections, 1939–40, for the Confidential Use of the Special Committee on Un-American Activities, 137.
48. Alwood, *Dark Days in the Newsroom*, 102.
49. Gordon's middle name was Alex; he merely dropped his first name and used it instead.
50. Among them were Bernard Segal, Medical Press's managing editor, Leo Schlessinger, a copy chief for William Douglas McAdams, and Gabriel Zakin, a copywriter there. Ray Lynch, "Max Gordon, Former Editor at Socialist 'Daily Worker,'" Memorandum from Supervisor in Charge, New York, to Director, FBI,

Subject: Changed, David Alex Gordon, 2–3. See also *The Sun-Sentinel* (Ft. Lauderdale, FL), January 19, 1990.

51. Sackler hoped *Medical Tribune* would become a daily but he never managed more than three times weekly. It fell off to twice monthly in the 1980s when there was considerably more competition from other journals. Letter from A. B. Magil to Professor Alan M. Wald, September 4, 1991, transcript provided to the author in an email from Professor Wald, March 27, 2017.
52. Jerry Schwartz, "A Life Tainted Red by McCarthyism Ends," *Courier-News* (Bridgewater, Somerset, New Jersey), July 26, 1998, Sunday Edition, 77.
53. Judy Klemesrud, "Woman Sets Fine Record," *Cumberland Evening Times* (Cumberland, Allegany, Maryland), May 21, 1969, 20; Testimony of William Marx Mandel (Accompanied by his counsel, Joseph Forer), Executive Sessions of the Senate Permanent Subcommittee on Investigations of the Committee on Government Operations, Vol. 2, 83rd Congress, First Session, 1953, 935–943; Institute of Pacific Relations; Hearings before the Subcommittee to Investigate the Administration of the Internal Security Act and Other Internal Security Laws of the Committee on the Judiciary, United States Senate, 82nd Congress, second session on the institute of pacific relations Part 8 (1952): I–XXXIV. As for Mandel's father, see Letter, Joseph M. Proskauer to Governor and Mrs. Herbert H. Lehman, March 26, 1942, City Housing Council of New York Collection, Columbia University. And see "'Mutual Admiration Society' of Browder, Senator Meets," *Florence Morning News* (Florence, SC), March 25, 1953, 5; "Reds' U.S. Boss," *Montgomery Advertiser* (Montgomery, AL), March 25, 1953, 2.
54. Haynes and Klehr, *Venona,* 79, 89–90; West, *Venona*, 279–80.
55. Memorandum from Supervisor in Charge, New York, to Director, FBI, Subject: Changed, David Alex Gordon, 5; Alwood, *Dark Days in the Newsroom,* 36, 42, 45.
56. Memorandum from Supervisor in Charge, New York, to Director, FBI, Subject: Changed, David Alex Gordon, 5.
57. Martí-Ibáñez used MD Publications to release Sigerist's writings, and sometimes was his coauthor. The reason the FBI took note was that Sigerist in his 1937 book, *Socialized Medicine in the Soviet Union,* presented the case that the Soviet medical system was a model for the world. https://philpapers.org/rec/SAUOTH.
58. Memorandum from Supervisor in Charge, New York, to Director, FBI, Subject: Changed, David Alex Gordon, 5.
59. Ibid., 6.
60. The three were Medical Science and Communications, World Wide Medical News Service, and Medigraphics. All moved in tandem in June 1955 to 130 East 59th Street. Another Sackler-controlled company, Medical Press, signed a lease there for three full floors (14–17). The William Douglas McAdams agency later also moved to East 59th Street. McAdams, *Medical Tribune*, and Medical Press all used PLaza 9-6300 (in Arthur's ever-changing name-swapping game, years later *Medical Tribune* became Avalon USA and then M.T. Business Corp.). The public listing for Medigraphics (MUrray Hill 6-2734) was also the number for Communications Associates, World Wide Medical News Service, and Sol Feuerman, a private person. Feuerman was a director of Medigraphics and a former film editor who had lost his job when it was disclosed he had signed a petition to place communist candidates on the New York ballot. See Signers of 1939–40 Communist Party Petitions for State and City Elections, Boroughs of New York City: Official Report, the Names and Addresses of the Signers of Petitions for Candidates

of the Communist Party for State and City Elections, 1939–40, for the Confidential Use of the Special Committee on Un-American Activities.

61. Arthur Sackler was chairman of the board for Medical Press, treasurer of World Wide Medical News Service, president of McAdams International, and had been secretary-treasurer at William Douglas McAdams before becoming its CEO. Although Arthur and his first wife, Else, had been divorced nearly eight years, she remained a director and shareholder at some of his firms. Else's friend, Helen Haberman, was a William Douglas McAdams vice president and part owner of the agency. Haberman was also a director of World Wide Medical News Service and McAdams International. Kefauver investigative committee staff notes on Haberman ownership stakes, in collection of author.
62. Incorporation and annual filings of corporations, in collection of author.
63. 270 Broadway, later to 1440 and then to 250 Broadway before the McAdams midtown Manhattan address.
64. Martin Greene was also a director.
65. See, for instance, Arthur M. Sackler, M.D. and Lawrence H. Sophian, M.D., "The Effects of the Ingestion of Amino Acid on Gastric Secretion, with Particular Reference to L-Lysine Monohydrochloride," *American Journal of Clinical Pathology*, Vol. 28, Issue 3, September 1, 1957, 258–63.
66. See Memo, Medical Tribune, From: Joseph Gennis, M.D., Executive Editor} and Frederick Silber, Managing Editor, To: Drs. Adriani, Bracelmld, Dameshek, Dubos} Master, Ochsner} Palmer, Rigler, Sabin and Schick, Subject: Report of Medical Tribune Advisory Board Meeting held in New York on January 13, 1967, collection of author.
67. Memorandum, from Supervisor Agent in Charge, New York, to Director, FBI, Subject: Mary Jane Keeney, May 17, 1950, 1 of 1, released to author by FOIA request from NARA, 101 HQ-467 v. 13, Serial 267. See also *The Competitive Status of the U.S. Pharmaceutical Industry: The Influences of Technology in Determining International Industrial Competitive Advantage*, Charles C. Edwards, Chairman, Lacy Glenn Thomas, Rapporteur, Prepared by the Pharmaceutical Panel, Committee on Technology and International Economic and Trade Issues, Office of the Foreign Secretary, National Academy of Engineering Commission on Engineering and Technical Systems, National Research Council (Washington, D.C.: National Academy Press, 1983). Arthur Sackler was one of twelve participants for the Committee on Technology and International Economic and Trade Issues.
68. Each was a Delaware corporation, where underlying ownership interest is confidential. The author obtained the "applications for authority" and "statements and designations" of the Delaware corporations to do business in New York from the New York Department of State. Each company was represented by, and the shares were held by, William Barnabas McHenry, an attorney at the blue-chip law firm of Lord Day & Lord. McHenry was a longtime Sackler family and company attorney, and listed as the CEO. He was at Lord Day from 1957 to 1962 before leaving to become the general counsel of *Reader's Digest*. The author uncovered a *Medical Tribune* memorandum from 1962 confirming the relationship between the five companies and Lord Day & Lord's McHenry.
69. The author, in certified copies of certificates and articles of association from the New York Department of State, discovered the Sacklers did not incorporate a new entity when they took control of the company in 1952, instead relying on its legal status in New York from a 1911 incorporation (DOS ID 30111). On paper

the owners were Louis Goldburt, an accountant, and two Brooklyn-born brothers and lawyers, Myron and Martin Greene. Goldburt and Martin Greene were listed for Purdue Frederick International, formally registered and filed with the state in 1957 (DDOS 163116). See also set 2 of the Kefauver investigative committee notes prepared for John Blair, under the heading "1955," page 3, collection of author.

70. Bard Pharmaceuticals, March 7, 1955, DOS ID 96706. Service of process was listed on the original incorporation papers on February 16, 1955, as Vard Pharmaceuticals. The author cannot find any evidence, aside from that listing, that there was a Vard Pharmaceuticals so it is almost certainly a typo.
71. Corporate History, "About Mundipharma," Timeline, described Mundipharma as an independently affiliated company with Purdue. Collection of author.
72. Dagrapharm was dissolved on September 30, 1991. Mundipharma is still active as of 2019. See Company Number 00553824, Incorporated August 26, 1955, London, UK. Documents in possession of author.
73. The Sacklers began the Swiss registration process a year after the launch of the U.K. companies, but the legal process was slow and the Basel Mundipharma branch did not open its doors until 1957. AG in its name is an abbreviation for Aktiengesellschaft, a term used in Germany, Austria, and Switzerland to indicate a company whose stock share might be publicly traded. SWISSFIRMS ID: 01201798, St. Alban-Rheinweg 74, 4000 Basel; Commercial register No. CH27030041559, No Crefo 406248151, No D-U-N-S 480045830, IDE No. CHE-107.788.217.
74. The shared office was on the ninth floor of New Zealand House, 80 Haymarket, London, SW1Y 4TQ.
75. Mundipharma AG was at St.Alban-Rheinweg, 74, Basel, 4020) Trademarks: XIUNIS SYNTHEBODY CARDOQUINA; Mundipharma Distribution GmbH (Switzerland, St.Alban-Rheinweg, 74, Basel, 4052); Mundipharma EDO GmbH (Switzerland, St.Alban-Rheinweg, 74, Basel, 4052); Mundipharma Holding AG (Switzerland, St.Alban-Rheinweg, 74, Basel, 4052); Mundipharma IT GmbH (Switzerland, St.Alban-Rheinweg, 74, Basel, 4052); Mundipharma IT Services GmbH (Switzerland, St.Alban-Rheinweg, 74, Basel, 4052); Mundipharma International Services GmbH (Switzerland, St.Alban-Rheinweg, 74, Basel, 4052); Mundipharma LATAM GmbH (Switzerland, St.Alban-Rheinweg, 74, Basel, 4052); Mundipharma Laboratories GmbH (Switzerland, St.Alban-Rheinweg, 74, Basel, 4052); Mundipharma MEA GmbH (Switzerland, St. Alban-Rheinweg, 74, Basel, 4052); branch Mundipharma Medical Company, Hamilton, Bermuda, Basel Branch (Switzerland, St.Alban-Rheinweg, 74, Basel, 4052); Mundipharma Medical GmbH (Switzerland, St.Alban-Rheinweg, 74, Basel, 4020); Mundipharma Near East GmbH (Switzerland, St.Alban-Rheinweg, 74, Basel, 4052); Mundipharma Pharmaceutical Company, Hamilton, Bermuda, Basel Branch (Switzerland, -24 Oct 2001); Mundipharma Pharmaceuticals GmbH (Switzerland, -29 Jun 2005, c/o Revinova Treuhand AG, Im Tiergarten, 7, Zürich, 8055); nonprofit Personalvorsorgestiftung der Mundipharma AG in Liquidation (Switzerland, c/o Mundipharma AG, St.Alban-Rheinweg, 74, Basel, 4052); Purdue Pharma GmbH in Liq. (Switzerland, -17 Sep 1999) Previously/Alternatively known as Mundipharma Products Gmbh.
76. Memorandum, from Supervisor Agent in Charge, New York, to Director, FBI, Subject: Mary Jane Keeney, May 17, 1950, 1 of 1, released to author by FOIA request from NARA, 101 HQ-467 v. 13, Serial 267.

Chapter 12: The Puppet Master

1. Win Gerson, a McAdams agency executive who later became its president, said, "In my mind, it was all Arthur. I guess legally you had to break it out into different 'affiliated companies,' and these are the legal entities. But, actually, to me, the whole thing was Arthur." Gerson quoted in Barry Meier's updated edition of *Pain Killer*, 54.
2. NYS corporation documents in collection of author.
3. United States Patent Tetracycline, Lloyd H. Conover, Oakdale, Conn, Application October 9, 1953, Serial No. 385,041, Patent issued US2699054A.
4. Tobbell, *Pills, Power and Policy*, 75–80; John Braithwaite, *Corporate Crime in the Pharmaceutical Industry* (New York: Routledge, 2013), 181.
5. L.W. Frohlich, "The Physician in the Pharmaceutical Industry in the United States," *Proceedings of the Royal Society of Medicine*, from April 11, 1960, London, Vol. 53, Sec. 1, August 1960, 586.
6. Ibáñez to Welch, 12/10/54, Box 1089, "Welch, Dr. Henry, FDA Materials Correspondence" (10 of 10), RG 46, NARA.
7. Letter from Ernest Jawetz to Martí-Ibáñez, February 7, 1956, Administered Prices Hearings before the Subcommittee on Antitrust and Monopoly of the Committee on the Judiciary, U.S. Senate, 86th Cong. 2nd sess., Part 23 (Washington, D.C.: Government Printing Office, 1957), 13025.
8. "Medicine: What the Doctor Ordered," *Time*. See also Li, *Triumph of the Heart*, 87.
9. "Administered Drug Prices," Report of the Committee on the Judiciary, Subcommittee on Antitrust and Monopoly, 145.
10. Dutfield, Intellectual Property Rights and the Life Sciences Industry.
11. Harry F. Dowling, "Tetracycline," *Medical Encyclopedia*, New York, 1955; U.S. Federal Trade Commission, "Economic Report on Antibiotics Manufacture," (Washington, D.C.: Government Printing Office, 1958), 245.
12. See U.S. Federal Trade Commission, "Economic Report on Antibiotics Manufacture," (Washington, D.C.: Government Printing Office, 1958), 250–57.
13. "Administered Drug Prices," Report of the Committee on the Judiciary, Subcommittee on Antitrust and Monopoly, 145.
14. Ibid., 145–46; Temin, "The Evolution of the Modern Pharmaceutical Industry," April 22, 1961.
15. Silberman, "Drugs: The Pace Is Getting Furious," 139.
16. Donohue, "A History of Drug Advertising," 668.
17. US. House, Committee on Government Operations, Subcommittee on Legal and Marketing Affairs (1958).
18. Richard Harris, *The Real Voice* (New York: MacMillan, 1964), 3–4, 6.
19. Victor Anfuso, "The Monopoly in the Antibiotic Field," *Congressional Record 101*, part 8 (1955): 10641–42.
20. Erythromycin was not a broad-spectrum antibiotic, but since it promised a better therapeutic response than penicillin it was a commercial success. A Lilly chemist, Abelardo Aguilar, working at a company lab in the Philippines, discovered it in 1949. Lilly obtained patent No. 2,693,892 on erythromycin on September 23, 1953, and cross-licensed it to Upjohn and Abbott.
21. Morton Meyers, *Happy Accidents: Serendipity in Modern Medical Breakthroughs* (New York: Arcade Publishing, 2007), Kindle Edition, 2153–81, 2221, 2250–51.
22. Podolsky, *Cures Out of Chaos*, 295–96, 307, 316, 321–23, 325.

23. The two were Gertrude Elion and George Hitchings, https://www.nobelprize.org/prizes/medicine/1988/press-release/. See also Podolsky, *Cures Out of Chaos*, 278–80.
24. Researchers at first thought interferon might be effective against a broad range of cancers, and even some viral infections. However, by the mid-1980s, it was only effective in fighting one form of leukemia. See Claudia Wallis, "Medicine: What's Become of Interferon? The once heralded wonder drug fulfills some of its promise," *Time*, July 1, 1985. For the discovery of interferon, see Sidney Pestka, "The Interferons: 50 Years after Their Discovery, There Is Much More to Learn," *Journal of Biological Chemistry*, Vol. 282, No. 28, July 13, 2007, 20047–51.
25. There was considerable legal and political fallout from that deadly mistake. The HEW division responsible for the oversight of vaccines tripled in size and budget. Hundreds of lawsuits resulted in product liability rulings that scared away many pharma companies from vaccine research and development. The potential costs and risks with vaccine production have resulted in annual shortages not only of the influenza vaccine, but the development of new ones to treat childhood diseases. Michael Fitzpatrick, "The Cutter Incident: How America's First Polio Vaccine Led to a Growing Vaccine Crisis." *Journal of the Royal Society of Medicine* 99.3 (2006): 156; Paul A. Offit, *The Cutter Incident: How America's First Polio Vaccine Led to the Growing Vaccine Crisis* (Hartford, CT: Yale University Press, 2007).
26. Offit, *The Cutter Incident*, 62–63.
27. Lilly also produced some of the polio vaccine. Neal Nathanson and Alexander D. Langmuir, "The Cutter Incident Poliomyelitis Following Formaldehyde-Inactivated Poliovirus Vaccination In The United States During The Spring Of 1955: I and 2, Background," *American Journal of Epidemiology*, Vol. 78, Issue 1, 1 July 1963, 16–28, 29–60. See also Offit, *The Cutter Incident*, 1080 of 2851.
28. Ibid., 2071 of 2851.
29. Senators Wayne Morse and Hubert Humphrey, "The Salk Vaccine," Congressional Record 101, pt. 6, 1955: 7115–19.
30. "Wire-Tapping Mystery: New York's Mayor O'Dwyer says enemies spied on him; they say his charges are attempt to cover up city graft," *Life*, November 28, 1955.
31. "Broady Found Guilty in Wiretapping Case," *New York Times*, December 9, 1955, 1, 56.
32. Long, *The Intruders*, 194–95. The dollar difference is purchasing power measured by inflation (www.in2013dollars.com).
33. See US v. Chas. Pfizer & Co., et al Defendants, United States District Court, Southern District New York, 367 F. Supp. 91 (1973), No. 61 Cr. 772, November 30, 1973.
34. *The Real Voice*, 81; "Administered Drug Prices," Report of the Committee on the Judiciary, Subcommittee on Antitrust and Monopoly, 146–47.
35. See for instance Agreement dated March 28, 1956, between Pfizer and Bristol Laboratories, submitted to the FTC in response to FTC data request, 1956: U.S. Federal Trade Commission, "Economic Report on Antibiotics Manufacture," (Washington, D.C.: Government Printing Office, 1958), 26–27; 254–57. See US v. Chas. Pfizer & Co., et al Defendants, United States District Court, Southern District New York, 367 F. Supp. 91 (1973), No. 61 Cr. 772, November 30, 1973. See also Braithwaite, *Corporate Crime in the Pharmaceutical Industry*, 186.
36. The nearly two dozen companies manufacturing antibiotics at the end of World

War II had been reduced by half in a decade. Those left, including Monsanto and Schenley Labs, were primarily manufacturers of industrial chemicals who had agreed to help the World War II crash program but had no intent of becoming pharmaceutical firms. One chemical company, Indiana-based Commercial Solvents, continued making antibiotics since it had a patent on a pioneering fermentation process. U.S. Federal Trade Commission, "Economic Report on Antibiotics Manufacture" (Washington, D.C.: Government Printing Office, 1958), 190–91.

37. Braithwaite, *Corporate Crime*, 175–76. "Administered Drug Prices," Report of the Committee on the Judiciary, Subcommittee on Antitrust and Monopoly, 147.
38. U.S. Federal Trade Commission, "Economic Report on Antibiotics Manufacture" (Washington, D.C.: Government Printing Office, 1958), 191–92.
39. Braithwaite, *Corporate Crime in the Pharmaceutical Industry*, 181. "Administered Drug Prices," Report of the Committee on the Judiciary, Subcommittee on Antitrust and Monopoly, 147.
40. Braithwaite, *Corporate Crime in the Pharmaceutical Industry*, 176.
41. Harris, *The Real Voice*, 26–30.
42. F. M. Scherer, "The F.T.C., Oligopoly, and Shared Monopoly," Faculty Research Working Paper Series, Harvard Kennedy School, September 2013, 4.
43. The year for comparison of profit share from tetracycline was 1957, in which $20 million of Pfizer's $23 million profit was from tetracycline. From 1946 to 1959, Pfizer's sales jumped from $39 million annually to $254 million. See Braithwaite, *Corporate Crime in the Pharmaceutical Industry*, 176; Podolsky, *The Antibiotic Era*, 37–38.
44. Thomas J. Winn, "The Antibiotics Market," *Drug and Cosmetic Industry* 67 (1950): 472.

Chapter 13: Fake Doctors

1. B. Ryman, "Infectious Diseases: 16th annual review of significant publications," *Archives of Internal Medicine* 87 1951:128.
2. Rosen, *Miracle Cure*, 272.
3. "Symposium on Antibiotics," *Journal of Pharmaceutical Sciences*, Vol. 45, Issue 6, June 1956.
4. Dr. Maxwell Finland, in testimony to the Senate, summarized in April 1961 report, 179.
5. "Symposium on Antibiotics," *Journal of Pharmaceutical Sciences*, Vol. 45, Issue 6, June 1956. See also Richard E. McFadyen, "The FDA's Regulation And Control Of Antibiotics In The 1950s," 166.
6. The student was Gideon Nachumi. He went on to become a respected psychiatrist in New York. Testimony of Gideon Nachumi, June 1, 1960, before the Committee on the Judiciary, Subcommittee on Antitrust and Monopoly, 86 and 87th Congress, NARA. See also Rosen, *Miracle Cure*, 273.
7. Joseph Hixson's confirmation to the Senate cited by Podolsky, *The Antibiotic Era*, 80–81, n. 39.
8. *Antibiotic Medicine*'s board consisted of twenty-five American and nine international editors, most recognized authorities in infectious diseases. A year after its successful debut, *Antibiotic Medicine* was renamed *Antibiotic Medicine and Clinical Therapy*. By then, MD Publications also published *The Quarterly Review of*

Pediatrics, Quarterly Review of Surgery, Obstetrics and Gynecology, International Record of Medicine, Journal of Clinical and Experimental Psychopathology, Quarterly Review of Psychiatry and Neurology, Antibiotic Medicine and Clinical Therapy, and *Antibiotics and Chemotherapy.* See Stengren, "He Takes Pulse of 150,000 U.S. Physicians." See also Rosen, *Miracle Cure*, 269, and Podolsky, *The Antibiotic Era*, 215.

9. Martí-Ibáñez also used *The Medical News Magazine MD* as a platform for long essays on his eclectic interests in "literature, love, art, travel, sports and gastronomics." The magazine was in print for six years and he later released the complete collection of 84 essays as a 712-page book, *The Crystal Arrow: Essays on Literature, Travel, Art, Love and the History of Medicine* (New York: C. N. Potter, 1964).
10. Stengren, "He Takes Pulse of 150,000 U.S. Physicians." See also Meier, *Pain Killer*, 214.
11. See "Circulation of Antibiotics: Journeys of Drug Standards, 1930–1970," papers presented from June 16–18, 2009, Madrid, Spain, European Science Foundation, Centro de Ciencias Humanas y Sociales Consejo Superior de Investigaciones Científicas (CSIC), edited by Ana Romero, Christoph Gradmann and Maria Santemases, Oslo, Norway, May 2010, 192–93, n. 52, 193. As for Welch's request, see Welch to Sackler, letter dated February 23, 1956, Box 3, ff 13, Records of the U.S. Senate, Committee on the Judiciary, Subcommittee on Antitrust and Monopoly, 86 and 87th Congress, RG 46.15, sub 13.115, NARA.
12. Harris, *The Real Voice*, 18–19.
13. "Circulation of Antibiotics: Journeys of Drug Standards, 1930-1970," papers presented from June 16–18, 2009, Madrid, Spain, European Science Foundation, Centro de Ciencias Humanas y Sociales Consejo Superior de Investigaciones Científicas (CSIC), edited by Ana Romero, Christoph Gradmann and Maria Santemases, Oslo, Norway, May 2010, 194.
14. Allen Weinstein and Alexander Vassiliev, *The Haunted Wood* (New York: Modern Library, 1999).
15. The description about the house was included in a later espionage indictment of the Sterns. Weinstein and Vassiliev, *The Haunted Wood.* Also https://www.geni.com/people/Alfred-Stern/6000000003301366250.
16. Besides L-Glutavite, Gray Pharmaceutical had Somatonin, a "tranquilizing preparation for use in the treatment of hypertension"; Lysidox, a general medicinal tonic; Therasalis, a "therapeutic saline and salt substitute"; and Lachrysol, an ophthalmic preparation. As for patents, there were eight related to the products.
17. Lear, "The Struggle for Control of Drug Prescriptions," 35.
18. Ibid.
19. Author interview with Richard Sperber, March 26, 2019.
20. Lear, "The Struggle for Control of Drug Prescriptions," 35.
21. Medical Promotion Production Inc, DOS ID #623501, Dissolved April 24, 1980, NY State, in collection of author.
22. In the mid-1960s, Sackler's MD Publications had launched a once-weekly edition of *Medical News* as a wholly owned subsidiary. Memo, Medical Tribune, From: Joseph Gennis, M.D., Executive Editor} and Frederick Silber, Managing Editor, To: Drs. Adriani, Bracelmld, Dameshek, Dubos} Master, Ochsner} Palmer, Rigler, Sabin and Schick, Subject: Report of Medical Tribune Advisory Board Meeting held in New York on January 13, 1967, collection of author.
23. 1. *Annals of Internal Medicine*, May, June 1958.

2. *New England Journal of Medicine*, June 5, 1958.
3. *American Journal of Medicine*, May, June 1958.
4. *American Journal of Psychiatry*, May, June 1958.
5. *American Journal of Clinical Nutrition*, May 1958.
6. *Mental Hospitals* (Hospital Journal of the American Psychiatric Association), Mar, May, June, Sept, Oct, Nov 1961.
7. *Journal of Chronic Diseases*, May, June 1958.
8. *Postgraduate Medicine*, May, June 1958.
9. *Clinical Medicine*, May, June 1958.
10. *General Practice*, Jan, Mar, May, July, Sept, Nov 1960.
11. *Geriatrics*, Feb, April 1962.
12. *Medical Times*, May, June 1958.
13. *Modern Medicine*, May 1, June 1, 1958.
14. *Hebrew Medical Journal*, Nov. 1959, May 1960, Jan. 1961.
15. *Factor*, Dec. 1959, Jan, Feb, Mar, April 1960.

See Lear, "The Struggle for Control of Drug Prescriptions," 35.

24. "Information, Workplace Health & Safety," *American Journal of Nursing*, November 1,1958, 32.
25. "Poor risk" covered those who did not respond to tranquilizers, or for whom tranquilizers had too many adverse effects, *The News* (Frederick, Maryland), "Medical Progress," May 22, 1958, 4.
26. See Emma Harrison, "Chemical In Juice Aids Mentally Ill; Aged Patients Are Reported Improved by Relative of Monosodium Glutamate," *New York Times*, April 20, 1958.
27. Official Summary of Security Transactions And Holdings, January 1968 United States Securities And Exchange Commission Washington, D.C. See also "Decline of Key Magazines Rocked Curtis Empire," *New York Times*, October 9, 1964, 64.
28. Lear, "The Struggle for Control of Drug Prescriptions."
29. From March 1955 through December, the Sacklers sold $499,148 worth of L-Glutavite; $511,782 worth in 1956, $443,668 worth in 1957; and $87,523 worth in the first two months of 1958.
30. "Official Summary of Security Transactions And Holdings," United States Securities And Exchange Commission (Washington, D.C.: Government Printing Office, 1968). See also Set 2, "Raymond and Mortimer Sackler," Kefauver investigative committee notes prepared for John Blair, page 2, collection of author; "Name of Zonite Products Changed to Chemway Corp.," *Central New Jersey Home News* (Brunswick, NJ), January 15, 1956, 37; "Zonite Products Will Change Name to Chemway Corporation," *Daily Home News*, November 4, 1955, 4. Also see "Decline of Key Magazines Rocked Curtis Empire"; Alexander B. Hammer, "Directors Approve Cooper Acquisition of Chemway Corp," *New York Times*, October 8, 1970; Jesse Bogue, "Banker Back of Big Merger," *San Francisco Chronicle*, January 27, 1962, 41.
31. "Excess Glutamate May Trigger Schizophrenia," *Medscape*, April 24, 2013.
32. Brennan was convinced that L-Glutavite had therapeutic properties but curing lifelong schizophrenics who had not responded to other treatments was not one of them. Kefauver committee investigative committee notes prepared for John Blair, page 2, collection of author.
33. U.S. Federal Trade Commission, "Economic Report on Antibiotics Manufacture," (Washington, D.C.: Government Printing Office, 1958).

34. FDC Reports, August 4, 1958, A4–16. Frohlich comments on competitiveness quoted later in L. W. Frohlich, "The Physician in the Pharmaceutical Industry in the United States," *Proceedings of the Royal Society of Medicine, from April 11, 1960, London,* Vol. 53, Sec. 1, August 1960, 586.
35. Braithwaite, *Corporate Crime in the Pharmaceutical Industry*, 184–86. See also US v. Chas. Pfizer & Co., et al Defendants, United States District Court, Southern District New York, 367 F. Supp. 91 (1973), No. 61 Cr. 772, November 30, 1973.
36. The SEC report was released in January 1959. The measurement was profits as a percentage of gross sales. The SEC finding reported in Tobbell, *Pills, Power, and Policy*, 90–91.
37. Frohlich, "The Physician in the Pharmaceutical Industry in the United States," 579, 582.
38. J. Greene and S. Podolsky, "Keeping Modern in Medicine: Pharmaceutical Promotion And Physician Education In Postwar America," *Bulletin of the History of Medicine,* 2009 Summer; 83(2):331–77.
39. Podolsky, *The Antibiotic Era*, 64–69.
40. See generally Frohlich, "The Physician in the Pharmaceutical Industry in the United States," 581.
41. Lear, "Taking the Miracle out of the Miracle Drugs," 36–38. Lear cited one instance in which penicillin was prescribed for a sprained toe. See also "New Investigation of Pharmaceutical Promotion Will Be Added to Govt. Pricing and Patent Probes: Result of Exposé Articles," FDC Reports, February 9, 1959, 12.
42. The five top selling drugs to pharmacies were antibiotics, tranquilizers, corticosteroids, hypotensive agents, and antihistamines. See Science Information Bureau, *Market Research Studies*, New York, 1960, figure 5.
43. Lear, "Taking the Miracle out of the Miracle Drugs," 37.
44. Davies and Davies, "Origins and Evolution of Antibiotic Resistance."
45. "Circulation of Antibiotics: Journeys of Drug Standards, 1930–1970," papers presented from June 16–18, 2009, Madrid, Spain, European Science Foundation, Centro de Ciencias Humanas y Sociales Consejo Superior de Investigaciones Científicas (CSIC), edited by Ana Romero, Christoph Gradmann and Maria Santemases, Oslo, Norway, May 2010, 191.
46. Lear, "Taking the Miracle out of the Miracle Drugs," 37–38.
47. Lear, "The Struggle for Control of Drug Prescriptions," 39.
48. Podolsky, *The Antibiotic Era*, 73.
49. Harris, *The Real Voice*, 18–19.
50. Ibid.
51. Lear, "Taking the Miracle out of the Miracle Drugs," 39–40.
52. Rosen, *Miracle Cure*, 267.
53. John Lear, "The Certification of Antibiotics," *Saturday Review,* February 7, 1959, 43–48.
54. Memo, George P. Larrick to Charles Miller, June 1, 1959, Administered Prices Hearings before the Subcommittee on Antitrust and Monopoly of the Committee on the Judiciary, U.S. Senate, 86th Cong. 2nd sess., Part 23 (Washington, D.C.: Government Printing Office, 1957), 12964.
55. John Lear, "Do We Need a Census of Worthless Drugs?" SR/Research/Science & Humanity, *Saturday Review*, May 7, 1960, 58.

Chapter 14: A "Sackler Empire"

1. It was formally the Select Committee to Investigate Crime in Interstate Commerce and its final report, published in 1951, was titled "Organized Crime in Interstate Commerce."
2. Harris, *The Real Voice*, 11.
3. *Time* was one of the advertising sponsors for the network coverage of the hearings. It promoted subscriptions to the magazine and they jumped after the hearings. "Crime Hunter Kefauver," *Time*, March 12, 1951.
4. Jackie Mansky, "How Watching Congressional Hearings Became an American Pastime," *The Smithsonian*, June 8, 2017.
5. See Daniel Scroop, "A Faded Passion? Estes Kefauver and the Senate Subcommittee on Antitrust and Monopoly," *Business History Conference*, Vol. 5, 2007, 4–6.
6. Sales data revealed that antibiotics accounted for most of the sales, about 40 percent for market leaders Lederle and Pfizer. David Schwartzman, *Innovation in the Pharmaceutical Industry* (Baltimore: Johns Hopkins Press, 1976), 124–26.
7. In terms of profits as a percentage of invested capital, from John Blair's compilation for the Kefauver committee, cited in Harris, *The Real Voice*, 33–34.
8. Harris, *The Real Voice*, viii.
9. Dixon, quoting conversation with Estes Kefauver, in Harris, *The Real Voice*, 47.
10. See December 7, 1959, hearing, testimony of Francis C. Brown, president of Schering, and December 9, testimony of John T. Connor, president of Merck, and December 12, E. Gifford Upjohn, president of Upjohn. Administered Drug Prices. Hearings Before the Subcommittee on Antitrust and Monopoly of the Committee on the Judiciary, United States Senate, 86th Congress, 2nd Session, Pursuant to S. Res. 238, Part 15 (Washington, D.C.: Government Printing Office, 1960).
11. John W. Finney, "Drug Output Curb Charged at Hearing," *New York Times*, December 9, 1959, 1, 36.
12. It was 17.9 cents for a single tablet that cost Schering 1.6 cents.
13. The scientists were Drs. Edward C. Kendall and Philip Hench, both of whom won the Nobel for the development of cortisone for Merck. John W. Finney, "Merck's Head Defends Drug Prices," *New York Times*, December 10, 1959, 1, 18.
14. "Drug Is Disputed at Senate Inquiry," *New York Times*, September 14, 1960, 47.
15. Maeder, *Adverse Reactions*, 160.
16. Ira Henry Freeman, "Drug Trade Held a 'Whipping Boy,' " *New York Times*, December 10, 1959, 19.
17. "Death costs about $900, and that does not include legal fees or doctor's fees, or the funeral director and the embalming service and the coffins and the monuments and the tombstones and the cemetery services." Smith testimony, Administered Prices. Part 22, The Food And Drug Administration: Part 19, 10615.
18. Scroop, "A Faded Passion? Estes Kefauver and the Senate Subcommittee on Antitrust and Monopoly," 11.
19. "Kefauver," John M. Blair, letter to the Editor in response to the review of Kefauver's book, *In a Few Hands: Monopoly Power in America* by Arthur Gass, *The New York Review of Books*, April 22, 1965.
20. The Senate Committee discovered that the government, from State Department to the Pentagon, was paying even more than the public, sometimes twice the price for the same drug. Rosen, *Miracle Cure*, 278; Harris, *The Real Voice*, 72–75.

21. Testimony of A. Dale Console, Administered Prices: Hearings Before the Subcommittee on Antitrust and Monopoly of the Committee on the Judiciary, United States Senate, 86th Congress, 2nd Session, Pursuant to S. Res. 238, Part 18, Apr. 13, 1960 (Washington, D.C.: Government Printing Office, 1960), 10390–91.
22. Stephen Mihm, "Employer-Based Health Care Was A Wartime Accident," *Chicago Tribune*, February 24, 2017.
23. Ibid.
24. M. Field and H. Shapiro, eds., "Origins and Evolution of Employment-Based Health Benefits," Institute of Medicine, *U.S. Committee on Employment-Based Health Benefits* (Washington, D.C.: National Academies Press, 1993), 2, 12, 34,
25. Elisabeth Rosenthal, "Insurance policy: How an industry shifted from protecting patients to seeking profit," *Stanford Medicine*: *Sex, Gender and Medicine*, Spring 2017. When Congress in 1954 rewrote the tax code, it enhanced the tax benefits for employer-provided health insurance.
26. Aaron E. Carroll, "The Real Reason the U.S. Has Employer-Sponsored Health Insurance," Upshot, https://www.nytimes.com/2017/09/05/upshot/the-real-reason-the-us-has-employer-sponsored-health-insurance.html.
27. Memorandum from John Blair, Chief Economist to Paul Rand Dixon, Counsel and Staff Director; Subject: Sackler Brothers, March 16, 1960, 4 pages, in collection of author (hereinafter Blair-Dixon Memorandum). The memo and eight pages of supporting evidence is disclosed for the first time in this book. The supporting evidence is handwritten notes and diagrams created by the investigative staff.

    Set 1 of notes consists of four pages titled on page 1 "Arthur Sackler Companies" and is a diagram flowchart of companies, with owners, shares, subsequent transfers, and other relevant ownership information, handwritten inside each company listing. Page 2 is titled "Raymond and Mortimer Sackler" and is a diagram flowchart of companies and ownership interests. Page 3 is untitled; it includes again company flowchart data, with "Marti Ibanez" and "L. W. Frohlich" listed. Page 4 is marked "R&D = Research and Development." Set 2 of notes consists also of four pages and is a flowchart of Sackler professional and corporate activity and roles in chronological order, listing activity under date headings for 1945, 1947–48, and 1952–59. Collection of author.
28. Blair-Dixon Memorandum.
29. John Lear concluded later that "The [Sackler] brothers cover every aspect of prescription medicine." See Lear, "The Struggle for Control of Drug Prescriptions," 35.
30. Blair-Dixon Memorandum, 1.
31. At the Pharmaceutical Research Center, Sackler signed the checks with the Italian-sounding name of Syngergiste, Latin for a bacterium species. Incorporation and annual state filings from Department of State, New York, in collection of author. Also, Blair-Dixon Memorandum, 2.
32. Ibid., 2–4.
33. "The Pharmaceutical Century—1950s."
34. Blair listed sixteen companies as "components of the Sackler empire."
35. Blair-Dixon Memorandum.
36. See assorted correspondence between Martí-Ibáñez and Welch and the Sacklers, Administered Prices, Part 22, The Food And Drug Administration: Dr. Henry Welch, 13139–64.
37. "Drug Aide Quits; Blames Politics," *New York Times*, May 19, 1960, 12.

38. Rosen, *Miracle Cure*, 270.
39. Ibid.
40. Letters from Dr. Henry Welch and Drs. Arnold S. Breakey and Willis S. Knighton, exhibits to Administered Drug Prices: Hearings Before the Subcommittee on Antitrust and Monopoly of the Committee on the Judiciary, United States Senate, Part 22, May 11, 1960, 11891, 11896, 13139–64.
41. "Drug Aide Quits; Blames Politics," *New York Times*, May 19, 1960, 12.
42. Memo, George P. Larrick to Charles Miller, June 1, 1959, Administered Drug Prices: Hearings Before the Subcommittee on Antitrust and Monopoly of the Committee on the Judiciary, United States Senate, Part 23, 12964. See also Thomas W. Ottenad, "Fleming Demands Immediate Resignation of Dr. Henry Welch," *St. Louis Post-Dispatch*, May 19, 1960, 4.
43. See McFadyen, "The FDA's Regulation And Control Of Antibiotics In The 1950s," 159–69.
44. Office of the Commissioner, "A Brief History of CDER." U.S. Food and Drug Administration. FDA, https://www.fda.gov/AboutFDA/History/VirtualHistory/HistoryExhibits/ucm325199.htm.
45. Maier, *Pain Killer*, 212.
46. "Early Chinese Art and Its Possible Influence in the Pacific Basin (published in two volumes). See also Lon Tuck, "Convictions of the Collector," *Washington Post*, September 21. 1986; Biography of Arthur M. Sackler, Drug Industry Antitrust Act, Hearings before the Subcommittee on Antitrust and Monopoly, Senate Committee on the Judiciary, Part 6 Document No. 6, January 30, 1962, 3064.
47. Blair-Dixon Memorandum.
48. Spencer Ante, *Creative Capital: Georges Doriot and the Birth of Venture* (Boston: Harvard Business Review Press, 2008).
49. The public association with *Medical Tribune* continued through the shareholder meeting for Doriot's American Research and Development Corporation (ARD) in 1963. See Frederick McCarthy, "American R. & D. Studying 30 New Venture Projects," *Boston Globe,* March 7, 1963, 14.
50. Doriot appointed John J. Snyder Jr., a noted American businessman, to *Medical Tribune*'s board to watch over the ARD investment (apparently $100,000 for a 5 percent stake). See, for instance, McCarthy, "American R. & D. Studying 30 New Venture Projects," 14.
51. Delaware Coporate ID 548703, 2/25/1960; Nevada 1964, permanently revoked 4/29/1993, and New York, DOS ID 127424, 3/22/60, all in archives of author.
52. Arthur Sackler, "One Man . . . And Medicine," *Medical Tribune*, December 20, 1972, 9. As for the publication about the earlier study by the Sackler brothers, it was "Quantitated identification of psychosis by blood sample. I. Instrumentation of ultrasound for biologic quantitation," *The Journal of Clinical and Experimental Psychopathology*, Vol. XII, No. IV, October–December 1951. The Sacklers were joined on that study by Martí-Ibáñez and two other Creedmoor physicians, W. Roth and F. C-Tui.
53. The quote from the American Association of Advertising Agencies executive and the background behind Arthur Sackler's reason to withdraw was set forth in an in-depth profile of Sackler by Robert Lenzner, "A Financial Man and the Fogg," *Boston Globe*, February 16, 1982, 45, 49. That profie caused a firestorm when it was published shortly after Arthur had made a $7 million bequest to Harvard for what would become the Alfred M. Sackler Museum. When Harvard temporarily

put the Sackler bequest on hold, Sackler's attorney wrote to the *Globe* claiming it had eleven "incorrect statements which require correction." Robert Kierstead, the paper's ombudsman, investigated and his results were published two months later under the title, "More Fact, Less Mystery" (April 5, 1982, 11). Kierstead concluded that "many of the complaints were justified. The writer was the victim of an inaccurate press release, a source who admittedly (but claimed inadvertently) misled him, as well as some insufficient reporting and use of questionable source material." The author has not cited nor relied on any of the reporting that Sonnenreich questioned. In instances in which Lenzner's article is cited, it is as a primary source—such as the only interview on the record with venture capitalist Georges Doriot—or the author has independently confirmed what Lenzner reported.

54. Ibid.
55. Doriot interviewed in Ibid.
56. Years later Doriot said he realized Sackler did not want the investment as much as he wanted "standing with the advertisers."
57. The executives included W. G. Malcolm, president of American Cyanamid Co., parent company of Lederle; Lyman Duncan, manager of Lederle Laboratories; Philip I. Bowman, president of Bristol Labs; Harry J. Loynd, president of Parke-Davis; and Eugene N. Beesley, president of Eli Lilly.
58. Kefauver, *In a Few Hands*, 34–35.
59. Ibid., 35–36.
60. "Nation's Largest Manufacturers," top 50 ranked by net profit as a percent of invested capital and as percent of sales, *Fortune*, December 1958.
61. Kefauver, *In a Few Hands*, 23.
62. Parke-Davis & Co. v. H. K. Mulford & Co., 189 F. 95 (C.C.S.D.N.Y. 1911) and Kuehmsted v. Farbenfabriken of Elberfeld Co., 179 F. 701 (7th Cir. 1910).
63. Kefauver, *In a Few Hands*, 37.
64. Richard Caves, Michael Whinston and Mark Hurwitz, "Patent Expiration, Entry, and Competition in the U.S. Pharmaceutical Industry," Brookings Papers: Microeconomics, 1991.
65. Alan M. Fisch, "Compulsory Licensing of Pharmaceutical Patents: An Unreasonable Solution to an Unfortunate Problem," 34 *Jurimetrics J.* 295, 316 (1994). The idea of compulsory licensing would again briefly become a hotly debated matter more than four decades later. See Debjani Roy, "In Search of the Golden Years: How Compulsory Licensing Can Lower the Price of Prescription Drugs for Millions of Senior Citizens in the United States," (2004) 52:3 *Cleveland State L Rev* 467.
66. Harris, *The Real Voice*, 116.
67. Ibid., 9.
68. Wayne Winegarden, "Price Controls Are Never the Answer," *Forbes*, April 1, 2019. See also Debjani Roy, "In Search of the Golden Years: How Compulsory Licensing Can Lower the Price of Prescription Drugs for Millions of Senior Citizens in the United States," 52:3 *Cleveland State Law Review*, 467, 2004.

Chapter 15: "Be Happy" Pills

1. Searle had introduced the progesterone-based Enovid in 1957 for menstrual disorders. Comprehensive overview by Nicholas Bakalar, "Birth Control Pills, 1957," *New York Times*, October 25, 2010.
2. As for the quandary the FDA faced in approving the contraceptive pill, see Carpenter, *Reputation and Power,* 183–88.
3. Barbara Seaman, *The Doctor's Case against the Pill* (Alameda, CA: Hunter House, 2000), 237–38.
4. "The FDA Approves the Pill," American Experience PBS, https://www.pbs.org/wgbh/americanexperience/features/pill-us-food-and-drug-administration-approves-pill/.
5. Elizabeth Siegel Watkins, "How the Pill Became a Lifestyle Drug: The Pharmaceutical Industry and Birth Control in the United States Since 1960," *American Journal of Public Health.* 102:8 (August 2012); 1462–72.
6. "Repackaging the Pill," *99 Percent Invisible,* July 10, 2017, https://99percentinvisible.org/episode/repackaging-the-pill/.
7. Dale Nouse, "Birth Control Ads Are Canceled in Big Magazine," *Detroit Free Press,* November 18, 2018, 1, 5.
8. Ibid.
9. Ibid.
10. "Freedom from Fear," *Time,* April 7, 1967, 78.
11. "Oral Contraceptives: The Liberator," *Economist,* December 31, 1999, 102.
12. The term "lifestyle drug" did not come into wide use in the industry until 1978.
13. "Searle and Enovid," *Investor's Readers,* March 1961.
14. Nicolas Rasmussen, "America's First Amphetamine Epidemic, 1929–1971: A Qualitative and Quantitative Retrospective with Implications for the Present," *American Journal of Public Health,* June 2008.
15. Shorter, *Before Prozac,* 433 of 4159.
16. Ibid., 469 of 4159.
17. One of the earliest advertisements for Dexamyl, *New York State Journal of Medicine* 50 (1950): 511.
18. Robins's rival combination was Ambar, a mix of methamphetamine and phenobarbital, while Abbott's Desbutal was a blend of amphetamine with pentobarbital. Rasmussen, "America's First Amphetamine Epidemic."
19. Ibid.
20. Pieter A. Cohen, Alberto Goday, and John P. Swann, "The Return of Rainbow Diet Pills," *American Journal of Public Health* 102.9 (2012): 1676–86.
21. Francisco López-Muñoz, Ronaldo Ucha-Udabe, and Cecilio Álamo, "The History Of Barbiturates A Century After Their Clinical Introduction," *Neuropsychiatric Disease and Treatment* 1(4), (December 2005), 329–43.
22. Ibid.
23. A problem that often proved fatal with barbiturates was that since the therapeutic threshold varied widely among patients, what helped relieve one's anxiety might kill another. Tone, *Age of Anxiety*, 24. See also Shorter, *Before Prozac*, 337 of 4159.
24. Charles Grutzner, "Grave Peril Seen in Sleeping Pills," *New York Times*, December 16, 1951, 1, 54.
25. Ibid.

26. "Report on Barbiturates," Committee on Public Health, Subcommittee on Barbiturates, *New York Academy of Medicine,* June 1956, 472–75.
27. *No Bromide and Acetanilid-Bromide 'Crusade' for FDA* 20 F-D-C. Reports/ Pink Sheet, at 6 (Sept. 16, 1957). See aso Federal Food, Drug, and Cosmetic Act amendments, 52 Stat. 1051, 21 U.S.C. Sec 353, Conditions for Dispensation of Certain Drugs, 21. U.S. C. Sec 352, Public Law 215, Chapter 578, October 26, 1951. See Donohue, "A History of Medical Advertising," 667.
28. *No Bromide and Acetanilid-Bromide 'Crusade' for FDA* 20 F-D-C Reports/Pink Sheet, at 6 (Sept. 16, 1957); Shorter, *Before Prozac,* 1273.
29. In 1936, the U.S. consumed 231,000 pounds of "barbituric acid and derivatives." By 1960, it had quadrupled to 852,000 pounds, enough for about six million pills. See Joel Fort, "The Problem of Barbiturates in the United States of America," *Bull on Narcotics* 16 (Jan.–Mar. 1964): 18.
30. It was then believed that if it were possible to slow the blood circulation of a violent or agitated mental patient, that would calm them. Dr. Benjamin Rush—one of the signers of the Declaration of Independence—designed a chair with leather straps to bind the chest and ankles, and a wooden box that fit over the top half of the patient's head, blocking their vision. Although his invention is barbaric by modern medical standards, Rush was considered humane at a time when many asylums handled patient outbursts with brutal and crude corporal punishment. "History of Pennsylvania Hospital," Penn Medicine, "Psychiatry," at *Pennsylvania Hospital History: Historical Collections—Psychiatry Exhibit.* N.p., n.d. Web. 13 July 2019.
31. Herzberg, *Happy Pills,* 228–29 of 3354.
32. Thomas Szasz, *Coercion as Cure: A Critical History of Psychiatry* (Abingdon, UK: Routledge, 2017), 167, 171.
33. Herzberg, *Happy Pills,* 220 of 3354.
34. Three thousand of the religious-based conscientious objectors in World War II had been committed to sixty-two mental institutions across the country. After the war, many made it their mission to expose the stomach-wrenching conditions they had seen in sections they dubbed "the hellholes," the "violent wards," and the "death house." Public health advocates demanded reform for psychiatric institutions that operated mostly in secrecy. A 1948 film, *The Snake Pit,* was a melodramatic rendition of the horrors inside a psychiatric asylum; still, it had a wide impact on forming public opinion about institutionalized care. Joseph Shapiro, "WWII Pacifists Exposed Mental Ward Horrors," NPR, *All Things Considered,* December 30, 2009, 2:00 PM ET.
35. "Drug Revolution," *Time,* January 30, 1956. Shortly after Thorazine went on sale, a similar hypnotic-sedative, Resperine, was introduced. It was the result of research by Dr. Nathan Kline, the director of Rockland State Hospital. Kline had arrived at Creedmoor shortly after the Sacklers had been dismissed for their left-wing political affiliations. The author's requests for an interview with Dr. Kline went unanswered. See also Milton and Lee, *Pills, Profits and Politics,* 12–13.
36. In 1957, three of the key psychiatric researchers behind the therapeutic use of Thorazine for treating schizophrenia, Henri Laborit, Pierre Deniker, and Heinz Lehmann, were awarded the prestigious Lasker Award, an acknowledgment of a significant contribution to medical science. Haddad, Peter, Robert Kirk, and Richard Green, "Chlorpromazine, The First Antipsychotic Medication: History, Controversy and Legacy," British Association for Psychopharmacology, Octo-

ber 31, 2016. See also Dowbiggin, *The Quest for Mental Health,* 147; Herzberg, *Happy Pills in America.*

37. Gilbert Cant, "Valiumania," *New York Times Magazine,* February 1, 1976.
38. "The Crazy Talk About Bringing Back Asylums," *New York Times,* June 2, 2018; Dowbiggin, *The Quest for Mental Health,* 177, 181.
39. Smith, Kline & French, "The Discharged Mental Patient . . . and Thorazine," *Journal of the American Medical Association* 187, no. 1 (January 1964): 18. Also see Guise-Richardson, "Protecting Mental Health in the Age of Anxiety," 287.
40. It would take nearly a decade before the FDA accumulated enough data to conclude that Thorazine sharply increased the risk of death for older adults with dementia. https://katherinegscott.wordpress.com/2011/02/03/a-short-history-of-thorazine/.
41. There were more adverse reactions reported in the U.S., mostly because American doctors prescribed larger doses, on average double that of their European counterparts. Dowbiggin, *The Quest for Mental Health,* 148.
42. Pharmaceutical companies certainly played a role in encouraging people to believe that they were living in an era of heightened anxiety. See Tone, *Age of Anxiety,* Kindle Edition, 197 of 6446.
43. Historian David Healy said that the NIH funding meant "Biological psychiatry had been capitalized." Healy quoted in Herzberg, *Happy Pills,* 249, 250–52 of 3354.
44. See Ban, Thomas A. "The role of serendipity in drug discovery," *Dialogues in Clinical Neuroscience,* 2006;8(3):338; D. W. Wooley and E. Shaw, "Biochemical and Pharmacological Suggestion About Certain Mental Disorders," Vol. 40 Communication, Rockefeller Institute for Medical Research, New York, Feburary 16, 1954, 228.
45. Frank Berger, "Anxiety and the Discovery of the Tranquilizers," *Discoveries in Biological Psychiatry,* Editors Frank Ayd and Barry Blackwell (Philadelphia: Lippincott Publishing, 1970), 119–21. Berger's mother was Czech, his father was German, and he was born in Pilsen, then in the Austro-Hungarian Empire.
46. Carter was in the middle of a fight with the FTC over therapeutic claims it made about its star product. That had begun in 1943 and would last for seventeen years (1959) when the FTC prevailed and Carter had to remove "Liver" as part of the product name. The more generic "Dr. Carter's Little Pills" never sold nearly as well. The original product was so successful that it was the basis behind a popular postwar statement, "He has more money than Carter has pills." "Trouble in Miltown," *Time,* February 8, 1960; Berger autobiography, 33.
47. Tone, *Age of Anxiety,* 39.
48. Ibid., 47.
49. Ibid., 52; Shorter, *Before Prozac,* 433.
50. An advertisement for Miltown, *New York State Journal of Medicine* 56 (1956): 5. Also, Shorter, *Before Prozac,* 595.
51. See Crocq M-A, "The history of generalized anxiety disorder as a diagnostic category," *Dialogues in Clinical Neuroscience,* 2017;19(2):107–16.
52. Crocq M-A., "A history of anxiety: from Hippocrates to DSM," *Dialogues in Clinical Neuroscience,* 2015;17(3):319–25.
53. Dr. Irvin Cohen quoted in Tone, *Age of Anxiety,* 180. Another psychiatrist estimated that upward of 60 percent of patients who went to doctors did not suffer from any organic illness but rather from psychoneurotic conditions.

54. Dowbiggin, *The Quest for Mental Health*, 147–48; Susan L. Speaker, "From 'Happiness Pills' to 'National Nightmare': Changing Cultural Assessment of Minor Tranquilizers in America, 1955–1980," *Journal of the History of Medicine and Allied Sciences*, Vol. 52, July 1997, 344.
55. Tallulah Bankhead said in jest that she had taken so many she feared she might have "to pay taxes in New Jersey." "Don't Give a Damn Pills," *Time*, February 27, 1956. For a thorough discussion of the extent to which Hollywood embraced Miltown, see Speaker, "From 'Happiness Pills' to 'National Nightmare,' " 338–76; Tone, *Age of Anxiety*, 54–61.
56. Speaker, "From 'Happiness Pills' to 'National Nightmare,' " 339.
57. Herzberg, *Happy Pills*, 321 of 3354.
58. " 'Behavior' Drugs Now Envisioned," *New York Times*, October 19, 1956, 29.
59. Tone, *Age of Anxiety*, 74 note 13.
60. "Miltown: a game-changing drug you've probably never heard of," CBC Radio, Special: On Drugs, August 7, 2017. See also Tone, *Age of Anxiety*, 27.
61. As for the cost, see "To Nirvana with Miltown," *Time*, July 7, 1958. As to how Gala Dali approached Berger with the idea of her husband's art, see interview with Frank Gerber, in Tone, *Age of Anxiety*, 76.
62. From *Time*: "What most visitors saw first walking through the caterpillar's insides was the figure of a gaunt man with porthole-sized gaps in his anatomy, holding a staff topped with a mostly black butterfly. This, said Dali in an explanatory blurb, 'portrays human anxiety.' Next on the way 'toward a harmonious tranquility' came a diaphanous female figure with a winged-egg head, who carried a staff with a crepuscular moth. The third figure was what Dali called 'the true butterfly of tranquility'—a maiden in yellow, with a head composed of blue, red and yellow flowers. For a finale, there was another maiden (with real hair) skipping rope on the way to the promised land of tranquility." Dali named his exhibit *Crisalida* and explained: "The outer structure of Miltown is that of a chrysalis, maximum symbol of the vital nirvana which paves the way for the dazzling dawn of the butterfly, in its turn the symbol of the human soul." "To Nirvana with Miltown," *Time*, July 7, 1958.
63. "Happiness by Prescription," *Time*, March 11, 1957. See also Tone, *Age of Anxiety*, 65–66.
64. "Trouble in Miltown," *Time*, February 8, 1960.
65. Ibid.
66. See Elena Conis, "Valium Had Many Ancestors," *Los Angeles Times*, February 18, 2008.
67. See Tone, *Age of Anxiety*, 90.
68. In 1960, the tranquilizer market reached forty million dollars in annual sales. That was impressive considering that market segment had not existed five years earlier. Still, it was only a tenth of antibiotic sales.
69. "Letdown for Miltown," *Time*, April 30, 1965.
70. Miltown was dealt a body blow when the *U.S. Pharmacopeia*—the official guide for pharmacists—dropped it in 1965 from its listing, concluding it was in fact a sedative rather than a tranquilizer. See "Miltown Off List of Tranquilizers," *The New York Times*, April 22, 1965, 34; "Happiness by Prescription," *Time*, March 11, 1957.
71. Andrea Tone, "Listening to the Past: History, Psychiatry, and Anxiety," *Canadian Journal of Psychiatry* 50:373–380, 2005, 377.

72. Sternbach had left Kraków University after earning his master's degree in pharmacy, because "I had no chance as a Jew." He moved to Switzerland, where he briefly worked in the labs at Zurich's Federal Institute of Technology before moving to Roche in 1940. Roche arranged Swiss passports for all the Jewish scientists it moved. The Swiss travel documents had the advantage of not listing nationalities or religion. See Siler, "Father and Son"; Ivan Oransky, "Leo H. Sternbach," *Lancet*, Vol. 366, October 22, 2005, 1430; Ian Sample, "Leo Sternbach," *Guardian* (UK), October 2, 2005; B. D. Cohen, "Adventurous Chemist and His Pill," *Washington Post*, January 20, 1980; B. D. Cohen, "Valium and Health," *Washington Post*, February 24, 1980, 1F.
73. B. D. Cohen, "Adventurous Chemist and His Pill," *Washington Post*, January 20, 1980.
74. Roche had by serendipity discovered that iproniazid, a tuberculosis treatment, showed promise for alleviating depression. It released it in 1957 under the brand name Marsilid as a depression treatment. It withdrew it in 1961 after an alarming number of reports of patients developing hepatitis. Although Roche was anxious to develop a Miltown competitor, Marsilid was not it. See generally Tone, *Age of Anxiety*, 176.
75. Sternbach quoted in B. D. Cohen, "Valium and Health," *Washington Post*, February 24, 1980.
76. Tone, *Age of Anxiety*, 175.
77. Sternbach quoted in B. D. Cohen, "Valium and Health," *Washington Post*, February 24, 1980.
78. Tone, *Age of Anxiety*, 176, note 22; Leo Sternbach, "The Benzodiazepine Story," *Journal of Medicinal Chemistry*, Vol. 22, 1979, 1–7.
79. The story that Earl Reeder discovered those flasks by accident has been repeated so many times it is even the official account in some medical histories about pharmaceutical discoveries. Only years later did Sternbach reveal how he orchestrated it to look like happenstance. B. D. Cohen, "Adventurous Chemist and His Pill," *Washington Post*, January 20, 1980; Ban, Thomas A., "The role of serendipity in drug discovery," *Dialogues in Clinical Neuroscience*. 2006;8(3):335–44.
80. See B. D. Cohen, "Adventurous Chemist and His Pill," *Washington Post*, January 20, 1980; Tone, *Age of Anxiety*, 129.
81. Thomas H. Maugh, "Leo Sternbach, 97; Invented Valium, Many Other Drugs," *Los Angeles Times*, October 1, 2005.
82. Cant, "Valiumania."
83. Milan Uskokovic, director of natural products research at Hoffmann-LaRoche, quoted in Oransky, "Leo H. Sternbach."
84. Tone, *Age of Anxiety*, 132.
85. Ibid., 133.
86. The FDA can order additional clinical testing if it has reason to believe the drug company is omitting key product information. This happened, for instance, with an antidepressant, reboxetine, that went on sale in Europe in 1997. The FDA ordered additional clinical testing that Pfizer failed to complete. In Europe the drug sold well until a German meta-analysis of clinical trials revealed Pfizer had left out data that showed the drug was no better than a placebo in treating depression and had far more side effects than Prozac. Ben Goldacre, *Bad Pharma: How Drug Companies Mislead Doctors and Harm Patients* (New York: Farrar, Straus & Giroux, 2013), Kindle Edition, 207–53 of 7421.

87. "Benzodiazepines Revisited," *British Journal of Medical Practitioners.* See also Boffey, "Worldwide Use of Valium Draws New Scrutiny"; Guise-Richardson, "Protecting mental health in the Age of Anxiety," vi.
88. Richard F. Squires, "Benzodiazepine Receptors in Rat Brains," *Nature,* Vol. 266, April 1, 1977, 732–34.
89. The questionnaire covered, among other items, anxious moods, fears, tension, depressed mood, insomnia, and difficulty in concentration. Each item was assigned a value ranging from *severe* (4) to *not present* (1).
90. Lucy Ozarin, "Hamilton: The Man Behind the Scale," *Psychiatric News*, October 18, 2002.
91. The McAdams Librium team mostly "had to generate our own data" about which doctors to target. Bill Frohlich's IMS shared information it had compiled from the early tranquilizer sales, but it was "very primitive." Looking back. Looking forward. (Interview with Irwin Gerson, chairman emeritus of Lowe McAdams Healthcare) (Agency CEO Perspectives), *Medical Marketing & Media,* April 1, 1998.
92. "Tranquil but Alert," *Time*, March 7, 1960, 47. The successful report about the Texas prison encouraged tranquilizer sales to state and local prisons. The experience was not always as positive as the one that Roche and Sackler had relied upon. At the Bronx House of Detention, for instance, 400 of 780 inmates were given Librium, Thorazine, and other tranquilizers. One corrections officer told *The New York Times* that the problem that developed was that some of the prisoners became so dependent on the tranquilizers, that they "will do anything when he can't get it." Ronald Smothers, "Muslims: What's behind the violence," *New York Times*, December 26, 1972, 18.
93. "New Way to Calm a Cat," *Life*, April 18, 1960, 93–95; "Tranquil but Alert."
94. Ibid.
95. Lilly pulled the drug, Oraflex, from the market only five months after it went on sale. There had been an unexpected flood of serious adverse reactions. Donohue, "A History of Drug Advertising," 675.
96. "New Way to Calm a Cat"; "Tranquil but Alert."
97. J. A. Greene, D. Herzberg, "Hidden in Plain Sight: Marketing Prescription Drugs to Consumers in the Twentieth Century," *American Journal of Public Health.* 2010;100(5):793–803. The Senate still censured Roche. *Time*, March 15, 1963, cited in US Senate, Committee on Government Operations, Subcommittee on Reorganization and International Organizations, Interagency Coordination in Drug Research and Regulation (Washington, D.C.: Government Printing Office, 1964), 1275–76, 1278–79, 1285.
98. See how *Cosmopolitan* was used in the Miltown campaign to pitch "perfect peace or calmness of mind" to its readers. Herzberg, *Happy Pills*, 527 of 3354.
99. Greene and Herzberg, "Hidden in Plain Sight." See Herzberg, *Happy Pills*, 353 of 3354; "Administered Drug Prices," Report of the Committee on the Judiciary, Subcommittee on Antitrust and Monopoly, 1455.
100. Being outpaced by Wyeth was not as terrible for Carter as it seemed; the licensing agreement had generous terms for Carter and the profits from that contract paid for all of Carter's manufacturing costs.
101. *JAMA*, March 12, 1960, cited in Drug Coordination Report, US Senate, Committee on Government Operations, Subcommittee on Reorganization and In-

ternational Organizations, Interagency Coordination in Drug Research and Regulation (Washington, D.C.: Government Printing Office, 1964), 1281–82.

102. Librium package insert, Manufacturers Files, AF14–324, Hoffmann-La Roche, FDA History Office; William D'Aguanno of the FDA Division of Pharmacology to J. D. Archer, FDA New Drug Branch, Apr. 7, 1961, Manufacturers Files, AF14–324, Hoffmann-La Roche, FDA History Office; Tone, *Age of Anxiety,* 266.
103. Stephens, C.R., et al., "Terramycin. VIII. Structure of Aureomycin and Terramycin," *Journal of the American Chemical Society,* 1952, 74: 4976–77; Donohue, "A History of Drug Advertising," 33.
104. For the Miltown side effects see Herzberg, *Happy Pills,* 469 of 3354.
105. The *Medical Letter* was founded in 1958 by Arthur Kallet and Dr. Harold Aaron. Kallet, who had used an alias to join the American Communist Party in the 1930s. They were also the cofounders of Consumers Union, publisher of *Consumer Reports.* The House Un-American Activities Committee later exposed Kallet's political association and branded Consumers Union "a communist-front organization." Hearings United States. Congress. House. Committee on Un-American Activities, January 1, 1949, 645.

    The *Medical Letter* concluded that doctors were probably better off prescribing the barbiturate phenobarbital, which was "much cheaper" than Miltown. Herzberg, *Happy Pills,* 474, 486 of 3354.
106. Dr. Nathan Kline, quoted in Cant, "Valiumania."
107. Drug Coordination Report, US Senate, Committee on Government Operations, Subcommittee on Reorganization and International Organizations, Interagency Coordination in Drug Research and Regulation (Washington, D.C.: Government Printing Office, 1964), 1280–81.
108. Tone, *Age of Anxiety,* 112.
109. Rasmussen, "America's First Amphetamine Epidemic."
110. Tone, *Age of Anxiety,* 154.
111. Roche promoted Sternbach as chief of a group of twenty PhDs and chemists in lab research. Not everyone was as happy as Sternbach. When Valium came off its patent in 1983, the company's revenues took a dive. It dismissed one thousand employees, including Reeder, Sternbach's loyal assistant. Reeder's name was listed on thirty patents and he considered himself the co-inventor of Librium and Valium. The sixty-one-year-old sued Roche for age discrimination and it settled by paying his salary for another four years (what would have been his retirement age). Tone, *Age of Anxiety,* 138 and note 42, and 265 (and 188 of 435 on pdf).
112. Tone, *Age of Anxiety,* 137, n41.
113. Michael Sternbach quoted in Tone, *Age of Anxiety,* 188.
114. Drug Coordination Report, US Senate, Committee on Government Operations, Subcommittee on Reorganization and International Organizations, Interagency Coordination in Drug Research and Regulation (Washington, D.C.: Government Printing Office, 1964), 1285.

Chapter 16: "The Therapeutic Jungle"

1. Gustav Drews, "Federal Drug Regulation Act," *Brooklyn Law Review* 29, no. 1, December 1962, 91.
2. Ibid., 91–97.

3. Alan M. Fisch, "Compulsory Licensing of Pharmaceutical Patents: An Unreasonable Solution to an Unfortunate Problem," 34 *Jurimetrics J.* 295, 316 (1994).
4. See Drews, "Federal Drug Regulation Act," 91–97; John Russell, "Lilly insulin prices come under microscope," *Indianapolis Business Journal*, August 25, 2017.
5. Drews, "Federal Drug Regulation Act," 93, 94.
6. "New Controls Proposed for Drug Industry," *CQ Almanac 1961*, 17th ed., 290–92 (Washington, D.C.: Congressional Quarterly, 1961).
7. Hugh Hussey, "Statement of the American Medical Association Re: S.1552, 87th Congress Drug Industry Antitrust Act," *JAMA*. 1961;177(3):190–95.
8. "New Controls Proposed for Drug Industry," 290–92.
9. FDC Reports, August 4, 1958, A4–16; "New Controls Proposed for Drug Industry," 290–92.
10. "Administered Drug Prices," Report of the Committee on the Judiciary, Subcommittee on Antitrust and Monopoly, pursuant to S. Red. 52, to Study the Antitrust Laws of the United States and Their Interpretation, Study of the Administered Prices in the Drug Industry, 87th Congress, 1st Session, June 27, 1961 (Washington, D.C.: Government Printing Office), 4; Braithwaite, *Corporate Crime*, 190.
11. Frank Cacciapaglia and Howard B. Rockman, "The Proposed Drug Industry Antitrust Act: Patents, Pricing, and the Public," *George Washington Law Review* 30 (5): 875–949, 894 (1961–1962); Kennedy, "Patent and Antitrust Policy–Acquisition of Patents by Fraud or by Unfair or Deceptive Acts or Practices," 35 *George Washington Law Review* 512, 531 (1966–1967); Stuart A. Laven, "Invalid Patents: Removing Statutory Protection from Improperly Granted Monopolies," *Case Western Reserve Law Review*, vol. 21, issue 2, 1970; Peter M. Costello, "The Tetracycline Conspiracy: Structure, Conduct and Performance in the Drug Industry," *Antitrust Law & Economic Review*, 1, 13–44 (1968).
12. "Administered Drug Prices," Report of the Committee on the Judiciary, 1961. Three senators dissented, Everett Dirksen, Roman Hruska, and Alexander Wiley. In their minority opinions attached as appendixes, they repeated almost all the pharmaceutical industry's defenses and excuses set forth during the hearings. Drug prices, they contended, were rising far slower than wages and construction costs. Their fellow senators did not have expertise to judge such scientific matters, and in any case, they warned, the proposed solutions might lead to socialized medicine and "will do little to enhance our reputation abroad." See Appendix A.
13. "Administered Drug Prices," Report of the Committee on the Judiciary, 1961, 3, 145.
14. Ibid., 3.
15. Hearings on Administered Prices in the Drug Industry before the Antitrust and Monopoly Subcommittee, 86th Cong, pt. 14, 7854.
16. "Administered Drug Prices," Report of the Committee on the Judiciary, 1961, Table 7, 27 and Table 8, 28, 29, Table 22A/B, 52–53, Chart 3, 54.
17. Ibid., 66.
18. Ibid., 55.
19. Ibid., 114.
20. Ibid., Table 1, 38, also 117–18.
21. Ibid., 139.
22. Ibid., 14. Belgium and Panama are the only two countries that offer patent protection comparable to America. Milton and Lee, *Pills, Profits and Politics*, 35.
23. "Administered Drug Prices," Report of the Committee on the Judiciary, 169.

24. Donohue, "A History of Drug Advertising."
25. It was their largest expense behind the cost of manufacturing the drugs. "Administered Drug Prices," Report of the Committee on the Judiciary, 157. See also Ruge, "Regulation of Prescription Drug Advertising," 7; Charles May, "Selling Drugs by Educating Physicians," *Journal of Medical Education,* Vol. 36, no. 1, 1960.
26. "Administered Drug Prices," Report of the Committee on the Judiciary, 165.
27. Greene and Podolsky, "Keeping Modern in Medicine," 362 note 122.
28. "Administered Drug Prices," Report of the Committee on the Judiciary, 198–99.
29. Ibid., 200, 221; Ruge, "Regulation of Prescription Drug Advertising." The pharma industry contended it was not a big deal to omit a drug's side effects in ads since all details were in the product inserts. However, those were not included with the samples detail men distributed to doctors like candy. Only pharmacists got the product inserts. Physicians wanting more information about side effects had to request the company mail a brochure. Only a couple of percent had ever done so.
30. Louis Goodman and Alfred Gilman, *The Pharmacological Basis of Therapeutics,* 2nd ed., Preface (New York: Macmillan, 1960).
31. "Administered Drug Prices," Report of the Committee on the Judiciary, 168, 170, 171.
32. Ibid., 190.
33. The medical director of the nation's Arthritis and Rheumatism Foundation testified that "puffery on brand name labels and advertisements" had persuaded many physicians to prescribe prescription medications although they "give no more relief than a nickel's worth of aspirin." The question about the relative efficacy of brand-name drugs versus "a nickel's worth of aspirin" was asked by Paul Dixon, the committee's counsel and staff director. See Hearings on Administered Prices, 8004–5; "Administered Drug Prices," Report of the Committee on the Judiciary.
34. "Administered Drug Prices," Report of the Committee on the Judiciary, 157–58, 338.
35. Ibid., 231.
36. Ibid., 192.
37. "Senate Drug Probers Call Ad Agency Officials Back," *Tucson Daily Citizen* (Tucson, AZ), February 1, 1962, 37.
38. Ibid.
39. "Administered Drug Prices," Report of the Committee on the Judiciary, 194. See also Rosen, *Miracle Cure*, 249.
40. "Administered Drug Prices," Report of the Committee on the Judiciary, 195.
41. Dr. Weinstein, cited in "Administered Drug Prices," Report of the Committee on the Judiciary, 182.
42. Dr. Console, cited in Ibid.
43. Felix Belair, Jr., "Inquiry on Drugs Enters New Area," *New York Times*, December 18, 1961, 38.
44. "Congress Tightens Drug Regulations," in *CQ Almanac 1962*, 18th ed., 05-197-05-210 (Washington, D.C.: Congressional Quarterly, 1963).

Chapter 17: "Paint the Worst Possible Picture"

1. Testimony of Arthur Sackler before the Judiciary Committee, Subcommittee on Antitrust and Monopoly, Legislative History of the Drug Amendments of 1962, P.L. 87-781 (1962).
2. "Stanley Wolder, 61, Law Firm Partner," *New York Times*, September 9, 1974.
3. Ben Harris, FOIA, 37–38.
4. Both died in Prague, Alfred Stern in 1986 and Martha Dodd in 1990. "Alfred K. Stern, Spy Suspect; Fled to Prague Over Charges," *New York Times*, June 24, 1986; Glenn Fowler, "Martha Dodd Stern Is Dead at 82; Author and an Accused Soviet Spy," *New York Times*, August 29, 1990.
5. Memo, Security Matter, February 25, 1955, Title and Synopsis of Facts is redacted, from production of FOIA to Ben Harris, 4, NARA.
6. Testimony of Arthur Sackler before the Judiciary Committee, bibliography introduced into the record, 3618–23.
7. Testimony of Arthur Sackler before the Judiciary Committee, 3625–29.
8. Among others a Johns Hopkins professor of medicine wrote about how Sackler's medical expertise ensured that his McAdams agency "deplores inaccuracies and bad taste in advertising," and Brooklyn's College of Pharmacy's Laboratories for Therapeutic Research had achieved international recognition, wrote its president, because of Sackler. Testimony of Arthur Sackler before the Judiciary Committee, 3630–31, 3632–33.
9. Testimony of Arthur Sackler before the Judiciary Committee, 3066.
10. Ibid., 3066–67.
11. Ibid., 3080.
12. Ibid., 3108.
13. Ibid., 3068.
14. The FDA had announced rules that drug inserts should be included on all packages, even samples, sent to pharmacists. However, physicians were still not covered. "Congress Tightens Drug Regulations," in *CQ Almanac 1962*, 18th ed., 05-197-05-210 (Washington, D.C.: Congressional Quarterly, 1963), 3070.
15. Testimony of Arthur Sackler before the Judiciary Committee, 3076.
16. Robert Warren Royle, *Upjohn Advertising: Then and Now*, Michigan State University thesis, 1964, in collection of author.
17. Testimony of Arthur Sackler before the Judiciary Committee, 3087–89.
18. Ibid., 3089, 3095.
19. Ibid., 3095.
20. Ibid., 3092.
21. Ibid., 3096–97.
22. Richard S. Gruner, *Corporate Criminal Liability and Prevention* (New York: Law Journal Press, 2004), 9–62 .
23. Kefauver, *In a Few Hands*, 61.
24. Wm. S. Merrell Co., Drug Warning—MER/29 (triparanol), Letter to Physicians, December 1, 1961. See also Paul D. Rheingold, "The MER/29 Story—An Instance of Successful Mass Disaster Litigation," *California Law Review*, Vol. 56, Issue 1, Article 9, 1968, 119–20.
25. Milton and Lee, *Pills, Profits and Politics*, 91.
26. Carpenter, *Reputation and Power*, 335.
27. Rheingold, "The MER/29 Story—An Instance of Successful Mass Disaster Liti-

gation," *California Law Review*, Vol. 56, Issue 1, Article 9, 1968. As for the costs of litigation, see Richard S. Gruner, *Corporate Criminal Liability and Prevention*, 961.

28. Testimony of Arthur Sackler before the Judiciary Committee, 3105.
29. Fortunately for Sackler, the Senate investigators had not uncovered two cases in which a six-year-old child and a twenty-three-year-old medical student, both on a low dose of MER/29, were diagnosed with cataracts. Kirby TJ. "Cataracts produced by triparanol, (MER-29)," *Transactions of the American Ophthalmological Society*. 1967;65:493–94.
30. Testimony of Arthur Sackler before the Judiciary Committee, 3100, 3102.
31. Ibid., 3111.
32. Ibid., 3083–84.
33. Ibid., 3105–9.
34. Ibid., 3110.
35. Ibid., 3119.
36. Ibid., 3113, 3117.
37. Ibid., 3131.
38. Ibid.
39. Ibid., 3131–32; see also Blair-Dixon Memorandum, 1–3.
40. Testimony of Arthur Sackler before the Judiciary Committee, 3132.
41. Ibid.
42. The senate investigative staff suspected Else Sackler had hidden equity stakes in several Sackler companies, including McAdams itself. Charts of 1960 investigative staff Senate into Sacklers, part of Blair-Dixon Memorandum.
43. Else Sackler was not the only one Arthur trusted as a proxy to hide his own shares. Bill Frohlich controlled the Medical Pharmaceutical Information Bureau, and Mortimer and Raymond owned Pharmaceutical Advertising Associates. Charts of 1960 investigative staff Senate into Sacklers, part of Blair-Dixon Memorandum. State of Delaware, Corporations Division, File Number 548703, Incorporation 2/25/1960, a general domestic corporation; NY State Division of Corporations, DOS ID 127424, Date of Filing, March 22, 1960, registered as a foreign business corporation, surrendered all rights to do business on August 30, 1993.
44. "Congress Tightens Drug Regulations"; Drug Industry Antitrust Act, Hearings before the Subcommittee on Antitrust and Monopoly, Senate Committee on the Judiciary, Part 6 Document No. 6, January 31, 1962, 3139–40.

Chapter 18: Thalidomide to the Rescue

1. "Congress Tightens Drug Regulations," in *CQ Almanac 1962*, 18th ed., 05-197-05-210 (Washington, D.C.: Congressional Quarterly, 1963).
2. Ibid.
3. Mintz, "'Heroine' of FDA Keeps Bad Drug Off Market."
4. Kimiya Sarayloo, "A Poor Man's Tale of Patented Medicine: The 1962 Amendments, Hatch-Waxman, and the Lost Admonition to Promote Progress," 18 *Quinnipiac Health Law Journal* (2015); Sam Peltzman, "An Evaluation of Consumer Protection Legislation: The 1962 Drug Amendments," 81 *J. POL. ECON.* 1049 (1973); Carpenter, *Reputation and Power*, 140–41; Rosen, *Miracle Cure*, 281.
5. Sarayloo, "A Poor Man's Tale of Patented Medicine"; Peltzman, "An Evaluation of Consumer Protection Legislation."

6. See James H. Kim & Anthony R. Scialli, "Thalidomide: The Tragedy of Birth Defects and Effective Treatment of Disease," 122 *Toxicological Sci.* 1, 1 (2011).
7. For a detailed review of Kelsey and Thalidomide, see Carpenter, *Reputation and Power*, 213–27 and 238–56.
8. Hawthorne, *Inside the FDA*, 1065 of 7181; WHO, "Drug Consumption," *WHO Chronicle* 25:458, 197.
9. Carpenter, *Reputation and Power*, 259.
10. Unnamed pharma executives told *The Wall Street Journal* their shift in strategies was because they "have no choice. . . . Our political situation has changed, we can't get anyone's ear in Washington." Carpenter, *Reputation and Power*, 260.
11. See Peter Matthiessen, *Courage for the Earth: Writers, Scientists, and Activists Celebrate the Life and Writing of Rachel Carson* (New York: Mariner Books, 2017).
12. Rachel Carson had created a widespread public distrust for new products hailed as breakthroughs by the chemical industry. The budding skepticism served as the seed for amateur health and consumer activists to form advocacy groups that lobbied the government as a counterweight to big industry. Ralph Nader's deconstruction of the American auto industry, *Unsafe at Any Speed*, gave impetus to the citizens groups. Although there were quickly as many goals as there were organizations, they all focused on some form of consumer safety. See generally Carpenter, *Reputation and Power*, 232–33.
13. Anna McCarthy, *The Citizen Machine: Governing by Television in 1950s America* (New York: The New Press, 2010), 50.
14. Gustav Drews, "Kefauver Loss: Amendment by Tennessean to Control Costs Is Killed," *Kansas City Times*, August 24, 1962, 1.
15. For instance, in one case four people had died from a tainted glucose and saline mixture from Cutter Labs, and, in another, Abbott Laboratories' barbiturate suppository that was used as a sedative for children had produced severe adverse reactions in several states. Carpenter, *Reputation and Power*, 147.
16. Donohue, "A History of Drug Advertising," 671.
17. Castagnoli, *Medicine Avenue*, 45.
18. See Podolsky, *The Antibiotic Era*, 74.
19. See Section 505 (b), (c) and (d). That was a considerable vote of confidence in the FDA. Carpenter, *Reputation and Power*, 257.
20. "Origins and Scope of the Drug Efficacy Study," *Drug Intelligence and Clinical Pharmacy*, Vol. 3, September 1969, 237.
21. As for drugs approved before the 1962 law, the Kefauver Amendments required the FDA to classify each medication as effective; probably effective; possibly effective; effective but not for all recommended uses; ineffective as a fixed combination; and ineffective. Rosen, *Miracle Cure*, 287. In 1966, James Goddard, the FDA commissioner, enlisted the help of the Division of Medical Sciences of the National Academy of Sciences and National Research Council on the agency's ambitious drug review project. Podolsky, *The Antibiotic Era*, 94. See also US Supreme Court, Weinberger v. Hynson et al., 412 US 609 (1973), Certiorari to the United States Court of Appeals for the Fourth Circuit, No., 72–394, decided, June 18, 1973.
22. The FDA inspection record has improved over the decades as it hired more inspectors. A problem it faces, however, is that it is also responsible for the safety of medications manufactured in foreign plants and then shipped to the U.S. More than half of all generics used in the U.S. are made in India, China, and Turkey. In

2018, an FDA report showed that the agency had increased its overseas inspections over four years from 993 to 1,245. However, that was at the cost of inspecting domestic facilities, which dropped from 1,869 to 1,662. See Ed Silverman, "FDA is Inspecting More Foreign Plants, But Fewer Domestic Facilities," *STAT*, September 10, 2019. See also John Lear, "Do We Need a Census of Worthless Drugs?" SR/Research/Science & Humanity, *Saturday Review*, May 7, 1960, 58; Scott Podolsky in *The Antibiotic Era*, 89.

23. Carpenter, *Reputation and Power*, 178–79.
24. Commissioner, Office of the. "A Brief History of CDER." *U.S. Food and Drug Administration*, FDA, A virtual history of the FDA, Food and Drug Administration, at https://www.fda.gov/AboutFDA/History/VirtualHistory/HistoryExhibits/ucm325199.htm.
25. Some included "The Guardian of the Drug Market" (*New York Times*); "Feminine Conscience of the FDA" (*Saturday Evening Post*); "Lady Cop" (*Newsweek*).
26. Katherine A. Helm, "Protecting Public Health from Outside the Physician's Office: A Century of FDA Regulation from Drug Safety Labeling to Off-Label Drug Promotion," *Fordham Intellectual Property, Media and Entertainment Law Journal*, Volume 18, Number 1, 2007, Article 9. As for the third and broadest phase of testing, an amendment that would have required extensive informed consent for all participants in any clinical trial was watered down in the final version of the Kefauver Amendments. Pharma successfully argued that such rigid centralized oversight would handicap American drug research. Podolsky, *The Antibiotic Era*, 92–93. Also struck from an early draft was a provision that would have allowed the clinical experience of doctors to be considered as part of a drug's efficacy profile along with controlled clinical studies. See Shorter, *Before Prozac*, 148 of 4159; Rosen, *Miracle Cure*, 288–90.
27. Koichi Mikami, "Orphans in the Market: The History of Orphan Drug Policy," *Social History of Medicine*, November 27, 2017.
28. Six competing brands touted as "synthetic penicillin" were distinctive only in how they were chemically modified during fermentation. Their only advantage was that they were absorbed in a full stomach as fast as earlier versions of penicillin had been absorbed in an empty stomach. The "faster absorption" antibiotics were in vogue from 1957 to 1960. The fillers included everything from phosphate, citric acid, to glucosamine. A subsequent investigation showed that in some cases the fillers had the opposite effect than was intended since they reacted with the antibiotics in the bloodstream to lower the drug's level. See Charles May, "Selling Drugs by Educating Physicians," 1, 3. Also, while the modifications were different for every class of drugs, all were subject to it. The only difference for some me-too allergy medications, for instance, was the use of sodium instead of potassium, both very similar alkaline metals. Tranquilizers that were chemically modified so as to have a butyl ester instead of propyl were judged distinct enough by the Patent Office for separate protection. It did not matter that the therapeutic improvements, to the extent they could be demonstrated, were minor. Milton and Lee, *Pills, Profits and Politics*, 39.
29. Milton and Lee, *Pills, Profits and Politics*, 40.
30. See generally Rosen, *Miracle Cure*, 290–94. Some research scientists at the drug companies complained to the management that their talents "should not be expended on patent-bypassing chemical manipulations." Milton and Lee, *Pills, Profits and Politics*, 40.

31. Report, Study Of "Interagency Coordination in Drug Research and Regulation," by the Subcommittee on Reorganization And International Organizations Of The Senate Committee On Government Operations, A Factual Survey on "The Nature and Magnitude of Drug Literature" by the National Library of Medicine, August 30, 1963 (Washington, D.C.: Government Printing Office). See generally "Kefauver Scores New Bill Regulating Drug Industry," AP Wire, August 1, 1962.
32. Humphrey's committee also addressed concerns that overlapping responsibilities of different agencies allowed the nontherapeutic use of antibiotics in agricultural feed to skate by virtually unregulated. Physicians' overreliance on pharma detail men was also highlighted as a systemic problem.
33. Greene and Podolsky, "Keeping Modern in Medicine," 339.
34. The National Academy of Sciences and the National Research Council tried helping out by forming the Drug Research Board in 1964. It was intended to advise doctors on drug policies, but its critics charged later it was too heavily influenced by pharma firms. Podolsky, *The Antibiotic Era*, 92–94.
35. Shorter, *Before Prozac*, 1029.
36. Carpenter, *Reputation and Power*, 367.
37. Ibid., 380.
38. Ibid., 365.
39. Ibid., 374; Tobbell, *Pills, Power and Policy*, 181–82. The largest falloff in new drug introductions was in the tranquilizer category. Some researchers cite the 1962 thalidomide scandal as having temporarily scared pharmaceutical companies away from developing central nervous system medications. Also, Roche had patented so many me-too chemical derivatives of its benzos it made it difficult for its rivals to develop a competitive drug.
40. Shorter, *Before Prozac*, 496, 505.
41. Joseph Sadusk, Jr., "The Impact of Drug Legislation on Clinical Evaluation of Drugs," paper presented by Sadusk at a symposium at the Gottlieb Duttweiler Institute, Zurich, August 28–29, 1969.
42. Larrick also expanded the agency's influence by allowing FDA science and medical employees to serve on dozens of prominent organizations from the American Cancer Society to the World Health Organization to the National Academy of Sciences. Carpenter, *Reputation and Power*, 135, 307.
43. "Engergizing FDA," *The Washington Post*, October 28, 1962, E6.
44. "Cold Cure Ban," Congressional Record, August 26, 1963, 15825.
45. "Administered Drug Prices," Report of the Committee on the Judiciary, 160–66.
46. Podolsky, *The Antibiotic Era*, 89.
47. "Antibiotics Use in Colds Backed," *Arizona Daily Star* (Tucson, AZ), December 15, 1975.
48. The members of the panel were infectious disease pioneers Harry Dowling and Max Finland, Cornell's Edwin Kilbourne, Yale's Paul Beeson, the University of Pennsylvania's Carl Schmidt, and the University of Virginia's William Jordon.
49. "Washington Proceedings," *New York Times*, June 18, 1964.

Chapter 19: The $100 Million Drug

1. It was another thirty years before the regulation of medical advertisement reached its zenith, with the FDA extending its reach to govern continuing medical education as well as even press releases from pharmaceutical firms. The industry suc-

cessfully fought most of that expanded power citing a First Amendment right to distribute "truthful and accurate" information. See Castagnoli, *Medicine Avenue*, 46.

2. The district court in 1963 ruled that the provision was contrary to the intent of the Kefauver Amendments. The Third Circuit reversed on procedural grounds, with the majority deciding there was no cause of action stated by the Pharmaceutical Manufacturers Association (PMA). The Supreme Court, in May 1967, reversed that decision and sent the case back to the Third Circuit for a decision on the substantive merits. The FDA and PMA settled before the appellate court ruled again. Ruge, "Regulation of Prescription Drug Advertising," 656.
3. Author interview with Karen Bush, November 7, 2016.
4. Interagency Coordination in Drug Research and Regulation: Review of Cooperation on Drug Policies Among Food and Drug Administration, National Institutes of Health, Veterans' Administration, and Other Agencies, Hearings Before the Subcommittee on Reorganization and International Organizations of the Committee on Government Operations, Senate, 87th Congress, 2nd Session. (Washington, D.C.: Government Printing Office, January 1964), 1281–82, 1429.
5. The study consisted of thirty-six patients on high doses of Librium, eight to twenty times Roche's recommended therapeutic range. When eleven were switched cold turkey to a placebo, most suffered from "agitation, insomnia, loss of appetite, and nausea." Two had seizures a week after they stopped taking Librium. Roche dismissed the study because it was small and the doses administered were so high. L.E. Hollister, F.P. Motzenbecker, and R.O. Degan, *Psychopharmacologia* (1961) 2: 63–68.
6. Interagency Coordination in Drug Research and Regulation, 1428.
7. Ibid., 1286.
8. Ibid., 691.
9. Shorter, *Before Prozac,* 1094 of 4159.
10. "Drug cannibalism" was what one psychiatrist called it, the idea that it was better for Roche to develop the medication that "devoured its younger brother." Dr. Mitchell B. Baiter, of the National Institute of Mental Health, quoted by Cant, "Valiumania," *New York Times Magazine*.
11. Miller, "Valium Inventor Earl Reeder," 9.
12. Tone, *Age of Anxiety*, 139.
13. Ibid., 138.
14. See Edward Shorter, *A Historical Dictionary of Psychiatry* (Oxford: Oxford University Press, 2005).
15. Tone, *Age of Anxiety*, 206.
16. Shorter, *Before Prozac,* 505 of 4159.
17. Interagency Coordination in Drug Research and Regulation. Hearings Before the Subcommittee on Reorganization and International Organizations of the Committee on Government Operations. Part 4, Review of Cooperation on Drug Policies Among the Food and Drug Administration, National Institutes of Health, Veterans Administration and Other Agencies. US Senate, 88th Congress, 1st Sess, (March 21, 1963):983, 990.
18. Interview with Irwin Gerson, chairman emeritus of Lowe McAdams Healthcare (Agency CEO Perspectives), *Medical Marketing & Media*, April 1, 1998.
19. Ibid.

20. Valium tablets did not have the coating that was applied to Librium. That meant patients felt the effects of Valium faster, which they interpreted as proof of its strength. Also, Roche won a narrow FDA approval for psychosomatic illnesses in which stress resulted in chronic physical symptoms. That made Valium the drug of first resort for patients whose complaint about some malady had been dismissed previously by family, friends, or even doctors as "it's all in your head." Guise-Richardson, "Protecting mental health in the Age of Anxiety," 291. See also Suzanne O'Sullivan, "Psychosomatic disorders: When illness really is all in the mind," *The Telegraph* (UK), May 30, 2015.
21. Shorter, *Before Prozac*, 105.
22. Ibid., 105 n.49.
23. Tone, *Age of Anxiety*, 155, 206.
24. Ibid., 206
25. When VHS tapes came into wide use in the early 1970s, more than seven hundred hospitals subscribed to a series of videos about different medical subjects, and often made them available to the community as an additional service. The cost ranged between $1,200 and $1,600 annually. Roche paid all expenses not covered by collecting subscription fees. "Competitive problems in the drug industry." Hearings before the Subcommittee on Monopoly of the Select Committee on Small Business, United States Senate, ninetieth Congress, first session on present status of competition in the pharmaceutical industry. Vol 30, 2, Washington: U.S. Govt. Print. Off., 1967. See generally Tone, *Age of Anxiety*, 211.
26. Cant, "Valiumania," 39; Tone, *Age of Anxiety*, 207, 210.
27. An exception was the April 1978 issue of the *American Journal of Psychiatry*, a special focusing on tranquilizers. That issue had sixty-four pages of tranquilizer ads, and Sackler ran several full pages promoting Valium.
28. Tone, *Age of Anxiety*, 207.
29. Gene Bylinsky, quoting an unnamed scientist in "A Preview of the 'Choose Your Mood' Society," *Fortune*, March 1977, 220.
30. Herzberg, *Happy Pills*, 356–61. The market for twenty-one minor tranquilizers peaked in the mid-1970s at just over 100 million. Herzberg, *Happy Pills*, 483 of 3354.
31. That compared at the same time to 30 million prescriptions for antidepressants and 25 million for antipsychotics. And Roche did not include in its Valium numbers the sales in bulk or from wholesalers to hospitals, nursing homes, and the U.S. military and Veterans Administration. Cant, "Valiumania," 31.
32. Ibid.
33. Most who heard the song and understood the connection to Valium realized it was not an ode to the drug but instead a snarky protest that middle-class mothers and fathers were downing prescription pills while condemning the use of illicit drugs by their children.
34. Tone, *Age of Anxiety*, 153.
35. Interview with Irwin Gerson, chairman emeritus of Lowe McAdams Healthcare, "Agency CEO Perspectives," *Medical Marketing & Media*, April 1, 1998.
36. Mickey C. Smith, *A Social History of the Minor Tranquilizers: The Quest for Small Comfort in the Age of Anxiety* (New York: Pharmaceutical Products Press, an imprint of The Haworth Press, 1991), 12.
37. Tone, *Age of Anxiety*, 153.
38. Cant, "Valiumania," 31.

39. Ibid. See also, Tone, *Age of Anxiety*, 222.
40. Cited in *Hoffmann-La Roche, Inc. v. Kleindist*, 478 F.2d 1 (1973).
41. Tone, *Age of Anxiety*, 142; Smith, *Small Comfort*, 30.
42. Author interview with Richard Sperber, March 26, 2019.
43. Tone, *Age of Anxiety*, 153.

Chapter 20: Legal but Somehow "Shifty"

1. Executive Order 11076—"Establishing the President's Advisory Commission on Narcotic and Drug Abuse," January 15, 1963. *The American Presidency Project*, January 15, 1963.
2. FDA Commissioner Larrick had issued estimates that as of 1960–61, barbiturates caused more overdose deaths than all other drugs combined. *Drug Abuse Control, 1965*, druglibrary.org/special/king/dhu/dhu26.htm.
3. Dodd had investigated juvenile delinquency in 1958; it was from there that he became a zealous antidrug crusader. Rasmussen, *On Speed*, 256–58.
4. Nancy E. Marion, Willard M. Oliver, *Drugs in American Society: An Encyclopedia of History, Politics, Culture, and the Law*, 3 Volumes (New York: ABC-Clio, 2014), 17; Rasmussen, "America's First Amphetamine Epidemic."
5. US Senate, Committee on Government Operations, Subcommittee on Reorganization and International Organizations, Interagency Coordination in Drug Research and Regulation (Washington, D.C.: Government Printing Office, 1964).
6. Thomas Hoving, *Making the Mummies Dance: Inside the Metropolitan Museum of Art* (New York: Simon & Schuster, 1994), 96.
7. Meyer and Brysac, *The China Collectors*, 23–24, 40.
8. Lutze, *Who Can Know the Other?*, 155.
9. According to Marietta, "We even had to call upon the resources of my factory in Germany [Dr. Kade Pharmaceutical] to store artifacts Arthur purchased in Communist China." It was illegal to import those goods into the U.S. until President Nixon opened diplomatic relations with China in the early 1970s. Arthur and Marietta were among the first Westerners permitted into the country. For information on continuing government control over the postcommunist art market in China, see generally Abigail R. Esman, "China's $13 Billion Art Fraud—And What It Means For You," *Forbes*, August 13, 2012; David Barboza, Graham Bowley, and Amanda Cox, "Forging an Art Market in China," *New York Times*, October 28, 2013; David Pilling, "CT Loo: champion of Chinese art . . . or villain?," *Financial Times*, April 24, 2014.
10. Letter to the Editor, "Not For Attribution," *New York*, December 4, 1978, 5.
11. Hoving, *Making the Mummies Dance*, 95.
12. Schwarcz, *Place and Memory in the Singing Crane Garden*, 196.
13. Lutze, *Who Can Know the Other?*, 147.
14. Meyer and Brysac, *The China Collectors*, 351. Lee Rosenbaum, *The Complete Guide to Collecting Art* (New York: Alfred A. Knopf, 1982).
15. Lutze, *Who Can Know the Other?*, 151. Sackler had found out about Singer in 1957 when Arthur bought nearly a hundred objects at a Parke-Bernet auction in New York. When Sackler noticed that thirty of the bronzes he had acquired came from one collector, Paul Singer, he met him and offered to deal directly with him, thereby cutting out the auction houses. See also Meyer and Brysac, *The China Collectors*, 349–50. In a 2012 tally of the collection of Asian art at the Freer/

Smithsonian, the curators counted the contributions: Freer, 3,270 pieces; Sackler, 812 pieces; Singer, about 5,000 pieces.

16. A self-taught psychiatrist leading the way for Sackler, a rich psychiatrist, struck some of the Metropolitan directors and trustees as the "blind leading the blind." "Brooklyn Museum Plans Indian Tour," *New York Times*, December 18, 1966, 84; Marvin D. Schwartz, "Antiques: A Flying Tour of Carpets," *New York Times*, April 29, 1967, 32; "Compatible Art Tastes Now Factor in Marriage," *New York Times*, March 17, 1960, 36; Meyer and Brysac, *The China Collectors,* 350–55, 352.
17. Meyer and Brysac, *The China Collectors,* citing a letter to James Cahill from Wen Fong in 1966.
18. Hoving, *Making the Mummies Dance*, 93.
19. Letter to the Editor, "Not For Attribution," *New York*, December 4, 1978, 5.
20. Lutze, *Who Can Know the Other?,* 164.
21. Set 2 of Kefauver investigative committee notes prepared for John Blair, under the heading "1955," page 3, collection of author; Goldburt was one of the original incorporators for Mortimer Sackler's Foundation.
22. See "Members of the Corporation Elected during the Year," Annual Report of the Trustees of the Metropolitan Museum of Art (111), 1980; 88–90; "Back Matter," *Metropolitan Museum of Art Bulletin* 23, no. 2, 1964: 95–108.
23. An art correspondent described Arthur's objects as "artistic treasures . . . a magnificent collection of ancient Chinese jade and bronze objects and Central and Western Asian bronzes." Sanka Knox, "Asian Treasures Lent Columbia for Public Exhibit and Research," *New York Times*, November 11, 1960. In addition to the public art exhibition, Sackler gave permission to university researchers to test the objects with a combination of metallurgical, spectrographic, and crystallographic analyses so historians and archaeologists might obtain a better understanding of the development of Eurasian cultures.
24. The Metropolitan will not confirm the amount of the gift. *The Boston Globe* later reported it as $250,000. However, Thomas Hoving, who replaced Rorimer as the Met's director, wrote in his memoir of his tenure at the museum that it was $150,000. Lenzner, "A Financial Man and the Fogg," and Hoving, *Making the Mummies Dance.*
25. According to Thomas Hoving, director of the Met from 1966 to 1976, when it came to the Rogers Fund, "strictly speaking, the funds were intended to be used *only* for acquisitions, not the extras. . . . Over the years we had been dipping in . . . to pay for restorations, frames, publications, and sometimes even expenses for the curators to travel to and from Europe to look at possible purchases" (emphasis in original). Hoving, *Making the Mummies Dance*, 291.
26. Morgan had one of the finest collections in private hands of master European paintings, rare manuscripts, Renaissance tapestries, and ancient sculpture. However, he did not leave any of it to the Metropolitan, which he led for nine years until his death in 1913. His son donated about 40 percent of his father's collection to the Metropolitan in 1917; it is still considered by the museum the most valuable bequest in its history. McDowall, Carolyn, and Carolyn McDowall FRSA, "The Metropolitan Museum of Art New York—Exalting the Arts." The Culture Concept Circle, July 17, 2012.
27. Hoving, *Making the Mummies Dance,* 94–95.
28. The museum deposited Sackler's gift into the account for the Rogers Fund, list-

ing it as a "replenishment," and that allowed it to make the attribution changes on some of the Rogers Fund collectibles. Lenzner, "A Financial Man and the Fogg."

29. Hoving, *Making the Mummies Dance*, 94.
30. Ibid.
31. Published accounts place the second Sackler request anywhere from the same day as he made the demands over the Rogers Fund, to early 1965. Thomas Hoving, who replaced Rorimer as director, says that it was in the same meeting in November 1963. Hoving, *Making the Mummies Dance*, 94.
32. Ibid.
33. Glueck, "An Art Collector Sows Largesse and Controversy."
34. "Even the Met curators needed permission to get in," said Professor James Cahill, a leading authority on Chinese art, "a situation unheard of in the history of great museums." Cahill quoted in Meyer and Brysac, *The China Collectors*, 352–53.
35. Noble quoted in Hoving, *Making the Mummies Dance*, 94.
36. "Guide to the Records of the Department of Asian Art 1925–2003," Brooklyn Museum, at https://d1lfxha3ugu3d4.cloudfront.net/archives/Asian_final.pdf.
37. When Singer died in 1997, his nearly six-thousand-piece collection, valued at $60 million, doubled the size of Sackler's Asian trove overnight. Meyer and Brysac, *The China Collectors*, 351. See also Lee Rosenbaum, "Private Boon or Private Reserve? The Met's Sackler Enclave," *ARTnews*, September 1978, 56–57.
38. Marion, and Oliver, *Drugs in American Society*, 87.
39. "The President's Advisory Commission on Narcotic and Drug Abuse," Final Report (Washington, D.C.: Government Printing Office, November 1963). See Exhibit 1, 6–7.
40. Ibid., 9.

Chapter 21: Targeting Women

1. "Psychotoxic," literally "mind poison," was coined during JFK's administration as a catchall. Rasmussen, *On Speed*, 259.
2. Ibid., 257–58.
3. Ibid.
4. Act of July 15, 1965 (Drug Abuse Control Amendments of 1965), Public Law 89-74, 79 *STAT* 226, a Bill to Protect the Public Health and Safety by Amending the Federal Food, Drug, and Cosmetic Act to Establish Special Controls for Depressant and Stimulant Drugs, and for Other Purposes.
5. Ibid.
6. Douglas Martin, "James L. Goddard, Crusading F.D.A. Leader, Dies at 86," *New York Times*, January 2, 2010.
7. George Larrick testimony, in Drug Abuse Control Amendments of 1965. Hearings Before the Committee on Interstate and Foreign Commerce, House of Representatives, 89th Congress, First Session, on H.R. 2. U.S., House of Representatives, at 33 (1965).
8. When Goddard took charge there was a vigorous debate inside the FDA over whether the Drug Abuse Control Amendments passed the previous year had empowered the agency to place sales restrictions on Miltown and Roche's blockbusters, Librium and Valium. Tone, *Age of Anxiety*, 225; Edward Shorter, "The Liberal State and the Rogue Agency: FDA's Regulation of Drugs for Mood Disorders,

1950s–1970s," *International Journal of Law and Psychiatry* 31.2 (2008): 126–35; Dowbiggin, *The Quest for Mental Health*, 150. See also Herzberg, *Happy Pills*, 1341–1345 of 3354.

9. Proposed Rule, Department of Health, Education and Welfare, Food and Drug Administration. Meprobamate: Proposed Findings of Fact and Conclusions and Tentative Order Regarding Listing Drug as Subject to Control 32 F.R. 5933 (1967).
10. "F.D.A. Head Urges Drug Producers to Curb Abuses; Tells Industry Meeting That Some Are More Interested in Gain Than in Patients," *New York Times*, April 7, 1966, 1.
11. Ruge, "Regulation of Prescription Drug Advertising: Medical Progress and Private Enterprise," 651; Donohue, "A History of Drug Advertising," 659–99.
12. "U.S. False Ad Drive Cite Journal of AMA," *Los Angeles Times*, March 4, 1966, 2.
13. Ruge, "Regulation of Prescription Drug Advertising," 661. The 1953 merger of Merck with Sharp & Dohme had pushed Merck ahead of Parke-Davis as the largest American drug company. In the U.S. and Canada, the new company used the trade name Merck while it was known as Merck Sharp & Dohme (MSD) everywhere else. "Merck's Merger," *Time*, March 16, 1953, 58.
14. "F.D.A. Head Urges Drug Producers To Curb Abuses," 1.
15. Martha Lear, a *New York Times Magazine* writer and editor, coined in a 1988 article the terms "first-wave feminism" and "second-wave feminism." First-wave covers the late nineteenth and early twentieth centuries, revolving around the suffragist movement and efforts to ensure women's legal rights in relation to property, marriage, and children.
16. Magazines reinforced many of the female stereotypes. *Newsweek* told women that "anatomy is destiny" and that those who went to college might only find it diminished their critical role as housewives and mothers. *Better Homes and Gardens* said that at the top of every woman's "to do" list was to "help their husbands decide where they are going and use their pretty heads to help them get there." *Esquire* thought working wives might constitute a "menace." See Tone, *Age of Anxiety*, 177.
17. A German psychoanalyst, Karen Horney (née Danielsen), is credited as the neo-Freudian founder of feminist psychology. Her seminal book, *Feminine Psychology*, was a collection of her essays over fifteen years. https://plato.stanford.edu/entries/feminism-psychoanalysis/.
18. Kate Millett, *Sexual Politics*; Phyllis Chesler, *Women & Madness: When Is a Woman Mad and Who Is It Who Decides?* (Garden City, NY: Doubleday, 1972); Juliet Mitchell, *Psychoanalysis and Feminism: Freud, Reich, Laing, and Women* (New York: Vintage Books, 1974); Carol Gilligan, *In a Different Voice: Psychological Theory and Women's Development* (Cambridge: Harvard University Press, 1982).
19. Half the chairs of academic psychiatric departments were Freudian psychoanalysts. Dowbiggin, *The Quest for Mental Health*, 89. Psychoanalysis had, concluded the feminist writers, put women in a permanently subordinate status while conditioning them to be content with a lowly stature. Parul Sehgal and Neil Genzlinger, "Kate Millett, Ground-Breaking Feminist Writer, Is Dead at 82," *New York Times*, September 6, 2017.
20. Dowbiggin, *The Quest for Mental Health*, 9–12.

21. Ibid., 68.
22. During the peak use of lobotomies, 60 percent were performed on women. Joel Braslow, *Mental Ills and Bodily Cures: Psychiatric Treatment in the First Half of the Twentieth Century* (Los Angeles: University of California Press, 1997), 153.
23. Lobotomizing men raised questions about whether the operations might permanently end a previously successful business career. The female stereotype meant doctors concluded that a woman had a remote chance of returning to her pre-illness "normal" life as a dutiful daughter or subservient wife. See generally Dowbiggin, *The Quest for Mental Health*, 119. For other analyses of ways that drugs were marketed historically to reinforce female stereotypes, see Charles Rosenberg and Carroll Smith-Rosenberg, "The Female Animal: Medical and Biological Views of Woman and her Role in Nineteenth-Century America," *Journal of American History*, 1973, 60, 332–56; Mary C. Howell, "What Medical Schools Teach About Women," *NEJM*, 1974, 291, 304–7; A. Mant and D. Darroch, "Media Images and Medical Images," *Soc. Sri. Med.*, 1975, 9, 613; J. Prather and L. Fidel, "Sex Differences in the Content and Style of Medical Advertisements," *Soc. Sri. Med.*, 1975, 9, 23; Mickey C. Smith and Lisa Griffin, "Rationality of Appeals Used in the Promotion of Psychotropic Drugs," *Soc. Sri. Med.*, 1977, 11, 409–14; E. H. Mosher, "Portrayal of Women in Drug Advertising: A Medical Betrayal," *J. Drug Issues*, 1976, 6, 72.
24. Tone, *Age of Anxiety*, 106.
25. A 1956 *Life* magazine interview with five male psychoanalysts summarized the then dominant psychiatric assessment: women with career ambition were more likely to have "mental illness . . . emotional conflict in their marriage, and had sons who were more likely to be adult homosexual." Bob Sipchen, "Women and Power in the U.S.: Life Asks, 'What If?,' " *Los Angeles Times*, May 21, 1992.
26. *Aspects of Society,* with a preface by C. H. Hardin Branch, Compliments of Roche Laboratories, (J. B. Lippincott, 1965). There are very few original copies of the book available from antiquarian bookdealers. Those in very good condition, with an intact jacket, and the attached sixteen-page insert with graphics, photos, and dispensing information, are priced between $300 and $500. The author obtained an intact copy from a California collector.
27. Still, Roche included a list of side effects in the last pages in case the FDA tried using the book as a test case for expanded enforcement authority.
28. Arthur M Sackler, Raymond R Sackler, Félix Martí-Ibáñez, and Mortimer D Sackler, "Contemporary Physiodynamic Trends in Psychiatry," *Journal of Clinical and Experimental Psychopathology and Quarterly Review of Psychiatry and Neurology*, I 15 (1954), 382–400; Eugene L. Bliss et al., "Reaction of the Adrenal Cortex to Emotional Stress," *Psychodynamic Medicine* 18 (1956), 56–76. See also William Malamud, "C. H. Hardin Branch, M.D. Eighty-Ninth President 1962–1963, A Biographical Sketch," *American Journal of Psychiatry*, Vol. 120, Issue 1, April 1, 2005, 12–15.
29. Marietta thought its heavy psychoanalytic undertone bore a striking similarity to much of the ad copy Arthur had previously written for Roche.
30. "Executive Neurosis" comes from William Whyte's 1956 *The Organization Man.*
31. Joseph V. Brady, "Ulcers in 'Executive' Monkeys," *Scientific American*, October 1958, 95–100; Conversation with Joseph V. Brady, *Addiction*, September 15, 2005.
32. *Aspects of Society*, 3943.

33. Supplement attached to *Aspects of Society*, unnumbered pages 6–7.
34. *Aspects of Society*, 40.
35. McNeil Laboratories, "When Nervous Tension Augments Family Problems," *JAMA* 187, No. 2, January 11, 1964, 228.
36. Tone, *Age of Anxiety*, 159.
37. Copy of full-page Roche advertisement titled "35, single and psychoneurotic," in collection of author.
38. Hugh J. Parry, "Use of Psychotropic Drugs by U.S. Adults," *Public Health Reports* 83 (Oct. 1968): 799; Edwin M. Schur, *Labeling Women Deviant: Gender, Stigma, and Social Control* (New York: Random House, 1984), 160, 195; Ruth Cooperstock, "Sex Differences in the Use of Mood-Modifying Drugs: An Explanatory Model," *Journal of Health and Social Behavior* 12, no. 3 (1971): 238–44.
39. Mary Sykes Wylie / Psychotherapy Networker, "Falling in Love Again: The Amazing History, Marketing, and Wide Legal Use of Today's 'Dangerous' Drugs," Alternet.org, August 18, 2014.
40. In 1987, American Home Products merged Ayerst with its other pharma subsidiary, Philadelphia-based Wyeth.
41. Joe Palca and Patricia Neighmond, "The Marketing of Menopause: Historically, Hormone Therapy Heavy on Promotion, Light on Science," NPR, August 8, 2002.
42. See R.A. Wilson, "The Roles of Estrogen and Progesterone in Breast and Genital Cancer," *JAMA*, 1962;182(4):327–31; and with his wife, Thelma Wilson, "The Fate Of The Nontreated Postmenopausal Woman: A Plea For The Maintenance Of Adequate Estrogen From Puberty To The Grave," *Journal of the American Geriatrics Society*, Vol. 11, Issue 4, April 1963.
43. Wilson, "The Roles of Estrogen and Progesterone in Breast and Genital Cancer."
44. The publisher was New York–based M. Evans and Company, an imprint formed in 1951. It offered a mix of self-help medical and diet books, histories of Freemasonry and the Knights Templar, and topics as far flung as collections of Jewish humor and manuals for surviving marriage and divorce. The company's biggest hit was a book by Robert Atkins, the New York doctor who single-handedly kicked off the low-carbohydrate diet craze with the pitch "the high calorie way to stay thin." British publisher Rowman & Littlefield bought M. Evans in 2007 for an undisclosed amount.
45. Gina Kolata With Melody Petersen, "Hormone Replacement Study A Shock to the Medical System," *New York Times*, July 10, 2002.
46. *The New Republic* and *The Washington Post* were the first in 1968 to publish reports of pharma money to Wilson's foundation. More evidence of the extent to which Wilson relied on drug money was disclosed in Morton Mintz, *The Pill: An Alarming Report* (New York: Beacon Press, 1970), and Barbara Seaman, *The Greatest Experiment Ever Performed on Women: Exploding the Estrogen Myth* (New York: Seven Stories, 2009). 222–23, 451.
47. Natasha Singer and Duff Wilson, "Menopause, as Brought to You by Big Pharma," *New York Times*, December 12, 2009.
48. Trisha Posner, *No Hormones, No Fear: A Natural Journey Through Menopause* (New York: Villard, 2003), 35–38.
49. Kolata and Petersen, "Hormone Replacement Study A Shock to the Medical System."
50. Gary Null and Barbara Seaman, *For Women Only!: Your Guide to Health Empowerment* (New York: Seven Stories Press, 1999), 751.

51. Ibid.
52. Posner, *No Hormones, No Fear,* 36.
53. Null and Seaman, *For Women Only!*, 752.
54. Martin J. Walker, "The Ghost Lobby and Other Mysteries of the Modern Physic: Wyeth Pharmaceuticals and New Labour," *Science and Democracy,* August 31, 2005.
55. D. W. Johnson, "Memorandum of Telephone Conversation" with Simon & Schuster counsel, Selig Levitan, June 19, 1967, New Drug Application 10-976, Vol. 131, Records Groups 88, NARA.
56. Gusberg quoted in Sandra Coney, *The Menopause Industry: A Guide to Medicine's 'Discovery' of the Mid-life Woman* (London: The Women's Press, 1995), 164.
57. Claudia Wallis, "The Estrogen Dilemma," *Time,* June 24, 2001.
58. Robert Metz, "Market Place," *New York Times,* November 12, 1975, 64. A later historical study of the estrogen and hormone markets concluded that Premarin had on average at least 70 percent of annual HRT sales. See Dianne Kennedy et al., "Noncontraceptive Estrogens and Progestins: Use Patterns Over Time," *Obstetrics and Gynecology* 65, March 1985, 444–45.
59. Carmel J. Cohen and Saul B. Gusberg, "Screening for Endometrial Cancer," *Clinical Obstetrics and Gynecology,* January 1976.

Chapter 22: Death with Dignity

1. Advocates for legalizing euthanasia were a minority but their view began showing wider support in opinion polls of British citizens. England's Catholic Church, backed by most traditional medical associations, led the fight against it. See "The Right to Die," *Observer,* January 21, 1967, 38; "Brass Tacks," *Observer,* July 27, 1980, 44; Marlise Simons, "Dutch Becoming First Nation to Legalize Assisted Suicide," *New York Times*, November 29, 2000.
2. Kübler-Ross relied on more than five hundred interviews with dying patients to contend that treatment in traditional settings such as hospitals or nursing homes should be replaced when possible with home care. In 1972, the U.S. Senate Special Committee on Aging recommended the government provide families of terminally ill patients assistance with home care and visiting nurses. "History of Hospice," National Hospice and Palliative Care Organization.
3. "Dame Cicely Saunders, Founder of the Modern Hospice Movement, Dies," *British Medical Journal*, July 14, 2005.
4. "Dame Cicely Saunders Biography" at https://cicelysaundersinternational.org/dame-cicely-saunders/.
5. Cicely Saunders, quoted in Beryl McAlhone, "You: No Screens Around the Bed," *Observer*, July 7, 1975, 18.
6. See "Dame Cicely Saunders, Founder of the Modern Hospice Movement, Dies."
7. Cicely Saunders, "The Treatment of Intractable Pain in Terminal Cancer," *Proceedings of the Royal Society of Medicine,* March 1963, 56(3): 195–97.
8. This was particularly true of injections or IV administration; doctors were somewhat more willing to administer morphine orally by tablets.
9. Saunders, "The Treatment of Intractable Pain in Terminal Cancer," 196.
10. Cicely Saunders and David Clark, *Cicely Saunders: Selected Writings 1958–2004* (Oxford, UK: Oxford University Press, 2006), 83.

11. Saunders, "The Treatment of Intractable Pain in Terminal Cancer," 196. Saunders quoted in "When Death Is Not Just a Release from a Life of Pain," *Guardian*, January 20, 1979, 8.
12. As she later reported in a paper to the Royal Society of Medicine, "pain of terminal disease can be controlled without any erosion of personality and alertness." Saunders quoted in "Dying Trends," *Guardian*, January 24, 1979, 8.
13. She eventually had 1,110 patients in her study.
14. Saunders, "The Treatment of Intractable Pain in Terminal Cancer," 196.
15. "Can Lives be Saved by Blocking Pain?" *Observer*, November 1, 1985, 14.
16. Saunders, "The Treatment of Intractable Pain in Terminal Cancer," 197.
17. Ibid.
18. Cicely Saunders, "The Last Stages of Life," *American Journal of Nursing*, Vol. 65, No. 3 (1965), 73–74.
19. Richard Carter, "Cicely Saunders—Founder of the Hospice Movement: Selected Letters 1959–1999." *Journal of the Royal Society of Medicine* Vol. 96,3 (2003): 149–51.
20. Richmond, "Dame Cicely Saunders, Founder of the Modern Hospice Movement, Dies."
21. Talk by Cicely Saunders at "The Right to Die" public forum, sponsored by the National Secular Society, Conway Hall, London, January 25, 1968.
22. R. G. Twycross, "Choice Of Strong Analgesic In Terminal Cancer: Diamorphine Or Morphine?" *Pain*, 1977 3; 93–104. Britain's National Health Service provided morphine and heroin as needed to patients in hospice care. From the government's perspective, either was acceptable since both were inexpensive. The pharmacy cost of heroin, for instance, was $0.4 per grain (60 mg), about 600 percent cheaper than in the United States for an equivalent dose. Patricia M. Wald, "Dealing with Drug Abuse," 257.
23. Hermann Richard Knapp dropped the *K* in the company's name under the belief that it was a simpler pronunciation for English-speaking customers. "Napp Pharmaceutical Holdings," *Sunday Times*, March 9, 2008.
24. "Britain's Economy: The Big Lie," *Spectator Archive*, March 11, 1966. See also Tejvan Pettinger, "UK Devaluation of Sterling," *Economics Help*, 1967; "Dr. Mortimer Sackler," *Telegraph*, April 27, 2010.
25. "Dr. Mortimer Sackler," *Telegraph*, April 27, 2010.
26. "Our History," BARD, http://bardpharmaceuticals.co.uk/our-company/our-history/.
27. Correspondence files are in Papers of Cicely Saunders, King's College, K/PP149 /3/4/27.
28. See communications and correspondence Saunders/Smith & Nephew, 1969–1970, Papers of Cicely Saunders, King's College, K/PP149/3/4/9.
29. H. J. Gallimore, Director, Smith & Nephew Pharmaceuticals Limited, to Dr. Cicely Saunders, September 23, 1969, in Papers of Cicely Saunders, King's College, K/PP149/3/4/9, folder 19791980.
30. Cicely Saunders to H. J. Gallimore, 1 page, September 27, 1969, Ibid.
31. See Postal Symposium "Dear Doctor" letter format, "Management of Terminal Illness," and six-page attached questionnaire; Postal Symposium No. 1, Management of Terminal Illness, Report No. 1—"Hospitalization," Report No. 2—"Home Care," Report No. 3—"Analgesic and Sedation," Report No. 4—"Does A Doctor Tell?," Report No. 5—"An Independent View," Report No. 6—"Religio Medici—

The Reflections of a Clergyman-Doctor," Confidential, K_P149_2_3_33, King's College, 1–3.

32. C.B. Pert and S.H. Snyder, "Opiate receptor: Its demonstration in nervous tissue," *Science*, 1973;179:1011–14.
33. The levels are low enough that there is never enough to risk an overdose. W.R. Martin et al., "The effects of morphine- and nalorphine-like drugs in the nondependent and morphine-dependent chronic spinal dog," *J. Pharmacol. Exp. Ther.* 197 (1976): 517–32. The general medical term for natural opiates produced by the brain is endogenous opioids (enkephalin). "The brain contains an endogenous constituent which acts as an agonist at morphine receptor sites. . . . This substance. . . . .we have termed enkephalin." J. Hughes et al. in *Life Sci.* XVI. 1753.
34. Trescot A, Datta S, Lee M, Hansen H., "Opioid pharmacology," *Pain Physician* 2008:11:S133–S153.
35. "Analysis: See How Deadly Street Opioids like 'elephant Tranquilizer' Have Become," *Washington Post.* And see Fiore, Kristina. "Patients Opt for Stronger Opioids," *MedPage Today: Medical News and Free CME*, February 25, 2015.
36. "It causes less hypotension and respiratory depression. Nausea, vomiting and constipation are rare." Annual Clinical Meeting, *British Medical Journal*, October 8, 1960, 14.
37. "Pain-Killing Drug Approved By F.D.A.," *New York Times*, June 27, 1967, 41.
38. Pentazocine hydrochloride label, at https://www.glowm.com/resources/glowm/cd/pages/drugs/p018.html; Fortral at https://www.myvmc.com/drugs/fortral/. And see Barnett, "Alternative Opioids to Morphine in Palliative Care: A Review of Current Practice and Evidence," *Postgraduate Medical Journal*, The Fellowship of Postgraduate Medicine, June 1, 2001.
39. "Oral pentazocine and phenazocine: A comparison in postoperative pain," *British Journal of Anaesthesia*, June 1971 43(5):486–95; JP Conaghan, "Pentazocine and phenazocine. A double-blind comparison of two benzomorphan derivatives in postoperative pain," *British Journal of Anaesthesia*, May 1966 38(5):345–54.
40. "Postal Symposium No. 1, Management of Terminal Illness, Interim Report based on Postal Questionnaire, Confidential, Smith & Nephew Pharmaceuticals Ltd, July 1970, 25 pages, Papers of Cicely Saunders, King's College, K/PP149/2/3/33.
41. Annual Clinical Meeting, *British Medical Journal*, October 8, 1960, 14. British spelling in original journal is retained in this selected material.
42. Papers of Cicely Saunders: papers relating to research on automated pain relief, 1979–1980, King's College, PP149/3/4/27.

Chapter 23: "Go-Go Goddard"

1. "National Center for Chronic Disease Prevention and Health Promotion (US) Office on Smoking and Health. The Health Consequences of Smoking—50 Years of Progress: A Report of the Surgeon General," Atlanta (GA): Centers for Disease Control and Prevention (US); 2014. 2, Fifty Years of Change 1964–2014. See also Federal Cigarette Labeling and Advertising, 15 U.S.C. §§ 1331–40; 21 U.S.C. § 387c.
2. Initially, the surgeon general's warning about the evidence establishing smoking and serious heath risks got a lot of media coverage but barely affected cigarette sales. "Tobacco: After publicity surge Surgeon General's Report seems to have little enduring effect," *Science*, 145:1021–22, Sept. 4, 1964, 1021.

3. David A. Kessler et al., "The Food and Drug Administration's Regulation of Tobacco Products," *New England Journal of Medicine*, September 26, 1996; 335:988–94.
4. Interview with William W. Goodrich, part of the FDA Oral History Program, October 15, 1986 1:4–5. 8.
5. Douglas Martin, "James L. Goddard, Crusading F.D.A. Leader, Dies at 86," *New York Times*, January 1, 2010.
6. Valerie J. Nelson, "Dr. James L. Goddard," *Chicago Tribune*, January 3, 2010.
7. "F.D.A. Head Urges Drug Producers To Curb Abuses; Tells Industry Meeting That Some Are More Interested in Gain Than in Patients," *The New York Times*, April 7, 1966, 1.
8. Ibid.
9. Ibid.; Martin, "James L. Goddard."
10. Statistic from Richard Lyons, "Goddard Expects Ban on 300 Drugs," *New York Times*, December 31, 1967, 1.
11. Report to the Ranking Minority Member, Special Committee on Aging, U.S. Senate, FDA's Reviews Of New Drugs, Changes Needed in Process for Reviewing and Reporting on Clinical Studies, General Accounting Office, September 1988.
12. Martin, "James L. Goddard."
13. The drug was Norlutin, a Parke-Davis hormone dispensed for gynecological disorders.
14. He had to settle for ramping up the number of "Dear Doctor" letters in which drug companies paid fines of $40,000 and sent letters to physicians correcting misleading promotion. Carpenter, *Reputation and Power*, 320–22. See also Nelson, "Dr. James L. Goddard," and Ruge, "Regulation of Prescription Drug Advertising," 668.
15. Doctors hoped to find ways to stimulate the body's immune response by studying how live cancer cells were dealt with by otherwise healthy patients, those with cancer, and patients with other serious diseases.
16. Elinor Langer, "Human Experimentation: Cancer Studies at Sloan-Kettering Stir Public Debate on Medical Ethics," *Science*, February 7, 1964: Vol. 143, Issue 3606, 551–53,
17. When *Science* magazine asked Southam if he had injected himself or any of his medical team with live cancer cells, he said he "would not have hesitated, but it would have served no useful purpose. . . . I did not regard the experiment as dangerous. But let's face it, there are relatively few skilled cancer researchers, and it seemed stupid to take even the little risk." See Langer, *Science*.
18. Allen M. Hornblum, "NYC's Forgotten Cancer Scandal," *New York Post*, December 28, 2013.
19. Ibid.
20. Pharma carried the day, in alliance with the AMA: full informed consent was unnecessary since physician investigators were bound to protect the rights of clinical trial participants. See Tobbell, *Pills, Power and Policy*, 172–77.
21. Holly Fernandez Lynch and I. Glenn Cohen, eds., *FDA in the Twenty-First Century: The Challenges of Regulating Drugs and New Technologies* (New York: Columbia University Press, 2015); Shorter, "The Liberal State and the Rogue Agency." See also "Origins and Scope of the Drug Efficacy Study," *Drug Intelligence and Clinical Pharmacy*, Vol. 3, September 1969, 237.
22. Podolsky, *The Antibiotic Era*, 94–95. Most observers expected the FDA would be

hard pressed not to follow any recommendations made by the panels of esteemed researchers assembled by the NAS and NRC.

23. After several administrative delays, the Drug Efficacy Study Implementation began in 1966. *Drug Efficacy Study* (DES), 45, and DES, 230, Archives, National Academy of Sciences. See also Carpenter, *Reputation and Power*, 315–16, 346–49.
24. Shorter, "The Liberal State and the Rogue Agency." See also "Origins and Scope of the Drug Efficacy Study," *Drug Intelligence and Clinical Pharmacy*, Vol. 3, September 1969, 237.
25. David Mantus, Douglas J. Pisano (eds), *FDA Regulatory Affairs: Third Edition* (Boca Raton, FL: CRC Press, 2014).
26. "Origins and Scope of the Drug Efficacy Study," *Drug Intelligence and Clinical Pharmacy*, Vol. 3, September 1969, 237.
27. Podolsky, *The Antibiotic Era*, 94–95, 97. A sixth category was later added, "ineffective with the following qualifications."
28. "Report Including Recommended Findings and Conclusions Re: Potential for Abuse of the Drugs Librium and Valium," Department of Health, Education, and Welfare, FDA, April 7, 1967, Manufacturers Files No. AF14–324, re Hoffmann-La Roche, Federal Drug Administration History Office.
29. Ibid.
30. Ibid.
31. Tobbell, *Pills, Power and Policy*, 168–69.
32. Ruge, "Regulation of Prescription Drug Advertising: Medical Progress and Private Enterprise," 672.
33. Ibid., 654.
34. Ibid. Anytime promotional films were screened at conventions and seminars, the major side effects of any featured drugs would have to be listed on-screen. Full labeling packets would also be distributed to the audience..
35. Ibid.
36. DeForest Ely, cited by Morton Mintz, "The Stuff Doctors Read," *Progressive* 33:31, April 1969.
37. Ruge, "Regulation of Prescription Drug Advertising: Medical Progress and Private Enterprise," 655.
38. Ibid., 653.
39. Milton and Lee, *Pills, Profits and Politics*, 76.
40. Edward Berkowitz, "Medicare and Medicaid: The Past as Prologue." *Health Care Financing Review* Vol. 27, 2 (Winter 2005): 11–23.
41. The life expectancy in America then was 70.2 years. Medicare was designed as a program to prevent enormous hospital bills from causing havoc in the last five years of patients' lives. Thomas Oliver, Phillip Lee, and Helene L. Lipton, "A Political History of Medicare and Prescription Drug Coverage," *Milbank Quarterly*, Vol. 82, No. 2, 2004, 283–354.
42. M. Gornick, "Twenty years of Medicare and Medicaid: Covered populations, use of benefits, and program expenditures." *Health Care Financing Review*, Vol. 2 Supp. 2 (December 1985): 13–59.
43. Ruge, "Regulation of Prescription Drug Advertising," 672.
44. See Tobbell, *Pills, Power and Policy*, 189–92.
45. Generics then had to demonstrate only that they were "chemical equivalents" of brand-name drugs in order to receive FDA approval. By the early 1970s, as more concerns mounted about the quality of generics, the FDA instituted a rule requir-

ing generic manufacturers to submit evidence that their drugs performed with a "biological equivalence" to brand-name medications. As for health care expenditure comparison, see U.S. Department of Health, Education, and Welfare, 1975, DHEW Publication (HRA) 76-1232, 70–71. Also see Tobbell, *Pills, Power and Policy*, 192–93.

46. Senator Nelson quoted in Tobbell, *Pills, Power and Policy*, 147.
47. Podolsky, *The Antibiotic Era*, 98.
48. As for the rest, 47 percent were classified as "possibly effective," and the remaining 41 percent were judged as "probably ineffective" or "clearly ineffective." See US Supreme Court, *Weinberger v. Hynson et al.*, 412 US 609 (1973). Certiorari to the United States Court of Appeals for the Fourth Circuit, No., 72-394, decided, June 18, 1973. See also Shorter, "The Liberal State and the Rogue Agency," 126–35.
49. Proposed Rule Making: Combination Drugs for Human Use [21 CFR Part 3] 36 FR 3126 (Feb. 18, 1971).
50. Shorter, "The Liberal State and the Rogue Agency," 126–35.
51. Milton and Lee, *Pills, Profits and Politics*, 123–24, 131.
52. National Academy of Sciences, Division of Medical Sciences, National Research Council, Drug Efficacy Study: Final Report to the Commissioner of Food and Drugs, Food and Drug Administration, at 7 (1969). See Paul A. Bryan and Lawrence H. Stern, "The Drug Efficacy Study, 1962–1970," FDA Papers, October 1970, 14–15, 17. Bryan was the director of the DESI and Stern the assistant director.
53. The drug companies with "probably effective" medications got an extra twelve months to submit improved clinical data; those with "possibly effective" drugs had six extra months; and those whose drugs were marked as "ineffective" had only thirty days to change the FDA's mind. See Herbert Ley and Louis Lasagna, "The Quality of Advice," in Joseph Cooper (ed.) *Philosophy and Technology of Drug Assessment*. Vol. 2 (Washington, D.C.: The Interdisciplinary Communication Associates, 1971), 156.
54. Milton and Lee, *Pills, Profits and Politics*, 132–33.
55. Abuse of Depressant and Stimulant Drugs Advisory Committee. Minutes of the Seventh Committee Meeting; Sept. 19, 1967.
56. Cohen, Pieter A., Alberto Goday, and John P. Swann, "The Return of Rainbow Diet Pills," *American Journal of Public Health* 102.9 (2012): 1676–86.
57. Press Release, U.S. Food and Drug Administration, March 21, 1968, Files, FDA History Office, Silver Spring, MD.
58. "Diet Pills Seized in 2 Cases," *Indianapolis Star*, January 24, 1968, 4. In April, Goddard would add to the ban any combination of thyroid with amphetamines. 33.Fed. Reg. 5616–17 (April 11, 1968).
59. Rainbow diet pills made a resurgence in the late 1990s, mostly packaged as over-the-counter weight loss dietary supplements; vitamins and supplements are not subject to FDA regulation. Pieter A. Cohen, Alberto Goday, and John P. Swann, "The Return of Rainbow Diet Pills," *American Journal of Public Health* 102.9 (2012).
60. Rasmussen, "America's First Amphetamine Epidemic 1929–1971." Susanna McBee, "The Dangerous Diet Pills: How Millions of Women Are Risking Their Health for 'Fat Doctors,' " *Life*, January 27, 1968.
61. Smith Kline had unsuccessfully sued Clark & Clark in 1945 for infringing its pat-

ent on amphetamines. See *Smith, Kline & French Laboratories v. Clark & Clark*, 62 F. Supp. 971 (D.N.J. 1945) US District Court for the District of New Jersey—62 F. Supp. 971 (D.N.J. 1945) September 1, 1945, 62 F. Supp. 971 (1945) No. C-2311.

62. The following March, the Senate Committee on Crime held hearings on whether diet pills and amphetamines were behind a jump in crime. Cohen et al., "The Return of Rainbow Diet Pills," 1676–86. PMC. Lee Belser), "Deaths of 12 Md. Women Attributed to Diet Pills," *News American* (Maryland), March 1, 1968, 1. See also "Crime in America—Why 8 Billion Amphetamines?" Hearings of the Senate Committee on Crime, 91st Cong, 1st Sess, November 18, 1969.
63. Quoted in Carpenter, *Reputation and Power*, 367.
64. Seizing on the developing rift between Goddard and the White House, pharmacists offered $100,000 to the Democratic Party's 1968 presidential campaign war chest. The offer was contingent on Goddard being replaced at the FDA. Douglas Martin, "James L. Goddard, Crusading F.D.A. Leader, Dies at 86," *New York Times*, January 2, 2010.
65. "Dr. Goddard Quits as Head of F.D.A.," *New York Times*, 1, 26.
66. Martin, "James L. Goddard, Crusading F.D.A. Leader, Dies at 86." See also Valerie Nelson, "Dr. James L. Goddard: 1923–2009," *Chicago Tribune*, August 25, 2018.
67. "New Warning Given on Antibiotic Drug," *New York Times*, May 13, 1968.
68. Morton Mintz, "FDA and Panalba: A Conflict of Commercial, Therapeutic Goals?" *Science*, August 29, 1969.
69. The delay surprised some medical researchers because *The New England Journal of Medicine* had published a 1960 editorial that raised early problems with fixed dose combination antibiotics. "Antibioitcs in Fixed Combinations," *NEJM*, 1960; 262:255–56.
70. In addition to Panalba, also high on the list of drugs prioritized for removal from the market was Lederle's Achrocidin, which the FDA had originally tried banning in 1963 but had to delay after a hard pushback from pharma. The third targeted drug was Squibb's Mysteclin-F, its hit mixture of tetracycline and the antifungal amphotericin. See Milton and Lee, *Pills, Profits and Politics*, 125; American Cyanamid Company, *Petitioner, v. Elliot L. Richardson, Secretary of Health, Education and Welfare, et al., Respondents*, 456 F.2d 509, No. 71-1388, United States Court of Appeals, First Circuit, Heard Dec. 14, 1971, Decided Dec. 16, 1971.
71. Podolsky, *The Antibiotic Era*, 95–97.
72. Patrick Clinton, "The Panalba Parable," *New Food Economy*, May 10, 2016.
73. Ibid. Also see *The Upjohn Company, Petitioner, v. Robert H. Finch, Secretary of Health, Education & Welfare, and Herbert L. Ley, Jr., Commissioner of Food and Drugs, Respondents*, 422 F.2d 944 (6th Cir. 1970), U.S. Court of Appeals for the Sixth Circuit—422 F.2d 944 (6th Cir. 1970), February 27, 1970, Order March 3, 1970.
74. The scientific panel also recommended, and the FDA agreed, that two less successful but related Upjohn fixed-dose antibiotic products be removed from the market: Albamycin-T (tetracycline and novobiocin) and Albamycin-GU (novobiocin and sulfamethizole). Howard Brody, M.D., "Health," *Lansing City Pulse*, November 17, 2004, http://lansingcitypulse.com/archives/041117/features/health.asp.
75. "Upjohn Advertising, Then and Now," Thesis for the Degree of M.A., Robert Warren Royle, Michigan State University, 1964,
76. Podolsky, *The Antibiotic Era*, 102.

77. The decision was 7–0. Justice Brennan did not take part in the consideration or decision and Justice Stewart did not take part in the decision. See US Supreme Court, *Weinberger v. Hynson, Westcott and Dunning*, 412 US 609 (1973). Certiorari to the United States Court of Appeals for the Fourth Circuit, No., 72–394, decided, June 18, 1973. See also USV Pharmaceutical Corp. v. Weinberger, 412 U.S. 655 (1971), No. 72-666, Argued April 17, 1973, Decided June 18, 1973, 412 U.S. 655; *Weinberger v. Bentex Pharmaceuticals*, 412 U.S. 645 (1973), No. 72-555, Argued April 17, 1973, Decided June 18, 1973, 412 U.S. 645; *Ciba Corp. v. Weinberger*, No. 72-528, Argued April 17, 1973, Decided June 18, 1973, 412 U.S. 640.
78. See U.S. Supreme Court, *Weinberger v. Hynson et al.*, 412 US 609. Certiorari to the United States Court of Appeals for the Fourth Circuit, No., 72–394, decided June 18, 1973.
79. FDA Regulatory Affairs, Third Edition, 5–6.
80. Shorter, "The Liberal State and the Rogue Agency."
81. In some cases, the same pharma firm produced a new version of a drug to replace one that the FDA decertified. Milton and Lee, *Pills, Profits and Politics*, 132.

Chapter 24: "Here, Eat This Root"

1. The first published reports about instances of resistance to penicillin were only four years after it came to the market. When medical journals later reported other case studies of patients whose underlying illness did not respond to an antibiotic, drug firms invariably were ready with a newer antibiotic. That meant a fresh patent, reinvigorated sales, and no drug resistance since it had not yet been administered to patients. Julian Davies, "Where Have All the Antibiotics Gone?," *Canadian Journal of Infectious Diseases & Medical Microbiology*, Vol. 17,5 (2006): 287–90.
2. Julian Davies and Dorothy Davies, "Origins and Evolution of Antibiotic Resistance," *Microbiology and Molecular Biology Reviews*, Aug. 2010, 74 (3), 424.
3. "SciTech Tuesday: Sir Alexander Fleming's Ominous Prediction," *The National WWII Museum Blog*, January 11, 2017.
4. Rosen, *Miracle Cure*, 305.
5. George Orwell, for instance, fell ill with tuberculosis shortly before he wrote his dystopian novel, *1984*. He died at the age of forty-six, only months after its publication. Researchers have concluded that Orwell did not respond to any treatment because he was infected with an antibiotic-resistant strain of *M. tuberculosis*. Davies and Davies, "Origins and Evolution of Antibiotic Resistance," 419–20; Frank Ryan, *The Forgotten Plague: How the Battle Against Tuberculosis Was Won—And Lost* (Boston, MA: Back Bay Books, 1994), 35, 41–42. There was no central database of incidents suspected as drug-resistant infections. Davies and Davies, "Origins and Evolution of Antibiotic Resistance," 419.
6. Professor Marlene Zuk quoted in Tara Parker-Pope, "Drug Resistance, Explained," *The New York Times*, March 27, 2008.
7. "The History of Medicine," *Western Journal of Medicine*, Vol. 176,1 (2002): 11.
8. Brad Spellberg et al., "Trends in Antimicrobial Drug Development: Implications for the Future," *Clinical Infectious Diseases* 38, No. 9 (2004): 1279–86.
9. V Stockwell, Duffy B., "Use of antibiotics in plant agriculture," *Rev Sci Tech.*; 31(1), April 2012, 199–210.
10. Frenkel and Paul Cook, "Current Issues in Approaches to Antimicrobial Re-

sistance," 48; Martin J. Blaser, *Missing Microbes, How the Overuse of Antibiotics Is Fueling Our Modern Plagues* (New York: Henry Holt and Company, 2014), 99–101.

11. A. Hicks, TH Taylor, Jr., R.J. Hunkler, "US outpatient antibiotic prescribing, 2010," 2013;368(15):1461–62. See also A. Huttner, S. Harharth, S Carleet, et al., "Antimicrobial Resistance: A Global View from the 2013 World Healthcare Associated Infections Forum," 2013;2(1):31. See also Blaser, *Missing Microbes*, 84–86; "Antibiotic Use in the United States, 2017: Progress and Opportunities," U.S. Department of Health and Human Services, Centers for Disease Control and Prevention; Atlanta, GA: 2017; Frenkel and Paul Cook, "Current Issues in Approaches to Antimicrobial Resistance," 48; Blaser, *Missing Microbes*, 99–101; Author interview with Barry Eisenstein, December 19, 2016; Author interview with Steven Projan, December 5, 2016.
12. Author interview with Barry Eisenstein, December 19, 2016. Cubist was founded in 1992 in order to develop biotech antibiotics. When Merck bought the company in 2014 for $9.5 billion, it slashed the company's anti-infective research and many of its 120 scientists left for other companies. See Derek Lowe, "What Became of Cubist?" In the Pipeline, Science Translational Medicine, *Science*, August 4, 2015.
13. Davies and Davies, "Origins and Evolution of Antibiotic Resistance"; Maria Ramirez et al., "Plasmid-Mediated Antibiotic Resistance and Virulence in Gram-negatives: The *Klebsiella pneumoniae* Paradigm," *Microbiology Spectrum* vol. 2,5 (2014): 1–15; Maria S. Ramirez et al., "The IncP-1 plasmid backbone adapts to different host bacterial species and evolves through homologous recombination," *Nature Communications*, 2011.
14. MRSA stands for methicillin-resistant Staphylococcus aureus. The scientists utilized DNA-mapping technology to compare the genetic similarities of sixty-three samples of MRSA, a superbug that is increasingly problematic at hospitals, where patients with compromised immune systems are attractive hosts for the pathogenic bacteria. See Richard Alleyne, "Widespread Antibiotic Use in 1960s Sparked MRSA," *Telegraph*, January 22, 2010.
15. Davies and Davies, "Origins and Evolution of Antibiotic Resistance," 417–43.
16. Experimental drugs were tested on "prisoner volunteers" at the Jackson County jail in Kansas City, and also an Italian research team tested on civilians in Ethiopia and Nigeria. All the test patients were either exposed to mosquitoes carrying the mutant malaria strain or were injected with blood contaminated with it. Richard D. Lyons, "Unusual Malaria Reported Cured," *New York Times*, December 9, 1967. See also Dondorp, Arjen M., et al., "Artemisinin Resistance in Plasmodium Falciparum Malaria," *New England Journal of Medicine* 361.5 (2009): 455–67, PMC. Web. 1 Aug. 2018.
17. Quoted in Parker-Pope, "Drug Resistance, Explained."

Chapter 25: "They Clean Their Own Cages"

1. "The Birth Control Pill: A History," Planned Parenthood, 2015.
2. *Planning Your Family*, G. D. Searle & Co, Chicago, 1967.
3. Ad Hoc Committee for the Evaluation of a Possible Etiologic Relation of Enovid with Thromboembolic Conditions: Final Report on Enovid, FDA, Washington D.C., September 12, 1963.

4. The FDA accepted the conclusion of a new advisory committee, this time under the aegis of Dr. Louis Hellman, later in charge of Population Affairs at HEW.
5. Jane E. Brody, "Birth Control Pills: A Balance Sheet on Their National Impact," *New York Times*, March 23, 1969, 60.
6. Two academic researchers with a Public Health Service grant had published a five-year review of women on the Pill. "Trends in Contraceptive Practice: United States, 1965–76," Data From the National Survey of Family Growth, Series 23, No. 10, DHHS Publication No. (PHS) 82-1986, U.S. Department of Health and Human Services, Public Health Service, Office of Health Research, Statistics, and Technology, National Center for Health Statistics, Hyattsville, Md., February 1982.
7. Dr. Elizabeth Connell of the New York Metropolitan Hospital and Dr. Hans Lehfeldt of Bellevue Hospital Contraceptive Clinic, quoted in Barbara Seaman, *The Doctors' Case Against the Pill* (New York: Peter H. Wyden, 1969), 10–11.
8. Null and Seaman, *For Women Only!*, 721.
9. Dr. David Clark, remarks at the American Academy of Neurology, Eighteenth Annual Meeting, Bellevue-Stratford Hotel, Philadelphia, April 28–30, 1966. See also Elaine Tyler May, "Promises the Pill Could Never Keep," *New York Times*, April 24, 2010.
10. Barbara Seaman, "The Pill and I: 40 Years On, the Relationship Remains Wary," *New York Times*, June 25, 2000, 38; See also Lara Marks, *Sexual Chemistry: A History of the Contraceptive Pill* (New Haven: Yale University Press, 2001).
11. Seaman, *The Doctors' Case Against the Pill*, 248.
12. An example of the FDA's irritation with Searle in this regard is Division of Case Guidance to Director, Bureau of Regulatory Compliance, January 4, 1967, "Proposed Prosecution of G. D. Searle & Col. For Alleged Misbrandings by Medical Journal Advertising and Promotional Labeling," New Drug Application 10-796, Vol. 124; Record Group 88, NARA.
13. Obstetricians wrote the most contraceptive prescriptions. Jane E. Brody, "Birth Control Pills: A Balance Sheet on Their National Impact," *The New York Times*, March 23, 1969, 1, 60; Lois R. Chevalier and Leonard Cohen, "The Terrible Trouble with the Birth-Control Pill: Should You Stop Taking Them Immediately," *Ladies' Home Journal*, July 1967, 44–45.
14. Chevalier and Cohen, "The Terrible Trouble with the Birth-Control Pill," 43. Discussed in Pamela Verma Liao and Janet Dollin, "Half A Century Of The Oral Contraceptive Pill: Historical Review And View To The Future," *Canadian Family Physician*, Vol. 58,12 (2012): e757–60. See also Beth Bailey, "Prescribing the Pill: Politics, Culture, and the Sexual Revolution in America's Heartland," *Journal of Social History* Vol. 30, No. 4 (Summer 1997), 827–56.
15. "Investigation of relation between use of oral contraceptives and thromboembolic disease," *British Medical Journal* 2, 1968: 199–205.
16. However, others contended the Pill's safety should be compared to risks of death from other contraceptive methods. In that matchup, the Pill still seemed dangerous.
17. Dr. Malcolm Potts quoted in Brody, "Birth Control Pills," 60.
18. Seaman, *The Doctors' Case Against the Pill*.
19. One article that raised warnings about the pill before 1969 ran in *Ladies' Home Journal* in July 1967, "The Terrible Trouble with the Birth Control Pill." Doctors ignored the two activist writers, Lois Chevalier and Leonard Cohen, since they

did not have medical pedigrees; and it was published in a women's general interest magazine. Readers of the article who were alarmed almost always were reassured by their physicians that the Pill was safe.

Seaman also highlighted that the Pill was not always effective, something that some women only discovered when they got pregnant while on it. If used as directed, only three out of one thousand women became pregnant in the first year on the Pill. For women who occasionally missed a daily dose, a much higher rate of nine out of one hundred became pregnant during the first year (Nelson & Cwiak, 2011). Seaman, *The Doctors' Case Against the Pill*. See also David Grimes, "History and Future of Contraception: Developments over Time," *Contraception Report* (2000), 10(6), 15–25.

20. For instance, one of the most alarming studies by Brody was "Oral Contraceptives and Cerebrovascular Complications" in *Radiology* in February 1969. It was not cited in other medical journals and only about 9,000 of the nation's 300,000 doctors subscribed to *Radiology*. A very small number prescribed contraceptives.
21. Jane Brody, "Study Links a Pre-Cancer Condition and Users of the Pill," *New York Times*, September 27, 1970, 1. *JAMA* printed in full the results of the Planned Parenthood–backed study the month before Brody's front-page story. Brody had first written about the pill the previous year in the *Times* ("Birth Control Pills: A Balance Sheet on their National Impact," *New York Times*, March 23, 1969, 60).

    The conclusions of the 1970 study's researchers were not as downbeat as Brody's report. Although women on the Pill did have a higher rate of precancerous uterine cell mutations, the study concluded it could not be certain there was a direct cause and effect between the Pill and those results. Other factors might be responsible, including the number of pregnancies and the age of first sexual activity. Subsequent backpedaling from the study's conclusion drew substantial criticism that "the investigation linking cancer and the pill was being suppressed by the *Journal of the American Medical Association*, supposedly from the drug companies making oral contraceptives." "The Pill and Cancer," *Newsweek*, August 11, 1969, 59.
22. Brody, "Birth Control Pills," 1, 60.
23. "The Pill and Cancer," *Newsweek*, August 11, 1969, 59.
24. Donald Drake, science editor for *The Philadelphia Inquirer*, on the conclusion from the May 1969 conference held in Washington, D.C.
25. Sumner Kalman quoted in "New Book Says Pill Ill-Conceived," *Indianapolis Star*, October 23, 1969, 9.
26. Columbia University gynecologist Dr. Harold Speert, in Seaman, *The Doctors' Case Against the Pill*, 25.
27. Chevalier and Cohen, "The Terrible Trouble with the Birth-Control Pill," 43.
28. Francis J. C. Roe, "The Pill: A Special Case Within Normal Safeguards Against All Carcinogens," *International Medical Tribune of Great Britain*, June 23, 1966, 125.
29. Seaman, *The Doctors' Case Against the Pill*, 28.
30. "Physicians Asked to Warn Patients," *Pomona Progress Bulletin* (Pomona, CA), June 6, 1969, 3.
31. Seaman, *The Doctors' Case Against the Pill*, 20.
32. Advisory Committee on Obstetrics and Gynecology, Food and Drug Administration, *Second Report on the Oral Contraceptives* (Washington, D.C.: Government Printing Office, August 1, 1969). See also Harold M. Schmeck, Jr., "Words on the Safety of the Pill," *New York Times*, January 18, 1970, 165.

33. Twenty-five of the drugs on the FDA's list had been voluntarily recalled by pharma companies. Those, however, were little used and generated small profits. "F.D.A. Cites Failures in Drug Withdrawal," *New York Times*, November 11, 1969, 12.
34. Richard D. Lyons, "Officials of the Food and Drug Agency Are Ousted as Wide Government Overhaul Begins," *New York Times*, December 11, 1969, 11. See also Douglas Martin, "Dr. Charles C. Edwards, Influential F.D.A. Commissioner, Dies at 87," *New York Times*, August 28, 2011.
35. "FOOD SAFETY: The Agricultural Use of Antibiotics and Its Implications for Human Health," Report to the Honorable Tom Harkin, Ranking Minority Member, Committee on Agriculture, Nutrition, and Forestry, U.S. Senate, United States General Accounting Office, April 1999.
36. Ibid.
37. Medical Device Amendments of 1976 to the Federal Drug and Cosmetic Act, Public Law 94-295, 90 Stat. 539, 94th Congress, May 28, 1976.
38. The battle over jurisdiction continued for decades and resulted sometimes in odd divisions of responsibility for food and drug safety. The FDA, for instance, regulates all drugs given to farm animals except for biologic ones that fall under the aegis of the Department of Agriculture. Agriculture oversees safety for meat eaten by humans while the FDA has responsibility for meat fed to other animals. The EPA handles all fish caught recreationally and the FDA takes over for fish sold commercially. As for genetically modified food crops, the FDA decides if it is safe to eat, the EPA controls pesticide levels, and the Agriculture Department handles all field testing. The FDA and Customs split responsibility over imported food safety. Even on medical devices the FDA must sometimes share authority. The Department of Energy has equal say over ultrasound equipment, and while the FDA regulates any nuclear radiation medical treatment, the Nuclear Regulatory Agency is tasked with approving any treatment. Compounding pharmacists are not under FDA authority but instead given to the DEA.

    Pizza is often cited as a prime example of how the divided authority can be confusing about which agency is in charge. The FDA is responsible for the safety of frozen pizza. If pepperoni is placed on it, it is considered to have "meat for consumption" and becomes the responsibility of Agriculture. See Hawthorne, *Inside the FDA*, 802, 882, 1320–22, 1324, 1454 of 7181. For examples of how the FDA's budget is split for its enforcement duties, see Fiscal Year 2018 FDA Budget, Details of Full Time Equivalent Employment, Supplementary Tables, Food and Drug Administration (Washington, D.C.: Government Printing Office), 239.
39. It was a topic that affected nine million women. It also fit broadly into the issue that ex–FDA commissioner James Goddard had raised about how pharmaceutical firms unfairly targeted women for products that either they did not need or were not safe. Barbara Seaman's book had convinced Nelson that a full investigation was needed into what had gone wrong for a decade at the government's drug watchdog agency.
40. "Senate Panel to Open Hearing on Birth Control Pill," *New York Times*, January 14, 1970, 13.
41. Harold M. Schmeck Jr., "Biologist Urges a Drive to Study Possible Genetic Peril in Drugs," *New York Times*, January 15, 1970, 1, 23.
42. Submitted statement of Herbert Ratner to the Senate Subcommittee on Monopoly, Select Committee on Small Business, "Competitive Problems in the Drug

Business," February 1970 (Washington, D.C.: Government Printing Office, 1970), 6719.

43. Testimony of Roy Hurtz, Regulatory Policies Of The Food And Drug Administration, Hearing Before A Subcommittee Of The Committee On Government Operations, House Of Representatives, Ninety-First Congress, Second Session, June 9, 1970, Printed for the use of the Committee on Government Operations, (Washington, D.C.: Government Printing Office, 1970).
44. "Poll on the Pill," *Newsweek*, February 9, 1970.
45. See "Notes on the Package Insert," *JAMA*, 207 (February 1969): 1335.
46. All the women who belonged to the group had previously been on the Pill. Part of their outrage was that their doctors, all men, had never warned about any health risks.
47. Seaman, "The Pill and I"; Tone, *Age of Anxiety*, 188.
48. "Defenders of the Pill floated the rumor that Nelson and I wanted to ban it," Seaman recalled years later. "We had no such intention; we just wanted women to have the information to make their own decisions." Seaman, "The Pill and I."
49. "Expert Decried 'Alarm' on Birth-Curb Pill," *New York Times*, February 26, 1970, 67.
50. Opening statement of Washington Women's Liberation at Women's Hearings on the Birth Control Pill, March 7, 1970.
51. "Senate Hearings on the Pill," *American Experience*, PBS, at https://www.pbs.org/wgbh/americanexperience/features/pill-senate-holds-hearings-pill-1970/.

    As for the poll reported in *Newsweek*, it was cited in Jane E. Brody, "Pregnancies Follow Birth Pill Publicity," *New York Times*, February 15, 1970, 28.
52. Intrauterine devices (IUDs) had only been introduced in the early 1960s and did not have the popularity yet of diaphragms.
53. Jane E. Brody, "Pregnancies Follow Birth Pill Publicity," 28.
54. Dr. Elizabeth Connell, an associate professor of obstetrics and gynecology at the Columbia College of Physicians and Surgeons, quoted in Richard D. Lyons, "Panic and Pregnancies Linked to Senate Inquiry on Birth Pill," *New York Times*, February 24, 1970, 28.
55. "Sen. Nelson Accused Of Creating A Fear Of Birth Control," *New York Times*, March 4, 1970, 22.
56. "Highlights of the Percy Skuy History of Contraception Gallery: Intrauterine device (IUD)," Case Western Reserve University, https://case.edu/affil/skuyhistcontraception/online-2012/IUDs.html.
57. Michael Ollove, "Destroyed By His Own Invention Hugh Davis Had It All: A Promising Career At Johns Hopkins, An International Reputation And A String Of Important Medical Discoveries. But The Dalkon Shield Scandal Broke Him—As A Scientist And As A Father," *The Baltimore Sun*, October 25, 1998, 1.
58. Medical Device Amendments of 1976, 94th Congress, Public Law 94-295, May 28, 1976. In June 2019, the FDA made public a database of some 10,000 malfunctions and injuries collected over twenty years and linked to 108 medical devices.
59. Dowbiggin, *The Quest for Mental Health*, 150.
60. In 1970, a study in *Cancer* identified a rare type of vaginal cancer, clear cell adenocarcinoma. The *NEJM* next demonstrated a link between that cancer and uterine exposure to DES. That prompted an FDA warning bulletin in late 1971 about possible DES problems and the agency for the first time advised against using it

during pregnancy. While so-called DES daughters suffered a wide array of adverse effects, recently a number of DES sons were also found to have higher incidences of reproductive tract abnormalities. In 1977, in large part because of the disasters with thalidomide and DES given to pregnant women, the FDA recommended against including women of childbearing age in any early phases of drug testing with an exception for life-threatening illnesses. Europe did not ban DES until 1978, and the following year the FDA finally prohibited its use in hormone-treated cattle and livestock. Susan L. Speaker, "From 'Happiness Pills' to 'National Nightmare': Changing Cultural Assessment of Minor Tranquilizers in America, 1955–1980," *Journal of the History of Medicine and Allied Sciences*, Vol. 52, Issue 3, July 1997, 366. See also "About DES; DES History," Centers for Disease Control, at https://www.cdc.gov/des/consumers/about/history.html.

61. *Our Bodies, Ourselves: A Book By and For Women* (Boston: Boston Women's Health, Book Collective, 1967). See also Rebecca M. Kluchin, *Fit to Be Tied: Sterilization and Reproductive Rights in America, 1950–1980* (New Brunswick, NJ: Rutgers University Press, 2009).
62. *HEW News*, June 9, 1970. See also Milton and Lee, *Pills, Profits and Politics*, 102.
63. A 2018 study covering all drugs, not just oral contraceptives, disclosed that 40 percent of patients reported that their physicians did not tell them about the side effects for the drugs they prescribed. "The Birth Control Pill: A History," Planned Parenthood Federation of America, at https://www.plannedparenthood.org/files/1514/3518/7100/Pill_History_FactSheet.pdf. See Kathy Oxtoby, "Over 40% Of Patients Not Told About Side Effects Of Their Medicines," *Pharmaceutical Journal*, June 18, 2018.
64. Edwards was also active on the "food" side of the FDA's responsibilities, pushing for the introduction of nutritional labels, and got a lot of press for his orders temporarily removing swordfish tainted with mercury and soup that carried botulism. Douglas Martin, "Dr. Charles C. Edwards, Influential F.D.A. Commissioner, Dies at 87," *New York Times*, August 28, 2011.
65. "9 Mouthwashes Held Ineffective: F.D.A., Citing Study, Asks End to Unscientific Ads," *New York Times*, August 4, 1970, 35.
66. "Mouthwash Ads Hit by FDA," *Anniston Star* (Anniston, Alabama), August 3, 1970, 7.
67. "Drugs Deemed Ineffective or Dangerous," *New York Times*, November 28, 1970, 38.
68. Purdue marketed it as Pharycidin Concentrate.
69. "Drugs Deemed Ineffective or Dangerous."
70. David Marcus, "The History of the Modern Class Action, Part I: Sturm Und Drang, 1953–1980," 90, *Washington University Law Review* 587 (201).
71. Elizabeth Siegel Watkins, "How The Pill Became A Lifestyle Drug: The Pharmaceutical Industry And Birth Control In The United States Since 1960." *American Journal Of Public Health* Vol. 102,8 (2012): 1462–72.
72. Barbara Seaman, "The Pill and I," 38.
73. Ibid.

Chapter 26: "Splashdown!"

1. Michael F. Flamm, *Law and Order: Street Crime, Civil Unrest, and the Crisis of Liberalism in the 1960s* (New York: Columbia University Press, 2005), 65.

2. Keith D. Harries, "The Geography of American Crime, 1968," *Journal of Geography*, 1971, 70:4, 204–13; see also Chris Barber, "Public Enemy Number One: A Pragmatic Approach to America's Drug Problem," June 29, 2016, Richard Nixon Public Library.
3. Barber, "Public Enemy Number One." Also, see "Excerpts From President's Message on Drug Abuse Control," *New York Times*, June 18, 1971, 22.
4. National Cancer Act of 1971, Senate Bill 1828—Enacted December 23, 1971 (P.L. 92-218).
5. "Special Message to the Congress on Crime and Law Enforcement 'To Insure the Public Safety,'" February 7, 1968, Public Papers of the Presidents of the United States, Lyndon B. Johnson 1968–69 (Book I—January 1 to June 30, 1968); (Washington, D.C.: Government Printing Office, 1970), 190.
6. LBJ merged the Treasury Department's Bureau of Narcotics, responsible for enforcing laws against opiates and marijuana, with the Bureau of Drug Abuse Control which had the authority for stimulants, depressants, and hallucinogens. It took four years before Congress passed a reorganization plan that eliminated the BNDD and created the Drug Enforcement Administration, empowered with greatly enhanced policing authority. Reorganization Plan No. 2 Of 1973; Eff. July 1, 1973, 38 F.R. 15932, 87 Stat. 1091, as amended Pub. L. 93–253, §1, Mar. 16, 1974, 88 Stat. 50, Prepared by the President and transmitted to the Senate and the House of Representatives in Congress assembled, March 28, 1973, pursuant to the provisions of Chapter 9 of Title 5 of the United States Code. Law Enforcement In Illicit Drug Activities.
7. Author interview with former business partner of Arthur Sackler, November 2018.
8. "Local Firm Acquired by Purdue Frederick," *The Progress-Index* (Petersburg, Virginia), March 30, 1966, 17.
9. Since Betadine was not a military or intelligence product, there was no need in Pentagon procurement for background and security checks that might have revealed the communist backgrounds for the Sacklers. Chris McGreal, *American Overdose: The Opioid Tragedy in Three Acts* (New York: PublicAffairs, 2018), 17.
10. Andrew Tarantola, "How NASA Prevents a Space Plague Outbreak," *Gizmodo*, September 2, 2012.
11. Mary Agnes Carey, "NASA Turned to Norwalk Firm to Kill Potential Moon Germs," *Hartford Courant*, July 23, 1992, C1-2.
12. Full-page advertisement, *American Journal of Pathology*, 3, in author's possession.
13. McGreal, *American Overdose*, 15.
14. Lutze, *Who Can Know the Other?*, 152, 159.
15. The author has compiled a list of the publications related to Arthur Sackler's work into the 1980s: A. M. Sackler et al., "Effects of methylphenidate on whirler mice: An animal model for hypokinesis,"*Life Sciences*, September 1985; "Behavior and endocrine effects of 3,4,5-trimethoxyamphetamine in male mice," *Experientia*, April 1976; "Some adrenal correlates of aggression in isolated female mice," *Life Sciences*, Jan. 1976; "Aggressive Behavior; Biochemical and endocrine differences between normotensive and spontaneously hypertensive rats," *Life Sciences*, Nov. 1974; "Laboratory animal science, Behavioral and adrenal relationships to audiogenic-seizure susceptibility in mice," *Life Sciences*, May 1974; "Adrenal relationships to aggressiveness in isolated female mice," *Experientia*, March 1974; "Behavioral and endocrine effects of ts for of amlodipine trlle (ADPN) in male

mice," *Pharmacology Biochemistry and Behavior*, March 1973; "Gonadal effects of vasectomy and vasoligation," *Science*, Feb. 1973; "Plasma protein and free fatty acid levels in male whirler mice," *Experientia*, Sep. 1971; "Acute effects of mescaline HCI on behavior, resistance, and endocrine function of male mice," *Experimental Medicine and Surgery*, Feb. 1971; "Effect of mescaline HCI on resistance of male mice to histamine stress," *Journal of Pharmaceutical Sciences*, Nov. 1970; "Metabolic and endocrine aspects of the whirler mutation in male mice," *Proceedings of The Society for Experimental Biology and Medicine*, Nov 1966, updated in *Journal of Experimental Zoology*, May 1967, updated again in *Acta endocrinologica*, July 1970; "Blood glucose and liver glycogen content in male whirler mice," *Experientia*, May 1970; "Effects of isolation stress on female albino mice," *Laboratory animal care*, Sep. 1968; "Effects of levels of audiogenic-seizure susceptibility on endocrine function of rats," *Physiology & Behavior*, March 1968; "Maternal effects on behavior and white blood cells of isolated female mice," *Life Sciences*, April 1970; "Metabolism rate, biochemical and endocrine alterations in male whirler mice," *Physiology & Behavior*, Feb. 1970; "Pre-maternal isolation effects on behaviour and endocrine function of offspring," *Acta endocrinologica*, Nov. 1969; "Mescaline hydrochloride effects on the endocrine activity of male albino mice," *Experimental medicine and surgery*, Feb. 1968; "Effects of isolation on maternal aggressiveness and body growth rates of offspring," *Experientia*, Oct. 1967; "Effects of isolation stress on peripheral leucocytes of female albino mice," *Nature*, July 1967; "Isolation stress on female albino mice," *Aerospace medicine*, Sep. 1966; "Endocrine and metabolic effects of Lysergic acid diethylamide on female rats," *Toxicology and Applied Pharmacology*, Sep. 1966; "Metabolic and endocrine effects of lysergic acid diethylamide (LSD-25) on male rat," *Journal of Endocrinology*, Feb. 1966; "Effect of lysergic acid diethylamide (LSD-25) on growth metabolism and the resistance of male rats to histamine stress," *Journal of Pharmaceutical Sciences*, Sep. 1965; "Effects of Lysergic Acid Diethylamide on the Total Leukocytes and Eosinophils of the Female Rat," *Nature*, Oct. 1963; "Effects of vibration on the endocrine system of male and female rats," *Aerospace medicine*, March 1966; "Effects of Lysergic Acid Diethylamide on Urinary Ketosteroid and 1Corticosteroid Levels of Female Rats," *Nature*, June 1963; "Effect of Age and Thymectomy on Urinary 17-Ketosteroid-levels In Male Rats," *Nature*, July 1962; "Effects of Thymectomy on the Resistance of Rats to Drowning and Histamine Stress," *Nature*, Dec. 1961; "Effects of handling on weight gains and endocrine organs in mature male rats," *Journal of applied physiology*, Aug. 1961; "Effect of Splenectomy on the Resistance of Rats to Histamine Stress," *Nature*, May 1961; "Comparative evaluation and the Influence of various factors on eye-irritation scores," *Toxicology and Applied Pharmacology*, April 1965; "The effects of reserpine on histamine tolerance and endocrine organs of the rat," *Acta endocrinologica*, Sep. 1960; "Endocrine changes due to auditory stress," *Acta endocrinologica*, Aug. 1959; "Biochemical Responses of Rats to Auditory Stress," *Science*, June 1959; "Effect of Tranquillizing Agents on the Resistance of Rats to Histamine Stress," *Nature*, April 1959; "Methylphenidate effects on whirler mice/ Endocrine differences and audiogenic seizure susceptibility between whirler and normal strains of female mice/male mice," *Acta endocrinologica*, June 1961, August 1962.

16. Arthur later created Therapeutic Research Press, Inc, to publicize the research trials. DOS # 481282, NY State Incorporation files.
17. Statement of A. Stanley Weltman, Vol. VII—Physiological and psychological ef-

fects, Oct 28–29, 1971, Conducted by the Office of Noise Abatement and Control January 1, 1972 U.S. Environmental Protection Agency us govt printing office.

18. Author collection of Sackler post-1965 articles, in *Experientia* and *Pharmacology Biochemistry and Behavior*.
19. Weltman testified after Arthur was called away at the last moment. Public Hearings on Noise Abatement and Control, Oct 28–29, 1971, Conducted by the Office of Noise Abatement and Control, division of the Environmental Protection Agency, Boston, Massachusetts.
20. "Survey Shows Shortage of Medical Technicians," *New York Times*, December 13, 1970, 85.
21. See M.G. Candau, World Heath Workplace, 1967, "A Mutual Task for All," Deutsche Schwesternzeitung 20(4): 167.
22. Two previous British studies undertaken for the Association for the Aid of Crippled Children (AACC) had demonstrated that environmental factors were instrumental in determining whether children had "retardation in both intellectual and social incompetence and in physical growth." Sackler wanted to conduct a trial that followed a group of children born in the same year to determine whether the original investigators had overlooked the importance of genetic variabilities. If he had gotten the AACC grant, Sackler intended to use it as the starting point to pursue federal funding for studies that might help programs such as Head Start develop better standards for assisting disadvantaged children in health and education. See Association for the Aid of Crippled Children, Annual Report, 1971–1972, Wm. F. Fell Company, Philadelphia, PA, 1972; Meetings of the Executive Committee, June 24, 1971, the Association for the Aid of Crippled Children, Association Offices, Room 700, 345 East 46th St., NY, NY, see page 6 of "Declinations." Both in collection of author.
23. "Scientists Advising Rats to Avoid Subway Rides," *New York Times*, April 15, 1976.
24. The Noise Pollution and Abatement Act of 1970 (Title IV to the Clean Air Amendment of 1970—PL 91-604) had required that the Environmental Protection Agency hold a series of eight public hearings. The seventh hearing was entitled "Transportation (Rail and Other), Urban Noise Problems and Social Behavior—Physiological and Psychological Effects."
25. "Scientists Advising Rats to Avoid Subway Rides."
26. The *Times* reported that: "Dr. Sackler conceded that the severity of the shaking given the rats, in proportion to their body size, was well beyond anything that people normally sustain on subways." Still, Arthur thought the results "merit additional attention and study."
27. See Raymond Raphael Sackler, Inventor, to Current Assignee Mundipharma AG Worldwide applications, 1966 GB Application GB5022966A events 1966-11-09, Application filed by Mundipharma AG. 1966-11-09; Priority to GB5022966A, 1969-09-24, Publication of GB1164808A, in collection of author.
28. Madelein Kleyn, "BEPS and Intangibles: How does it impact IP tax structures?," *Chair of Intellectual Property* (CIP), February 1, 2018.

Chapter 27: "Tell Him His Lawyer Is Calling"

1. The court upheld the FDA's authority to restrict Miltown to a maximum of five refills; before the FDA ruling it had been unlimited. Carter-Wallace, Inc., Petitioner, v. John W. Gardner, Secretary of Health, Education, and Welfare, and

James L. Goddard, Commissioner of Food and Drugs, Respondents, 417 F.2d 1086 (1969).

2. Ibid.
3. Ibid.
4. Yvonne Shinhoster Lamb, "Devoted Jew Combined Faith, Progress," *Washington Post*, October 16, 2005.
5. Michael Sonnenreich, interview with author, January 19, 2019.
6. Before getting a thirty-hour-a-week job at the university's Hydrobiology Lab, he had worked as "a drugstore soda jerk and then a short order cook. Listen to me, never send food back to the kitchen. Don't ever, ever do that. I know what happens to that food before it goes back to the diner." He also wrote for the school newspaper and conducted interviews for the campus radio station (including one with Frank Lloyd Wright). Michael Sonnenreich, interview with author, January 19, 2019.
7. Sonnenreich says it was a marriage that the families wanted. Some of her family was in Canada, which resulted in "us having a service in Toronto with three rabbis." They are still married. Michael Sonnenreich, interview with author, January 19, 2019.
8. Ibid.
9. While at Charlottesville, he sometimes combined his legal knowledge with his experience in Spain. Typical was a review he wrote for the *Military Law Review* about a book in Spanish covering the history of the country's right-wing military. Michael R. Sonnenreich, Second Lieutenant, Book Review, (Foreign Periodical): *Revista Espanola de Derecho Militar*, by the Instituto Francisco de Vitoria. 27/153, Vol. 81, *Military Law Review*.
10. Michael Sonnenreich, interview with author, January 19, 2019. Also see Walter Powell, *From Patrician to Professional Elite* (New York: Russell Sage Foundation, 1989), 76.
11. After the Hoffa trial, Robert Kennedy brought Bittman from the U.S. Attorney's Office in Chicago to the Justice Department in Washington. Bittman led the successful prosecution later against Bobby Baker, the secretary of the Senate that *The Washington Post* described as "a protege of Lyndon Johnson." J. Y. Smith, "Lawyer William O. Bittman Dies," *Washington Post*, March 3, 2001.
12. Michael R Sonnenreich, *Handbook of Federal Narcotic and Dangerous Drug Laws* (Washington, D.C.: Government Printing Office, 1969).
13. Dean and Sonnenreich became good friends. After Dean divorced his first wife in 1970, he met Maureen (Mo) Kane. She was looking for work in the government and Sonnenreich found her a spot in his office doing advance work for Department of Justice trips. Michael Sonnenreich, interview with author, January 19, 2019.
14. The Boggs Act Amendment to the Narcotic Drugs Import and Export Act, 82nd Congress, Public Law 82-255, November 2, 1951.
15. Note 16: Traffic in Narcotics, Barbiturates and Amphetamines in the United States Amendment to the Internal Revenue Code of 1954 and the Narcotic Drugs Import and Export Act, 84th Congress, Public Law 728-81, January 1, 1956. "This Act may be cited as the 'Narcotic Control Act of 1956.'"
16. In 1965 Congress passed the Drug Abuse Control Amendments (DACA). It created the Bureau of Drug Abuse Control (BDAC) inside the Department of Health, Education, and Welfare.

17. Michael Sonnenreich, interview with author, January 19, 2019.
18. Ibid. Sonnenreich was an advocate for limiting some controlled substances to no more than three refills in six months. The rules ultimately put in place were not as strict for those listed on Schedules III and IV. They got a "five time rule," no more than five refills in six months. A physician cannot call those prescriptions in to a pharmacy but must handwrite each on an original prescription pad. Schedule II medications, mostly narcotic painkillers, stimulants, and barbiturates, cannot be refilled. A new prescription must be written every time it is dispensed. Code of Federal Regulations, Title 21, Volume 9; 21CFR1306.22 and 21CFR1308.S.
19. As for his salary, Sonnenreich recalled "That's what I earned when I started at Justice because I was in the top 10 percent of my class. If I had been in the bottom 10 percent I would have been earning $7,200."
20. Some published reports say the Controlled Substances Act was drafted by Sonnenreich's boss, John Ingersoll, the director of the Bureau of Narcotics and Dangerous Drugs, as well as with John Dean. Sonnenreich told the author, "Dean did not write one word of the act and Ingersoll never saw it until I was finished."
21. See 1970 guidelines of the WHO Committee on Addiction-Producing Drugs; WHO Expert Committee on Addiction-Producing Drugs. Thirteenth report. Geneva, World Health Organization, 1964 (WHO Technical Report Series, No. 273).
22. See Hoffmann-La Roche, Inc., Petitioner, v. Richard G. Kleindienst, Attorney General of the United States, and John E. Ingersoll, Director, Bureau Of Narcotics and Dangerous Drugs, United States Department of Justice, respondents, 478 F.2d 1 (3d Cir. 1973).
23. Herzberg, *Happy Pills*, 142.
24. Ibid. Also, in response to considerable criticism about the unfairness of mandatory minimum sentences, the final bill passed by Congress and signed by Nixon made possession of controlled substances for personal use on Schedules III to V, and also marijuana, a misdemeanor. Judges were given the discretion to sentence first-time-possession defendants to probation. "Drug Scheduling: Drug Schedules," Drug Enforcement Administration, https://www.dea.gov/drug-scheduling. See also Calcaterra NE, Barrow JC, "Classics in Chemical Neuroscience: Diazepam (Valium)." *ACS Chemical Neuroscience*. 2014;5(4):253–60. Shorter, *Before Prozac*, 351 of 4159.
25. Michael Sonnenreich, interview with author, January 19, 2019.
26. Ibid.
27. Ibid.
28. Ibid.
29. Daniel Bessner, "National Commission on Marihuana and Drug Abuse," in *Encyclopedia of Drug Policy*, Edited by: Mark A. R. Kleiman & James E. Hawdon (Sage Publications, 2011).
30. Eric Sterling, "Shafer Commission Report on Marijuana and Drugs, Issued 40 Years Ago Today, Was Ahead of Its Time," *Huffington Post*, May 21, 2013.
31. Michael Sonnenreich, interview with author, January 19, 2019.
32. Sonnenreich coined the phrase "drug abuse industrial complex" for all the agencies that had a role in regulating and enforcing drug laws. Michael R. Sonnenreich, "Discussion of the Final Report of the National Commission on Marijuana and Drug Abuse," *Villanova Law Review*, 18:817–27 May 1973, 818.
33. Michael Sonnenreich, interview with author, January 19, 2019.
34. Sterling. "Shafer Commission Report on Marijuana and Drugs."

35. Elizabeth Hlavinka, "Can Cannabis Replace Opioids for Pain?" *MedPage*, September 7, 2019. See Skye Gould and Jeremy Berke, "Illinois just became the first state to legalize marijuana sales through the legislature—here are all the states where marijuana is legal," *Business Insider*, June 25, 2019.
36. Sterling, "Shafer Commission Report on Marijuana and Drugs."
37. "L. W. Frohlich; Led Ad Agency," *New York Times*, September 29, 1971. Among the dozen radio stations Frohlich acquired were WNCN in New York, KMPX in San Francisco, and WDHF in Chicago. Pasadena's KPPC-FM was at the forefront of counterculture politics and music in the late 1960s. Frohlich acquired it in 1969, at the height of its loyal underground following. Film director Francis Ford Coppola bought San Francisco's KMPX after Frohlich's death. See *SF Examiner*, Aug 27, 1975, and October 9, 1976. See also "Closed Circuit," *Broadcasting*, Vol. 85, No. 14, October 1, 1973, 48.
38. By then named L. W. Frohlich/Intercon International. At the time of his death, Frohlich had earned a reputation every bit the rival of Arthur Sackler's. He served as a trustee of Columbia College of Pharmaceutical Sciences, London's Royal Society of Medicine, New York's Pratt Institute, the American Council for Health and Education of the Public, the International Medical Congress, and the National Foundation of Science. Five years before his death he had funded the L.W. Frohlich Research Study Center, a think tank on the Italian island of Elba designed to speed scientific and medical innovation. Frohlich had built a grand villa there overlooking the sea for his own getaways (it was half a mile from where Napoleon Bonaparte had been exiled).

    Not even in death did Frohlich or his sister, Ingrid, acknowledge the family's Jewish heritage. The standing-room-only crowd of nine hundred at the memorial service was at one of Manhattan's top Episcopal churches, St. Bartholomew's. "L. W. Frohlich; Led Ad Agency," *New York Times*, September 29, 1971; Tanner, *Our Bodies, Our Data*, 28; "Frohlich Funeral Service Is Attended by 900 Here," *New York Times*, October 2, 1971.
39. "Dr. Felix Marti-Ibanez Is Dead; Psychiatrist and Publisher, 60," *New York Times*, May 25, 1972, 48.
40. Sterling. "Shafer Commission Report on Marijuana and Drugs."

Chapter 28: A New Definition of Blockbuster

1. Emily P. Walker, "Since 1970s, 'Unimagined Progress' Seen in Cancer Research," *MedPage Today*, September 20, 2011.
2. Appropriations History by Institute/Center, 1938 to 2019, National Institutes of Health, Office of the Budget, at https://officeofbudget.od.nih.gov/approp_hist.html.
3. Vincent T. DeVita Jr. and Edward Chu, "A History of Cancer Chemotherapy," *Cancer Research*, November 2008, Vol. 68, Issue 21, 8643–53.
4. Bernard Fisher et al., "L-Phenylalanine Mustard (L-PAM) in the Management of Primary Breast Cancer—A Report of Early Findings," *NEJM*, 1975; 292:117–122. See also L. Turner et al., "Radical versus modified radical mastectomy for breast cancer," *Annals of the Royal College of Surgeons of England*, 1981, 63(4), 239–43.
5. DeVita and Chu, "A History of Cancer Chemotherapy."
6. Lawrence H. Einhorn et al., "Cis-Diamminedichloroplatinum, Vinblastine, and Bleomycin Combination Chemotherapy in Disseminated Testicular Cancer,"

Annals of Internal Medicine, 1977;87(3):293–98; See "Cancer Progress Timeline; Major Milestones Against Cancer 1975–1980," *American Society of Clinical Oncology*, at https://www.asco.org/research-progress/cancer-progress-timeline.

7. Alfonso Gambardella, *Science and Innovation: The US Pharmaceutical Industry During the 1980s* (Cambridge, UK: Cambridge University Press, 1995), 25.
8. When the angiotensin-converting enzyme (ACE) is overactive, it creates hypertension. ACE inhibitors relax blood vessels and counteract the blood pressure increase.
9. Capoten was approved in 1981 for severe hypertension and in 1985 for both congestive heart failure as well as milder forms of high blood pressure. Gambardella, *Science and Innovation*, 93–94; Packer M et al., Comparative effects of low and high doses of the angiotensin-converting enzyme inhibitor, lisinopril, on morbidity and mortality in chronic heart failure. ATLAS Study Group. Circulation 1999; 100:2312–18; Jenny Bryan, "From snake venom to ACE inhibitor—the discovery and rise of captopril," *Pharmaceutical Journal*, April 17, 2009.
10. Popular competitors to Capoten included Lotensin (benazepril), Vasotec (enalapril), Fosinopril, Prinivil, Zestril (Lisinopril), Univasc (Moexipril), Aceon (perindopril), Accupril (quinapril), Altace (ramipril), and Mavik (Trandolapril). Nearly thirty years later, ACE inhibitors came under scrutiny for a possible link to an increased recurrence of breast cancer in women older than sixty-six years, Lu Chen et al., "Antihypertensive Drugs & Breast Cancer: Use Of Antihypertensive Medications And Risk Of Adverse Breast Cancer Outcomes In A SEER-Medicare Population," *American Association for Cancer Research: Cancer Epidemiol Biomarkers*, August 14, 2017.
11. Discovered and marketed by Indiana's Miles Laboratories. Bayer bought the single-product company in 1977 for $253 million, then the most expensive acquisition in the U.S. by a foreign drug company.
12. *The Discovery of Histamine H_2-Receptor Antagonists,* The American Chemical Society and The Royal Society of Chemistry, 1999. (Subscript used in title.)
13. The receptor is called the H2.
14. "Antihistamine" is a simple description of what Bovet had discovered. He had created an inactive version of a specific histamine molecule that he wanted to target. That inactive molecule (the antihistamine) then stimulated the receptor site involved in a disease, and thereby blocked the active histamine from attaching to the receptor. See generally Church, Martin K and Diana S Church, "Pharmacology of antihistamines," *Indian Journal of Dermatology* vol. 58,3 (2013): 219–24. "Daniel Bovet, Biographical," at https://www.nobelprize.org/prizes/medicine/1957/bovet/biographical/.
15. Gambardella, *Science and Innovation*, 24–25.
16. The disorder was agranulocytosis and was not completely unexpected by the H2-Receptor team.
17. Black and his team performed the equivalent of molecular surgery, substituting cyanoguanidine moiety for the compound's thiourea group.
18. It took ten years for Tagamet to reach the billion-dollar mark in the U.S.
19. Joseph A. DiMasi and Cherie Paquette, "The economics of follow-on drug research and development: trends in entry rates and the timing of development," *PharmacoEconomics* 2, 2004, Supp 2, 1-14.
20. Henry Grabowski, "The Evolution of the Pharmaceutical Industry Over the Past

50 Years: A Personal Reflection," *International Journal of the Economics of Business*, vol. 18, iss. 2, 2011, 169.

21. Berg spliced a tiny amount of a bacterial virus (lambda) into the DNA of a simian virus (SV40).
22. Stanley Cohen et al., "Construction of Biologically Functional Bacterial Plasmids In Vitro (R factor/restriction enzyme/transformation/endonuclease/antibi otic resistance," *National Academy of Sciences,* Vol. 70, No. 11, November 1973, 3240–44.
23. Paul Berg et al., "Potential Biohazards of Recombinant DNA Molecules," *Science* July 26, 1974: Vol. 185, Issue 4148, 303.
24. A comprehensive history of the debate that led to the moratorium is in S. Krinsky, *Genetic Alchemy: The Social History of the Recombinant DNA Controversy* (Cambridge, MA: MIT Press, 1982); Kathi E. Hanna, Ed., *Biomedical Politics* (Washington, D.C.: The National Academies Press, Division of Health Sciences Policy Committee to Study Biomedical Decision Making, Institute of Medicine, 1991).
25. On the company website Dr. Kade welcomed Arthur Jr. as "the fourth generation of the Lutze family." He took over a company whose top sellers were Sanostol, a line of pediatric vitamins, Riopan, an antacid, and Posterisan, a hemorrhoid suppository. The author discovered that in 1975 Arthur Jr. and his sister, Denise Marika Sackler, were appointed managing partners. In the 1980s, Arthur Jr. wanted sole control of the firm. An attorney familiar with what happened told the author that "Denise and Marietta were ready to throw him out. They [Denise and Marietta] put a fast stop to that." Arthur Jr. remained at the firm but as co-director. Denise died at sixty-three in 2018. Her mother, Marietta, died in 2019, at the age of ninety-nine. Arthur Jr. now runs Dr. Kade. Author interview with friend of Marietta Sackler, November 2018. "Denise Marika, 1955–2018," *Boston Globe*, August 5, 2018. Lutze, *Who Can Know the Other?*, 145; see also https://www.kade.com/company/history/.
26. Milton and Lee, *Pills, Profits and Politics*, 31; John Schoen, "Here's How an Obscure Tax Change Sank Puerto Rico's Economy," CNBC, September 26, 2017.
27. Author interview with Richard Sperber, March 26, 2019.
28. "Improvements in novel mercury compound," DE FR GB GB1093971A Mortimer David Sackler Mundipharma Ag, Priority 1965-12-23 • Filing 1966-02-15 • Publication 1967-12-06

    - "Amine sennosides," DE DE1793321A1 Alfred Halpern Mundipharma Ag, Priority 1968-08-31, Filing 1968-08-3, Publication 1971-09-02;
    - "Novel Quaternary Compounds," US AT BE CH DE DK FI FR GB NL NO OA SE GB1178724A Alfred Halpern Mundipharma Ag, Priority 1966-03-15, Filing 1967-01-27, Publication 1970-01-21;
    - "Quaternary ammonium salt," Mundipharma A.G. 27 Jan., 1967 [15 March, 1966], No. 4139/67; "Ammoniated mercury compounds and pharmaceutical compositions containing the same," AU174866A Raymond R. Sackler Alfred Halpern Mortimer D. Sackler Mundipharma Ag, Filing 1966-02-17, Publication 1967-08-17;
    - "Novel Hydrogen-Bonded Compounds and Pharmaceutical Compositions Prepared," GB GB1164808A Raymond Raphael Sackler Mundipharma Ag, Priority 1966-11-09, Filing 1966-11-09, Publication 1969-09-24;

- "Suppositories," Mundipharma A.G., 9 Nov., 1966, No. 50229/66, Heading A5B. [Also in Division C3]; "A process for preparing quin polygalacturonate," US CH DE GB CH489500A David Sackler Mortimer Mundipharma Ag, Priority 1966-08-08, Filing 1967-07-28, Publication 1970-04-30;
- "A process for the preparation of a mixture of sennosides A and B," US DE DK FR GB NL DK124819B A Halpern Mundipharma Ag, Priority 1962-06-04, Filing 1966-04-15, Publication 1972-11-27.

29. The author found "sustained release pharmaceutical compositions" was also in the patent filings of American Home Products and Smith Kline French (1960), A. H. Robins Co (1965), and Forest Laboratories (1967). In the 1970s, special projects that focused on "sustained release capsules" got under way at Hoffmann-La Roche, Johnson & Johnson, and Ciba Geigy. See:

    - Pharmaceuticals with delayed release, US3074852A Mayron David American Home Prod Priority 1960-06-06 • Filing 1960-06-06 • Grant 1963-01-22 • Publication 1963-01-22;
    - Method of preparing sustained release pharmaceutical tablets, US3148124A William E Gaunt William E Gaunt Priority 1962-06-12 • Filing 1962-06-12 • Grant 1964-09-08 • Publication 1964-09-08;
    - Method of preparing high dosage sustained release tablet and product of this . . . , US US3108046A Keith B Harbit Smith Kline French Lab Priority 1960-11-25 • Filing 1962-10-17 • Grant 1963-10-22 • Publication 1963-10-22;
    - Compressible sustained release pharmaceutical tablet lipid-colloidal silica gel . . . , US3400197A Lippmann Irwin Robins Co Inc A H, Priority 1965-01-26 • Filing 1965-01-26 • Grant 1968-09-03 • Publication 1968-09-03;
    - Sustained action dosage form, US3634584, A John W Poole American Home Prod, Priority 1969-02-13 • Filing 1969-02-13 • Grant 1972-01-11 • Publication 1972-01-11;
    - Slow release bolus, US4066754, A Shih-Toon Chou Ralston Purina Company, Priority 1976-04-26 • Filing 1976-04-26 • Grant 1978-01-03 • Publication 1978-01-03;
    - Sustained release pharmaceutical capsules, US4126672A Prabhakar R. Sheth Hoffmann-La Roche Inc., Priority 1976-02-04 • Filing 1977-09-19 • Grant 1978-11-21 • Publication 1978-11-21;
    - Process for the production of antidiarrheal agents, GB1595021A Ciba Geigy Ag, Priority 1977-01-07 • Filing 1978-01-05 • Publication 1981-08-05;
    - Coated 1-(2-chlorodibenzo[b,f]oxepin-10-yl)-4-methylpiperazine compositions, US4180559A Harold E. Huber Richardson-Merrell Inc., Priority 1978-01-05 • Filing 1978-12-01 • Grant 1979-12-25 • Publication 1979-12-25;
    - Delbarre tablet with a controlled Science, FI76691B Hans Hess Ciba Geigy Ag, Priority 1979-08-16 • Filing 1980-08-13 • Grant 1988-08-31 • Publication 1988-08-31.

30. Halpern's professional affiliation was listed in the publication for a National Academy of Sciences conference, "Use of Human Subjects in Safety Evaluation of Food Chemicals," Washington, D.C., November 29–30, 1966.
31. See "Pharmaceutical Composition in Solid Dosage Form, and Process for Its Production," European Patent Office EP0013131A2, assignee Mundipharma AG.
32. "Front Matter," *British Medical Journal (Clinical Research Edition)* 293, no. 6540 (1986).
33. See *Napp Pharmaceutical Holdings Limited and Subsidiaries v. Director General of Fair Trading*, In the Competition Commission, Appeal Tribunal, before Sir Christopher Bellamy, Professor Peter Grinyer, and Harry Colgate, New Court, London, Case No 1001/1/01, January 15, 2002.
34. Napp had also developed a suspension formula of MST Continus, and Purdue sold that version as well in the U.S. It could be dissolved in water for patients who had difficulty swallowing pills. And the company sold a controlled release suppository. MS Contin (morphine sulfate), Package label insert. Stamford, CT: Purdue Frederick; 2004; C. Boroda et al., "Comparison of the bioavailability of aminophylline in a conventional base and in a continuous-release base," *J Clin Pharmacol.* 1973;13:383–87; S. Leslie, "The Contin delivery system: Dosing considerations," *J Allergy Clin Immunol.* 1986;78:768–73; G. K. Gourlay, "Sustained relief of chronic pain pharmacokinetics of sustained release morphine," *Clin Pharmacokinet*, 1998;35:173–90; C. M. Amabile et al., "Oral modified-release opioid products for chronic pain management," *Ann Pharmacother*, 2006;40:1327–35.

Chapter 29: "Kiss the Ring"

1. Sonnenreich recalled his initial impressions of Arthur's brothers. "I had met Mortie and Ray right when I met Arthur. Mortie I got along with instantly. Raymond was more laid-back, the quieter one because Arthur used to beat him up verbally. Mortie, however, he would stand up for himself. He was very bright." Michael Sonnenreich, interview with author, February 23, 2019.
2. Michael Sonnenreich, interview with author, February 23, 2019.
3. Lutze, *Who Can Know the Other?*, 144.
4. Michael Sonnenreich, interview with author, January 19, 2019.
5. Ibid., and February 23, 2019.
6. Ibid., January 19, 2019.
7. Ibid.
8. The National Coordinating Council on Drug Education was formed in 1968 and is a coalition of religious, youth, service, professional, and law enforcement organizations. More than 130 groups are included, as diverse as the Boys and Girls Clubs of America to the American Bar Association. Its mission is to find ways to enhance education to assist in preventing and reducing drug abuse. See "Drugs," Debbie Wilder (1973) National Coordinating Council on Drug Education, *School Health Review*, 4:5, 11–19.
9. See "Marijuana Research and Legal Controls." Hearings before the Subcommittee on Alcoholism and Narcotics of the Committee on Labor and Public Welfare, United States Senate, Ninety-third Congress, Second Session, November 19, 20, 1974; United States Congress Senate Committee on Labor and Public Welfare Subcommittee on Alcoholism. United States Congress, 1975; "Narcotics," United States Congress Senate Committee on Labor and Public Welfare Subcommittee

on Alcoholism and Marihuana (Washington, D.C.: Government Printing Office, 1975).

10. Duff Wilson, "Sheldon Gilgore, Physician Who Led Drug Giants Pfizer and Searle, Dies at 77," *New York Times,* March 1, 2010, A25.
11. Jerry Schwartz, "A Life Tainted Red by McCarthyism Ends," *Courier-News* (Bridgewater, Somerset, New Jersey) July 26, 1998, Sunday Edition, 77. See Letter from A. B. Magil to Professor Alan M. Wald, September 4, 1991, transcript provided to the author in an email from Professor Wald, March 27, 2017.
12. "J-school students refuse to 'scab,'" *Columbia Daily Spectator*, Volume CII, Number 87, 27 March 1978.
13. Michael Sonnenreich, interview with author, February 23, 2019.
14. "Advertising: President of Frohlich Resigns," *New York Times,* January 25, 1972, 43.
15. "Ex-Frohlich Executives Form a Health Agency," *New York Times,* April 10, 1972, 76.
16. "New Goals for Pharmaceuticals," *New York Times,* July 8, 1975.
17. "The Boom Years," Industry Chronology of the Medical Advertising Hall of Fame, at https://www.mahf.com/industry-chronology.
18. "Ex-Frohlich Executives Form a Health Agency."
19. "New Goals for Pharmaceuticals."
20. Michael Sonnenreich, interview with author, January 19, 2019.
21. Ibid.
22. "Advertising: Donnelley Introduces First Lady," *New York Times*. March 10, 1972, 60.
23. Michael Sonnenreich, interview with author, January 19, 2019.
24. When journalist Adam Tanner called Raymond Sackler years later to ask about the arrangement between the Sacklers and IMS and Frohlich, Raymond said he could not remember any of the details of the IMS deal. See Adam Tanner, "This Little-Known Firm Is Getting Rich Off Your Medical Data," *Fortune*, February 9, 2016; Tanner, *Our Bodies, Our Data,* n. 20, 175–76. See also Matter of Estate of Sackler, 149 Misc.2d 734, 564 N.Y.S.2d 977, 980 (N.Y. Surrogate Court. 1990); Matter of Sackler, (9-28-2007), 2007 NY Slip Op 33226(U) (N.Y. Misc. 2007).
25. Michael Sonnenreich, interview with author, January 19, 2019.
26. Ibid.
27. Ibid.

Chapter 30: The Temple of Dendur

1. "W. T. Grant Estate Sold," *New York Times*, June 3, 1973, 397.
2. "Buyers Scarce When the Price Is $1.8 Million, Hospital Finds," *New York Times*, January 21, 1973.
3. "Ex-W.T. Grant Tract Sold for $1.3 Million," *Bridgeport Post* (Bridgeport, CT), May 24, 1973.
4. "W. T. Grant Estate Sold," 397.
5. Ibid.
6. Ibid.
7. Lutze, *Who Can Know the Other?*, 136.
8. Michael Sonnenreich says that both Senokot and Betadine were Arthur Sackler's ideas; interview with author, January 19, 2019. See also Mary Agnes Carey,

"NASA Turned to Norwalk Firm to Kill Potential Moon Germs," *Hartford Courant* (Hartford, CT), July 23, 1992, C1-2.

9. *The Boston Globe* reported gross billings for McAdams of $50.3 million in 1980, and estimated a gross income of $7.55 million. Lenzner, "A Financial Man and the Fogg," 1, 49.
10. Adam Tanner, based on his interviews with former executives at Frohlich businesses, concluded that Frohlich owned a 50 percent interest in the international editions of *Medical Tribune*. See Tanner, *Our Bodies, Our Data*, 175.
11. Lenzner, "A Financial Man and the Fogg."
12. Bill Ingram, managing editor of the *Medical Tribune*, to Lenzner, "A Financial Man and the Fogg."
13. Medical Tribune International Inc., January 31, 1968, New York State incorporation, DOS ID # 219254; Excalibur International Inc and Exclaibur International Group, September 14, 1989.
14. Harry Henderson, a widely published author and journalist, was key in the successful rollout of the *Medical Tribune* magazine supplements. Henderson had interviewed Sackler in the early 1950s for a *Collier's* article that addressed alternatives to electroshock therapy for the mentally ill. He thought Arthur was "one of the most fascinating 'Renaissance men' to straddle several worlds at the same time." In 1956, he went to work for him and stayed twenty-three years, the last eight as the editor-in-chief of *Medical Tribune* and its subsidiary publications. Besdies developing the supplements, Henderson produced a dozen films for Sackler, mostly about problems in psychiatric institutions. See "Harry Henderson 1914–2003," http://harryhenderson.com/harry_henderson-biopage.html; Elaine Woo, "Harry B. Henderson, 88; Writer Drew Attention to African American Artists," *Los Angeles Times*, September 12, 2003.

    As for *Sexual Medicine Today*, its complete but seldom cited title was *Sexual Medicine Today and Therapacia*. See J. S. Groden, "Do Sore Nipples Inhibit Sexual Foreplay?," *Sexual Medicine Today*, July 1976; H. Gillespie and C. LaPointe, "Physicians' Marriages in Crisis: Sex and Love at Midlife," *Sexual Medicine Today*, October 1979; G. Bachman and S. Leiblum, "Sexual Expression During the Climacteric Years," *Sexual Medicine Today*, February 1985; J. Griffiths, "Reducing the Medical Risk of Teenage Pregnancy," *Sexual Medicine Today*, October 1977. See also the accumulated forty-three issues of *Sexual Medicine Today* by International Medical News Service, Washington, D.C., 1980.
15. A marble plaque at the entrance to the school reads, "Dedicated to Mankind for the Health of All People in Honor of Our Parents, Isaac and Sophie Sackler by Raymond R. Sackler, MD; Mortimer D. Sackler, MD; Arthur M. Sackler, MD." See https://en-med.tau.ac.il/Application-Process_5992.
16. "Sackler School of Medicine Celebrates 50 Years of Impact," Tel Aviv University, https://english.tau.ac.il/sackler_medicine_faculty_celebrates_50_years.
17. The Met's most serious contenders were the Smithsonian and the Boston Museum of Fine Arts. The Met argued that Dendur's sandstone would deteriorate quickly along the shores of either the Potomac or Charles Rivers.
18. Diana Craig Patch, "A Monumental Gift to The Met," Lila Achseson Wallace Curator in Charge, Department of Egyptian Art, https://www.metmuseum.org/about-the-met/curatorial-departments/egyptian-art/temple-of-dendur-50/gift-to-the-met .

19. "[Lyndon] Johnson Gives Egyptian Temple to Metropolitan Museum," *New York Times*, April 30, 1967, 81.
20. The Met has gotten stricter in giving away naming rights. Cosmetics tycoon Leonard Lauder gave the museum seventy-eight Cubist paintings and sculptures in 2013, valued at more than $1 billion. Although he said the gift was without any conditions, there is considerable speculation in the art world that if the Met does not finish its $600 million wing for contemporary and modern art, and name it for Lauder before 2025, he might regift the art elsewhere. Robin Pogrebin, "Putting Doubts to Rest About Leonard Lauder's Gift to the Met," *New York Times*, July 4, 2017.
21. Hoving, *Making the Mummies Dance*, 239.
22. Today, the original galleries Sackler had designated in 1963 with Rorimer and the adjacent exhibition gallery he arranged with Hoving are the centerpieces of the Sackler Wing, Galleries 223–31, with 232 a reading room. Marietta thought that Arthur's naming of the gallery after her was his attempt to make up for their strife at home.
23. Hoving, *Making the Mummies Dance*, 240.
24. Author interview with Michael Sonnenreich, February 23, 2019.
25. The agreement between Sackler and the Met for Dendur was signed in June 1974, after the Art Commission had already given its approval. Gross, *Rogue's Gallery*, 344.
26. Marietta said that even when it came to buying art, Arthur "made payment arrangements for his art purchases that usually extended over many years." Lutze, *Who Can Know the Other?*, 207; Author interview with Michael Sonnenreich, February 23, 2019.
27. Hoving, *Making the Mummies Dance*, 241.
28. Gallery 401 on Metropolitan Museum maps.
29. Gross, *Rogue's Gallery*, 343–44.
30. Rosenblatt oral history transcript, cited by Michael Gross, *Rogue's Gallery*, 344. The Metropolitan has made it difficult for researchers and journalists to access its oral history transcripts. See Michael Gross, "Oral-gate: The Secret History of the Metropolitan Museum," *Huffington Post*, July 5, 2010, updated May 25, 2011.
31. Calvin Tomkins, "The Importance of Being Élitist," *New Yorker*, Nov 24, 1997, 75.
32. Paul Richard, "Mixing It Up at the Metropolitan," *Washington Post*, February 1, 1987.
33. Gross, *Rogue's Gallery*, 346.
34. Ibid.
35. The six-story Neo-Georgian brick townhouse at 124 East 80th comprises the Clarence Dillon House, named after the younger Dillon's father. It is one of four adjoining townhomes built in the 1920s and designated landmarks in 1980 by the National Register of Historic Places. Dillon's original neighbors in the adjoining townhouses were Vincent Astor and George Whitney.
36. Author interview with Michael Sonnenreich, February 23, 2019.
37. Ibid.
38. Michael Sonnenreich, interview with author, January 19, 2019. Not every Jewish pharmaceutical executive ran into the prejudice Sackler encountered. Richard Sperber, who began his career at Schering-Plough in 1969, told the author he did not encounter "a smidgen of anti-Semitism." Sperber was at Schering when

its president was German-born Willibalb Conzen, and when he later worked at American Homes/Wyeth/Ayerst, "it was dominated by WASPs."

39. Michael Sonnenreich, interview with author, February 23, 2019.
40. "Princeton Gains Rare Chinese Art," *New York Times*, June 25, 1968, 38. See also Rosenblatt oral history transcript, cited by Michael Gross, *Rogue's Gallery*, 345.
41. John L. Hess, "Can the Met Escape King Tut's Curse!," *New York*, November 13, 1978, 79–80, 82, 85. Also see Carter B. Horsley, "Metropolitan Museum Haul of More Chinese Art Makes The Front Page of The New York Times But Some Details Are Missing," http://www.thecityreview.com/tang.htm.
42. Sackler also gave etchings and drawings by the eighteenth-century engraver and architect Giovanni Battista Piranesi to Columbia University's Avery Architectural Library. Sanka Knox, "Asian Treasures Lent Columbia For Public Exhibit and Research," *New York Times*, November 11, 1960. See also Sanka Knox, "Rare Chinese Manuscript Shown at Museum," *New York Times*, June 25, 1968. Sackler sent some of his collection from the Met and Princeton for an exhibit at the Philbrook Art Center in Oklahoma. "Philbrook to Show Rare Chinese Art," *Tulsa Tribune*, January 9, 1976; Grace Glueck, "An Art Collector Sows Largesse and Controversy," *New York Times*, June 5, 1983.
43. Solomon H. Snyder, "Arthur M. Sackler and Science," Proceedings of the National Academy of Sciences, September 25, 2001, 98 (20) 10994–95; https://doi.org/10.1073/pnas.211417398.
44. With Arthur, Mortimer and Raymond funded the Sackler School of Medicine at Tel Aviv University and the Sackler School of Biomedical Sciences at Tufts University. Snyder, "Arthur M. Sackler and Science." Outside the U.S., Mortimer took the lead and much of the philanthropy went to prestigious art, cultural, and educational institutions in the U.K. They include the Sackler Courtyard at London's Victoria and Albert Museum, the Sackler Gallery at The Serpentine, a Sackler Hall at the Museum of London, the Sackler Pavilion at the National Theatre, Sackler Studios at Shakespeare's Globe, a Sackler Crossing at the Kew, where the nation's archives are maintained, even the Sackler Escalators at the Tate Modern. Millions in bequests also went to the Royal College of Art, King's College, University College of London, and Oxford University, among others. From 2013 to 2018, Mortimer and Raymond donated $110 million to elite schools and cultural instituions worldwide. See David Cohen, "The Opioid Timebomb: The Sackler Family And How Their Painkiller Fortune Helps Bankroll London Arts," *Evening Standard*, March 19, 2018,
45. See Meier, *Pain Killer*, 60–61.
46. James Fallows, "When the Top U.S. Tax Rate Was 70 Percent—or Higher," *The Atlantic*, January 25, 2019.
47. Sam Roberts, "Raymond Sackler, Psychopharmacology Pioneer and Philanthropist, Dies at 97," *New York Times*, July 10, 2017.
48. Lutze, *Who Can Know the Other?*, 142.

Chapter 31: "Valiumania"

1. Television host Dick Cavett was the only other defendant besides Sackler who was not a museum official. The attorney general charged that he had received "unique and irreplaceable" museum artifacts without paying for them. Cavett returned the objects shortly after the attorney general's filing. Lee Rosenbaum,

"Private Boon or Private Reserve? The Met's Sackler Enclave," *ARTnews*, September 1978, 57; C. Gerald Fraser, "Court Acts on Indian Museum," *New York Times*, June 28, 1975, 60; Fred Ferretti, "Dealer's Papers Sought In Indian Museum Case," *New York Times*, February 26, 1975, 22; "Museum of the Indian Picks Chairman and Administrator," *New York Times*, December 1, 1975, 39; Grace Glueck, "Court Orders an Inventory Of Indian Museum Objects," *New York Times*, September 6, 1975, 11; Fred Ferretti, "State Investigates American Indian Museum," *New York Times*, October 3, 1974.

In 1992, Elizabeth, Arthur's daughter from his first marriage, incorporated the American Indian Ritual Object Repatriation Fund, a charitable foundation headquartered at the East 57th Street townhouse her father had bought in 1960. Sotheby's had ignored pleas from the Hopi and Navajo tribes to cancel the auction of three American Indian masks of spiritual importance. In her first ever auction bid, Elizabeth bought the masks for $39,000 and returned them to the tribes. http://sacredland.org/american-indian-ritual-object-repatriation-foundation. See also Ali Maloney, "Art and activism: The compass points of Elizabeth Sackler's storied career," *Women in the World*, January 8, 2016.

2. Marietta later recalled this period as one during which Arthur "worked harder at his office, taxing himself to extraordinary degrees." It was the only way, she said, that he could "meet his obligations. . . . With some people, they might slow collecting in order to pay existing bills, but not Arthur. Every purchase was like a carrot that made him work harder to earn the money with which to purchase more." Lutze, *Who Can Know the Other?*, 162.
3. Barry Blackwell, "Minor Tranquilizers: Use, Misuse or Overuse?" *Psychosomatics*, Vol. 16, Issue 1, 1975, 28–31.
4. The number of prescriptions is from Philip Boffey, "Worldwide Use of Valium Draws New Scrutiny," *New York Times*, October 13, 1981, C1, 2. According to B. D. Colen, "America's Psychic Aspirin: Valium: Problems with America's 'Perfect Drug,'" *Washington Post*, January 21, 1980, there were 53 million prescriptions in 1975.
5. According to Sonnenreich, Sackler bought stock in Roche, Ciba, and Sandoz. Both also "bought a lot of Pfizer." Author and Trisha Posner interview with Michael Sonnenreich, February 23, 2019.
6. "Danger Ahead! Valium—The Pill You Love Can Turn on You," *Vogue*, February 1975.
7. Tone, *Age of Anxiety*, 156.
8. Phyllis Chesler, *Women & Madness: When Is a Woman Mad and Who Is It Who Decides?* (Garden City, NY: Doubleday, 1972).
9. Roland H. Berg, "The Over-Medicated Women," *McCall's*, September 1971, 109–11; Carl D. Chambers and Dodi Schulz, "Women and Drugs: A Startling Survery," *Ladies' Home Journal*, November 1971, 191.
10. Boffey, "Worldwide Use of Valium Draws New Scrutiny," C2.
11. "Danger ahead! Valium—The Pill You Love Can Turn on You," 152–53.
12. Deborah Larned, "Do you take Valium?," *Ms. Magazine* 4 (1975), 26–29. See also John Pekkanen, "The Tranquilizer War: Controlling Librium and Valium," *New Republic*, July 19, 1975, 17–19. The major newsweeklies periodically continued their coverage about the dangers of Valium into the late 1970s. See, for example, Penelope McMillan, "The Prisoner of Pills," *Newsweek*, April 24, 1978, 77.
13. Cant, "Valiumania," *New York Times Magazine*, February 1, 1976.

14. Ibid.
15. Adding to the speculation about Morrison was that there was no autopsy. A friend of Morrison, the manager of Paris's Rock & Roll Circus Club claimed Morrison died in a bathroom at the club from heroin he bought and snorted. The dealer who had given him the heroin, said the club manager, helped bring Morrison back to his apartment. It was there, in his bathtub, where his girlfriend found him dead the following morning. See Elizabeth Goodman, "Jim Morrison's Death May Be Reinvestigated," *Rolling Stone*, July 10, 2007.
16. If Nyswander was correct, where was the evidence of the Valium overdoses? The medical examiners for Los Angeles and New York, when asked by *The New York Times*, said they had never seen a single case in which the drug was the cause of death.
17. Marcus A. Bachhuber et al., "Increasing Benzodiazepine Prescriptions And Overdose Mortality In The United States, 1996–2013," *American Journal of Public Health*, Vol. 106, Issue 4, April 1, 2016, 686–88). See also Andrea Tone, "Valium Celebrates 40th, but not with a Bang," *Times Colonist*, July 21, 2003: D4.
18. Marilyn Goldstein, "Society Is Still Coping with Valium," *Newsday* (New York), January 26, 1988, 4A. Follow-up stories included William Nolen, "Tranquilizer use and abuse," *McCall's*, May 1976, 94; "What's Good About Tranquilizers," *Vogue*, April 1976, 221.
19. The problem with withdrawal dependence had been raised only a year after Librium's release. It had taken almost fifteen years to get the FDA to act on its more popular cousin, Valium. See Leo Hollister et al., "Withdrawal Reactions from Chlordiazepoxide (Librium)," *Psychopharmacologia* 2 (1961): 63–68. Also John Pekkanen, "The Tranquilizer War: Controlling Librium and Valium," *New Republic*, July 19, 1975, 17–19.
20. Hoffmann-La Roche, Inc., Petitioner, v. Richard G. Kleindienst, Attorney General of the United States, and John E. Ingersoll, Director, Bureau Of Narcotics and Dangerous Drugs, United States Department of Justice, respondents, 478 F.2d 1 (3d Cir. 1973), US Court of Appeals for the Third Circuit—478 F.2d 1 (3d Cir. 1973), Argued June 25, 1971. Decided March 28, 1973. As Amended July 3, 1973.
21. When the Drug Enforcement Administration (DEA) was created in 1973, it took over all enforcement duties.
22. Virgil Van Dusen, "An Overview and Update of the Controlled Substances Act of 1970," *Pharmacy Times*, February 1, 2007.
23. Schedule IV is where all other benzos and mild tranquilizers got listed. The good news for Roche was that the government put barbiturates on Schedule III in 1970 and then moved them to the more stringent Schedule II in 1972. The restricted barbiturate prescribing unintentionally expanded a larger market for the benzodiazepines and other mild tranquilizers. "Drug Scheduling: Drug Schedules," Drug Enforcement Administration, https://www.dea.gov/drug-scheduling. See also Calcaterra NE, Barrow JC. "Classics in Chemical Neuroscience: Diazepam (Valium)." *ACS Chemical Neuroscience*. 2014;5(4):253–60. doi:10.1021/cn5000056; Shorter, *Before Prozac*, Kindle Edition, 351 of 4159.
24. See *State of Illinois v. Leslie Audi*, 392 N.E. 2d 248. *Rufus C. Cockrell v. State*, 392 So. 2d 541. See also Tone, *Age of Anxiety*, 203–4, 279.
25. Robert Reinhold, "U.S. Wins Agreement on Warning to Doctors on Use of Tranquilizers," *New York Times*, July 11, 1980, A1; "An Anxious History of Valium."

26. Valium label at https://www.accessdata.fda.gov/drugsatfda_docs/label/2016/013263s094lbl.pdf.
27. Tone, *Age of Anxiety*, 204.
28. Mickey Smith, *Small Comfort*, 218–23.
29. Shorter, *Before Prozac*, 1610 of 4159.
30. Andrea Tone and Elizabeth Siegel Watkins (eds.), *Medicating Modern America, Prescription Drugs in History* (New York: New York University Press, 2007), 69–71.
31. Kenneth J. Ryan, "Cancer Risk and Estrogen Use in the Menopause," *New England Journal of Medicine*, December 4, 1975, 293:1199–200. Donald Smith et al., "Association of Exogenous Estrogen and Endome-trial Carcinoma," *New England Journal of Medicine* 293 (December 4, 1975), 1164–67; Harry Ziel and William Finkle, "Increased Risk of Endometrial Carcinoma Among Users of Conjugated Estrogens," *New England Journal of Medicine* 293 (December 4, 1975), 1167–70.
32. Smith et al., "Association of Exogenous Estrogen and Endome-trial Carcinoma," 1164–67; Ziel and Finkle, "Increased Risk of Endometrial Carcinoma Among Users of Conjugated Estrogens," 1167–70.
33. "Estrogen is Linked to Uterine Cancer," *New York Times*, December 4, 1975. Two studies the following year added to the evidence of the cancer risk posed by Prempro. Thomas Mack et al., "Estrogens and Endometrial Cancer in a Retirement Community," *New England Journal of Medicine* 294 (June 3, 1976): 1262–67; Noel Weiss et al., "Increasing Incidence of Endometrial Cancer in the United States," *New England Journal of Medicine* (June 3, 1976): 1259–62.
34. "Estrogen is Linked to Uterine Cancer," *New York Times*.
35. Elizabeth Siegel Watkins, " 'Doctor, Are You Trying To Kill Me?': Ambivalence about the Patient Package Insert for Estrogen," *Bulletin of the History of Medicine* 76 (Spring 2002), 84–104.
36. Robert Wilson is quoted in Null and Seaman, *For Women Only!*, 752.
37. Ryan, "Cancer Risk and Estrogen Use in the Menopause," 1199–200. Smith et al., "Association of Exogenous Estrogen and Endome-trial Carcinoma," 1164–67; Harry Ziel and William Finkle, "Increased Risk of Endometrial Carcinoma Among Users of Conjugated Estrogens," *New England Journal of Medicine* 293 (December 4, 1975): 1167–70.
38. By 1980 Premarin sales went from 28 million to 14 million. Kennedy et al., "Noncontraceptive Estrogens and Progestins," 443.
39. "History of Cancer Screening and Early Detection," American Cancer Society, June 12, 2014.
40. Posner, *No Hormones, No Fear*, viii.
41. See for instance "Bazaar's Over-40 Guide on Health, Looks, Sex," *Harper's Bazaar*, August 1976.
42. Every year during the 1990s, Premarin was number one or number two; it only dropped to third in 2001 after Lipitor, Parke-Davis's hit statin, went on sale. By 2000 Premarin was dispensed 38 million times, 35 percent more than its best year in the 1970s (28 million prescriptions). Elizabeth Siegel Watkins, "Hormone Replacement," chapter 3 in Tone and Watkins (eds.), *Medicating Modern America*, 69–71; See Diane Wysowski et al., "Use of Menopausal Estrogens and Medroxyprogesterone in the United States, 1982–1992," *Obstetrics & Gynecology* 85 (1995).

43. Kennedy et al., "Noncontraceptive Estrogens and Progestins." 443.
44. Watkins, "Hormone Replacement," citing data through 1999 from *American Druggist's* annual list of top 200 prescription drugs. From 2000 on the data is from a list of top 200 drugs published at RxList, http://www.rxlist.com/top200.htm. The change in sources was because *American Druggist* ceased publication in 2000.
45. In 2002, the Women's Health Initiative, a federally funded randomized double-blind controlled trial with 16,000 participants, halted its study midway after startling results showed that HRT increased risk for heart disease, blood clots, strokes, and breast cancer. That news was worldwide front-page news. Gina Kolata, "Study Is Halted Over Rise Seen In Cancer Risk," *The New York Times,* July 9, 2002, 1. One year after that news, Prempro's sales had dropped by two thirds and Premarin by a third. They never again broke into the top ten bestselling drugs. Watkins, "Hormone Replacement," 93–94.
46. Robert A. Wilson and Thelma A. Wilson, "The Fate Of The Nontreated Post-menopausal Woman: A Plea For The Maintenance Of Adequate Estrogen From Puberty To The Grave," *Journal of the American Geriatrics Society*, April 1963.
47. Higano, R., W.N. Robinson, and W.D. Cohen. 1960. "Effects of long-term administration of estrogens on serum lipids of postmenopausal women," *New England Journal of Medicine* 293 (December 4, 1975): 828–31.

Chapter 32: Swine Flu

1. "Polio Elimination in the United States," Centers for Disease Control and Prevention, November 28, 2017.
2. Maggie Fox, "CDC says polio-like disease is puzzling. These doctors disagree," NBC News, October 25, 2018; AFM Investigation, CDC Investigation Updates, CDC, https://www.cdc.gov/acute-flaccid-myelitis/afm-surveillance.html.
3. Helen Branswell, "Despite high hopes for polio eradication, discouraging news is piling up," *STAT*, April 12, 2018. Another WHO goal was eradicating smallpox, an infectious virus that had killed millions. In 1980, the WHO certified that smallpox had been eliminated. The last known case was diagnosed in October 1977. Production of the vaccine stopped in 1982.
4. A. Hashim, "Pakistan's polio problem and vaccination danger," *Al Jazeera*, March 28, 2015; H. J. Warraich, "Religious opposition to polio vaccine," *Emerging Infectious Diseases*, 2009;15:978; Brian Krans, "Anti-Vaccination Movement Causes a Deadly Year in the U.S.," *Healthline*, December 3, 2013.
5. S. Plotkin, "Polio vaccine was not the source of human immunodeficiency virus type 1 for humans," *Vaccines*, 2001;32:1068–84; Warraich, "Religious opposition to polio vaccine." A.S. Jegede, "What led to the Nigerian boycott of the polio vaccination campaign?" *PLOS Medicine*, 2007;4:0417–22.
6. The only "evidence" was that the vaccinations had taken place before parents noticed any developmental regression. Maybe, the authors speculated, the vaccines had disrupted the digestive system and thereby affected brain development, causing ileal-lymphoid-nodular hyperplasia, nonspecific colitis, and pervasive developmental disorder in children. A.J. Wakefield et al., *Lancet*, Feb. 28, 1998; 351(9103):637–41.
7. The Generation Rescue website promotes the theory that the vaccine manufacturers are hiding the truth about how their products cause autism. It is a group

founded by actors Jenny McCarthy and Jim Carrey. For more, see "The MMR vaccine and autism: Sensation, refutation, retraction, and fraud," *Indian journal of psychiatry* vol. 53,2 (2011): 95–96. See also Michael J. Smith, Susan S. Ellenberg, Louis M. Bell, David M. Rubin, "Media Coverage of the Measles-Mumps-Rubella Vaccine and Autism Controversy and Its Relationship to MMR Immunization Rates in the United States," *Pediatrics*, April 2008, Vol. 121 / Issue 4; Jefferson, T., "Real or perceived adverse effects of vaccines and the media—a tale of our times," *Journal of Epidemiology & Community Health* 2000;54:402–3.

8. Committee on Safety of Medicines. Report of the Working Party on MMR vaccine London: May 1999.
9. "Lancet retracts 12-year-old article linking autism to MMR vaccines," *CMAJ: Canadian Medical Association Journal*, vol. 182,4 (2010): E199-200.
10. S.H. Murch et al., "Retraction of an interpretation," *Lancet*. March 6, 2004; 363(9411):750.
11. "Lancet retracts 12-year-old article linking autism to MMR vaccines."
12. Wakefield had falsely reported the sampling as consecutive although it was instead selective. His ethical violation was that he had not obtained any necessary clearances before performing the invasive investigations on the children. "Lancet retracts 12-year-old article linking autism to MMR vaccines."
13. F. Godlee, "The fraud behind the MMR scare," *British Medical Journal*, 2011;342:d22; B. Deer, "Secrets of the MMR scare. The Lancet's two days to bury bad news," *British Medical Journal*, 2011 Jan 18; 342():c7001.
14. "Andrew Wakefield struck off register by General Medical Council," *Guardian*, May 24, 2010; see also Andy Hayes and Greg Heffner, "Jacob Rees Mogg Apologises for Comparing Doctor to Disgraced Anti-Vaxxer," *Sky News*, September 5, 2019.
15. Letter, Pontificia Academia Pro Vita to Debra Vinnedge, Children of God For Life, June 9, 2005, CBS Evening News with Jeff Glor, March 20, 2019.
16. J.C. Gaydos et al., "Swine influenza A at Fort Dix, New Jersey (January–February 1976). II. Transmission and morbidity in units with cases," *Infect Dis*. 1977 Dec; 136 Suppl():S363–68; "Swine Flu," CBS *60 Minutes*, Mike Wallace, November 4, 1979.
17. Fifteen of the nineteen cultures were either the Victoria or Port Chalmers virus, which had been the dominant bugs for nearly a decade. Scientists were unsure about the others. Richard E. Neustadt and Harvey V. Fineberg, "The Swine Flu Affair Decision-Making on a Slippery Disease," U.S. Department of Health, Education, and Welfare, Washington, D.C., U.S. Government Printing Office, 1978, 4. See Swine Flu Chronology January 1976–March 1977 at https://www.ncbi.nlm.nih.gov/books/NBK219595/.
18. "Trends in recorded influenza mortality: United States, 1900–2004," *American Journal of Public Health*, Vol. 98,5 (2008): 939–45.
19. Harvey V. Fineberg, "Swine Flu of 1976: Lessons from the Past," *Bulletin of the World Health Organization*, Vol. 87, No. 6, June 2009, 405–84. Also see Lessler, Justin, et al., "Transmissibility of swine flu at Fort Dix, 1976," *Journal of the Royal Society*, Interface vol. 4,15 (2007): 755–62; Patrick Di Justo, "The Last Great Swine Flu Epidemic," *Salon*, April 28, 2009.
20. Its scientific name is Influenza A virus subtype H1N; it had jumped species from birds to pigs and then to humans. It was not until 1997 that Defense Department researchers found fragments of the genetic material from the Spanish flu

in a formaldehyde-soaked scrap of lung tissue preserved from a twenty-one-year-old soldier who had died of it. Investigators hoped that by deciphering its genetic code they might better prepare for future pandemics. See Gina Kolata, "Genetic Material of Virus From 1918 Flu Is Found," *New York Times*, March 21, 1997. The matter was resolved by Reid et al. (1999, 2000), who identified the swine flu virus as the cause of the 1918–19 pandemic, using tissues recovered from victims interred in Alaskan permafrost. Kolata 2000; Yewdell and Garcia-Sastre 2001.

21. The Spanish Flu killed so many younger Americans that once it was over the average lifespan in the U.S. dropped by twelve years. Joan Trossman Bien, "The Swine Flu Vaccine: 1976 Casts a Giant Shadow," *Pacific Standard*, December 4, 2009, updated June 14, 2017.
22. D.J. Sencer and J. Millar, "Reflections on the 1976 Swine Flu Vaccination Program," *Emerging Infectious Diseases*, 2006;12(1):29–33.
23. See Gaydos et al., "Swine Influenza A Outbreak, Fort Dix, New Jersey, 1976." See also Lessler et al., "Transmissibility of swine flu at Fort Dix, 1976," 755–62.
24. Harold M. Schmeck, Jr., "U.S. Calls Flu Alert On Possible Return Of Epidemic's Virus," *New York Times*, February 20, 1976, 1.
25. Steffan Foss Hansen, "The Precautionary Principle and Unnecessary Precautionary Actions," Technical University of Denmark, November 6, 2014, 45, https://www.researchgate.net/publication/267376224.
26. Schmeck, "U.S. Calls Flu Alert On Possible Return Of Epidemic's Virus."
27. Memorandum for the Honorable F. David Matthews, Secretary of Health, Education and Welfare, From Jim Cannon, Subject: Swine Flu Statement, August 7, 1976, 1–8, Box 34, Swine Flu (6), James M. Cannon Files, Gerald R. Ford Presidential Library.
28. One committee member suggested that instead of dispensing the vaccine when it was ready, it might be wiser to simply stockpile it for future outbreaks. Feinberg, "Swine Flu of 1976: Lessons from the Past." See also M. Goldfield et al., "Influenza in New Jersey in 1976: isolations of influenza A/New Jersey/76 virus at Fort Dix," *J Infect Dis*. 1977;136:S347–55.
29. Although the World Health Organization stayed on the sidelines during the 1976 swine flu outbreak it took a much more proactive position during a 2009 outbreak. It alone concluded in 2009 that swine flu was about to become a global epidemic and it encouraged governments to order record amounts of vaccine from pharmaceutical manufacturers. The epidemic turned out to be much less extensive and deadly than the WHO predicted. A year later, the *British Medical Journal* and London's Bureau of Investigative Journalism exposed that many top WHO advisors had financial ties to the drug companies that made the high-demand vaccines. Tiffany O'Callaghan, "BMJ: WHO Swine Flu Advisors Had Drug Company Ties," *Time*, June 4, 2010 (orig source BMJ). Fineberg, "Swine Flu of 1976: Lessons from the Past."
30. Neustadt and Fineberg, "The Swine Flu Affair."
31. Sencer emphasized the potential human toll from inaction: "There is evidence there will be a major flu epidemic this coming fall. The indication is that we will see a return of the 1918 flu virus that is the most virulent form of flu. In 1918, a half million people died [in the U.S.]. The projections are that this virus will kill one million Americans in 1976." Laurie Garrett, "The Next Pandemic," *Foreign Affairs*, July/August 2005. Also see G Dehner (2010) "WHO Knows Best?:

National and International Responses to Pandemic Threats and the 'Lessons' of 1976." *J Hist Med Allied Sci.* 65(4): 478-513.

32. In addition to Salk and Sabin, the group included Dr. Edwin Kilbourne, a leading influenza specialist, Dr. Frederick Davenport, an esteemed virologist, Maurice Hilleman, the head of Merck's virology labs, and Dr. Reul Stallones, dean of the University of Texas's Public Health School. See Sencer, David J., and J. Donald Millar, "Reflections on the 1976 Swine Flu Vaccination Program," *FDA Consumer*, v. 12, no. 1 (January 2006): 29–33.
33. The drug companies used hens to make the year's current vaccine against the more commonplace influenza. Late each spring, they slaughtered the roosters used to inseminate the hens. However, the CDC had notified the advisory panel that the hens were still alive. If they were killed, manufacturing the vaccine would be delayed several months. Neustadt and Fineberg, "The Swine Flu Affair," 13–14.
34. Boffey [1976], *Science*.
35. Ibid.
36. Jeffrey Jones, December 29, 2006, "Gerald Ford Retrospective, Approval ratings low by historical standards," https://news.gallup.com/poll/23995/gerald-ford-retrospective.aspx.
37. Iowa (January 19), New Hampshire (February 24), Massachusetts (March 2), Vermont (March 2), Florida (March 9), and Illinois (March 16).
38. President Gerald R. Ford's Remarks Announcing the National Swine Flu Immunization Program, March 24, 1976; The President spoke at 4:50 p.m. to reporters in the White House Briefing Room. Following the remarks, a briefing on the subject was held by David Mathews, Secretary, Dr. Theodore Cooper, Assistant Secretary for Health, Dr. David J. Sencer, Director, Center for Disease Control, Department of Health, Education, and Welfare, and Dr. Jonas Salk and Dr. Albert B. Sabin, https://www.fordlibrarymuseum.gov/library/speeches/760257.asp.
39. In addition to the funding for the swine vaccination program, Public Law 94-266 included "emergency supplemental appropriations" of $300 million for the EPA, $528 million for the Employment and Training Act, $55 million for the Older Americans Act, and $23 million for Community Services Act.
40. Neustadt and Fineberg, "The Swine Flu Affair," 109.
41. Memorandum for the President, F. David Mathews, July 20, 1976, Box 34, Swine Flu (6), James M. Cannon Files, Gerald R. Ford Presidential Library, 2, https://www.fordlibrarymuseum.gov/library/document/0039/16989155.pdf. Two weeks after the bill was signed, "HEW Press Analysis tracks news coverage from 111 newspapers in 60 cities; shows that editorial response to the swine flu program in April has been 88 percent favorable." See Neustadt and Fineberg, "The Swine Flu Affair," 109.
42. Alice Park, "How Fast Could a Swine Flu Vaccine Be Produced?" *Time*, April 29, 2009.
43. Neustadt and Fineberg, "The Swine Flu Affair," 111.
44. Bien, "The Swine Flu Vaccine: 1976 Casts A Giant Shadow."
45. *Reyes v. Wyeth Laboratories*, 498 F.2d 1264 (5th Cir. 1974), cert. denied, 419 U.S. 1096 (1974).
46. Neustadt and Fineberg, "The Swine Flu Affair," 108.
47. The House Committee on Appropriations for the Subcommittee on Labor-Health, Education and Welfare, had unanimously sponsored an indemnification resolu-

tion on March 30, just a week before the House passed the bill in a voice vote. Neustadt and Fineberg, "The Swine Flu Affair," 107.

48. Memorandum for the President, Jim Cavanaugh, Re: Swine Flu Letter to Paul Rogers, July 23, 1976, Box 34, Swine Flu (6), James M. Cannon Files, Gerald R. Ford Presidential Library, 1-4; Neustadt and Fineberg, "The Swine Flu Affair," 113–15.
49. Memorandum for the Honorable F. David Mathews, Secretary of Health, Education and Welfare, From Jim Cannon, Subject: Swine Flu Statement, August 7, 1976, 1–8; President, Jim Cavanaugh, Re: Swine Flu Letter to Paul Rogers, July 23, 1976, Box 34, Swine Flu (6), James M. Cannon Files, Gerald R. Ford Presidential Library, 1–4.
50. Memorandum for the President, F. David Mathews, July 20, 1976, Box 34, Swine Flu (6), James M. Cannon Files, Gerald R. Ford Presidential Library, 1, https://www.fordlibrarymuseum.gov/library/document/0039/16989155.pdf.
51. Neustadt and Fineberg, "The Swine Flu Affair," 110.
52. Lawrence K. Altman, "In Philadelphia 30 Years Ago, an Eruption of Illness and Fear," *New York Times*, August 1, 2006. See also Laurie Garrett, *The Coming Plague: Newly Emerging Diseases in a World Out of Balance* (New York: Penguin, 1995), 172; https://www.cdc.gov/about/facts/cdcfastfacts/legionnaires.html.
53. Lawrence K. Altman, "In Philadelphia 30 Years Ago, an Eruption of Illness and Fear," *New York Times*, August 1, 2006.
54. See, for instance, Text of a Letter From the President to the Speaker of the House of Representatives and the Honorable Mike Mansfield, From The White House, President Gerald R. Ford, August 4, 1977, Box 34, Swine Flu (6), James M. Cannon Files, Gerald R. Ford Presidential Library, 1–2.
55. Memorandum for the Honorable F. David Mathews, Secretary of Health, Education and Welfare, From Jim Cannon, Subject: Swine Flu Statement, August 7, 1976, 1–8, Box 34, Swine Flu (6), James M. Cannon Files, Gerald R. Ford Presidential Library.
56. The White House, Statement by the President, Office of the White House Press Secretary, For Immediate Release, August 6, 1976, 1–2, Box 34, Swine Flu (6), James M. Cannon Files, Gerald R. Ford Presidential Library.
57. "Doubts About Swine Flu," *New York Times*, August 9, 1976, 16.
58. The Senate passed the bill by voice vote and the House followed at 8:30 p.m. by a floor vote of 250 to 83, with two voting "present"; Harold M. Schmeck, "Congress Votes Flu Vaccine Liability Bill," *New York Times*, August 11, 1976, 1, 30; National Swine Flu Immunization Program of 1976, Pub. L. No. 94-380, 90 Stat. 1113 (1976) (the Swine Flu Act).
59. Pub. L. No. 94-380, 90 Stat. 1113 (1976) (the Swine Flu Act), https://www.gpo.gov/fdsys/pkg/STATUTE-90/pdf/STATUTE-90-Pg1113.pdf.
60. Interview with David Sencer, former Director of the CDC, "Swine Flu," CBS *60 Minutes*, Mike Wallace, November 4, 1979.
61. National Swine Flu Immunization Program of 1976, Pub. L. No. 94-380, 90 Stat. 1113 (1976) (the Swine Flu Act); Garrett, *The Coming Plague*, 173.
62. Ibid., 175.
63. "Legionella (Legionnaires' Disease and Pontiac Fever): History, Burden and Trends," Centers for Disease Control and Prevention, at https://www.cdc.gov/legionella/about/history.html.
64. The CDC had even investigated suspicious outbreaks in Taiwan and the Philip-

pines, but they turned out not to be the swine virus. Interview with David Sencer, former director of the CDC, "Swine Flu," CBS *60 Minutes*, Mike Wallace, November 4, 1979.

65. Harold M. Schmeck, "Swine Flu Program Is Halted in 9 States as 3 Die After Shots," *New York Times*, October 13, 1976, 1.
66. Bien, "The Swine Flu Vaccine: 1976 Casts A Giant Shadow."
67. Garrett, *The Coming Plague*, 175.
68. Ibid., 179.
69. Albert Sabin, "Washington and the Flu," *New York Times*, November 5, 1976, 21.
70. "Guillain-Barré syndrome and Flu Vaccine," Centers for Disease Control, https://www.cdc.gov/flu/prevent/vaccine/guillainbarre.htm.
71. Much has changed since then. Genetic advances have given researchers new ways of developing vaccines. At that time, pharmaceutical companies used the entire virus to stimulate the human immune system. Today, tiny genetic extracts from infectious bugs activate immunity without as high a risk of an unwanted infection. Park, "How Fast Could a Swine Flu Vaccine Be Produced?"
72. Interviews with David Sencer, former director of the CDC, and Dr. Michael Hattwick, CDC Vaccination Surveillance Team, "Swine Flu," CBS *60 Minutes*, Mike Wallace, November 4, 1979.
73. Gina Kolata, *Flu: The Story of the Great Influenza Pandemic of 1918 and the Search for the Virus That Caused It* (New York: Farrar, Straus and Giroux, 1999), 182–85.
74. Sencer and Millar, "Reflections on the 1976 Swine Flu Vaccination Program."
75. A later study demonstrated that those who had been vaccinated were about ten times more likely to come down with Guillain-Barré syndrome than the rest of the population. Garrett, *The Coming Plague*, 181.
76. Harry Schwartz, "Swine Flu Fiasco," *New York Times*, December 21, 1976, 33.
77. Rebecca Kreston, "The Public Health Legacy of the 1976 Swine Flu Outbreak," *Discover*, September 30, 2013.
78. Paul D. Rheingold and Clifford J. Shoemaker, "The Swine Flu Litigation," *Litigation*, Vol. 8, No. 1, 1981, 28.
79. Ibid.; Garrett, *The Coming Plague*, 181–82.
80. Rheingold and Shoemaker, "The Swine Flu Litigation."
81. In 1993, a Maryland federal district court judge ruled that those claiming injury from the 1960s were not barred by the statute of limitations. The Justice Department settled five of the early polio cases for "seven-figure sums" and the court sealed the details. Garrett, *The Coming Plague*, 182.
82. Gaydos et al., "Swine Influenza A Outbreak, Fort Dix, New Jersey, 1976."
83. Garrett, *The Coming Plague*, 182.
84. Brigit Katz, "New York County Bans Unvaccinated Children From Public Places," *Smithsonian*, March 27, 2019.
85. Katie Shepherd, "An Oregon Lawmaker Wants To Repeal Personal Vaccine Exemptions As Measles Outbreak Grows," *Willamette Week*, February 9, 2019.
86. Ann Smajstrla, "CDC: Number of measles cases in U.S. second-highest since 2000," *Atlanta Journal-Constitution*, April 16, 2019.
87. Seema Yasmin and Madhusree Mukerjee, "The Dengue Debacle," *Scientific American*, April 2019, 39–47. They were Connaught Laboratories, Lederle-Praxis Biologicals, Merck, and Wyeth-Ayerst. Garrett, *The Coming Plague*, 182.
88. Lorraine Johnson, "Lyme disease costs may exceed $75 billion per year," Lyme Disease.Org, July 19, 2018. H. B. Noble, "3 Suits say Lyme vaccine caused severe

arthritis," *New York Times*, June 13, 2000; S. A. Plotkin, "Need for a new Lyme disease vaccine," *New England Journal of Medicine*, 2016; 375:911–13. See G. A. Poland, "Vaccines Against Lyme Disease: What Happened And What Lessons Can We Learn?" *Clin Infect Dis.* (2011) 52 (suppl 3): s253–58.

89. Kolata, *Flu: The Story Of The Great Influenza Pandemic Of 1918.*

Chapter 33: "Black River"

1. Until 1976 the DRC was Zaire.
2. Donald G. McNeil, Jr., "Earlier Ebola Outbreaks, and How the World Overcame Them," *New York Times*, July 17, 2019.
3. Between 1908 to 1960, the Democratic Republic of the Congo was the Belgian Congo. After independence in 1960, the new country maintained close ties to Belgium, so it is not surprising that the blood sent abroad for testing went to an institute in Antwerp before any arrived at the CDC. Helen Branswell, "History credits this man with discovering Ebola on his own. History is wrong," *STAT*, July 14, 2016.
4. Ibid.
5. Lawrence K. Altman, "The Doctor's World; Battle-Scarred Veteran Is General in Global War on AIDS," *New York Times*, July 21, 1998, F1.
6. N.J. Cox et al., "Evidence for two subtypes of Ebola virus based on oligonucleotide mapping of RNA." *J Infect Dis*. 1983; 147: 272–75.
7. In parts of Africa, bush meat is cooked and consumed as are dried remains of wild animals, from bats to chimpanzees. It is a multigenerational tradition and also a key source of protein in a region where protein is scarce. See Abby Phillip, "Why West Africans keep hunting and eating bush meat despite Ebola concerns," *Washington Post*, August 5, 2014.
8. Charlie Cooper, "How the Ebola Virus Got its Name and How We Caught it From Animals," *Independent*, October 2, 2014.
9. Feldmann H, Geisbert TW (March 2011). "Ebola haemorrhagic fever." *Lancet*. 377 (9768): 849–62. See also "Ebola Virus Disease," World Heath Organization at http://www.who.int/news-room/fact-sheets/detail/ebola-virus-disease.
10. Cooper, "How the Ebola Virus Got its Name and How We Caught it From Animals."
11. "What happens to your body if you get Ebola," *Conversation*, June 17, 2014.
12. E. Stimola, *Ebola* (New York: Rosen Publishing, 2011), 31, 52.
13. Bahar Gholipour, "How Ebola Got Its Name," *LiveScience*, October 9, 2014.
14. Ibid.
15. In 1973, the international committee with oversight for such naming had proposed Congo-Crimean hemorrhagic fever virus. The Soviets, who had isolated the virus in Crimea, insisted on Crimean-Congo hemorrhagic fever. They prevailed. Onder Ergönül and Charles Whitehouse, *Personal Reflections, Congo Hemorrhagic Fever: A Global Perspective*, Netherlands: Springer, 2007, 23.
16. Only later did the doctors realize the map they had picked was not very precise; Ebola was not the river nearest to the infected village. In 2005, two British medical researchers caused an uproar by publishing a thesis that the fourteenth-century Black Plague that killed some 25 million Europeans was not a flea-borne bubonic disease but rather an early version of Ebola. It took researchers five years of DNA analysis to convincingly disprove that. Peter Piot, *No Time to Lose: A Life*

in Pursuit of Deadly Viruses (W. W. Norton & Company, 2012). Christopher J. Duncan and "Congo ebola epidemic becomes second worst outbreak ever," SKY News, March 25, 2019.

17. "A HIV/AIDS Timeline: The Origins of HIV/AIDS," 5th Edition, An Albion Center Publication, Australia, 2007, in collection of author.
18. Pneumocystis carinii was long classified as a protozoan and many journalists and authors list it as such. In fact, DNA sequencing analysis has in recent years confirmed it is a fungus. The parasitic microorganism had first been isolated in guinea pigs in 1910 by a Brazilian researcher, and then French scientists subsequently identified it in Parisian sewer rats. See Ann E Wakefield, "Pneumocystis carinii: Role in childhood respiratory infections," *British Medical Bulletin*, Volume 61, Issue 1, March 1, 2002, 175–88; M. T. Cushion, "Pneumocystis carinii Pneumonia," *Transmission and Epidemiology*, September 1994; 123–37.
19. Altman, "The Doctor's World."
20. Randy Shilts, *And the Band Played On: Politics, People and the AIDS Epidemic* (London: Souvenir Press, 2011), 6.
21. Ibid., 20. See also Y. Chang et al., "Identification of herpesvirus-like DNA sequences in AIDS-associated Kaposi's sarcoma," *Science*. 266 (5192), 1994: 1865–69. See also "A HIV/AIDS Timeline: The Origins of HIV/AIDS."
22. Some researchers believe the first case of AIDS in the U.S. was confirmed by a preserved tissue sample to be a sixteen-year-old African American who died in St. Louis in 1969. Others contest that finding, citing that the brand of test kit used was one that had a high rate of false positives, and aside from Kaposi sarcoma, none of his symptoms were typical of AIDS patients. See generally "A HIV/AIDS Timeline: The Origins of HIV/AIDS."
23. "Charles Richard Drew—'Father of the Blood Bank,'" *American Chemistry Society*, at https://www.acs.org/content/acs/en/education/whatischemistry/african-americans-in-sciences/charles-richard-drew.html.
24. Douglas P. Starr, *Blood: An Epic History of Medicine and Commerce* (New York: Perennial, 2002), 216.
25. "The Blood, Plasma, and Related Programs in the Korean War," Chapter 20 from "The Blood Program in World War II," at http://hcvets.com/data/military/1948_korea_military_blood_supply.htm.
26. Starr, *Blood*, 219.
27. Paolo Caraceni et al., "Clinical use of albumin." "Blood transfusion," *Trasfusione del Sangue* Vol. 11 Suppl 4, Suppl 4 (2013): s18–25.
28. Starr, *Blood*, chapter 12.
29. Starr, *Blood*, 178.
30. Ibid.
31. D. J. Wallace, "Apheresis for lupus erythematosus," *Lupus* (1999) 8, 174–80.
32. Factor VIII was a glycine-precipitated plasma fraction.
33. There are two types of hemophiliacs, A and B; both are mostly men whose blood fails to produce sufficient proteins required for clotting. Factor VIII treated only hemophilia A. A different treatment, Factor IX, was later developed for hemophilia B. See generally Starr, *Blood*, chapter 12.
34. The first crude method developed around 1940 to separate plasma from blood was dubbed fractionation. When the liquid plasma was then centrifuged, the first fractionation produced a small pebble-sized piece of clotting protein (mostly fibrinogen, called Factor I).

35. Hemophiliacs, who had a short life expectancy then of only forty-two years, were more than willing to pay several thousand dollars for a year's supply.
36. See Albert Farrugia and Josephine Cassar, "Plasma-derived medicines: access and usage issues," *Blood Transfusion*, vol. 10,3 (2011): 273–8.
37. Starr, *Blood*, 178, 186.
38. "National Research Council Committee on AIDS Research and the Behavioral, Social, and Statistical Sciences, Chapter 5, AIDS and the Blood Supply," in *AIDS: The Second Decade*, H. G. Miller, C. F. Turner, and L. E. Moses, eds. (Washington, D.C.: National Academies Press, 1990).
39. *JAMA*, Feb 5, 1968: Vol 203, No 6.
40. Starr, *Blood*, 256–57. In 1975 a new hepatitis screening test was 40 percent effective.
41. Cutter Laboratories and Armour Labs had separated blood and plasma during World War II. Armour was a drug spinoff of the meatpacking giant. The others were Courtland Laboratories (later Alpha Therapeutics) and Hyland (owned by Baxter Labs).
42. Donna Shaw, "On The Trail Of Tainted Blood—Hemophiliacs Say U.S. Could Have Prevented Their Contracting Aids," *Philadelphia Inquirer*, April 16, 1995, 1.
43. Gilbert M. Gaul, "How blood, the 'gift of life,' became a billion-dollar business," *Philadelphia Inquirer*, March 12, 1989, 1.
44. The U.S. drug market was largely self-regulated through the 1990s. Those three giant blood bank organizations are registered nonprofits, but all derive significant annual profits from their blood business. They simply mark it as "excess over expenses" and then bank it against future losses. Gaul, "How blood, the 'gift of life,' became a billion-dollar business."
45. The United Nations Organization in the Congo was the sponsor for the project. U.N. secretary-general Dag Hammarskjöld was trying to mediate the armed conflict when he was killed on September 18, 1961. His chartered DC-6 crashed in the Congo. To this day there are conflicting theories about whether the fatal crash was an accident or the result of ground fire. For those who believe it was intentional, different conspiracy theories put the blame on black nationalists, white mercenaries, Western intelligence agencies, and even colonial-era mining syndicates. Rick Gladstone and Alan Cowell, "More Clues, and Questions, in 1961 Crash That Killed Dag Hammarskjold," *New York Times*, February 17, 2019.
46. In the 1960s there were an estimated 4,500 and the number increased by another 1,500 in the 1970s.
47. Regine Jackson, "The Failure of Categories: Haitians in the United Nations Organization in the Congo, 1960–1964," *Journal of Haitian Studies*, Vol. 20, No. 1 (Spring 2014), 34–64.
48. Gorinsteen had incorporated the company in Florida on August 11, 1970 (Document Number 368180). Werner H. Thill was the only technical director. See Richard Severo, "Impoverished Haitians Sell Plasma for Use in the U.S.," *New York Times*, January 28, 1972; Jacques Pepin, *The Origin of AIDS* (Cambridge: Cambridge University Press), 2012, 201.
49. Duvalier liked the nickname. He was a physician before he was elected Haiti's president in 1957 running on a black-nationalist-populist campaign. He considered himself the father of independent Haiti and the "Doc" was a reference to his medical degree.
50. Severo, "Impoverished Haitians Sell Plasma for Use in the U.S."; Pepin, *The Origin of AIDS*, 201–2.

51. Ibid., 202.
52. Ibid., 201–2.
53. Francis B. Kent, "Rising Criticism—Haiti: Jobless, Poor Line up to Sell Blood," *Los Angeles Times*, January 27, 1972, 1; Severo, "Impoverished Haitians Sell Plasma for Use in the U.S."
54. Pepin, *The Origin of AIDS*, 201.
55. The pharmaceutical/biologic companies were Armour Pharmaceutical, Cutter Laboratories, Hyland Labs, Dow Chemical, and Dade Reagent. Hemo-Caribbean also sold to pharmaceutical and biologic companies in Germany and Sweden. Severo, "Impoverished Haitians Sell Plasma for Use in the U.S."
56. Ibid. The FDA has a rule from 1984 banning cash payments in the U.S. to blood donors, but there are numerous examples of how little it is enforced; blood banks are supposed to only give small token rewards including such items as movie tickets, gift cards, and T-shirts. Elizabeth Preston, "Why You Get Paid To Donate Plasma But Not Blood," *STAT News*, January 22, 2016.
57. Severo, "Impoverished Haitians Sell Plasma for Use in the U.S."
58. "Haiti: Jobless, Poor Line Up to Sell Blood," Representative Victor V. Veysey, Congressional Record, February 3, 1972, 2563–64.
59. Not only was the Biologics Division unable to say whether infected Hemo-Caribbean plasma fractions were sold in the U.S., it could not track where the plasma was distributed after it entered the country. The government agency tasked with protecting the American blood did not even know how much Haitian plasma had been imported into the U.S. The National Blood Bank Act, HR 11828, that in 1973 established inspection and licensing of all blood banks and importers.
60. Author interview with former assistant manager at Hemo-Caribbean, July 8, 2017.
61. Francis B. Kent, "Rising Criticism—Haiti: Jobless, Poor Line up to Sell Blood," *Los Angeles Times*, January 27, 1972.
62. Author interview with former assistant manager at Port-au-Prince Hemo-Caribbean, November 1971 to August 1972, name withheld on request, in Miami, June 28, 2017. While it is not possible to know with certainty what caused the instances of vomiting or breathing problems, a known rare adverse effect with blood donors is "citrate reaction," in which a donor reacts badly to the body's temporary loss of calcium.
63. Report of the United Nations AIDS report, Country: Haiti. See http://www.unaids.org/en/regionscountries/countries/haiti.
64. Dr. Jacques Pepin, an infectious disease specialist who has written extensively about HIV/AIDS, believes that Hemo-Caribbean "could have been the perfect venue for the rapid parenteral amplification of a strain of HIV-1. . . . Hemo-Caribbean operated in 1971 and 1972, at exactly the right time, after the virus had been imported into Haiti." Pepin, *The Origin of AIDS*, 205.
65. B. Liautaud et al., "Kaposi's Sarcoma In Haiti: Unknown Reservoir Or A Recent Appearance?" *Ann Dermatol Venereol*. 1983;110(3):213–19. There are no written records of donors from which to compare to the earliest identified HIV patients.
66. Mirko Gmek, *History of AIDS: Emergence and Origin of a Modern Pandemic* (Princeton, NJ: Princeton University Press, 1990), 37.
67. H. Luke Shaefer and Analidis Ochoa, "How Blood-Plasma Companies Target the

Poorest Americans: The industry's business model depends on there being plenty of people who need cash quickly," *Atlantic*, March 15, 2018.

Chapter 34: "Everything Can Be Abused"

1. The Sacklers had incorporated Napp Chemicals in Delaware in 1970, but its name changed by 1978. Besides its U.S. branch, the Sacklers used the name in a series of UK companies, all slight variations of the original 1966 Napp Pharmaceutical Group Limited (company #00884285). Among them are Napp Research Centre Limited, co. #01837276 (1984); Napp Pharmaceutical Research Limited, co. #4608592 (1985); Napp Pharmaceutical Holdings Limited, co. #03486244 (1997); and Napp Pharmaceuticals Limited, co. #03690299 (1998). Files in collection of author.
2. The Mortimer Sackler and Sackler Family Foundations use the same address and telephone number to this day. When Michael Sonnenreich began working as an attorney for Arthur Sackler in 1973, his office was at 15 East 62nd Street. He told the author he does not remember Greene there in 1978, suggesting Greene might have only used it as a mail drop. Tax Return of Private Foundation, Mortimer D. Sackler Foundation, EIN: 23-7022461. 19 pages, Form 990-PF, 2013, in collection of author.
3. Edward Shorter, *A Historical Dictionary of Psychiatry* (Oxford, UK: Oxford University Press, 2005).
4. Carol Brennan, "Valium," at https://www.benzo.org.uk/valium3.htm.
5. Author interview with former business partner of Arthur Sackler, November 2018.
6. Marilyn Goldstein, "Society Is Still Coping with Valium," *Newsday* (New York), January 26, 1988, 4A.
7. Barbara Gordon, *I'm Dancing as Fast as I Can* (New York: Harper & Row, 1979). See Tammy Faye Baker, "Mother's Little Helper: Valium at 35," ABC News, December 17, 1998, and for Elizabeth Taylor, Robin Marantz Henig, op-ed, "Valium's Contribution to Our New Normal," *New York Times*, September 29, 2012.
8. The Memphis medical examiner concluded that Elvis died of natural causes, a cardiac arrhythmia caused by "polypharmacy" (drug interaction). That ruling eliminated any possible prosecution against Dr. Nick for murder or manslaughter. Three years after Presley's death, the Tennessee Board of Medical Examiners gave Dr. Nick a three-month suspension but cleared him of more serious charges of unethical conduct and medical malpractice. The following year, state prosecutors filed a 14-count indictment for overprescribing thousands of stimulants, barbiturates, and painkillers to Elvis, Jerry Lee Lewis, and eight others. A jury acquitted Dr. Nick on all counts. In 1992, a tougher Tennessee Board of Medical Examiners charged him again, this time with reckless overprescribing. It took three years before the state prevailed and stripped Dr. Nick of his medical license. See "Presley's Doctor on Trial Over Prescriptions," *New York Times,* September 30, 1981, A22; Adam Higginbotham, "Doctor Feelgood," *Guardian*, August 10, 2002; see Dr. Nick interviewed in Gerald Posner, "Elvis's Doctor Speaks," *Daily Beast*, August 14, 2009.
9. The fourth benzodiazepine discovered by Leo Sternbach was Dalmane, which Roche released in 1970 as a sleep aid. It was marketed as a hypnotic and had little effect on Valium sales.

10. "Lorazepam (Ativan)," History, Ativan Drug Project, at https://ativandrugproject.weebly.com/structure-and-history.html.
11. Shahrzad Salmasi et al., "Interaction and medical inducement between pharmaceutical representatives and physicians: a meta-synthesis," *Journal of Pharmaceutical Policy and Practice*, vol. 9, no. 37, November 17, 2016. See also Hneine Brax et al., "Association between physicians' interaction with pharmaceutical companies and their clinical practices: A systematic review and meta-analysis," *PloS One* (Public Library of Science), vol. 12, iss 4, April 13, 2017.
12. Sackler hoped that Valium might also be helped unintentionally by the chief of the Office of Drug Abuse whom Jimmy Carter had selected earlier that year. Arthur knew Dr. Peter Bourne, a London-born, American-educated psychiatrist, who made barbiturates his number one target for the most abused prescription category in the U.S. That took the federal spotlight temporarily off benzodiazepines.
13. Nicholas E Calcaterra and James C Barrow. "Classics in Chemical Neuroscience: Diazepam (Valium)." *ACS Chemical Neuroscience* vol. 5, no. 4 (2014): 253–60.
14. Matthew Herper, "Slide Show: America's Most Popular Psychiatric Drugs," *Forbes*, September 17, 2010.
15. Boyce Rensberger, "Abuse of Prescription Drugs: A Hidden but Serious Problem for Women," *New York Times*, April 19, 1978, A12; also Myra MacPherson and Donnie Radcliffe, "Betty Ford Says That She Is Addicted to Alcohol," *Washington Post*, April 22, 1978, 1.
16. Arnie Cooper, "An Anxious History of Valium," *Wall Street Journal*, November 15, 2013, 1; Dowbiggin, *The Quest for Mental Health*, 161.
17. Stephen Cohen, "It's a Mad, Mad Verdict: Hinckley Got Off, But the Verdict on the Insanity Defense Is Guilty," *New Republic*, July 12, 1982.
18. Author interview with former business associate of Arthur Sackler, November 2018.
19. The generic name was triazolam.
20. *An Assessment of Data Adequacy and Confidence. Halcion: An Independent Assessment of Safety and Efficacy Data*. Institute of Medicine (US) Committee on Halcion (Washington, D.C.: National Academies Press, 1997, introduction, 1.
21. FDA Approval for "Type 1—New Molecular Entity, alprazolam," drug application from Pharmacia and Upjohn, NDA 018276, FDA action date October 16, 1981.
22. J. Angs, "Panic Disorder: History and Epidemiology," *Eur Psychiatry*. 1998;13 Suppl 2:51s–55s.
23. Matthew Herper, "America's Most Popular Mind Medicines," *Forbes*, September 17, 2010.
24. Dowbiggin, *The Quest for Mental Health*, 188–89.
25. The FDA approval for Xanax to treat panic disorder did not come until 1990. However, psychiatrists and general practitioners had been prescribing it off-label for that from since its 1981 introduction.
26. Cooper, "An Anxious History of Valium"; Tone, *Age of Anxiety*, 213.
27. Shorter, *Before Prozac*; George Stein and Brett Chase, "Pharmacia & Upjohn, Monsanto to Merge in $26.5-Billion Deal," *Los Angeles Times*, December 20, 1999; Matthew Herper, "Pfizer Buys Pharmacia For $60 Billion," *Forbes*, July 15, 2002.
28. Dowbiggin, *The Quest for Mental Health*, 174–76.

29. Arthur Kleinman quoted in Ashley Pettus, "Psychiatry by Prescription," *Harvard Magazine*, July–August 2006.
30. Peter Kramer quoted in Jonathan Rosen, "The Assault on Antidepressants," *Atlantic*, July/August 2016.
31. C. Karestan Koenen et al., "Persisting Posttraumatic Stress Disorder Symptoms and their Relationship to Functioning in Vietnam Veterans: A 14-Year Follow-up," *Journal of Traumatic Stress* vol. 21, no. 1 (2008): 49–57.
32. Smith, *A Social History of the Minor Tranquilizers*, 1.
33. Leo Sternbach quoted in B. D. Cohen, "Valium and Health," *Washington Post*, February 24, 1980.
34. Author interview with former business partner of Arthur Sackler, November 2018.

    Eventually there was a scientific pushback against the offensive on Valium. Heinz Lehmann, a psychiatrist considered the "father of modern psychopharmacology," had predicted in 1960 Senate testimony that the overprescribing of mild tranquilizers would create a dependence crisis. Two decades later he had concluded that "sensational horror stories" had unfairly maligned Valium. A *JAMA* editorial later asked, "Where are all the tranquilizer junkies?," questioning whether the great scare about the addictiveness of the benzos was mostly wrong. E. R. González, "Where are all the tranquilizer junkies?," *JAMA*, May 20, 1983;249(19):2603–4; Andrea Tone, "Listening to the Past: History, Psychiatry, and Anxiety," *Canadian Journal of Psychiatry*, June 2005.

Chapter 35: The Age of Biotech

1. Searches by the author for "valium" in LexisNexis and newspapers.com show 32,769 print articles in the United States from 1975 through 1980.
2. Oversight and Review of Clinical Gene Transfer Protocols: Assessing the Role of the Recombinant DNA Advisory Committee. Committee on the Independent Review and Assessment of the Activities of the NIH Recombinant DNA Advisory Committee, Board on Health Sciences Policy, Institute of Medicine (Washington, D.C.: National Academies Press 2014).
3. With the end of the moratorium, the NIH became the unofficial biotech regulator and benefactor. Its National Medical Library was an unmatched knowledge base through which researchers shared information. And, most important, it opened its peer-review pipeline for federal grants to encourage cutting-edge research and sponsored the doctoral and postdoctoral studies of young biologists and scientists. Fredrickson quoted in Nell Henderson and Michael Schrage, "The Roots of Biotechnology: Government R&D Spawns a New Industry," *Washington Post*, December 16, 1984, 5.
4. Ibid.
5. The change was proposed in 1979 but it took until 1981 for it to become effective. Private companies were mostly uncertain about how much of what they discovered would be theirs under a patent that had been financed by the government. For the first decade, on average there were a dozen private companies that applied annually for research grants, in contrast to the approximately twenty thousand nonprofit applications every year.
6. History of Congressional Appropriations, National Institutes of Health, 1960–1969,

at https://officeofbudget.od.nih.gov/pdfs/FY08/FY08%20COMPLETED/appic3806%20-%20transposed%20%2060%20-%2069.pdf.

7. If, for some reason, the university did not patent its NIH-funded discovery, the government could patent it and the royalties would go the Treasury Department. The NIH created the Office of Medical Applications of Research in 1977 and it was responsible for recommending whether something developed by an academic research center should be patented by the government.
8. Swanson called Boyer in April 1976; the moratorium was not lifted until July.
9. Kleiner Perkins was the firm, based in Menlo Park. Kleiner was a cofounder of Fairchild Semiconductor.
10. It was Stanford's director of Technology Licensing that convinced a reluctant Cohen to file for the patent. Their original application was split into three parts, two of them for products produced in different cell lines and the other a process patent for the mechanics they used.
11. S. S. Hughes, "Making dollars out of DNA. The first major patent in biotechnology and the commercialization of molecular biology, 1974–1980," *Isis*, 92(3), September 2001: 541–75.
12. Doogab Yi, "Who Owns What? Private Ownership and the Public Interest in Recombinant DNA Technology in the 1970s," *Isis*, 102(3), September 2011: 446–74
13. Marie Godar, "Humble Beginnings: The Origin Story of Modern Biotechnology," *LabBiotech,* November 17, 2005.
14. "Gobind Khorana and the Rise of Molecular Biology," MIT School of Science/Research and Academics, at https://science.mit.edu/gobind-khorana-molecular-biology/.
15. Nathan Rosenberg, Annetine Gelijns, and Holly Dawkins, ed., "Sources of Medical Technology: Universities and Industry," Chapter 7 in vol. 5, Committee on Technological Innovation in Medicine, Institute of Medicine (Washington, D.C.: National Academy Press, 1995).
16. Ibid., 168.
17. Ibid., 169–70, and Biogen: Company History Overview, at https://www.biogen.com/en_us/history-overview.html.
18. Stephan S. Hall, *Invisible Frontiers: The Race to Synthesize a Human Gene* (New York: Atlantic Monthly Press, 1987).
19. Quoted in "Cloning Insulin," Genentech, April 7, 2016, at https://www.gene.com/stories/cloning-insulin.
20. There were over four thousand biotech start-ups in the coming decades. Most were one-product firms and more than 80 percent never brought a drug to market. Gary P. Pisano, "Can Science Be a Business?: Lessons from Biotech," *Harvard Business Review*, October 2006.
21. Henderson and Schrage, "The Roots of Biotechnology," 5.
22. Robert J. Cole, "Genentech New Issue, Up Sharply," *New York Times,* October 15, 1980, D1.
23. Stelios Papadopoulos, "Evolving paradigms in biotech IPO valuations," *Nature Biotechnology*, Volume 19, BE18–BE19 (2001).
24. A miscalculation by Wall Street was the belief that the FDA approval process for biopharmaceuticals would be much speedier than the one for traditional drugs. A 2005 study showed that over thirty years the biotech industry had attracted $300 billion in venture capital. Although the sector had gone from zero revenues

in 1975 to $40 billion, only a handful of companies earned profits. The most successful firms were the earliest ones, Genentech, Amgen, Chiron, Genzyme, and Biogen. Stelios Papadopoulos, "Evolving paradigms in biotech IPO valuations"; Pisano, "Can Science Be a Business?"

25. Bogle quoted in *The Wall Street Reporter*, May 1980; see also Wayne Duggan, "John Bogle's Biggest Investing Mistake And What He Learned From It," *Benzinga*, June 11, 2005, in which Bogle referred to market bubbles such as biotech, and later the dot-com companies, "Each stock looked really great, but anybody would know that all of them cannot succeed."
26. Activase is the brand name for the first drug to utilize tissue plasminogen activator (TPA), an enzyme that dissolves blood clots. The stock dropped from 48.25 to 36.75 for a paper loss of $930 million. Carpenter, *Reputation and Power*. For FDA approval, see License 1048, Application No.:103172-Supplement 1055, generic name Alteplase, tradename: Activase, June 18, 1996.
27. The next rally would not happen until congressional Republicans killed Bill Clinton's sweeping proposed health care legislation in 1995, easing concerns that there could be price controls. Biotech would suffer the most from such limits since its successful products are by a wide margin the most expensive in the industry.
28. For a few examples of institutional buy recommendations followed by drops of 80 percent or more in share price within a week of bad news, see DOV Pharma in 2005; Threshold Pharmaceuticals and Valentis in 2006; Casey Murphy, "The Ups and Downs of Biotechnology," *Investopedia*, updated October 16, 2019; Heidi Ledford, "Blood Money: The Biotech Debacle of Theranos on Screen," *Nature*, April 2, 2019.

Chapter 36: A "Gay Cancer"

1. Randy Shilts, *And the Band Played On: Politics, People, and the AIDS Epidemic*, 20th-Anniversary Edition (New York: St. Martin's Griffin, 2007), Kindle Edition, 11. See also Bill Van Niekerken, "Rainbow Gold Mine: Early SF Pride Parade Photos Rediscovered in Archive," *San Francisco Chronicle*, June 26, 2019.
2. The Bay Area's burgeoning gay community had social and political influence. One of those who had arrived in the migration to San Francisco was Harvey Milk; he made history in 1977 when he ran and won a seat on the city's board of supervisors. Milk was California's first openly gay elected official. When he and the city's progressive mayor were assassinated by a disgruntled former supervisor the following year, Milk's death was a chilling reminder that although tremendous gains had been made in only a few years, homophobia still flourished. Dudley Clendinen and Adam Nagourney, *Out for Good: The Struggle to Build a Gay Rights Movement in America* (New York: Simon & Schuster, 1999) 151–55; Shilts, *And the Band Played On*, 15–17; Jennifer Robison, "What Percentage of the Population Is Gay?" Gallup Poll, October 8, 2002.
3. Randy Shilts, broadcast commemorating Stonewall, June 22 1979, Bay Area Television Archive, KQED Collection, (Public Television, San Francisco), San Francisco State University.
4. The Consenting Adult Sex Bill did not repeal the state's sodomy and oral copulation laws, but instead excluded private consensual activity between adults over the age of eighteen. See Assembly Bill 489, January 15, 1975.
5. Clendinen and Nagourney, *Out for Good*, 151.

6. Among two dozen San Francisco bathhouses was the Bulldog Baths, the world's largest in the seedy Tenderloin district. It was a two-story bondage/leather reproduction of nearby San Quentin prison. In 2012, the shuttered building was listed in the National Register of Historic Places. The decision to list the building on the federal government's register of historic places was not without controversy. Some leaders of the San Francisco gay community thought the Bulldog's contribution to gay history was not one that deserved historic recognition. On the other hand, Back2Stonewall, a popular online LGBT news site, wrote at the time: "The Bull Dog was an architectural playground for the fantasies of gay sexual desires. It is a historic place in gay history and it's good to see that the National Registry of Historic Places recognizes that even though many in our own community won't." Will Kohler, "National Register of Historic Places Recognizes San Francisco's Bulldog Baths With Historical Plaque," Back2Stonewall, September 22, 2012. Miller HG, Turner CF, Moses LE, editors.
7. David Cheng, "Amyl Nitrites: A Review of History, Epidemiology, and Behavioral Usage," *Journal of Student Research*, vol. 2, no. 1, 2013; 17–21.
8. Sevgi O Aral et al., "Sexually Transmitted Diseases In The USA: Temporal Trends," *Sexually Transmitted Infections* vol. 83, no. 4 (2007): 257–66.
9. Dale O'Leary, "The Syndemic of AIDS and STDS among MSM [men who have sex with men]," *Linacre Quarterly,* vol. 81, no. 1 (2014): 12–37.
10. "AIDS and the Blood Supply," chapter 5 in *AIDS: The Second Decade* (National Research Council, Committee on AIDS Research and the Behavioral, Social, and Statistical Sciences), (Washington, D.C.: The National Academies Press, 1990).
11. William J. Woods et al., "Facilities and HIV Prevention in Bathhouse and Sex Club Environments," *Journal of Sex Research* 38, no. 1 (2001): 68–74; see also Shilts, *And the Band Played On,* 19.
12. Thomas R. Blair, "Safe Sex in the 1970s: Community Practitioners on the Eve of AIDS," *American Journal of Public Health* 107, no. 6 (June 1, 2017): 872–79.
13. Giving credence to the idea that sex acts could be considered part of the political Gay Liberation movement, a left-wing alternative Toronto newspaper hailed rimming as "a revolutionary act."
14. Shilts, *And the Band Played On*, 18–19.
15. Janice Hopkins Tanne, "Fighting AIDS: On the Front Lines Against the Plague," *New York*, January 12, 1987, 24–25.
16. Donna Mildvan quoted in Ibid., 25.
17. Ibid., 27.
18. Harry Mobley, "How Do Antibiotics Kill Bacterial Cells But Not Human Cells?" *Scientific American,* March 13, 2006.
19. Iulia Filip, "Avoiding the Black Plague Today," *Atlantic*, April 11, 2004.
20. Joan Trossman Bien, "The Swine Flu Vaccine: 1976 Casts A Giant Shadow," *Pacific Standard*, December 4, 2009; "Why Can't We Beat Viruses?," BBC News, January 24, 2013.
21. Lawrence K. Altman, "Rare Cancer Seen in 41 Homosexuals," *New York Times*, July 3, 1981. In a 2014 interview, Altman told *The Atlantic* that he had been intending to write a story in the spring, but it got delayed to the summer because he had been assigned to cover the attempted assassination of Pope John Paul II that May. See Cari Romm, "'The Disease of the Century': Reporting on the Origin of AIDS," *Atlantic*, December 5, 2014.
22. Romm, "'The Disease of the Century.'"

23. Tanne, "Fighting AIDS," 25.
24. The first medical paper about the symptoms and cases that would later be identified as AIDS was in December 1981: M. S. Gottlieb et al., "Pneumocystis Carinii Pneumonia And Mucosal Candidiasis In Previously Healthy Homosexual Men: Evidence Of A New Acquired Cellular Immunodeficiency," *NEJM*, December 10, 1981, 305(24):1425–31. As for the early descriptions of the mystery illness as being unique to the gay community, see André Picard, "How the Advent of AIDS Advanced Gay Rights," *Globe and Mail* (Canada), August 15, 2014, updated May 12, 2018; "News From the Front Lines of the AIDS Fight," Newscenter, Univeristy of Rochester, December 1, 2016. See Myrna Watanabe, "AIDS 20 Years Later," *Scientist*, June 11, 2001. See also "July 2, 1981, Bay Area Reporter" listing in 1981 on the Timeline of HIV and AIDS at HIV.gov.
25. Dr. Samuel Broder, Oral History Collection, National Institutes of Health, Historical Office, U.S. National Library of Medicine. Bethesda, MD, February 5, 1997. The medical records for that first paitent were subsequently "lost, misplaced, or something happened to them."
26. The CDC description of what was now believed to be a new virus was "A disease at least moderately predictive of a defect in cell-mediated immunity, occurring in a person with no known cause for diminished resistance to that disease." See the September 24 listing in 1982 on the Timeline of HIV and AIDS at HIV.gov.
27. Tom Curtis, "The Origin of AIDS," *Rolling Stone*, issue 626, March 19, 1992; see also Tom Curtis Papers, The Wittliff Collections, Texas State University; David Secko, "Polio Vaccine-AIDS Theory Dead," *Scientist*, April 21, 2004; M. Worobey et al., "Origin of AIDS: Contaminated Polio Vaccine Theory Refute; Kisangani Chimpanzees Contain a Virus Unrelated to HIV-1," *Nature*, Vol. 428 [6985], April 22, 2004; Mitch Leslie, "Study Pushes AIDS Origins Back to 1930s," *Science*, June 9, 2000; Jon Cohen, "Vaccine Theory of AIDS Origins Disputed at Royal Society," *Science*, Vol. 289, Issue 5486, September 15, 2000; Stanley A. Plotkin and Hilary Koprowski, "Responding to The River," *Science*, Vol. 286, Issue 5449, 2449, December 24, 1999; Jon Cohen, "Disputed AIDS Theory Dies its Final Death," *Science*, Vol. 292, Issue 5517, April 27, 2001. And see Richard Horton, "New Data Challenge OPV Theory of AIDS Origin," *Lancet*, Vol. 356, Issue 9234, September 16, 2000; Sarah Ramsay, "Cold Water Downstream from *The River*," *Lancet*, Vol. 357, Issue 9265, April 28, 2001; Helen Branswell, "HIV's Genetic Code, Extracted From A Nub Of Tissue, Adds To Evidence Of Virus' Emergence In Humans A Century Ago," *STAT*, July 16, 2019.
28. Herpes, which was possibly the most widespread sexual disease in the 1970s, was the same DNA family from which Kaposi sarcoma and cytomegalovirus developed. High rates of parasitic infections added to the overall toll on the immune system. Infectious disease experts later concluded that unprotected anal intercourse was the highest sexual risk factor for HIV. John Tierney, "The Big City; In 80's, Fear Spread Faster Than AIDS," *New York Times*, June 15, 2001. And see Trenton Straube, "Against All Odds: What Are Your Chances of Getting HIV in These Scenarios?" *POZ*, March 26, 2014.
29. Altman quoted in Cari Romm, "'The Disease of the Century': Reporting on the Origin of AIDS," *Atlantic*, December 5, 2014.
30. Another key person was Dr. Bruce Chabner, chief of the Division of Cancer Treatment.
31. Broder says most scientists who steered clear of AIDS did not want to risk their

reputations. They thought the pressure from HIV/AIDS activists meant they would have to rush. Instead, their attitude was, "A cure or nothing. Give me 20 years and I'll give you a cure." Dr. Samuel Broder, Oral History Collection, NIH.

32. Tanne, "Fighting AIDS."
33. Filip, "Avoiding the Black Plague Today."
34. "Pneumocystis Carinii Pneumonia Among Persons With Hemophilia A," *Morb Mortal Wkly Rep*. 1982;31:365–67; Gilbert C. White, II, "Hemophilia: An Amazing 35-Year Journey From The Depths Of HIV To The Threshold Of Cure," *Transactions of the American Clinical and Climatological Association* vol. 121 (2010): 61–73; see figure 1.
35. Dr. Samuel Broder, Oral History Collection, NIH.
36. Renowned sex researchers William Masters and Virginia Johnson wrote a book, *Crisis: Heterosexual Behavior in the Age of AIDS*, in which they warned that AIDS could be potentially caught from a public toilet seat. Another pioneer sex therapist, Helen Singer Kaplan, published *The Real Truth About Women and AIDS*, in which she warned that condoms might not provide protection against infection and claimed even kissing was risky. Dr. Samuel Broder, Oral History Collection, NIH. See also Tierney, "The Big City; In 80's, Fear Spread Faster Than AIDS."
37. Simon Garfield, "The Rise And Fall Of AZT," *Independent* (UK), May 2, 1993.
38. Broder quoted in Ibid.
39. Broder quoted in Celia Farber, "AIDS and the AZT Scandal: SPIN's 1989 Feature, 'Sins of Omission,'" *SPIN*, October 5, 2015.
40. At the peak of the AIDS epidemic, July of 1988, the New York City health commissioner, Dr. Stephen Joseph, reduced the city's estimate of infected New Yorkers from 400,000 to 200,000. The leaders of ACT UP, the AIDS Coalition to Unleash Power, were furious, convinced he lied to cover up the gravity of the epidemic and thereby cut city funding to battle it. Activists demanded his resignation and dogged him at public appearances. They picketed at his home and spray-painted his car. Police protection was assigned after he got death threats. Dr. Joseph rescinded his reduced estimate and restored it to 400,000. Thirteen years later *The New York Times* reported: "Now it turns out that Dr. Joseph's estimate [of 400,000] was actually too high. It might have been twice the actual figure, according to a new report from the American Council on Science and Health, a science advocacy group. The total number of AIDS cases diagnosed in New York City from 1981 through early 2000 was less than 120,000." Tierney, "The Big City; In 80's, Fear Spread Faster Than AIDS."
41. Picard, "How the Advent of AIDS Advanced Gay Rights."
42. Daniel J. DeNoon, "AIDS Worse Than Black Death," WebMD, January 25, 2002.
43. Matt Ridley, "Apocalypse Not: Here's Why You Shouldn't Worry About End Times," *Wired*, August 17, 2012.
44. The Health Department investigator was Anastasia Lekatsas, whom the *New York Times* journalist John Tierney dubbed "America's most dogged street detective of AIDS." Lekatsas had examined the New York Health Department's NIR cases (no identified risk). "If a man claimed to have gotten AIDS from a woman, she would visit him, revisit him, interview his family and friends—and eventually she would almost always find that he'd been sharing needles or having sex with men." Regarding the eight men listed by the New York Health Department as having been infected as heterosexuals, she told the *Times*, "I have doubts about seven of them, but we couldn't prove anything." See Tierney, "The

Big City; In 80's, Fear Spread Faster Than AIDS." See also K. G. Castro et al., "Investigations of AIDS Patients With No Previously Identified Risk Factors," *JAMA*, 259(9), 1988,1338–42.

45. Tierney, "The Big City; In 80's, Fear Spread Faster Than AIDS."
46. Patrick J. Buchanan and J. Gordon Muir, "Gay Times and Diseases," *The American Spectator*, August 1984.
47. Ronald Reagan, Appointment of Patrick J. Buchanan as Assistant to the President and Director of Communications Online by Gerhard Peters and John T. Woolley, The American Presidency Project, https://www.presidency.ucsb.edu/node/259289.
48. Picard, "How the Advent of AIDS Advanced Gay Rights," and see "Homophobia and HIV," *Avert*, at https://www.avert.org/professionals/hiv-social-issues/homophobia.
49. "Some people had hoped that AZT would be a cure," says Broder. "No one at NIH ever said that it would be. . . . We always chose our words cautiously and specifically. It was simply a starting point. But without AZT . . . we would have been very hard pressed to make any progress in the therapy of the AIDS virus." D. Fajardo-Ortiz et al., "The Emergence and Evolution of the Research Fronts in HIV/AIDS Research," *PLoS One*. 2017;12(5); Ghobad Moradi et al., "Health Needs of People Living with HIV/AIDS: From the Perspective of Policy Makers, Physicians and Consultants, and People Living with HIV/AIDS," *Iranian Journal of Public Health* vol. 43,10 (2014): 1424; Dr. Samuel Broder, Oral History Collection, NIH.
50. Alice Park, "The Story Behind the First AIDS Drug," *Time*, March 19, 2017.
51. Farber, "AIDS and the AZT Scandal."
52. "AZT's Inhuman Cost," *New York Times* editorial, August 28, 1989, A16.
53. Ibid.
54. Garfield, "The Rise And Fall Of AZT."
55. Harry Jupiter, "18 Protestors Arrested at AIDS-Drug Firm," *San Francisco Examiner*, January 25, 1988, B1.
56. Victoria F. Zonana, "Firm to Offer AIDS Drug Free in Critical Cases," *Los Angeles Times*, July 14, 1989, 1, 39.
57. Mikami, "Orphans in the Market," 609–30.
58. Ibid.
59. Sarah Jane Tribble and Sydney Lupkin, "Drugs For Rare Diseases Have Become Uncommonly Rich Monopolies," *NPR Morning Edition*, January 17, 2017; Michael Henry Davis et al., "Rare Diseases, Drug Development and AIDS: The Impact of the Orphan Drug Act," 73 *Milbank Quarterly* 231 (1995). See also Mikami, "Orphans in the Market."
60. Davis et al., "Rare Diseases, Drug Development and AIDS."
61. Malorye A. Branca, "How the Orphan Drug Act Changed the Development Landscape," *BioPharma Dive*, April 10, 2017.
62. Tribble and Lupkin, "Drugs For Rare Diseases Have Become Uncommonly Rich Monopolies."
63. Davis et al., "Rare Diseases, Drug Development and AIDS."
64. See generally P. S. Arno et al., "Rare Diseases, Drug Development, And AIDS: The Impact Of The Orphan Drug Act," *Milbank Q*. 1995;73(2):231–52.
65. Davis et al., "Rare Diseases, Drug Development and AIDS."
66. Off-label dispensing is legal, set out in the Food, Drug, and Cosmetic Act of 1938.

That was the same law that empowered the FDA to regulate drugs, medical devices, food, and cosmetics. See D. C. Radley et al., "Off-Label Prescribing Among Office-Based Physicians." *Arch Intern Med* 2006 May 8;166(9):1021–26.

67. The generic is a combination of emtricitabine and tenofovir disoproxil fumarate. The FDA's approved label indication for the orphan on September 28, 2017, is "DESCOVY, indicated in combination with other antiretroviral agents, for the treatment of HIV-1 infection in adults and pediatric patients weighing at least 35 kg and also indicated, in combination with other antiretroviral agents other than protease inhibitors that require a CYP3A inhibitor, for the treatment of HIV-1 infection in pediatric patients weighing at least 25 kg and less than 35 kg."
68. Christopher Rowland, "An HIV Treatment Cost Taxpayers Millions. The Government Patented It. But a Pharma Giant Is Making Billions," *Washington Post*, March 26, 2019.
69. Robert M. Grant et al., "Preexposure Chemoprophylaxis for HIV Prevention in Men Who Have Sex with Men," *NEJM*, December 30, 2010, 363:2587–99.
70. James Krellenstein, Aaron Lord, and Peter Staley, "Why Don't More Americans Use PrEP?," *New York Times*, July 16, 2018.
71. Ibid.

Chapter 37: "None of the Public's Damned Business"

1. The Martha Graham Dance Company performed before two thousand guests.
2. It was a far cry from an ostentatious seventieth birthday gala that Mortimer hosted for himself a decade later at the Temple of Dendur. The highlight was a four-foot-high cake resembling a Sphinx with Mortimer's face. In a cringeworthy rambling speech, he said that collecting art was like masturbation, an orgasm could only be delayed so long. Arthur told another guest it "was vulgar." His friends recalled that on his seventieth birthday a few years earlier, he had marked it with a private dinner for some close friends. Author interview with business partner of Arthur Sackler, December 2018.
3. The forty-one-year-old Montebello was a surprise choice after a special committee of six trustees spent nearly six months conducting an intensive international search for a new director. He transformed the museum in his thirty-one-year tenure, the longest in the institution's history. Leah Shanks Gordon, "Help Wanted at the Met," *New York Times*, June 26, 1977; Calvin Tomkins, "The Importance of Being Élitist," *New Yorker*, Nov 24, 1997, 75; Charles McGrath, "Twilight of the Sun King," *New York Times*, July 29, 2007.
4. Arthur complained constantly that Montebello was defiling Dendur's "sacred" enclosure by using it as the setting for dinner parties. Arthur griped that a Diana Vreeland fete for fashion designer Valentino was "disgusting." Worse was a dinner for designer Pierre Cardin that drew Norman Mailer, Andy Warhol, Estée Lauder, Betsy Bloomingdale, Atlantic Records president Ahmet Ertegun, and talent agent Swifty Lazar, among others. "It was an everybody-who-is-anybody guest list," wrote John Duka in the next day's *New York Times*. Duka was a style and fashion industry reporter and Sackler pointed to that as the epitome of what was wrong with how Montebello used the family's wing. McGrath, "Twilight of the Sun King."
5. Lee Rosenbaum, "The Met's Sackler Enclave: Public Boon or Private Reserve?"

ARTnews, September 1978, 56–57; John L. Hess, "Can the Met Escape King Tut's Curse?," *New York*, November 13, 1978, 82.

6. Hess, "Can the Met Escape King Tut's Curse?," 83.
7. Ibid., 79.
8. Hoving File memo, Dec. 29, 1982, and memos to Phil Herrera, Jan. 1, 2, 1983, Hoving Papers, cited in Michael Gross, *Rogues' Gallery: The Secret Story of the Lust, Lies, Greed, and Betrayals That Made the Metropolitan Museum of Art* (New York: Random House, 2009), Kindle Edition, 346. The New York State attorney general ultimately found no liability for Sackler, but sharply chastised the Met for the arrangement. Testimony of Sol Chaneles, chairman of Rutgers University Department of Criminal Justice, cited in Hess, "Can the Met Escape King Tut's Curse!," 86. Chaneles had been on assignment for *ARTnews* when he uncovered the secret Sackler storage room at the Metropolitan. The Society of Silurians, a distinguished press club of veteran reporters and editors, awarded *ARTnews* a journalism award for Lee Rosenbaum's two-part "The Care and Feeding of Donors" and "The Met's Sackler Enclave." Grace Glueck, "An Art Collector Sows Largesse and Controversy," *New York Times*, June 5, 1983; "Protecting the Public Interest in Art," *The Yale Law Journal*, Vol. 91, No. 1 (November 1981), 121–43. See also Milton Esterow, "Reflections on Three Decades at the Helm of ARTnews," *ARTnews*, November 1, 2002.
9. Gross, *Rogues' Gallery*, 338–39. Also, author interview with Sonnenreich, February 23, 2019.
10. Lutze, *Who Can Know the Other?*, 165.
11. Press reports often spell the name as Gillian. The same spelling was used in court litigation in the 1990s. However, in an announcement from the Smithsonian about a $5 million endowment she made in 2012, it was Jillian. In her own public statements it is Jillian, which is the one in this book.
12. "Design Notebook: A Remarkable Maisonette on Park Ave," *New York Times*, July 16, 1981. Jillian Sackler lives there today. See also Christopher Gray, "The Real 666 Park Avenue," *New York Times*, September 27, 2012.
13. Glueck, "Art Collector Sows Largesse and Controversy."
14. George Bulanda, "The Legacy of Charles L. Freer," *Detroit Hour*, February 7, 2008.
15. Meyer is the author of a dozen books. He was a foreign affairs reporter before serving on the *New York Times* and *Washington Post* editorial boards.
16. British architect James Stirling was retained to complete the Sackler Museum and also to renovate the Fogg Museum, directly across the street. Grace Glueck, "Sackler Art Museum To Open At Harvard," *New York Times*, October 18, 1985.

Chapter 38: A Pain Management Revolution

1. "John Bonica, Pain's Champion and the Multidisciplinary Pain Clinic," Relief of Pain and Suffering, John C. Liebeskind History of Pain Collection, Box 951798, History & Special Collections, UCLA Louise M. Darling Biomedical Library, Los Angeles, CA.
2. Ibid.
3. Medical historians pick that time as the unofficial beginning of the pain management field.
4. Frank Brennan, "Decade on Pain Control and Research 2001–2011: A Review,"

Journal of Pain & Palliative Care Pharmacotherapy, (2015) 29:3, 212–27; Edward Helmore, "Enduring Pain: How A 1996 Opioid Policy Change Had Long-Lasting Effects," *Guardian*, March 30, 2018.

5. Victor Cohn, "Study Lowers Estimate Of Prescription Drug Toll," *Washington Post*, February 28, 1977, A3.
6. "Addiction Rare in Patients Treated With Narcotics," Correspondence, *NEJM*, January 10, 1980, Vol. 302, No. 2, 123.
7. Sarah Zhang, "The One-Paragraph Letter From 1980 That Fueled the Opioid Crisis," *Atlantic*, June 2, 2017.
8. Ibid.
9. The number of times it was subsequently cited is evidence of its impact. In comparison, there were eleven other letters published in that same *NEJM* issue; they were cited on average fewer than ten times each. Pamela T. M. Leung et al., "A 1980 Letter on the Risk of Opioid Addiction," *NEJM*; June 1, 2017, 376:2194–95.
10. Ibid. Before the Jick-Porter letter, a 1977 study about drugs that treated chronic headache sufferers had sometimes been cited for the thesis that powerful pain relievers were not terribly addictive. That study was not persuasive, however, since its statistics did not support the "low risk of addiction" theory. Fifty-five patients had taken a combination of nonnarcotic analgesics and barbiturates or codeine. The report listed eight as "dependent," six physically addicted, two "psychologically dependent," and five as "abusers." See Jose L. Medina and Seymour Diamon, "Drug Dependency in Patients with Chronic Headaches," presented at the eighteenth annual meeting of the American Association for the Study of Headache, Dallas, Texas, June 26, 1976.
11. Leung et al., "A 1980 Letter on the Risk of Opioid Addiction," and "Painful Words: How A 1980 Letter Fueled The Opioid Epidemic," Associated Press, *STAT News*, May 31, 2017.
12. Ronald Melzack, "The Tragedy of Needless Pain," *Scientific American*, February 1990, Vol. 262, No. 2, 27, 29.
13. Sam Allis, "Less Pain, More Gain," *Time*, June 24, 2001.
14. The WHO report was the product of a commission of anesthesiologists, neurologists, pharmacologists, and oncologists. It warned that "not enough is done to control pain in cancer patients" and that an underlying reason for "unsatisfactory" pain management was "fears concerning 'addiction' both in cancer patients and in the wider public." Cancer Pain Relief, World Health Organization, Geneva, 1986, 79 pages, publication in collection of author.
15. A UCLA researcher, John Liebeskind, coined the term "non-malignant chronic pain" to describe persistent pain in patients who did not have cancer. He contended that most doctors were "dangerously wrong" in not appreciating that "pain can devastate lives . . . kill by leading to suicide" and "accelerate tumor growth." R. K. Portenoy and K. M. Foley, "Chronic Use of Opioid Analgesics in Non-Malignant Pain: Report of 38 Cases," *Pain*, 25(2):171–86, May 1986; "Pain can kill!" later draft, 1990, John C. Liebeskind History of Pain Collection, History & Special Collections, UCLA Louise M. Darling Biomedical Library.
16. "At Work: Neurologist Kathleen Foley," Memorial Sloan Kettering Cancer Center, at https://www.mskcc.org/experience/physicians-at-work/kathleen-foley-work.
17. Portenoy and Foley, "Chronic Use of Opioid Analgesics in Non-Malignant Pain."
18. Ibid.
19. Oral history interview of Dr. Kathleen Foley, by Marcia L. Meldrum, in the

Liebeskind History of Pain Collection, History & Special Collections, UCLA Louise M. Darling Biomedical Library.

20. Portenoy had become acquainted with the benefits of opioid painkillers for cancer patients at Memorial Sloan Kettering Hospital in New York. Portenoy and Foley, "Chronic Use of Opioid Analgesics in Non-Malignant Pain."
21. Portenoy, as of 2019, is executive director and chief medical officer of the Institute for Innovation in Palliative Care at the MJHS, a not-for-profit Brooklyn health care organization. He is also a neurology professor at the Albert Einstein College of Medicine. Foley, after eight years running the George Soros–funded Project on Death in America, is an attending neurologist in the Pain and Palliative Care Service at Memorial Sloan Kettering Cancer Center.
22. Max quoted in Joseph R. Schottenfeld et al., "Pain and Addiction in Specialty and Primary Care: The Bookends of a Crisis," *The Journal of Law, Medicine and Ethics*, July 17, 2018. vol 46, no. 2: 220–37.
23. That was a concept light-years removed from the early-nineteenth-century medical view that since "pain was one of God's punishments for the wicked and purifying trials for the good," doctors should not interfere by treating it. Natalia E Morone and Debra K Weiner, "Pain As The Fifth Vital Sign: Exposing The Vital Need For Pain Education," *Clinical Therapeutics*, November 2013, vol. 35, no. 11 (2013): 1729.
24. The Veterans Administration adopted it in 1999. "At Work: Neurologist Kathleen Foley," Memorial Sloan Kettering Cancer Center, https://www.mskcc.org/experience/physicians-at-work/kathleen-foley-work. See *State of Indiana v. Purdue Pharma L.P. et al.*; Brennan, "Decade on Pain Control and Research 2001–2011"; Morone and Weiner, "Pain As The Fifth Vital Sign."
25. S. A. Dunbar et al., "Chronic Opioid Therapy For Nonmalignant Pain In Patients With A History Of Substance Abuse: Report of 20 Cases," *J Pain Symptom Management* 1996;11:163–71; D. T. Cowan et al., "A Randomized, Double-Blind, Placebo-Controlled, Cross-Over Pilot Study To Assess The Effects Of Long-Term Opioid Drug Consumption And Subsequent Abstinence In Chronic Noncancer Pain Patients Receiving Controlled-Release Morphine," *Pain Med* 2005; 6:113–21; F. S. Tennant Jr. et al., "Narcotic Maintenance For Chronic Pain. Medical And Legal Guidelines." *Narc Maintenance* 1983;73:81–94; F. S. Tennant et al., "Chronic Opioid Treatment Of Intractable, Nonmalignant Pain," *Pain Management* 1988;Jan/Feb:18–26; A. Taub et al., Opioid Analgesics In The Treatment Of Chronic Intractable Pain Of Non-Neoplastic Origin," *Narcotic Analgesics in Anesthesiology* 1982:199–208; R. K. Portenoy, Chronic Opioid Therapy In Nonmalignant Pain, *J Pain Symptom Management* 1990;5:46–62; F. S. Tennant et al., "Chronic Opioid Treatment Of Intractable, Nonmalignant Pain." *NIDA Res Monogr* 1988;81:174–80; G. Schaffer-Vargas et al., "Opioid for Non-Malignant Pain Experience," 9th World Congress on Pain, 1999;289:345; B. J. Urban et al., "Long-Term Use Of Narcotic/Antidepressant Medication In The Management Of Phantom Limb Pain," *Pain* 1986;24:191–96; M. Zenz et al., "Long-Term Oral Opioid Therapy In Patients With Chronic Nonmalignant Pain," *J Pain Symptom Management* 1992;7:69–77; K. Milligan et al., "Evaluation Of Long-Term Efficacy And Safety Of Transdermal Fentanyl In The Treatment Of Chronic Noncancer Pain," *J Pain* 2001;2:197–204; D. E. Moulin et al., "Randomised Trial Of Oral Morphine For Chronic Non-Cancer Pain," *The Lancet* 1996;347:143–47; J. Porter and H. Jick. "Addiction Rare In Patients Treated With Narcotics," *NEJM*

1980; 302:123; N. Doquang-Cantagrel et al., "Tolerability And Efficacy Of Opioids In Chronic Nonmalignant Pain," *Addiction* 1991; 722:129; A. J. Bouckoms et al., "Chronic Nonmalignant Pain Treated With Long-Term Oral Narcotic Analgesics," *Ann Clin Psychiatry* 1992;8:185–92; R. N. Jamison et al., "Opioid Therapy For Chronic Noncancer Back Pain. A Randomized Prospective Study," *Spine* 1998;23:2591–600; R. D. France et al., "Long-Term Use Of Narcotic Analgesics In Chronic Pain," *Soc Sci Med* 1984;19:1379–82; M. J. Kell, "Long-Term Methadone Maintenance For Intractable, Nonmalignant Pain: Pain Control And Plasma Opioid Levels," *AJPM* 1994;4:10–16; D. T. Cowan et al., "A Survey Of Chronic Noncancer Pain Patients Prescribed Opioid Analgesics," *Pain Med* 2003; 4:340–51; W. S. Mullican and J. R. Lacy, "Tramadol/Acetaminophen Combination Tablets And Codeine/Acetaminophen Combination Capsules For The Management Of Chronic Pain: A Comparative Trial," *Clin Ther* 2001;23:1429–44.

26. Some studies were more than sixteen weeks; three followed patients for twenty-four months. Mark D Sullivan and Catherine Q Howe, "Opioid Therapy For Chronic Pain In The United States: Promises And Perils," *Pain* vol. 154 Suppl 1,0 1 (2013), 94–100.
27. The medical description given was "an iatrogenic syndrome resulting from poorly treated pain" where the patient exhibits behavior of "psychological dependency." D. E. Weissman and J. D. Haddox, "Opioid Pseudoaddiction—An Iatrogenic Syndrome," *Pain* 1989 Mar;36(3):363–66.
28. "Definitions Related to the Use of Opioids for the Treatment of Pain," Consensus Statement of the American Academy of Pain Medicine, the American Pain Society, and the American Society of Addiction Medicine, approved by the American Academy of Pain Medicine Board of Directors on February 13, 2001, the American Pain Society Board of Directors on February 14, 2001, and the American Society of Addiction Medicine Board of Directors on February 21, 2001 (replacing the original ASAM Statement of April 1997), published 2001.
29. The study's researchers did not find empirical data to support the pseudoaddiction theory. Marion S Greene and R. Andrew Chambers, "Pseudoaddiction: Fact Or Fiction? An Investigation Of The Medical Literature," *Curr Addict Rep* (2015) 2:310–17. Other prominent pain specialists offered theories as to why opioids had what they considered an undeservedly bad reputation. Several experts in 1988 concluded that "mental disorders" of some chronic pain patients "had led to substance abuse among prescription opioid users [rather] than prescription opioids themselves." The 2008 article has a comprehensive discussion of previous studies as well as the underlying theory. Mark J. Edlund et al., "Do Users of Regularly Prescribed Opioids Have Higher Rates of Substance Use Problems Than Nonusers?" *Pain Medicine*, Vol 8, no. 8, November 2007, 647–56.
30. Sidney H. Wanzer et al., "The Physician's Responsibility toward Hopelessly Ill Patients. A Second Look," *NEJM*, March 30, 1989, 320(13):844–49.
31. Others include federal Intractable Pain Regulation (1974); and the state laws in Virginia (1988), Texas (1989), California (1990), Colorado (1992), Washington (1993), and Florida (1994).
32. R. K. Portenoy, "Appropriate Use Of Opioids For Persistent Non-Cancer Pain," *Lancet*, August 28, 2004, vol. 364, no. 9436, 739–40.
33. For some historical overview on the debate over whether there should be a maximum dose, see L. R. Webster and P. Fine, "Approaches To Improve Pain Relief While Minimizing Opioid Abuse Liability," *J Pain*. 2010;11(7):602–11.

34. The pain reevaluation proponents are similar to today's cannabis advocates who push for much wider acceptance of medical or recreational marijuana. Will it be the panacea that some predict or will it turn into diversion to the illicit market and abuse resulting in human and financial costs from accidents, lost productivity, hospitalizations, and yet-to-be-discovered adverse effects of long-term use? As with opioids, it might take twenty years to get the definitive answer. And as with opioids, the experiment will be run with millions of patient guinea pigs. The difference is that no matter what the potential downside of the widespread dissemination of legalized marijuana, it is unlikely to be lethal on its own.
35. Thomas Catan and Evan Perez, "A Pain-Drug Champion Has Second Thoughts," *Wall Street Journal*, December 17, 2012; "ASPMN Backs Pain Champion: Russell Portenoy," *Pain Management Nursing*, Vol. 14, Issue 1, 1–2.
36. The rivals with opioid painkillers in the 1990s were Johnson & Johnson, Janssen, Mylan, and Endo.
37. The American Society for Pain Management Nursing, in 2012, said: "It is not only repugnant but deeply disturbing to link Pharma monies to pro-opioid proselytizing; impugning both the science and merit of the subsidized research." "ASPMN Backs Pain Champion: Russell Portenoy," *Pain Management Nursing*, March 2013 vol. 14, no. 1, 1–2.
38. Russell Portenoy on ABC's *Good Morning America*, July 20, 2010.
39. Catan and Perez, "A Pain-Drug Champion Has Second Thoughts." That interview with the other physician was videotaped. Dr. Portenoy refused the author's requests for an interview or to answer questions by email.

Chapter 39: Enter Generics

1. Ron A. Bouchard et al., "Empirical Analysis of Drug Approval-Drug Patenting Linkage for High Value Pharmaceuticals," 8 *Nw. J. Tech. & Intell. Prop*. 174 (2010). See also Austin Frakt, "How Patent Law Can Block Even Lifesaving Drugs," *New York Times*, September 28, 2015.
2. The Hatch-Waxman Act of 1984 attempted to correct some of the time lost while drugs were pending approval, but it gave five additional years only when a drug qualified as a "new chemical entity," words that sometimes got mired in years of litigation. Garth Boehma, LixinYaoa Liang, Hanab Qiang Zhengac, "Development of the generic drug industry in the US after the Hatch-Waxman Act of 1984," Acta Pharmaceutica Sinica B, Volume 3, Issue 5, September 2013; Kesselheim, "The High Cost of Prescription Drugs in the United States: Origins and Prospects for Reform," *JAMA*, 861.
3. Kesselheim, "The High Cost of Prescription Drugs in the United States." As of 2018 it was as high as twelve years. Katherine Ellen Foley, "Big Pharma Is Taking Advantage of Patent Law to Keep OxyContin From Ever Dying," *Quartz*, November 18, 2017.
4. It has ballooned to $2.7 billion on average in 2018.
5. It is the same in the U.K., a twenty-year patent protection from the date of discovery, and instances in which some drugs took a decade or more before approval and the start of public sales. See "Briefing for the Public Relations Committee," Subject: Wholly Owned National Private Pharmaceuticals, PE1608, August 16, 2016, Scottish Parliament Information Centre. See also T. H. Stanley, "The History Of Opioid Use In Anesthetic Delivery," Chapter 48 in Eger EI II, Saidman

LJ, Westhorpe RN (eds): *The Wondrous Story of Anesthesia* (New York: Springer, 2014).

6. Matthew Herper, "Solving The Drug Patent Problem," *Forbes*, May 2, 2002.
7. Katie Thomas, "Pfizer Races to Reinvent Itself," *New York Times*, May 1, 2012.
8. Those were Pfizer, Abbott Laboratories, Johnson & Johnson, Eli Lilly, Merck, and Bristol-Myers Squibb.
9. The pharma firms that were the most active buyers of biotech companies were Novartis, Pharmacia & Upjohn, Warner-Lambert, Glaxo-Wellcome, Smith-Kline Beecham, and Hoechst-Marion Roussel. "Conference Proceedings—Consolidation in the Pharmaceutical Industry," *Semantic Scholar*, 2001.
10. Kelli Miller, "Off-Label Drug Use: What You Need to Know," WebMD, June 2009.
11. Darshak Sanghavi, "Cooking The Books: The Statistical Games Behind 'Off-Label' Prescription Drug Use," *Slate*, December 21, 2009.
12. That becomes somewhat alarming in light of a study that later demonstrated more than half of the off-label use "may have insufficient scientific support . . . [and] may result in inadequate efficacy or an unjustified risk of harm to the patient." D. C. Radley et al., "Off-Label Prescribing Among Office-Based Physicians," *Arch Intern Med* 2006;166: 1021–26.
13. Meyers, H*appy Accidents*, 4688 of 6459; Henry Grabowski, "The Evolution of the Pharmaceutical Industry Over the Past 50 Years: A Personal Reflection," *Int. J. of the Economics of Business* vol. 18, no. 2, July 2011, 16.
14. A. S. Kesselheim and J. Avorn, "Pharmaceutical Promotion to Physicians and First Amendment Rights," *NEJM*, 2008;358(16): 1730.
15. M. S. Kinch et al., "An Overview Of FDA-Approved New Molecular Entities: 1827–2013," *Drug Discovery Today*. 2014 Aug;19(8):1033–39; Kesselheim, "Pharmaceutical Promotion to Physicians," 1730.
16. Kesselheim, "Pharmaceutical Promotion to Physicians."
17. See Rebecca Dresser and Joel Frader, "Off-Label Prescribing: A Call For Heightened Professional And Government Oversight," *The Journal Of Law, Medicine & Ethics* (The American Society Of Law, Medicine & Ethics) vol. 37,3 (2009): 476–86, 396. See also Kesselheim, "Pharmaceutical Promotion to Physicians.".
18. Ajaj Raj, "How A Doctor's Chance Appointment With A Hairy Woman Led To The Discovery of Rogaine," *Business Insider*, September 26, 2014.
19. Gina Kolata, "Hair-Growth Drug Approved, The First Cleared in the U.S.," *New York Times*, August 18, 1988, A1. Author interview with Bill Winkowski, retired pharmacist, about the standard practice of extracting minoxidil by crushing hundreds of Loniten tablets, April 2, 2019.
20. Abraham Morgentaler, *The Viagra Myth: The Surprising Impact On Love And Relationships* (San Francisco: Jossey Bass, 2003).
21. Lisa Beebe, "Viagra Turns 20: The History Of The 'Little Blue Pill,' " *Romanhood*, February 12, 2018.
22. Ibid., and see "Rogaine—Pharma's Biggest Flops," *Fierce Pharma*.
23. A pharmacist, Gavin Herbert Sr., had started Allergan in 1950 in a room above his drugstore. It was named after an anti-allergy nose drop developed by his business partner, Stan Bly, a chemist. "Taking A Chance On Botox Paid Off For Allergan," *Ocular Surgery News*, U.S. Edition, June 10, 2018.
24. Dr. Alan Scott quoted in "Botox: A Story With a Few Wrinkles," CBS News, April 15, 2002.
25. "The Government has approved a type of food poisoning bacteria for use as a

treatment for two eye muscle disorders." "Eye Drug Approved By F.D.A.," *New York Times*, January 9, 1990, C6.

26. Lucy Rock, "Is America Developing a 'Crack-Like Addiction' to Botox Beauty?" *Observer* (UK), January 7, 2017.
27. It is such a powerful toxin that even today powdered botulinum toxin the size of a pea is enough to supply all the Botox dispensed worldwide. Cynthia Koons, "The Wonder Drug for Aging (Made From One of the Deadliest Toxins on Earth)," *Businessweek*, October 26, 2017.
28. See generally "Pharmacia & Upjohn Company to pay the largest criminal fine ever imposed in the U.S.," *Medical Life Sciences*, October 19, 2009.
29. Joseph G. Contrera, "The Food and Drug Administration and the International Conference on Harmonization: How Harmonious Will International Pharmaceutical Regulations Become?" 8 *Admin. L.J. Am. U.* 1995; (927), 934 n.26.
30. E. Colman, "Anorectics on Trial: A Half Century of Federal Regulation of Prescription Appetite Suppressants," *Annals of Internal Medicine* 2005;143(5):380–85.
31. "The future of Pfizer's $5bn Lyrica brand is in jeopardy," *Pharmaceutical Technology*, November 21, 2018; Ben Hirschler, "Pfizer Loses Drug Patent Fight in UK Top Court, May Face Claims," Reuters, November 14, 2018.
32. C. W. Goodman and A. S. Brett, "A Clinical Overview of Off-label Use of Gabapentinoid Drugs," *JAMA Intern Med.* 2019;179(5):695–701.
33. Jane Brody, "Millions Take Gabapentin for Pain. But There's Scant Evidence It Works," *New York Times*, May 20, 2019.
34. As for its worldwide ranking, it was at #9 for 2012–2014, #10 in 2017 and 2018, #11 in 2011, #12 in 2016, and #13 in 2015. See "Lyrica, The Top Pharma List: Top 50 pharmaceutical products by global sales ranking is compiled from GlobalData." *PMLive*.
35. See generally Comprehensive Drug Abuse Prevention and Control Act, Pub. L. 91-513, 84 Stat. 1242 (1970) (codified as amended at 21 U.S.C. §§ 801-971).
36. Robin Feldman et al., "Empirical Evidence of Drug Pricing Games—A Citizen's Pathway Gone Astray," (September 1, 2016). 20 *Stan. Tech. L. Rev.* 39 (2017).
37. "How Much Haven for Drug Pioneers?," Editorial, *New York Times,* June 25, 1984, 33.
38. William Haddad, president of the Generic Trade Association, quoted in Philip M. Boffey, "Accord May Lead to Cheaper Drugs," *New York Times,* June 2, 1994.
39. Ibid.
40. Richard Lyons, "Demoralized FDA Struggles to Cope," *New York Times,* March 14, 1977.
41. Thomas Ascik, "Report: The Drug Regulation Act, (S.2755–H.R. 11611), The Heritage Foundation, June 21, 1978.
42. Philip J. Hilts, "F.D.A. Commissioner Reassigned In Aftermath of Agency Scandals," *New York Times*, November 14, 1989, B13.
43. Harry Low and Tom Heyden, "The Rise and Fall of Quaaludes," *BBC News Magazine,* July 9, 2015.
44. Lee Linder, "Quaalude Manufacturer: Image Hurt By Street Use," *Lawrence Journal-World* (Lawrence, KS), May 28, 1981, 6.
45. Boffey, "Accord May Lead to Cheaper Drugs."
46. *Roche Prods. Inc. v. Bolar Pharm. Co.*, 733 F.2d 858 (Fed. Cir. 1984), cert. denied, 469 U.S. 856 (1984), 860. See also *Hoffmann-La Roche, Inc. v. Weinberger*, 425 F. Supp. 890, 892–93 (D.D.C.) 1975.

47. Stuart Diamond, "Upjohn Cuts Price of Top-Selling Drug," *New York Times*, July 12, 1984; Boffey, "Accord May Lead to Cheaper Drugs."
48. *FDA Consumer* Vol. 19, U.S. Department of Health, Education and Welfare, Public Health Service, FDA, (Washington, D.C.: Government Printing Office, 1985), 28.
49. Tamar Levin, "Drug Makers Fighting Back Against Advance of Generics," *New York Times,* July 28, 1987, 1.
50. Boffey, "Accord May Lead to Cheaper Drugs."
51. Milt Freudenheim, "Executive Changes at LaRoche," *New York Times*, December 5, 1992.
52. Levin, "Drug Makers Fighting Back."
53. Stuart Diamond, "Upjohn Cuts Price of Top-Selling Drug," D5.
54. Public Law 98-417. It passed 362–0 in the House, and in the Senate by a voice vote, with a notation of not a single "nay" vote.
55. Nearly twenty years later (2013), the percentage of physicians with a negative opinion of generics was still at 50 percent. Katie Thomas, "Why the Bad Rap on Generic Drugs," *New York Times*, October 5, 2013.
56. Aaron S. Kesselheim et al., "Clinical Equivalence Of Generic And Brand-Name Drugs Used In Cardiovascular Disease: A Systematic Review And Meta-Analysis." *JAMA* vol. 300,21 (2008): 2514–26.
57. Levin, "Drug Makers Fighting Back."
58. Sales dropped from $294 million in 1984 to $185 million in 1986. Ibid.
59. The figures are from Arthur D. Little.
60. "We're not anti generic," said Martin Brodie, the director of the Epilepsy Institute, "we believe that people who start on generics should stay on them. But based on the anecdotes we've heard, we are concerned about switching." Levin, "Drug Makers Fighting Back."
61. "Seminar Briefs Lawmakers On How Prescription Drug Reimbursement Affects Access To Care," *American Journal of Hospital Pharmacy*, Vol 44, no. 10, October 1, 1987, 2197–98.
62. M. J. Grinfeld, "Ex-Profs Charged in Psych Department Research Scam," Vol. 14, no. 4, *Psychiatric Times*, April 1, 1997; "Drug Money: Medical Trials Run Without Real Doctors," reported by Laura Spencer, *48 Hours*, CBS News, July 31, 2000. See also Steve Stecklow and Laura Johannes, "Drug Makers Relied on Two Researchers Who Now Await Trial," *Wall Street Journal*, August 18, 1997, A1.
63. Ibid.
64. Borison's colleague, pharmacologist Bruce Diamond, was convicted and given a five-year sentence, and CBS's *48 Hours* dubbed Borison "the mastermind." "Drug Money," CBS News.
65. When generics are available, patients select them 94 percent of the time. Two of the largest ten generic manufacturers are subdivisions of traditional drug firms, the Sandoz division of Novartis is third and Pfizer is fourth. See generally Kathlyn Stone, "Top Generic Drug Companies," *The Balance*, May 10, 2018. Author interview with former business partner of Arthur Sackler, November 2018.

Chapter 40: Selling Hearts and Minds

1. Roy Vagelos and Louis Galambos. *Medicine, Science, and Merck* (New York: Cambridge University Press, 2004), 142.

2. Gambardella, *Science and Innovation*, 95.
3. Ibid.
4. From $570.1 million to $229.2 million. *Moody's Industrial Manual*, 1989.
5. In 1991, for instance, Zantac was the top selling drug in America, with $3 billion in revenues and a 10 percent annual growth rate. Tagamet was still a big seller, the seventh best with $1 billion. It had a negative growth rate, however, of 2.2 percent. The gap between the two grew during the 1990s. "Top Ten Pharmaceutical Products in 1991," *Financial Times*, 1992.
6. As Smith Kline cut back, it no longer attracted the best research scientists. Another blow came when Dr. James Black, a Scottish pharmacologist who led the team that developed Tagamet, and later won a Nobel for that breakthrough, left the company.
7. Don Kazak, "Syntex Lays Off 1,000 Employees," *Palo Alto Online*, January 18, 1995; see also Gambardella, *Science and Innovation*, 93–102.
8. Vagelos and Galambos, *Medicine, Science, and Merck*, 56–57, 208–9.
9. His full name was Pindaros Herodotus Vagelos. Roy is the anglicized version of his middle name. He liked pointing out that he was born only three weeks before the 1929 stock market crash, so his parents were under financial distress from his birth. While he was at the University of Pennsylvania, he interned at the Merck laboratory in Rahway, New Jersey, for what he later described as "one unexciting summer."
10. Vagelos and Galambos, *Medicine, Science, and Merck*, 101.
11. John Simon, "The $10 Billion Pill: Hold the fries, please: Lipitor, the cholesterol-lowering drug, has become the bestselling pharmaceutical in history. Here's how Pfizer did it," *Fortune*, January 20, 2003.
12. It was Aspergillus terreus.
13. Merck licensed the active drug in Pepcid, the first time the company had not released a drug that was developed from inception inside its lab. It had lost several years of getting into the ulcer treatment field by pursuing a different line of research that proved fruitless. Vagelos and Galambos, *Medicine, Science, and Merck*, 130–31. Its one billion a year in revenue included later OTC sales in a partnership with consumer goods giant Procter & Gamble.
14. Peter A. Kreckel, "The First Billion-Dollar Drug," Vol. 162, no. 1, *MJH Life Sciences*, January 11, 2018.
15. Gina Kolata, "Companies Search for Next $1 Billion Drug," *New York Times*, November 28, 1988, D1.
16. John A. Byrne, "The Miracle Company," *Businessweek*, October 19, 1987, 88.
17. Vagelos and Galambos, *Medicine, Science, and Merck*, 250.
18. Transcript of speech by George W. Merck, "Medicine Is for the Patient, Not for Profits," December 1, 1950, available in full at https://www.merck.com/about/our-people/gw-merck-doc.pdf.
19. Luke Whelan, "This Company Gave Away a Drug That Just Won the Nobel Prize and Helped Millions," *Mother Jones*, October 5, 2015.
20. Vagelos and Galambos, *Medicine, Science, and Merck*, 193–94.
21. Kolata, "Companies Search for Next $1 Billion Drug."
22. "Mega-Merger Mania Hits Pharmaceutical Industry," *The Pharma Letter* (TPL), March 2, 1998; Melody Petersen, "Pfizer Gets Its Deal to Buy Warner-Lambert for $90.2 Billion," *New York Times*, February 8, 2000.
23. Vagelos and Galambos, *Medicine, Science, and Merck*, 208–9.

24. Ibid., 200.
25. Scott Holleran, "The History of HMOs," *Capitalism Magazine*, November 1, 1999.
26. Transcript of taped conversation between Richard Nixon and John Ehrlichman (1971), University of Virginia—February 17, 1971, 5:26 pm–5:53 pm, Oval Office Conversation 450-23. Tape rmn_e450c.
27. The idea of partial coverage for a limited number of medications was borrowed from inpatient prescription formulary lists developed originally by hospitals. Robert Goldberg, "Managing the Pharmacy Benefit: The Formulary System," *Journal of Managed Care Pharmacy*, Vol. 3, No. 5, September/October 1992, 565.
28. N. R. Kleinfield, "The King of the H.M.O Mountain," *New York Times*, July 31, 1983, 132, 153.
29. "History of the Kaiser Permanente Medical Care Program," *Kaiser Thrive* at http://www.kaiserthrive.org/kaiser-permanente-history/.
30. Vagelos and Galambos, *Medicine, Science, and Merck*, 201.
31. Helene L. Lipton et al., "Pharmacy Benefit Management Companies: Dimensions of Performance," *Annual Review of Public Health* 1999 20:1, 361–401.
32. Ellen Schultz, "Merck Is No. 1 For The Second Year In A Row, IBM Falls Out Of The Magic Circle To No. 32, And Two Tobacco Companies Make It Into The Top Ten For The First Time," *Fortune*, January 18, 1988.
33. Jennifer Reese, "America's Most Admired Corporations: What Lies Behind A Company's Good Name?" *CNN Money*, February 8, 1993.
34. Carpenter, *Reputation and Power*, 666. Gardiner Harris, "How Merck Survived While Others Merged—Drug Maker Relied on Inspired Research," *Wall Street Journal*, January 12, 2001.
35. Barry Werth, *The Billion-Dollar Molecule* (New York: Simon & Schuster, 1995).

Chapter 41: "No One Likes Airing Dirty Laundry in Public"

1. In fact, by the time MS Contin went on sale, there was already competition from a rival morphine pill boasting its version of a time release delivery. Fortunately for Purdue, an independent clinical trial compared the two and concluded that MS Contin was by far the more effective drug. L. M. Sherman, "The use of sustained-release morphine in a hospice setting." *Pharmatherapeutica*, 1987;5(2):99–102.
2. In the U.K., Napp's exclusive patent was issued in 1980 and was set to expire in 1992. The drug accounted for more than half of Napp's income, although it had (and would) release seven other painkillers. See "Decision Of The Director General Of Fair Trading No Ca98/2/2001 in the matter of Napp Pharmaceutical Holdings Limited And Subsidiaries (Napp)," pursuant to the Competition Act 1998, March 30, 2001, 72 pages, in collection of author; Katherine Ellen Foley, "Big Pharma Is Taking Advantage of Patent Law to Keep OxyContin From Ever Dying," *Quartz*, November 18, 2017.
3. Herper, "Solving The Drug Patent Problem."
4. Kesselheim et al., "The High Cost of Prescription Drugs in the United States," 861. See also Joanna Shepherd, "The Prescription for Rising Drug Prices: Competition or Price Controls?" 27 *Health Matrix* 315 (2017).
5. The cost of discovering, developing, testing, and getting approval for a new class of drugs was prohibitively expensive. Large pharmaceutical firms avoided medications they thought had potential sales of less than $200 million. That was the market Purdue and smaller drug firms targeted. Stanley, "The History Of Opioid

Use In Anesthetic Delivery"; Deposition of Richard Sackler, Commonwealth of KY v. Purdue Pharma L.P., August 28, 2015, 14–17 (hereinafter Richard Sackler Deposition). See also Theodore H. Stanley, "The Fentanyl Story," *The Journal of Pain*, vol 15, no 12 (December), 2014: 1215–26.

6. *City of Jersey City, New Jersey v. Purdue Pharma L.P. et al.*, District of New Jersey, njd-2:2018-cv-11210, Complaint, filed June 28, 2018, 13.
7. Deposition of Richard Sackler, 17.
8. Ibid., 17–18.
9. One had settled on morphine and the other utilized hydromorphone, a semisynthetic opioid.
10. On the patent applications reviewed by the author, in the instances in which rights were assigned to Euro-Celtique (sometimes spelled Euroceltique), the assignors were Mortimer and Raymond Sackler, joined sometimes by Dr. Alfred Halpern, and occasionally Sackler-owned companies also assigned their interests. Those firms included Purdue Frederick, Gray Pharmaceutical, and Synergistics. The eighteen patents located by the author for the Mundipharma or Euro-Celtique transfers included five from U.S. See generally U.S Patent Office applications 3440320, 4954351, 3325472, 3471617, 3360535.
11. FDA Statement quoted in Miranda Hitti, "Palladone Pain Drug Pulled Off the Market," *WebMD*, July 14, 2005. Besides Palladone, other Napp painkillers consisted of oxycodone and dihydrocodeine, a weaker synthetic opioid based on codeine as well as buprenorphine, which has antagonist properties that can wean addicts from opioids. Napp also produced nonnarcotic painkillers, Remedeine and Remedeine Forte, a combination of acetaminophen and dihydrocodeine. Decision Of The Director General Of Fair Trading No Ca98/2/2001 in the matter of Napp Pharmaceutical Holdings Limited.
12. R. F. Kaiko et al., "The United States Experience With Oral Controlled-Release Morphine (MS Contin Tablets). Parts I And II. Review Of Nine Dose Titration Studies And Clinical Pharmacology Of 15-Mg, 30-Mg, 60-Mg, And 100-Mg Tablet Strengths In Normal Subjects," *Cancer*, 1989 Jun 1;63(11 Suppl):2348–54.
13. Deposition of Richard Sackler, 20.
14. Author interview with former Purdue assistant marketing manager, February 2017 and July 2018.
15. Philip J. Hilts, "F.D.A. Commissioner Reassigned In Aftermath of Agency Scandals," *New York Times*, November 14, 1989, B13.
16. Starr, *Blood*, 317.
17. Ibid.
18. Author interview with former Purdue assistant marketing manager, Feburary 2017.
19. Marie Curie was the only other person to win Nobels in two different fields (chemistry and physics). Frederick Sanger and John Bardeen were awarded two Nobels each, but in the same field, Sanger in chemistry and Bardeen in physics.
20. Michael Sonnenreich told the author that Sackler never complained about his health and seemed to be one "of the healthiest guys I knew." In the few weeks before his death, Sonnenreich recounted that Arthur was depressed and agitated over scathing reviews of a jewelry exhibition he held in London. Sonnenreich believes the stress from Sackler's first ever bad reviews contributed to his unexpected death. Sonnenreich interview 2-23-2019; Grace Glueck, "Dr. Arthur Sackler Dies at 73; Philanthropist and Art Patron," *New York Times*, May 27, 1987, B8.

21. Although the sales of SSRIs were double that of antianxiety medications in the 1990s, some firms bent the rules to sell even more. In 2010, Forest Laboratories pled guilty to a criminal count that it illegally promoted Celexa, its best-selling antidepressant, to children despite the FDA having blocked it for such use. Forest paid $313 million to settle those claims, and others against its successor SSRI, Lexapro. That fine was a fraction of what Forest had earned in profits on the two SSRIs. Herper, "America's Most Popular Mind Medicines." Sonnenreich interview 2-23-2019; Shorter, *Before Prozac*, 1383–87).
22. Arthur Sackler Probate Litigation; author interview with Sonnenreich, February 23, 2019.
23. Ibid.
24. Deirdre Carmody, "The Media Business; Springer's Medical Tribune To Start Publishing Today," *New York Times*, April 5, 1990, D22.
25. In The Matter Of The Estate Of Arthur M. Sackler, Deceased, Surrogate's Court, Nassau County, 145 Misc.2d 950 (N.Y. Misc. 1989).
26. Ibid.
27. In The Matter Of The Estate Of Arthur M. Sackler, Deceased, Surrogate's Court, Nassau County, 149 Misc.2d 734 (N.Y. Misc. 1990).
28. In The Matter Of The Estate Of Arthur M. Sackler, Deceased. Gillian T. Sackler, Respondent; Else Sackler, Appellant, Et Al., Respondent, Appellate Division of the Supreme Court of New York, Second Department.·193 A.D.2d 806 (N.Y. App. Div. 1993). Note that all litigation files have Jillian Sackler spelled as Gillian Sackler.
29. In The Matter Of The Estate Of Arthur M. Sackler, Deceased. Gillian T. Sackler, Respondent; Else Sackler, Appellant, Et Al., Respondent, Appellate Division of the Supreme Court of New York, Second Department.·192 A.D.2d 660 (N.Y. App. Div. 1993).
30. In The Matter Of The Estate Of Arthur M. Sackler, Deceased. Gillian T. Sackler, As Executor Of Arthur M. Sackler, Deceased, Appellant; Breed, Abbott Morgan, Respondent, Et Al., Respondents, 222 A.D.2d 9 (N.Y. App. Div. 1996).
31. In The Matter Of The Estate Of Arthur M. Sackler, Deceased. Gillian T. Sackler, Respondent; Else Sackler, Appellant, Et Al., Respondent, Appellate Division of the Supreme Court of New York, Second Department.·192 A.D.2d 536 (N.Y. App. Div. 1993).
32. In The Matter Of The Application Of The Final Account And Supplemental Account Of Carol Master, Arthur F. Sackler, Gillian T. Sackler And Michael R. Sonnenreich, And Carol Master And Elizabeth A. Sackler, As Executors Of The Estate Of Arthur M. Sackler, Deceased, John B. Riordan, Judge. 2008 [This case is unpublished, copy in collection of author]. See also Dec. No. 466, same judge, in 2007.
33. In The Matter Of The Settlement Of The Final Account And Supplemental Account Of Carol Master, Arthur F. Sackler, Gillian T. Sackler And Michael R. Sonnenreich, And Carol Master And Elizabeth A. Sackler, As Executors Of The Estate Of Else Sackler, As Executors Of The Estate Of Arthur M. Sackler, Deceased, Surrogate's Court, Nassau County, 2007 NY Slip Op 33226(U) (N.Y. Misc. 2007).
34. Author interview with Sonnenreich, Febraury 23, 2019.
35. Ibid.
36. "Arthur would have expected that Mortie and Ray would do the right thing," Sonnenreich believes. "He had always taken care of them since they were kids. He

expected they would have been fair with his children, no question in my opinion that he would have done it for them." Author interview with Sonnenreich, February 23, 2019.

37. As quoted by Barry Meier in *Pain Killer* and confirmed to the author by Sonnenreich.
38. The details only became public in an Audited Combined Financial statement of Purdue LP and associated companies, PRA holdings, Inc. and subsidiaries, Purdue Pharma Inc., AB Generics LP, Purdue Associates Inc., Purdue Associates LP, and Norwell Land Company, years ended Dec 31 1997 and 1996.

    A footnote on page 9 of a twenty-two page report of the independent auditors, Ernst & Young, dated April 9, 1998, states: "The note payable to the Estate of A.M. Sackler, MD bore interest at approximately 14% per annum, payable quarterly through November 13, 1996, at which time the interest rate decreased to 11.75% per annum through November 13, 1997. The note was secured by 250 shares of PRA Holdings, Inc.'s common stock and Mortimer D Sackler M.D. and Raymond R. Sackler M.D. each guaranteed one-half of all amounts due. The balance of the note was paid off on November 14, 1997." This footnote refers to a line item below "Number 6, Debt," showing a debt as of December 31, 1996 to AM Sackler estate of $19,654,000 and then nothing due as of the end of December 31, 1997.

    Some opioid case plaintiffs tried bringing Arthur Sackler's estate into the litigation by contending it profited from some Oxy money since the $22 million installment buyout of his Purdue share extended a year past the drug's sale date. However, the author has verified there was more than enough profit from other Purdue Frederick products to make the final installments to the estate without the need to rely on any OxyContin profits.

Chapter 42: "The Sales Department on Steroids"

1. Deposition of Richard Sackler, 19.
2. "Purdue Pharma Inc.'s 1991 filings with the Secretary of State of Connecticut state that it was incorporated in New York on October 2, 1990. Richard, Ilene, Jonathan, and Kathe Sackler are all listed as directors on the earliest (1991) report. Ilene and Kathe are Mortimer's daughters with his first wife. Dr. Muriel Lazarus Sackler. Beverly, Mortimer, and Theresa all appear on the 1995 report. *Commonwealth of Massachusetts v. Purdue Pharma L.P., et al.* Superior Court, C.A. 1884-cv-01808 (BLS2) (hereinafter *Massachusetts v. Purdue*). See also Jared S. Hopkins, "OxyContin Made The Sacklers Rich. Now It's Tearing Them Apart," *Wall Street Journal*, July 13, 2019, 1.
3. Purdue paid for and directed the trial on women recovering from gynecological and abdominal surgeries at two hospitals in Puerto Rico. Ninety women received one dose of OxyContin while the other patients got immediate release painkillers or placebos. Ryan, Harriet, Lisa Girion, and Scott Glover, "'You Want A Description Of Hell?' OxyContin's 12-Hour Problem," *Los Angeles Times*, May 5, 2016.
4. Deposition of Richard Sackler, 20–21.
5. Starting with this chapter, unless specified otherwise, Purdue refers to both Purdue Pharma Inc. and Purdue Pharma LP. Purdue Pharma Inc. is a New York company with its principal place of business in Stamford, Connecticut. Purdue Pharma LP is a Delaware limited partnership with its operating office at the same Connecticut address. As for Purdue Frederick acting as the holding company for

Purdue Pharma Inc. and Purdue Pharma LP, see Deposition of Richard Sackler, 20.

6. Deposition of Richard Sackler, 22.
7. Ibid., 22–24.
8. Ibid., 20.
9. Incorporation documents and Articles of Incorporation in collection of author.
10. A review by the author of the company's audited financial statements for the year in which the family members assumed director's positions reveals they held control over a consortium of companies beyond those with "Purdue" in the title. Some associated companies over which they exerted control through PRA Holding Company included AB Generics, Norwell Land, PF Laboratories, and Blair Labs. See Audited Combined Financial statements, Purdue LP and associated companies, PRA holdings, Inc. and subsidiaries, Purdue Pharma Inc., AB generics LP, Purdue Associates Inc., Purdue Associates LP, and Norwell Land Company, years ended Dec 31 1997 and 1996, Report of the independent auditors Ernst & Young dated April 9, 1998, 22 pages, in collection of author.

    Richard Sperber, himself a marketing executive at publicly traded pharmaceutical companies, did business with many privately held drug and biotech firms. "Purdue was always tightly controlled," he told the author. "However, almost all those family-held companies were like that, they always thought they knew how to run it better than anyone else." Sperber says that based on his experience, the most control was usually exerted when the companies were run by doctors, as was the case with the Sackler brothers and Richard Sackler taking the lead for the next generation of the family. "They are the worst because they are obnoxious and think they know how to do marketing," Sperber says. Colleagues of his at private companies often shared stories about how the founders micromanaged the business. Author interview with Richard Sperber, March 26, 2019.
11. By 2000, only three of the top ten pharma companies had not been involved in any mergers or acquisitions. Anna Bonomi and Oana Pop, "Implications of Consolidation in the Pharma & Biotech Sector," *Sustainalytics*, December 12, 2018.
12. On average, $138 million in the 1970s and approximately $800 million in the early 1990s.
13. Pisano, "Can Science be a Business?"
14. "1980s: Arteries, AIDS and Engineering," part of "Ten Decades of Drug Discovery, The Pharmaceutical Century," *ACS Publications*.
15. Grabowski, "The Evolution of the Pharmaceutical Industry," 169.
16. Ibid.
17. Raymond had persuasively made the case that the name should include "contin" since MS Contin had earned a good reputation among dispensing doctors and was recognized as a Purdue product. "Oxy" was an abbreviated way of signaling the active ingredient was oxycodone, not morphine.
18. Paul Goldenheim sworn declaration, 2003, cited in Ryan, Girion, and Glover, "You Want A Description Of Hell?"
19. Patent 5,549,912, filed November 25, 1992, granted on August 27, 1996, in collection of author.
20. In 2001, *The Medical Letter on Drugs and Therapeutics* concluded OxyContin offered no therapeutic advantage over equivalent doses of immediate release opioids. In 2003, that was confirmed in randomized double-blind studies that compared OxyContin and comparable opioids for chronic back pain and can-

cer pain. R. Kaplan et al., "Comparison Of Controlled-Release And Immediate-Release Oxycodone In Cancer Pain," *J Clin Oncol* 1998;16:3230–37; T. Heiskanen et al., "Controlled-Release Oxycodone And Morphine In Cancer Related Pain," *Pain* 1997;73:37–43; P. Mucci-LoRusso et al., "Controlled-Release Oxycodone Compared With Controlled-Release Morphine In Treatment Of Cancer Pain: A Randomized, Double-Blind, Parallel-Group Study," *Eur J Pain* 1998;2:239–249; B. S. Berman et al., "Randomized, Double-Blind, Cross-Over Trial Comparing Safety And Efficacy Of Oral Controlled-Release Oxycodone With Controlled-Release Morphine In Patients With Cancer Pain," *J Clin Oncol* 1998;16:3222–29; J. E. Staumbaugh et al., "Double-Blind, Randomized Comparison Of The Analgesic And Pharmacokinetic Profiles Of Controlled- And Immediate-Release Oral Oxycodone In Cancer Pain Patient," *J Clin Pharmacol* 2001;41:500–506; "Oxycodone and OxyContin," *Med Lett Drugs Ther* 2001, 43:80–81; "New Drug Application for OxyContin." Purdue Pharma, Stamford, CT, December 1995.

21. In addition to the six controlled clinical trials, the company did four less rigorous studies and fourteen pharmacokinetic studies. More than seven hundred subjects were involved in all. See "Approval Package for: Application Number: NDA 20-553/S-002, Trade Name: OXYCONTIN 80 mg, Generic Name: (oxycodone hydrochloride controlled release tablets), Sponsor: Purdue Pharma LP, Approval Date: December 9, 1996, Indication: Provides for 80 mg green colored tablets as a line extension to the approved 10, 20 and 40 mg tablets," Center For Drug Evaluation And Research, FDA. See also Ryan, Girion, and Glover, "You Want A Description Of Hell?"
22. Pat Beall, "Purdue Pharma Plants The Seeds Of The Opioid Epidemic In A Tiny Virginia Town And Others," Investigation: "Igniting the Heroin Epidemic," *The Palm Beach Post*, January 31, 2019.
23. Raymond Sackler, the author learned, liked to say, only partly in jest, that Purdue's marketing department would have been hard pressed to outdo the persuasive presentations of their star lecturers. United Food and Commercial Workers Health Fund of Northeastern Pennsylvania v. Purdue Pharma et al., case 2:17-cv-05078-TJS, filed 11/09/17, Document 1, 42–46.
24. "Prescription Drugs: OxyContin Abuse and Diversion and Efforts to Address the Problem," Washington, DC: General Accounting Office; December 2003. Publication GAO-04-110.
25. Andrew Joseph, "Purdue Cemented Ties With Universities And Hospitals To Expand Opioid Sales, Documents Contend," *STAT*, January 16, 2019.
26. "In 1980, three Sackler brothers, through a very large payment, established the Sackler School of Graduate Biomedical Sciences. Later, in 1999, the Sackler family made a more targeted gift, establishing Tufts Masters of Science in Pain Research, Education, and Policy." *Massachusetts v. Purdue*, 93; Rick Seltzer, "'Deeply Troubling' Allegations," *Inside Higher Ed*, January 21, 2019.
27. In March 2019, Tufts retained Donald Stern, a former U.S. attorney, to conduct an independent investigation of whether Purdue had manipulated Tufts to promote its narcotic painkillers. Andrew Joseph, "'We Owe Much to the Sackler Family': How gifts to a top medical school advanced the interests of Purdue Pharma," *STAT*, April 9, 2019. In December, the school announced it would remove the Sackler name from all buildings and programs.
28. Michael Joyce, "Pharma Backing of Advocacy Groups: A Call for Transparency," *Health News Review*, March 7, 2018.

29. *County Of Wayne and Country of Oakland v. Purdue Pharma*, USDC Eastern District of Michigan, 17-cv-13334-JCO-EAS, Exhibit 57, General Financial Information for the American Pain Foundation.
30. John Fauber, "Academics Profit By Making the Case for Opioid Painkillers," *MedPage Today*, April 3, 2011.
31. Ibid. From 2009 to 2012, Purdue gave the American Pain Society nearly $500,000 and the American Academy of Pain Medicine more than $400,000. Purdue gave APS another $500,000 and AAPM more than $700,000 between 2012 and 2017.
32. *ProPublica*'s database is at https://projects.propublica.org/docdollars/. The partial listing of 2009 to 2013 payments is at https://projects.propublica.org/d4d-archive/.
33. In 2019, a respected group of international researchers proposed a revised definition of pain. The International Association for the Study of Pain suggested changes that would cover situations in which the discomfort was not simply from a physical cause but might also be the result of "an aversive sensory and emotional experience." Emotional or mental connections to pain would not need opioid medications for treatment, a goal of the proposed changes. See Dawn Rae Downtown, "Who Is Really Behind a Proposed New Definition of Pain?" *STAT*, September 5, 2019.
34. Gigen Mammoser, "Is OxyContin Losing Its Luster?" *Healthline*, February 21, 2018.
35. Tony Dokoupil, "America's Long Love Affair With Anti-Anxiety Drugs," *Newsweek*, January 21, 2009.
36. They were all men then, the first detail women started in the late 1950s. Carl Elliott, "The Drug Pushers," *The Atlantic*, April 2006; see Tone, *Age of Anxiety*, 72,
37. Goldacre, *Bad Pharma*, 89 of 7421.
38. Email from Russell Gasdia, Purdue vice president, 02-07-2012, *Massachusetts v. Purdue*, document LPC012000368569.
39. Ryan, Girion, and Glover, "You Want A Description Of Hell?".
40. Ibid.
41. Holcomb B. Noble, "A Shift in the Treatment of Chronic Pain," *New York Times*, August 9, 1999.
42. Urging patients to "overcome" any "concerns about addiction" was the main message on the Purdue-sponsored website, In The Face of Pain, 14.
43. Purdue internal strategy presentation, *Massachusetts v. Purdue*, 2009-11 FACETS, slide 9, document PTN000006436.
44. "Website capture, In the Face of Pain, 2011-10-24," *Massachusetts v. Purdue*, document PVT0033890–891.
45. "Exit Wounds (2009), pg. 107," and "Opioid Prescribing: Clinical Tools and Risk Management Strategies (2009), pg. 12," *Massachusetts v. Purdue*, documents PTN000023114 and WG000242087.
46. Art Van Zee, "The Promotion And Marketing Of OxyContin: Commercial Triumph, Public Health Tragedy," *American Journal Of Public Health* vol. 99,2 (2009): 221–27.
47. Sales reps told doctors that in instances in which some patients "became physiologically dependent . . . addiction is rare." *Massachusetts v. Purdue*, "Opioid Prescribing: Clinical Tools and Risk Management Strategies (2009), pg. 12," document PWG000242087.
48. See for instance, "I Got My Life Back," Purdue Pharma LP, transcript of video

presentation by Dr. Alan Spanos, 1998; *Massachusetts v. Purdue*, document PDD9521403504. See also Barry Meier, *Pain Killer*, 99.

49. *The Anatomy of Sleep, Roche Laboratories*, Div of Hoffmann-LaRoche Inc (Roche: Nutley, NY, 1966), 111, in collection of author.
50. Resource Guide for People with Pain (2009), pg. 8, *Massachusetts v. Purdue*, document PVT0037321.
51. Beall, "Purdue Pharma Plants The Seeds Of The Opioid Epidemic."
52. See email from John Stewart, senior Purdue executive, later CEO, 2008-02, *Massachusetts v. Purdue*, document PPLPC012000172201. See also two Purdue studies published in 2013 regarding "abuse potential" of crushed or altered OxyContin, documents PTN000002031-2034 and PTN000002031-2044. Purdue revised its OxyContin label to refer to those studies.
53. Kelly R. Cohen et al., "Relationship Between Drug Company Funding And Outcomes Of Clinical Psychiatric Research," *Psychological Medicine*, 36(11), 1647–56, 2006.
54. Ibid. And see L. Bero et al., "Factors Associated with Findings of Published Trials of Drug–Drug Comparisons: Why Some Statins Appear More Efficacious than Others," *PLOS Medicine* 2007 Jun 5;4(6): e184.
55. Handwritten interview notes of Purdue sales manager Bill Gergely obtained by investigators for the Attorney General of Florida, Interview Notes 2/21/2003, 2 pages, included in litigation files in "Purdue And The OxyContin Files," *Kaiser Health News,* June 23, 2018.
56. The study David Sackler referred to was a meta-analysis of 6,164 articles and 12 studies involving more than 300,000 participants. The surprising conclusion was that when opioids were dispensed to treat pain, the "incidence of opioid dependence or abuse [was] 4.7%." C. Higgins et al., "Incidence Of Iatrogenic Opioid Dependence Or Abuse In Patients With Pain Who Were Exposed To Opioid Analgesic Therapy: A Systematic Review And Meta-Analysis," *British Journal of Anaesthesia*, vol 120, no. 6, 1335–44. In any case, David Sackler said "the FDA approved this medication," so it was their responsibility to protect patients, not an obligation of Purdue. See also Bethany McLean, " 'We Didn't Cause The Crisis': David Sackler Pleads His Case On The Opioid Epidemic," *Vanity Fair*, August 2019.
57. Author interview with assistant marketing manager, July 2018.
58. P. R. Chelminski et al., "A Primary Care, Multi-Disciplinary Disease Management Program For Opioid-Treated Patients With Chronic Non-Cancer Pain And A High Burden Of Psychiatric Comorbidity," *BMC Health Serv Res.* 2005;5(1):3; M. F. Fleming et al., "Reported Lifetime Aberrant Drug-Taking Behaviors Are Predictive Of Current Substance Use And Mental Health Problems In Primary Care Patients," *Pain Med*, 2008;9(8):1098–1106.
59. See joint statement, "Use of Opioids For The Treatment Of Chronic Pain. A Consensus Statement From The American Academy Of Pain Medicine And The American Pain Society," *Clin J Pain.* 1997;13(1):6–8.
60. Joyce, "Pharma Backing of Advocacy Groups: A Call for Transparency."
61. That incredibly low figure was simply a calculation of the numbers in the letter to the *NEJM* sixteen years earlier (four cases of addiction out of 11,882 patients). By the time of the joint statement, while the details of the *NEJM* letter had been forgotten, what stuck was its dramatic conclusion. It had become so enshrined as an accepted fact inside the emerging pain management field that no

one challenged it. Dr. J. David Haddox, the inventor of pseudoaddiction, chaired a joint commission. By this time, Haddox, with dual specialities in anesthesiology and behavioral medicine and psychiatry, was one of the most successful lecturers in Purdue's speaker's bureau. Another successful Purdue-sponsored lecturer, Dr. Portenoy, was retained by the two pain societies as their single consultant to help draft the joint language.

62. Zoe Matthews, "AG: North Andover doctor was top prescriber of OxyContin," *Eagle Tribune* (North Andover, MA), February 6, 2019. See also Patrick D. Wall and Ronald Melzack. *Textbook of Pain*. 3rd ed. Edinburgh; Churchill Livingstone, 1994, 341; Dennis C. Turk and Ronald Melzack, eds. *Handbook of Pain Assessment.* New York, Guilford Press, 1992, 262.
63. The contract was between Purdue Pharma LP and IMS Health Strategic Technologies, a wholly owned subsidiary of IMS. See "Purdue Pharma Selects IMS HEALTH Strategic Technologies to Enhance Sales and Marketing Effectiveness, CORNERSTONE(TM) 3.0 Automation Solution to Support Purdue Pharma Sales Representatives," *PR Newswire*, September 14, 1998.
64. Elliott, "The Drug Pushers."
65. Also included in the prescribing habits was a new drug, Ultram, released the previous year by Ortho-McNeil. It was a weaker chemical cousin to oxycodone.
66. "OxyContin Marketing Plan, 1996," Purdue Pharma, Stamford, CT; Stolberg S, Gerth J., "High-tech stealth being used to sway doctor prescriptions," *New York Times,* November 16, 2000; Van Zee, "The Promotion and Marketing of OxyContin."
67. *Massachusetts v. Purdue*, paragraph 113, 39.
68. "Purdue Pharma Selects IMS HEALTH Strategic Technologies."
69. Author interview with assistant marketing manager, July 2018. Also, the Sacklers were irked that IMS sold its much more accurate prescribing info to any drug company that paid its asking price. "The result was an arms race of pharmaceutical gift-giving," wrote Carl Elliott, a physician and distinguished professor of bioethics, "in which reps were forced to devise ever-new ways to exert influence." Elliott, "The Drug Pushers."
70. "Treatment Options: A Guide for People Living with Pain," pg. 15, *Massachusetts v. Purdue*, document PWG000243995.
71. If pressed, the sales reps were instructed to backpedal slightly and declare that OxyContin provided a "quality of life we deserve." See "Treatment Options: A Guide for People Living with Pain," pg. 15, *Massachusetts v. Purdue*, document PWG000243995.
72. The marketing team developed some "reminder items" for the detail force visits to nursing and long-term-care facilities. For patients who had previous problems with opioids or were too ill for OxyContin, the sales reps were told to push Ryzolt, Purdue's brand name for tramadol, a less potent narcotic-like medication. Finally, since one of the most common side effects from opioids is constipation, the sales reps were reminded to sell Purdue Frederick's Senokot laxatives and Colace stool softener.
73. Purdue also underwrote a website promoting the book and its central theses. The author was a decorated Iraq combat veteran, Derek McGinnis, who had lost a leg in combat and suffered himself from chronic pain. The book was *Exit Wounds: A Survival Guide to Pain Management for Returning Veterans and Their Families.*

74. Jenni B. Teeters, "Substance Use Disorders In Military Veterans: Prevalence And Treatment Challenges," *Subst Abuse Rehabil* 2017: 8: 69–77.
75. Some of the publications included *Providing Relief, Preventing Abuse: A Reference Guide to Controlled Substance Prescribing Practices; Resource Guide for People with Pain; Clinical Issues in Opioid Prescribing; Opioid Prescribing: Clinical Tools and Risk Management Strategies; Responsible Opioid Prescribing.* One of their main websites was In the Face of Pain. As for the curriculums at schools, some included Purdue's underwriting of the Massachusetts General Hospital Purdue Pharma Pain Program and a complete degree program at Tufts University. See Joseph, "Purdue Cemented Ties With Universities And Hospitals To Expand Opioid Sales, Documents Contend," and Seltzer, " 'Deeply Troubling' Allegations."
76. An executive director of a leading California treatment center noted that medical schools spent so little time on the subject that "if you miss the three hours they spend on pain management, you've missed the entire curriculum." Kathryn Weiner, Executive Director of the American Academy of Pain Management, quoted in Doris Bloodsworth, "Pain Pill Leaves Death Trail," *Orlando Sentinel*, October 19, 2003, A19, A22.
77. Pat Anson, "Purdue Pharma's 'Misleading' Websites," *Pain News Network*, August 21, 2015; NY State AG filing on 2015. After the New York attorney general filed a complaint against Purdue for the misleading information on its In the Face of Pain website, Purdue subsequently closed it. All that remains as of 2019 is a single page that says in full: "Dear Pain Advocates: In the Face of Pain has been proud to serve the pain community since 2001. Please note that we have deactivated the website on October 1, 2015. It is our sincere hope that the information and materials available on this website have informed, equipped, and inspired you on your pain advocacy journey. With gratitude, Your Patient & Professional Relations Team at Purdue Pharma L.P."

    The date of the rollout, 2001, was early in what would become the dominance of the internet for consumers who wanted to quickly obtain information about health-related matters. There were more than thirty thousand websites devoted to health as of 2000 and by 2002, two thirds of respondents to a nationwide poll reported they went online to get health information. Fox and Fallows, 2003, Internet Health Resources, Pew Internet and American Life Project, Washington DC, July 16, 2004.
78. "Partners Against Pain's Pain Management Kit," *HCP Live Network*, August 21, 2011.
79. Review of five thousand pages of Purdue marketing documents released pursuant to Orlando Sentinel Freedom of Information lawsuit, detailed in Bloodsworth, "Pain Pill Leaves Death Trail,"
80. Sergey Motov, "Is There a Limit to the Analgesic Effect of Pain Medications?" *Medscape*, June 17, 2008.
81. Scott E. Hadland, "Association of Pharmaceutical Industry Marketing of Opioid Products to Physicians With Subsequent Opioid Prescribing," *JAMA Intern Med.* 2018;178(6):861–63. Seven hundred and thirty thousand Americans have died of drug overdoses from 1999 through 2018. That includes everything from heroin to mixtures of barbiturates and cocaine. The lethal overdoses involving only opioids account for about two thirds of the total. About half of all the opioid-related fatalities are from legally dispensed prescriptions. "Overdose Death Rates," National Institute on Drug Abuse, National Institutes of Health, revised January

2019. German Lopez and Sarah Frostenson, "How The Opioid Epidemic Became America's Worst Drug Crisis Ever, In 15 Maps And Charts," *Vox*, March 29, 2017.

82. 2011-10 Guidelines on Product Promotion: Comparative Claims Workshop, slide 12, *Massachusetts v. Purdue*, 67, 68.
83. "Partners Against Pain's Pain Management Kit."
84. Olga Khazan, "The New Heroin Epidemic," *The Atlantic*, October 30, 2014, and Beall, "Purdue Pharma Plants The Seeds Of The Opioid Epidemic." According to *Dopesick*: "$300,000 worth of OxyContin-branded scroll pens, $225,000 worth of OxyContin resource binders, and $290,000 worth of 'Pain: The Fifth Vital Sign' wall charts and clipboards," 28. See Purdue budgets in *Massachusetts v. Purdue*, each year presented with original slides at board meetings for which the Sackler-family directors voted to approve them. For example, 2015-11 budget for 2016, slides 24, 26, 49, documents PPLPC011000069975, -69977, -70000.
85. Bert Spilker, "The Benefits And Risks Of A Pack Of M&Ms," Narrative Matters, *Health Affairs*, March/April 2002; Goldacre, *Bad Pharma*, 4277 and 4291 of 7421. See also Elliott, "The Drug Pushers"; A. Fugh-Berman et al., "Following The Script: How Drug Reps Make Friends And Influence Doctors," *PLoS Med* 4(4): e150 (2007).
86. "Follow the Money: Pharmaceutical Manufacturer Payments and Opioid Prescribing Patterns in New York State," Report, New York State Health Foundation, June 12, 2018.
87. Hadland, "Association of Pharmaceutical Industry Marketing of Opioid Products to Physicians With Subsequent Opioid Prescribing."
88. Kanner was the chairman of Long Island Jewish Medical Center's Department of Neurology.
89. Portenoy and four other doctors are cited as "KOL, Key Opinion Leaders" in many of the lawsuits filed against Purdue. The theory is that their prominence helped make OxyContin widely acceptable to dispensing physicians. As of 2019, Portenoy had evidently agreed to help the plaintiffs in the litigation against Purdue in the hope he would be excluded as a party in any litigation. Larry McShane, "How Big Tobacco-Style Marketing Propels U.S. Opioid Crisis—And Powers $400B Pharma Industry," *New York Daily News*, June 24, 2017, and "Portenoy Opioid Talk Sparks Controversy," *Medpage Today*, September 29, 2014.
90. The authors revealed that in a recent survey more than half of physicians said they had decided not to dispense opioids since they were controlled substances. They worried that prescribing opioids might subject them to "regulatory scrutiny or . . . possibility of investigation." Portenoy and Kanner, *Pain Management: Theory and Practice*, 253, 254, 364–65.
91. In concluding a discussion about whether the drugs should be dispensed more widely, the two doctors admitted "this approach . . . is controversial." That did not prevent them from a "tentative" endorsement of "long-term opioid therapy for chronic nonmalignant pain." Their only caveat was the need for "appropriate controlled clinical trials." Portenoy and Kanner, *Pain Management*, 258–59, 268.
92. Ibid., 258–59.
93. "Pain and the Dying: The Hospice Movement and the Work of Cicely Saunders," Relief of Pain and Suffering, John C. Liebeskind History of Pain Collection.

Chapter 43: "$$$$$$$$$$$$$ It's Bonus Time in the Neighborhood!"

1. "New Hope for Millions of Americans Suffering from Persistent Pain," *PR Newswire*, May 31, 1996, exhibits to litigation, in collection of author.
2. Full-page advertisements in medical journals left no doubt about how long a single dose was supposed to last. "Remember, Effective Relief Just Takes Two." A spotlight lit two prescription cups, one labeled 8 AM and the other 8 PM. Ryan, Girion, and Glover, "You Want A Description Of Hell?"
3. "New Hope for Millions of Americans Suffering from Persistent Pain."
4. See as an example what happened in one state, Massachusetts, with the Purdue sales representatives and the targeted doctors. *Massachusetts v. Purdue*, para. 112–16, 39.
5. Ibid., para. 33, 12
6. Ibid., 114, 39.
7. Elliott, "The Drug Pushers."
8. 2018-02-18 deposition of Catherine Yates Sypek pg. 120; 2018-03-01 deposition of Timothy Quinn pg. 99, part of the court record in *Massachusetts v. Purdue.*
9. "If Only I Had a Brain," Planning and Effective Presentation, from Training and Development to Entire Field Force, Dept. Sales-9521, November 4, 1996, 3 pages.
10. Ryan, Girion, and Glover, "You Want A Description Of Hell?"
11. Wild interview in Greg Crister, *Generation Rx: How Prescription Drugs Are Altering American Lives, Minds, and Bodies* (New York: Houghton Mifflin Harcourt, 2005), 100.
12. Summary Review for Regulatory Action, from Sharon Hertz, MD, re Division Director Summary Review, Purdue Pharma, NDA 22272/027, Center for Drug Evaluation and Research, FDA, copy in collection of author.
13. 2013-10-29 Sales & Marketing presentation to the Board, *Massachusetts v. Purdue*, document PPLP004409989.
14. See chart "OxyContin Prices," *Massachusetts v. Purdue* para 68, 22. And Ryan, Girion, and Glover, "You Want A Description Of Hell?"
15. 2002-03-21 email from Merle Spiegel, *Massachusetts v. Purdue*, document PPLPC023000014497.
16. 2016-04-13 April Board meeting Commercial Update, slide 74, *Massachusetts v. Purdue*, document PPLPC016000286167.
17. Beall, "Purdue Pharma Plants The Seeds Of The Opioid Epidemic."
18. Ryan, Girion, and Glover, "You Want A Description Of Hell?"
19. Thomas Landon Jr., "Maker of OxyContin Reaches Settlement With West Virginia," *New York Times,* November 6, 2004.
20. "Is It Pain (2011)?," slide 6, *Massachusetts v. Purdue*, document PTN000007194.
21. 2013-08-27 Opioid dosage data press release, PWG000216270; 2012-10-01 internal Purdue analysis, pg. 22, *Massachusetts v. Purdue*, document PWG000226041.
22. 2013-07 Publication Plan for Long-Term Opioid Therapy for Chronic Non-Cancer Pain, 3, *Massachusetts v. Purdue*, document PWG000323550.
23. "An Assessment of Opioid-Related Overdoses in Massachusetts 2011–2015," Massachusetts Department of Public Health, August 2017.
24. "Prescription Drugs: OxyContin Abuse and Diversion and Efforts to Address the Problem," December 2003.
25. 2012-02-15 10-Year Plan, slide 33, *Massachusetts v. Purdue*, document PWG00016 4240.

26. 2012-11-01 Board report, pg. 31, *Massachusetts v. Purdue*, document PWG00041 4917.
27. Haddox quoted in Macy, *Dopesick*, 20–21. Haddox told an addiction conference in New York in 2003: "If I gave you a stalk of celery and you ate that, it would be healthy. But if you put it in a blender and tried to shoot it into your veins, it would not be good." Patrick Radden Keefe, "The Family That Built an Empire of Pain," *New Yorker*, October 23, 2017.
28. Haddox left Purdue in October 2018. He now is with Opos Consulting, which describes itself on its website as "Opioid Management Strategies and Solutions."
29. Purdue promoted its unorthodox view in publications it distributed directly to doctors and in bulk at medical conventions and to hospitals. Some included *Medication Therapy Management*; *Providing Relief, Preventing Abuse: A Reference Guide to Controlled Substances Prescribing Practices;* and *Responsible Opioid Prescribing.* 2007-11 Medication Therapy Management: Opportunities For Improving Pain Care, slide 31, PTN000006105; see also, Clinical Issues in Opioid Prescribing (2008), pgs. 1–3, *Massachusetts v. Purdue*, document PWG0000058054-055.
30. Morphine gets to the brain slightly slower than either oxycodone or heroin and as a result has never become a preferred drug for street addicts. "New Drug Application to FDA for OxyContin, Pharmacology Review: 'Abuse Liability of Oxycodone.'" Purdue Pharma, Stamford, CT, 1995.
31. OxyContin prescription insert, page 4, 1996, in collection of author.
32. CDC Guideline for Prescribing Opioids for Chronic Pain (2016), at https://www.cdc.gov/mmwr/volumes/65/rr/rr6501e1.htm.
33. Van Zee, "The Promotion and Marketing of OxyContin," 224.
34. Meier, "F.D.A. Bars Generic OxyContin."
35. Barry Meier, "Origins of an Epidemic: Purdue Pharma Knew Its Opioids Were Widely Abused," *New York Times*, May 29, 2018.
36. Richard Sackler, while the Senior Vice President for Sales, quoted at the OxyContin launch event, *Massachusetts v. Purdue*, document PKY180280951.
37. Gigen Mammoser, "Is OxyContin Losing Its Luster," *Healthline*, February 21, 2018.
38. In another two years, during which time Purdue doubled its sales force and distributed tens of thousands of discount or free prescription coupons, prescriptions surpassed six million annually. Ryan, Girion, and Glover, "You Want A Description Of Hell?"; "Prescription Drugs: OxyContin Abuse and Diversion and Efforts to Address the Problem," 2003. Van Zee, "The Promotion and Marketing of OxyContin," 221–22; Joanna Walters, "America's Opioid Crisis: How Prescription Drugs Sparked A National Trauma," *Guardian*, October 25, 2017.
39. "OxyContin Marketing Plan, 2002," 47 pages, Purdue Pharma, Stamford, CT, 2002, contributed to Document Cloud by Fred Shulte, *Kaiser Health News*,
40. From its first sales in 1996 through 2018, OxyContin brought $39 billion in revenue for Purdue. "Prescription Drugs: OxyContin Abuse and Diversion and Efforts to Address the Problem." See also Gigen Mammoser, "Is OxyContin Losing Its Luster."

Chapter 44: Talking Stomachs and Dead Presidents

1. Weissman et al., 2003; Molly M. Ginty, "Drug Ads Targeting Women Called Health Hazard," *We News*, November 14, 2006.

2. Damian Garde, "Direct-to-Consumer Drug Advertising, Explained," *STAT*, September 5, 2019.
3. May, "Selling Drugs by 'Educating' Physicians."
4. The authority of OTC ads to the FTC was part of the 1938 Wheeler-Lea Act. See Address of R. E. Freer, Commissioner, Federal Trade Commission, before the annual convention of The Proprietary Association, Biltmore Hotel, New York, NY, May 17, 1938, regarding The Wheeler-Lea Act.
5. The Kefauver legislation required the FDA to draft advertising guidelines. It took the agency seven years to publish them.
6. Donohue, "A History of Drug Advertising."
7. Code of Federal Regulations (CFR), Title 21, FDA, Drugs for Human Use, 202.1; C. Lee Ventola, "Direct-to-Consumer Pharmaceutical Advertising: Therapeutic or Toxic?" *Pharmacy and Therapeutics*, 2011 Oct; 36(10): 669–74.
8. CFR 21 314.81(b)(3)(I).
9. The volume of drug ads increased annually. Ad revenue at Arthur Sackler's *Medical Tribune* and its dozen publications doubled every year for a decade. Wayne L. Pines, "A History and Perspective on Direct-to-Consumer Promotion," Food and Drug Law Journal, vol. 54, no. 4, 1999, pp. 489–518.
10. Donohue, "A History of Drug Advertising," 671.
11. Ibid., 662.
12. Michael K. Paasche-Orlow et al., "National Survey of Patients' Bill of Rights Statutes," *Journal of General Internal Medicine*, 2009 Apr; 24(4): 489–94.
13. Donohue, "A History of Drug Advertising," 672.
14. Ibid., 673.
15. Elizabeth Watkins, "Expanding Consumer Information: The Origin of the Patient Package Insert," *Advancing the Consumer Interest*, (1998) 10(1), 20–26, and "Doctor, Are You Trying to Kill Me?": Ambivalence about the Patient Package Insert for Estrogen," *Bulletin of the History of Medicine* (2002): 76(1), 84–104.
16. David Kessler and W. Pines, "The Federal Regulation Of Prescription Drug Advertising And Promotion," *JAMA*, 1990 Nov 14;264(18):2409–15.
17. L.K. Harvey and S.C. Shubat, "Physician and Public Opinion on Health Care Issues," *American Medical Association*, April 1991.
18. See Arthur Hull Hayes Jr., "Remarks by Arthur Hull Hayes, Jr.," the Pharmaceutical Advertising Council, Inc., New York, February 18, 1982, copy in collection of author.
19. A Gallup poll showed that 58 percent of the public thought that Reagan's proposed cuts were either "about right" or "too low." Voters mostly believed Reagan's argument that he was cutting only duplication and pork, and all the agencies would function just as well on lower budgets. Lydia Saad, "Spending Cuts Popular in Reagan's 1981 Budget," *Gallup Vault*, May 25, 2017.
20. Dingell to Hayes, Letter via Messenger, March 9, 1982, "Prescription Drug Advertising To Consumers," Staff Report Prepared For The Use Of The Subcommittee On Oversight And Investigations Of The Committee On Energy And Commerce," House Of Representatives, 98th Congress, 2nd Session, September 1984 (Washington, D.C.: U.S. Government Printing Office), 17–18.
21. Ventola, "Direct-to-Consumer Pharmaceutical Advertising."
22. Comments of the staff of the FTC Bureau of Consumer Protection before the FDA in the matter of Request for Comments on Consumer-Directed Promotion, Docket 2003N-0344, December 1, 2003.
23. Donohue, "A History of Drug Advertising," 679.

24. Staff Report, "Prescription Drug Advertising To Consumers," 1984.
25. "Direct-To-Consumer Advertising Of Prescription Drugs: Withdrawal Of Moratorium," Food and Drug Administration, Federal Register, 1985.
26. Steven Woloshin et al., "Direct-To-Consumer Advertisements For Prescription Drugs: What Are Americans Being Sold?" *Lancet*, 358, no. 9288, October 6, 2001, 1141–46.
27. Edmund L. Andrews, "F.D.A. Inquiry on Generic Drugs Focuses on Changes in Ingredients," *New York Times*, July 31, 1989, 1.
28. Michael F. Mangano, "A Multi-Disciplinary Approach to Problem Solving: The Generic Drug Scandal," *The Government Accountants Journal*, Fall 1992.
29. Bill Clinton reappointed Kessler in 1994. For overview of Kessler tenure at the FDA see Marian Burros, "F.D.A. Commissioner Is Resigning After 6 Stormy Years in Office," *New York Times*, November 26, 1996, A1.
30. Ibid. Kessler had worked in the early 1980s as a consultant on food additive safety and tobacco regulation for Utah senator Orrin Hatch. It was Hatch who had suggested to President Bush that Kessler be appointed the FDA commissioner. However, once he was in charge at the FDA, Hatch became a critic. "If I have a big criticism of David, it is that he loves publicity and seeks it."
31. Warren E. Leary, "Citing Labels, US Seizes Orange Juice," *New York Times*, April 25, 1991, A18.
32. "Independent Review Group, Silicone Breast Implants: The Report of the Independent Review Group," Institute of Medicine Committee on the Safety of Silicone Breast Implants, issued July 8, 1998; see also B. Diamond et al., "Silicone Breast Implants in Relation to Connective Tissue Diseases and Immunologic Dysfunction," Report by a National Science Panel to the Honorable Sam C. Pointer Jr., Coordinating Judge for the Federal Breast Implant Multi-District Litigation, November 30, 1998.
33. Kessler was the first commissioner since James Goddard in the late 1960s to go after Big Tobacco. Kessler issued the so-called FDA Rule by which the agency attempted to restrict tobacco advertising since children were susceptible to it. Nicotine, he said, was a drug responsible for over 400,000 deaths annually. Big Tobacco brought the FDA to federal court. It took four years before a bitterly divided Supreme Court ruled 5–4 in favor of the tobacco industry. Two moderate justices joined with three conservatives for the slim majority. Sandra Day O'Connor wrote the majority decision, joined by Anthony Kennedy, Antonin Scalia, Clarence Thomas, and Chief Justice William Rehnquist.

    Kessler's desire for the FDA to have jurisdiction over tobacco came to fruition in 2010 when Congress expanded the FDA's authority in the Family Smoking Prevention and Tobacco Control Act. See *FDA v. Brown & Williamson Tobacco Corp.*, 529 U.S. 120 (2000).
34. Congress passed protections in the Patient Self Determination Act in 1989 and the 1996 Health Insurance Portability and Accountability Act (HIPAA). See S. J. Nass, Levit L, Gostin L, eds, "Beyond the HIPAA Privacy Rule: Enhancing Privacy, Improving Health Through Research," Institute of Medicine (US) Committee on Health Research and the Privacy of Health Information (Washington, D.C.: National Academies Press, 2009).
35. Donohue, "A History of Drug Advertising," 680, 682.
36. Leslie Weiss, "Radical Plan From Newt Gingrich's Think Tank To Gut FDA," *Mother Jones*, September/October 1995.

37. Burros, "F.D.A. Commissioner Is Resigning After 6 Stormy Years in Office."
38. Also coming up were: loratidine (OTC in 2002), omeprazole (2004), orlistat (2007), and cetirizine (2008).
39. Rich Thomaselli, "Ten Years Later: Direct to Consumer Drug Advertising," *Adage*, October 1, 2006.
40. Ibid. And see GAO report number GAO-03-177, "Prescription Drugs: FDA Oversight of Direct-to-Consumer Advertising Has Limitations," released December 4, 2002.
41. Michael C. Gerald, "The Rise and Fall of Celebrity Promotion of Prescription Products in Direct-to-Consumer Advertising," *Pharmacy in History*, Vol. 52, No. 1 (2010), 13–23.
42. Ibid. See also M. S. Wilkes et al., "Direct-To-Consumer Prescription Drug Advertising: Trends, Impact, And Implications," *Health Aff*, 2000, 19:110-28; David Herzberg, "Will Wonder Drugs Never Cease. A Prehistory of Direct-to-Consumer Advertising," *Pharmacy in History* 51 (2009): 47–56.
43. Gerald, "The Rise and Fall of Celebrity Promotion of Prescription Products in Direct-to-Consumer Advertising." See "The Impact Of Direct-To-Consumer Drug Advertising On Seniors' Health And Health Care Costs," Hearing before Special Committee On Aging, United States Senate, 109th Congress, First Session (2005).
44. Warner-Lambert had developed Lipitor and was ready to sell it in 1996. At the last moment it reached a marketing agreement with Pfizer, whose sales force was considered one of the industry's best.
45. Pfizer cut Jarvik loose (but let him keep his $1.35 million fee) and instead went to a subdued ad featuring a San Francisco talent agent who had gone on Lipitor after surviving a heart attack. Although the dustup did not hurt Lipitor's sales, it did revive doubts about the accuracy of drug television ads. Gerald, "The Rise and Fall of Celebrity Promotion of Prescription Products in Direct-to-Consumer Advertising."
46. Mark Morford, "Giant Floating Purple Pills / Are Those Creepy Prescription-Drug Commercials On TV Trying To Kill You?," *San Francisco Chronicle*, November 21, 2003.
47. Jim Edwards, "Lies, Damned Lies, and Drug Advertising: Judge Turns Blind Eye to AZ's 'Deceptive' Purple Pill Ads," Moneywatch, CBS News, May 11, 2010.
48. Years later, even after Nexium's patent protection had expired, AstraZeneca battled to keep the capsule's color exclusive. When India-based Dr. Reddy's Laboratories released a generic with two shades of purple in September 2015, AztraZeneca sued, claiming that patients would be confused by the similarity of the brand name's color. The case was settled out of court when Dr. Reddy's changed the color of its generic to blue. See El Silverman, "Maker of Generic Version of Nexium Goes to Blue to Settle Litigation," *Stat*, January 4, 2016.
49. Kesselheim, "The High Cost of Prescription Drugs in the United States," 862–65.
50. Herper, "The Best-Selling Drugs In America."
51. Edwards, "Lies, Damned Lies, and Drug Advertising"; Stuart Elliott, "AstraZeneca Sued Over Advertising," *New York Times*, October 19, 2004.
52. Ginty, "Drug Ads Targeting Women Called Health Hazard"; Jin In, "Marketing Mother's Little Helper," *We News*, June 23, 2002.
53. Scott Hensley, "Remember Vioxx? Merck Settles Marketing Charges From Way Back," NPR, November 22, 2011; Snigdha Prakash and Vicki Valentine, "Time-

line: The Rise and Fall of Vioxx" in "Special Series, Vioxx: The Downfall of a Drug," NPR, November 10, 2007.

54. Thomaselli, "Ten Years Later: Direct To Consumer Drug Advertising." Direct-to-consumer ads "had gotten away from us," Kessler later said.
55. Donohue, "A History of Drug Advertising."
56. Pharma spending on consumer ads skyrocketed. One year after the fallout over the Vioxx ads had caused a momentary hiccup, drug firms spent $4.2 billion on DTCA, 40 percent of all industry promotion. As of 2019, a study in *JAMA* reported that DTCA had reached $9.6 billion annually, "mostly TV commercials and glossy magazine ads." It was another record for consumer ads. L. M. Schwartz and S. Woloshin, "Medical Marketing in the United States, 1997–2016," *JAMA* 2019;321(1):80–96. Separately, pharma spent $20 billion on marketing to doctors and health care professionals.

Chapter 45: "We Have to Hammer on the Abusers"

1. The six states were Kentucky, West Virginia, Ohio, Pennsylvania, Maine, and Virginia. See for example Karin Meadows, "Alcohol, Drugs May Be Culprits in Deaths in Leesburg," *Orlando Sentinel,* December 30, 1998, 1.
2. "Prescription Drugs: OxyContin Abuse and Diversion and Efforts to Address the Problem," 2003, 9.
3. "Overview of the Public Health Burden of Prescription Drug and Heroin Overdoses: How We Got to Now?" National Center for Injury Prevention and Control Division of Unintentional Injury Prevention, CDC, July 1, 2015. As for the ER cases treated, see Sujata S. Jayawant and Rajesh Balkrishnan, "The Controversy Surrounding Oxycontin Abuse: Issues And Solutions," *Therapeutics And Clinical Risk Management* vol. 1,2 (2005), 80.
4. "Diversion here was, at least in part," concluded Passik, "a matter of self-medicating loss of hope, feeding one's family and seeking escape run amok. It could have been OxyContin, it could have been anything else." Steven Passik, "Same As It Ever Was? Life After the OxyContin Media Frenzy," *Journal of Pain and Symptom Management,* Volume 25, Issue 3, March 2003, 199–201.
5. "OxyContin Diversion and Abuse," Information Bulletin, National Drug Intelligence Center, U.S. Department of Justice, Product No. 2001-L0425-001, January 2001, 3. See also Substance Abuse and Mental Health Services Administration, Drug Abuse Warning Network, 1997-1998: Area Profiles of Drug-Related Mortality. HHS Publication No. (SMA) 12-4699, DAWN Series D-3 (Rockville, MD: Substance Abuse and Mental Health Services Administration, 1999).
6. "Oxycontin: Balancing Risks And Benefits," Hearing Of The Committee On Health, Education, Labor, And Pensions, U.S. Senate, 107th Congress, Second Session; "On Examining The Effects Of The Painkiller OxyContin, Focusing On Federal, State And Local Efforts To Decrease Abuse And Misuse Of This Product While Assuring Availability For Patients Who Suffer Daily From Chronic Moderate To Severe Pain," February 12, 2002, Senate Committee on Health, Education, Labor, and Pensions (Washington, D.C.: U.S. Government Printing Office, 2002).
7. Statement and Testimony of Jay P. McCloskey for the Hearing Before the Committee on the Judiciary, United States Senate on "Evaluating the Propriety and Adequacy of the OxyContin Criminal Settlement," July 31, 2007 (hereinafter "McCloskey Judiciary Committee Statement and Testimony 2007").

8. 1999-06-17 email from Michael Friedman, reference #228728.1 and 1998-09-28 email from Richard Sackler, *Massachusetts v. Purdue* document PDD17015 46497.
9. "OxyContin Marketing Plan, 2002." Purdue Pharma, Stamford, CT, 2002; Van Zee, "The Promotion and Marketing of OxyContin."
10. McCloskey Judiciary Committee Statement and Testimony 2007.
11. "OxyContin: Balancing Risks And Benefits," Senate, 2002, 57.
12. McCloskey Judiciary Committee Statement and Testimony 2007.
13. McCloskey summary of the meeting, Ibid.
14. Meier, "Origins of an Epidemic."
15. J. C. Crews and D. D. Denson, "Recovery Of Morphine From A Controlled-Release Preparation: A Source Of Opioid Abuse," *Cancer* 1990;66:2642–44.
16. McCloskey Judiciary Committee Statement and Testimony 2007.
17. Van Zee, "The Promotion and Marketing of OxyContin."
18. Jared S. Hopkins, "OxyContin Made The Sacklers Rich. Now It's Tearing Them Apart," *Wall Street Journal*, July 13, 2019. According to Hopkins, "some people close to the family said Mortimer opposed tapping Raymond's son Richard Sackler to be president in 1999 . . ."
19. All opioid overdoses were less than half of the reported four thousand Americans who died of drugs in 1999, and OxyContin was only one of the opioid-based painkillers on the market. See "Opioid Overdose Death Rates and All Drug Overdose Death Rates per 100,000 Population (Age-Adjusted)," 1999, State Facts, Kaiser Family Foundation.
20. Summary Review. Application number: 022272Orig1s027 (OxyContin). Center For Drug Evaluation And Research, FDA.
21. Jayawant and Balkrishnan, "The Controversy Surrounding OxyContin Abuse: Issues And Solutions," 77–82.
22. James Inciardi and Jennifer Goode, "OxyContin and Prescription Drug Abuse," *Consumer's Research*, July 2003, 17.
23. Purdue's new phase of promotion targeted arthritis sufferers and resulted in the FDA's first complaint filed against the company. It charged the ad addressed conditions for which it was not approved. Purdue was prepared to contest it but general counsel Howard Udell convinced the Sacklers it was not worth souring their relationship with the chief regulatory agency that up to that time had been accommodating. Purdue voluntarily withdrew the advertisement. "Opioids and Women: From Perspective to Addiction," *National Women's Health Network*, May 2018.
24. Purdue company statement quoted in Barry Meier, "At Painkiller Trouble Spot, Signs Seen as Alarming Didn't Alarm Drug's Maker," *New York Times* , December 10, 2001, 1.
25. Inciardi and Goode, "OxyContin and Prescription Drug Abuse," 21.
26. 1997-02-27 email from Robert Kaiko, document PDD1701345999; 1997-03-02 email from Richard Sackler, *Massachusetts v. Purdue* document PDD1701345999.
27. 2000-11-30 email from Michael Friedman, *Massachusetts v. Purdue* document PDD1706196247.
28. 2000-12-01 email from Mortimer D. Sackler, *Massachusetts v. Purdue* document PDD1706196246.
29. Author interview with former Purdue assistant marketing manager, February 2017.

30. Inciardi and Goode, "OxyContin and Prescription Drug Abuse." As for the figure of twenty-fold in four years, see the GAO report of December 2003, "Prescription Drugs: OxyContin Abuse and Diversion and Efforts to Address the Problem."
31. R. Lagos et al., "The Face Of Hillbilly Heroin And Other Images Of Narcotic Abuse," *West Virginia Medical Journal*, 2010;106(4 Spec No):34-37. Fox Butterfield was the first *New York Times* reporter to use the term in a July story, "Theft of Painkiller Reflects its Popularity on the Street," July 7, 2001, A5. For other slang for OxyContin, see Jayawant and Balkrishnan, "The Controversy Surrounding OxyContin Abuse."
32. Julian Borger, "Hillbilly Heroin: The Painkiller Abuse Wrecking Lives In West Virginia," *Guardian* (UK), June 24, 2001. As for the average annual incomes in those states, $24,500 in Kentucky in 2000: https://www.statista.com/statistics/205414/per-capita-personal-income-in-kentucky/. And in West Virginia it was $22,000: https://www.statista.com/statistics/205577/per-capita-personal-income-in-west-virginia/. A later study that evaluated data from West Virginia's Controlled Substance Monitoring Program showed that Medicaid patients had "substantially higher" opioid prescription rates than those privately insured; also the rate of opioid misuse was higher than the state average. See G. L. Peirce et al., "Doctor and Pharmacy Shopping for Controlled Substances," *Med Care*, 50(6):494–500, June 2012.
33. Drugstores in southeast Kentucky, for instance, could not keep pill crushers in stock. Francis X. Clines and Barry Meier, "Cancer Painkillers Pose New Abuse Threat," *New York Times*, February 9, 2001, 1, 115.
34. Borger, "Hillbilly Heroin."
35. Famularo and Haddox quoted in Clines and Meier, "Cancer Painkillers Pose New Abuse Threat."
36. 2001-02-08 email from Richard Sackler, *Massachusetts v. Purdue* document PDD8801151727.
37. Author interview with former assistant production manager, February 2017.
38. M. N. Pastore et al., "Transdermal Patches: History, Development And Pharmacology," *British Journal Of Pharmacology* (2015), 172(9), 2179–2209. See also Julia Lurie, "A Brief, Blood-Boiling History of the Opioid Epidemic: From OxyContin Coupons To Fentanyl-Laced Heroin, This Is How The Crisis Unfolded," *Mother Jones*, Jan/Feb 2017.
39. J. Suzuki and S. El-Haddad, "A Review: Fentanyl And Non-Pharmaceutical Fentanyls," *Drug Alcohol Depend*. 2017 Feb 1;171:107–16.
40. John Carreyrou, "Narcotic 'Lollipop' Becomes Big Seller Despite FDA Curbs," *Wall Street Journal*, November 3, 2006, 1.
41. Jerald King v. Frank Baldino, Civil Action No. 08-54-GMS-MPT, In the United States District Court for the District of Delaware, ruling issued August 26, 2009. See also Carreyrou, "Narcotic 'Lollipop' Is Big Seller Despite FDA Curbs"; Jim Edwards, "Judge Revisits Cephalon's Off-Label Madness: Actiq is 'an ER on a Stick!'" *CBS News Moneywatch*, September 2, 2009; "Lollipop Made With Powerful Opioid Fentanyl Was Illegally Marketed, Ex-Pharma Rep Says," CBS News, "Whistleblower," June 28, 2019.
42. Inciardi and Goode, "OxyContin and Prescription Drug Abuse."
43. "OxyContin Diversion and Abuse," Information Bulletin, National Drug Intelligence Center, U.S. Department of Justice, Product No. 2001-L0425-001, January 2001, 3.

44. 2001-02-01 email from Richard Sackler, Massachusetts v. Purdue document PDD8801133516.
45. "Abusers aren't victims; they're victimizers," Sackler wrote that same month to an acquaintance.
46. Frank Berger, the scientist who discovered Miltown, told a congressional committee that "Alcohol, when used improperly, can be habit forming. But you don't find a warning to that effect on a bottle of beer." He told *The New York Times* the problem was that users abused it. "One just expects it will be used properly." Benedict Carey, "Frank Berger, 94, Miltown Creator, Dies," *New York Times*, March 28, 2008.
47. Barry Meier and Melody Petersen, "Sales of Painkiller Grew Rapidly, But Success Brought a High Cost," *New York Times*, March 5, 2011, 1, 61.
48. Ibid.
49. Ibid.
50. When the *Times* article ran, the amount paid by drug companies to physicians for speaking engagements was not public knowledge. Later, some of what Purdue paid became public as a result of litigation discovery. Since 2010, companies are required to report their payments. In the years since disclosure, the annual reported payments have varied from $12 million to $24 million. https://projects.propublica.org/docdollars/company/purdue-pharma-l-p.
51. Inciardi and Goode, "OxyContin and Prescription Drug Abuse."
52. DuPont had released naltrexone under the brand name Trexan in 1984 for opioid dependence. Clinical trials later demonstrated it was also useful in reducing alcohol cravings. Elaine A. Moore, *The Promise of Low Dose Naltrexone Therapy: Potential Benefits in Cancer* (Jefferson, NC: McFarland Books, 2008).
53. "Decision Of The Director General Of Fair Trading No Ca98/2/2001 in the matter of Napp Pharmaceutical Holdings Limited And Subsidiaries (Napp)," pursuant to the Competition Act 1998, March 30, 2001, 72 pages, in collection of author.
54. Laura Nagel, Deputy Assistant Administrator, Drug Enforcement Administration, Speech to American Association for the Treatment of Opioid Dependence, Washington, D.C., April 14, 2003.
55. Meier, *Pain Killer*, 53.
56. "Summary: Health Impact Of The Napp Technologies Fire," Division of Environmental and Occupational Health Services, New Jersey Department of Health and Senior Services, April 1997.
57. "Lodi Plant Faces Fines for Fatal Blast," *Ashbury Park Press*, October 19, 1995, 6; "Chemical Explosion Kills Four at New Jersey Plant," *Capital Times* (New Jersey), April 22, 1995, 8; "4 Killed in Lodi Explosion," *Ashbury Park Press*, A1, A7.
58. "Lodi Plant Faces Fines for Fatal Blast."
59. Author interview with former Purdue assistant marketing manager, July 2018.
60. *Massachusetts v. Purdue* 186, n. 85, citing Meier, *Pain Killer*, 158.
61. Udell quoted in Meier, *Pain Killer*, 111.
62. 2014-02-14 email from Russell Gasdia, *Massachusetts v. Purdue* document PPLPC012000464424.
63. "Prescription Drugs: OxyContin Abuse and Diversion and Efforts to Address the Problem," 2003.
64. Author interview with former DEA official involved in the original OxyContin investigation, February 28, 2019.

65. Jayawant and Balkrishnan, "The Controversy Surrounding OxyContin Abuse."
66. Benjamin Lesser, Dan Levine, Lisa Girion, and Jaimi Dowdell, "How Judges Added To The Grim Toll Of Opioids," A Special Investigation, Hidden Injustice, Reuters, June 25, 2019.
67. Ashanti M. Alvarez, "Arrests Heighten Battle Over Pain Killer," *The Record*, New Jersey, July 6, 2001, A1, A18.
68. Ibid.
69. Ibid.
70. "Did the FDA Ignite the Opioid Epidemic?" *60 Minutes*, February 24, 2019.
71. FDA Issues New Warnings on Painkiller OxyContin, *WebMD*, July 26, 2001.
72. Author interview with former Purdue assistant marketing manager, July 2018.
73. Caitlin Esch, "How One Sentence Helped Set Off The Opioid Crisis," *Marketplace*, December 13, 2017.
74. "Prescription Drugs: OxyContin Abuse and Diversion and Efforts to Address the Problem," 2003.
75. Ibid., Appendix II: Summary of FDA Changes to the Original Approved OxyContin Label," 48–52.
76. "Did the FDA Ignite the Opioid Epidemic?"
77. "Prescription Drugs: OxyContin Abuse and Diversion and Efforts to Address the Problem," 48–52.
78. David Kessler interviewed in "Did the FDA Ignite the Opioid Epidemic?"
79. Andrew Kolodny interviewed in Ibid.
80. Ed Thompson interviewed in Ibid.
81. "Did the FDA Ignite the Opioid Epidemic?"
82. "OxyContin: Its Use And Abuse," House of Representatives, Committee on Energy and Commerce, Subcommittee on Oversight and Investigations, Serial 107-54, August 28, 2001, 107th Congress, First Session.
83. Purdue's Totowa, New Jersey, plant was 110 miles away from the Cardinal Health recipient in Swedesboro, New Jersey. Connected by I-95, the typical travel time is two hours. In the case of the missing OxyContin, a truck brought the Oxy to Newark International Airport where it was transferred to another truck that then drove it to Philadelphia. From there it was loaded on a cargo plane for Dayton, Ohio, after which it was flown back to Philadelphia. When the crate was opened on the truck that took it on its last leg to Swedesboro, the OxyContin was missing. "$800,000 in Painkilling Pills Disappear on a Zigzag Route," *New York Times*, December 22, 2001.
84. Randolph Lievertz prescribed six times as much OxyContin as the next biggest dispenser in Indiana. The prescriptions he wrote were for so many pills that patients would have had to take thirty-one OxyContin tablets every twelve hours instead of the one approved by the FDA. Barry Meier, "Doctor to Face U.S. Charges in Drug Case," *New York Times*, December 23, 2001.
85. Caryn James, "Television Review; A Painkiller's Double Life as an Illegal Street Drug," *New York Times*, December 12, 2001.
86. Pain management advocates always pushed back against state prescription-monitoring systems. They contended such systems created undue fear among doctors and therefore punished chronic pain sufferers. By the time OxyContin was released in 1996, only fourteen states had prescription-monitoring systems. That made it impossible in the other thirty-six to determine if a patient obtained multiple prescriptions from different doctors and filled them at separate

pharmacies. Melody Petersen and Barry Meier, "Few States Track Prescriptions As Way to Prevent Overdoses," *New York Times*, December 21, 2001.

87. Peter Provet, President, Odyssey House, "OxyContin Abuse," Letters to the Editor, *New York Times*, December 27, 2001.
88. Hutchinson testimony before the House Appropriations Subcommittee on Commerce, Hearings on OxyContin Abuse, Decemeber 11, 2001, at https://www.c-span.org/video/?167770-1/oxycontin-abuse. See also Barry Meier, "Official Faults Drug Company For Marketing of Its Painkiller," *New York Times*, December 12, 2001.
89. Goldenhiem testimony before the House Appropriations Subcommittee on Commerce, Hearings on OxyContin Abuse, December 11, 2001, at https://www.c-span.org/video/?167770-1/oxycontin-abuse.
90. Meier, "Official Faults Drug Company For Marketing of Its Painkiller."
91. Inciardi and Goode, "OxyContin and Prescription Drug Abuse."
92. Elliott, "The Drug Pushers"; Meyers, *Happy Accidents*, 4693 of 6459.
93. Jayawant and Balkrishnan, "The Controversy Surrounding Oxycontin Abuse."
94. Purdue also distributed one of the few sets of good statistics. The National Institutes of Health's Monitoring the Future survey had since 1975 assessed annually the extent of prescription drug abuse and illegal drug use among eighth- through twelfth-grade students (mostly fourteen to eighteen years). The survey conducted in 2002 added for the first time some questions about OxyContin. Less than 4 percent of the students admitted to trying OxyContin and fewer than half of 1 percent said they had taken it to get high. Nearly 10 percent had tried other opioids such as Percocet, Lortab, or Vicodin. Inciardi and Goode, "OxyContin and Prescription Drug Abuse."

Chapter 46: "Giving Purdue a Free Pass"

1. Fred Schulte, "Internal Documents: Purdue Pharma Knew OxyContin's Risks, Pushed It Anyway," *Kaiser Health News*, June 13, 2018.
2. Meier, "At Painkiller Trouble Spot." Also see "Pulse Check. Trends in Drug Abuse. January–June 2001 Reporting Period. Special Topic: Synthetic Opioids," Office of National Drug Control Policy, Washington, D.C., 2001.
3. It was $300,000 more than any other sales territory. See Meier, *Pain Killer*, 40.
4. Meier, "At Painkiller Trouble Spot."
5. Author interview with former Purdue assistant marketing manager, February 2017.
6. Alabama, Arkansas, Kentucky, Indiana, Louisiana, Michigan, Mississippi, North Carolina, Ohio, Oklahoma, South Carolina, Tennessee, and West Virginia had between 96 and 143 prescriptions written per 100 people. See IMS, National Prescription Audit, 2012.
7. The Centers for Disease Control in 2006 started compiling annual opioid prescribing statistics by county. See also Julie Appleby and Elizabeth Lucas, "Doctors Can Change Opioid Prescribing Habits, But Progress Comes In Small Doses," *Kaiser Health News*, August 14, 2019.
8. Katherine Hoover was the West Virginia doctor. German Lopez, "This Doctor Wrote 130 Opioid Prescriptions A Day. She Says She Did Nothing Wrong," *Vox*, September 26, 2018.

9. Zoe Matthews, "AG: North Andover Doctor Was Top Prescriber Of OxyContin," *Eagle Tribune* (North Andover, MA), February 6, 2019.
10. Andover's Dr. Walter Jacobs, for instance, received $50,000 to talk to other physicians about opioids and pain treatment. Meanwhile, Purdue netted an estimated $3 million from the OxyContin he prescribed. 2001-06-25 spreadsheet attached to email from Kathy Doran (re Thought Leaders), Document PPLPC012000038726; 2010-10-06 Consultant Services Agreement signed by Russell Gasdia and Walter Jacobs, *Massachusetts v. Purdue* document PPLP003479945.
11. 2012-10-02 email from Yoni Falkson, *Massachusetts v. Purdue* document PLPC012000392932. "Purdue Pharma Family Sought To Profit Off Opioid Crisis, Filing Alleges," *PBS News Hour*, February 1, 2019.
12. Meier, "Origins of an Epidemic."
13. *Massachusetts v. Purdue*, para 135–37, 45–46.
14. See "Prescription Drugs": OxyContin Abuse and Diversion and Efforts to Address the Problem," GAO Report, 2003.
15. Four months earlier, the DEA's director, Asa Hutchinson, had testified to Congress that there had been 282 OxyContin overdose deaths. Purdue dismissed that conclusion and attacked the media reports of abuse and diversion as fake news.
16. The author also obtained a twenty-page printout of a related but streamlined PowerPoint presentation by Laura Nagel's Office of Diversion Control at the sixty-fourth annual meeting of the College on Problems of Drug Dependence. It was held June 8–13 in Quebec City, Canada.
17. Author interview with former DEA official involved in the original OxyContin investigation, February 28, 2019.
18. David V. Gauvin, Christine Sannerud, Frank Sapienza, "Two-Year Incidence of Fatal Adverse Drug Events Associated with Single-Entity Oxycodone Products: A Review of 1,304 Cases." From the Drug and Chemical Evaluation Section, Office of Diversion Control, Drug Enforcement Administration, Washington, D.C., undated, twenty-six pages, in collection of author.
19. All of the descriptions of the DEA presentation and its findings are from the author's review of David V. Gauvin, Christine Sannerud, and Frank Sapienza, "Two-Year Incidence of Fatal Adverse Drug Events Associated with Single-Entity Oxycodone Products: A Review of 1,304 Cases."
20. Lev Facher, "Fentanyl And Other Synthetic Opioids Contributed To More Overdose Deaths In 2016 Than Prescription Painkillers," *STAT*, May 1, 2018.
21. "Meeting, Presentation: DEA, Headquarters, 2002, Present: DEA Staff, Dr. Debra Leiderman FDA, Friedman, Udal [*sic*] Dr. Goldenheim, in collection of author.
22. DEA notes of April 2002 meeting, in collection of author.
23. Years later the FDA complained the DEA had not shared the 1,304 death records, while the DEA said the records were available for review, but no one had done so. Meier, "At Painkiller Trouble Spot."
24. Author interview with former DEA official involved in the original OxyContin investigation, February 28, 2019.
25. Barry Meier, "OxyContin Deaths May Top Early Count," *New York Times*, April 15, 2002.
26. Author interview with former DEA official involved in the original OxyContin investigation, February 28, 2019.
27. Notes from DEA officer regarding submission to *NEJM*, in collection of author.

28. "Evaluating the Propriety and Adequacy of the OxyContin Criminal Settlement," Hearing before the Committee on the Judiciary, US Senate 110th Congress, first session July 31, 2007 (US Government Printing Office, Washington: 2008), 15.
29. United States Attorney's Office for the District of Columbia archive by year, www.justice.gov/usao-dc.
30. Daniel C. Richman, "Political Control of Federal Prosecutions: Looking Back and Looking Forward," 58 *Duke L. J.* 2087 (2009).
31. "Evaluating the Propriety and Adequacy of the OxyContin Criminal Settlement," Senate 2008, 15.
32. The paper's public editor, Daniel Okrent, had extensively addressed Purdue's complaints in a December 21, 2003, column, "You Can Stand on Principle and Still Stub a Toe." Okrent noted that the paper's written policy was that "staff members must never give an impression that they might benefit financially from the outcome of news events." Okrent said "after talking to authorities both parties directed me to, I believe Meier's reporting was generally accurate and fair, even if the way some of the pieces were played—placement, headline, frequency, etc.—sometimes seemed the work of an especially ferocious terrier that had gotten its teeth into someone's ankle." According to Okrent, "Even if Barry Meier was not going to see dollars pouring in from writing about OxyContin, and even if he was the *Times* reporter who knew the most about oxycodone-based painkilling medication, and even if Udell's demand was perceived as a disingenuous effort to intimidate the paper into altering its coverage—despite all this, there did exist the appearance of a conflict."
33. Stuart Baker's law firm, Chadbourne & Parke, was one of the two that advised on the early litigation defense. The other was Atlanta's King & Spaulding. Meier, *Pain Killer*, 144.
34. Udell quoted in Ibid. Udell told *Corporate Counsel Business Journal* in September 2002 that Purdue had spent $45 million on legal expenses and the bills were escalating at $3 million per month. Macy, *Dopesick*, 68.
35. Author interview with former Purdue assistant marketing manager, February 2017.
36. John Solomon and Matthew Mosk, "The Importance of Being Rudy," *Seattle Times*, May 15, 2007.
37. 2008-01-15 Board report, pgs. 4, 22, 24, *Massachusetts v. Purdue* document PDD8901733977.
38. Solomon and Mosk, "The Importance of Being Rudy."
39. Nagel quoted in Ibid.
40. Tandy became the DEA director in January 2003 when Hutchinson went to run the Border and Transportation Security division at the newly created Department of Homeland Security.
41. Kerik quoted in Chris Smith, "American Idol," *New York*, September 6, 2002. Kerik was sentenced to four years in prison in 2010 after he pled guilty to eight felonies, ranging from lying to White House officials tax fraud. Sam Dolnick, "Kerik Is Sentenced in Corruption Case," *New York Times*, February 16, 2010.
42. Author interview with former DEA official involved in the original OxyContin investigation, February 28, 2019.
43. David Kessler, the crusading chief of the FDA, was not involved with OxyContin's approval when he ran the agency in 1996. This was when the Sackler directors shuffled some of their own corporate titles. Richard Sackler, for instance, resigned

as CEO and appointed as his replacement his trusted, longtime colleague Michael Friedman. However, the swapping of titles was mostly window dressing that hid the extent to which the family continued to run the firm.

44. The investigation was the Florida attorney general's office File No. L01-3-2535; from that investigation, Kaiser Health News has published Purdue's internal budget documents from 1996 to 2002 online at https://khn.org/news/purdue-and-the-oxycontin-files/.
45. Author interview with former Purdue assistant marketing manager, July 2018. See "OxyContin Abuse Shatters Drug Company's Low Profile," *Hartford Courant*, September 2, 2001, 1, 26.
46. Ethan Barton, "American Cartel: Here Are The Politicians That Took Opioid Tycoons' 'Dirty, Bloody Money,' " Investigative Group, *Daily Caller*, March 14, 2008.
47. Matthew Perrone and Ben Wieder, "Pro-Painkiller Echo Chamber Shaped Policy Amid Drug Epidemic," Part 2 of 3, The Center for Public Integrity copublished with The Associated Press, September 19, 2016; IMS Health and citation for FEC for chart "The Politics of Pain." The spending was during the decade 2006 to 2016.
48. Ibid., Perrone and Wieder, "Pro-Painkiller Echo Chamber."
49. Agreement dated November 1, 2002, between the Office of the Attorney General, Department of Legal Affairs, State of Florida, and Purdue Pharma L. P. and Purdue Frederick Company, 9 pages, and Exhibits A and B and a 3-page amendment dated April 25, 2003, in files of author.
50. Lizette Alvarez, "Florida Shutting 'Pill Mill' Clinics," *New York Times*, August 31, 2011.
51. Barry Meier, "Opioid Makers Are the Big Winners in Lawsuit Settlements," *New York Times*, December 26, 2018.
52. See "OxyContin: Balancing Risks and Benefits," Senate Hearing before the Committee on Health, Education, Labor and Pensions, 107th Congress, second session, February 12, 2002.
53. Purdue contributed $10,000 to Senator Dodd in 2002, more than any other federal politician. Barton, "American Cartel."
54. The 257 cases resulted in 302 arrests and $1 million in fines, separate from the civil settlement with Purdue. Solomon and Mosk, "The Importance of Being Rudy." See also "In fiscal years 2001 and 2002, GAO's report noted, the Drug Enforcement Administration initiated 257 OxyContin related abuse and diversion cases, which resulted in 302 arrests and about $1 million in fines," "FDA Approves Generic OxyContin," *American Journal of Health-System Pharmacy*, April 23, 2004.
55. Author interview with former Purdue assistant marketing manager, February 2017.
56. Sam Dolnick, "Kerik is Sentenced in Corruption Case," *New York Times*, February 18, 2010, A1.

Chapter 47: "You Messed with the Wrong Mother"

1. Some had also been filed by OxyContin patients who claimed the drug had been falsely marketed since it did not provide a full twelve hours of pain relief. See Ryan, Girion, and Glover, "You Want A Description Of Hell?"; Bob Braun, "A Chilling Attempt at Damage Control," *Star-Ledger* (Newark, NJ), March 5, 2003.

2. Giovanna Fabiano, "Dangers of Painkiller Highlighted by Fatality," *The Courier-News* (Bridgewater, NJ), September 15, 2002, 22.
3. Marianne was divorced from her first husband. She also had raised a son from that marriage. He was nineteen when his sister died.
4. Fabiano, "Dangers of Painkiller Highlighted by Fatality."
5. Marianne Skolek Perez, "You Messed with the Wrong Mother: One mother's 17-year personal account exposing Purdue Pharma, maker of OxyContin in fueling the 'manufactured' opioid epidemic crippling the U.S.," unpublished manuscript, cited here by courtesy of author. Bob Considine, "Readington Family Finds Justice, But Seeks More," *Courier-News* (Bridgewater, NJ), June 4, 2007, A1, A4.
6. Marianne Skolek Perez, "You Messed with the Wrong Mother."
7. Fabiano, "Dangers of Painkiller Highlighted by Fatality."
8. Ibid.
9. The task force was based in Hunterdon County, NJ. See Marianne Skolek, "The Citizens of Ohio Deserve Better in Dealing with Your Epidemic of Drugs," *Salem-News* (Salem, OR), March 18, 2010.
10. Marianne Skolek Perez, "You Messed with the Wrong Mother."
11. Ibid.
12. Ibid.
13. Considine, "Readington Family Finds Justice."
14. See, for example, "Griffith Hopes for Better Regulation of Painkiller," *Quad-City Times* (Davenport, Iowa), November 11, 2002, 16.
15. Marianne Skolek, "Mom Vows to Fight Heroin Epidemic," *Courier-News* (Bridgewater, NJ), March 31, 2001, A9.
16. Braun, "A Chilling Attempt at Damage Control."
17. "Prescription Drugs: OxyContin Abuse and Diversion and Efforts to Address the Problem," 2003.
18. It was founded in 1992 by former HEW secretary Joseph Califano Jr.
19. Marianne Skolek Perez, "You Messed with the Wrong Mother."
20. Bob Braun, "A Chilling Attempt at Damage Control."
21. Marianne Skolek Perez, "You Messed with the Wrong Mother."
22. Ibid.
23. Giovanna Fabiano, "Woman Who Lost Daughter Targets Painkiller," *The Courier-News* (Bridgewater, NJ), November 17, 2002, A6.
24. Braun, "A Chilling Attempt at Damage Control."
25. Ibid.
26. Ibid.
27. Ibid.
28. Marianne Skolek Perez, "You Messed with the Wrong Mother."
29. Ibid.
30. Hogen quoted in Bob Braun, "A Chilling Attempt at Damage Control" and "Inappropriate Comment," *Star-Ledger*, March 18, 2003.
31. Considine, "Readington Family Finds Justice."
32. Ibid.
33. Ibid.
34. Ibid.
35. Mark I. Pinsky, "Right Too Soon: The Orlando Sentinel On Opioid Epidemic," *Columbia Journalism Review*, August 23, 2017.

36. One of the lead characters in the *Sentinel* series was described, for instance, as an "accidental addict" whose "idyllic life was ruined by OxyContin." It turned out he had a federal conviction for conspiracy to distribute cocaine and a history of financial problems and domestic abuse allegations. See Dan Tracy and Jim Leusner, "Sentinel Finishes Report About OxyContin Articles," *The Orlando Sentinel*, February 24, 2004. See also Pinsky, "Right Too Soon: The Orlando Sentinel On Opioid Epidemic."
37. Ibid., Pinsky, "Right Too Soon: The Orlando Sentinel On Opioid Epidemic."
38. "Orlando Sentinel Reporter Resigns, Two Editors Reassigned In OxyContin Story Fallout," *Orlando Business Journal*, February 27, 2004.
39. T. Cicero et al., "Trends In Abuse Of OxyContin And Other Opioid Analgesics In The United States: 2002–2004," *J Pain* 2005;6:662–72.
40. Author interview with former assistant production manager, February 2017. See also Cicero, "Trends In Abuse Of OxyContin And Other Opioid Analgesics In The United States."
41. A. G. Lipman, "Pain as a human right: the 2004 Global Day Against Pain," *J Pain Palliat Care Pharmacother*. 2005;19(3):85–100. The WHO declaration led to initiatives in some countries to address pain as a basic human right. See F. Brennan et al., "Pain Management: A Fundamental Human Right," *Anesth Analg*. 2007 Jul;105(1):205–21. In 2010, six years after the WHO conference, at the International Pain Summit Of The International Association For The Study Of Pain in Montreal, the delegates adopted what became known as the "Declaration of Montreal." It stated that "access to pain management is a fundamental human right" and urged that all nations provide "access to pain management without discrimination . . . on the basis of age, sex, gender, medical diagnosis, race or ethnicity, religion, culture, marital, civil or socioeconomic status, sexual orientation, and political or other opinion." Declaration at https://www.iasp-pain.org/DeclarationofMontreal. See also International Pain Summit Of The International Association For The Study Of Pain, *J Pain Palliat Care Pharmacother*. 2011; 25(1):29–31.
42. Meier, "Origins of an Epidemic."
43. Barry Meier, "Why Drug Company Executives Haven't Really Seen Justice for Their Role in the Opioid Crisis," *Time*, June 15, 2018.
44. Meyer, "Origins of an Epidemic."
45. Chris McGreal, "Rudy Giuliani Won Deal For OxyContin Maker To Continue Sales Of Drug Behind Opioid Deaths," *Guardian*, May 22, 2018.
46. Meier, "Origins of an Epidemic."
47. Andrew Good, attorney for Dr. Goldenheim, interviewed in Meier, "Origins of an Epidemic."
48. What Is a Serious Adverse Event? Reporting Serious Problems to the FDA, Safety Information and Adverse Event Reporting Program, FDA, at https://www.fda.gov/safety/reporting-serious-problems-fda/what-serious-adverse-event.
49. 2008-01-15 Board report, pgs. 16, 24, PDD8901733989, -997.
50. 2007-07-15 Board report, pgs. 33, 41, 54, *Massachusetts v. Purdue* document PWG000300817, -825, -838.
51. Barry Meier reported in 2018 "top Justice Department officials in the George W. Bush administration did not support the move [for the serious felony counts], said four lawyers who took part in those discussions or were briefed about them." Meier, "Origins of an Epidemic."

52. Author interview with retired criminal investigator, DOJ, June 2018.
53. Rannazzisi interviewed in Meier, "Origins of an Epidemic."
54. 2006-10-25 Board minutes, *Massachusetts v. Purdue* document PKY183307486; see also 2006-10-25 agreement, PPLP004031281.
55. According to a complaint filed in January 2019 by the Massachusetts attorney general against Purdue and the eight living Sackler family members who had served as company directors. Bob Considine, "Readington Family Finds Justice, But Seeks More," *Courier-News*, June 4, 2007, A4; *Massachusetts v. Purdue* 61.
56. 2007-05-09 Agreed Statement of Facts, paragraph 20, available at https://www.documentcloud.org/documents/279028-purdue-guilty-plea.
57. "The Purdue Frederick Company, Inc. And Top Executives Plead Guilty To Misbranding OxyContin; Will Pay Over $600 Million," News Release from the United States Attorney's Office, Western District of Virginia, May 10, 2007. The plea deal allowed the Purdue executives to plead guilty only to misdemeanors.
58. 2007-05-09 Plea Agreement; 2007-05-04 Associate General Counsel's Certificate, *Massachusetts v. Purdue* document PDD1712900054.
59. 2007-05-15 Consent Judgment, *Massachusetts v. Purdue* document 07-1967(B).
60. 2007-05-09 Plea Agreement; 2007-05-04 Associate General Counsel's Certificate, *Massachusetts v. Purdue* document PDD1712900054.
61. David Sackler quoted in Bethany McLean, "'We Didn't Cause The Crisis': David Sackler Pleads His Case On The Opioid Epidemic," *Vanity Fair*, August 2019.
62. Marianne Skolek Perez, "You Messed with the Wrong Mother."
63. Considine, "Readington Family Finds Justice."
64. "Evaluating the Propriety and Adequacy of the OxyContin Criminal Settlement," Hearing before the Committee on the Judiciary, US Senate 110th Congress first session July 31, 2007 (US Government Printing Office, Washington: 2008).
65. Nagel quoted in Solomon, "The Importance of Being Rudy."
66. Marianne Skolek Perez, "You Messed with the Wrong Mother."
67. Testimony of Marianne Skolek, July 31, 2007, before the Senate Judiciary Committee, 110th Congress, first session, July 31, 2007.
68. Skolek became an investigative reporter for *The Washington Standard* and *Salem-News* and also has served as a consultant to plaintiff's attorneys suing Purdue.

Chapter 48: Profits and Corpses

1. "Instead of reporting dangerous prescribers, or even directing sales reps to stop visiting them, the Sacklers chose to keep pushing opioids to whoever prescribed the most," *Massachusetts v. Purdue*, 65, and para 112–53, 39–50.
2. The estimate for 2007 profits was presented in a July 2007 board meeting, and the figures on net sales were in a January 2008 board meeting. 2007-07-15 Board report, pg. 46, *Massachusetts v. Purdue* document PWG000300830 and 2008-01-15 Board report, pgs. 4, 22, 24, *Massachusetts v. Purdue* document PDD8901733977, -995, -997. Net sales are the sum of a company's gross sales minus its returns, allowances, and discounts. Revenues reported on the income statement often represent net sales.
3. 2007-10-28 attachment to email from Edward Mahony, *Massachusetts v. Purdue* document PPLPC012000159170.
4. In 2008, the detail team had four hundred employees; in 2009, just under five

hundred; 2010, six hundred; and in 2014, it surpassed seven hundred. That remained consistent until 2017 when Purdue thought the opioid market in the U.S. was saturated and the company was under increasing legal attack for its marketing of OxyContin. In February 2018 the detail squad was back to three hundred. In June 2018, Purdue laid off the remainder of its once high-flying detail team. 2007-07-15 Board report, pg. 46, *Massachusetts v. Purdue* document PWG000300830; 108 2007-07-15 Board report, pg. 52, *Massachusetts v. Purdue* document PWG000300836. See Nate Raymond, "OxyContin maker Purdue Pharma cuts remaining sales force," Reuters, June 20, 2018.

5. "The Sacklers' micromanagement was so intrusive that staff begged for relief," *Massachusetts v. Purdue*, 63. Richard Sackler was often involved in minutiae and details of marketing OxyContin. The complaints of those who worked for him and had to constantly accede or fend off his directives are recounted in the emails and memos produced by Purdue later as part of litigation discovery. See 2012-02-07 email from Russell Gasdia, *Massachusetts v. Purdue* document PPLPC012000368569.
6. Barry Meier, "Ruling Is Upheld Against Executives Tied to OxyContin," *New York Times*, December 15, 2010. The law firm was originally Washington, D.C.'s, Hogan & Hartson. Seven months before the 2010 ruling that rejected the appeal to overturn the ban on the three executives, Hogan & Hartson merged with London's Lovells. The new firm had forty-nine offices worldwide. It represented Mylan Pharmaceuticals when that company was later named a defendant in the consolidated opioid litigation. See for instance Washington County, Virginia v. Purdue Pharma, L.P. et al, US District Court, Western District of Virginia, case number 1:18-cv-00046-EKD-PMS, filed 12/13/2018.
7. Russell Gasdia, Purdue's vice president of sales and marketing, wrote to Michael Friedman, the CEO, about Richard Sackler: "Anything you can do to reduce the direct contact of Richard into the organization is appreciated." 2012-02-07 email from Russell Gasdia, *Massachusetts v. Purdue* document PPLPC012000368569.
8. *Massachusetts v. Purdue*, para 227, 74.
9. Tom Loftus, "Tighter Rein on Controlled Drugs Urged," *Lexington Courier-Journal*, September 19, 2001, 1, 5.
10. Remedica was an offshoot of a successful Cyprus drug company of the same name; Mortimer Sackler had come across it not long after it opened in the U.K. See "Brief History Of Remedica, A Leading Pharmaceutical Company In The European Union," at https://www.remedica.eu/about-us/history/.
11. There were then 142 accredited colleges of pharmacy nationwide.
12. His "relevant financial relationships" were: Abbott, Adolor, Alpharma, Anesiva, Archimedes Pharma, Ascent Biomedical Ventures, Aveva Drug Delivery, Baxter, Bayer, BioDelivery Sciences, Biometrix, Biovail, Cephalon, CombinatroRx, Cytogel, Endo Pharmaceuticals, Fralex, Genentech, GlaxoSmithKline, Globomax, GPC Biotech, GW Pharmaceuticals, Janssen/Ortho-McNeil, Johnson & Johnson, King Pharmaceuticals, Ligand Pharmaceuticals, Merck, Nektar Therapeutics, Neuromed, Novartis, Organon, Painceptor, Pfizer, Pharmos, PPD, Progenics, Sarentis, United Biosource Corp, Valeant Pharmaceuticals North America, Wyeth, Xenome, and Xenon Pharmaceuticals.
13. "Screening and Stratification Methods to Minimize Opioid Abuse in Cancer Patients," Lynn Webster, *Advances in Pain Management*, Volume 2, Number 1, 2008, 4–8.

14. *Salt Lake County v. Purdue Pharma, et. al.*, Third District Court for Salt Lake County, State of Utah, paragraph 12.
15. CDC Guideline for Prescribing Opioids for Chronic Pain (March 18, 2016), available at https://www.cdc.gov/mmwr/volumes/65/rr/rr6501e1.htm. See also Jesse Hyde and Daphne Chen, "The Untold Story Of How Utah Doctors And Big Pharma Helped Drive The National Opioid Epidemic," *Deseret News*, October 26, 2017.
16. In the few instances that *Pain Management* acknowledged there were "some endemic areas of high [opioid] abuse," it put the blame on "inadequately trained clinicians trying to do the right thing . . ." In a widely disseminated "lead article" published a year after Purdue's guilty plea, it explained, for instance, that the "myth [that] the mere exposure to an opioid leads to addiction" had given way to the "new thought [that] patients function well on opioids and rarely show addictive behavior." The same was true for the myth that "opioids should be only used to treat severe pain." It had given way to the idea that "treating pain early and aggressively leads to better quality of life" (the idea expressed often by Richard Sackler). See generally Ricardo Cruciani, "Treatment of Pain with Opioids and the Risk of Opioid Dependence: The Search for a Balance"; Steven D. Passik, "Appropriate Prescribing of Opioid and Associated Risk Minimization"; Lynn Webster, "Screening and Stratification Methods to Minimize Opioid Abuse in Cancer Patients," all three articles in *Advances in Pain Management*, Volume 2, Number 1, 2008.
17. *Salt Lake County v. Purdue Pharma, et. al.*, Third District Court for Salt Lake County, State of Utah, para 11–12, 56.
18. Ibid. See also Kristen Steward and Jennifer Dobner, "Utah Doctors Paid $25.8 Million By Drug Companies," *Salt Lake Tribune*, March 12, 2013.
19. His conviction was upheld on appeal. The People of the State of New York, v. Ricardo Cruciani, Supreme Court, New York County, New York, 1734-2018, January 23, 2019.
20. Steward and Dobner, "Utah Doctors Paid $25.8 Million By Drug Companies."
21. Salt Lake County v. Purdue Pharma, et. al., Third District Court for Salt Lake County, State of Utah, para 13.
22. 2008-04-18 email and attached memo from Richard Sackler, *Massachusetts v. Purdue* document PDD9316300629-631.
23. Chart titled "The Sacklers Paid Themselves Billions of Dollars," AGO graphic based on Purdue's internal Board documents, covering from April 2008 through 2016. *Massachusetts v. Purdue*, board minutes cited in note 154, 79.
24. Jared S. Hopkins, "OxyContin Made The Sacklers Rich. Now It's Tearing Them Apart," *Wall Street Journal*, July 13, 2019.
25. 2008-10-15 Board report, pgs. 19, 24, 28, *Massachusetts v. Purdue* document PDD9316101020, -025, 029.
26. 2009-03-05 Board minutes, *Massachusetts v. Purdue* document PKY183212 703-711.
27. 2009-07-30 Board report, pg. 16, *Massachusetts v. Purdue* document PPLPC01200 0233246; 2009-06-26 Board minutes, *Massachusetts v. Purdue* document PKY183 212742.
28. David Sackler did not become a Purdue director until 2012. McLean, " 'We Didn't Cause The Crisis.' "
29. "Numerous studies have shown that the most common route by which drugs of

abuse are administered is ingestion, followed by snorting and injection, with the percentage of those ingesting the drugs ranging from 64 percent to 97 percent, depending on the population studied. Certain medications are more likely than others to be snorted or injected." "Many Doctors Misunderstand Key Facets of Opioid Abuse." Survey by Bloomberg School of Public Health, Johns Hopkins, June 23, 2015.

30. 2008-02-22 email from John Stewart, *Massachusetts v. Purdue* document PPLPC012000172201.
31. Introducing Opioids with Abuse-Deterrent Properties (OADP), *Massachusetts v. Purdue* document PVT0024614.
32. Three Purdue-sponsored articles ran in *The Atlantic*. The company's campaign built around the tamper-resistant formulations ran in medical journals, medical education courses, and on the website In the Face of Pain. Some of the Purdue publications included: *Providing Relief, Preventing Abuse: The Resource Guide for People with Pain*; *Exit Wounds*; *Opioid Prescribing: Clinical Tools and Risk Management; Strategies For Responsible Opioid Prescribing*; and *Clinical Issues in Opioid Prescribing*. See Introducing Opioids with Abuse-Deterrent Properties (OADP), PVT0024614.
33. 2010-07-22 questions during Board meeting, *Massachusetts v. Purdue* document PPLPC012000283167.
34. 752,417 visits in 2012, and 744,777 visits in 2013. See the following Purdue board of director meeting reports, all documents in *Massachusetts v. Purdue*: 2010-02-01 Board report, 23, PPLPC012000252797; 2011-05-02 Board report, 3, PPLPC012000322128; 2012 01 30 Board report, 3, PPLPC012000374793; 2013-05-13 Board report, 7, PPLP004367546.
35. Richard Sackler complained, for instance, that they were slightly under their quotas for doctor visits and did not forcefully present the benefits of opioid pain treatment. He was particularly incensed that managers had allowed many visits to "non-high potential prescribers." 2011-06-16 email from Richard Sackler, *Massachusetts v. Purdue* document PPLPC012000329706.
36. See the following Purdue board of director meeting reports, all documents in *Massachusetts v. Purdue*: 2010-02-04 Board minutes, PKY183212818-820; 2010-04-01 Board minutes, PKY183212829; 2010-12-02 Board minutes, PKY183212869-70. In 2010-07-27 Board report, pg. 18, PWG000422494, the staff reported to the Sacklers "that Purdue had paid their family $389,000,000 in the first six months of 2010," *Massachusetts v. Purdue*, para 317, 107.
37. 2010-06-24 Purdue Pharma 2010 10-Year Plan, 1-15, Key Assumptions 6, *Massachusetts v. Purdue* document PPLPC012000277155-169, 217.
38. Walters, "America's Opioid Crisis: How Prescription Drugs Sparked A National Trauma."
39. *Massachusetts v. Purdue*, para 335–37, 113.
40. Purdue contended its promotion of Oxy was "consistent with FDA-approved product labeling. And doctors at all times have had access to FDA-approved label, which is crystal clear about the risk of abuse and addiction." *Massachusetts v. Purdue*, Purdue's Memorandum Of Law In Support Of Its Motion To Dismiss Amended Complaint, 20–21.
41. Ryan, Girion, and Glover, "More than 1 Million OxyContin Pills Ended up in the Hands of Criminals and Addicts."
42. According to the complaint filed in *Massachusetts v. Purdue*, the attorney general

charged, "The Sacklers knew these employees were aware of misconduct because they had directed it," para 334, 112. See also 2011-01-20 Board minutes, *Massachusetts v. Purdue* document PKY183212882-892. And Ryan, Girion, and Glover, "More than 1 Million OxyContin Pills Ended up in the Hands of Criminals and Addicts."

43. Joseph Rannazzisi quoted in Ryan, Girion, and Glover, "More than 1 Million OxyContin Pills Ended up in the Hands of Criminals and Addicts."
44. Ibid.
45. Phil Strassburger quoted in Ibid.
46. Rannazzisi was featured as a whistleblower in a 2017 joint investigation by *60 Minutes* and *The Washington Post*. "Ex-DEA agent: Opioid crisis fueled by drug industry and Congress," CBS *60 Minutes*, October 15, 2017. See also Scott Higham and Lenny Bernstein, "Who is Joe Rannazzisi: The DEA man who fought the drug companies and lost," *Washington Post*, October 15, 2007.
47. "Ex-DEA agent: Opioid crisis fueled by drug industry and Congress"; Nate Raymond, "Mckesson To Pay $37 Million To Resolve West Virginia Opioid Lawsuit," Reuters, May 2, 2019. See Sara Randazzo, "Last-Minute Opioid Deal Could Open Door to Bigger Settlement," *Wall Street Journal*, October 21, 2019.
48. Matthew Herper, "David Graham On The Vioxx Verdict," *Forbes*, August 19, 2005.
49. Derek Lowe, "500,000 Excess Deaths From Vioxx?," *In the Pipeline* (AAAS), May 30, 2012.
50. Since Vioxx was not a Controlled Substances Act scheduled drug, Merck was spared parallel investigations by the DEA and FBI, and criminal probes by state attorneys general and federal prosecutors. Because of Purdue's great success with OxyContin, the Sacklers believed that politicians and law enforcement had unfairly put most of the blame for the abuse and addiction epidemic on the company. See differences with a drug not a controlled substance in "Merck Settles Vioxx Claims for $4.85 Billion," Reuters, November 9, 2007.
51. "Ex-DEA Agent: Opioid Crisis Fueled By Drug Industry And Congress," CBS *60 Minutes*, October 15, 2017.
52. Author interview with former attorney for Purdue, January 2019.
53. Jef Feeley, "J&J Labeled 'Kingpin' of US Opioid Drug Epidemic by Oklahoma," *Bloomberg*, March 12, 2019; Jan Hoffman, "Johnson & Johnson Ordered to Pay $572 Million in Landmark Opioid Trial," *New York Times*, August 26, 2019, 1; Colin Dwyer and Jackie Fortier, "Oklahoma Judge Shaves $107 Million Off Opioid Decision Against Johnson & Johnson," *NPR*, "All Things Considered," November 15, 2019.
54. 2011-11-09 Board report, pg. 26, *Massachusetts v. Purdue* document PWG00041 9328.
55. 2012-04-20 email from David Rosen, *Massachusetts v. Purdue* document PPLPC0 12000374532.
56. 2013-07-05 email from Edward Mahony, *Massachusetts v. Purdue* document PPL PC012000431312-313.
57. Paul D. Thacker, "Senators Hatch And Wyden: Do Your Jobs And Release The Sealed Opioids Report," *Stat*, June 27, 2016.
58. Charles Ornstein and Tracy Weber, "The Champion of Painkillers," *ProPublica*, December 23, 2011.
59. Charles Ornstein and Tracy Weber, "American Pain Foundation Shuts Down

as Senators Launch Investigation of Prescription Narcotics," *ProPublica*, May 8, 2012.

60. Thacker, "Senators Hatch And Wyden: Do Your Jobs And Release The Sealed Opioids Report." See also Jason Smith, "OxyContin, Heroin, and the Sackler-Sinaloa Connection," Part I: The Come Up, September 25, 2015, 20, initially published online on therealedition.com but not available as of 2019. Smith has written about that article, "Of anything I've ever written, I may be most proud of this piece," Medium.com, September 10, 2015.
61. 2012-04-20 email from David Rosen, *Massachusetts v. Purdue* document PPLPC0 12000374532.
62. The FDA had approved generic OxyContin in 2003 and Purdue had agreed for several years to limited competition, but the competitors had difficulties duplicating the extended release coating. There were many generic oxycodone tablets on the market, but they were all instant release, short relief. FDA Actions on OxyContin Products, 4/16/2013, at https://www.fda.gov/drugs/information-drug-class/fda-actions-oxycontin-products-4162013.
63. Nancy Shute and Audrey Carlsen, "FDA's Rejection of Generic OxyContin May Have Side Effects," *NPR News*, April 18, 2003.
64. The arguments before the FDA had made for some odd allies. In opposing any generics Purdue was joined by some state attorneys general who decided it was better to allow Purdue to keep prices high and feed its profits than to allow cheap generics to flood the market and almost certainly fuel the illicit street trade. McLean, "'We Didn't Cause The Crisis'"; See also Barry Meier, "F.D.A. Bars Generic OxyContin," *New York Times*, April 16, 2013.
65. Shute and Carlsen, "FDA's Rejection of Generic OxyContin May Have Side Effects."
66. Meier, "F.D.A. Bars Generic OxyContin."
67. Ibid.
68. 2013-08-08 Identifying Granular Growth Opportunities for OxyContin: Addendum to July 18th and August 5th Updates, *Massachusetts v. Purdue* document PPLP004409892.
69. 2014-01-30 memo from Edward Mahony, *Massachusetts v. Purdue* document PPLPC020000756513.
70. 2013-08-08 Identifying Granular Growth Opportunities for OxyContin: Addendum to July 18th and August 5th Updates, *Massachusetts v. Purdue* document PPLP004409896-897.
71. The exact amount was $399,920,000. 2013-11-01 Board report, pgs. 3, 6, *Massachusetts v. Purdue* document PPLPC002000186913, -916.
72. 2013-12-04 email from David Rosen, *Massachusetts v. Purdue* document PPLPC012000454676; 500 2014-01-03 email from Burt Rosen, *Massachusetts v. Purdue* document PPLPC020000748356 ("I spoke to Richard just before the year end and raised concerns over our internal documents.").
73. "I think my dad's vision was that I would replace him at some point," said David Sackler, "as his health continued to decline." McLean, "'We Didn't Cause The Crisis.'"
74. Alex Morrell, "The OxyContin Clan: The $14 Billion Newcomer to Forbes 2015 List of Richest U.S. Families," *Forbes*, July 1, 2015.
75. Ibid.
76. McLean, "'We Didn't Cause The Crisis.'"

Chapter 49: Gaming the System

1. See Benjamin M. Craig and Scott A. Strassels, "Out-of-pocket Prices of Opioid Analgesics in the United States, 1999–2004," *Pain Med.* 2010;11(2):240–47.
2. Kesselheim, "The High Cost of Prescription Drugs in the United States: Origins and Prospects for Reform."
3. "Pain Management and the Opioid Epidemic: Balancing Societal and Individual Benefits and Risks of Prescription Opioid Use," National Academies of Sciences, Engineering, and Medicine; Health and Medicine Division; Board on Health Sciences Policy; Committee on Pain Management and Regulatory Strategies to Address Prescription Opioid Abuse; (Phillips JK, Ford MA, Bonnie RJ, editors) (Washington, D.C.: National Academies Press, July 2017).
4. Dan Mangan, "US Often Pays Much More Than Other Countries For Prescription Drugs, Surgery," CNBC, July 19, 2016.
5. Ben Hirschler, "How the U.S. Pays 3 Times More for Drugs," *Scientific American*, October 13, 2015.
6. Kefauver, *In a Few Hands*, 6.
7. Dan Mangan and Anita Balakrishnan, "Mylan CEO Bresch: 'No One's More Frustrated Than Me' About Epipen Price Furor," CNBC, August 25, 2016.
8. Michael A. Carrier and Carl J. Minniti III, "The Untold Epipen Story: How Mylan Hiked Prices By Blocking Rivals," *Cornell Law Review*, Vol. 102:53, 2017, 53–72.
9. Cynthia Koons and Robert Langreth, "How Marketing Turned the EpiPen into a Billion-Dollar Business," *Businessweek*, September 23, 2015.
10. As with most drug company settlements, it admitted no guilt. Ibid. See also David Lazarus, "Always look on the bright side of life, says CEO who raised EpiPen price by more than 400%," *Los Angeles Times*, June 5, 2018.
11. A snapshot of the industry in 2014 was skewed by the sale of just four prescription drugs that had been approved recently to treat hepatitis C. Gilead Sciences had Harvoni and Sovaldi, AbbVie sold Viekira Pak, and Janssen had Olysio. If their combined 2014 sales of $14 billion were removed from the $265 billion prescription market, the industry's total growth rate would have been 7.6 percent instead of 12.2 percent. Even the lower rate would have been nearly triple the annual inflation rate. See Charles Roehrig, "The Impact Of New Hepatitis C Drugs On National Health Spending," *Health Affairs*, December 7, 2015.
12. Helene L. Lipton et al., "Pharmacy Benefit Management Companies: Dimensions of Performance," *Annual Review of Public Health* 1999 20:1, 361–401.
13. Vagelos and Galambos, *Medicine, Science and Merck*, 202–3.
14. C. Woolsey, "Any adverse effects? Drug industry mergers invite more scrutiny of plan costs," *Business Insurance*, July 18, 1994, 1.
15. Some examples include the purchase of Caremark by MedPartners, a physician practice management firm, for $2.5 billion. The following year, RxAmerica, a PBM owned by American Stores, a national retail pharmacy, merged with Integrated Health Concepts, a PBM owned by Long's Drugstores. PCS Health Systems acquired Managed Prescription Services, Inc., a PBM owned by Humana Health. Also in 1997 the national hospital chain Columbia HCA bought Value Health, Inc., the parent of ValueRx, for $1.1 billion. A year later, Columbia sold ValueRx to Express Scripts, an independent PBM, for just under half a billion. Lipton et al., "Pharmacy Benefit Management Companies."

16. Medicare Prescription, Drug, Improvement, and Modernization Act of 2003, 108th Congress, Public Law 108-173.
17. Sidney Lupkin, "5 Reasons Prescription Drug Prices Are So High in the U.S.," *Money, Kaiser Health News*, August 23, 2016.
18. "Fact Sheet: How Much Money Could Medicare Save By Negotiating Prescription Drug Prices?," *Committee for a Responsible Budget*, April 11, 2016.
19. Brittany Hoffman-Eubanks, "The Role of Pharmacy Benefit Managers in American Health Care: Pharmacy Concerns and Perspectives: Part 1," *Pharmacy Times*, November 14, 2017.
20. "While PBMs Market Themselves As Being Well-Positioned To Bring Savings To Plans And Consumers, A Lack Of Transparency In Their Practices Enables Them To Wield Their Power To Increase Their Profits, Often At The Expense Of The Consumer," *PBM Watch*, Winter 2018.
21. "CMS Updates Drug Dashboards with Prescription Drug Pricing and Spending Data," Centers for Medicare & Medicaid Services, March 14, 2019, and Jacqueline Renfrow, "Kentucky Officials: Pbms Earned $123M Last Year Through Spread Pricing In State's Medicaid Program," *Fierce Healthcare*, February 25, 2019; Susan Jaffe, "No More Secrets: Congress Bans Pharmacist 'Gag Orders' on Drug Prices," *Kaiser Health News*, October 10, 2018.
22. Rabah Kamal et al., "What Are the Recent and Forecasted Trends in Prescription Drug Spending," Health System Tracker, *Kaiser Family Foundation*, 2018, 21.
23. "An Overview of the Medicare Part D Prescription Drug Benefit," *Kaiser Family Foundation*, October 12, 2018.
24. Veterans Affairs has the discretion to exclude some of the budget-busting drugs from its formulary.
25. "Prices for Brand-Name Drugs Under Selected Federal Programs," A CBO Paper, Congressional Budget Office, June 2005.
26. Katherine Young et al., "Medicaid's Most Costly Outpatient Drugs," *Kaiser Family Foundation*, July 15, 2016; see also "Medicaid Spending for Prescription Drugs," Report of Medicaid and CHIP Payment and Access Commission, January 2016.
27. "An Overview of the Medicare Part D Prescription Drug Benefit."
28. The federal government pays for drugs under Social Security Disability, Veterans Affairs, TRICARE, the civilian health program of the U.S. military and State Department, and FEHB, which provides civilian health coverage for all other divisions in the federal government. Kesselheim, "The High Cost of Prescription Drugs in the United States," 859.
29. M.R. Trusheim et al., "Stratified Medicine: Strategic and Economic Implications of Combining Drugs and Clinical Biomarkers," *Nature Reviews: Drug Discovery* 6, no. 4 (2007): 287–93.
30. David Dayen, "The Hidden Monopolies That Raise Drug Prices," *American Prospect*, March 28, 2017.
31. Separate contracts mean that insurance companies cannot determine what percentage of what they pay to a PBM for a drug is reimbursed to the pharmacist at the bottom of the pharma distribution chain. Insurers also have no idea of what the PBM paid for a drug; the pharma company might have discounted the list price or effectively reduced it by offering a rebate. Since pharmacists do not know what insurance companies paid to the PBMs for the drug, when they finally re-

ceive their payment there is no way to tell whether the PBM passed along most of the insurance reimbursement or retained an outsized share as its profit.

32. It is not even certain whether PBMs keep all profits from spread pricing or share some with private insurers in order to get them to issue the highest reimbursement rates without asking any questions.
33. Robert Langreth et al., "The Secret Drug Pricing System Middlemen Use to Rake in Millions," *Bloomberg*, September 11, 2018.
34. "Study shows PBMs skimming big markups," *National Community Pharmacists Association*, January 25, 2019.
35. Review of costs from 1987 to 2014, CMS Updates Drug Dashboards with Prescription Drug Pricing and Spending Data, Centers for Medicare & Medicaid Services, March 14, 2019.
36. Ibid.
37. "Feeling The Pain Of Rising Drug Prices? Blame The Middle Man," CBS News, September 20, 2018.
38. Hirschler, "How the U.S. Pays 3 Times More for Drugs."
39. Testimony of Heather Bresch, "Reviewing The Rising Price Of Epipens," Hearing Before The Committee On Oversight And Government Reform House Of Representatives, 114th Congress, second session, September 21, 2016.
40. Deposition of Richard Sackler, 41.
41. Listed are the three hypertension drugs, year of first approval in the U.S., and the price increase from 2008 to 2015: isoproterenol (1947), 2,500 percent; nitroprusside (1955), 1,700 percent; digoxin (1949), 687 percent. *JAMA*, 860—n 23; see "Escalating Prices Of Generic Drugs In The US," *Generics and Biosimilars Initiative*, March 15, 2019.
42. Hirschler, "How the U.S. Pays 3 Times More for Drugs."
43. I. Papanicolas et al., "Health Care Spending in the United States and Other High-Income Countries." *JAMA*, 319(10), 2018:1024–39.
44. Nicholas Florko, "Federal judge blocks Trump rule to require drug prices in TV ads," *STAT*, July 8, 2019.
45. "Sweeping Lawsuit Accuses Top Generic Drug Companies, Executives of Fixing Prices," CBS News, *60 Minutes*, May 12, 2019.
46. Nicholas Florko and Lev Facher, "Pelosi's Drug Pricing Plan Is More Aggressive than Expected," *STAT*, September 9, 2019. See also Johnathan Gardner, "Medicare Would Negotiate Prices for 250 Drugs Under House Democrats' Plan," *BioPharma Dive*, September 10, 2019; Shraddha Chakradhar, "Battle Set in Washington Over Competing Drug Price Bills," *STAT*, December 9, 2019; "Health Care: See Where the 2020 Democrats Stand," Tracking the Issues in the 2020 Election, Special Series, NPR, September 10, 2019. See also Jay Hancock, "Talk About Déjà Vu: Senators Set To Re-Enact Drug Price Hearing Of 60 Years Ago," *Kaiser Health News*, February 22, 2019.

Chapter 50: Billion-Dollar Orphans

1. The per capita health care costs were compared in the U.S. and Australia, Canada, France, Germany, the Netherlands, Norway, Sweden, Switzerland, and the U.K. The Swiss came in second, at $783 per person, and Sweden was the lowest at $351. Austin Frakt, "Something Happened to U.S. Drug Costs in the 1990s," *New York Times*, November 12, 2018.

2. Sarah Jane Tribble and Sydney Lupkin, "Drugs For Rare Diseases Have Become Uncommonly Rich Monopolies," *NPR, Morning Edition*, January 17, 2017.
3. Paul Melmeyer, Director of Federal Policy for the National Organization of Rare Disorders, quoted in Malorye A. Branca, "How the Orphan Drug Act Changed the Development Landscape," *BioPharma Dive*, April 10, 2017; see also Sarah Jane Tribble and Sydney Lupkin, "How Drugmakers Manipulate Orphan Drug Rules to Create Prized Monopolies," *California Healthline*, January 18, 2017.
4. Kaiser Health Report 2017. See also Stephen Barlas, "The Push for Additional Orphan Drugs," *P&T Community*, 2016;41(11): 667.
5. FDA's Orphan Drug Database, *Kaiser Health News*, Tribble and Lupkin, "How Drugmakers Manipulate Orphan Drug Rules to Create Prized Monopolies."
6. In 2015, orphan drugs accounted for 47 percent of FDA approved medicines, up from 29 percent in 2010. In 2016, nine more orphans were approved, 40 percent of the total.
7. Andrew Pollack, "AstraZeneca Pushes to Protect Crestor From Generic Competition," *New York Times*, June 27, 2016.
8. The seven orphan drugs in the top ten were Humira (2), Enbrel (3), Remicade (5), and 7 through 10 were Rituxan, Neulasta, Revlimid, and Copaxone.
9. Nigel Walker, "Where Do Orphan Drugs Go From Here?," *Pharma's Almanac*, May 24, 2019.
10. Michael G. Daniel et al., "The Orphan Drug Act: Restoring the Mission to Rare Diseases," *American Journal of Clinical Oncology*: April 2016, Volume 39, Issue 2, 210–13.
11. "Orphan Products: Hope for People With Rare Diseases," Drug Information for Consumers, FDA, March 1, 2018.
12. Coté quoted, and Coté Orphan website, in Tribble and Lupkin, "Drugs For Rare Diseases Have Become Uncommonly Rich Monopolies."
13. Ibid.
14. "I was responsible for the administration of the US Orphan Drug Act—the first in the world," Haffner says on her LinkedIn profile. https://www.linkedin.com/in/marlene-haffner-299b3b22/.
15. In 2013, Haffner opened a new LLC with Lisa Beth Ferstenberg, the medical director of Sequella, a small biotech.
16. Subsequently, the FDA has given Genentech and Biogen separate orphan status on even smaller subclasses of follicular B-cell non-Hodgkin's lymphoma: diffuse large B-cell lymphoma and lymphocytic leukemia.
17. MedStats and Kiplinger (2017); Megan Brooks, "Cancer Drugs Dominate Top 10 Best-Selling Drugs in 2018," *Medscape*, March 19, 2019.
18. Bill Saporito, "Hospitals Furious at Cancer-Drug Price Hikes," *Time*, October 27, 2014.
19. Measuring the number of people affected with FH has proven difficult and is the subject of academic studies that have attempted to standardize the measurements and factors. Leo Akioyamen et al., "Estimating The Prevalence Of Heterozygous Familial Hypercholesterolaemia: A Systematic Review And Meta-Analysis," *BMJ* vol. 7, no. 9, September 1, 2017. The FH Foundation provides this information: "Worldwide, 1 in every 200–500 people has FH. Certain populations display a higher prevalence of FH, such as the French Canadian, Ashkenazi Jew, Lebanese, and South African Afrikaner populations. In these populations, 1 in every 67 people are found to have FH." Marie Louise Brumit, "How Common Is Famil-

ial Hypercholesterolemia?" News & Blogs, The FH Foundation, December 24, 2014.

20. Anne C. Goldberg and Samuel S. Gidding, "Knowing the Prevalence of Familial Hypercholesterolemia Matters," *Circulation*, March 15, 2016, vol 133, no. 11.
21. The more common FH includes all instances in which a child inherits only one dominant gene from one parent. That is classified as Heterozygous familial hypercholesterolemia, HeFH. See "Repatha (Evolocumab) for the Treatment of Heterozygous and Homozygous Familial Hypercholesterolemia," *Clinical Trials Arena*, at https://www.clinicaltrialsarena.com/projects/repatha-evolocumab-treatment-heterozygous-homozygous-familial-hypercholesterolemia.
22. Some researchers who worked on the development of Repatha were surprised that Amgen applied for orphan status. Steven Nissen, the chairman of Cardiovascular Medicine at the Cleveland Clinic, had run one of the largest clinical trials. "It's certainly not considered by any of us [researchers] to be an orphan drug." Nissen quoted in Sarah Jane Tribble and Sydney Lupkin, "Drugs For Rare Diseases Have Become Uncommonly Rich Monopolies," NPR, Morning Edition, January 17, 2017.
23. Anthony Wang et al., "Systematic Review of Low-Density Lipoprotein Cholesterol Apheresis for the Treatment of Familial Hypercholesterolemia," *Journal of the American Heart Association* vol. 5, no. 7, July 6, 2016,
24. Pediatric Device Consortia Grants Program, Section: "Developing Products for Rare Diseases & Conditions," FDA, September 20, 2018.
25. "To Accelerate The Discovery, Development, And Delivery Of 21st Century Cures, And For Other Purposes" (this Act may be cited as the "21st Century Cures Act"), H.R.24, 114th Congress, second session, January 4, 2016.
26. Pollack, "AstraZeneca Pushes to Protect Crestor From Generic Competition."
27. Ibid.
28. "Csrxp Statement On Astrazeneca Seeking 'Orphan Drug' Designation For Widely-Used Cholesterol Drug Crestor," The Campaign for Sustainable Rx Pricing, September 2016.
29. Crestor's patent now expires on May 27, 2023, unless AstraZeneca can extend it even further by finding another rare disease that Crestor could treat.
30. It was in December 1999 for the "Treatment of patients with pancreatic cancer that overexpress p185HER2, a monoclonal antibody," and in December 2009 for "Treatment of HER2-overexpressing advanced adenocarcinoma of the stomach, including gastroesophageal junction."
31. Christopher T. Chen and Aaron S. Kesselheim, "Journey of Generic Imatinib: A Case Study in Oncology Drug Pricing," *Journal of Oncology Practice* 2017 13:6, 352–55.
32. Gleevec's patent included a pediatric exclusivity extension, an additional six months of protection for drug companies that conduct a clinical trial in pediatric patients. It also got a patent term restoration of 586 days.
33. Chen and Kesselheim, "Journey of Generic Imatinib."
34. See Orphan Designations under Generic Name Imatinib and Imatinib Mesylate, FDA, ranging from January 21, 2001 to December 19, 2005.
35. Abbott got Humira when it bought BASF Pharma. See Dyke Hendrickson, "Birth Of A Blockbuster: Abbott Mounts Humira's Marketing Campaign," *Boston Business Journal*, October 20, 2003.
36. Ibid.

37. Lipitor is #1 by a healthy margin, more than $150 billion in sales.
38. Two approvals for juvenile rheumatoid arthritis (2005); pediatric Crohn's disease (2006); pediatric ulcerative colitis (2011); chronic noninfectious anterior uveitis (2014); moderate to severe hidradenitis suppurativa (2015); and severe hidradenitis suppurativa (2015). US FDA Orphan Drug Designations and Approvals.
39. "Humira: The Highs And Lows Of The World's Best-Selling Drug," *Pharmaceutical Technology*, September 5, 2018.
40. Allergan was spun off from SmithKline Beecham and was looking for ways to build a business beyond its mainstay allergy eye and nose drops and eye care products. Between 1986 and 1991, there had been five double-blind, placebo-controlled studies of botulinum toxin protein on patients with a rare disorder, cervical dystonia. The trials, sponsored by academic institutes and the NIH, had produced promising results. Marius Nicolae Popescu et al., "Injecting Botulinum Toxin Into The Treatment Of Blepharospasm," *Romanian Journal of Ophthalmology* 62(2), April–June 2018, 162–65. See also Leslie Berkman, "Shareholders OK SmithKline Deal Spinning Off Beckman, Allergan," *Los Angeles Times*, July 27, 1989.
41. "Allergan Agrees to Plead Guilty and Pay $600 Million to Resolve Allegations of Off-Label Promotion of Botox," Press Release, Department of Justice, September 1, 2010.
42. Ibid.
43. It took until 2013 for the FDA to approve Botox for the mass-market treatment of lateral canthal lines, so-called crow's-feet wrinkles near the eyes.
44. When it comes to treating upper limb spasticity, the FDA approved muscles and doses are biceps brachii (100 units to 200 units divided in four sites); flexor carpi radialis (12.5 units to 50 units in 1 site); flexor carpi ulnaris (12.5 units to 50 units in 1 site); flexor digitorum profundus (30 units to 50 units in 1 site); flexor digitorum superficialis (30 units to 50 units in 1 site); adductor pollicis (20 units in 1 site); and flexor pollicis longus (20 units in 1 site).
45. "Botox Approval History, Treatment for: Hyperhidrosis, Cervical Dystonia, Urinary Incontinence, Migraine Prevention, Upper Limb Spasticity, Lower Limb Spasticity, Blepharospasm, Strabismus" at https://www.drugs.com/history/botox.html.
46. They include corticobasal degeneration, a progressive neurological disorder marked by cell loss and deterioration of areas of the brain; essential tremor, an involuntary, rhythmic spasm of the hands; Frey syndrome, affecting ability to form saliva; gastroparesis, slow emptying of food from the stomach; hereditary leiomyomatosis and renal cell carcinoma, smooth muscle growths on the uterus and kidneys; hereditary spastic paraplegia, difficulty walking; laryngeal dystonia, chronic voice disorder caused by uncontrolled spasms of the larynx muscles; multiple system atrophy, which causes Parkinson's-type symptoms; necrotizing fasciitis, a decaying infection of the fascia; Niemann-Pick disease Type C, an inability of the body to transport cholesterol; pantothenate kinase-associated neurodegeneration, a neurological movement disorder; primary orthostatic tremor, a rapid uncontrolled trembling in the leg when standing. See Rare Disease Database, National Organziation for Rare Disorders. See also Antigone S Papavasiliou et al., "Safety of botulinum toxin A in children and adolescents with cerebral palsy in a pragmatic setting," *Toxins* vol. 5(3), March 12, 2013, 524–36.
47. When the Orphan Drug Act passed in 1983, it had been less than a year since the

FDA approved Genentech's Humulin, the first ever genetically engineered drug. Biotechnology since then has changed the world of orphan drugs.

48. "Atypical hemolytic-uremic syndrome," Genetics Home Reference, U.S. National Library of Medicine, October 29, 2019.
49. Chuck Dinerstein, "Why Is Soliris The Most Expensive Drug In The US?," *American Council on Science and Health*, May 27, 2017.
50. The orphan illness was biallelic RPE65-mediated inherited retinal disease.
51. The drug was only approved for children under the age of two. See Joshua Cohen, "At Over $2 Million Zolgensma Is The World's Most Expensive Therapy, Yet Relatively Cost-Effective," *Forbes*, June 5, 2019; Hannah Kuchler, "Novartis Wins Approval For World's Most Expensive Drug," *Financial Times*, May 24, 2019.
52. Berkeley Lovelace Jr., and Angelica LaVito, "FDA Approves Novartis' $2.1 Million Gene Therapy—Making It The World's Most Expensive Drug," CNBC, May 24, 2019.
53. Robert Weisman, "New Genzyme Pill Will Cost Patients $310,250 A Year," *Boston Globe*, September 2, 2014.
54. Tim Coté, the ex-FDA orphan drug director and founder of Coté Orphan, told NPR when asked about Kalydeco's price: "The price point is justified because actually it has a dramatic effect on the children. Dead children . . . people are willing to pay a lot to prevent that. And that's a real good thing that we have this drug. OK?" Coté quoted in Tribble and Lupkin, "Drugs For Rare Diseases Have Become Uncommonly Rich Monopolies."
55. John Farber, a specialist researcher on cystic fibrosis, organized the petition. For more on the pricing controversy see Ed Silverman, "Vertex Faces More Pressure Over Pricing, But One Analyst Does Not Expect Any Movement," *Stat*, January 28, 2019.
56. Megan Thielking, "NIH Funding Contributed To 210 Approved Drugs In Recent Years, Study Says," *Stat*, February 12, 2018.
57. Mariana Mazzucato, "How Taxpayers Prop Up Big Pharma, And How To Cap That," *Los Angeles Times*, October 27, 2015.
58. On the few occasions in which the FDA tried to limit some of the orphan abuses, it was not successful. Depomed, a small California pharmaceutical company, tried in 2010 to get orphan approval for "management of postherpetic neuralgia" (a complication of shingles). Depomed's once-a-day pill was based on gabapentin, the same active ingredient in Pfizer's Neurontin. The FDA approved Depomed's pill but denied it the seven-year exclusive selling period since there was no proof its product was any better than others. Depomed sued the FDA, contending the Orphan Drug Act did not require a drug to be better, only effective. The courts agreed and the drug, Gralise, became one of the small company's best-selling drugs at $100 million annually. Tribble and Lupkin, "Drugs For Rare Diseases Have Become Uncommonly Rich Monopolies"; Monica Holmberg, "New FDA Actions: Depomed Inc's Gralise," *Pharmacy Times*, 2012-01-09 09:45:51.
59. Pollack, "Questcor Finds Profits, at $28,000 a Vial."
60. Michael Gibney, "H.P. Acthar Gel–Questcor/Mallinckrodt," *FiercePharma*, 2019.
61. Pollack, "Questcor Finds Profits, at $28,000 a Vial."
62. Gibney, "H.P. Acthar Gel."
63. In 2006, for example, Questcor lost $10.1 million on revenues of $12.8 million.
64. Don Bailey quoted in Pollack, "Questcor Finds Profits, at $28,000 a Vial."

65. David White, "Questor Pharmaceuticals: Quickly Building A Multi-Billion Dollar Business," *Seeking Alpha*, January 17, 2012.
66. Historical share price of QCOR at https://www.historicalstockprice.com/qcor-historical-stock-prices/.
67. Sergio Hernandez and Wayne Drash, "How CNN Reported on Acthar," CNN, June 29, 2018.
68. Andrew Pollock and Chad Bray, "Mallinckrodt Pharmaceuticals to Buy Questcor for $5.6 Billion," *New York Times*, April 7, 2014.
69. Hernandez and Drash, "How CNN Reported on Acthar."
70. S. Shakil and Redberg RF, "New (Very High) Prices on Old Drugs," *JAMA Intern Med.* 2017;177(11):1568.
71. Bourdette quoted in Linette Lopez, "The Most Respected Medical Journal In The US Just Eviscerated A Drug That's Cost Taxpayers Over $1 Billion," *Business Insider*, September 12, 2017.
72. Matt Novak, "Drug Company to Pay Just $15.4 Million Over Doctor Bribery Scandal Involving Medicine That Brings in $1 Billion a Year," *Gizmodo*, June 5, 2019.
73. Shakil and Redberg, "New (Very High) Prices on Old Drugs," 1568.
74. Novak, "Drug Company to Pay Just $15.4 Million Over Doctor Bribery."
75. Beth Mole, "The 5,000 percent price hike that made Martin Shkreli infamous is no longer paying off," *ARSTechnica*, July 19, 2018; Scarlet Fu, "Drug Goes From $13.50 to $750 Overnight," *Bloomberg*, September 21, 2015.
76. Only 27 percent had a positive view while 58 percent had a negative opinion. Americans ranked even the federal government ahead of pharma. Justin McCarthy, "Big Pharma Sinks to the Bottom of U.S. Industry Rankings," *Gallup News*, September 3, 2019.
77. Stephanie M. Lee, "Here's How Big Pharma Plans To Clean Up After Martin Shkreli," Science, *BuzzFeed*, January 10, 2017.
78. Tom Hays and Colleen Long, " 'Pharma Bro' Martin Shkreli cries in court, is sentenced to 7 years for securities fraud," Associated Press, March 9, 2018.
79. " 'Pharma Bro' Shkreli Is In Prison, But Daraprim's Price Is Still High," *Kaiser Health News*, May 4, 2018.
80. Lee, "Here's How Big Pharma Plans To Clean Up After Martin Shkreli."
81. Marlene Haffner told NPR: "People have played games with the Orphan Drug Act since it was passed. It's the American way, I don't mean that in a nasty way. But we take advantage of what's in front of us."
82. Quoted in "How Pharma Companies Manipulate Orphan Drug Rule to Create Monopolies P&T Community," https://www.ptcommunity.com/news/20170117/how-pharma-companies-manipulate-orphan-drug-rule-create-monopolies.

Chapter 51: The Coming Pandemic

1. "Antimicrobial Resistance: Tackling a crisis for the health and wealth of nations," *The Review on Antimicrobial Resistance*, December 2014.
2. "In 15 European countries more than 10 percent of bloodstream Staphylococcus aureus infections are caused by methicillin-resistant strains (MRSA), with several of these countries seeing resistance rates closer to 50 percent." See European Centre for Disease Prevention and Control Antimicrobial Resistance Interactive Database (EARS-NET) data for 2013. See also R. Monina Klevens et al., "Inva-

sive Methicillin-Resistant *Staphylococcus aureus* Infection in the United States," *JAMA* 298, no. 15 (2007): 1763–71; Gregory A. Filice et al., "Excess Costs and Utilization Associated with Methicillin Resistance for Patients with *Staphylococcus aureus* Infection," *Infection Control and Hospital Epidemiology* 31, no. 4 (2010): 365–73.

3. "Antimicrobial Resistance: Tackling a crisis for the health and wealth of nations," 5. See also *Antibiotic Resistance Threats in the United States, 2013*, U.S. Department of Health and Human Services, Center for Disease Control and Prevention, https://www.cdc.gov/drugresistance/pdf/ar-threats-2013-508.pdf.
4. Referring to a 2015 WHO report, in "Doctors Urged to Stop Prescribing Antibiotics for Colds and Flus," CBS/AP, January 19, 2016.
5. L.A. Hicks, TH Taylor, Jr., and R.J. Hunkler, "US outpatient antibiotic prescribing, 2010," 2013;368(15):1461–62. See also A. Huttner et al., "Antimicrobial Resistance: A Global View from the 2013 World Healthcare Associated Infections Forum," 2013;2(1):31; Blaser, *Missing Microbes*, 84–86.
6. Another Obama administration health priority in 2015 was passing the Drug Supply Chain Security Act. It sought to upgrade the safety of compounded medicines following a severe outbreak of fungal meningitis that killed sixty-four people. It also sought to better track the distribution of prescription drugs through the supply chain in the hope of cutting back on stolen, counterfeit, and contaminated medications. Sabrina Tavernise and Michael D. Shear, "Obama Seeks to Double Funding to Fight Antibiotic Resistance," *New York Times*, March 27, 2015. As for 30 percent of antibiotics dispensed to Americans being unnecessary, see "Antibiotic Use in the United States, 2017: Progress and Opportunities," U.S. Department of Health and Human Services, Centers for Disease Control and Prevention; Atlanta, GA: 2017.
7. Nick Cumming-Bruce, "W.H.O. Plan Aims to Combat Resistance to Antibiotic Drugs," *New York Times*, May 25, 2015.
8. Ibid.
9. Morbidity and Mortality Weekly Report, Centers for Disease Control, Vol. 68, 2019. By 2019, some infectious disease specialists called on countries to list antibiotic resistance as a cause of death on official certificates. Doing so would provide researchers with more accurate data and also bring attention to the health crisis. Sarah Newey, "Superbugs Should Be Entered as a Cause of Death on Death Certificates, Say Experts," *The Telegraph* (U.K.), November 21, 2019.
10. "Antibiotic/Antimicrobial Resistance (AR/AMR) Biggest Threats and Data," Report of the Centers for Disease Control, 2013 (the CDC website says it "is working towards releasing an updated AR Threats Report in fall 2019").
11. Many of the most "dangerous pathogens were hiding in plain sight," said the CDC's deputy director. Eleven percent of the health care workers screened carried the superbugs although they were asymptomatic. The concern at the CDC is that while those people might have a natural immunity they could be carriers that infect others, especially immunosuppressed patients. Alexandra Sifferlin, "CDC Finds 'Nightmare Bacteria' Across the U.S. Here's What That Means," *Time*, April 3, 2018.
12. The CDC's official position is: "Like in humans, giving antibiotics to food animals will kill most bacteria, but resistant bacteria can survive. When food animals are slaughtered and processed, resistant germs in the animal gut can contaminate the

meat or other animal products. Resistant germs from the animal gut can also get into the environment, like water and soil, from animal manure. If animal manure or water containing resistant germs are used on fruits, vegetables, or other produce as fertilizer or irrigation, then this can spread resistant germs." https://www.cdc.gov/drugresistance/food.html.

13. Thomas P. Van Boeckel et al., "Reducing Antimicrobial Use In Food Animals," *Science,* September 29, 2017. 1350–52. See J. O'Neill, "Antimicrobials In Agriculture And The Environment: Reducing Unnecessary Use And Waste," *Review on Antimicrobial Resistance*, 2016.
14. "Fact Sheet: Veterinary Feed Directive Final Rule and Next Steps," FDA, July 29, 2019.
15. Andrew Jacobs, "Citrus Farmers Facing Deadly Bacteria Turn to Antibiotics, Alarming Health Officials," *New York Times*, May 17, 2019.
16. "Antimicrobial Susceptibility Testing of Human Bacterial Pathogens to Antibiotics Used as Pesticides," Report to EPA, May 11, 2017, in collection of author.
17. Erik Wistrand-Yuen et al., "Evolution Of High-Level Resistance During Low-Level Antibiotic Exposure," *Nature Communications*, 2018; 9 (1).
18. Jacobs, "Citrus Farmers Facing Deadly Bacteria Turn to Antibiotics, Alarming Health Officials."
19. Ibid.
20. "Antibiotic Resistance Threats in the United States, 2019," U.S. Department of Health and Human Services, Centers for Disease Control and Prevention, November 2019, 1–143.
21. Jason Gale, "The Deadly African Virus That's Killing China's Pigs," *Washington Post*, May 2, 2019.
22. Author interview with Karen Bush, November 7, 2016. See also David Shlaes, "The Abandonment of Antibacterials: Why and Wherefore?," *Current Opinion in Pharmacology* 3, no. 5 (2003): 470–73; Steven Projan, "Why is Big Pharma Getting Out of Antibacterial Drug Discovery?," *Current Opinion in Microbiology* 6, no. 5 (2003): 428; see H. W. Boucher et al., "Bad Bugs, No Drugs: No ESKAPE! An Update From The Infectious Diseases Society Of America," *Clin Infect Dis.* 2009 Jan 1;48(1):1–12.
23. The first new drug in the class was Pharmacia's Zyvox. Milton and Lee, *Pills, Profits and Politics*, 33.
24. Amy Nordrum, "Antibiotic Resistance: Why Aren't Drug Companies Developing New Medicines To Stop Superbugs?" *International Business Times*, March 3, 2015. At present, this approach has remained essentially unchanged. See Andrew Pollock, "Antibiotic Subsidies Weighed by US," *New York Times*, November 6, 2010. See also, "Tracking the Pipeline of Antibiotics in Development," Antibiotic Resistance Project, The Pew Charitable Trusts, 2015.
25. J. Sun et al., "A systematic analysis of FDA-approved anticancer drugs," *BMC Syst Biol.* 2017;11(Suppl 5):87. October 3, 2017.
26. Forty-five percent of cancer patients are expected to survive at least ten years, compared with 23 percent in the 1970s. Matthew Weaver, "Cancer Survival Rates Have Doubled Since 1970s, Research Shows," *Guardian*, July 12, 2010.
27. A good example of misplaced priorities was Upjohn. It depended on antibiotic sales for almost half its gross revenues from the early 1950s through the mid-1960s. During World War II when penicillin revolutionized the pharma market,

Upjohn had twelve scientists researching those drugs. In 1970, it had more than four hundred scientists, but fewer than a dozen were assigned to antibiotics. Author interview with Barry Eisenstein, December 19, 2016. See also "Report: Bad Bugs, No Drugs: As Antibiotic R&D Stagnates A Public Health Crisis Brews," *Infectious Disease Society of America*, 2004.

28. Author interview with Mike Skoien, December 21, 2016.
29. Author interview with Barry Eisenstein, December 19, 2016.
30. Author interview with Steven Projan, December 5, 2016.
31. Author interview with Barry Eisenstein, December 19, 2016.
32. Author interview with Karen Bush, November 30. 2016.

Chapter 52: "Essentially a Crime Family"

1. Hadland, "Association of Pharmaceutical Industry Marketing of Opioid Products to Physicians With Subsequent Opioid Prescribing."
2. Walters, "America's Opioid Crisis: How Prescription Drugs Sparked A National Trauma."
3. In 1993, life expectancy declined by 0.3 percent. See Lopez and Frostenson, "How The Opioid Epidemic Became America's Worst Drug Crisis Ever."
4. Ibid. The attraction for many was that the price of heroin was cheap compared to high-dosage opioids and it was often easier to obtain than dealing with the increasing restrictions on prescriptions in some states. For the Veterans Administration, see "Calculating Total Daily Dose Of Opioids For Safer Dosage," CDC.
5. Lopez and Frostenson, "How The Opioid Epidemic Became America's Worst Drug Crisis Ever," and German Lopez, "The Opioid Epidemic, Explained," *Vox*, December 21, 2017.
6. Survey: Many Doctors Misunderstand Key Facets of Opioid Abuse, Johns Hopkins Bloomberg School of Public Health, June 23, 2015. Purdue was not the only drug company selling opioids and breaking the rules on promotion and marketing. Insys Therapeutics, founded in 2013, was a one-drug company. Its future depended on a single opioid drug approved for "breakthrough" pain in terminal cancer patients. The small detail team used an updated version of Purdue's playbook. Insys sales reps pitched it for everything from regular back pain to arthritis, even treating depression. Doctors who prescribed the most drugs, and at the highest dosages, were rewarded with lucrative contracts for the company's "Speakers Bureau." Many times, the physicians never even gave a talk but got paid anyway (that is illegal, since federal regulations require at least two doctors to be at a public event; otherwise the "speaker's fee" is judged a bribe). Doctors whose prescribing dropped off were struck from the speaker's bureau. And Insys set a new low for their detail team. The company hired as a supervisor in sales a former exotic dancer who had no prior experience in pharmaceuticals. Dubbed "a closer" inside the company, at least once she did a lap dance on a physician in order to encourage him to write more prescriptions. The results of all the shady and unauthorized marketing? Over three years, the company's opioid sales went from seven thousand annual prescriptions to sixty thousand. That pushed the stock price up from $5 in 2015 to a high in late 2017 of $44.92, making its owner a billionaire. As of January 2019, Kapoor and four Insys sales managers were charged with criminal racketeering and conspiracy. Insys's stock price had crashed, down by 95 percent. All five were convicted of conspiracy and racketeer-

ing on May 2, 2019. Each faces up to twenty years in prison. "'We Owe Much to the Sackler Family.'"

7. The CDC is considered the most reliable source of opioid overdose death figures. It collects underlying data from the National Vital Statistics System, a web-based "Injury Statistics Query and Reporting System," and an online database that the CDC says provides "data from a variety of trusted sources." See generally https://www.cdc.gov/drugoverdose/data/statedeaths.html.
8. In November 2017 four West Virginia cities filed a class action lawsuit against the Joint Commission, alleging that when it issued its pain management standards in 2001 it had deliberately underplayed the dangers of opioids. See Joint Commission Statement on Pain Management, April 18, 2016,
9. Sarah Varney, "Beset by Lawsuits and Criticism in U.S., Opioid Makers Eye New Market in India," *Kaiser Health News*, August 28, 2019.
10. "We're only just getting started" according to one Mundipharma promotional video. "Pharma Leader Series: Top 50 Generic Drug Manufacturers 2012–2022," CISION PR Newswire, Macy 2, 2012; Harriet Ryan, Lisa Girion, and Scott Glover, "OxyContin Goes Global—'We're Only Just Getting Started,'" *Los Angeles Times*, December 18, 2016.
11. Ryan, Girion, and Glover, "OxyContin Goes Global."
12. Max Blau, "Opioids could kill nearly 500,000 Americans in the next decade," *STAT*, June 27, 2017.
13. "Put another way, opioids could kill nearly as many Americans in a decade as HIV/AIDS has killed since that epidemic began in the early 1980s." Blau, "Opioids could kill nearly 500,000 Americans in the next decade."
14. "Purdue Pharma Promoted OxyContin for Years. Now, It Is Combating the Opioid Crisis," *PBS NewsHour*, March 14, 2018.
15. W. Timothy Coombs, Texas A&M Professor of Crisis Communications, quoted in "Purdue Pharma Promoted OxyContin for Years. Now, it is Combating the Opioid Crisis.".
16. Ibid.
17. "Cure to the Crisis?" *NBC Weekend National News*, March 18, 2018. See also Walters, "America's Opioid Crisis: How Prescription Drugs Sparked A National Trauma."
18. The network of Sackler Mundi companies operating from Bermuda included Mundipharma International, Mundipharma Pharmaceutical Company, Mundipharma Medical Company, Mundipharma International Holdings, Mundipharma Laboratories, Mundipharma International Corporation, Mundipharma Research Company, Mundipharma Company, and Rooksnest Estate and Merganser Ltd. The companies used the same address on Par-la-Ville Road in Hamilton, Bermuda. Tax experts who looked at the arrangement for Britain's *Evening Standard* estimated that based on the amount of OxyContin Napp sold, it had saved over $1.4 billion in taxes over a quarter century. It was technically legal since it took advantage of a loophole in the U.K. tax law that was closed after the Sackler revelations.

    The author found an overlap between the directors of half a dozen Mundipharma companies and some of the firms listed in the *Evening Standard* exposé, including Merganser Limited and Rooksnest Estate Limited. Documents released as part of the leak of papers from the Bermuda law firm, Appleby, referred to as the Paradise Papers, available as a searchable database maintained by the International Constortium of Investigative Journalists (ICIJ).

The Sackler family's only statement to the *Evening Standard* was through a spokesman: "The late Dr Mortimer Sackler paid full UK taxes, including on all UK-sourced income, capital gains and monies remitted to the UK. His heirs also pay the full amount of UK taxes as required by law." See David Cohen, Special Investigation, "Opioid Timebomb Series"—"Revealed: Tax Secrets of the Opioid Billionaires"; "Revealed: Sackler Family Linked To Worldwide Drugs Crisis Saves Millions Using Offshore Haven And Non-Dom Status"; "Prescriptions Are Double What the Government Told Us"; "Taxman Criticised for Letting Sackler Firms 'Dodge Corporation Tax' "; "How a Painkiller Addiction Cost This Man Everything"; "The Sackler Family And How Their Painkiller Fortune Helps Bankroll London Arts"; "Princes's Trust Stops Taking Donations from Sackler Family," May 11, 2018 through September 2019.

19. Author review of Registry and Company files in the U.K.
20. Renae Reints, "Family Behind Purdue Pharma and OxyContin Faces Multiple Lawsuits," *Fortune*, November 19, 2018.
21. Judge Dan A. Poster, of the Federal District Court in Cleveland, oversees the multidistrict litigation. Matthew Goldstein, Danny Hakim, and Jan Hoffman, "Sacklers vs. States: Settlement Talks Stumble Over Foreign Business," *New York Times*, August 30, 2019.
22. It was an amended complaint of the original submitted by Massachusetts for the multidistrict litigation against the company and some individual directors and Sackler family members. *Massachusetts v. Purdue*, C.A. 1884-cv-01808 (BLS2), Filed January 31, 2019.
23. Since the Massachusetts suit, nineteen other states have named the Sacklers as defendants through September 2019, and others are expected to do so. Joel Achenbach, "Purdue Pharma Reaches Tentative Deal in Federal, State Opioid Lawsuits," *Washington Post*, September 11, 2019, 1; Jesse Paul, "Colorado expands lawsuit against opioid-maker Purdue Pharma to include its owners, the Sackler family," *Colorado Sun*, July 1, 2019.
24. Joanna Walters, "Sackler Family Members Face Mass Litigation And Criminal Investigations Over Opioids Crisis," *Guardian*, November 19, 2018.
25. In mid-August, the New York attorney general subpoenaed banking institutions and money managers who had worked with the Sacklers. See David Robinson, "NY AG subpoenas financial advisers, banking institutions tied to Sacklers, Purdue, opioids," *Lohud*, August 16, 2019; Morrell, "The OxyContin Clan: The $14 Billion Newcomer to Forbes 2015 List of Richest U.S. Families." As for the billion dollars transferred through Swiss banks, see Danny Hakim, "New York Uncovers $1 Billion in Sackler Family Wire Transfers," *New York Times*, September 13, 2019, 1.
26. Walters, "Sackler Family Members Face Mass Litigation And Criminal Investigations Over Opioids Crisis."
27. Expert Report Of Professor John C. Coffee, Jr., Matter Of: Purdue Pharma L.P., et al, DCP Case No. 107102, July 12, 2019, in collection of author.
28. Benjamin Sutton, "Elizabeth A. Sackler Supports Nan Goldin in Her Campaign Against OxyContin," *Hyperallergic*, January 22, 2018. One criticism of Elizabeth Sackler was that the foundation for her uncle Mortimer Sackler had made a $500,000 gift to the Brooklyn Museum, designated for the Elizabeth A. Sackler Center for Feminist Art. Mortimer's wealth was largely built on the success

of OxyContin. See Ethan Barton, "Opioid Billionaires' Niece Denounces Family Company After Her Art Center Took $500,000," *Daily Caller*, January 18, 2018.

29. Jillian Sackler, "Stop Blaming My Late Husband, Arthur Sackler, For The Opioid Crisis," *Washington Post*, April 11, 2019.
30. See also "Disclaimer—Statement by Jillian Sackler," http://www.sackler.org/about/, and Barton, "Opioid Billionaires' Niece Denounces Family Company After Her Art Center Took $500,000."
31. From 1999 to 2017, there were 218,000 deaths. That included prescription as well as illegal opioids as the cause of death. Another 72,000 died in 2018 and the federal government lists 68,588 as of August 4, 2019. The most recent annual statistics represent the first time in over a decade that the number of opioid-related overdose deaths declined. Experts are divided about whether it is the beginning of a trend or a onetime anomaly in the epidemic. See NCHS, National Vital Statistics System. Estimates for 2018 and 2019 are based on provisional data. See also R. A. Rudd et al., "Increases in Drug and Opioid-Involved Overdose Deaths—United States, 2010–2015," *MMWR Morb Mortal Wkly Rep* 65(5051):1445–52. 2016.
32. "I admire Nan Goldin's commitment to take action and her courage to tell her story. I stand in solidarity with artists and thinkers whose work and voices must be heard." Elizabeth Sackler statement issued to *Hyperallergic*. Benjamin Sutton, "Elizabeth A. Sackler Supports Nan Goldin in Her Campaign Against OxyContin."
33. Laura Strickler, "OxyContin maker Purdue Pharma agrees to $270M settlement with Oklahoma: source," NBC News, March 26, 2019 (confirmed and announced publicly on March 28).
34. J&J's share price rose the next day as Wall Street investors had expected a judgment of about $1 billion. The trial judge lowered it to $465 million in November 2019, but the company has appealed the verdict. Hoffman, "Johnson & Johnson Ordered to Pay $572 Million in Landmark Opioid Trial." As for the public nuisance laws, see Henry Gass and Christa Case Bryant, "When It Comes to Opioid Crisis, What Does Justice Look Like?," *Christian Science Monitor*, August 28, 2019. Scott Higham and Lenny Bernstein, "Drug Companies Seek Removal of Judge in Landmark Opioid Case," *Washington Post*, September 14, 2019.
35. James McClain, "OxyContin Heir David Sackler Spends $22.5 Million In Bel Air," *Dirt*, March 7, 2018.
36. David Sackler is listed as the CEO of Summer Road LLC, which according to the *Palm Beach Post* is "an entity that manages the Sacklers' fortune." Summer Road LLC is listed on state records as the purchaser on July 31, 2019, of the Glidden Spina Architecture building at 207 Sixth St, West Palm Beach. Summer Road LLC moved into that building, and the *Palm Beach Post* reports that David Sackler and his wife, Joss, moved into the "sprawling mansion" in Boca Raton. See Alexandra Clough, "Purdue Pharma Family Office Move To WPB Is 'Salt In The Wounds,' Lawyer Says," *Palm Beach Post*, September 18, 2019, 1; Alexandra Clough, "EXCLUSIVE: Sackler Family Company Pays $7 Million For Mansion Near Boca Raton," *Palm Beach Post*, October 25, 2019, 1.
37. When news of the Florida purchases became public in late September, one lawyer representing Palm Beach County in its lawsuit against Purdue and some of the former Sackler-family directors told the *Palm Beach Post* that "It's rubbing salt in

the wounds." Hunter Shkolnik interviewed in Clough, "Sackler Family Company Pays $7 Million For Mansion Near Boca Raton."

38. McLean, "'We Didn't Cause The Crisis.'"
39. Chris Spargo, "Heir to $13B OxyContin Fortune Says Son, 4, Asked if Family Kills People, Rejects Blame for Opioid Crisis and Plays Victim in Interview," *Daily Mail*, June 28, 2019.
40. The top selling drug companies for opioids from 2006 to 2012 were two generic firms, Actavis Pharma and Mallinckrodt's subsidiary, SpecGx. "Opioids Market Size, Share & Trends Analysis Report By Product (IR/ Short-acting, ER/ Long-acting), By Application (Pain Relief, Anesthesia), By Region, And Segment Forecasts, 2019–2026," Grand View Research, April 2019, 1–113. See also "Common Myths About OxyContin® (oxycodone HCl) Extended-Release Tablets CII," Purdue Pharma at https://www.purduepharma.com/news-media/common-myths-about-oxycontin/. For David Sackler, see McLean, "'We Didn't Cause The Crisis.'" See also David Armstrong and Jeff Ernsthausen, "Data Touted by OxyContin Maker to Fight Lawsuits Doesn't Tell the Whole Story," *ProPublica*, September 9, 2019.
41. RICO, passed in 1970, is used more frequently now for civil cases, where it allows for triple damages, than in criminal cases. Walter Pavlo, "Once Meant To Nail Mobsters, RICO Sees Resurgence In Civil Cases In 2018," *Forbes*, Octrober 31, 2018. Ohio Judge Dan Aaron Polster did not dismiss racketeering and fraud claims filed by the Ohio cities of Akron and Cleveland and counties of Cuyahoga and Summit. Polster ruled that key claims made in pending lawsuits should proceed to trial and denied the requests of drug manufacturers and distributors that the charges be dropped. In Re: National Prescription Opiate Litigation, This Document Relates To, The County of Summit, Ohio, et al. v. Purdue Pharma L.P., et al., Case No. 18-op-45090 (MDL 2804), Case No. 1:17-md-2804,
42. That was a far cry from the estimate nine months earlier by Mike Moore, the former Mississippi attorney general, that a complete settlement of all opioid litigation would top $100 billion. "Purdue Pharma Promoted OxyContin for Years. Now, It Is Combating the Opioid Crisis," *PBS News Hour*, March 14, 2018. See also Walters, "Sackler Family Members Face Mass Litigation And Criminal Investigations Over Opioids Crisis."
43. Jef Feeley and Riley Griffin, "Sackler Family Backs $11.5 Billion Purdue Opioid Settlement," *Bloomberg*, August 27, 2019.
44. There is precedent for such an arrangement. Both Halliburton and W. R. Grace had separate trusts established and managed by court-appointed trustees to settle claims from asbestos litigation. See Feeley and Griffin, "Sackler Family Backs $11.5 Billion Purdue Opioid Settlement"; Mike Spector and Jessica DiNapoli, "Exclusive: OxyContin maker prepares 'free-fall' bankruptcy as settlement talks stall," Reuters, September 3, 2019.
45. And see ibid.
46. Jared S. Hopkins and Sara Randazzo, "Proposed Opioid Deal With Purdue Drawing Pushback From States," *Wall Street Journal*, August 29, 2019, 1.
47. Mundipharma's own website listed its value at $7 billion in 2017. It is almost impossible to get a fair market value since all Mundipharma firms operate separately as private companies and there are no unified sales and profits numbers.
48. The Sacklers agreed to pay $500 million the first year, then $300 million from years two through six, and the final $1 billion in the seventh year. Lenny Bern-

stein et al., "OxyContin Owners May Retain The Bulk Of Their Billions," *Washington Post*, August 31, 2019.

49. Bernstein, "OxyContin Owners May Retain The Bulk Of Their Billions."
50. Feeley and Griffin, "Sackler Family Backs $11.5 Billion Purdue Opioid Settlement."
51. Joel Achenbach, "Purdue Pharma Reaches Tentative Deal in Federal, State Opioid Lawsuits," *Washington Post*, September 11, 2019, 1.
52. Ed Silverman, "Purdue Pharma's newly created subsidiaries raise questions over attempts to shield assets from bankruptcy," *STAT*, April 1, 2019.
53. Adam Geller, "Where Did the Sacklers Move Cash From Their Opioid Maker?" *Associated Press*, September 2, 2019.
54. The Sackler directors voted themselves over $4 billion in OxyContin profits from 2008 through 2016. Based on information received from subpoenas, New York State investigators tracked a billion dollars in transfers suggesting some family members tried shielding their wealth in case of an adverse litigation ruling. Some Oxy profits passed through a Swiss bank account located in the Channel Islands before getting transferred to a series of trusts (Millborne Trust Company, Heatheridge Trust Co., and Purdue Pharma Trust MDAS). Hakim, "New York Uncovers $1 Billion in Sackler Family Wire Transfers." Profit statistics are from the office of the Massachusetts attorney general and based on Purdue's board documents. See Tom Maloney and Jef Feeley, "Sacklers to Remain Billionaire Family If Purdue Settles Opioid Lawsuits," *Bloomberg*, August 28, 2019.
55. Author's review of registry and company files.
56. McClain, "OxyContin Heir David Sackler Spends $22.5 Million In Bel Air."
57. Geller, "Where Did the Sacklers Move Cash From Their Opioid Maker?" See also David Crow, "Billionaire Sackler family owns second opioid drugmaker," *Financial Times*, September 15, 2018.
58. On some figures there was mutual agreement. Purdue's cash balance was $500 million. Its largest asset is a group of liability insurance policies worth approximately another $500 million. The policies provide $725 million in coverage but the plaintiffs expect the insurance companies to deny full coverage by insisting that any intentional acts of fraud are outside the coverage terms. A settlement with the insurance companies is expected to bring in two thirds of the face value of the policies. A sale of Purdue's headquarters, manufacturing facilities, and patents would bring an estimated $750 million. Author interview with a party familiar with the negotiations, September 5, 2019. Bernstein et al., "OxyContin owners may retain the bulk of their billions."
59. Bernstein, "OxyContin Owners May Retain Bulk of Their Billions." See also Jared S. Hopkins and Andrew Scurria, "Sacklers Received $12 Billion to $13 Billion in Profits from OxyContin Maker Purdue Pharma," *Wall Street Journal*, October 4, 2019, 1.
60. Ibid.
61. "FDA approves first generic naloxone nasal spray to treat opioid overdose," FDA News Release, April 19, 2019.
62. Achenbach, "Purdue Pharma Reaches Tentative Deal in Federal, State Opioid Lawsuits."
63. Feeley and Griffin, "Sackler Family Backs $11.5 Billion Purdue Opioid Settlement."
64. After news had broken of the proposed settlement, Connecticut attorney general

William Tong issued a statement: "Connecticut demands that the Sacklers and Purdue management be forced completely out of the opioid business, domestically and internationally, and that they never be allowed to return." Bernstein, "OxyContin Owners May Retain The Bulk Of Their Billions."

65. That is the estimated value of an immediate auction of the company's assets, including the $500 million in cash. Bernstein, "OxyContin Owners May Retain The Bulk Of Their Billions." See also Spector and DiNapoli, "Exclusive: OxyContin maker prepares 'free-fall' bankruptcy as settlement talks stall."
66. Sarah Skidmore Sell, Geoff Mulvihill, and Adam Geller, "What a Purdue Bankruptcy Means for the Sackler Family," *Washington Post*, September 12, 2019.
67. Sara Randazzo and Jared S. Hopkins, "OxyContin Maker Purdue Pharma Files for Bankruptcy Protection," *Wall Street Journal*, September 16, 2019. See Spector and DiNapoli, "Exclusive: OxyContin maker prepares 'free-fall' bankruptcy as settlement talks stall"; Bernstein et al., "OxyContin owners may retain the bulk of their billions"; and Joel Achenbach, "Purdue Pharma Reaches Tentative Deal in Federal, State Opioid Lawsuits," *Washington Post*, September 11, 2019, 1.
68. Dan Mangan, "Economic cost of the opioid crisis: $1 trillion and growing faster," CNBC, February 13, 2018.

INDEX

ABOUT THE AUTHOR

GERALD POSNER is an award-winning journalist who has written twelve books, including the Pulitzer Prize finalist *Case Closed* and multiple national bestsellers. His 2015 book, *God's Bankers*, a two-hundred-year history of the finances of the Vatican, was an acclaimed New York Times bestseller. Posner has written for many national magazines and papers, including the *New York Times*, *The New Yorker*, *Newsweek*, and *Time*, and he has been a regular contributor to NBC, the History Channel, CNN, CBS, MSNBC, and FOX News. He lives in Miami Beach with his wife, author Trisha Posner.